WORD
BIBLICAL
COMMENTARY

WORD
BIBLICAL
COMMENTARY

VOLUME 36

(John)

GEORGE R. BEASLEY-MURRAY

WORD BOOKS, PUBLISHER • WACO, TEXAS

Word Biblical Commentary
JOHN
Copyright © 1987 by Word, Incorporated

Library of Congress Cataloging in Publication Data
Main entry under title:

Word biblical commentary.

Includes bibliographies.
1. Bible—Commentaries—Collected works.
BS491.2.W67   220.7′7   81–71768
ISBN 0–8499–0235–5 (vol. 36) AACR2

Printed in the United States of America

Scripture quotations in the body of the commentary marked RSV are from the Revised Standard Version of the Bible, copyright 1946 (renewed 1973), 1956, and © 1971 by the Division of Christian Education of the National Council of the Churches of Christ in the USA and are used by permission.

The author's own translation of the text appears in italic type under the heading "Translation."

7898 FG 987654321

To
Laurence Cobb
whose endurance of suffering
enables him to enter into this Gospel
more than most

Contents

Editorial Preface	ix
Author's Preface	x
Abbreviations	xii
Commentary Bibliography	xxvi
General Bibliography	xxviii
INTRODUCTION	xxxii
THE ENIGMA OF THE FOURTH GOSPEL	xxxii
THE ORIGIN OF THE FOURTH GOSPEL	xxxv
The Relations of the Fourth Gospel with the Synoptic Gospels	xxxv
The Literary Sources of the Fourth Gospel	xxxviii
The Tradition behind the Fourth Gospel and Its Development	xliv
The Religious Relations of the Fourth Gospel	liii
Hellenistic Traditions	liii
Philo	liv
Gnosticism	lv
The Hermetic Literature	lvi
Mandaism	lvii
Jewish Traditions	lviii
The Old Testament in the Gospel	lix
Rabbinic Judaism	lx
The Qumran Literature	lxi
Samaritan Religion	lxiii
Conclusion	lxv
THE AUTHORSHIP OF THE FOURTH GOSPEL	lxvi
The External Evidence	lxx
The Internal Evidence	lxxv
THE DATE AND PLACE OF WRITING OF THE FOURTH GOSPEL	lxxxi
ASPECTS OF THE THEOLOGY OF THE FOURTH GOSPEL	lxxxi
Christology	lxxxi
Soteriology	lxxxiv
Eschatology	lxxxv
THE PURPOSE OF THE FOURTH GOSPEL	lxxxviii
THE STRUCTURE OF THE FOURTH GOSPEL	xc
THE GOSPEL OF JOHN	
I. The Prologue (1:1–18)	1
II. The Public Ministry of Jesus (1:19–12:50)	18
A. Testimonies to Jesus: The Witness of John the Baptist and the Early Disciples (1:19–51)	18
B. The Revelation of the New Order in Jesus (2:1–4:42)	31

1. The Beginning of the Signs: Water into Wine (2:1–12)   32
2. The Cleansing of the Temple (2:13–22)   37
3. The Nicodemus Discourse (2:23–3:36)   43
4. Jesus and the Samaritans (4:1–42)   56
C. Jesus the Mediator of Life and Judgment (4:43–5:47)   66
D. Jesus the Bread of Life (6:1–71)   81
E. Jesus the Water and the Light of Life (7:1–8:59)   100
    1. Jesus the Water of Life (7:1–52)   100
    2. Jesus the Light of Life (8:12–59)   123
    3. A Woman Caught in Adultery (7:53–8:11)   143
F. Jesus the Light and Shepherd of Humankind (9:1–10:42)   148
    1. Jesus the Light of the World That Brings Judgment to the World (9:1–41)   149
    2. Jesus the Shepherd and Son of God (10:1–42)   162
G. Jesus the Resurrection and the Life (11:1–54)   180
H. Jesus the King, Triumphant through Death (11:55–12:50)   201
III. The Passion and Resurrection of Jesus (13:1–20:31)   222
A. The Ministry of Jesus to the Disciples in the Upper Room (13:1–17:26)   222
    1. The Footwashing and the Betrayal of Jesus (13:1–30)   227
    2. The Departure and the Return of Jesus (13:31–14:31)   240
    3. Jesus the True Vine—The Hatred of the World for the Church—The Joy That Overcomes Tribulation (15:1–16:33)   265
    4. The Prayer of Consecration (17:1–26)   291
B. The Death and Resurrection of Jesus (18:1–20:31)   308
    1. The Passion Narrative: The Arrest, Trial, Crucifixion, and Burial of Jesus (18:1–19:42)   308
    2. The Resurrection of Jesus (20:1–31)   364
IV. Epilogue: The Mission of the Church and Its Chief Apostles (21:1–25)   392

Indexes   419

Editorial Preface

The launching of the *Word Biblical Commentary* brings to fulfillment an enterprise of several years' planning. The publishers and the members of the editorial board met in 1977 to explore the possibility of a new commentary on the books of the Bible that would incorporate several distinctive features. Prospective readers of these volumes are entitled to know what such features were intended to be; whether the aims of the commentary have been fully achieved time alone will tell.

First, we have tried to cast a wide net to include as contributors a number of scholars from around the world who not only share our aims, but are in the main engaged in the ministry of teaching in university, college, and seminary. They represent a rich diversity of denominational allegiance. The broad stance of our contributors can rightly be called evangelical, and this term is to be understood in its positive, historic sense of a commitment to scripture as divine revelation, and to the truth and power of the Christian gospel.

Then, the commentaries in our series are all commissioned and written for the purpose of inclusion in the *Word Biblical Commentary*. Unlike several of our distinguished counterparts in the field of commentary writing, there are no translated works, originally written in a non-English language. Also, our commentators were asked to prepare their own rendering of the original biblical text and to use those languages as the basis of their own comments and exegesis. What may be claimed as distinctive with this series is that it is based on the biblical languages, yet it seeks to make the technical and scholarly approach to a theological understanding of scripture understandable by— and useful to—the fledgling student, the working minister as well as to colleagues in the guild of professional scholars and teachers.

Finally, a word must be said about the format of the series. The layout in clearly defined sections has been consciously devised to assist readers at different levels. Those wishing to learn about the textual witnesses on which the translation is offered are invited to consult the section headed "Notes." If the readers' concern is with the state of modern scholarship on any given portion of scripture, then they should turn to the sections on "Bibliography" and "Form/Structure/Setting." For a clear exposition of the passage's meaning and its relevance to the ongoing biblical revelation, the "Comment" and concluding "Explanation" are designed expressly to meet that need. There is therefore something for everyone who may pick and use these volumes.

If these aims come anywhere near realization, the intention of the editors will have been met, and the labor of our team of contributors rewarded.

General Editors: *David A. Hubbard*
Glenn W. Barker †
Old Testament: *John D. W. Watts*
New Testament: *Ralph P. Martin*

Author's Preface

The Gospel of John has been well served by commentators, from Origen in the third century of our era to the present day. It is likely that it claims the attention of more scholars at the present time than any other book of the Bible. In 1967 Eduard Malatesta issued a substantial work, consisting of a classified bibliography of books and periodical literature on our Gospel published during the period 1920–65 (*St. John's Gospel*, Analecta Biblica 32 [Rome: Pontifical Biblical Institute]). It listed 3120 works, with more than 1800 book reviews that had appeared mainly in the "Elenchus Bibliographicus," vols. 1–47. When Hartwig Thyen, in a series of articles in the *Theologische Rundschau* (1974, 1977, 1978, 1979) reviewed literature on the Fourth Gospel that had appeared in the previous twenty years, his bibliography of books and articles for the five years 1966–71 comprised 34 pages of closely printed small type. That is an indication of the interest, even fascination, that the Fourth Gospel awakes in New Testament scholars. Naturally the Gospel was not written for the benefit of the academic community; couched in the simplest language possible, it was written to provide the Church with an exposition of the Good News of Jesus, the Christ and Son of God, and to show inquirers into the Christian faith the way to life through him (20:30–31). The young believer finds in it an enthralling exposition of the faith that he or she has embraced; the mature Christian receives from it an illuminating revelation of the person of the Redeemer who is the subject of the book; the aged saint gains from it comfort and a glimpse of the glory of God that irradiates life's eventide; and Christians departing from this world take with them the word of life and peace given by the Shepherd of souls. The very nature of the work as a product of preaching and teaching makes it the preacher's Gospel *par excellence*.

The writer of this commentary has passed through most of these stages in his own experience (the last is yet to come!). Converted to the Christian faith in his teens, he found this Gospel a thrilling book, though at that time he found the opening sentences quite baffling (how could a Word be God?). As a theological student he discovered unsuspected depths in the book, but found some aspects of the critical treatment of the Gospel difficult to appreciate. On becoming a pastor in the midst of World War 2 he learned the comfort of this book to those who were shattered by the tragedies enacted around them and the power of its presentation of the Good News of Christ for those who had neither faith nor hope. It was as a young pastor that he listened to the crystal-clear exegesis of the Gospel by C. H. Dodd (and incidentally learned to what heights lecturing could attain). At the same time he was guided in his studies by that stern disciplinarian, P. Gardner-Smith, who had a special interest in the Fourth Gospel. Through them he was introduced to the work of E. C. Hoskyns, and from him he learned that a New Testament commentary should both do justice to the theology of the book and withal impart something of the spiritual experience that lay behind it. It was Hoskyns who made known to the writer the existence of Adolf Schlatter and led him to explore the writings of that kindred spirit far beyond the Johannine corpus. So he was prepared to engage with Bultmann, and incidentally to understand what it was that those two diametrically opposed exegetes (Schlatter and Bultmann) had in common—a passionate desire to demonstrate that the gospel was not only to be believed but to be lived. Returning to Barrett's commentary one appreciated its commonsense stance. And it was intriguing to realize that the two most influential recent commentaries on the Gospel are by Roman Catholic scholars—Raymond Brown in the U.S.A. and Rudolf Schnackenburg in Germany: the former work is splendid for the pastor in his preaching; the latter is an unprecedented mine of information (many mines!) and contains a constant flow of insights into the meaning of the text.

This personalized description of works on John's Gospel could continue, lengthily, and might well lead to the question, Why, then, yet another commentary on it? One supreme consideration weighed with the writer in his decision to embark on this work. He knows well that average ministers are far too busily engaged in their diverse responsibilities to attempt to cope with Hoskyns and Bultmann, with Barrett and Dodd, with Schnackenburg and Haenchen, etc.—still less to examine the endless stream of articles and monographs on varied aspects of the Fourth Gospel. It seemed that there was room for an attempt to pass on some of the treasures of modern study of this Gospel and with them to combine one's own findings and convictions. It has been an immeasurable enrichment of mind and heart to prepare for and write this exposition of the so-called "spiritual Gospel." To study the book with integrity, openness and with expectation of the guidance of the Paraclete-Spirit can and should be a spiritual adventure for anyone. It will lead the reader to a more profound understanding of him of whom it tells— Jesus, the Christ, the incarnate Son of God, Word of God, Son of Man, and Savior of the World; and, if the purpose of its composition is fulfilled in him, it will lead to a deeper faith in and knowledge of that same Jesus, and a more adequate witness to him before the world.

It remains for me to express my thanks and appreciation to Dr. Larry Kreitzer, formerly a student at Louisville and now at Regent's Park College, Oxford, for his work in compiling the indexes.

GEORGE R. BEASLEY-MURRAY

Hove, E. Sussex

Abbreviations

A. General Abbreviations

A	Codex Alexandrinus	in loc.	*in loco,* in the place cited
ad	comment on	Jos.	Josephus
Akkad.	Akkadian	Lat.	Latin
א	Codex Sinaiticus	LL.	Late Latin
Ap. Lit.	Apocalyptic Literature	LXX	Septuagint
Apoc.	Apocrypha	M	Mishna
Aq.	Aquila's Greek Translation of the Old Testament	masc.	masculine
		mg.	margin
		MS(S)	manuscript(s)
Arab.	Arabic	MT	Masoretic text
Aram.	Aramaic	n.	note
B	Codex Vaticanus	n.d.	no date
C	Codex Ephraemi Syri	Nestle	Nestle (ed.) *Novum Testamentum Graece* revised by K. and B. Aland
c.	*circa,* about		
cf.	*confer,* compare		
chap., chaps.	chapter, chapters		
cod., codd.	codex, codices	no.	number
contra	in contrast to	NS	New Series
CUP	Cambridge University Press	NT	New Testament
		obs.	obsolete
D	Codex Bezae	OL	Old Latin
DSS	Dead Sea Scrolls (see **F.**)	OS	Old Syriac
ed.	edited, edition, editor; editions	OT	Old Testament
		p., pp.	page, pages
e.g.	*exempli gratia,* for example	*pace*	with due respect to, but differing from
Egyp.	Egyptian		
et al.	*et alii,* and others	par.	paragraph
et passim	and elsewhere	Pers.	Persian
ET	English translation	Pesh.	Peshitta
EV	English Versions of the Bible	Phoen.	Phoenician
		pl.	plural
f., ff.	following (verse or verses, pages, etc.)	Pseudep.	Pseudepigrapha
		Q	Quelle ("Sayings" source in the Gospels)
fem.	feminine		
FS	Festschrift	q.v.	*quod vide,* which see
ft.	foot, feet	rev.	revised, reviser, revision
gen.	genitive	Rom.	Roman
Gr.	Greek	RVm	Revised Version margin
Heb.	Hebrew	Samar.	Samaritan recension
Hitt.	Hittite	sc.	*scilicet,* that is to say
ibid.	*ibidem,* in the same place	Sem.	Semitic
id.	*idem,* the same	sing.	singular
i.e.	*id est,* that is	Sumer.	Sumerian
impf.	imperfect	s.v.	*sub verbo,* under the word
infra.	below	Syr.	Syriac

Symm.	Symmachus	viz.	*videlicet,* namely
Targ.	Targum	vol.	volume
Theod.	Theodotion	v, vv	verse, verses
TR	Textus Receptus	vs.	versus
tr.	translation, translator, translated	vg	Vulgate
		WH	Westcott and Hort, *The*
UBS	The United Bible Societies Greek Text		*New Testament in Greek*
		x	number of times words
Ugar.	Ugaritic		occur
u.s.	*ut supra,* as above	§	section

B. Abbreviations for Translations and Paraphrases

AmT	Smith and Goodspeed, *The Complete Bible, An American Translation*	TLB	The Living Bible
		Moffatt	J. Moffatt, *A New Translation of the Bible*
ASV	American Standard Version, American Revised Version (1901)	NAB	The New American Bible
		NASB	New American Standard Bible
AV	Authorized Version	NEB	The New English Bible
Beck	Beck, *The New Testament in the Language of Today*	NIV	The New International Version
BV	Berkeley Version (The Modern Language Bible)	Ph	J. B. Phillips, *The New Testament in Modern English*
GNB	*Good News Bible*	RSV	Revised Standard Version
JB	The Jerusalem Bible	RV	Revised Version—1881–1885
JPS	*Jewish Publication Society Version of the Old Testament*	TEV	Today's English Version
		Wey	R. F. Weymouth, *The New Testament in Modern Speech*
KJV	King James Version		
Knox	R. A. Knox, *The Holy Bible: A Translation from the Latin Vulgate in the Light of the Hebrew and Greek Original*	Wms	C. B. Williams, *The New Testament: A Translation in the Language of the People*

C. Abbreviations of Commonly Used Periodicals, Reference Works, and Serials

AAS	*Acta apostolicae sedis*	AGJU	Arbeiten zur Geschichte des antiken Judentums und des Urchristentums
AASOR	Annual of the American Schools of Oriental Research		
		AH	F. Rosenthal, *An Aramaic Handbook*
AB	Anchor Bible		
ABR	*Australian Biblical Review*	AHR	*American Historical Review*
AbrN	*Abr-Nahrain*	AHW	W. von Soden, *Akkadisches Handwörterbuch*
ACNT	Augsburg Commentary on the New Testament		
		AION	*Annali dell'istituto orientali di Napoli*
AcOr	*Acta orientalia*		
ACW	Ancient Christian Writers	AJA	*American Journal of Archaeology*
ADAJ	Annual of the Department of Antiquities of Jordan		
		AJAS	*American Journal of Arabic Studies*
AER	*American Ecclesiastical Review*		
AFER	*African Ecclesiastical Review*	AJBA	*Australian Journal of Biblical Archaeology*
AfO	*Archiv für Orientforschung*		

AJSL	*American Journal of Semitic Languages and Literature*	ATANT	Abhandlungen zur Theologie des Alten und Neuen Tetaments (AThANT)
AJT	*American Journal of Theology*		
ALBO	Analecta lovaniensia biblica et orientalia	ATD	Das Alte Testament Deutsch
ALGHJ	Arbeiten zur Literatur und Geschichte des hellenistischen Judentums	*ATR*	*Anglican Theological Review*
		AUSS	*Andrews University Seminary Studies*
ALUOS	Annual of Leeds University Oriental Society	*BA*	*Biblical Archaeologist*
AnBib	Analecta biblica	BAC	Biblioteca de autores cristianos
AnBoll	Analecta Bollandiana		
ANEP	J. B. Pritchard (ed.), *Ancient Near East in Pictures*	*BAR*	*Biblical Archaeology Review*
		BASOR	*Bulletin of the American Schools of Oriental Research*
ANESTP	J. B. Pritchard (ed.), *Ancient Near East Supplementary Texts and Pictures*	*BASP*	*Bulletin of the American Society of Papyrologists*
ANET	J. B. Pritchard (ed.), *Ancient Near Eastern Texts*	BBB	Bonner biblische Beiträge
		BCSR	*Bulletin of the Council on the Study of Religion*
ANF	The Ante-Nicene Fathers		
Ang	*Angelicum*	BDB	E. Brown, S. R. Driver, and C. A. Briggs, *Hebrew and English Lexicon of the Old Testament*
AnOr	Analecta orientalia		
ANQ	*Andover Newton Quarterly*		
Anton	*Antonianum*		
AOAT	Alter Orient und Altes Testament	BDF	F. Blass, A. Debrunner, and R. W. Funk, *A Greek Grammar of the NT*
AOS	American Oriental Series		
AP	J. Marouzeau (ed.), *L'année philologique*	BDR	F. Blass, A. Debrunner, and F. Rehkopf, *Grammatik des neutestamentlichen Griechisch*
APOT	R. H. Charles (ed.), *Apocrypha and Pseudepigrapha of the Old Testament*	*BeO*	*Bibbia e oriente*
		BETL	Bibliotheca ephemeridum theologicarum lovaniensium
ARG	*Archiv für Reformationsgeschichte*		
ARM	Archives royales de Mari	BEvT	Beiträge zur evangelischen Theologie (BEvTh)
ArOr	*Archiv orientální*		
ARSHLL	Acta Reg. Societatis Humaniorum Litterarum Lundensis	BFCT	Beiträge zur Förderung christlicher Theologie (BFCTh)
ARW	*Archiv für Religionswissenschaft*	BGBE	Beiträge zur Geschichte der biblischen Exegese
ASNU	Acta seminarii neotestamentici upsaliensis	BGD	W. Bauer, F. W. Gingrich, and F. Danker, *Greek-English Lexicon of the NT*
ASS	*Acta sanctae sedis*		
AsSeign	*Assemblées du Seigneur*	*BHH*	B. Reicke and L. Rost (eds.), *Biblisch-Historisches Handwörterbuch*
ASSR	*Archives des sciences sociales des religions*		
ASTI	*Annual of the Swedish Theological Institute*	*BHK*	R. Kittel, *Biblia hebraica*
		BHS	*Biblia hebraica stuttgartensia*
ATAbh	Alttestamentliche Abhandlungen	BHT	Beiträge zur historischen Theologie (BHTh)

Bib	*Biblica*	CAT	Commentaire de l'Ancien
BibB	Biblische Beiträge		Testament
BibLeb	*Bibel und Leben*	*CB*	*Cultura bíblica*
BibOr	Biblica et orientalia	*CBQ*	*Catholic Biblical Quarterly*
BibS(F)	Biblische Studien (Freiburg,	CBQMS	Catholic Biblical
	1895–) (BSt)		Quarterly—Monograph
BibS(N)	Biblische Studien (Neukir-		Series
	chen, 1951–) (BibSt)	CCath	Corpus Catholicorum
BibZ	*Biblische Zeitschrift*	CChr	Corpus Christianorum
BiTod	*Bible Today*	*CH*	*Church History*
BIES	*Bulletin of the Israel*	*CHR*	*Catholic Historical Review*
	Exploration Society (= *Yediot*)	CIG	*Corpus inscriptionum*
BIFAO	*Bulletin de l'institut français*		*graecarum*
	d'archéologie orientale	*CH*	*Corpus inscriptionum*
BJRL	*Bulletin of the John Rylands*		*iudaicarum*
	University Library of	CIL	*Corpus inscriptionum*
	Manchester		*latinarum*
BK	*Bibel und Kirche*	CIS	*Corpus inscriptionum*
BKAT	Biblischer Kommentar:		*semiticarum*
	Altes Testament	*CJT*	*Canadian Journal of Theology*
BL	*Book List*	*ClerRev*	*Clergy Review*
BLE	*Bulletin de littérature*	CNT	Commentaire du Nouveau
	ecclésiastique		Testament
BLit	*Bibel und Liturgie*	ConB	Coniectanea biblica
BNTC	Black's New Testament	*ConNT*	*Coniectanea neotestamentica*
	Commentaries (=HNTC)	*Corp Herm.*	Corpus Hermeticum
BO	*Bibliotheca orientalis*	*CQ*	*Church Quarterly*
BR	*Biblical Research*	*CQR*	*Church Quarterly Review*
BS	*Biblische Studien*, Freiburg	*CRAIBL*	*Comptes rendus de l'Académie*
BSac	*Bibliotheca Sacra*		*des inscriptions et belles-*
BSO(A)S	*Bulletin of the School of*		*lettres*
	Oriental (and African)	*CrQ*	*Crozier Quarterly*
	Studies	CSCO	Corpus scriptorum
BT	*The Bible Translator*		christianorum orientalium
BTB	*Biblical Theology Bulletin*	CSEL	Corpus scriptorum
BTS	*Bible et terre sainte*		ecclesiasticorum latinorum
BU	Biblische Untersuchungen	*CTA*	A. Herdner, *Corpus des*
BVC	*Bible et vie chrétienne*		*tablettes en cunéiformes*
BWANT	Beiträge zur Wissenschaft		*alphabétiques*
	vom Alten und Neuen	*CTJ*	*Calvin Theological Journal*
	Testament	CTM	Concordia Theological
BZ	*Biblische Zeitschrift*		Monthly
BZAW	Beihefte zur ZAW	*CurTM*	*Currents in Theology and*
BZET	Beihefte z. Evangelische		*Mission*
	Theologie		
BZNW	Beihefte zur ZNW	*DACL*	*Dictionnaire d'archéologie*
BZRGG	Beihefte zur ZRGG		*chrétienne et de liturgie*
		DBSup	*Dictionnaire de la Bible,*
CAD	*The Assyrian Dictionary of the*		*Supplément*
	Oriental Institute of the	*DISO*	C.-F. Jean and J. Hoftijzer,
	University of Chicago		*Dictionnaire des inscriptions*
CAH	*Cambridge Ancient History*		*sémitiques de l'ouest*

DJD	Discoveries in the Judean Desert	GKC	*Gesenius' Hebrew Grammar,* ed. E. Kautzsch, tr. A. E. Cowley
DOTT	D. W. Thomas (ed.), *Documents from Old Testament Times*	GNT	Grundrisse zum Neuen Testament
DS	Denzinger-Schönmetzer, *Enchiridion symbolorum*	*GOTR*	*Greek Orthodox Theological Review*
DTC	*Dictionnaire de théologie catholique (DTHC)*	*GRBS*	*Greek, Roman, and Byzantine Studies*
DTT	*Dansk teologisk tidsskrift*	*Greg*	*Gregorianum*
DunRev	Dunwoodie Review	*GThT*	*Geformelet Theologisch Tijdschrift*
EBib	Etudes bibliques (EtBib)	*GuL*	*Geist und Leben*
EBT	*Encyclopedia of Biblical Theology*	*HALAT*	W. Baumgartner et al., *Hebräisches und aramäisches Lexikon zum Alten Testament*
EDB	L. F. Hartman (ed.), *Encyclopedic Dictionary of the Bible*		
EHAT	Exegetisches Handbuch zum Alten Testament	HAT	Handbuch zum Alten Testament
EKKNT	Evangelisch-katholischer Kommentar zum Neuen Testament	HDR	Harvard Dissertations in Religion
EKL	*Evangelisches Kirchenlexikon*	*HeyJ*	*Heythrop Journal*
EncJud	*Encyclopaedia judaica* (1971)	*HibJ*	*Hibbert Journal*
EnchBib	*Enchiridion biblicum*	HKAT	Handkommentar zum Alten Testament
ErJb	*Eranos Jahrbuch*		
EstBib	*Estudios biblicos*	HKNT	Handkommentar zum Neuen Testament
ETL	*Ephemerides theologicae lovanienses (EThL.)*	HNT	Handbuch zum Neuen Testament
ETR	*Etudes théologiques et religieuses (EThR)*	HNTC	Harper's NT Commentaries
EvK	*Evangelische Kommentar*	*HR*	*History of Religions*
EvQ	*The Evangelical Quarterly*	HSM	Harvard Semitic Monographs
EvT	*Evangelische Theologie (EvTh)*		
Exp	*The Expositor*	HTKNT	Herders theologischer Kommentar zum Neuen Testament (HThKNT)
ExpTim	*The Expository Times*		
FBBS	Facet Books, Biblical Series	*HTR*	*Harvard Theological Review*
FC	Fathers of the Church	HTS	Harvard Theological Studies
FRLANT	Forschungen zur Religion und Literatur des Alten und Neuen Testaments	*HUCA*	*Hebrew Union College Annual*
FTS	Frankfurter Theologischen Studien	*HUTh*	*Hermeneutische Untersuchungen zur Theologie*
		IB	*Interpreter's Bible*
GAG	W. von Soden, *Grundriss der akkadischen Grammatik*	*IBD*	*Illustrated Bible Dictionary,* ed. J. D. Douglas and N. Hillyer
GCS	Griechische christliche Schriftsteller	ICC	International Critical Commentary
GeistLeb	*Geist und Leben*		
GKB	Gesenius-Kautzsch-Bergsträsser, *Hebräische Grammatik*	*IDB*	G. A. Buttrick (ed.), *Interpreter's Dictionary of the Bible*

IDBSup	Supplementary volume to *IDB*	JQRMS	Jewish Quarterly Review Monograph Series
IEJ	*Israel Exploration Journal*	*JR*	*Journal of Religion*
Int	*Interpretation*	*JRAS*	*Journal of the Royal Asiatic Society*
ITQ	*Irish Theological Quarterly*		
		JRE	*Journal of Religious Ethics*
JA	*Journal asiatique*	*JRelS*	*Journal of Religious Studies*
JAAR	*Journal of the American Academy of Religion*	*JRH*	*Journal of Religious History*
		JRS	*Journal of Roman Studies*
JAC	Jahrbuch für Antike und Christentum	*JRT*	*Journal of Religious Thought*
		JSJ	*Journal for the Study of Judaism in the Persian, Hellenistic and Roman Period*
JAMA	*Journal of the American Medical Association*		
JANESCU	*Journal of the Ancient Near Eastern Society of Columbia University*	*JSNT*	*Journal for the Study of the New Testament*
		JSOT	*Journal for the Study of the Old Testament*
JAOS	*Journal of the American Oriental Society*	*JSS*	*Journal of Semitic Studies*
JAS	*Journal of Asian Studies*	*JSSR*	*Journal of the Scientific Study of Religion*
JB	A. Jones (ed.), *Jerusalem Bible*		
		JTC	*Journal for Theology and the Church*
JBC	R. E. Brown et al. (eds.), *The Jerome Biblical Commentary*	*JTS*	*Journal of Theological Studies*
		Judaica	*Judaica: Beiträge zum Verständnis . . .*
JBL	*Journal of Biblical Literature*		
JBR	*Journal of Bible and Religion*		
JCS	*Journal of Cuneiform Studies*		
JDS	Judean Desert Studies	*KAI*	H. Donner and W. Röllig, *Kanaanäische und aramäische Inschriften*
JEA	*Journal of Egyptian Archaeology*		
JEH	*Journal of Ecclesiastical History*	*KAT*	E. Sellin (ed.), Kommentar zum A. T.
JEOL	*Jaarbericht . . . ex oriente lux*	KB	L. Koehler and W. Baumgartner, *Lexicon in Veteris Testamenti libros*
JES	*Journal of Ecumenical Studies*	*KD*	*Kerygma und Dogma*
JETS	*Journal of the Evangelical Theological Society*	KJV	King James Version
		KIT	Kleine Texte
JHS	*Journal of Hellenic Studies*		
JIBS	*Journal of Indian and Buddhist Studies*	LCC	Library of Christian Classics
		LCL	Loeb Classical Library
JIPh	*Journal of Indian Philosophy*	LD	Lectio divina
JJS	*Journal of Jewish Studies*	*Leš*	*Lešonénu*
JMES	*Journal of Middle Eastern Studies*	*LLAVT*	E. Vogt, *Lexicon linguae aramaicae Veteris Testamenti*
JMS	*Journal of Mithraic Studies*	*LPGL*	G. W. H. Lampe, *Patristic Greek Lexicon*
JNES	*Journal of Near Eastern Studies*		
		LQ	*Lutheran Quarterly*
JPOS	*Journal of the Palestine Oriental Society*	*LR*	*Lutherische Rundschau*
		LSJ	Liddell-Scott-Jones, *Greek-English Lexicon*
JPSV	*Jewish Publication Society Version*	*LTK*	*Lexikon für Theologie und Kirche (LThK)*
JQR	*Jewish Quarterly Review*		

LUÅ	Lunds universitets årsskrift	NIDNTT	C. Brown (ed.), *The New International Dictionary of New Testament Theology*
LW	*Lutheran World*		
		NKZ	*Neue kirchliche Zeitschrift*
McCQ	*McCormick Quarterly*	NorTT	*Norsk Teologisk Tidsskrift (NTT)*
MDOG	Mitteilungen der deutschen Orient-Gesellschaft		
		NovT	*Novum Testamentum*
MeyerK	H. A. W. Meyer, Kritischexegetischer Kommentar über das Neue Testament	NovTSup	Novum Testamentum, Supplement
		New Docs	*New Documents Illustrating Early Christianity*, A Review of Greek Inscriptions etc. ed. G. H. R. Horsley. North Ryde, NSW, Australia
MGWJ	*Monatsschrift für Geschichte und Wissenschaft des Judentums*		
MM	J. H. Moulton and G. Milligan, *The Vocabulary of the Greek Testament*	NPNF	Nicene and Post-Nicene Fathers
		NRT	*La nouvelle revue théologique (NRTh)*
MNTC	Moffatt NT Commentary		
MPAIBL	*Mémoires présenté à l'Académie des inscriptions et belles-lettres*	NTA	*New Testament Abstracts*
		NTAbh	Neutestamentliche Abhandlungen
MPG	*Patrologia Graeca*, ed. J. P. Migne, 1844 ff.		
		NTD	Das Neue Testament Deutsch
MScRel	*Mélanges de science religieuse*		
MTZ	*Münchener theologische Zeitschrift (MThZ)*	NTF	Neutestamentliche For-schungen
		NTS	*New Testament Studies*
MUSJ	*Mélanges de l'université Saint-Joseph*	NTSR	The New Testament for Spiritual Reading
MVAG	Mitteilungen der vorder-asiatisch-ägyptischen Gesellschaft	NTTS	New Testament Tools and Studies
		Numen	*Numen: International Review for the History of Religious*
NAB	*New American Bible*		
NAG	*Nachrichten von der Akademie der Wissenschaften in Göttingen*	OCD	*Oxford Classical Dictionary*
		OIP	Oriental Institute Publi-cations
NCB	New Century Bible (new edit.)		
		OLP	Orientalia lovaniensia periodica
NCCHS	R. C. Fuller et al. (eds)., *New Catholic Commentary on Holy Scripture*	OLZ	*Orientalische Literaturzeitung*
		Or	*Orientalia (Rome)*
NCE	M. R. P. McGuire et al. (eds.), *New Catholic Encyclopedia*	OrAnt	*Oriens antiquus*
		OrChr	*Oriens christianus*
		OrSyr	*L'orient syrien*
NClB	New Clarendon Bible	ÖTKNT	Ökumenische Taschenbuch-Kommentar zum NT
NEB	*New English Bible*		
NedTTs	*Nederlands theologisch tijdschrift* (NedThTs)	OTM	Oxford Theological Monographs
Neot	*Neotestamentica*	OTS	Oudtestamentische Studiën
NFT	New Frontiers in Theology		
NHS	Nag Hammadi Studies	PAAJR	Proceedings of the American Academy of Jewish Research
NICNT	New International Commentary on the New Testament		
		PC	Proclamation Commentaries

PCB	M. Black and H. H. Rowley (eds.), *Peake's Commentary on the Bible*	*RevExp*	*Review and Expositor*
		RevistB	*Revista biblica*
		RevScRel	*Revue des sciences religieuses*
PEFQS	*Palestine Exploration Fund, Quarterly Statement*	*RevSém*	*Revue sémitique*
		RevThom	*Revue thomiste*
PEQ	*Palestine Exploration Quarterly*	RGG	*Religion in Geschichte und Gegenwart*
PG	*Patrologia graeca*, ed. J. P. Migne		
		RHE	*Revue d'histoire ecclésiastique*
PGM	K. Preisendanz (ed.), *Papyri graecae magicae*		
		RHPR	*Revue d'histoire et de philosophie religieuses (RHPhR)*
PhEW	*Philosophy East and West*		
PhRev	*Philosophical Review*		
PJ	*Palästina-Jahrbuch*	RHR	Revue de l'histoire des religions
PL	*Patrologia Latina*, J. P. Migne		
		RivB	*Rivista biblica*
PNTC	Pelican New Testament Commentaries	RNT	Regensburger Neues Testament
PO	Patrologia orientalis	RQ	*Revue de Qumrân*
PRU	*Le Palais royal d'Ugarit*	RR	*Review of Religion*
PSTJ	*Perkins (School of Theology) Journal*	RSO	*Rivista degli studi orientali*
		RSPT	*Revue des sciences philosophiques et théologiques (RSPhTh)*
PVTG	Pseudepigrapha Veteris Testamenti graece		
PW	Pauly-Wissowa, *Real-Encyklopädie der klassischen Altertums-wissenschaft*	RSR	*Recherches de science religieuse (RechSR)*
		RscPhTh	*Revue des Sciences Philosophiques et Théologiques*
PWSup	Supplement to PW		
		RSV	Revised Standard Version
QDAP	*Quarterly of the Department of Antiquities in Palestine*	RTL	*Revue théologique de Louvain (RThL)*
		RTP	*Revue de théologie et de philosophie (RThPh)*
RA	*Revue d'assyriologie et d'archéologie orientale*	RTR	*The Reformed Theological Review*
RAC	*Reallexikon für Antike und Christentum*	RUO	*Revue de l'université Ottawa*
RArch	*Revue archéologique*	RV	Revised Version
RB	*Revue biblique*		
RBén	*Revue bénédictine*	SacPag	*Sacra Pagina*
RCB	*Revista de cultura biblica*	SAH	*Sitzungsberichte der Heidelberger Akademie der Wissenschaften (phil.-hist. Klasse),* 1910 ff.
RE	*Realencyklopädie für protestantische Theologie und Kirche*		
RechBib	Recherches bibliques	SANT	Studien zum Alten und Neuen Testament
REg	*Revue d'égyptologie*		
REJ	*Revue des études juives*	SAQ	Sammlung ausgewählter kirchen- und dogmen-geschichtlicher Quellen-schriften
RelArts	Religion and the Arts		
RelS	*Religious Studies*		
RelSoc	*Religion and Society*		
RelSRev	*Religious Studies Review*	SE	Sources bibliques
RES	*Répertoire d'épigraphie sémitique*	SBFLA	*Studii biblici franciscani liber annuus*
RestQ	*Restoration Quarterly*	SBJ	*La sainte bible de Jérusalem*

SBLASP	Society of Biblical Literature Abstracts and Seminar Papers	SPAW	Sitzungsberichte der preussischen Akademie der Wissenschaften
SBLDS	SBL Dissertation Series	SPB	Studia postbiblica
SBLMasS	SBL Masoretic Studies	SR	Studies in Religion/Sciences religieuses
SBLMS	SBL Monograph Series		
SBLSBS	SBL Sources for Biblical Study	SSS	Semitic Study Series
		ST	Studia theologica (StTh)
SBLSCS	SBL Septuagint and Cognate Studies	STÅ	Svensk teologisk årsskrift
		StBibT	Studia Biblica et Theologica
SBLTT	SBL Texts and Translations	STDJ	Studies on the Texts of the Desert of Judah
SBM	Stuttgarter biblische Monographien	STK	Svensk teologisk kvartalskrift
SBS	Stuttgarter Bibelstudien	Str-B	[H. Strack and] P. Billerbeck, Kommentar zum Neuen Testament
SBT	Studies in Biblical Theology		
SC	Sources chrétiennes		
ScEs	Science et esprit	StudNeot	Studia neotestamentica, Studia
SCR	Studies in Comparative Religion	StudOr	Studia orientalia
Scr	Scripture	SUNT	Studien zur Umwelt des Neuen Testaments
ScrB	Scripture Bulletin		
SD	Studies and Documents	SVTP	Studia in Veteris Testamenti pseudepigrapha
SE	Studia Evangelica I, II, III (= TU 73 [1959], 87 [1964], 88 [1964], etc.) (StEv)	SWJT	Southwestern Journal of Theology
		SymBU	Symbolae biblicae upsalienses (SyBU)
SEÅ	Svensk exegetisk årsbok		
Sef	Sefarad		
SeinSend	Sein Sendung	TAPA	Transactions of the American Philological Association
Sem	Semitica		
SHAW	Sitzungsberichte heidelbergen Akademie der Wissenschaften	TBC	Torch Bible Commentaries
		TBI	Theologische Blätter (ThBl)
		TBü	Theologische Bücherei (ThBü)
SHT	Studies in Historical Theology	TBT	The Bible Today
SHVL	Skrifter Utgivna Av Kungl. Humanistika Vetenskapssamfundet i Lund	TD	Theology Digest
		TDNT	G. Kittel and G. Friedrich (eds.), Theological Dictionary of the New Testament
SJLA	Studies in Judaism in Late Antiquity	TextsS	Texts and Studies
		TF	Theologische Forschung (ThF)
SJT	Scottish Journal of Theology		
SMSR	Studi e materiali di storia delle religioni	TGI	Theologie und Glaube (ThGI)
SNT	Studien zum Neuen Testament (StNT)	Th	Theology
		ThA	Theologische Arbeiten
SNTSMS	Society for New Testament Studies Monograph Series	ThBer	Theologische Berichte
		THKNT	Theologischer Handkommentar zum Neuen Testament (ThHKNT)
SO	Symbolae osloenses		
SOTSMS	Society for Old Testament Study Monograph Series	TLZ	Theologische Literaturzeitung (ThLZ)
SPap	Studia papyrologica		

TNTC	Tyndale New Testament Commentary	*VoxEv*	*Vox Evangelica*
		VS	Verbum salutis
TP	*Theologie und Philosophie (ThPh)*	*VSpir*	*Vie spirituelle*
		VT	*Vetus Testamentum*
TPQ	*Theologisch-Praktische Quartalschrift*	VTSup	Vetus Testamentum, Supplements
TQ	*Theologische Quartalschrift (ThQ)*	WA	M. Luther, Kritische Gesamtausgabe
TRev	*Theologische Revue*		(= "Weimar" edition)
TRu	*Theologische Rundschau (ThR)*		
TS	*Theological Studies*	WBC	Word Biblical Commentary
TSK	*Theologische Studien und Kritiken (ThStK)*	WC	Westminster Commentary
		WDB	*Westminster Dictionary of the Bible*
TT	*Teologisk Tidsskrift*		
TTKi	*Tidsskrift for Teologi og Kirke*	*WHAB*	*Westminster Historical Atlas of the Bible*
TToday	*Theology Today*		
TTS	Trierer Theologische Studien	WMANT	Wissenschaftliche Monographien zum Alten und Neuen Testament
TTZ	*Trierer theologische Zeitschrift (TThZ)*	*WO*	*Die Welt des Orients*
TU	Texte und Untersuchungen	*WTJ*	*Westminster Theological Journal*
TynB	*Tyndale Bulletin*		
TWAT	G. J. Botterweck and H. Ringgren (eds.), *Theologisches Wörterbuch zum Alten Testament (ThWAT)*	WUNT	Wissenschaftliche Untersuchungen zum Neuen Testament
		WZKM	*Wiener Zeitschrift für die Kunde des Morgenlandes*
TWNT	G. Kittel and G. Friedrich (eds.), *Theologisches Wörterbuch zum Neuen Testament (ThWNT)*	*WZKSO*	*Wiener Zeitschrift für die Kunde Süd- und Ostasiens*
TZ	*Theologische Zeitschrift (ThZ)*		
		ZA	*Zeitschrift für Assyriologie*
UBSGNT	United Bible Societies Greek New Testament	*ZAW*	*Zeitschrift für die alttestamentliche Wissenschaft*
UF	*Ugaritische Forschungen*	*ZDMG*	*Zeitschrift der deutschen morgenländischen Gesellschaft*
UNT	Untersuchungen zum Neuen Testament		
US	*Una Sancta*	*ZDPV*	*Zeitschrift des deutschen Palästina-Vereins*
USQR	*Union Seminary Quarterly Review*	*ZEE*	*Zeitschrift für evangelische Ethik*
UT	C. H. Gordon, *Ugaritic Textbook*	*ZHT*	*Zeitschrift für historische Theologie (ZHTh)*
UUÅ	Uppsala universitetsårsskrift	*ZKG*	*Zeitschrift für Kirchengeschichte*
VC	*Vigiliae christianae*	*ZKNT*	*Zahn's Kommentar zum NT*
VCaro	*Verbum caro*	*ZKT*	*Zeitschrift für katholische Theologie (ZKTh)*
VD	*Verbum domini*		
VF	*Verkündigung und Forschung*	*ZMR*	*Zeitschrift für Missions-kunde und Religions-wissenschaft*
VKGNT	K. Aland (ed.), *Vollständige Konkordanz zum griechischen Neuen Testament*	*ZNW*	*Zeitschrift für die neutestamentliche Wissenschaft*

ZRGG	Zeitschrift für Religions-und Geistesgeschichte	ZTK	Zeitschrift für Theologie und Kirche (ZThK)
ZST	Zeitschrift für systematische Theologie (ZSTh)	ZWT	Zeitschrift für wissenschaftliche Theologie (ZWTh)

D. Abbreviations for Books of the Bible, the Apocrypha, and the Pseudepigrapha

OLD TESTAMENT

Gen	2 Chr	Dan
Exod	Ezra	Hos
Lev	Neh	Joel
Num	Esth	Amos
Deut	Job	Obad
Josh	Ps(Pss)	Jonah
Judg	Prov	Mic
Ruth	Eccl	Nah
1 Sam	Cant	Hab
2 Sam	Isa	Zeph
1 Kgs	Jer	Hag
2 Kgs	Lam	Zech
1 Chr	Ezek	Mal

NEW TESTAMENT

Matt	1 Tim
Mark	2 Tim
Luke	Titus
John	Philem
Acts	Heb
Rom	James
1 Cor	1 Peter
2 Cor	2 Peter
Gal	1 John
Eph	2 John
Phil	3 John
Col	Jude
1 Thess	Rev
2 Thess	

APOCRYPHA

1 Esd	1 Esdras	Ep Jer	Epistle of Jeremy
2 Esd	2 Esdras	S Th Ch	Song of the Three Children
Tob	Tobit		(or Young Men)
Jud	Judith	Sus	Susanna
Add Esth	Additions to Esther	Bel	Bel and the Dragon
Wisd Sol	Wisdom of Solomon	Pr Man	Prayer of Manasseh
Sir	Ecclesiasticus (Wisdom of Jesus the Son of Sirach)	1 Macc	1 Maccabees
		2 Macc	2 Maccabees
Bar	Baruch		

E. Abbreviations of the Names of Pseudepigraphical and Early Patristic Books

Adam and Eve	Books of Adam and Eve	T. 12 Patr.	Testaments of the Twelve Patriarchs
2–3 Apoc. Bar.	Syriac, Greek Apocalypse of Baruch	T. Benj.	Testament of Benjamin, etc.
Apoc. Abr.	Apocalypse of Abraham		
Apoc. Mos.	Apocalypse of Moses	T. Levi	Testament of Levi, etc.
Asc. Isa.	Ascension of Isaiah	Acts Pil.	Acts of Pilate
As. Mos.	Assumption of Moses	Apoc. Pet.	Apocalypse of Peter
Bib. Ant.	Ps.-Philo, Biblical Antiquities	Gos. Eb.	Gospel of the Ebionites
		Gos. Eg.	Gospel of the Egyptians
1–2–3 Enoch	Ethiopic, Slavonic, Hebrew Enoch	Gos. Heb.	Gospel of the Hebrews
		Gos. Naass.	Gospel of the Naassenes
Ep. Arist.	Epistle of Aristeas	Gos. Pet.	Gospel of Peter
Ep. Diognetus	Epistle to Diognetus	Gos. Thom.	Gospel of Thomas
Jub.	Jubilees	Prot. Jas.	Protevangelium of James
Mart. Isa.	Martyrdom of Isaiah		
Odes Sol.	Odes of Solomon	Barn.	Barnabas
Pss. Sol.	Psalms of Solomon	1–2 Clem.	1–2 Clement
Sib. Or.	Sibylline Oracles	Did.	Didache
T. Abr.	Testament of Abraham	Diogn.	Diognetus

Herm. Man.	Hermas, Mandates	*Smyrn.*	Ignatius, Letter to the
Sim.	Similitudes		Smyrnaeans
Vis.	Visions	*Trall.*	Ignatius, Letter to the
Ign. *Eph.*	Ignatius, Letter to the		Trallians
	Ephesians	*Mart Pol.*	Martyrdom of Polycarp
Magn.	Ignatius, Letter to the	Pol. *Phil.*	Polycarp to the
	Magnesians		Philippians
Phld.	Ignatius, Letter to the	*Adv. Haer.*	Irenaeus, Against All
	Philadelphians		Heresies
Pol.	Ignatius, Letter to	*De Praesc.*	
	Polycarp	*Haer.*	Tertullian, On the
Rom.	Ignatius, Letter to the		Proscribing of Heretics
	Romans		

F. Abbreviations of Names of Dead Sea Scrolls and Related Texts

CD	Cairo (Genizah text of the) Damascus (Document)	1QM	*Milhāmāh* (*War Scroll*)
		1QS	*Serek hayyahad* (*Rule of the Community, Manual of Discipline*)
Hev	Nahal Hever texts		
Mas	Masada texts	1QSa	Appendix A (*Rule of the Congregation*) to 1QS
Mird	Khirbet Mird texts		
Mur	Wadi Murabba'at texts	1QSb	Appendix B (*Blessings*) to 1QS
p	Pesher (commentary)		
Q	Qumran	3Q15	Copper Scroll from Qumran Cave 3
1Q, 2Q, 3Q, etc.	Numbered caves of Qumran, yielding written material; followed by abbreviation of biblical or apocryphal book		
		4QFlor	*Florilegium* (or *Eschatological Midrashim*) from Qumran Cave 4
		4QMess ar	Aramaic "Messianic" text from Qumran Cave 4
		4QPrNab	Prayer of Nabonidus from Qumran Cave 4
QL	Qumran literature		
1QapGen	*Genesis Apocryphon* of Qumran Cave 1	4QTestim	*Testimonia* text from Qumran Cave 4
1QH	*Hôdāyôt* (*Thanksgiving Hymns*) from Qumran Cave 1	4QTLevi	*Testament of Levi* from Qumran Cave 4
		4QPhyl	Phylacteries from Qumran Cave 4
1QIsa^{a,b}	First or second copy of Isaiah from Qumran Cave 1	11QMelch	*Melchizedek* text from Qumran Cave 11
1QpHab	*Pesher on Habakkuk* from Qumran Cave 1	11QtgJob	*Targum of Job* from Qumran Cave 11

G. Abbreviations of Targumic Material

Tg. Onq.	*Targum Onqelos*	*Tg. Ps.-J.*	*Targum Pseudo-Jonathan*
Tg. Neb.	*Targum of the Prophets*	*Tg. Yer. 1*	*Targum Yerušalmi I* *
Tg. Ket.	*Targum of the Writings*	*Tg. Yer. 11*	*Targum Yerušalmi II* *
Frg. Tg.	*Fragmentary Targum*	*Yem Tg.*	*Yemenite Targum*
Sam. Tg.	*Samaritan Targum*	*Tg. Esth I,*	*First or Second Targum of*
Tg. Isa.	*Targum of Isaiah*	*II*	*Esther*
Pal. Tgs.	*Palestinian Targums*		
Tg. Neof.	*Targum Neofiti I*	* optional title	

H. Abbreviations of Other Rabbinic Works

ʾAboṭ	ʾAbot de Rabbi Nathan	Pesiq. Rab Kah.	Pesiqta de Rab Kahana
ʾAg. Ber.	ʾAggadat Berešit	Pirqe R. El.	Pirqe Rabbi Eliezer
Bab.	Babylonian	Rab.	Rabbah (following
Bar.	Baraita		abbreviation for biblical
Der. Er. Rab.	Derek Ereṣ Rabba		book: Gen. Rab. [with
Der. Er. Zuṭ.	Derek Ereṣ Zuṭa		periods] = Genesis
Gem.	Gemara		Rabbah)
Kalla	Kalla	Sem.	Semaḥot
Mek.	Mekilta	Sipra	Sipra
Midr.	Midraš; cited with usual	Sipre	Sipre
	abbreviation for biblical	Sop.	Soperim
	book; but Midr. Qoh. =	S. ʿOlam Rab.	Seder ʿOlam Rabbah
	Midraš Qohelet	Talm.	Talmud
Pal.	Palestinian	Yal.	Yalquṭ
Pesiq. R.	Pesiqta Rabbati		

I. Abbreviations of Orders and Tractates in Mishnaic and Related Literature

ʾAboṭ	Pirqe ʾAbot	Nazir	Nazir
ʿArak.	ʿArakin	Ned.	Nedarim
ʿAbod. Zar.	ʿAboda Zara	Neg.	Nega ʿim
B. Bat.	Baba Batra	Nez.	Neziqin
Bek.	Bekorot	Nid.	Niddah
Ber.	Berakot	Ohol.	Oholot
Beṣa	Beṣa (= Yom Tob)	ʿOr.	ʿOrla
Bik.	Bikkurim	Para	Para
B. Meṣ.	Baba Meṣi ʿa	Pe ʾa	Pe ʾa
B. Qam.	Baba Qamma	Pesaḥ.	Pesaḥim
Dem.	Demai	Qinnim	Qinnim
ʿEd.	ʿEduyyot	Qidd.	Qiddušin
ʿErub.	ʿErubin	Qod.	Qodašin
Giṭ.	Giṭṭin	Roš. Haš.	Roš Haššana
Ḥag.	Ḥagiga	Sanh.	Sanhedrin
Ḥal.	Ḥalla	Šabb.	Šabbat
Hor.	Horayot	Šeb.	Šebi ʿit
Ḥul.	Ḥullin	Šebu.	Šebu ʿot
Kelim	Kelim	Šeqal.	Šeqalim
Ker.	Keritot	Soṭa	Soṭa
Ketub.	Ketubot	Sukk.	Sukka
Kil.	Kilʾayim	Ta ʿan.	Ta ʿanit
Ma ʿaś.	Ma ʿaśerot	Tamid	Tamid
Mak.	Makkot	Tem.	Temura
Makš.	Makširin (= Mašqin)	Ter.	Terumot
Meg.	Megilla	Ṭohar.	Ṭoharot
Me ʿil.	Me ʿila	T. Yom	Tebul Yom
Menaḥ.	Menaḥot	ʿUq.	ʿUqṣin
Mid.	Middot	Yad.	Yadayim
Miqw.	Miqwaʾot	Yebam.	Yebamot
Moʿed	Moʿed	Yoma	Yoma (= Kippurim)
Moʿed Qat.	Moʿed Qaṭan	Zabim	Zabim
Ma ʿas. S.	Ma ʿaśer Šeni	Zebaḥ	Zebaḥim
Našim	Našim	Zer.	Zera ʿim

J. Abbreviations of Nag Hammadi Tractates

Acts Pet. 12		Melch.	Melchizedek
Apost.	Acts of Peter and the Twelve Apostles	Norea	Thought of Norea
		On Bap. A	On Baptism A
Allogenes	Allogenes	On Bap. B	On Baptism B
Ap. Jas.	Apocryphon of James	On Bap. C	On Baptism C
Ap. John	Apocryphon of John	On Euch. A	On the Eucharist A
Apoc. Adam	Apocalypse of Adam	On Euch. B	On the Eucharist B
1 Apoc. Jas.	First Apocalypse of James	Orig. World	On the Origin of the World
2 Apoc. Jas.	Second Apocalypse of James	Paraph. Shem	Paraphrase of Shem
Apoc. Paul	Apocalypse of Paul	Pr. Paul	Prayer of the Apostle Paul
Apoc. Pet.	Apocalypse of Peter	Pr. Thanks	Prayer of Thanksgiving
Asclepius	Asclepius 21–29	Prot. Jas.	Protevangelium of James
Auth. Teach.	Authoritative Teaching	Sent. Sextus	Sentences of Sextus
Dial. Sav.	Dialogue of the Savior	Soph. Jes. Chr.	Sophia of Jesus Christ
Disc. 8–9	Discourse on the Eighth and Ninth	Steles Seth	Three Steles of Seth
		Teach. Silv.	Teachings of Silvanus
Ep. Pet. Phil.	Letter of Peter to Philip	Testim. Truth	Testimony of Truth
Eugnostos	Eugnostos the Blessed	Thom. Cont.	Book of Thomas the Contender
Exeg. Soul	Exegesis on the Soul		
Gos. Eg.	Gospel of the Egyptians	Thund.	Thunder, Perfect Mind
Gos. Phil.	Gospel of Philip	Treat. Res.	Treatise on Resurrection
Gos. Thom.	Gospel of Thomas	Treat. Seth	Second Treatise of the Great Seth
Gos. Truth	Gospel of Truth		
Great Pow.	Concept of our Great Power	Tri. Trac.	Triparite Tractate
Hyp. Arch.	Hypostasis of the Archons	Trim. Prot.	Trimorphic Protennoia
Hypsiph.	Hypsiphrone	Val. Exp.	A Valentinian Exposition
Interp. Know.	Interpretation of Knowledge	Zost.	Zostrianos
Marsanes	Marsanes		

Note: The text upon which this volume is based is that of the United Bible Societies' *Greek New Testament*, [3]1975. The textual notes and numbers used to indicate individual manuscripts are those found in the apparatus criticus of that work.

Commentary Bibliography

Barclay, W. *The Gospel of John.* 2 vols. Edinburgh: St. Andrew Press, 1956. **Barrett, C. K.** *The Gospel According to St. John.* London: SPCK, [2]1978. **Bauer, W.** *Das Johannesevangelium.* HNT 6. Tübingen: J. C. B. Mohr, 1925. **Becker, J.** *Das Evangelium des Johannes.* 2 vols. OTKNT 4/1, 2. Gütersloh: G. Mohn, 1979, 1981. **Bernard, J. H.** *The Gospel According to St. John.* 2 vols. Ed. A. H. McNeile. ICC. Edinburgh: T. & T. Clark, 1928. **Blank, J.** *The Gospel According to St. John,* vols. 2–3. NTSR 8–9. New York: Crossroad, 1981. **Boice, J. M.** *The Gospel of John.* Grand Rapids: Zondervan, 1979. **Boismard, M. E.,** and **Lamouille, A.** *L'évangile de Jean.* Paris: Cerf, 1977. **Bouyer, L.** *The Fourth Gospel.* Tr. P. Byrne. Westminster, MD: Newman Press, 1964. **Brown, R. E.** *The Gospel According to John.* 2 vols. AB. New York: Doubleday, 1966 and 1970. **Bruce, F. F.** *The Gospel of John.* Basingstoke: Pickering & Inglis, 1983. **Büchsel, F.** *Das Evangelium nach Johannes.* NTD 4. Göttingen: Vandenhoeck & Ruprecht, [5]1949. **Bultmann, R.** *The Gospel of John.* Oxford: Blackwell, 1971. **Dodd, C. H.** *The Interpretation of the Fourth Gospel.* Cambridge: CUP, 1953. 289–453. **Edwards, R. A.** *The Gospel According to St. John: Its Criticism and Interpretation.* London: J. Clarke, 1954. **Fenton, J. C.** *The Gospel According to John.* NClB. Oxford: Clarendon, 1970. **Findlay, J. A.** *The Fourth Gospel: An Expository Commentary.* London: Epworth, 1956. **Gnilka, J.** *Johannesevangelium.* Neue Echter Bibel. Würzburg: Echter Verlag, 1983. **Godet, F.** *Commentary on the Gospel of St. John.* 3 vols. Edinburgh: T. & T. Clark, 1899–1900. **Grundmann, W.** *Das Evangelium nach Johannes.* Berlin: Evangelische Verlagsanstalt, 1968. **Haenchen, E.** *Das Johannesevangelium.* Ed. U. Busse. Tübingen: Mohr, 1980. ET: *A Commentary on the Gospel of John.* 2 vols. Hermeneia. Philadelphia: Fortress, 1984. **Heitmüller, W.** *Das Evangelium des Johannes.* Die Schriften des NT 2. Göttingen: Vandenhoeck & Ruprecht, 1908. **Hendriksen, W.** *Exposition of the Gospel According to John.* 2 vols. Grand Rapids: Baker, 1954. **Hobbs, H. H.** *An Exposition of the Gospel of John.* Grand Rapids: Baker, 1968. **Hoskyns, E. C.** *The Fourth Gospel.* Ed. F. N. Davey. London: Faber & Faber, [2]1947. **Howard, W. F.** *The Gospel According to John.* IB 8. Nashville and New York: Abingdon, 1952. **Huckle, J.** and **P. Visokay.** *The Gospel According to St. John.* NTSR 1. New York: Crossroad, 1981. **Hull, W. E.** *John.* Broadman Bible Commentary 9. Nashville: Broadman, 1970. **Hunter, A. M.** *The Gospel According to John.* CBC. Cambridge: CUP, 1965. **Kysar, R.** *John.* ACNT. Minneapolis: Augsburg, 1986. **Lagrange, M. J.** *Évangile selon Saint Jean.* Paris: Gabalda, [8]1948. **Lightfoot, R. H.** *St. John's Gospel: A Commentary.* Oxford: OUP, 1956. **Lindars, B.** *The Gospel of John.* NCB. London: Oliphants, 1972. **Loisy, A.** *Le quatrième évangile.* Paris: Nourry, [2]1921. **MacGregor, G. H. C.** *The Gospel of John.* MNTC. London: Hodder & Stoughton, 1928. **MacRae, G. W.** *Invitation to John: A Commentary on the Gospel of John.* New York: Doubleday, 1978. **Marsh, J.** *The Gospel of St. John.* PNTC. Harmondsworth: Penguin Books, 1968. **Morris, L.** *The Gospel According to John.* NICNT. Grand Rapids: Eerdmans, 1971. **Newbigin, L.** *The Light Has Come: An Exposition of the Fourth Gospel.* Grand Rapids: Eerdmans, 1982. **Richardson, A.** *The Gospel According to Saint John.* TBC. London: SCM, 1959. **Sanders, J. N.,** and **B. A. Mastin.** *A Commentary on the Gospel According to St. John.* BNTC. London: A. & C. Black, 1968. **Schlatter, A.** *Das Evangelium nach Johannes.* Erläuterungen zum Neuen Testament, pt. 3. Stuttgart: Calwer, [4]1928. ———. *Der Evangelist Johannes: Wie er spricht, denkt und glaubt: Ein Kommen-*

tar. Stuttgart: Calwer, [2]1948. **Schnackenburg, R.** *The Gospel According to St. John.* 3 vols. HTCNT. London: Burns & Oates, 1968, 1980, 1982. **Schneider, J.** *Das Evangelium nach Johannes.* NTD 4. Göttingen: Vandenhoeck & Ruprecht, 1972. **Smith, D. M.** *John.* PC. Philadelphia: Fortress, 1976. **Strachan, R. H.** *The Fourth Gospel: Its Significance and Environment.* London: SCM, [3]1941. **Strathmann, H.** *Das Evangelium nach Johannes.* NTD 4. Göttingen: Vandenhoeck & Ruprecht, 1968. **Tasker, R. V. G.** *The Gospel According to St. John.* TNTC. London: Tyndale Press, 1960. **Temple, W.** *Readings in St. John's Gospel.* 2 vols. London: Macmillan, 1939, 1940. **Tenney, M. C.** *John: The Gospel of Belief.* Grand Rapids: Eerdmans, 948. **Wellhausen, J.** *Das Evangelium Johannes.* Berlin: Reimer, 1908. **Westcott, B.** *The Gospel According to St. John.* London: Murray, [2]1881. ———. *The Gospel According to St. John: The Greek Text with Introduction and Notes.* 2 vols. London: Murray, 1908. **Wikenhauser, A.** *Das Evangelium nach Johannes.* RNT. Regensburg: Pustet, [6]1961. **Zahn, T.** *Das Evangelium des Johannes ausgelegt.* Leipzig: Deichert, [5]1921.

General Bibliography

Abbott, E. A. *The Son of Man.* Cambridge: CUP, 1910. **Barrett, C. K.** "The Theological Vocabulary of the Fourth Gospel and the Gospel of Truth." *Current Issues in New Testament Interpretation.* FS O. A. Piper. Ed. W. Klassen & G. F. Snyder. London: SCM, 1962. 111–23. ———. "John and the Synoptic Gospels." *ExpTim* 85 (1974) 228–33. ———. *The Gospel of John and Judaism.* Tr. D. M. Smith. London: SPCK, 1975. **Blank, J.** *Krisis. Untersuchungen zur johanneischen Christologie und Eschatologie.* Freiburg: Lambertus, 1964. **Borgen, P.** *Bread from Heaven: An Exegetical Study of the Concept of Manna in the Gospel of John and the Writings of Philo.* NovTSup 10. Leiden: Brill, 1965. ———. "Some Jewish Exegetical Traditions in the Fourth Gospel." *L'Evangile de Jean: Sources, rédaction, théologie.* BETL 44, 1977. 243–58. **Bowker, J. W.** "The Origin and Purpose of St. John's Gospel." *NTS* 11 (1964–65) 398–408. ———. *The Targums and Rabbinic Literature.* Cambridge: CUP, 1969. **Bowman, J.** "Samaritan Studies." *BJRL* 40 (1958) 298–327. **Brown, R. E.** *The Community of the Beloved Disciple.* New York: Paulist Press, 1979. **Brownlee, W. H.** "Whence the Gospel according to John?" *John and Qumran.* Ed. J. H. Charlesworth. London: Chapman, 1972. 166–94. **Bruns, J. E.** *The Art and Thought of John.* New York: Herder & Herder, 1969. **Buchanan, G. W.** "The Samaritan Origin of the Gospel of John." *Religions in Antiquity.* Ed. J. Neusner. Leiden: Brill, 1968. 149–75. **Carson, D. A.** "Current Source Criticism of the Fourth Gospel: Some Methodological Questions." *JBL* 97 (1978) 411–29. ———. "Historical Tradition in the Fourth Gospel: After Dodd, What?" *Gospel Perspectives, Studies of History and Tradition in the Four Gospels, II.* Ed. R. T. France & D. Wenham. Sheffield: JSNT Press, 1981. 83–145. ———. "Understanding Misunderstandings in the Fourth Gospel." *TynB* 33 (1982) 59–91. **Charlesworth, J. H.** "A Critical Comparison of the Dualism in 1QS iii, 13–14, 26 and the 'Dualism' Contained in the Fourth Gospel." *NTS* 15 (1968–69) 389–418; also in *John and Qumran.* Ed. J. H. Charlesworth. London: Chapman, 1972. 107–36. **Colpe, C.** "Gnosis, I. Religionsgeschichtlich." *RGG* 3d. ed. Tübingen: Mohr, 1958. II, 1648–52. **Cribbs, F. L.** "A Reassessment of the Date of Origin and Destination of the Gospel of John." *JBL* 89 (1970) 38–55. **Cullmann, O.** *The Johannine Circle.* Tr. J. Bowden. London: SCM, 1976. **Culpepper, R. A.** *The Johannine School: An Evaluation of the Johannine School Hypothesis Based on an Investigation of the Nature of Ancient Schools.* SBLDS 26. Missoula: Scholars Press, 1975. ———. "The Pivot of John's Prologue." *NTS* 27 (1980) 1–31. ———. *Anatomy of the Fourth Gospel: A Study in Literary Design.* Foundations and Facets: New Testament. Ed. R. W. Funk. Philadelphia: Fortress, 1983. **Dahl, N. A.** "The Johannine Church and History." *Current Issues in New Testament Interpretation.* FS O. A. Piper. Ed. W. Klassen & G. F. Snyder. London: SCM 1962. 124–42. **Demke, C.** "Der sogenannte Logos Hymnus im johanneische Prolog." *ZNW* 58 (1967) 45–58. **Dodd, C. H.** *The Interpretation of the Fourth Gospel.* Cambridge: CUP, 1953. ———. "The Prophecy of Caiaphas: John xi. 47–53." *Neotestamentica et Patristica.* FS O. Cullmann. Ed. W. C. van Unnik & B. Reicke. Leiden: Brill, 1962. 134–43; also in *More New Testament Studies.* Manchester: Univ. Press, 1968. 58–68. ———. *Historical Tradition in the Fourth Gospel.* Cambridge: CUP, 1963. ———. "The Portrait of Jesus in John and in the Synoptics." *Christian History and Interpretation.* FS John Knox. Ed. W. R. Farmer, C. F. D. Moule, R. R. Niebuhr. Cambridge: CUP, 1967. 183–88. ———. "A l'arrière plan d'un dialogue johannique." *RHPR* (1957) 5–17. ———. "Behind a Johannine Dialogue." *More New Testament Studies.* 41–57. ———. "A Hidden Parable in the Fourth Gospel." *More New Testament Studies.* 30–40. **Filson, F. V.** "The Gospel of Life: A Study of the Gospel of John." *Current Issues in New Testament Interpretation.* FS O. A. Piper. 111–23. **Fortna, R. T.** *The Gospel of Signs: A Reconstruction of the Narrative Source underlying the Fourth Gospel.* SNTSMS 11. Cambridge: CUP, 1970. **Freed, E. D.** "Did John Write His Gospel Partly to Win Samaritan Converts?" *NovT* 12 (1970) 241–56. **Gardner-Smith, P.** *Saint John and the Synoptic Gospels.* Cambridge: CUP, 1938. **Green-Armytage, A. H. N.** *John Who Saw: A Layman's Essay on the Authorship of the Fourth Gospel.* London: Faber, 1952. **Haenchen, E.** "Aus der Literatur zum Johannesevangelium 1928–1956." *TRu* 23 (1955) 295–335. ————. "Gnosis und Neues Testament." *RGG* 3d. ed. Vol. 2. 1653–56. **Hare, D. R. A.** *The Theme of Jewish Persecution of Christians in the Gospel According to St Matthew.* SNTSMS 6. Cambridge: CUP, 1967. **Hartingsveld, L. van.** *Die Eschatologie des Johannesevangeliums.* Assen: van Gorcum, 1962. **Holland, H. S.** *The Fourth Gospel.* Ed. W. J. Richmond. London: Murray, 1923. **Hegermann, H.** "Er kam in sein Eigentum: Zur Bedeutung des Erdenwirkens Jesu im vierten Evangelium." *Der Ruf Jesu und die Antwort der Gemeinde.* FS J. Jeremias. Ed. E. Lohse, C. Burchard, B. Schaller. Göttingen: Vandenhoeck & Ruprecht, 1970. 112–31. **Howard, W. F.** *The Fourth Gospel in Recent Criticism and Interpretation.* London: Epworth, [3]1945; revised by C. K. Barrett, 1955. ————. *Christianity according to St. John.* London: Duckworth, 1943. **Hunter, A. M.** *According to John: A New Look at the Fourth Gospel.* London: SCM, 1968. **Jaubert, A.** *Approches de l'Evangile de Jean.* Paris: Seuil, 1976. ————. "The Calendar of Qumran and the Passion Narrative." *John and Qumran.* Ed. J. H. Charlesworth. 62–75. **Jeremias. J.** "The Revealing Word." *The Central Message of the New Testament.* London SCM, 1965. 71–90. **Jocz, J.** *The Jewish People and Jesus Christ.* London: SPCK, 1954. **Jonge, M. de,** ed. *L'évangile de Jean: Sources, rédaction, théologie.* BETL 44. Louvain: University Press, 1977. ————. *Jesus: Stranger from Heaven and Son of God.* Tr J. E. Steely. SBLSBS 2. Missoula: Scholars Press, 1977. **Käsemann, E.** "Ketzer und Zeuge, zum johanneischen Verfasserproblem." *ZThK* 48 (1951) 292–311. ————. *The Testament of Jesus: A Study of the Gospel of John in the Light of Chapter 17.* London: SCM, 1968. ————. "The Structure and Purpose of the Prologue to John's Gospel." *New Testament Questions of Today.* London: SCM, 1969. 138–67. **Kilpatrick, G. D.** "The Religious Background of the Fourth Gospel." *Studies in the Fourth Gospel.* Ed. F. L. Cross. London: Mowbray, 1957. 36–44. ————. "What John Tells Us about John." *Studies in John.* FS J. N. Sevenster. Leiden: Brill, 1970. 75–87. **Kragerud, A.** *Der Lieblingsjünger im Johannesevangelium.* Oslo: Universitäts Verlag, 1959. **Kümmel, W. G.** *Introduction to the New Testament.* Tr. H. C. Kee. London: SCM, 1975. ————. *Theology of the New Testament.* Tr. J. E. Steely. Nashville: Abingdon, 1973. **Kysar, R.** *The Fourth Evangelist and His Gospel: An Examination of Contemporary Scholarship.* Minneapolis: Augsburg, 1975. ————. *John, The Maverick Gospel.* Atlanta: Knox, 1976. ————. "The Source Analysis of the Fourth Gospel—a Growing Consensus?" *NovT* 15 (1973) 134–52. **Léon-Dufour, X.** "Le mystère du pain de vie (Jean VI)." *RSR* 46 (1958) 481–523. ————. "Towards a Symbolic Understanding of the Fourth Gospel." *NTS* 27 (1981) 439–56. **Lindars, B.** *Behind the Fourth Gospel.* London: SPCK, 1971. ————. "Traditions behind the Fourth Gospel." *L'Evangile de Jean, Sources, rédaction, théologie.* Ed. M. de Jonge. 107–24. **Lohmeyer, E.** *Die Offenbarung des Johannes.* HNT. Tübingen: Mohr, 1953. **Lorenzen, T** *Der Lieblingsjünger im Johannesevangelium.* Stuttgart: Katholisches Bibelwerk, 1971. **Macdonald, J.** *The Theology of the Samaritans.* London: SCM, 1964. **Macdonald, J.** & **Higgins, A. J. B.** "The Beginnings of Christianity according to the Samaritans: Introduction Text, Translation, Notes and Commentary." *NTS* 18 (1971) 54–80. **MacRae, G. W.** "The Ego-Proclamation in Gnostic Sources." *The Trial of Jesus.* FS C. F. D. Moule. Ed. E. Bammel. SBT, 2d ser. 13. London: SCM, 1970. 122–34. **Malatesta, E.** *St. John's Gospel: 1920–1963: A Cumulative and Classified Bibliography of Books and Periodical Literature on the Fourth Gospel.* AnBib 32. Rome: Pontifical Biblical Institute, 1967. **Manson, T. W.** "The Fourth Gospel." *BJRL* 30 (1946–47) 312–29. ————. *On Paul and John: Some Selected Theological*

Themes. Ed. M. Black. SBT 38. London: SCM 1963. **Martyn, J. L.** "Glimpses into the History of the Johannine Community." *L'Evangile de Jean, Sources, rédaction, théologie.* Ed. M. de Jonge. 149–75. ———. *History and Theology in the Fourth Gospel.* Nashville: Abingdon, [2]1979. **Meeks, W. A.** *The Prophet-King.* Leiden: Brill, 1967. ———. "The Man from Heaven in Johannine Sectarianism." *JBL* 91 (1972) 44–72. **Michaelis, W.** *Einleitung in das Neue Testament.* Bern: Berchtold Haller, 1954. **Miranda, J. P.** *Die Sendung Jesu im vierten Evangelium: Religions-und theologiegeschichtliche Untersuchungen zu den Sendungsformeln.* SBM 87. Stuttgart: Katholisches Bibelwerk, 1977. **Moffatt, J.** *An Introduction to the New Testament.*[3] Edinburgh: T. & T. Clark, 1918. **Moule, C. F. D.** "A Neglected Factor in the Interpretation of Johannine Eschatology." *Studies in John.* FS J. N. Sevenster. Leiden: Brill, 1970. ———. "The Individualism of the Fourth Gospel." *NovT* 5 (1962) 171–90. **Munck, J.** "The New Testament and Gnosticism." *Current Issues in New Testament Interpretation.* FS O. A. Piper. 224–38. **Mussner, F.** *The Historical Jesus in the Gospel of St. John.* Quaestiones Disputatae no. 19. London: Burns and Oates, 1967. **Neirynck, F.** *Jean et les Synoptiques: Examen critique de l'exégèse de M.-E. Boismard.* Leuven: 1979. **Nicol, W.** *The Semeia in the Fourth Gospel.* Leiden: Brill, 1972. **Odeberg, H.** *The Fourth Gospel Interpreted in Its Relation to Contemporaneous Religious Currents in Palestine and the Hellenistic-Oriental World.* Uppsala: 1929. **Pancaro, S.** "'People of God' in St. John's Gospel." *NTS* 16 (1969–70) 114–129. ———. "The Relationship of the Church to Israel in the Fourth Gospel." *NTS* 21 (1975) 396–405. **Pollard, T. E.** *Johannine Christology and the Early Church.* SNTSMS 13. Cambridge: CUP, 1970. **Porsch, F.** *Pneuma und Wort. Ein exegetischer Beitrag zur Pneumatologie des Johannesevangeliums.* Frankfurt: Knecht, 1974. **Robinson, J. A.** *The Historical Character of St. John's Gospel.* London: Longmans-Green, 1908. **Robinson, J. A. T.** *Twelve New Testament Studies.* SBT 34. London: SCM, 1962. ———. "The Relation of the Prologue to the Gospel of St. John." *NTS* 9 (1962–63) 120–29. ———. *Redating the New Testament.* London: SCM, 1976. ———. "The Place of the Fourth Gospel." *The Roads Converge.* Ed. P. Gardner-Smith. London: Arnold, 1963. 49–74. ———. *The Priority of John.* Ed. J. F. Coakley. London: SCM, 1985. **Roloff, J.** "Der johanneische 'Lieblingsjünger' und der Lehrer der Gerechtigkeit." *NTS* 15 (1968–69) 129–51. **Ruckstuhl, E.** *Die literarische Einheit des Johannesevangeliums.* Freiburg: Paulus, 1951. ———. *Chronology of the Last Supper.* New York: Desclée, 1965. **Sanders, J. N.** *The Fourth Gospel and the Early Church.* Cambridge: CUP, 1943. ———. "St. John on Patmos." *NTS* 9 (1962–63) 75–85. **Sanders, J. T.** *The New Testament Christological Hymns.* SNTSMS 15. Cambridge: CUP, 1971. **Schottroff, L.** *Der Glaubende und die feindliche Welt: Beobachtungen zum gnostischen Dualismus und seiner Bedeutung für Paulus und das Johannesevangelium.* WMANT. Neukirchen: Neukirchener Verlag, 1970. **Schweizer, E.** *Ego Eimi.* Göttingen: Vandenhoeck, 1939. ———. "Jesus der Zeuge Gottes. Zum Problem des Doketismus im Johannesevangelium." *Studies in John.* FS J. N. Sevenster. 161–86. **Scobie, C. H. H.** "The Origins and Development of Samaritan Christianity." *NTS* 19 (1972–73) 390–414. **Sevenster, G.** "Remarks on the Humanity of Jesus in the Gospel and Letters of John." *Studies in John.* FS J. N. Sevenster. Leiden: Brill, 1970. 185–93. **Smalley, S. S.** *John: Evangelist and Interpreter.* Exeter: Paternoster, 1978. **Smith, D. M., Jr.** *The Composition and Order of the Fourth Gospel: Bultmann's Literary Theory.* Yale Publications in Religion 10. Ed. D. Herne. New Haven: Yale University Press, 1965. ———. "The Sources of the Gospel of John: An Assessment of the Present State of the Problem." *NTS* 10 (1964) 336–51. **Solages, B. de.** *Jean et les Synoptiques.* Leiden: Brill, 1979. **Thyen, T.** "Aus der Literatur zum Johannesevangelium." *TRu* 39 (1975) 1–69, 222–52, 289–330; 42 (1977) 211–70; 44 (1979) 97–134. ———. "Entwicklungen innerhalb der johanneischer Theologie und Kirche im Spiegel von Joh 21 und der Lieblingsjünger Texte des Evangeliums." *L'Evangile de Jean: Sources, rédaction, théologie.* Ed. M. de Jonge. 259–99. **Teeple, H. M.** "Methodology in Source Analysis of the Fourth Gospel." *JBL* 81 (1962) 279–86. ———. *The Literary Origin of the Gospel of John.* Evanston:

Religion and Ethics Institute, 1974. **Thüsing, W.** *Die Erhöhung und Verherrlichung Jesu in Johannesevangelium.* NTAbh 21/1–2. Münster: Aschendorff, 1960. **Titus, E. L.** "The Identity of the Beloved Disciple." *JBL* 49 (1950) 323–28. **Torrey, C. C.** "The Aramaic Origin of the Fourth Gospel." *HTR* 16 (1923) 305–44. **Unnik, W. C. van.** "The Purpose of St. John's Gospel." *The Gospels Reconsidered.* Papers read at the Congress on the Four Gospels in 1957. Oxford: OUP, 1960. 167–96. **Wiles, M. F.** *The Spiritual Gospel: The Interpretation of the Fourth Gospel in the Early Church.* Cambridge: CUP, 1960. **Wilkens, W.** *Die Entstehungsgeschichte des vierten Evangeliums.* Zollikon: Evangelischer Verlag, 1958. **Wilson, R. McL.** *Gnosis and the New Testament.* Oxford: Blackwell, 1968. **Windisch, H.** *Johannes und die Synoptiker.* Leipzig: 1926. ———. *The Spirit-Paraclete in the Fourth Gospel.* Philadelphia: Fortress, 1968. **Yamauchi, E.** *Pre-Christian Gnosticism: A Survey of the Proposed Evidence.* London: Tyndale, 1973.

Introduction

I. THE ENIGMA OF THE FOURTH GOSPEL

The last of the four Gospels appears among the rest in a manner reminiscent of the appearance of Melchizedek to Abraham: "without father, without mother, without genealogy" (Heb 7:3). Everything we want to know about this book is uncertain, and everything about it that is apparently knowable is matter of dispute. The Gospel is anonymous; argument about its traditional ascription to the apostle John has almost exhausted itself. We cannot be sure where it was written, or when. We are uncertain of its antecedents, its sources, and its relationships. This includes its relations with the synoptic Gospels and with the religious movements of its day. Whereas many scholars have spoken of it as the gospel for the Greek world, others have seen it as firmly rooted in Judaism by upholding the good news of Christ among Christians from the Synagogue.

Issues of this kind admittedly are problems for the academic community, and they provide wonderful subjects for Ph.D. dissertations. But the question of how to square the presentation of Jesus in the Fourth Gospel with those provided by the other three is a very serious one, and it concerns every preacher of the gospel and every student of the life of Jesus. The elements of contrast are well known and do not require detailed description here. Let it suffice to mention the opening of the Gospel and its subsequent narrative matter and teaching (the passion narrative is significantly closer to those of the synoptics). The prologue to the Gospel provides a theological statement about the activity of the Logos in the universe that would magnificently open an epistle; set as it is at the beginning of the Gospel, it provides an interpretation of the story of Jesus before the story is told. This "story" unfolds almost entirely in Judea, chiefly in Jerusalem (Jesus operates in Galilee only in 2:1–12, 4:43–54, and chap. 6; in most of chap. 4 he is in Samaria). This complicates the picture of the ministry considerably. Whereas the synoptic account of the Galilean ministry of Jesus begins after John the Baptist is imprisoned, in the Fourth Gospel Jesus and the Baptist exercise concurrent ministries in Judea. The feasts in the temple of Jerusalem feature prominently in John; no less than three Passovers are mentioned, which entail a ministry of at least two years and are consonant with a longer one, in contrast to the synoptic account of the work of Jesus in Galilee, which could be comprised of less than a year. The teaching of Jesus in the synoptics is characterized by his parables and collections of sayings, nearly all of which are related to the theme of the kingdom of God. In John there is little parabolic teaching (it has to be uncovered by the scholars), but there are many discourses, with dialogues and monologues, largely relating to the overarching theme of the transcendent significance of the mission of Jesus, and all are stamped with the style of the Evangelist.

How to account for these phenomena constitutes the major problem of the Fourth Gospel. Earlier apologetic emphasized the *historical* nature of the synoptic presentations of Jesus, in contrast to the *theological* interpretation provided by John. That distinction can no longer be maintained. We now realize that the synoptic Evangelists are also theologians, and that each presents Jesus from the vantage point of his own theological interests and in the light of the needs of his community. It is particularly instructive to compare Mark with John. Early in his career C. H. Dodd pointed out that Mark and John have one basic feature in common: both concentrate on presenting Jesus in the kerygma, without diverting into the "didache" (instruction) which Matthew and Luke provide (*The Apostolic Preaching and Its Developments*,[2] [1944], 54–55). Kähler's famous definition of a gospel as a passion narrative with an introduction applies particularly well to Mark and John, although both seek to set forth the eschatological significance of the total messianic ministry of Jesus, and both view the whole as illuminated by the Resurrection (without the Easter illumination, a gospel would be inconceivable). There is, however, ground for affirming that the process of interpretation and clarification of the kerygma which Mark began in relation to his own church's situation was carried to its logical conclusion in the Fourth Gospel.

It was the merit of two English scholars earlier in this century, J. Armitage Robinson (*The Study of the Gospels*, 123–131; *The Historical Character of St. John's Gospel*, 14–18) and H. Scott Holland (*The Fourth Gospel*, 1–27) to emphasize how sorely this process of elucidation was needed. Holland was especially trenchant in his exposition of this theme. To him the enigma was attached less to the Fourth Gospel than to the three synoptics. He affirmed, "They raise problems for which they offer no solution. They provoke questions which they never attempt to answer. They leave off at a point where it is impossible to stop" (2). They make known, for example, Jesus' proclamation of the kingdom of God and the necessity of his death, but they offer little indication of the link between them. Nor is it entirely clear why Jesus is so emphatic that he will be seized by the Jewish leaders and handed over to death when he goes to Jerusalem; nor why, when he is there, he does not preach the kingdom of God. Rather he weeps over the city and declares the impending day of the Lord on the city and its temple and its people. On this Holland comments: "He does not go to offer his gospel to Jerusalem, to give it its chance of salvation. *All that is over.* The decision has been taken. Jerusalem has given its verdict. It was pronounced irrevocably against him. If he challenges them, he knows what it will be." When was the offer made and the verdict given? "The synoptics cannot tell. Apparently they do not know" (30–31). What the synoptics do not know or tell is a major theme of the Fourth Gospel, from its prologue to its end: the tragedy of the rejection of the Christ by his own people, in his own place. Jesus had ministered in Jerusalem time and again, and the result was a decision that "one man must die for the people that the whole nation should not perish" (John 11:50).

This is but one aspect of the wider context in which the story of Jesus is set in the Fourth Gospel. The real enigma, as Holland confessed, was not the incompleteness of the synoptic Evangelists nor the special interpretation in the Fourth Gospel, but Jesus himself. Who could hope to explain him adequately? What we find in the Fourth Gospel is a development of earlier lines of understanding which seem to be demanded by the traditions themselves. If Mark's Gospel be viewed as a passion narrative provided with an introduction, it may be said that John's is all passion narrative. And we do not forget that a passion narrative includes the resurrection of the crucified. Accordingly, in John the lifting up of the Son of Man on his cross reaches to the throne of heaven; and as the shadow of the cross marks the entire story of Jesus, so the glory of the Resurrection event suffuses every hour of his ministry, and even reaches back to the morning of creation. The eschatological glory for which creation was made was brought to actuality in the deeds and words of Jesus.

Now, while no synoptic evangelist unequivocally makes that claim, the teaching that each presents points in that direction. The tension between Jesus' proclamation of the presence of the kingdom and its revelation in the future was scarcely appreciated before the present century, and some of the most influential New Testament scholars even of our time have persisted in denying it. Schweitzer, Bultmann, and Conzelmann, for example, undeviatingly rejected the view that Jesus declared the presence of the kingdom in and through his ministry, despite the apparently plain meaning of such passages as Matt 11:5; 11:12; 12:28. Not even they, however, could mistake it in the Fourth Gospel; there the eschatological hope has become reality in the deeds and words of the Word made flesh. While the kingdom of God is hardly mentioned at all, every line of the Fourth Gospel is informed by it. But a "translation" has taken place. In accordance with the Evangelist's emphasis on the personal nature of faith and appropriation of salvation, the key term is *life*, or eternal life, and that, of course, denotes life in the kingdom of God. And as the resurrection glory of the Christ suffuses the whole Gospel, so the resurrection life which Christ bestows through his Spirit is a present reality for every believer.

The implications of such teaching for the understanding of him through whom eternal life is gained are evident, and they are the supreme theme of John's Gospel. These will occupy our attention, alike in the further introduction and in the exegesis of the text. The Church through the ages has believed that John's interpretation is not an imposition of a view foreign to the earlier traditions, but one that is implicit in them. The uncovering of the creedal statements and Christological hymns in the NT letters (e.g., Phil 2:6–11; Col 1:15–20), may be said to vindicate this conviction. Not infrequently the same admission is made from a quite different viewpoint. There are scholars who believe that the Christological titles accorded to Jesus in the synoptic Gospels reflect early church terminology rather than his own language, but they go on to affirm that the "implicit Christology" of Jesus was bound to produce such thoughts, for it went even beyond them. So, for example, Reginald H. Fuller writes: "An examination of Jesus' words . . . forces upon us the conclusion that underlying his word and work is an implicit Christology. *In Jesus as he understood himself, there is an immediate confrontation with 'God's presence and his very self,' offering judgment and salvation*" (*Foundations of New Testament* Christology, 106). To pursue the study of the Gospel that seeks to make that plain is one of the most rewarding exercises a Christian believer can undertake. And not only Christians. The instinct which leads Christians to hand on a copy of this Gospel to those who do not share the Christian faith is related to that of the dying believer who turns to it in his latest hours, and that of the Christian preacher who expounds it in order to deepen the experience and understanding of Christ among his or her congregation. The power of this Gospel's testimony to Christ is an experienced fact. Archbishop Frederick Temple attested this from his own experience; writing to his son, who was finding philosophic difficulties in his attempts to grasp the Christian faith, he stated: "I am obliged to confess that from seventeen to five and twenty I indulged largely in such speculations. But I felt all along like a swimmer who sees no shore before him after long swimming, and at last allows himself to be picked up by a ship that seems to be going his way. . . . My passing ship was St. John" (cited by J. A. Robinson, *Historical Character of St. John's Gospel*, 27). It would appear that son William was picked up by the same boat!

II. The Origin of the Fourth Gospel

There was a time when the subject indicated by the above title would have been considered superfluous; for the tradition was unquestioned that the Gospel was composed by the apostle John on the basis of his own memories, with no other assistance than the prompting of his friends and colleagues to set down in writing his recollections of Jesus. The question of authorship, however, is not so simple; the answer has to take into account evidence relating to other sources of information about Jesus and considerations that arise from the book itself. We shall therefore postpone discussion on the authorship of the Gospel till we have considered the wider questions of relationships to other writings and traditions about Jesus, the religious thought of the Evangelist's time, and the circumstances of the church or churches to which he belonged, which may have prompted and determined the nature of the writing of this Gospel.

1. The Relations of the Fourth Gospel with the Synoptic Gospels

It has been almost universally believed that our Gospel is the latest of the four canonical Gospels; since Mark has been generally dated shortly after the deaths of Peter and Paul, possibly during the Jewish war with Rome in the late sixties of the first Christian century, it was assumed that the Fourth Evangelist must have known it, and that he probably knew Matthew and Luke also. When the relationships of the synoptic Gospels were critically investigated and it was concluded that Matthew and Luke used Mark, it was natural to ask whether John did the same. The general consensus of critical opinion was that he did. C. K. Barrett states the case as follows: "The facts which have convinced most students of the synoptic problem that Mark (or a document closely resembling it) was used by Matthew and Luke are the occurrence in Matthew and Luke of Marcan episodes in the Marcan order, and the use by Matthew and Luke of Marcan language. Analogous facts may, to a smaller extent, be observed in regard to John" (*John*, 45). Barrett gives a lengthy list of such episodes, which convinced him that the Fourth Evangelist did, in fact, use Mark as a source for his own Gospel; it appears to him likely that John also used Luke's Gospel, though to a lesser degree.

This critical consensus was challenged by P. Gardner-Smith, in a little volume devoted to the issue (*Saint John and the Synoptic Gospels*). He drew attention to the neglect of two factors in this discussion: first, the existence of continuing oral tradition at the time when the Gospel was written, which renders the argument for John's dependence on the synoptics less compelling; second, the concentration of critics on points of agreement between the Fourth Gospel and the synoptics and their overlooking of the significance of the differences. Examples of the latter, discussed by Gardner-Smith, include the call of the disciples, which has no point of contact in John with the synoptic narratives; Peter's confession of Jesus as the Holy One of God (John 6:66–71; contrast Mark 8:27–29); the report of the trial of Jesus, which describes his appearance before Annas, but not before Caiaphas (John 18:13–24); the lengthy account of the trial by Pilate (18:28–19:16); and the Resurrection scenes, notably the bestowal of the Holy Spirit, set in the Easter narratives rather than at Pentecost (chap. 20). Gardner-Smith's point was that in these and many other narratives there can be no question of the Evangelist deliberately changing the representations of the synoptic writers for his own purposes; it is far more likely that he was reflecting independent sources of information.

The effect of this little work on the academic world was startling. It converted to his viewpoint Gardner-Smith's more famous colleague at Jesus College, Cambridge, C. H. Dodd, and a good many others too. Robert Kysar, writing in 1975, speaks of "the near demise of the proposition that the Fourth Evangelist was dependent upon one or more synoptic gospels" in the decade prior to his own writing (*The Fourth Evangelist and His Gospel*, 45). This conviction of John's independence of the synoptics is reflected in most recent commentaries, e.g., those of R. Bultmann, R. E. Brown, R. Schnackenburg, L. Morris, J. N. Sanders & B. A. Mastin, B. Lindars. The most notable treatment of the issue is that of C. H. Dodd (in *Historical Tradition in the Fourth Gospel*). As the title indicates, Dodd was especially concerned to investigate the historicity of the Fourth Gospel, but for him this was bound up with the nature of the traditions that lay behind it. He had long been convinced that the period of oral tradition did not subside when written gospels began to appear, but rather that the oral tradition continued to be an important factor through and beyond the New Testament period. The question he raised was whether we can recover a tradition lying behind the Fourth Gospel which is distinctive and independent of other traditions known to us. To this end he examined the Gospel meticulously, beginning with the passion narrative and working backwards to the beginning of the Gospel. His conclusion at the end of the investigation was: "Behind the fourth gospel lies an ancient tradition independent of the other gospels, and meriting serious consideration as a contribution to our knowledge of the historical facts concerning Jesus Christ" (423).

Great as Dodd's contribution is, the discussion of the issue has by no means abated. Since the appearance of Kysar's review of Johannine studies, the "near demise" of the view that John was dependent upon the synoptics has been followed by a resurrection. Barrett, in the second edition of his commentary, has reaffirmed and elaborated his earlier convictions. He urges that there is repeated evidence in the Gospel that the Evangelist knew traditional material that was either Mark, or something much like Mark, and he adds: "Anyone who after an interval of nineteen centuries feels himself in a position to distinguish nicely between 'Mark' and 'something much like Mark' is at liberty to do so. The simpler hypothesis, which does not involve the postulation of otherwise unknown entities, is not without attractiveness" (45). The Belgian scholar F. Neirynck energetically pursues the advocacy of John's dependence on all three synoptic Gospels (*Jean et les Synoptiques*).

What may be described as a mediating view has been advocated by some recent writers. Sanders and Mastin agreed that the evidence does not compel us to believe that Mark is a source for John, but they suggested that John must have known Mark, and may have had it in mind as he wrote his own Gospel. "But knowing Mark, and using it as a source, are two different things" (10). De Solages has elaborated that view in a full scale monograph, urging that while John knew the synoptics he did not use them as sources; he did, however, take them into account, and in his writings he confirmed them, completed them, illuminated them, and rectified them (*Jean et les Synoptiques*). Similarly D. Moody Smith, in a review of the problem, admitted that while it appeared to him simpler to assume that John did not know the synoptics, he was beginning to be able to conceive a scenario in which John knew, or knew of the synoptics, and yet still could produce his very different Gospel. This "scenario" was one in which an independent tradition of the miracle stories circulated in John's community along with a collection of sayings of Jesus, which had become greatly modified through use in preaching and in controversies. Meanwhile the Gospels of Mark, Luke, and Matthew (in that order) became known to the members of John's church, but they had not yet been fully absorbed by them. Since John's concerns were different from those of the synoptics, his Gospel does not reflect the others in a manner comparable to the use of Mark by Matthew and Luke. Nevertheless while the Fourth Evangelist did not use any of the synoptics as his sources, neither did his Gospel take shape in isolation from them.

If it be asked what difference this view makes for understanding the Gospel over against the postulate of John's independence of the synoptics, Smith answers frankly, "Not much"! But he adds:

> In neither case does one simply assume that the base-line or material which John employs and from which he takes his departure is the synoptics as such. In either case, the direction or development of his gospel is taken to be relatively independent of the synoptics. The Johannine gospel would then reflect a distinct set of circumstances and perspective on them. In neither case is there warrant for treating any divergence from the synoptics as *prima facie* a deliberate and intentional departure. On the other hand, in neither case will it be possible to ignore the content of the synoptics in interpreting John, particularly in the parallel pericopes. This means in effect that on either side the question of the mode of the relationship should remain open in principle. (*John and the Synoptics*, 443–44)

This may be as wise a solution as any in the present stage of the debate.

2. The Literary Sources of the Fourth Gospel

The search for sources behind the Fourth Gospel has been intensified in recent years as belief in the independence of the Gospel in relation to the synoptics has increased.

Earlier attempts to solve the problem concentrated on the endeavor to unearth a foundation document within the Gospel which could have been extended by successive writers (for an account of such attempts see Howard, *Fourth Gospel*, 74–83, 258–63). These efforts found their culmination in Bultmann's analysis of the literary strata of the Gospel. He was encouraged in this undertaking by the structure of the prologue (1:1–18), which appeared to be based on a poetic source in vv 1–5, 9–12, interrupted by the prose section of vv 6–8. He postulated that the prologue originally introduced a source of *revelation-discourses*, composed in poetic style in Aramaic, which came from a group of adherents of John the Baptist. Their ultimate origin was a form of Gnosticism such as that adopted by the Baptist sect. Along with the revelation-discourses was a *signs source*; this was a propaganda document drawn up by former disciples of the Baptist, now disciples of Jesus, through whom the Evangelist was converted. It had a naive understanding of miracles, which attested Jesus as a *theios aner*, a divine-man of the kind known in the Hellenistic world; this concept the Evangelist rejected, for he viewed the signs as symbolic representations of Jesus as the Revealer, and the signs as calling for decision regarding Jesus. A *passion source*, independent of the passion narratives of the synoptic Gospels, was further distinguished, and other lesser sources and traditions, which included such narratives as the temple cleansing, the entry into Jerusalem, and the footwashing. Finally Bultmann proposed a main redactor of the Gospel, termed by him *the Ecclesiastical Redactor*, since his modifications of and additions to the text were especially characterized by ecclesiastical interests; chief among these additions were sacramental interpolations (e.g., ἐξ ὕδατος καί in 3:5; 6:51b–58; 19:34b–35), others reflecting apocalyptic eschatology (e.g. 5:28–29, and references to resurrection in the last day in 6:39, 40, 44, 54), and certain representations of the Beloved Disciple, whom the Evangelist had created as an ideal figure, but who was regarded as an historical person by the redactor (the references to him in 19:35 and the whole of chap. 21 were viewed as composed by the redactor). Not the least achievement of the redactor, in Bultmann's view, was his rearrangement of the Gospel, which is to be regarded as a *dis*arrangement, and which requires fresh sorting out by the student of the Gospel. (A brief summary of these views is provided by W. Schmithals in the English version of Bultmann's commentary on the Gospel, 6–7, 10–11; they are fully described and evaluated by D. M. Smith in his *Composition and Order of the Fourth Gospel.*)

All subsequent discussions of the sources of the Fourth Gospel have to relate to Bultmann's proposals, whether positively or negatively. J. Becker, a pupil of Bultmann, is one of the comparatively few scholars who have adopted, with little modification, Bultmann's view of the sources (*NTS* 16, 130–48), and H. M. Teeple expounded a theory of the sources akin to that of Bultmann (*Literary Origin of the Gospel of John*). The majority of scholars have been skeptical of the proposed Revelation-Discourses source. It is regarded as misleading to make the prologue a starting point for such source criticism, since it is a unique composition in relation to the Gospel, and in all probability is based on a hymn which has been enlarged for the purpose of introducing the Gospel; nothing comparable to it can be found in the rest of the work. The idea that the foundation of the Gospel's teaching is a pagan Gnostic work is a difficult notion to accept in the light of the actual teaching of the Gospel. Bultmann viewed the same document as lying behind 1 John; Käsemann pointed out that that suggestion involves the incredible notion that the doctrine of justification by faith of one who is at once righteous and a sinner originated in pagan Gnosis (*ZTK* 48 [1951] 306 n. 2; see Smith's discussion, 57–63).

It is especially in the area of language and style that the debate on the sources has been prolonged. Before Bultmann's commentary was published, E. Schweizer tested partition theories of earlier critics in the light of the characteristics of speech and style in the Johannine literature. He found that these characteristics are scattered throughout the proposed sources and redactional elements of the Gospel. Schweizer did not conclude on that account that the Evangelist could not have used sources, but he affirmed that any such sources could not be recovered on stylistic grounds (*Ego Eimi*, 82–112). E. Ruckstuhl followed up Schweizer's work in an examination of Bultmann's source analysis. He maintained that whereas Bultmann had established stylistic criteria for the Evangelist, those of his alleged sources do not adequately distinguish themselves from those of the Evangelist. He took Schweizer's list of thirty-three characteristics of the Evangelist's style and increased their number to fifty; applying these to Bultmann's sources he again found them distributed through the sources, and drew the conclusion that all such theories were untenable (*Einheit des Joh-Ev.*, 203–19).

While Bultmann's attempt to disentangle a Revelation-Discourse source suffered a battering from the critics, his postulate of a Signs-Source has fared better. R. T. Fortna and W. Nichol independently sought to set the existence of such a source on a firm foundation. Fortna laid great stress on the "aporiai" of the Gospel, i.e., apparent points of disagreement with other elements of the context (see, e.g., 3:26 and 4:1–2); these he saw as the key to the sources, on the ground that they betrayed different hands in the writing of the Gospel. He claimed that Ruckstuhl's stylistic tests actually support the existence of a signs-source, since they are less frequent in that stratum than elsewhere in the Gospel. He further proposed to extend the source to include the ministry of John the Baptist and the call of the first disciples, and also the passion narrative, thereby producing a complete gospel, a kind of Proto-John. This early form of the Gospel had affinity with the synoptic Gospels; in it Jesus was presented as a "divine-man," working miracles of the order of Elijah and Elisha. The purpose of the source was to present Jesus as the Messiah (see *The Gospel of Signs*, esp. 204–32). By contrast Nichol rejected the idea that the signs-source included the Passion, as also that the Hellenistic notion of the "divine-man" was applied in it to Jesus; in his view the fundamental typology of the source was Moses and the salvation from Egypt; it was as a second Moses, working signs as Moses did in the achievement of a second exodus, that the source presented the Messiah Jesus (*Semeia in the Fourth Gospel*, 48–91).

Not a few scholars view this proposal of a signs-source with a sympathetic eye, and some advocate it with enthusiasm. It has the advantage of explaining the tension in the Gospel between the emphasis on signs as revelations of the messiahship of Jesus (e.g., 2:11) and the apparent devaluation of faith in Jesus based on signs (e.g., 2:23–25); the statement of purpose in 20:30–31 is then understood as relating to the signs document, and not to the Gospel as a whole. Nevertheless, resistance to the hypothesis remains widespread, especially on the European scene. Ruckstuhl examined in detail Fortna's endeavor to utilize his stylistic data to establish the signs-source, and he concluded that the attempt gives "a strong impression of a poor result." He maintained: "Almost all of the usages are distributed throughout both strata of the gospel, or are confined to the source because of subject matter. In the latter case they are characteristic of the source but do not point to an author different from the Evangelist" ("Johannine Language and Style" *L'évangile de Jean*, ed. M. de Jonge [Louvain: University Press, 1977] 141). Other scholars are impressed with the way some at least of the signs and discourses are woven together; they are so closely related they can hardly be viewed as two independent sources. In this connection it is noteworthy that along with the term "sign" the term "work" occurs in a related sense; but the latter embraces not only the *miraculous* deeds of Jesus, but the entire ministry of deed and word which God had commissioned him to achieve (cf. 4:34; 9:4; 14:10; 17:4); such "works" extend to power to raise the dead and to exercise judgment over mankind (5:17, 19–23). In harmony with this we find some discourses introduced by significant miraculous acts (so chaps. 5, 6, 9, 11), whereas the discourse of chap. 12 is introduced by two significant non-miraculous acts (the Anointing of Jesus and the Entry into Jerusalem); the discourses of chaps. 3–4 are introduced by one significant miracle (the Changing of Water into Wine) together with one significant non-miraculous event (the Cleansing of the Temple); the lengthy discourse of chaps. 7–8 to no small degree is conditioned by the presence of Jesus at the Feast of Tabernacles and its significant *rituals*, akin to which is the discourse given in chap. 10 at the Feast of Dedication. All this raises the question whether the setting of the ministry of Jesus under the rubric of "signs" (12:37 and 20:30) may have a more extensive significance than that commonly attributed to it, and whether therefore the separation from the rest of the Gospel of a source consisting of miracles only accords with the mind of the Evangelist and with the structure of his Gospel.

The conjecture of an independent source for the passion narrative in our Gospel does not raise the same objections as the notions of Revelation-Discourse and a signs-source, since it has long been believed that accounts of the Passion must have been compiled from a very early time in the Church's life. Moreover, the broad outline of John's passion narrative is remarkably close to that of the synoptics. There are, of course, marked divergences from the synoptic accounts, notably the date of the Last Supper and the death of Jesus, and their relation to the Passover; the absence of mention of the eucharistic actions in the meal is striking, yet there is a lengthy elaboration of conversations within it, introduced by the description of the footwashing; the trial narrative, wherein the brief appearance before Annas (not Caiaphas!) serves merely to formulate a charge to Pilate; the trial before Pilate is recounted in detail and centers on the kingship of Jesus, reflecting the charge that Jesus claimed to be king of the Jews; the account of the crucifixion has various independent elements, above all the piercing of his side (19:31–37); and the Resurrection narratives have contacts with the synoptics, yet appear to reflect independent traditions (above all in the bestowal of the Spirit in 20:22).

The suggestion that an "Ecclesiastical Redactor" has extensively edited the Evangelist's work is a more debatable matter. The sacramental element of the Gospel cannot be eliminated by the excision of a phrase from John 3:5 ("of water and") and of 6:51b–58. The interest in baptism is pervasive in the first three chapters of the Gospel, whatever may be thought about the rest of the book; and there is strong reason for seeing in the entire material of 6:31–58 reflections of a Jewish exegetical tradition, which continues without a break into vv 51b–58 (see P. Borgen, *Bread from Heaven,* 20–26, 33–35, 41–42). The excision of "apocalyptic" elements from the Gospel so as to leave a purely realized eschatology is equally questionable, since the tension between "realized" and "futurist" eschatology applies to all the elements of eschatological hope in the Gospel. The belief that an editor has been at work on the text of the Gospel is not an unreasonable one, and is accepted by most students of the Gospel in recent years. It is not plausible, however, to ascribe to such an individual major changes which *seriously* modify the teaching of the Gospel and its presentation of the ministry of Jesus, least of all when the supposed modifications create an inconsistent picture of the instruction and labors of Jesus.

It is the conviction of not a few that we do well to think in terms of *traditions* available to the Evangelist rather than literary *sources.* Barrett summarily affirmed that, beyond the Evangelist's use of the synoptics, "all source criticism of John is guesswork" (17). A comparison of attempts to delineate the supposed sources tends to bear out that judgment. It led D. A. Carson to appeal for a "probing agnosticism regarding sources of the Fourth Gospel" (*JBL* [97] 428). To surmise the existence of *traditions* about Jesus, both oral and written, can hardly be viewed as guesswork in light of the synoptic Gospels and the epistles of the New Testament; it is their precise identification and delimitation in given texts that involves speculation, especially when supported by tenuous proof. By contrast, Dodd's work on the *Historical Traditions of the Fourth Gospel* is an impressive and sober attempt to trace traditions behind the Gospel. The existence of distinctive Johannine traditions is increasingly accepted by contemporary scholars. Some, indeed, stress the distinctiveness to the point of viewing the community from which it came as an isolated conventicle, critical of the rest of the Church. Cullmann's suggestion is more justifiable, that in this Gospel there are reflected traditions common to all branches of Christianity, together with a separate tradition that was handed on in the circle known to the Evangelist (*The Johannine Circle,* 7).

A helpful approach to the composition of the Gospel, having a great measure of plausibility, postulates that the organizing of the traditions to form the Gospel took place through preaching, especially the preaching of the

Evangelist. The suggestion appears to have occurred spontaneously to a number of students of the Gospel. The thought came to me when, as a student, I listened to Dodd expound his understanding of the structure of John's "Book of Signs" (chaps. 2–12). He believed that each episode of this part of the Gospel consists of sign(s) plus discourse and that *each presents the Gospel in its wholeness,* namely, Christ manifested, crucified, risen, exalted, and communicating life (see Dodd, *Interpretation,* 383–86). To me this was as scales falling from the eyes, for this arrangement of the evangelic material was in all probability due to the Evangelist's use of it in his preaching, as he presented the episodes of the ministry in the light of their end in the redemptive death and resurrection of the Lord. No doubt the synoptic Gospels reflect a like process, but the Fourth Gospel is supremely the preacher's gospel—every episode in the book shouts out to be preached—and it is so because it is the product of a highly effective preacher's proclamation of Christ in the Gospel. R. H. Strachan, who labored through most of his years to elucidate this Gospel, was convinced that the Upper Room discourses were formed from meditations uttered by the Evangelist at celebrations of the Lord's Supper (*The Fourth Gospel,* 274–77). Comparable views regarding preaching and the Gospel have been expressed by various critics and exegetes in recent years, including Michaelis (*Einleitung,* 111), Nichol (*Semeia,* 5), Barrett (26), Brown (1:xxxiv–v), Martyn ("History of the Johannine Community," 151), and notably Lindars (*Behind the Fourth Gospel,* 27–42, and "Traditions Behind the Fourth Gospel," 107–24).

Brown's view of the evolution of the Gospel is of particular interest in the context of our discussion. He posits the prior existence of an independent tradition of the words and works of Jesus; this was developed into Johannine patterns through preaching and teaching over several decades; the material at length was organized by the Evangelist into a gospel; subsequently the Gospel was revised by the Evangelist himself to meet different needs of the churches (e.g., the excommunication of Christians from the synagogues, reflected in 9:22–23); a final edition was made by a redactor, who incorporated all available Johannine material that had not been previously used in the Gospel (1:xxxiv–ix). The significant features of this reconstruction is the suggestion that the chief redactor of the Gospel was none other than the Evangelist, and that the final redactor incorporated authentic Johannine material (including 6:51b–58). The difficulty about it is how confident we can be that the Evangelist's additions to the Gospel took place in a specific subsequent revision, rather than that they represent reflections at various stages during which the Gospel was composed. It illustrates the inherent difficulties in all reconstructions of the process of composition of the Gospel.

Related to the discussion of the sources of the Gospel is the problem of the original order of its material. Many students of our Gospel have been struck by the unexpectedness of certain sequences in its narrative; it has led them to conclude that the Gospel at an early date became disarranged, possibly through leaves of the manuscript becoming displaced before being sewn together. The most comprehensive attempt to put the elements of the Gospel into "logical" order is that of Bultmann, whose rearrangement includes not merely page lengths of text but sentences and short paragraphs. The "disorder" which compels such dealing, in his view, was the work of the ecclesiastical redactor; Bultmann attempted to redress the wrong, and his commentary on the Gospel is an exposition of the Gospel according to his rearrangement of the text (the fresh ordering of the segments of the Gospel is indicated on p. xiii of his commentary; the justification for each transposition is given in the introduction to each section). Few have followed Bultmann in his elaborate reconstruction of the Gospel, but many scholars have considered that some reordering of the text is necessary. While their suggestions are often plausible, the fact remains that the text as it stands appears to have reason for its order at all times. This may be illustrated from the most popular of all suggested changes of order in the Gospel, namely the inversion of chaps. 5 and 6. In 4:54 Jesus is located in Galilee; in 5:1 he goes up to Jerusalem, and in 6:1 he crosses the sea of Galilee, though no mention is made of his leaving Jerusalem; in 7:1 it is said that Jesus went about in Galilee, because the Jews in Judea were seeking to kill him. The narrative would be eased considerably if chap. 6 were placed before chap. 5; we would then read of Jesus in Galilee (4:54), who crosses the sea (6:1), then goes up to Jerusalem (5:1), and departs again to Galilee for safety (7:1). Now while that makes admirable sense as a narrative, it has problematic effects on the teaching material in the text; for the discourse of 5:10–29 most plausibly develops the significance of both the healing of the officer's son (4:46–54) and the healing of the paralytic beside the pool (5:1–9); moreover, Moody Smith considers that the discussion of the works of the Father and the Son in chap. 5 forms the proper background for the interpretation of 6:28–29 (*Composition*, 130). From the viewpoint of *content* the present order of text is comprehensible, and it would seem best to leave it as it is. Similar observations can be made about most of the transpositions of text suggested by advocates for reordering. There are, however, some features of the text which lend plausibility to a suggestion, frequently put forward, that the Gospel was left by the Evangelist in an unfinished state. The outstanding example of such a possibility is the Upper Room discourses, with their repetitions of thought in chaps. 14–16, and above all the conclusion in 14:25–31 (on this see Moody Smith, 239). Where this possibility appears in the text we shall recall it in our exposition, but on the whole the Gospel is a remarkably unified and well integrated document. It is well to bear in mind Dodd's judgment when commencing his exposition of the thought of the Fourth Gospel:

> I conceived it to be the duty of an interpreter at least to see what can be done with the document as it has come down to us before attempting to improve upon it. . . . If the attempt to discover any intelligible thread of argument should fail, then we may be compelled to confess that we do not know how the work was originally intended to run. If on the other hand it should appear that the structure of the gospel as we have it has been shaped in most of its details by the ideas which seem to dominate the author's thought, then it would appear not improbable that we have his work before us substantially in the form which he designed. (*Interpretation*, 290)

That procedure we ourselves shall follow in the commentary on the text.

3. THE TRADITION BEHIND THE FOURTH GOSPEL AND ITS DEVELOPMENT

It is evident that the fundamental tradition of the Fourth Gospel is the kerygma of *the Church,* not simply that of the Johannine community (or communities). This is apparent not only from John 3:16, but from the relationship between John and the synoptic Gospels and the records of the kerygma recoverable from the *Acts* and *Epistles* (see C. H. Dodd, *The Apostolic Preaching and its Developments*). Yet 3:16 itself, in the context of the Gospel, has overtones which go beyond the primitive kerygma of the churches, and it is these features of the Fourth Gospel which it is our task to investigate.

Earlier in this century it was common to view the Fourth Gospel as the gospel for the Greeks, and so emanating from a center of contemporary Hellenistic culture. By contrast, a strong movement today seeks to relate the Gospel with Judaism and Jewish communities; the work is viewed as the product of an isolated Jewish-Christian church, oppressed by hostile policies of the Jewish community of which it formed part. The experiences of this community are believed to have strongly influenced the presentation of Jesus in the Gospel. This view is most plausibly expounded in the writings of J. L. Martyn (especially *History and Theology in the Fourth Gospel* and "Glimpses into the History of the Johannine Community") and of W. A. Meeks (*The Prophet-King* and "The Man from Heaven in Johannine Sectarianism"). In the latter article Meeks calls attention to the social significance of the Jewish myths in the Johannine church; the Gospel, he maintains, was written to provide reinforcement for the community's social identity in its isolation from society; this is observable in the descent-ascent concept, which is applied exclusively to Jesus as the Stranger: "Wherever it occurs, it is in contexts where the inability of men of this world to understand and accept Jesus is in mind" (58). So also "above" and "below" relate exclusively to the Son of Man, and to the disciples as God's gift to him. "The Fourth Gospel functions for its readers in the same way as the epiphany of its hero functions in narratives and dialogues" (68–69).

Now while there is truth in these contentions, their significance has surely been exaggerated. The Evangelist and his community were not so isolated as has been suggested, and their view of Jesus does not betray a beleaguered sectarian group reacting negatively to the society in which it is set. The Christology characteristic of the Gospel has affinity with that of churches of both Palestinian and Hellenistic provenance, as the Christological confessions and hymns of the Epistles show (e.g., 1 Tim 3:16; Phil 2:6–11; Col 1:15–20; Heb 1:1–3), and the prologue has affinities to the contemporary religious scene generally. Moreover the relation of the Gospel to the Book of Revelation should be accorded adequate recognition. While there is no question of the two works having a common author, the contacts between them, alike in terminology and certain theological concepts, are such that one must postulate contact between the authors, probably as fellow members of a Johannine "school"; this demands as a corollary a relationship between the Johannine community (or communities) and the churches of Roman Asia to which the Revelation was addressed. Not the least significance of this observation is the likelihood that by the end of the first Christian century, with the eclipse of the church of Jerusalem, the center of the primitive Church moved to Asia Minor, which was the most strongly Christianized province of the Roman empire, "the Christian country κατ᾽ ἐξοχήν" (Lohmeyer, *Die Offenbarung des Johannes*, 43). The author of Revelation, while addressing his work to Seven Churches, will have had in view also other churches in Roman Asia (cf. the repeated refrain "He who has an ear, let him hear what the Spirit says to the churches"), and almost certainly he will have desired that the book be heeded by the churches of Christendom generally. Will the author of the Fourth Gospel, while having in view the needs of his own constituency, have wished for a less audience? His consciousness of the unity of the Church, possessing a universal destiny and calling, counterbalances the dualism manifest in the Gospel and makes difficult the notion that the work was the product of a little community burdened with an inferiority complex.

In writing thus we are conscious of leaping ahead in the discussion, for the root of the Gospel would appear to be in traditions emanating from Palestine. The prominence in the Gospel of Judea, and of Jerusalem in particular, suggests a tradition linked with the city. But if the tradition was Judean, it was not Judaistic. While the Galilean ministry is given little space in the Fourth Gospel, its significance is acknowledged: unlike the Judeans, the Galileans welcomed Jesus, and the first two significant miracles recorded by John were performed in Galilee; the movement from Galilee to Jerusalem, the city that rejects its King, is as important to John as to the synoptics (see Dodd, *Fourth Gospel*, 384–85). Similarly there is acknowledgment of the relation between Jerusalem and Samaria, which is given a prominence approached among the other Gospels only in Luke. Meeks has drawn attention to the suggestion of K. Kundsin, that the topographical notes in the Fourth Gospel were the product of local traditions maintained by Palestinian communities; while Jerusalem undoubtedly dominates the Gospel, many of the Johannine traditions were shaped in communities in Samaria and Galilee (*Topologische Überlieferungsstoffe im Johannesevangelium*, 1925). Meeks himself concludes, "The peculiarities of the Johannine material result from a period of consolidation of Palestinian Christianity, with an accompanying juxtaposition and partial assimilation to one another of several stands of tradition" (*Prophet-King*, 318). We should further recall that the church at Jerusalem from its beginning included Hellenist Christians (Acts 6). When account is taken of the links in the Gospel with the outlook characteristic of the Qumran community, and the tendency of Judea to despise Galilee and Samaria, there is much to be said for Cullmann's view that the Jewish heritage that lay back of the Fourth Gospel reflects "nonconformist" elements in Judaism, and that the Hellenist Christians in Jerusalem, who had sympathy with the Samaritans (cf. Acts 8), had a major influence on the Johannine traditions (*The Johannine Circle*, 30–53). There will, of course, have been not a few *non*-Hellenist Jews who had sympathies with the Qumran outlook and joined the Church; converts from the followers of John the Baptist will probably have been among such. The presentation of Jesus in this Gospel was evidently formulated in Palestine among Christians maintaining traditions about Jesus, drawn from a variety of areas, with elements of Judaism alien to the prevailing religious establishment. Judging from the glimpses in Acts of Palestinian churches maintaining close relations with institutional Judaism (cf. above all Acts 21:20–24), it is likely that the Johannine church(es) also remained in fellowship with the synagogue, viewing themselves as people of God who confessed Jesus as their promised Messiah, but developing independently the theology which such a confession entailed. As with all Christian churches in Palestine, this created tensions between believers in Jesus and their fellow Jews who were not Christians, and such tensions will have oscillated in severity from time to time.

The Jewish war with Rome will have caused as much upheaval for the Christian communities as for the rest of Jews in Palestine. It is probable that the Evangelist migrated to Roman Asia about that time, and with him a number of Christians of his group. In their new surroundings they will have sought to maintain relations with their fellow Jews who were not believers in Jesus as Messiah. In this post-war period, however, wherein Pharisaic Judaism came to ascendancy, the relations between synagogue and church became increasingly strained, even in the Dispersion. We see a glimpse of such a situation in the Gospel of Matthew, which is likely to have emanated from Syria, a Gentile country adjacent to Israel's territory and having many Jews among its populace. Matthew's Gospel is notable for its maintenance of a continuing sense of responsibility for witness to Jews as well as mission to the nations. In the discourse of chap. 10 there is reflected a clear consciousness of continuing mission to Israel (in vv 5–15, 17–23, especially v 23), maintained in conditions of acute opposition (see especially vv 16, 24–31, 32–38). Matthew's church may well have experienced the effects of the policies determined by the Pharisaic decision-making in Jamnia. Foremost among these was the inclusion of Christians among heretics on whom damnation was called in the twelfth of the Eighteen Benedictions. These prayers were to be said, in full or abbreviated, by every Jew each day, and in every synagogue service. No Christian could utter benediction no. 12:

> For apostates let there be no hope, and the dominion of arrogance do thou speedily root out in our days; and let the Nazarenes and heretics perish as in a moment, let them be blotted out of the book of the living and let them not be written with the righteous. Blessed art thou, O Lord, who humblest the arrogant.

The date when this form of the benediction was promulgated is uncertain, but it illustrates the hostility of Pharisaic Judaism to the Christians. Matthew's Gospel may well have been written with the revision of Judaism that was going on in Jamnia in mind (see W. D. Davies, *The Setting of the Sermon on the Mount* [Cambridge: CUP, 1964] 256–315).

Two interesting examples of the increasing hostility of Jews toward Christians occur in the Book of Revelation, addressed to churches in the area wherein the Fourth Gospel emanated. The church at Smyrna is addressed as hard-pressed and poor, though rich in the spiritual sphere. The Lord of the church continues, "I know how you are slandered by those who claim to be Jews but are not—they are Satan's synagogue. Do not be afraid of the suffering to come. . . . Only be faithful to death and I will give you the crown of life" (Rev 2:9–10).

Yet more pertinent is the letter to the church at Philadelphia (Rev 3:7–13). The Christ who speaks is described as he "who holds the key of David; when he opens none may shut, when he shuts none may open." The key of David is the key that opens the door into the kingdom of God, and so to life in that kingdom. When the Christ opens for his followers the door to the kingdom, none can shut them out, and when he shuts the door on those who oppose, none can open the door and enter. This is the "open door, which no one can shut," which the Lord has set before the members of the Philadelphia church; in all probability the allusion here is to the denial by Jews of their right to the kingdom of God; their doom is to be blotted out of the book of the living and not be written with the righteous! But the message to the church goes on to announce an unexpected reversal of prophecy: "I will make those of Satan's synagogue, who claim to be Jews but are lying frauds, come and fall down at your feet"; the homage which these Jews expected Gentiles to pay them (Isa 60:14) they will pay to the Christians, to whom they denied a place in the kingdom. Significantly, it is added: "they shall know that *you* are my beloved people"; the Christians are the real people of the Messiah!

By the time that the Fourth Gospel was finally composed it is likely that a situation akin to those reflected in Matthew and in Revelation had come about. In Matthew's area, doors of conversation between Christians and non-Christian Jews were probably still open; the call could still be made to Jews to rise to the fulfillment of their divine vocation through Jesus, the Son of David and Son of God. In the Book of Revelation the doors may well have been locked, though of this we cannot be sure; there is no further polemic against the Jews in the book, and the "synagogues of Satan" may have been viewed by the Seer as exceptional. In John there is reflection of debates between church and synagogue; it is possible that such discussions were continued in the period of the Gospel's composition, despite the implications of John 16:1–4; violence against Christians in the name of the Lord was known from the time of Stephen, but the witness went on, till at length the Church itself changed its attitude. We are not persuaded that that stage had been reached when the Gospel was composed.

The presentation of Jesus in the Fourth Gospel, then, was adapted for the guidance and encouragement of the Church within its concrete situation. Its theological understanding of Jesus will occupy us later. Here we draw attention to a feature of the Gospel which more than any other gives it its unique form. *The Evangelist sets the historical ministry of Jesus in Palestine in indissoluble relation to the ministry of the risen Lord in the world.* The continuity of the ministry of Jesus with that of the Risen Lord will have been assumed by the synoptists. The Book of Acts has been termed "the Acts of *the Risen Lord.*" Various recent writers, however, have pointed out an instructive difference between Luke and John: whereas Luke wrote an account of the origins of the Christian Church in *two* volumes, the first, of Jesus at work with his disciples in Palestine and the second, of the risen Christ at work through the disciples in the world, John writes *one* book, wherein Jesus after the flesh and Jesus the risen Lord are presented together in a single perspective (so Cullmann, *Circle,* 14; Martyn, *History and Theology,* 129; D. M. Smith,

John, Proclamation Commentaries, 55–56). This could be thought to be a highly contrived way of presenting the story of Jesus, and one difficult to accomplish. From the Evangelist's viewpoint it is comprehensible that he should endeavor to carry it through, since for him the relations of Jesus with his disciples and his people during his ministry were continuous with the relations of the Lord with his Church and nation after the Resurrection. They were determined by the unity of Jesus in the flesh and the risen Christ, the unity of the mission of Jesus to his people and the mission of the risen Lord to the nation and the wider world, and the fact that in both eras *he* is the focal point of faith and of opposition. The disciples are inextricably linked with Jesus in his destiny; if his mission in the days of his flesh provoked faith and fury, the Church likewise received converts to Jesus as Christ and Lord and opposition from those who rejected their testimony.

Now this is no novel insight. It was set forth long ago by E. F. Scott, though he was inclined to speak of *two* revelations—of the Jesus of history and the Christ of religious experience—an interpretation strictly inharmonious with the Paraclete doctrine (*The Fourth Gospel,* 358–59). When, however, Scott came to deal with the discourses of the Gospel he could see only *the Church* in the debate with the synagogue:

> The writer is carrying back into the Gospel period the discussion of his own age. He is thinking not of the actual opposition which scribes and Pharisees offered to Jesus, but of the attacks directed in the present against the Christian Church (68–70).

Since Scott's time this position has become virtually axiomatic in Johannine studies; New Testament scholars generally assume it as self-evident that the controversies in the Fourth Gospel reflect the tensions that prevailed between the Johannine community and the synagogue in the period when the Gospel was written. The contention is undoubtedly correct, but to state it without qualification is to deny the unity of perspective maintained in the Gospel relating to Jesus at work in Judea, Samaria, and Galilee *and* to the risen Lord at work through the Spirit. In Scott's view, indeed, the actual assailants of Jesus had been forgotten by the time the Gospel was written; only the fact remained that Jesus had been opposed by his countrymen and that they had brought about his death (68–70). Such a suggestion seems to us the height of improbability. That traditions of hostile encounters of Jesus with Pharisees and Sadducees were kept alive in the churches is seen in the records of the other three Gospels, the latest of which will have been written about the same time as the Fourth Gospel. The preservation of this element of the Jesus tradition was inevitable. The Palestinian churches were constantly faced with problems similar to those which Jesus encountered, for their lives were passed in Jewish communities which centered in the synagogues, and they were as truly part of the synagogue as their non-Christian compatriots. No aspect of the ministry of Jesus was more pertinent, more "actual" to them than this one. How Jesus dealt with his opponents regarding the interpretation of the Torah was of crucial importance to them, even as it was to know how the chief priests came to the decision that he must be put to death. Our real concern, however, is to stress that the fundamental issue that determined the form of the Fourth Gospel is the theological one, namely, the unity of Christ's action in the flesh and in the Spirit. It calls for recognition of *both* components of the Lord's work and their mutual relations. In John's thought and writing their unity and distinctiveness are held in balance.

Various writers have sought to elucidate this understanding of the Gospel. X. Léon-Dufour approached the subject from the point of view of symbolism. He observed that the ambivalence of language in the Fourth Gospel is due to its coming from two different origins, that of the Jewish cultural milieu in which Jesus lived and the Christian cultural milieu of John's time and area. Both have their own means of symbolic representation; e.g., among the Jews bread is symbolic of heavenly food, among the Christians it becomes linked on another level with the Eucharist. Since John sought to unite the two milieux in one written text, we should not look for two different readings in his text but a unified one: "The only viable reading is . . . the one which, from the Christian point of view, discovers the relationship between the present reality of the Spirit and the times past of Jesus of Nazareth." The acknowledgment of this relationship then demands that "the singularity and the proper weight of the one and of the other" be respected. According to Léon-Dufour the main obstacle in the way of doing this is the exegete's temptation to bring the Easter perspective prematurely into play, a temptation which must be resisted. In John, as well as in the synoptics, Jesus proposes a revelation which must have a meaning from the Jewish point of view. "John wants to show how Jesus came to offer to his contemporaries the fulfillment of their beliefs and of their traditions by showing that they were indeed fulfilled in his person." It is therefore incumbent on the exegete to discover the coherence of the dialogues and the relevance of the speeches to the particular Jewish context described by the Evangelist: "If we end up failing to recognise all this, it is because we allow ourselves to be dazzled by the light of Easter. The Christian present would contribute to erasing the roots of the Christian faith in that unique event which was the encounter of Jesus with men." Along with this we must acknowledge that John has actualized the past of Jesus by showing its relevance for the present time; the reading of the Gospel, accordingly, consists not of bringing the past into the present, but in developing a deeper understanding of the present in the light of the past ("Towards a Symbolic Reading of the Fourth Gospel," 440–46).

J. Louis Martyn seeks to elucidate this combination of the history of Jesus with the activity of the risen Lord by adducing the idea of a drama presented on a two-level stage (in *History and Theology of the Fourth Gospel*). The narrative of the healing of the man born blind in John 9 provides an ideal test case for the thesis. Martyn sees in vv 1–7 a typical miracle story, which sets forth the *"einmalig"* or single, non-recurring event, while in vv 8–41 Jesus represents the Christian preacher; the two sections are not rigidly divided between past and present, the whole chapter participates in the two-level drama. Martyn comments: "Confronted by a blind beggar near the Temple, Jesus takes the initiative to heal him. However, the work of him who is the Light of the world (8:12, etc.) is not terminated in that deed. Through a faithful witness in the Johannine church, the healing power of Jesus touches a poor Jew, afflicted many years with blindness" (30). Whether, on the contemporary level, the blindness is to be thought of as physical as well as spiritual, Martyn leaves open, citing 2 Cor 3:12–18. The important issue is the twofold relation of the event as described: "Presented as a formal drama, and allowed to mount its actors, so to speak, on a two-level stage so that each is actually a pair of actors playing two parts simultaneously, John 9 impresses upon us its immediacy in such a way as strongly to suggest that some of its elements reflect actual experiences of the Johannine community" (37). Martyn acknowledges that it is a bold step that John takes in "doubling" Jesus with the figures of Christian witnesses in his own community, but this is how the Evangelist avoids a two-volume work of Jesus and his Church such as Luke has given, and shows instead the unity of the present activity of the risen Christ with the ministry of Jesus in the flesh. The key to the procedure is the doctrine of the Paraclete: the paradox of Jesus' promise that his work on earth will be continued because he is going to the Father is solved by his return in the person of the Paraclete. "It is therefore precisely the Paraclete who creates the two-level drama" (148).

This approach to the Fourth Gospel is ingenious and illuminating, even if at times one may wish to apply the principle differently from Martyn. It is hardly necessary, for example, to see at all times *individual* counterparts in the second level to those of the first. Narratives like the healing of the son of the king's officer, the paralytic of Bethesda, the man born blind, and the raising of Lazarus can be compared in a more general way with the activities of the post-Pentecostal Church and the controversies into which they were drawn. Hoskyns expressed precisely such a view: "By a natural and unconscious symbolism the traditional narratives of his miraculous actions were related in such a way as to identify the converts with those who had originally been healed, and the later opponents of Christianity with the original opponents of Jesus. The earlier narratives tended to become more and more clearly symbolical of the later experiences of the Christians, the original history providing the framework within which reference was made to contemporary history, and the materials out of which narratives and discourses could be constructed" (362). This accords with the understanding of the Gospel by Léon-Dufour, and especially with the concept embodied in John 14:12–13: the works of Jesus in his ministry are to be continued by his disciples after his death, and yet greater things achieved, since Jesus will be with the Father. "Jesus with his Father" signifies not absence from the earth scene, but Jesus occupying the place of power and glory, so that when the disciples pray in his name, *he* will act. The disciples thus become agents of the risen Lord for performing "greater things" than he did in the days of his flesh. In the Resurrection era and the presence of the Spirit, the spiritual realities signified by the "signs" become available to men. They may take bread of life, not simply bread that perishes, and the life of the eternal kingdom, of which recovery from sickness or even resuscitation from the grave are but reflections.

F. Mussner made yet another approach to the dual form of the Fourth Gospel, of which we must take note (*The Historical Jesus in the Gospel of St. John*). Mussner examined the nature of John's "historical knowledge" of Jesus through an analysis of his "gnoseological terminology"; this indicates that the terms for seeing, hearing, coming to know, knowing, testifying, and remembering all relate to the seeing, hearing, knowing, etc., of apostolic witnesses in the past, transposed kerygmatically into the present (cf., e.g., the "we have seen" of John 1:14; 1:34; 4:42; 6:40; 20:29). The Johannine mode of vision is that of a believing and informed witness who "sees" his subject in such a way that the hidden mystery of the latter becomes "visible" and expressible for the Church in the kerygma In the act of vision the time horizons merge, but in the merging, the past is not annulled, and the questions of the present provide the angles from which the historical material is focused. "To put it concretely, Jesus of Nazareth is so expressed by John in his act of vision, that the history of Christ projected and presented by him simultaneously gives an answer to the Christological questions of the time of its composition" (46). Hearing his words, the Church shares in the Evangelist's "act of vision." The Lord himself comes before them in the words of the Gospel and speaks to them through the Paraclete, and the latter through the Evangelist. So the Evangelist becomes the inspired mouthpiece of the glorified Christ; he lends him his tongue, so that the Christ speaks to the Christian community in Johannine language

The key to this process lies in the Paraclete doctrine. Here John 14:26 is especially significant: "The Paraclete . . . will teach you all things, and will call to mind all that I have told you." In this Gospel διδάσκειν, "teach," nearly always denotes "reveal" (cf. 8:28); the teaching like the recalling which immediately follows, is a rendering present that at the same time implies interpretation. The Paraclete thus is the instrument of the glorified Christ; he preserves Jesus' words and work for the Church, renders them present, and interprets them. This is stated yet more plainly in 16:12–15: "I have many things still to say to you, but you cannot endure them now. But when he, the Spirit of truth comes, he will guide you in the entire truth; for he will not speak on his own authority, but will tell only what he hears. . . ." The fullness of truth into which the Spirit guides is the word of Jesus, continuing in the word of the glorified Christ in an unbroken process of instruction. "The word transmitted through the Spirit is no other than the word of the Lord himself, and as a consequence in the Gospel of John the word of the earthly and of the exalted Christ can no longer be distinguished at all; for the Spirit . . . operates particularly in the inspired word of the Evangelist, who presents to the Church Jesus' words as the words of the glorified Christ" (63). Thus the Johannine mode of vision and the work of the Paraclete belong inseparably together.

Mussner's exposition of this theme may be said to complement those of Léon-Dufour and Martyn, although his work antedated their publications. In one respect, however, Mussner appears to have overstated his case, namely, in claiming that "the word of the earthly and of the exalted Christ can no longer be distinguished *at all*."

The researches of C. H. Dodd (in *Historical Tradition in the Fourth Gospel*) are a massive attempt to do precisely the opposite, namely, to lay bare words of the earthly Jesus in this Gospel. A notable example of the possibility, and desirability, of doing this may be seen in John 1:29. It is likely that the original testimony of John the Baptist is that recorded in 1:36, "Look, the Lamb of God!" In v 29 the continuation of the saying "who takes away the sin of the world" is the Evangelist's interpretative addition to ensure that readers understand that Jesus is not simply the leader of God's flock who came to exercise judgment and rule (the apocalyptic concept, which John the Baptist would have shared), but the One who fulfills the hope of a second Exodus by carrying out the function of God's passover Lamb, so achieving a universal redemption for the world. A more complex procedure is observable in chap. 3 of the Gospel. Nicodemus comes to Jesus by night for a conversation. Where does the conversation end? It is generally (and rightly) acknowledged that vv 16–21 are a group of sayings brought together by the Evangelist which look back on the completed life, death, and resurrection of Jesus and incorporate the kerygma of the churches. Possibly we must go back further and recognize vv 14–15 as set by the Evangelist in this context (it is the first "lifting up" saying) to indicate how the birth from above becomes possible, and v 13 as a comment upon v 12. We now move in an area where Mussner's dictum holds good! Similar observations may be made as to the latter half of the chapter: vv 31–36 have been set after the final testimony of John the Baptist to Jesus; while there is no indication that John has ceased to speak, it is transparently clear that his testimony ends with the climactic word of v 30 and that vv 31–36 are the Evangelist's reflections, setting forth the ultimacy of the word of God through Jesus. A further example of this procedure is seen in 12:36b–43, where the Evangelist looks back on the public ministry of Jesus as he draws his record of it to a close.

Admittedly chap. 3 is unique in the Gospel as to its form, but it perfectly illustrates the point we are seeking to make and that from another perspective: the whole narrative of the chapter and its accompanying teaching form a presentation of the kerygma of the Incarnate Christ with a view to the production of faith. W. Wilkens seized on this characteristic of the Fourth Gospel as a whole in his treatment of the raising of Lazarus, which he saw as written with that same end in view. It led him to speak of the Johannine portrayal of history as "kerygmatic history." It is kerygma in the form of history, but a history in no way to be distinguished from historical event, "for Jesus and Christ cannot be torn asunder, because the Word has become flesh and is attested to the world ever and again in concrete historical situations as the One become flesh." From this Wilkens proceeds to affirm the viewpoint we have been expounding:

> The kerygmatic historical declaration in the Fourth Gospel therefore bears a double character: it is directed to the saving event at a specific time in the past and testifies to the Word of God become flesh; at the same time it turns to man here and now and leads him into the discipleship of Christ. This double character of the Johannine representation of history is ultimately grounded in the presence of the exalted Lord, who is identical with the Word of God become flesh ("Die Erweckung des Lazarus," *ThZ* 15 [1959] 38–39).

This reminder that the Gospel in all its parts is written "that you may believe" is of fundamental importance, and of course is stated by the Evangelist himself (20:30–31).

This conception of the nature of the Fourth Gospel inevitably raises a question: can we take its testimony to Jesus seriously? Mussner affirmed: "The word transmitted through the Spirit is no other than the word of the Lord himself," and he added, "The Spirit operates in the inspired word of the Evangelist." He appears to answer our question with a resounding "yes." His response contrasts with the tendency of some scholars to discuss the contents of the Gospel as they would archaeological exhibits in a museum of anthropological antiquities. It is, of course, possible to treat the "theory" of the Paraclete-Spirit in the Fourth Gospel as some in fact do, just as one may discuss Paul's "theory" of justification by faith and the primitive Church's "opinion" that "Christ died for our sins according to the Scriptures, that he was buried, and that he has been raised from the dead on the third day according to the Scriptures" (1 Cor 15:3–4). Such language is comprehensible on the lips of people standing outside the Christian faith, or in discussions of the phenomenology of religion, but in expounding the Word of God some elements of faith may be assumed as given points of departure for the journey of understanding the Word through Christ. One of these cherished by the Church is that the Fourth Gospel is a supreme example of the truth and application of the Paraclete doctrine which it contains. It is a disturbing fact that the effect of more than a little contemporary scholarly discussion on the Fourth Gospel is to confuse both laity and clergy; it leads some to disregard the Gospel's significance for life and for ministry and others to reject the insights of scholarship in a desperate endeavor to save the message of the Gospel. Both these reactions are unfortunate. The patient labors of scholars have enabled us to perceive more clearly than ever before the intention of the Evangelist in writing his Gospel, his mode of interpretation, and his message for his own contemporaries and for our times. Of this result the great commentaries on the Gospel in the past fifty years bear eloquent testimony, some of which are among the greatest expositions of the Word of God that have ever appeared. We may with confidence seek the guidance of the Spirit in our own endeavors to understand the Gospel.

4. The Religious Relations of the Fourth Gospel

The term "relations" is preferable to "background," since it is likely that the Evangelist may have wished to relate the Gospel to groups with religious concepts and traditions other than his own. It is desirable, accordingly, to distinguish among traditions common to John and religious groups in the Jewish and Hellenistic world of his time—those which were fundamental to his thought and those which he used as vehicles of address in the service of the Gospel.

(1) Hellenistic Traditions

Since the Gospel was written in Greek for Greek-speaking people, we consider first its relationship to the religious traditions of the Hellenistic world. It may be noted at the outset that the significance of the fact that the Fourth

Gospel was written in Greek is an ambivalent factor. The Septuagint was also written in Greek! G. D. Kilpatrick observed that while the rendering of the Old Testament into Greek represented the migration of a religion and theology from one language to another, the effect of the Jewish scriptures on the Greek language was even more notable than the effect of the Greek language and culture on Judaism. He was prepared to affirm the like of the Fourth Gospel: "John represents a stage in the invasion of Hellenistic paganism by Judaism and later by Christianity, and not an invasion of the Biblical religion by the pagan world" ("The Religious Background of the Fourth Gospel," 40–41). Our task is to weigh the extent of the influences upon and from the Fourth Gospel.

(i) Philo

This writer has long been viewed, and rightly so, as the supreme example of a Jew seeking to understand his faith in the light of Hellenistic culture and to explain it to the Gentile world. Both aspects are observable in his writings—the comprehension and the proclamation. Philo treated the Old Testament in a manner similar to the treatment of Homer by Greek teachers— he allegorized the Scriptures. In this respect he differed from John, whose treatment of the OT is more in line with Palestinian traditions of exegesis. Philo's use of symbolism is more significant for his relations with the Fourth Evangelist; Dodd cites three features of special importance in this area; namely, God as Light, as Shepherd, and as the Fountain of living water, all of which, of course, feature in the OT Scriptures (*Interpretation*, 53–58).

The most significant point of contact between Philo and John lies in their use of the concept of the Logos. Philo borrowed from the Stoics the notion of Logos as the principle of reality. He interpreted the concept in the light of God as Creator; the Logos, like wisdom, was viewed as God's medium of creation and governance of the world and of revelation to the world. As such the Logos is termed the image of God and the First-born Son of God. Since he is the medium through which the world approaches God, he is also termed the High Priest, the Paraclete for the forgiveness of sins and the bestowal of God's blessings on man (*De Vita Mos.* 2:134). Philo also conjoins with the Logos the Platonic notion of the archetypal man, who is contrasted with the earthly man of Gen 2, in whom *nous* is mingled with earth (*Leg. All.* 1:31–32). Some see in this concept of the archetypal man a close approach to the treatment of the Son of Man in the Fourth Gospel (so, for example, Dodd, *Interpretation*, 69–71).

The links between Philo and John are undoubtedly remarkable and extend beyond these examples. They are the more significant when it is recognized that Philo was not an isolated phenomenon, but a spokesman for other likeminded men of his race, whose thoughts he appears to have utilized. There is no evidence that John had ever studied Philo's writings. The declaration of John 1:14 and the function of the prologue to the Gospel as introducing the revelation and redemption of the Logos within the concrete situations of a local history were beyond Philo's horizon. Nevertheless, it is entirely plausible that the Evangelist's formulations of this story will have been made with people in view who shared the convictions of the man who sought to bridge the world of the Bible with the religious thought of the Hellenistic world.

(ii) Gnosticism

The relations between the Fourth Gospel and Gnosticism are still in debate and are far from settled. It will be recalled that in Bultmann's view a major source of the Gospel was the Revelation-Discourses, which were derived from a Baptist Gnostic sect and which embodied the Gnostic Redeemer myth. The fundamental elements of this system are cosmic dualism, redemption from the demonic powers of earth, and Gnosis from the Revealer, by which the way of salvation is known. These determine the form of the Redeemer and the nature of redemption. The cosmic dualism forbids him to belong to the inferior creation; he is an Envoy sent down from heaven, commonly in disguise that the hostile powers may not recognize him, and he returns thither after achieving his redemptive task; since his ascension concludes his work, eschatological hope is drastically modified. All this is thought to be utilized and adapted in the Fourth Gospel. It is urged that the dualism is marked (cf. 8:23, "You are from below [ἐκ τῶν κάτω], I am from above [ἐκ τῶν ἄνω]"); the Redeemer descends from heaven to bring the revelation of the truth (3:13), and ascends to heaven from his cross (12:31–32); the future eschatology of the Church is transformed to a wholly realized eschatology (5:24); the Christ is the Logos-Redeemer, God walking about the earth in the guise of a man. Käsemann, interpreting the Gospel on this basis, maintains that the Evangelist presents a Christology of glory with which the Passion is hardly reconcilable; hence the Gospel has no real theology of the cross and exemplifies a naive docetism (*Testament of Jesus*, 27; cf. 7 and 51). In like vein L. Schottrof describes the Fourth Gospel as "the first system known in detail to us of a Gnosticism which adapts the Christian tradition" (*Der Glaubende und die feindliche Welt*, 295).

Most Johannine scholars consider that this judgment overshoots the mark. That the Gospel employs a dualism is evident—its nature and origin we may for a moment leave in abeyance; the descent and ascent of the Redeemer is undoubtedly of primary significance—though it may not be overlooked that the Redeemer ascends via his grave; the subordination of futurist eschatology to one of present realization is also of major importance, and we may not minimize the fact that the Christ is presented as the Logos "walking about the earth." But all this gives no warrant for playing down the significance of the enfleshment of the Word in 1:14, or for diminishing the importance to the Evangelist of the death of Jesus, or for denying the genuine eschatology of hope in the Gospel, and for representing the Christology of the Gospel as docetic. The thoroughgoing Gnostic interpretation of the Fourth Gospel is in no small degree due to a scholarly minimizing of the Jewish relations that it exhibits, and that we must shortly consider. Setting aside for a moment leading themes in the Gospel that are not common in Gnostic thought, such as the second Exodus motif, why do enthusiasts for the Gnostic relations of the Fourth Gospel have to be so exclusive, dismissing, for example, the importance of Ezekiel 34 and other related OT passages about God as the Shepherd of his people when citing the Hellenistic parallels to the discourse of John

10? Why are the precedents of the "I am" sayings in Deutero-Isaiah relegated to a buried past in favor of parallels in the Nag Hammadi literature, when the former tradition is so plainly alive in the Book of Revelation, which emanates from a group closely related to that which produced the Fourth Gospel? And how does one relate the fiercely *anti-Gnostic* document, 1 John, to the allegedly Gnostic Fourth Gospel, which also emanates from the circle that produced the Gospel, and which seeks to expound the thought of the Gospel? There are sober scholars who are ready to acknowledge positive relations of the Fourth Gospel to the contemporary religious movements that inspired the Gnosticism of the second century without the one-sided emphasis some enthusiasts for Gnosticism are making. C. K. Barrett's comment, concluding a study of the theological vocabulary of the Fourth Gospel and the Gospel of Truth, is worthy of note: "It is difficult to doubt that John detected real theological appropriateness in the words he used, that in fact he was giving a Christianized—and that meant often an inverted—and always historicized version of a way of thinking that was not simply too popular but also too near to and too far from the truth to be ignored. Gnosticism raised questions that the theologian could not ignore" ("The Theological Vocabulary of the Fourth Gospel and the Gospel of Truth," 223). In reality, the conviction has become increasingly adopted that the Evangelist, by his use of Gnostic categories, gave the completest answer to Gnosticism. He had defeated the Gnostics with their own weapons (so Barrett, *Commentary*, 134).

(iii) The Hermetic Literature

The writings purporting to convey the instruction of Hermes Trismegistos (= the Egyptian God Thoth) are in the Gnostic tradition (some of them are in the Nag Hammadi library), and are generally dated in the second and third century A.D. While the dualism that is characteristic of Gnosticism is found in these writings also, it is modified by their belief that the cosmos is related to God, and may be called the Son of God, and that man knows God through its agency. Significantly, man is also represented as the image of God in so far as he partakes of *nous*, which is the soul of God. The man of *nous* is τέλειος ἄνθρωπος, "perfect man," sent down by God into the world to adorn it: because he has received *nous* he is one with God and immortal; knowing for what purpose he has come from God, he also knows that he will ascend to God. C. H. Dodd, comparing such ideas with what is said about the Son of Man in the Fourth Gospel (e.g., John 13:3; 1:32–34; 10:30; 20:17) considers that the latter figure has more in common with the Anthropos of Poimandres than with the Son of Man of Jewish Apocalyptic (*Interpretation*, 43–44).

The Logos doctrine is not so prominent in the Hermetic literature as it is in some Gnostic writings. As the thought of God it is a cosmological principle, but in man it is a psychological faculty of hearing and seeing, and is the offspring of God (*Poimandres* 1.6). Dodd considered that the conception of Christ in the Fourth Gospel has combined the roles assigned in the Poimandres tractate to four distinct beings: the divine Revealer (Poimandres), the prophet himself, the heavenly Anthropos, and the Logos (*Interpretation*, 33).

A further point of contact with this same tractate concerns its teaching on regeneration: a man who gains the knowledge of God becomes divine and is declared to have been born again; he becomes one with God through the indwelling of the Logos and passes from the realm of the physical to that of *nous*.

As so often in discussions relating to Gnosticism, the age at which this thinking circulated in these groups is uncertain. The writings in their present form are generally dated in the second to the fourth centuries. Dodd, who would place the Poimandres tractate early in the second century, or even before, nevertheless is cautious in his judgment on the relation of this litera-ture to the Fourth Gospel: "It seems clear that as a whole they (the Hermetic writings) represent a type of religious thought akin to one side of Johannine thought, without any substantial borrowing on one side or the other" (*Interpre-tation*, 53). At most we would be justified in affirming that the Evangelist is concerned to convey the gospel of the Word made flesh to the kind of pagan reader who is acquainted with thought embodied in the Hermetic writings (so Schnackenburg, 1:138).

(iv) Mandaism

In no area of the investigation of the religious relationships of the Fourth Gospel is the confusion so great and difficult to disentangle as in discussions relating to Mandaism. The origin of the Mandaic traditions is still disputed. Bultmann considered that the Mandaic literature exhibited a form of the Redeemer myth *prior to* the rise of Christianity, and Cullmann has supported this view throughout his career. The English-speaking world has tended to be skeptical of this estimate. H. E. W. Turner wrote in 1954, "The attempt to derive the Fourth Gospel from Mandaean sources is already a curiosity of scholarship" (*The Pattern of Christian Truth*, 113). In the light of publications that appeared shortly after that date, W. Schmithals affirmed to the contrary in 1969, "The early dating of the beginnings of the Mandaean literature in the pre-Christian and early Christian period is less disputed today than ever" (*The Office of Apostle in the Early Church*, 185). The lateness of the present form of the texts is admitted; there are references to Mohammed in the Haran Gawaita, which lead some to date the Mandaic canon *ca*. A.D. 700 (so Dodd, *Interpretation*, 115). The oldest extant manuscript of the Mandaic scrip-tures comes from the sixteenth century, and most of the rest belong to the eighteenth and nineteenth centuries. On the other hand, there is a colophon in the canonical Mandaean Prayer-book, published in 1959, which lists the copyists of the manuscript; if genuine, it would lead us to date its composition in the second half of the third century A.D. The account given in the Haran Gawaita of the history of the Mandaeans is quite fantastic; R. Macuch, who takes the work with seriousness, admits that it may be 95 percent legendary (*Anfänge der Mandäer*, 117, cited by E. Yamauchi, *Pre-Christian Gnosticism*, 127). The question arises as to what truth there may be in the connection claimed with John the Baptist and his ministry. Contrary to Bultmann, there is a strong tendency to view this as a late development in the sect's progress.

There is ground for believing that the Mandaeans began as one of the many baptizing sects in the Jordan valley in the first century of our era and that they developed their peculiar beliefs after migrating to Mesopotamia.

Yamauchi postulated the following evolution of the sect: the Mandaeans were non-Jews who were superficially acquainted with the Old Testament and spoke an Aramaic dialect; they probably lived in Transjordan and worshiped the god of the Hauran range east of Galilee; they had no firsthand knowledge of Christ or Christianity; the attacks of the Jews on Gentiles on the eve of the war with Rome (A.D. 66) may have forced them to the area of Antioch, where they may have accepted the Gnostic views of Menander, attracted by his teaching on achieving immortality through baptism; seeking a place where they could be free from domination, they departed east to the region of Adiabene, but owing to the influence of Christians and Jews there they moved on to southern Mesopotamia, where they converted the indigenous Aramaean population; the Mesopotamian tradition had no hope for life after death, so immortality through Gnosis would have been good news to the people. "It was this fruitful union of the vitality of Gnosticism and the tenacity of Mesopotamian cult and magic that resulted in the birth of a hardy new religion, perhaps by the end of the second century A.D." (*Pre-Christian Gnosticism*, 141–42).

Mandaism presents a radical dualism of light and darkness, of the heavenly and earthly realms. Escape from the latter is possible for those who carry out the Mandaic ritual, the chief element of which is baptism (frequently repeated). Baptism entails the re-enactment of the myth of the descent of Manda d'Hayye (= "knowledge of life") and ascent to the realm of light and reunion with the Great Life and heaven. In the elaboration of the doctrine a polemic against Judaism and Christianity, and even Mohammedanism, is apparent. The realm of darkness is ruled over by the Holy Spirit; Adonai is an evil power which brought the Jews out of Egypt and gave the Law; Christ is identified with Hermes, a planet that deceives men by calling himself Jesus, Savior, and Son of God; and Mohammed is yet another deceiver. The true deliverer is Enosh-Uthra, who is identified with John the Baptist, but this identification appears to be a secondary adaptation of the myth in the light of the Christian proclamation of Jesus. G. Quispel wrote, "The Gospel of John, more than any other writing of the NT, has stylistic and conceptual parallels with Mandaean literature. Even if Mandaeism turns out to be neither so old nor of Palestinian origin, obligatory reading of Mandaean writings could serve students of the NT as good preparation for the right understanding of the Fourth Gospel" ("Gnosticism and the New Testament," *The Bible and Modern Scholarship*, 266).

(2) Jewish Traditions

The Jewish cast of the Evangelist's mind and his Jewish training were expounded long ago by B. F. Westcott. He instanced familiarity with Jewish thought and religious observance, the Hebraic style of the writer, the acknowledgment of Judaism as the divine starting point of the Christian faith ("salvation is of the Jews," 4:22), the Evangelist's knowledge of Palestine and of festival customs belonging to the Temple worship, agreements with the Hebrew Old Testament as against the LXX, and Hebraic ideas behind the Logos doctrine (x–xxxix). We should speak now of the Semitic rather than simply Hebraic style of the Evangelist, for both Aramaic and Hebrew are reflected in the Gospel. Whether the Semitisms are due to sources or to the writer's thinking in terms of Semitic idiom while writing in Greek (an issue not necessarily requiring an either/or pronouncement, as with the Book of Revelation), the evidence for an underlying Semitic idiom, as Dodd pointed out, is irresistible: "This in itself brings the gospel back into a Jewish environment" (*Interpretation*, 75).

(i) *The Old Testament in the Fourth Gospel*

There is little in John's Gospel to compare with Matthew's abundant citation of OT testimonies to Christ. Doubtless John would have acclaimed the principle enshrined in Matt 5:17—Jesus came not to destroy but to fulfill Law and Prophets; and since his overriding interest was Christological, his use of the OT, like Matthew's, is chiefly in Christological texts, but more particularly in their typological application. This may be instanced in his citation from the OT in John 19:37: it would seem that Exod 12:46 is primarily in view, hence that Jesus in his death is viewed as God's Passover Lamb; if the Evangelist was at the same time conscious of the echo of Ps 34:20, then he recognized that it is the Christ who fulfills the role of the Righteous Man of the Psalms who by his death brings about the second Exodus.

A great deal of the OT language employed in the Gospel is bound up with the concept of Jesus as One greater than Moses, who achieved the redemption anticipated in the second Exodus The theme is alluded to even in 1:14, where the language used of the incarnation of the Logos is reminiscent of the dwelling of the Shekinah among the people of God in the wilderness (ἐσκήνωσεν ἐν ἡμῖν), and in 1:17 (the Law came through Moses, grace and truth through Jesus Christ). The Lamb of God theme is announced in 1:29, doubtless in relation to the concept of the Warrior Lamb who delivers the flock of God and establishes his kingdom, but modified by the concept of the death that is exaltation to sovereignty, as in 3:14 and 12:31. Just as the Son of Man brings a revelation beyond that vouchsafed to Moses, 3:13, so his "lifting up" on the cross is the means of a more complete healing and gift of life than that given through the lifting up of the snake in the desert (3:14 f.). Similarly the discourse on the bread of life sets out from a reference to the gift of manna in the time of Moses to expound the realization of hope of its return in the gift of "true' manna through Christ, which results in eternal life in the kingdom of God (6:30–59). With this theme is linked the representation of Jesus as the fulfiller of the meaning of the Feasts of Israel—Passover (chap. 6), Tabernacles (chap. 7), and Dedication (chap. 10).

There are various elements of imagery and modes of speech in the Gospel for which Hellenistic parallels can be adduced as well as from the OT, but in view of the importance of the OT to the writer, the latter must be given due weight, without excluding consciousness of the former. One thinks of the discourse of the shepherd and the sheep in John 10, and the allegory of the vine in chap. 15, as also the 'I am" sayings of the Gospel, which could scarcely have been penned without reference to such passages as Isa 41:4; 43:10–13 (cf. Deut 32:39). The like must be said of the concept of wisdom, which runs through the Gospel as a kind of ground bass. Doubtless in the first century of our era, wisdom had already been influenced by Hellenistic thought, as is apparent from the so-called *Wisdom of Solomon,* but its basic Semitic root should be acknowledged (a root that reaches back beyond the beginnings of Israel). While in early Israel wisdom was primarily concerned with the laws of life and of the world, in post-exilic Israel it came to be a kind of umbrella concept beneath which the centralities of faith were brought. Von Rad pointed out that while this is a comparatively late development in Israel, "the conviction that perfect wisdom is with God alone was certainly inherent in Jahwism from the beginning" (*Old Testament Theology* 1:441–42). When Prov 3:19 states that God founded the earth "by wisdom," and the heavens "by understanding . . . ," it approaches the concept of wisdom as the instrument of creation, which is spelled out in later writings, e.g., Wisd Sol 9:1–4. In the praise of wisdom in Wisd Sol 7:22–8:1, we see a coalescence of Semitic and Greek thought, wherein the principle of creation becomes the expression of the glory of the Almighty, pervading the whole creation and the souls of men. This concept plays a major part in the formulation of the hymn within the prologue, but it also is a major constituent in the Christology of the Gospel as a whole.

All in all, it is difficult to challenge the propriety of Schnackenburg's summary of his discussion on the OT in the Fourth Gospel: "This gospel would be unthinkable without the OT basis which supports it" (1:124).

(ii) Rabbinic Judaism

The clearest evidence of the Evangelist's acquaintance with Rabbinic thought is seen in his reflection of rabbinic understanding of some of the OT texts he has cited. For fuller exposition of such sayings the reader is referred to the present commentary, and still more to that of Strack-Billerbeck. Here we content ourselves with brief mention of some examples of the Evangelist's knowledge of rabbinic interpretation of the Scriptures.

The key saying of John 1:51, which anticipates the whole course of the ministry of Jesus, rests on a resolution of the ambiguity in the statement as to whether the angels ascend and descend on the ladder or on Jacob. The Hebrew term סלם (*sûllām*), "ladder," is masculine, so בו (*bô*) can mean either "on *him*" or "on *it*." The LXX decides for the latter rendering בו as ἐπ᾽ αὐτῆς agreeing with κλίμαξ, ladder. The rabbis discussed the matter and differed in their judgment of it. In stating that the angels will be seen ascending and descending *on the Son of Man,* John 1:51 represents the Son of Man as replacing *Jacob,* and as becoming the place of mediation to man of the revelation and redeeming powers of the kingdom of God.

John 5:17 entails two extraordinary claims: that God still works though it is his Sabbath, and that Jesus as the Son of God likewise works on the Sabbath. According to the rabbis, the works of God after creation, when God entered upon his Sabbath, are restricted to anticipating his judgment on the wicked in the future, and the rewards he will give to the righteous. So also, reports the Evangelist, the Son, like the Father, gives *life* to whom he will and has authority to exercise *judgment* (vv 21–22). The dialogue is related to the healing of a paralytic on the Sabbath (5:1–9). The same event is referred to in 7:21–23, where the healing of a man on the Sabbath is justified by the custom of carrying out circumcision on the Sabbath. The rabbis explicitly required that eighth day circumcision be performed on the Sabbath, even though it broke the law of Sabbath rest. The contrast between circumcision and a *whole* man reminds one of the saying of R. Eleazar (*ca.* A.D. 100): "If circumcision, which concerns one of man's 248 members, overrides the Sabbath, how much more must his whole body override the Sabbath?" But of course Jesus carried the principle beyond the point to which the rabbis were prepared to go.

John 8:56 reflects a rabbinic interpretation of the clause in Gen 24:1, "Abraham entered into the days" (= Abraham was advanced in years), as meaning that Abraham in vision entered the future, and so enjoyed a vision of the days of the Messiah (so R. Akiba, in opposition to Johanan ben Zakkai).

The employment of the term "law" in the Gospel is characteristic of its use among rabbis, including the narrower use to denote the Mosaic law (1:17) and its extension to include the Scriptures as a whole (12:34). The observation in 5:39 is a perfect mirror of the conviction of the rabbis as to the duty of man to be occupied with the law, and the reward that such study brings ("life!"). By contrast, the contempt of the learned for the common people, who were ignorant of contemporary expositions of the law, is equally well expressed in 7:49.

In the light of our earlier observations on the twofold relation of the Gospel record to the ministry of Jesus and to the time of the Evangelist it will be seen that these reflections on the reference of the words and acts of Jesus to Pharisaic and rabbinic views will have been of great significance to the earliest readers of the Gospel, as the divide between Christians and the synagogue deepened.

(iii) *The Qumran Literature*

That close contacts exist between the literature of the Qumran sect and the Fourth Gospel is common knowledge, but how to evaluate them is variously estimated. A. M. Hunter said of these writings, "For the first time they give us a body of thought which may provide an actual background for the fourth gospel, both in date and place (southern Palestine in the first century B.C./A.D.) and in basic theological affinity" (*According to John,* 27). A similar assessment of the evidence is given by R. Brown (lxiii–iv). On the other hand W. G. Kümmel concluded, "John and Qumran presuppose a common background, but the thought world of Qumran cannot be the native soil of the Johannine thought forms" (*Introduction,* 158). The elements within this "common background" are numerous and striking. The differences between a group awaiting the messianic deliverance and one for whom the Messiah has come and wrought redemption are bound to be also considerable.

(a) Stress is laid in the Qumran writings on the importance of the community itself. The penitent who has received understanding of the truth is cleansed and made holy "that he may be joined with thy sons of truth and with the lot of thy saints" (1QH 11:10–12). Characteristic of the life of the community are the daily ablutions, the first of which appears to have the significance of baptism into the Covenant and the community (1QS 3:1–12), and participation in its sacred meals.

(b) Highly significant for comparison with the Fourth Gospel is the critical attitude of the sect to the Temple and its priesthood, which led to the view of the community as the true temple of God; the concept is frequently expressed, but most succinctly in 1QS 9:6: ". . . the men of the community shall separate themselves as a sanctuary for Aaron, to be united as a holy of holies and a house of the community for those in Israel who walk in perfection" (cf. John 2:19–21).

(c) While the community is characterized by a vivid eschatological hope, it appears that its members viewed themselves as possessing the blessings of the kingdom in advance of its full revelation. This finds expression in the Hymns of Thanksgiving, wherein H.-W. Kuhn traced the following elements of salvation: rescue from death and introduction into eternal life; cleansing from sins and the concept of new creation; entry into the inheritance of God's people and the "lot of the angels"; the gift of the Holy Spirit of the last days; the possession of knowledge which is the experience of salvation (see, e.g., 1QH 3:19–23; 11:7–14; 16:8–12; and 1QS 11:2–9). These passages fall short of the realized eschatology of the Fourth Gospel, but they are a unique anticipation within Judaism of that teaching.

(d) Reference has already been made to the Holy Spirit as the gift of the kingdom, given in advance to the people of the Covenant. Concerning the frequent mention of this theme we may cite 1QS 3:6–8 by way of example: "By this Spirit of true counsel concerning the ways of man shall all his sins be atoned when he beholds the light of life. By the Holy Spirit of the community, in his truth, shall he be cleansed of all his sins; and by the Spirit of uprightness and humility shall his iniquity be atoned." Or again, 1QH 16:11–12: "I know that no man beside thee can be just. And I therefore entreat thee, through the Spirit which thou didst put in me, to bring unto fulfillment the lovingkindness thou hast shown unto thy servant. . . ." Since the Spirit is also called "the Spirit of truth" and is named in parallelism with the Prince of Light and the Angel of Truth (1QS 3:21–24), it is often considered that the Paraclete doctrine of John is rooted in the Qumran teaching. "Rooted" is probably too strong a term; "related" is more fitting, for the notion of witness-bearing to the first Paraclete, Jesus the Messiah, is far removed from the horizon of the scrolls.

(e) Most important of all is the dualism in the Qumran literature. The teaching is expounded at length in 1QS 3:15–4:26. It begins with an affirmation which rules out an absolute dualism: "From the God of Knowledge comes all that is and shall be." Then follows a description of the two Spirits apportioned to man: "He allotted unto man two Spirits that he should walk in them until the time of his visitation; they are the Spirits of truth and perversity. The origin of truth is in a fountain of light, and the origin of perversity is from a fountain of darkness. Dominion over all the sons of righteousness is in the hand of the Prince of light; they walk in the ways of light. All dominion over the sons of perversity is in the hand of the Angel of darkness; they walk in the ways of darkness." It is explained that while the sons of righteousness go astray because of the Angel of darkness and the spirits of his lot, "the God of Israel and his Angel of truth succour all the sons of light." It is precisely in this passage that some of the most characteristic linguistic parallels between the Qumran writings and the Fourth Gospel occur. On these J. H. Charlesworth observed, "These similarities are not close enough nor numerous enough to prove that John directly copied from 1QS. But on the other hand they are much too close to conclude that John and 1QS merely evolved out of the same milieu" ("Dualism," 103).

(*f*) It is known that the Qumran sect, with certain other Jews of their time, uniformly celebrated Passover on a Tuesday evening—Wednesday, on the basis of a solar calendar. A. Jaubert has suggested that John's account of the Last Supper and the events leading to the death of Jesus indicates that the Evangelist represented Jesus as observing the Passover according to the Qumran calendar (for a brief statement of her thesis see "The Calendar of Qumran and the Passion Narrative in John," 62–75; its cogency is strongly contested).

The deductions to be drawn from this evidence are variously stated by students of the Fourth Gospel, but there is little doubt that associations between the thought of the Qumran Community and that of the Evangelist must be taken into account in the explanation of the Gospel.

(*iv*) *Samaritan Religion*

Awareness of connections between the Fourth Gospel and Samaritan religious traditions is a comparatively recent development in Johannine studies. The Evangelist's interest in the Samaritans is evident as soon as the attention that he gives them is compared with that which appears in the synoptic Gospels: Mark does not so much as mention Samaritans; Matthew reproduces Jesus' command to his disciples on their mission to Israel not to be deflected into Samaria (10:5); Luke is sympathetic to the Samaritans, so while recording the hostility of a Samaritan village toward Jesus and his followers he notes the rebuke of Jesus for his disciples' rage (9:51–55). John, by contrast, records that Jesus saw the Samaritan "fields" as "white unto harvest" (4:35); he describes how Jesus led a Samaritan woman of doubtful morality to faith and reports the confession of the inhabitants of Sychar, "We know that this is indeed the Savior of the world" (4:42). That testimony amounts to an affirmation that Jesus is the fulfillment of the hopes of Samaritan religion, as for those of all other peoples.

The major issue, however, is the extent to which Samaritan religious traditions are reflected in the Gospel. J. Bowman pointed out that the Samaritans early developed a creed with five points: belief in God, in Moses, in the Scriptures, in Mount Gerizim, and in the Day of Vengeance. Apart from the fourth item these are basic beliefs shared with the Jews. The Samaritan tenth commandment includes a statement that Mount Gerizim is the place where God is to be worshiped and an appendix on the coming of one like Moses, the *Taheb* (the Coming One). Precisely these two items figure in the conversation of the woman at the well with Jesus, reflecting their link in the mind of a Samaritan. The picture of the Samaritans in their adherence to their faith and response to the fuller revelation in Christ compares well with that of the Jews in John 5:34–47 (see Bowman, "Samaritan Studies," 310–14). But it is the Samaritan belief in Moses that is of special importance for the student of John's Gospel.

The figure of Moses attains quite staggering proportions in Samaritan religion. J. MacDonald gives an outline of Samaritan beliefs about Moses under the significant title "Moses, Lord of the World" (*Theology of Samaritans*, 147–222). If the Christian view of Jesus was decisively affected by the resurrection on the third day, the Samaritan view of Moses was especially conditioned through the ascent of Moses to the mount of God at the giving of the Law, interpreted as an ascent to God *in heaven*. "The great prophet Moses ascended to the level of the Divine One and was honoured on Mount Sinai" (Cowley, *The Samaritan Liturgy*, 877.28; cited in Macdonald, *The Theology of the Samaritans*, 181). Moses thus becomes the Revealer of God, the Prophet par excellence, beside whom there is no other. From this point one can move backward to creation and forward to the end of time. From the primordial light that preceded creation the creative Word fashioned the preordained image in Moses. He was the prototype of all human beings, and in due time he became identified both with the Word and with the Light, and participated in Creation. Moses is the Savior of Israel (the Samaritans!). As Lawgiver he gave Israel the way of salvation; his words are life, and a medicine to cure all who are sick ("Exalted is the mighty prophet Moses, whose every word is life and blessing," *Memar* 4:1). The narrative of Exod 34 encouraged the thought of Moses as the Intercessor between God and humankind, the Reconciler through whom humans can have communion with God. Such a role Moses maintains to the end, even in the day of judgment and resurrection. It was inevitable that the *Taheb*, the Samaritan Messiah, who was viewed as the prophet to come in the likeness of Moses (Deut 18:15, 18), was frequently viewed as Moses *redivivus*. So Markah: "The great prophet Moses . . . spoke concerning Israel words of blessing. . . . He will come . . . and seek out their enemy and deliver Israel" (*Memar* 3:3).

Many of these features of Moses' exaltation can be paralleled in rabbinic haggada (see W. Meeks, *The Prophet-King*, 176–215): there, too, Moses is viewed as supreme Prophet, King, Intercessor, the Shepherd of Israel, the Redeemer who serves as the prototype of the second Redeemer, and his ascent to heaven at the giving of the Law is stressed. But Moses is not the solitary mediator as in Samaritanism; if by some he is expected to come at the end of the age, it will be to precede the Messiah or accompany him, but not *as* Messiah (any who set their hope on Moses rather than the Messiah were out of step with Israelite tradition generally).

Since Samaritanism has evolved continuously from centuries before Christ to the present day, it is not easy to date with precision the stages of development of the Mosaic doctrine. Macdonald considers that Christianity exercised a powerful influence on the development of this religion; in his view Samaritanism is "Pentateuchal religion evolved along lines influenced by Christianity" (32), and in this process the Fourth Gospel had a decisive influence. Without doubt Samaritan literature has been influenced by varied streams of religious thought, including Christianity; nevertheless, it is likely that its beliefs about Moses began to be formulated earlier than the documents of the New Testament, as parallels in Philo, Josephus, and rabbinic haggada intimate (see Meeks, *Prophet-King*, 239–40; G. W. Buchanan, "The Samaritan Origin of the Gospel of John"; E. D. Freed, "Did John Write His Gospel Partly to Win Samaritan Converts?," and C. H. H. Scobie, "Origins and Development of Samaritan Christianity").

The Fourth Gospel appears to relate both positively and negatively to Samaritan views of Moses. Meeks has sought to show that the presentation of Jesus in the Fourth Gospel has been largely determined by the conviction that Jesus is the one of whom Moses speaks—the ultimate Prophet and Messianic King, whose signs attest his sending from God. Miracles were characteristic of the Mosaic redeemer, not the Davidic Messiah. In this presentation Jesus is viewed not as a second Moses, but as the greater than Moses. If Moses was the representative of God, even at times accorded the name Elohim (on the basis of Exod 7:1), how much more does that hold good for Jesus! So it may be said of all the functions and attributes of Moses: it is Jesus who is "the Man" (a title of Moses in the *Memar Markah*) the Word, the Light, the Savior, the Paraclete, the Revealer. Significantly, when Mosaic traditions are corrected in the Gospel, this is done in the same spirit as corrections of false estimates of John the Baptist. Far from denigrating Moses, Jesus adduces him as a witness on his behalf Israel's Advocate becomes the Samaritans' opponent when they reject the word of Jesus, since in rejecting him they refuse Moses' testimony to him in the Law (5:45–47).

In so far as these traditions about Moses were shared by Jews, the positive and negative relations to Mosaic "christology" hold good of their beliefs also. It was Bowman's conviction that the Evangelist, through his Gospel, sought to bridge the divide between Jews and Samaritans in Christ ("Samaritan Studies," 302). E. D. Freed endeavored to substantiate that position, and urged that John was seeking to make Christianity appeal to Samaritans as well as to Jews, in the hope of winning converts from both ("Did John Write the Gospel Partly to Win Samaritan Converts?," 241–56). That is not an impossible thesis, but it must be acknowledged that the Christology of the Fourth Gospel cannot be wholly comprehended under the Moses traditions. That the latter form an important ingredient is a significant insight, but the key elements of Johannine Christology are the Son of Man and Son of God concepts, and these have not been formed through the Mosaic traditions. Nor, indeed, should one attempt to assign the concepts of Logos, Light, Savior, Paraclete, Apostle, Shepherd primarily to Mosaism, any more than one can Messiah and King. Samaritanism would appear to be one of the sources that fed the Johannine reservoir—admittedly a neglected one, but not on that account to be magnified beyond warrant.

5. Conclusion

From the foregoing review it is evident that the religious relations of the Fourth Gospel are complex. The links traceable between the Gospel and diverse Hellenistic and Semitic traditions make it implausible to settle for any one of them to the exclusion of the rest. It is, accordingly, as inadmissible to view the Fourth Gospel as emanating from a Gnostic enclave as it is to view it as emerging from a group of Christian rabbis. The breadth of the Evangelist's sympathies is demonstrable above all through his employment of the Logos concept in the prologue. The attempt should never be made to explain it on the basis of Hellenism or Judaism alone. Its roots are in the ancient religions of the nearer Orient in which ancient Israel was set, and from which the Greeks themselves learned. The powerful and creative Word of Marduk, Ellil, Ptah, Re is to be compared with the mighty and creative Word of Yahweh in the OT, which merged with the Wisdom of ancient tradition, blossomed in later Judaism, and was fused with the Torah. Yet Greek readers would not have read the prologue without recalling some of the primary elements of the Logos concept in their own traditions, even though they had never read a philosophical book or heard a lecture on philosophy (how many moderns who use the word "evolution" have read Darwin?). Its use in Hellenistic religion was, as we have seen, widespread, popularized through Philo, the forerunners of Gnosticism, and the Hermetica. The hymn of Col 1:15–20 shows how the concept without the term could be in circulation at an early date. John's employment of the concept to introduce the story of Jesus was a master-stroke of communication to the world of his day. What he achieved in the prologue to the Gospel he did in the body of the Gospel; the bells he had set ringing in the minds of his readers in the first eighteen verses of his book continued to ring out the message with a multitude of associations that helped to commend and interpret the good news he sought to convey. If it has made the task of interpretation more difficult for modern readers, it will not have been so for its earliest readers. Few of them, doubtless, will have caught *all* the associations present in the text, any more than moderns do. This is the gospel that speaks accordingly as the hearers and readers can receive it. That applies equally to the ignorant and the learned who seek God through its pages.

III. THE AUTHORSHIP OF THE FOURTH GOSPEL

W. G. Kümmel pointed out that, from earliest times, discussion of this subject has been conditioned by two questionable presuppositions: on the one hand, the belief that the apostle John wrote the Fourth Gospel has been passionately upheld, as though the authority of the Gospel depended on its composition by John; on the other hand, the tradition has been as strongly attacked, under the conviction that its incorrectness carried with it the untrustworthiness of the Gospel (*Introduction to the NT*[3], 234). Neither notion, of course, can stand. The evidence must be weighed as dispassionately as possible. Where it is ambiguous the ambiguity should be acknowledged and conclusions drawn with appropriate reserve.

1. THE EXTERNAL EVIDENCE

The most important witness in the early Church as to the authorship of our Gospel is Irenaeus, bishop of Lyons in the last quarter of the second century. He wrote: "John, the disciple of the Lord, who leaned on his breast, also published the gospel while living at Ephesus in Asia" (*Adv. Haer.* 3.1,2). The "disciple" is clearly the apostle John, who is identified with the "beloved disciple" of the Gospel. Irenaeus also acknowledged the authority of the church in Ephesus, since "it was founded by Paul, and John lived there till the time of Trajan" (3.3,4). This testimony is the more significant in view of Irenaeus' acquaintance with Polycarp, who was martyred in his old age in A.D. 155. Irenaeus referred to this in a letter to his friend Florinus; he reminded him of their endeavors as boys to gain the appprobation of the aged saint, and in this connection spoke of his memory of those days: "I am able to describe the very place in which the blessed Polycarp sat as he discoursed, and his goings out and his comings in, and the manner of his life, and his physical appearance, and his discourses to the people, and the accounts which he gave of his intercourse with John and with others who had seen the Lord" (cited by Eusebius, *H.E.* 5.4–8). Here we have a man who, toward the end of the second century, is able to claim a link with the apostle John through the mediation of a single individual, who was a teacher of the Church through the first half of the second century.

Polycrates, bishop of Ephesus, in a letter to Pope Victor I *ca.* A.D. 190, refers to the "great lights" who were buried in Asia, awaiting the resurrection; among these were Philip, one of the apostles, and his three daughters (one of whom "lived in the Holy Spirit"), and "John, who was both a witness and a teacher, who reclined upon the bosom of the Lord, and being a priest wore the sacral plate; he sleeps at Ephesus" (Eusebius, *H.E.* 3.31.3).

Clement of Alexandria made a famous statement about the Gospel: "Last of all John, perceiving that the bodily facts had been made plain in the gospel, being urged by his friends, and inspired by the Spirit, composed a spiritual gospel" (Eusebius, *H.E.* 4.14.7). He also reported that the Apostle John went to Ephesus after Domitian's death, and went about the surrounding country appointing bishops and consolidating the churches (*Quis dives salvetur,* 42:1 f.).

The Muratorian Canon, generally dated about A.D. 180–200, expanded Clement's references to John's "friends" who urged him to write the Gospel: "The fourth gospel is by John, one of the disciples. When his fellow-disciples and bishops exhorted him he said, 'Today fast with me for three days, and let us recount to each other whatever may be revealed to each of us.' That same night it was revealed to Andrew, one of the apostles, that John should write down all things under his name, as they all called them to mind. So although various points are taught in the several books of the gospels, yet it makes no difference to the faith of believers, since all things in all of them are declared by one supreme Spirit. . . ." John's Gospel is thus represented as a joint production of a number of the apostles, with John as their spokesman.

The anti-Marcionite prologue to Luke states that John the Apostle wrote the Apocalypse on the island of Patmos and wrote the Gospel afterwards. The prologue to the Fourth Gospel states: "According to Papias, the dear disciple of John, in his five exegetical books, this gospel was published and sent to the churches of Asia by John himself during his lifetime."

While this testimony in the churches to the authorship of the Fourth Gospel by the apostle John appears impressive, it becomes evident on examination that it is marred by unwarranted elaborations and confusions concerning those of whom it speaks. One such confusion is seen in the anti-Marcionite reference to Papias as "the dear disciple of John," a mistake shared by Irenaeus, who also called Papias "a hearer of John and companion of Polycarp" (*Adv. Haer.* 5.33.4). This reflects a misunderstanding of Papias, already pointed out by Eusebius, who makes it clear that Papias had to rely on presbyters for his information about the teaching of the apostles, and who referred to the *presbyter* John as a contemporary of his (see below). The anti-Marcionite prologue confuses Philip the apostle with Philip the Evangelist, whose daughters were prophetesses (Acts 21:8–9). The Muratorian Canon has reproduced sheer legend in suggesting that a group of the original Apostles, with Andrew in particular, shared with the apostle John in the writing of the Fourth Gospel; the motive for this is clearly to reinforce the authority of the Gospel by adducing joint apostolic production of it—an early example of the tendency to confuse apostolic authority with apostolic authorship. The notion voiced by Clement of Alexandria that John the Apostle went to Ephesus from Patmos after Domitian's death and pursued an active ministry in the surrounding area is elaborated in the anti-Marcionite prologue by the assertion that the Apostle wrote the Apocalypse on Patmos and then wrote the Gospel in Ephesus. The Apostle would have been nearly a hundred years old when he exercised this ministry of preaching and writing. Such a ministry is comprehensible of John the Prophet who wrote the Book of Revelation on Patmos (Rev 1:1–3; 22:9, 18), but hardly of the Apostle of that name.

All this combines to make the testimony of Irenaeus concerning the traditions about the Fourth Evangelist very uncertain. There is no reason to doubt his veracity in recounting to Florinus his memories of Polycarp, but there is ground for questioning his understanding as a boy of Polycarp's references to "John." Here we must consider briefly his understanding of Papias' witness. This has been preserved for us by Eusebius and has been repeated *ad nauseam* by writers on this subject, but we have to adduce it again. Papias, in his *Exposition of the Oracles of the Lord,* wrote: "I shall not hesitate to append to the interpretations all that I ever learned from the presbyters and remember well, for of their truth I am confident. . . . If ever anyone came who had followed the presbyters, I inquired into the words of the presbyters, what Andrew or Peter or Philip or Thomas or James or John or Matthew, or any other of the Lord's disciples, had said, and what Aristion and the presbyter John, the Lord's disciple, were saying. For I did not suppose that information from books would help me so much as the word of a living and surviving voice" (Eusebius, *H.E.* 3.39.3 f.). Had Papias set out to formulate a puzzle to confuse future generations he could not have produced a better one than the last two sentences. Nevertheless it seems reasonably clear that he intended to distinguish between what "Andrew . . . or any other of the Lord's disciples" had said *in the past,* and what "Aristion and the presbyter John" were saying *in his day.* John the Apostle is named in the first group, John the presbyter in the second. Moreover, it looks as though Papias had not been instructed by the presbyter John himself, but that he had learned of his teaching through "anyone who had *followed* the presbyters." From the description of this presbyter John as "the Lord's disciple" it would appear that this presbyter had been a personal disciple of Jesus. That is a noteworthy point; it could have contributed to the confusion of Irenaeus concerning the John who had seen the Lord.

There are certain features that are constant in the external tradition: the exile of John on Patmos; the identification of this John with the author of Revelation; his return to Ephesus to guide the churches after the death of Domitian (i.e., after A.D. 98); the affirmation that the same John wrote the

Fourth Gospel; the belief that he was John the Apostle, the son of Zebedee. Let us acknowledge immediately that there is no ground for questioning the name of the author of the Book of Revelation as *John;* virtually all are agreed that there is no case for pseudonymity in the Book of Revelation. This John, to judge from the book, must have been a man of great authority among the churches of Roman Asia. He makes no attempt to distinguish himself from any other Christian leader by the same name. He never calls himself an apostle. There is, however, no possibility that this writer shortly after completing the Revelation wrote the Fourth Gospel. Admittedly, the famous Cambridge trio of Westcott, Lightfoot, and Hort attempted to preserve the identity of authorship of the two works by postulating that John the Apostle wrote the Revelation in the confused period at the end of Nero's life, A.D. 68, and that he wrote the Gospel *thirty years later,* so giving time to the Apostle to improve his Greek. But this suggestion brings in a fresh and formidable set of problems concerning the two books. After pondering the Book of Revelation for a considerable period I came to the conclusion that the two great Johannine writings have one feature in common: they express to an unusual degree the characters, personalities, and ways of thinking of their respective authors. We have already affirmed the conviction that the Evangelist had reflected on his material and used it in preaching over many years; it proceeds from prolonged consideration of the gospel traditions. So also the Revelation exhibits the thought of a Christian apocalyptist. It is the product of a mind soaked in the Old Testament, to a degree to which no other work in the New Testament approximates. Moreover, the prophet is so much at home in Jewish apocalyptic literature that he finds it natural to express the Christian message through this mode of writing, and he freely utilizes oracles from other apocalyptic works. A striking example of this is seen in a comparison of Rev 12:1–17 with John 12:23–26, 31–32. The theology of the two passages is fundamentally the same: the dethronement of the devil and the enthronement of the Christ occur through the Redeemer's death and exaltation to heaven, which yet entails kindred suffering for the followers of the Lord. But the modes of expression stand in great contrast: the Evangelist combines synoptic-like sayings of Jesus with a quasi-apocalyptic utterance, while the prophet takes over and adapts a Jewish oracle, which itself had adapted an Ancient Near Eastern myth, to express the victory of the Messiah and his people over heathen oppressors and the coming of the divine kingdom. The Evangelist and the prophet have minds made in different molds. The difference in their modes of presenting the common faith is matched by the differences in their language—differences the more striking in that both authors appear to think in Aramaic and write in Greek, though they do so in consistently different ways.

A solution of the problem posed by the statements of early Christian writers concerning the activity of John of Ephesus would be to recognize that the tradition arose out of the activity of *John the prophet* in Roman Asia. He it is who was banished to Patmos and composed the Book of Revelation; and it is entirely comprehensible that he was released from his exile in the reign of Trajan, and continued his ministry among the churches in Roman Asia. On one basis alone would it be possible to combine this tradition with that of the residence of John the Apostle in Ephesus, namely, if indeed John the Apostle were the author of the Book of Revelation. Such a postulate would be in harmony with the synoptic picture of John "the son of Thunder," but there is not a hint in the Revelation that it was written by an apostle; the connection between the twelve tribes of Israel and the twelve apostles of the Lamb in the Jerusalem from heaven (Rev 21:13–14) suggests a detached view of the apostles from one who stands outside the apostolate. Since John the prophet is almost certainly a Palestinian, his migration to Ephesus could well have been the beginning of the confusion that attributed the move to John the Apostle. But the resolution of that issue is inseparably bound up with the identity of the Beloved Disciple, and to that we must turn.

2. THE INTERNAL EVIDENCE

Westcott's presentation of the internal evidence relating to the authorship of the Fourth Gospel is justly famous and worthy of mention. By a series of arguments that move in narrower concentric circles he sought to show that (*i*) the author was a Jew, (*ii*) the author was a Jew of Palestine, (*iii*) the author was an eyewitness of what he describes, (*iv*) the author was an apostle, (*v*) the author was the apostle John (lii–lix). The last two affirmations depend on the belief that only an apostle could have been an eyewitness on some of the occasions delineated, especially in the Passion and Resurrection narratives, and that the disciple whom Jesus loved must have been the apostle John. It is this last issue, however, on which discussion has most vigorously centered in recent times.

"The disciple whom Jesus loved" is first mentioned in John 13:23–26, and thereafter in 19:25–27; 20:1–10; 21:1–14, 20–24. With these passages it is commonly believed that 19:34–37 should be grouped as referring to the same individual, possibly also 18:15–16, and with greater hesitation, 1:35–40. We shall briefly look at these texts to see what can be learned from them concerning the author of the Gospel.

The Beloved Disciple emerges into clear view in 13:23. His presence at the Last Supper in Jerusalem, and later in the Passion and Resurrection narratives, claims him as an eyewitness of these crucially important events. No indication, however, is given as to his identity, certainly not in chap. 13. While we tend to assume that only the Twelve were gathered with Jesus for the Last Supper (cf. Mark 14:17 par.), John does not say so; in 13:1 he subsumes the group under the expression "his own," and later refers to them as "disciples." For our purpose two observations may be made: "the disciple whom Jesus loved" is not a natural self-designation for an author to use of himself, were he portraying the event of 13:21–26; second, the phrase ἐν τῷ κόλπῳ τοῦ Ἰησοῦ in v 23 appears to be an echo of εἰς τὸν κόλπον τοῦ πατρός in 1:18; it is apparently intended to convey the idea that as Jesus was in closest fellowship with the Father and so was able to "make him known" with peculiar authority, so the Beloved Disciple was in closest fellowship with Jesus and therefore able to make *him* known with very special authority. Such language is understandable from others about a disciple of Jesus, but inconceivable from the disciple himself.

Again, a prime element of the significance of 19:25–27 is the presence of a disciple of Jesus at the scene of the crucifixion. From 16:32, to say nothing of the evidence of the synoptic Gospels, we may assume that the disciples of Jesus forsook him at the end; but here is a "disciple" who did not do so, and to him Jesus commits his mother. It is unlikely that we are intended to view him as one of the Twelve. There may be a nuance here that as Jesus committed his mother to the Beloved Disciple, so the followers of Jesus should resort to him for knowledge of him (so Schnackenburg, 3:457, following Schürmann).

While the disciple who witnessed the spear thrust in 19:34–37 is in no way identified, the proximity of the scene to that recorded in 19:25–27 and the similarity of language used in vv 34–37 with that in 21:24 make it probable that the Beloved Disciple is in mind. His function as witness to the actuality and significance of the Gospel events is heavily emphasized: he attests the reality of the humanity and the death of Jesus, and the meaning of the latter as the sacrifice of the Lamb of God, through whom the redemption of the second Exodus is achieved.

John 20:1–10 describes the race of Peter and the Beloved Disciple to the tomb of Jesus. The latter reaches the tomb first, but Peter enters before him, and departs without comprehending what he has seen; the Beloved Disciple, on the contrary, sees and "believes" (v 9).

The superiority of the insight of the Beloved Disciple appears again in chap. 21; he recognizes the figure of the risen Christ standing on the shore and makes it known to Peter (v 7). The situation is more complex in vv 20–23. Peter has been restored to ministry for his Lord and his martyrdom obliquely made known, and he receives the command from the risen Christ, "Follow me." His query as to what is to happen to the Beloved Disciple is countered by the question "If it is my will that he remain until I come, what is that to you?" (v 23). This enables the writer to allude to the misapprehension commonly spread abroad that Jesus said that the Beloved Disciple should survive until the Parousia, and so he repeats again the precise words of the Lord. From this we deduce: (*i*) the Beloved Disciple was probably dead at the time of the writing, and the passage was intended to allay the disappointment of the community; and (*ii*) the repetition of the words of the risen Lord in v 23, coupled with the present tense of v 24, "who is bearing witness . . . ," suggests that the Beloved Disciple "remains" in the witness he continues to bear; Peter has glorified Christ through a martyr's death, and the Beloved Disciple continues his function of testimony through the Gospel.

What, then, are we to make of v 24: "This is the disciple who is bearing witness to these things, *and who has written these things*"? Dodd considered that the reference was solely to the preceding paragraph, vv 20–23, or that at most it extends to the whole of chap. 21 (*Historical Tradition*, 12). The contention is possible, but unnatural. The immediate sequence of "who has written these things" in v 24 by the "many other things" which Jesus did and which could hardly be written (v 25) leads the reader to relate the statement to chaps. 1–20 as well as to chap. 21. The Gospel, then, in v 24 is put to the account of the Beloved Disciple, and an attestation is added, "we know that his testimony is true." This led Westcott to believe that the sentence was added by the elders of the church at Ephesus, so making it our earliest (external) witness to the authorship of the Gospel. On the contrary, there is no ground for separating v 24 from its context; rather it forms the climax of the narrative and is most naturally seen as deriving from the author of the chapter. But the author has so written it as to indicate that the Beloved Disciple is now deceased! In that case v 24 cannot be intended to ascribe direct authorship of the Gospel to the Beloved Disciple; the emphasis of the statement is on the *witness* of the disciple (ὁ μαρτυρῶν . . . ἡ μαρτυρία . . .), and the term γράψας either has a causal meaning ("caused these things to be written") or signifies "wrote about these things." The Beloved Disciple, accordingly, is represented as providing the witness which chap. 21 and the preceding chapters embody.

Strictly speaking, we must acknowledge that this representation comes from *the writer of chap. 21;* there is uncertainty as to the origin of the passage, whether it is a postscript or an epilogue, whether it is added by the Evangelist or by a redactor. Such considerations raise the possibility that the author of the chapter had one view of the Beloved Disciple and the Evangelist another. H. Thyen supplies yet another possibility: chap. 21 is an epilogue to balance the prologue (1:1–18); both were written by the redactor, who was responsible for *all* the passages relating to the Beloved Disciple and whose editorial labors were such that *he* should be viewed as the evangelist! (*L'Evangile de Jean,* 267). At this point we content ourselves with noting the closeness of relation between chap. 21 and chaps. 1–20, which suggests that, on the least estimate, the author of chap. 21 belonged to the same circle as that of 1–20, and he is unlikely either to have misunderstood or diverged from the Evangelist's view of the Beloved Disciple (so Schnackenburg, 3:453).

We still do not know who the Beloved Disciple is. The episode of 21:1–14 tells of an appearance of Jesus to seven disciples, among whom was the Beloved Disciple. Simon, Thomas, and Nathanael are named, then the sons of Zebedee, and "two others of his disciples"; but there is nothing to indicate which of the unnamed *four* is the Beloved Disciple.

It would aid us if we could be confident that 18:15–17 relates to the Beloved Disciple; in favor of that identification is the manner in which "the other disciple" is spoken of, in association with Peter, in v 16, just as the Beloved Disciple is in 20:2, 4, 8 (cf. also 21:21–23). This "other disciple," who followed Jesus to the High Priest's house and had Peter brought into the court, is described as ὁ γνωστὸς τοῦ ἀρχιερέως; this does not simply mean an *acquaintance* of the High Priest, but, in C. H. Dodd's estimate, one who stood in intimate relations with the High Priest's family, possibly a relative and of priestly birth (*Historical Tradition,* 86–87). This would exclude the possibility of identifying this "other" disciple with one of the Twelve. His presence as a disciple in the priestly circles of Jerusalem is of more than ordinary interest, not least as a possible source for certain of the traditions relating to the passion of Jesus.

If we were to include 1:35–40 among the Beloved Disciple texts, its implication would be considerable, both from the viewpoint of his earlier background in the circle of John the Baptist's disciples and his knowledge of the beginnings of the (Judean) ministry of Jesus.

Admittedly, there are numerous uncertainties here, but it would appear that the texts relating to the Beloved Disciple hold well together and present a consistent picture. If chap. 21 was written by another author than the Evangelist, he appears to have shared the tradition relating to the disciple without modification. On the basis of these texts it is possible to make some tentative statements concerning the Beloved Disciple and his relation to the author of the Fourth Gospel.

(a) The Beloved Disciple is presented as a historical figure among the early disciples of Jesus and in the continuing Church. We acknowledge that this has been disputed at times. Bultmann, for example, believed that the Evangelist intended us to see in the Beloved Disciple a purely ideal figure, but that he was "historicized" by the redactor of chap. 21 (483–84). H. Thyen, however, affirmed that recent Johannine research shows "a growing and by no means uncritical consensus that to the literary figure of the Beloved Disciple on the textual level must correspond, on the level of the real history of Johannine Christianity, a concrete person" ("Aus der Literatur zum Johannesevangelium," *TRu* 42/3, 223). That the Beloved Disciple served a representative and symbolic function is entirely consistent with his being a real disciple of Jesus, as with other figures of the Gospel like Nicodemus, the Samaritan Woman, Lazarus—or even the pool of Siloam!

(b) The Beloved Disciple is not a member of the Twelve, nor a well-known person in the early Church. It is difficult to supply a cogent reason for the Evangelist consistently and completely hiding his identity if he were a prominent leader like John the Apostle or Paul, or a well-known individual like John Mark or Lazarus. By contrast the anonymity is understandable if the designation were the common mode of referring to a leader within the Johannine churches not known elsewhere; there would be no need to name the beloved leader.

(c) The Beloved Disciple is not the author of the Gospel—neither of chaps. 1–20 nor of chap. 21. This we deduced from the first mention of his name in 13:23 and from the implications of 21:21–24, despite the first impression which 21:24 may make. The texts in which the disciple features present him as *the witness* on which the Gospel rests, not its author.

(d) The Beloved Disciple is presented as an eyewitness of certain crucial events in the Gospel, notably in connection with the end of the ministry of Jesus and the resurrection appearances. If 1:35–40 and 18:15–16 were included in the relevant texts, this would greatly strengthen the impression, gained from the other passages, that the disciple was a Judean and therefore able to narrate elements in the ministry of Jesus in the south of Palestine and in Jerusalem in particular. His participation in the movement of John the Baptist and his involvement in the Jerusalem priestly circles would shed light on various elements in the background of the Fourth Gospel, including its basic theological thrust.

(e) The authority of the Beloved Disciple extends beyond the events which he may have witnessed. The implication of 13:23 leads to a view of the disciple as an authoritative interpreter of Jesus, not simply of the course of events at the close of the ministry of Jesus. He is the prime source of the traditions about Jesus in the Johannine circle. J. Roloff illuminatingly compared the role of the Beloved Disciple with that of the Teacher of Righteousness in the Qumran Community; both figures are anonymous, and both had decisive influence in their respective communities as interpreters and exegetes ("Der Johanneische Lieblingsjünger," 129–51). While, however, the role of the Teacher of Righteousness was to be an interpreter of the OT for his community, that of the Beloved Disciple was to be an interpreter of Jesus and his revelation (*Jesus* was the interpreter of the OT!). This was beautifully and succinctly expressed by Yu Ibuki: "The revelation of the one loved by the Father takes place through the one loved by the Son. Hence the gospel of John can be described as the gospel of the Beloved according to the Beloved" (*Wahrheit* 271, cited by H. Thyen, *TRu* 42/3:260–61).

(*f*) The relationship of the Beloved Disciple to Peter requires examination in the exegesis of the passages. Here it suffices to note that if the superiority of the Beloved Disciple's insight is stressed, there is no suggestion of a polemic against Peter. If there is any thought in the background that Peter represents the official ministry within the churches and the Beloved Disciple the charismatic ministries of the Spirit, both ministries are admitted as complementary within the Church of the Lord. Primarily, however, the authority of the Beloved Disciple within the Johannine communities is in view, possibly with an eye on the deviations that were arising from the teaching he communicates through the Gospel.

(*g*) As the authority figure to which the Johannine communities looked, the Beloved Disciple appears to have had a group of teachers about him. The existence of a Johannine literature alongside the Gospel, including the three epistles and the Book of Revelation, points to a group of teachers having a common center of loyalty, with a diversity not too great to be contained within the unity. Cullmann postulates that this group consciousness goes back to very early days within the life of the Church (*The Johannine Circle*, 39–56). R. A. Culpepper has filled out the thesis of a Johannine school by giving a detailed comparison with comparable "schools" in the ancient world (*The Johannine School*, 1975). It is important to recognize that this school, though distinctive within early Christianity, was broad enough to include apocalyptic Christianity as well as a nonapocalyptic presentation of the kerygma, and that these coexisted under the greater unity of faith in the incarnate Word, who through his redeeming acts has brought the life of the kingdom of God to man.

(*h*) The identity of the leader of this group remains the secret of the Evangelist. There has been no lack of suggestions as to who he may have been: after John the Apostle, Lazarus is a favorite nomination (cf. 11:5, 36); in addition, John Mark, Matthias, Paul, the Presbyter John, [a symbol for] Gentile Christianity or free charismatic Christianity have all been proposed. Most recently H. Thyen has argued in favor of the elder who wrote 2 and 3 John as the Beloved Disciple (*L'Evangile de Jean*, 296–98). In the end we have to admit that these are all guesses, some with less and some with more plausibility. As with the Beloved Disciple, so with the Evangelist: we do not know his name. But our ignorance of his identity entails no detriment to the value of his work. Those who, like the *Alogi* of the second century, have rejected the Fourth Gospel as a profound interpretation of Jesus have thereby passed judgment on themselves. The Church through the ages has recognized in the Evangelist a unique theologian taught by the Spirit of truth. Perhaps we should extend the range of that judgment and view the Evangelist as a master interpreter of the school of the Beloved Disciple, among whom the Spirit showed his activity in large measure. The Fourth Gospel is a monument to the presence of the Paraclete in the Church of the Word made flesh. The work of the Evangelist is an encouragement to every believer to look to that same Paraclete to guide into all the truth attested in the Gospel.

IV. THE DATE AND PLACE OF WRITING OF THE FOURTH GOSPEL

Traditionally the Gospel has been viewed as the last of the canonical Gospels, and this has remained the general opinion of most scholars to this day. In the nineteenth century and the earlier part of this, it became fashionable to assign a very late date to our Gospel; authorities can be cited for placing it in virtually every decade of the second century to its last quarter (e.g., O. Holtzmann and A. Jülicher assigned it to A.D. 100–125, T. Keim and P. W. Schmiedel to 130–140, G. Volkmar and E. Schwartz to 140–155, F. C. Baur and Bruno Bauer to 160–170; see J. Moffatt, *Introduction to the NT,* 580–81). The reasons for such late dating were diverse, but, above all, scholars were impressed with the lack of clear knowledge of the Fourth Gospel by early Christian writers and the advanced nature of the theology of the Gospel. The former factor is certainly puzzling; to this day scholars differ as to whether the Fourth Gospel can be clearly traced in 1 Clement, the Epistle of Barnabas, the Didache, Ignatius, the Shepherd of Hermas, or even the Odes of Solomon; most are inclined to a negative verdict, but remain uncertain about Ignatius (the evidence is conveniently assembled by Barrett, 109–15). Even the apparent use of John 3:3 by Justin Martyr (καὶ γὰρ ὁ Χριστὸς εἶπεν. Ἂν μὴ ἀγεννηθῆτε οὐ μὴ εἰσέλθητε εἰς τὴν βασιλείαν τῶν οὐρανῶν, I Apol. 61) is disputed by some as a Johannine reminiscence. The first clear citation of the Gospel by name is from Theophilus of Antioch, *ca.* A.D. 180, but Tatian used it, along with the three synoptic Gospels, in his Harmony of the Gospels, which was probably compiled in Syriac *ca.* A.D. 160, and then in Greek A.D. 170. The Valentinian Gnostics used and prized the Gospel at an earlier date, as may be seen in *The Gospel of Truth,* possibly written by Valentinus himself, *ca.* A.D. 150.

All this discussion, however, has been put in the shade by the publication of two papyrus fragments, the Egerton Papyrus 2, published under the title *Fragments of an Unknown Gospel and other Early Christian Papyri* (H. I. Bell and T. C. Skeat, London: British Museum, 1935), which appears to have used the Fourth Gospel along with other Gospel traditions, and P[52], a fragment which includes John 18:31–33, 37–38. This latter papyrus was dated by F. C. Kenyon as "early second century" (*Text of the Greek Bible,* 75), and more recently by K. Aland as "the beginning of the second century" ("Neue Neutestamentliche Papyri II," *NTS* 9 [1962–63] 307); on the basis of this papyrus Bultmann concluded that the Gospel must have been known in Egypt *ca.* A.D. 100 (270, n.4; Schmithals, writing on Bultmann's behalf an introduction to the English translation of the commentary, curiously pushes the date of the final redaction of the Gospel on to A.D. 120, p. 12).

In recent years there has been a reaction on the part of a number of scholars to assigning a late date to the Gospel, believing it to be either contemporary with or earlier than the synoptic Gospels, but in any case prior to A.D. 70. The reasons for this are varied, but chief among them are the conviction as to the independence of the Fourth Gospel of the other three; certain primitive traits in the portrayal of Jesus, such as the regular use of the name Jesus, Rabbi, teacher, and emphasis on the role of Jesus as the prophet like Moses; the presentation of the message of Jesus as a genuine extension of Judaism, reflecting the Christian faith as still contained within Judaism; allusions to the Temple and other buildings in Jerusalem as still standing (e.g., 5:2), along with absence of any hint that Jerusalem and its Temple have been destroyed; the marked influence of the Qumran group, which ceased to exist by A.D. 70; the reflection of concerns of the Church during the period A.D. 40–70 rather than a 70–100 date (e.g., the polemic against John the Baptist, presupposing a continuing strength of his movement at the time of writing; the commitment of mission to Israel, reflecting continuing relations between Temple and Church); the inexplicable gap between the primitive traditions behind the Fourth Gospel and their publication if the Gospel was written at the end of the first century (on these arguments see R. M. Grant, *A Historical Introduction to the NT* [London: Collins, 1963] 152–53, 160; F. L. Cribbs, "A Reassessment of the Date of Origin and the Destination of the Gospel of John," 38–55; L. Morris, 30–35; J. A. T. Robinson, *Redating*, 254–84).

Most scholars find this position difficult to accept. Many are ready to acknowledge the early date of the *traditions* utilized in the Gospel, but they believe that their final embodiment in the Gospel will have taken place at a later date. The moot point is how much later; how long does it require for the theological maturity of the Fourth Gospel to develop? Centuries could roll by without its emergence, but the early Christological hymns of the NT, like Phil 2:6–11 and Col 1:15–20, show what can happen within a single generation, and the minds behind the Fourth Gospel were not ordinary. The final chapter of the Gospel (21) appears to reflect the passing of the Beloved Disciple, but again that cannot of itself determine the date at which it happened, though it suggests one not earlier than A.D. 70. Most important are the relations between the synagogue and the Christian communities reflected in the Gospel. F. L. Cribbs maintains that the Gospel assumes they are open, whereas J. L. Martyn holds that by the time of the final redaction of the Gospel they have become irreparably broken off. The problem is posed by the references in the Gospel to the Jews making confessors of Jesus as Messiah ἀποσυνάγωγοι (9:22; 12:42; 16:2). It is urged that these passages presume not a disciplinary exclusion from the synagogue (for a short time, till amendment is evident), but ejection from the synagogue, carrying with it exclusion from the community life of the Jews. W. Schrage, for example, in his article on ἀποσυνάγωγος, writes: "Plain in all three references is the fact that an unbridgeable gulf has now opened up between Church and Synagogue, so that exclusion on the part of the latter is total. To think in terms of the lesser synagogue ban is a trivializing; this is no mere excommunication but total expulsion, a result of the *birkath ha-minim*" (*TDNT* 7:852; similarly Str-B 4:331, followed by most commentators). This "blessing about the heretics," ironically so termed, relates to an addition to the Eighteen Benedictions, which constituted the daily prayers of all pious Jews and were repeated in every synagogue service. The Twelfth Benediction reads: "For the apostates let there be no hope, and let the arrogant government be speedily uprooted in our days. Let the Nazarenes and the heretics be destroyed in a moment, and let them be blotted out of the book of life and not be inscribed together with the righteous Blessed art thou, O Lord, who humblest the arrogant." The tractate *Ber.* 28b declares that the benediction was composed in Jamnia by Samuel the Small, in response to a request by Gamaliel II for someone to word a benediction relating to the "minim." From the first the "minim" (= heretics) probably denoted the Christians, for in Jewish eyes they were the arch-heretics, and the most dangerous; it is likely that the prayer mentioned them alone when it was first composed, and that later "the Nazarenes" was added to make the reference explicit (so Jocz, *Jewish People*, 56–57). The date when this version of the "blessing" was composed is commonly put at A.D. 85, possibly a few years later. J. L. Martyn makes this event the fixed point in his reconstruction of the composition of the Fourth Gospel, and the development of synagogue-church relations reflected in it. In his view the story in John 9 of the man born blind is recounted in such a manner as to mirror the contemporary situation of Jewish Christians, excommunicated from the synagogue, and to encourage them to stand firm in their faith; the wording of 16:2 reflects an advance on that, when Jewish leaders, in their determination to stop the proselytizing by Jewish Christians in their midst, began to exact the death penalty on Christian activists (see "History of the Johannine Community," 149–75, more fully in *History and Theology of the Fourth Gospel*). On this basis the Fourth Gospel cannot be dated earlier than the decade 90–100, and toward its end rather than its beginning. That is, indeed, the date favored by most Johannine scholars, and this appears to have set it on a firm foundation.

The foundation, however, may not be as firm as many assume. Not a few Johannine scholars remain unconvinced that the Twelfth Benediction is in view in the Evangelist's employment of the term ἀποσυνάγωγος, partly by reason of the similar situation envisaged in Luke 6:22, and partly through the record of the treatment of Jewish Christians in Acts (e.g., of Stephen, chaps. 6–7, and of Paul, 13:50) and Paul's own references to like experiences (see especially 1 Thess 2:14–16. For this understanding of the setting of the Johannine community see Dodd, *Historical Tradition*, 410; Sanders, 242; D. R. A. Hare, *The Theme of Jewish Persecution of Christians in the Gospel of Matthew*, 48–56; F. L. Cribbs, 53–54; J. A. T Robinson, *Redating*, 273–74). More importantly, perhaps, it has been urged that the attitude of the Jewish authorities in the Fourth Gospel reflects a gathering opposition which *led to* the formulation of the Twelfth Benediction of Jamnia (so R. Kysar, *The Fourth Evangelist*, 171; W. H. Brownlee, "Whence the Gospel of John?," 182). W. A. Meeks, who is in sympathy with Martyn's views, stated, "I doubt whether the separation can be identified specifically with the *birkath ha-minim* promulgated at Yavneh, and whether that decree itself can be dated so precisely"

("Man from Heaven," 55, n.40). Meeks considers that the Jewish record of the scenes in *T. Ber.* 28 "portray as punctiliar events in Gamaliel's time what was actually a linear development stretching over a lengthy period and culminating in the pertinent formulation of the *birkath ha-minim*" (in a written communication to Martyn, cited in *History and Theology,* 55, n.69). Martyn also reports a comparable correspondence with Morton Smith, who holds that Gamaliel is likely to have instituted the *birkath* after similar moves had been made in Jewish communities and that it should be placed in the second century; while not convinced, Martyn states his readiness to entertain the whole period between A.D. 80 and 115 for the composition of the Benediction, but preferring the earlier to the latter part of the period (*History and Theology,* 57, n.75).

It seems that more caution is required about this issue, and that the date of the Fourth Gospel is less capable of precise determination than is frequently represented. But that is nothing new in Gospel criticism! The dates of the synoptic Gospels are uncertain; there is not one of them for which we can set a date of composition with complete confidence. Whereas it was common to date Mark A.D. 65–67 (shortly after the deaths of Paul and Peter), it is now fashionable to set it shortly after the Jewish war, on the ground that Mark 13 was composed to moderate the apocalyptic fever caused by the fall of Jerusalem; one would have thought, however, that the apocalyptic fever would be no less intense in the early days of that war, and as it moved toward its climax. Matthew is frequently dated about A.D. 90, on the ground of its reflection of the deliberations of Jamnia and the *Birkath ha-minim* in particular. And Luke must be set about the same time through its relations with Matthew. If it be so that the Fourth Evangelist was acquainted with the synoptic Gospels but did not use them, this is not without significance for us. One is reminded of the simile that Austin Farrer used when discussing the date of the Book of Revelation: "The datings of all these books (i.e., Revelation and the gospels) are like a line of tipsy revellers walking home arm-in-arm; each is kept in position by the others and none is firmly grounded" (*The Revelation of St. John the Divine* [Oxford: Clarendon Press, 1964] 37). When one considers the other companions of the Fourth Gospel, namely, the three epistles of John and their authors, it is clear that unusual care is required in our estimates, or the whole lot will fall down!

What is eminently plausible is the origin of the *traditions* of the Fourth Gospel at an early date, and their development over a considerable period. A process akin to that proposed by R. E. Brown and O. Cullmann is most likely: an early tradition within the Johannine community became crystallized in the preaching and teaching of the Beloved Disciple, and it was taken up by the Evangelist and embodied in his own way in the Gospel. The *Birkath ha-minim* may be viewed as an indicator of the tensions between the Jewish Christians and their non-Christian compatriots presupposed by the Evangelist, but not as a chronological marker that had already been passed. A date around A.D. 80 would satisfy the evidence, but we admit that to be no more than a plausible guess.

No less than four areas have been suggested as a possible venue for the writing of the Fourth Gospel.

Ephesus has been traditionally viewed as the place of its composition, owing to the testimony of the Fathers (e.g., Irenaeus: "John, the disciple of the Lord . . . published the gospel while living at Ephesus in Asia," *Adv. Haer.* 3.1.2). As we saw in our consideration of the authorship of the Gospel, this tradition appears to have been primarily determined by the ministry of John the prophet, who wrote the Book of Revelation and sent it to the churches of Roman Asia. Whether or not John the prophet was identical with John the Apostle, he cannot be viewed as the author of the Fourth Gospel.

While there is more than this to be said in favor of the Ephesian origin of the Gospel, it was this confusion of the tradition relating to John the prophet in Ephesus that caused Kirsopp Lake to regard the persistent linking of the Fourth Gospel with Ephesus as a curiosity of criticism. Observing that "the gospel is extremely Philonic," he thought it likely that it came from Alexandria (*Introduction to the NT*, 53). J. N. Sanders was earlier attracted to this idea, and supported it by pointing out the affinities of the Gospel with the Epistle of Barnabas and that to Diognetus, its use by the Egyptian Gnostics, and the early circulation of the Gospel in Egypt as attested by the papyri Egerton 2 and P^{52} (*The Fourth Gospel in the Early Church*, 85–86). W. H. Brownlee likewise lent his support to the Alexandrian origin of the Gospel; he drew attention to the large Jewish and Samaritan populations in the city, terming it "a little Palestine" in which most of the parties to which the Fourth Gospel was addressed were found, and the fanaticism of the city, where such passages as John 8:58 ff.; 10:29–30; 16:2 would have a comprehensible setting ("Whither the Gospel according to John?" 189–90). These arguments are interesting, but hardly compelling. Sanders later abandoned the Alexandrian hypothesis in favor of the Ephesian tradition ("St. John on Patmos," *NTS* 9 [1962–63] 75–85). It may be pointed out that the Egyptian sands have preserved for us papyri of all the Gospels and fragments of almost all the books of the NT, and we may yet hope to recover further remains of them all.

Early in this century F. C. Conybeare drew attention to a statement, attributed to Ephraem the Syrian, in the Armenian version of his commentary on the Diatessaron: "John wrote in Antioch where he lived till Trajan's time" ("Ein Zeugnis Ephraims über das Fehlen von C.1 und 2 im Texte des Lukas," *ZNW* 3 [1902] 193). The claim sounds suspiciously like an accommodation of a different tradition due to local Syrian patriotism, and its authenticity has been disputed. Nevertheless, the suggestion that the Gospel originated in Syria has attracted a number of scholars, including C. F. Burney, E. Schweizer, E. Haenchen, and W. G. Kümmel. In its favor can be urged the Aramaic tradition behind the Greek text of the Gospel, its close affinities with Ignatius, bishop of Antioch, and with the *Odes of Solomon*, and the kinship of the discourse material with Syrian Gnosticism (so especially Bultmann-Schmithals, 12). There is no denying the attractiveness of this view. One must acknowledge, however, that it is difficult to define precisely the locality of the type of Gnosticism with which the Fourth Evangelist was confronted; in the Nag Hammadi gnostic writings of Egypt, the Gospel of Truth, which shows conspicuous connections with the Fourth Gospel, also has affinities with the *Odes of Solomon*.

Of late there has been an interest in locating the Gospel in Palestine, not least in view of the nature of its contacts with Qumran, with Samaritan religion, and with varied other strains of Judaism. J. L. Martyn has urged this from the point of view of the relations between the Synagogue and the Church reflected in the Gospel. He would see the Gospel as rooted in a purely Jewish city, subject to the authority of the synagogue and of the council of Jamnia. He traces a developing situation in the Gospel: (a) the believers in Jesus are part of the synagogue, they are Christian Jews in the strictest sense, and the Gentile mission is not on their horizon; (b) the believers are forced to separate from the synagogue through excommunication, which leads to the infliction of the death penalty on some of its leaders; (c) a movement to firm social and theological configurations ("History of the Johannine Community," 151–75).

We have already discussed some of the issues bound up with this view. That the Fourth Gospel has its roots in Palestine is virtually certain. That the entire development of the Johannine tradition up to its publication took place in Palestine is less certain. The Gospel suggests wider horizons than purely Jewish communities in Israel's land. It is doubtful that the prologue would ever have been formulated in its present terms in an exclusively Jewish setting in Palestine. We need to recall at this point our review of the religious relations of the Fourth Gospel, which are uncommonly wide for a document of the NT. The relation of the incarnation, ministry, death, and exaltation of Jesus to the cosmos similarly needs to be taken into account; it is false to the heart of the Fourth Gospel to minimize the significance of John 3:16, with kindred passages like 12:20–23, 31–32; 11:50–52; the implications for mission of 10:16; 17:20–23; 20:21 (cf. 17:18; 21:1–11), and the eschatological significance of 4:23–24, 42. The Evangelist may have subordinated the expression "kingdom of God" to the more personal one of "life," but the reality is fundamental to the Gospel; and it is an impossible idea that in the Fourth Gospel the kingdom that came in the redemptive ministry of Jesus is restricted to a Jewish horizon. That representatives of the Gospel could be subject to disciplinary measures of Jewish courts outside Palestine is evident from the Book of Acts and the letters of Paul.

It would seem desirable, then, to acknowledge the growth of the Fourth Gospel as a process indebted to more than one area. Its origin in a form of Palestinian Judaism which was open to influences other than Pharisaism is clear; we have already recognized its links with the Qumran sect and Samaritanism, as well as with rabbinic and hellenistic Judaism. In view of the nearness of Syria to the Jewish homeland, and the growth of the Church in Damascus and Antioch especially, it would not be surprising if Syrian thought left its stamp on the Johannine tradition. But Ephesus cannot be dismissed, not simply by reason of the external tradition of John's domicile in the city, but because of the presence of the Johannine school in that area, to which the Book of Revelation bears witness. We have clear attestation within the NT of Gnosticizing activities in Roman Asia, as is evident from the letter to the Colossians, 1 and 2 Timothy, the Johannine letters, Revelation 2–3 (which also attest intense opposition between Jews and Christians, 2:9 and 3:9), and possibly 2 Peter and Jude.

This solution of the problem was tentatively adopted by T. W. Manson.

He suggested that the Fourth Gospel originated in a tradition which had its home in Jerusalem, and was taken to Antioch; there it influenced literature connected with that city, the liturgical usage of the Syrian church, the teaching of missionaries who went out from it (e.g. Paul) and its later leaders (e.g., Ignatius); from Antioch it was taken to Ephesus, where "the final literary formulation was achieved in the Gospel and Epistles attributed to John" ("The Fourth Gospel," 320). With Manson, R. H. Lightfoot (5–6) and Schnackenburg (152) expressed agreement.

V. Aspects of the Theology of the Fourth Gospel

The theme of the Fourth Gospel is Christ. The aphorism of Zinzendorf might have been uttered by the Evangelist, "I have but one passion: that is he, only he" (cited by Käsemann, *Testament of Jesus*, 38). The controlling theological concern, accordingly. is Christology; all other theological concerns such as salvation, eschatology, Church, world, Holy Spirit, are aspects of the one great theme, and all are viewed in the light of the dualism that characterizes the Christology. We shall therefore examine at greater length the Christology of the Gospel and look more briefly at the important themes of salvation and eschatology.

1. Christology

There is an astonishing variety of ways in which Jesus is confessed and described in this Gospel. The most important are the following (the references adduced are only examples):

The Word (1:1,14)
μονογενὴς θεός (? or μονογενὴς υἱός [1:18])
μονογενὴς υἱός (3:16, 18)
Son of God (with varied nuances, 1:34; cf. 1:49; 11:11, 20, 31)
The Son (3:17, 36; 5:19–27)
Son of Man (1:51 etc.)
A teacher come from God (3:2)
A prophet (4:19; 9:19)
The prophet that should come into the world (6:14; cf. 7:40)
The Messiah (1:41; 4:29; 11:11, 20, 31)
King of Israel (1:49; cf. 6:15; 12:13)
King of the Jews (19:19)
The Holy One of God (6:69)
The Lamb of God (1:29, 36)
The Coming One (12:13)
The Man (19:5)
The Sent One of God (3:16–17, 34; 5:30; 7:16–18; especially 10:36)
ἐγώ εἰμι (8:24, 28, 58; with predicates the Bread of Life [chapter 6], the Good Shepherd [chapter 10], the Resurrection [11:25], the Way, the Truth, the Life [14:6], the true Vine [15:1–10])
A Paraclete (14:16)
Rabbouni (20:16)
The Lord (20:18; 21:7; cf. 6:68)
My Lord and my God (20:28, cf. 1:1)

The remarkable feature of this list is not alone the titles that are unique to this Gospel, but the accent given to those that do occur elsewhere.

That Jesus is "a teacher come from God," for example, is true beyond the comprehension of Nicodemus (3:2), for Jesus is the Revealer from Heaven to bring the ultimate truth of God to man. Similarly the recognition of Jesus as "a prophet" (4:19; 9:19) is inadequate, but it is an important motif that Jesus is "the prophet who should come into the world" in the last times, for he is the prophet like Moses, yet greater than Moses; he performs greater works in a greater exodus for redemption unto life in the kingdom of God (3:14–15; 6:32–58). While the related terms "Messiah," "King of Israel," "Son of God" are all rooted in Israel's religion and eschatological hope, they acquire deeper dimensions in the Fourth Gospel; so also the significant variants of Messiah, "Lamb of God" (the Warrior Lamb of apocalyptic tradition transformed into the Passover Lamb of God); "the Holy One of God" (6:69), and (at least in Samaritan thought) "the Savior of the world" (4:42). "The King of Israel" is expounded in terms of the king who has come into the world to bear witness to the truth (18:37), and the expression "Son of God" is lifted to a new plane through the concept of the sending of the Son from the presence of God.

It is generally acknowledged that the most characteristic elements of Johannine Christology are bound up with the last-named concept, "the Son (of God)." It is the outstanding feature of the revelation of God as Father in the Fourth Gospel. A few statistics will illustrate this. According to T. W. Manson πατήρ as a name for God attributed to Jesus occurs 4 times in Mark, 8 or 9 in Q, 6 in Luke, 23 in Matthew (of which 17 fall in the Sermon on the Mount), and 107 times in John (*On Paul and John*, 129). Of these over half in the Fourth Gospel denote the relation of Jesus to the Father. The absolute use of "the Son" with reference to Jesus occurs once in Mark (13:32) and once in Q (Matt 11:27 = Luke 10:22), then in the trinitarian baptismal formula in Matthew's resurrection narrative (28:19); the term occurs 18 times in John (plus 1:18), along with "his μονογενής son" (3:16), and certain occurrences of "Son of God" used in an identical sense as "the Son" (e.g., the μονογενής "Son of God" in 3:18, following on 3:16 and 17, and "Son of God" in 5:25 in the midst of a series of references to the Son in 5:19–24, 26). Accordingly Schnackenburg affirmed, "The 'Father-Son' relationship is the key to the understanding of Jesus as portrayed by the Evangelist, and of his words and actions as interpreted by him" (2:172). That relationship is grounded in a unity between the Father and the Son "before the world was" (17:5, 24). The "sending" of the Son by the Father, accordingly, is for a redemption through incarnation and death (3:16–17), the purpose of which is a gathering into that unity of all who respond to the word of his revelation (17:20–23; 11:51–52).

A striking feature of the presentation of the Son in the Gospel is its close liaison with the Son of Man. Such a relationship is adumbrated in the synoptic Gospels (see, e.g., Mark 8:38 and 13:32), but in the Fourth Gospel the mission of the Son virtually merges with the functions of the Son of Man. The representation in Dan 7 of the coming of one like a Son of Man with the kingdom of God pervades the synoptic Gospels. It is the link which binds the synoptic sayings on the Son of Man; in his authoritative ministry of word and deed, in his dying and rising, and in his Parousia he is the instrument of the kingdom of God that brings salvation and judgment to mankind. It is highly significant that the first statement relating to the Son of Man in the Fourth Gospel (1:51) announces the mediation of the redemptive powers of heaven through the Son of Man; the sayings concerning the "lifting up" of the Son of Man for the life and the judgment of the world (3:14–15; 12:31) strongly remind us of the synoptic passion predictions (Mark 8:31, etc.), while 12:31 also calls to mind the utterance of Jesus before the High Priest in Mark 14:62. The interpenetration of the mission of the Son (of God) with that of the Son of Man works in both directions. It appears most plainly in 5:17–29: the Son performs the works which the Father has continued from the creation and will conclude in the last day, namely, those of giving life and exercising judgment (vv 17, 19–23, 25–26); in v 27 the judgment that accompanies the coming of the kingdom of God is stated to be the prerogative of the Son "because he is the Son of Man'; so also it is assumed in vv 28–29 that the resurrection for the judgment that determines entry into or exclusion from the kingdom of God is by the agency of the Son who is also Son of Man. In 3:14–15 the gift of life through the lifting up of the Son of Man is expounded in terms of the sending of the Son for life and judgment (3:16–21); the reverse phenomenon is observable in 12:27–28, 31–34. Ultimately the works of the Son who is Son of Man are those of God through him. Hence his unity with the Father is stressed—in terms of the Son in 10:30 ("I and the Father are One," cf. v 29), and of the Son of Man in 8:28 ("When you have lifted up the Son of Man you will know that *I am*").

In the light of the foregoing it is evident that the exposition in the prologue of the Son in terms of "the Word" is in harmony with the Christology of the Gospel. It makes explicit what is implicit in the body of the Gospel. If, as I do not doubt, the term "Logos" is used as "an attention catcher" (Filson, 111), its importance is not on that account to be minimized. The prologue provides, as T. E. Pollard expressed it, an overture to the Gospel in which its main themes are announced (*Johannine Christology*, 14). The ruling concept is that of the Word as Mediator—in creation (vv 1, 10), in revelation (vv 4, 5, 9, 18), and in salvation (vv 12, 13, 16), and its climax is reached in the declaration of incarnation in v 14, which Thyen considers to be the climactic utterance of the whole Gospel also (*TRu* 39 [1975] 222). Admittedly, the impersonal concept of "Word" cannot represent all that the man Jesus is set forth in the Gospel to be, but neither can any other term do that, not even "the Son." If, as Pollard rightly suggested, the Fourth Gospel is preeminently "the Gospel of the Father and the Son" (the title of a book by W. F. Lofthouse), it is also true that the term "the Son" itself needs to be complemented with all that the other titles attributed to Jesus in this Gospel signify. That has many implications, but one in particular may be mentioned at this point: the frequently reiterated obedience of the Son to the Father (e.g., 4:34; 5:19; 8:29), whom he acknowledges to be "greater than I" (14:28), requires complementation by the statements in the prologue such as καὶ θεὸς ἦν ὁ λόγος (1:1), and (if it be the correct reading) μονογενὴς θεὸς ὁ ὢν εἰς τὸν κόλπον τοῦ πατρὸς ἐκεῖνος ἐξηγήσατο (1:18), together with the climactic confession in the Easter narrative, ὁ κύριός μου καὶ ὁ θεός μου (20:28). Such is the content which the Evangelist would have his readers import into the declaration of faith, "Jesus is the Christ, the Son of God" (20:31). Then, moreover, it becomes evident that the exposition of the Son in the Fourth Gospel cannot be justly viewed as "functional Christology." Doubtless the prime interest of a gospel, including the one we are discussing, is to set forth the *action* of God in Christ for the fulfillment of his purpose of grace, whether that be described in terms of new creation or saving sovereignty (both are present in John). We have already acknowledged that, for the Evangelist, salvation, eschatology, God's dealings with his people and the world, and the mission of the Holy Spirit are all set in relation to Christ, and so are aspects of the function of the Christ. But the unremitting concentration of the Evangelist on the person through whom God acts makes it plain that for him "function and person are inseparable" (J. Blank, *Krisis*, 36; see also the review of recent discussion in Kysar, *Fourth Evangelist*, 200–206). "John clarifies the relation of Jesus to God," wrote Barrett (54). Such was the Evangelist's intention, and such was his achievement.

2. Soteriology

In the light of the preceding discussion it is not surprising that one should affirm that the Christology of the Fourth Gospel is "essentially ordained to soteriology" (Schnackenburg, on 20:31). This, as Kümmel pointed out, is the primary import of the "I am" sayings in the Gospel; for while a few of them are without a predicate (so 6:20; 8:28, 58), most point to an aspect of the salvation which Jesus is and brings: he is Bread of Life (6:35), Light (8:12), the Door to life (10:7), the Shepherd (10:11), the Resurrection (11:25), the Way, the Truth and the Life (14:6), the Vine (15:1). In these sayings "Jesus bestows life as only God can" (see Kümmel, *Theology of the NT*, 283–86).

It is no accident that the first Christological utterance after the prologue is the Baptist's cry, "See, the Lamb of God who takes away the sin of the world" (1:29). The famous declaration of John 3:16 links the incarnation of the Son of God with his death for the life of the world; thus his "sending" was "soteriologically determined" (Miranda, *Die Sendung Jesu*, 15 f.). The peculiar Johannine mode of representing the redemptive death of Jesus as the "lifting up" of the Son of Man (3:14 f.; 8:28; 12:31; 13:31) is no exception to this. Apart from the linguistic association of the Aramaic term *zeqaph* (to "lift up," to "crucify"), the background to this concept is to be sought in Isa 52:13, the opening sentence of the fourth Servant Song: "See, my servant will act wisely [mg: will prosper]; he will be raised and lifted up and highly exalted" (NIV). The LXX omits the first of the three verbs in the second clause and renders the rest: καὶ ὑψωθήσεται καὶ δοξασθήσεται σφόδρα, which is very "Johannine" language (cf. John 13:31 f.)! In the Song, the Servant's "lifting up" for glory *follows* his sufferings to death—it is the outcome of his yielding up of himself to the Lord for others. In the Gospel the "lifting up" *coincides* with the death of the Son of Man; it is the supreme moment of his obedience which reconciles the world to God and is one with the Resurrection which brings life to the world. The language of exaltation via death to the Father's presence, inspired by the Servant Song, should lead neither to a minimizing of the vicarious nature of the death endured (see, e.g., 1:29; 6:51; 12:23–24; 17:19), nor to an elimination of the concept of resurrection to glory (see, e.g., 2:19–22; 10:17–18). The lifting up of the Son of Man also entails the judgment of the godless world that refuses the light of God's revelation and of the "prince" of this world (12:31; cf. 3:16–21), but the emphasis in the Gospel is on the deliverance from sin and death for life in the new creation, for salvation is above all *life* (3:14–16, 36; 5:24; 6:33, 40, 47–51, 58, 68, etc.).

It is in this context that the sacraments of baptism and the Lord's Supper may fitly be mentioned, for the only clear allusions to both are precisely in relation to the life of the new world. The "new beginning" in a human life, by which it is possible for one to enter the kingdom of God (3:3) takes place "through water and the Spirit" (3:5). The exposition will give reason for believing that the text is authentic as it stands, for interpreting its historical background in terms of a baptism of repentance and the eschatological hope of the Spirit, and will seek to explain their relation in the Evangelist's perspective in an era initiated by the lifting up of the Son of Man (3:14 f.) and the sending of the Spirit (7:39). Similarly the discourse of chapter 6 in its entirety is oriented to the gift of life through the Son of Man, who gives his flesh for the life of the world (6:27, 31–33, 39 f., 49–51, 53–58); that revelation stands in its integrity apart from the Lord's Supper, but its reality is at the heart of the Supper, to which the discourse is manifestly oriented.

3. Eschatology

The purpose of the incarnation, death, and resurrection of Christ is that humankind may have life (see, e.g., 3:14–16; 10:10; 20:31). Self-evidently this "life," or life eternal, is life in the "eternal age," i.e., life in the kingdom of God (for an extended example of this concept in the synoptic Gospels see Mark 10:17, 21, 23, 27, 29–30). That this was axiomatic for the Fourth Evangelist is apparent in the Nicodemus discourse; its theme is the experience of or entry into the kingdom of God (3:3, 5), and it reaches its climax in the earliest statements of the Gospel concerning the gift of eternal life through the redemption of Christ, the alternative to which is judgment (3:14–15, 16–21). It is probable that the utterances of John 3:3 and 5 are themselves rooted in eschatology. To see or enter the kingdom of God it is necessary to be born ἄνωθεν, that is, as the context makes clear, "from above," from God, by the Spirit who is poured out in the new age. The concept of a new beginning or new creation from God applied primarily to the cosmos in Jewish and Stoic thought; it had in view a new world that replaces the old one, although in Jewish thought the destruction of the old world was not as radical as in Stoicism. (Philo used the term παλινγενεσία of the new world into which Noah and his sons stepped, *Vit. Mos.* 2.65, and Josephus of the renewal of the Jewish πατρίς when the Jews returned to the homeland after the Babylonian exile, *Ant.* 11.2.) In Matt 19:28 παλινγενεσία denotes the new age or new world, when the apostles will sit as assessors with Christ in the judgment of Israel. Alike in Hellenistic and in Jewish thought the concept of the new beginning or new creation was applied to the individual also (see the discussion in J. Ysebaert, *Greek Baptismal Terminology* [Nijmegen: Dekker & Van der Vegt, 1962] 93–129). The context of this application in the Fourth Gospel (kingdom of God, agency of the Holy Spirit, exaltation of the Son of Man for life and judgment) indicates that the eschatological significance has been retained. Hegermann is right, therefore, in affirming that salvation in the Fourth Gospel is "miraculous new creation" ("Er kam in sein Eigentum," 120). Paul's teaching on the believer as a new creation in Christ (2 Cor 5:17), given in a context of God's reconciling activity in Christ, is a close parallel to the Johannine teaching, but without the concept of new birth.

The Evangelist consistently represents the new existence in Christ by the Spirit to be a *present* reality. Life in the kingdom of God or new creation is *now*, not a hope reserved for the future. The strongest statement of this occurs in 5:24: the believer μεταβέβηκεν ἐκ τοῦ θανάτου εἰς τὴν ζωήν, he "has made the transition out of death into life." Undoubtedly this is in harmony with the representations in the synoptics of the presence of the kingdom of God with and through the ministry, death, and resurrection of Jesus (cf. the parables of Mark 4, the Q sayings Matt 11:5–6 = Luke 7:22–23; Matt 12:28 = Luke 11:20; Matt 11:12–13 = Luke 16:16), but what in the synoptics has to be searched out lies on the surface in the Fourth Gospel. The strongest statement of the eschatological action of God in Christ in present time is John 12:31: *"Now* the judgment of this world takes place, *now* the prince of this world will be thrown out; and I, if I am lifted up from the earth, will draw to myself all people." This emphasis on the future in the present finds a unique expression in the Evangelist's teaching that the believer knows *resurrection* in and through Christ in the present time. This is most clearly exemplified in 5:21, 24 and 11:25. It would appear to be the result of the Evangelist's taking with rigorous seriousness the eschatological significance of the life, death, and resurrection of Jesus Christ, and the presence of the risen Christ with his people. Through Christ the new age of life eternal has come and the new creation is here; as all know, participation in both is through resurrection; since the giver of life is the risen Lord, and he is *the Resurrection* (11:25), ipso facto life in Christ is *resurrection life.*

In view of all this, what are we to make of expressions of future eschatology in the Gospel? We read of a future resurrection in 5:28–29, the refrain of 6:39, 40, 44, 54 ("I will raise him up at the last day"), of a judgment in the last day (12:48), and of what appears to be an assertion of the Parousia in 14:3, explicitly asserted in 21:21–23. Bultmann's view has won many adherents: these affirmations of traditional eschatology are, in his estimate, the work of a later redactor, bringing the Gospel into harmony with the views of the Church at large, while such a statement as 14:3 is commonly interpreted in the light of the realized eschatology of the Gospel. For Bultmann John 12:31 alone settles the matter: "The turn of the ages results now. . . . Since this 'now' the 'prince of the world' is judged (16:11); the destiny of man has become definitive, according as each grasps the meaning of this 'now,' according as he believes or not (1:36; 5:25). *No future in this world's history can bring anything new, and all apocalyptic pictures of the future are empty dreams"* (431). Despite the popularity of this view, it fails to do justice to the evidence. If any of these expressions of future eschatology are due to a redactor, they are in harmony with the fundamental theology of the Evangelist. For the latter takes with seriousness not alone the consequences for present time of the work of the incarnate Lord, not alone the present activity of the risen Lord, but also *the present action of the risen Lord that extends to the future horizons,* as 5:17 intimates. The key saying on Christ and the resurrection is 11:25, the primary reference of which is to *future* resurrection, though it covers *also* present resurrection; Christ as the Resurrection gives hope for the future life, and the reality of that life in the present. The same applies to judgment; 3:16 implies a future judgment—God gave his Son that humankind "should not perish," while vv 18–21 speak of a present process of judgment with a view to its revelation at the last day (3:21; cf. 3:36: the unbeliever *"will not see life,* but the wrath of God *remains* on him"; i.e., he will be excluded from the life, and the wrath that is upon him now will continue to remain on him). So also with the Parousia. For the Evangelist it is an adaptable concept, like resurrection. The statement in 14:18 "I will not leave you as orphans; I am coming to you" is to be interpreted of the resurrection of Christ at Easter, when the disciples will come to know the real relation of Jesus to the Father and the mutual indwelling of Christ in them and they in Christ (v 20). This theme of the "coming" of the Lord at Easter and its consequences for the disciples is unmistakably expanded in 16:16–24. Its extension in 14:21, how-ever, is generalized in a significant manner: "He who loves me will be loved by my Father, and I will love him and will manifest (ἐμφανίσω) myself to him." The verb ἐμφανίζειν is used in Matt 27:53 of appearances of the dead to the living. Judas (not Iscariot) takes the statement to denote an outward revelation of Jesus to the disciples (v 23), but the Evangelist clearly intends it to be understood of an inward revelation, comparable to the disciples' Easter experiences. The saying, accordingly, is freshly stated to clarify its meaning: "If anyone loves me he will keep my word, and my Father will love him, and *we will come* to him and make our dwelling with him" (v 23). Here the same reality is stated in terms of a private parousia, with an anticipa-tion of the promise to the disciples that they will occupy the μοναί prepared for them in the Father's house in virtue of the death of Jesus (v 3). Observe, however, that v 23 no more nullifies the anticipation of the ultimate Parousia of Jesus at the end than v 21 nullifies the reality of the "coming" of Jesus from the hiddenness of God at Easter. The Easter "coming" was the revelation of the exaltation of Jesus and of the new creation opened up for believers; the "coming" to believers who receive the word of Christ and "love" him initiates the "quickening" (5:21) that brings life from the dead and abiding in the Father through the Son; the "coming" at the Parousia completes the process in the "welcome" (παραλήμψομαι) to the Father's house of those who, though they have died, enter upon the life of shared glory with the Son (cf. 17:21). This is a perfectly perspicuous view, and it is characteristic of the Johannine emphasis on the future in the present that does not abandon hope for the future. It is not to be truncated in the interest of an exclusive stress on the present or the future, still less by appeal to the use of sources or intervention of redactors having different eschatologies. The Johannine eschatology is explicable through the Evangelist's grasp of the insight that *eschatology is Christology.* To the Son is committed the carrying out of the eternal purpose of the Father; this he has achieved, he is achieving, and he shall achieve εἰς τέλος.

VI. THE PURPOSE OF THE FOURTH GOSPEL

Earlier discussions on the purpose of the Gospel frequently were dominated by a concern to determine whether the Fourth Gospel was written to supplement the other three, or to interpret them, or even to correct them. Clement of Alexandria's statement "John, perceiving that the bodily facts had been made plain in the gospel . . . composed a spiritual gospel" would possibly include the first two alternatives. Windisch gave striking expression to the last view; convinced that John wrote to supersede the other Gospels, he set at the beginning of his work *Johannes und die Synoptiker* the saying of John 10:8, "All others who have come before me are thieves and robbers." Yet there is no hint in the Gospel that the Evangelist adopts any stance toward the synoptic Gospels. The most that we can say with confidence is that he writes to provide an authoritative interpretation of the *traditions* concerning Jesus current in his own communities, whether oral or written. In so doing he is concerned above all to impart an adequate understanding of the person, words, and deeds of Jesus the Christ and Son of God.

The last sentence consciously alludes to the Evangelist's own statement of purpose that he provided in 20:30–31: "There are many other signs which Jesus did. . . . These have been written that you may believe that Jesus is the Christ the Son of God, and that through believing you may have life in his name." Unfortunately there lies an ambiguity in the phrase "that you may believe," and it is compounded by uncertainty as to whether the original text read ἵνα πιστεύσητε or ἵνα πιστεύητε; the former could suggest the making of an act of faith, the latter a continuing in faith, the former a missionary purpose, the latter an instructional or parenetic purpose, the former that the Gospel was directed to outsiders, the latter that it was directed to those within the Church. Whether in reality such distinctions can be justly maintained on the basis of the difference between an aorist and a present subjunctive is dubious; nevertheless, the majority of recent scholars incline to the latter view. It finds expression in Neugebauer's rendering of the text: "This has been written that you may continue in believing that Jesus is the Christ, the Son of God, and that as those continuing to believe in his name you may hold on to (the) life" (*Die Entstehung des Johannesevangeliums* [Stuttgart: Calwer, 1968] 12). In support of this it has been urged that the language of the passage reflects the Church's catechetical teaching rather than the language of mission, and that the Christology of the Gospel seems to have been formed in order to illuminate the Church in its struggle with opponents and those who misrepresent the faith, rather than to convert people outside the Church (so, e.g., de Jonge, 2–3). One is constrained to ask whether we have an either-or choice here. If the language of 20:30–31 reflects the catechesis of the Church, it is equally true that it echoes the missionary preaching as recorded in Acts (so van Unnik, *The Gospels Reconsidered,* 180–82). The clause "That you may, through believing, have life in his name" is especially suitable to evangelistic proclamation, and while it may doubtless be adapted to the Church's parenesis, it would appear to have been formulated in the first instance in relation to the former, as 3:14–15, 16 suggest. Moreover, in the Fourth Gospel "the Jews" are not uniformly opposed to Jesus. Frequently they are shown to be divided between the uncommitted and the hostile to Jesus; if the Christology is framed to rebut the objections of the latter, it would at the same time help the former to advance to faith in Christ. Similar considerations apply to all the polemical aims of the Gospel; in so far as they are intended to instruct and warn Christians, they could also conceivably help to win those maintaining false or inadequate views of Jesus.

There is ground therefore for thinking that the Fourth Gospel was written with both evangelistic and didactic aims in view. Such is the conviction of several, among whom Barrett may be cited as representative. In his view John "attempted and achieved the essential task of setting forth the faith once delivered to the saints in the new idiom, for the winning of new converts to the church, for the strengthening of those who were unsettled by the new winds of doctrine, and for the more adequate exposition of the faith itself" (26).

This reference to the "new winds of doctrine" raises the issue of the polemical aims of the Fourth Gospel. That such aims were in the Evangelist's mind is not to be doubted, but they were not all of equal importance. Of the less urgent kind is the polemic against contemporary views of John the Baptist. The poem cited in the prologue is interrupted with a statement on the purpose of John's ministry and its limitations ("He was not that light, but came to bear witness to the light," v 8). Other reports of John's teaching, especially in 1:19–23, 29–31; 3:25–30, bear a similar slant and suggest that the Evangelist had a subsidiary purpose in correcting current tendencies to elevate the role of John the Baptist in relation to the kingdom of God. This would have applied primarily to disciples of John (cf. Acts 19:1–7), but also perhaps to Jews in their polemic against Christians; these may have made capital out of the divergence between John and Jesus, charging Jesus with initiating a breakaway from the teaching of John.

More important in the Gospel is the polemic against "the Jews." The record of the acts and teaching of Jesus in the Gospel is to no small degree determined by objections against Jesus voiced by Jewish leaders in his time and by Jewish opponents of the Church in the Evangelist's day. This we have already discussed in connection with the form of the Gospel. Here we observe that when "the Jews" are spoken of in a pejorative manner, the term generally denotes the Jewish leaders (especially Pharisees) in their opposition to Jesus and his followers; because of that they have become the prime representatives of the (godless) world that stands in opposition to God. John writes to expose the nature of this hostility to the Son of God, to elucidate the revelation brought by Jesus and how it answers the Jewish objections, to encourage Christians to maintain their Christian confession despite the sufferings they endure from Jewish opponents, and to provide an appeal to Jews to give heed to the witness to Jesus borne by Moses and the prophets and the signs which Jesus did (cf. 5:19–47).

The possibility of an anti-Gnostic polemic in the Gospel has been discussed over many years, accentuated through the clear intention of the Johannine epistles to correct docetic views of Jesus. That the Gospel was used alike by Gnostics, and by orthodox in refuting Gnosticism, suggests that the Evangelist was concerned to win as well as refute those who held such views. It is also possible that the polemic against docetism had in view members of the Johannine communities who had withdrawn from the Church on the basis of their Christology and who were posing a threat to those who remained (note the contemporary relevance of 6:60–69). That the Evangelist himself was inclined to a docetic view of Jesus, maintaining, as Käsemann put it, a "naive docetism," is excluded by the language of the Gospel. The celebrated statement of 1:14 "The Word became flesh, and dwelt among us, and we looked on his glory" goes beyond a mere assertion of the Logos *coming* among men that they might see his glory; rather the σὰρξ ἐγένετο signifies *becoming* something that the Logos was not beforehand, namely, *flesh*. It is a real incarnation of the Logos that is asserted here, rendering impossible the notion of at least one influential stream of docetism, that the Logos was not truly one with the man Jesus (cf. 1 John 4:2). A like assertion of the unity of the heavenly redeemer with the flesh and blood of the man Jesus is at the heart of the discourse in chap. 6, most strongly expressed in 6:51–58. And the most natural interpretation of 19:34 is to see it as possessing an anti-docetic intention (cf. 1 John 5:6–8), along with its theological purposes in relation to the OT scriptures (see the important discussion in Thyen, *TRu* 39 [1975] 224–29, 236–41).

VII. THE STRUCTURE OF THE FOURTH GOSPEL

The fundamental plan of the Gospel is plain, and it is acknowledged by most exegetes: after the prologue of 1:1–18 an account is given of the public ministry of Jesus to the end of chap. 12; the latter half of the Gospel portrays the last week of the life of Jesus, including his ministry to the disciples in the Upper Room, his arrest, trial, death, and resurrection, and an epilogue in chap. 21. C. H. Dodd, along with other writers, is content to divide the Gospel into two main sections: viewing chapter 1 as introductory, he describes chaps. 2–12 as the Book of Signs and chaps. 13–20 as the Book of the Passion (*Interpretation*, 289). R. E. Brown follows suit, preferring to use the nomenclature "Book of Signs" and "Book of Glory" (1:cxxxviii–ix). This division is helpful, since it calls attention to the importance of the "signs" in the ministry of Jesus, with which most of the discourses are linked, as also to the extended treatment of the passion of Jesus, viewed as his glorification. Nevertheless, it is necessary to bear in mind that in the passage that describes the purpose of the book, 20:30–31, the *whole* work is viewed as a book of signs. This remains true, even if, as some contend, 20:30–31 originally related to a collection of signs that Jesus performed; the Evangelist has chosen to set the statement at the climactic point in his account of the passion and resurrection of Jesus, with the intention, presumably, of including the "lifting up" of the Son of Man as the ultimate sign of the Christ for man. Likewise, while the anticipation of the passion and glory of Jesus is so vivid in chaps. 13–17 that the hour is viewed as having arrived, the anticipation of that passion and glory dominates the account of the two signs in the programmatic chap. 2, and it is so prominent from 1:29 on that *the whole Gospel* may be said to be the story of the passion and glory of Jesus. It is also important to recognize that the structure of sign and discourse in chaps. 2–12 is interlaced with another prime theme of John namely, the fulfillment of the feasts of the Jews in the ministry of Jesus. This occupies the field entirely in chaps. 7–8, where the narration of signs performed by Jesus is replaced by the rites of the Feast of Tabernacles, which the Evangelist does not trouble to describe, but whose significance he expounds in relation to Jesus in the developing discourse. In chap. 6 the exposition of the two signs of the multiplication of the loaves and the walking on the water is *combined* with the theme of Jesus as the fulfillment of Passover while in 10:22–38 there are overtones from the sign of the healing of the man born blind in the exposition of Jesus as the fulfillment of the feast of the Dedication of the Temple. Accordingly we must be sure that our desire for attractive or attention-drawing analyses of the Gospel does not detract from the emphases that the Evangelist himself makes in his Gospel.

By contrast there is no warrant for dismissing the existence of a clear groundwork or plan of the Gospel. Not infrequently, mention is made of the so-called "chaotic" state of the text of the Gospel (in relation to its present order), and warnings are given not to read the Gospel too schematically. From the point of view of structure, however, there appear to be signs of careful thought by the Evangelist as to the form of his work. J. H. Bernard drew attention to the way John brings to a climax the conclusions of major sections of his Gospel; notably 1:18, the conclusion of the prologue; 12:36b–50, the climax of his description of the public ministry of Jesus; 20:30–31, the conclusion of the resurrection narratives and of the Gospel itself; and 21:24–25 at the end of the epilogue (xxiii). The like is observable in the sections that fall within the major divisions: the testimonies to Jesus of chap. 1 head up to the climactic 1:51; the section 2:1–4:42 comes to a climax in the notable confession of 4:42; the signs and discourse of 4:43–5:47 in the forceful passage 5:45–47; the account of chap. 6 in the dramatic 6:66–70; the controversial chaps. 7–8 in the astonishing 8:58–59; chaps. 9–10 in the not unrelated 10:40–42; the sign of chap. 11 in vv 43–44, and the high-priestly plot in the suspense of 11:55–57; the instruction of the Upper Room discourses in the triumphant 16:33; the prayer in the peace and assurance of 17:24–26; the account of the passion in the dramatic episode of Thomas, 20:24–28, the beatitude of v 29, and the conclusion of vv 30–31. Whatever the antecedent traditions the Evangelist worked with, or whatever may be said in favor of transpositions of the text delivered to us, there can be little doubt that the account of the ministry that lies before us in the Fourth Gospel displays signs of most careful construction.

Without going into detail the following analysis of the Gospel may be considered as a basis for exposition:

I. 1:1–18:	THE PROLOGUE
II. 1:19–12:50:	THE PUBLIC MINISTRY OF JESUS
A. 1:19–51:	*Testimonies to Jesus*
	The Witness of John the Baptist and the Early Disciples.
B. 2:1–4:42:	*The Revelation of the New Order in Jesus*
	Two signs exhibiting the new order, the water into wine and the cleansing of the

                                        temple (chap. 2); the Nicodemus dis-
                                        course answering to the former (chap.
                                        3); the Samaritan discourse answering
                                        to the latter (chap. 4).

C. 4:43–5:47:   *Jesus the Mediator of Life and Judgment*
                                        Two signs, the healing of the officer's
                                        son and the paralytic at Bethesda, with
                                        discourse elucidating their significance
                                        in relation to Jesus' eschatological task.

D. 6:1–71:   *Jesus the Bread of Life*
                                        Two signs, the feeding of the multitude
                                        and Jesus' walking on the water, with a
                                        discourse expounding their significance
                                        and revealing Jesus as the fulfillment of
                                        the Passover feast.

E. 7:1–8:59:   *Jesus the Water and Light of Life*
                                        Jesus as the fulfillment of the Feast of
                                        Tabernacles; the conflict between the
                                        representatives of God and the world.

F. 9:1–10:42:   *Jesus the Light and Shepherd of Humankind*
                                        The sign of the healing of the man
                                        born blind, the discourse on the Good
                                        Shepherd, and Jesus as the fulfillment
                                        of the feast of the Dedication of the
                                        Temple.

G. 11:1–54:   *Jesus the Resurrection and the Life*
                                        The sign of the healing of Lazarus and
                                        the plot of the high priests against
                                        Jesus.

H. 11:55–12:50:   *Jesus the King, Triumphant through Death*
                                        Two significant acts, the anointing of
                                        Jesus and his entry into Jerusalem, with
                                        a discourse on his glorification and epi-
                                        logue to his ministry.

III. 13:1–20:31:   THE PASSION AND RESURRECTION OF JESUS
     A. 13:1–17:26:   THE MINISTRY OF JESUS TO THE DISCIPLES
                                        IN THE UPPER ROOM
        1. 13:1–30:   *The Foot Washing*
                                        A sign of cleansing through the death
                                        of Jesus and example to be followed.

        2. 13:31–14:31:   *The Departure and the Return of Jesus*
        3. 15:1–17:   *Jesus the True Vine*
        4. 15:18–16:4a: *The Hatred of the World for the Church*
        5. 16:4b-33:   *The Joy That Overcomes Tribulation*
        6. 17:1–26:   *The Prayer of Consecration*
     B. 18:1–20:31:   THE DEATH AND RESURRECTION OF JESUS
        1. 18:1–11:   *The Arrest of Jesus*
        2. 18:12–27:   *The Trial before the High Priest*
        3. 18:28–19:16a: *The Trial before Pilate*
        4. 19:16b-42:   *The Crucifixion and Burial of Jesus*
        5. 20:1–31:   *The Resurrection of Jesus*
IV. 21:1–25:   EPILOGUE: THE MISSION OF THE CHURCH
                                        AND ITS CHIEF APOSTLES

John

I. The Prologue (1:1–18)

Bibliography

Aland, K. "Eine Untersuchung zu Joh 1, 3.4." *ZNW* 59 (1968) 174–209. **Borgen, P.** "Observations on the Targumic Character of the Prologue of John." *NTS* 16 (1969–70) 288–95. ———. "The Logos Was the True Light. Contributions to the Interpretation of the Prologue of John." *NovT* 14 (1972) 115–30. **Boman, T.** *Das hebräische Denken im Vergleich mit dem Griechischen.* Cöttingen: Vandenhoeck & Ruprecht, 1954. 45–56. (ET: *Hebrew Thought Compared with Greek.* Tr. Jules L. Moreau. Philadelphia: Westminster, 1960. 58–69.) **Culpepper, R. A.** "The Pivot of John's Prologue." *NTS* 27 (1980–81) 1–31. **Demke, C.** "Der sogenannte Logos Hymnus in Johanneische Prolog." *ZNW* 58 (1967) 45–68. **Dodd, C. H.** *Interpretation of the Fourth Gospel*, 263–85, 294–96. ———. "The Prologue to the Fourth Gospel and Christian Worship." *Studies in the Fourth Gospel.* Ed. F. L. Cross. London: Mowbray, 1957. 9–22. **Hooker, M. D.** "John the Baptist and the Johannine Prologue." *NTS* 16 (1969–70) 354–58. ———. "The Johannine Prologue and the Messianic Secret." *NTS* 21 (1974–75) 40–58. **Jeremias, J.** "The Revealing Word." *The Central Message of the New Testament.* London: SCM, 1965. 71–90. **Käsemann, E.** "The Structure and Purpose of the Prologue to John's Gospel." *New Testament Questions of Today.* London: SCM, 1969. 138–67. **Richter, G.** "Die Fleischwerdung des Logos im Johannes-Evangelium." *NovT* 13 (1971) 81–126; 14 (1972) 257–76. **Robinson, J. A. T.** "The Relation of the Prologue to the Gospel of St. John." *NTS* 9 (1962–63) 120–29. **Sanders, J. T.** *The New Testament Christological Hymns.* SNTSMS 15. Cambridge: CUP, 1971. 29–57. **Thyen, H.** "Aus der Literatur zum Johannesevangelium." *TR* 39 (1975) 53–69, 222–52.

Translation

¹ *In the beginning was the Word,*
and the Word was with God,
and the Word was God.
² *This was in the beginning with God.*
³ *Everything came into existence through him,*
and apart from him not a thing came into being.[a]
⁴ *What has come into being had*[b] *its life in him,*
and the life was the light of men;
⁵ *And the light shines on in the darkness,*
and the darkness did not grasp it.

⁶ *There came on the scene a man sent from God whose name was John;* ⁷ *he came for witness, to bear testimony concerning the light, in order that all might believe through him.*
⁸ *He was not the light, but came to bear testimony about the light.* ⁹ *This was the authentic light, which enlightens every man by his coming into the world.*
¹⁰ *He was in the world,*
and the world came into existence through him,
and the world did not know him.
¹¹ *He came to his own domain,*
and his own people did not accept him.

¹² *But to all who did accept him*
he gave authority to become God's children,
namely to those who believe on his name, ¹³ *who were begotten* ^c *not from*
humans' blood, nor out of the desire of the flesh, nor out of the desire of a
man, but of God.
  ¹⁴ *And the Word became flesh*
and pitched his tent among us,
and we gazed on his glory,
glory such as belongs to the only Son from the Father,
full of grace and truth.
¹⁵ *John bears testimony concerning him, and in his proclamation said, "This is he*
of whom I said, 'He who comes after me ^d *has become before me,' for he existed*
prior to me."
  ¹⁶ *For a share of his fullness we all received, even grace upon grace.*
¹⁷ *For the law was given through Moses; grace and truth were established through*
Jesus Christ.
  ¹⁸ *God no one has ever seen. The only Son,* ^e *by nature God, who is ever close*
to the Father's heart, has brought knowledge of him.

Notes

^a There is uncertainty whether the second line of v 3 should end with οὐδὲ ἕν or with ὃ γέγονεν. The majority of early writers, both orthodox and Gnostic, adopted the former alternative; but the use of the statement by the Arians and Macedonians to prove on that basis that the Holy Spirit was a created being led the orthodox to favor the second way of reading the sentence. Most moderns consider the former to be intended, on the grounds of rhythmical balance of the clauses; the "staircase parallelism," characteristic of vv 1–5, is then preserved. For the ambiguity of the term ζωή on this reading see *Comment.*

^b Since the perfect tense of γέγονεν is naturally followed by a present, some authorities (notably ℵ D OL MSS), read ἐστιν in v 4 instead of ἦν. The external attestation for ἦν is slightly better than for ἐστιν; the latter is probably due to accommodating ἦν to γέγονεν; moreover the occurrence of ἦν in the next line indicates that such was read also in the first.

^c All Gr. manuscripts, virtually all of the early versions and most of the Fathers read in v 13 οἳ οὐκ ἐγεννήθησαν, agreeing with the τοῖς πιστεύουσιν of v 12. The OL MS b reads *qui natus est,* reflecting ὃς οὐκ ἐγεννήθη, supported by, among others, Tertullian, who charged the Valentinians with responsibility for altering the sing. reading to the pl. The external evidence for the pl. is overwhelming, and most adopt it without hesitation. Nevertheless many modern critics and exegetes have accepted the originality of the sing. (including Burney, Boismard, Dupont, F. M. Braun, P. Hofrichter, whose researches persuaded Thyen of its rightness), and it is incorporated into the JB. The conviction, voiced by many, that the pl. was changed to the sing. to make it refer to the Virgin Birth of Jesus is reversed by Hofrichter; in his view the sing. was altered to a pl. because it appears to *exclude* the virgin birth through a denial that Jesus was begotten ἐξ αἱμάτων, which includes the blood of Mary! The decision is more difficult than is generally acknowledged, and we leave it open.

^d Various attempts were made by copyists to improve the rough Gr. of v 15a. Note especially the reading of the first hand of Sinaiticus, which omits the grammatically offensive relative clause and makes a single statement: οὗτος ἦν ὁ ὀπίσω μου ἐρχόμενος ὃς ἔμπροσθέν μου γέγονεν. The reading adopted in the UBS and Nestle editions of the Gr. NT should be accepted.

^e The decision as to whether μονογενὴς θεός or μονογενὴς υἱός in v 18 is the original reading is difficult. Both readings are consistent with Johannine theology, and both have good external attestation, though the support of P⁶⁶ and P⁷⁵ gives advantage to the former. The difference in the uncials would be minimal, ΘΣ or ΥΣ (both abbreviations were usual). While υἱός seems more natural in view of the following εἰς τὸν κόλπον τοῦ πατρός, it should, perhaps for that very reason, be viewed as the easier reading and so yield to the more difficult θεός. In that case θεός must be viewed as in apposition to μονογενής and be understood as "God by nature" as in v 1c

(so Schnackenburg, 1:280). Lindars, in agreement, comments, "The harder reading has the merit of bringing the thought back to v 1, and so constitutes another case of the Johannine *inclusio*. 'God' here has the same meaning as and the Word was God' (1c)" (99).

Form/Structure/Setting

1. THE COMPOSITION OF THE PROLOGUE

The poetic quality of the prologue is observable, even in translation. C. F. Burney maintained that a retroversion of the passage into Aramaic reveals the form of a hymn consisting of eleven couplets, interspersed with comments; this hymn he saw preserved in vv 1–5, 10–11, 14, 16–17 (*Aramaic Origin*, 40–41). The suggestion of an Aramaic original, while accepted by Bultmann, has been widely rejected, but the basic idea of a poem concerning the Logos has found general acceptance.

Bernard's comments are worthy of note; he pointed out that the hymn does not consist only of couplets but contains also triplets (in vv 1, 10, 18) and even single lines (vv 2, 14e); he omitted vv 16–17 from the hymn and considered that it concluded with v 18; the remaining verses give comments from the Evangelist: 6–8, 15 on the witness of John the Baptist; 12–13 correct the notion that no one recognized the Word; and 16–17 illustrate the grace and truth of 14 (I cxliv–vii).

Variations in attempts to delimit the postulated poem have strengthened the skepticism of some as to whether any such poem ever existed. Barrett, for example, prefers to describe the prologue as "rhythmical prose" (150), as also does Lindars (80–82). Interestingly, Haenchen accepts the idea of an original poem, but in his desire to recognize its freedom of construction (over against Bultmann's postulate of couplets only) he construes the poem as "rhythmical prose"! (137). It is not difficult to observe the difference between the lyrical prose of 1 Cor 13 and the more formal poetry of such hymn citations as 1 Tim 3:16; 2 Tim 2:11–13. It is noteworthy that Phil 2:6–11 and Col 1:15–20 are closely related to the prologue in theology, and both are commonly regarded as Christological hymns. The balance of vv 1–5 in the prologue favors their origin in a hymnic composition, as also vv 10–12. But there is a tendency among scholars to restrict the further extent of the poem. Various writers wish to omit v 2 from it, on the ground that there is a smooth transition from v 1 to v 3, and that v 2 explains the application of θεός to the Logos in v 1c (so C. Demke, *Logos Hymnus* 54; also Käsemann, *Structure*, 151; Schnackenburg, 1:227; Thyen *TR* [39] 58); yet these reasons are hardly strong enough to require the elimination of v 2 from the poem, and most regard 1–5 as a unity. V 9 is commonly linked with 6–8a as explanatory comment from the Evangelist. More importantly, 14–18 are frequently separated from 1–5, 10–12b on the grounds that the later verses have in mind the Sinai tradition rather than the wisdom tradition of the earlier verses, and that whereas the poem is written in the third person, 14–15 are uttered in the first person and appear to be in the nature of a confession, forming the church's responsive praise to the affirmations of the hymn to the Logos (so Demke, *ibid.;* Käsemann, 150–52; Boismard, *Saint Luc et la rédaction*, 206–210; Thyen claims that the majority of exegetes now adhere to this position, *TR* [39] 222, 246). It is not an easy question to determine. Vv 1–5, 10–12b give the impression of being incomplete excerpts from the original hymn, calling for a climax such as 14 provides; 10–12b are best interpreted as relating (in the poem) to the preincarnate ministry of the Logos, *anticipating* the incarnation rather than being a statement of it; and v 14 consists of balanced

clauses like the former verses! If indeed 14–18 are to be viewed as elements of
the Church's confession of faith, like 3:16, this would underscore what in any
case is implied in the postulate of a hymn at the base of the prologue, that the
theology of the Logos incarnate was not the product of a single theological genius,
as the Church has generally viewed the Evangelist, but a fundamental tenet of a
church (or group of churches) of which the Evangelist was a prominent leader,
whose gospel is its definitive exposition.

2. THE STRUCTURE OF THE PROLOGUE

If from one point of view the prologue may be viewed as a poem provided
with explanatory comments, from the literary viewpoint it is a closely knit
composition, constructed with consummate artistry.

This latter aspect has been emphasized by some scholars, who hold that the
text is the result of an intricate process, whereby an extended chiasmus has been
fashioned. Attempts to display such a structure are described by R. A. Culpepper
("The Pivot of John's Prologue," 2–6); he himself sets forth an analysis wherein
vv 1–2 are balanced by v 18, 3 by 17, 4–5 by 16, 6–8 by 15, 9–10 by 14, 11 by
13, 12a by 12c, so resulting in 12b as the pivot of the chiasmus: "He gave them
authority to become the children of God." Impressive as this examination is, I
find it difficult to accept. The commencement and conclusion of the prologue are
crucial for this view; it is urged that in the beginning the Logos is in heaven with
God, and at the end of the redemptive process he is "in the bosom of the Father,"
i.e., again in heaven with God; the prologue exemplifies the descent-ascent theology
of the Redeemer. This is surely a misunderstanding of the passage. It begins by
declaring the unity of the Logos with God and his role as the instrument of God
in the act of creation; in that capacity *he remains active within the created order,* and
is the source of life in the world; as "the light of men" he continues to shine,
even in the presence of uncomprehending darkness. This continued ministry of
the Logos in the world is underscored if (as most believe) the poem in 10–12
relates to the preincarnate work of the Logos. As there is no "descent" (not even
for incarnation!) neither is there ascent here; for the assertion in v 18 most naturally
relates to the authoritative revelation of the Father given by the Incarnate Son.
Since he is ever "in the bosom of the Father," he knows the Father's heart and
mind, and out of that intimate fellowship he "gave an exposition of him." The
imagery is applied later to the Beloved Disciple, who in 13:23 is said to have
reclined "in the bosom of Jesus," and so was able to learn the mind of the Lord—
a comment which may well extend to the revelation of which the Gospel is the
distillation and record. With this Schnackenburg agrees, pointing out that the prologue, unlike other NT hymns to Christ, does not conclude with a celebration of
the Lord's heavenly exaltation, but with "a pointed statement of the one historical
revelation brought by the unique Son of God" (1:224). Apart from this vital consideration, the parallels between 3 and 17, and between 4–5 and 16 seem fragile. Moreover, the references to the testimony of John the Baptist owe their position not
to the necessities of a chiasmus structure but to the interpretation of the context
in which each reference is placed (see *Comment*). For the Evangelist it would
appear that the account of the prologue moves to the statement of v 14; by virtue
of its theological significance *it* forms the center of gravity of the prologue, and
indeed of the Gospel itself.

As to its subject matter, there is widespread agreement on the division of
the prologue, though the exegetes use various ways of describing the sections.
It divides naturally into four, which may be enumerated as follows:

(*i*) vv 1–5, *The Word and Creation;* (*ii*) vv 6–8, *The Witness to the Word by John the Baptist;* (*iii*) vv 9–13, *The Reactions to the Word in the World;* (*iv*) vv 14–18, *The Confession of the Word by the Church.*

3. THE FUNCTION OF THE PROLOGUE

It is evident that the prologue is more than a preface, such as that which Luke provides for his Gospel, explaining how he came to write his work. The explanation for the writing of the Gospel is left to its conclusion (20:30–31). The prologue is "a directive to the reader how the entire Gospel should be read and understood" (Thyen, *TR* [39] 223). As the Gospel is wholly concerned with Jesus, so the prologue is wholly taken up with him. The Evangelist does not feel it necessary to commend the story of Jesus to his readers. Rather he prepares for the story by describing the Son of God in terms that rivet the attention of his readers, and so encourages them to read the story for themselves. The remarkable feature of this presentation is that it employs categories universally known, possessing universal appeal, which would attract and have attracted alike Jews, Christians and pagans, Hellenists and Orientals in their varied cultures, followers of ancient and modern religions, philosophers and people of more humble status who were yet seekers after God.

The prologue has frequently been likened to an overture to an opera. The comparison is apt, since an overture is calculated to whet the appetite of the hearers, preparing them for the work to be presented and bringing together themes developed in it. On the latter point one may, for example, recall how the Gospel makes mention of the preexistence of the Son of God (e.g., 17:5), the giving of the μονογενής in incarnation and death (3:16), his function as the light of the world (8:12) and its life (11:25), the manifestation of his glory (2:11), the unbelief of the world in face of it (12:41; 16:8–11), and the trust of those drawn by it (6:67–69; 12:31–2; 17:6–19). The declaration of purpose in 20:30–31 has a fundamental connection with the punch line of the prologue in 1:14; the latter affirms the reality of the incarnation of the Logos in humanity, and 20:30 records the intention of establishing that Jesus is the Christ and Son of God in the sense confessed by Thomas ("my Lord and my God").

Despite its simplicity of language the prologue is far from simple. Bultmann asserted that it is more a mystery than a key to the Gospel and is comprehensible only to one who knows the whole Gospel (13). The truth in that assertion lies in the profundities which inhere in the terms and concepts used in the prologue (word, life, light, glory, grace, truth, revelation), and which gain their fullest significance in the light of the story of the incarnate Logos that follows. Nevertheless, despite the measure of enigma in the prologue, it does prepare the way for the exposition of the profundities it so tersely declares. This Hoskyns perceived and characteristically stated: "In the course of his gospel the Evangelist draws out what is involved in Jesus as the Word of God. . . . The figure of Jesus as the embodiment of the glory of the Word of God controls the whole matter of the Christian religion" (162).

4. The Origin of the Logos Concept

There is a famous passage in the *Confessions* of Augustine wherein, during a recital to God of his spiritual pilgrimage, he wrote,

> Thou procuredst for me, by means of one puffed up with most unnatural pride, certain books of the Platonists, translated from Greek into Latin. And therein I read, not indeed the very words, but to the very same purpose, enforced by many and diverse reasons, that In the beginning was the Word, and the Word was with God, and the Word was God: the same was in the beginning with God: all things were made by Him, and without Him was nothing made: that which was made by Him is life, and the life was the light of men, and the light shineth in the darkness, and the darkness comprehended it not. And that the soul of man, though it bears witness to the light, yet itself is not that light; but the Word of God, being God, is that true light that lighteth every man that cometh into the world. And that He was in the world, and the world was made by Him, and the world knew Him not.

"But," observed Augustine, "that He came unto his own, and his own received Him not; but as many as received Him, to them gave He power to become the sons of God, as many as believed in his name; this I read not there." Similarly after citing a version of John 1:13, he added, "that the Word was made flesh, and dwelt among us, I read not there" (*Confessions* 9.13, 14, translated by E. B. Pusey [London: Dent, 1907] 129–31). Whether one is impressed more by what Augustine found in the Platonists or did not find in their writings depends perhaps on the interests in a given moment. Doubtless there will have been many besides Augustine in the early centuries of our era who were struck by the relationships between the prologue and Hellenic and Hellenistic traditions, and there was much to encourage comparison in these areas.

For Heraclitus the Logos is "the omnipresent wisdom by which all things are steered"; it is the divine word received by the prophet, which becomes almost equivalent to God (see J. Adam, *The Religious Teachers of Ancient Greeks*, 216–34). For the Stoics, the Logos is the common law of nature, immanent in the universe and maintaining its unity, the divine fire, the soul of the universe. Philo of Alexandria exploited the concept in a striking fashion. He saw the Logos as *the agent of creation*, distinguishing between the Logos as a *thought* in the mind of God, his eternal wisdom, and its *expression* in making formless matter a universe. The Logos is *the medium of divine government of the world;* it is "the captain and pilot of the universe." The Logos is *the means by which man may know God,* for God is unknowable by the mass of mankind; they can know him only in and through the Logos: "The Logos is the God of us imperfect men, but the primal God is the God of the wise and perfect"; accordingly the Logos is viewed as the High Priest through whom men come to God, an Advocate (παράκλητος) for the forgiveness of sins. And the Logos is identified with the *Perfect Man,* the man of Gen 1, made in the image of God, as distinct from the man of the earth of Gen 2; he is the Father's "eldest Son," his "Firstborn." These contacts of Philonic thought with the Fourth Gospel are the more significant in view of the independence of the two authors, for they clearly reflect related traditions and modes of thinking. To some extent a similar observation may be made regarding Gnostic representations of the Logos as an intermediary figure between God and the world; through the Logos God is able to make a material world, and through him man has the possibility of deliverance from this world. The concepts of creation and redemption are, of course, quite different from the biblical concepts. For the Gnostic the Logos is the Redeemer who descended into the lower world in human form, deceiving the demonic powers, and made it possible for man to follow him into the higher world of God. Here the Logos is called the Son of God, the μονογενής, the Image of God, the demiurge, even a δεύτερος θεός, and also Man ('Ανθρωπος). In the *Odes of Solomon*, the parallels to the picture of the Logos in the prologue are particularly interesting, especially in *Ode* vii:

> He became like me, in order that I might receive him,
>   he appeared in likeness as myself, in order that I might put
> him on.
> And I trembled not when I saw him,
>   for he is my grace. . . .
>
> He gave himself to be seen by those who are his,
>   in order that they should know him who made them
>   and that they should not think that they came of themselves.

To what extent the Odist has been influenced in his language by the Evangelist is difficult to determine, but the Odes as a whole are not, apparently, Christian.

Where did these ideas emanate from? Their history stretches beyond the confines of Greek culture. The opening words of the prologue give the clue: *"In the beginning was the Word. . . ."* The statement recalls the first word of the Hebrew Bible, בְּרֵאשִׁית (*bᵉrešit*), rendered in the LXX, as in the Gospel, ἐν ἀρχῇ. The association was the more evident to the Jews, since they referred to books of the Bible by their opening words, and so "In the beginning" was the Jewish name for "Genesis." In that beginning God *spoke*, and the universe was created (Gen 1:3, 6, 9, etc.). This representation was entirely comprehensible to Jews, since to them, as to other peoples throughout the ancient Orient, the Word, especially the Word of God, was not so much an expression of thought as a powerful *action*, a concept not native to Greeks. So we read in Ps 33:6: 'By the word of the Lord the heavens were made, and all their host by the breath of his mouth." This delineation of the creative power of the word of God is observable in much of the literature of the ancient nearer Orient. In Assyrian and Babylonian thought the word of God is a cosmic power, compared in the Ellil hymns to a raging storm, a bursting dam, a snare in the forest, a net stretched out over the sea which nothing can escape:

> The word of Ellil, heaven cannot endure it.
> The word of Ellil, earth cannot endure it.

L. Dürr, from whom these references are cited, emphasizes that in the hymns that tell of the power of the divine Word, the beneficence and life-giving activity of the Word in creation are also celebrated (see *Die Wertung des göttlichen Wortes*, 12–14). In Egypt the power of creation and the maintenance of the universe are attributed to the divine Word; here the Word is viewed as an ever-active substance that flows out of the mouth of the deity. The OT representations of creation as taking place through the mighty utterance of the Word of God are clearly characteristic of Near Eastern thought, but there is one important difference: in the OT the Word is never spoken of in terms of an emanation, but always of God sovereignly acting on the world through his Word. This creative action of God by the Word is fundamentally the same as that by which God brings to pass his purpose in history by the Word which he makes known to his prophets (see e.g. Isa 55:11, and T. Bowman's comments, *Das hebräische Denken*, 47–48; ET *Hebrew Thought Compared with Greek* [London: SCM, 1960]).

It is important to observe that the development of the concept of the Word of God in the OT and later Judaism is similarly related to that among Israel's neighbors. This applies to the association of Word and Wisdom. The connection of Wisdom with the creative Word is already assumed in Prov 8:22-31 (note especially vv 27–31). In Wisd 9:1 there is an explicit identification of Wisdom and the Word: "God of our fathers, and Lord who keepest mercy, who madest all things by thy *word,* and by thy *wisdom* formedst man. . . ." This can be paralleled in varied ancient texts of countries with which Israel was in contact. In Egypt, Thoth is alike the Word and the god of wisdom. In the Ras Shamra texts the word and wisdom of El are linked together: "Thy word, O El, is wisdom, wise art thou eternally" (II AB IV, 41 f.). It is perhaps not without significance that the clearest approach to the hypostatizing of the Word occurs in the *Wisdom of Solomon,* wherein Wisdom is also presented in a highly developed fashion. Describing the slaying of the firstborn in Egypt the writer proceeds: "All things were lying in peace and silence, and night in her swift course was half spent, when thy almighty Word leaped from thy royal throne in heaven into the midst of the doomed land like a relentless warrior, bearing the sharp sword of thy inflexible decree, and it stood and filled it all with death, his head touching the heavens, his feet on earth" (18:14–16). The imagery is consonant with the tradition of the powerful, and even terrible, action of the Word in and upon the world. A more characteristic element in the poetry of Wisdom is to depict her as descending from heaven to seek a place of welcome in the earth and finding none. A late expression of that concept is seen in Enoch 42:2:

> Wisdom went forth to make her dwelling among the children of men,
>   and found no dwelling place;
> Wisdom returned to her place,
>   and took her seat among the angels.

By contrast Sir 24:6–8 tells of the home that was appointed for her:

> The waves of the sea, the whole earth,
> every people and nation were under my sway.
> Among them all I looked for a home:
> in whose territory was I to settle?
> Then the Creator of the universe laid a command upon me;
> my Creator decreed where I should dwell.
> He said, "Make your home in Jacob;
> find your heritage in Israel."

Here, however, the author has given a significant twist to the ancient tradition, for what he has in mind is none other than the Torah, the Law, with which Wisdom has been identified. It was an extraordinary, though comprehensible, development in a context wherein the Word of God was understood as revealed in the Law. The term תורה (*tôrāh*) is itself many hued; it could denote the word of God, the will of God concretely embodied in the Law, and divine instruction (especially in the Book of Proverbs). In due time it became identified with Wisdom itself, and so gained the theological and cosmological associations of Wisdom and the Word. The passage above cited from Sir 24 begins with a declaration of Wisdom:

> I am the word which was spoken by the Most High;
> it was I who covered the earth like a mist . . . ,

an utterance clearly due to the approximation of Wisdom to the creative Word of God. The passage concludes with the statement, "All this is the covenant book of God Most High, the law which Moses enacted." This notion of Torah was developed by the rabbis. The opening word of Genesis. *bereshith*, can signify *"in* the beginning" or *"by* the beginning." *Gen. Rab.* 1 comments thus: "Through the beginning God created the heaven and the earth; the 'beginning' is nothing other than the Torah, as it says in Prov 8:22, Yahweh created me as the beginning of his way." The citation is instructive, for Prov 8:22 speaks of Wisdom, but for the rabbis Wisdom is the Law, the creative Word.

Distinctively Jewish as this development of the Wisdom-Word concept is, it is important to bear in mind its origins in the early dynamic concepts of Word and Wisdom of God in creation. It is significant that this thinking is most characteristically expressed in poetic utterance. Apart from the later Wisdom writings there are the Wisdom psalms of the OT, which are believed to preserve a tradition of composition which originated and was maintained in circles of the "wise men." Of them, S. Mowinckel affirmed, "From of old these 'learned' or 'wise' men used to cultivate a special kind of literature, 'the poetry of wisdom,' which was cultivated all over the Orient, and had a common, markedly international, character, in Egypt, Babylonia, and Canaan" (*Psalms and Wisdom* 206–71). J. T. Sanders considers this tradition to be the fount of the NT Christological hymns, with its most notable expression in the prologue to the Fourth Gospel (see *The New Testament Christological Hymns,* chap. 8).

Here then we have a fascinating example of an ancient religious tradition from the area in which Israel's faith was cradled, accommodated to the monotheistic and historic nature of the revelation in Israel, spread through the Western world and taken up in its developing religious and philosophical traditions, and finally given a new orientation within the Gospel. T. Bowman, assured as he was of the oriental origin of the concept of the Word and its decisive significance within the OT and Judaism, believed that the Greek tradition must not be discounted within the prologue, but rather that the two streams must be seen as flowing together in it. He illustrated this from the convergence and divergence of the meanings of the Hebrew דבר (*dābār*) and the Greek λόγος:

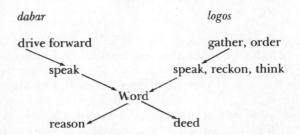

The famous scene in Faust, therefore, where Faust reflects on how to translate *Logos* in John 1:1 and decides on "In the beginning was the *deed"* is one-sided. What we have in the prologue is a coming together of notions buried deep in the cultures of East and West. The result, as Boman suggested, should be compared with the effect of the ringing of many bells together; the OT tone sounds most powerfully in the assertions of the *action* of the Word, but the affirmations of the *nature* of the Word comport with the characteristic Greek emphasis on being (55). Here one should heed the words of J. B. Skemp, a classicist, regarding the prologue and the Gospel it introduces: "It may be possible as a *tour de force* to prove that everything in it could stem from pure Hebrew antecedents, but it will never be possible to prove that its hearers heard it with minds and hearts uninfluenced by Hellenistic meanings of the words they heard read to them" (*The Greeks and the Gospel* [London: Carey Kingsgate, 1964] 56).

But a further factor calls for consideration. Among Christians the expression "the Word" was laden with a special meaning: it denoted the good news of God's revelation and redemption in Christ. The four Gospels present it as God's word spoken *through* Christ and *about* Christ. This prompted Hoskyns to assert: "That Jesus once spoke is more fundamental for the understanding of the Logos than is the history of Greek philosophy, or the story of the westward progress of oriental mysticism, more fundamental even than the first chapter of Genesis or the eighth chapter of Proverbs" (137). In so writing, Hoskyns almost certainly would have united the speech of Jesus in word and deed. In that wider sense he insisted on linking the identification of Jesus as the Logos with other images used of Jesus— the Life, Light, Truth, Way, Door, Bread, Resurrection (see 139). C. H. Dodd made the same point, as the present writer once heard him say: "As Jesus gives life and is life, raises the dead and is the resurrection, gives bread and is bread, speaks truth and is the truth, so as he speaks the word he is the Word."

The employment of the Logos concept in the prologue to the Fourth Gospel is the supreme example within Christian history of the communication of the gospel in terms understood and appreciated by the nations. As Paul stood on Mars Hill and declared, "That which you worship but do not know, I now proclaim" (Acts 17:23), so the Evangelist set forth to the world of his day thoughts familiar to all about the Logos in relation to God and the world, startlingly modified by the affirmation of the Incarnation, and then went on in the Gospel to tell how the Word acted in the words and deeds of Jesus and brought about the redemption of the nations.

Comment

THE WORD OF GOD AND CREATION (1:1-5)

1 "In the beginning" recalls Gen 1:1. But it relates here not to the act of creation, but to what existed when creation came into being, namely the Word, who was with God and was God. As Haenchen pointed out (116), the subject is surprising; one expects to read, "In the beginning . . . God," but it is "the Word"; yet it would be impossible to read in its place any other title that has been appropriated for Jesus, e.g., "In the beginning was *the Christ*," or "the Son," or "the Son of Man." Not even the lofty title "the Lord" or the more ancient "the Wisdom" could adequately convey the associations of the following utterances, for the connotation of "the Word" is unique; and it is without parallel in the languages of modern culture. Its richness has to be searched out and conveyed by explanation (see above, pp. 6–10). πρὸς τὸν θεόν = "with God," in the sense of "in the presence of God" (cf. Mark 6:3), or "in the fellowship of God" (1 John 1:2–3), or even (as the next clause suggests) "in union with God." καὶ θεὸς ἦν ὁ λόγος: θεός without the article signifies less than ὁ θεός; but it cannot be understood as "*a god*," as though the Logos were a lesser god alongside the supreme God; nor as simply "divine," for which the term θεῖος was well known (in 2 Pet 1:4 believers are said to be θείας κοινωνοὶ φύσεως, "sharers of the divine nature"); nor as indicating the exercise of divine *functions* without possessing the divine nature; rather it denotes *God in his nature*, as truly God as he with whom he "was," yet without exhausting the being of God (observe that the Evangelist did *not* write καὶ λόγος ἦν ὁ θεός ("and God was the Word"). The divine nature of the Logos is seen in his activity in creation (1–5), revelation (5, 9–12, 18) and redemption (12–14, 16–17); in all these God expresses himself through the Word, hence the dictum of Bultmann, "From the outset God must be understood as the 'one who speaks,' the God who reveals himself" (35).

2 The statement of v 2 emphasizes, through repetition, (*i*) that the Word, and none other (οὗτος), was with God in the beginning; (*ii*) that he was with God before all times and did not come into being at the "beginning" (contrast the ἐγένετο of vv 3 and 6); and (*iii*) the paradox of the Word who was God, and yet in fellowship with God.

3 For the punctuation of the sentence see the *Notes*. The Logos is asserted to be the Mediator of creation, positively and negatively ("Everything by the Logos, nothing without him," Bultmann, 37). In view of 1c the concept of the Logos as *Mediator* must be distinguished from that of an *intermediary* between God and creation, as though the Logos were a species of demiurge, doing something in and for the world which God in his glory would not do; the creative activity of the Logos is the activity of *God* through him (so Pollard, 20).

4 The Logos is Mediator not only in the act of creation, but in its continuance. Hence ζωή (life) and φῶς (light) include the life and light which come to man in *both* creation *and* new creation. Our Gospel emphasizes the latter aspect, since it is concerned with the saving action of the Logos-Son for humankind, but the new creative work presupposes the original creative action of the Logos and is its goal.

5 The present φαίνει is unexpected; it embraces history and the present time of the Evangelist. The light of the Logos shone in the primal darkness at creation, and continued amidst the darkness of fallen mankind; it shone with greater brilliance in the glory of the Incarnate One; and it shines on in the era of the Resurrection, which is the time of the Paraclete. Similarly the verb οὐ κατέλαβεν includes the past of the preincarnate Logos, as of the Incarnate Logos, and extends into the era of the Church's witness to the Logos made flesh. καταλαμβάνειν can mean "grasp" in the sense of makes one's own (cf. Phil 3:12), understand (Eph 3:18), overcome or overtake (12:35, cf. 1 Thess 5:4). The context (cf. 10–12) suggests that acknowledging and receiving the truth of the revelation is primarily in view here.

The Witness to the Word of God by John the Baptist (1:6–8)

6 An account of John the Baptist's ministry formed the commencement of the kerygma (Acts 10:37; Mark 1:1, 4; similarly in this Gospel, immediately following the prologue, 1:19 ff.). The Evangelist interrupts his citation from the Logos hymn in order to present the Baptist's testimony to "the Light," i.e., to the Logos incarnate in Jesus. It is possible that in the Evangelist's time there were followers of John who claimed that *he* was the Light, i.e., the Light of Salvation, the Deliverer of God's people. The mistake is effectively rectified: John's appearance (ἐγένετο, "came on the scene") was in response to a commission from God to be a witness to the one and only Light of the world. This, in the purpose of God, was the supreme end of his proclamation and baptism. (The passage following the prologue will expand this theme, especially vv 19–37.)

THE REACTIONS TO THE WORD OF GOD IN THE WORLD (1:9–13)

9   In face of false claims (concerning John or any other alleged prophet-redeemer) the authentic Light is affirmed to be the Word who illumines the existence of every man (positively *and* negatively, for salvation and judgment; see 3:19–21). The statement is ambiguous, inasmuch as the phrase "coming into the world" can relate to the Light ("through his coming into the world") or to every person ("every person born into the world"). The expression "all who come into the world" was common among Jews to denote everyone, but it did not include the generic term "man." We cannot be sure what was intended here. Either reference makes sense, and is harmonious with the context. It is perhaps preferable to connect the phrase with the coming into the world of the Logos. The question then arises: *When* does he come? The writers to whom Augustine referred will have naturally thought in terms of the universal ministry of the Logos in the world; incarnation of the Logos was not within their horizon. It is likely that such was the intention of the poem here cited, and vv 10–12 are wholly comprehensible in this sense. But 10–12 also summarize admirably in retrospect the ministry of Jesus, and 12–13 seem to have the gospel of new life in view. Dodd's interpretation has much to commend it: the Evangelist (as distinct from the poet) holds both references together. "The life of Jesus is the history of the Logos as incarnate, and this must be, upon the stage of limited time, the same thing as the history of the Logos in perpetual relations with man and the world. . . . The whole passage from v. 4 is *at once* an account of the relations of the Logos with the world *and* an account of the ministry of Jesus Christ, which in every essential particular reproduces those relations" (*Interpretation*, 284).

10   Here we meet for the first time in this Gospel the term κόσμος, "world." In 10a it denotes the world inhabited by humankind, in 10b the world including human beings, in 10c humanity, fallen and in darkness, yet remaining the object of the love of God (3:16). The utterance is akin to Jewish sayings regarding the unresponsiveness of humankind to Wisdom (cf. Enoch 42:2, "Wisdom went forth to make her dwelling among the children of men, and found no dwelling place").

11   The statement is viewed by Bultmann as precisely parallel to 10: εἰς τὰ ἴδια, lit., "to his own (property)" = the world of men; οἱ ἴδιοι, lit., "his own (people)" = humankind in its entirety; therefore human beings, not Israel, are in view (56). If this should correspond to the intention of the original hymn, the Evangelist almost certainly saw the saying as relating especially to Israel in its resistance to the Word of God (Israel is the people peculiarly "God's own"; see Exod 19:5; cf. Rom 15:8; John 4:22).

12 The positive aspect of the ministry of the Logos is here described: there were those who "received" the Logos, i.e., welcomed the Word in faith. To them he gave authority to become God's children; they were not so by nature (contrary to the Gnostics!), but became such by authorization of the Logos. This implies a concept of adoption, which in v 13 gives way to that of regeneration (the theme is developed in 3:1–21). If, as Bultmann thought, the Evangelist inserted the term ἐξουσία (authority) into the hymn (in Semitic language]ת) (*nātan*), "to give," itself can mean "give permission"; see e.g. Rev 2:7; 3:21), then the insertion emphasizes the action of the Logos. We observe that believers are called τέκνα θεοῦ, *children* of God; unlike Paul, the Evangelist never refers to them as υἱοὶ θεοῦ, *sons* of God; like the Seer of Revelation, he reserves the expression *Son* (of God) for Jesus.

Believing "in the name of Jesus" is found only in John and 1 John; it implies "acceptance of Jesus to the full extent of his revelation" (Schnackenburg, 1:263). Later we learn that the Father has given to the Son to share *his* name (17:11; cf. 6:20; 8:58).

13 To "become children of God" is a work wholly of God's operation. The successive phrases contrast birth from God with human begetting, and emphasize the inability of men and women to reproduce it. The plural αἵματα (commonly = "drops of blood") alludes to the blood of the parents who beget and give birth; the "will of the flesh" denotes sexual desire; the will of "a male" (ἀνδρός) has in view the initiative generally ascribed to the male in sexual intercourse; here it extends to human initiative as such.

On the possibility of v 13 relating to the birth of Jesus (reading ὃς οὐκ . . . ἐγεννήθη) see the *Notes*. The singular reading would emphasize the Incarnation of the Logos as wholly due to the miracle of divine action, and as such anticipates the μονογενής of v 14. Hoskyns rejected the singular reading but saw in it a clue to the unusual wording of the sentence. He suggested that the Evangelist deliberately employed language suggestive of the Virgin Birth when describing the new birth of believers the miracle of regeneration is thus patterned on and determined by the miracle of the Incarnation (164–65). Even if a reference to the *Virgin* Birth be questioned (there is no clear reference to it in the Gospel), the idea of relating "birth from God" (3:3) to the Incarnation is entirely possible, and theologically sound.

THE CONFESSION OF THE WORD OF GOD BY THE CHURCH (1:14–18)

14 ὁ λόγος σὰρξ ἐγένετο, "the Word became flesh," is the controlling utterance of the sentence. It is not to be subordinated to the third clause, as though it signified only the condition for manifesting the glory of God in the world (*contra* Käsemann, "Prologue to John's Gospel," 158–59). Σὰρξ ἐγένετο is more emphatic than the related ἐφανερώθη ἐν σαρκί, "who was manifested in the flesh," of 1 Tim 3:16. On ἐγένετο Richter commented: "The verb γίνομαι in connection with a predicative noun expresses that a person or a thing changes its property or enters into a new condition, becomes something that it was not before" (*Fleischwerdung*, 88). In this context that "something" is *flesh*. The assertion excludes any notion of Docetism, "naive" or otherwise. The Logos in becoming σάρξ participated in man's creaturely weakness (the characteristic meaning of "flesh" in the Bible).

Into that condition of human weakness the Logos "pitched his tent" (ἐσκήνωσεν, from σκηνή, "tent") and revealed his glory (cf. *shekinah*, having the same consonants as the Greek σκηνή). The language is evocative of the revelation of God's glory in the Exodus—by the Red Sea, on Mount Sinai, and at the tent of meeting by Israel's camp (especially the last; see Exod 33:7–11; for the glory in and upon the Tabernacle cf. Exod 40:34–38). The Exodus associations are intentional, and are part of the theme of the revelation and redemption of the Logos-Christ as fulfilling the hope of a *second* Exodus.

ἐθεασάμεθα, *"we* gazed on," represents the taking up by the Church into its confession the testimony of the eyewitnesses of the ministry of the Christ. It connotes more than contemporary spiritual insight of faith, though it doubtless includes it. The Evangelist will have had in mind the glory of the Christ which the witnesses saw in the signs he performed (e.g., 2:11), in his being lifted up on the cross (19:35), and in the Easter resurrection (20:24–29). It was a revelation of glory such as could proceed alone from the "μονογενής from the Father," i.e., *God's* only Son (not "as of an only son of his father" in a generic sense).

Μονογενής, lit., "the only one of its kind," unique in its γένος, in the LXX frequently translates יָחִיד (*yaḥîd*), used of an only or beloved child (as in Judg 11:34, of Jephthah's only daughter). It is therefore parallel to ἀγαπητός, "beloved," an alternative rendering of יָחִיד in the LXX. Significantly, in Gen 22:2, 12, 16, ἀγαπητός in the LXX renders יָחִיד with reference to Isaac, Abraham's "only" son; Heb 11:17, alluding to the same passage, uses μονογενής of Isaac. The use of ἀγαπητός in the synoptic accounts of the baptism of Jesus (e.g., Mark 1:11) accordingly, may be compared with μονογενής, despite the difference of scriptural backgrounds, and the same would apply to John 3:16, 18, and 1 John 4:19. Μονογενής also appears in Greek religious literature. Bultmann adduces examples of the term applied to divinities in the sense of "begotten by one alone" (i.e., by one father, without the assistance of a mother), a significance which Hofrichter would adopt for this passage also, in view of its proximity to 1:13 (139 ff.). While that meaning would suit nicely the singular reading of 1:13, the associations of the term with יָחִיד and ἀγαπητός suggest that the Johannine community had the latter meaning ("only") in mind in the confessional statements of 1:14 and 3:16, which will have been formulated without reference to 1:13.

χάρις καὶ ἀλήθεια, "grace and truth," = the common וֶאֱמֶת חֶסֶד (*hesed we²emet*), frequently rendered in the LXX by ἔλεος καὶ ἀλήθεια to describe the covenant mercy of God (cf. Exod 34:6). This "gracious constancy" of God is manifest in its fullness in the Logos-Son. χάρις occurs in the Fourth Gospel in this paragraph alone (14, 16, 17) but its threefold repetition here reflects its importance in the confessional theology of the Johannine church. By contrast, ἀλήθεια, "truth," is a key Johannine term, in which the Hebrew and Greek concepts of truth come together. אֱמֶת (*²emet*) represents firmness, stability, and of persons, steadfastness or trustworthiness; among Greeks ἀλήθεια denotes that which *really* is; in this Gospel it often represents "eternal reality as revealed to men—either the reality itself or the revelation of it" (Dodd, *Interpretation*, 177). Here the personal nature of the reality of God and the revelation is to the fore.

15 An anticipation of 1:30, this statement is a Johannine interpretive representation of a well known saying in the primitive Church, recorded in Mark 1:7, but closer in form to Matt 3:11. The Messiah is superior to John in "might," in that he has been accorded a *priority of status* (ἔμπροσθέν μου γέγονεν) in accordance with his *priority in time* (πρῶτός μου ἦν). The Logos-Christ participates in the eternal priority of God. The mixture of tenses in the saying reflects its frequent citation; the past tense represents what John *used to say*, but the present μαρτυρεῖ ("witnesses") indicates that John's testimony to Christ continues in the kerygma. Its pertinence here is its confirmation of the truth affirmed in v 14, along with the implicit rejection of any claim made on John's behalf that he was greater than the Messiah Jesus (cf. 1:6–8).

16 The saying relates immediately to v 14 (v 15 is parenthetic). The Word made flesh was full of grace and truth, *for* "in his fullness we all have shared, even (καί resumptive) grace after grace." ἀντί appears to indicate that fresh grace replaces grace received, and will do so perpetually, the salvation brought by the Word thus is defined in terms of inexhaustible grace, a significant feature in view of the absence of further mention of χάρις in the Gospel.

17 The grace that characterizes the revelation and redemption of the μονογενής is underscored by a comparison with the old covenant mediated through Moses. The deliverance under the "first Redeemer" (as the rabbis viewed Moses) issued in the gift of the Law; this was "given," not as a burden, but as a revelation of God's will for his people (there is no hint of polemic against the Law). The redemption brought about by the "second Redeemer," the Logos-Christ, occasioned a revelation of God and an experience of salvation characterized by "grace and truth." By this means the earlier revelation of the covenant faithfulness of God was brought to an eschatological fulfillment; the second Exodus under the Logos-Christ led to the new order of the eternal kingdom of God.

18 In view of the Exodus associations of vv 14 and 17, "No one has ever seen God" will have in view not only deliverers and prophets of Hellenistic religions and of the OT generally, but most especially Moses. He witnessed the theophany at Sinai, but his request to look directly on the glory of God was denied: "No mortal man may see me and live" (Exod 34:18–20). The principle was recognized by contemporary Judaism. A blind man of great learning said to Rabbi Chijja: "You have greeted one who is seen and does not see; may you be counted worthy to greet him who sees and is not seen" (Hag. 5b, 32; cited Str-B 2:362–63). Moses saw no more than God's back (Exod 34:21–23), and out of that encounter issued the revelation of *the Law;* claimants to open visions and revelations from God must be judged in the light of such facts. By contrast, however, the only Son, who shares the nature of God (ὁ μονογενὴς θεός), has given an authentic exposition of *God* to man.

The term ἐξηγήσατο is related to the English term "exegesis"; in Josephus it is the technical term for the exposition of the Law by the rabbis. The object of the exposition from the Logos-Son is the Father. This "exegesis" is peculiarly authoritative by virtue of the unity of the Son with God, expressed in the phrase "who is in the bosom of the Father," i.e., in closest fellowship with him (cf. 13:23). The prime reference is to the relationship to God of the Son in his life of flesh and blood, but it naturally extends to his pre-existent and post-Resurrection relationship to the Father. The finality of the revelation of God through the Logos-Son could hardly be more strongly expressed.

Explanation

1. The life of Jesus, of whom the Gospel will tell, is set in relation to the God of eternity, who is the Lord of the ages, Creator of all, Sustainer of all, and Redeemer of all. He in whom the Word took flesh is presented as the divinely appointed Mediator in all the works of God: he is Mediator of creation and new creation, and in and through both, the Mediator of revelation.

2. The appearance of the incarnate One is set in relation to all previous revelatory and redemptive acts of God as their consummation and perfection. That such revelatory and redemptive works took place within Israel's history is taken as axiomatic; the Evangelist sees in Jesus the fulfillment of all intimations of "grace and truth" made known to Israel. The same applies in principle to the revelation of God in the world beyond Israel. The Logos is the source of all life and light in the world. The response among the nations to the activity of the Logos was, alas, no more fruitful than it was among Israel; one may also add that it was no less positive among them than in Israel! But the Logos was not discouraged; on the contrary, he involved himself with the life of the world in an ultimate manner: he became flesh that the glory of God might be revealed to *all* flesh. So through the universal embrace of his incarnate life and ministry, the way was made for the scattered children of God in all the earth to be united into one (cf. 11:52; 12:31–32).

3. The death and resurrection of Jesus find no mention in the prologue, but that twin event stands as the presupposition of its every line, so surely as the incarnation of the Logos is presupposed through the whole. The Word of whom the prologue speaks is the Christ who revealed the divine glory in his living and dying and rising. As the risen Lord he is active still among the nations by his Spirit. Of this the Church is the sign, even as it is his instrument (15:1–17) and the voice of the Paraclete (15:26–27). The Fourth Gospel is the proclamation of the Lord of life—the Lord from whom life takes its beginning, because he is the Mediator of creation; and the Lord from whom life takes a *new* beginning, because he is the Mediator of the new creation, manifest in his resurrection (20:22). The prologue introduces the story of the Word made flesh, climaxed in the revelation of his Easter glory; without the Easter glory there would have been no prologue. We are reminded at the beginning of the Gospel never to forget its issue: Christ with God and life through his name (20:31).

4. If the prologue is the supreme example of the communication and commendation of the gospel to the world, it also provides immense encouragement to believers who read the story again. For the Lord they serve and adore is the ultimate revelation of the Father, sharing with him the sovereignty of the ages and bringing into reality the divine purpose for the ages. They have learned from bitter experience that the darkness still rejects the light, and threatens life itself (cf. 16:2). But does that matter? The Light shines on, more brightly than on the day of creation, and the life is bestowed which gives entrance to the new creation. Expectation of future glory is not a theme of the prologue; rather the emphasis lies on the revelation of the glory awaited from the future made in the present. The glory of the Second Exodus has come about because the redemptive event has happened, and in it the glory has been revealed as infinite grace. It follows that the grace that has been established as divine reality through incarnation, cross, and resurrection is a continuing reality for all who know him. The Resurrection is nothing if it is not the triumph of love with power. In the knowledge and experience of that reality, through the presence of the Spirit of the risen Lord, the believing reader anticipates with eagerness the "exegesis" of that boundless grace in the flesh and blood of Jesus, the Christ and the Son of God.

II. The Public Ministry of Jesus

A. Testimonies to Jesus: The Witness of John the Baptist and the Early Disciples (1:19–51)

Bibliography

Bammel, E. "The Baptist in Early Christian Tradition." *NTS* 18 (1971–72) 95–128. **Barrett, C. K.** "The Lamb of God." *NTS* 1 (1954–55) 210–18. **Berger, K.** "Zum traditionsgeschichtlichen Hintergrund christologischer Hoheitstitel." *NTS* 17 (1970–71) 391–425. ———. "Die königlichen Messiastraditionen des Neuen Testaments." *NTS* 20 (1973–74) 1–44. **Cullmann, O.** "ὁ ὀπίσω μου ἐρχόμενος." *Coniectanea Neotestamentica* 21. FS A. Fridrichsen. Lund: Gleerup, 1947. 26–32. **Dodd, C. H.** *Interpretation of the Fourth Gospel*, 302–12. ———. *History and Tradition in the Fourth Gospel*, 248–80. **Hulen, A. B.** "The Call of the Four Disciples in John 1." *JBL* 67 (1948) 153–57. **Iersel, B. M. F. van.** "Tradition und Redaktion in Joh 1, 19–36." *NovT* 5 (1962) 245–67. **Jonge, M. de.** "Jesus as Prophet and King in the Fourth Gospel." *Jesus: Stranger from Heaven and Son of God*. Missoula, MT: Scholars Press, 1977. 49–76. ———. "Jewish Expectations about the 'Messiah' according to the Fourth Gospel." *Ibid.* 77–116. **Kraeling, C. H.** *John the Baptist.* New York/London: Scribners, 1951. **Moule, C. F. D.** "A Note on 'Under the Fig Tree' in Jn. II:48, 50." *JTS* ns 5 (1954) 210–11. **O'Neill, J. C.** "The Lamb of God in the *Testaments of the Twelve Patriarchs*." *JStNT* (1979) 2–30. **Painter, J.** "Christ and the Church in John 1, 45–51." *L'Evangile de Jean.* Ed. M. de Jonge. BETL 44. 1977. 359–62. **Robinson, J. A. T.** "Elijah, John and Jesus: An Essay in Detection." *NTS* 4 (1957–58) 263–81. **Scobie, C. H. H.** *John the Baptist.* London: SCM, 1964. 73–79, 142–62. **Smalley, S. S.** "Johannes 1, 51 und die Einleitung zum vierten Evangelium." *Jesus und der Menschensohn.* FS A. Vögtle. Ed. R. Pesch and R. Schnackenburg. Freiburg: Herder, 1975. 300–313. **Williams, F. E.** "Fourth Gospel and Synoptic Tradition: Two Johannine Passages." *JBL* 86 (1967) 311–19. **Wink, W.** *John the Baptist in the Gospel Tradition.* SNTSMS 7. Cambridge: CUP, 1968. 87–115.

Introduction

The initiatory character of this record of the ministry of John the Baptist is unmistakable; it reads, as Hoskyns remarked, like a second, though subsidiary, introduction to the Gospel as a whole (167). Smalley indeed holds that the whole of chap. 1 forms the introduction to the Gospel; the two halves of the chapter belong together, so that the prologue to the Gospel really ends not with v 18 but with the Christological utterance of v 51 ("Joh. 1:51 und die Einleitung zum vierten Evangelium," esp. 304). Certainly 1:19–51 is closely linked with the prologue through its expansion of the theme of John's witness to Jesus (cf. 6–8, 15) and its Christological declarations. It may be viewed as a bridge from the purely theological affirmations of the prologue to the account of the ministry of Jesus, which itself is accompanied by a perpetually recurring Christological ground bass.

Translation

19 And this is the witness of John, when the Jews[a] sent to him priests and Levites from Jerusalem to question him, "Who are you?" 20 He confessed, and did not deny it; he confessed, "I am not the Christ." 21 And they asked him, "Well then, are you Elijah?" And he said, "I am not." "Are you the prophet?" And he replied, "No." 22 They said then to him, "Who are you?—that we may give an answer to those who sent us. What do you say about yourself?" 23 He declared, "I am—

'a voice of one calling out in the wilderness[b]
"Make straight the Lord's highway,"'

as Isaiah the prophet said."
24 Now those who had been sent[c] included some Pharisees. 25 They questioned him and said to him, "Why then are you baptizing if you are not the Christ, nor Elijah, nor the prophet?" 26 John replied to them, "I baptize only with water; among you stands[d] one whom you do not know, 27 one who comes after me;[e] I am not worthy to undo the strap of his sandal." 28 These things took place in Bethany, on the far side of the Jordan,[f] where John used to baptize.
29 On the next day John sees Jesus coming to him, and he says, "Look, the Lamb of God, the one who takes away the sin of the world! 30 This is he of whom I said, 'After me comes a man who has taken precedence over me, for he existed prior to me.' 31 And I did not know who he was, but I came, baptizing in water, for the purpose of his being revealed to Israel." 32 And John bore witness and said, "I saw the Spirit coming down as a dove from heaven, and it remained upon him; 33 and I did not know him, but he who sent me to baptize in water said to me, 'You will see the Spirit coming down and remaining on someone; this is the one who is to baptize in Holy Spirit.' 34 And I have seen it, and borne witness that this man is the Son[g] of God."
35 The next day John was again standing there with two of his disciples, 36 and looking at Jesus as he was walking by, he said, "Look, the Lamb of God!" 37 And his two disciples heard him say this, and they followed Jesus. 38 But when Jesus turned and saw them following he said to them, "What are you looking for?" They said to him, "Rabbi (which is translated 'Teacher'), where are you staying?" 39 He says to them, "Come, and you will see." They came therefore and saw where he was staying, and they stayed on with him that day, for it was about four in the afternoon.[h]
40 Andrew, Simon Peter's brother, was one of the two who heard John and followed him; 41 the first thing he did[i] was immediately to find his brother, Simon, and he said to him, "We have found the Messiah (which is translated 'Christ')"; 42 he led him to Jesus. Jesus fixed his gaze upon him and said, "You are Simon, the son of John;[j] you will be called Kepha (which is translated 'Rock')."
43 On the next day he decides to go off into Galilee, and he finds Philip. Jesus

*says to him, "Follow me." *[44]* Now Philip was from Bethsaida,*[k]* the town of Andrew
and Peter. *[45]* Philip finds Nathanael and tells him, "We have found the one of
whom Moses wrote in the Law, and of whom the prophets wrote. It's Jesus, the son
of Joseph, a man from Nazareth." *[46]* And Nathanael said to him, "Nazareth? Can
anything good come out of that place?" Philip says to him, "Come and see."*
[47] Jesus saw Nathanael coming to him, and he says about him, "Look, a true
Israelite—and there's no deceit in him!"*
[48] Nathanael says to him, "How in the world do you know me?" Jesus replied
to him, "Before Philip called you, while you were under the fig tree, I saw you."
[49] Nathanael answered him, "Rabbi, you are the Son of God, you are the King of
Israel!" *[50]* Jesus replied to him, "Are you believing because I told you that I saw
you beneath the fig tree? You will see greater things than that."*
[51] And he said to him, "Amen, amen,*[l]* I say to you all: you will see heaven
standing open, and the angels of God going up and coming down to the Son of
Man."*

Notes

[a] The expression "the Jews" has a peculiar place in the Fourth Gospel; in Mark it occurs six
times, five of which are in the phrase "king of the Jews" (in Matt five occurrences, four of
them in "king of the Jews," in Luke five occurrences, three in "king of the Jews"), whereas it
occurs seventy times in John. To Bultmann the Jews in this Gospel are representatives of unbelief
toward Jesus, and so the unbelieving world as such (186–87). This is largely true, but countered
by such passages as 4:22 ("salvation is of the Jews"), and passages in which "the Jews," meaning
Jewish *people*, are distinguished from "the Jews," meaning Jewish *rulers* (e.g., 7:11–13). We must
distinguish, therefore, between the Jews in an ethnic and historical sense (e.g., 3:1, 25; 4:9),
Jewish people who *reject* the claims of Jesus (6:41; 7:11; 8:22), and Jewish rulers, especially
Pharisees, who *oppose* Jesus (10:24, 31; 18:14, 31, 36, 38). The Evangelist's usage may have
been prompted by the conduct of Jewish leaders of his time who opposed the Church, and
whom he views as the spiritual descendants of the Jewish authorities who contended against
Jesus in his ministry and sought his death (Brown, 1:lxxii).
[b] The citation from Isa 40:3 in v 23 follows the punctuation in the LXX and Targum. The
Massoretic Heb. text understands it as, "Prepare the Lord's *highway in the wilderness*," rather
than relating the voice to "in the wilderness." John carries out his appointed task in the wilderness,
in accordance with the second Exodus typology.
[c] Some texts insert οἱ before ἀπεσταλμένοι, understanding the envoys of v 19 as sent by the
Pharisees, an unlikely situation, since Pharisees generally were laymen. The article is omitted
by most MSS, indicating that Pharisees were included in the deputation, or possibly formed a
second one.
[d] The perfect ἕστηκεν signifies, "There is one who has taken his stand in your midst"; the
hidden Messiah is present in Israel! Other readings (στήκει pres., εἱστήκει plupf.) are inadequately
supported.
[e] ὁ ὀπίσω μου ἐρχόμενος may reflect the messianic expression (hardly a title) ὁ ἐρχόμενος; cf.
the message from John in Matt 11:3, which echoes the messianic interpretation of Ps 118:26,
cited in the accounts of the Triumphal Entry into Jerusalem (Mark 11:9 par), and which should
be rendered:

> "Blessed in the name of the Lord
> (is) the Coming One."

As to the sandals, cf. the dictum of Rabbi Jehoshua b. Levi: "All works which a slave performs
for his master a disciple should do for his teacher, except undoing shoe straps" (*Keth.* 96a,
Str-B 1:121).
[f] Bethany "on the far side of Jordan" is distinguished from Bethany near Jerusalem. Origen,

unable to locate this Bethany, adopted a reading found in a few MSS *Bethabara;* this he viewed as admirable, since "House of Preparation" was an apt name for the baptism which prepared for Christ! But it is not to be accepted.

ᵍ Some MSS, chiefly Western, read in v 34 ὁ ἐκλεκτός instead of ὁ υἱὸς τοῦ θεοῦ. Many exegetes accept the variant, on the ground that it would be far more likely to be changed to ὁ υἱὸς τοῦ θεοῦ than that the reverse should happen (so e.g. Barrett Becker, Brown, Sanders, Schnackenburg). Textual critics tend to adhere to the more strongly supported reading ὁ υἱὸς τοῦ θεοῦ (so Metzger ed. for the UBS; and Bernard, Bultmann, Lodd, Haenchen). The variant could have occurred through the influence of an early tradition of the baptism of Jesus (Bultmann), or through reflection on Isa 42:1 (Haenchen), but uncertainty remains as to the original reading.

ʰ The tenth hour will have been reckoned from dawn, generally assumed to be about 6:00 A.M., hence it stands for 4:00 P.M., toward the end of a working day.

ⁱ πρῶτον, most widely attested in the textual tradition, indicates that Andrew, before doing anything else, found Simon. πρῶτος is also found, implying that Andrew was the *first* follower of Jesus to lead another to him. A few Lat. MSS read *mane* = πρωΐ, early, i.e., in the morning of the day following that mentioned in v 39.

ʲ Instead of son of *John* ('Ιωάννου) many MSS read "son of *Jonah*" ('Ιωνᾶ), a reflection of Matt 16:17. Some MSS even read son of Joanna ('Ιωαννᾶ, cf. Luke 8:3, 24:10). κηφᾶς is the Gr. form of the Aram. כֵּיפָא (*kēphā'*) (Gr. adds the "s," to avoid it sounding like a feminine name). Πέτρος is a translation of כֵּיפָא, and it should be *translated* into English ("Rock"), not *transliterated* ("Peter").

ᵏ *Bethsaida*, "place of the fishery," lay on the eastern bank of Jordan, strictly in Gaulanitis, but popularly viewed as in Galilee. There is evidence that from the commencement of the Jewish war, A.D. 66, the whole area round the lake was known as Galilee; the Evangelist follows contemporary usage (Barrett). In Mark 1:29 the home of Simon and Andrew is given as Capernaum, perhaps indicating a later move.

ˡ 'Αμήν, ἀμήν will have sounded as strange in Gr. ears as it does in English, and should not be translated ("verily, verily" etc.). It was an unusual usage, and occurs only in John (the synoptists have some sayings with a single ἀμήν). Among the Jews *amen* was used to affirm a prayer; a few instances of its occurrence in statements are found in the Qumran literature, but at the end of a sentence (e.g., 1QS 1:20; 12:10). Jesus used it to introduce important statements, implying that behind them stands the authority of "the God whose name is Amen" (Isa 65:16 NEB; note the name "the Amen," applied to Jesus in Rev 3.14).

Some MSS add to "you shall see" the phrase ἀπ' ἄρτι, reflecting the influence of Matt 26:64; contrary to some exegetes, this copyist's mistake is not to be viewed as a pointer to the meaning of the saying.

Form/Structure/Setting

1. The narrative is characterized by a certain repetitiveness (cf. v 27 with 30) and lack of continuity (cf. 25–26, unexpectedly separated from 33). Such features have led to various attempts to reconstruct an original source and to reorder the present text.

Bultmann held that in the original text of vv 19–34 (the most "disturbed" section of 19–51) 21 was followed by 25, 26, 31, 33–34, and 28–30 concluded the paragraph; the remaining vv 22–24, 27, 32 were added from the synoptic tradition by the ecclesiastical redactor (84–85). Van Iersel followed on Bultmann's reconstruction, but he placed 24–25a after 19b, then continued with 19c–22a, 25b–26, 31, 33b–34, 28, 35–36; the modifications of the source he considered to be due to the introduction of material from the synoptic tradition (known orally) and to the desire to present in one paragraph information concerning John, the first witness to Jesus the Son of God (*Tradition und Redaktion*, 160–77). F. E. Williams believed the opening paragraph, 19–28, to be a Johannine dramatization of Luke 3:15 f., which drew on material from Peter's confession of Jesus as the Messiah (Mark 8:27–30), Luke's version of John's embassy to Jesus (7:18–30) and Mark 1:3, a hypothesis with a high degree of improbability (see *The Fourth Gospel and Synoptic*

Tradition, 311–12, 317–19). More recently J. Becker expounded the view that vv 19–51 are based on the Signs Source and the Evangelist's own material; assuming that 2:1–11 comes from the Signs Source, he observed that that passage needs 35 ff. to precede it, and the latter similarly requires 19 ff.; but 29–34 is formed by the Evangelist, with elements from the Signs Source and from the Ecclesiastical Redactor (see his commentary, 87–90). Boismard forsakes the postulate of sources and suggests that the Evangelist wrote *three* different accounts for the opening of his Gospel, two of which were closely parallel and contained both common material and doublets (e.g., common material in 19–21, parallels in 25–26, 31 with 22–23, 30b, 33); these varied accounts were combined into one by a later editor (*Les traditions johanniques,* 5:42).

Space forbids individual examination of these attempts to account for and improve upon the Evangelist's report on the ministry of John (a lucid discussion of those that appeared before 1966 will be found in Brown, 1:67–71). That the Evangelist employed earlier traditions is evident, but the judgments of the critics on the materials of 19–51 are sometimes highly subjective and less convincing to readers than to those who propound them. If the Evangelist or a subsequent editor had wished to clarify the narrative with the aid of the synoptic material, it would have been simple enough to record (discreetly, had he so wished) the baptism of Jesus by John; the allusions to the event are too plain to justify the idea that the Evangelist suppressed it on polemical or theological grounds. The account reads more consistently than some allow, and it is not difficult to see reasons for the Evangelist's handling of his material. In v 26, for example, the balancing clause of "I baptize with water" is delayed till 33b, until the revelation is given as to who the Baptizer in Spirit is; 26c is allowed to remain as a brief allusion to the presence of the hidden Messiah, and the answer (to 25) completed when the fuller testimony of John is recorded in 30–34. (On these and kindred issues see the lengthy discussion by Dodd, *Historical Tradition,* 248–301.)

2. The structure of the section is determined by the witness theme already announced in vv 6–8, 15 of the prologue. We have here recorded: (*i*) the witness of John to *Jewish leaders* ("the Jews of Jerusalem," 19), first negatively (19–24), then positively (25–28); (*ii*) 29–34, the witness of John to *people who came to hear him;* (*iii*) 35–50, the witness of John to certain *disciples,* resulting in their following Jesus and the call of others through their witness, the whole providing a chain of testimonies concerning Jesus; (*iv*) a concluding statement, v 51, which, though following that to Nathanael, is addressed in the plural to the disciple group (it would have been an originally independent saying). The relation of the section to references to John in the prologue is clear: "He came for witness" (7a) governs the whole passage; "he was not that light" (8a) is elaborated in 19–28, "he came to bear witness about the light" (8b) in 29–34, "that all might believe through him" (7c) in 35–50. Haenchen is right in discerning a "dramatic development" in the unfolding of events in 19–51 (165). If the variant reading "the Chosen One of God" be accepted in v 34 the following acclamations concerning Jesus are made: (1) the Lamb of God, (2) the Chosen One of God, (3) Rabbi, (4) the Messiah, (5) the Son of God, (6) the King of Israel, (7) the Son of Man. The closing statement directly leads into the narrative that follows, and covers the presentation of Jesus in the entire Gospel to its last sentence.

3. The narrative provides an account which (a) clarifies the nature of John's ministry and its relation to that of Jesus, and (b) describes the call of the

first disciples and their earliest confessions of faith in Jesus. Both these elements will have been of importance to the Church of the Evangelist's time. The former will have gained increased actuality through the existence of a community of disciples of John which continued after his death (cf. Acts 18:24–19:7), and which was bound to be in uneasy relation to the Church. In the face of inevitably growing adulation of John in a movement sprung from him, it is made plain that John was no rival to Jesus; he made no messianic claims for himself, but functioned supremely as the great Witness for Jesus. The Church itself is reminded that through his witness to Jesus and his pointing the earliest disciples to him, the Church had its roots in the work and witness of John to Jesus. In turn the Church is instructed how to act toward the community (or communities) that followed the teaching of John: the followers of the Christ should make known to them what John actually said to Jesus and should seek to win them, even as John pointed disciples of his to Jesus.

This interpretation of the Evangelist's characterization of John is admittedly milder than is frequently represented. The rivalry and even hostility that later sprang up between the Baptist movement and the Church, as witnessed in the *Clementine Recognitions,* is often read into the situation of the Evangelist's time, leading to a constant insinuation of sharp polemic against John's community in the Evangelist's words. This is an exaggeration of the situation. There is not the slightest hint of John being viewed as a false prophet or pseudo-Messiah, nor of hostility toward his followers (contrast the representations of "the Jews"); rather there is apparent a profound respect towards John, which is consonant with a hope that his later followers might yet be won to the Church (on this see Scobie, *John the Baptist,* 154–56; Wink, 102–5).

The call of the first disciples and their confessions of faith in Jesus will have been similarly instructive for the later Church, precisely because of the representative capacity of the disciples. Their declarations of faith were spontaneous—and inadequate; they required the complementation of a greater revelation through the total ministry of Jesus, which is indeed promised in 1:51.

Comment

THE WITNESS OF JOHN TO THE JEWISH LEADERS (1:19–28)

19 The deputation is not recorded in the synoptic Gospels. We are to assume that the reports of John's activities and popular speculations concerning him prompted the investigation from Jerusalem.

20 John's denial that he was the Messiah is unusually emphatic. The language is reminiscent of Christian vocabulary concerning confessing and denying Christ (cf. Mark 8:38; Luke 12:8–9), but here it is used by John to confess that he was *not* the Messiah and to deny any suggestion that he was (for the need, cf. Luke 3:15).

21 The question, "Are you Elijah?" arises from Mal 4:5 (cf. 3:1), promising the sending of Elijah before the Day of the Lord that Israel might avert its wrath (cf. Sir 48:10). J. A. T. Robinson thought that John denied that he was Elijah because he believed that his task was to prepare for Elijah's coming,

and that Jesus at first accepted this Elijah role ("Elijah, John and Jesus,"
264 f., 270). The notion is unlikely. Popularly it was believed that Elijah
would anoint the Messiah, and thereby reveal his identity to him and to
Israel (see Justin, *Apology* 35.1). It is possible that the Evangelist reports John
as denying that he was Elijah because such a view of the Messiah was unthinkable, alike in John's preaching and in Christian thought (so de Jonge, *Jesus,
Stranger from Heaven*, 89).

As to "the prophet," cf. the formula in 1QS 9:11: ". . . until the coming
of the prophet and the Messiahs of Aaron and Israel." The coming of the
prophet was generally viewed as the fulfillment of Deut 18:15, 18, though
Becker suggests (95) that the type of the Exodus prophet, who repeats the
miracles of the Exodus and conquest of the land, may have been in mind
(cf. the "prophets" of whom Josephus reports, *Ant.* 20.5.1 f.; 21.38).

24–25 The question "Why then are you baptizing" hardly proceeds from
the view that the Messiah, or Elijah or the prophet, will baptize at their
appearing (*contra* Bultmann, 88), but seeks to know John's authority for calling
on *Jewish* people to be baptized for the kingdom of God, a demand by no
means acceptable to Pharisees or Sadducees.

26–27 John's reply indicates that his baptism is a preparation for the
appearance of the hidden Messiah, who already stands in Israel's midst and
is about to fulfill his Messianic task. V 26 therefore has a significance independent of v 31, but it finds its completion in that saying: the identity of the
Messiah was hidden even from John, but through a vision of the Spirit (at
the baptism of Jesus) it was revealed that Jesus was to fulfill the role of the
Lamb of God. In that revelation, and the witness it made possible, John
found the *raison d'être* of his baptism (on this see below, p. 25).

THE WITNESS OF JOHN TO THE PEOPLE (1:29–34)

29 The audience is unnamed, but the mention of "the next day" shows
that the embassy has departed and John speaks to the people about him.
The cry of v 29 must be seen in conjunction with v 36 and the intervening
paragraph; vv 32–34 make it clear that the revelation of Jesus as the Lamb
of God is consequent on his baptism, and is not proclaimed while Jesus advances
to his baptism. The basis of v 29 is the cry of v 36: "Look, the Lamb of
God!" Taking the relevant evidence into account, we conclude that there is
little doubt as to what figure is in mind: the Baptist has in view the Lamb
who leads the flock of God, and who delivers them from their foes and
rules them in the kingdom of God.

Such a figure appears in the *Testament of Joseph* 19:8 f., where a lion and a
lamb appear together, the former the Messiah from Judah, the latter the Messiah
from Aaron (so reads the present text; J. C. O'Neill has suggested that the original
text spoke of one animal only: "a lamb . . . like a lion," *The Lamb of God*, 5). It is
said, "And all the beasts rushed against him (the lamb), and the lamb overcame
them, and destroyed them, and trod them underfoot. And because of him the
angels and men and all the earth rejoiced. . . . His kingdom is an everlasting
kingdom, which shall not pass away." A further reference to the lamb of God
occurs in the *Testament of Benjamin* 3; O'Neill has given strong reasons for believing
both references to be pre-Christian (1–27). More important still is the vision of

the Lamb in Rev 5. There the Christ is depicted as the Lion of Judah who has conquered, then as a Lamb with seven horns who has won the right to open the scroll, representing the covenant of God to give the kingdom. These portrayals of the Christ as Lion and as Lamb are not paradoxical but parallel, since seven horns signify immense strength—the Lamb is a powerful *Ram!* But he must be presented as Lamb, for "he stands as one that has been slaughtered." He *stands,* for he is the Living One who died and is alive for ever (Rev 1:18); and he was *slaughtered* in sacrifice, specifically as God's Passover Lamb, to bring about the new Exodus for the liberty and life of the kingdom of God (the Book of Revelation is controlled from its first to last pages by the Exodus typology). In this work from the Johannine circle, then, we have an apocalyptic representation of the Christ adapted to the Christian doctrine of redemption; the mighty Christ wins salvation for the world through his sacrificial death. Precisely the same has taken place in John 1:29.

The proclamation of John the Baptist identifies Jesus as the powerful Lamb of God, whose task is to bring about the judgment of the wicked and the salvation of the righteous (cf. Matt 3:7–12 par.). The identification and the role are retained in the Johannine circle, but these are modified in the light of the redemptive event and the revelation of its meaning: the Lamb of God brings deliverance through submission to death as the Passover Lamb (see 19:31–37) and his rising to life with the Father in heaven. Since this understanding of Jesus as the Lamb of God belongs to the Johannine circle, and so is a community tradition and not the invention of the Evangelist, it is at least possible that other elements of Jewish and Christian tradition will have been linked with the figure, notably the submissive lamb of Isa 53 (cf. Acts 8:32–35) and the lamb provided by God at the intended sacrifice of Isaac (Gen 22:10–13). As various streams of thought flow together in the concept of the Word of God in the prologue, a similar development could have happened with this one.

30 See the comment on 1:15, and note Cullmann's suggestion, that by the form of this statement the Evangelist responds to the Baptist community's application of the maxim that one who *precedes* is greater than his successor ("ὁ ὀπίσω μου ἐρχόμενος," 26–32).

32 The language is reminiscent of the common tradition regarding the divine response to the baptism of Jesus: the Spirit of the age to come descends from an opened heaven and remains on Jesus, just as the prophets of the OT anticipated the Spirit to rest on the Messiah (cf. Isa 11:1–2; 42:1). The Father's voice declares him to be not simply a man of the Spirit, but the *Baptizer* with the Spirit; the witness in v 26 is thus completed, for the revelation has been made as to who the Baptizer with the Spirit is.

34 The witness of John to Jesus comes to its climax in the confession: "This man is the Son of God." As with the Lamb of God, so the expression Son of God is differentiated according to speaker and context. "Son of God" was more prevalent in Judaism than has generally been allowed. Israel is God's first-born son (Exod 4:22 f.); David's progeny is owned by God as his son in 2 Sam 7:14, a deeply influential passage (cf. Ps 2:7; 89:26 f.) which came to be interpreted messianically. The "righteous" are spoken of as God's sons in Sir 4:10; Wisd Sol 2:18; Jub 1:24 f.; for Qumran views cf. 4QFlor 1:6 f.; 1QSa 2:11 ff., and the reference to the Son of God in the Daniel

apocryphon of Cave 4. "Son of God" was applied also to miracle workers
and charismatic figures (see D. Flusser, *Jesus,* 93–94; Vermes, *Jesus the Jew,*
206–10; Hengel, *The Son of God,* 42–43). The differentiation between the
expression applied prior to and after the ministry of the Revealer is clear,
but the significance of the confession is equally evident: the Jews, the Church,
the contemporary movement of John the Baptist, the world itself are called
on to listen to the witness of the last of the prophets of the old order: Jesus
is *the* Son of God!

If the confession of v 34 is to be read, "This man is *the Elect One* of God" (see
Notes), the essential testimony remains. The term is reminiscent of the first Servant
Song (Isa 42:1), but it is not thereby to be automatically interpreted in the light
of the last Servant Song (Isa 52:13–53:12), as though John viewed the Elect as
the suffering Servant; the name is applied to the Son of Man in the judgment
scenes of the Similitudes of Enoch, e.g., Enoch 49:2–4:

> The Elect One standeth before the Lord of Spirits,
> And his glory is for ever and ever,
> And his might unto all generations . . .
> And he shall judge the secret things,
> And none shall be able to utter a lying word before him;
> For he is the Elect One before the Lord of Spirits according to his
>   good pleasure.

Again, however, one must distinguish between the use of the title in an apocalyptic
setting and in the Christian, and specifically Johannine, tradition.

THE CALL AND WITNESS OF THE FIRST DISCIPLES (1:35–51)

36–39   The cry, "Look, the Lamb of God," is a directive to the two disciples
of John to follow Jesus. In 37 ἠκολούθησαν, "they followed," is literally
meant, but the nature of the narrative indicates it as a first step towards
becoming disciples of Jesus. The Evangelist would have *all* the followers of
John in his day to listen to their master and follow the Lamb.

The first words of Jesus in this Gospel are, "What do you want?" On this
Bultmann observed, "It is the first question which must be addressed to anyone
who comes to Jesus, the first thing about which he must be clear" (100). A
secondary significance of μένειν, "to stay," in 38–39 (cf. 14:2–3, 23) is less
obvious, as also the tenth hour ("the hour of fulfillment," Bultmann). The
hour mentioned suggests time for conversation, perhaps even that the disciples
stayed overnight with Jesus. At all events they became convinced of the truth
of John's witness (41).

Andrew is named as one of the two disciples; but who is the other? Commonly he has been thought of as the Beloved Disciple, and this may be
right—but not his identification with John, the son of Zebedee (see above,
pp. lxx–lxxi). A plausible alternative is Philip, a guess supported by the conjunction of Andrew and Philip elsewhere in the Gospel (6:58; 12:21–22, see
A. B. Hulen, 151–53; Schnackenburg's acceptance of this view led him to
regard v 43 as an addition of the redactor, 1:310). Andrew finds his brother,
who is referred to first as *Simon Peter,* as in all the Greek-speaking churches;
then as *Simon,* his given name; finally it is reported how he came to be known

as *Kepha,* "Rock." Since knowledge of these early disciples is clearly assumed, we may view v 42 as recording the *source* of Simon's new name, not the *time* when it was given. Its inclusion here may suggest that the Evangelist saw in the call of the first disciples an anticipation of the formation of the later Church (Schnackenburg, 1:313).

43–46 That Jesus "finds" Philip emphasizes his call to be a disciple. Only in this Gospel do we hear anything of his doings (6:5–8; 12:21–22; 14:8–10); in the synoptics his name occurs only in lists of the twelve apostles. Nathanael is not even mentioned in the other Gospels; expositors therefore have sought to supply him with another name—from the lists of the Twelve! (Bartholomew is the favorite identification.) The assumption, however, that all the early followers of Jesus had to be apostles is as gratuitous as the notion that all the books in the NT had to come from pens of apostles. Nathanael's expostulation at the idea that the Messiah could come from Nazareth is comprehensible, for Nazareth was utterly insignificant; it has no mention in the OT, the Talmud or Midrash, or in any contemporary pagan writings (Str-B cite one reference to Nazareth from a Jewish writer *ca.* A.D. 800). The residence of Jesus in Nazareth is akin to his birth in a stable; it is part of the offense of the incarnation. Philip therefore can only reply, "Come and see"; the answer to the offense of the incarnation is Jesus himself.

47–50 Nathanael is greeted by Jesus as "an Israelite in whom is no deceit." Why "no deceit"? There may be an echo of Ps 32:2, spoken of one who is acceptable to God: οὐδέ ἔστιν ἐν τῷ στόματι αὐτοῦ δόλος, "there is no deceit in his mouth." It is likely, however, that Nathanael is regarded as a descendant of Jacob-Israel who does not share in the notorious deceit of his ancestor (cf. Gen 27:35, ἐλθὼν ὁ ἀδελφός σου μετὰ δόλου ἔλαβεν τὴν εὐλογίαν σου, "Your brother came with deceit and took your blessing.") Nathanael's surprised question, how Jesus should know him, is answered by an even more surprising affirmation: Jesus saw him "under the fig tree" when Philip called him (no hidden subtlety here, just a statement of place where the two met). Is this, as has been frequently suggested, an instance of Jesus being viewed as a "divine man," possessing magical powers, such as the Hellenistic world knew? No, the OT is familiar with this kind of phenomenon among the prophets (cf. 2 Kings 6:8–12; Ezek 8:1–18; 21:21–23). Jesus has insight beyond that of the prophets, he is the Revealer to whom and through whom God communicates; hence, Nathanael confesses him as Son of God and King of Israel (on Nathanael's lips the two titles are virtually synonymous, see on v 34). It is possible that we have here a reflection of the Wisdom tradition wherein the "Son of God" is marked as having wisdom from God; the Son has received from God his Father knowledge and revelation, of which Solomon, the Son of David, the supremely wise man, was the model; he who knows the hearts possesses wisdom. Solomon had this gift (Wisd 7:20), and it is manifested in yet greater measure in Jesus; hence, Nathanael acknowledges Jesus as *Son of God* and *King of Israel* (for a comparable recognition of Jesus cf. 4:19, 29, and see Berger's discussion, "Die königlichen Messiastraditionen," 4–5, 22–41). But Nathanael is to see "greater things" than this example of Jesus' knowledge; he is to witness *signs* that reveal Jesus as the Son of God and mediator of the kingdom to Israel.

51 The Evangelist adds a saying addressed to all the disciples. Its imagery is complex; Jacob's dream is clearly in the foreground, but there are reminiscences of the baptism of Jesus, possibly of his temptation (see Bammel, 111), and of the eschatological and apocalyptic picture language used of the Son of Man, such as appears in the synoptic Gospels. In Jacob's dream a ladder is set up between earth and heaven, and angels ascend and descend on— "it"? or upon Jacob? The point was discussed by later rabbis; in *Ber. Rab.* 70:12 the angels "were ascending on high and looking at his εἰκών (image), and then descending below and finding him sleeping" (see Burney, *Aramaic Origin,* 116). The natural reading of v 51 is that the angels ascend to heaven, and descend *to* the Son of Man (ἐπὶ τὸν υἱὸν τοῦ ἀνθρώπου); he is the point of contact between heaven and earth, the locus of the "traffic" that brings heaven's blessings to mankind. "You shall see" relates not to a future beyond the death of Jesus (as in Mark 14:62), but to the entire gamut of the action of the Son of Man for the kingdom of God: from the heaven that became open at his baptism, the blessings of the saving sovereignty will be poured out through him—in the signs he performs, the revelation of his word, the life that he lives, the death and resurrection that he accomplishes (his "lifting up"), till the goal is attained when the Son of Man welcomes the redeemed to the Father's house (14:3). This affirmation is a summary of the ministry of the Son of Man for the achievement of the divine purpose; it embraces the intent of the whole sweep of the Son of Man sayings in the synoptic Gospels, including those relating to the ministry of the Son of Man (e.g., Mark 2:10, 28; Matt 11:18–19; Luke 19:10), his death and resurrection (e.g., Mark 8:31, etc.), and his ultimate Parousia (e.g., Mark 14:62; Matt 25:31–46). It is characteristic of the difference in the emphases of the Gospels that while the synoptists give prominence to the future revelation of the Son of Man, the Fourth Evangelist stresses the revelation of the divine sovereignty in the incarnate life of the Son of Man, culminating in his exaltation to heaven via the cross. But not even he can forget the ultimate end (e.g. 5:21–29), and it should not be eliminated from the prospect in 1:51.

Explanation

1. The theme that binds together 1:19–51 is that of witness to Jesus. It is written from the perspective of the completed ministry of Jesus, with its revelation through word and sign, cross and resurrection, and illumination of the Spirit-Paraclete. The witness of the Baptist accordingly is viewed against the background of the achieved sacrifice of Christ and the light of Easter upon it. So also the confessions of the disciples are taken up into the fullness of the revelation through the Son of Man. The whole is written in the light of the destiny of Jesus to suffer rejection and condemnation by the "world," and of the Church's experience of like opposition from authorities of the same order.

2. Witness is a central theme of the Fourth Gospel as a whole, and it is developed in harmony with the fundamental idea of the term. For witness is basically an attestation of facts that have bearing on a case presented in a law court, and by natural extension it denotes attestation of convictions held

to be true. The concept is strikingly developed in the writings of Deutero-Isaiah, wherein Yahweh confronts a disbelieving world in a kind of trial relating to his claims to be the sole and sovereign God; the prophet who is his mouthpiece is instructed in the revelation (Isa 50:4), and the people of Israel are his witnesses (Isa 43:10–13; 44:7–9). So in the Fourth Gospel the whole story of Jesus is shot through with trial motifs; witnesses are called, witness is borne, and the testimony is constantly questioned and rejected by opponents of Jesus, till at length he undergoes a final trial. Through it all Jesus himself appears as the Witness to the revelation from God; he bears testimony to what he has seen and heard from the Father (3:32), and in support thereof he adduces the ultimate witness—that of the Father, who bore witness to Jesus through John, through the works he gave Jesus to do, and through the Scriptures of the OT (5:31–47); the process reaches its end in the exaltation of Jesus to the Father's presence in heaven (13:32; 17:1). Accordingly the world that accused Jesus and passed sentence on him has sentence passed on it as having been the tool of the devil (12:31–32). It has been overcome by the Son of God (16:33), and through the witness of the Church it becomes the object of the Paraclete's convicting exposure (16:8–11).

The significance of this for our passage is that the latter commences with a report of John's witness when questioned by emissaries of the Jews in Jerusalem. The scene is set as an interrogation of John by the authorities, i.e., the same authorities who will later interrogate Jesus. In response to their question he gives clear witness, both as to who he is *not* and as to who he *is;* his task is to straighten a path for "the Lord," and his baptism is a preparation for him who baptizes with Spirit. This witness to the interrogators is followed by the prophetic witness recorded in 1:29–36, which declares Jesus to be the Lamb of God and the Son (or Elect) of God, and directs men to follow him.

3. This representation of the nature and significance of John's ministry has been severely criticized by recent scholars. They maintain that to reduce John's role to that of a "mere witness" to Jesus is to distort the history of John for the sake of the theology of Jesus. This is a questionable position to take; whoever adopts it is likely to extend it to the whole Gospel. The Evangelist did not set out to tell the whole story even of Jesus, but to give a key to its understanding. His narrative had a limited aim, and he concentrated attention on achieving it (20:30). So also is evident that the Evangelist knew a good deal more about John than he recorded; for example, 1:32–33 reflects knowledge of an early tradition of John's baptism of Jesus; he alludes to it but he does not describe it. On the other hand the synoptists themselves reflect a conviction that John came as witness as well as forerunner (see e.g. Matt 3:11–12, 11:2–3, 12–13). The tradition reproduced by the Fourth Evangelist about John itself contained this theme of John's witness to Jesus, as the Lamb of God saying indicates (we have already noted its currency in the Johannine circle before the Evangelist, pp. 24–25). We may well believe that the Evangelist in the prologue crystallized the belief of his contemporaries when he summarized John's function as: "He came for witness, to bear witness to the Light." In the perspective of the Church the role of John as witness to Jesus may be compared with the claim that the Scriptures serve as witness to Jesus,

the Son of God (cf. 5:39–40); the Scriptures contain more than that, but the church confesses without hesitation that this is their supreme function. The Church itself, with all its variety of functions, concurs with this Gospel that it is sent into the world for the same purpose—to bear witness by word and deed to the Son of God, as he was sent into the world to bear witness to the Father (20:17).

4. John's witness under interrogation was highly relevant for the Johannine group that received the Book of Revelation; for that whole work is characterized as "the witness of Jesus" (Rev 1:2), and Jesus is described in its opening greeting as "the faithful Witness" (1:5). Having exemplified faithfulness as a witness under trial (cf. the tradition in 1 Tim 6:13), he now bears witness to the word and promise of God for the encouragement of churches called to endure a like passion as he did. The community of the Evangelist stands in need of just such encouragement, and in the Gospel it receives it.

It needs hardly to be remarked that this motif applies to multitudes of Christians in the world today who find themselves in situations comparable to those of the Johannine communities. They know what it is to bear witness under interrogation, sometimes extremely hostile. To such the witness of John, of Jesus, of the earliest churches, and of the Gospel speaks powerfully, frequently leading them to follow the example and declare the witness in a manner unmatched by churches in more tolerant areas. Nevertheless those of us who live where Jesus is of small concern to the populace ("They wouldn't hurt a hair of him, they only let him die") have need to ponder John's witness. For an affluent and materialist generation needs as urgently as any the witness to the Lamb of God who takes away the sin of the world.

5. The witness of John in chapter 1 gives way to that of the early disciples. Here is a series of enthusiastic testimonies to Jesus, covering a wide spectrum of the contemporary Church's witness to its Lord. The "Rabbi" is confessed as the Messiah, as the One who fulfills the Law and the Prophets, as the Son of God and the King of Israel. All these are valid confessions of faith, and they are especially pertinent for the Church's witness to the synagogue. But they all require to be filled with greater meaning than they have in Judaism. It has often been observed that the "Messianic Secret" is lacking in this chapter. In reality the Evangelist has his own version of it: first impressions of Jesus have to grow under the impact of the revelation that comes through him. All Jewish understandings of the Anointed One are inadequate to describe the Incarnate One sent from the Father; they require the depth and height and breadth of the witness of Jesus—hence the relevance of the additional logion about the Son of Man in 1:51. In this Gospel Son of Man and Son of God are complementary concepts; they flow into one another. The saying forms the climax of the introduction to the story of the Word made flesh; it illuminates the Gospel, and it continues to speak to the Church, not alone of the Evangelist's time but to that of every generation. For the Son of Man is still the meeting point of heaven's fullness and earth's need, even in the midst of the bustle and noise of our modern world. So Francis Thompson (*The Kingdom of God*) saw, and bore his witness:

The angels keep their ancient places;
Turn but a stone, and start a wing!
'Tis ye, 'tis your estrangèd faces
That miss the many sp endoured thing.

But (when so sad thou canst not sadder)
Cry; —and upon thy sc sore loss
Shall shine the traffic of Jacob's ladder
Pitched betwixt Heaven and Charing Cross.

B. The Revelation of the New Order in Jesus (2:1–4:42)

Introduction

It is evident that the second chapter is linked with the account of the call of the disciples in chap. 1 through the reference in 2:1 to the *third* day; the promise in 1:51 is given its first fulfillment in the miracle of the water into wine. But it is equally plain that the sign described in vv 1–11 is the first of the series of signs incorporated in chaps. 2–12 as examples of the deeds of the Redeemer-Revealer, hence that a new start is being made at 2:1. It commences the account in this Gospel of the public ministry of Jesus. The chapter naturally has a completeness of its own. It conjoins a significant miraculous deed with a significant non-miraculous act. The placing of the latter (the cleansing of the temple) at the beginning of the ministry, in striking contrast to the synoptic accounts, is almost certainly due to a decision of the Evangelist, through which the peculiar significance of the event in the temple is underscored. By this conjunction of the sign of Cana and the cleansing of the temple he has created a diptych to form a prelude to his story of the ministry of Jesus (so Bultmann, 112). The chapter has a programmatic significance: *whoever understands the miracle of the wine and the cleansing of the temple has the key to the ministry, death, and resurrection of Jesus and their outcome in the salvation of the kingdom and existence of the Church.*

But further: as the chapter is linked in its opening with chap. 1, so it is bound with the Nicodemus discourse of chap. 3 by the paragraph 2:23–25. The discourse may be seen as a drawing out of aspects of the signs of chap. 2. But only aspects. A major feature of the cleansing of the temple finds its exposition in chap. 4, namely the new order of worship brought into being through the redemptive presence and action of Christ. This was perceived by C. H. Dodd, who saw chaps. 2–4 (specifically 2:1–4:42) as bound together by a single theme: "The old things have passed away, see, the new have come!" (2 Cor 5:17). The three chapters together present the replacement of the old purifications by the wine of the kingdom of God, the old temple by the new in the risen Lord, an exposition of new birth for new creation, a contrast between the water of Jacob's well with the living water from Christ, and the worship of Jerusalem and Gerizim with worship "in Spirit and in truth" (see *Interpretation*, 297). It is well to keep in mind these wider horizons as we study the narratives of chap. 2.

1. The Beginning of the Signs: Water into Wine (2:1–12)

Bibliography

Boismard, M. E. *Du Baptême à Cana.* 33–59. **Brown, R. E.** "The 'Mother of Jesus' in the Fourth Gospel." *L'Évangile de Jean.* 307–10. **Derrett, J. D. M.** "Water into Wine." *BZ* 7 (1963) 80–97; also in *Law in the New Testament.* 228–46. **Dodd, C. H.** *Historical Tradition.* 223–28. **Geyser, A.** "Semeion." *Studies in John.* FS J. N. Sevenster. 12–21. **Lindars, B.** "Two Parables in John." *NTS* 16 (1969–70) 318–29 (especially 318–24). **Linnemann, E.** "Die Hochzeit zu Kana und Dionysios." *NTS* 20 (1974) 408–18. **Noetzel, H.** *Christus und Dionysus.* Stuttgart: Calwer Verlag, 1960. **Rissi, M.** "Die Hochzeit in Kana Joh 2, 1–11." *Oikonomia.* FS O. Cullmann. 76–92. **Schnackenburg, R.** *Das erste Wunder Jesu.* Freiburg: Herder, 1951. **Temple, S.** "Two Signs in the Fourth Gospel." *JBL* 81 (1962) 169–74. **Theissen, G.** *Urchristliche Wundergeschichten.* Gütersloh: Mohn, 1974; *The Miracle Stories of the Early Christian Tradition.* Tr. F. McDonagh. Ed. J. Riches. Edinburgh: T&T Clark, 1983.

Translation

2:1 *And on the third day a wedding took place in Cana of Galilee, and the mother of Jesus was there.* 2 *Jesus was also invited to the wedding, together with his disciples.* 3 *When the wine ran short the mother of Jesus says to him, "They have no wine left."*[a] 4 *Jesus says to her, "What have we to do with one another, woman? My hour has not yet arrived."*[b] 5 *His mother says to the servants, "Whatever he tells you, do."* 6 *Now there were standing there, in accordance with the purification requirements of the Jews, six stone water jars, each one holding from twenty to thirty gallons.* 7 *Jesus says to them, "Fill the jars with water." And they filled them up to the brim.* 8 *And he says to them, "Now draw some, and take it to the man in charge of the feast." And they took it.* 9 *But when the man in charge of the feast tasted the water that had become wine (not knowing where it had come from, though the servants who had drawn the water knew), he called the bridegroom* 10 *and said to him, "Everybody serves the good wine first, and when people are drunk the inferior kind; you have kept the good wine till now!"*

11 *Jesus did this as the beginning of his signs in Cana of Galilee and revealed his glory, and his disciples believed in him.*

12 *After this he went down to Capernaum, he and his mother and his brothers and his disciples,*[c] *and there they remained not many days.*

Notes

[a] After the concluding statement, some OL MSS and syr[hmg] add: ὅτι συνετελέσθη ὁ οἶνος τοῦ γάμου· εἶτα, "since the wine for the wedding was used up; then. . . ." This appears to be a secondary explanation, but it is adopted in the text of the JB.

[b] Grammatically it is possible to understand οὔπω ἥκει ἡ ὥρα μου as a question: "Has not my hour now arrived?" The "hour" would then unambiguously relate to the messianic task of Jesus, and the difficulty that Jesus responds to Mary's request, in spite of an apparent rebuff, would be removed. For this reason it is favored by some early Fathers and some recent Roman Catholic exegetes, but the principle of *difficilior lectio potior* should be applied here and the words read as a statement.

^c καὶ οἱ μαθηταὶ αὐτοῦ is omitted by א W, some OL MSS and the Armenian. This strengthened Lindars in his belief (following Bultmann) that in the original narrative no mention was made of the disciples of Jesus; the incident was related as occurring while Jesus lived at home, and is to be classed with the folk legends recounted in the apocryphal gospels (127, 132). These speculations are scarcely warranted by the textual phenomena of v 12. For a different deduction, see Barrett, 194. ἔμεινεν instead of ἔμειναν is read in p⁶⁶ᶜ and some later MSS. It is favored by Bultmann and Barrett, but it could be due to the influence of the sing. verbs that precede and follow this one (κατέβη . . . ἀνέβη . . .).

Form/Structure/Setting

1. A miracle story is related, comparable to those described in the synoptic Gospels, but unknown to them. As throughout this Gospel, the miracle is termed a σημεῖον, a "sign" (the word δύναμις, "act of power, miracle" does not occur in this Gospel). The concept of *sign* is familiar in the OT (commonly אוֹת, *'ôt*); it is used especially of events, both normal and supranormal, that demonstrate the truth of God's word through his prophet (e.g. Exod 3:12; 1 Sam 10:1–9) and so authenticate the prophet himself (e.g. Exod 4:1–9); it also denotes events that herald things to come, especially in relation to the eschatological future (e.g. Isa 7:10–16). As in the synoptic Gospels so in the Fourth Gospel, the miraculous deeds of Jesus attest that the promises relating to the kingdom of God are actualized in and through Jesus. Our evangelist goes one step further in viewing the miracles as *parables* of the kingdom which comes through the total work of the Son of God. If the works of the present are manifestations of the kingdom that now is, they are also anticipations of the "greater things" (14:12) of the kingdom that comes in the death and resurrection of the Christ, the sending of the Spirit and the Parousia for final judgment and resurrection. As in the OT the coming of God for his kingdom results in the gathering of the Gentiles to see his glory, and their proclamation of it to nations that have not seen it (Isa 66:19), so the σημεῖα of Jesus are revelations of *his* glory. For the divine *basileia* is God sovereignly acting in judgment and salvation through the Son; accordingly the kingdom that comes through the Son is the kingdom of *God in Christ*. Of this the σημεῖα are revelations.

2. The structure of the narrative is clear. The situation is described in vv 1–3a; the need for an intervention is made known in 3b–5, entailing a dialogue between the mother of Jesus and Jesus himself; in 6–8 a miracle occurs, as servants obediently carry out the commands of Jesus; in 9–10 the miracle is attested through the master of the feast, as he compliments the bridegroom on the excellence of the wine. A comment is added in v 11, emphasizing that it was the first of the signs of Jesus, and clarifying its function as a revelation of the glory of Jesus and a strengthening of the faith of his disciples.

3. This mention of the *first* of the signs done in Cana calls to mind the statement in 4:54, that the healing of the royal official's son was the *second* sign performed by Jesus on coming from Judea into Galilee, ignoring thereby the reference in 2:23 to the signs done by Jesus in Jerusalem. This linking of the signs led to the postulate of a Signs Source, which contained all seven of the signs narrated in the Gospel (with possibly a good deal more material utilized) and concluded with 20:30–31 (so Bultmann, whose views

on this were developed by R. T. Fortna and W. Nichols, see pp. xxxix–xl).
The theory entails formidable difficulties, but it is not impossible that the
Evangelist was acquainted with a source that contained the two signs of Cana.
That he should have stressed this sign as the beginning of self-revelation of
Jesus given through the signs is natural (Schnackenburg, 1:323), not least
in view of the significance which he wished us to see in it.

Comment

1 The mention of the third day has led to various attempts to read a
symbolic meaning into the date. For some it is allusion to Easter: the miracle
anticipates the manifestation of Christ's glory in the Resurrection (Dodd,
Interpretation, 300). Others note that 1:19–2:1 implies the passage of a week;
they see here a comparison of the first week of the *new* creation with the
work of creation (Boismard, *Du baptême à Cana,* 15). A simpler interpretation
is preferable: "The promise made by Jesus in 1:50 or 51 was fulfilled very
soon" (Schnackenburg, 1:325).

2–3 The disciple group invited with Jesus will have been viewed as his
family, for whose contributions to the marriage feast he will have been responsible. It is a natural assumption that this motivated Mary's drawing the attention
of Jesus to the lack of wine—not that she hoped for a miracle, but that his
presence with the disciples, jointly embarked on a mendicant ministry which
rendered them unable to fulfill the obligation of guests, contributed to the
embarrassing situation (for customs on the obligations of wedding guests
and their relation to this event see Derrett, *Law in the NT,* 228–38).

4 It is not impossible that this verse was inserted by the Evangelist into
his "signs source"; the passage would read more smoothly without it. By
contrast Becker claims that the thought is characteristic of the Signs Source
itself (he notes 5:6; 6:5 ff.; 7:6 ff.; 11:6 ff.). It is wiser to retain the narrative
in its wholeness.

τί ἐμοὶ καὶ σοί; is a well known but ambiguous expression, which can express
a hostile or peaceful attitude (contrast Judg 11:12 with 2 Chron 35:21). 2
Kgs 3:13 is of interest, in that it expresses rejection, yet the prophet gives
what is asked; so here is an apparent rejection of Mary's initiative, yet a
granting of the request for intervention. The question may, however, have
a gentler tone; an analogical expression from east Syrian "Chaldean" suggests
not division but unity of thought, which could here be rendered, "Why are
you speaking to me of this need? With you, I understand it" (see Derrett,
241–42).

γύναι has caused needless perplexity. While it is an unusual mode of address
to one's mother, it also may be affectionate. Apart from John 19:26, which
cannot be intended to express distance, a significant occurrence of the term
is found in Josephus, *Ant.* 17.74: the wife of Pheroras tells Herod (the Great)
how her husband summoned her in his illness, beginning his statement with
"Woman." The example is important, since Pheroras had great affection for
his wife; he refused Herod's request that he send her away, and his persistence
in keeping her led to a rupture of relations between the two men.

In this Gospel the "hour" of Jesus commonly denotes his death and glorification (see 7:30; 8:20; 13:1; 17:1). An *immediate* reference to that hour is scarcely thinkable in this context; it must relate to the service of the divine sovereignty on which Jesus now embarks, which will (as the Evangelist knows) culminate in the "lifting up" on the cross. (If the saying was in the source it would clearly have related to the beginning of the redemptive ministry, and was interpreted by the Evangelist in the light of its end, since the ministry was an indivisible unity.) The import of the statement is to declare that Jesus' service for the kingdom of God is determined solely by his Father; into that area not even his mother can intrude (cf. 7:3–9 and Mark 3:31–35, and see the excellent discussion of Schnackenburg, 1:327–31).

6 The Jewish requirements for which the jars were used included ritual cleansing of the hands through pouring water on them and washing of vessels (cf. Mark 7:3–4, and for the regulations Str-B 1:695–705). The jars were of stone, since stone vessels did not contract uncleanness. Their large size was natural, but the sequel suggests that the great quantity they contained reflected the fullness of Christ's grace, in contrast to the limitations of the old covenant (John 1:16–17).

8 Jewish sources do not enable us to be certain whether the ἀρχιτρίκλινος was a guest chosen to supervise the feast ("the president of the banquet," Barrett) or a servant appointed for the task (a "butler," Lindars). The issue is secondary; whether guest or servant, he acted as master of ceremonies.

10 The statement to the bridegroom is neither a proverb nor a rule; it may be an ironical or humorous or simply shrewd comment on human conduct. For the Evangelist it serves as a testimony to the perfection of the sign performed by Jesus.

11 The miracle of the wine revealed the *glory* of Jesus. We are to recall 1:14 and 1:51: the Word made flesh, the only Son of the Father, who is the Son of Man, manifested his creative *power*. Does that exhaust the content of the sign? To what end does he use his power and glory?

Some scholars view the glory of Jesus here set over against that claimed for Dionysus, the provider of wine, and the fullness of life experienced in intoxication. Various stories were told of this provision, such as the placing of three empty basins at night in the temple at Elis and finding them to be full of wine the next day; or of the spring of wine that flowed in the temple of Bacchus in Andros on the festal day known as *Theodosia* (see Dodd, *Historical Tradition*, 224–25). An exhaustive examination of the evidence relating to such parallels was made by H. Noetzel (*Christus und Dionysus*); he has convinced most scholars that the parallels are insufficient to support the claims made for them. In particular the motif of *changing* water to wine is not present in the Dionysus legends; the jugs of Elis, for example, were not filled with water but were empty, and the fount of wine in Andros did not replace one of water. To suggest that the Evangelist or his source wished to demonstrate through the Cana miracle that a greater than Dionysus has appeared is a speculation without warrant.

The notion that at Cana the superiority of Jesus to Melchizedek was evidenced was earlier suggested by C. H. Dodd. In contrast to the Ammonites and Moabites, who refused Israel bread and water in the wilderness, Melchizedek, said Philo, "shall bring forth wine instead of water and give our souls a pure draught, that they may become possessed by that divine intoxication that is more sober than sobriety itself; for he is the priest-logos, and has for his portion the Self-existent" (*Leg. Alleg.* 3.79 ff.: see Dodd, *Interpretation*, 298 f.). The parallel is interesting, but insufficient to account for the Cana narrative. Dodd later maintained that the story could have evolved from a *parable* of Jesus which had the setting of a wedding feast; it could have begun, "A certain man made a wedding feast," and ended, "You have kept the good wine till now" (*Historical Tradition*, 227). On this Haenchen commented, "In that case Jesus would have had to recount between that beginning and this end about a miracle of wine, and who should have performed that?" (193).

Most writers acknowledge that in the Johannine narrative there is an implicit contrast between water used for Jewish purificatory rites and the wine given by Jesus; the former is characteristic of the old order, the latter of the new. There can be little doubt that the change of which the miracle is a sign is the coming of the kingdom of God in and through Jesus. The picture of the kingdom of God as a feast is prominent in Judaism and in the synoptic teaching (see, e.g., Matt 5:6; 8:11–12; Mark 2:19; Luke 22:15–18, 29–30a), and abundance of wine is a feature of the feast (e.g. Isa 25:6). The glory of Jesus, manifest in Cana was a sign of his mediating the grace of the kingdom of God in his total ministry. The glory of God is seen precisely in God's bestowal of life in his kingdom, and this he gives through the Son.

Explanation

1. This first of the signs of Jesus is depicted as the first public act of the ministry of Jesus. As a revelation of the divine intervention that then began and continued throughout his ministry, it is significant that it was perceived by very few persons and its meaning understood only by the closest associates of Jesus.

2. The hour of Jesus in Cana was less a symbol of his timeless redemptive action than a representation of the eschatological moment which, itself full of glory, leads to a glorious future. We may here recall a different but related use of "hour" in this Gospel: "the hour comes and now is" (4:23; 5:25), which refers to eschatological realities of the kingdom of God which are now in process of actualization and are moving to a climax in the near future.

3. The hour that struck in Cana leads on inexorably to the moment of the exaltation of the Son of Man to heaven via his cross, when the wine of the kingdom of God was made available to the whole world (12:30–31). Its anticipation runs through the whole Gospel till the triumphant *tetelestai*, "It is finished!" rings out from the cross (19:30). While we do not consider that the statement of time in 2:1 has relation to the third day of the Resurrection, there is no doubt that the narrative is suffused with the Easter faith and is to be understood in its light. The event sheds light on the time of the Church as well as on the historic ministry of Jesus.

4. For this reason the gift of wine instead of water was crucially important for the earliest readers of this Gospel. They must grasp the superiority of the Son of God and his gift to the mediator of the old covenant and its gifts (1:17). It is their privilege to rejoice in the possession of the life of the kingdom of God, and to persist in their adherence to its Lord and Giver in face of those who champion the old order and glory in its mediator. Of this gift every celebration of the Eucharist is a standing reminder.

5. The reality and the gift remain through every succeeding generation, till the last hour strikes and the ultimate gift of life through Christ is his gift to all who do not reject the revelation in him (5:21–29).

2. The Cleansing of the Temple (2:13–22)

Bibliography

Braun, F. M. "L'expulsion des vendeurs de Temple." *RB* 38 (1929) 178–200. **Buse, I.** "The Cleansing of the Temple in the Synoptics and in John." *ExpTim* 70 (1958–59) 22–24. **Cullmann, O.** "L'Opposition contre le Temple de Jérusalem." *NTS* 5 (1958–59) 157–73; ET in *ExpTim* 71 (1959–60) 8–12, 39–43. **Dodd, C. H.** *Interpretation,* 300–303. ———. *Historical Tradition.* 89–91. **Hiers, R. H.** "The Purification of the Temple: Preparation for the Kingdom of God." *JBL* 90 (1971) 82–90. **Léon-Dufour, X.** "Le signe du Temple selon saint Jean." *RSR* 39 (1951) 155–75. **Mendner, S.** "Die Tempelreinigung." *ZNW* 47 (1956) 93–112. **Roloff, J.** *Das Kerygma und der irdische Jesus.* 89–110. **Scott, E. F.** *The Crisis in the Life of Jesus.* New York: Scribners, 1952. **Trocmé, E.** "L'expulsion des marchands du Temple." *NTS* 15 (1968–69) 1–22. **Vögels, H.** "Die Tempelreinigung und Golgotha (Joh 2 19–22)." *BZ* 6 (1962) 102–7. **White, H. J.** "On the Saying Attributed to Our Lord in John II.19." *ExpTim* 17 (1919) 415–23.

Translation

[13] *Now the Jewish passover*[a] *was near, and Jesus went up to Jerusalem.* [14] *And he found in the temple*[b] *people selling cattle and sheep and doves, and the money-changers*[c] *sitting at tables.* [15] *So he made a whip*[d] *out of cords and he threw them all out of the temple, including the sheep and the cattle;*[e] *he scattered the coins of the money-changers and overturned their tables,* [16] *and to those who were selling doves he said, "Stop making the house of my Father a house of trade."* [17] *His disciples remembered that it is written, "Zeal for your house will destroy*[f] *me."* [18] *The Jews therefore answered him, "What sign can you show us as authority for doing these things?"* [19] *Jesus replied to them, "Destroy this temple, and in three days I will raise it up."* [20] *The Jews therefore said, "This temple has taken forty-six years to build,*[g] *and are you going to raise it up in three days?"* [21] *But he was speaking about the temple of his body.* [22] *When therefore he had risen from the dead*[h] *his disciples remembered that he had said this, and they believed the scripture and the words that Jesus had spoken.*

Notes

[a] τὸ πάσχα strictly denotes the Passover celebration held on the night of 14–15 Nisan, which was followed by the Feast of Unleavened Bread, 15–21 Nisan. In later Judaism the two feasts were combined under the one term and called the Passover.

[b] τὸ ἱερόν = the whole temple complex, including the sanctuary, ancillary buildings, and courts (here the courts are in mind, probably the court of the Gentiles, cf. Mark 11:17). The sanctuary proper = ὁ ναός, as in vv 19–20.

ᶜ Money changers were required, since Jews were not allowed by the Romans to issue their own coins, and Rom. coins bore images of their rulers with (to Jews) blasphemous claims of rule and divinity. The Jewish rulers therefore decreed that the temple tax and sacrifices be paid for in Tyrian coinage.

ᵈ p⁶⁶ and p⁷⁵ and some other MSS prefix ὡς to φραγέλλιον, "a kind of whip." Despite the age of these witnesses the addition looks like an attempt to tone down the action of Jesus.

ᵉ τά τε πρόβατα καὶ τοὺς βόας is frequently viewed as "a poor apposition to πάντας" (so Bultmann, 123 n.8), but that is an impossible meaning in this context, since πάντας must include the sellers of v 14. It is a construction according to sense (though see Schnackenburg on the Evangelist's use of τε, 1:346 n.15), drawing attention to the fact that Jesus drove out the sacrificial animals as well as those who sold them.

ᶠ καταφάγεται "will consume," not in a psychological sense, but more drastically *"will destroy"*; cf. Rev 11:5; 12:4; 20:9.

ᵍ οἰκοδομήθη, not a completed act lying in the past, for the building operations continued on the temple until A.D. 63.; rather a past process viewed from the present. Bernard (after Alford) cites Ezra 5:16 as a remarkable parallel, also relating to the temple: ἀπὸ τότε ἕως τοῦ νῦν ᾠκοδομήθη καὶ οὐκ ἐτελέσθη, "From that time until now building has gone on and it is not yet finished."

ʰ ἠγέρθη is passive in form, but can have intransitive as well as passive sense. In view of ἐγερῶ in v 19 and the parallel concept in 10:17–18 the intransitive sense is more suitable here.

Form/Structure/Setting

1. It has been pointed out (by Schnackenburg, 1:344) that our passage is strikingly like a diptych (a double altarpiece on two leaves hinged together): we have (*i*) the action of Jesus, vv 14–15; words of Jesus, v 16; "remembering" of disciples, v 17; (*ii*) action of the Jews, v 18; words of Jesus, v 19; misunderstanding of the Jews and comment of Evangelist, vv 20–21; "remembering" of disciples, v 22.

2. Of these two sections the former, describing the cleansing of the temple, is also related to the synoptic accounts of the event, though independent of them, whereas the second, narrating a dialogue of Jesus with Jewish authorities, has considerable differences. Interestingly enough, there is ground for viewing the accounts of the cleansing both in John 2:14–16 and Mark 11:15–19 as apothegms (for the former see Becker, 1:122–23; for the latter Trocmé, "L'expulsion des marchands," 10–11). This suggests that the dialogues had a separate existence from the action. Certainly the saying of Jesus in v 19, circulated independently in varied (and garbled!) forms, gained notoriety (see Mark 14:58//Matt 26:61 and Mark 15:29//Matt 27:40). Trocmé pointed out that the corresponding dialogue in Mark 11:27–33 is more closely bound with the controversies recorded in Mark 12:13–37 than it is with the temple event. It would appear that the two halves of the accounts, alike in John and the synoptics, had independent circulation, or at least embodied material that circulated independently.

3. The relationship of the accounts of the cleansing of the temple in the Fourth Gospel and in the synoptics has been endlessly discussed, with all possible variety of options put forward by exegetes. There is reasonably widespread agreement now that: (*i*) the event happened only once, not twice (at the beginning and end of the ministry of Jesus); (*ii*) it took place in the last week of the life of Jesus; (*iii*) the Fourth Evangelist had no intention of correcting the timing of the event, but set his account at the beginning of

the ministry of Jesus to highlight its significance for understanding the course of the ministry. It provides a vital clue for grasping the nature and the course of our Lord's work, his words and actions, his death and resurrection, and the outcome of it all in a new worship of God, born out of a new relation to God in and through the crucified-risen Christ. (For a comparable procedure of an evangelist transferring to an earlier point a well known event in the life of Jesus, note Luke's setting his report of the visit of Jesus to Nazareth at the beginning of the Galilean ministry, Luke 4:16–30; this Luke did because what then took place presaged the outcome of the entire ministry of our Lord in the Jewish rejection of him and his acceptance among the Gentiles, so preparing for volume 2 of Luke's story of Jesus and his Church.)

Comment

13 That the evangelist speaks of the ' Passover *of the Jews*" indicates that the Church no longer observes the feast; this is not through hostility (to it, or to any other Jewish feast, *contra* Haenchen, 198), but because the Passover has been fulfilled in and through Jesus (cf. 19:31–37). The question arises as to which Passover is in mind, for that in which the temple was cleansed was at the end of the Lord's ministry. Did Jesus also go to Jerusalem for a Passover at this early date? The indications of time in 2:1, 23; 3:22; 4:1 suggest that he did. It was the period when the ministries of Jesus and John overlapped.

14–17 The ejection from the temple of traders, with their beasts and birds for sacrifice and the scattering of their money, is an act of wrath which the traders were powerless to resist. Observe that the wrath was directed not against those engaged in or leading worship, but against those detracting from it. The motives and significance of the action are hinted at in vv 15–17.

(*i*) The trade in the temple was viewed as an act of desecration: "Stop making the house of my Father a house of trade." There is probably an allusion here to the final words of Zechariah's vision of the kingdom of God: "No trader shall again be seen in the house of the Lord of Hosts." Jesus is taking action to bring about the eschatological order wherein God will be glorified in his house and in the worship of his people (see R. H. Hiers, "The Purification of the Temple," 83–90; Dodd, *Interpretation*, 300). The expression "house of my Father" instead of "house of the Lord of Hosts" is typically Johannine, but equally typical of Jesus (cf. Luke 2:49 and his teaching on God as Father). (*ii*) The eschatological order is achieved not through the ejection of traders but through that to which the action leads: the death of the Father's Son. So Ps 69:9 is quoted, a psalm of the Righteous Sufferer, frequently cited in the NT with reference to Christ's death. The discourse that follows (as the rest of the Gospel) will show that this death will be for the glory of God and the redemption of man. (*iii*) That the action in the temple can be characterized as "zeal for your house" suggests a positive attitude to the temple, and not one of total rejection (contrary to a frequently held opinion). "Jesus purified the temple, showing thereby that he had come to remove all barriers to the true worship of God" (E. F. Scott, *The Crisis in the*

Life of Jesus, 19). That is, stated positively, Jesus had come to open up the way to the true worship of God, and this motif lies at the heart of the narrative and dialogue. (*iv*) The curious structure of v 15b, which overloads the sentence, draws attention to the expulsion of the sacrificial beasts. This comports with the thought that in the temple of the eschatological order sacrificial worship will have no place. This again is to be understood in terms of eschatological fulfillment rather than condemnation of the old order of worship; for the death that puts an end to all sacrifices is one with the exaltation of the Christ to Lordship and leads to the age of the Spirit. This, too, is assumed in the enigmatic utterance of v 19.

18 The demand by the Jewish interrogators for a sign to legitimate the outrageous action and teaching of Jesus is in harmony with Jewish ideas of testing prophets (cf. Deut 18:20–22 and 13:1–5; the latter could have a threatening application). Similar demands for a sign are related in the synoptic Gospels (cf. Mark 8:11; Luke 23:8–9, and especially Matt 12:38–40//Luke 11:29-30, where the sole sign to be given is that of the resurrection of Jesus).

19–21 The response of Jesus to the demand for a legitimating sign is given in the form of a *māšāl,* a riddle which at the same time is parabolic.

Mendner vehemently protested its absurdity (particularly in the light of v 21), citing scholarly criticisms of it as "an unsuitable and thoroughly incomprehensible answer," "thoroughly unworthy, and also unfair," "a blow in the air," giving rise to "suspicion that Jesus has megalomania" ("Die Tempelreinigung," 99–101). These citations are given by Mendner not to discredit Jesus, but in an endeavor to prove that Jesus could not have made such an utterance. On the contrary, virtually all agree that Mark 14:58//Matt 26:61 and Mark 15:29//Matt 27:40 show that Jesus did make some such statement, and there is increasing recognition that John 2:19 is its most primitive form (so e.g. Bultmann, 126 n.1; Lindars, 142; Sanders, 119; Becker, 125). And is the answer so incomprehensible as Mendner made out? This logion is one of the clearest examples in this Gospel of its composition on two planes for two stages of history (or, as Léon-Dufour put it, of the author playing on two keyboards at the same time). The clue to its meaning is not in determining the appropriate signification of the ambiguous terms "destroy," "temple," "raise," "body" (in v 21), but to distinguish between what the *hearers* could and should have understood and what the *readers* are to understand (see Léon-Dufour, "Le signe du Temple," 156–57, and his exposition of the passage on this basis). In its context, "destroy the temple" does not convey a challenge to the Jewish leaders to tear down the stones of the temple; more plausibly it is an ironical call for them to carry on their behavior to its limit, which will end in the destruction of the temple of which they are guardians (for such prophetic irony Bultmann cites Amos 4:4; Isa 8:9; Jer 7:21; Matt 23:32 is particularly apposite: "Go on then, finish off what your fathers began!", followed by the prophecy of doom in vv 35–36). In such circumstances the sign demanded will be given in raising the temple of the new age in three days (i.e., shortly). This would accord perfectly with contemporary Jewish ideas of the new or glorified temple in the kingdom of God. But Jesus is more than a Jewish apocalyptist. The expression "within three days" points to a meaning of the words closely in harmony with the unique ministry of Jesus. "After three days" or "on the third day" and the like denotes in Jewish tradition the time when God may be counted on to deliver his people from their troubles. The Midrash on Gen 42:17 contains the dictum, "The Holy One, blessed be he, never leaves the righteous in distress more than three days," and in its comment on Gen 22:4, it lengthily elaborates the principle from the OT. So explicit was this tradition in Israel that K. Lehmann concluded that the third day was not simply a short time, but a time stamped with special meaning: "The third day brings the turning to something new and better. God's mercy and righteousness creates a new 'time' of salvation, of life, of victory; the third day brings a difficult circumstance from decision, through God's saving action, to a final solution which is creative of history" (*Auferweckt am Dritten Tag*, 181). It is not to be wondered at that Jesus incorporated the expression in his reference to his destiny of death and resurrection (Mark 8:31, etc.). If, then, the saying of v 19 promises a creative intervention of God through his Son, it is seriously to be considered that the "destruction" of the temple which it rectifies may be of a moral kind, a degradation that destroys the nature of the temple as the temple of the covenant of Israel. The OT is acquainted with such thinking; cf. Ezekiel's denunciation of the profanation of the temple (e.g. chap. 8) and his description of the glory of God forsaking the temple and city of Jerusalem, rendering the temple meaningless (Ezek 10:15–19; 11:22–23); it has a vivid counterpart in Matt 23:38: "Look, there is your temple, *forsaken by God!*"

The Jewish leaders understand, or rather misunderstand, the saying of Jesus in terms of demolishing and re-erecting buildings (for this feature of Jewish misunderstanding in the Gospel see O. Cullmann, "Der johanneische Gebrauch doppeldeutiger Ausdrücke als Schlüssel zum Verständnis des vierten Evangeliums," *TZ* 4 [1948] 360–72; D. A. Carson, "Understanding Misunderstandings in the Fourth Gospel," *TynB* 13 [1982] 59–91; H. Leroy, *Rätsel und Missverständnis: Ein Beitrag zur Formgeschichte des Johannesevangeliums*). Commonly in the Gospel such misunderstandings are corrected by further exposition from Jesus (as in 3:4–12). Here the Evangelist does it with a single comment: "He was speaking about the temple of his body." This is not a denial of the contextual interpretation of v 19, but a clarification of its nature as sign and a pointer to its mode of fulfillment: the "destruction" of the temple is completed in the destruction of the body of Jesus, and the building of the new temple takes place through the resurrection of Jesus. The Jews will accomplish the former; Jesus will accomplish the latter. This is the interpretation on the second plane, understood in the light of Easter. The risen Lord is the "place" where the glory of God is revealed, where his forgiveness and renewal are experienced, and where fellowship with God is grounded and forever maintained. Note that the temple of the new age is Christ, not the Church (cf. Bultmann: "It is not possible that σῶμα should refer to the community in a Pauline sense, since the object of λύειν and ἐγείρειν must be one and the same," 127–28 n.6). The same concept of the risen Christ as the new temple is exemplified in John 7:37–38, with its reference back to Ezek 47:1–12 (cf. Rev 21:22; 22:1–3; see further Bultmann, 127–29; Schnackenburg, 1:352–56; Léon-Dufour, 169–72; Lindars, 144; Gärtner, *Temple and Community*, 120–22).

22 The "scripture" which the disciples believed after the Resurrection is presumably Ps 69:9, mentioned in v 17, which enabled them to relate the temple cleansing to the death of Christ; the "word" of Jesus is that of v 19, which enabled them to grasp the significance of his resurrection in relation to the temple.

Explanation

1. The cleansing of the temple is a sign of the nature of Christ's mediatorial work as Revealer and Redeemer. For those who witnessed the event and heard the explanatory word (of v 19) it contained a message alike of rebuke and promise, with evident threat of judgment for those responsible for the desecration of the "place" of the Holy One of Israel. The perspective opened up by the ministry of Jesus shows that its full significance, and the fulfillment of the thing signified, were accomplished in the offering of the body of Christ and his rising from the dead. If the true nature of the profanation of God's name and place was thereby exposed, with threat of judgment for those who persisted in the same, the primary thrust of the sign is nevertheless fulfillment of promise. For Jesus came not to destroy Judaism, but to bring it to its destined goal in the eschatological order of worship in the new creation, initiated through and in his deed and presence as the crucified and resurrected Lord.

2. The new temple is precisely the crucified and risen Son of God. In this concept there is both close relation with and distinction from the contemporaries of the Evangelist with whom he had most in common. The Qumran community, a group of priests zealous for the Kingdom of God and its new order of worship, protested at the unworthy service of God in the temple and viewed themselves as the new temple, to which the presence and glory of God proper to the old temple had been transferred. In the letters of the NT, that presence and glory were seen as inhering in the Church, the Body of Christ and the temple of the Spirit of Christ. The difference between the Qumran writings and the NT letters is the relation to the Messiah, who has brought into full actuality by his redemptive work and the sending of the Holy Spirit that which the Qumran covenanters were seeing as dawning. The Fourth Evangelist concentrates attention on that point of difference: the glory of God and the presence of God are revealed in the only Son and his redemptive acts; it is in and through him that mankind experiences that presence, is transfigured by that glory, and offers a worship worthy of his name. All that Paul seeks to convey by his images of the Church as temple of the Spirit and the Body of Christ is assumed by the Evangelist, but he refrains from the use of such expressions. It is natural that in the context of the cleansing of the temple the idea of Christ as the new temple should bring to consciousness the elements for which the ancient temple stood and the prospect of their consummation in the new age in the unveiled glory of God and the universal enjoyment of his presence. The Evangelist, who also looked forward to the resurrection of the last day, will have recognized that there remain elements of that ultimate glory yet to come, but he emphasizes that they have become an abiding actuality in the risen Lord and by the Spirit whom he has sent (so 4:21–26).

3. The ultimate significance of the temple cleansing is therefore Christological, not ecclesiological. As throughout this Gospel forgiveness, unity with the Father, and life under the saving sovereignty of God and all that flows from it are the fruit of his redemptive action. It is experienced in union

with the Son, and its end is the glory of God—in him and in those united with him.

3. The Nicodemus Discourse   (2:23–3:36)

Bibliography

Beasley-Murray, G. R. *Baptism in the New Testament,* 67–72, 226–32. **Becker, J.** "Joh 3, 1–21 als Reflexion johanneischer Schuldiskussion." *Das Wort und die Wörter.* FS G. Friedrich. 85–95. **Blank, J.** *Krisis.* 56–108. **Boismard, M. E.** "Les traditions johanniques concernant le Baptiste." *RB* 70 (1963) 25–80. **Borgen, P.** "Some Jewish Exegetical Traditions in the Fourth Gospel." *L'Evangile de Jean.* Ed M. de Jonge. Louvain: Univ. Press. 243–58. **Dodd, C. H.** *Interpretation.* 279–87. ———. *Historical Tradition,* 357–59. **Guthrie, D.** "Importance of Signs in the Fourth Gospel." *VoxEv* (1967) 72–83. **Jonge, M. de.** "Nicodemus and Jesus: Some Observations on Misunderstanding and Understanding in the Fourth Gospel." *Jesus Stranger from Heaven,* 29–47; also in *BJRL* 53 (1971) 337–59. **Kraeling, C. H.** *John the Baptist.* 123–57. Lindars, B. "Two Parables in John." *NTS* 16 (1969–70) 324–29. **Odeberg, H.** *The Fourth Gospel.* 48–71. **Potterie I. de la.** "Naître de l'eau et naître de l'esprit." *ScEc* 14 (1962) 417–43. **Richter, G.** "Zum sogenannten Taufetext Joh 3, 5." *Studien zum Johannesevangelium.* 327–45. **Schnackenburg, R.** *Die Sakramente im Johannesevangelium.* 1946. **Stauffer, E.** "Agnostos Christos. Joh 2,24 und die Eschatologie des vierten Evangeliums." *The Background of the NT and Its Eschatology.* FS C. H. Dodd. 281–309. **Thüsing, W.** *Erhöhung und Verherrlichung Jesu im Johannesevangelium.* NTAbh 21, Münster: Aschendorff, 1960. 4–14, 31–37. **Topel, L. J.** "A Note on the Methodology of Structure Analysis in John 2:23–3:21." *CBQ* 33 (1971) 211–20.

Translation

[23] *Now while he was in Jerusalem for the feast of the Passover many came to believe in his name, for they saw the signs that he was performing.* [24] *But Jesus himself did not trust himself to them,* [25] *because he knew all men, and because he had no need that anyone should give evidence about man, for he himself knew what was in man.*
[3:1] *Now there was a Pharisee named Nicodemus,[a] a member of the Jewish ruling council.* [2] *He came to him at night and said to him, "Rabbi, we know that you have come from God as a teacher, for no one can perform the signs that you are doing unless God is with him."* [3] *Jesus said in reply to him, "Amen, amen I tell you, unless one is begotten from above[b] he cannot see the kingdom of God."* [4] *Nicodemus says to him, "How can one be born when he is old? He can't enter a second time into his mother's womb and be born, can he?"* [5] *Jesus replied, "Amen, amen I tell you, unless one is begotten of water and Spirit he cannot enter the kingdom of God.[c]* [6] *What is begotten of flesh is flesh, and what is begotten of Spirit is spirit.* [7] *Do not be astonished that I said to you, 'You people must be begotten from above.'* [8] *The wind[d] blows where it wants to, and you hear its sound, but you do not know where it is coming from and where it is going to; so it is with*

everyone who is begotten of the Spirit." [9] *Nicodemus said in reply to him, "How can these things happen?"* [10] *Jesus answered him, "You are the teacher of Israel, and you do not understand these things?* [11] *Amen, amen I tell you, we are talking about what we know, and we are testifying to what we have seen, and you people are not accepting our testimony.* [12] *If I told you about earthly things and you all are unbelieving, how will you believe if I tell you about heavenly things?"*

[13] *Now no one has gone up to heaven except the one who came down out of heaven, the Son of Man.*[e]

[14] *And as Moses lifted up the snake in the desert, so the Son of Man must be lifted up,* [15] *in order that everyone who believes may have in him*[f] *eternal life.*

[16] *For God loved the world so greatly that he gave the only Son, in order that everyone who believes in him may not be lost but have eternal life.*

[17] *For God did not send the Son into the world in order to condemn the world, but that the world might be saved through him.* [18] *He who believes in him is not condemned, but he who does not believe stands already condemned, because he has not believed in the name of God's only Son.* [19] *And this is the ground of condemnation, that the light has come into the world and men loved the darkness more than the light because their deeds were evil.* [20] *Everyone who practices wickedness hates the light and does not come to the light in case his actions should be exposed,*[g] [21] *but he who does the truth comes to the light in order that it may be revealed that his acts are performed through God.*

[22] *After this Jesus came into the Judean country with his disciples, and there he stayed with them and baptized.* [23] *But John also was baptizing in Aenon, near Salim, because plenty of water was there, and people were coming to him and getting baptized.* [24] *For John had not yet been thrown into prison.*

[25] *An argument arose between disciples of John and a certain Jew*[h] *about ritual cleansing.* [26] *They came to John and said to him, "Rabbi, that man who was with you the other side of Jordan, to whom you bore witness, look, he's baptizing, and everyone is going to him!"* [27] *John said in reply, "A man can have nothing unless it be given him from heaven.* [28] *You yourselves bear me witness that I have said to you, 'I am not the Christ,' but rather, 'I am the one sent ahead of him.'* [29] *It is the bridegroom who has the bride; but the bridegroom's friend, who stands by and listens for him, is overjoyed when he hears the bridegroom's voice. That is the joy I have, and I have it to the full.* [30] *He must grow greater, but I must grow less."*[i]

[31] *He who came from above is over everything. He who is born of the earth belongs to the earth, and talks on the earthly level. He who comes from heaven [is over everything.* [32] *He]*[j] *bears witness to what he has seen and heard, and his witness no one accepts.* [33] *Whoever has accepted his witness has set his seal to the fact that God is true.* [34] *For the one whom God sent speaks the words of God, for he*[k] *does not give the Spirit in a limited measure (to him).* [35] *The Father loves the Son, and has placed everything in his hand.* [36] *Whoever believes in the Son has eternal life; but whoever disobeys*[l] *the Son will not see life, but the wrath of God remains upon him.*

Notes

[a] Nicodemus, a Gr. name, was adopted by the Jews in the form of Naqdemon. A man of this name is mentioned in Josephus, *Ant.* 14.37, as an envoy of Aristobulus to the Roman

general Pompey. Later a certain Gorion, son of Nicodemus, negotiated with the Romans for the conclusion of the war of A.D. 66–70. The Nicodemus of our narrative could have been a member of the same family (for details see Schlatter, 84).

[b] ἄνωθεν can mean "from above" and "again, anew." Westcott (1:136) and Bultmann (135) insisted on the latter meaning here, Bernard (1:102) and Schnackenburg (1:367–68) affirmed that it must mean the former; others consider that both meanings are intended (e.g., Bauer, *Lexicon*, 77; Dodd, *Interpretation*, 303). In this context "from above" in the sense of "from God" appears to be primarily in mind (this is its meaning elsewhere in the Gospel, including 3:31), the other meaning is naturally subsumed under its primary emphasis.

Since ἄνωθεν relates to God's action it is best to translate γεννηθῇ as "be begotten," rather than "be born" (used of birth from a mother).

[c] For τὴν βασιλείαν τοῦ θεοῦ, some cursives and numerous Fathers read τὴν βασιλείαν τῶν οὐρανῶν. This may be due to the known frequency of the expression in Matt, "to enter the kingdom of heaven" (Matt 5:20; 7:21; 18:3; 19:23).

[d] The play on the two meanings attaching both to רוח (*rûah*) and to πνεῦμα of "wind" and "spirit" cannot be reproduced in English, but it makes possible the production of this very illuminating simile (A. M. Hunter views it as a parable, *According to John*, 79).

[e] Many authorities add at the end of the verse the phrase "who is in heaven"; some alter it to "who was in heaven," and yet others to "who is *from* heaven." The omission is supported by p[66] and f[75], א B L. The early attestation of the shorter reading inclined the UBS editors to follow it (Metzger, 203–4); but v 13 is probably a Johannine reflection on the preceding dialogue, and the very difficulty of the phrase, felt by later copyists, suggests that it may well be original to the Gospel (so, e.g., Schlatter, 94–95; Hoskyns, 218; Barrett, 213; Brown [hesitantly], 133).

[f] The expression ὁ πιστεύων ἐν αὐτῷ has caused confusion in the textual tradition. The text is read in p[75] B, whereas p[66] reads ἐπ᾽ αὐτῷ, p[63] (apparently) א and most MSS read εἰς αὐτόν, and A reads ἐπ᾽ αὐτόν. In this Gospel πιστεύειν is always followed by εἰς (34 times). Both the unusualness and the ambiguity speak for the originality of ἐν αὐτῷ; in that case it must be viewed as an adverbial phrase, linked with ἔχῃ: "may in him have life eternal" (so Metzger, 204, and most recent commentators).

[g] Some MSS, including p[66], add to the verse ὅτι πονηρά ἐστιν ("because [or "that"] they are evil"). There appears to be no obvious reason for the deletion of the phrase; it could have been added from v 19 (cf. also 7:7).

[h] In v 25 the attestation for μετὰ Ἰουδαίου and μετὰ Ἰουδαίων is about equal (e.g. p[75] and B for former, p[66] and א* for latter). It is perhaps more likely that the sing. was changed to pl. than that the reverse happened. Many scholars are attracted to the conjectural alternative μετὰ Ἰησοῦ or τοῦ Ἰησοῦ or τῶν Ἰησοῦ. In Dodd's view such emendation is arbitrary and uncalled for (*Historical Tradition*, 280 n.2).

[i] αὐξάνειν, "grow greater," ἐλαττοῦσθαι, "grow smaller," were used specifically of the rising and setting of stars. The Fathers saw in this language an image of the waxing and waning of the sunlight. Becker interprets, "Jesus, according to divine decision, must rise like a star; John however must decrease, or go down" (*Johannes*, 155).

[j] ἐπάνω πάντων ἐστίν is omitted by p[75] D OL OS. The phrase could have been carelessly repeated by a scribe after the first clause, or it could have been viewed as needless after that clause, and so omitted. If the phrase be omitted we should translate, "He who comes from heaven bears witness. . . ."

[k] In the second clause a number of MSS insert ὁ θεός as the subject of δίδωσιν. It would appear to be secondary, but serves to clarify (correctly) the question as to who gives the Spirit in this context, God or "the one whom God sent."

[l] ἀπειθεῖν = be disobedient; it is tempting to view it here as "not to believe" (so the Lat. tradition; Barrett, 227; Lindars renders, "refuse to believe," 171), but it is better to retain its proper meaning; the disobedience to the gospel here mentioned is parallel to the disobedience to God's commands in vv 19–21 (Brown, 158)

Form/Structure/Setting

1. Just as 2:1 harks back to the events of chap. 1 yet commences a new division of the Gospel, so 2:23–25 is linked with the setting of the previous

episode yet belongs essentially with chap. 3, since it provides a context for
the Nicodemus narrative and an important clue to its understanding. The
chapter opens with a dialogue between Nicodemus and Jesus concerning
participation in the kingdom of God. The address of Jesus in the second
person ends in v 12; it yields in vv 13–21 to a meditation on the ascent
(ἀναβαίνειν) of the Son of Man (v 13) which entails his "exaltation" (ὑψωθῆναι),
i.e., his crucifixion-resurrection (vv 14–15); this in turn leads to a confessional
summary of the Gospel in v 16, and kerygmatic reflections on the saving
intent of the mission of the Son of God, with its concomitant of judgment
on those who reject the redemptive revelation made known therein (vv 17–
21).

2. The structure of 3:22–36 conforms to that of 2:23–3:21. In 3:22–24
we have an introduction, providing the setting for the dialogue of vv 25–
30; the latter tells of a controversy concerning ritual washings and the final
testimony of John the Baptist to Jesus; vv 31–36 give a summary of the
witness of the One who comes from above.

3. The close parallelism of structure between the two halves of the chapter
has been stressed by H. Thyen. Following a suggestion of Yu Ibuki he adopted
the following analysis of the discourse:

A (1) 2:23–25, a *Report* which also provides the key to the dialogue that
follows; (2) 3:1–12, *Dialogue* of Jesus with Nicodemus; (3) 3:13–21, *Monologue*,
giving "the voice of Christ."

B (1) 3:22–24, *Report;* (2) 3:25–30, *Dialogue* of John the Baptist with Disciples; (3) 3:31–36, *Monologue,* giving "the voice of Christ" ("Aus der Literatur
zum Johannesevangelium," *TR* 44 [1979] 112). While this makes the structure
of the passage crystal clear, it is doubtful that the Evangelist wished his readers
to understand vv 13–21 and 31–36 as spoken by Jesus (with the possible
exception of v 14); the sayings in both paragraphs look back on the completed
work of Christ, and are most certainly self-conscious reproductions of kerygmatic declarations which circulated in the Johannine churches as the essence
of the Gospel.

4. Some exegetes, recognizing the affinity of vv 13–21 and 31–36, have
sought to link them more closely. Bernard considered that vv 31–36 were
meant to follow vv 16–21 (1:xxiii); Bultmann in his commentary treated them
in juxtaposition; Schnackenburg does the same, but reverses their order (v
31: this suits the responses of Nicodemus well!). Brown maintains that 3:13–
21, 31–36 and 12:44–50 are three variant discourses as from Jesus on identical
themes; and that 3:22–30 belong to the testimony of John given in 1:19–34
and originally *preceded* that passage (160); this again has the effect of placing
3:31–36 in immediate juxtaposition with vv 13–21. This procedure fails to
observe the relationship of the two paragraphs 3:1–12 and 25–30; it can
hardly be an accident that the baptisms of John and Jesus are central to the
thought of both sections, and that they are immediately followed by expositions
of the redemptive significance of Jesus in the Gospel. Dodd expressed similar
convictions in affirming that vv 31–36 are not an appropriate continuation
of vv 13–21, and that vv 22–30 have their place in the flow of thought of
the chapter relating to baptism; for him vv 31–36 are less a continuation of
the preceding discourse than a recapitulation of its leading ideas (*Interpretation*,
309).

Comment

INTRODUCTION TO THE DISCOURSE TO NICODEMUS (2:23–25)

The impression is given that the context is the Passover at which Jesus cleansed the temple. This caused Tatian, who compiled a gospel harmony in the second century, to set the Nicodemus passage in the last week of Jesus in Jerusalem, a precedent that has attracted some moderns (e.g. Bernard, 1:98). More probably we are dealing with a visit of Jesus to Jerusalem for a Passover festival, without closer definition of time.

The comment in v 24 indicates the inadequacy of the faith of those who believed in Jesus solely because of "signs": "Jesus did not trust them" (Haenchen). This does not mean that faith prompted by the miracles of Jesus is spurious, rather that "such faith is only the first step towards Jesus; it has not yet seen him in his true significance, and it is therefore not yet fully established" (Bultmann, 131). It is noteworthy that the unsatisfactory nature of faith that rests on signs, recorded here in an introduction to a baptismal discourse, is reiterated later in a context that has strong associations with the Lord's Supper (6:14–15, 25–27); in both cases the inadequacy of such faith is countered by pointing to the redemptive activity of the Son of Man (3:13–21; 6:32–40, 51–58).

Mek. Exod. 15:32 (59b) has a comment that sheds light on v 25: "Seven things are hidden from man—the day of death, the day of consolation, the depths of judgment, one's reward, the time of restoration of the kingdom of David, the time when the guilty kingdom (i.e., Rome) will be destroyed, and *what is within another.*" Scripture proof for this last "unknown" is given in *Gen. Rab.* 65 (41b) and *Midr. Qoh.* 11:5: "I the Lord search the heart" (Jer 17:10); on this Billerbeck comments, "Thereby he (Jesus) is set on the side of God" (*Kommentar*, 2:412).

THE DIALOGUE OF JESUS WITH NICODEMUS (3:1–12)

2 That Nicodemus came to Jesus "by night" is less likely to be due to fear than to desire for uninterrupted conversation. If "night" has a symbolical overtone (see especially 11:10 and 13:30), it hints of the darkness in which Nicodemus stood ("a dangerous position betwixt and between"! Hoskyns, 211); whereas de Jonge insists that we are to understand that Nicodemus never got out of it (29–42), other references to him suggest a happier outcome (7:50; 19:38–40).

3 Frequently v 3 is viewed as a Johannine development of Matt 18:3 (cf. Mark 10:15), or a logion similar to it but independent of it (Dodd, *Historical Tradition*, 359). Yet a saying similar to vv 3 and 5 was cited by Justin: ἂν μὴ ἀναγεννηθῆτε οὐ μὴ εἰσέλθητε εἰς τὴν βασιλείαν τῶν οὐρανῶν (*Apol.* 61); since Justin shows no other knowledge of our Gospel, the logion evidently circulated freely. It is likely that the Evangelist found the saying in an earlier source (Becker thinks that both vv 3 and 5 were current before the Evangelist, who commented on v 3 in v 7 and on v 5 in v 8, *Johannes*, 134). The concept of being begotten from above is not a simple translation of becoming *as* a child, but an adaptation of the Jewish hope of a new creation. The Jews became

familiar with the application of this concept to people, even in noneschatologi-
cal contexts (e.g. God is said to make men "new creatures" when he heals
them of their infirmities; Str-B, *Matthäus,* 420–23), but in the tradition stem-
ming back to Jesus the eschatological element was constant. In Matt 19:28
the familiar βασιλεία is replaced by παλιγγενεσία, "regeneration," Matthew's
equivalent of "new world" or "new age." The LXX renders Job 14:14, "All
the days of my service I would wait, till my release should come," ὑπομενῶ
ἕως ἂν πάλιν γένωμαι, literally, "I will endure till I 'become again,' " i.e. until
I live again through resurrection; πάλιν γίνεσθαι is a verbal form of the noun
παλιγγενεσία. While 1 Pet 1:23 repeats the verb "begotten anew" of Christians
(ἀναγεγεννημένοι), Paul prefers the category of new creation (2 Cor 5:17;
Gal 6:15). Titus 3:5 combines the two images; "He saved us through the
washing characterized by the παλιγγενεσία and ἀνακαίνωσις that the Holy Spirit
effects." The saying in v 3 declares that it is those whom God makes new
who will "see" (= experience) the new age. Naturally this saving sovereignty
of God will be thought of as coming in the future, as in the Beatitudes of
Matt 5:3–12. In the perspective of the Gospel, however, the saving sovereignty
has come into being through the redemptive activity of the Redeemer (cf.
vv 13–16), and those whom God renews experience it now.

5   In the face of the incredulous expostulation of Nicodemus in v 4 the
expression "to be begotten *from above"* is expounded as being begotten *of
water and Spirit.* What is the relation of "water" and "Spirit"? Origen suggested
that here "water" differs from "Spirit" only in ἐπίνοια, i.e., in "notion," not
in ὑπόστασις, "substance" (*Commentary,* 2:249 ff. in A. E. Brooke's edition). Calvin
in like fashion interpreted water and Spirit as meaning the same thing,
comparable to "Spirit and fire" in the preaching of John the Baptist (*John,*
1:64–65). Odeberg held that water stands for the celestial waters, viewed in
mystical Judaism as corresponding to the semen of the fleshly being; to be
begotten "of water and Spirit" therefore means rebirth of spiritual seed, as
in 1 John 3:9 (*The Fourth Gospel,* 63). A popular interpretation has it that
water represents human birth, whether semen of man or waters in the womb,
in contrast to birth from the Spirit; this, however overlooks that the *whole*
expression "of water and Spirit" defines the manner in which one is born
from above. Suggestions like these do not do justice to the text and have
not commended themselves to scholarly opinion. It would seem that the text
relates birth from above to baptism and the Holy Spirit. In the estimate of
some interpreters this is an intrusion, alien to the flow of thought in the
passage; they therefore regard ὕδατος καί as either an interpolation from an
early copyist or, more popularly, from the hand of a redactor who sought
to make the Gospel acceptable to the churches (so Bultmann, 139, and recently
Haenchen, 218, 227). More cautiously Bernard viewed the addition of ὕδατος
καί as due to the Evangelist himself (1:104–5), a suggestion that has been
widely taken up of late. De la Potterie holds that the earliest Johannine cate-
chism spoke only of regeneration by the Spirit, which could reflect what Jesus
actually said, but in the light of the baptismal commission of the risen Lord
and the Christian practice of baptism; the Evangelist added ὕδατος καί by
way of commentary, to indicate how the new life of the Spirit is gained
("Naître de l'eau et naître de l'esprit," 424–25). The suggestion is plausible,

but unprovable. If the text is to be read as it stands, there is much to be said for the interpretation enunciated by Bengel, and characteristic of British exposition: "Water denotes the baptism of John into (i.e., preparing for) Christ Jesus" (*Gnomon* 2:275). Such a view assumes that entry into the kingdom of God requires baptism of water and of the Spirit. The conjunction of water and Spirit in eschatological hope is deeply rooted in the Jewish consciousness, as is attested by Ezek 36:25–27 and various apocalyptic writings (e.g., *Jub.* 1:23; *Pss. Sol.* 18:6; *Test. Jud.* 24:3), but above all the literature and practices of the Qumran sectaries, who sought to unite cleansing and the hope of the Spirit with actual immersions and repentance in a community beginning to "see" the kingdom of God (cf. 1QS 3:6–9; 1QH 11:12–14).

The need for cleansing and expectation of the renewal of the Spirit, accordingly, was in the air in the period of Jesus and the early Church. The Evangelist's setting of the dialogue with Nicodemus alongside a second section concerned with the relation of John's baptism to that promoted by Jesus (vv 25–30) indicates how he wished the first to be understood: Pharisees like Nicodemus should not stand aloof from the call to repentance for the kingdom of God issued by John the Baptist and by Jesus, for *all* stand in need of God's forgiveness and the recreating work of the Holy Spirit, which is as imminent as the kingdom itself. In Nicodemus's situation these gifts are separated, but it is a division determined by the tension within the ministry of Jesus of the "now and not yet," or better the link of "is coming and now is" of the saving sovereignty, and by the fact that the sending of the Spirit awaits the "lifting up" of the Son of Man (7:39) In the time of the Church the gifts are conjoined, since the Lord by his death and resurrection has achieved a once-for-all cleansing and sent the Spirit of the kingdom: he who is baptized in faith in the Son of Man, exalted by his cross to heaven, becomes a new creation by the Spirit, "sees" the kingdom, and in Christ has life eternal (vv 14–15).

6–8 The radical nature of the birth from above is emphasized by the contrast of flesh and Spirit, v 6. "Flesh" speaks of the weakness of man as creature, "Spirit" of the power of the God of heaven at work in the world below (cf. Isa 31:1–3, and for the thought, John 1:13). The parabolic saying of v 8 exemplifies the reality yet also the incomprehensibility of the work of the Spirit in man: the wind is invisible and mysterious, yet known in experience. "So it is with everyone begotten of the Spirit" implies, "What those who have been born of the Spirit are, whence they come and whither they go, is incomprehensible to the world; as incomprehensible as Jesus himself is to the Jews" (Hoskyns, 215).

11–12 Nicodemus is manifestly addressed as representative of his people (λέγω σοι . . . εἶπον ὑμῖν) by the Revealer, who represents all who bear witness to the authentic word of God. The "we know" of Nicodemus (v 2) is tacitly corrected by the "we know" of the Redeemer (οἴδαμεν), who bears unique witness to heavenly realities (ὃ ἑωράκαμεν), and of the Church that perpetuates his testimony. Tragically the refusal of the witness by Nicodemus is also representative of its rejection by his generation, as by that of the Evangelist's day (οὐ λαμβάνετε . . . οὐ πιστεύετε).

The "earthly things" of which Nicodemus has heard, but which he does

not believe, must denote the teaching on the birth from above, recorded in
vv 3–8. It is "earthly" in that it relates to man's situation in the world and
his incapability to "see" the kingdom. The "heavenly things" which have
not been declared to Nicodemus will relate to the eschatological dimension
of the salvation which the Redeemer brings through his "descent" and "ascent"
to heaven via the cross; these form the subject of the reflections that follow in
vv 13–21 and 31–36 (see further Bultmann, 147–49; Blank, *Krisis*, 62–63).

THE REDEMPTION OF THE REVEALER (3:13–21)

13   The Evangelist's extension and exposition of the preceding dialogue
begins with an ambiguous saying. Most commonly it is considered to be directed
against all claims made by or on behalf of individuals who are supposed to
have ascended to heaven and received revelations to make known to the
world below, whether apocalyptic seers or (especially and above all) Moses
(see especially W. Meeks, *The Prophet-King*, 295–301; P. Borgen, "Some Jewish
Exegetical Traditions," 243–58). Barrett states, "The Son of Man descends
from heaven in order to convey ἐπουράνια to men." But Bultmann is surely
right in pointing out that the ascent itself is one of the "unbelievable ἐπουράνια,"
and that in v 13 "his exaltation is the fulfilment of the work of salvation by
which he draws his own to himself" (151). The descent is mentioned in v
13 as the presupposition of the ascent (via the cross) for the salvation of
humankind. This is the task of the Son of Man, who alone by virtue of his
descent from heaven is authorized and empowered by the Father to achieve
the salvation of the divine sovereignty (so essentially Schnackenburg, 1:302;
Blank, 77–80; Becker, 1:140–41).

14–15   The brief kerygmatic formula of vv 14–15 makes evident the presuppositions of v 13. It is closely related to the synoptic predictions of the
Passion (Mark 8:31, etc.), but illuminates the meaning of the Passion by the
incident of Moses lifting up a bronze snake for the healing of Israelites bitten
by snakes (Num 21:4–9). To the lifting up of the snake on a pole that all
may live corresponds the lifting up of the Son of Man on a cross that all
may have eternal life. The term ὑψωθῆναι is associated with δοξασθῆναι, "be
glorified," (cf. 12:23; 13:31 f.). The opening sentence of the last Servant
Song in Isa 52:13 is clearly in mind: Ἰδοὺ συνήσει ὁ παῖς μου καὶ ὑψωθήσεται
καὶ δοξασθήσεται σφόδρα (LXX), "My servant will be wise and exalted and greatly
glorified." This anticipates the Servant's vindication *consequent* on his sufferings
(so Phil 2:9), but the Evangelist consistently applies ὑψοῦν to the death of
the Son of Man (cf. 8:28; 12:31). Curiously several Semitic terms encourage
this procedure. The Aramaic אזדקף (*'ezdᵉqeph*) means "lift up," literally, and
secondarily in the sense of "lift up one bowed down," and specifically "lift
up on a cross, crucify" (see Bertram, *TDNT* 8:610); אשתלק (*ištᵉlaq*) = "be
lifted up," and "depart, die"; אָרִים (*'ārîm*) = "lift up," and "remove." In
Gen 40 Joseph tells two prisoners, "within three days Pharaoh will lift up
your head"; one is raised to his former office, the other is decapitated! (Dodd,
Interpretation, 377). More significant than these linguistic phenomena is the
simple fact that the Evangelist views the death and resurrection of Christ as

indissolubly one. The redemptive event is the crucifixion-resurrection of the Son. Accordingly it is *in* the risen, crucified Lord that the believer has eternal life (v 15).

16 A confessional summary of the Gospel follows: it originates in the love of God for a disobedient world, it centers in the giving of the only Son to and for the world, and its end is that people may not be lost but live under the saving sovereignty of God. The giving of the only Son clearly embraces both incarnation and vicarious death; it is the entire mission of the Son that is in view. If, as many think, the language echoes Abraham's *giving* his *only son*, whom he *loved* (Gen 22), the event in view is vaster. Here alone in the Fourth Gospel the love of God for the rebellious *world* is stated to be the reason for the incarnation and death of Christ; more characteristically love for the disciples and the evil of the world are stressed. That is no reason for diminishing the importance of this statement; it is the fundamental summary of the message of this Gospel and should therefore be seen as the background of the canvas on which the rest of the Gospel is painted. Becker points out that this "comprehensive horizon" appears elsewhere (e.g., 1:7, 9; 12:32), and suggests that the Evangelist consciously resisted the tendency in the Church to isolationism (145).

17–21 If the purpose of the mission of the Son is that people may live and not be lost, the possibility of both destinies is clearly implied, and God in his love stands behind both. This dual possibility is expounded in vv 17–21. The positive purpose of the mission is unambiguously stated in v 17: it is that the world be saved. The incarnation, death, and resurrection of the Son of God were directed to the salvation of all humanity, not to a segment of it. But since this salvation is found in the Son (v 15), and so through faith's acknowledgment of the Revealer and his redemption (v 16), the coming of the Son for *salvation* can be turned into the occasion of *judgment*, and that possibility is present for all who hear the gospel (v 18). The process is described in vv 19–21. Here the key term is κρίσις, "judgment," and it is used in its twofold sense of separation and condemnation. The Redeemer has come into the world as Light in a dark place, clearly to bring the "light" of salvation. But before that Light men separate themselves; they either approach it or move away from it. The former move into the light of salvation, the latter depart from it into deeper darkness. This is a different image from that of judgment as separation of sheep from goats (Matt 25:31–33), but it sets forth the same fundamental reality, humankind dividing before the representative of God. The striking difference in the Evangelist's picture is its relation to the present situation of humankind: the separation is taking place now, and its results are felt in the present. But the tragedy of the separation is also underscored: God's great saving act has become a means of judgment through the perverted reaction of people. What causes the wrong decisions? "Men loved the darkness more than the light because their deeds were evil." They who love darkness hate the light. Their deeds express their perversity; hence, they keep far from the Light to avoid exposure. Conversely the believer, here defined as "he who does the truth" i.e. acts in accordance with the truth, comes to the Light, for his acts have been achieved through the grace of God in Christ, and he would acknowledge it before God and the world. In short, "In the decision of faith or unbelief it becomes apparent what man really is and what he always was" (Bultmann, 159).

THE BAPTIZING MINISTRY OF JESUS (3:22–24)

22 Jesus comes into the Judean γῆ; this most naturally means the area of Judea into which Jesus came from outside (from Galilee?). But 2:23–3:12 are set in Jerusalem: either Jesus leaves the city for the Judean *countryside,* or the tradition relates to another occasion.

Here alone (with the sentence following the discourse, 4:1–2) do we read of Jesus baptizing—or authorizing baptism—during his ministry. Moreover he is said to have done this at the same time as John was preaching and baptizing, and with even greater success (4:1). While at one time a number of scholars considered this a reflection back into the ministry of later rivalry between the Church and the followers of John, most now see this as a remnant of primitive tradition unknown to the synoptists. We know that Jesus approved of John's baptism (Mark 11:30), and submitted to it himself. If, as many believe, Jesus was baptized expressing solidarity with his people as his first step of bringing the kingdom, it is not surprising that he called on them to be baptized with a view to their entering it. Remembering 3:3 and 5, and such statements as 7:34, we shall not attempt to identify such a baptism with later Christian baptism. Yet neither was it identical with the baptism of John. Oriented to the coming of the kingdom, like John's baptism it gained special significance as obedient response to him who was in the process of bringing the saving sovereignty (see Dodd, *Historical Tradition,* 285–86; Schlatter, 106; Schnackenburg, 1:411–12).

23 Aenon, "place of springs," is of uncertain site (suggestions are northeast of the Dead Sea; near Sychem in Samaria; in the Jordan valley of Samaria, south of Scythopolis); the importance of the note is to show that John moved from the south to the north, leaving Jesus to baptize in the area not distant from Jerusalem.

THE FINAL WITNESS OF JOHN TO JESUS (3:25–30)

25–26 If there is any real connection between v 25 and v 26, other than editorial, the dispute περὶ καθαρισμοῦ will not concern the relative merits of Jewish cleansing rites and John's baptism, but the merits of John's baptism and that of Jesus. Since Jesus was baptizing at a distance from John, the report of his success will be secondhand—perhaps from the Jew. The discussion and the report would be more comprehensible if he had been baptized by (the disciples of) Jesus.

27–29 The principle enunciated is capable of general application, and in 19:11 it is applied to Pilate. Here the powerful ministry of Jesus is in view, which John acknowledges to be due to the gift of God ("from heaven"). This should be no matter of surprise to John's disciples in view of his earlier confession as to his own God-given task (cf. 1:19–23). His role is likened to that of the bridegroom's "friend" at a wedding. Among the friends of the bride and groom (in Judea, at least), two had a position of trust regarding them and had to watch over the sexual relations of the young couple; they led the bride to the groom and kept watch outside the bridal chamber. The "voice of the bridegroom" is thought to be "the triumph shout by which the bridegroom announced to his friends outside that he had been united to a virginal bride" (Schnackenburg, 1:416: see further Str-B 1:45–46, 500–501). The picture indicates John's selfless joy in learning of the people of God flocking to Jesus (v 26). While no allegory s in mind, the Evangelist and his readers will be conscious of the use of the picture in the OT for Israel as the bride of God (Isa 62:4–5; Hos 2:14–20) and in the NT of the Church as the bride of Christ (Eph 5:25–27; Rev 19:7; 21:2, 9–10; 22:17).

30 The last and most magnificent words of testimony from John. Coming from the last of the prophets they indicate, in Bultmann's words (174), "The old epoch of the world has run its course, the eschatological age is beginning." For the Evangelist's contemporaries, the whole passage is significant as showing the character and role of this man: he was no rival to the Christ but his "friend"; the followers of the "friend" should then be won to allegiance to the real Christ.

THE WITNESS OF THE ONE FROM HEAVEN (3 31–36)

31 If, as we believe, this paragraph consists of reflections of the Evangelist and his community, comparable to vv 13–21, it is doubtful that its opening sentence has the purpose of contrasting the exaltation and exalted position of the Son of God and the revelation through him with the merely earthly ministry and teaching of John. Rather the discourse draws to its climax with declarations of the supremacy of the revelation through the Christ over all other prophets and prophecies. Having come from above he is over "all," i.e., "the whole realm of man" (Brown, 157), whereas those who *originate* from the earth are purely of earthly *kind* and can therefore speak only of the earthly *plane*.

32 The testimony of the One from above accordingly, derives from "what he has seen and heard." The language appears to include reminiscence of preincarnate existence; yet such passages as 5 19–20, 30 speak of a continuous fellowship between Father and Son as the source of all his speech and action. The mysteries of incarnation and Trinity are alike involved here.

There is a tension entailed in the "everyone" of v 26 and "no one" of v 32, which is eased in v 33. The first statement relates to the success and the superiority of Jesus in his ministry over that of John, the second to the tragedy of Israel's rejection of Jesus, which however has at no time been complete (v 33, cf. 1:5, 10–13). The historic situation of Jesus' ministry is repeated in the time of the church, not least in the experience of the Johannine community.

33–35 A seal was used to secure (Matt 27:66), conceal (Rev 22:10), and authenticate (John 6:27); here the last meaning is in view (Hoskyns, 230). Observe that the believer affirms the truthfulness of *God,* since the Son bears witness to what God has given him to say. This the Son can do since the Father has given him the Spirit "without measure," and the Spirit to the Jew is supremely the Spirit of prophecy. The saying of R. Aha (*Lev. Rab.* 15.2) is often cited: "The Holy Spirit who rests on the prophets, rests on them only by measure," for one writes only one book another writes more.

To the immeasurable gift of the Spirit to the Son of God corresponds the perfection of the revelation through him. If such a thought is in mind, the perfection of the revelation through the Son is clearly the result of the immeasurable gift of the Spirit to him. While it is possible grammatically to view the subject of δίδωσιν to be "the one whom God sent," and so to see the Son as the giver of the Spirit, the context demands that the Son is here the receiver of the Spirit. This is confirmed in the next sentence: the Father has given "all things" into his hand, i.e., bestowed on him authority alike in revelatory speech and action. Compare Matt 11:27; but this saying will extend beyond words of God to redemptive deeds of God for the salvation of humankind in his kingdom.

36 Fittingly, the ultimate significance of the Son for salvation and judgment concludes the discourse. Since life eternal is "in" the Son (v 15), the believer possesses that life when he is united to him by faith. By the same token, to reject the Son is to cut oneself off from the life, and such disobedience puts one under the wrath of God. The future "will not see life" hints of denial of the future life in the perfected kingdom of God, as the "remaining" of the wrath of God anticipates its non-removal in the future. Present eschatological realities anticipate a future eschatological consummation.

Explanation

1. Some of the fundamental themes of the Fourth Gospel appear in the Nicodemus discourse. It begins with a reference to unsatisfactory faith and concludes with an exposition of faith's true goal and the importance of decision for personal destiny. In this setting it is fitting that baptism should be treated, for baptism relates to the gospel and to faith's response to it. Nicodemus lived in a time of baptismal revival, and the Johannine churches were also acquainted with various baptisms. The Evangelist sets forth a baptism that links a person with the kingdom of God by relating it to the recreating Spirit, the Lord of the cross and the resurrection, and the faith which acknowledges Jesus as the Revealer-Redeemer from God. No less than Paul, the Fourth Evangelist firmly sets baptism in the context of the gospel.

2. The concept of the "lifting up" of Christ occurs for the first time in our passage. Exaltation and glorification are intertwined in this Gospel in a manner unique in the NT. Whereas other writers view the death of Jesus as deepest humiliation, reversed by the divine action in raising him on high (e.g., Phil 2:6–11), the Evangelist sees the death on the cross as itself participating in the glorification of Jesus. This is not due to viewing the crucifixion as the "noblest hour" of Jesus but rather to seeing in a new way its powerful meaning. As the climax of his obedient self-offering, it led to the Father's presence. But wherever this thought is voiced (e.g., in 13:31 f.; 17:1, 5), it implies the Father's glorifying the Son by raising him to the height of his own glory. It is the end result of the Evangelist's seeing the cross and resurrection of Jesus as *one redemptive event.* The Church as a whole has yet to follow him in grasping this concept and working out its implications for thought and life.

3. The Nicodemus discourse also gives us a clear exposition of the presence

of the kingdom of God through the redemptive action in the Son (vv 14–16), and its counterpart in present judgment, determined by response to the proclamation of Christ in the gospel (vv 17–21). This phenomenon characterizes the time of the Church as an eschatological hour, wherein the realities of the end are perpetually present. We do well to receive this teaching as it is presented, and not assume that it eliminates all expectation of future salvation and judgment. Life under the divine sovereignty revealed in Christ looks to future resurrection, just as repudiation of that sovereignty leads to divine rejection. Since the sovereignty is manifested alike in salvation and judgment, those who proclaim it have an urgent responsibility to declare it adequately, and those who hear it to give an appropriate response, both in the light of the eschatological present and future.

4. The Evangelist's concern to relate events of the historic ministry of Jesus and the contemporary needs of the churches is evident here. Nicodemus is a spokesman for many Jews in Jerusalem who believed on the name of Jesus by reason of the signs that he performed; their faith was inchoate rather than the full trust of 3:14–16, and they needed to advance to faith-commitment based on a genuine grasp of the revelation in Christ. Similarly, in the situation of the contemporary church Nicodemus becomes the representative of Jews (and others) who found the Christian proclamation hard to receive because of the necessity for submission to baptism as *sinners* needing regeneration if they would attain the kingdom. The Evangelist therefore concentrates on the question, "How can these things be?" (v 9). They happen because the Son of Man has descended from heaven in order to achieve a redemption which makes that recreation possible (v 13); through his "lifting up" on his cross and by resurrection to heaven, eternal life becomes a present reality to every believer in him (vv 14–16).

The dialogue of John the Baptist with his disciples has a different issue in view: in the light of the continued existence of communities claiming to follow John the Baptist, it was essential that the Johannine churches understood the significance of John's ministry and baptism; both were ordained by God for Christ's sake and both were ordained to end for his sake. Baptism in the name of Jesus had a profounder significance than that in the name of John; inasmuch as the Bridegroom is superior to the Bridegroom's friend, the Incarnate Son of God is greater than the witness who precedes him.

5. The peculiar authority of the revelation through the Son is here clarified. Strictly speaking there is no revelation *by* the Son, as though it originated in him; rather in Christ we see the revelation of God *through* him. The uniqueness of this revelation of the Father (who has made himself known throughout the ages) lies in the origin of the Son "from above" and his unprecedented "possession" of the Holy Spirit of revelation, which we must interpret in terms of his unique relation to the Holy Spirit. Setting 3:13–16 alongside 3:31–35, it is evident that the revelation includes the redemptive action of the Father in and through the Son, which reaches its climax in the Crucifixion-Resurrection. The revelation of God in Christ is in word and deed, and is conditioned by the mysteries of the incarnation and Trinity.

6. The two Christological passages 3:13–21 and 31–36 set forth an element in the revelation of God that tends to be passed over: they both expound

the eschatological polarity inherent in the Christ event. The redemptive revelation took place that men may have life under the saving sovereignty of God; the inexorable complement of that is judgment, entailing exclusion from the saving sovereignty for such as reject the revelation and spurn the Redeemer. "Universalism and particularism cannot here be soberly separated from one another," wrote Haenchen. "It must not be forgotten: only he avoids this dilemma who allows the divine will to be wholly vague" (233). This element of the revelation according to the Fourth Gospel challenges our contemporary tendencies to a comfortable "vagueness" in interpreting and proclaiming Christ and the gospel.

4. Jesus and the Samaritans   (4:1–42)

Bibliography

Argyle, A. W. "A Note on John 4:35." *ExpTim* 82 (1971) 247–48. **Bowman, J.** "Early Samaritan Eschatology." *JJS* 16 (1955) 63–72. **Bligh, J.** "Jesus in Samaria." *HeyJ* 3 (1964) 329–46. **Braun, F. M.** "Avoir soif et boire (Jn 4, 10–14; 7, 37–39)." *Mélanges Béda Rigaux.* Leuven; Duculot, 1970. 247–58. **Cullmann, O.** "Samaria and the Origin of the Christian Mission." *The Early Church.* 183–92. ———. *The Christology of the New Testament.* 241–45. **Daube, D.** "Jesus and the Samaritan Woman: The Meaning of συνχράομαι." *JBL* 69 (1950) 137–47. **MacDonald, J.** *The Theology of the Samaritans.* 362–71. **Marshall, I. H.** "The Problem of NT Exegesis (John 4:1–45)." *JEvThS* 17 (1974) 67–73. **Porsch, F.** *Pneuma und Wort.* 137–60. **Robinson, J. A. T.** "The 'Others' of John 4:38: A Test of Exegetical Method." *SE* 1 (1959) 510–15; also in *Ten NT Studies.* 61–66. **Walker, R.** "Jüngerwort und Herrenwort: Zur Auslegung von Joh 4:39–42." *ZNW* 57 (1966) 49–54. **Watson, W. G. E.** "Antecedents of a NT Proverb." *VT* 20 (1970) 368–70. **Wedel, A. F.** "John 4:5–26." *Int* 31 (1977) 406–12.

Translation

[1] *When therefore Jesus*[a] *knew that the Pharisees heard that he was making and baptizing more disciples than John—*[2] *although Jesus himself used not to baptize but his disciples did*[b]*—*[3] *he left Judea and went off again into Galilee.* [4] *This meant that he had to go through Samaria.* [5] *He comes therefore to a town in Samaria called Sychar,*[c] *near the plot of ground that Jacob gave to his son Joseph. And Jacob's well was there.*[d] [6] *Jesus, therefore, tired by reason of the journey, sat down by the well. It was about twelve noon.*[e] [7] *A Samaritan woman comes to draw water. Jesus said to her, "Give me a drink";* [8] *for his disciples had gone off to the town to buy food.* [9] *The Samaritan woman therefore says to him, "How is it that you, a Jew, are asking for a drink from me, when I'm a Samaritan woman?" (for Jews do not have anything to do with Samaritans).*[f] [10] *Jesus replied to her, "If you knew the gift of God, and who it is who is saying to you, 'Give me a drink,' you would have been the one to ask, and he would have given you living water."* [11] *The woman says to him, "Sir, you haven't a bucket, and the well is deep; where are*

you going to get the living water from? [12] You aren't greater than our father Jacob, are you, who gave us the well and drank from it, as well as his sons and his flocks?" [13] Jesus replied, "Everyone who drinks this water will become thirsty again, [14] but whoever drinks the water that I shall give him will never become thirsty anymore, but the water that I shall give him will become a fountain of water in him, perpetually flowing for eternal life." [15] The woman says to him, "Sir, give me this water, that I may not become thirsty nor keep coming here to draw water." [16] He says to her, "Go and call your husband, and come back here." [17] The woman replied to him, "I haven't any husband." Jesus says to her, "You are right in saying, 'I haven't a husband.' [18] For you have had five husbands, and the man you have now is not your husband. In saying this you have told the truth."

[19] The woman says to him, "Sir, I can see that you are a prophet. [20] Our fathers worshipped on this mountain; and you Jews say that the place where people should worship is in Jerusalem." [21] Jesus says to her, "Believe me, woman, the hour is coming when you people will worship the Father neither in this mountain nor in Jerusalem. [22] You worship what you do not understand; we worship what we know, because salvation comes from the Jews. [23] But the hour is coming, and it is here already, when the genuine worshippers will worship the Father in the Spirit and in the truth; for the Father indeed is seeking just such people to worship him. [24] God is Spirit, and those who worship him must worship in the Spirit and in the truth." [25] The woman says to him, "I know that the Messiah (i.e., the Anointed) is coming; when he comes he will make everything known to us." [26] Jesus says to her, "I am (he), I who am speaking to you."

[27] At that moment his disciples came, and they were amazed that he was talking with a woman; no one, however, asked, "What do you want?"g or, "What are you talking to her about?" [28] The woman then left her water-jar and went off to the town, and she said to the men, [29] "Come and see a man who told me everything I've ever done. Could this man possibly be the Christ?"h [30] They went out from the town and made their way toward him.

[31] In the meantime his disciples were asking him, "Rabbi, have something to eat." [32] But he said to them, "I have food to eat that you do not know about." [33] The disciples therefore were saying to one another, "Surely no one has brought him anything to eat?" [34] Jesus says to them, "My food is to do the will of him who sent me and to accomplish the work he gave me to do. [35] You say, don't you, 'Four months more and harvest comes'? Look, I tell you, lift up your eyes and gaze on the fields; they are white, ready for harvest. [36] Alreadyi the reaper is receiving his wages and is gathering a crop for life eternal, so that the sower and the reaper may rejoice together. [37] For in this regard the saying is true, 'One man is the sower and another the reaper.' [38] I sent you to reap a crop for which you have not toiled; others have worked away, and you have entered into the results of their work."

[39] Many of the Samaritans of that town believed in him because of what the woman said when she testified, "He told me everything I had ever done." [40] When therefore the Samaritans came to him they requested him to stay with them, and he stayed there two days. [41] And many more believed because of what they heard from him, [42] and they said to the woman, "No longer is it because of what you said that

we believe, for we have heard him for ourselves, and we know that this man is in truth the Savior of the world."

Notes

^a Some authorities (including P⁶⁶ P⁷⁵ B) read ὁ κύριος instead of ὁ Ἰησοῦς (א and Western tradition). The former is less likely, since scribes would not correct κύριος to Ἰησοῦς; moreover, apart from the doubtful 6:23, κύριος for Jesus occurs only at 11:2 prior to the resurrection narrative. Possibly ἔγνω originally was without a subject and ὁ Ἰησοῦς and ὁ κύριος were supplied to clarify the statement.

^b The parenthesis is commonly believed to be an insertion by a later editor, possibly to avoid Jesus being viewed as merely another baptizer like John, or even his imitator (in Haenchen's view, because baptism prior to the sending of the Spirit was meaningless to the Evangelist). Such scruples are needless. The tradition of Jesus baptizing need not be resisted (see on 3:22). That Jesus remitted the task of baptizing to his disciples is comprehensible. Paul did the same (1 Cor 1:14–17). But the structure of the sentence in vv 1–3 is admittedly awkward. It is really an itinerary fragment, and in v 3 it has a significant parallel in Matt 4:12. The Evangelist may have reproduced an early datum of the ministry of Jesus and preferred to modify the text instead of rewriting it (so Dodd, *Historical Tradition*, 237).

^c Sychar is usually identified with Askar, a mile distant from Jacob's well. The OS reflects the reading Συχέμ = Shechem, which Jerome believed correct; Jacob's well is immediately outside it. Albright urged that this must be right and that Συχάρ was due to the influence of the immediately preceding Σαμαρεία (twice! see "Recent Discoveries in Palestine," in *The Background of the NT*, FS C. H. Dodd, 160). If the common reading be accepted, the woman must have walked the extra distance because of the purity of the water of Jacob's well (Lindars, 178–79, following G. A. Smith).

^d Jacob's well is perhaps the most identifiable site in modern Israel connected with the ministry of Jesus. It stands at the foot of Mt. Gerizim and is very deep. To this day the traveller (or tourist!) may drink from it.

^e Literally, "about the sixth hour," reckoning the day beginning at 6:00 A.M. The mention of time explains the tiredness and thirst of Jesus.

^f It was urged by D. Daube that συνχρῶνται must mean "do not use (vessels for food and drink) together" ("Jesus and the Samaritan Woman," 137–47), an interpretation adopted in the NEB. This is questionable, since the verb would then require an object, which is not given. The meaning "to have dealings with" is well attested and may be adopted here (so Bauer's *Lexicon*, 775; Schnackenburg, 1:425 n.18; Lindars, 181; Haenchen, 240).

^g Bernard, 152, with Tatian and other ancients, thought that the first question was addressed to the woman, and that τί λαλεῖς addressed to Jesus means "*Why* do you talk with her?" Most moderns consider the two questions to be addressed to Jesus and τί as having the same meaning in both cases.

^h μήτι need not imply a negative answer but "puts a suggestion in the most tentative and hestitating way" (Moulton, *Prolegomena*, 193). The suggestion may be so phrased because it is so astounding, but its language is in keeping with the woman's understanding of the "Taheb" (cf. v 25).

ⁱ ἤδη could well conclude the preceding sentence (v 35), and is so construed in most ET. It accords more with the Evangelist's style, however, to view it as commencing the next sentence (v 36), and is so understood in א D OS, some OL MSS, Boh, and the UBS edition of the Gr. NT.

Form/Structure/Setting

1. While 4:1–42 apparently forms an independent unit, it is closely linked with the events of chap. 2 (and chap. 3; see Introduction to chap. 2). As the sign at Cana entails a contrast between the water of Jewish purification and the wine of the kingdom brought by Jesus, so the water of Jacob's well is contrasted with the living water given by Jesus. The Evangelist will have

been familiar with the concept of water as a symbol for the Torah (the saying in Yalkut Shimoni 2, 480 is strikingly apposite: "The words of Torah are received (into the heart) till the Torah becomes a flowing spring," cited Odeberg, 160). As the wine of Cana symbolizes the gift of the kingdom of God, so the water from Jesus symbolizes the life and salvation of the kingdom (vv 14–15). Similarly, as the cleansing of the temple entails a contrast between the old temple and the new temple of Christ's Body, carrying with it a contrast between the old order of worship and that of the new age initiated through the death and resurrection of Christ, so the worship of Jerusalem and Gerizim is declared to be superseded by the worship of the new age introduced by Christ and the Spirit he sends. The form is thus controlled by the preceding signs, but is set in a new dimension of mission to non-Israel.

2. The passage has a clear structure, dominated by two dialogues of Jesus. After the introduction in vv 1–6 we have in 7–26 the dialogue of Jesus with the Samaritan Woman. This contains two distinct themes; in 6–18 the living water from Christ, in 19–26 the worship that the Father seeks. The dialogue of Jesus with the disciples in 31–38 is set between two paragraphs, 27–30 describing the witness of the Samaritan woman to the people of Sychar, and 39–42 recounting their conversion. The dramatic nature of the second episode is frequently noted. Dodd likened it to a drama with action taking place on two stages, one front and the other back. On the front stage Jesus converses with his disciples (31–38), while on the back stage the woman speaks to the townsfolk of Sychar, and persuades them to come and see Jesus (28–30, 39). The two groups then come together and move to the town; the scene concludes with a declaration of the men of Sychar, like the final chorus of a Greek play, summing up the movement of the whole (*Interpretation*, 315).

3. The setting is provided in the introductory paragraph of vv 1–6. The Pharisees (of Jerusalem?) learn of the extraordinary success of Jesus in his preaching and baptizing ministry (1–2). This causes Jesus to withdraw from Judea to Galilee, presumably to avoid a conflict which could lead to a premature end to his ministry (Jesus is "under the 'law of the hour' which the Father has fixed for him," Schnackenburg, 1:422). Jesus therefore "had to go through Samaria." There is an interesting coincidence of language between v 4 and a statement of Josephus: "It was absolutely necessary for those who would go quickly to pass through that country (Samaria), for by that road you may, in three days, go from Galilee to Jerusalem" (*Vita*, 269). In this Gospel, however, as in the synoptics, necessity laid on Jesus generally hints of the divine will for him: he goes through Samaria not only for safety, but to accomplish the work assigned to him by the Father (vv 32, 34). The mission to the Samaritans was unplanned by Jesus but willed by God.

The arrival at Jacob's well (5–6) sets the stage for the meeting of Jesus with the woman of Sychar and the developments that ensue from it. (For varied analyses and reconstructions of traditions lying behind the composition of the section see Bultmann, 175; Lindars, 174–76; Haenchen, 252–56; Becker, 1:165–68; for discussions on the historicity of the narrative see Schnackenburg, 1:458–60; Brown 1:175–76; Cullmann, *Johannine Circle*, 48, 90; Haenchen, 248–52.)

Comment

THE DIALOGUE OF JESUS WITH THE WOMAN OF SYCHAR (4:7–26)

Living Water (4:7–18)

9 The antipathy between Jews and Samaritans was deeply rooted, going back to the origins of the Samaritans as a mixed race, settled in the northern kingdom by the king of Assyria (see the account in 2 Kings 17:24–41). The Samaritans nevertheless viewed themselves as true Israel, and heirs of the promises of God to Israel, and their version of the Pentateuch as the original one, direct from Moses! The explanatory parenthesis in v 9 has survived as a proverb, and is used by people of various creeds when, for example, they fall out over business transactions or castigate the dishonest actions of others (Bultmann, 178 n.6).

10 The "gift of God" denotes the salvation of God in an inclusive sense. The "living water" from Jesus is here virtually equated with it. "Living water" is a common expression for flowing or spring water, distinct from still water, as of a cistern or well, and so for fresh water as compared with brackish. The woman's understanding in the setting by the well is perfectly comprehensible. The absolute necessity of water for life caused it to become a wide-ranging symbol in religious thought. In the OT, it is applied to God, "the fountain of living waters" (Jer 2:13; 17:13); in Judaism to the Law ("As water is life for the world, so are the words of the Torah life for the world," SDt 11, 22, 48 [84a]), to wisdom (e.g. Sir 24:21, 24–27), to the Holy Spirit ("As water is given to dry land and is led over arid land, so will I give my Holy Spirit to your sons and my blessings to your children's children," *Tg. Isa.* 44:3), and even (by Philo) to the Logos, which is said to flow like a stream from Wisdom (*De somn.* 2.242; for further illustrations see Str-B 2:433–36). In view of the contemporary Jewish emphasis on the Torah as life for the world, it is tempting to view the "living water" in our passage as relating primarily to the revelation brought by the Revealer, or the gift bestowed by the revelation (see Bultmann, 181–87). But what, then, is the gift? We cannot forget the related symbol of bread, to be expounded in chap. 6: Jesus *is* the living bread that came down from heaven, and yet he also *gives* the bread (6:51); in 6:35 the two symbols of bread and water are brought together. Apparently we are intended similarly to interpret Jesus as both the living water and he who *gives* water of life to believers. But again we note that in 7:37–38 Jesus is the source of living waters, and he invites the thirsty to come to him and drink: to this the Evangelist adds the comment, "This he said of the Spirit, which those who believe on him should receive" (7:39). It is evident that "living water" has a variety of nuances that must be taken into account; chiefly it appears to denote *the life mediated by the Spirit sent from the (crucified and exalted) Revealer-Redeemer.*

11–12 The woman's response is controlled by her misunderstanding of the statement in v 10, and this leads Jesus to elaborate the image he has used.

13–14 The restatement inevitably calls to mind Sir 24:21, where Wisdom cries, "Whoever feeds on me will be hungry for more, and whoever drinks from me will thirst for more." On this Bultmann observed, "The meaning of these apparently contradictory sayings is the same! Once a man has tasted this drink, he will never seek any other means of quenching his thirst; his need is past." He adds that the Evangelist does not suggest that the believer must not again and again "drink" from the revelation, so surely as the branch must "abide" in the vine (15:4 ff.; *Comm.* 186–87). The believer, then, has an inexhaustible well within him; that it flows εἰς ζωὴν αἰώνιον means not that he may have eternal life, but simply "for ever" (so Schnackenburg, 1:431. Contrary to Haenchen, 241, who appeals to 7:37–38, the believer is not said to be a source of water for others; the use of the figure in 7:37–38 is quite different, for there *the Christ* is the source of a river of living waters for the world. Here the believer's possession of the life of the kingdom of God is alone in view).

15–18 The woman's misunderstanding becomes crass. She asks for the *magic water* that Jesus has, so that she may not have to come daily for ordinary water! Jesus' request for her to bring her husband leads to a revelation of her immoral life. This is not an example of the Evangelist presenting Jesus as a "divine man," of which contemporary paganism spoke (that is to step alongside the woman!); the prophetic insight which e.g. characterized Ezekiel's ministry is understood by the Evangelist to be uniquely present in the Revealer (cf. 1:48; 2:25; 11:14; 13:38). Technically it was not contrary to the Mosaic law for a woman to be married five times, but Jewish teachers forbade a woman to be married more than twice—or at most (in the eyes of some) three times; this woman must have had a series of divorces and now lived with a man without marriage. If the woman evades the issue, Jesus does not return to it. (The notion has long survived that the five husbands = the five gods of the nations that entered Samaria, and that the sixth = Yahweh, who was no "husband" of the Samaritans hence "the woman's private life corresponds with the history of her people" [Hoskyns, 243]. This exegesis is not to be countenanced; 2 Kings 17:30 f. mentions seven gods, not five, but more importantly the Evangelist does not allegorize in this manner.)

True Worship (4:19–26)

19 The woman's recognition of Jesus as a prophet leads her to raise the most burning issue between Samaritans and Jews, namely the place where God should be worshipped. The command in Deut 12:1–14 to worship God in the place that he will show follows the command to pronounce a blessing from Mt. Gerizim and a curse from Mt. Ebal (Deut 11:29). In the Samaritan Pentateuch of Deut 27:3 the place where an altar is to be built on arrival in the promised land is Gerizim, not Ebal as in the MT. That could conceivably be right, the text possibly having been changed through anti-Samaritan motives. References in the later books of the OT to worship in Jerusalem would not have been viewed by the Samaritans as authoritative, since the Pentateuch alone was binding for them. In the Persian period a temple was built on Gerizim; it was destroyed by John Hyrcanus in 128 B.C., but the Samaritans continued to worship on the sacred site.

21 Jesus champions neither Jerusalem nor Gerizim, for "the hour is coming"—the eschatological hour, initiating the new age of the kingdom of God—when worship of the Father will be tied to no place (cf. Rev 21:22, an example of the positive relations between the two major Johannine works, for Jews looked for the temple to be the focus of the divine glory in the kingdom, as their daily prayers constantly reminded them).

22 The object of worship (neuter for the Person of God, Schlatter, 125) the Samaritans do not understand; the Jews do, for they were elected as the people from whom the salvation of the world would come, i.e., through the Messiah. The saying is not an editorial intrusion, as is often maintained. The Evangelist rejects neither Moses and the prophets, nor Judaism as such; it is the unbelieving leaders of Israel against whom he polemizes.

23 The unique Johannine expression "The hour is coming and now is" brackets future and present without eliminating either. The saving sovereignty of the future is in process of being established through the Christ, and it is moving to its ordained climax in his redemptive death and resurrection, but not to its conclusion at that point, for the final resurrection is yet to take place, even after Easter (so 5:25; cf. 5:28–29). Since the kingdom of God is the age of the Spirit's outpouring, true worshippers will worship the Father in virtue of the life, freedom, and power bestowed by the Spirit, and in accordance with the redemptive revelation brought by the Redeemer.

24 "God is Spirit" defines God, not in his metaphysical being, but "according to his work in the world." The clause is parallel in this respect with 'God is light' (1 John 1:5) and 'God is love' (1 John 4:8); "All these statements describe *God's mode of action and working*" (Schlatter, 126. So also Bultmann: "The πνεῦμα is God's miraculous dealing with man which takes place in the revelation. . . . 'God is πνεῦμα' defines the *idea* of God by saying what God *means*, viz., that for man God is the miraculous being who deals wonderfully with him, just as the definition of God as ἀγάπη refers to him as the one who deals with men out of his love and in his love," 190–92).

25 This authoritative declaration on worship leads the woman to play her last card: "The Messiah is coming, and will tell us everything." This is a faithful reflection of the Samaritans' messianic expectation, which was defined not by the prophetic books but by the Pentateuch, notably Deut 18:15–18. The *Taheb*, as another Moses, would have the task of restoring true belief in God and the true worship of God, and to this end he would reveal the truth (see J. MacDonald, *Theology of the Samaritans*, 362–65).

26 On the woman's affirmation of this hope in the Messiah, Jesus reveals himself to her: Ἐγώ εἰμι, "I am," which may be completed with "he"; for the Evangelist, however, the formula has the overtone of the absolute being of God (cf. 6:20; 8:28, 58).

THE WITNESS OF THE WOMAN OF SYCHAR (4:27–30)

27 The disciples were shocked, not because Jesus was talking with *the* woman (KJV)—a Samaritan—but with *a* woman! That is characteristic of attitudes to women reflected in Jewish rabbinical writings. Billerbeck cites, among other extraordinary examples, *'Abot* 2 (1d): "One should not talk with a woman on the street, not even with his own wife, and certainly not with somebody's else's wife, because of the gossip of men," and *Qidd.* 70a: "It is forbidden to give a woman any greeting" (*Kommentar* 2:438).

28–29 The woman left her jar—in haste, and because she intended to come back at once with others! Her deduction that Jesus was the "Messiah" by reason of his revelation of her past life is consonant with the Samaritans' understanding of the role of the "Taheb" as restorer and revealer of the truth (but cf. also 1:48–49).

A DIALOGUE OF JESUS WITH HIS DISCIPLES (4:31–38)

31–34 These verses form a distinctive paragraph, which moves from the misunderstanding by the disciples of Jesus' answer to their request. Barrett points out that the woman misunderstood what Jesus said about living water, and the disciples misunderstood what he said about food (240). But observe the difference: she did not grasp what Jesus had to give *her;* they did not grasp what Jesus *himself* lived by—the satisfaction of doing his Father's will and carrying out to the finish the work given to him to do. One may see here a parallel to the answer of Jesus to the first temptation, recorded in Matt 4:1–4 (Dodd, *Historical Tradition,* 325–26). The entire ministry of Jesus is represented by the Evangelist as obedience in action, which leads him finally to the surrender of himself in death (cf. 17:4).

35–38 The paragraph is composed of two sets of sayings relating to harvest, both apparently consisting of a proverb (35a, 37) provided with comment (35b–36, 38). "Four months more and harvest comes" could relate to the precise time of speaking, or signify a common observation on the interval between sowing and reaping, but most consider it to be a current proverb (Argyle strongly argued that the iambic rhythm of Greek statement was in keeping with its nature as a proverb, and that it had penetrated Galilee like a good deal else of Greek tradition, "A Note on John 4:35," *ExpTim* 82, 247–48. The Semitic form of the saying, however, is commonly accepted; see Schlatter, 131). The period between sowing and harvest was usually thought of as six months, but the interval from the latest date of sowing to the beginning of harvest was four months (Str-B 2:439–40). The point of citing the proverb is to contrast it with the present situation: the waiting time is over, the time of harvest has arrived! Since harvest is a common eschatological symbol (e.g., Isa 27:12; Joel 4:13; Mark 4:1–9, 26–29; Matt 13:24–30; Rev 14:14–16), the saying of Jesus represents the gathering of people into the kingdom of God. It is closely similar to Matt 9:37, but more emphatically asserts the arrival of the harvest; indeed, the call, "Look at the fields, they are white for the harvest!" could refer to the approaching Samaritans (dressed in white) as exemplifying the presence of the harvest. The arrival of harvest is underscored in v 36: the harvester is *already* receiving his "wages" and gathering produce "for life eternal"; i.e., he is bringing men and women under the saving sovereignty that has arrived, that they may enjoy the life eternal of the kingdom. (Note: it is unnatural to interpret 35–36 as meaning that in the eschatological situation there is no time between sowing and reaping, since they take place together; Bultmann, 196–98. The point of the sayings is to indicate the critical nature of the present: sowing has taken place and the anticipated harvest has now come.)

37–38 Another proverb, anciently attested, is cited in v 37, but applied very differently from its ancient use. The proverb generally had a negative connotation, expressing cynicism, depression, or even threat of judgment, as, e.g., in Mic 6:15: "You will sow, but never reap" (cf. also Lev 26:16; Deut 28:30; Matt 25:26). Its use is illustrated in a Ras Shamra letter from King Iturlim to the king of Ugarit, objecting to men from Ugarit crossing the border and sowing grain on his territory: "If I enter your territory and sow then you can harvest; and (now) you have entered my territory and I can reap"; the latter clause implies, "That's what I'll certainly do!" (see W. G. E. Watson, "Antecedents of a NT Proverb," 368–70).

By contrast Jesus uses the saying to indicate the difference of roles in the service of the kingdom of God. The part that each plays is important for the mission of the kingdom in the world, and each worker may rejoice in the success that "the Lord of the harvest" gives to their labors.

The interpretation of v 38 has been rendered needlessly complex through stumbling at the aorist ἀπέστειλα, "I sent." It is pointed out that no mention has been made of Jesus sending the disciples on mission. They have not been sent to Samaria; nor can they be said in this context to be reapers. Either then Jesus projects himself into the future and looks back on the mission on which they will engage (Schnackenburg, 1:452), or the statement is a post-Resurrection utterance, made perhaps in the light of the mission to Samaria by Philip and other Hellenist Christians (Cullmann, *The Early Church*, 186). That the Evangelist will have had in mind the later Samaritan mission is entirely probable; but the pressing of the terms in v 38 is illegitimate, for the Evangelist has almost certainly brought together from various contexts sayings relating to the kingdom and the mission. He has done the like elsewhere, a particularly clear example being 12:24–26. There, too, sayings relating to sowing and reaping have been assembled, having parallels in different settings in the synoptic Gospels. In the context of the ministry of Jesus, the "others" who labored are likely to denote primarily John the Baptist and Jesus, and others who spread their message, such as the woman at Sychar (cf. v 39).

THE CONVERSION OF THE PEOPLE OF SYCHAR (4:39–42)

39 Many of the Samaritans believed through the *testimony* that the woman bore: that, as Barrett points out, is the task of a disciple! She joined with John the Baptist as a witness to Jesus before the disciples bore any testimony to her people; that made possible the difference between the welcome to Sychar and the experience of Jesus and the disciples recorded in Luke 9:53. Not that Jesus stayed there long—two days only were spared. But they were sufficient for the people of Sychar to grasp for themselves that the testimony of the woman was right, and they bore their own witness to him: "We know that this man is in truth *the Savior of the world.*" That is a notable confession, worthy to be placed alongside the declarations about Jesus in chap. 1. It is difficult to be certain whether the Samaritans did actually use the term "Savior" of Jesus, or whether John is giving an equivalent term (as he replaced the term "Taheb" by Messiah in vv 25, 29). Jews did not apply the term "Savior" to the Messiah; they reserved that for God. As a divine title it is frequent in the latter chapters of Isaiah (e.g., Isa 43:3 11; 63:8–9); Isa 45:21–22 sets forth the concept of God as Savior of the world without using the expression. The title "Savior" was freely applied by Christians to the Christ (e.g., Acts 5:31; 13:23; Phil 3:20, and especially the Pastoral Epistles) for they saw him as the representative of God the Savior, and the Mediator of the kingdom of God, which means salvation and life. The traditions of the Samaritans prepared them for the understanding of the Messiah enunciated in v 42. Their term "Taheb" is generally defined as the Coming or the Returning One. Since the Samaritan expectation is rooted in the promise of Deut 18:15–18, he is thought of as another Moses, or even as Moses returned (so the Memar Markah 111.3). With his appearance begins the period of the "divine favor," which comes not for Israel alone but for the world (cf. Samaritan prayer cited by MacDonald, 365): "Happy the world when he who brings peace with him comes and reveals the divine favor and purifies Mount Gerizim"). MacDonald records that in a letter to Kautsch the Samaritans (of modern times) explained the term *Taheb* as meaning "Converter" (i.e., of the nations), and he draws attention to the suitability of this definition to the acclamation of John 4:42 (*Theology of the Samaritans*, 367). If the men of Sychar believed first through the witness of the woman they knew, and then after hearing Jesus for themselves it is comprehensible that they should have acknowledged him as the Converter, or Deliverer, or Savior of the world. The Evangelist, writing at a time when the title Savior of the World was applied to certain deities in the pagan world and was claimed by the Emperor of Rome, was affirming in the Samaritans' confession of Jesus in these terms both that the title rightly belongs to Jesus alone and also that, as Redeemer and Lord, Jesus fulfills the hopes of Samaritans, Jews, and the world of nations.

Explanation

The concerns of the episode at Sychar are threefold: the gift of "living water," the worship of the Father in Spirit and in truth, and mission to non-Jews. They are bound together by the action of Jesus Christ, which encompasses the tasks of Revealer, Redeemer, and Mediator of the divine sovereignty. Eschatological gift and action are at the heart of all three concerns.

1. The woman of Sychar had no understanding of what it means to drink the living water till it dawned on her, however inadequately and crudely, that she was face to face with the one who "will make known everything to us"—the Messiah. We are intended to understand that she "drank" the water, and that her fellow townsmen did as well. Yet the reader recognizes that the formula "the hour is coming and now is" applies here, equally as to the worship in the Spirit; the fullness of the revelation and the life by the Spirit could not be known till the Redeemer who worked by the Spirit should send the Spirit of life to the redeemed. Of this cardinal gift of Christ, the Johannine community was very much aware. The Church of succeeding times needs to know its reality and power in like measure.

2. "The hour is coming and now is" is first used in relation to the worship of the Father in Spirit and in truth. It is possible only by reason of the action of the Christ who brings in the new age, wherein the temple of Jerusalem

becomes as irrelevant as the sacred site of Gerizim. Jesus can say, "and *now is*," because he is the Bearer of the Spirit, and speaks the word of the kingdom, and performs the signs of the kingdom by his ceaseless aid. What is begun in Judea, Samaria, and Galilee comes to fuller realization when the Bearer of the Spirit is "lifted up" to heaven as the Lord of the kingdom and bestows the Spirit of the new age (cf. 1:33). Then worship "in spirit and in truth" becomes the mark of the Church that is baptized by the Spirit. That the historic Church through the ages can claim that that mark is evident in its worship is questionable, even if in the mercy of God it is not bereft of the Spirit and still has the truth. Contemporary striving after its fuller recovery is laudable, and should be directed "in the Spirit and in the truth."

3. The Fourth Gospel is not infrequently considered to reflect an inward-looking community, concerned rather to survive than to evangelize, and with a negative view both of the Jewish people and the world of nations. That is a curious interpretation in light of the prologue, the celebrated v 3:16, and 12:20–32. But chap. 4 is also unique among the four Gospels, in its depiction of the compassion and patience of Jesus in dealing with a Samaritan woman, his willingness to minister to a Samaritan community, and the confession arising from their experience of him: "This man is in truth the Savior of the world." It is a great insight from a little people. Almost certainly the Fourth Evangelist will have viewed this breaking down of walls between Jew and Samaritan as Luke viewed Philip's evangelism of Samaria: a major step in the Church's advance to mission to the world. The later advance is embodied in the peculiarly Johannine version of the Easter commission in 20:21 and exemplified in the epilogue of chap. 21. The spirit in which it should be undertaken was marvelously captured by the early commentator on Tatian's Harmony of the Gospels, Ephraem the Syrian: "Jesus came to the fountain as a hunter. . . . He threw a grain before one pigeon that he might catch the whole flock. . . . At the beginning of the conversation he did not make himself known to her, but first she caught sight of a thirsty man, then a Jew, then a Rabbi, afterwards a prophet, last of all the Messiah. She tried to get the better of the thirsty man, she showed dislike of the Jew, she heckled the Rabbi, she was swept off her feet by the prophet, and she adored the Christ" (cited by J. A. Findlay, *Comm.*, 61). That imaginative description grasps the essential burden of the chapter, namely to reveal the Christ in action and the growth of faith responsive to the revelation. We do well to go and do likewise.

C. Jesus the Mediator of Life and Judgment (4:43–5:47)

Bibliography

Blank, J. *Krisis*. 109–82. **Bligh, J.** "Jesus in Jerusalem (John 5)." *HeyJ* 4 (1963) 115–34. **Dodd, C. H.** "A Hidden Parable in the Fourth Gospel." *More New Testament Studies.*

30–40. ———. *Interpretation*. 318–22. ———. *Historical Tradition*. 188–95, 174–80.
Feuillet, A. "La signification théologique du second miracle de Cana (Jo. IV.46–54)."
RSR 48 (1960) 62–75. **Fortna, R. T.** *Gospel of Signs*. 38–48 especially. **Gaechter, P.**
"Zur Form von Joh 5, 19–20." *Neutestamentliche Aufsätze*. FS J. Schmid. Regensburg:
Pustet, 1963. 65–68. **Jeremias, J.** *The Rediscovery of Bethesda*. Louisville: Southern Baptist
Theological Seminary, 1966. **Kilpatrick, G. D.** "John iv:51, ΠΑΙΣ or ΥΙΟΣ?" *JTS* 16
(1965) 448–49. **Kümmel, W. G.** "Die Eschatologie der Evangelien." *Heilsgeschehen
und Geschichte*. 48–66, esp. 60–66. **Léon-Dufour, X.** "Trois chiasmes johanniques."
NTS 7 (1960–61) 253–55. **Lohse, E.** "Jesus Worte über den Sabbat." *Die Einheit des
NT* 62–72. **Moreton, M. J.** "Feast, Sign, and Discourse in John 5." *SE* 4 (1968) 209–
13. **Nicol, W.** *Semeia in the Fourth Gospel*. Leiden: Brill 1972. 41–48. **Schulz, S.** *Untersuchungen zur Menschensohn-Christologie im Johannesevangelium*. 109–14, 128–39.
Schweizer, E. "Die Heilung des Königlichen. Joh 4, 46–54." *EvTh* 11 (1951) 64–71;
also in *Neotestamentica*. 407–15. **Temple, S.** "The Two Signs in the Fourth Gospel."
JBL 81 (1962) 169–74. **Vanhoye, A.** "La composition de Jn 5, 19–30." *Mélanges B.
Rigaux*. 259–74. **Wieand, D. J.** "John 5:2 and the Pool of Bethesda." *NTS* 12 (1966)
392–404.

Introduction

As with chaps. 2–4, the connections of this section with what has gone before
are evident. Both the beginning and the end of the second Cana narrative (4:46–
54) make reference to the first sign performed in Cana (2:1–11). This has understandably led some exegetes to consider that 4:46–54 is essentially bound up with
the preceding episode ("from Cana to Cana"). Yet a similar phenomenon was
observed in the account of the first Cana miracle, in that 2:1 is clearly linked
with 1:19–51; that caused some to bracket the narrative with the foregoing section
and to separate it from the account of the Cleansing of the Temple; to us, on the
contrary, it seems more plausible that the Evangelist set together the two signs of
chap. 2 to form a programmatic beginning of his presentation of the ministry of
Jesus (hence the drastic step of transferring the report of the cleansing from the
end of the ministry to its beginning), and to make them serve as introductions to
the discourses of chaps. 3 and 4, with which they are thematically bound. The
same reasoning applies to the section 4:43–5:47. While the two Cana signs could
well have once circulated as twin narratives in the oral tradition of the Johannine
communities, the Evangelist appears to have conjoined the two healing miracles
of 4:46–54 and 5:1–9 and made them introduce the discourse of 5:17–47, for
they embody the primary theme of 5:17–47: "Jesus the one who gives life to
those whom he wishes" (5:21). (Such is the view of exegetes as varied as Heitmüller,
111–12; Bultmann, 203; Hoskyns, 249; Dodd, *Interpretation*, 318; Feuillet, 62–75;
Brown, 197, who, however, equally emphasizes the link with chaps. 2–4. On the
question as to the original order of chaps. 5 and 6, see the Introduction to the
Gospel, p. xlii–xliii.)

Translation

[43] *After the two days he departed from that place to Galilee* [44] (*for Jesus himself
testified that a prophet has no honor in his own country*). [45] *When therefore he
arrived in Galilee the Galileans welcomed him, because they had seen all that he
had done in Jerusalem during the festival, for they too had gone to the festival.*
[46] *He came therefore again into Cana of Galilee, where he had made the water
wine. And there was in Capernaum a certain officer in the royal service*[a] *whose*

son was ill. ⁴⁷ When this man heard that Jesus had arrived in Galilee from Judea he went to him and asked that he should come down and heal his son, for he was at the point of death. ⁴⁸ Jesus therefore said to him, "Unless you people see signs and portents you will never believe!"ᵇ ⁴⁹ The officer says to him, "Sir, come down before my little boy dies." ⁵⁰ Jesus says to him, "Go; your son lives." The man believed the word that Jesus said to him, and he set off for home. ⁵¹ But while he was on his way down his servants met him and told him that his boyᶜ was living. ⁵² He inquired therefore at what time he began to recover; they said to him, "Yesterday, at one in the afternoonᵈ the fever began to leave him." ⁵³ The father therefore knew that it was in that hour that Jesus had said to him, "Your son lives," and he became a believer, along with his whole household. ⁵⁴ This was the second sign that Jesus performed after coming from Judea into Galilee.

⁵:¹ After this there was aᵉ festival of the Jews, and Jesus went up to Jerusalem. ² Now there is in Jerusalem by the sheepgate a poolᶠ which is called in Hebrew Bethesda,ᵍ having five colonnades. ³ In these a crowd of sick people was lying— blind, lame, and paralyzed.ʰ

⁵ One man was there who had been ill for thirty-eight years; ⁶ Jesus, on seeing this man lying there, and knowing that he had already been ill for a long time, says to him, "Do you want to become well?" ⁷ The sick man answered him, "Sir, I have nobody to put me into the pool when the water is disturbed, but while I'm on my way someone else goes down before me." ⁸ Jesus says to him, "Stand up, take your mattress, and walk." ⁹ And immediatelyⁱ the man became well, and he took up his mattress and started walking.

Now that day was a sabbath. ¹⁰ The Jews therefore said to the man who had been healed, "It is the sabbath, and it is against the law for you to carry your mattress."ʲ ¹¹ But he replied to them, "The man who made me well told me, "Take up your mattress and walk." ¹² They questioned him, "Who is the man who said to you, 'Take it up and walk'?" ¹³ But the man who had been healed did not know who it was, for Jesus had slipped away as there was a crowd in the place. ¹⁴ Later Jesus found him in the temple and said to him, "Look, you have become well; don't continue sinning any longer, in case something worse should happen to you." ¹⁵ The man went off and reported to the Jews that it was Jesus who had made him well. ¹⁶ It was on this account that the Jews used to persecute Jesus, because he used to do such things on the sabbath. ¹⁷ But Jesusᵏ answered them, "My father has been working until now, and I also am working." ¹⁸ On this account therefore the Jews were the more seeking to kill him, because he not only used to break the sabbath, but he also used to call God his own Father, making himself equal to God.

¹⁹ Jesus gave them this answer. "Amen, amen I tell you, the Son can do nothing by himself, only what he sees the Father doing; for what he does, the Son does likewise. ²⁰ For the Father loves the Son, and shows him everything that he himself does, and he will show him greater works than these that you may be amazed. ²¹ For as the Father raises the dead and gives them life, so also the Son gives life to those whom he wishes. ²² Indeed, the Father judges no one, but he has given all judgment to the Son, ²³ so that all should honor the Son, just as they honor the Father. ²⁴ Amen, amen, I say to you, he who hears my word and believes him who sent me has eternal life; he does not come to judgment but has crossed over from death to life. ²⁵ Amen, amen I say to you, the hour is coming and now is when the

dead will hear the voice of the Son of God, and they who hear will live. [26]*For just as the Father has life in himself, so also he has granted the Son to have life in himself;* [27]*and he gave him authority to pass judgment, because he is the Son of Man.* [28]*Do not be amazed at this, because the hour is coming in which all who are in the grave will hear his voice* [29]*and come forth; those who have done what is good will rise for life, those who practiced what is wicked will rise for judgment.* [30]*I can do nothing by myself; it is as I hear that I judge, and my judgment is just, because I do not seek my own will, but the will of him who sent me.*

[31]*"If I bear witness about myself my witness is not valid;*[1] [32]*there is Another who bears witness about me, and I know*[m]*that the witness which he bears for me is true.* [33]*You have sent to John, and he has borne witness to the truth.* [34]*I myself do not receive witness from man, but I say these things that you may be saved.* [35]*He was a lamp which burns and brightly shines, and you were willing to exult for an hour in his light.* [36]*But I have witness greater than John's, for the works that the Father has given me to carry through to the end, the very works that I do bear witness concerning me that the Father has sent me.* [37]*And the Father who sent me has borne witness concerning me; his voice you have never heard, nor have you seen his form,* [38]*and his word has no lodging in you, for you do not believe the one whom he sent.* [39]*You search the Scriptures, because you suppose that you have eternal life in them; and it is they that bear witness about me,* [40]*and you are unwilling to come to me that you may have life.*

[41]*"I do not accept honor from men,* [42]*but I know you people—I know that you do not have the love of God*[n]*in you.* [43]*I have come in the name of my Father and you do not accept me; if another should come in his own name you will accept him.* [44]*How can you believe, when you accept honor from one another, but do not seek the honor that is from the only God?*[o] [45]*Do not suppose that I shall be the one to accuse you before the Father; the one who accuses you is Moses, on whom you have set your hope.* [46]*For if you were believing Moses, you would now be believing me, for he wrote about me.* [47]*But if you are not believing his writings, how will you believe my words?"*

Notes

[a] βασιλικός as an adjective = royal, as a noun = a relative or official of a king (Bauer, *Lexicon*, 136). Schlatter points out that Josephus uses the term to describe all the relatives and officials of the Herods, and their troops (137). If the narrative records the same incident as that in Matt 8:5–13//Luke 7:1–10 we may view him as an officer in the army of Herod Agrippa.

[b] The answer of Jesus is treated as an exclamation in JB, as a question in the NEB. Note that most recent exegetes view Matt 8:7 as a question, implying an objection.

[c] παῖς is read by P[66*] P[75] ℵ A B C Origen, υἱός by P[66c] D[gr] and other Western representatives, and Origen. Kilpatrick thinks that the former is due to the influence of Matt and Luke, and so selects the latter as original; the UBS committee views the latter as due to scribal assimilation to the context (cf. vv 46, 47, 50, 53), and so favors the former.

[d] Lit., the *seventh* hour, beginning the day at 6:00 A.M.

[e] ἑορτή without the article is generally acknowledged to be better attested than ἡ ἑορτή; the latter will have been due to the assumption that the feast was the Passover, *the* great festival of the Jews.

[f] The opening phrase is ambiguous because our earliest MSS frequently do not employ the iota subscript, and so leave it uncertain whether a nominative or dative is intended, and there is on any interpretation a word missing. If we may assume ἐπὶ τῇ προβατικῇ to refer to ἡ πύλη ἡ προβατική of Neh 3:1 we may translate, "There is in Jerusalem *by the sheepgate* a pool." It is

possible to view κολυμβήθρα as a dative and render "There is *by the sheep pool* (a place)." א* and other authorities omit the preposition and read, "There is in Jerusalem a sheep pool." Most critics view the first possibility as original and the others due to scribal attempts to clarify the text (Metzger, 207–8).

ᵍ The "Hebrew" (= Aram.) place name appears in various forms in the MSS. βηθζαθά (א), βηξαθά (L // Betzetha, it), βελζεθά (D), βηθσαϊδα (p⁷⁵ B = βηδσαϊδα in p⁶⁶), βηθεσδά (A C and most later MSS). A majority of the UBS committee favored the first variant, of which the following two are alternative spellings; the third is thought to be due to assimilation to Bethsaida by Galilee, mentioned in 1:44. There is strong reason, however, for favoring the last, since *Bethzatha* is an Aramaic equivalent of Bethesda, and a copper scroll of Qumran has a reference to the pool *Bethesdatayin*. Whereas Bethesda has been popularly viewed as Heb. for "the house of mercy" (a suitable name for this story), the Aram. term appears to have the less attractive meaning, "place of poured out water." *Bethesdatayin* is a dual form, denoting *two* pools. The site of the two pools with four enormous porticoes surrounding them and one dividing them has been unearthed at the church of St. Anna in Jerusalem (see the account in Jeremias, *The Rediscovery of Bethesda,* and the discussion of Wieand, 394–95).

ʰ Our earliest textual authorities end v 3 with the term ξηρῶν, "crippled" or "paralyzed" (so p⁶⁶ p⁷⁵ א A* B C* etc.). The mass of later MSS add "awaiting the movement of the water," and append a further statement (v 4): "For the angel of the Lord from time to time used to come down into the pool and disturb the water; the first one therefore to get in after the disturbance of the water became healed of whatever disease he suffered." While this may reflect an old tradition it formed no part of the text of the Gospel (see the discussion in Metzger, 209).

ⁱ While the term εὐθέως is omitted by א and the Western text, the evidence for its inclusion is overwhelming.

ʲ Among the 39 chief works which were forbidden on the sabbath, according to the Jewish tractate *Sabbath,* the carrying of articles from one place to another was very precisely determined; the removal of a bed is specifically included, but if a man is lying on it no offense is incurred! (See the lengthy discussion narrated in Str-B 2:454–61.)

ᵏ The name Ἰησοῦς is read by p⁶⁶ A D K etc., κύριος by Syrˢ (Ἰησοῦς κύριος by syrᵖᵃˡ), and no subject by p⁷⁵ א B W etc. The UBS committee recognized the uncertainty of the reading and set Ἰησοῦς in brackets.

ˡ ἀληθής in v 31 is best rendered "valid." The statement is based on the principle of witness in Deut 19:15. In Jewish legal procedure it was witnesses, not the accused, who were examined; hence the statement in *Keth.* 2.9: "A man is not attested through himself (i.e., through his own testimony). . . . . A man cannot bear witness for himself" (Str-B 2:466).

ᵐ οἶδα is read by the great majority of MSS. A few read οἴδαμεν (cf. 3:2; 4:42 etc.); οἴδατε appears in א* D and other Western MSS, which strengthens the argument ("You know that God's testimony about me is true!"), but is not to be accepted (contrast v 37).

ⁿ τὴν ἀγάπην τοῦ θεοῦ. Is the genitive objective—"love *for* God," or subjective—"love that God exercises"? The latter is in harmony with the entire NT, but such love naturally is the spring of love within man; "the love that corresponds to God's love" is near the mark (cf. 1 John 3:17; 4:7–12).

ᵒ θεοῦ is omitted in p⁶⁶ p⁷⁵ B W, but surely by accident. ΘΕΟΥ is usually shortened to $\overline{\text{ΘΥ}}$; the text will have read ΤΟΥΜΟΝΟΥΘΕΟΥ, from which it will have been easy to omit ΘΥ. The term is required in the context. "The only God" reflects the Jewish confession of faith, rooted in the *Shema* in Deut 6:4.

Form/Structure/Setting

1. As stated in the Introduction to this section, we understand 4:43–5:47 as a connected whole, consisting of two "signs," both healing miracles, and a discourse primarily on the theme of Jesus, the Mediator of Life and Judgment.

2. 4:43–45 is a transitional paragraph, similar to 2:23–25, introducing the rest of the section. Within the paragraph v 44 is a saying that existed in isolation in the Johannine tradition.

3. 4:46–54, the Healing of an Officer's Son, has been taken from a source that contained the first Cana miracle. If, as is often thought, 2:12 formed the introduction to the second miracle, the latter will have been seen in close proximity to the former. The statement in 4:54 that this was the *second* sign that Jesus did on coming from Judea into Galilee has led to the postulate of a "signs source," which included all the seven reproduced in the Fourth Gospel (plus a great deal more, according to Bultmann and Fortna). This is not impossible, but it is a large leap from vv 46 and 54 to that conclusion; the two statements primarily connect the *two* narratives.

The relationship between the Johannine narrative of the healing of the king's officer's son and that of the Centurion's son (or παῖς/servant), recounted in the Q source (Matt 8:5–13 // Luke 7:1–10), has been much discussed. Whereas earlier writers tended to view them as different events most recent scholars agree that they represent independent accounts of the same happening (for a careful discussion of the issue see Schnackenburg, 1 471–75). From the point of view of form, the accounts in John and Matthew are remarkably similar. The simple form of a healing miracle (circumstances of need; description of healing; effect of the miracle) is elaborated in an unusual manner. The father's statement of his boy's illness and appeal for healing is in both accounts followed by an unexpected rebuff, followed by a renewal of the father's request; instead of going off to the child Jesus makes a declaration of healing (John 4:50, "Go, your son lives"; in Matt 8:13, "Go, as you believed, let it happen for you"); the father believes and returns to his house in Luke 7:10, as in John 4:51 ff., and confirmation of the miracle is given by those in the home. Within that common form different expressions occur. Matt 8:7 should probably be rendered, "Am *I* to come and heal him?," with the implication that a Gentile should know better than to ask a Jew to break Jewish laws by entering his house. John 4:48 laments the lack of faith without seeing "signs and wonders," but it is couched in the *plural*—addressed to the *public* through the officer (cf. Mark 9:19 for a remarkable parallel, addressed to a father requesting his son's healing). In the Q account the father's response is an expression of great faith in Jesus, on which Jesus comments that he had *not found such faith in Israel*, and he speaks the word of healing. The father's faith is differently described in John 4:49 ff.: on hearing the word of healing he "believes," and on meeting his servants his faith is brought to maturity: he becomes a believer (i.e., in Jesus), and so do the members of his household. We should recall here the Markan story of the healing (at a distance) of the Syro-Phoenician woman's daughter (Mark 7:24–30), which has a similar form and content; the approach of the woman meets with an apparent objection from Jesus, but is followed by affirmation of faith and the granting of healing. In view of these parallels the common notion that the Evangelist was responsible for modifying a straightforward narrative by his insertion of vv 48–49 is to be queried; the motifs and vocabulary are akin to synoptic traditions and are likely to have existed in that handed on to the Evangelist (so Dodd, *Historical Tradition,* 192–93; Becker, 185).

4. 5:1–9, The Healing at Bethesda, is one of several healing narratives in the Gospels in which Jesus took the initiative (instead of others approaching him with requests to heal a sick person). Curiously these events commonly take place on the sabbath, as the present one (see also Mark 3:1–6; Luke 13:10–17; 14:1–6). The narrative is simple in form: the setting and circumstance of the man in need are described (1–5); Jesus sees the man (cf. Luke 7:13; 13:12), questions his willingness to be healed, then speaks a healing command; the man is instantly cured, as his picking up and carrying his mattress demonstrates.

It is characteristic of this Gospel that the emphasis in both signs recorded at this point lies on the sovereign power of Jesus. The synoptic account of the Centurion's boy stresses the man's faith, so that it has become the center of the story; in the Fourth Gospel the father's faith is made plain, but the weight falls on the life-giving word of Jesus ("Your son *lives!*"). So also in the second sign the paralytic appears as a colorless individual, without faith or hope; the intervention of Jesus in his condition of living death makes it an ideal exemplification of the teaching in the discourse that follows.

5. 5:9c–18, The Dialogue on the Sabbath, has in all likelihood expanded an originally brief indication that the previous healing took place on the sabbath. One sabbath healing becomes an example of the recurring controversy of the Jews with Jesus about the Sabbath, and it enabled the Evangelist to make plain why Jesus so acted, and the nature of the Jewish opposition to him in the light of his teaching.

6. 5:19–30, A Discourse on Jesus the Life-Giver and Judge, is an exposition of v 17 and of the signs that preceded it, and at the same time takes up the charge of the Jews that Jesus "made himself equal to God" (v 18). Some of its sayings may have earlier circulated independently, but the section is closely interwoven. Both Léon-Dufour ("Trois chiasmes johanniques," 253–55) and Vanhoye ("La composition de Jn 5, 19–20") see in the passage a chiasmus, and the latter maintains that the composition of the whole is modeled on the proceedings of biblical parallelism.

7. 5:31–47 adduces witnesses to Jesus in the face of Jewish unbelief. Haenchen maintained that the passage has come from the Redactor, who tried to defend Jesus against the charge of self-witness in vv 19–30; the reference to the Father as the third witness, coming after John the Baptist, is thought to be out of place, and the appeal to works does not fit the Evangelist's view of signs (296–98). This should be linked with Haenchen's view of the whole chapter, which he saw as a good example of the three hands in the Gospel: (*i*) 1–9 gives a crude story of Jesus provoking a sabbath controversy by healing a man and telling him to walk about carrying a bed; (*ii*) the Evangelist retells the story and draws out the lesson in ἔγειρε, "Rise" (v 8): Jesus does the works of his Father, vv 19–21, 24–26, 30a; (*iii*) the Redactor seeks to make this teaching compatible with that of the Church, vv 22–23, 27–29, 30b (286). Haenchen uses an unfortunate technique of exaggeration to buttress his viewpoint; in reality the chapter is more compact and consistent with the Evangelist's mode of writing and theology than he allowed.

8. The setting of chap. 5 is a feast of Jerusalem, with which the Galilean sign of the Officer's son is conjoined by reason of its pertinence to the discourse of 5:19–30. If the unnamed feast were Pentecost it would particularly well suit the closing section of the discourse, since Pentecost had become for the Jews the celebration of the giving of the Law at Sinai (see J. H. E. Hull, *The Holy Spirit in the Acts of the Apostles* [London: Lutterworth, 1967] 53–55); the witness of Moses *for* Jesus and *against* the Jews would have been very powerful in that context. For the Johannine community the conflict of the Jerusalem Jews with Jesus had strong pertinence; the sabbath issue, and the claims of and on behalf of Jesus in that connection, were perpetually debated. The discourse will have both provided guidance for and reflected the contemporary

controversy between the Christians and the Jews (for a more specific suggestion as to a contemporary setting for chap. 5, see J. L. Martyn, *History and Theology,* 68–73).

Comment

Jesus Comes to Galilee (4:43–45)

44 The saying in v 44 had evidently become isolated in the tradition (in *P. Oxyr.* 1 and *Gos. Thom.* 31 it has a double form; the latter reads, "No prophet is welcome in his native village, no physician heals those who know him"). Its significance in this context is uncertain. The notion that vv 43 and 45 imply that the Evangelist viewed Jesus' πατρίς as Jerusalem (so, e.g., Dodd, *Historical Tradition,* 240 n.2; Barrett, 246; Lindars, 201) is hardly to be received in view of 1:46; 7:52. The γάρ ("for") shows that we must take the sentence, along with 4:1, as indicating the reason for the journey to *Galilee:* Jesus withdrew to Galilee to be less conspicuous to the Jewish leaders, yet to continue his ministry to his people (is there a contrast here with his ministry to Samaria just described?). But he anticipated that there would be no tumultuous welcome on arrival there, in accord with his understanding and experience of the Galileans (for a *wrong* kind of following that he subsequently gained there, and from which he fled, cf. 6:15).

45 Jesus was in fact welcomed by the Galileans who had seen his signs in Jerusalem; but cf. 2:23–25; 3:2–3.

Healing of the King's Officer's Son (4:46–54)

On the relation between this narrative and that in Q (Matt 8:5–13; Luke 7:1–10), see p. 71. The unexpected v 48, addressed to *people* (plural) who demand miracles before believing, could, like v 44, have been an isolated saying placed here by the Evangelist, but cf. Mark 9:19; if original here it must be viewed in the light of 2:4; Mark 7:27; Matt 8:7 as a test of faith.

54 The clue to the Evangelist's purpose in the narrative, its "sign" value, lies in the threefold reference to the statement of Jesus to the officer: ὁ υἱός σου ζῇ, "Your son lives" (vv 50, 51, 53). The healing of the boy is a sign of the power of Jesus to give life, which in the discourse that follows will be defined as "eternal life" (5:24) and even life from the dead, resurrection life (5:21, 25–26, 28–29). Its appropriateness to the latter aspect is clear in the light of 4:47—the boy was at the point of death. Along with the emphasis on the word of Jesus, the narrative reveals a corresponding progression in the officer's faith (vv 48, 50, 53). These two features, the authoritative word of the Lord and the faith of the officer, provide "the form by which the final eschatological truth is made known and apprehended" (5:24; so Hoskyns, 262).

The Healing of a Paralytic at Bethesda (5:1–9b)

The healing, like that of the Officer's son, is a sign of the life-giving power of Christ—the key term is Ἔγειρε, v 3 (cf. 5:21, ὥσπερ ὁ πατὴρ ἐγείρει τοὺς νεκροὺς . . . οὕτως καὶ ὁ υἱὸς . . . , "As the Father raises the dead . . . so also the Son . . . "). The helpless man is given power to obey the word of Christ to stand up and begin to live (v 9).

6–8 In this man there is no such faith as that of the king's officer; on the contrary when Jesus tests the man's will to gain health, which is one aspect of faith, the sick man's only answer is a complaint (so Dodd, *Historical Tradition*, 177). The command to take up the mattress and walk is not to be regarded as a provocation of the Jews through an ostentatious sabbath-breaking (Strathmann, 101; Haenchen, 269 f.), but as a sign of the man's restoration to health: "he became fit, he took up his mattress, and he made his way" (v 9).

DIALOGUE ON THE SABBATH WORK OF JESUS (5:9c–18)

13 It is extraordinary that the healed paralytic had no idea of the identity of his benefactor—so little did he "believe"! It is equally extraordinary that the Jewish leaders had no regard for the healing of a man who had been crippled for almost a lifetime; their sole concern was for the breaking of a sabbath rule as defined in their tradition.

14 Μηκέτι ἁμάρτανε, "Do not continue sinning any longer," could imply that the man's illness was connected with his sinful ways; yet 9:1–4 forbids any facile connection between sin and disease. As in Mark 2:5 the sin of the paralytic appears to be viewed as of major importance; the "something worse" that could happen to the man would be to finish up in Gehenna. Hoskyns comments: "There is a more serious disease than lameness or paralysis; there is a more serious possibility of judgment, and there is a righteousness that sets men free" (253). The saying of v 14 has pertinence in the light of vv 17–30: Jesus carries out the work of God in deliverance from sin and death for life eternal.

17–18 The statement "My Father has been working until now" must be set in the context of Jewish exposition of the Scriptures. The Jews understood Gen 2:2 as implying that God's sabbath following creation continues to the present—his works are *finished*. But that raises a difficulty: how can God be said in the Scriptures to be active, if he keeps sabbath? One answer ran: God rested from work on the world, but not from his work on the godless and the righteous: "He works with both of them, and he shows to the latter something of their recompense, and to the former something of *their* recompense" (*Gen. Rab.* 11.8c; see Str-B 2:461–62 for further examples of this thinking). Accordingly God blesses the righteous in anticipation of their gaining the life of the kingdom of God, and brings judgment on sinners in anticipation of their exclusion from it. Here we see the significance of "I also am working." Jesus as the Son of God does the works of God, even on the sabbath. The signs just narrated indicate that he brings to men no mere *anticipation* of the saving sovereignty of God but its *reality*—life from the dead; and he declares judgment on rejectors of the word of God which the Last Judgment will confirm. Such is the theme of vv 19–30, but it is slanted to meet the major Jewish objection to Jesus: "He called God his own Father, making himself equal to God" (v 18). Is the latter a correct deduction from the former? Bultmann answered, Yes. "The Jews rightly understand that Jesus makes himself equal to God in these words, and so for their ears it is an insane blasphemy." Bultmann, however, went on to point out that the Jews failed to grasp that Jesus is the *Revealer;* second, they made the mistake of viewing equality with God as independence from God, whereas for Jesus it meant total dependence on God (244). In the light of these (undoubtedly correct) observations, the expression "equal to God" is a misleading interpretation of the declaration of Jesus. That Jesus spoke of God as his *own* Father rightly points to his unique relation to God, and it is the Evangelist's concern to make plain the nature of that relationship. But in vv 19–30 we see a twofold emphasis that exists in tension: on the one hand there is the acknowledgment by Jesus of the total dependence of the Son on the Father, and on the other a consciousness of the Father's appointment of the Son to perform on his behalf works that God alone has the right and power to execute (vv 19–20, 21, 22, 26–27, 30). It is perhaps not irrelevant to note that the Jews were ready, when they wished, to recognize that in certain conditions men could be spoken of as God. For example they viewed Ps 82:6, "I said you are gods, sons of the Most High all of you," as relating to the people of Israel. And they gloried in the fact that in Exod 7:1 God states that he has made Moses as God to Pharaoh, whereas since Pharaoh made himself as God he had to learn that he was nothing (*Tanh.* B § 12 in Str-B 2:462–64). It would seem that in their eyes God could exalt a man to be as God, but whoever *made himself* as God called down divine retribution on himself. They saw Jesus in the latter category.

Jesus the Life-Giver and Judge (5:19–30)

19 The opening clause links on to v 17: "My Father works . . . I also work . . . "; hence, "The Son can do nothing . . . only what he sees the Father doing."

The suggestion has been made (apparently independently by Dodd, "A Hidden Parable," 30–40, and Gaechter, "Zur Form von Joh 5, 19–20," 65–68) that a parable lies embedded in vv 19–20a; it depicts a son apprenticed to his father's trade; he watches the father at work and copies everything that the father does, who in turn shows the boy all the secrets of his craft; the passage beginning at v 20b then allegorizes various elements of the picture. It is an attractive idea, but it seems to the present writer that there are too many statements in the Gospel in the same vein to make it probable. See, e.g., 8:28, spoken with reference to the prospect of the Son of Man being "lifted up": "Then you will know that I am, and that I do nothing by myself, but I speak these things just as the Father taught me." A similar claim is stated concerning Jesus *saying* nothing ἐξ ἑαυτοῦ, other than what the Father commands him, 12:49; and 14:10 conjoins the *words and acts* of Jesus as done not ἀφ᾽ ἑαυτοῦ, but of the Father who dwells in him. So also Jesus has not *come* ἀφ᾽ ἑαυτοῦ, but has been *sent;* hence he speaks and acts according to the direction of the Father who sent him, 7:28. All this suggests that vv 19–20 originate not in a generalized parable that depicts the relation of any son to his father, but in a deep consciousness of the unique relation of the Son to the Father, sent to be the instrument of God's final purpose for humankind. So we may see v 19a as not simply an expression of the humility of Jesus; when the first clause is taken in conjunction with the second, it is recognized as an assertion of identity of action of the Son and the Father. It is this kind of action that the Son cannot do "by himself."

20   The "seeing" of the Son in v 19 has its counterpart in the "showing" by the Father in v 20. It is an image of the perpetual communion of the Son with the Father in his day-by-day life (*not* in his pre-existence). The source of that communion, and its illumination and direction, is the Father's love for the Son. This is to be seen in the "greater works" that will be shown to the Son, and that will cause the Jews to marvel. Precisely because these works can be seen by the Jews and move them to astonishment, they must denote the greater signs that Jesus will perform in his ministry; naturally they will also point to the greater realities of the kingdom of God, which however the Jews will not be able to perceive.

21–23   Bultmann understands vv 21–23 as setting forth a single thought; Jesus fulfills on behalf of the Father the office of the eschatological Judge, with power to give life and to condemn. This does not do justice to the emphasis in the passage on the *redemptive* action of the Son. The two signs of 4:46–5:9 exemplify the power of the Son to "quicken" the helpless and those near to death. So here the Son performs the works of the Father in giving life; it is that aspect of the work of the Son which is to the fore in vv 24–26. True, the Father has committed the responsibility of judgment to the Son (v 22), for the entire eschatological process has been remitted to his hands; but the emphasis here, as throughout the Gospel, is on the divine will for the salvation of the world, not its condemnation (cf. 3:16–21).

The consequence of this good pleasure of the Father (ἵνα is consecutive rather than purposive) is that "all should honor the Son as they do the Father." It follows from the completeness of the Son's representation of the Father (for the Jews "One sent is as he who sent him") and the Son's accomplishment of the Father's works (raising the dead and judgment are the exclusive prerogatives of God, see Str-B 1:523, 895 and 4:pt. 2, 1199–1212). The inclusive language of vv 21–23 embraces resurrection, judgment, and honor due to the Son, alike in the present and the future, but the context has the present primarily in mind. With the advent of the Son of God, the new age has come; hence he brings to men the life of the new age in the present one; likewise he mediates its corollary of judgment in this time (cf. 9:39–41; 12:31–32). Accordingly the honor that belongs to the mediator of life and judgment belongs to the Son even in this present time.

24   The declaration of v 24, as Schnackenburg observes, contains the essential Johannine kerygma (cf. 3:16, 36) adapted to the present context (2:108). The promise of life is for him who *hears the word of the Son* and *believes the Father who sent him*. The promise becomes immediately effective; the hearer-believer *has* eternal life *now*. He has the judgment behind him, not before him, since judgment is for unbelief (3:18, 36), and he has crossed over from the realm of death into the sphere of the divine sovereignty, the characteristic of which is life for all who enter it (cf. Col 1:13). This is the strongest affirmation of realized eschatology applied to the believer in the NT, as 12:31–32 is the strongest expression of its cosmic aspect.

25   The truth of v 24 is projected on a vast scale. The "hour" that is coming is that of the eschatological future, to which the resurrection of the dead belongs; but it has already entered the present, since the Christ who raises the dead is here. His voice sounds out (cf v 8: Ἔγειρε, "Rise"!) that the "dead" (the mass of humankind, who exist in a condition of spiritual death) may live. The eschatological future which has come into the present bursts on the world through the lifting up of the Christ and embraces the resurrection hour of vv 28–29, for the Christ-event divides and determines all ages (see Blank, *Krisis*, 134–43).

26–27 This eschatological miracle is possible because (*a*) the Father has given the Son to have life "in himself," so that he not only possesses it but can communicate it; and (*b*) the Son exercises the functions of the Son of Man. The assertion is illuminated less by contemporary Jewish apocalyptic literature (contrary to Schulz, 91, and his *Untersuchungen zur Menschensohn-Christologie*, 111–13) than by the teaching of Jesus in the synoptic Gospels relating to the Son of Man. For while Jesus manifestly has in view the vision of the one like a son of man in Daniel 7, he goes far beyond it in subsuming the whole eschatological process of mediating the kingdom of God and the judgment in the present and the future under the function of the Son of Man (see, e.g., Matt 8:20; 11:18–19; Mark 8:31; 8:38 // Luke 12:8–9; Mark 14:62; Matt 25:31–46).

28–29 "Do not be amazed"—at what? At what has been said in vv 25–27, that in this life Jesus the Son, in his capacity as Son of Man, raises the "dead" and exercises judgment. But more is to follow. An amazing future follows the amazing present! The same Son of God–Son of Man is to speak a word that will quicken "all in the graves," and raise them for life in the kingdom of glory or for condemnation. This is in no way an accommodation of the revolutionary eschatology of vv 24–27 to that of Jewish apocalyptic, but rather a logical development that must be strictly interpreted in the light of the foregoing. The spiritually dead who "hear" the voice of the Son of God in the days of their flesh and are raised by him to life will hear that voice again, calling them to enter upon the fullness of resurrection life for the kingdom of glory. Similarly those who are deaf to the voice of the Son of God in life must in the end respond to that voice, and rise to hear the word of condemnation pronounced upon them. The resurrection of the last day reveals the decision that each has made in life. The "works" of good and evil, alluded to in v 29, flow from the acceptance or rejection of the word of the Redeemer-Revealer, as in 3:16–21. The judgment of those who have not heard that word is not in view in this passage; it is intended for the encouragement or warning of those who have heard it. (Concerning the authenticity of vv 28–29, see the discussion of Schulz, *Untersuchungen*, 110–11, and his *Commentary*, 91; for their exposition Blank, *Krisis*, 172–82.)

30 The eschatological disclosure concludes by returning to its beginning, v 19. The dependence of the Son on his Father applies to the highest reach of his activity for the Father: the Father's will determines the judgment by the Son—on the last day and every day. His judgment therefore is always just, for it reveals the truth about everyman and fulfills the Father's will in relation to every man.

Witness to Jesus in Face of Jewish Unbelief (5:31–47)

The train of argument in this section is like a court scene, reminiscent of the trial scenes in the OT, when witnesses are summoned by Yahweh to testify on behalf of the gods of the nations in the face of the manifest truth of the only God, whose witnesses his people are (see esp. Isa 43:8–13; 44:6–11). Here Jesus stands opposed by the Jews, who demand witnesses to justify the claims of Jesus in his teaching. Jesus proceeds to call them, beginning with "Another," an unnamed person but one whose witness he knows to be true (v 32). That "Other" is God himself, who has provided the witnesses that follow: John the Baptist (33–35), the man sent from God for witness to the Light (1:6–7); the works of Jesus, which the Father had given him to do (36); and the word of God, which the Father attests through the Scriptures (37–40). This is followed by an indictment of the Jews for their rejection of the witness which God has borne to Jesus (41–47); the tables are turned, Jesus stands vindicated and the Jews condemned. With the thought of the passage cf. 1 John 5:8–12.

31–32 The opening sentence invites comparison with 8:13–18; there it is said that Jesus' self-testimony is in fact true, for he speaks what the Father communicates to him (8:16, 28; 12:49). Therefore, his self-testimony is in reality the joint testimony of the Father and the Son (8:17–18). The same thought lies behind the present passage. The Father's testimony is the only witness that matters, but in the trial setting envisaged, Jesus acknowledges the principle of Deut 19:15; since the Jews do not know the voice and form of the "other" Witness, he adduces three ways in which the Father bears a witness that the Jews can understand.

33–35 John the Baptist is named first, since Jewish representatives were sent to examine him (1:19–28). In contrast to 1:19–36 John's witness is played down here, for Jesus is dealing with those who rejected it; he adduces it, though it be but the witness of a man, in hope that the Jews might think on it again and be saved (v 34). Note the perfect μεμαρτύρηκεν; John's witness *remains* as evidence. For the image of the lamp, cf. 2 Sam 21:17; Ps 132:17–18.

37–40 The Father's witness is not to be thought of as immediate and separate from those named (e.g., the voice at the baptism and the transfiguration of Jesus, neither of which finds mention in this Gospel). The clue to what is in mind is seen in what follows: though the Jews acknowledged that they had not seen the form of God, they prided themselves on being the nation that heard the voice of God—at the giving of the Law at Sinai (Exod 19:16–25; Deut 4:11–12, 33). Jesus denied that claim to his contemporaries, for they do not have the word of God abiding in them (v 38), as is evident in their rejection of him whom the Father sent, to whom the Scriptures bear witness. The Father's witness in this paragraph is *his word in the Scriptures* (so Schlatter, 157; Bultmann, 266; Hoskyns, 273).

Ἐραυνᾶτε in v 39 should be taken as indicative, as δοκεῖτε: "You search the Scriptures because you suppose you have in them eternal life." The conviction is expressed frequently in rabbinic writings. *Pirqe ʾAbot* 27 reports Hillel as saying, "If a man . . . has gained for himself words of the Law, he has gained for himself life in the world to come." R. Akiba's witness is particularly significant; living after the destruction of the temple, his faith was essentially faith in the Scriptures. He stated, "God said: the word is not an 'idle' thing for you, Deut 32:47; and if it is idle for you, why is it so? Because you do not know how to search it, for you do not energetically occupy yourself with it. For it is your life. When is it your life? When you exert yourself with it" (*Gen. Rab.* 1.19, cited by Schlatter, *Der Glaube im NT,* 57). V 39 constitutes a denial of this view: "You suppose *wrongly* that you have life in them." The Scriptures were given by God to witness to the Christ, that his people might come to *him* and *through him* gain the life of which they give promise. To search the Scriptures and reject their testimony to Christ is to frustrate the purpose of God in giving it them.

41–44 The Jews addressed by Jesus have neither the word of God in them (v 38), nor the life of God (v 40), nor the love of God (v 42). Since this is so, they do not accept the one who comes in the name of God (v 43), though they are ready to accept one who comes in his own name. The language in v 43b is general; it is unlikely to refer to a particular individual, such as the Antichrist, the Devil, or some notorious figure of history.

45–47 The indictment closes with an astonishing statement, befitting the "amazing" revelations in the earlier part of the discourse (cf. v 28). For the Jews believed that as Moses acted as their intercessor at their apostasy over the golden calf (Exod 32:30–32), so he continued to intercede for them in heaven (see, e.g., *As. Mos.* 12:6: Joshua lamented Moses' impending departure, since Israel would have no advocate with God. Moses assured him, "The Lord hath on their behalf appointed me to pray for their sins and make intercession for them"). There is evidence that Jews looked for Moses to act as their intercessor in the final judgment (Meeks, *The Prophet-King,* 161); thus they "set their hope on him" (v 45). Jesus stated that, on the contrary, Moses would be their accuser, not defender; for "he wrote of me," and "you neither believe him nor me." The reference is not so much to any particular passage, such as Deut 18:15–18, but to the revelation of the divine will and promise in the Pentateuch as a whole (so most exegetes).

Explanation

1. The theme of 4:46–5:47 is Jesus as Mediator of Life and Judgment; that is, Christology and eschatology in their inseparable relationship. It is generally acknowledged that vv 17–30 are of crucial importance to both subjects. Haenchen considered that theologians of former years were singularly blind to the significance of the passage, and that not a few still have not grasped it, including Käsemann, with his view of the Christ of the Fourth Gospel as "God striding about the earth." The Evangelist reveals to us a Christ who, on the one hand, can neither utter a word nor perform an act without the Father's direction and enabling, and on the other, by virtue of that direction and enabling, performs the works of God, including the ultimate works of raising humanity for life in the perfected kingdom of God and for judgment. The polarities of the concept of Jesus as the Son of the Father are seen here with clarity: as the Son he owes his Father total obedience, but as the Son he is one with the Father. The paradox runs through the Gospel and appears most starkly expressed in the utterances of 14:28 and 10:30: "The Father is greater than I"; "I and the Father are one."

2. An important aspect of the relationship of the Son to the Father and to humanity is expressed in his function as Son of Man (v 27). For the Son

of Man in this Gospel is the Son in his role as eschatological Redeemer; he mediates the blessings of the kingdom to man (1:51), gives himself in death, and is exalted in resurrection to bring to a climax the mediation of the kingdom of God begun in his ministry in Judea and Galilee (see 3:14–16; 12:31–34). Admittedly there is no mention in our passage of the "lifting up" of the Son of Man to the throne of God, but the entire discourse (as all the discourses of the Gospel) moves on the assumption of the unity of the Son in his ministry with the Son in his exaltation. Indeed, the Evangelist in his reproduction of the discourse has in view the full sweep of the relationship of the Son to the Father as he carries out the ministry of the Son of Man. The Son gives life to whom he wills (v 21), alike in the days of his flesh, in the exaltation of his resurrection, and in the culmination of the ages, because the Father has given him to have "life in himself," just as the Father has life in himself (v 26). This implies both an ineffable communion of the Son and the Father, and a unique fellowship of the Son with human beings, whereby "life" for them means life *in the Son*. We are driven back to the thought of the prologue, where the Logos is one with God and Mediator of creation, so that in him was the life of humanity; so also the Son in his ministry in the flesh and in the Spirit is mediator of the new creation (1:3–4). The signs in the ministry of Jesus, not least those of 4:46–5:9, are pointers to the life which the Son of God gives, especially in the age initiated by Easter and the Spirit, in anticipation of resurrection to the fullness of being of which vv 28–29 speak. This last passage, we observed, is no intrusion of an alien hope; that hope is envisaged in 5:25, as in 11:25, and represents the culmination of the mediation of the Son of God–Son of Man. Every aspect of this Christology and Eschatology is foreshadowed in the synoptic Gospels (e.g., Matt 11:27//Luke 10:22; Mark 13:32; Luke 22:29; Mark 8:38 with its Q parallel Luke 12:8–9; Matt 10:32–33; Matt 25:31–46). But what for the latter is latent is for the Evangelist patent: Christology is the root of eschatology; eschatology is the outworking of the Christology of the only Son of the Father.

3. We have earlier observed that everything in this Gospel has been preached—and countless times! We may assume that 5:17–30 owes its present shape to its use in the defense and proclamation of Johannine preachers to Jews, who assailed the Christians for their understanding of the sabbath and still more their beliefs about Jesus. Similarly we may see in 5:31–47 a prime example of the missionary apologetic of Christians to Jews, who wanted to know on what basis they maintained their belief in Jesus as the promised Messiah of God. As in all such biblical testimony, appeal is made to the evidence of reason, but its end is the decision of faith. The witness of John the Baptist to Jesus has no power for the person who is deaf to the voice of prophecy, but it is of great moment to those who recognized in John a man sent from God. The "works," as signs authorized by the Father and performed by his power, were of greater significance to contemporary Jews, as may be seen in 2:23–32; 4:45. Their inclusion in this list of witnesses to Jesus is of importance as indicating the Evangelist's understanding of the validity of signs. Far from being of small value (as some exegetes maintain), they proceed from the Father's command and aid—they are *his* works, performed by the Son he has sent, and as such are revelations of the Father's will to save and

the nature of his salvation. For this reason they are set above the testimony of John, but their purpose is frustrated entirely if they do not lead to the obedience of faith. In this respect they are to be compared with the revelation of God in the Scriptures; they, too, are given as witnesses in order to lead to Christ.

The reference to the purpose of the Scriptures in vv 39–40 will have been of critical importance to the early Church. It entails a Christological interpretation and evaluation of the OT. This did not justify the creation of farfetched typologies, or mechanical listing of prophecies with fulfillments in the ministry of Jesus, though in the nature of things such activities were inevitable. It does affirm, however, that the intent of the entire Law (and Prophets and Psalms, Luke 24:44) finds its fulfillment and goal in Jesus, and that their purpose is realized when those who read them put their trust in the Christ to whom the OT bears witness, and so gain from him the life of which they give promise. This makes of the OT a different book for Christians from what it is for Jews; for the Christians see therein a revelation whose lines lead to the culmination of revelation in Jesus the Son of God, and through him they seek the fulfillment of the promises. In a very real way they endeavor to read the OT as the Evangelist bids us read the story of Jesus in the Gospel: to hear therein the testimony of the Father, to acknowledge its meaning for us today, to have trust in the Revealer, and to receive the blessings of the divine sovereignty. The Scriptures of both covenants bear testimony to Christ. That is their glory. It is also their limitation. They point to him, who alone can bind us to the Father and give the life.

D. Jesus the Bread of Life (6:1–71)

Bibliography

Barrett, C. K. "Das Fleisch des Menschensohnes." *Jesus und der Menschensohn.* FS A. Vögtle. 342–54. **Bligh, J.** "Jesus in Galilee." *HeyJ* 5 (1964) 3–21. **Borgen, P.** "The Unity of the Discourse in John 6." *ZNW* 50 (1959) 277–78. ———. "Observations on the Midrashic Character of John 6." *ZNW* 54 (1963) 232–40. ———. *Bread from Heaven: An Exegetical Study in the Concept of the Manna in the Gospel of John and the Writing of Philo.* Leiden: Brill, 1965. **Bornkamm, G.** "Die eucharistische Rede im Johannesevangelium." *ZNW* 47 (1956) 16–69. **Brooks, O. S.** "The Johannine Eucharist: Another Interpretation." *JBL* 82 (1963) 293–300. **Brown, R. E.** "The Eucharist and Baptism in John." *New Testament Essays.* Milwaukee: Bruce, 1968. 108–131. **Dunn, J. D. G.** "John 6: A Eucharistic Discourse?" *NTS* 17 (1971) 328–38. **Feuillet, A.** "The Principal Biblical Themes in the Discourse on the Bread of Life." *Johannine Studies.* Tr. Thomas E. Crane. Staten Island, N.Y.: Alba House, 1965. 53–128. **Fortna, R. T.** *The Gospel of Signs.* 55–70. **Gärtner, P.** *John 6 and the Jewish Passover.* ConNT 17. Lund: Gleerup, 1969. **Giblet, J.** "The Eucharist in St. John's Gospel." *Concilium* 4 (1969) 10/32–42. **Giffort, G.** "ἐπὶ τῆς θαλάσσης." *ExpTim* 40 (1928–29) 236. **Horsley, R. A.** "Popular Messianic Movements around the Time of Jesus." *CBQ* 46 (1984) 471–95. **Howard, J. K.** "Passover and Eucharist in the Fourth Gospel." *SJT* 20 (1967) 329–

37. **Jeremias, J.** "Joh. 6.51c–58—redaktionell?" *ZNW* 44 (1953) 256–57. ———. *The Eucharistic Words of Jesus.* Tr. N. Perrin. London: SCM, 1966. 106–8. **Johnston, E. D.** "The Johannine Version of the Feeding of the Five Thousand—An Independent Tradition?" *NTS* 8 (1961–62) 151–54. **Kilmartin, E. J.** "Liturgical Influence on John 6." *CBQ* 22 (1960) 183–91. **Klos, H.** *Die Sakramente im Johannesevangelium.* Stuttgart: Katholisches Bibelwerk, 1970. **Leenhardt, F. J.** "La structure du chapître 6 de l'Evangile de Jean." *RHPR* 39 (1959) 1–13. **Léon-Dufour, X.** "Le mystère du pain de vie (Jean VI)." *RSR* 46 (1958) 481–523. **Lindars, B.** "Word and Sacrament in the Fourth Gospel." *SJT* 29 (1976) 49–63. **MacGregor, G. H. C.** "The Eucharist in the Fourth Gospel." *NTS* 9 (1962–63) 111–19. **Malina, B. J.** *The Palestinian Manna Tradition.* Leiden: Brill, 1968. 42–93, 102–6. **Mollat, D.** "The Sixth Chapter of Saint John." *The Eucharist in the New Testament.* Tr. E. M. Stewart. Baltimore: Helicon, 1964. 143–56. **Montefiore, H.** "Revolt in the Desert." *NTS* 8 (1961–62) 135–41. **Porsch, F.** *Pneuma und Wort.* Frankfurt: Knecht 1974. 161–210. **Roloff, J.** *Das Kerygma und der irdische Jesus.* Göttingen: Vandenhoeck & Ruprecht, 1970. 237–69. **Schnackenburg, R.** "Das Brot des Lebens." *Tradition und Glaube.* FS K. G. Kuhn. Göttingen: Vandenhoeck & Ruprecht, 1971. 328–42. **Schürmann, H.** "Joh 6, 51c—ein Schlüssel zur grossen johanneischen Brotrede." *BZ* 2 (1958) 244–62. ———. "Die Eucharistie als Representation und Applikation des Heilsgeschehens nach Joh 6,53–59." *TTZ* 68 (1959) 30–45, 108–18; revised in *Ursprung und Gestalt.* Düsseldorf: Patmos, 1970. 167–84. **Schweizer, E.** "Das johanneische Zeugnis vom Herrenmahl." *Neotestamentica.* Zürich: Zwingli, 1963. 371–96. **Thyen, H.** "Aus der Literatur zum Johannesevangelium." *TR* 44 (1979) 97–110.

Translation

¹ *After this Jesus went off to the farther side of the Sea of Galilee*[a] (*i.e., Tiberias*), ² *and a large crowd was following him, because they were seeing the signs that he performed on the sick.* ³ *Jesus then went up the hillside and there he sat down with his disciples.* ⁴ *The Passover, the great festival of the Jews, was near. Jesus therefore,* ⁵ *raising his eyes and seeing that a great crowd was coming to him, says to Philip, "Where are we to buy bread that these people may eat?"*[b] ⁶ *But he said this to test him, for he himself knew what he was about to do.* ⁷ *Philip answered him, "Two hundred denarii worth of loaves is not enough for them that each may receive a little."* ⁸ *One of his disciples, Andrew, Simon Peter's brother, says to him,* ⁹ *"There's a little boy here who has five barley loaves*[c] *and two fishes, but what are they for so many?"* ¹⁰ *Jesus said, "Make the people sit down." Now there was much grass in the place.*[d] *The men therefore sat down, their number about five thousand.* ¹¹ *Jesus therefore took the loaves, and after giving thanks he distributed them to those who were sitting down, and the same with the fish, as much as they wanted.* ¹² *And when they were full he said to his disciples, "Collect up the pieces left over, so that nothing perish."* ¹³ *They collected them, therefore, and they filled twelve baskets with the pieces of the five barley loaves left over by those who had eaten.*

¹⁴ *When the men saw the sign*[e] *that he had performed they said, "This is in truth the prophet who was to come into the world."* ¹⁵ *Jesus therefore, knowing that they were about to come and seize him to make him king, fled*[f] *again to the hill country by himself, alone.*

¹⁶ *When it had become late his disciples went down to the sea,* ¹⁷ *and getting into a boat they set out for Capernaum, the other side of the lake. It had by now become dark and Jesus had not yet come to them;* ¹⁸ *moreover the sea was becoming whipped up, since a strong wind was blowing.* ¹⁹ *After rowing for about twenty-*

five or thirty stadia[g] *they see Jesus walking upon the sea and coming near the boat, and they became terrified.*

[20] *But he says to them, "I am (he), don't be afraid."* [21] *So they were ready to take him into the boat, and at once the boat came to the shore to which they were journeying.*

[22] *On the next day the crowd was standing on the far side of the sea. They knew that only one boat*[h] *had been there, and no other, and that Jesus had not entered with his disciples into the boat, but his disciples had gone off alone;* [23] *other*[i] *boats*[j] *from Tiberias came to land near the place where they ate the bread after the Lord had given thanks.*[k] [24] *When therefore the crowd saw that Jesus was not there, nor his disciples, they themselves got into boats and came to Capernaum, searching for Jesus.*

[25] *When they found him on the other side of the sea they said to him, "Rabbi, when did you get here?"* [26] *Jesus replied to them, "Amen, amen I tell you, you are searching for me not because you saw signs, but because you ate the loaves and had all you wanted.* [27] *You should work not for food that perishes but for food that lasts for eternal life, which the Son of Man will give*[l] *to you; for the Father has set his seal on him."* [28] *They said therefore to him, "What are we to do to work the works God wants?"* [29] *Jesus said in reply to them, "This is the work that God requires, to believe in him whom he sent."* [30] *They therefore said to him, "What sign then are you doing, that we may see it and believe you? What are you working?* [31] *Our fathers ate the manna in the desert, as it stands written, 'He gave them bread from heaven to eat.'"* [32] *Jesus said to them, "Amen, amen I tell you, it was not Moses who gave you the bread from heaven, but my Father gives you the true bread from heaven;* [33] *for God's bread is the bread that*[m] *comes down from heaven and gives life to the world."*

[34] *They said therefore to him, "Sir, give us this bread always."* [35] *Jesus said to them, "I am the bread of life; he who comes to me will never become hungry, and he who believes in me will never again become thirsty.* [36] *But as I told you, 'You have both seen me*[n] *and yet you do not believe.'* [37] *Everything that the Father gives me will come to me, and anyone who comes to me I shall not reject,* [38] *because I have come down from heaven not to do my own will but the will of him who sent me; and this is the will of him who sent me:* [39] *that I should lose nothing of what he has given me, but raise it on the last day.* [40] *For this is my Father's will, that everyone who sees the Son and believes in him should have eternal life, and I shall raise him on the last day."*

[41] *The Jews therefore were grumbling about him because he said, "I am the bread which came down from heaven,"* [42] *and they were saying, "This is Jesus, the son of Joseph, isn't it, whose father and mother*[o] *we know? How is he now saying, 'I have come down from heaven'?"* [43] *Jesus replied to them, "Do not keep on grumbling with one another.* [44] *Nobody can come to me unless the Father who sent me draws him, and I shall raise him up on the last day.* [45] *It stands written in the prophets, 'And they shall all be taught by God'; everyone who has heard from the Father and learned from him comes to me.* [46] *Not that anyone has seen the Father, other than he who is from God, he has seen the Father.* [47] *Amen, amen I tell you, he who believes*[p] *has eternal life.* [48] *I am the bread of life.* [49] *Your fathers ate the manna in the desert, and they died.* [50] *This is the bread which comes from heaven, that one may eat it and not die.* [51] *I am the living bread which came down from*

heaven; if anyone eats this bread he will live for ever; and the bread that I shall give is my flesh—given for the life of the world."

[52] *At this the Jews strove with one another, as they said, "How can this man give us his flesh to eat?"* [53] *Jesus therefore said to them, "Amen, amen I tell you, unless you eat the flesh of the Son of Man and drink his blood you do not have life in you.* [54] *Whoever eats my flesh and drinks my blood has eternal life, and I shall raise him up on the last day;* [55] *for my flesh is real*[q] *food, and my blood is real*[q] *drink.* [56] *Whoever eats my flesh and drinks my blood dwells in me and I in him.*[r] [57] *Just as the living Father sent me and I live because of the Father, so whoever eats me will live because of me.* [58] *This is the bread that came down from heaven, not as the fathers*[s] *ate and died; whoever eats this bread will live forever."*

[59] *These things he said while teaching in the synagogue in Capernaum.* [60] *Many of his disciples, accordingly, on hearing them said, "This teaching is impossible, who can listen to it?"* [61] *But Jesus, knowing in himself that his disciples were grumbling about this, said to them, "Does this create an offense for you?* [62] *What then will you do if you see the Son of Man ascending where he was formerly?* [63] *It is the Spirit who gives life, the flesh is useless; the words that I have spoken to you are Spirit and life.* [64] *But there are some among you who are not believing." For from the beginning Jesus knew who were not believing, and who was the one who would betray him.* [65] *And he said, "On this account I have told you, 'No one can come to me unless it be given him from the Father.' "*

[66] *From this time many of his disciples turned back and no longer continued to associate with him.* [67] *Jesus therefore said to the Twelve, "You men—you do not wish to go away also, do you?"* [68] *Simon Peter answered him, "Lord, to whom are we to go? You have words of eternal life,* [69] *and we have come to believe and to know that you are the Holy One*[t] *of God."* [70] *Jesus answered them, "I chose you, the Twelve, didn't I? Yet one of you is a devil."* [71] *But he was speaking about Judas, son of Simon Iscariot,*[u] *for he was about to betray him, one of the Twelve.*

Notes

[a] Some MSS omit τῆς Γαλιλαίας to avoid the double naming of the sea, others (including D θ) add after Γαλιλαίας, εἰς τὰ μέρη "to the regions of Tiberias," which changes the siting of the feeding miracle.

[b] Cf. the question of Moses in Num 11:13.

[c] Barley loaves are the bread of the poor; cf. 2 Kings 4:42.

[d] The mention of grass confirms the note in v 4: it was spring.

[e] p[75] B it[a] read ἀ . . . σημεῖα, pl. instead of sing., due presumably to the influence of 6:2.

[f] ℵ* with OL MSS vg etc., read φεύγει, "flees," instead of ἀνεχώρησεν, "withdrew." The UBS committee considered that the support for the former reading is too slender for its adoption (Metzger, 211–12), but most modern commentators hold that the common reading is an obvious softening of φεύγει (so, e.g., Hoskyns, 290; Bultmann, 214; Barrett, 278; Brown, 235; Schnackenburg is cautious—it "could well be original," 2:445, n.48).

[g] A stadion = 185 metres, roughly a furlong. According to Jos. the lake was 40 stadia wide and 140 long (*War* 3:506); it is now 61 stadia wide and 109 long, i.e., 7 miles by 12. The disciples had evidently been driven off course by the storm. For a suggestion as to their direction and position see Schnackenburg, 2:446 n.65.

[h] After ἐν a number of MSS read, with variations, "into which his disciples had entered," an attempted clarification of the text.

[i] Instead of ἄλλα ("other") many translators prefer to read ἀλλά ("however").

[j] For the confused alternative readings relating to the phrase πλοι[άρι]α ἐκ Τιβεριάδος, and the deductions that can be drawn from them, see Brown, 257–59.

k Some Western MSS omit "after the Lord had given thanks." While Western omissions are significant, the UBS committee was reluctant to omit the phrase (see Metzger, 212).

l For δώσει א D etc. read δίδωσιν, an assimilation to v 32b?

m ὁ καταβαίνων may be rendered "he who comes down," but the context favors referring it to ὁ ἄρτος τοῦ θεοῦ. The application to Jesus becomes evident in vv 35, 41.

n Some early authorities (א A it[a,b,e,q] OS) omit με, indicating thereby that "you have seen and do not believe" relates explicitly to the sign(s) seen by the hearers. The retention of με in this context would not entail a very different meaning.

o καὶ τὴν μητέρα is omitted by א* W etc., possibly accidentally, or in order to conform with the preceding clause ("Is not this the son of Joseph?").

p The reading ὁ πιστεύων without εἰς ἐμέ is supported by a formidable array of our earliest MSS. Metzger comments: "The addition . . . was both natural and inevitable; the surprising thing is that relatively many copyists resisted the temptation" (213).

q p[66] and many other authorities read ἀληθῶς instead of ἀληθής, but the latter is more strongly supported, and as the more difficult reading is to be accepted.

r After the end of the sentence D adds a typical Western expansion of the text: "As the Father is in me, I also am in the Father. Truly, truly I say to you, if you do not receive the body of the Son of man as the bread of life, you have no life in him" (cf. v 53 and 10:38).

s After οἱ πατέρες D adds ὑμῶν, other authorities further add τὸ μάννα, and some Syr. and Coptic MSS continue with ἐν τῇ ἐρήμῳ. These all appear to have been inspired by v 49.

t The variants of the title "Holy One of God" are a standing model of assimilation of texts in the Gospels. Tertullian reads instead ὁ Χριστός (= Mark 8:29); p[66] ὁ Χριστὸς ὁ ἅγιος τοῦ θεοῦ, combining Mark and John; Koine MSS have ὁ Χριστὸς ὁ υἱὸς τοῦ θεοῦ τοῦ ζῶντος (= Matt 16:16); Cyprian ὁ υἱὸς τοῦ θεοῦ (cf. John 1:29); some Caesarean MSS have ὁ Χριστὸς ὁ υἱὸς τοῦ θεοῦ, again reflecting Matt 16:16. The text adopted is read by p[75] א B C D L W etc.; it is unique in the gospel tradition, and is universally accepted today.

u Ἰσκαριώτου, agreeing with Σίμωνος, is read by p[66] p[75] B C L W etc., and is to be accepted rather than Ἰσκαριώτην, agreeing with Ἰούδαν. The name probably reproduces the Heb. אִישׁ קְרִיּוֹת (ʾîš qᵉrîyôt) "man of Kerioth," a Judaean town (cf. Josh 12:25), hence it could apply to both father and son. For other suggestions as to the name see Schnackenburg, 2:78.

Form/Structure/Setting

1. The chapter records two signs, the Feeding of the Multitude, vv 1–15, and the Walking on the Sea, 16–21; two dialogues, connected with a search for Jesus, 22–26, and a demand for a sign from heaven, 27–31; a discourse on the Bread of Life, 32–59; and finally two more dialogues, one with defecting disciples, 60–65, and the other with the Twelve, 66–71.

2. The two signs are nature miracles, the first of which is more fully described than the second. The narration of the Feeding miracle includes a statement of time and place of the event, 1–5a; a dialogue between Jesus and his disciples on meeting the need of the people, 5b–9; the action of Jesus, 10–11; its sequel in gathering the fragments left over, which confirmed the greatness of the miracle, 12–13; and the effect on the crowd, 14–15. The Walking on the Lake is more briefly described, and in contrast to the synoptic account is narrated from the point of view of the disciples. Their plight on the lake is described in 16–18, the appearance of Jesus to them, 19–21, and the sequel in an immediate landing, v 21. No comment is made as to the effect of this upon the disciples (contrast Mark 6:51, and still more Matt 14:33).

3. The discourse can be divided in many ways, as a perusal of the literature on it will show. Schürmann is content with two divisions, vv 26–51, 52–58 ("Joh 6:51c—ein Schlüssel," 244–45); Léon-Dufour also recognizes two sections, but makes them 35–47, 48–58 since they manifest a clear parallelism

("Pain de vie," 507–9). Leenhardt proposes a highly ingenious division of
three: the true Bread of heaven, 22–35; the true subjects and the true messianic
King, 36–47; the departure and return of the Son of Man, 48–71. These
three correspond to three episodes in 1–21, viz., the miracle of the loaves,
1–13; the attempt to make Jesus king, 14–15; the crossing of the sea, 16–
21. They also correspond to the three temptations of Jesus, as reported in
Luke 4:1–12 ("La structure du chapître 6," 1–13). A less sophisticated analysis
of the discourse is desirable. If we separate the two dialogues of 22–26, 27–
31 from the discourse proper we then observe that the paragraphs 32–35
and 48–51 are parallel and form a natural inclusion, so giving a certain unity
to this section. On this basis the following analysis may be offered:

    1a.   6:22–26: The search for Jesus.
    1b.   6:27–31: The demand for a sign from heaven and citation of Exod 16:15 in
           support.
    2a.   6:32–35: The true meaning of the Scriptures: Jesus the real Bread of Life.
    2b.   6:36–40: The demand for faith.
    2c.   6:41–47: The grumbling of the Jews and reiterated call for faith.
    2d.   6:48–51: Jesus the Bread of Life from heaven.
    2e.   6:52–59: The life-giving flesh and blood of Jesus.
     3.   6:60–71: The result of the revelation: defection from and confession of Jesus.

    4. While the discourse conforms to the pattern of sign(s) and discourse
observable elsewhere in the Gospel, it is primarily taken up with the significance
of the feeding miracle. Yet the meaning of the walking on the lake is also
presupposed; the main emphasis throughout the discourse is Christological;
Jesus is the Bread of Life precisely because he can utter the affirmation
Ἐγώ εἰμι (v 20).
    5. A curious feature of the discourse is that it begins by the lake (v 25)
and ends in the synagogue of Capernaum (v 59). This is consonant with the
mention of different groups in the audience: the crowd beside the lake, some
at least of which were present at the feeding miracle (25–26); the grumbling
"Jews" (41, 52); disciples of Jesus (61, 66); and the Twelve (67–71). It is
possible that the crowd of 25–27 was different from that of 30–31, hence
the request for the miracle of the manna to be repeated, in accordance with
the expectation that the Messiah would do that at his coming (so Brown,
following Boismard, 259)—but the issue is unclear. What is virtually certain
is that the discourse has been composed of sayings from various contexts
(and sources?), brought together to form a continuous whole.
    6. The connection of the discourse with the feeding miracle is complicated
by another feature, expounded at length by P. Borgen. He urges that from
v 31 onward we have a typical midrashic exposition of Scripture: Exod 16:15
is cited in v 31 to establish a position; the questioners' understanding of the
Scripture is corrected by Jesus (31–33); the clause "He gave them bread
from heaven" is expounded in 34–40; an exegetical debate follows, initiated
through an objection registered by hearers, wherein a further Scripture is
cited to strengthen the exposition already provided (41–48); the remainder
of the discourse elaborates the concept of "eating" the bread from heaven

(49–58). Borgen concludes from this that while the discourse draws on different sources it forms a unity in the midrashic tradition of interpreting the Scriptures (see Borgen's monograph, *Bread from Heaven,* and the two articles cited in the *Bibliography*). This view of the form of the discourse has commanded widespread assent, although it is also acknowledged that other factors have to be taken into account in the composition of the discourse, not least the influence of the Lord's Supper tradition, notably in vv 51–58. The belief that 51–58 represents a sacramental exposition *added* to the original discourse is maintained by many scholars from various viewpoints, some holding it to be from a later editor (as, e.g., Bultmann, 218–21; Haenchen, 331; Becker, 219–21), and others viewing it as an addition from the Evangelist himself (Brown, e.g., views 51–58 as a rewriting of the earlier discourse, 35–50, on the basis of a Johannine narrative of the institution of the Lord's Supper, 285–91). To us the whole chapter of signs and discourse appears to present a unity in progression, and so indicates the single hand of the Evangelist; this should become apparent as we move through the exposition and the *Explanation.*

7. The setting of the chapter is variously indicated "the other side of the Sea of Galilee/Tiberias," vv 3 and 15; the hill country (τὸ ὄρος), but close to the lake, v 15; Capernaum, v 24; and more specifically the synagogue in Capernaum, v 59. The "desert place" as scene of the feeding (Mark 6:31, 32, 36) is not mentioned by the Evangelist: the idea that the feeding miracle is a repetition of the nourishment of Israel in the wilderness gives way to the controlling thought of the miracle as a sign of the fulfillment of the hope of the new Exodus brought about by Jesus. The mention of the proximity of the Passover in v 4 naturally includes this concept, but yet more strongly hints of the sacrificial death of the Lamb of God, which is fundamental to vv 51–58. (So Hoskyns: "The movement from the miracle to the discourse, from Moses to Jesus [vv 32–35, cf. 1:17], and, above all, from *bread* to *flesh,* is almost unintelligible unless the reference in v 4 to the Passover picks up 1:29, 36, anticipates 19:36 [Exod 12:46; Num 9:12], and governs the whole narrative" [281].)

8. Here the relation of the chapter to the synoptic accounts should be considered. An unusual number of contacts between chap. 6 and the synoptic narratives are observable. In Mark 6 the feeding of the five thousand is immediately followed by the walking on the sea, as in John 6. Mark's second feeding narrative (8:1–8) is followed by a demand from Pharisees for a sign from heaven (8:11), which is closely related to John 6:30, and a dialogue on "leaven" and "bread," which alludes to the meaning of the feeding miracles (8:14–21), and Peter's Confession of Jesus as the Messiah (8:27–30), which forms an equivalent of Peter's confession in John 6:66–71. There are also striking contacts in the descriptions of the two "signs" in the synoptics and the Fourth Gospel (for comparative statements of these see Dodd, *Historical Tradition,* 196–211; Brown, 236–50). These comparisons have led many scholars to assume a dependence of the Fourth Evangelist on the records of the other three evangelists (a view vigorously maintained by Barrett, 271); more recently, however, the conviction has increased that John was dependent rather on traditions parallel to those of the synoptists rather than on any or all of the

three synoptic accounts (see, e.g., Bultmann, 210; Dodd, *Historical Tradition*, 196–222; Schnackenburg, 2:21–23, 28; Fortna, 63, 66).

Comment

THE FEEDING OF THE MULTITUDE (6:1–15)

That the event was an act of compassion on the part of Jesus is not mentioned by John (contrast Mark 8:2–3), but may have been assumed. The Christological emphasis within the chapter is emphasized from the outset in the initiative taken by Jesus (v 5), his knowledge of what he intends to do (v 6), and even his distribution of the bread and the fish (v 11; no mention is made of distribution through the apostles).

The statement as to the nearness of the Passover (v 4), the identification of Jesus as the prophet who should come (cf. Deut 18:15), and the discussion on the bread from heaven within the discourse (vv 31–33) combine to indicate that the feeding miracle is understood as falling within the fulfillment of the hope of a second Exodus. This flows together with the thought of the event as a celebration of the feast of the kingdom of God, promised in the Scriptures (Isa 25:6–9). The eschatological significance of the sign is thus doubly underscored, and is part of its fundamental connection with the Lord's Supper, which also is eschatologically oriented (cf. especially Luke 22:16, 18, 20, 29–30; within the discourse vv 39, 40, and esp. 54).

14–15 That the feeding was not a purely natural event, prompted for example through an encouragement to share available resources, but an act of God is assumed throughout the narrative, and underscored by the response of the crowd described in vv 14–15. It is scarcely to be doubted that the Evangelist viewed the attempt to make Jesus king as causally connected with the sign. The step from a prophet like Moses (v 14), the first Redeemer and worker of miracles, to a messianic deliverer was a short one for enthusiasts in contemporary Israel to make. Horsley has traced popular messianic movements in Israelite history that reflected the continuity of the hope among the populace, especially the peasantry, of a king who should lead them in a movement of liberation from their oppressors—from the kind of tyrant that Herod was, as well as from the Romans in the time of Jesus. Josephus speaks of leaders of popular revolts in this era, who "donned the diadem" or "claimed the kingship" or "were proclaimed king" by their followers; these, comments Horsley, were "clearly messianic pretenders, to be understood against the background of longstanding Jewish tradition of popular anointed kingship" ("Popular Messianic Movements around the Time of Jesus," 484). Montefiore, in an article linking these expectations to the feeding miracle, suggested that the falling away of the disciples in 6:66 is strongly connected with this feature; Jesus' refusal to accede to the multitude's demands must be reckoned as one of the turning points in his ministry, for from this time Jesus and the crowds parted company ("Revolt in the Desert?" 140–41). Dodd strongly supported this understanding of the event; he suggested that the danger of Jesus being made a leader of a movement of revolt by the turbulent Galileans was a feature that the evangelists preferred to gloss over, but which John chose to preserve (*Historical Tradition*, 213–15, 221–22). In that the Evangelist did choose to mention it, the function of the discourse to reveal the nature of Jesus' messiahship and his function as giver of *spiritual* bread of the kingdom of God is very much in place. This may well have contributed to the Evangelist's decision to place the sacramental teaching in this setting and not in the Upper Room.

The Walking on the Sea (6:16–21)

The reason for the disciples' departure alone is not stated by the Evangelist in v 16, but it is fairly evident: they were sent by Jesus out of the dangerous situation described in v 15. The disciples, too, were Jews, sharing their contemporaries' understanding of the Messiah and his work, and they needed to be prevented from becoming embroiled in a threatened messianic uprising.

19 Contrary to Bernard (185) and many others since his writing, we are not to understand that when the disciples saw Jesus walking ἐπὶ τῆς θαλάσσης, he was walking beside the sea. Certainly we read in 21:1 an appearance of the risen Lord ἐπὶ τῆς θαλάσσης, where the context makes it plain that Jesus was on the shore (21:4 states that Jesus stood εἰς τὸν αἰγιαλόν, "on the beach"). Mark 6:47 uses precisely the same wording as the Fourth Evangelist, following the declaration that the boat was "in the midst of the sea" (6:47); Matthew writes first that Jesus was walking ἐπὶ τὴν θάλασσαν (accusative), then that he was walking ἐπὶ τῆς θαλάσσης (Matt 14:25). Had our Evangelist wished to correct an earlier misstatement or misunderstanding of the event, he could easily have written that Jesus was walking παρὰ τὴν θάλασσαν (so Giffort, "ἐπὶ τῆς θαλάσσης," 36; for examples of that phrase cf. Mark 1:14; Acts 10:6). In reality he was concerned to do something quite different, as v 20 makes plain; there he records Jesus as appearing to his disciples on the sea with the words Ἐγώ εἰμι. He may have had in mind Job 9:8, but more obviously Ps 77:16, 19, which speaks of God coming in powerful theophany to the aid of his people at the Exodus: "The waters saw thee, O God, they saw thee and writhed in anguish. . . . Thy path was through the sea, thy way through mighty waters. . . ." The Evangelist was describing an event in which he saw Jesus as the revelation of God coming to his disciples in distress—*in the second Exodus!*

20 For the meaning of Ἐγώ εἰμι, see the lengthy note of Bultmann, 225–26, in which he conveniently summarizes the ways in which the phrase was used in the ancient world. He distinguishes four chief usages: (*i*) as a *presentation formula*, which replies to the question, "Who are you?" and in which the speaker introduces himself as so and so; (*ii*) as a *qualificatory formula*, which answers the question, "What are you?", to which the reply is, "I am that and that"; (*iii*) as an *identification formula*, in which the speaker identifies himself with another person or object; (*iv*) as a *recognition formula*, answering the question, "Who is the one expected, asked for, spoken to?", to which the reply is, "I am he." In this last, unlike the previous three, the ἐγώ is predicate, not subject. In Bultmann's view, the Ἐγώ εἰμι statements of John 6:35, 41, 48, 51; 8:12; 10:7, 9, 11, 14; 15:1, 5 employ the recognition formula, while those of 11:25 and 14:6 are probably an identification formula.

The absolute use of the expression is particularly striking (in 6:20; 8:24, 28, 58; 13:19). While it is clear that in 6:20 Jesus is identifying himself to the fearful disciples, the usage in the passages just mentioned indicates a unique relation to God, recalling the divine name in Exod 3:14 and the affirmations of Deutero-Isaiah (e.g., 43:10–11; 45:5–6, 18, 21–22). In these affirmations of Jesus we find not identification of himself with God, but an expression of himself as "God's eschatological revealer in whom God utters himself" (Schnackenburg, 2:88). The combinations of Ἐγώ εἰμι with various symbols (Jesus as the bread of life, light of the world, door (of the sheep), the good shepherd, the resurrection, the way, the truth and the life, the vine—seven utterances!) may be said to summarize his role in revelation and in salvation. For further discussions Isa 43:10 is particularly significant in this regard: "You are my witnesses, says the Lord . . . that you may know and believe me and understand that *I am he*." This last phrase, in Hebrew אֲנִי הוּא (ʾanî hûʾ), is rendered in the LXX as ἐγώ εἰμι. In this context "I am he" is an abbreviation for the expression in the next line, "I, I am the Lord"; not surprisingly אֲנִי הוּא "I am he," can appear as a substitute for אֲנִי יְהוָה (ʾanî Yhwh), "I am the Lord." There is indeed evidence that the expression אֲנִי הוּא came to be regarded as the name of God. Isa 43:25, "I, I am he who blots out your transgressions" appears in the LXX as ἐγώ εἰμι ἐγώ εἰμι ὁ ἐξαλείφων τὰς ἀνομίας σου, "I am 'I AM,' who blots out your transgressions." There were other related developments in the use of the divine name among the Jews which must be noticed later; it suffices here to observe that there was a direct line from אֲנִי הוּא through the LXX ἐγώ εἰμι to the ἐγώ εἰμι of the Fourth Gospel (so E. Zimmermann, "Das absolute Ἐγώ εἰμι," 270–71). The occurrences of ἐγώ εἰμι in sayings of Jesus indicate not an identification of himself with God but a solidarity or union with him, expressions of himself as "God's eschatological Revealer in whom God utters himself" (Schnackenburg, 2:88). The combinations of ἐγώ εἰμι with various symbols may be said to summarize his role in revelation and salvation. For further discussions concerning the expression see E. Schweizer, Ἐγώ εἰμι (Göttingen: Vandenhoeck, 1939); D. Daube, "The 'I am' of the Messianic Presence," *The New Testament and Rabbinic Judaism*, 325–29; Dodd, *Interpretation*, 93–96, 349–50; H. Zimmermann, "Das absolute Ἐγώ εἰμι als die ntliche Offenbarungsformel," *BZ* NF 4 (1960) 54–69, 266–76; Brown, 533–38; Schnackenburg, 2:79–89.

THE SEARCH FOR JESUS (6:22–26)

The statement in vv 22–24 is difficult to unravel with certainty. While some would explain it by attributing vv 22 and 25 to the original source and 23–24 to the Evangelist or another hand (see Bultmann, 217; Fortna, 68), it is perhaps simplest to view v 23 as a parenthesis. The statement serves as an indirect confirmation of the sign of the crossing of the lake; the crowd knew that one boat only was at the place where the disciples had embarked and that jesus did not go with them; hence, they were perplexed as to what had happened to Jesus. This "crowd," of course, is not to be identified with the entire multitude that had been present at the feeding miracle; it was not an armada that crossed the Lake to find Jesus!

26 The reply of Jesus to the question of those who sought him is brusque: they had searched for him, not because they "saw signs" but because they had full bellies and wanted more. Having failed to see the meaning of the feeding miracle, they had simply been mystified by the disappearance of Jesus.

THE DEMAND FOR A SIGN FROM HEAVEN (6:27–31)

27–31 The thought of the paragraph is controlled by the terms "work" and "bread." Hoskyns observed that the discourse sets out from the straightforward fact that Galilean peasants worked to get their bread (292). That is hardly the case. Jesus told the people to "work" for "bread that lasts for eternal life," i.e., that results in obtaining eternal life. The "work" of which Jesus speaks is of a spiritual kind that can receive the spiritual bread. This the Son of Man alone can give, since God has "set his seal on him," i.e., as the Mediator of the kingdom of redemption. The hearers, as they were Jews, interpret the "works which God demands" as works of the Law, which God will reward with life eternal. They learn, however, that the "work" God wants is faith in the one whom God has sent. Their response to this affirmation is nothing less than a challenge: "What are *you* 'working' to warrant such belief? What accrediting sign have you to show that you are from God?" Their citing of the Scripture that speaks of God giving Israel "bread from heaven" (Exod 16:15, modified by Neh 9:15 and Ps 78:24) presupposes the current teaching that the Messiah, the "second Redeemer" (after Moses, the first Redeemer), will at his coming restore the manna to Israel (so *Midr. Qoh.* 1:9, "As the first Redeemer brought down the manna . . . so will also the last Redeemer cause the manna to come down"). The implication is plain: if Jesus be God's deliverer, let him perform *that* sign!

The reader may well ask: How can people who experienced the miracle of the loaves ask for that sign, since in essence it had already been given! Some observations may be to the point here. Jesus in v 26 declares that those who sought him had not "seen" the sign of the loaves; they had merely experienced full stomachs and gotten excited. The interlocutors of v 30 may well not have been present at the miracle, but merely heard about it (note the interruptions in vv 41 and 52 of hostile 'Jews," who rejected the entire teaching of the discourse). Moreover the characterization of the bread-manna as "from heaven" is significant; Jesus, in the view of the questioners, had given mere bread in the wilderness (or so people said). "Let the *manna from heaven* rain down again upon us" reminds of the request of Pharisees, recorded at this point in Mark 8:11, for a sign 'from heaven:" they were not satisfied with an act that could be inspired "from below," i.e. by Beelzebub (cf. Mark 3:22); they wanted a demonstration that was clearly "from heaven," i.e., from God.

THE REAL BREAD OF LIFE (6:32–35)

32–33 The first thing that Jesus does (in harmony with Jewish exegetical method, see Borgen, *Bread from Heaven*, 61–67) is to correct the erroneous interpretation of the Scripture cited: (*i*) Contrary to contemporary assumptions, the bread from heaven was given not by Moses but by the Father (note the language of the Midrash: "As the first Redeemer *brought down* the manna . . . so will the last Redeemer. . . .") (*ii*) The Father gives the *true* bread from heaven, and he gives it now. (*iii*) This bread of God is "that which comes down from heaven and gives life to the world," i.e., it gives the life of the age to come, the kingdom of God.

34–35   With v 34, a typical "Johannine misunderstanding," cf. 4:15. Bread for the stomach is still in mind! The misunderstanding is corrected in v 35, which unveils the truth of the two signs narrated in vv 1–21: "I am the Bread of Life." This is the first of the seven Ἐγώ εἰμι sayings with a predicate in the Gospel. Jesus is the Bread which gives and sustains "life," the life of the kingdom of God. This he bestows on those who "come" to him and who "believe" in him—the synonymous parallelism is unmistakable. One who so "comes" and "believes" will "never hunger" and "never, never thirst" (the negatives οὐ μή and οὐ μή πώποτε are very strong). For this use of the symbolism of eating and drinking, cf. Isa 55:1, of the eschatological salvation through the word of God; Prov 6:5, of wisdom; and especially Sir 24:21:

> Whoever feeds on me will be hungry for more,
> and whoever drinks from me will thirst for more.

Here, too, wisdom is in mind, although the writer significantly immediately identifies it with the Torah. Jewish teachers frequently spoke of the Law as "bread"; there are indications that some at least also identified the manna with the Torah (so Philo in *Mut.* 253–63; and especially *Mek. Exod.* 13:17: "The Holy One, blessed be he, said, 'If I now suffer Israel to enter the land, then they will at once seize each his field and each his vineyard and be idle in the study of the Torah. Instead I will lead them about in the desert for forty years that they may eat manna and drink the water of the well and (thereby) the Torah will be united [= assimilated] with their body,' " cited in Odeberg, 243). If this interpretation was current in the first century of our era, as is likely, v 35 may yet be another example of the maxim, "The Law was given through Moses, grace and truth came through Jesus Christ" (1:17; so Dodd, *Interpretation,* 336–37).

THE DEMAND FOR FAITH (6:36–40)

36–37   The passage begins with a charge that the hearers of Jesus have "seen" yet not believed. They had witnessed the miracle, but they did not believe, for they saw nothing beyond loaves and power. To see and not believe is tantamount to a refusal of faith. But there are those whom the Father "gives" to Jesus; they are "given," since "faith is God's work" (Schlatter, 175). Such are not "cast out" (contrast Matt 8:12), for Jesus pledges his care for them; it is possible that the image of the shepherd and his flock is in view at this point, cf. 10:9–11, 26–30.

38–40   Herein lies the reason for his "descent," i.e. for his Incarnation; he is charged to lose none of those given him by the Father, but to give them eternal life now and to raise them in the last day. There is no contradiction between the gift of life now and resurrection in the future. The duality of present and future participation in the kingdom of God is fundamental to the proclamation of Jesus in all four Gospels, in this no less than in the other three, as also in the proclamation about Jesus in the rest of the NT. Contrary to Bultmann and many of his followers, no redactor is needed to account for the references to the last day in this discourse (vv 39, 40, 44, 54).

A Reiterated Call to Grumblers (6:41–47)

41 "Grumbling" at God and his messengers was characteristic of the Jews in their wilderness wanderings. It is recorded that they grumbled about the water they had to drink (Exod 15:24), at their lack of bread (Exod 16:2) and water (Exod 17:3), at their hardships in the desert (Num 11:1), at the difficulties in occupying the promised land (Num 14:1–3), and even against the manna (Num 11:4–6). The psalmist, singling out the last item, saw it as a rejection of the voice of the Lord, i.e., of God himself; so here the grumbling against the message of Jesus is a rejection of Jesus himself. The objection voiced is against his claim to be the bread come down from heaven. The feature of "bread" is not at this point contested; it is the claim to have come down "from heaven" that appears impossible, as vv 38 and 41 make clear. The Incarnation of the Son of God in Jesus was and remains the great stumbling block in Christianity for the Jews.

44 To this Jesus replies, in harmony with vv 37 and 39, that only they whom the Father "draws" can come to him; in them the promise of Isa 54:13 is fulfilled—they are "taught of God." This leads Bultmann to interpret the "drawing" by God as taking place when man abandons his own judgment and "hears" and "learns" from the Father, and so allows God to speak to him: "The 'drawing' by the Father occurs not, as it were, *behind* man's decision of faith, but in it" (232). Like the related Jer 31:34, the quoted prophecy relates to the knowledge of God in the last days. They have arrived! Those who listen to the Father "come" to the Son, since he, and he alone, has seen the Father (1:18). For such, v 47 contains a word of promise; to the "grumblers" it is an implicit appeal to receive the word, to believe, and so to gain the life (cf. 5:39–40).

Jesus the Bread of Life from Heaven (6:43–51)

The paragraph returns to the theme of vv 32–35; it thus forms with the latter an inclusion for the whole passage (32–51), and develops its thought with reference to the purpose of the Incarnation and death of Christ. While the "Bread from heaven" of Exod 16:15 is again to the fore (cf. v 31) the emphasis now falls on *eating* the bread. Strangely, the term "eat" has not been mentioned since the Scripture citation in v 31; it now appears in vv 49, 50, 51 and in each sentence of the next paragraph other than v 55, where it is also presupposed.

49–51 Whereas the Jews of the wilderness generation ate the manna and died in the desert (v 49), the bread of heaven which is Jesus has appeared that people may eat and *not* die (v 50). Whoever eats it will live "unto the age," and so enjoy the eternal life of the kingdom of God (v 51). The contrasting statements serve to warn the hearers (and readers!) lest they share the fate of the forefathers and to appeal to them to "eat" and live. The latter alternative is possible on two grounds: (*i*) the "living bread" has descended from heaven, i.e., he is the Incarnate One who has life in himself for others (cf. 5:26); (*ii*) the "bread" is the flesh of the Incarnate One which he is to give on behalf of the life of the world, i.e., he is to die that the world may live.

The "bread" is defined as "flesh" rather than the "body," almost certainly

by reason of the Evangelist's insistence that the Word became *flesh* (1:14).
But the conjunction of the terms "give," "flesh," and "on behalf of" in v
51c strongly suggests a sacrificial death for the sake of others (observe the
use of ὑπέρ of the death of Christ in 10:11, 15 on behalf of the flock; in
11:50–51 on behalf of the Jewish people; in 11:52 on behalf of the nations;
in 17:19 on behalf of the disciples). We should also recall the Passover context
for the feeding of the multitude (v 4): he who is the Living Bread is to die
as the Lamb of God for the sin of the world (1:29). It is characteristic of
this Gospel, however, that the emphasis in the passage falls not on Christ's
death *for sin* but on his death for *life:* "my flesh . . . for the life of the world."
The death of the Redeemer is a "lifting up" for the purpose of drawing all
men to himself, and so into his eternal glory (12:31).

The question whether v 51c completes the foregoing section or begins a new
one ending at v 58 has been much debated. A majority of scholars decide for the
latter alternative, convinced that 51c is a Johannine version of Jesus' saying about
the bread at the Last Supper (cf. Luke 22:19; 1 Cor 11:24), and that it fittingly
introduces a eucharistic discourse in vv 53–58. Schürmann, while agreeing that
53–58 form a eucharistic discourse, views 51c as bringing to a conclusion the "metaphorical discourse" of 26–51 through an adaptation of the "bread-word" of the
Eucharist. He rightly points out that in this Gospel the concept of the Incarnation
tends to the thought of the death of the Incarnate One, as in 3:13–16; from this
viewpoint he urges that a discourse without allusion to the saving death of Christ
would hardly be a Johannine revelation discourse ("Joh 6,51c—ein Schlüssel zur
grossen johanneischen Brotrede," 245–57). Whether indeed 53–58 should be
sharply separated from 32–51 is a moot point, but the suitability of 51c to bring
to a climax the preceding train of thought is clear (so Sanders, 192–94; Lindars,
253; Schnackenburg, 2:54–55; Bruce, 158).

The idea that the term "flesh" in 51c reflects the original use of the Aramaic
בשרא (bisrā') "flesh" in the original tradition of the Institution of the Lord's Supper
is widespread (see e.g. Jeremias, *Eucharistic Words of Jesus,* 198–201). Schürmann,
in another context, has given weighty reason to doubt the notion (see his *Einsetzungs-
bericht Lk 22: 19–20,* pt. 2 [Münster: 1955]). The Evangelist's use of σάρξ reflects
his emphasis on the reality of the Incarnation, and so on the reality of the death
of the Incarnate One, as in 19:34.

THE LIFE-GIVING FLESH AND BLOOD OF JESUS (6:52–59)

52 Schnackenburg (2:60) points out that the Exodus narrative records
that the Jews not only *grumbled* at God and his servants for their hardships
(see *Comment* on v 41), but also *strove* with them (e.g. Exod 17:2, against
Moses; Num 20:3, against the Lord; the Hebrew term is ריב (rîb) often
translated by μάχεσθαι, which is here used). In like manner, their successors
first grumble at Jesus, then in their fury "fight" over his words. In colloquial
American, they were "mad" at him! (Were there some who supported Jesus
in the quarrel? We cannot tell.)

53 The saying in v 53 expresses the thought of v 51 in a negative form
(Barrett, 298), but it advances on the former by paralleling eating the flesh
of Jesus with drinking his blood. This may be viewed as a development of v
35 in the light of v 51: he who "comes" never *hungers,* and he who "believes"
never *thirsts.* Coming and believing are replaced by eating and drinking, and
the satisfaction of hunger and thirst with possession of life within, for the

object of faith is Christ in his sacrificial offering of body and blood for the life of the world. So interpreted the saying is strictly in line with the development perceptible in vv 35, 40, 50, 51, the image of eating the bread of life increasing in intensity. Accordingly it is not necessary to interpret the statement exclusively in terms of the body and blood of the Lord's Supper. Nevertheless it is evident that neither the Evangelist nor the Christian readers could have written or read the saying without conscious reference to the Eucharist; to say the least, they would have acknowledged it as supremely fulfilled in the worship event. This twofold reference of the words, however, should guard us against deducing from them the unconditional necessity of eating and drinking the eucharistic elements in order to "have eternal life in yourselves" (a view maintained alike by many Catholics and by certain critical exegetes who reject the teaching as contrary to that of the Evangelist).

54 The term τρώγω is often used of animals gnawing, nibbling, or munching food, but it is used also of ordinary human eating. It is common to view the use of the term here as emphasizing a genuine eating of the flesh of Christ in the Lord's Supper, in conscious opposition to the Docetists, who denied that such was possible. (Schnackenburg cites Ignatius on his Docetist opponents: "They keep away from the Eucharist and prayers because they do not admit that the Eucharist is the flesh of our Redeemer Jesus Christ which suffered for our sins," *Smyrn.* 7:1.) The anti-Docetist slant of the passage is apparent, but is not the supposed meaning of τρώγω. It has been noted frequently that the term ἐσθίω occurs in none of the Johannine writings; its place, as frequently in other writings, is taken by τρώγω as the present tense of the aorist ἔφαγον. So we find in John 13:18 that the citation from Ps 40:10, ὁ ἐσθίων ἄρτους μου is replaced by ὁ τρώγων μου τὸν ἄρτον, where no more than a symbol of friendship is in view. An insistence therefore on the eucharistic emphasis of τρώγω here does not accord with the linguistic evidence. (Note that in v 58 ἔφαγον and τρώγων are set in synonynous parallelism.)

55 "Real" (ἀληθής) here denotes "really are what flesh and blood should be," i.e., in fulfilling the ideal function of food and drink in giving eternal life (Barrett, 299).

56 The eating and drinking of Christ's flesh and blood result in mutual "abiding" of the believer and Christ. This is very close to the Pauline conception of κοινωνία (cf. Gal 2:19–20), and indicates a personal relationship of faith. Schlatter's statement on this passage warrants pondering: "What we have to do with his flesh and blood is not chew and swallow, but that we recognize in his crucified body and poured out blood the ground of our life, that we hang our faith and hope on that body and blood and draw from there our thinking and our willing" (*Das Evangelium nach Johannes,* Erläuterungen 3:116).

57 The relation to Christ of the believer who so "eats" is analogous to that of the Son and the Father. As the Son lives "through the Father," i.e., has his life from and is sustained by the Father, so the believer has life from and is sustained by the Son. This is the consequence for humanity of the Son acting as the Mediator between God and man; the Father has given to the Son to have life in himself, and through him alone can that divine life be known by man.

58 The discourse concludes with a summary statement that harks back to its beginning (v 31): the bread from heaven is the Christ in his incarnate life and redemptive death, alike Revealer and Redeemer, giving life where death reigned. The saying refers back to vv 32–35 and also gathers up the thought of vv 53–57. While we may not be so confident as Schnackenburg that the primary allusion of the statement is to the Eucharist, and therefore that "life" is obtained through Christ "in faith and in the eucharist" (2:64), we may readily concur with him in his final statement on the issue; "The eating of the eucharistic bread is the final acting out of the eating mentioned in the text of 31" (2:65).

THE RESULT OF THE REVELATION: DEFECTION AND CONFESSION (6:60–71)

The teaching of the discourse is declared to be "impossible," not only by Jewish opponents and spectators but also by disciples of Jesus, who share in the general "grumbling." The reference in v 62 to the "ascent" of the Son of Man, the counterpart of the descent, to which objection is made in vv 41–42, indicates that these disciples share the Jewish objection to this teaching, as well as to that concerning the flesh and blood of the Son of Man in vv 53–58. The "impossible teaching," accordingly, embraces the whole discourse from v 35 onward.

62   The reply of Jesus in v 62 carries a dual application. They who stumble at the doctrine of the descent of one who calls himself the Living Bread, who gives himself for the life of the world, are to be confronted with a terrible and awesome phenomenon: they will see the Son of Man ascend where he was before. We have learned about this event earlier. The Son of Man is to be "lifted up" (3:14), and the world will be divided before him (12:31–32). They who deny the descent will look upon it as the final ground of rejection, whereas they who can "see" signs may see in this event the ultimate sign which illuminates all their problems; for that "lifting up" by human hands of Jesus on a cross will be recognized as the exaltation by God of the Son of Man, via resurrection, to the throne of God, so making possible a blessed eating and drinking of the flesh and blood of the Son of Man. We may be sure that the Evangelist will have had in mind here, as throughout the discourse, disciples in the church who found this teaching difficult: for them vv 62–63 could lead to the falling of scales from the eyes.

63   Following on vv 53–58 this saying is startlingly unexpected. It is wholly implausible to view it as a repudiation of all sacramentalism, particularly of that represented in the previous paragraph (in the view of some, it provides evidence that 53–58 come from a later hand). The accent in the saying falls on the life-giving Spirit. The flesh alone, even of the Son of Man, does not achieve the end which God has purposed, namely of giving life to the world (= "profits nothing"). Just as the Incarnation of the Son of God is not to be abstracted from its end in crucifixion-resurrection for the life of the world, so both are bound up with the sending of the Spirit for the union of God and man in Christ in the kingdom of God. As Schürmann observed: "It is not simply as $\sigma\acute{\alpha}\rho\xi$, as the Incarnate One who goes to his death, that Jesus is $\acute{o}$ $\ddot{\alpha}\rho\tau os$ $\tau\hat{\eta}s$ $\zeta\omega\hat{\eta}s$; exaltation and sending of the Spirit must also take place" (259). The words of Jesus in the discourse are "Spirit and life"—for those who receive them in faith, since they who accept them and believe in the Son receive the Spirit and the life of which he speaks (5:39–40 and 7:37–39).

66 The explanation in vv 62–63 fails to satisfy the "grumbling" disciples; like the grumbling Jews (vv 41, 52), they reject the teaching of Jesus and desert him. This represents an extraordinary reversal of the excitement engendered by the feeding miracle. The crowds who wanted to make Jesus king melt away when he makes it plain that his kingdom is not of this world, and the disappointed disciples who cannot stomach his teaching join them. P. J. Temple comments: "Those who wanted a temporal king who would give them food for the body turned their backs on the King's Son when he promised a banquet truly royal for the soul" ("The Eucharist in John 6," 451).

67–69 The context of Peter's confession of Jesus as the Sent One of God is more dramatic than that in the synoptics and reflects the deep tension of the situation (Dodd held this to be an authentic reminiscence of an all-but-forgotten tradition of the crisis in the ministry of Jesus: *Historical Tradition,* 220–22). The negative force of μή in Jesus' question conveys a certain pathos, which should be retained: "You (plural) also do not wish to go away, do you?" Peter's reply on behalf of the Twelve yields three separable assertions: (*i*) There's no one else to go to! They who have (truly) seen and (truly) heard Jesus know that there is none beside him (cf. Isa 46:9; Acts 4:12). (*ii*) Jesus speaks words that give to those who receive them the life of the world to come. (*iii*) The early enthusiastic expression of faith and hope has grown to fuller faith and knowledge (observe the perfect tense in v 69, πεπιστεύκαμεν and ἐγνώκαμεν); they now really believe and have come to know that Jesus is "the Holy One of God."

The title is no ordinary messianic designation. That is "holy" which belongs to God; hence, "Jesus stands over against the world simply as the One who comes from the other world and belongs to God" (Bultmann, 449). Standing in that unique relation to God, he embodies the holiness of God, whom Israel confessed as "the Holy One of Israel." To confess Jesus as the Holy One of God accordingly is to give faith's response to the utterance of Jesus in v 21: "I am." In the context of the Gospel as a whole, the Holy One of God, who has been consecrated by the Father and sent into the world (10:36), brings his mission to its God-ordained culmination in consecrating himself as a sacrifice for the world (17:19). He is the holy Redeemer.

70–71 As in Mark 8:33, the acknowledgment of Jesus as the One sent of God to bring life through his death ends on a note of profound disturbance: an apostle makes himself an agent of the devil. Here, however, it is Judas, not Peter who is so described. The reason for the Evangelist's procedure may not have been primarily to spare Peter. He has almost certainly transferred to this point an element of the Last Supper narrative (cf. 13:2, 21–30) to highlight the ultimate end of the apostasy described in 6:66, which in all likelihood was being repeated in the churches of the Johannine circle (cf. 1 John 2:18–27; 3:7–10; 4:1–6). The Church must abide in the apostolic confession and not join the company of Judas.

Explanation

1. The Feeding Miracle is presented by the Evangelist as a sign of the gift by Jesus of the bread of life, through which a man may live and not

die. The context within the chapter gives depth to this presentation. It is Passover season, with its associations of sacrifice, redemption, cultic meal, and eschatological deliverance. The people are looking for the return of the manna with the Messiah and the kingdom of God. Jesus, unlike Moses, gives the *true* bread from heaven, for with him comes the kingdom, and through him will come resurrection in the last day. All this suggests that the feeding miracle is understood as a celebration of the feast of the kingdom of God in the present, anticipating its continual celebration in the Church's worship and its ultimate fulfillment in the last day.

2. The Walking on the Sea is portrayed by the Evangelist as a sign of Jesus, Master of the threatening waters, coming to his followers in distress, and so a revelation of Jesus exercising sovereignty over the seas which appertains to God. Hence the climactic "I am," which prepares for the later "I am the living bread which came down from heaven."

3. The signs are linked to the discourse through the demand for Jesus to produce a sign from heaven, on the order of the awaited bestowal of the manna in the last times. The failure of the questioners to understand that this has already been given in sign form enables the discourse to unfold the nature of the true bread from heaven, and what must take place for it to become available for all humankind.

4. The unity of the discourse has been questioned, chiefly through isolating certain segments and contrasting them with each other. That the Evangelist drew on disparate sources should not lead to the denial of a harmonious development of thought through the chapter. This is done when the link between the concept of Bread of Life in v 35 and Jewish thought on Wisdom and Law prompts an exclusively sapiential interpretation of the passage, and again when the eucharistic terminology of vv 51–58 leads to an exclusively sacramental interpretation of that paragraph, viewed as at variance with what has preceded.

The difficulties in relating the two sections of the discourse have encouraged a variety of approaches to it. Some have interpreted the whole discourse as purely metaphorical, with no relation to the Lord's Supper; others have proceeded in the reverse direction and affirmed that the entire discourse is sacramental in nature; the majority of interpreters have viewed the discourse as progressing from a metaphorical to a sacramental understanding of Jesus as the Bread of life. It seems to us that the material we have reviewed demands a fourth approach, admittedly close to the last one mentioned, namely that *the entire chapter,* including signs and discourse, exhibits metaphorical *and* sacramental features, while yet manifesting a progression to an increasingly sacramental emphasis. This is by no means a new approach (see, e.g., C. H. Dodd, *Interpretation,* 333–45, and esp. X. Léon-Dufour, "Le Mystère du pain de vie," 481–523), and it has the merit of being able to embrace the historical context of the ministry of Jesus and the interpretation needful for the church of the Evangelist's day. H. Thyen stated tersely, "The theme of John 6 is Christology" (*TR* 44, 109). That is manifestly true of the Feeding Miracle ("The miracle is above all the occasion of manifesting the mystery of the person of Jesus"; so Léon-Dufour, 494); it is equally true of the Walking on the Lake, with its climactic Ἐγώ εἰμι; and it is the central meaning of the entire discourse. The metaphorical interpretation of Jesus as the living Bread come down from heaven is transparent; it is related not only to Jewish thought, but to other cultures of the nearer and remoter east. While its typological background is evident, that should not be allowed to blind us to a fundamental element in the concept; *bread* is *necessary for life!* E. M. Sidebottom cites Appasamy's observation that for the Indian, Bhaktas God is milky sugar-cane, nectar, luscious fruit, the finest delicacies, whereas for John, Christ is water and bread; "What the Bhaktas desire is rapture, ecstasy, flights of emotion reserved for the few and that in extraordinary hours. What the Fourth Evangelist emphasizes is the moral strength which all men and women need to exercise every day of their lives" (*Christianity as Bhakti Marga,* 145–46, cited in Sidebottom, *The Christ of the Fourth Gospel,* 130 n.6). The acknowledgment of this is fully consonant with the naturalness of meditating on John 6:32–35 in the Christian Lord's Supper. So also we readily acknowledge the pertinence of vv 52–58 to the Supper. Christians of today can hardly read the passage without thinking of that supreme moment of worship, and it is altogether fitting that they should do so in the service itself, as we may be sure the churches of the Evangelist's day did. Nevertheless it must be recognized that hearers of those words in the first century were well able to make sense of them without knowledge of the Christian Eucharist (despite John 6:52!).

The standard rabbinic interpretation of Eccl 8:15, "Nothing is better than for man to eat and drink and enjoy himself . . . ," related the saying to the study of the law and engaging in good works (Str-B, 2:485). A closer parallel to the heart of John 6 is a statement of a certain Rabbi Hillel, son of Gamaliel III (not the famous teacher of that name), which outraged his contemporaries. He said, "There shall be no Messiah for Israel, because they have already eaten him in the days of Hezekiah" (*Sanh.* 99a). What motived Hillel to say that is uncertain; he may have wished to counteract the apocalyptic enthusiasm of some of his fellow Jews, or the beliefs of the Christians, but it would appear that he denied a future Messiah for Israel by identifying him with King Hezekiah. For our own interest it is noteworthy that Jewish translations of the Talmud into English substitute the term "enjoyed" for "have eaten"; the blessings awaited from the Messiah were *enjoyed* by Israel through King Hezekiah's rule.

It is well to bear in mind, in connection with the discourse, that modern man is more acquainted with the metaphor of eating and drinking than we sometimes allow; we "devour" books, "drink in" a lecture, "swallow" a story (if we swallow an insult we forbear to reply!); we may "ruminate" on an idea or poem (ruminate = chew the cud), we "chew over" a matter, we "stomach" something said, or find ourselves unable to do so (cf. John 6:60, NEB), and sometimes we have to eat our own words! I have heard fond grandmothers declare they could "eat up" their grandchildren (i.e., love them to death!), whereas to bite someone's head off conveys a different notion! Further examples of these metaphors will come to mind. It is, however, significant that the profound saying in the heart of the so-called sacramental discourse, i.e., v 57, interprets the language of eating the Son of God in terms of ultimate *koinonia* such as exists between the Father and the Son. Léon-Dufour therefore appears to have ground for his affirmation that chap. 6 deals not *successively* with faith and the Eucharist, but *simultaneously* with both ("Pain de vie," 489).

5. It is important to remember that the chapter does not cease at the close of the discourse, but with the narration of its effects: the disciples of Jesus cannot endure it, and forsake him; the Twelve attain the climax of their growing faith, and confess Jesus as the Holy One of God. The original readers were placed by the Evangelist before the same choice. So are readers of every age. Neutrality on the question, "Who do you say that I am?" is not allowed. The answer determines life now and hereafter.

E. Jesus the Water and the Light of Life
(7:1–8:59)

Introduction

Chapters 7 and 8 are bound together by their relation to the Feast of Tabernacles, and they should be viewed as forming a single section of the Gospel. This has been obscured through the insertion between the two chapters of the narrative of the Woman Taken in Adultery (7:53–8:11). This story originally formed no part of our Gospel. A discussion of the textual evidence for the passage and of the various locations in which it has been placed in the Gospels is given on pp. 143–44.

The circumstances of Jesus' attendance at the festival are described in the opening paragraph of chap. 7: Jesus declines to go to the festival at the urging of his brothers, but later travels to Jerusalem privately, and halfway through the festival begins to teach the crowds in the temple. This precipitates a series of encounters between him and the hostile Jewish leaders, as well as with various elements in the crowd, and the narrative concludes with a brief statement as to the departure of Jesus from the temple (8:59). Some of the most characteristic teaching of the Gospel is contained in this section, notably with regard to the fulfillment of the Jewish festivals in the ministry of Jesus and the nature of that ministry as a mission from the Father to the world through the incarnate Son.

For convenience of reference the detailed discussion and exposition of the two chapters will be given separately, but the treatment of their *Form/Structure/Setting* has to be one in view of the continuity of the whole section.

Observe that consideration of the narrative of the Adulterous Woman (7:53–8:11) is set after the conclusion of the section, i.e., pp. 143–47, to enable the account of Jesus in the Feast of Tabernacles to be followed without a break, as the Evangelist intended.

1. Jesus the Water of Life   (7:1–52)

Bibliography

Allen, W. C. "St. John 7:37–38." *ExpTim* 34 (1922–23) 329–30. **Blenkinsopp, J.** "The Quenching of Thirst: Reflections on the Utterance in the Temple, Jn 7:37–39." *Scr* 12 (1950) 39–48. ———. "John 7:37–39: Another Note on a Notorious Crux." *NTS* 6 (1959–60) 95–98. **Boismard, M. E.** "De son ventre couleront des fleuves d'eau (Jn 7,38)." *RB* 65 (1958) 523–46. **Braun, F. M.** "Avoir soif et boire: Jn 4,10–14; 7:37–39." *Mélanges B. Rigaux.* 247–58. **Burney, C. F.** "Our Lord's Old Testament Reference in John 7:37–38." *Exp* 20 (1920) 385–88. ———. "The Aramaic Equivalent of ἐκ τῆς κοιλίας in Jn 7:38." *JTS* 24 (1922–23) 79–80. **Cortes, J. B.** "Yet Another Look at John 7:37–38." *CBQ* 29 (1967) 75–86. **Cottam, T.** "At the Feast of Booths (John 7:1–10, 21)." *ExpTim* 38 (1936–37) 45. **Daniélou, J.** "Joh 7, 38 et Ezéch 47, 1–11." *SE* 2 (1961) 158–63. **Dekker, C.** "Grundschrift und Redaktion in Johannesevangelium." *NTS* 13 (1966–67) 66–80. **Fee, G. D.** "Once more: John 7:37–39." *ExpTim* 89 (1978) 116–18. **Grelot, P.** "De son ventre couleront des fleuves d'eau: La citation scriptuaire de Jean 7, 38." *RB* 66 (1959) 369–74. ———. "A propos de Jean 7, 38." *RB* 67 (1960) 224–25. ———. "Jn 7, 38: Eau du rocher ou source du temple?" *RB* 70 (1963) 43–51. **Hahn, F.** "Die Wörte vom lebendigen Wasser im Johannesevangelium." *God's Christ and His People.* FS N. A. Dahl, ed. J. Jervell and W. A. Meeks: Oslo: Universitets-forlaget 1977. 51–70. **Harris, R.** "Rivers of Living Water." *Exp* 20 (1920) 196–202. **Hooke, S. H.** "'The Spirit Was Not Yet' (Jn 7:39)." *NTS* 9 (1962–63) 372–80. **Jonge, M. de.** *Jesus: Stranger from Heaven and Son of God.* 77–116. **Kilpatrick, G. D.** "The Punctuation of Jn 7:37–38." *JTS* 11 (1960) 340–42. **Kuhn, K. H.** "St. John 7:37–38." *NTS* 4 (1957–58) 63–65. **Macrae, G. W.** "The Meaning and Evolution of the Feast of Tabernacles." *CBQ* 22 (1960) 251–76. **Martyn, J. L.** *History and Theology in the Fourth Gospel.* 73–89. **Oke, C. C.** "At the Feast of Booths: A suggested rearrangement of John VII–IX." *ExpTim* 47 (1935–36) 425–27. **Schneider, J.** "Zur Komposition von Joh. 7." *ZNW* 45 (1954) 108–19. **Smith, C. W. F.** "Tabernacles in the Fourth Gospel and Mark." *NTS* 9 (1962–63) 130–46. **Smothers, E. R.** "Two Readings in Papyrus Bodmer II." *HTR* 51 (1958) 109–11. **Turner, C. H.** "On the Punctuation of John 7:37–38." *JTS* 24 (1922–23) 66–70. **Woodhouse, H.** "Hard Sayings—IX: 'The Holy Ghost Was Not Yet Given' (Jn 7:39)." *Theol* 67 (1964) 310–12.

Translation

[1] *And after this Jesus went about in Galilee; for he did not wish [a] to stay in Judea, because the Jews were seeking to kill him.* [2] *Now the Jews' festival of Tabernacles was near.* [3] *His brothers therefore said to him, "You should leave this area and go off to Judea, that your disciples also may observe the works you are doing;* [4] *for nobody acts in secret and at the same time seeks to be in the public eye.[b] If you are doing these things, show yourself to the world."* [5] *For even his brothers did not believe in him.* [6] *Jesus therefore says to them, "The (right) [c] time for me has not yet arrived, but the (right) time for you is always ready.* [7] *The world cannot hate you, but it hates me because I bear witness concerning it that its works are evil.* [8] *You yourselves go up to the festival; I myself am not [d] going up to this festival, because the right time for me has not yet fully come."* [9] *After saying this he [e] stayed behind in Galilee.*

[10] *When however his brothers had gone up to the festival he himself also went up, not publicly but (as it were) [f] in secret.* [11] *The Jews therefore were looking for him in the festival and were saying, 'Where is he?"* [12] *And there was a lot of secret discussion going on about him among the crowds; [g] some were saying, "He is a good man," but others were saying, "No, on the contrary he is leading the people astray."* [13] *Nobody, however, was talking publicly about him for fear of the Jews.*

[14] *But halfway through the festival Jesus went up to the temple and taught.* [15] *The Jews therefore were astonished, and they said, "How does this man have such learning [i] when he hasn't had an education?"* [16] *Jesus said in reply to them, "My teaching is not mine, but it comes from him who sent me.* [17] *If anybody is willing to do his will, he will know about this teaching, whether it comes from God or whether I am talking on my own initiative.* [18] *He who talks on his own initiative seeks his own honor; but he who seeks the honor of the one who sent him is true, and there is nothing false in him.* [19] *Moses gave you the Law, didn't he? yet none of you is keeping the Law. Why are you seeking to kill me?"* [20] *The crowd answered, "You have a demon; who is trying to kill you?"* [21] *Jesus replied to them, "I performed one work, and you are astonished.* [22] *Moses gave you circumci-*

sion—*not that it came from Moses but from the Patriarchs—and on that account you circumcise a man on the sabbath.* [23] *If a man receives circumcision on the sabbath in order that the law of Moses may not be broken, are you angry with me because I healed a man's whole body on the sabbath?* [24] *Stop judging according to appearances, but let your judgment ever be just."*

[25] *Some of the people of Jerusalem therefore were saying, "This is the man they were seeking to kill, isn't it?* [26] *And look, he's talking publicly, and they aren't saying anything to him! Can it possibly be that the rulers have really found out that he is the Christ?* [27] *Yet we know where this man comes from; when the Christ comes no one knows where he is from."* [28] *Jesus then, while teaching in the temple, cried aloud and said, "You both know me, and know where I come from. I have not come of my own accord, but the one who sent me is true, and him you do not know;* [29] *but I know him, because I am from him, and he it is who sent me."* [30] *So they sought to seize him, but nobody laid a hand on him, because his hour had not yet come.* [31] *Many of the crowd, however, believed in him, and they said, "When the Christ comes, he won't do more signs than those which this man has done,* [i] *will he?"*

[32] *The Pharisees heard the crowd secretly discussing these things about him, so the chief priests and the Pharisees sent temple police to arrest him.* [33] *Jesus therefore said, "For a little longer time I am with you, and then I am going away to the one who sent me.* [34] *You will look for me, but you will not find (me),* [j] *and where I am you are unable to come."* [35] *The Jews therefore said to one another, "Where is this man about to go that we shall not find him? Surely he's not going to the Dispersion among the Greeks,* [k] *and teach the Greeks, is he?* [36] *What does this statement mean that he made, 'You will look for me and you will not find (me),' and, 'Where I am you cannot come'?"*

[37] *On the last day of the festival, the greatest day, Jesus stood and cried aloud, saying, "If anyone is thirsty, let him come to me,* [l] *and let him drink* [38] *who believes in me. As the scripture said, 'Rivers of living water will flow from his heart.'"* [39] *Now he said this about the Spirit which they who believed* [m] *in him were to receive, for the Spirit* [n] *was not yet (present) because Jesus was not yet glorified.*

[40] *Some of the crowd, after hearing these words, said, "This man is truly the prophet."* [41] *Others were saying, "This man is the Christ." But others were saying, "The Christ doesn't come from Galilee, does he?* [42] *Didn't the scripture say that it is from David's family, and from Bethlehem, the village where David was, that the Christ comes?"* [43] *A division therefore took place among the people because of him.* [44] *And some of them were wanting to seize him, but nobody laid hands on him.*

[45] *The temple police therefore came to the chief priests and Pharisees, and these said to them, "Why did you not bring him?"* [46] *The police officers replied, "Never has a man spoken like this man."* [o] [47] *The Pharisees then answered them, "You also haven't been led astray, have you?* [48] *None of the rulers or of the Pharisees have believed on him, have they?* [49] *But this mob which doesn't know the Law are cursed."* [50] *Nicodemus, the man who came to him formerly, and was one of their number, said to them,* [51] *"Our law doesn't judge a man, does it, before first hearing from him and knowing what he is doing?"* [52] *They replied to him, "You, too, aren't from Galilee, are you? Search and see; the prophet* [p] *does not arise out of Galilee."*

Notes

ᵃ For ἤθελει, read by the majority of our earliest MSS, εἶχεν ἐξουσίαν occurs in W, some OL MSS and syrˢ (the expression is in 10:18; 19:10). The latter is preferred by many critics as the more difficult reading, but is rejected by the UBS committee.

ᵇ P⁶⁶ B W read αὐτό, in evident agreement with the foregoing τι, instead of αὐτός, and neither occurs in some OL, OS, and Coptic MSS. But the attestation for αὐτός is good and the construction regular.

ᶜ καιρός can mean a simple point of time, but it is frequently used of an *opportune* time which calls for decisive action, "the decisive moment, plucked out of the stream of time (χρόνος), which is favorable for a particular action" (Bultmann, 292). In typical Gr. thought the opportune time was considered to be determined by fate, in the biblical revelation it is determined by God.

ᵈ Some of our earliest MSS read οὔπω "not yet" (so P⁶⁶ P⁷⁵ B etc.) rather than οὐκ, the simple negative. Whereas the former reading is all but universally considered to be a correction of the latter, to remove the inconsistency between vv 8 and 10, Haenchen demurs: If Jesus does not know when his time is fulfilled and the Father calls him to Jerusalem (to die?) then logically he cannot say "not," but must say, as in v 6, 'not yet' (346). Haenchen's equation of καιρός here with ὥρα in 2:4 is questionable, but the logic remains.

ᵉ αὐτός is replaced by αὐτοῖς in P⁷⁵ B Dᵗ etc., by Ἰησοῦς in itᶜ Chrys, and simply omitted (as superfluous) in others; αὐτός, however, is well attested and is in accordance with the Evangelist's style.

ᶠ A significant minority of MSS omit ὡς (ℵ D OL OS Coptic); while most MSS include it, the term could have been added to soften the "contradiction" with v 8, hence it is set in brackets in the UBS text.

ᵍ τοῖς ὄχλοις (P⁷⁵ B etc.) is less common in the Fourth Gospel than τῷ ὄχλῳ (read by P⁶⁶ ℵ etc.), but it is strongly attested and may well be original (it is given only a D reading in the UBS edition of the NT).

ʰ γράμματα εἰδέναι in ordinary Gr. means either to be able to read and write (through an elementary education, γράμμα is a letter of the alphabet) or to be an educated person (through receiving a higher education). The latter meaning will be in mind here, for most Jewish boys were taught to read the Scriptures (= the Law). In a Jewish environment, however, where literature means the Holy Scriptures, to be educated will have reference to a correct understanding of the Bible such as could be obtained from a rabbi within his group of followers. The objection to Jesus is that he had not received a rabbinic education nor was accredited by a Jewish teacher.

ⁱ For ἐποίησεν (read by P⁶⁶, P⁷⁵ ℵᶜ B L etc.) some authorities have the present ποιεῖ (ℵ*D θ etc.). Apart from the superior MSS attestation of the former, the latter looks like a correction, to avoid giving the impression that Jesus no longer performed miracles.

ʲ The second με in the sentence is omitted by P⁶⁶ ℵ D L W etc., but included in P⁷⁵ B N T etc. The meaning is the same on either reading (Lagrange's notion that the expression is intentionally vague, and that the Jews will seek the one who Jesus is, i.e., the Messiah, is implausible).

ᵏ ἡ Διασπορὰ τῶν Ἑλλήνων = the Diaspora *among* the Greeks, the genitive denoting the geographical area; the second mention of the Greeks indicates the persons whom (it is thought) Jesus may teach.

ˡ πρός με is included by the great majority of MSS, but omitted by a few—through an oversight?

ᵐ πιστεύσαντες, aorist participle in agreement with εἶπεν. Many MSS read οἱ πιστεύοντες, some Coptic MSS οἱ πιστεύσοντες, to relate the saying to the time of the Church.

ⁿ The laconic οὔπω γὰρ ἦν πνεῦμα, "the Spirit was not yet," caused trouble for copyists. Many added the familiar ἅγιον, "holy"; others extended either πνεῦμα or πνεῦμα ἅγιον with δεδομένον ("given"), to avoid the idea that the Holy Spirit did not yet exist; D achieved the same end with τὸ πνεῦμα ἅγιον ἐπ' αὐτοῖς ("the Holy Spirit was not yet upon them"), while Ethiopic has the term "came" (upon them).

ᵒ The pithy statement of the temple police (text as in P⁶⁶ᶜ P⁷⁵ ℵᶜ B L T W etc.) is filled out variously in the MSS traditions to express the thought "as this man speaks."

ᵖ For προφήτης P⁶⁶* and apparently P⁷⁵ read ὁ προφήτης, namely the prophet like Moses (Deut 18:15), which many moderns consider to be the original reading. See *Comment*.

Form/Structure/Setting

1. The setting of chaps. 7 and 8 determines in a peculiar way the form and structure of the passage. Unlike previous episodes narrated we do not have sign(s) plus discourse, but we do have a narrative with a core of teaching significantly related to its setting. The Feast of Tabernacles is taking place in Jerusalem. Prior to it Jesus is itinerating in Galilee, since the "Jews" in Judea are seeking to kill him. In the eyes of his brothers Jesus is living in obscurity (ἐν κρυπτῷ) when he ought to be active in public (ἐν παρρησίᾳ), and so should go to Jerusalem. Jesus does in fact go to the festival, not at their bidding, nor "publicly" (ἐν παρρησίᾳ) but still "in obscurity (ἐν κρυπτῷ, v 10). At length he emerges in the temple and teaches "publicly" (παρρησίᾳ v 26). So begins a series of controversies between Jesus and "the Jews" which become ever more severe and into which the participants of the festival are drawn. It is a story of κρίσις, a separation before the revelation of the Christ, wherein the hearers by declarations of faith and unbelief divide, and so pass judgment on themselves and come under the judgment of God. The story ends with Jesus withdrawing from his assailants and departing from the temple (8:59). Thus the narrative begins and ends with the murderous hostility of the Jews and the hiddenness of Jesus, from which he emerges to make known the revelation he has been sent to declare and then retires. Moreover, certain features of the festival and its ritual are applied to Jesus in such a way as to make them signs of the kingdom of God, comparable to the miracles earlier recounted, and leading to further dialogues. There is ground therefore for viewing the narrative and teaching elements in chaps. 7–8 as parallel to the signs plus discourse structure characteristic of the Book of Signs (so Dodd, *Interpretation,* 351–52). The comparison of structure is more evident in relation to chaps. 9, 10, 11, where the narrative and discourse are not separate but interwoven, and dialogue is frequently more prominent than discourse.

2. In chaps. 7–8 the comparatively lengthy discourses, such as we see in chaps. 5–6, are replaced by a series of brief dialogues. Questioning, challenging, and objecting on the part of hearers are characteristic of the whole section, and at times the field is taken by the objectors rather than by Jesus (in 7:40–52 the entire debate takes place among members of the crowd at the festival and then among the Jewish leaders in council). While dialogue is a feature of the Fourth Gospel its domination in this section makes it unique within the Gospel. The succession of controversial interchanges between Jesus and the Jewish authorities reminds us of the series of controversies recorded in the synoptic Gospels (especially in Mark 2:1–3:6 and 11:27–12:40). In all probability these go back to the period of oral collections of the teaching and acts of Jesus. Their grouping in this manner will have served the early Christian churches as guidance in their debates with contemporary synagogue rulers, and were so incorporated by Mark in view of the large number of Jewish members of the churches and the continuing relations with the synagogues even outside Palestine. So also the Fourth Evangelist has assembled materials from various contexts that set forth the conflict between Jesus and the Jewish authorities, both to illuminate the historical situation which eventu-

ally led to the death of Jesus and to guide the churches in their own confrontations with Jewish teachers and rulers. It would appear that in the Johannine circle the controversy had become more urgent and intense than in the churches to which the synoptic Gospels were addressed, and this is reflected in the Evangelist's presentation of the material. It helps to account for some of the surprising sequences in the narrative and dialogues, especially in chap. 8, where the materials are very compressed.

Similar considerations are germane regarding other passages of uncertain position. Without doubt 8:21–22 is extraordinarily close in thought and language to 7:33–36. Common to both are the expressions: "I am going away" (8:21; 7:33); "You will look for me" (8:21; 7:34); "Where I am going you cannot come" (8:21; 7:34); a misunderstanding of the Jews, in 8:22, "Will he kill himself?", in 7:35, "Is he going to the Dispersion among the Greeks?"; and the puzzling statement of Jesus, again echoed by them, "Where I am you cannot come" (8:22; 7:36). Brown thinks that the Evangelist has preserved two forms of the same scene (349); Bultmann believes simply that he has twice employed the same saying. The Evangelist is evidently concerned that the reader has before him in this context yet another point of controversy, wherein Jesus warns the Jews that they will die in their sins if they persist in rejecting the word he brings (8 21, 24), and repetition to him is of little consequence. For this reason Bultmann's procedure of dissecting the elements of chap. 8 and scattering them to what he judged to be more suitable contexts in various chapters of the Gospel (see his analysis of chap. 8, 312–15) is quite mistaken. We are intended to hold these dialogues together, just as Mark wished his readers to gain a perspective on the conflicts of Jesus and the Jewish leaders in 2:1–3:6 and 11:27–12:40 of his Gospel. It is particularly evident in the long section 8:31–59 that separate issues have been brought together, resulting in a fearful picture of the gulf between Jesus and his Jewish opponents. On the relation between the historical situation of Jesus in his ministry and that of the early Church see the *Comment* and the *Explanation* sections.

3. The division of the material in chaps. 7–8 is by topic, and since overlapping occurs, especially in chap. 8, any analysis is somewhat arbitrary, but the following may serve as a guide to the contents of the section.

7:1–13	Jesus and the question of attendance at the festival
7:14–18	Jesus the teacher: qualified or unqualified?
7:19–24	Jesus and the Law
7:25–31	The origin of Jesus
7:32–36	The impending departure of Jesus
7:37–39	Jesus the Source of Living Water
7:40–44	Division among the people
7:45–52	Division among the authorities
8:12–20	Jesus the Light of the World
8:21–29	Jesus the One from the World Above
8:30–36	The freedom of Jesus and the slavery of the Jews
8:37–40	The real children of Abraham
8:41–47	The children of God and the children of the devil
8:48–59	The priority of Jesus over Abraham and the prophets

Comment

Jesus and the Question of Attendance at the Festival (7:1–13)

1 The threat to the life of Jesus in v 1 sounds a note of opposition and danger like a continuing ground bass, extending through the whole of chap. 7. The term Ἰουδαῖοι has the characteristic Johannine meaning of Jewish *authorities;* in v 26 it is defined as the rulers, in vv 32b and 45 as the chief priests and Pharisees. Vv 32a and 47–52 indicate that the Pharisees are especially prominent in the events narrated. Observe the distinction between them and the Jewish "crowds" in vv 12–13: the Jewish people at the festival dared not speak openly about Jesus "for fear of the Jews"! The term used in this sense in vv 1 and 13 makes the passage (1–13) an inclusion, so delimiting it as an introduction to the following narrative.

2 The Festival or Feast of Tabernacles was the most popular of Jewish annual gatherings in the temple (so Jos. *Ant.* 8.100). *Tabernacle* is an old English term derived from the Latin *tabernaculum,* a diminutive of *taberna,* "hut or booth," and means a tent or booth or shed. The celebration was popularly known as the Feast of Tents (ἡ ἑορτὴ τῶν σκηνῶν) or, here, the setting up of tents (ἡ σκηνοπηγία), since the participants in the festival camped out in homemade shelters of leafy branches, erected on rooftops or about the houses or in fields. Lev 23:34–36 enacts that the festival is to be held for seven days, beginning with a sabbath convocation on the fifteenth day of the seventh month (i.e., *Tishri* = September-October) and ending with another holy convocation on the *eighth* day. Primarily a thanksgiving for the harvests of wine, fruit, and olives, it was conjoined with a remembrance of the mercies of God during the forty years of wilderness wanderings and an anticipation of their return at the second Exodus when the kingdom of God should come. The most outstanding features of the festival were the camping out in the huts, the ceremonial drawing of water each morning from the pool of Siloam (reflected in 7:37–38) and the rejoicing at night in the light of the enormous candelabras set up in the court of the women (cf. 8:12; for a detailed description of the festival rituals, see Str-B 2:774–812; more briefly G. W. MacRae, "The Meaning and Evolution of the Feast of Tabernacles," 251–76).

3–5 The brothers of Jesus (cf. Mark 6:3) urge him to go to "Judea" and use the opportunity provided by the festival to perform more miracles, and so encourage his disciples. The impression is given that the "disciples" are those in Judea, which is not impossible in the light of 3:26; 4:1, but since pilgrims would be present at the festival from all parts of the country no such limitation is necessary. Barrett suggests that the disciples who forsook Jesus in Galilee (6:60–66) are primarily in mind, with the implication that Jesus could recover them as well as win others by a public display of power (311). The brothers seem not to question the ability of Jesus to perform miracles, and assume that he wishes to become a successful figure. Their estimate of success, however, and the way to secure it has already been presented to Jesus—by the Tempter in Matt 4:5–7. The concurrence of their advice with the Tempter's voice leads the Evangelist to characterize them as unbelievers (v 5; cf. the related event in Mark 3:20–21 and the response of Jesus in 3:32–35). The "success" that Jesus seeks and his mode of attaining it are of a different order from their imaginings (cf. 12:23–24, 31–32).

6–7 If in Greek thought the "decisive moment" (καιρός) was determined by fate, in the biblical revelation it is determined by God. Jesus awaits an intimation from the Father as to the right time for action. The relation of the καιρός to the ὥρα (hour) of Jesus is plain: the latter is the climactic decisive moment of his death, but this is not to the fore at this point. By contrast the καιρός of the brothers of Jesus is "always present"; since they neglect God's καιροί, they determine their own lives, and so lead a meaningless existence in the world of which they are a part. That is why the world cannot hate them; the world loves its own (15–19).

8 The brothers' advice is declined because "the right time for me has not yet fully come." No evasion is intended here, any more than there was in 2:4. Jesus is represented as not yet having received word from God as to his next move ("He refuses in the plainest terms to comply with human— and unbelieving—advice, acting with complete freedom and independence with regard to men, but in complete obedience to his Father," Barrett, 313). The ancient interpretation of the words, "I am not going up," as signifying the ascension of Jesus via his cross to heaven (cf. 20:17) is hardly to be received (it was advanced by Ephraem in his commentary on the Diatessaron, 14.28, and by Epiphanius, *Panarion* 51.25.6, and is endorsed by some moderns, e.g., Hoskyns. 313; Brown, 308); it appears to be another endeavor to eliminate the supposed contradiction between v 8 and v 10.

10 That Jesus eventually goes to the festival ἐν κρυπτῷ is to be interpreted strictly in relation to v 4: he journeys quietly to Jerusalem, without making any ostentatious entry into the city or drawing attention to himself on arrival at the festival.

11–12 The "Jews" who seek him in the festal crowd are apparently the Jewish leaders bent on his arrest (cf. 13b, 25, 32). Whereas γογγυσμός in 6:41, like the verb γογγύζω in 6:61. represented a grumbling against Jesus, here (as in v 32) the term indicates a "restless muttering" (Hoskyns, 313), or "undercover talk" (Schnackenburg, 2:143). Some of this talk was sympathetic to Jesus ("He is a good man"), and some of it hostile ("He is leading the people astray"). The latter charge is a serious one in Jewish law, and if established could lead to capital punishment. It is early exemplified in Deut 13:1– 6 (LXX), which states that a false prophet must die, "because he spoke so as to lead you astray (πλανῆσαι) from the Lord your God." The allegation that Jesus sought to lead astray the people remained firm in Jewish tradition. It is cited by Justin in his dialogue with Trypho the Jew ("They dared to call him a magician and one who leads the people astray [λαοπλάνον]" *Dialogue*, 69), and it is preserved in a famous passage in the Talmud: "It was taught: On the eve of the Passover they hanged Yeshu. And an announcer went out in front of him for forty days saying: 'He is going to be stoned, because he practiced magic and enticed and led Israel astray. Anyone who knows anything in his favor, let him come and plead in his behalf.' But not having

found anything in his favor, they hanged him on the eve of the Passover"
(*Sanh.* 43a; there are further references to this in *Sanh.* 107a and *Sota* 47a,
see Str-B 1:1023–24).

JESUS THE TEACHER: QUALIFIED OR UNQUALIFIED? (7:14–18)

14–15 Not till halfway through the festival does Jesus emerge and begin
to teach in the Temple. It will have been the first occasion for many to hear
him teaching in the temple courts, hence their astonishment. Their amazement
links with other testimonies to the effect of Jesus' teaching on his contemporaries (cf. esp. Mark 1:22 and Luke 4:22). Authority and graciousness were the
marks of his speech, but both in Nazareth and in Jerusalem it caused anger
(for "amazement" in a pejorative sense cf. v 21). That he taught "not as the
scribes," i.e. without appeal to rabbinic authorities ("Rabbi A. B. said in the
name of Rabbi C. D. . . ."), and that he had not served as a disciple of an
acknowledged rabbinic master are one. If this fresh mode of teaching delighted
the crowds, it scandalized the Jerusalem elite ("the Jews," v 15). *Sota* 22a
Bar has the statement, "Who is one of the people of the land (ʿ*am* haʾ*ares*)?
The others (= the school of Rabbi Meir) said: 'If anyone has learned the
Scripture and the Mishna but has not served as a student of the Learned he
is one of the people of the land. If he has learned the Scripture but not the
Mishna he is an uneducated man. If he has learned neither the Scripture
nor the Mishna the Scripture says of him: "I sow the house of Israel and
the house of Judah with seed of men and seed of cattle" ' " (i.e., he is reckoned
as an animal!). So Str-B 2:486. This view finds clear expression in v 49 of
this chapter.
   16–17 The reply of Jesus to the criticism of the Jewish teachers is simple:
"If others drew their teaching from a rabbinic lecture room, he brought his
from his Father" (Barrett, 318). Jesus adds that the truthfulness of this affirmation will become evident to anyone who "wills to do his will," i.e., his Father's
will. We should here recall the insistence of Jesus that his whole concern
was to do the Father's will (5:30); it is therefore a question of sharing Jesus'
mind, of being similarly devoted as he to discovering and doing the will of
God; the claim is made that whoever walks that path will understand that
the teaching of Jesus is none other than revelation from God. It is, of course,
a matter of faith rather than logic, of being "attuned to God's voice in order
to recognize one who speaks for God" (Brown, 316). But the invitation so
to learn was given, and remains.
   18 A principle is then enunciated in general terms. A person who represents none but himself and talks on his own initiative is naturally anxious to
win the approval of others; but one who seeks the honor of the one he
represents is truthful and not false. Lindars suggests that the first half of
the statement categorizes "the blinding ambition of the rabbis," in contrast
to which the unselfishness of Jesus' motive is the proof of the integrity of
his teaching (289). It is assumed that one who advances in the knowledge
of the teaching of Jesus, in accordance with v 17, will recognize that v 18b
is true of him.

JESUS AND THE LAW (7:19–24)

Jesus has stated that one who wills to do God's will is able to discover whether his teaching is from God, since he himself is devoted to doing God's will. He is aware, however, that the Jews are accusing him of setting aside the Law of God. He does two things therefore: he declares that it is his detractors who break the Law, and he reveals the reasoning behind his sabbath deeds.

19 Moses gave the Law—the Moses whose proud disciples his hearers claim to be (9:28), and in whom they trust (5:45). Yet none of them keeps the Law, as is evident in their rejection of Moses' testimony to Jesus (5:45–46) and still more in their desire to kill him to whom Moses bore witness.

20 The crowd appears to be ignorant of the intention of their leaders to get rid of Jesus and therefore reject the charge as absurd. They retort, "You have a demon," which appears to signify what others later allege: "He has a demon *and is mad*" (10:20). That is, they charge Jesus of cherishing insane imaginations, an idea voiced on other occasions (8:48–59, cf. Mark 3:21; the allegation that he was in league with the devil and worked by his power, Mark 3:22, is of a different order and much more serious).

21–23 The threat to the life of Jesus is not the product of a diseased imagination. Jesus therefore returns to the issue that caused the wrath of the Jewish leaders—the healing of a cripple at the pool of Bethesda on a sabbath (5:1–9, 10–18). *"One work I did,"* said Jesus—*one!* And they were horrified! "But," said Jesus, "you *perpetually* break the Law by circumcising boys whose eighth day of life falls on the sabbath" (note the present continuous tense, περιτέμνετε).

To the modern Western mind this may sound a curious charge of sabbath breaking, but the Jews were very conscious that this is precisely what they were doing (on the basis of their understanding of keeping the sabbath). "One can do anything that is necessary for circumcision on the sabbath," *Šabb.* 19:2. Rabbi Jose said, "See how beloved (in the sight of God) is the command of circumcision, for it supersedes the sabbath" (*Tanh* 19b see Str-B 2:487). For them, therefore, it was sufficient to recognize the superiority of the circumcision law over the sabbath law. But Jesus has something profounder in mind. He points out that if circumcision, which is performed on a single part (*membrum virile*) of a male, is allowed on the sabbath, how much more it is to heal a man's *whole* body. In principle this was acknowledged by more than one Jewish teacher. Str-B cite two different rabbis who made similar comments on this issue in the same era as the Evangelist: R. Eliezer about A.D. 90 affirmed that not to perform circumcision on the sabbath day would be to incur the judgment of God; "And does not that justify a conclusion from the less to the greater? If one supersedes the sabbath on account of one of his members, should he not supersede the sabbath for his whole body (if in danger of death)?" (*T. Šabb.* 15, 16). In *Yoma* 85b a more explicit statement of the same principle is made by R. Eliezer ben Azariah about A.D. 100: "If circumcision, which affects one of man's two hundred and forty-eight members, supersedes the sabbath, how much more must his whole body (if his life is in danger of death) supersede the sabbath?" In the eyes of the Jewish teachers this reasoning can apply only when someone is in danger of death. Jesus allows no such limitation, any more than in the application of circumcision. But he goes a stage further by uncovering the reason for Moses re-enacting the circumcision law given to the Patriarchs: *"On this account* Moses gave you circumcision . . . and you circumcise on the sabbath . . . ,"* namely, by implication, that it may point to God's redeeming purpose for man; or as Hoskyns expressed it, "that it should be a type and anticipation of that greater and entire healing by the Christ, which also of necessity displaces the sabbath" (316). Barrett's comment is noteworthy: "This gives a striking and important turn to the sabbath controversy which plays so large a part in the synoptic gospels but is never really explained in them. Jesus' attitude is not a sentimental liberalising of a harsh and unpractical law . . . nor the masterful dealing of an opponent of the Law as such; it is rather the accomplishment of the redemptive purpose of God towards which the Law had pointed" (320–21).

THE ORIGIN OF JESUS (7:25–31)

Here only and in Mark 1:5 do we read of οἱ Ἱεροσολυμῖται, "the Jerusalemites," the inhabitants of Jerusalem. The Evangelist apparently distinguishes them from the pilgrims who have come to the feast; they would have been better informed than the latter as to the hostile intentions of the Sanhedrin (contrast v 20). There is no hint in vv 25–27 that they were in sympathy with Jesus over against the Sanhedrin. On the contrary, they have their own objection to him (v 27), and at length want to lay hands on him to deliver him to the Sanhedrin (v. 30), in contrast to the ὄχλος, many of whom are drawn to Jesus through his σημεῖα (v 31).

26–27 The hesitant, not to say incredulous question of v 26, is put forward on the supposition that the members of the Sanhedrin, who had wanted formerly to kill Jesus, may have received fresh information that led them to believe that Jesus is, after all, the Messiah. To the men of Jerusalem one item of doctrine alone suffices to put that out of court: "We know where this fellow comes from, but no one knows where the Messiah comes from" (v 27).

One could be puzzled by this bit of messianic dogma. What about Bethlehem (Mic 5:2; cf. Matt 2:4–6)? Or what about the teaching that the Messiah comes from the presence of the Ancient of Days (Dan 7:13)? Do these people reject all such traditions? Naturally not. Ultimate origin of the Messiah is not in their minds. Contrary to the belief of Bultmann and others, it is unlikely that these Jews cherished the apocalyptic conception, expressed in the *Similitudes of Enoch,* that the messianic Ruler and Judge has been "chosen and hidden before him, before the creation of the world and for evermore" (Enoch 48:6, cf. also 4 Ezra 13:51–2). E. Sjöberg, in his investigation of this apocalyptic idea of the Messiah, maintained that it is rare in rabbinic writings and alien to the typical rabbinic understanding of the Messiah (*Der verborgene Menschensohn in den Evangelien* [KHV: Lund, 1955] 41–98). The Jerusalemites will have held to the common notion of the Messiah, that he will be born of flesh and blood but wholly unknown until the time of his appearing for Israel's redemption. The doctrine is assumed—and opposed—in various passages in the synoptic Gospels (cf. Mark 13:21–22; Matt 24:26–27 // Luke 17:23–24), and is set by Justin in the mouth of Trypho the Jew, at least in one form current in the second century: "Christ—if he indeed has been born, and exists anywhere— is unknown, and does not even know himself, and has no power until Elijah comes to anoint him and make him manifest to all" (*Dialogue,* 8). Over against that kind of teaching the Jerusalemites set the simple fact that everybody knows where Jesus comes from, namely from Nazareth, whence he launched out on an itinerating ministry. No doubt their objection was echoed frequently by Jewish contemporaries of the Evangelist in their polemic against the Christians' proclamation of Jesus as Messiah.

28–29 The Evangelist, in reporting this use of Jewish messianic dogma against Jesus, will have seen the irony in it: these opponents of Jesus were more right than they could have realized, and yet they could not have been more wrong (the more so had the Evangelist known that Jesus was born in Bethlehem! See comment on v 42). "You know me, and you know where I come from" is an admission that the Jews are right, in so far as they know Jesus was reared in Nazareth, of the family of Joseph and Mary. But the further declaration, "I have not come of my own accord, but the one who sent me is true," specifies something that has not dawned on their horizon. Not only did Jesus not venture forth from Nazareth on his own volition; the starting point of his mission to Israel was elsewhere. He came from "the Faithful and True One," Someone who is very real, whom you do not know" (AmT). In the Evangelist's vocabulary ἀληθινός denotes an attribute of God (17:3); the point of origin of Jesus' mission was with God. Hence he could say, "I know him," for his knowledge is based on his relationship to God. His Jewish opponents, on the contrary, do not know God, or they would grasp that Jesus had come from him, and if they would only listen to him they would begin truly to know God. This statement of origin of Jesus is reiterated even more plainly in v 29. "I know him because I am from him and he sent me."

Westcott, in agreement with earlier interpreters, appears to distinguish between "I am from him" and "he sent me": "The continuance of being and the historic mission are set side by side; and both are referred to God" (273). It is better to see both as relating to the origin of the mission of Jesus: he both *came from* God and *was sent by* God. Schnackenburg is justified in affirming, "Jesus' coming forth from God (cf. 8:42; 17:8) always means, in John, his mission in historical time" (2:147); but that mission begins with God in heaven. Hence the ultimate difference between the sending of prophets by God (including that of John the Baptist, 1:6) and that of Jesus: he comes "from above," that is "from heaven," and so is qualitatively different from "him who is from the earth" (3:31). Herein lies the mystery of the Incarnation: the man of Nazareth is from heaven. The messianic dogma proclaimed by the men of Jerusalem had greater truth than they knew, but their interpretation of it kept them from recognizing the Messiah when he came among them. It illustrates how dogma, even about the Christ, can hide the truth from the people of God if it is not subject to the revelation made known through the Christ who came in the flesh.

30–31 The final sentences of the paragraph provide an example of the process which takes place throughout this record of Jesus at the festival, as throughout the record of the ministry as a whole: the people are divided in their response to Jesus. The men of Jerusalem wanted to seize him, but "his hour had not yet come." The one from whom Jesus came permitted none to bring the mission to an end before the time he himself had appointed— an illustration of the words of Jesus: "He who sent me is with me!" By contrast, "many of the crowd believed in him." They did so because they could not imagine even the Messiah doing more "signs" than Jesus had done and was doing. Here the pilgrims are echoing a different contemporary messianic dogma. Whereas traditionally miracles were not associated with the Messiah in his coming, the merging of the expected prophet like Moses with the Messiah as the "second Redeemer" led to anticipation of the miracles of Moses in the Exodus finding a repetition in the greater than Moses at the second Exodus (see Meeks, *The Prophet King*, 162–64). Hence these members of the festival crowd were open to attend sympathetically to the words and deeds of Jesus, and were impressed by them.

THE IMPENDING DEPARTURE OF JESUS (7:32–36)

The Pharisees, as they mingle with the crowd, become aware of the widespread discussions that are taking place concerning Jesus. As usual they take the initiative in action against Jesus, and they persuade the priestly authorities, who were in charge of the temple, to have Jesus arrested (the ὑπηρέται are "servants" at the disposal of the Sanhedrin, having various duties, "half cultic officials and half police" [Bultmann, 306 n.6]). Whether these police officers were instructed to arrest Jesus at once we are not told; it is feasible that they were ordered to watch for a favorable opportunity to arrest him without creating an uproar (cf. Mark 14:1–2).

33–34   Into this context of heightened tension Jesus speaks. The irony of his statements is even more marked than in v 27. The Jews are intent on getting rid of him, and their desire will be fulfilled in "a little while," (how it will happen is not said). But his departure will signal his return to the One who sent him. The language of v 33 constantly reappears in the Upper Room discourses (for ὑπάγω of the departure of Jesus from this world to the Father see 13:3, 33–36; 14:4, 28; 16:5, 10, 17; for the "little while," see the exposition of it in 16:16–22, and for the return to the Father, chap. 17). In these circumstances it is unexpected that Jesus states that the day will come when the Jews seeking his death will "look for" him. Since they will look for him in vain, and cannot follow him to the place to which he has gone, the seeking must relate not to a change of heart in the course of ordinary life but to a desperate desire in the judgment, when the opponents of the Messiah who compassed his death will seek for salvation from the exalted Lord and will not find it. The thought of "too late," which is implied in these words, appears in a version of the saying in the *Gos. Thom.*, 38: "Many times have you desired to hear these words which I say to you, and you have no other from whom to hear them. There will be days when you will seek me (and) you will not find me." Remoter parallels to the idea may be seen in the portrayal of the wicked and the Righteous Man in Wisd Sol 2:10–24 and 5:1–5, and the judgment of the kings and the mighty in *Enoch* 62:1–10.

35–36   The complete misunderstanding of these words on the part of the hearers is as ironical as the sayings they misunderstood. Like Caiaphas advocating the death of Jesus in the Sanhedrin (11:49–50), they unwittingly utter a prophecy of the future activity of Jesus among the nations. The critics of Jesus think in terms of his forsaking his country and settling among the Jews scattered in various parts of the empire, and teaching not Jews but Greeks. But that appeared to them a preposterous idea: if Jesus could not succeed among his people in the Holy Land, how should he be successful among Jews abroad? And since the critical attitude of Greeks to Jewish traditions was known to Jews everywhere, what hope should Jesus have of winning them to his cause? (Note the use of μή before the question of v 35b, presuming a negative answer.) At this point the original readers of the Gospel could have been forgiven a smile. To the enemies of Jesus it sounded an absurd notion to think of Jesus embarking on a mission to the Greeks, but it happened! And it had marvelous success among peoples of *many* nations! Most astonishingly of all, it came to pass through the Jewish authorities achieving their aim and putting him to death! For it was in his "departure" that the Christ achieved a salvation for all nations, and from his enthroned glory with the Father he bestowed on his followers the Holy Spirit who is the Spirit of Mission, and through his disciples he made known to the nations the revelation and salvation his own people neglected.

JESUS THE SOURCE OF LIVING WATER (7:37–39)

The saying of vv 37–38 is an outstanding example of a characteristic of the Fourth Gospel, in that a saying or episode embodies memory of the great deeds of God in the past and anticipation of the saving acts of God in the future, both united in an affirmation of their fulfillment in Jesus in the here and now. John 6:35, "I am the Bread of life . . . ," forms a close parallel, alike in form and content, to vv 37–38, but without the high drama which the context of the festival bestows on the latter.

It is virtually certain, despite the denial by Hoskyns (320–21), that the passage assumes the rite of water-drawing that took place on each of the seven days of the festival proper. The pilgrims entered into the procedures with greatest delight; in *Sukk.* 5:1 it is stated, "He who has not seen the joy of the water-drawing has not seen joy in his whole lifetime." At the break of day priests processed from the temple to the pool of Siloam. There they filled a golden pitcher with water and bore it back to the temple. On approaching the watergate on the south side of the inner court the *shophar* (trumpet) was sounded three times—joyous blasts which were explicitly related to Isa 12:3, *"With joy* you will draw water from the wells of salvation." The priests bearing the water then processed around the altar, watched by the pilgrims, while the temple choir sang the Hallel (i.e., Pss 113–18). When the opening words of Psalm 118 were reached, "Give thanks to the Lord," every man and boy shook the *lulab* (a bunch of willow and myrtle tied with palm) with his right hand and held aloft citrus fruit in his left hand (a sign of the harvest gathered in), and the cry "Give thanks to the Lord" was repeated three times. The same thing happened at the cry "O Lord save us!" of Ps 118:25. Since all this took place at the time of the daily offering, the water was offered to God in connection with the daily drink-offering (of wine). A chosen priest mounted the altar on which stood two silver bowls, one for the reception of the drink-offering and the other for the water. When the priest had poured the wine and the water into their respective bowls, they were then poured out as offerings to God. The crowd then called out, "Lift up your hand!" The demand was made as a sign that the rite was properly fulfilled, since the Sadducees objected to the rite on the ground that it was not prescribed in the Law. Accordingly the priest had to raise his hand aloft to show that he had faithfully discharged his duty.

The ideas behind the rite were complex. Since the festival was essentially bound up with the agricultural year, prayer for the sending of rain, a highly uncertain element in Palestinian weather, was a prime factor in the performance of the rite. There appears to be a reference to this significance of the rite in the prophecy of Zech 14:16–17. Indeed, if rain fell during the festival it was regarded as a sign of the plentiful rains that would be given in the coming agricultural year. Since Tabernacles was also a celebration of the blessings of God upon Israel during the nation's forty years sojourn in the wilderness, the water-drawing served as a reminder of the water that came from the rock smitten by Moses, when the people were in danger of perishing from thirst (Exod 17:1–6). According to rabbinic exposition, the rock remained with the people throughout their wilderness journeyings (cf. 1 Cor 10:4). Furthermore the rite was also linked with the anticipation of the abundant gift of living water flowing from Jerusalem when the kingdom of God comes (with Isa 12:3, cf. esp. Ezek 47:1–12 and Zech 14:8, both passages being read during the festival). The associations of the ceremony with the salvation of God, past, present, and future were accordingly evident to the people at the festival.

37   The "last day, the greatest day of the festival," is an ambiguous designation. Whereas the festival proper is spoken of as seven days in Deut 16:13, 15; Ezek 45:25; *Jub.* 16:20–31; an eighth day, a sabbath, is reckoned in Lev 23:34–36 (cf. Num 29:12–39; 2 Macc 10:6). For the rabbis "the last day" of the festival was the eighth day, but they never spoke of it as the *greatest* day. Since the water-drawing rite and the dancing in the light of the great menoras were omitted on the eighth day, the description of "the greatest day" is thought by many to denote the seventh day, when the priests processed around the altar with the water drawn from Siloam not once but *seven* times. Certainly if Jesus "stood and cried out" at the moment when the priest at the altar had lifted up his hand to signify the completion of the rite, the effect of the cry on the multitude would have been as a thunderclap from heaven. Everybody would have known whose cry it was, and its significance, namely that everything embodied in that rite of past experience of salvation, present prayer, and future hope was available and offered through Jesus. The Evangelist's description of the effect of the cry upon the crowd and upon the temple police (vv 40–43, 46) would have been entirely comprehensible. Nevertheless one must acknowledge that it is not stated that such was the moment when Jesus made his great declaration, though it is not to be ruled out as fanciful. It is also to be recognized that the invitation would have been equally relevant on the eighth day, which was celebrated as a sabbath with appropriate ceremonies and was attended by a great congregation. The water-drawing ceremony was not enacted on that day; if the cry of vv 37–38 was uttered when the sign of past and hoped-for salvation was noticeably absent, the declaration of its presence in and through Jesus, with invitation to receive it from him, will have been a striking and powerful announcement. Moreover the occasion of the sabbath would have provided Jesus with a natural opportunity to expound the central thought of the saying, which again would have given sufficient cause for the deep impression made upon the hearers and the expostulation of the police to the hierarchy (v 46).

37–38   The actual rendering of the saying in vv 37–38 and its construction have been disputed throughout Christian history.

The punctuation of the text in the UBS Greek NT represents the understanding of most of the Eastern Fathers, including Origen: "If anyone is thirsty let him come to me and drink"; there follows an assurance, in accordance with the scripture, that the believer whose thirst is slaked will become a source of living water to others. That rendering of the text is followed in the majority of Bible translations and by a number of modern exegetes (e.g., Rengstorf, Barrett, Lightfoot, Lindars, Haenchen). Blenkinsopp supported this view, but regarded the phrase "he who believes in me" as an editorial explanatory expansion. The saying of Jesus, in his view, is limited to the words, "If anyone thirsts, let him come to me and drink," and an interpretation is added, "(This is) as the scripture text says: Rivers of living water shall flow from his side" ("John VII:37–39," 95–96). If the living waters symbolize the revelation of God through Jesus, this would not be an impossible interpretation; it would then signify that one who received the revelation from Jesus would then become a source of it to others. There is little doubt, however, in view of the Evangelist's interpretative comment in v 39, relating the living water to the Spirit bestowed by the Lord on the thirsty, that he himself did not so understand the saying. The difficulty is diminished if a full point is placed after the first clause and ὁ πιστεύων εἰς ἐμέ is viewed as a nominative absolute, beginning a fresh sentence, thus: "As for the one who believes in me, as the scripture says, rivers of living water will flow from his (viz., the Lord's) heart." This was Bauer's solution (108), and is accepted by Schnackenburg (2:154). Kilpatrick achieves the same end by viewing ὁ πιστεύων εἰς ἐμέ as forming, with ἐάν τις διψᾷ, the subject of the verbs ἐρχέσθω πρός με καὶ πινέτω: "If anyone is thirsty, let him who believes in me come to me and drink" ("The Punctuation of John VII 37–38," 341). While this is grammatically possible, it hardly appears to be a natural reading of the text.

The mode of understanding the text that commends itself to the majority of recent exegetes follows on the recognition by many western Fathers that the source of the living waters is Christ alone, and that the key utterance should be read as a couplet:

> ἐάν τις διψᾷ ἐρχέσθω πρός με,
> καὶ πινέτω ὁ πιστεύων εἰς ἐμέ,
> If anyone is thirsty let him come to me,
> and let him drink who believes in me.

The OT citation that follows provides an encouragement to the thirsty believer to come and drink, on the ground that the OT type and promise of the gift of living water has now been realized and is available to all mankind through the Redeemer. Admittedly the chiasmus is unusual for the Evangelist, since it sets in parallelism "let him come" and "let him drink," as also "he who thirsts" and "he who believes"; in the closely related John 6:35 "he who comes" and "he who believes" are placed in parallelism, and "will not hunger" and "will not thirst." While the parallelism is different in the two sayings, the thought and language are strikingly similar. In John 7:37–38 the thirsty one is a believer convinced that Jesus can satisfy his thirst, and so he comes and drinks. In John 6:35 we have the double picture of hunger assuaged and thirst slaked. It is assumed that one comes to Jesus because he is hungry, and one who believes in him is thirsty; hence the hungry one *comes and eats* and the thirsty one *believes and drinks*. The fundamental concept is precisely the same in the two passages, apart from the doubling of the picture in John 6:35, and its emphasizing the availability of bread for the hungry, whereas John 7 has in view water for the thirsty. But the same salvation of God in the past and the same eschatological gift in the future and the same offer of grace in the present are the substance of both utterances.

On the basis of this last reading, the essential call of Christ is the couplet of vv 37a–38b. It is not impossible that this alone is the saying of Jesus which passed on in the tradition of his words, and that v 38b, "as the scripture said . . . ," is the comment of the Evangelist, relating the logion to the OT history and promise which lay at the heart of the festival, even as v 39 is his explanation of the water symbolism in the light of the saving events of the cross and resurrection and sending of the Spirit by Christ. Of this we cannot be sure, since Jesus himself was not unaccustomed to using the OT in a creative manner in relation to the salvation of the kingdom of God. In any case we take it that the OT scripture affords the basis for the invitation: the thirsty believer may come and drink because "rivers of living water will flow out of his κοιλία," i.e., from the κοιλία of the Christ. There is no OT scripture that explicitly states that, but it is likely that a multiple allusion to pertinent scriptures is in mind. Those would be passages that were of prime significance for the meaning of the festival and that were read at it: chief among them were the record of the gift of water from the rock in the desert, Exod 17:1–6 (cf. also Pss 78:15–16; 105:40–41), the flowing of the river of living water from the temple in the kingdom of God, Ezek 47:1–11, and the waters that flow in the new age from Jerusalem to the eastern and western seas, Zech 14:8. The picture of Ezekiel is taken up in a similar sense in the description of the City of God in Rev 22:1–2: the river of water of life is said to flow from "the throne of God and the Lamb." This statement is followed by a citation from Zech 14:11, "There shall no longer be any curse," and in the immediately ensuing epilogue (v 17) there is a similar invitation to that given in John 7:37–38:

> Let him who is thirsty come,
> let him who wishes take the water of life freely.

Thus the remembrance of divine intervention in the past is conjoined with the promise of eschatological fullness of blessing in the coming kingdom of God, in order to show the realization of both in the present through Jesus.

Why are the waters said to flow "out of his κοιλία"? The term can be used as a synonym for καρδία, "heart," and occasionally is so employed in the LXX. From ancient times to the present readers have recalled that a Roman soldier pierced the side of the crucified Jesus with a lance, "and immediately blood and water came out" (John 19:34). It is suggested that the Evangelist by the use of κοιλία was pointing to that event as the occasion when the living waters began to flow; the Lord becomes the source of living water when he is "lifted up" on his cross and so to heaven. While this is theologically correct, it is our belief that a different concern motivated the Evangelist in the record of 19:31–37, and that we should dissociate it from the logion of vv 37–38. A simpler explanation, favored by many exegetes, sees in κοιλία a rendering of the Aramaic term גוף, גופא (gûph, gûph[ā']), which, while originally meaning "cavity," is used to denote "body" or "person," and even as a substitute for the personal pronoun, so that מן־גופא simply means "from him" (so Str-B 2:492; Jeremias, *Golgotha*, 82; Bultmann, 303–4 n.5; Schnackenburg, 1:156). It is not impossible that the term גוף, "cavity, self," may provide a link between the remembrance of water from the rock in the wilderness and the expectation of water from the temple in the new age, and Jesus as its source, if it is assumed that the living waters are to flow from a cavity in *the rock in the temple* (of which rock the Jews were ever aware). We recall the teaching of 2:17–19, that the new temple is the Lord in his exaltation, and the identification, early made, of the rock in the wilderness with Christ (see Daniélou, "Joh 7.38 et Ezéch 47.1–11," 161).

39 The Evangelist adds that the living waters represent the Spirit, which Jesus was to send when he was glorified. This connects with both Jewish and Christian convictions. Jewish teachers interpreted Isa 12:3 in its relation to the water-drawing rite; *Sukk.* 5:55a cited Jehoshua ben Levi: "Why did they call it (the court of the women) the place of drawing water? Because it was from there that they drew the Holy Spirit, according to the word: 'With joy you will draw water. . . .'" More importantly, the Evangelist's comment assumes the basic doctrine that the Holy Spirit is the Spirit of the kingdom of God, and that while Jesus was the instrument of the kingdom through his whole ministry, the crucial event whereby the saving sovereignty came among men was the crucifixion-resurrection of Jesus. The kingdom having come, the Spirit was sent by the exalted Lord (20:22), and so the Spirit's ministry in the world is especially directed to that of communicating the life of the kingdom of God to humankind (see John 3:3, 5, 6, 8). It is *this* all-important work of the Spirit in the world that prompted the Evangelist's observation, "The Spirit was not yet, because Jesus was not yet glorified" (compare further the teaching on the Paraclete-Spirit in chaps. 14–16).

DIVISION AMONG THE PEOPLE (7:40–44)

The declaration of Jesus in vv 37–38, with whatever else he may have added by way of explanation, evokes instant responses among the crowd, both favorable and hostile.

40–41 Some exclaim, "This man is truly the prophet," i.e. the prophet like Moses of Deut 18:15, 18. Others affirm, "This man is the Messiah." We should like to know precisely how different these judgments were intended to be. The prophet like Moses was viewed as a figure belonging to the end time of salvation, as we see from the formula in use among the Qumran Community, whose organization held good "until the coming of the Prophet and the Anointed Ones of Aaron and Israel" (1QS 9:11). This formula, however, *distinguishes* the Prophet from the two (priestly and royal) Messiahs expected by the community. The same distinction is assumed in the question of the Pharisees in John 1:25. Yet we know that the distinction came to be blurred in the minds of not a few, especially in the light of the enhancement of Moses and his powerful deeds and the elaboration of the second Exodus motif, as a result of which the awaited Prophet like Moses became in the minds of many, at least a messianic figure, if not redeemer (among the Samaritans the identification became complete). J. L. Martyn considers that the evidence of the Fourth Gospel, and of our passage in particular, "reflects the easy modulation from the Mosaic Prophet to the Mosaic Prophet-Messiah" (*History and Theology in the Fourth Gospel*, 113–14), and Bultmann affirmed, "Both titles refer to the eschatological bringer of salvation, and the two-fold statement serves only to illustrate the uncertainty of Messianic doctrine" (305 n.4). On such an interpretation the first two groups expressed the same conviction in different terms. We may recall the similar reactions of the crowd to the feeding miracle in 6:14–15: those who witnessed it said, "This is truly the prophet that should come into the world," and "they" were about to seize Jesus and make him king. This could indicate the equivalence of Mosaic Prophet and King Messiah in the minds of those concerned, or it could connote two views among them, namely that Jesus was the Prophet like Moses, and that Jesus was the man designated to be the warrior King Messiah. The ambiguity applies to 7:40–41 also, and we cannot be certain of its resolution. It is of interest to observe that the reactions to Jesus at the feeding miracle and at Tabernacles have to do with events connected with Moses, namely the descent of the manna and the gift of water from the rock; the same gifts were expected of the Messiah, namely the return of the manna (see *Comment* on 6:31) and the gift of abundant water. The latter is attested in *Midr. Rabba* on Eccl 1:9, "As the first redeemer made a well to rise, so will the second Redeemer bring up water, as it is stated, 'And a fountain shall come forth from the house of the Lord . . .' (Joel 3:18)" (cited Brown, 329).

41 A third group objects to any claims that Jesus is the Messiah, on the ground that he comes from Galilee, whereas the Scripture says that the Messiah is to be of David's line and town, i.e., Bethlehem. The "scripture" is Mic 5:2, which is cited to the same effect in Matt 2:5–6. Curiously the text was much more commonly used among Christians than among Jewish teachers for this purpose, but it seems to have been acknowledged by the latter as affirming the Messiah's birth in Bethlehem (it is so interpreted in the Targum on the passage: "You, Bethlehem Ephratha . . . from you shall proceed forth to me the Messiah, in order to exercise rule over Israel . . ." (similarly *Pirqe R. El.* 3[2b]; *J. Ber.* 5a; *Midr. Rabb.* 51 on Lam 1:16, see Str-B 1:83; R. E. Brown, *The Birth of the Messiah*, 513 n.2). Characteristically the Evangelist makes no comment on the objection. Is this because, in Bultmann's words, "The Evangelist knows nothing or wants to know nothing of the birth in Bethlehem" (306 n.6)? That conclusion goes beyond the evidence. Doubtless the place of Jesus' birth is for the Evangelist altogether less important than his heavenly origin, but it is likely that we have here a typical instance of Johannine irony, similar to that displayed in connection with the related objection to Jesus as Messiah in vv 26–27. There the fact that Jesus came from Nazareth is contrasted by certain people with the doctrine of the unknown origin of the Messiah, little knowing that their doctrine was truer of Jesus than they imagined—his origin was in reality *"hidden"*—it was from God in heaven! So here as the Evangelist records the Jewish objection to Jesus as coming from Nazareth instead of Bethlehem, he knows that his Christian readers are aware that Jesus was born in Bethlehem, and more importantly that he was the Word made flesh, whose "origins," in truth, were "from of old, from ancient times" (Mic 5:2). The reasonableness of this interpretation is seen in the early attestation in Christian tradition of the Davidic ancestry of Jesus, (cf. especially the confessional fragments in Rom 1:3 and 2 Tim 2:8), the unlikelihood that the Evangelist would have so lightly dismissed an objection based on the scriptures, and the doubtfulness that the birth of

Jesus in Bethlehem was a fiction based on Mic 5:2, current in the limited circles to which Matthew and Luke belonged. See Schnackenburg, 2:158–59, and Brown's excursus, "The Birth at Bethlehem," in *The Birth of the Messiah*, 513–16.

43–44   The occurrence of a division among the crowd because of Jesus provides a further instance of "the critical function of Jesus' word of revelation" (Schnackenburg, 2:159). People confronted with the revelation of God in Christ are not allowed to remain neutral; they divide before him as before the judgment seat of God (cf. 3:19–21; 12:31–32, 46–49, and for further instances of such division see vv 12–13, 30–31; 9:16; 10:19). With v 44 cf. v 30 and the *Comment* thereon, also 8:20, 59; no one could lay hands on Jesus prior to his "hour," but contrast 13:1; 17:1.

DIVISION AMONG THE AUTHORITIES (7:45–52)

45–46   The officers' reaction to Jesus is a prime example of the impression that Jesus made on people from the commencement of his ministry to its close: "The people were astounded at his teaching, for, unlike the doctors of the law, he taught with authority' (Mark 1:22; the saying is aptly placed by Matthew immediately following the Sermon on the Mount, Matt 7:28–29; for the same phenomenon at the close of the ministry of Jesus, cf. Mark 12:17b, 32–34, 37b; John 8:7–9). The officers were not simply helpless to lay hands on a numinous man (cf. 18:3–6), but were awed by the incomparable authority of his speech, above all as manifest in the declaration of vv 37–38. Convinced of the truth of his proclamation (cf. v 47), they refused to obey the orders of the Jewish authorities and arrest him. The unadorned dictum of v 46 may be compared with the utterance of an even humbler group of people in 4:42, which history has vindicated as it has this one. Two thousand years later, with the cultures of the whole world available to us, it remains true: "No man has ever spoken like this man."

47–48   Significantly it was the Pharisees in the Sanhedrin who responded to the statement of the officers. They were the authorized teachers of the Law (= the Bible in Jewish eyes). To them it was outrageous that these men, set under the authority of the supreme council of the Jews, should have turned from the true interpreters of the Law and allowed themselves to be persuaded by a deceiver, who ought to die for his deception of the people (see the *Comment* on v 12). They tell the officers that none of the rulers or Pharisees have believed on him (the question of v 48 expects the answer, "No"). This is a further instance of the Evangelist's irony, for he has earlier recounted the meeting with Jesus of a "ruler of the Jews," whom Jesus described as *"the* teacher of Israel," and who confessed that Jesus was "a teacher sent from God" (3:1–10) and the Evangelist is about to tell of the same man's intervention on behalf of Jesus in the council (cf. also the Evangelist's summation of the public ministry of Jesus to the Jews in 12:37–43: *"Many* of the rulers believed on Jesus").

49   The dictum of v 49 has become a celebrated utterance, as perfectly expressing the attitude of the Pharisees to the common people. Str-B pointed out that the phrase "this crowd that doesn't know the Law" paraphrases the rabbinic expression עַם הָאָרֶץ (‘am hā’āreṣ) "the people of the land." It has an ancient history, denoting first the whole nation of Israel (e.g., Ezek 22:29), then the people in distinction from the rulers (Jer 1:18), and after the exile the mixed population that settled in the land as distinct from the returned Jewish exiles (Ezra 10:2, 11). Among the rabbis the expression signifies those who do not know the Law and therefore do not live according to it; since for them the Law signifies the Mosaic Law as interpreted in the developed oral tradition, this included the mass of ordinary people, who could not attain to it. Even the liberal-minded Hillel could say, "An uneducated man is not slow to sin, and no people of the land (‘am hā’āreṣ) is righteous" (’Abot 2.5). This classic saying was paraphrased by G. F. Moore as, "It takes education to make a saint," which was true to Jewish thought when "education" was precisely instruction in the right understanding of the Law. Where compassion ruled the Pharisees, this could inspire a desire to instruct all and sundry, but unfortunately it led to an attitude of despising the ignorant, so that "the people of the land" became virtually a term of abuse, as in v 49, and as Billerbeck's lengthy assembling of material from rabbinic literature illustrates (Str-B 2:494–519). Since those who did not know the Law were assumed not to fulfill the Law, the Pharisees doubtless classed them among the breakers of the Law on whom the curses of Deut 27:15–26 should fall. Hence the statement in v 49, and the attitude expressed in *Midr. Sam* 5.9: "It is forbidden to have mercy on one who has no knowledge." This sentiment was rigidly taken up by the Qumran community, as may be seen in 1QS 10:19–21, wherein the perfect sectary asserts:

> As for the multitude of the men of the Pit,
> I will not lay hands on them till the day of vengeance,
> but I will not withdraw my anger far from perverse men. . . .
> I will be without malice and wrath towards those that are
>   converted from rebellion,
> but merciless to those that have turned aside from the way;
> I will not comfort them that are smitten until their way is perfect.

In their attitudes to the common people of Israel, Jesus and the Pharisees stood at opposite poles, for which reason Jeremias affirmed, "The good news was a slap in the face to all the religious feelings of the time" (*NT Theology*, 118). The Pharisees were enraged, and hit back!

50–51 Nicodemus raises his voice on behalf of Jesus. He points out that the Law does not pass sentence on a man before giving him an opportunity to speak for himself. This was true, despite the primary importance of the testimony of witnesses in law courts (cf. Deut 19:15–19), as Deut 1:16–17 and 17:2–5 show. It is attested variously in rabbinic writings, e.g., *Exod. Rab.* 21:3: "Men pass judgment on a man if they hear his words; if they do not hear his words they cannot establish judgment on him." On this basis the protest of Nicodemus carries the implication that, in refusing to listen to one who challenged their mode of interpreting the Law, the members of the Sanhedrin are setting themselves against the Law and consequently are law-breakers—like the people of the land!

52 The Sanhedrin responds to this intervention with a biting attack on Nicodemus, on the assumption that only a Galilean would listen to *this* Galilean! For Galilee was despised as an area that did not keep the Law with the scrupulousness of Judea. The challenge to "search," i.e., the Scriptures, should not be interpreted as establishing that the Bible shows that no prophet ever comes from Galilee, since the Evangelist would not impute to these scholars of the Law ignorance of the fact that the prophet Jonah, son of Amittai, hailed from Gath-hepher in Galilee (2 Kings 14:25). Indeed, about the time when this Gospel was written R. Eliezer maintained, "Thou hast no single tribe in Israel from which a prophet has not come forth" (*Sukk.* 27b). That assertion is echoed in S. *'OlamRab.* 21: "Thou hast no city in the land of Israel in which there has not been a prophet" (Str-B 2:519). The alternative reading in P[66] and P[75] is increasingly viewed as authentic: "Search, and see that *the* prophet does not arise . . . ," i.e., the prophet like Moses, awaited to appear in the last times. As everyone knows that there is no statement in the Bible that the Prophet would come out of Galilee, so everyone knows that Galilee is not godly enough to produce that Prophet! Only Judea could be his *patris!* If we are intended to hear in this an echo of the objection recorded in vv 41–42, the same Johannine irony would be present as in that passage.

Explanation

Two themes dominate chap. 7, namely Jesus as the fulfillment of the Feast of Tabernacles and the κρίσις precipitated by his mission to Israel. The two themes are bound together, for it is precisely because Jesus proclaims that Israel's faith, embodied in its festivals, finds its fulfillment in him that the nation is compelled to make a *decision* relating to him, and in so doing they *divide* according as they *judge* (all three meanings are included in the term κρίσις, which denotes *separation, decision, judgment*). The gravity of the process lies in the ultimacy of the revelation in Jesus: the fulfillment of Israel's faith and its feasts is the coming of the kingdom of God—to Israel and therefore to mankind; hence the judgment upon Jesus by those to whom he is sent partakes of the eschatological nature of the judgment and salvation that he brings. This theme we shall see unfolded in the remaining chapters of the Gospel. It is the leading motif in chap. 7 from the first sentence to the last, and it continues into chap. 8.

The situation of danger for Jesus in Judea is mentioned at the outset (v 1): "the Jews" intend to bring him to justice (!). They have made up their minds that he is a heretic and a law-breaker, and that he must be put to death. When Jesus decided to go to Jerusalem he would have been aware that his every word and movement would be scrutinized. And so it was. As he stepped into the glare of publicity at the festival, it was as though he stepped into a public trial. That, certainly, is how the Evangelist represents the events at the festival. When Jesus appears before the people, a series of charges are brought against him, of greater and less gravity, but all with a view to discrediting his ministry. They may be enumerated as follows: (*i*) Jesus is a deceiver of the people (vv 12, 47); (*ii*) he is an ignorant layman, lacking the education and training essential for a teacher of the law, hence without authority to teach (v 15); (*iii*) his healing of the cripple at Bethesda shows that he flouts the sabbath laws (v 21); (*iv*) his messianic claims are false, since everyone knows where Jesus comes from, but the Messiah's origin is unknown until his revelation to Israel; (*v*) the Scripture teaches that the Messiah is born in Bethlehem, whereas Jesus hails from Nazareth (v 42; the point is alluded to in v 52, where the Galilean origin of the Messiah is said to be impossible).

These charges are dealt with *seriatim,* with a good deal of irony which allows the Evangelist to leave his reader with knowledge of the facts to judge for himself. No attempt is made to rebut the first charge, but it is met by the answer given by Jesus to the second one: his teaching has a higher authority than a master rabbi could convey, for it comes from the One who sent him, namely God (v 17), and since he seeks the glory of him who sent him, not his own, there is no question of his being a deceiver (v 18). The answer to (*iii*) assumes the exposition given of God's way of keeping sabbath in 5:17–30, for Jesus' actions are of the kind that fulfill God's purpose in instituting the sabbath (vv 22–23). The objections to his being the Messiah are answered in an oblique manner, for Jesus does not openly declare to the crowds that he is the Messiah; he emphasizes rather that he has been sent by the One who is ultimately Real and True. Hence his origins are as unknown to them as God himself is unknown by them. If faith alone can attain to the truth of that claim (vv 28–29), its proclamation in terms of Jesus as the fulfiller of all that Tabernacles stands for bears it own authenticity (vv 37–38), and compels a response from those who hear (vv 40–43).

It is evident that the Evangelist in this presentation does not represent Jesus as standing pathetically before the bar of his people and their rulers; on the contrary his answers to their charges raise the question of *their* integrity, and confront them with a revelation that demands an answer from them. *His* trial becomes *their* trial! The crowd questions whether Jesus, by healing a paralytic on the sabbath, breaks the law of the sabbath; Jesus declares that none of *them* keeps the Law of Moses, as is evidenced by their desire to put him to death (v 19). Nicodemus courageously tells the members of the Sanhedrin that in condemning Jesus without giving him a hearing they become law-breakers and are in danger of standing condemned by the Law. The rejection of the revelation brought by Jesus on the ground of current messianic dogmas again implies a willful deafness to the word of God and blindness to the significance of deeds wherein it is expressed (the "signs"). Hence the demand of Jesus in v 24: "Stop judging according to appearances, and let your judgment ever be just."

There is little doubt that this whole presentation of Jesus at the feast of Tabernacles had profound relevance for the churches for which the Evangelist wrote. We may be sure that every one of the charges against Jesus mentioned in chap. 7 was repeated by Jews in their opposition to Jewish Christians, who remained loyal to the synagogue while yet confessors of Jesus as the Christ and worshiped in Christian communities (a situation that held good in all Palestine and in many areas of the Dispersion in the world of the first century of our era). The pressures brought upon Jesus by the populace, the threat of emissaries of the authorities, and above all the hostility of the powerful Pharisees were experienced by many of the followers of Jesus in the primitive church and especially among the Johannine communities. J. L. Martyn sees in chap. 7 a clear example of what he calls the two-level drama presented in the Gospel: the strictly unrepeatable story of Jesus in his ministry and the strangely similar experiences of the followers of Jesus in settings where Jewish influences prevailed. Martyn saw as the counterpart to Jesus in his ministry Jewish-Christian evangelists, to the Sanhedrin in Jerusalem the local "Gerousia" (council), to the temple police sent to arrest Jesus the beadles of the local court sent to arrest Christian workers (*History and Theology*, 82–89). Whether or not the detailed correspondences were actually in the Evangelist's mind, the *general* correspondence of situation is entirely plausible and calls for taking seriously both the history which the Evangelist records and the application to the constituency amongst whom this history was being repeated and for which the words of Jesus were vitally relevant.

The pertinence of the record for us who live in the wholly different contexts of Gentile nations, dominated by a multiplicity of religions and ideologies and in the different climates of thought of the modern world, is not so immediate in its application, but its message is no less relevant. For the revelation of God in Christ is directed to our age no less than to people in the first century of our era. He who fulfilled the festival of Tabernacles can quench the thirst of every human being in our time. And the challenge of Jesus' claim to be the bearer of the revelation of God and the instrument of his redemption demands of every one of us an answer that we can give before the judgment seat of God, for that is what in the end will be required of us. The call comes to us, accordingly, as to the crowd in the temple at Tabernacles and the recipients of the Gospel fifty years later: "Stop judging according to appearances, but let your judgment ever be just."

2. Jesus the Light of Life   (8:12–59)

Bibliography

Blank, J. *Krisis.* 183–251. **Charlier, J. P.** "L'exégèse johannique d'un precepte legal: Jean VIII 17." *RB* 67 (1960) 503–15. **Dahl, N. A.** "Der erstgeborene Satans und der Vater des Teufels (Polyk. 7:1 und Joh 8:44)." *Apophoreta.* FS Haenchen, Berlin: Töpelmann, 1964. 70–84. **Dodd, C. H.** "A l'arrière plan d'un dialogue johannique." *RHPR* 37 (1957) 5–17; Translated in *More New Testament Studies.* 41–57. **Dupont, J.** "Jésus Christ, Lumière du monde." *Essais sur la Christologie de St Jean.* Bruges: Saint-André, 1951. 61–105. **Funk, R. W.** "Papyrus Bodmer II (P66) and John 8, 25." *HTR* 51 (1958) 95–100. **Kern, W.** "Der symmetrische Gesamtaufbau von Joh 8, 12–58." *ZKTh* 78 (1956) 451–54. **Lategan, B. C.** "The Truth That Sets Man Free: John 8:31–36." *Neot* 2 (1968) 70–80. **Riedl, J.** "Wenn ihr der Menschensohn erhöht habt, werdet ihr erkennen (Joh 8, 28)." *Jesus der Menschensohn.* FS A Vögtle. 355–70. **Smothers, E. R.** "Two Readings in Papyrus Bodmer II." *HTR* 51 (1958) 111–22. **Thüsing, W.** *Die Erhöhung und Verherrlichung Jesu im Johannesevangelium.* 15–22.

Translation

[12] *Again Jesus spoke to them and said, "I am the light of the world; he who follows me will never walk in the dark, but will have the light of life."* [13] *The*

Pharisees therefore said to him, "You are testifying about yourself; your testimony is not valid." [a] [14] *Jesus said in reply, "Even though I am testifying about myself my testimony is valid,* [a] *because I know where I come from and where I am going to. You do not know where I come from and where I am going to.* [15] *You judge in accordance with human standards, I do not judge anyone.* [16] *But even if I do judge, my judgment is authentic,* [a] *because it is not I alone who judges but I and the Father who sent me.* [17] *In your own law it stands written that the testimony of two men is valid;* [a] [18] *I am one who testifies about myself and the Father who sent me bears testimony about me."* [19] *They said therefore to him, "Where is your Father?" Jesus replied, "You know neither me nor my Father; if you knew me you would know my Father also."* [20] *Jesus said these things in the treasury,* [b] *while he was teaching in the temple; but no one arrested him, because his hour had not yet come.*

[21] *He said to them again, "I am going away, and you will look for me and will die in your sin; where I am going you cannot come."* [22] *The Jews therefore said, "Surely he is not going to kill himself, is he? Is that why he said, 'Where I am going you cannot come'?"* [23] *He said to them, "You are from below, I am from above; you have your origin in this world, I do not have my origin in this world.* [24] *This is why I said to you that you will die in your sins, for if you do not believe that 'I am (he)' you will die in your sins."* [25] *They said therefore to him, "Who are you?" Jesus said to them, "Just what I am telling you.* [c] [26] *I have many things to say about you—and to judge; but he who sent me is truthful, and what I have heard from him I speak to the world."* [27] *They did not know that he was speaking to them about the Father.* [28] *Jesus therefore said to them, "When you lift up the Son of Man, then you will know that 'I am (he),' and that I do nothing of my own accord, but speak only those things the Father has taught me.* [29] *And he who sent me is with me; he has not left me alone, for I always do what is pleasing to him."*

[30] *As he was saying these things many came to believe in him. Jesus therefore said to the Jews who had put their trust in him, "If you continue in the revelation I have brought you really are my disciples,* [32] *and you will come to know the truth, and the truth will set you free."* [33] *They replied to him, "We are Abraham's descendants, and have never been slaves to anybody; how is it that you are saying, 'You will become free'?"* [34] *Jesus answered them, "Amen, amen I tell you, everyone who commits sin is a slave of sin,* [d] [35] *but the slave does not remain in the house forever; the son does remain forever.* [36] *If therefore the son sets you free, you certainly will be free.*

[37] *"I know that you are Abraham's descendants; but you are intent on killing me, because my teaching has not penetrated you.* [38] *I am speaking what I have seen in the presence of (my)* [e] *Father; and you are doing what you have heard* [f] *from (your) father."* [39] *They said in reply to him, our Father is Abraham." Jesus says to them, "If you really were Abraham's children you would be doing what Abraham did.* [g] [40] *But now you are intent on killing me, a man who has proclaimed to you the truth which I heard from God; this Abraham did not do.* [41] *You are doing what your father does."*

They said therefore to him, "We have not been born as a result of fornication; we have one Father only, that is, God." [42] *Jesus said to them, "If God were your Father you would love me, for I proceeded and have come here from God; for I have not come of my own accord, but he sent me.* [43] *Why do you not understand*

my language? Because you are incapable of heeding my revelation. [44] *You belong
to your father the devil, and you are willing to carry out the wishes of your father.
He was a murderer from the beginning, and never did stand* [h] *in the truth, because
there is no truth in him. Whenever he lies he talks according to his nature, because
he is a liar and the father of lying.* [45] *But because I am speaking the truth you do
not believe me.* [46] *Which of you can convict me of any sin? If I am telling the
truth, why are you not believing me?* [47] *He who belongs to God listens to God's
words; the reason why you are not listening is because you do not belong to God."*

[48] *The Jews said in reply to him, "Are we not right in saying that you are a
Samaritan and are demon-possessed?"* [49] *Jesus replied, "I am not demon-possessed,
but I honor my Father, and you dishonor me.* [50] *I am not seeking my glory; there
is one who is doing that, and he is the one who judges.* [51] *Amen, amen I say to
you, if anyone holds to my revelation he will never, never see death."* [52] *The Jews
said, "Now* [i] *we really know that you are possessed. Abraham died, and so did the
prophets, and you are saying, 'If anyone holds to my revelation he will never,
never taste death'!* [53] *You aren't greater than our father* [j] *Abraham, who died,
and the prophets, who died, are you? Who are you making yourself out to be?"*
[54] *Jesus answered, "If I glorify myself my glory is nothing; it is my Father who
glorifies me, of whom you say, 'He is our* [k] *God.'* [55] *And you do not know him, but
I know him. If I were to say that I did not know him I should be like you, a liar;
but I know him, and I hold to his revelation* [56] *Abraham your father exulted that
he should see* [l] *my day, and he saw it and was glad."* [57] *The Jews therefore said to
him, "You are not yet fifty years old, and you have seen Abraham?"* [m] [58] *Jesus
said to them, "Amen, amen I tell you, before Abraham came into existence I am."*
[59] *They picked up stones therefore to throw at him; but Jesus hid himself and went
out of the temple.* [n]

Notes

[a] In vv 13, 14, 17 testimony that is, or is not ἀληθής is spoken of, in v 16 the judgment of
Jesus is ἀληθινή; while some view the two terms in this context as interchangeable it is better to
understand the former as "true," in the sense of "valid," and the latter as "just" or "authentic,"
as having behind it the verdict of God himself.

[b] γαζοφυλάκιον can mean a receptacle in which "treasure" can be placed, i.e., a collecting
box (as in Mark 12:41), or a place where treasure is kept. Jos. speaks of several rooms in the
temple where valuables were kept, but it is likely that the hall in which the thirteen trumpet-
shaped collection boxes stood was so named it was evidently in the court of the women, since
they had access to it, and is here mentioned to identify the scene for the utterance of v 12.

[c] V 25b is the most obscure sentence in the Gospel and the most uncertain how to translate.
On the basis that τὴν ἀρχήν is an adverbial accusative the following options have been proposed:
(i) ὅτι introduces a question: "Why do I speak to you at all?" So the Gr. Fathers, a majority of
recent scholars, and NEB. As a variant of this ὅτι is taken as = מה (māh): "That I speak to you
at all!" A rebuke is in mind in either case (cf. Mark 9:19). (ii) Most read ὅτι as ὅ τι. Bernard
then renders τὴν ἀρχήν as "primarily," or essentially: "Primarily what I am telling you" (II 301).
(iii) Understanding τὴν ἀρχήν as "from the beginning," Barrett (343) translates, "(I am) from
the beginning what I tell you" (cf. 1:1). (iv) More commonly on this basis the clause is rendered,
"(I am) what I have been telling you from the beginning" (RSV, JB, GNB, NIV). To this it is
objected that λαλῶ is present, and the sentence would need the aorist; but cf. 15:27: ἀπ' ἀρχῆς
μετ' ἐμοῦ ἐστε. Does however τὴν ἀρχήν = ἀπ' ἀρχῆς? (v) P66 prefaces the clause with εἶπον ὑμῖν.
R. W. Funk ("Papyrus Bodmer II and John 8:25") and E. R. Smothers ("Two Readings in
Papyrus Bodmer II") both hold this reading to be original; Bruce (194) thinks that it points in
the right direction and renders, "I told you at the beginning that which also I am speaking to

you (now)." (*vi*) Lat. versions translate, "I am the beginning, that which I am saying to you" (*principium quia [quod] et loquor vobis*), an interpretation also in the Ethiopic: "I am the beginning, and I told you so."

Apart from (*vi*), which is a clear misunderstanding of the Gr., all these are possible. The difficulty of (*i*) is the continuation of Jesus' address to his opponents, both positively and negatively; (*iii*) appears to me doubtful; if the reading of P[66] is not accepted (*v*) is difficult to justify. With greatest hesitation I favor a variant of Bernard's view (*ii*) mentioned by Zerwick (*Biblical Greek* [4th ed.] par. 222), retaining the crispness of the sentence and the full force of the present tense: "*Just what I am telling you*," which would reiterate the affirmation in the preceding sentence: ὅτι ἐγώ εἰμι.

[d] τῆς ἁμαρτίας is omitted by some Western MSS (D etc.); the omission is adopted by various exegetes, but it may be a stylistic improvement (so UBS committee).

[e] The statement without personal pronouns (μου after τῷ πατρί, ὑμῶν after τοῦ πατρός) is commonly felt to be the best attested in the MS tradition, but it is ambiguous. The affirmation may be understood as referring to God the Father in both clauses, and ποιεῖτε be viewed as an imperative (so Moulton, *Grammar of NT Greek* 1:85; Brown, 356; Metzger, 225); but v 41 seems to demand that ποιεῖτε be viewed as indicative, in which case the pronouns μου and ὑμῶν, though not original, rightly interpret the saying.

[f] Instead of ἠκούσατε many authorities, including P[66] ℵ* D, read ἑωράκατε. This however appears to be due to the notion that the same term should appear in both clauses.

[g] The text as read is a mixed conditional sentence, ἐστε (instead of ἦτε) perhaps giving a stronger sense: "If you really are Abraham's children, you will be doing the works of Abraham" (so Metzger, 225). Some MSS correct ἐστε to ἦτε, and others (including P[66] B*) read ποιεῖτε, an imperative, "If you are children of Abraham, do the works of Abraham"; while this latter reading is well possible, the conditional sentence perhaps suits the context better.

[h] οὐκ ἔστηκεν, read by P[66] ℵ B* C D etc., is the imperfect of στήκω, lit. "was not standing," describing a perpetual condition. οὐχ ἔστηκεν, read by P[75] B[3] K P etc., is the perfect of ἵστημι with a present meaning, "does not stand." The former is not to be interpreted as referring to a fall of Satan, which would be more fitly expressed through an aorist; such a thought lies outside the scope of the saying.

[i] νῦν here has the force of "now really"; so Bauer, *Lexicon* (2nd ed.), 545–46, section 2.

[j] πατρὸς ἡμῶν is omitted in some Western MSS (D etc.), perhaps through a feeling that the statement clashes with v 44.

[k] ἡμῶν is direct discourse, ὑμῶν indirect; the former is more likely to be original (Metzger, 226).

[l] ἠγαλλιάσατο ἵνα is rendered by Blass-Debrunner (§ 392, 1a): "He longed with desire, rejoiced that he was to see," and is so adopted by most recent scholars and in most recent translations. Others view the ἵνα as explaining the ground of the joy: "he rejoiced in that he saw," or "he rejoiced to see" (so Bauer, 131; Hoskyns, 347; Barrett, 351, who cites the modern Gr. χαίρομαι να σε θωρῶ, "I'm glad to see you"). Turner's view is similar, regarding it as an instance of the causal use of ἵνα: "rejoiced because he saw" (Moulton, *Grammar* 3:102).

[m] A few MSS (including P[75] ℵ*) read ἑωράκέν σε instead of ἑώρακας: "has Abraham seen you?" It is generally agreed that this represents an attempt to make the sentence more completely match the previous one: "Abraham rejoiced to see . . . and he saw . . . ." The MSS attestation of the usual reading is far superior.

[n] The best attested text ends the sentence with ἱεροῦ. Some MSS, however, add διελθὼν διὰ μέσου αὐτῶν (taken from Luke 4:30), and yet others give a further addition, καὶ παρῆγεν οὕτως, so anticipating 9:1. There is no warrant for these additions.

Comment

JESUS THE LIGHT OF THE WORLD (8:12–20)

12 We note immediately that the declaration, "I am the Light of the World . . ." is one of the ἐγώ εἰμι sayings of the Gospel; Jesus is the Light of the World, as he is the Bread of Life, the Door, the Good Shepherd, etc.

It is a revelatory declaration. But the context is of vital importance for its understanding. The narrative begins, *"Again* Jesus spoke to them . . . ." The last utterance of Jesus recorded by the Evangelist is 7:37–38. Jesus had no part in the discussions recorded in 7:40–52, and 7:53–8:12 did not exist for the Evangelist. The setting is Jesus in the Feast of Tabernacles. As 7:37–38 had immediate reference to the water-drawing ceremony of the festival, and showed Jesus as fulfilling all that it signified of Israel's experience of and hope for the salvation of God, so 8:12 has immediate reference to the joyous celebration each night in the light of the lamps, with all that it connoted of Israel's experience of the shining of God upon them for their deliverance and hope of future salvation.

The saying of *Sukk.* 5.1, "He who has not seen the joy of the place of water-drawing has not seen joy in his whole life-time," immediately precedes the description of the lighting of the four huge lamps in the court of the women and what took place thereafter. It reads:

> Towards the end of the first day of the feast of Tabernacles, people went down into the court of the women, where precautions had been taken [to separate the men from the women]. Golden lamps were there, and four golden bowls were on each of them, and four ladders were by each; four young men from the priestly group of youths had jugs of oil in their hands containing about 120 logs and poured oil from them into the individual bowls. Wicks were made from the discarded trousers of the priests and from their girdles. There was no court in Jerusalem that was not bright from the light of the place of drawing [water]. Men of piety and known for their good works danced before them [the crowd] with torches in their hands, and sang before them songs and praises. And the Levites stood with zithers and harps and cymbals and trumpets and other musical instruments without number on the 15 steps, which led down from the court of the Israelites into the court of the women and which corresponded to the 15 songs of the steps in the psalms.

From other references to this procedure it is clear that this took place each night of the feast (except on an intervening sabbath). The dancing and singing lasted all night till dawn, and it was the endeavor of the pious not to sleep any night of the feast. It evidently did not lack the element of entertainment; it is recorded that Rabbi Simeon ben Gamaliel (a son of Gamaliel, the elder, who belonged to the leading men prior to the destruction of Jerusalem) "danced with eight lighted torches without any one of them touching the ground"! The nightly celebration ended with two appointed priests with trumpets slowly descending the steps to the court of the women. At the Nicanor door of the temple they turned towards the shrine and said, "Our fathers who were in this place turned their backs to the temple of God and their faces eastward and threw themselves down eastward before the sun; but we direct our eyes to Yahweh." R. Jehuda later said, "They repeatedly called out, 'We are Yahweh's, and our eyes are directed to Yahweh!'" This may have been to dissociate the celebration of the Lights from sun worship and to make clear that it was for the Lord. (For the text and its interpretation see Str-B 2:805–7.)

As with the water-drawing ceremony, the celebration in the light of the lamps will have been associated with recollection of the nation's experience at the Exodus and the hope for a second Exodus. In the wilderness wanderings, the presence of the Lord with his people was manifested in the Shekinah cloud—the pillar of cloud by day and the pillar of fire by night—which saved them from would-be-destroyers (Exod 14:19–25) and guided them through the wilderness to the promised land (Exod 13:21–22). It is linked with the OT faith in the Lord as the Light of his people (Ps 27:1), which for the Jew connoted not so much the being of God as his saving activity. "Light is *Yahweh in action*," said Conzelmann (*TDNT* 9:320). Ps 44:3 gives a remarkable expression of this concept, and it was ever before the eyes of the Israelites in the representations of theophany, both for revelation (Ezek 1:4, 13, 26–28) and for salvation (Hab 3:3–4). God's "shining" for their salvation at the Exodus encouraged prayers for the like "shining" of his face in the predicaments of the faithful (e.g., Ps 80:1–7, 14–19), and was matched by their expectation of that same light shining for their salvation in the coming kingdom of God (e.g., Isa 60:19–22). Zech 14:5b–7 is especially important here, for the description of the continual light of "that day" is immediately followed by that of the living waters that are to flow from Jerusalem, a passage read at Tabernacles and one of those assumed in the saying of 7:37–38.

This festival background for 8:12 does not, of course, exhaust the meaning of the saying, but it does indicate the starting point for its understanding. Had it been uttered in a synagogue, it would have awakened in the people familiar associations (not to say astonishment and outrage!), for contemporary Judaism spoke not only of God as the Light of the world but also of the Torah, and the Temple, and Adam (to whom Prov 20:27 was applied), and even of at least one of its great teachers, Johanan ben Zakkai (see Str-B 1:237 for citations). When, however, the utterance is set in the celebration of salvation history and eschatological expectations of Tabernacles, the application assumes greater proportions, and the relation to the cry of 7:37–38 is clear. In the context of the Gospel, the saying takes on a cosmic scope. It expresses, in the words of J. Blank, "the universal saving character of the revelation and the universal saving significance of the Person of Jesus" (*Krisis*, 184). That would have been quite comprehensible to readers of the Fourth Gospel, reared in the faiths of the Hellenistic world, for the thought of God as Light and his messengers as bringers of light to the world was familiar (see Dodd, *Interpretation*, 201–8; Odeberg, 286–92; Bultmann, 40–44, 342–43). They would also have recognized in these words an exclusive claim that permitted no rival, but through the doctrine of the Logos would have been equally ready to see in Jesus the completion of their former glimpses of truth and the fulfillment of their earlier hopes and longings.

When the original setting of 8:12 is seen in the Feast of Tabernacles, it is understood why the imagery of "following" the Light is employed instead of *receiving* it, or *walking in* it, or the like: this is what Israel did in the wilderness! The people followed the Light as it led from the land of slavery through the perilous wilderness to the promised land. The picture harmonizes perfectly with the call of Jesus to "follow" him as disciples, but makes plain its soteriological and eschatological dimensions: following Jesus, the Light of the World, gives to the believer assurance of avoiding the perils and snares of the darkness and the promise of possessing "the light of life," i.e., liberation from the realm of death for life in the kingdom of light. Since Jesus *is* the Light of life (1:4), the promise carries the reality now, in anticipation of its fullness in the glory of the kingdom to be revealed (cf. 11:25). That the "following" takes the believer along a path that leads to the glory via Golgotha is yet to be made known (cf. 12:24–26), but the Christian reader, acquainted with the kerygma, understands that already (cf. Mark 8:34; 2 Tim 2:11–13).

13 No mention is made of positive reactions to v 12, such as those to 7:37–38 (cf. 7:40–41a, 46), but an effect of the assertion in the saying is at once perceptible (as indeed throughout the chapter): it belongs to the function of the Light to discriminate and judge (3:19–21). The Pharisees object that Jesus is bearing witness to himself; in view of Deut 19:15, that is not allowed in Jewish law. Hence Jesus' testimony is invalid (cf. *Ketub.* 2.9: "No man is authenticated through his own testimony. . . . No man can bear testimony on his own behalf").

14 The reply of Jesus is unexpected: his testimony concerning himself is valid, because he knows his origin and his destiny, whereas his opponents do not. His origin and destiny, of course, are in God, from whom he comes and to whom he goes (cf. 13:3), who moreover is *with him* (v 16). The testimony of Jesus therefore is grounded in his unity with the Father, from whom his revelation is derived. This has the consequence of identifying the revelation of God with the (self-) testimony of Jesus. (Note: in 5:31 Jesus proceeds on the basis of the legitimacy of the Jewish use of Deut 19:15 and so adduces the testimony of "Another," i.e., God, given through varied means. Here he makes a different use of that law, to affirm that his own testimony was not simply his own but was from God, in God, and with God, hence ἀληθής, "valid"! Despite the different applications of the Deuteronomic law, the result is really the same.)

15–16 With the charge that the Pharisees judge κατὰ τὴν σάρκα, cf. 7:24: "Do not judge κατ' ὄψιν (according to appearance)." κατὰ τὴν σάρκα, however, indicates a criterion of judgment fashioned by men of this world not subject to the Spirit, and therefore motivated by unbelief (cf. 3:3–7). Unlike the Pharisees Jesus does not judge; that is not the purpose of his ministry as Revealer and Redeemer (3:17), but it forms an inevitable consequence of it by reason of the resistance to it of man (3:19, cf. also 9:39). "Even if I do judge" of v 16 should be compared with "Even if I do bear testimony concerning myself" of v 14: the testimony and the judgment of Jesus are alike rooted in God. Hence his judgment is "authentic," as manifesting the good-pleasure of the Father, just as his testimony reveals the word of the Father.

17–18 In the light of the preceding utterances, the adducing of the law of two witnesses in Deut 19:15 must be viewed as "an analogical mode of speech" (Blank, *Krisis,* 221). For the Father who "sent" Jesus is "with" him, not to declare publicly his agreement with what Jesus independently says (an impossible notion!), but to reveal to him what to say, alike in judgment and testimony (see 5:30 and 7:16–17). Two complementary ideas are presented here: on the one hand the unity of the Father and the Son in the testimony and judgment declared by the Son and on the other hand their distinction. Blank observed: "The revelation-testimony corresponds in eminent fashion to the principle of two witnesses; for that which is there only externally attained, the agreement of two different persons, is here given with an inner necessity, and conditions the material as well as the logical structure of the revelation-statement" (*Krisis,* 223).

19 "Where is your father?" expresses another "Johannine misunderstanding." They think of another man they could question ("We can't see him and we haven't got his evidence!" so Schnackenburg, 2:195). Since they are incapable of recognizing in Jesus the one sent of God, it is deduced that they know neither him nor the Father. "As in 5:37, the claim is made that when men shut themselves off from Jesus' witness it is a sign that God has shut himself off from them" (Bultmann, 283).

20 That no one seized Jesus at this point indicates a desire to do so; cf. 7:28–30, which relates similar teaching and a similar response.

JESUS THE ONE FROM THE WORLD ABOVE (8:21–29)

21–22 The passage is reminiscent of 7:33–34, but more threatening. Jesus is to "depart," i.e., to the Father's dwelling (14:2), and the Jews who opposed him will "seek" him. This may be meant ironically: they will seek what he proclaimed as God's gift through him, but in vain, for they will die in their sin, i.e., the sin of unbelief (cf. 16:8–9). This represents the opposite of what is proclaimed in 8:12; whereas followers of the Christ walk in the Light, in possession of and with hope for the eternal life of the kingdom of God, unbelievers walk in the darkness of this age to "death," i.e., exclusion from the kingdom of God.

That Jesus might kill himself would, in Jewish thought, put him beyond "finding," since the suicide goes to "darkest Hades" (so Jos., *BJ*, 3.375; Jewish teachers deduced from Gen 9:5 that God would "require" of the suicide his own blood). If in 7:35 there is an ironical reflection of the mission of Jesus (through his Church) to the nations, so here it is possible that 8:22 is seen (somewhat as 11:49–50) as an unwitting prophecy, even if a caricature, of Jesus laying down his life for others (so Hoskyns, 334; Bultmann, 283; Barrett, 341, etc.).

23–24 Far from Jesus being doomed to the nether world, he declares that he is "from above," the heavenly world, whereas his detractors are "from below," i.e., this world, alienated from God and subject to the "ruler of this world" (12:31; 16:11). Since Jesus is from God, his destiny is to return to God, but the Jews addressed will "die in their sins," and so miss the new world of the kingdom of God, if they do not believe that "I am he" (ἐγώ εἰμι). The converse is not stated but assumed: if they do believe, they will find what they seek.

There appears to be little doubt (see the *Comment* on 6:20) that ἐγώ εἰμι is an OT revelation formula. It is especially common in Deutero-Isaiah, and Isa 43:10 is of particular significance for the present passage: "You are my witnesses, says the Lord, and my servant whom I have chosen, that you may know and believe and understand that *I am He*" (Hebrew אני הוא [ʾanî hûʾ] rendered in the LXX as ἐγώ εἰμι). The phrase is equivalent to "I am the Lord," which occurs in the sentence that follows (Isa 43:11). Schnackenburg points out the excellence of the connection between Isa 43:10 and v 24: "Jesus is in a lawsuit with the 'world' (vv 14–18), and in him God testifies that he is the eschatological helper and savior who turns darkness into light and wants to bring every human being into the light of life (8:12). The Jews should put themselves on God's side, accept his testimony and believe that in Jesus God says his 'It is I.' Then they too would win a share in God's eschatological salvation" (2:200).

Further, C. H. Dodd pointed out that "I am He," אני הוא, gave rise to a peculiar variation, "I *and* He," אני והוא, which was treated as the name of God, and interpreted as expressing the, close association, almost identification, of God with his people. This name was used at the Feast of Tabernacles by the priests when they chanted the Hosanna from Ps 118:25; instead of "I am Yahweh," they sang "I and He," אני והוא (*Interpretation*, 93–96). It is significant that the absolute ἐγώ εἰμι should occur twice in this paragraph: in the context of the feast and in the related "I am" of v 58. It certainly indicates the unity of Jesus as Revealer and Redeemer with God the Father; it conceivably could also carry the further implication of Jesus as the representative of God's people binding them to the Father (so Bruce, 193).

26–29 "The Jews demand . . . that a definite predicate be provided for the 'I am'" (Hoskyns, 335). Hence their question, "Who are you?" Jesus simply replies, "Just what I am telling you" (see note on v 25). If he declines to define further the ἐγώ εἰμι at this point, he gives not the least suggestion of refusal to speak further about it. On the contrary he has "many things" to say about the Jews, and to judge, i.e., to show their wrong and their guilt, and he will continue to tell them what he hears from him who sent him to them (v 26). When incomprehension again greets him (v 27), Jesus informs them of the time and the event when they will know the truth and meaning of his claim, ἐγώ εἰμι: "When you lift up the Son of Man, then you will know. . . ."

28 The saying cannot be dissociated from 3:14–15; 12:31–32 (34).

(*i*) In 3:14 and 12:32 the verb ὑψοῦν, "lift up," is in the passive voice, probably examples of the so-called divine passive; it is God who will lift up the Son of Man.

(*ii*) The term "lift up" is closely associated with "glorify" (δοξάζω) cf. especially 12:23, with 13:31–32; 17:1. The lifting up of Jesus on the cross is one with his exaltation to heaven, and the *whole* event reveals his glory. The language reflects Isa 52:13: "My servant ὑψωθήσεται καὶ δοξασθήσεται σφόδρα," i.e., will be exalted and greatly glorified.

(*iii*) In v 28 *the Jews* will "lift up" Jesus; clearly the death of Jesus is in view; but that does not exclude the element of departure to the Father, and therefore exaltation, any more than the decision of the Jews to have Jesus put to death excludes the will of the Father. "You will know" is consequent on the total act of Christ's death and resurrection to glory.

(*iv*) That the "Son of Man" is the object of the "lifting up" is due to the event in view. The use of this expression in redemptive and, therefore, eschatological contexts derives from Dan 7:13, where "one like a son of man" appears as the representative of the kingdom of God and its lord (possibly agent too). In the synoptic predictions of the Passion (notably Mark 8:31; 9:31; 10:32), which are closely related to the Johannine lifting up sayings, the Son of Man suffers, dies, and rises as the instrument of the kingdom of God. This Christological, soteriological, and eschatological tradition is assumed in the Johannine counterparts.

(*v*) The unique element in v 28 is its statement that the Jews responsible for the death of Jesus will afterwards know who he is, his relation to the Father, and the character of his ministry, for v 29 continues the flow of thought in v 28. In the view of many, the context demands that the saying be seen as a prophecy of doom, like Mark 14:62: the Jews will come to know the identity of Jesus too late; they will know, and be judged (so Bultmann, 349–50; Barrett [hesitantly], 344; Blank, 329–30; Brown, 351. Haenchen following Bernard, 2:303] refers it to the time of judgment in the destruction of Jerusalem, 369). Others point out that γινώσκω in relation to Jesus is nowhere else in John used in a purely negative way (contrast 7:17; 8:32; 10:38; 14:31), and that the immediate effect of vv 28–29 is indicated in v 30: "Many believed in him." Moreover in this Gospel the offer of God in the Christian proclamation is always one of salvation, and it is changed to judgment only through man's unbelief. Hoskyns therefore takes this as a prophecy of conversion (337), while Schnackenburg (202–3), followed by Becker (296), recognizes in the saying the possibility of both salvation and judgment. Riedl urges that justice is done to the saying when one "leaves it in the twilight." ("Wenn ihr den Menschensohn erhöht," 365, citing without reference Heer). This is surely right. Two considerations must be borne in mind: (a) since the knowledge of Jesus represented in εγώ εἰμι is consequent on his exaltation, it falls in the age of the Spirit-Paraclete; (b) it is therefore also dependent on the proclamation of the gospel by the Church. Of this the Evangelist is aware; he has in view the Jews of his own generation, and not least the readers of his Gospel. The lifting up of the Son of Man sets in a position of decision not only the contemporaries of Jesus but every generation till the end.

THE FREEDOM OF JESUS AND THE SLAVERY OF THE JEWS (8:30–36)

The opening sentence poses a problem that involves the whole section 8:30–59. In the words of C. H. Dodd: "A group of Jews described as believers are accused of attempted murder and roundly denounced as children of the devil" ("Behind a Johannine Dialogue," 42). Scholars have been hard put to it to solve the problem.

(i) It is suggested that we should distinguish πιστεύω εἰς in v 30 from πιστεύω with the dative in v 31: in v 30 true believers in Christ are spoken of, whereas in v 31 we see Jews impressed with the teaching of Jesus but speedily offended by his further instruction (so, e.g., Westcott, 2:14; Moulton, *Grammar* 1:67–68; Bernard, 2:304; W. F. Howard, *According to John,* 88). There appears to be no real foundation for this distinction in our Gospel (see esp. Bultmann, 252 n.2).

(ii) The believers of vv 30 and 31 have no more than a sham faith. It is akin to that in 2:23, and those who profess it here are of the same kind as there: Jesus doesn't trust them, and with good reason—they eventually pick up stones to kill him! The purpose of this discourse is to expose this false belief (strongly advocated by Hoskyns, 336–37; also Bultmann, 433; Haenchen, 369–70; Becker, 293). On the contrary, the belief in v 30 is called forth by the *word* of Jesus, not by miracles; 4:41 is more pertinent here than 2:23.

(iii) In Dodd's view, these believers are what Acts 10:45 terms "believers in the circumcision," like the myriad Jewish believers "all zealous for the law" in Acts 21:20. They represent the Judaizing Christians, such as Paul knew, who threatened the integrity of the gospel and the mission of the Church. The Evangelist's attitude to them was like Paul's in Gal 1:6–9: "Let them be *anathema*—accursed!" Vv. 30–59 reflect the Johannine churches' struggle against Judaizers ("Behind a Johannine Dialogue," 43–47). In our judgment it is implausible that the Evangelist should so represent Jewish *Christians* of his time, nor is it clear that his circle was endangered by them.

(iv) We should recognize that there is not a hint in vv 30–32 that the faith of the believers is inadequate or insincere. By contrast the would-be murderers of Jesus are told in v 37, "My word οὐ χωρεῖ ἐν ὑμῖν," which means that it has not begun to penetrate their minds (see Schnackenburg, 490 n.82); their unbelief makes them wholly resistant to the word of Jesus. Hence in v 43 they are said to be incapable of "giving heed" to his word. After the depiction of people becoming believers in vv 30–32, the entire passage is punctuated by objections to faith in Jesus—vv 33, 41, 48, 52, 57. Since the objectors in the last three passages are termed "the Jews," i.e., Jewish opponents of Jesus, it is reasonable to assume that they are the protesters also in vv 33 and 41. In that case we are presented in 8:30–59 with a typical statement of Jews coming to faith in Jesus; they are instructed by him as to what true discipleship means and there follows a mass of typical Jewish propaganda calculated to destroy faith in Jesus. The *Sitz im Leben* of this composition is not a controversy with Judaizers, but the conflict with Judaism that was a perpetual threat to Jewish believers. Such is Schnackenburg's conclusion: in 8:30–59 "the attempt to confirm Jews who had become believers in loyalty to Jesus combines with the polemic against the Judaism of John's time, which was mounting violent attacks on the Messiahship of Jesus. The polemical aspect predominates in the rest of the section because a rebuttal of the Jewish counter-arguments had become a necessity for the sake of the Jewish Christians, who had become insecure" (2:205). Needless to say the twofold perspective or two-level drama characteristic of the Gospel is much in evidence in this passage.

31–32 The primary duty of a believer is indicated in the exhortation of Jesus, "Remain in my word." That is the mark of a real disciple. Μείνητε signifies a settled determination to *live* in the word of Christ and by it, and so entails a perpetual listening to it, reflection on it, holding fast to it, carrying out its bidding. In 15:7 it is represented as letting the word abide in us, which puts the same thing in another figure, and it leads to living (abiding) in Christ and Christ in us. If being a disciple is to be a learner in the presence of Christ, that is the counterpart in the post-Easter situation to the experience of the disciples in the earthly ministry. The process entails a *coming to know the truth*, that is, a grasping of the revelation of God in Christ (cf. v 28, "You will know that I am he"), and so the salvation of the kingdom which he brings. As the revelation in Christ is inseparable from his redemptive action, the knowledge of the truth is not alone intellectual, but existential; hence it is *life* under the saving sovereignty of God (on this see Bultmann, 434–35). That " the truth will set you free" follows from this as the day the night, for the revelatory redemption initiates an *Exodus* on the grand scale. As the Exodus under "the first Redeemer" was a release from the slavery of Egypt's land for the freedom of the people of God in the promised land, so the great Exodus under "the second Redeemer" is for the emancipation of a new people of God, drawn from all nations of the earth, for the freedom of the kingdom of God. While the Evangelist is sparing in his use of the expression "kingdom of God," his characterizing the new life as life through the Spirit in the age ushered in by the glorification of Christ (7:39) denotes exactly the same reality.

33 The first objection to the teaching of Jesus in the dialogue that follows rests on a double misunderstanding, namely on the meaning of freedom in Jesus' proclamation and on the identity of Abraham's children. The first is clarified in vv 34–36, the second in vv 37–40. "We have never been slaves to anybody" is a curious claim in view of Israel's experience in Egypt, their deportation to Babylon, and their present subjection to Rome. But the accent falls on "We are Abraham's descendants." It was the boast of rabbis, "All Israelites are sons of kings" (i.e., of Abraham, Isaac, and Jacob), and in their view the merits of Abraham covered all their demerits, hence the dictum, "The circumcised do not go down to Gehenna" *Exod. Rab.* 19.81c; see Str-B 1:116–21 for examples of these convictions). Israelites are "sons of the kingdom" (cf. Matt 8:12).

34–36 Jesus explains the assumption of v 32. There is a slavery from which Abraham's descendants are not exempt and which Abraham's merits cannot affect: bondage to sin is a reality for every one who sins, including Abraham's children. Unlike slavery that is external, this is an inward condition from which one cannot flee, with its roots in a wrong relation to God. Such a slave needs a redeemer! Vv. 35–36 indicates his presence and how he operates. The imagery changes in v 35: a slave has no permanent place in a household (he can be sold at any time); the son of a houseowner has such a place, for manifestly he ever remains a son with inheritance rights. If the parable were independent, it could simply depict the differing situations of people, with the unspoken possibility of change from the worse to the better (so Dodd, *Historical Tradition,* 381–83; Lindars, 325; Bruce, 197). One may so interpret in this context: the Son (of God, v 36, not of the houseowner, v 35) has come to liberate the slaves and give them the freedom of sons. It is likely, however, that we are intended to see the Son of v 36 in the son of v 35: as the only Son of the Father, he offers the slaves a new relation to God and a share in the inheritance which is his in the Father's house; slaves redeemed into *that* relationship *really* know freedom!

THE REAL CHILDREN OF ABRAHAM (8:37–40)

37–38 The claim of the Jews in v 33a is now dealt with: "We are Abraham's descendants." Jesus acknowledges it: "I know!" But something is drastically wrong: (*a*) they are trying to kill him, (*b*) they have no place for the revelation from God that Jesus brings. This is in crass contradiction to their status. It appears that a different father is involved here. On the one hand, Jesus is an obedient and responsive son to his Father, since he speaks and does what the Father tells him (see vv 28–29); yet on the other hand, the same applies to the Jews respecting their father! But he is not named—yet! The language is veiled.

39–40 The Jews repeat their claim: "Abraham is our Father." This time Jesus denies it, in that he distinguishes between Abraham's "descendants" (σπέρμα) and Abraham's "children" (τέκνα), implying that the latter category is the important one: Abraham's *children* act like their father. This is similar to Paul's teaching in Rom 2:28–29; 9:6–8; it was forcibly expressed by John the Baptist (Matt 3:9), and by Jeremiah much earlier (9:25–26), and finds occasional mention in the Talmud (e.g., "He who has compassion on men certainly belongs to the descendants of our father Abraham, but he who has no compassion on men certainly does not belong to the descendants of our father, Abraham," *Beṣa* 32b), but this failed to impress the Jews generally. Jesus applies it to his hearers: their endeavor to kill a righteous man, and that because he spoke God's truth, is totally opposed to everything known about Abraham, whose life was marked by faith in and obedience to God's word (cf. Gen 12:1–4; 22:15–18).

The Children of God and the Children of the Devil (8:41–47)

41 Jesus has stated that the works of his Jewish opponents show that their father is not Abraham but another, as yet unnamed. To this they reply that they are not spiritual bastards but the children of God. Their language echoes that of Hosea, who had likened Israel's idolatry to spiritual harlotry and described the individual Israelites as "children of fornication" (τέκνα πορνείας). These Jews dissociate themselves from that judgment, and affirm "We have *one* Father, God," thereby conjoining the Shema (Deut 6:4) with OT affirmations of Israel as the son of God (see esp. Exod 4:22; Deut 14:1–2).

From Origen on it has been thought that *"we* are not born of fornication" is a counterattack on Jesus, whose birth was suspicious, and so assumed to be "of fornication" (so the opponent of Christianity, Celsus, in Origen's *Contra Celsum,* 1.28; the allegation is also in the late Jewish writing *Toledoth Jeshu*). Among moderns this is held by Hoskyns, 324; Barrett, 348; Brown, 357; Sanders, 230; Lindars (possibly), 328. The context and OT background, however, sufficiently account for the language; the allusion is very indirect and not followed up; the Jews are defending themselves (so Schnackenburg, 2:212).

42–43 The claim is rejected: if God were their Father they would recognize him as one come from God and sent by him, and so love him instead of hating him (cf. 1 John 5:1). As it is they do not understand the message that he brings; his *language* is incomprehensible because they cannot "hear" the *revelation* he brings, i.e., receive it with faith. This is inevitable: if they listen to their father (v 38) they can only reject in unbelief the message of the Son of God (cf. Blank, 238, "From a not wanting to hear develops a not able to hear, an incapability of giving a hearing to the message of Jesus. Unbelief has become an attitude of life in self-enclosure, a hardening or stubbornness").

44 Such conduct shows that these men are not children of God but children of the devil. They carry out what he wants, and that above all is to kill, for (*a*) he was a murderer from the beginning, (*b*) he is a liar, and (*c*) he is the father of lying. The saying reflects the narrative of the fall in Gen 3 (rather than that of the first murder, Gen 4; cf. Wisd 2:24: "It was the devil's spite that brought death into the world, and the experience of it is reserved for those who take his side"). All this is the opposite of Jesus and his works, since he came (*a*) to bring life to the world, (*b*) to reveal truth, and (*c*) to enable mankind to share in its reality and power. As the devil opposes the word and works of the Christ, so the Jewish opponents of Jesus are his willing instruments, in particular they are ready to contrive his death.

The structure of the first and last clauses of v 44 is unexpected. They could (Bultmann: "they *should*") be rendered as, "You are of the father of the devil . . . he is a liar, and so is his father." Early Christian teachers had to face the Gnostic interpretation of this as the Demiurge (the supposed inferior god who created the evil world of matter), who was the father of the devil and the grandfather of the Jews! Bultmann ascribed the ambiguous language to a Semitic original misleadingly translated (318–19). Westcott wished to translate the final clause: "Whenever *a man* speaks a lie he speaks of his own, for his father also is a liar" (2:22–23). Attractive as this is, it is hardly warrantable to introduce a different subject into the final clause; the subject of the whole second sentence is ἐκεῖνος, i.e., the devil.

45–47 Precisely because Jesus speaks the truth, i.e., the revelation of God, the Jews, prompted by the father of lies, do not believe him. But their rejection of the truth and murderous hostility to him provoke a question: "Which of you can expose a sin in me?" This is not a general but specific question: what action of Jesus can justify their attitude and behavior toward him? Wherein has he sinned that they should want to put him to death? His life and his teaching are one—he embodies in life the truth he proclaims from God. Why then do they not believe him? The issue of the righteousness of Jesus over against allegations made against him is presented to the Jewish leaders by none other than Pilate (18:38b; 19:4–6), but more strikingly as an element of the work of the Spirit, who is to expose the world as to its sin of unbelief and the truth of the righteousness of Jesus (16:8–9). The question, "Why then do you not believe?" is answered in v 47: it is the one begotten by God through the Spirit who listens to God. They who surrender themselves to the father of lies render themselves insensible to the truth, and so manifest their real paternity (cf. 1 John 4:5–6).

The Priority of Jesus over Abraham and the Prophets (8:48–59)

48 The charge that Jesus is a Samaritan is unique to this passage, and its precise significance uncertain. Note the following points: (*a*) Samaritans were viewed by the Jews as heretics, since they rejected the worship at Jerusalem and asserted their own as God ordained. (*b*) Jews seem to have associated Samaritans with magic. In *Soṭa* 22a, one who studies the Bible and the Mishna but has not studied with a rabbi is described by one teacher as one of "the people of the land," by another as a Samaritan, and by another as a magician (Str-B 2:524–25). J. L. Martyn sees in v 48 another instance of the Jewish allegation that Jesus was a magician and a deceiver of the people (see *History and Theology*, 77–78). (*c*) Samaritans were known for prophets who made great claims, notably Dositheus, who said he was the Son of God, and Simon Magus, who claimed to be "the Great Power." Justin viewed these men as demon possessed (*Apol* 26:1, 4–5), and Origen reported that the Jews regarded them as mad (*Contra Celsum*, 6.11). These examples, of course, are later than Jesus, but would pertain to the period of the Evangelist. (*d*) The Jews may have called Jesus a Samaritan because they recognized an affinity between his teaching and that of the Samaritans (so J. W. Bowman, "Samaritan Studies," 298–308; Cullmann, *The Johannine Circle*, 50, 90). It is clear that the charges of being a Samaritan and of being possessed were linked, and were prompted by the denials of Jesus that these Jews were children of Abraham and of God as well as his own claim to being the One Sent by God.

49–50 Jesus ignores the former charge and denies the latter. He "honors" his Father, i.e., by carrying out his commission to declare the truth he has been given, while the Jews dishonor him through rejecting it. Contrary to their unbelief, the Father honors Jesus, and "he is the one who judges." This latter clause is reminiscent of OT passages in which the righteous commit their cause to God the Judge, that he may vindicate them and condemn their unjust oppressors (so, e.g., Ps 7:9–11; 35:22–28; see Blank, *Krisis*, 241). Jesus depicts a court scene in which he and his adversaries appear before

God; since God even now "honors" him, he will certainly vindicate the truth of his testimony and condemn his accusers for rejecting it. The picture receives a universal setting in 16:9–11, after the world has given its judgment upon Jesus through the cross and he has ascended to the Father.

51 The promise relates to one who "keeps" the word of Jesus, i.e., who believes it, holds on to it, carries out its demands, and so lives by it; it is the equivalent to "abiding" in his word (v 31) and is common in Johannine writings (in 1 John usually of obedience to commands, e.g., 1 John 2:3–5, but in Revelation as in the Gospel; cf. Rev. 1:3; 3:8; 22:7, 9). Such a person will "never, never see death" (οὐ μή goes with εἰς τὸν αἰῶνα). The assurance relates to life which physical death cannot extinguish, and so to the death of the spirit; the believer receives eternal life, i.e., the life of the kingdom of God, over which death has no power and which is destined for resurrection. The thought is exactly that of 11:26 and is otherwise expressed in 5:24; 6:47, and assumed in 6:63, 68. The occurrence of the expression "not see death" in Ps 89:48 (LXX 88:49) is in striking contrast to the logion of Jesus.

The suggestion that the saying is a Johannine equivalent of Mark 9:1 (H. Leroy, *Rätsel und Messverständnis*, 76–80; Haenchen, 373; Lindars, 332) is needless and quite implausible. The language is biblical (cf. Luke 2:26; Heb 11:5), and the thought is fundamental to this Gospel, and set forth, as we have seen, in a variety of ways. It is an expression of the theological axiom that the kingdom of God has come in the life, ministry, death, and resurrection of Jesus and sending of the Spirit, and is open to all who believe

The Jews misunderstand the saying as relating to physical death, and so find in it a confirmation of their charge of madness ("Their νῦν ἐγνώκαμεν, 'now we know,' is the counterpart to the ἐγνώκαμεν of the faithful community, 6:69, 1 Jn 3:16, 4:16," Bultmann, 325). Strangely their version of the logion, replacing "see" by "taste," coincides with the related saying which occurs at the beginning of the Gospel of Thomas: "Everyone who finds the explanation of these words will not taste death," but the two terms are interchangeable (Thomas has "*see* death" in logia 18, 19, and 85). The craziness of the saying is emphasized by the Jews in adducing the holiest of their forefathers, Abraham, and all who have spoken in God's name, as men who yet experienced death like the rest of humankind. Whom then is Jesus making himself? Observe that this is more than asking, "Who does he think he is?" It is a case of what he is exalting himself to be. They had an answer earlier: he was making himself equal to God (5:18). God alone is eternal and can give eternal life. Jesus then is verging on blasphemy. Schnackenburg thinks that the Jews by their question are trying to push Jesus one stage further to open blasphemy by an outright claim to divine status, which will justify stoning him (2:220). With the question, "You aren't greater than our father Abraham and the prophets, are you?" (cf. 4:12), the Evangelist expects his readers to answer in both cases, "Yes, of course!"

54–55 To the question "Whom are you making yourself," Jesus answers, "I'm not making myself anybody" (cf. the response to 5:18 in 5:19, 30). Jesus is not seeking his own glory (v 50), and if he were to do so it would be worthless (v 54a); it is the Father who glorifies him. The reader who knows how that will happen (3:14; 12:23–24, 31–33) realizes the gulf between

Jesus and the Jews in their understanding of God and of him. God's mode of glorifying Jesus, through self-sacrifice in shameful death, is as distant from self-glorification as heaven is from hell. It is this incomprehension of God's ways that makes Jesus say, "You do not know him," and to affirm, "I do know him and I keep his word."

To say, with Bultmann, that Jesus' knowledge of God is "no more nor less than his knowledge of his own mission" (301) is surely insufficient. Blank points out (as Schlatter did before him, *Der Glaube,* 219) that the Fourth Gospel never speaks of Jesus *believing in* God, but always of his *knowing* him, and he cites Thomas Aquinas, that Jesus knows God "as God knows himself" (*Krisis,* 245 and n.48). The strong asseveration to the Jews, that to say he did not know God would make him "a liar like you," implies that they are not merely *mistaken* about their supposed knowledge of God but *lying*. That is manifest in their rejection of the revelation of God through Jesus and their hatred of the messenger.

56 In sharpest contrast to the rage of the Jews, Jesus says that Abraham "exulted to see my day." In Jewish terminology "the day" usually signifies the appearance of the Messiah in the last days, but here, as in the Gospel generally, it will denote the ministry of Jesus in its totality as Revealer and Redeemer, through which the saving sovereignty of God comes. The saying primarily relates to vv 52–53: Abraham, seeing the day of salvation as the day of Jesus, acknowledged that the Son of God–Redeemer, not himself, was the means of bringing to pass the divine purpose for blessing the nations. He did not begrudge that Jesus was greater than he, but *exulted* in his work— the verb is expressive, "he was overjoyed." What a contrast, not to say gulf, between Abraham and these descendants of his!

The main import is clear, some of the details less so. That Abraham was given to see the future was a commonplace among Jews. The mysterious vision of Gen 15:17–21 was interpreted by Johanan ben Zakkai as showing: "God revealed this world to Abraham; but the world to come he did not reveal." Akiba differed: "Both this world and the world to come he revealed to him" (including therefore the days of the Messiah; *Gen. Rab.* 44.28a). 4 Ezra 2:14 also states, "Him (Abraham) you loved, and to him alone, secretly at dead of night, you showed how the world would end. You made an everlasting covenant with him. . . ." Gen 24:1 reads, "Abraham was old, *well advanced in years,"* lit., "went into the days." This was literally understood, as in *Tanḥ B.* 6 (60a): R. Johanan said, "He came to the curtain of this world" (i.e., that separated it from the coming world); R. Eliezer added, "In this world and in the future world." The joy of Abraham is referred to in *Sanh.* 38b: Gen 15:1 teaches that God showed Abraham every generation and every teacher that was to come, and he rejoiced over Akiba's knowledge of the law and said, "How dear to me are your friends, O God!" (Ps 139:17, Midrash). Schlatter accordingly commented that to say that Abraham saw the Messiah was neither new nor offensive to Jewish teachers; it was its application to Jesus that was unbelievable (220).

That Abraham "rejoiced" could allude to his laughter at the prospect of his having a son (Gen 17:17 was interpreted as signifying his joy, not scorn, at the announcement). Or it could relate to the birth of Isaac, whose name means "laughter." Bruce thinks of the finding of the ram to save Isaac in Gen 22, since the event was so important to Jewish understanding of atonement. If the first clause be translated, "Abraham exulted *that he should see* my day," the occasion is distinguished from that of the second clause: Abraham saw that the promise was to be fulfilled. "He saw it and was glad" then relates to a later occasion of vision. A number of scholars (among them recently Lindars, 335; Haenchen, 371) understand this second clause of Abraham in Paradise seeing Jesus in his ministry; in view of the Jewish background of prophetic vision and the implications of vv 57–58, this is unlikely.

57–58 The Jews realized that v 56 goes beyond a mere deduction from the Scriptures; it implies that Jesus observed Abraham's faith and hope in him, hence their shocked question. "Not yet fifty years" is not intended to suggest that Jesus was almost that age, as Irenaeus thought (*Adv. Haer.* 2.22.6; Chrysostom and others read the number forty, due to an attempt to reconcile the statement with Luke 3:23). It simply indicates the common view of the end of a man's working life (see Num 4:2–3, 39; 8:24–25); Jesus has not yet reached seniority, and he claims to have seen Abraham!

"Before Abraham came into existence I am" expresses "the contrast between the existence initiated by birth and an absolute existence" (Hoskyns, 349). The statement implies a real pre-existence, and is possible because the "I" of Jesus is one with the "I" of the divine Logos. The form is reminiscent of Ps 90:2 (LXX 89:2):

> Before the mountains were born
> or you brought forth the earth and the world,
> from everlasting to everlasting συ εἶ—*You are!*

This use of ἐγώ εἰμι is slightly different from that in vv 24 and 28, where "I am he" is clearly in mind, whereas no predicate is intended here. Nevertheless the OT revelation formula is in the background. Blank regards the "I am he" and "I am who I am" utterance as finding their "fulfillment" in Christ: "It is as if Jesus said, 'I am the revelation of God. I am the place of the divine presence and revelation in history!' The formula is not only 'expression' of the revelation, but it says itself what the revelation is and that it is here. . . . Those who debate with Jesus have to do it with the Ἐγώ εἰμι himself, with the historical revealer and representative of Yahweh, and thus with Yahweh himself" (*Krisis*, 246). The intention of the saying, however, is primarily what Jesus means for salvation, rather than of his being. Schnackenburg rightly points out that in Exod 3:14 Yahweh reveals not his metaphysical nature, but his steadfastness and faithfulness and his promise to help his people. The same is even more apparent in the "I am he" sayings of Deutero-Isaiah (see especially 43:11–13; 46:4; 48:12). In this context the assertion "Before Abraham was, I am," forms the basis of the promise of salvation to God's people. This is why Jesus can give the true freedom (v 31) and the life that overcomes death (v 51) (see Schnackenburg, 2:88–89, 223–24).

Is then the statement an assertion that Jesus is God? Not in terms of identification. It is an affirmation of Jesus as the revelation of God, and so a fresh expression of the Logos theology. As such it entails *unity* with God, as John 1:1. Consider Bultmann's statement: "The *ego* which Jesus speaks as the Revealer is the 'I' of the eternal Logos, which was in the beginning, the 'I' of the eternal God himself" (327). It is that because Jesus is the Revealer. Bultmann nevertheless is mistaken in denying a connection here with the OT revelation formulas "I am he" or "I am who I am." If it were an echo of the latter, he urged, it would mean that the *ego* would have to be both subject and predicate (n.5, 327–28). This is by no means obvious. The saying is kin in spirit to Isa 46:4, ἕως γήρους ἐγώ εἰμι, καὶ ἕως ἂν καταγηράσητε, ἐγώ εἰμι, "Until old age I am, and till you grow old, I am," and Isa 48:12, ἐγώ εἰμι πρῶτος, καί ἐγώ εἰμι εἰς τὸν αἰῶνα, "I am the first, and I am forever" (lit. unto the age). These are related to John 8:58, but not the same, since the latter appears to include remote past and remote future in an existence superior to time. The revelation utterance of v 58, accordingly, is one with the Logos theology of the prologue in declaring the Son to be the authentic revealer of the Father and his unity with him beyond all times.

59 The Jews respond to what they viewed as the blasphemy of Jesus with stones that lay at hand from the builders of the outer court, but they were unable to hurl them. On this Augustine commented, "As man he flees from the stones, but woe to those from whose hearts of stone God flees!" (cited in Schnackenburg, 2:224).

Explanation

The two dominant themes in chap. 8 are those of chap. 7, namely Christology and *krisis* (judgment). Both themes are developed in depth and intensity.

1. The presentation of Jesus as fulfilling the faith and hope of Israel expressed in the Feast of Tabernacles is continued from chap. 7 in the first utterance of Jesus in chap. 8, and its presuppositions are exposed in the subsequent dialogues. It should not be overlooked that in these sayings Jesus presents himself to the people as Messiah and offers them the blessings associated with the messianic age, but in terms quite different from those of popular messianic ideas. Nothing could be further from Zealotic hopes than 7:37–38 and 8:12, yet both sayings are rooted in biblical prophecy and contemporary yearnings that lay at the heart of the festival. The basis for this proclamation is seen in the ἐγώ εἰμι sayings of vv 24, 28, 58, which again are linked with the festival celebrations through the "I and he" formula in the Psalms singing each day, and which form part of the background and meaning of Jesus' ἐγώ εἰμι utterances. If, as we have good reason to believe, the Light of the world saying of 8:12 relates to the theophanic presence of Yahweh with his people in their journeyings through the wilderness, it too has close relation with the fundamental meaning of the ἐγώ εἰμι without predicate of vv 24, 28, 58. The judgment and testimony themes of vv 13–20 are similarly related, since they are both grounded in the presence of the Father with the Son (vv 14, 16; v 19 presupposes the unity of the Father and the Son).

Powerful as these expressions of Christology are, we are constantly to bear in mind that they are all linked with the soteriological interest of the Evangelist. This applies, as we saw, even to the "I am" sayings of vv 24, 28, 58, rooted as they are in the OT revelation of God, in contexts of assurance of the care of God for his people and his sovereign and exclusive power to save. In them we see again the thrust in this Gospel of salvation as life through Christ, made possible for the world through the "lifting up" of Christ (v 28). From beginning to end, the Fourth Gospel is concerned to set forth Jesus as the Revelation of the Father and one with the Father, but always with a view to making plain his role as Mediator of salvation—and of judgment, where man so insists.

2. The term κρίσις, "judgment," occurs only once in chap. 8, namely in v

16, though the verb κρίνω, "to judge," appears four times in significant ways (vv 15, 16, 26, 50). But as Blank pointed out, "*Krisis* is less terminologically present than in its execution. It is the controversy about Jesus which is to the fore here. . . . The *krisis* of Israel or of the Jews stands in a special way in the center of the passage before us" (*Krisis*, 231). In what sense is it represented here? Becker speaks for others when he asserts that an anti-Jewish line, elsewhere observable in Christianity of the third generation, is sharpened by the Evangelist: "While for the Evangelist in general the One who is sent by the Father brings the possibility of faith and so of salvation for all men, in chap. 8 Judaism is excluded from this generality and instead is totally and irrevocably assigned to the devil" (300). This surely represents a misunderstanding of the purpose of chap. 8. The passage is not an isolated segment but is bound to chap. 7 within the festival of Tabernacles, and the *krisis* motif dominates chap. 7 also; there the aspect of *krisis* most apparent is that of division—between those who believe and those who oppose Jesus. This feature is visible in chap. 8; the Light of the World saying produces objection on the part of the Pharisees, who are perplexed by the further teaching of Jesus, but some Jews believe. The encouragement given to them to advance in faith is again met by protests from hearers, from which point the controversy becomes sharper till it ends in uproar. The primary element in the *krisis* depicted in chap. 8 is seen in v 50, where the imagery of a court of law is used. The Judge is none other than the Father, and since he affirms the revelation of Jesus, it is clear that he is to vindicate him before his opponents and condemn them for their belief.

But who are they who face this judgment? The Jewish nation in its entirety? Naturally not. The Evangelist who composed the narrative of chaps. 7–8 was not schizophrenic, incapable of writing a coherent narrative of that length. In chap. 7 the *krisis* divides Jews into believers and unbelievers; the Evangelist does not suddenly change his mind and present Israel as an indivisible *massa perditionis*. The grave mistake that makes the contrary idea feasible is the assumption that the faith response recorded in 8:30–32 is viewed by the Evangelist as sham faith, and that he writes the rest of the account to expose its falsity. In so doing he is made to appear an inconsistent and implausible writer. It is this as much as anything else that made the sober F. C. Burkitt comment on the representation of Jesus in the Fourth Gospel, "There is an argumentativeness, a tendency to mystification, about the utterances of the Johannine Christ which, taken as the report of actual words spoken, is positively repellent" (*The Gospel History and Its Transmission* [1906] 227; see also idem, 228, on chap. 8). We have sought to show the weakness of this understanding of vv 30–32 in their context, not least as illuminated by the experience of the Johannine community. The parallel between 7:37–44 and 8:12–20, 30–32 should suggest caution before judging harshly the believers of 8:30–32. Since chap. 8 is composite, it is not inconceivable that vv 30–32 were earlier more closely associated with v 12 than they are now. Moreover we have cited Mark 2:1–3:6; 11:27–12:37 as parallels to John's bringing together elements of Jewish controversy with Jesus. The series of woes on the Pharisees in Matt 23 is an even more instructive parallel to 8:33–59; for while the effect of assembling judgments on the opponents of Jesus is overwhelming

in both passages, it is reasonably clear that the judgments on the Pharisees
in Matt 23 do not carry with them the exclusion of all Jews from the salvation
of the kingdom of God, despite vv 34–36. The like observation applies to
John 8, which begins by recording objections of the Pharisees to the revelatory
saying of v 12. That the chap. so begins is a pointer to the way we should
understand who the objectors are in v 33 to the Lord's saying in vv 30–32,
especially in view of their desire to kill Jesus (v 37), and the description of
them in vv 48, 51, 57 as "the Jews" (cf. the usage of this name in 7:13, 15,
[19], 35). Note further the abortive attempt of the Pharisees and other Sanhedrin members to arrest Jesus, 7:32, 45–46 and their rage in 7:46–52.

We may add that the idea of Christ as the fulfillment of Judaism is not
set forth in the Gospel to destroy Judaism and the Jews, but to carry forward
the OT revelation to its conclusion in the revelation and redemption of Christ,
issuing in the kingdom of God for all nations, including the Jews, as 7:37–
38, 8:12 make plain. The emphasis in chap. 8 admittedly is not on salvation
but on judgment, but it begins with salvation and is compelled by the response
of the hearers to concentrate on the judgment theme. The whole section
chaps. 7–8 may be viewed as an extensive illustration of the teaching in
3:17–21.

That this exposition of *krisis* in Israel was written with the controversy in
mind between Christians and Jews in the Evangelist's time may be taken as
certain (just as Matt 23 has in view the increasing opposition to the churches
from Pharisaic Judaism in the post–A.D. 70 period leading up to, if not actually
concurrent with, the deliberations of Jamnia). The *Sitz im Leben* of increasing
pressure from the Jews on the Johannine churches illuminates the necessity
for such a presentation of the issues between Christianity and Judaism. But
in seeking to deduce from chap. 8 the relations between the Johannine
churches and the Jews of the synagogue with whom they were in contact, it
is essential not to isolate 8:33–59 from the whole section, chaps. 7–8, and to
bear in mind the complex significance of *krisis* in the passage—division as
well as decision and condemnation. The description of the opponents of
Jesus as children of the devil should no more be viewed as reflecting the
Evangelist's estimate of all Jews in his time than the comparable description
in the Book of Revelation of the persecuting Jews of Smyrna and Philadelphia
as the synagogue of Satan (Rev 2:9; 3:9) can be held to reflect the Seer's
view of all Israel. The Seer's visions of judgment and salvation in the kingdom
of God simply do not allow that conclusion, nor does the theology of the
Evangelist allow the application of 8:44 to all Jews. The twofold perspective
of the Evangelist in relation to the story of Jesus and the situation of the
Church holds good in chap. 8 and chap. 7: the Jewish teachers and leaders
in Jerusalem did, in fact, become implacably opposed to Jesus in the latter
part of his ministry, and he in turn exposed their errors and their hypocrisy,
as the synoptic Gospels make plain. It is integral to the tragic history of
Jewish-Christian relations that that clash was repeated in the time of the
Church from its earliest days on, and it reached a bitter stage in the latter
part of the first century of our era. That the relations of Church and Synagogue
persisted in estrangement and mutual anathemas for so many centuries is
an even greater tragedy, but that they have radically changed for the better

is one of the signs of the times—surely of God's times. That the grace of God will be ever more manifest, in Church and Synagogue, is the Christian's hope and confidence as he anticipates the triumph of the kingdom of God and of his Christ.

3. A Woman Caught in Adultery (7:53–8:11)

Introduction

It is universally agreed by textual critics of the Greek NT that this passage was not part of the Fourth Gospel in its original form. The evidence may be summarized as follows. (*i*) It is omitted from our earliest copies of the Greek NT. (*ii*) In the East it is not found in the oldest form of the Syriac version, the Sahidic and sub-Achmimic, the oldest Bohairic MSS, some Armenian MSS, and the older Georgian version. In the West it is not in some Old Latin MSS and not in the Gothic version. (*iii*) No Greek commentator on the Gospel before Euthymius Zigabenus (twelfth century) discusses the passage, and Euthymius stated that the accurate copies of the Gospel do not contain it. (*iv*) No Eastern Fathers cite the passage prior to the tenth century. The earliest Western Fathers, Irenaeus, Tertullian, Cyprian, also make no reference to it. (*v*) The passage is found in the MS D, and in the mass of later Koine MSS, in some old Latin MSS, the Latin Vulgate, the Ethiopic version and a few MSS of other versions, the writings of Ambrose and Augustine; Jerome said that it was in many Greek and Latin codices. (*vi*) Many of the MSS which have the passage have asterisks or obeli, showing that the scribes knew the uncertainty of its status. (*vii*) There is an extraordinary number of variant readings in the passage. (*viii*) While most of the Greek MSS that include it set it in its present position, in the Ferrar group of cursives it follows Luke 21:38, in 225 it comes after John 7:36, in the Sinai Georgian MS 16 it follows 7:44, and a number of MSS, including the Armenian, set it after 21:25. (*ix*) The style and language are more akin to the synoptic Gospels than to the Fourth Gospel.

There are some uncertainties in the evidence. Eusebius states that Papias, writing in the mid-second century, "told another story about a woman who was accused of many sins in the presence of the Lord, a story which is contained in the Gospel according to the Hebrews" (*H.E.* 3.39.17); this could relate to the same episode as that in John 7:53–8:11, but of that we cannot be sure (see Vielhauer in Hennecke's *New Testament Apocrypha* 1 [Tr. R. McL. Wilson. London: Lutterworth, 1963] 121–22). More important is the reference in the Syriac Didascalia vii, of the early third century: bishops dealing with repentant sinners are admonished to do "as he also did with her who had sinned, whom the elders set before him, and leaving the judgment in his hands, departed." We cannot know where the author found the story, whether in a canonical or uncanonical gospel or in some other kind of writing.

It is clear that the story was not penned by the Fourth Evangelist (or any of the other three Gospel writers), yet there is no reason to doubt its substantial truth. The saying that it preserves is completely in character with what we know of our Lord, and quite out of character with the stern discipline that came to be established in the developing Church. (Augustine tells of the fear of some believers that the story would give their wives encouragement to sin with impunity! This led him to believe that this was the reason for its *removal* from the Gospel, *de coniug. adult.* 2.6.) We may regard the story as one those incidents in the life of our Lord that circulated in the primitive Church and did not come to the notice of our Evangelists (unless the fear that Augustine mentions led them to keep it out of their Gospels!—an unlikely eventuality); it was saved from oblivion by some unknown Christian, who wrote it down. If we ask why it was set in its present place, the answer must be a genuine sense of fitness of context. The theme of judgment is strong in chaps. 7–8; the story could well be regarded as illustrative of 7:24 and 8:15–16; and we note the opposition of the Pharisees to Jesus in 7:46–52 and 8:13.

Bibliography

Becker, U. *Jesus und die Ehebrecherin.* BZNW 28. Berlin: Töpelmann, 1963. **Blinzler, J.** "Die Strafe für Ehebruch in Bibel und Halacha. Zur Auslegung von Joh viii 5." *NTS* 4 (1957–58) 32–47. **Campenhausen, H. von.** "Zur Perikope von der Ehebrecherin (Joh 7:53–8:11)." *ZNW* 68 (1977) 164–75. **Coleman, B. W.** "The Woman Taken in Adultery, Studies in Texts: Jn 7:53–8:11." *Theol* 73 (1970) 409–10. **Derrett, J. D. M.** "Law in the New Testament: The Story of the Woman Taken in Adultery." *NTS* 10 (1963–64) 1–26. **Jeremias, J.** "Zur Geschichtlichkeit des Verhors Jesu vor dem hohen Rat." *ZNW* 43 (1950–51) 148–50. **Manson, T. W.** "The Pericope *de Adultera* (Joh 7,53–8,11)." *ZNW* 44 (1952–53) 255–56. **Osborne, R. E.** "Pericope Adulterae." *CJT* 12 (1966) 281–83. **Riesenfeld, H.** "Die Perikope von der Ehebrecherin in der frühkirchlichen Tradition." *SEÅ* 17 (1952) 106–11. **Schilling, F. A.** "The Story of Jesus and the Adulteress." *ATR* 37 (1955) 91–106. **Stauffer, E.** *Jesus war ganz anders.* Hamburg: Wittig, 1967. 123–42. **Trites, A. A.** "The Woman Taken in Adultery." *BS* 131 (1974) 137–46.

Translation

   [7:53] *And they went, each to his own home,* [8:1] *but Jesus went to the Mount of Olives.* [2] *At daybreak he appeared again in the temple, and all the people were coming to him, and he sat down and began teaching them.* [3] *The scribes and the Pharisees bring a woman caught in adultery,*[a] *and after setting her in the midst* [4] *they say to him, "Teacher, this woman was caught in the very act of adultery;* [5] *in the Law Moses commanded us to stone such women; now what do you yourself say?"* [6] *They said this as a test, so as to frame a charge against him. But Jesus bent down and started writing on the ground with his finger.* [7] *As they persisted in questioning him he sat upright and said to them, "Let the man among you who is without sin be the first to throw a stone at her."* [8] *And again he bent down and continued writing on the ground.*[b] [9] *But on hearing that, they went out one by one,*[c] *beginning with the oldest,*[d] *and he was left alone, while the woman was still standing in the midst.* [10] *He sat up and said to her, "Women, where are they? Did nobody condemn you?"* [11] *She answered, "Nobody, sir." And Jesus said, "Nor do I condemn you; go, and from this time on don't sin any more."*

Notes

[a] Instead of μοιχείᾳ D reads ἁμαρτία, "an act of sin." This has encouraged the belief that the story about the woman accused of "many sins" before the Lord, ascribed by Eusebius to the *Gospel according to the Hebrews,* was this narrative.

ᵇ Some MSS add after the end of v 8, ἑνὸς ἑκάστου αὐτῶν τὰς ἁμαρτίας, "the sins of each one of them."

ᶜ Many MSS add: ὑπὸ τῆς συνειδήσεως ἐλεγχόμενοι, "being convicted by their conscience."

ᵈ After πρεσβυτέρων some MSS add ἕως τῶν ἐσχάτων, "to the youngest," others πάντες ἀνεχώρησαν, "so that all went out."

Form/Structure/Setting

The setting has been discussed in the *Introduction* to the section. Since the narrative takes place during a period when Jesus was staying in Jerusalem, and on an occasion when he was teaching in the temple, it is natural to link it with the controversy stories of Mark 11:27–12:37; accordingly it is frequently classed as a controversy dialogue (so, e.g., Lindars, 308; Gnilka, 64). Since however the weight of the story falls on the saying of Jesus in v 7, it may be better to view it as a (biographical) apothegm (a saying set in a brief context), written down for the instruction of the Church in its treatment of offenders (so Bultmann, *History of the Synoptic Tradition*, 63; Schnackenburg, 2:169; Becker, 281).

Comment

7:53–8:3 The opening sentences are uncommonly reminiscent of Luke 21:37–38; they are similarly akin to the situation described in Luke 19:47–48, which finds instant illustration in Luke 20:1–2. This has confirmed many in their belief that the incident concerning the adulterous woman took place about the same time in the ministry of Jesus. Curiously v 3 is the only mention of the scribes in the present text of the Gospel, which is a reminder that for reasons of his own the Evangelist left them out of his account of the story of Jesus.

The woman was caught in the act of adultery. Was she married, or single? Billerbeck, followed by Jeremias, maintained the latter, on the ground that the Mishnah prescribes the more lenient form of execution by strangling for intercourse between a married woman and a man other than her husband, whereas the more serious punishment of stoning was meted out to a couple, one of whom was a betrothed woman (the evidence in Str-B 2:519–20). This has the startling effect of making the "woman" a girl, not less than twelve years of age but not more than twelve years and six months old (one less than twelve years old would go unpunished as a minor, one more than twelve-and-a-half would be strangled). Jeremias was prepared to maintain this, and it adds an almost unbearable pathos to the story and a shocking reflection on the Pharisees (*Parables of Jesus*, 1st Eng. ed., 158 n.96). In his revised edition of the *Parables*, however, he withdrew that idea, presumably in the light of the information given by Blinzler, who discussed in detail the evidence for the various modes of punishment for immorality among Jews in the time of Jesus. The chief points made by Blinzler related to the term μοιχεύειν and its derivatives, which in the LXX and related Greek writings were used exclusively of adulterous actions of *married* persons, and the evident fact that the prescriptions in the Mishnah for the punishment of immoral sexual acts did not apply to the time of our Lord; the woman brought to Jesus for his judgment was married (see "Die Strafe für Ehebruch," 34–47).

4–6 The Pharisees used this occasion of proved adultery to "test" Jesus and to have ground for a "charge" against him. If the time was near the end of Jesus' ministry they would have known of his proclamation of the kingdom of God to the poor and the sinners, his compassion on the disreputable of society, and even his eating with them, thereby showing complete indifference to the ritual laws as currently understood. Well, here was a *real* sinner, and the Law demands that she should die for her wickedness. What does he think about it? There is no question of their seeking his advice; they simply wish to discredit him publicly. If he upholds the Law, he contradicts his way of life and his preaching; if he maintains his outlook and preaching regarding sinners and denies Moses, he shows himself a lawless person and perverter of the people who must be brought to justice.

Jesus declines to give an immediate answer. Instead he bent down (presumably still seated in his teaching position) and drew on the dusty ground with his finger. Thereby he set an unanswerable conundrum for exegetes of all time. What did he write? We cannot tell, but that does not prevent the exegetes from guessing! A number have thought that Jesus was simply doodling, whether to calm his anger at the action of the Pharisees or simply for time to think (Brown reports examples from Arabic literature of the Semitic custom of doodling when distraught, 334). T. W. Manson, with others, cited the custom of Roman judges writing out their decision on a case before announcing it ("The Pericope *de Adultera*," 255–56), but that may be less relevant in a Palestinian context. Derrett offered an ingenious suggestion, based on the conviction that an adultery that was witnessed by two men looking on was likely to be a framed affair, probably through the connivance of the husband. As Jesus was seated, he could write only a limited number of letters in a row without moving, sixteen Hebrews characters in fact. The first sentence that Jesus wrote, and that suits that length, could have been Exod 23:1b: "You shall not support a wicked man (as a malicious witness)"; the second, Exod 23:7, "From a false matter keep far," a text quoted in the comparable story of Susanna ("The Story of the Woman . . . ," 18–20). The suggestion is entirely possible, though as little provable as others. From ancient times the pertinence of Jer 17:13 to this incident has been noted: "Those who turn away from you will be written in the dust, because they have forsaken the Lord, the spring of living water." It is suggested that this writing in the dust by Jesus was an example of his parabolic actions, reminding the woman's accusers of this scripture, as though to say "You are those of whom the scripture speaks," and a silent call to repentance (so Jeremias, *Parables*, 228). On this understanding the writing need not have been of actual words; the gesture would have been sufficient.

7–9 If to us the symbolic action of Jesus is ambiguous, his spoken word was devastatingly clear. Its immediate application will have been to the witnesses, since in a death by stoning, they had to throw the first stones. On Derrett's view they had been party to a disgusting conspiracy, but in any case had apparently made no attempt to prevent the adulterous act. Speculation apart, the word of Jesus challenged their behavior, their motives, and their life in the sight of God, and they failed the test. But they were not the only sinners present, as everyone involved in the case was quick to realize.

They all left, convicted by their consciences, as some early scribes recognized (see *Notes* on v 9). And the readers of the narrative know themselves to be included; the saying of Jesus, "Do not judge, or you too will be judged" (Matt 7:1), reminds us of our own sinfulness in the sight of God that could rightly be visited upon us.

10–11 Not till the accusers had departed did Jesus address the woman, and that presumably was to put her at ease and encourage her to speak to him (he knew that they had all gone!). What she said was little, but it led Jesus to utter a word of liberation: "Neither do I condemn you." Coming from the man whom people called *the* prophet (6:14; 7:40), and some the Messiah, but who in reality was the Redeemer-Revealer with authority bestowed by God, it was an assurance of the mercy of God upon her. But that was not all; he added another statement: "From this time on, do not continue in sin"—neither that for which she had been brought to judgment, nor any other deed of defiance against God. Mercy from God calls for life unto God.

Explanation

The story is a superb illustration of the dictum of 3:17, of which (with the continuing vv 18–21) the whole account of Jesus at Tabernacles in chaps. 7–8 may be viewed as exposition. It serves both as a model for the Church's attitude to prodigal sons and daughters and as an illustration of the gospel. As Schnackenburg saw, "The point is not the condemnation of sin but the calling of sinners: not a doctrine but an event. Jesus accepts sinners in God's name; his will is not to judge but to save" (2:168). From this point of view it has often been subject for comment that no record is given of the woman's acknowledging of her sin or repentance for it. Yet the Lord's, "Neither do I condemn you," must be taken as a declaration of forgiveness in the name of God. He saw her need and addressed himself to it. Whoever first recounted the story intended us to understand the word of forgiveness as a means of release for new life. Grace, by definition, is always undeserved. Here we see it in its starkest application (the same principle is embodied in the healing of the paralytic in Mark 2:1–12, and will have been the reason for its inclusion in the Gospel). If this is *kerygma* in its essentials, it is not left without *didache* (teaching). Release from life contrary to the will of God is always with a view to life according to the will of God. That is the fundamental principle of Christian ethics, as is set forth with plainest clarity in Rom 12:1–2; coming after the sustained doctrinal exposition in chaps. 1–11, the latter summarizes the content and motive of Christian living and is expounded in the chapters that follow. Here the notion is expressed in a sentence. In the nature of the case the power of the command is unexpressed, but the Gospel in which the incident has been set makes it clear that the grace of forgiveness is accompanied by the grace of new life by the Spirit. The Lord lifted up to heaven for the sin of the world sent the promised Spirit to enable the righteousness of God to be lived in the world. Life in the Kingdom of God is for kingdom of God *living*. To that the woman was sent into the world, as is every justified sinner.

F. Jesus the Light and Shepherd
of Humankind   (9:1–10:42)

Introduction

It is unlikely that the opening phrase of 9:1 implies unbroken continuity
in time between the temple discourse of 8:31–59 and the healing of the
man born blind (cf. the use of παράγω in Mark 1:16; 2:14). Yet the continuity
of thought in the two chapters is given in 9:5; the healing of the blind man
and its consequences form a concrete example and exposition of 8:12: Jesus
is Light for the world, revealing God to man and exposing the darkness of
the heart that rejects the revelation.

By contrast, chap. 9 flows into chap. 10 without a break. Bultmann viewed
9:39–41 as providing the introduction for the discourse that follows (329);
that some early readers of the Gospel thought in a similar manner is seen
in lectionaries that apportion 9:1–38 as one reading and 9:39–10:9 as the
next. But it is not alone vv 39–41 that introduce the discourse of 10:1–21;
the whole narrative of Jesus making the blind to see and the hostile actions
of the Pharisees provide the context for the parabolic discourse of the Shepherd
and the Sheep. Hoskyns observed: "The blind man—who obeys the command
of Jesus, is put forth from the synagogue of the Jews, and recognizes and
believes in Jesus as Lord and Son of Man—reappears in the description of
the sheep who hear the voice of the shepherd, are put forth from the various
folds in which they have awaited his call (10:4, 16), and form a new flock,
secure in the care of the One Good Shepherd. Similarly the Pharisees, who
strove energetically to disturb the relationship between the blind man and
Jesus, reappear in the company of thieves and robbers and hirelings, who
either have no care for the sheep or attempt to steal and murder and destroy
them. . . . The two chapters therefore stand in the closest possible relationship,
and the Evangelist presupposes the ability of his readers to recognize it"
(366).

On the other hand, 10:22–39 is set in the feast of Dedication, three months
after Tabernacles. Yet in this discourse there are clear echoes of the Shepherd
discourse; indeed vv 26–29 may be viewed as continuing the thought of the
earlier discourse. This has led to attempts to reconstruct the chapter to "improve" its order, and even to place the whole chapter within the feast of
Dedication. Recognizing, however, that the Evangelist here, as elsewhere,
has brought together originally discrete materials, and that the flow of thought
through chaps. 9 and 10 is so transparent, it is difficult not to see the whole
as due to his ordering. This becomes even more plain in the light of the
fact that the ideas within chap. 10 are related *both* to the feast of Tabernacles
and to that of the Dedication of the Temple, in some respects yet closer to
the latter than the former. R. E. Brown pointed out that the Jews themselves
related the two feasts: "For them Dedication was another Tabernacles, only
celebrated in the month of Chislev (2 Macc 1:9)"; he suggested that the
succession of events in chaps. 9–10 is to be understood as indicating what

took place shortly after Tabernacles (i.e., chap. 9), and prior to the feast of Dedication (10:1–21), moving into the Dedication feast itself (10:22–39) (388–90). C. H. Dodd expressed himself similarly, viewing 9:1–10:21 as a single episode, and 10:22–39 as an appendix or epilogue (*Interpretation*, 356). To us it seems right to regard the two chapters as forming a continuous whole in the Evangelist's intention, coming to a climactic utterance in 10:30, just as chaps. 7–8 move to the climax of 8:58, both declarations resulting in rage on the part of the hearers and an attempt to stone Jesus.

1. Jesus the Light of the World That Brings Judgment to the World (9:1–41)

Bibliography

Bligh, J. "The Man Born Blind." *HeyJ* 7 (1966) 129–44. **Bornkamm, G.** "Die Heilung des Blindgeborenen (Joh 9)." *Geschichte und Glauben.* Vol. 2. München: Kaiser Verlag, 1971. 65–72. **Carroll, K. L.** "The Fourth Gospel and the Exclusion of the Christians from the Synagogue." *BJRL* 40 (1957) 19–32. **Dodd, C. H.** *Historical Tradition in the Fourth Gospel.* 181–88. **Feuillet, A.** "The Composition of Chapters IX–XII." *Johannine Studies.* 129–47. **Fortna, R. T.** *The Gospel of Signs.* 70–74. **Horbury, W.** "The Benediction of the *Minim* and Early Jewish-Christian Controversy." *JTS* 33 (1982) 19–61. **Jocz, J.** *The Jewish People and Jesus Christ.* London: SPCK, 1949. 51–57. **Kimelman, R.** "Birkat Ha-Minim and the Lack of Evidence for an Anti-Christian Jewish Prayer in Late Antiquity." *Jewish and Christian Self-Definition.* Ed. E. P. Sanders, A. I. Baumgarten, A. Mendelson. London: SCM Press, 1981. 226–44. **Kuhn, K. G.** *Achtzengebet und Vaterunser und der Reim.* Tübingen: Mohr, 1950. 18–21. **Martyn, J. L.** *History and Theology in the Fourth Gospel.* 24–62. **Mollat, D.** "La guérison de l'aveugle-né." *BVC* 23 (1958) 22–31. **Müller, K.** "Joh 9:7 und das jüdische Verständnis des Siloh-Spruches." *BZ* 13 (1969) 251–56. **Porter, C. L.** "John 9:38, 39a: A Liturgical Addition to the Text." *NTS* 13 (1967) 387–94. **Roloff, J.** *Das Kerygma und der irdische Jesus.* 135–41. **Schrage, W.** τυφλός. *TDNT* 8 (1972) 270–94.

Translation

[1] *And as he passed by he saw a man blind from birth.* [2] *His disciples questioned him and asked, "Rabbi, who sinned, this man or his parents, that caused him to be born blind?"* [3] *Jesus answered, "Neither did this man sin nor his parents, but it happened that the works of God might be displayed [a] in him.* [4] *We [b] must work the works of him who sent me[b] while it is day; night is coming, when no one can work.* [5] *While I am in the world I am the light of the world."* [6] *After saying this he spat on the ground, and made mud with his saliva, and smeared [c] the man's eyes with the mud,* [7] *and said to him, "Go and wash in the pool of Siloam" (which means "Sent"). He went away therefore and washed, and he came away seeing.*

[8] *The neighbors therefore, and those who saw him formerly when he was a beggar, said, "This is the man who used to sit and beg, isn't it?"* [9] *Some said, "He is the man." Others said, "No, but it is someone like him." He himself said, "I am the*

man!" [10] They said therefore to him, "How did your eyes get opened?" [11] He replied, "The man called Jesus made mud and smeared my eyes with it, and said to me, 'Go to Siloam and wash yourself.' I went off therefore, and I washed, and I was able to see." [d] [12] They said to him, "Where is that man?" He said, "I don't know."

[13] They bring to the Pharisees the man who once was blind. [14] Now it was a sabbath day when Jesus made the mud and opened his eyes. [15] Again therefore the Pharisees questioned him how he gained his sight. He said to them, "He put mud on my eyes, and I washed, and I see." [16] Some of the Pharisees therefore were saying, "He is not from God, this man, because he does not keep the sabbath." But others were saying, "How can a sinful man do signs like this?" And there was a division among them. [17] They spoke again therefore to the blind man: "What do you yourself say about him, regarding the fact that he opened your eyes?" He said, "He is a prophet."

[18] The Jews did not believe the report about him, that he had been blind and gained his sight, till they called the parents of the man who had gained his sight, [19] and they questioned them, "Is this your son? Do you say that he was born blind? How then is it that he now sees?" [20] His parents answered, "We know that he is our son, and that he was born blind, [21] but how it is that he now sees, we don't know, and we don't know who opened his eyes; question him, he is of age, he should speak for himself." [22] His parents said this because they were afraid of the Jews, for the Jews had already agreed that anyone who confessed him as the Christ should be expelled from the synagogue. [23] That is why his parents said, "He is of age, question him."

[24] So they called a second time the man who had been blind and said to him, "Give glory to God! [e] We know that this man is a sinner." [25] He replied, "Whether this man is a sinner I don't know; one thing I do know: whereas I used to be blind I now see." [26] They said therefore to him, "What did he do to you? How did he open your eyes?" [27] He answered them, "I've told you already and you didn't listen. Why do you want to hear it again? You don't want to become his disciples, do you?" [28] They then abused him and said, "You are that fellow's disciple, but we are disciples of Moses. [29] We know that God has spoken to Moses, but as for this fellow, we do not so much as know where he comes from." [30] The man replied to them, "Why this is an amazing thing! You don't know where he comes from, yet he opened my eyes! [31] We know that God doesn't listen to sinners, but if anyone is a worshipper of God [f] and does his will, he listens to him. [32] Not since time began has it been heard that somebody opened the eyes of a man born blind. [33] If this man were not from God he couldn't do anything." [34] They replied to him, "You were born in utter sin, and are you trying to instruct us?" And they threw him out.

[35] Jesus heard that they had thrown him out, and when he found him he said, "Do you believe in the Son of Man [g]?" [36] He replied, "Who is he, sir? Tell me, that I may believe in him." [h] [37] Jesus said to him, "You have seen him; it is he who is speaking to you." [38] He said, "I believe, Lord." And he prostrated himself before him. [i]

[39] Jesus said, "It is for judgment that I came into this world, that those who do not see might see, and that those who see might become blind." [40] Some of the Pharisees who were near him heard this, and they said to him, "Surely we aren't

blind, are we?" [41] *Jesus said to them, "If you were blind you would not be guilty of sin, but now you are saying, 'We see'; consequently your guilt remains."*

Notes

[a] Grammatically ἵνα φανερωθῇ could be construed as an imperative: "Let the works of God be displayed in him!" For such a construction cf. Mark 5:23; Eph 5:33; 2 Cor 2:7; possible Johannine instances are 14:31; 15:25; see C. F. D. Moule, *An Idiom Book of NT Greek* [Cambridge: CUP 1953] 144–45, with literature there cited, and N. Turner in Moulton's *Grammar of NT Greek* 3:95. The chief reason for hesitating to adopt this rendering is the comparable thought in 11:4.

[b] ἡμᾶς (δεῖ) is better attested than ἐμέ and was more likely to be altered than vice versa. By contrast πέμψαντος ἡμᾶς instead of πέμψαντός με appears to be due to assimilation to ἡμᾶς δεῖ.

[c] ἐπέχρισεν is replaced by ἐπέθηκεν in B, Diatessaron, perhaps because the former term has associations too sacred for use with mud! Ephraem's Commentary on the Diatessaron has an extraordinary reading: "He made eyes from his clay," reflecting a thought, frequent among Patristic commentators, that a creative act was here involved, as in Gen 2:7.

[d] ἀναβλέπειν strictly means either "to look *up*" or "to see *again*," and so *recover* sight. Its use in relation to the gaining sight of one who has never seen is comprehensible, and is attested in profane Gr. (Bauer's *Lexicon*, 51.2β).

[e] "Give glory to God" can serve as an exhortation to praise, but in a context such as this it is a charge to confess sin that has been committed; the Pharisees are assuming that the man has lied concerning his alleged blindness and healing by Jesus (cf. Josh 7:19. The idiom was continued in Judaism: e.g., criminals about to be executed were asked to confess their sin to the honor of God, and so gain part in the world to come, Str-B 2:535).

[f] θεοσεβής occurs here only in the NT and = "god-fearing, devout." The term seems to have been applied especially to Jews by Greeks; Deissmann reproduces an inscription on a theatre seat in Miletus "Place of the Jews, who are also called God-fearing (θεοσεβῶν; *Light from the Ancient East*, 446). The Evangelist will have seen the fitness of the term on the lips of the blind man confessing his faith to worshippers of God revealed in Christ, cf. 4:22–24.

[g] Instead of τὸν υἱὸν τοῦ ἀνθρώπου (P[66] P[75] ℵ B D W etc.) many MSS (e.g., A L Θ ψ f.1, 13) read τὸν υἱὸν τοῦ θεοῦ. This is a classic instance of *difficilior lectio probabilior;* while the impulse to change the former to the latter will have been strong, the reverse change was unthinkable (in the later Church "Son of Man" came to be viewed as connoting the humanity of Christ, in contrast to "Son of God" as expressing his deity).

[h] The variations in the text chiefly relate to the order of words and are unimportant; the wording adopted in the UBS text is "typically Johannine and the most widely attested" (Metzger, 229).

[i] Some early MSS (P[75] ℵ * W it[b] cop[ach]) omit v 38 and the opening clause of v 39 (καὶ εἶπεν ὁ Ἰησοῦς). C. L. Porter ("John ix.38,39a: A Liturgical Addition to the Text," 387–94), following on a suggestion of Brown (375), argued strongly that the omitted passage was added through the use of chap. 9 in baptisms. In early lectionary usage the lesson extended from 9:1 to 9:38; it is suggested that v 38 reflects the confession of one being baptized (in the Hippolytan rite "I believe" was confessed by the baptized three times as he was immersed three times), while "And Jesus said" was added to begin the following lection, 9:39–10:9. In view of the early attestation for omission the suggestion could be correct. The Diatessaron, however, omits the *whole* of vv 38–39; this points to the omission as likely due to a textual accident (vv 37 and 39 both begin with εἶπεν ὁ Ἰησοῦς) or to early editing.

Form/Structure/Setting

1. A sign is narrated in vv 1–7, the consequences of which are reported in the rest of the chapter. The essential action of the miracle is recounted in vv 1, 6, 7, with a dialogue set in vv 2–5. Critics differ on how to account

for the elements of the dialogue. Dodd, noting the difference of the symbol
of "day(light)" in vv 4 and 5, viewed vv 3–4 as a recasting by the Evangelist
of earlier material (he regarded v 4 as originally of general application, expressing the sentiment of the well-known saying of Rabbi Tarphon: "The day is
short and there is much work to be done; the workers are lazy, and the
reward is great, and the Master of the house is urgent," *Pirqe ʾAbot* 2.15; the
disciples are told that it was not the sinfulness of the blind man that should
concern them but his need, which challenged their faith and willingness to
use *their* limited opportunities of doing God's work; *Historical Tradition*, 186–
87). J. Bligh limited the insertions of the Evangelist into the narrative to vv
4–5, which gave the true interpretation of the event ("The Man Born Blind,"
132–33). With this Haenchen agreed; he regarded the whole chapter as taken
from a source, to which the Evangelist added vv 4–5 and 39–41, thereby
changing the nature of the story from a demonstration that Jesus had come
"from God" (cf. 3:2; 20:30–31) to a sign of Jesus as the Light of the world
who has come for judgment (384). Fortna, in line with his view of a signs
source behind the miracle stories of the Gospel, sees in vv 1–7(8) a conflation
of a healing and a pronouncement story, with remnants of a tradition in v
8 of the effect of the miracle on others (*The Gospel of Signs*, 71).

It is, of course, impossible to dogmatize on the constituent elements of a
brief narrative like this. The dialogue in vv 2–3 is likely to be a feature of
the original story, and is wholly characteristic of Jesus (cf. Luke 13:1–5).
The limitation of the period wherein Jesus can work is fundamental to this
Gospel (cf. the "hour" to which he advanced) and is expressed in 11:9, primarily
with reference to Jesus, though again extending to others since it is a general
statement. V 5 certainly could have been inserted by the Evangelist as providing
the essence of 8:12 and the clue to the meaning of the narrative. That he
did this to transform an unacceptable interpretation of his source, as suggested
by Haenchen, is dubious. We are not convinced of the hypothesis of a signs
source, containing a theology alien to that of the Evangelist, which he found
it necessary perpetually to correct.

2. The structure of the chapter is clear. After the sign in vv 1–7 the controversy occasioned by the healing is described, at the center of which stands
the blind man. He is subjected to a series of interrogations:

vv 8–12   Questioning by his neighbors.
vv 13–17   Interrogation by the Pharisees.
vv 18–23   Interrogation of the man's parents by the Pharisees.
vv 24–34   Further interrogation of the man by the Pharisees.
vv 35–38   Jesus seeks him and leads him to full confession of faith.
vv 39–41   Aftermath of the sign: Jesus declares the purpose of his coming in
            making the "blind" to see and the "seeing" blind.

It will be observed that the chapter thus divides itself into seven sections.
This gratified J. L. Martyn, who treats the chapter as a drama, wherein the
rule is largely followed of two active characters only on the stage at one
time, and arrives at the same analysis (*History and Theology in the Fourth Gospel*,
26–27).

3. The *historical* setting appears to be in the period shortly after Tabernacles. In fact, no mention of time or place is given, but the following points should be noted. (*i*) Since the neighbors of the blind man after his healing speak of him as one who "sat and begged," we may take it that his pitch was near one of the temple gates in Jerusalem, and that Jesus and his disciples saw him there. (*ii*) The blind man is directed by Jesus to the pool of Siloam (v 7). (*iii*) It is unlikely that the meeting of 9:1 and the events that followed took place immediately after Jesus' departure from the temple, when the Jews attempted to stone him. (*iv*) No mention of the presence of the disciples with Jesus is made in chaps. 7–8. (*v*) The rift between Jesus and the Pharisees became radically deepened during the feast (so chaps. 7–8), and this is reflected in the opposition of the Pharisees in chap. 9. We may assume therefore that the occasion is shortly after the feast of Tabernacles, in the vicinity of the temple, prior to Jesus' return to Galilee.

4. The question of the *contemporary* setting of the scene is raised by the observation in v 22: "The Jews had already agreed that anyone who confessed him as the Christ should be expelled from the synagogue." On this Barrett commented, "According to Mark, Jesus was not during his ministry publicly confessed as Messiah (except by demons) That the synagogue had already at that time applied a test of Christian heresy is unthinkable" (361). He concurs therefore with the current trend of scholars to see in v 22 a reflection of the (ironically called) *birkath ha-minim*, "The benediction of the heretics," which is the twelfth of the Eighteen Benedictions, said thrice daily at that time by all pious Jews. The benediction runs: "For the apostates let there be no hope, and let the arrogant government be speedily uprooted in our days. Let the Nazarenes and the Minim [heretics] be destroyed in a moment, and let them be blotted out of the book of life and not be inscribed with the righteous. Blessed art thou, O Lord, who humblest the proud." J. L. Martyn has urged that the expression, "The Jews had already agreed . . ." shows that the expulsion from the synagogues was the result of a formal decision of an authoritative Jewish body; that is likely to have been the one taken by the Pharisees at Jamnia, during their reformulation of Judaism under the leadership of Rabban Gamaliel. According to *Ber.* 28b it was in response to an appeal by Gamaliel that Samuel the Small composed the twelfth benediction; Martyn sets that somewhere in the period A.D. 80–115, "with an inclination toward the earlier part of that period" (56). It is assumed therefore either that the Evangelist (or editor) updated the story of John 9 in the light of the situation that arose from this decision at Jamnia (so Bultmann, 335 n.5; Brown, 380), or that the story as a whole was composed in order to take into account this situation. It is on the basis of the latter interpretation that Martyn formulated his idea of the chapter as presenting the story of Jesus as a drama enacted on two stages simultaneously; the actors represent both Jesus and the blind man and a Christian evangelist and an individual in dire need; the expulsion from the synagogue relates to the fate of the latter (*History and Theology*, 30–36).

That the narrative has been composed with the contemporary church in mind is not to be doubted, but the interpretation sketched in the foregoing lines does not sufficiently take into account the complexity of the circumstances.

On the one hand, we must remember that the followers of Jesus suffered much in the manner of the blind man from the time of Jesus on. And, contrary to Barrett, we must not forget that Jesus himself enunciated the crucial test of discipleship as confession of him before men as Son of Man (Luke 12:8–9 = Matt 10:32–33; cf. John 9:35); the emphasis in Mark 8:37 on not being ashamed to confess Jesus doubtless expresses the concern in Mark's church of the danger of denial in face of external pressures. Equally significant is the last beatitude in Matt 5:11–12, coming from the later period of Jesus' ministry, the parallel to which in Luke 6:22–23 is remarkably close to John 9: "Blessed are you when men hate you, and when *they exclude you and insult you and cast out your name as evil,* because of the Son of Man." Paul knew what it was to be thrown out of synagogues on mission (Acts 13:50), and he was not alone in that experience. Moreover, the twelfth benediction did not occur to Samuel the Small without cause. It would appear that there had long been recited in synagogues a benediction against heretics, sometimes alone and also in combination with other benedictions; it will have been this that Samuel incorporated into his revision of the twelfth benediction. W. Horbury, in an exhaustive examination of the evidence, affirmed that the twelfth benediction did not and could not of itself bring about the enforced separation of Christians from Jewish synagogues; "it simply reinforced an earlier, more drastic exclusion of Christians" ("The Benediction of the Minim," 38, 50–52). The "updating" of the story of the Evangelist may have been less drastic than that suggested by Martyn and others. Nor can we be *certain* that the benediction in question had been formulated in Jamnia and made known through the Jewish dispersion by the time the Gospel was written. The decision of the Pharisees in 9:22 should be viewed as typical of what took place in varied localities prior to Jamnia's promulgation of the twelfth benediction; it will have been by no means universally observed, or regarded as irrevocable when taken. The last point will clearly follow if Horbury's contention be established, that the *Sitz im Leben* of the twelfth benediction was the *presence of non-Jews in synagogues, for whose allegiance the church and the synagogue both vied;* i.e., it expressed Judaism's concern not alone for heresy but also for mission, which probably included a counter-mission to the Christians ("Benediction . . . ," 51–53). This may require a fresh estimate of the element of witness to Christ which is so plain and appealing in John 9. The church of the Evangelist's day does not simply have its back to the wall; it proclaims Christ and the gospel—to the Jew first, and also to the Greek!

Comment

THE SIGN (9:1–7)

2   The question of the disciples is typical of the outlook of the ancient world (cf. Job's friends and their addresses to him). That the sins of parents could be "visited" on children is contained on the Decalogue (Exod 20:15 = Deut 5:9). The Jerusalem Targum on Deut 21:20 bids parents who bring a rebellious boy to the elders to say: "We have transgressed the Memra [word] of Yahweh, *therefore* this our son has been born to us, who is unruly and rebellious. . . ." The possibility of a child sinning before birth was discussed by the rabbis, not in respect of a pre-existent life (Wisd Sol 8:19–20 reflects Alexandrian, not Palestinian Judaism), but of life in the womb. Gen 25:22, telling of the twins Jacob and Esau struggling in Rebecca's womb, provoked some interesting explanations. Rabbi Laqish said, "This one ran round to kill that one, and the other ran round to kill him." R. Bekehja said in the name of R. Levi: "When she [Rebecca] walked past synagogues and houses of instruction, Jacob struggled to get out, in accordance with Jer 1:5: 'Before I formed you in your mother's womb I knew you.' And when she passed idol temples Esau ran and struggled to get out, in accordance with Ps 58:4, 'The godless go astray from the womb' " (*Gen. Rab.* 63:[39c]; see further Str-B 2:527–29).

3 The answer of Jesus does not have in view human suffering generally but this particular individual in relation to his mission. So Bornkamm: "It is he who does God's works, and the works of the Father have basically one meaning: to show and to glorify him as Revealer and Bringer of salvation. It would therefore be a mistake to make out of the saying of Jesus a general truth, an all-too-cheap pastoral 'recipe,' which as a timeless theory always tastes like the theology of Job's friends" ("Die Heilung des Blindgeborenen," 68). For the possibility of interpreting v 3b as an imperative, see *Note* on v 3.

4 The collocation of plural and singular verbs is significant: "*We* must work the works of him who sent *me*. . . ." Jesus associates his disciples with him in his mission in the present, as he will do in the future (14:12; 20:21). The limitation of time in which to fulfill it applies to him and to them ("while it is day"). Both he and they have an "hour" appointed by the Father, which imparts assurance and urgency to their service of God and man.

5 The saying "I am the light of the world," enunciated in 8:12 with universal application, is here applied to a concrete instance. The miracle about to be narrated is a sign that Jesus is the source of light for *all* humankind.

6 The procedure of Jesus with this blind man reminds us of Mark 8:23 (cf. also Mark 7:33). Saliva was regarded as having healing properties—under certain circumstances (cf. *B. Bat.* 126b: "The saliva of the firstborn of a father heals [diseases of the eye], but the saliva of the firstborn of the mother does not heal"). But the frequent connection of saliva with magical practices caused its use to be forbidden by later rabbis (so explicitly Akiba, *Tos. Sanh.* 12:10, Str-B 2:15). The making of "clay" from the earth was frequently compared by early Church Fathers with the creation of man from the earth in Gen 2:7; this prompted Irenaeus to comment, "That which the artificer—the Word—had omitted to form in the womb he supplied in public, that the works of God might be manifested in him" (*Adv. Haer.* 15.2).

7 Jesus sends the blind man to wash in the pool of Siloam, as Elisha sent Naaman to wash in the Jordan for the healing of his leprosy (2 Kings 5:10–14). Siloam is the LXX translation of the Hebrew *Shilôah* (שלח as in Isa 8:6, שילוח in the copper roll of Qumran). The verb שלח = "to send"; construed as a Hebrew participle שילוח it = "sent," and so denotes in this context a discharge of waters. The Evangelist, as Chrysostom observed, sees Jesus the Sent One as "the spiritual Siloam" (*Hom. in Ioan.* 9.6.7); the blind man gains his sight as he washes in the pool of Siloam, but he actually received it through the power of the Sent One. This identification of Jesus with Siloam, i.e., Shilôah, may well have been suggested through the messianic interpretation of Gen 49:10, "The sceptre shall not depart from Judah until Shiloh comes" (see von Rad, *Genesis* [Philadelphia: Westminster, 1961] 419–21). It is conceivable that the actions of Jesus, including the command to wash in Siloam, were signs to aid the blind man's faith; they undoubtedly served as evidence to the man's interrogators that he had gained his sight through Jesus, cf. vv 11, 15.

QUESTIONING BY NEIGHBORS (9:8–12)

The healed man's neighbors find it difficult to believe that the man who stood among them really was their neighbor, formerly so pitiable in his helplessness and poverty. Their perplexity, uncertainty as to his identity, and desire to learn what had taken place all attest the extraordinary reality that had happened to one of their number. At the same time their probing of the man, and his ready and consistent witness to "the man called Jesus," run through the whole narrative in its varied changes of scene. He becomes a sign that something not of this world is active within the world through the One who gave him sight. For this reason, as Blank points out, a latent tension is observable in the text: "It is not the healed man who stands in the centre of the discussion; he is only the occasion and the stone of offence; in the centre stands Jesus; he is in the entire narrative, although outwardly he is absent, yet as present as he alone can be" (*Krisis,* 255).

QUESTIONING BY PHARISEES (9:13–17)

The neighbors bring the formerly blind man to the Pharisees. Why? Presumably because the Pharisees were their religious leaders, and should know about this extraordinary event; as religious experts they would doubtless understand what had taken place. There is no need to assume hostility on the neighbors' part. They were not to know that bringing the healed man to the Pharisees would result in his undergoing a trial and expulsion as a sinful man. Bligh considers the scene an exemplification of Jesus' saying in Matt 23:13 = Luke 11:52 ("The Man Born Blind," 137).

14–16 The comment that the event took place on a sabbath is viewed by some as an intrusion (e.g., Becker, 315), but the suggestion is needless. The fact that the healing took place on the sabbath controls much of the discussion and course of events. As Bultmann perceived, the healing *on the sabbath* made what was a source of amazement a source of offense, and the Pharisees were faced with a dilemma: on the one hand the miracle shows Jesus as a man accredited by God, but on the other the breach of the Sabbath shows him to be a sinner (334). In this they were controlled by the interpretation of the sabbath law in the oral tradition. Therein it was frequently acknowledged that intervention may be made on the sabbath to save a man's life when it was in danger (cf. R. Samuel, "Man shall live through the precepts of the Torah [Lev 18:5], but he should not die in consequence of the same!"), but the blind man was not in that predicament. *B. ʿAbod. Zar.* 28b relates contrary ideas about anointing an eye on the sabbath (R. Jehuda said it was permitted to do so; R. Samuel declared it was not, but when his own eyes gave him trouble he asked the former if it was allowable, and Jehuda said it was so for others, but not for *him!*). But it is expressly stated in *J. ᶜAbod. Zar.* 14d that fasting spittle must not be put on eyes on the sabbath. And *Šabb.* 7.2 prohibits kneading on the sabbath; Jesus' mixing a paste out of saliva and earth would fall in this category. Jesus, accordingly, in the eyes of the Pharisees would have been a sabbath-breaker They would have looked on his miracle(s) in the light of Deut 13:1–5: a miracle worker who teaches people to go after other gods and so encourages rebellion against God must be rejected and executed. Sabbath-breaking will have put Jesus in that class; hence he is "not from God." Some Pharisees, however, were uneasy at this judgment: "How," they asked, "can a sinful man do signs *like this?*" Hence the division that so frequently arose among Jews over Jesus (cf. 6:66–69; 7:12–13, 30–31, 43; 10:19) now takes place among the Pharisees. The *krisis* of the world is again anticipated (12:31–32).

17 The answer of the formerly blind man to what he thought of the one who had healed him is to be compared with the declaration of the woman of Samaria: "He is a prophet" (cf. 4:19). His eyes were opening wider! Not all prophets performed signs, and not all miracle workers were prophets, but no Jew could forget that Moses was the greatest of all prophets and that his miracles in the Exodus were the greatest of all wonders (Deut 34:10–12). It was this, linked with the promise of Deut 18:15, 18, that led to the belief that the prophet of the end time, who was associated with and even identified with the Messiah, would perform miracles like those of Moses at the Exodus. The healed man had not yet attained to this perception, but he was on the way.

QUESTIONING OF THE PARENTS (9:18–23)

18–21 The "Pharisees" of vv 13, 15, 16 have now become "the Jews." This reflects the Evangelist's own terminology, and not least his tendency to vary his terms (cf. a comparable exchange of the two names in 7:13, 32, 47; 8:13, 22, 48, 57). The authorities, in deciding to call the parents of the man before them, are doubtless actuated by a suspicion that a miracle had not actually taken place (as appears in the next paragraph). But for the reason given in vv 22–23, the parents refuse to be drawn. They willingly affirm that this man is their son and that he was born blind, but since they have no firsthand knowledge of how he came to see, they cannot testify about it. "He is of age" signifies that he has passed his thirteenth birthday, and so attained the age of legal responsibility (Str-B 2:534–35).

22–23 The parents' fear of "the Jews" (they were themselves Jews!) would have been groundless had they viewed Jesus as a mere miraclemonger, without authorization from God. But it was their son who had been healed; and we are to assume that they were awed at what had happened to him and were ready to recognize with him that Jesus was a prophet, but they were afraid of the consequences. On the historical problem entailed in the expulsion from the synagogue of those who confessed Jesus as Messiah, see the *Notes* on v 22 (pp. 153–54). It is possible that the Evangelist, in describing the situation, "speaks of the cost of discipleship in terms of the conditions with which his readers were familiar" (Lindars). The Evangelist wishes to inspire the readers of the Gospel to a courageous confession like that of the healed blind man.

FURTHER INTERROGATION BY THE PHARISEES (9:24–34)

24–25 "Give glory to God" is a command to the man to confess his sin, i.e. the sin of lying as to his blindness and subsequent healing by Jesus, and to admit that the authorities are right and that Jesus is a sinner. The formerly blind man obliges: he gives glory to God—not by denial, but by fearlessly reiterating the truth that he knows and has experienced. Of the alleged sinfulness of Jesus he knows nothing; but one thing he does know, and not even the Pharisees can shake its certainty: once he was a blind man, and now he can see. And as he and they know perfectly well, that sets in question the assertion that Jesus is a sinful man.

26–29 The request that the man repeat his story may have been to confuse him, and to see if he contradicted his first statement, which would discredit his evidence. The man in the dock, however, is unabashed. He rises to the height of irony when he asks whether the authorities were anxious to know more in order to become disciples of Jesus! At this all pretense to impartiality on their part disappears: "We *know* that this man is a sinner." No evidence can alter that conviction! They are disciples of Moses; and they know that God spoke to Moses face to face and gave him the Law (Exod 33:11). But they do not know where Jesus came from, and therefore who authorized him; however (it is implied) they do know that he did not come from God.

Here we have the heart of the opposition of Judaism to Christianity: Moses and the Law are set over against Jesus and his teaching; the authority of Moses is indisputable, the authority of Jesus is spurious.

In *Yoma* 4a there is an instructive example of the Pharisees claiming to be Moses' disciples over against the Sadducees. In *'Abot* 5:19 the Jews are referred to as disciples of Abraham, the Christians as disciples of "Balaam the wicked" = Jesus! (Str-B 2:535). But the reader of this Gospel knows the flaw in this argument: Moses is not an opponent of Jesus but a witness to him, and therefore a witness against the Jews who reject Moses' testimony to Jesus in the Law (cf. 5:45–46). Ignorance as to the origin of Jesus is the fount of their misguided opposition to Jesus; he comes from God with a revelation from God, and so with God-given authority (cf. 7:14–16; 8:23–29 and 3:31–34).

30–33 The man on trial becomes more bold. "Here is a truly amazing thing"—not that he should believe Jesus to be a prophet, but that the religious leaders should be so ignorant of Jesus and so *disbelieving!* The "amazing thing" is not faith, but unbelief! Jesus opened his eyes; everybody knows that God responds to the prayers of righteous men, not sinners; Jesus therefore is a righteous man, and it was God who gave him power to open his eyes. Moreover, this power was unique: to restore sight to one who had lost it was miraculous enough, but to give it to one who never had it is unheard of. This unprecedented act therefore shows that God is with Jesus in an unprecedented way. Hoskyns observed: "If once it be assumed that a miracle proclaims the presence of a prophet, a miracle without parallel since the world began proclaims the presence of the Christ." (The conclusion is not yet explicitly drawn, but it will be, v 35: Hoskyns, 358.)

34 The outraged Pharisees refuse the instruction of the healed man in words which, without realizing it, condemn their stratagem to deny the miracle: "You were born in utter sin!" Then the man *was* born blind! And Jesus *did* open his eyes! But they reject the man, and the miracle, and the One through whom God wrought it. In so doing they reject the shining of the Light upon them, and plunge further into their darkness. They illustrate the perpetual truth of 1:3–4 and the contemporary truth of 3:19–21.

THE BLIND MAN'S FULL EMERGENCE INTO LIGHT (9:35–38)

35–36 Jesus finds the man whom the Pharisees had thrown out, since he urgently needs help, and above all needs to know the identity of the one who had healed him and whom he had steadfastly refused to deny. The question that Jesus directs to him does not mean, "Do you believe in the existence of the Son of Man?", but rather, "Do you put your trust in the Son of Man?", as in 3:14–15 (cf. 3:16, 28, 36, etc.). We may compare Jesus' questioning the disciples in Mark 8:27 (cf. Matt 16:13!); here, as there, the Lord leads his follower(s) to a fuller revelation of himself and a more adequate confession of faith in him. On this occasion Jesus employs the expression "Son of Man" (as in Mark 8:31): this is not simply in anticipation of his role in judgment (vv 39–41), but more positively as the one who mediates the salvation of the kingdom of God, which in this Gospel is chiefly represented as eternal life; his function as executor of the judgment which accompanies the revelation of the divine sovereignty, now and in the future, naturally goes along with this (so in 5:26–27; 12:31–32; see Martyn, *History and Theology*, 134; Barrett, 364; Schnackenburg. 2:253).

37–38 The response of the man, "Who is he . . .?", should be compared with the same question in 12:34, where it is spoken in a querulous manner, and to which Jesus responds with a warning to give heed to the light, lest those who so asked be engulfed in darkness. Here, on the contrary, Jesus gives an answer such as he rarely gave to anyone: "You have seen him; it is he who is speaking to you." The latter clause is almost identical with the statement of Jesus to the Samaritan woman in 4:26 (the third person in the latter passage accords with the fact that a statement regarding the Son of Man has to be in the third person). But there is a poignancy in the words to the formerly blind man; this is the first time he has been able to see the face of Jesus; and he learns that he is actually looking on the Son of Man! The effect of this revelation is as overwhelming as that to the Samaritan woman: the latter runs to her village to proclaim the advent of the Messiah, the former prostrates himself before Jesus.

προσεκύνησεν is commonly translated, "he worshiped him" (so KJV, RSV, JB, NIV, etc.), but this is doubtful. κυνέω means "to kiss," its extension in προσκυνέω reflects the Eastern custom of prostrating oneself before a person and kissing his feet, especially of one viewed as belonging to the supernatural world, e.g., a deified king (see Bauer's *Lexicon*, 716). Its use in the synoptics is instructive; in Matt 8:2 it replaces Mark's γονυπετῶν, of the leper "kneeling down" before Jesus (Mark 1:40), and in Matt 9:18 it represents Mark's πίπτει πρὸς τοὺς πόδας αὐτοῦ, "he falls at his feet" (Mark 5:22). Note also Acts 10:25, and Rev 3:9, which is significant in

view of the frequent and consistent use of the term in Revelation for the worship
of God or pseudo-divinities. It would seem that in John 9:38 the healed man is
ascribing honor to the Redeemer from God, which is beyond that due to other
men but short of that due to God Almighty. We have not yet reached the stage
of revelation represented in 2:28. So Schnackenburg: "The man's action is not
the expression of formal adoration of Jesus, but of the honor due to the God-
sent bringer of salvation which itself gives honor and adoration to God. It shows
the man's advance from his Jewish faith (vv 31–33) to Christian faith" (2:254).

DIVISION BETWEEN THE BLIND AND THE SEEING (9:39–41)

39   The opening sentence in v 39 draws the lesson from the story narrated in
vv 1–38. It makes the healing of the man born blind a symbol of the grace
and judgment which Jesus brings into the world (Bornkamm, "Die Heilung
des Blindgeborenen," 71). The assertion "I came . . ." reminds of related
statements in the synoptic Gospels that speak of the purpose of Jesus' mission
(e.g., Mark 2:17; Matt 5:17; Luke 12:49), and links up with sayings which
speak of Jesus as Son of Man (cf. Mark 10:45; Luke 19:10; see Blank, *Krisis,*
262–63). "I came for judgment" reads strangely contradictory to 3:17 ("God
did not send his son to judge . . . but to save . . ."). The latter expresses
the primary purpose of Christ's coming, as the Evangelist emphasizes through
this Gospel, but since faith and obedience are involved in salvation, judgment
on rejectors and the willful is an unavoidable concomitant of God's will to
save, as 3:18–21 go on to affirm.

Bultmann well observes: "This is the paradox of the revelation, that in order
to bring grace it must also give offence, and so can turn to judgment. In order to
be grace it must uncover sin; he who resists this binds himself to his sin, and so
through the revelation sin for the first time becomes definitive" (341–42). We
have already observed this in the twofold role of the Son of Man, who comes to
mediate the kingdom of God and all it connotes of salvation, and at the same
time the judgment of God on the godless. The statement as to the purpose of
Christ's coming relates both to the sign of the blind man's healing and the symbolism
of v 5. The blind are in darkness, and therefore lost; the Lord comes to bring
them "light," and so enable them to "see" and to receive the salvation of God.
The picture includes all humankind, but it assumes a distinction between those
who are blind and know it and want to see, and those who do not acknowledge it
and reject the revelation that would lead them into light. Jesus comes to give
sight to the former and to condemn the latter to their darkness.

41   This is further brought out in v 41. To the Pharisees, who objected
to the notion that they were blind, believing that they above all men saw,
Jesus states that if they were truly blind, and so ignorant of the truth of
God, they would not "have sin," i.e., they would not be guilty of the sin of
unbelief (cf. 16:8–9). But their insistence that they "saw" made their position
serious. For they certainly saw Jesus at work and heard his proclamation,
but because they thought that they had the light, they refused to acknowledge
that his works and word were from God. "Had they wished, they could have
seen what they really should have seen: the presence of the revelation in
Jesus Christ. Their not seeing is a guilty *not wanting to see,* and that is sin"
(Blank, *Krisis,* 263). Accordingly, since they continue in their unbelief, their
sin "remains"; i.e., they remain in their guilt of rejection of the Light, and
so condemn themselves to their self-chosen darkness.

Explanation

1. The narrative of chap. 9, as Blank pointed out, embodies two motifs, closely interwoven, which are fundamental to this Gospel, namely, that of revelation and that of *krisis* (judgment). The former is highlighted in v 5, the latter in v 39, but both motifs pervade the narrative as it unfolds. The blind man healed by Jesus beomes a sign of the revelation, and this in turn precipitates a *krisis,* which both divides those involved in the event and brings judgment on those who reject the sign and the revelation embodied in it (see Blank's exemplary exposition, *Krisis,* 252–63). The two features of revelation and judgment develop side by side, and so compel recognition that the event does not simply set forth Jesus as the Light of the world, but rather exemplifies what happens when the Light shines in the world: the saving power of the divine sovereignty becomes active through its representative and agent, bringing the light of life to any responsive to him. At the same time it exposes and judges the sin of those who reject the revelation and the redemption brought by the Redeemer. The Light by its shining accordingly creates judgment; in the very act of bringing salvation into the world, it divides the world. This it does not alone by revealing who receive it and who refuse it, but by transforming the former by the light (anticipating the resurrection) and by abandoning the latter to their self-chosen darkness (ending in death). The processes find illustration in what happens to the blind man and his judges. The former gains first his sight, and then increasing insight as he progresses from referring to "the man called Jesus," whose whereabouts he does not know (vv 11–12), to declaring him to be a prophet (v 17), then one sent from God (v 33), and finally confessing him as Son of Man and *kurios* ("Lord," vv 37–38). The Pharisees by contrast assert that Jesus is not from God (v 16) and that he is a sinner, and they deny the miracle (v 24); they do not know where he is from, nor the origin of his teaching and authority (v 29); they eject the man from their midst, and in so doing they reject Jesus (v 34); finally they are pronounced to be culpably blind and remaining in sin (39–41). The narrative thus exemplifies the continuing operation of the Logos as the Life which is the Light of men, whose light cannot be extinguished by the agents of darkness (1:4–5), and illustrates the process of salvation and judgment enunciated in 3:17–21.

2. The motif of witness is exceptionally plain in this narrative. The sign itself is a powerful witness to Jesus as the One sent of God for the salvation of a world in darkness. It is further reinforced by the courageous testimony of the blind man now healed. His dogged persistence in declaring the facts about his blindness and his healing by Jesus, and still more his bold resistance of attempts by the religious authorities to discredit Jesus are remarkable. Unlike his parents, he shows himself as one who refuses to be browbeaten by the Jewish opponents of Jesus and who is ready to risk rejection rather than deny him. The example he provides to readers of the Gospel in the Evangelist's day is evident, and is especially pertinent to those facing the possibility of similar treatment by Jewish leaders through confession of Jesus as Messiah. From time to time through subsequent centuries, Christians have had to endure this kind of rejection by family and society for the sake of

Christ, and have courageously made the same choice as the blind man. The theme provides a powerful basis on which preachers in societies that couldn't care less about religion may preach the gospel which offers the light of life and reveals the peril of choosing to remain in darkness.

3. Does the healing of the blind man portray the significance of baptism? From early times there have been those who saw in it the passage of the convert from darkness to life and from spiritual blindness to illumination by Christ in baptism. Tertullian began his work on baptism, "Happy is the sacrament of our water, it that by washing away the sins of our early blindness we are set free unto eternal life" (*De Bapt.* 1). Augustine also wrote, "It is not sufficient for the catechumens to hear that the Word was made flesh; let them hasten to the laver if they seek light" (*In Ioan. Ev. Tract.* 9.1). Such an understanding of the chapter is very common today (e.g., it is lengthily elaborated by Brown, 380–82). Whereas, however, the story could plausibly be used as illustrative of conversion that finds completion in baptism, it is doubtful that the Evangelist had any such thought in mind, not even when narrating about the man washing his eyes in the water of Siloam. That act is part of the whole process adopted by Jesus for the healing of this man; it has as little allegorical significance as Jesus' saliva, or the mud that was made with it (contrary to those who thought that Jesus created eyes from the mud, on the analogy of Gen 2:7, or those who adduce the latter text to speak of recreation through baptism). The Evangelist's profound use of symbolism in his delineation of the word and works of Jesus should not be extended to an allegorizing of details of which the Evangelist himself provides no hint. (On this see the critical discussion on the baptismal interpretation of John 9 by Schnackenburg, 2:257–58.)

2. Jesus the Shepherd and Son of God (10:1–42)

Bibliography

Ackermann, J. S. "The Rabbinic Interpretation of Psalm 82 and the Gospel of John." *HTR* 59 (1966) 186–91. **Bammel, E.** "John Did No Miracles: John 10:41." *Miracles. Cambridge Studies in their Philosophy and History.* Ed. C. F. D. Moule. London: Mowbrays, 1965. 197–202. **Birdsall, J. N.** "John x.29." *JTS* 11 (1960) 342–44. **Bishop, E. F. F.** "The Door of the Sheep: John x.7–9." *ExpTim* 71 (1959–60) 307–9. **Boismard, M. E.** "Jésus, le prophète par excellence, d'après Jean 10,24–39." *Neues Testament und Kirche.* FS R. Schnackenburg. Freiburg: Herder, 1974. 160–71. **Bruns, J. E.** "The Discourse of the Good Shepherd and the Rite of Ordination." *AER* 149 (1963) 386–91. **Cerfaux, L.** "Le thème parabolique dans l'évangile de saint Jean." *ConNT* 11. FS A. Fridrichsen. Lund: Gleerup, 1947. 15–25. **Derrett, J. D. M.** "The Good Shepherd: St. John's Use of the Jewish Halakah and Haggadah (John 10:1–18)." *ST* 27 (1973) 25–50. **Emerton, J. A.** "Some New Testament Notes, I: The Interpretation of Psalm 82 and John 10." *JTS* 11 (1960) 329–32. ———. "Melchizedek and the Gods: Fresh Evidence for the Jewish Background of John X.34–36." *JTS* 17 (1966) 399–401. **Feuillet, A.** "The Composition of Chapters IX–XII." *Johannine Studies.* 129–47.

George, A. "Je suis la porte des brebis (John 10.1–10)." *BVC* 51 (1963) 18–25. **Giblet, J.** "Et il y eut la dedicacé, Jn 10, 22–39." *BVC* 66 (1965) 17–25. **Hahn, F.** "Die Hirtenrede in Joh 10." *Theologia Crucis—Signum Crucis.* FS E. Dinkler. Tübingen: Mohr, 1979. 185–200. **Hanson, A. T.** "John's Citation of Psalm 82." *NTS* 11 (1964–65) 158–62. ———. "John's Citation of Psalm 82 Reconsidered." *NTS* 13 (1967) 363–67. **Jeremias, J.** "θύρα." *TDNT* 3:173–80. ———. "ποιμήν." *TDNT* 6:485–502. **Martin, J. P.** "John 10:1–10." *Int* 32 (1978) 171–75. **Meyer, P. W.** "A Note on John 10:1–18." *JBL* 75 (1956) 232–35. **Minear, P. S.** *Images of the Church in the New Testament.* 84–92. **Mollat, D.** "Le bon pasteur (Jean 10:1–18, 26–30)." *BVC* 52 (1963) 25–35. **Pollard, T. E.** "The Exegesis of John x.30 in the Early Trinitarian Controversies." *NTS* 3 (1956–57) 334–49. **Quasten, J.** "The Parable of the Good Shepherd: John 10:1–21." *CBQ* 10 (1948) 1–12. **Robinson, J. A. T.** "The Parable of John 10:1–5." *ZNW* 46 (1955) 233–40; also in *Twelve New Testament Studies.* 2d ed. London: SCM, 1965. 67–75. **Schneider, J.** "Zur Komposition von Joh.10." *ConNT* 11. FS A. Fridrichsen. Lund: Gleerup, 1947. 220–25.

Translation

[1] *"Amen, amen I tell you, he who does not enter the sheepfold through the door, but climbs in by some other way, is a thief and a robber;* [2] *but he who enters through the door is the shepherd of the sheep.* [3] *The doorkeeper opens the door for him, and the sheep listen to his voice; he calls his own sheep by name and leads them out.* [4] *When he has brought out all his own sheep he goes before them, and the sheep follow him, because they know his voice;* [5] *but a stranger they will never follow, but will run away from him, because they do not know the voice of strangers."*

[6] *Jesus told them this parable,[a] but they did not understand what he was saying to them.*

[7] *Jesus therefore spoke again to them, "Amen, amen I tell you, I am the door[b] of the sheep.* [8] *All whoever came before me[c] are thieves and robbers, but the sheep did not listen to them.* [9] *I am the door; whoever enters through me will be saved, and will go in and out and will find pasture.* [10] *The thief comes only to steal and slaughter and destroy; I have come that they may have life, and have it in its fullness.*

[11] *"I am the good shepherd. The good shepherd lays down[d] his life for the sheep.* [12] *The hired hand, since he is not a shepherd and the sheep do not belong to him, sees the wolf coming and leaves the sheep and runs away—and the wolf ravages and scatters them.* [13] *He does this because he is simply a hired man and the sheep do not matter to him.* [14] *I am the good shepherd; I know mine and mine know me,* [15] *as the Father knows me and I know the Father; and I lay down my life for the sheep.*

[16] *"There are other sheep of mine which do not belong to this fold; those also I must bring, and they will listen to my voice. So they will become[e] one flock, with one shepherd.* [17] *For this reason my Father loves me, because I lay down my life, in order to take it again.* [18] *Nobody takes it away[f] from me, but I lay it down of my own accord. I have authority to lay it down, and I have authority to take it again. This command I received from my Father."*

[19] *Again a division took place among the Jews on account of these sayings.* [20] *Many of them were saying, "He has a demon and is raving; why are you listening to him?"* [21] *Others were saying, "These words are not from a demon-possessed man; a demon cannot open the eyes of blind people, can he?"*

[22] *The festival of the Dedication then[g] took place in Jerusalem.* [23] *It was winter,*

and Jesus was walking in the temple area, in the Colonnade of Solomon.[h] *24 The Jews therefore surrounded him and said to him, "How long are you going to provoke us? If you are the Christ, tell us plainly."* *25 Jesus answered them, "I told you, and you do not believe; the works that I am doing in my Father's name bear witness about me.* *26 But you do not believe because you are not my sheep.*[i] *27 My sheep listen to my voice, and I know them, and they follow me,* *28 and I give them eternal life and they will never, never be lost, and no one will snatch them out of my hand.* *29 My Father, who has given them to me, is greater than all,*[j] *and no one can snatch them out of the Father's hand.* *30 I and the Father are one."*

31 The Jews again fetched stones to stone him. *32 Jesus answered them, "Many noble works of power I have set before you from the Father;*[k] *for which of them are you going to stone me?"* *33 The Jews replied to him, "It is not for a noble work that we are going to stone you but for blasphemy, and because you, though you are but a man, are making yourself God."* *34 Jesus replied to them, "It is written in your Law,*[l] *isn't it, "I said you are gods"?* *35 If the Scripture called them 'gods' to whom the word of God came—and the Scripture cannot be set aside— 36 do you say regarding the one whom the Father consecrated and sent into the world, 'You are blaspheming,' because I said, 'I am the Son of God'?* *37 If I am not doing my Father's works do not believe me;* *38 but if I am doing them, even if you do not believe me, believe the works, that you may know and come to grasp*[m] *that the Father is in me and I am in the Father."* *39 Again therefore they attempted to seize him, and he slipped away out of their hands.*

40 And he went away again across the Jordan to the place where John was first baptizing, and he remained there. *41 Many came to him, and they said, "John did no sign at all, but everything that he ever spoke about this man was true."* *42 And many came to believe in him there.*

Notes

[a] παροιμία commonly = "proverb." In the LXX it appears with παραβολή to translate משל, *māšāl*. But *māšāl* denotes (*i*) proverb, (*ii*) parable or allegory, (*iii*) riddle; the enigmatic quality of the last tends to adhere to the first two (in Ps 78:2 משל and חידה, "riddle," appear in parallelism; LXX renders the former by παραβολή, Symm. by παροιμία, showing that the two terms were viewed as synonymous; so also in Sir 39:3, the scholar researches into "the hidden sense of proverbs," ἀπόκρυφα παροιμιῶν, and ponders "the obscurities of parables," ἐν αἰνίγμασιν παραβολῶν). Jesus' use of the *māšāl* to convey the message of the kingdom of God is in line with that of the prophets (cf Isa 5) and of apocalyptists (cf. the "Similitudes" of Enoch, chaps. 37–71); in the synoptics the term is always παραβολή (παροιμία does not occur in them), in the Fourth Gospel only παροιμία (παραβολή does not occur in it). Observe John 16:25; the saying can be extended to the teaching of Jesus generally in this Gospel, in contrast to its promised illumination by the Paraclete after the Lord's resurrection (see Cerfaux, "Le thème parabolique," 20).

[b] ἡ θύρα is replaced by ὁ ποιμήν in P75 and various Coptic MSS. C. C. Torrey thought that this reading was correct; he suggested that the Aram. statement אנא אחית רעהון די ענא "I came as Shepherd of the sheep," was read as אנא אתי תרעהון די ענא, "I am the Door of the sheep" (*Our Translated Gospels*, 111–12; Black has a similar solution, *Aramaic Approach*, 193 n.1); attractive as this is, it entails viewing v 9 as an interpolation (so Torrey), or v 7 as an assimilation to v 9. Clearly ἡ θύρα is the more difficult reading and should be retained.

[c] πρὸ ἐμοῦ is omitted by P45vid P75 א * E F G, most minuscules and many MSS of versions. The position also varies before or after ἦλθον. Normally this would suffice to indicate that the expression is a later insertion; but some early MSS also omit πάντες (D itbd vgmss). It looks as though both omissions were made to soften the strong meaning of the statement, which may have been

interpreted by some as a condemnation of all OT leaders and prophets. The UBS therefore includes the phrase, but in brackets.

d Instead of τίθησιν some early MSS (P⁴⁵ א* D etc.) read δίδωσιν; but the former with τὴν ψυχήν is a common expression in the Fourth Gospel (10:15, 17; 13:37, 38; 15:13); the latter reading is likely to have been influenced by Mark 10:45.

e γενήσονται has stronger attestation than the singular γενήσεται; the latter appears to be "a stylistic correction" (Metzger, 230).

The tr. of μία ποίμνη as "one fold" (KJV, Douay etc.) goes back to Jerome's rendering in the Lat. vg *unum ovile;* this is less likely to be due to a mistake than to a Gr. text reading αὐλή.

f A few early MSS (P⁴⁵ א* B) read ἦρεν instead of αἴρει; while it is the more difficult reading the greater attestation of the latter led the UBS editors to retain it (Lagrange, 283; Barrett, 377; Lindars, 364, accept the former reading).

g Both τότε and δέ after ἐγένετο are well supported; the former is appropriate to the context, but Sanders argues persuasively for the omission of both (254, n.1).

h A colonnade surrounded the entire outer court of the temple; according to Jos. (*Ant.* 15.396–97, 20.9.7) that known as Solomon's (alleged to have been built by him) was on the eastern side. It became a meeting place for the early Jerusalem church (Acts 5:12).

i After ἐμῶν many MSS add καθὼς εἶπον ὑμῖν, probably without warrant (though no earlier saying of Jesus states that the Jews did not belong to the sheep of Jesus!).

j The text of the first clause is uncertain. The chief readings are:

(i)   ὃ δέδωκέν μοι πάντων μεῖζον ἐστιν, B*.

(ii) ὃς δέδωκέν μοι μεῖζον πάντων ἐστιν, θ.

(iii) ὁ δεδωκώς μοι πάντων μείζων ἐστιν, D.

(iv) ὃ δέδωκέν μοι πάντων μείζων ἐστιν, א W.

(v)   ὃς δέδωκέν μοι μείζων πάντων ἐστιν, Koine MSS.

The UBS committee viewed (i) as best accounting for the other readings: "As to my Father, that which he has given to me is greater than all"; since, however, "that which he has given to me" appears to be the sheep, the statement is surely improbable. (ii) finds wide support; Barrett renders it, "My Father who gave (them) me is a greater power than all, and no one can snatch them out of the hand of the Father." J. N. Birdsall accepts the reading but renders it, "My Father, in regard to what he has given me is greater than all," viewing the subject as "the unassailability of the flock of God because of his guardian power" ("John x.29," 344); in this he is followed by Brown, 403; Lindars, 370; Schnackenburg, 2:307–8. The simplest reading is undoubtedly (v), which we now find to be supported by P⁶⁶ (but reading ἔδωκεν instead of δέδωκεν). Bultmann considered it to be the only reading that made sense; but one must ask if it was original, how did the variants arise? Bernard thought that the ὁ was due to the influence of 6:39; 17:2, and so μεῖζον was written to agree with it (2:348); Bultmann suggested that μεῖζον was due to a copyist's mistake through expecting an object after δέδωκεν, and so the relative was altered in agreement with it (336 n.2); Schlatter thought that ὁ supplied the object and μεῖζον agreed therewith (242). The issue is uncertain; the simplest reading may be, after all, the correct one (so Dodd, *Interpretation,* 433, n.1; Bruce, 232).

Most later MSS add μου to πατρός, but it is omitted by P⁶⁶ P⁷⁵ᵛⁱᵈ B L Origen, and is likely to be an addition, possibly made independently by various copyists.

k The same comment applies to the appearance in many MSS of μου after τοῦ πατρός.

l ὑμῶν is omitted after τῷ νόμῳ in P⁴⁵ א* D etc., perhaps because it seemed strange for Jesus so to refer to the OT; but it appears similarly in 8:17 and should be retained here.

m καὶ γινώσκητε is omitted by D OL syrˢ, and replaced by πιστεύσητε in many more MSS (πιστεύητε in א), probably for the identical reason, namely that the term appears needless after γνῶτε, but its attestation is good and early (P⁴⁵ P⁶⁶ P⁷⁵ B L etc.), and is to be accepted.

Form/Structure/Setting

1. The chapter consists primarily of a discourse on the Shepherd and his Flock, vv 1–18, and a dialogue between Jesus and the Jews during the Festival

of the Dedication, vv 22–39. The former is followed by a note on a division among the Jews occasioned by Jesus' teaching, vv 19–21, and the latter by a report of Jesus withdrawing to the other side of the Jordan, vv 40–42. Since vv 19–21 make mention of the healing of the blind man, it is often thought that the passage should immediately follow 9:39–41; and as vv 26–29 develop the theme of the Shepherd and his Flock, it is also proposed that vv 22–29 should immediately follow 19–21. The effect of this is to set the entire narrative of chap. 10 within the Festival of the Dedication.

This suggested transfer of 10:19–29 before vv 1–18 was proposed by F. Warburton Lewis in his work *Disarrangements in the Fourth Gospel* (Cambridge: CUP, 1910) (his findings are discussed by Howard, *The Fourth Gospel in Recent Criticism,* 133–41). It was adopted by Moffatt, in his translation of the NT, and by Bernard in his commentary (1:xxiv–xxv; 2:341–66). Bultmann accepted the revised order, but set vv 11–13 prior to 1–10, seeing in 11–13 and 1–5 a double parable, the former a parable of the Good Shepherd, the latter a *paroimia* contrasting the Shepherd with thieves and robbers. Vv 7–10 are then viewed as an explanatory gloss on 1–5, and 14–18 explanatory glosses on the whole two-part parable (358–60). Commentators of late have been more cautious. Many are ready to acknowledge that vv 1–18 probably had a separate existence prior to their incorporation into the present narrative, and that vv 19–21 and 22–39 may well have come from a source that included the controversy-dialogues of chaps. 7–10 (see especially Dodd, *Interpretation,* 355; Sanders, 246). Nevertheless, they also acknowledge that the present order makes sense, both in relation to chap. 9 and internally, and they assign the redaction of the whole to the Evangelist himself. In this respect the analysis of J. Schneider is particularly instructive. He sees in vv 1–5 a *paroimia* that needs explanation; this is given according to a clear plan, which links on to the words that stand at the center of the parable, namely (*i*) the door, (*ii*) the Shepherd, (*iii*) his own sheep. Vv 7–10 stand under the doubly formulated sentence, "I am the door" (vv 7, 9); vv 11–18 are controlled by the statement twice made, "I am the good shepherd" (vv 11, 14), together with the thrice repeated "I lay down my life for the sheep" (11, 15, 17, and cf. v 18); vv 27–30 expand the concept "his own sheep": they hear his voice and follow him, he knows them and gives them life, and they shall never perish. The last passage (26–29) has been placed by the Evangelist in a different context to illuminate that context; the question of the Messiah is at the center, and the saying in v 26, "You do not believe because you are not of my sheep," gives the Evangelist the possibility of placing the last section of the Shepherd discourse here (see "Zur Komposition von Joh. 10," 220–25). This is a plausible interpretation of the schema of the chapter, and is in harmony with the convictions of other exegetes who decline to reverse the present order of the text (see Feuillet in his *Johannine Studies,* 137–38; Jeremias, *TDNT* 6:494–95; Barrett, 366–68; Brown, 388–90; Schnackenburg, 2:276–78; Haenchen, 395–96. Becker, while agreeing with this position, emphasizes the independence of 10:1–18 from its context, and with Langbrandtner (*Weltferner Gott oder Gott der Liebe*) regards it as an addition by the "ecclesiastical redactor," 311–12).

2. The integrity of the parable in vv 1–5 has been questioned by several scholars, notably by J. A. T. Robinson. He argued that the parable is a fusion of two parables on related themes: vv 1–3a are concerned with two figures, a bandit and a shepherd, who seek to enter a sheepfold; the porter opens to the latter alone; vv 3b–5 points to the difference in relationship between the sheep with a stranger and with their own shepherd. The latter parable relates to the claims of Jesus in his teaching, which is repudiated by scribes

and Pharisees, but recognized by the true people of God. The Jewish leaders are condemned as ἀλλότριοι, foreigners to God's people, and this accords with the setting of John 10. The parable of vv 1–3a is built around the contrast between the bandit and the shepherd, both of whom seek to gain access to the courtyard; here the central figure is not the shepherd but the gatekeeper (cf. the θυρωρός, the porter of synoptic parables, e.g. Mark 13:34; Luke 12:36). This parable, like the latter, warns the Jewish leaders of the urgency of the present eschatological situation, and challenges them to open up to the true Shepherd of God's Flock ("Parable of the Shepherd," 68–72). With this analysis Dodd was basically in agreement, though he acknowledged that the joining of the two parables will have shortened both ("We have in vv 1–5 the *wreckage* of two parables fused into one, the fusion having partly destroyed the original form of both," *Historical Tradition*, 383). Brown is able to build his exposition on the basis of this postulate of the two parables (391–93). It appears to us, however, that the distinction drawn between the two halves of vv 1–5 is somewhat tenuous. Becker points out that the positive statement within the parable is actually in vv 2–4, which is framed through the negative contrast in vv 1 and 5. The shepherd comes to the sheep (1–3a) and then leads them to pasture (3b–5); the events stand in good succession, and are held together through the essential statement that the sheep know the shepherd's voice and follow him. Vv 1–5 therefore are explicable as a unity and should not be dissected into several parables (see Becker, 325). This seems the most natural way of construing the parable, as the majority of exegetes agree. That which follows the parable in vv 7–18 forms a meditation on the parable, directing attention especially to "the door" and "the Shepherd," at the same time taking into account the feature of the "thief" or "stranger," and the contrast between their relation to the sheep and that of the shepherd to them.

Accepting then the present order of text, we propose that 10:1–21 is set in close association with the narrative of the healing of the blind man in the period following the Festival of Tabernacles, while 10:22–39 falls within the Festival of Dedication, shortly after the preceding events. We are evidently intended to assume that Jesus spent the time between the two festivals in the area of Jerusalem. The Dedication festival, with its celebration of the deliverance from the tyrant Antiochus Epiphanes and the rededication of the profaned temple, forms a suitable background for "the Jews" to question Jesus whether he is the Messiah, and for the discussion it provoked.

3. The following analysis of the chapter will provide the basis for our exposition:

1. 10:1–21: Discourse on the Shepherd and the Flock
   i. 10:1–6: The Parable of the Shepherd, the Flock, and the Robber
   ii. 10:7–18: Meditation on the parable
   iii. 10:19–21: Division among the hearers
2. 10:22–42: Jesus at the Festival of the Dedication
   i. 10:22–30: Jesus the Messiah
   ii. 10:31–39: Jesus the Son of God
   iii. 10:40–42: Jesus' withdrawal to Transjordan

Comment

THE DISCOURSE ON THE SHEPHERD AND THE FLOCK (10:1–21)

The Parable of the Shepherd, the Flock, and the Robber (10:1–6)
The parable in essence depicts a shepherd as one having authorized access to his flock, in contrast to a thief, who must steal clandestinely into the fold; the shepherd, unlike the thief, has an established relationship with the sheep— he knows them, and they recognize him, and so they follow him as he leads them out to pasture, whereas they run away from a stranger.

The assumptions of the picture are reasonably clear. The sheep are kept at night in a fold, either one erected in the open country or in a yard surrounded by a wall adjacent to a house. It is possible that several flocks share the one fold. The shepherd arrives in the morning and gathers his own sheep, calling to them individually, and leads them out to pasture. On this "gathering," "calling," and leading of the sheep, cf. the remarks of G. A. Smith: "On the boundless Eastern pasture . . . the shepherd is indispensable. With us sheep are often left to themselves; I do not remember to have seen in the East a flock without a shepherd. In such a landscape as Judea, where a day's pasture is thinly scattered over an unfenced tract, covered with delusive paths, still frequented by wild beasts, and rolling into the desert, the man and his character is indispensable. . . . Sometimes we enjoyed our noonday rest beside one of those Judean wells, to which three or four shepherds come down with their flocks. The flocks mixed with each other, and we wondered how each shepherd would get his own again. But after the watering and the playing were over the shepherds one by one went up different sides of the valley, and each called out his peculiar call; and the sheep of each drew out of the crowd to their own shepherd and the flocks passed as orderly as they came" (*Historical Geography of the Holy Land,* 25th ed. [London: Fontana] 210–11).

The Evangelist describes this as a παροιμία (see *Notes* on the passage). Fundamentally it is a parable rather than an allegory (so Bultmann, 371); nevertheless it has within it features that recall to any Jew a wealth of biblical associations that make certain applications of imagery almost inevitable. Four elements in its background may be distinguished. (*i*) Of the many relevant OT passages the polemical discourse in Ezekiel 34 is outstanding; Israel's leaders are condemned for neglecting the sheep, for slaughtering them and leaving them as prey to the wild beasts; the Lord declares that he will be their Shepherd, that he will gather his scattered sheep and pasture them on the mountains of Israel, and set over them as shepherd "my servant David," i.e., the Messiah. (*ii*) The use of the imagery of shepherd and sheep in the synoptic teaching of Jesus is inevitably recalled, especially the parable of the one lost sheep, which depicts the care of God for the lost and justifies Jesus' seeking them (Luke 15:1–7; Matt 18:12–14), and Mark 14:27, which links the death and resurrection of Jesus the shepherd with Zech 13:7–9. (*iii*) The immediately foregoing narrative of the healing of the man born blind, culminating in his ejection by the Pharisees, finds a reflection in the contrast between the "thief and robber" and the good shepherd in their respective attitudes to the sheep. (*iv*) As throughout the Gospel, the circumstances of the church contemporary with the Evangelist are also in mind: the original readers will have recognized in the thief and robber, who is a stranger to the sheep, Jewish opponents who seek to draw them away from their Shepherd, and possibly also schismatic leaders who appeal to them to forsake the orthodox Church (cf. 1 John 2:18–22; 4:1–6).

1 The mention of the "thief and robber" (a single figure, as ἐκεῖνος shows) *prior* to the shepherd in the parable is significant, following as it does immediately on 9:40–41.

2–4 The shepherd enters the fold as of right, for the sheep are his. The doorkeeper has no function other than to open the door to him (contrast the figure in Mark 13:34–36; Luke 12:35–38). The repetition of ἴδια in vv 3–4 (τὰ ἴδια πρόβατα . . . τὰ ἴδια πάντα) prompts the thought that more than one flock is in the fold, and that the shepherd calls "his own" from among the others. He calls them κατ᾽ ὄνομα, not necessarily by different names (though such is not unknown), but "individually" (such is the meaning of κατ᾽ ὄνομα in 3 John 15; see Dodd, *Historical Tradition*, 384 n.4). As is customary in Palestine, the sheep *follow* the shepherd (it is the butcher who drives them!); following the shepherd makes the picture peculiarly apt to Christian discipleship.

Meditation on the Parable (10:7–18)

7–10 "I am the Door" is to be retained as the authentic text (see *Notes* on v 7). Chrysostom's comment is basically correct: "When he brings us to the Father he calls himself a Door, when he takes care of us, a Shepherd" (cited by Hoskyns, 373). It should be noted, however, that the symbol of the shepherd is more comprehensive than that of the door, since it includes the thought of bringing people to God and caring for them (v 16, hence the importance of the shepherd laying down his life for the sheep, vv 11,15). The saying is parallel to 14:6, "I am the Way, the truth, and the life; no one comes to the Father except through me." Jesus is the Door to the life of the kingdom of God, which is given to those who come to the Father through him.

Various writers, familiar with life in the nearer Orient, have drawn attention to statements of shepherds virtually identical with v 7b. They speak of themselves as a "door of the sheep," since they habitually lie down across the open entry of a sheepfold, and their body forms a barrier to intruders, whether thieves or wild beasts (E. F. F. Bishop recounts in detail two such instances, "The Door of the Sheep," 307, and L. Morris cites another told by G. A. Smith to G. Campbell Morgan, 507 n.30). It is an attractive interpretation and conceivably could have been so understood by readers of the Gospel familiar with such pastoral settings, but they would have been few; more importantly, the idea does not comport with vv 2–3, which have in view an actual door in the wall or fence, guarded by a gatekeeper.

As the figure of a Shepherd was widely taken up in Oriental thought and religion, so was that of Door. Barrett marshalls an interesting array of evidence for the latter (372), some of which could have been familiar to some early readers of our Gospel. Curiously Barrett fails to mention the most likely precedent for the figure, namely Ps 118:20: "This is the gate of the Lord, the righteous shall enter through it." The whole passage is capable of messianic application (esp. vv 22–27, elements of which feature prominently in the NT, e.g., Mark 12:10–11 par; 11:9 par; Acts 4:11; 1 Pet 2:4, 7). It is most natural to interpret the Door here in relation to the sheep, who enter by the Redeemer into the salvation of the kingdom of God. This is preferable to the commonly espoused view that in v 7 Jesus is the Door *to* the sheep, whereby true (Christian) shepherds may have access to the sheep, while in v 9 he is the Door *for* the sheep (so, e.g., Schneider, 222–23; Brown, 371; Morris, 506). Some make no distinction between the two sayings and understand the Door to be the means by which the shepherds and sheep alike enter (e.g., Westcott, 2:53; Lagrange, 282; Hoskyns, 373; Barrett, 371). Schnackenburg dismisses the notion of Christian shepherds as in view here and wishes to keep the figure strictly in line with vv 2, 3, 8: the Door represents a "symbol of the entrant's legitimacy, the proof of the Shepherd's right"; hence it rules out all other claimants to being saviors of humankind (2:289). Perhaps this is a little too rigid; if we take the simpler view of Jesus as the Door to the salvation of the kingdom of God, on the analogy of Ps 118:20, the claimants in view in vv 8 and 10 are automatically eliminated, and the "I am . . ." of vv 7, 9, and 11 is allowed its positive and exclusive significance.

Needless to say, the sweeping affirmation of v 8 does not have in mind the notable figures of the OT, since in the Gospel they are spoken of as witnesses to Jesus, as truly as John the Baptist is. The saying is directed against those who claim to be mediators of salvation. As such it would embrace false messiahs within Judaism and redeemer gods of the pagan world, and in the present context, perhaps even more obviously, Pharisees who claimed to hold the keys of the kingdom (cf. Matt 23:13 = Luke 11:52) and in the perspective of the Gospel their successors in contemporary Judaism (so Schnackenburg, 2:291).

The positive aspect of v 10 is to be emphasized as an expression of the message of this Gospel: Jesus has come that all in the world may have life in its fullest sense—the eternal life of the kingdom of God (20:30–31).

11–13 The "noble" (καλός) shepherd virtually = ὁ ποιμὴν ὁ ἀληθινός, the "genuine" shepherd, since he contrasts with all who claim, or are claimed to be, the shepherds of humankind but are powerless to save. Here, however, καλός relates primarily to the readiness of the shepherd to lay down his life for the sheep. The comparison with the "hireling," who neither owns the sheep, nor cares for them, nor defends them from marauding beasts (vv 12–13), invites translating τὴν ψυχὴν αὐτοῦ τίθησιν as "*risks* his life" for the sheep. Again, however, the continuing context demands a more emphatic rendering. V 15 speaks explicitly of the Shepherd laying down his life for the sheep, and vv 17–18 that he does this in obedience to the command of the Father. The language of metaphor thus gives way to kerygmatic affirmation.

14–15 In vv 14–15 we have a good example of how concepts in different languages can draw close, yet still require discrimination. In the Greek tradition knowledge is thought of as analogous to *seeing*, with a view to grasping the nature of an object; for the Hebrew, knowledge means *experiencing* something. In the area of religion, therefore, knowledge of God for the Greek is primarily contemplation of the divine reality; for the Hebrew it means entering into a relationship with God. This latter is vividly, if not shatteringly, illustrated in Amos 3:1–2. On this background vv 14–15 have a clear meaning: the mutual knowledge of the Shepherd and his "sheep" denotes an intimate relationship which reflects the fellowship of love between the Father and the Son. (In 17:21 it not only *reflects* but is *rooted in* that relationship, expressed in terms of the Son being "in" the Father and the believers "in" the Son.) Hellenistic Judaism prepared the ground for Greeks to approach this way of thinking, so that in the Hermetic literature knowledge of God means mystical communion with God. Bauer adduces, in illustration of vv 14–15, a well-known prayer in a magical papyrus, thought to be taken from a Hermetic cult liturgy: "I know you, Hermes, who you are and whence you are. I also know your barbarous names. . . . I know you, Hermes, and you know me. *I am you and you are I"* (Bauer, 137). The last sentence, however, indicates a wholly different religion from the Johannine revelation, which emphasizes a union initiated by the Creator in his redeeming love and by the creature in responsive love through the Christ, in whom God and man alone are one.

16 In v 16 return is made again to the parable of vv 1–5, where the "fold" to which the Shepherd comes is that of Israel. If salvation is "of the Jews" (4:22), it must first come to the Jews, and then proceed from them to the nations (significantly it was in that context that Jesus was described by Samaritans as the Savior of the world, 4:42). So here, in the context of Jesus as the Shepherd of God's flock and in conjunction with his intention to lay down his life for the sheep, we learn that he has sheep of other folds than Israel's. The death of the Shepherd embraces all people (cf. 11:50–52, also 3:16; 6:51; 12:20, 24, 31–32). The sheep are his before they hear his voice, for they have been given him by the Father (cf. v 29, and the repeated similar affirmations in chap. 6—vv 37–39, 44–45, 64–65). Who, then, is to gather them? None other than the Shepherd himself! "*I* must bring them . . . and they shall hear *my* voice." The mission to the nations is that of Jesus, continuing his mission to Israel's fold. As he was sent by the Father on mission to Israel, so he will conduct his mission to the nations through his disciples (so 20:21; the thought is embodied in Matt 28:18–20, "Go, and make disciples of all nations . . . See, I am with you always . . ."; similarly in terms of action, in the longer ending of Mark at 16:20). The sheep of the different folds are not to remain in their separateness, but "they shall become one flock," under the care of the one Shepherd. Their unity is the fruit of his solitary sacrifice (vv 15, 17–18) and his unique relation to God and man (vv 14–15a) as the Pauline epistles joyfully proclaim (Rom 5:12–21; 2 Cor 5:14–21; Eph 2:11–18).

17–18 The theme of the Shepherd's death, announced in vv 11 and 15, is now elaborated, but without reference to the pastoral imagery. The main statement is in v 17, which is amplified in v 18. Two points are made.

(*i*) The Father's love for the Son is linked with the Son's death for the world. This event is naturally not represented as the origin of that love but its supreme manifestation and enactment. The Father willed that the Son should lay down his life for humankind (v 18), and the Son obeyed, in freedom, and with sovereign authority from the Father. The mutual love of the Father and Son thus was seen in a deed of love for the world, in which the Father in love willed to save all and the Son in love freely gave his all.

The significance of the statement was well perceived by Hoskyns:

The love of the Father for the Son is set in the context neither of the original creation nor of a relationship which existed before the world was made, but of the love of the Father for the world of men and women. . . . The love of the Father is directed towards the Son, because by him, by his voluntary death, the obedience upon which the salvation of men depends has been accomplished (379).

(*ii*) Jesus lays down his life in order to take it again. Here two thoughts coalesce: the unity of the death and resurrection of the Son for the salvation of the world, and the attribution of the resurrection to the Son. Both are characteristic of this Gospel (cf. the "lifting up" sayings, 3:14–15; 8:28; 12:31–32; and 2:19–21), but not inharmonious with the others. In the Markan predictions of the passion (Mark 8:31; 9:31; 10:32), the death of the Son of Man is conjoined with his resurrection not, as is often alleged, as a mere prophecy after the event, but because the death of the Son of Man in his service for the kingdom of God is inconceivable without his resurrection for the same end, and because the latter is God's act, not alone to vindicate the Son of Man but in God's completing his work of establishing his saving sovereignty through the Son of Man. So also in the Fourth Gospel the Resurrection is the completion of the works given by the Father to the Son to do; but like the rest of those works it is ultimately the work of the Father through the Son (the principle is applied in 5:19–30 to the resurrection and judgment of the world). Accordingly, "When, in rising from the dead, Jesus takes up his life again, nothing occurs other than that the Father glorifies him" (Schnackenburg, 2:302). For the death of the Son is his return to the Father, and the resurrection his glorification by the Father (17:1, 5, 11).

Division among the Hearers (10:19–21)

This further occasion for division arose "among the Jews," which appears to mean the people and not the rulers. The ambiguity of the term has been seen in 7:11–13: the Jews were looking for Jesus in the temple, but were afraid to speak openly of him "because of the Jews," and a division among them took place (7:31, 32, 40–43). Here, as there, the division was occasioned through the *sayings* of Jesus (7:40–43); it is unlikely therefore that the paragraph was intended to follow 9:40–41. The mention at this point of the healing of the blind man is natural, since it took place in Jerusalem (observe that it is referred to again in 11:37). The mention of the division indicates the uncertainty and tension in the situation, and so prepares for the following section, where the uncertainty and tension reach explosion point (vv 24–39).

JESUS AT THE FESTIVAL OF THE DEDICATION (10:22–42)

Two closely related subjects (or, as we may say, two aspects of one theme) are dealt with in vv 22–39. Jesus is asked whether he is *the Messiah* (v 24). He replies in terms reminiscent of the Shepherd discourse of vv 1–18, culminating in the utterance of v 30, "I and the Father are one." The second part of the discussion sets out from that statement, and by reference to Ps 82 justifies Jesus' claim that he is *the Son of God* (v 36). The terms in which the latter statement is enunciated may have in view the significance of the Dedication festival in relation to the mission of Jesus.

Jesus the Messiah (10:22–30)

22–23 The institution of the Festival of Dedication is described in 1 Macc 4:59. Antiochus Epiphanes, in pursuance of his policy to establish one religion throughout his empire, had forbidden the Jews to maintain their ancestral religion and laws, and ordered them to conform to the pagan worship of Zeus. The climax of his attempt to eradicate the Jewish worship was to set on the altar in the Jerusalem temple a pagan altar, probably with an image of Zeus in his own likeness, and on the 25th. Kislev (= December 167 B.C.) sacrifice was offered on this altar. In a heroic series of military encounters Judas Maccabaeus led the Jews to victory over the forces of Antiochus; the desolated temple was cleansed and refurbished, and on the 25th. Kislev 164 B.C., sacrifice was offered "as the Law commands" on the newly built altar of burnt offering. The people joyously celebrated the rededication of the altar for eight days, and it was decreed that a like festival be held each year for eight days, beginning on the 25th. Kislev (see 1 Macc 4:36–59). It is likely that in earlier times a festival celebrating the winter solstice had been held on that date; its purpose was now adapted to commemorate the deliverance from Antiochus and renewal of the temple worship.

The festival was marked by its use of lights. Josephus called it φῶτα, "The Festival of Lights," "because . . . such a freedom shone upon us" (*Ant.* 12.325). In 2 Macc 1:9 it is called "the Festival of Tabernacles of the month Kislev." 1 Macc 1:9 mentions the lighting again of the temple lamps at the Rededication, as the later rabbis did yet more emphatically. Unlike Tabernacles, the festival could be celebrated at home. A lampstand with eight lamps was used; according to Shammai, the eight lamps were lighted on the first day, and one light was extinguished each day until there were none, but according to Hillel, one lamp should be lighted on the first day and one added each day till all eight were alight. Rejoicing was the keynote of the festival, and no mourning was allowed during its observance (for the customs of the festival and their explanations accorded them by the rabbis see Str-B 2:539–41).

The mention that it was "winter" could relate to the immediately following clause. It was wintry weather; hence Jesus moved about in Solomon's Porch, which gave shelter from the cold winds (cf. the significance of χειμῶνος in Mark 13:18). It may, however, relate to the spiritual climate (cf. ἦν δὲ νύξ in 13:30). A great deliverance from an Antichrist and the triumph of true religion was being celebrated, but the frosty temperature without corresponded to the frozen spirits of "the Jews." For them there was no sign of the Deliverer, but among them stood Jesus, whom many of the populace regarded as the Messiah, but who did not observe the Law as the sacred tradition demanded, and whose speech and actions were tantalizing.

24 Despite all that Jesus is recorded as saying to the Jews, including the immediately preceding chapters, he had never publicly stated that he was the Messiah (the admission to the Samaritan woman was no public proclamation). His claims to being the source of living water (7:37–38), Light for the world (8:12), the Shepherd of the sheep (10:11) were certainly astonishing, but was he prepared to affirm that he was *the Anointed of God,* and so the King of the coming Kingdom of God? That was the crucial matter.

If it be asked why the Jewish leaders posed the question, it is unlikely that they wished to know the answer of Jesus in order to acknowledge him as Messiah, if he so confessed it. While the clause Ἕως πότε τὴν ψυχὴν ἡμῶν αἴρεις; is commonly translated, "How long are you keeping us in suspense?", Barrett cites authorities in both ancient and modern Greek for the meaning, "How long do you intend to *annoy* or *provoke* us?" (380). The similarity between vv 24–25 and the synoptic trial narrative in Mark 14:61–62 and especially Luke 22:67 has often been noticed. It has prompted the question whether a common source lies behind the Fourth Gospel and the others, and if so whether the Fourth Evangelist has antedated the proceedings in the trial or the synoptics have transferred earlier material to the later time (see the discussions in Dodd. *Interpretation,* 361–62; *Historical Tradition,*

92; Brown, 405; Schnackenburg, 2:306). We have no means of settling that issue; the differences among the accounts suggest that these exchanges occurred both prior to and during the trial, but the similarities strengthen the view that the passage before us represents a hostile intent, reflecting a desire of the Jewish leaders to discredit Jesus rather than to follow him. This accords with the reply of Jesus that follows: he perceived the real motive of his questioners.

25 Jesus characteristically answers the question in an indirect manner. (The Fourth Evangelist has his own way of representing the messianic reserve of Jesus.) But what does he mean by, "I have *told* you"? No such clear statement has been hitherto recorded. The affirmation may mean, "My teaching makes the answer plain enough for those with eyes to see and ears to hear"; in which case Jesus asserts that his words and his works set forth who he is (so, e.g., Westcott, 65; Hoskyns, 387). Or we must understand that the works done in the Father's name tell the Jews what they want to know, since they bear clear witness to him (so Bultmann, 362; Schnackenburg, 2:305–6; Barrett, 378).

26–30 The Jewish leaders do not believe, because they do not belong to the flock of Jesus; i.e., they have not been "given" to Jesus by the Father (cf. 6:36–37, 44). But note the appeal in vv 37–38 to renounce unbelief and to believe in Jesus as the Son of God; the two aspects of election and responsible hearing of the revelation are maintained. In v 27 the thought of vv 14–15 is echoed: Christ's sheep listen to his voice; he *knows* them and they *follow* him, for they too know him. The emphasis falls on the Shepherd's calling and establishing a relationship with the sheep. He gives eternal life to the sheep, for he lays down his life for them that he may take it again (vv 16–17). The reverse aspect of this is that they shall never be "lost" or "destroyed" (with reference to the last day? but cf. v 10), and no one can tear them out of his hand, i.e., by attacks upon them (cf. v 12). The assurance is reinforced in the sentence that follows: the Father who gave the sheep to the Son is greater than all powers in the universe, and none can tear them out of *his* hand. That is why Jesus can say that none can rob him of his sheep, for *he and the Father are one*.

The setting of v 30 in relation to vv 28–29 shows that a functional unity of the Son and the Father in their care for the sheep is in mind. From earliest times it has been observed that Jesus says, "I and the Father are ἕν," not "εἷς," i.e., one in action, not in person. Fundamentally the issue would not be different if it be postulated that the Evangelist's source followed vv 24–25 with v 30 without a break; for then we have the familiar assertion that the works done in the Father's name show who Jesus is, with the added observation that he and the Father are one in their action. In either case we are presented again with the theology of 5:17–30 (so emphatically Schlatter, 242; Sanders, 258; Haenchen, 392; Becker, 337–38). Nevertheless the observation is justified that in v 30 we have a glimpse of "the metaphysical depths contained in the relationship between Jesus and the Father" (Schnackenburg, 2:308), so long as it is recognized that the Evangelist has not spelled out the nature of those "metaphysical depths." The sentence in v 30 played an important role in the early Church controversies on Christology and the doctrine of the Trinity; these are reviewed by T. E. Pollard in his article "The Exegesis of John x.30 in the Early Trinitarian Controversies," but it is evident that the conclusions drawn from the statement by many of the early Fathers were far from the mind of the Evangelist.

Jesus the Son of God (10:31–39)

31–32 The response of the Jews to Jesus' utterance in v 30 confirms the doubtful motives in their question (v 24) and Jesus' observation as to their unbelief (vv 25–26). We recall the reaction to his statement in 8:58. Unlike that occasion, however, Jesus does not immediately withdraw, but challenges their violent action. His question in v 32 is deeply ironical: he performed many ἔργα καλά "from the Father." Which of them were blasphemous, calling for lynching? The relevance of the question is clear: those "works" were done at the command and by the power of the Father through the agency of the Son, and therefore bear witness to the unity mentioned in v 30; and second, the works are one with the words given by the Father to the Son, and attest the truth of v 30. (For the unity of words and works of the Father through Jesus see 14 10–11; for the nuance of "beautiful, fine, noble" in the expression ἔργα καλά, see Mark 14:6; Luke 8:15; 1 Tim 4:6, and in this context 10:11, 14.)

33 The anger of the Jews blinds them to the issues in Jesus' question; they assert that he has uttered blasphemous words and therefore he should die. This is the sole passage in the Gospel where Jesus is alleged to have blasphemed. Later Jewish ruling held that blasphemy was committed only when the sacred name of God was mentioned, but the charge that Jesus "made himself God" and therefore blasphemed reflects contemporary thought, and is in line with the judgment scene in Mark 14:61–64. The High Priest's pronouncement that Jesus had blasphemed was not on the basis of his confession to being the Messiah, but through his explanatory addition, "You shall see the Son of Man *sitting at the right hand of power*," so sharing the power and glory of God, which no human being can do, and *"coming with the clouds of heaven,"* i.e., in a theophany proper alone to God. In the present context the accusation, "You make yourself God," is that of 5:17–18, which is rebutted in the answer of Jesus in 5:19–30. That answer is pertinent in relation to v 30: his unity with the Father is not a self-exaltation, but proceeds from the Father, who gives him power and authority, and so unity of action and being, with himself.

34–36 Jesus defends his utterance by citing Ps 82:6, which with the sentence that follows, reads:

> I said, "You are gods;
>   you are all sons of the Most High."
> But you will die like mere men;
>   you will fall like any prince.

It is plain from the course of the argument, as well as from usual Jewish assumptions in quoting the Bible, that the second line is assumed along with the first (the whole passage was well known to the hearers, for its meaning was frequently discussed). A single clear idea is in mind as Jesus cites this scripture: In the "Law" (i.e., the OT, of which the Law is the chief part; cf. 12:34; 15:25), the term "god" is applied to others than God himself; if those addressed by God in this passage can be called gods (and sons of God), how much more can he whom the Father consecrated and sent into the world be so termed?

So much is plain, and admitted by all. There are, however, considerable differences in interpreting who are addressed in the psalm. The possibilities of interpretation were all represented in early Judaism.

(*i*) The psalm has in view *Israel's judges,* who fail to maintain justice in their courts (cf. vv 1–4); they are called "gods" by virtue of their exercise, through God's appointment, of the divine function of judgment. The Midrash on Ps 82 comments on v 1, "These words are to be considered in the light of Moses' charge to the judges of Israel (i.e., in Deut 1:17); hence the verse 'He is a judge among *Elohim*' is to read 'He is a judge among judges.' What can *Elohim* signify except judges?" (so rendered by W. G. Braude, Yale Judaica Series 13; see also *Sanh.* 6b–7a; *Soṭa* 47b; *Tg. Ps.-J.*).

(*ii*) Ps 82:6 is addressed to *the people of Israel at the giving of the Law. Tanḥ. B.* 9(13a) recounts that God spoke to the Angel of Death, "When I created you, I created you for the nations of the world, but not for my sons; for these I have made gods, as it says, 'I myself have spoken: You are gods and sons of the Most High, all of you.'" *ʿAbod. Zar.* 5a and *Midr. Rab. Exod* 32:7 make it plain that it was at the giving of the Law that the people were declared to be gods, and that had they remained obedient to it they would not have died; their disobedience however, was almost immediately manifested in the making of the golden calf, and so they became subject to death (hence Ps 82:6–7, "I said, You are gods . . . nevertheless you shall die like men. . . .").

(*iii*) Those addressed as "gods" are *angelic powers* who had authority over the nations but misused it. J. A. Emerton has shown that such was the probable understanding of the LXX translators in their rendering of Ps 82, and quite certainly that of the Peshitta translators, who rendered *El* in v la and *Elohim* in 1b by the term *malke,* "angels" ("Some New Testament Notes," 331). Fundamentally this was adopted in the Qumran community, but with an astonishing modification: the opening sentence of the psalm is viewed as spoken by Melchizedek. The Melchizedek fragment reads, ". . . it is written concerning him in the hymns of David, who says, '*The heavenly one standeth in the congregation of God; among the holy ones he judgeth,*' and concerning him he says, '*Above them return thou on high; God shall judge the nations.*' And that which he says: '*How long will ye judge unjustly and accept the persons of the wicked? Selah*': its interpretation concerns Belial and the spirits of his lot . . ." (translation by de Jonge and van der Woude, "11Q Melchizedek and the New Testament," 303). In this passage Melchizedek is viewed as an ̇angel, with the title of God; and those addressed as "gods" and "sons of the Highest," but who act unjustly in the world, are apparently evil angels ("Belial and the spirits of his lot").

Emerton was strongly inclined to see this third understanding of the text as assumed in John 10:34–36: if angels, fallen or unfallen, could be termed "gods," how much more rightly Jesus! ("Melchizedek and the Gods," 399–401). The interpretation would be strengthened if the contrast included that between Jesus and Melchizedek: the latter, who is above the other angels, is expected by the Qumran monks to destroy the powers of evil and save the people of God, but Jesus is greater than Melchizedek, and is the true Son of God, one with God. De Jonge and van der Woude, in their discussion of the Melchizedek text, consider this possibility, but reject it by reason of a serious difficulty: the context in the Fourth Gospel makes no mention of angels. V 33 makes a clear contrast between god and men, but nowhere in this Gospel do heavenly beings, like those portrayed in 11QMelch, play a role of any importance (unlike, e.g., the Letter to the Hebrews; see "11Q Melchizedek," 313–14).

The relation of the passage to Israel's judges is also unlikely; in John 10:35

the recipients of the saying, "I said, You are gods" are said to be, "those to whom the word of God came (ἐγένετο)"; this is best understood as describing Israel's gathered tribes about Mount Sinai, as virtually all the Rabbis believed. In this connection we should recall the importance to the Jews of Exod 4:21–22, "Israel is my first-born son. . . . Let my son go that he may serve me." The citation of Ps 82:6 in the context before us accordingly is thoroughly comprehensible in a discussion between Jesus and Jewish teachers and leaders (as also between Christian Evangelist and later Jewish opponents of the Church). The parallelism within Ps 82:6, "You are gods, you are all sons of the Most High," explains the reproduction of v 30 ("I and the Father are one") in the changed form of v 36 ("I said, 'I am God's Son'"). If the thought of Jesus as the representative Son of the people called to be sons of God may be assumed in the context, the "how much more" of v 36 is yet more understandable.

A. T. Hanson has modified this third interpretation by suggesting that the "Word of God" in v 35 is *the pre-existent Logos;* the expression in v 35 "to whom the word of God *came*" means "to whom the pre-existent Word *spoke*" (after Westcott, 2:70). The argument then runs: "If to be addressed by the pre-existent Word justifies men in being called gods . . . far more are we justified in applying the title Son of God to the human bearer of the pre-existent Word, sanctified and sent by the Father as he was, in unmediated and direct presence" ("John's Citation of Psalm 82," 159–61); the argument is later elaborated in the light of the Melchizedek fragment ("John's Citation of Psalm 82 Reconsidered," 363–67). Attractive as this is, it is hardly likely to be in the Johannine text. The phrase "to whom the word of God came (ἐγένετο)" is most naturally to be understood as those to whom *the message* was spoken, and is frequently so used in the OT prophets, especially in Jer and Ezek).

The application of the term ἡγίασεν ("consecrated") to Jesus occurs here and in 17:17, 19 only, the latter in the sense of consecration unto death. The concept of Jesus as the one sent by the Father into the world is frequent in the Fourth Gospel; that Jesus is described as "he whom the Father *consecrated and sent* . . .*"* in the context of the festival commemorating the dedication or consecration of the temple is highly significant. It suggests that the meaning of the Festival of the Dedication, like that of the Tabernacles and Passover, finds its ultimate fulfillment in the mission of Jesus.

Hoskyns points out that variants of the term τὰ ἐγκαίνια ("The Dedication," v 22) appear in the LXX to describe the dedication of the altar in the Tabernacle (Num 7:10–11), of the temple of Solomon (1 Kgs 8:63), and of the temple built after the return from the Babylonian captivity (Ezra 6:16; LXX, 7:7), and he comments, "The Feast therefore called to mind the whole dignity of Hebrew worship in the commemoration of a particular episode in Jewish history" (385). The concept of the fulfillment of the Dedication festival in the redemptive revelation in Jesus thus has profound depth. The admitted allusiveness of the reference in v 36 is in line with the allusiveness of the other references to Jesus as fulfilling the feasts of the Jews (e.g., in 6:4; 7:37–38; 8:12; 19:31–37 is more explicit, yet also ambiguous); the cumulative effect of their testimony is nevertheless clear (so Lightfoot, 211–12; Brown, 404, 411; Marsh, 407; Lindars, 375; Newbigin, 136).

37–39 A renewed appeal is made to recognize the testimony of the "works" of Jesus as pointing to his unity with the Father. That unity, however, is now defined in terms of mutual indwelling, "the Father in me and I in the Father." The expression conveys the thought of completest unity, a relation *sui generis;* nevertheless we learn later that it forms the basis of a union between

God and man through the Son by virtue of the redemptive event (cf. 14:10–11, and especially 17:21). The fulsome expression, "that you may know and come to grasp" (ἵνα γνῶτε καὶ γινώσκητε) intimates that the knowledge in view is no mere cognizance of a dogma, but an experience attainable only in faith.

39 The scene ends as in 8:59; the Shepherd, like his sheep, is in the almighty Father's hand till his hour strikes (cf. 7:30; 8:20).

Jesus' Withdrawal to Transjordan (10:40–42)

The departure of Jesus from Jerusalem to the territory east of Jordan was doubtless prompted by the virulent opposition of the Jewish leaders. In going to the place where John the Baptist first baptized and bore his decisive witness to Jesus (i.e., Bethany, see 1:28–34), the wheel has come full circle (Sanders, 261). Here the memory of John was still fresh. Those who had known and heard him recalled his testimony concerning Jesus, and what they said was remarkable in more than one respect. "John did no sign"; this in itself is notable, in the light of John's reputation. E. Bammel pointed out that, in contemporary Judaism, a sign was considered decisive for the recognition of a prophet; indeed, "the praise of a man of God who did *not* perform miracles was completely unknown in Jewish sources" ("John Did No Miracles," 190–91). But these people added, "Everything that he ever spoke about this man was true," That was said in the light of subsequent history; the word and the signs of Jesus confirmed the word without signs of John the Baptist. Accordingly the hearers of John at once confirmed the authenticity of John as a prophet and the superior authority of Jesus, in a context of unqualified appreciation of the former. Not surprisingly, "Many believed on him there." We recall what is said of John in the prologue (1:7) and are prepared for the last and greatest sign of Jesus which is about to be narrated (cf. Schnackenburg, 2:315: "The reader already senses the renewed swell of the movement of faith which will be the outcome of the Lazarus miracle, 11:45; 12:9, 17–19)."

Explanation

The Christological issue is again to the fore, and dominates both the Shepherd discourse and the dialogue in the Dedication festival. Again the dual perspective of the Evangelist is apparent: Jesus in Jerusalem, in dialogue with Jewish leaders, whose hostility bursts into threatened violence, and the Evangelist with his churches, opposed by leaders of the synagogue because of the claims made on behalf of Jesus.

The Shepherd imagery is peculiarly apt to set forth the significance of Jesus, since it was well known to both Jews and Gentiles as a picture of Leadership and Salvation for humanity; in the Christian setting it has the deeper dimension of mediation of the Rule and Redemption of the Lord of the universe. In the discourse of Ezek 34 it is God who takes upon himself the role of Shepherd of the flock, and this he does in view of the faithlessness of the shepherds of Israel; in place of their devastating rule he brings salvation to the flock. In the time of Jesus these false shepherds would be seen as primarily the spiritual guides of Israel, especially the Pharisees, but the picture of the Door and the destroyers of the flock would extend their application to the whole gamut of religious rulers, teachers, messianic prophets, and Zealotic leaders of the people. In the time of the Evangelist and his church, the picture would go beyond them to the pantheon of savior gods, divinized men, and powers of the Gnostic pleroma. But the attention paid to the Jewish leaders surrounding Jesus in 10:21–39 and the biblical exposition in response to their charge of blasphemy, together with the congruence of the passage with chaps. 5–8, suggest that post–A.D. 70 Jamnian Pharisaism is to the fore in the Evangelist's mind. Not exclusively so, of course, for the Johannine letters and the Apocalypse, also produced in the Johannine circle, show that the Johannine communities were threatened by the cults of the Mediterranean world, including that of the worship of the Emperor, and more dangerous still the Gnosticism that threatened to attack the heart of the Christian revelation and redemption like a cancer (cf. 1 John 2:18–24; 4:1–6).

The exposition of the relation of Jesus to God and to Israel and the nations provides a definitive answer to these varied movements. Negatively, the picture of the Door excludes all others who claim (or for whom claims are made) to open the way to God and to bring salvation to the world. Positively, we observe that Jesus as the Good Shepherd is related more closely to God who acts as Shepherd than to "David," as he is depicted in Ezek 34. The prophetic allegory is one with OT messianic teaching generally in representing God as the Deliverer of his people, gathering them into their land, giving them salvation in his kingdom, and *then* providing them with the Messiah who shall act as Shepherd on his behalf. In the Shepherd discourse of John 10, the saving activity of God takes place *through* his representative Jesus; in the Father's name he cares for the sheep of Israel's flock, he gathers the sheep of the Gentile folds, and he lays down his life and takes it again for the redemption of all mankind, that they all may become one flock under one Shepherd.

For this reason it is fitting that the question as to whether Jesus is the Messiah is answered in broad terms: he is the Messiah who is the Son of God and one with the Father. Dodd saw in the Evangelist's exposition of this theme an advance from Israelite to Hellenistic thought (*Interpretation*, 361); while that is evident, the relation between the two is closer than is often recognized. The representation of Jesus as the Son of God, spelled out with reference to Ps 82, has affinity with a stream of thought within Judaism that emphasized the relation of Israel to God, and especially the righteous of Israel, in terms of sonship to God, a relation which naturally applied especially to the Messiah (see, e.g., Sir 4:10; Wisd Sol 2:18; *Jub.* 1:24 f.; for the Qumran development in this direction cf. 4QFlor 1:6 f.; 1QSa 2:11 f., and the references to the Son of God in the Daniel apocryphon of Cave 4; for the application of Son of God to miracle workers and charismatic figures in Israel see G. Vermes, *Jesus the Jew* [New York: Macmillan, 1983] 206–10, and M. Hengel, *The Son of God* [Philadelphia: Fortress, 1976] 42–43). We are now realizing that the assumed equation of Messiah and Son of God in the High Priest's question to Jesus, Mark 14:61, is wholly compatible with contemporary Jewish thought, though for Caiaphas it will have remained on the plane of representative and adoptive relation to God. The equation in Jesus' answer of Son of God and Son of Man seated at the right hand of God is more important (it is assumed also in Mark 8:38; 13:32). Here is a primary root of the Johannine development of Jesus as the Son, for throughout this Gospel Son of God and Son of Man are one, and the significance of both is deepened by the concept of incarnation. It appears that in John 10 it is the function of Christ who *acts* as Son of God, Shepherd of man, and Door to the kingdom that is to the fore, even in v 30, while the inner relation to the Father is set forth in v 38 and reflects back on the preceding passage.

It is not without interest that later Pharisaism retreated from the developments that had earlier taken place in the concept of the Messiah as Son of God, almost certainly through controversy with the Church and the Christian proclamation of Jesus as the Messiah and Son of God. This finds a well-known illustration in the polemic of Rabbi Abbahu. He said, "If a man say to you, 'I am God,' he is a liar; 'I am the Son of Man,' he will finally regret it; 'I ascend into heaven,' he may say it, but he will not accomplish it." And again, in a comment on Exod 20:22: "It is like a king of flesh and blood, who can rule as king while he has a father or a brother or a son. But God says, 'With me that is not so. "I am the First," Isa 44:6, for I have no Father; "and I am the Last," for I have no brother; "and besides me there is no God," for I have no Son' " (cited Str-B 2:542). Abbahu lived in Caesarea *ca.* A.D. 300, long after the composition of the Fourth Gospel, but one sees in him the kind of opposition that came to be expressed against Christians when the controversy with the Church reached its climax in the ascendancy of Pharisaic Judaism.

The interpretation of Jesus continues to remain the supreme issue separating Jews from Christians, but the discussion may now be conducted in a very different spirit from that of earlier times. The Christian debt to Judaism is widely acknowledged in the churches, and an increasing number of Jews are drawn to Jesus, recognizing in him a Son of their people who opened up to the world the revelation made known to their Fathers. It remains for the followers of Jesus to demonstrate, in life as well as in teaching, how that revelation reaches its true culmination in Jesus *the* Son of God.

G. Jesus the Resurrection and the Life (11:1–54)

Bibliography

Bammel, E. " 'Ex illa itaque die consilium fecerunt . . .' (John 11:53)." *The Trial of Jesus.* FS C. F. D. Moule. Ed. E. Bammel. SBT 2d ser. 13. London: SCM, 1970. 11–40. **Barker, M.** "John 11–50." *The Trial of Jesus.* Ed. E. Bammel. 41–46. **Bevan, E.** "Note on Mark i.41 and John xi.33, 38." *JTS* 33 (1932) 186–88. **Bonner, C.** "Traces of Thaumaturgic Technique in the Miracles." *HTR* 20 (1927) 171–81. **Braun, F.-M.** "Quatre 'signes' johanniques de l'unité chrétienne." *NTS* 9 (1962–63) 147–55. **Cadman, W. H.** "The Raising of Lazarus." *SE* (1959) 423–34. **Daube, D.** *Collaboration with*

Tyranny in Rabbinic Law. London: Oxford, 1966. **Dodd, C. H.** *Historical Tradition in the Fourth Gospel*. 228–32. ———. "The Prophecy of Caiaphas: John 11:47–53." *More New Testament Studies*. Manchester: Univ. Press, 1968. 58–68. **Dunkerley, R.** "Lazarus." *NTS* 5 (1958–59) 321–27. **Foretell, I. T.** "I Am the Resurrection and the Life." *Contemporary New Testament Studies*. Ed. Rosalie Ryan. Collegeville, MN: Liturgical Press, 1965. 99–104; also in *BiTod* 1 (1963) 331–36. **Fortna, R. T.** *Gospel of Signs*. 74–87. **Fuller, R. H.** *Interpreting the Miracles*. London: SCM, 1963. 105–8. **Grimm, W.** "Das Opfer eines Menschen: Eine Auslegung von Joh 11, 47–53." *Israel hat dennoch Gott zum Trost*. FS S. ben Chorin. Ed. G. Müller. Trier: Paulinus, 1978. 61–82. **MacNeil, B.** "The Raising of Lazarus." *Dunwoodie Review* 92 (1974) 269–75. **Martin, J. P.** "History and Eschatology in the Lazarus Narrative, John 11:1–44." *SJT* 17 (1964) 332–43. **Nicol, W.** *Semeia in the Fourth Gospel*. 37–38, 109–11. **Osborne, B.** "A Folded Napkin in an Empty Tomb: John 11:44 and 20:7 Again." *HeyJ* 14 (1973) 437–40. **Pancaro, S.** "'People of God' in St. John's Gospel?" *NTS* 16 (1969–70) 114–29. **Reiser, W. E.** "The Case of the Tidy Tomb: The Place of the Napkins of John 11:44 and 20:7." *HeyJ* 14 (1973) 47–57. **Romaniuk, K.** "'I am the Resurrection and the Life'; John 11:25." *Concilium* 6 (1970) 68–77. **Sanders, J. N.** "Those Whom Jesus Loved: St. John xi.5," *NTS* 1 (1954–55) 29–41. **Sass, G.** *Die Auferweckung des Lazarus: Eine Auslegung von Johannes 11*. Neukirchen-Vluyn: Neukirchener Verlag, 1967. **Stenger, W.** "Die Auferweckung des Lazarus (John 11:1–45) *TTZ* 83 (1974) 17–37. **Trudinger, P.** "The Raising of Lazarus—a Brief Response." *Dunwoodie Review* 94 (1976) 187–90. **Wilcox, M.** "The 'Prayer' of Jesus in John xi.41b–42." *NTS* 24 (1977–78) 128–32. **Wilkens, W.** "Die Erweckung des Lazarus." *TZ* 15 (1959) 22–39.

Translation

[1] *Now there was a certain man who was ill, Lazarus from Bethany,*[a] *the village of Mary and her sister Martha.* [2] *It was the Mary who anointed the Lord with ointment and wiped his feet with her hair, whose brother was ill.*[b] [3] *The sisters therefore sent to him, saying, "Master, we want you to know that the one whom you love*[c] *is ill."* [4] *But Jesus, on hearing it, said, "This illness is not with a view to death, but for the sake of the glory of God, that the Son of God may be glorified through it."*

[5] *Now Jesus loved Martha and her sister and Lazarus.* [6] *When therefore he heard that he was ill he continued to remain in the place where he was for two days.* [7] *After this he says to the disciples, "Let us go to Judea again."* [8] *The disciples say to him, "Rabbi, the Jews were just now trying to stone you, and are you going back there again?"* [9] *Jesus replied, "There are twelve hours in the day, aren't there? If anyone walks in the day he does not stumble, because he sees the light of this world.* [10] *But if anyone walks in the night he stumbles, because the light is not in him."* [11] *This he said, and afterwards told them, "Our friend Lazarus has fallen asleep, but I am going to wake him out of sleep."* [12] *The disciples therefore said to him, "Master, if he has fallen asleep he will get well."* [13] *But Jesus had spoken about his death. They however supposed that he had been talking about sleep in the sense of slumber.* [14] *Then Jesus told them plainly, "Lazarus has died.* [15] *And I am glad for your sakes that I was not there, so that you may believe. But let us go to him."* [16] *Thomas, called the Twin, said therefore to his fellow disciples, "Let us also go, that we may die with him."*

[17] *When Jesus arrived he found that he had already been in the tomb for four days.*[d] [18] *Now Bethany was near Jerusalem, about fifteen stadia distant.*[e] [19] *Many*

of the Jews had come to Martha [f] *and Mary in order to console them concerning their brother.* [20] *When therefore Martha heard that Jesus was coming she went out to meet him, but Mary continued to sit in the house.* [21] *Martha therefore said to Jesus, "Master, if you had been here my brother would not have died;* [22] *(but) even now I know that whatever you ask of God, God will give you."* [23] *Jesus says to her, "Your brother will rise to life."* [24] *Martha says to him, "I know that he will rise in the resurrection at the last day."* [25] *Jesus said to her, "I am the resurrection (and the life);* [g] *whoever believes in me, even though he dies, will come to life,* [26] *and everyone who lives and believes in me will never, never die. Do you believe this?"* [27] *She says to him, "Yes, Master; I have come to believe that you are the Christ, the Son of God, He who comes into the world."*

[28] *After she had said this Martha went off and called her sister Mary, and said to her privately, "The Teacher is here and is calling for you."* [29] *When she heard that she got up quickly and made her way to him;* [30] *but Jesus had not yet come into the village, but was still in the place where Martha had met him.* [31] *The Jews therefore who were with her in the house and were consoling her, on seeing that Mary had arisen quickly and had gone out, followed her, supposing* [h] *that she had gone off to the tomb in order to weep there.* [32] *Mary therefore, when she came where Jesus was and saw him, fell at his feet and said to him, "Master, if you had been here my brother would not have died."* [33] *When Jesus saw her weeping, and the Jews who had come with her weeping, he became angry in spirit and very agitated,* [i] [34] *and he said, "Where have you laid him?" They said to him, "Master, come and see."* [35] *Jesus burst into tears.* [36] *The Jews therefore were saying, "Look, how he loved him!"* [37] *But some of them said, "Surely he who opened the eyes of the blind man was able to do something to prevent this man from dying?"*

[38] *Jesus therefore, again in a state of anger within, comes to the tomb. Now it was a cave, and a stone was lying against it.* [j] [39] *Jesus says, "Remove the stone." Martha, the sister of the dead man, says to him, "Master, by now he stinks, for it is the fourth day!"* [40] *Jesus says to her, "I told you, didn't I, that if you believed you would see the glory of God?"* [41] *They therefore removed the stone. But Jesus raised his eyes upward and said, "Father, I thank you that you heard me.* [42] *But I knew that you always do hear me; but this I said because of the crowd that is standing by, that they may believe that you have sent me."* [43] *And after saying this he shouted with a loud voice, "Lazarus, come out here!"* [44] *The dead man came out, his feet and hands bound with strips of linen and his face covered with a cloth. Jesus says to them, "Release him, and let him go."*

[45] *Many of the Jews therefore who had come to Mary and seen the things that he had done* [k] *believed in him;* [46] *but some of them went off to the Pharisees and told them what Jesus had done.* [47] *The chief priests and the Pharisees therefore gathered the Sanhedrin together and said, "What are we going to do?* [l] *For this man is performing many signs.* [48] *If we let him go on in this way everybody will believe in him, and the Romans will come and take away from us both the (holy) place and the nation."* [49] *But one of them, Caiaphas, who was high priest that year, said to them, "You know nothing at all,* [50] *nor do you realize that it is to your* [m] *advantage that one man should die for the people, and that the whole nation should not perish."* [51] *He did not say this of his own accord, but as he was high priest during that year he prophesied that Jesus was about to die for the nation,* [52] *and not only for the nation, but that he should gather into one the*

children of God who were scattered abroad. [53] *From that day therefore they made a resolution to put him to death.*

[54] *Jesus accordingly no longer went about publicly among the Jews, but departed from that place to the territory near the wilderness, to a town called Ephraim,*[n] *and there he stayed with the disciples.*

Notes

[1] Lazarus is the Lat. (and virtually Gr.) form of the Heb. *Lazar,* an abbreviation of Eleazar (= "he whom God helps"). Bethany lies east of Jerusalem, and is now called El-azariyeh, in honor of Lazarus. The tomb, said to be that of Lazarus, lies within the village but will have been outside its original borders (graves were set outside inhabited areas to avoid possible uncleanness through contact with the dead). Bethany is denoted as "the village of Mary and Martha" to distinguish it from the Bethany of 1:28, which was in Perea.

[b] Lazarus is identified as the brother of Mary and Martha, since the latter were well known in Christian circles (neither has been mentioned thus far in this Gospel, but cf. Luke 10:38–42).

[c] The description of Lazarus as "he whom you love" has led to the conjecture that he was "the Beloved Disciple" of this Gospel; it is an attractive but hardly compelling speculation; v 5 suggests that we should think of the "beloved family" and not simply of the beloved brother. (On the issue see J. N. Sanders " 'Those whom Jesus loved': St John xi.5," and the discussion in the *Introduction,* pp. lxx–lxxv.)

[d] The MSS tradition shows curious variations as to the place where ἤδη should occur in the expression τέσσαρας ἤδη ἡμέρας (whether in the first, second, or third place, or even omitted). The issue is unimportant, but it provides an instructive instance as to how variants in the text arise (see Metzger, 233).

[e] 15 stadia = 1¾ miles.

[f] The definite article τήν before Μάρθαν καὶ Μαριάμ governs both names; not surprisingly it is omitted in D and in some MSS of most versions. P[45vid] A C³ K Δ Θ etc. read τὰς περὶ Μάρθαν, due to interpreting τήν as the *household* of Mary and Martha (cf. Acts 13:13), but it is unlikely to have come from the Evangelist; the simpler reading is the best supported in the textual tradition (P[66] P[75vid] א B C* L W etc.).

[g] In P[45vid] it[1] syr[s] Origen Cyprian Titus-Bosra καὶ ἡ ζωή is omitted, leaving the simpler but striking saying, "I am the Resurrection." On the basis of *brevior lectio potior* this short reading could be original, in which case "and the Life" would probably reflect a marginal comment, explaining "the Resurrection" as meaning "the Life"; yet it is difficult to resist the support for the longer reading in the mass of early MSS, and the two clauses could be viewed as expounding the two fundamental elements, Resurrection and Life. The omission is generally viewed as accidental, or possibly due to the fact that v 24 mentions only the Resurrection (Metzger, 234).

[h] δόξαντες is read by א B C* D L W X etc., but λέγοντες occurs in P[66] A C² K Δ Θ Π etc. P[75] has the impossible reading δοξάζοντες, evidently written by a scribe when he nodded, but it actually supports δόξαντες, which should be accepted as the best attested reading.

[i] The main sentence (ἐνεβριμήσατο . . . καὶ ἐτάραξεν ἑαυτόν) is the strongest statement in the Gospels relating to the emotions of Jesus, and from ancient to modern times has led to endeavors to weaken its apparent meaning (see the *Comment*). One such endeavor appears in the reading ἐταράχθη τῷ πνεύματι ὡς ἐμβριμούμενος, given in P[45] P[66(?)] D f1 it[p] cop[sa ach] arm; this is clearly "a secondary improvement, introduced from a sense of reverence for the person of Jesus" (so the UBS Committee, Metzger, 235).

[j] If the rock tomb had a horizontal shaft λίθος ἐπέκειτο ἐπ᾽ αὐτῷ = "a stone lay *against* it," if it had a vertical shaft the clause = "a stone lay *over* it."

[k] ἃ ἐποίησεν, read by P[45], P[66] א A* K L W etc., is unexpected, inasmuch as the context concerns a single deed of Jesus and its effect on the witnesses (θεασάμενοι ἃ . . .). The singular ὃ ἐποίησεν accordingly is read by P[66vid] A[c] B C* D etc. That the latter may be due to accommodating the statement to the context is indicated by C², which reads ὃ ἐποίησεν σημεῖον (cf. the interesting alternative in P[66c] ὅσα ἐποίησεν). The pl. reading suggests that the raising of Lazarus was the *culminating* sign that led the Jews in question to believe in Jesus.

¹ τί ποιοῦμεν is not a deliberative subjunctive (which would be τί ποιῶμεν) but a present indicative. Whereas the latter *can* be the equivalent of the former, signifying "What are we to do?", it is better to retain the indicative meaning. It either asks, "What are we doing?", assuming the answer, "Nothing at all, our efforts have been to no avail"; or, with a future slant, "What are we going to do? We must act."

ᵐ ὑμῖν is read by P⁴⁵ P⁶⁶ B D L X etc., and is more in keeping with the arrogance of Caiaphas, expressed in the preceding clause, than ἡμῖν, read by A K W Δ Θ Π Ψ etc. (In ℵ and some Coptic MSS neither pronoun appears, possibly because of the influence of 18:14.)

ⁿ Ephraim is commonly identified with the village Et-Taiyibe, about 12 miles northeast of Jerusalem and 4 miles from Bethel. The change of name was due to Arabs, to whom the later form of the name *Afra* indicated the idea "misfortune," or "evil spirit"; hence, they changed it to Et-Taiyibe = "good," i.e., "the place with a good name" (see Schnackenburg, 2:351).

Form/Structure/Setting

1. The difference of form and structure in chap. 11 from that in the earlier sections of the Gospel has been frequently remarked on; instead of a narrative followed by a discourse on its meaning, we have a narrative interspersed with elements of dialogue that bring out its significance. Dodd, in his earlier work, *Interpretation of the Fourth Gospel,* stated that the interweaving of narrative and dialogue in this chapter is complete, so that one cannot isolate a piece of pure narrative; "There is no story of the Raising of Lazarus— or none that we can now recover—separable from the pregnant dialogues of Jesus with his disciples and with Martha" (363). In his later work, however, Dodd modified this position; he observed that the narrative begins and ends in a manner appropriate to a healing pericope; it commences with "A certain man was ill," gives some additional details about the patient, and ends with his restoration, a note on its effect on spectators, and an indication of its remoter results. He concluded, "The Story of Lazarus . . . is not an original allegorical creation. Fundamentally it belongs to the same genre as the two Marcan narratives (the Epileptic Boy, Mark 9:14–27, and Jairus' Daughter, Mark 5:21–43) . . . . There is good reason to believe that, like the Marcan pericopae, it has behind it a traditional narrative shaped in the course of Christian teaching and preaching, and then remolded by our evangelist to convey his own special message" (*Historical Tradition in the Fourth Gospel,* 232). Much labor has been spent by other scholars to uncover that "traditional narrative" and the nature of the "remoulding" carried out by the Evangelist.

While the account of the Lazarus episode certainly gives the impression of an interweaving of narrative and discourse, examination reveals rather a narrative interspersed with dialogues at two major points: in vv 7–16 we have brief elements of conversation between Jesus and his disciples subsequently expanded, and in vv 20–27 the crucially important dialogue between Jesus and Martha, followed by the briefer exchange with Mary (vv 28–32); with these are to be conjoined the saying in v 4, which supplies the key to the entire narrative, and the prayer of Jesus just before its conclusion (vv 41–42). Many scholars who hesitate to acknowledge a signs source behind the Gospel nevertheless tend to recognize a simpler narrative here, shorn of the specifically Johannine passages such as those mentioned in the previous sentence. When these are abstracted, we find a narrative that tells of the illness of Lazarus (v 1), a message sent to Jesus about it (v 3), a delay in the response of Jesus (v 6), his announcement to the disciples of Lazarus' illness and death and his intention to go and "awake" him (11–15), the arrival at Bethany (vv 17–19), the lamentation of the mourners and Jesus' anger, his arrival at the grave and demand to remove the stone (vv 33–39a), his calling Lazarus from death to life, and Lazarus' emergence from the tomb (vv 43–44). With variations, such an outline is advocated by Bultmann, 395–96; Fortna, *Gospel of Signs*, 74–86; Nicol, *Semeia in the Fourth Gospel* 37–39; Fuller, *Interpreting the Miracles*, 105; Schnackenburg, 2:320, 341.

The process of development in the tradition is a subject for further speculation. Bultmann (395 n.4), Fortna (75) and Becker (2:344) postulate an older form of the story before it was taken up in the signs source. W. Wilkens offers a different suggestion as to the postulated threefold strata of the chapter. He takes as his cue the presumption that Lazarus was not the brother of the two sisters (cf. 12:2), and that Lazarus was the central point of interest in the narrative, not the two sisters, who play such a leading role in the Johannine revision. On this basis he finds first a *Johannine foundational story* in vv 1, 3–4, 11–15, 17, 32–34, 38–39, 41–44; this was not the earliest form of the story, but the version within the foundation document which formed the basis of the present Gospel of John. To discover the *primitive* form of the story it is necessary to strip away all the sentences of a Johannine character. When this is done we find a narrative consisting of the following: vv 1, 3, 17, 33–34, 38–39, 41a, 43–44. This form of the story sets forth Jesus as Lord over death, before whose majesty death must depart, and it gave the Evangelist the opportunity to make it the high point of the signs and to raise the question of faith. The accent in the revision contained in the foundation document can be seen in v 4: Lazarus' illness is for the glory of God and the Son, made manifest through the powerful deed of Jesus. For the *Evangelist* this actually relates to the glory of Jesus on the cross; Jesus is glorified through the raising of Lazarus because he raises him in the authority and power of his cross-glory. Accordingly the Evangelist inserts into his foundation document further passages, namely vv 2, 5–6, 7–10, 16, 18–30, 35–37. The teaching that provides the real meaning of the sign is in this way set prior to the narration of the sign, above all in the conversation of Jesus with Martha, with which must also be seen the emphasis on faith, especially in the weeping of Jesus through lack of it in those around him. Thus the Evangelist sets the "Christ-word" alongside the "Christ-deed" ("Die Erweckung des Lazarus," 33).

Following on this contribution, and taking the work of his predecessors into account, W. Stenger sought to further the investigation of the Lazarus story along related lines. He distinguishes between the outer and the inner redaction. The former makes the raising of Lazarus the immediate cause of the passion of Jesus (vv 46–53); where the passion theme sounds out, there the Johannine redaction may be presumed, viz., in vv 7–10, 16, 18, 28, 30. "The redactional binding of the Lazarus pericope and the passion is a means of mutual contextual interpretation. Jesus, who goes to death, awakes a dead man. His life-giving work becomes the occasion of his giving up his life" ("Die Auferweckung des Lazarus," 22). The inner redaction is indicated in an apparently insignificant mention of Mary and Martha in v 1 (in that order), the attention given to Mary in v 2, and the fact that the Jews come to comfort *Mary* in v 45. In vv 5 and 19, however, Martha is mentioned before Mary; the revelation embodied in the story is made known to her (vv 20–27), and she informs Mary of the arrival of Jesus (v 28). Stenge observes that the dialogue of 20–27 is clearly redactional; if one follows v 17 with 20a and replaces the name of Martha with that of Mary, leaving out also the stress on the presence of Mary in the house, the narrative tells of Jesus' arrival, of *Mary's* hearing of it, and of *her* telling Jesus, "If you had been here my brother would not have died." In the original story, then, Martha occupied a subordinate position, not the prominent one given her by the redaction. The original story is located in vv 1, 3, 6, 11–15, 17, 20–21 (relating to Mary), 33–35, 38–39, 43–44, 45. The most important mark of its structure is the delay of Jesus; it causes Lazarus to die, and excludes all doubt as to the finality of his death. Everything is directed to the form of the miracle worker and his superhuman abilities; there is no suggestion of the miracle as the beginning and prolepsis of the kingdom of God; the story manifests a Christological concentration, which is due to the *Sitz im Leben* of missionary preaching. In the Johannine redaction Martha is introduced as the believer whose faith in the God-given power of Jesus does not waver in face of her brother's death. Her conversation with Jesus gives the story of a new center; whereas the high point of the source was the miracle, this gives another one and interprets the story: the Revealer is identified with the eschatological blessings of salvation and makes them present in his own person (28–30).

The postulate of a primitive narrative of the Raising of Lazarus, comparable in its brevity to other Johannine "sign" narratives, having contacts with miracle stories in other traditions (such as the Raising of Jairus' Daughter and the Epileptic Boy), developed within the Johannine circle, and finally related by the Evangelist in accordance with his profound theological insight is wholly comprehensible and by no means to be dismissed. It is, however, unnecessary in developing this thesis to seek to strengthen it by exaggerating the differences between the postulated strata. There is no real evidence that the story ever circulated among the churches to show Jesus simply as a wonder-worker. Indeed, the notion that Jesus was conceived of as a θεῖος ἀνήρ, a "divine man" such as the pagans glamorized, or that the miracle stories ever circulated without reference to their eschatological significance is highly debatable; the message of the kingdom of God manifest in Jesus and awaited through Jesus was too deeply rooted in the evangelic traditions and in the churches' kerygma and catechesis for that ever to have happened, as every identifiable source within the synoptic Gospels illustrates. The estimates of Jesus among imperfectly instructed believers, such as we glimpse in the Fourth Gospel and in some of the Pauline letters, must not lead to the notion that the churches' leaders and teachers so interpreted him. That the Fourth Evangelist had a firmer grasp of the theological significance of the signs, and developed it in a more profound manner than his contemporaries, gives to this Gospel its peculiar value, but we need not on this account exaggerate the distance between him and his fellow Christians.

It is also not to be overlooked that certain of the narrative elements classed as Johannine are likely to have been known in the circle to which he belonged, for example, knowledge of Mary and Martha, their relation to Lazarus, and their part in the whole episode of his illness and death and its sequel. We must not forget that this Gospel reflects Jerusalem traditions, which will almost certainly have contained this story, as well as the narrative concerning the judgment of Caiaphas and the Sanhedrin (vv 47–53). We may, accordingly, hold in view the strong probability of the development of the tradition relating to the death and recall to life of Lazarus, but be modest in our claims to delimit the strata in the tradition and to define their precise relations to one another.

2. The setting of the Lazarus account is not stated within the narrative itself; the Evangelist places it within the period following the Feast of Dedication (chap. 10) and before the last Passover of Jesus (11:55–57). Whether that was the actual time of the event, and if so how close it was to either Festival named, or whether it was placed here thematically is debated. The Evangelist presents it as the last of the signs of Jesus, which brought to a climax all that preceded it and precipitated his own death and resurrection.

This is underscored by the report of the meeting of the Sanhedrin, given in vv 46–53, as also of the immense interest in Lazarus among the pilgrims at the Passover (12:9–10, 17–19). The Sanhedrin decision nevertheless need not have been taken immediately prior to the Passover. Note especially that the plot against Jesus, mentioned in Mark 14:1–2, two days before the Passover, is not an alternative account of John 11:46–53 but *presupposes* such an earlier meeting of the Sanhedrin. Jesus' withdrawal to Ephraim, mentioned in 11:54, was for an undefined length of time, but it can hardly have been for a long period. We must be content to acknowledge a certain indefiniteness as to the time when the raising of Lazarus took place, but that it probably occurred in the period leading up to the final Passover.

3. The contents of the chapter yield a simple division of the material: 1–16, The Illness and Death of Lazarus; 17–27, The Revelation of Jesus as the Resurrection and the Life; 28–37, the Wrath of the Revealer in the Presence of Unbelief; 38–44, The Raising of Lazarus to Life; 45–53, The Decision of the Sanhedrin to put Jesus to Death; 54, The Retreat of Jesus to Ephraim by the Wilderness.

Comment

The Illness and Death of Lazarus (11:1–16)

1–2 The narrative begins without reference to preceding events or the circumstances of Jesus; it simply introduces a person in dire need, Lazarus of Bethany. He is identified with reference to two well-known members of the circle of Jesus' friends. The identification of Mary in v 2 as the woman who anointed Jesus is made prior to the account of the anointing (12:1–8), on the assumption that all Christians know of that event. The sentence is commonly viewed as an explanatory gloss by an editor (cf. 4:2; 6:22–23); it could be such, but there are other comments that interrupt the story and that come from the Evangelist (e.g., vv 5, 13, 18, 30), and this could be another.

4 The thought is akin to that in 9:3—the illness of Lazarus is not for the purpose of death (for the disciples it was a temporary illness, for Jesus a temporary death), but for the purpose of God's manifesting his glory in powerful and compassionate action through the Son ($\pi\rho\delta\varsigma$ and $\dot{\upsilon}\pi\epsilon\rho$ have a similar meaning in this context). The immediate reference is to the raising of Lazarus from death to life. But the event is to be a *sign*. The Evangelist makes it plain in the course of the narrative that the end of the story of Lazarus is the death of Jesus himself (cf. the hints in vv 8–9, 16, and the appended report on the meeting of the Sanhedrin that resolves on the execution of Jesus, vv 46–53). In the chapters that follow, the glory of God in Christ is bound up with the death and resurrection of Jesus (see esp. 12:23, 27–28, 31–32; 13:31–32; 17:1). The statement, "This illness is . . . for the sake of the glory of God, that the Son of God may be glorified through it," finds its ultimate meaning in the glorifying of God through the death and resurrection of Jesus and the glorifying of the Son through God's exalting him to his right hand. This glorifying action of God in Christ is the means whereby the revelation in vv 25–26 becomes actualized—the basis of hope for all the world. The statement in v 4 accordingly may be viewed as an extended title of the story of Lazarus and the key to its meaning.

5–6 If v 6 was part of the primitive account, the assurance in v 5 was certainly needed, for the statement in v 6 appears to be contrary to the character of Jesus: Jesus really *did* love Mary and Martha and Lazarus! Yet, curiously, the insertion of v 5 serves to make v 6 the more astonishing. Various motifs are entailed in the remark. The knowledge of Jesus as to the death of Lazarus, made known in v 14, should be assumed here also; v 17 implies that Lazarus had died by the time the message of his illness reached Jesus (four days—one for the journey to Jesus, two while he remained where he was, one for the journey to Bethany), hence Jesus did not refrain from setting out in order to give time for Lazarus to die (Barrett, 391). Second, v 6 has reference to the reiterated dependence of Jesus on his Father, whose will takes precedence over his own and over that of all others (cf. Schlatter, 248: "Jesus dealt with this request in accordance with the rule by which he refused his Mother, 2:4," and cf. also 7:3–9 regarding his brothers' advice). Jesus in his ministry is prompted at all times by his Father (5:19–20). Third, the issue of faith is prominent in this chapter; the disciples are to have their faith strengthened through the revelation of the glory of God consequent on Lazarus' death (v 15), while the sisters of the dead man are to have theirs tested to the utmost, prior to its being vindicated (vv 21–22, 26b–27, 32). Alike in the death and recall to life of Lazarus, and the death and resurrection of the Christ which it adumbrates, men are sifted accordingly as they believe or reject the glory of God in Christ manifest in the sign (vv 45–46; 12:31–32).

7–8 Jesus calls on his disciples to accompany him to Judea. The disciples are aghast; so recently as the Festival of the Dedication had Jewish opponents tried to stone him (10:31, 39); how foolish then to risk his life again! And how needless, since Lazarus' illness is not "for death"!

9 Jesus replies through a simile. A day has twelve hours (in all seasons, however short or long daylight may last, for the hours are contracted or expanded according to need); it has therefore both opportunity and limitation. One can walk in the day without stumbling, because one is aware of the light of this world (the sun) shining on one's path. This is true of people generally, and of Jesus in particular; he must "walk" in the (limited) time appointed for him; while he does so he knows that he will not "stumble," for he is under the protection of God. If v 10a is applicable to Jesus in his ministry, v 10b indicates that the thought is applied to others, especially to the disciples; whoever walks in the dark stumbles over unseen obstacles, for he is without the Light of the World (Jesus) shining within him; the application within the context is the necessity of the disciples to keep in his company, even though he does advance toward danger and death (Hoskyns, 400).

11–12 A typical "Johannine misunderstanding": an ambiguous statement of truth is misunderstood by the hearers, which leads to a clarification that opens up fuller revelation. That Lazarus has "fallen asleep" employs a familiar image of death, but in the Hebrew heritage it chiefly connoted a sleep from which there is no awakening (cf. the familiar formula in the books of Kings and Chronicles, "so-and-so slept with his fathers," and note Job 14:11–12: "As waters fail from a lake, and a river wastes away and dries up, so man lies down and rises not again; till the heavens are no more he will not awake or be roused out of his sleep"). The apocalyptic concept of death as a sleep from which one awakes (Dan 12:2) had by no means seized the minds of the people, though there are some striking expressions of it among Israel's later teachers (cf. Pauly, *Real-Encyclopädie,* 32: "Sleep in the night is like this world, and waking in the morning is like the world to come," cited by Balz, *TDNT* 8:552). With Jesus the thought is fundamental, bound up with the relation of God to his people (cf. Mark 12:24–27) and his own role as the Son who is Son of Man (cf. 5:21, 26–27). Hence he declares, "Lazarus has fallen asleep; *I am going to wake him out of sleep!*" The same outlook on death is seen in Mark 5:39, as Jesus advances to wake a child from death, just as he was to wake Lazarus. The idea was as ridiculous to the mourners for the child as it was distant from those who mourned Lazarus (v 33). In this context the implication of v 11 should be taken with utmost seriousness, particularly in light of vv 25–26: believers are to view death as a sleep from which they shall be awakened through Jesus.

12   The misunderstanding is couched in intriguing terms: "If he has fallen alseep *he will be saved* (σωθήσεται)." It is doubtful, however, that we are intended to read into this statement a secondary meaning that expresses the truth beyond the disciples' grasp; but contrast Mark 5:23, 34; 10:52, where the play on the meaning of σωθῆναι, "to recover" from illness and "to be saved" in a soteriological sense, is deliberate.

14–15   Having spoken plainly, Jesus expresses his gladness that he was not with Lazarus. His disciples are manifestly unprepared to endure the shock of faith that lies ahead of them; the awakening of Lazarus from his death will grant them a fresh vision of his glory, and after their trial enable them to grasp the meaning of it all.

16   Thomas summons his fellow disciples to accompany Jesus and die with him. An utterance of blind devotion, it expresses more than he realizes: for Jesus the journey will be for death, but one that will mean life for the world; and the Church that arises through the death and resurrection of Jesus is called to make the journey like its Lord, bearing a cross and revealing thereby the life that conquers death (cf. Mark 8:34; 2 Cor 4:10). The summons of Thomas accordingly is addressed to every reader of the Gospel.

THE REVELATION OF JESUS AS THE RESURRECTION AND THE LIFE (11:17–27)

17   The news that Lazarus was now four days in the tomb indicates that he was buried on the day of his death, as was customary in Israel, but its mention shows that he was dead beyond all doubt. In *Sem.* 8 it is said that one should visit a burial place of one newly buried for three days to ensure that the person was really dead. Why three days? *Gen. Rab.* 100 (64a) supplies the answer: "Bar Qappara taught, The whole strength of the mourning is not till the third day; for three days long the soul returns to the grave, thinking that it will return (into the body); when however it sees that the color of its face has changed then it goes away and leaves it" (Str-B 2:544–45). Four days in the grave establishes that all was over.

18–19 The mention of the proximity of Jerusalem to Bethany suggests that the "many Jews" who came to comfort the sisters were from the capital city. To console the bereaved was an acknowledged duty, but the Evangelist draws attention to the presence of these sympathizers, since they are to become witnesses of what happened to Lazarus.

20 While Martha hastened to Jesus, Mary "sat in the house." Schlatter observed, "Sitting belongs to mourning," citing *Ruth Rab.* 2:14 (252).

21–22 Martha's words are not intended as a reproach to Jesus, but simply express her grief; she does not doubt that had he been present he would have saved Lazarus from death. Does her added statement in v 22 imply a conviction that even now Jesus could and should pray that Lazarus be restored to life, since God would do what he asked? Many exegetes think so (it led Sanders to write: "John conveys a wonderfully life-like portrait of a faithful, but rather managing woman"!). This is a doubtful interpretation; Martha's horrified reaction in v 39 shows that she does not expect Jesus to recall her brother from his tomb. At this point she affirms her continued confidence in the power of Jesus' intercession for all eventualities. Her brother's death has not destroyed her faith in Jesus.

23–24 Here is another ambiguous saying of Jesus. It can relate to the recall of Lazarus to life about to take place, or to his resurrection in the end time. For the Evangelist it will have included both, but for Martha it meant the latter only: Lazarus will rise at the end of the age for life in the kingdom of God. (Our Evangelist alone among NT writers uses the expression "in the last day," as in 6:39, 40, 44, 54; 12:48. The more common formula, "in the last days," generally refers to the times *preceding* the end, as in Acts 2:17; 2 Tim 3:1; James 5:3.)

25–26 Martha has stated the belief of her people (the Sadducees alone denied it according to Mark 12:18–27); Jesus gives her a new and startling revelation: "*I am* the Resurrection and the Life!" It signifies not so much a rejection of Martha's faith (contrary to Bultmann, 403; Haenchen, 406) as an extension of it and a setting of it on a sure foundation. The eschatological rule of God for which Martha hopes, with all its blessings for humankind, is vested in Jesus. The greatest gift of God's saving sovereignty is precisely *life eternal* under that sovereignty and entry upon it through *resurrection*. The power to initiate it resides in Jesus ("the Resurrection") and to grant it in its fullness ("the Life"). Both elements of this function are his by God's appointment (5:21, 26). The meaning of this primary statement in v 25a is drawn out in the two parallel clauses that follow.

The parallelism is not synonymous, despite frequent assertions to the contrary (e.g., by Bultmann, 403; Cadman, "The Raising of Lazarus," 431; Schnackenburg, 2:331; Becker, 2:359–61). The first clause takes up the affirmation, "I am the Resurrection," the second "I am the Life" (Dodd, *Interpretation*, 365). While it is possible to translate v 25b, "He who believes in me, though he is dead, he *will live on*" (so R. A. Knox in his translation of the NT), it is altogether more likely that it should be rendered "will come to life" (so NEB; Dodd, *Interpretation*, 365; Brown, 421; Barrett, 396). This is its meaning in 5:25 (for the use of ζήσεται of the resurrection of Jesus cf. the confessional statement in Rom 14:9: Χριστὸς ἀπέθανεν καὶ ἔζησεν; Rev 2:8 ὃς ἐγένετο νεκρὸς καὶ ἔζησεν; also the Satanic imitative Antichrist, Rev 13:14 ὃς ἔχει τὴν πληγὴν τῆς μαχαίρης καὶ ἔζησεν. In Rev 20:4–5 ἔζησαν is used of the Christian dead in "the first resurrection"). The plain meaning of the first clause in John 11:25 is a promise of the future resurrection of the believer through Christ the Resurrection. The second clause advances on this: "Whoever lives and believes in me shall never die." What is the force of "lives"? Commonly ὁ ζῶν is identified as a living person who believes, so defined in the light of "even though he dies" in the previous line. But what other kind of person believes besides one who lives? ὁ πιστεύων in v 25 is any and every believer, and all such die; if πᾶς ὁ ζῶν καὶ πιστεύων is also any and every believer, the term ζῶν is superfluous. By contrast, however, the ὕδωρ ζῶν (living water) of 4:10–11; 7:38 and ὁ ἄρτος ὁ ζῶν (living bread) of 6:51 relate to the ζωὴ αἰώνιος of the kingdom of God; so also "the *living* Father" is the Fount of Life, whose relation to the Son forms the pattern of the Son's relation to the believer (6:57). Throughout 5:21–29, which is the background of 11:25–26, ζωή is consistently the life of the divine sovereignty. Accordingly v 26a appears to affirm that *everyone who has the life of the kingdom of God* and believes on Jesus shall never die. As the clause follows on one relating to ὁ πιστεύων it is not surprising that the subject of the next clause is described as ὁ ζῶν καὶ πιστεύων, the more so, in that the topic is the nature of the life that the believer has, namely one that death cannot destroy since the believer is in union with him who is the Life.

A close parallel to the ambiguity of language and thought of this passage is in 2 Cor 5:14–15: "One man died on behalf of all, hence all died; and he died for all in order that οἱ ζῶντες should no longer live to themselves . . . ." NEB renders the latter clause, ". . . that *men, while still in life,* should cease to live for themselves." But Paul's thought has a more comprehensive meaning than this; οἱ ζῶντες are surely *the dead who have come to life* through the risen Christ, who in v 17 are described as new creatures living in the new creation. J. Héring translates οἱ ζῶντες in v 15 as "they who have the life" (*La seconde épître de saint Paul aux Corinthiens* [Neuchâtel, 1958] ad loc), and Lietzmann paraphrases, "He has given us new life through his resurrection . . . so that we may lead this new life in the practice of pneumatic love" (*An die Korinther I–II,* 4th ed. rev. by W. G. Kümmel [Tübingen, 1949], 124–25). Paul's understanding of life in and through the risen Lord is virtually identical with that in the Fourth Gospel.

The revelation to Martha thus is an assurance of resurrection to the kingdom of God in its consummation through him who is the Resurrection, and of life in the kingdom of God in the present time through him who is the Life. Both aspects of the "life" are rooted in the understanding of Jesus as the Mediator of the divine sovereignty in the present and in the future, whose mediatorial work in earthly ministry reaches its climax in his death and exaltation to the throne of God, whereby the sovereignty of God is established in redemptive power for all humanity and the Spirit of the age to come is released for the world. (This interpretation is in harmony with that given by Westcott, 2:90–91; Bernard, 389; Schlatter, 253; Dodd, *Interpretation,* 364–66; Brown, 434; Bruce, 244–45.)

26b–27 The question, "Do you believe this?", is asked in the light of the context of vv 25–26, namely the death of Lazarus, which tested Martha's faith, and the binding of the revelation to the person of the Revealer. It is essential for Martha to grasp and receive this if she is to understand what Jesus is about to do for her brother. Her reply goes beyond a simple "Yes."

It is a fully fledged confession of faith in Jesus, the wording of which is frequently thought to reflect the contemporary Church's baptismal confession of faith (so Bultmann, citing with approval Dibelius, 404 n.5; Bornkamm, *Gesammelte Aufsätze* 2 [1970] 192; Lindars, 396). In acknowledging Jesus to be the Christ, the Son of God, the declaration echoes earlier confessions in the Gospel (1:42, 49) and anticipates the statement of its purpose in 20:30–31. The third element, "He who comes into the world," takes up the messianic expression (hardly a title) derived from Ps 118:26, which is applied to Jesus by others (see especially Matt 11:3 and the cry of the crowds in John 12:13 par.); it is possible that the Evangelist intends it to be interpreted in the light of the coming of the Christ and Son of God into the world from heaven (cf. 3:31; 6:33, 51; see Barrett, 397).

THE WRATH OF THE REVEALER IN THE PRESENCE OF UNBELIEF (11:28–44)

28–32 Martha's "secrecy" in speaking to Mary is natural and has no secondary significance (such as a reflection of the secrecy surrounding Jesus' miracles [Barrett, 398] or concern for the safety of Jesus [Sanders, 270]); it will have been to enable Jesus to speak to Mary alone, away from the people surrounding her. The privacy, however, was short-lived. Mary repeats the words of Martha to Jesus (cf. v 21), but without any affirmation of continued faith; no revelation from Jesus is given her, and no confession of faith elicited from her. It is hardly just, however, to conclude from this, "Mary gives the impression of being nothing but a complaining woman" (Schnackenburg, 2:333). Her statement to Jesus does, after all, reflect faith in the Lord's power to heal, but grief clouds her vision, and the arrival of the "consolers" prevents further conversation.

33 The rendering of the main clause, "Jesus . . . became angry in spirit and very agitated" requires discussion, not to say justification, in view of its departure from most English translations. There has been an unusual disagreement between the English and German traditions of understanding this passage. "He *groaned in the spirit* and was troubled" (AV/KJV, RV) set the pattern for English translations. It is echoed by NEB, "He *sighed heavily* and was deeply moved." This latter rendering of ἐτάραξεν ἑαυτόν has, however, been appropriated for ἐνεβριμήσατο τῷ πνεύματι in most recent English translations; e.g., RSV "He was *deeply moved* in spirit and troubled" (similarly Ph, NASV, NIV; other renderings are variants of this, e.g., JB, Jesus spoke "*in great distress*," GNB, "*his heart was touched*"). This understanding of ἐμβριμᾶσθαι has controlled the expositions of Bernard, Temple, Strachan, Sanders, Morris, Marsh, Lindars, Bruce, as also of Lagrange and F. M. Braun. By contrast Luther's rendering, "*Er ergrimmte im Geist und betrübte sich selbst,*" i.e., "He was *angry* in the spirit and distressed," has controlled German interpretation to the present day, which generally departs from it only by way of stronger expression (cf. the Zürich Bible: "*Er ergrimmte im Geist und empörte sich*" = "He became angry in the spirit and was disgusted"; Heitmüller, "*Er ergrimmte innerlich und brachte sich in Harnisch*" = "He was inwardly angry and became enraged"). Such is the interpretation followed by Bultmann, Büchsel, Strathmann, Schnackenburg, Schulz, Haenchen, and Becker in their commentaries. The treatment of the term in Bauer's *Lexicon of the Greek NT* is revealing. Bauer cites evidence from Lucian, LXX and the synoptic Gospels (Mark 1:43; Matt 9:30; Mark 14:5; Matt 12:18 in Egerton no. 2) for translating ἐνεβριμήσατο τῷ πνεύματι in John 11:33 "*bei sich unwillig werden,*" *innerlich ergrimmen,"* "be indignant (or displeased) in oneself, be inwardly angry." The translators of Bauer's *Lexicon* into English, however, have changed this to "be deeply moved." If the reader will consult the latest edition of BGD for the comparative use of the term, he may well come to the conclusion, with the present writer, that the evidence supports the contention of Schnackenburg: "The word ἐμβριμᾶσθαι . . . indicates an outburst of anger, and any attempt to reinterpret it in terms of an internal emotional upset caused by grief, pain, or sympathy is illegitimate" (2:335). With that Westcott, Hoskyns, Barrett, and Brown among English-speaking commentators agree.

(Matthew Black has no doubt that such is the meaning of the *Greek* term, but he considers it to be a "Syriacism"; i.e., that it represents a Syriac expression *'eth'azaz b'ruha*, which has a wider sense in Syriac than its Greek counterpart; in the Syriac versions of the Bible it is used to express the thought of being deeply moved, but that is also the equivalent of the following phrase ἐτάραξεν ἑαυτόν. Black therefore suggested that the Greek text of v 33b is a combination of two translation variants of a single Aramaic expression, which simply recorded that Jesus was deeply moved in his spirit [*Aramaic Approach*, 2d ed. 174–77; 3d ed. 240–43]. This solution is learned and ingenious, but an appeal to Syriac and Aramaic origins of the Greek text which makes the latter mean something for which there is no evidence in Greek literature that it can is dubious. That the two verbs in v 33b provide a fulsome expression may be acknowledged. All critics who see in John 11 an amplification of a shorter earlier narrative agree that ἐνεβριμήσατο was in the primitive source; in that case it was probably the Evangelist who added to the earlier form of the narrative the expression καὶ ἐτάραξεν ἑαυτόν, which he elsewhere employs in connection with inner disturbances of Jesus; see especially the narrative of the "Johannine Gethsemane" in 12:27 and 13:21; 14:1, 27. Such is Schnackenburg's conclusion, 2:335.)

Granting that the Evangelist reports Jesus as *angry*, what was the cause of his anger? V 33 makes it plain: *"When Jesus saw her weeping and the Jews who came with her weeping . . ."* They sorrowed, as Paul put it, "like the rest of men, who have no hope" (1 Thess 4:13), which is irreconcilable with faith in the resurrection. Despite the testimony of the Bible, despite the signs of Jesus wrought among them, which all bore witness to the life of the divine sovereignty that had come into the world through him, and despite the word that he proclaimed, with its emphasis on the promise of life now and hereafter, they mourned "like the rest of men." It was this unbelief of the people of God in the presence of him who is the "Resurrection and the Life," arrived among them to call their friend and brother from the grave, that made Jesus angry. The contrast between the Revealer who brought the word of God and lived by it and the recipients of it is startlingly exemplified here. The comment of G. Sass is in point: "So seen, the anger of Jesus becomes a question to our own faith" (*Die Auferweckung des Lazarus*, 53).

35 How, then, are the tears of Jesus to be interpreted? Certainly not through grief for Lazarus: his illness and death had been stated to be for the glory of God (v 4), and Jesus was now advancing to his tomb to call him from it, not to weep beside it. It is possible that the tears were motivated by the unbelief that caused him anger (as Hoskyns strongly contended, 405). It is, however, perhaps more likely that they were brought about by the sight of the havoc wrought among people through sin and death in this world. It would be harmonious with what we know of Jesus in this Gospel if anger by reason of unbelief was balanced by grief over the tragedy of the human situation, from which not even the people of God can extricate themselves.

So Schnackenburg: "The weeping here has no connection with the surge of anger." Comparing such passages as Heb 5:17; Rev 7:17; 21:4 he sees the reason for the tears to be the sadness and darkness of the present world, but compares it with the calm prayer of v 41, just as the agitation of 12:27a gives way to the triumphant prayer of 12:27b (2:336–37).

36–38 The Jews from Jerusalem accompanying Mary and Martha failed to understand the tears of Jesus; they did not perceive that the tears were more over them than over Lazarus! The query raised in v 37 will have come from a section of Jews other than those of v 36; it appears to be less expressive of faith in Jesus as a miracle worker (as Sanders, 273, and Barrett, 401, maintained) than a criticism of Jesus for not preventing the death of Lazarus; hence the further mention of the anger of Jesus as he made his way to the tomb (v 38a).

39–40 Martha is alarmed at the request of Jesus that the stone be removed from the tomb; she assumes that on this, the fourth day since Lazarus' death (see *Comment* on v 17), decomposition will have set in—"he stinks!" The aromatic spices and unguents used for the dead were intended to counteract the odor from decomposing bodies, in contrast to the Egyptians' procedures to preserve them (Sanders, 274 n.1). Jesus' reminder that Martha would see the glory of God if she believed must relate to vv 23, 25–26, but its echo of v 4 causes the whole narrative to be set within the framework of a revelation of the glory of God in Christ.

41–42 The opening words of the prayer in v 41b assume that Jesus has already prayed concerning Lazarus and his recall to life. M. Wilcox has pointed out the striking similarity of these words to Ps 118:21: "I thank thee that thou hast answered me" (LXX ἐξομολογήσομαί σοι ὅτι ἐπήκουσάς μου; the Targum renders it, "I give thanks before thee that thou hast received my prayer"). Wilcox comments, "In both the psalm and the Targum the concept of prayer is made explicit," and he suggests that v 41b is traceable to an old tradition ("The 'Prayer' of Jesus in John xi. 41b–42," 128–32). The second clause of the prayer, "I knew that you always do hear me," implies a perpetual union with the Father, on the basis of which his continuing prayers are ever heard and therefore granted.

R. H. Fuller perceptively commented on this prayer: "Jesus lives in constant prayer and communication with his Father. When he engages in vocal prayer, he is not entering, as we do, from a state of non-praying into prayer. He is only giving overt expression to what is the ground and base of his life all along. He emerges from non-vocal to vocal prayer here in order to show that the power he needs for his ministry—and here specifically for the raising of Lazarus—depends on the gift of God. It is through that prayer and communion and constant obedience to his Father's will that he is the channel of the Father's saving action. That is why the prayer is thanksgiving rather than petition . . . Here we have the most profound aspect of John's treatment of the miracles. It places Jesus poles apart from the mere wonder-workers, and seeks to penetrate into the mystery of how he, though to all outward appearance an ordinary (or perhaps extraordinary) human being, is the one in whom is disclosed God's presence and his very self in saving action" (*Interpreting the Miracles,* 107–8).

43–44 The event for which all that has preceded in the chapter has prepared us is described with the greatest economy of words: a loud cry of Jesus to Lazarus quickens him and brings him forth from the tomb. We are reminded of 5:25, 28–29; the raising of Lazarus is a sign authenticating the truth of those utterances and of the revelation given in vv 24–25.

The details of Lazarus' appearance, bound with linen strips and a napkin on his face, have prompted much discussion. How did he move, so bound? Basil's comment has been taken up by many: it was θαῦμα ἐν θαύματι, "a miracle within a miracle" (*Corderius-Catena,* 295), but that was hardly the Evangelist's intention. Contrary to pagan customs, the Jews did not tie up the dead to ensure that they did not return to life. Sanders stated: "The corpse would have been placed on a strip of linen, wide and long enough to envelop it completely. The feet would be placed at one end, and the cloth would then be drawn over the head to the feet, the feet would be bound at the ankles, and the arms secured to the body with linen bandages, and the face bound round with another cloth to keep the jaw in place . . . So bound up, a man could not possibly *walk.* Hence Jesus' final command, when Lazarus struggled out of the tomb. But he could at least have shuffled to the entrance, and it is absurd to imagine that a subsidiary miracle was necessary to waft him from the tomb" (276; on Jewish burial attire see further Blinzler, *Der Prozess Jesu,* [3]1960, 292–93). That the napkin was to hold the jaw in place is doubtful; wealthier Jews used to dress the dead very expensively until R. Gamaliel II (*ca.* A.D. 90), but whereas the rich used not to cover the face, the poor had to do so because it became black (through lack of money); in order to avoid shaming the poor it was ordered that the face of all the dead should be covered (Str-B 1:1048, 2:545). W. E. Reiser drew attention to the contrast between Lazarus emerging from the tomb with the napkin on his face and the empty tomb of Jesus containing the linen bands *and the napkin folded separately* (John 20:6–7); to him this signified that Lazarus from the grave still stands related to death, whereas the removal by Jesus of his own napkin was a sign that death had no more claim on him ("The Case of the Tidy Tomb . . ." 47–57, esp. 54). With this B. Osborne agreed, but he thought that the attention paid to the napkin in John 11 and 20 was due to the importance to the Jews generally and to the Evangelist of Isa 25:6: "He will swallow up (destroy) on this mountain the face of the covering that covers all peoples, the veil that is spread over all nations; he will swallow up death for ever." In the Hebrew text "face" means "surface," but in the Aramaic Targum it is interpreted as "person," thus: "On this mountain will be swallowed up the face of the Great One who is great over all peoples and the face of the King who is powerful over all kingdoms. . . ." In rabbinic interpretation "the Great One," "the King who is powerful," is viewed as the Angel of Death, and is linked with Satan and the "evil impulse" that leads to sin and death. Osborne concludes that the Evangelist wishes to say: "Lazarus comes forth from the tomb with his head still wrapped in a veil because he is still subject to the power which the Angel of Death, Satan, and the evil impulse will have over all mankind until this power has been destroyed in the days of the Messiah. Lazarus has been brought to life, but he will die again. Christ, however, removes the napkin from his face as he rises from the dead. He has conquered death definitively himself and will never die again . . . The folded napkin tells (the Evangelist) that the prophecy of Isaiah has been fulfilled: God has swallowed up death for ever" ("A Folded Napkin in an Empty Tomb . . .", 437–40). If such a nuance was in the mind of the Evangelist it would, of course, be recognizable only by those versed in Jewish exegetical traditions.

THE DECISION OF THE SANHEDRIN TO PUT JESUS TO DEATH (11:45–54)

45–46   The deeds and words of Jesus commonly created a division among
the Jews (cf, e.g., 6:14–15, 24–33, 66–69; 7:10–13, 30–32, 40–44, 45–52). It
was so on this occasion, but this time the Evangelist observes, *"Many* of the
Jews . . . believed in him; but *some* of them went off to the Pharisees." The
movement toward Jesus in Jerusalem became unprecedentedly strong; according to the Evangelist it led to the great welcome accorded to Jesus by the
people from the city on Palm Sunday (see 12:9–13, 17–19).
47–48   The news alarmed the Jewish leaders, and a meeting of the Sanhedrin was called. Strictly speaking the High Priest alone was responsible
for convening the council, but the expression "the chief priests" denotes
both the High Priest and members of the prominent priestly families. While
some of the latter will have included Pharisees, the term "Pharisees" in this
context will have referred mainly to the scribes ("The Pharisaic party in the
Sanhedrin was composed entirely of scribes"; so Jeremias, *Jerusalem in the
Time of Jesus* [London: SCM, 1969] 236). The fears of the members of the
Sanhedrin show that they had as little understanding of Jesus as the people
who tried to compel Jesus to be king and from whom he fled (6:15). Observe,
however, what it was that they feared (v 49): not that "the Romans will come
and *destroy* both our holy place and our nation" (so RSV, NEB, JB, GNB, and
among expositors, Bernard, 403; Bultmann, 410; Barrett, 406; Sanders, 278;
Schnackenburg, 2:346–48); rather it was that "the Romans will come and
take away from us both the place and the nation" (so Hoskyns, 410; Haenchen,
422; Becker, 367–68). Bammel states, "It would be the deposition of the
priests that is envisaged by these words. And indeed nothing is said of the
destruction of the temple . . . The consideration that 'the Romans might
take away from us . . .' must continually have been in the minds of those
who collaborated with them" ("Ex illa itaque die consilium fecerunt . . .",
23–24). The concern of the rulers, accordingly, was primarily for their own
position, not for the temple and the people. (For τόπος meaning temple, cf.
Acts 6:13; and 2 Macc 5:19, in a paragraph relating to the temple: "The
Lord did not choose the nation because of the place, but he chose the place
because of the nation.")
49–50   Caiaphas' counsel was given with arrogance typical of Sadducean
tradition. Josephus wrote of the Sadducees: "The behavior of the Sadducees
one towards another is in some degrees wild; and their conversation with
those that are of their own party is as barbarous as if they were strangers to
them" (*Wars,* 2.166). "It is to your advantage that one man should die for
the people"; was this remark based on purely political motivation? Such was
the conviction of Bultmann: "Political sagacity requires that the lesser evil
be preferred to the greater, and it demands that the fundamental principle
be put into effect that the individual be sacrificed in the interest of the nation"
(411). Or was it a matter of "lust for glory and power" (Schnackenburg,
2:348)? The latter perhaps suits the context (cf. v 48) more than the former.
It is possible that an echo of tradition may be faintly heard in Caiaphas'
judgment. Str-B cite two passages from *Gen. Rab.:* "It is better that one life
be in uncertain danger of death than all be in (danger of) certain death"

(91, 58a); "It is better that this man be killed than the totality be punished on his account" (94, 60a). D. Daube has devoted a book to the discussion of what lies behind such judgments. Jewish authorities decreed that if a company of Jews walking on the road were threatened by heathens who say, "Give us one of you that we may kill him, otherwise we shall kill you all," they must rather all be killed. If, however, the demand is for a *named* individual, like Sheba son of Bichri (2 Sam 20:1), then to avoid wholesale slaughter he should be surrendered. In this Daube distinguishes two situations; the first has in view thugs assaulting a group of Jews, the second a demand of heathen authorities for a specific individual. The latter ruling is based on the case of Sheba, son of Bichri; he was "a worthless fellow" (2 Sam 20:1), who led a revolt against David; on fleeing to the city Abel of Beth-maacah, Joab proceeded to attack it, and a "wise woman" protested at its threatened destruction; Joab said that he would withdraw if Sheba was given up; the woman persuaded the citizens to do so, and the head of Sheba was tossed over the wall. The event was widely discussed by the rabbis, especially through the cruel experiences of the Jews after the Jewish war; significantly Resh Laqish sought to delimit the circumstances in which a named Jew could be given up: "only if he is deserving of death" (see Daube, *Collaboration with Tyranny*, esp. 18–47). This is all later than Caiaphas, and relates to situations where *heathen* authorities make demands on Jews, but clearly the appeal to Sheba was old; was the precedent of this "worthless fellow" not sufficient to show how to deal with Jesus?

The observation relating to Caiaphas in v 49 (and v 51), "who was high priest that year" has raised questions. Does the Evangelist wish it to be understood that the office of high priest in Jerusalem was held for one year? Many have answered in the affirmative, and found therein confirmation of the Evangelist's ignorance of Palestinian affairs; it is assumed that he was misled by the annual appointment of pagan high priests in Syria and Asia Minor to believe that the same applied to the High Priest in Jerusalem (so Bauer, 151; Bultmann, 410 n.10; Haenchen, 423; Becker, 2:369). Barrett thought that if the Evangelist did so believe, he could not have been a Jew, but he adopted the suggestion that John meant that Caiaphas was high priest "in that memorable year of our Lord's passion" (406; similarly Bernard, 2:404; Hoskyns, 411; Brown, 440; Lindars, 406; Schnackenburg, 2:348–49; the interpretation is as old as Origen, *In Jo.* 28.12). It is, however, possible that the Evangelist *did* intend to convey the impression that the High Priest of Jerusalem held office for a year, and that he was in general right. Schlatter stated, "The uncertainty that attached to the high-priestly office was known to John. The High Priest at that time was exposed to deposition if a single action of his displeased the ever watchful governor of Caesar. The people emphatically experienced that under Pilate's predecessor, Gratus, since Gratus repeatedly deposed high priests after a short length of office. Pilate never clashed with Caiaphas, so the latter only lost his office at the same time as Pilate lost his" (258). W. L. Knox, on reviewing the situation of the Jewish high priests during the period of the Roman praetors up to A.D. 70 came to the same conclusion. He affirmed: "It seems not unreasonable to suppose that there was a general view in Roman official circles interested in the government of

Judea that the high priest should be changed annually, with occasional extensions of office for a second year, and that it was carried out with sufficient regularity to make it appear at certain periods, even to the Jewish mind, that the high-priesthood had in fact become an annual office" (*St. Paul and the Church of Jerusalem*, 64). Bammel strongly supported this view.

51–52 Caiaphas in his declaration had in view the benefit of the death of Jesus for the Jewish people: it would avert disaster for the nation and, by implication, leave the rulers secure. The Evangelist saw a more profound meaning in his words: the death of Jesus would benefit not alone Jews, but "the people of God" drawn from all nations, and the "benefit" would be nothing less than the salvation of the kingdom of God.

For the association of the gift of prophecy with the High-Priestly office, see the material assembled by Dodd, "The Prophecy of Caiaphas," 63–65. As to the concept of unconscious prophecy, Billerbeck cites rabbinical discussions that support the surprising conviction, "All prophets who have prophesied have not known what they prophesied; only Moses and Isaiah knew it" (*Mek Ex* 15, 17 (41a); see Str-B 2:546). The Evangelist frequently recognizes a primary and a secondary meaning of sayings of Jesus (cf. 2:19); in the case of Caiaphas' utterance he makes it explicit; Caiaphas uttered a *prophecy*, which said more than he knew. Jesus must die ὑπὲρ τοῦ λαοῦ. The preposition ὑπέρ is associated with the idea of a λύτρον, an "equivalent payment" or "ransom" (its purely secular use is illustrated in the gift given by Eleazar, guardian of the temple treasures, to Crassus, who had his covetous eyes on the whole treasure; Eleazar gave him a beam of solid beaten gold as a λύτρον ἀντὶ πάντων, i.e., in order to spare the rest; see Josephus, *Ant.* 14.107). For Caiaphas the death of Jesus will save the people from the judgment of the Romans; for the Evangelist it connoted a death which would avert the judgment of God (3:16), and open the door of the saving sovereignty to all nations (12:31–32).

Again, for Caiaphas the death of Jesus was on behalf of "the people" (λαός), that "the whole nation" (ἔθνος) should not perish; for him the two terms were used synonymously to denote the Jewish nation. In view of the Evangelist's habit of using alternative terms to avoid undue repetition he may have done the like here, as most believe. S. Pancaro, however, considers that the usage of the two terms in the LXX and the NT warns against too readily accepting their equivalence here; in both testaments λαός is a technical term for Israel, but the NT goes further in identifying the λαὸς τοῦ θεοῦ with the Church; in Caiaphas' statement the λαός on the first level means the Jews; on the second level it denotes the whole people of God, believing Israel and believing Gentiles (" 'People of God' in St. John's Gospel"). Jesus dies "on behalf of the (Jewish) nation" (ὑπὲρ τοῦ ἔθνους); but not for the nation only but for "the scattered children of God." For Jews this last expression designated Jews of the dispersion, in contrast to those who lived in the mother-land, but like λαός, the concept was appropriated by Christians to denote the Church, consisting of both Jews and Gentiles, scattered through the world (cf. 1 Pet 1:1). But more, the scattering anticipates a gathering; the Jews looked for the dispersed members of their race to be brought home to share in the kingdom of God in the promised land; Christians looked to the Lord in his parousia to gather into one the redeemed children of God of all nations for life in the kingdom of God (cf. Mark 13:27; 1 Thess 4:17; 2 Thess 2:1; in the Book of Revelation it is for life in the City of God, the Jerusalem that descends from heaven, Rev 21:2–4). The Evangelist sees this "gathering" of the redeemed into one as the ultimate purpose of the death and resurrection of Jesus (see esp. John 17:24).

53 The advice of Caiaphas was accepted, and action determined on. ἐβουλεύσαντο ἵνα is more specific than "they took counsel that . . ."; it signifies rather "they resolved" (BGD, 145). Bammel cites K. Bornhäuser's rendering, "They passed a resolution on that day" ("Ex illa itaque," 30 n.102); noting v 57 he comments, "It seems that Jesus is not to be captured in order to be tried. The decision has been made already; it is only the carrying out of the judgment which is still to come" (35). Precisely that is the position assumed in Mark 14:1–2: the decision has been made; all that remains is to find a way to accomplish their purpose.

54 Jesus now leaves Bethany, close as it was to Jerusalem, and withdraws to the mountainous area northeast of Jerusalem, to a town called Ephraim. No more do we read of many Jews resorting to him and believing on him (cf. 10:41–42). Apart from the final week in Jerusalem his public ministry was over. It was no intention of his to allow the Sanhedrin to take him unawares; *he* determined the time of his departure, not they (10:17–18). Since he had been sent to accomplish a second and greater Exodus, it was fitting that that should be achieved in the celebration of the first one; this time the redemption would be on behalf of *all* nations, that all who would be free might enter into the "promised land" of the kingdom of God.

Explanation

1. Whenever the Lazarus story is discussed the question of its historicity arises. Three points especially come to the fore: (*i*) the extreme nature of the event—Lazarus' *four* days in the tomb—arouses the suspicions of many; (*ii*) the synoptic Gospels appear to leave no room for the miracle, since in Mark the cleansing of the temple appears to be the final factor in the decision of the Jewish leaders to put Jesus to death; (*iii*) the contacts with the parable of the Rich Man and Lazarus in Luke 16:19–31 suggest to some that the narrative of the raising of Lazarus has come into being through a historicizing of the parable.

To attempt to prove the historicity of this or any other miracle of Jesus in the Gospels is beyond the scope of our discussions. That the raising of the dead belonged to the early traditions of the ministry of Jesus is exemplified in the answer of Jesus to John the Baptist (Matt 11:5), apart from narratives such as those in Mark 5:21–43 and Luke 7:11–17. A heightening of features in a tradition does not, of course, demand a rejection of the tradition itself. One should, however, keep steadfastly in mind that he who wrote the Gospel of the Word *made flesh* viewed history as of first importance; he would never have related a story of Jesus, still less created one, that he did not have reason to believe took place.

The silence of the synoptic Gospels concerning Lazarus is less important than it used to appear through the recognition that the Markan outline is based on kerygmatic rather than chronological considerations. Moreover the synoptic traditions are largely Galilean, the Johannine largely Judean, with special links to Jerusalem; hence the knowledge and interests of Mark and our Evangelist inevitably differed.

The relationship of the Lukan parable with the Lazarus event in John 11 is certainly remarkable: both center on a man named Lazarus who dies; in the parable the request that he be sent to the living to convince them of the reality of judgment beyond death is denied, on the basis that they who reject the testimony of the scriptures will not believe though one should rise from the dead; in the narrative one did rise, and some were confirmed in unbelief, even to the extent of determing on the death of Jesus. The features in common, however, must be set alongside the contrasts. The parable takes up the old Egyptian story of Satme Khamuas, which reveals the differences between the fate in the world beyond of a pious poor man and an impious rich man. No less than seven different forms of the story have been traced in rabbinic writings, the best known one relating the contrasting destinies of a poor student of the Law and a wealthy publican, Bar Maj'an (the story is translated in F. Ll. Griffith's *Stories of the High Priests of Memphis* [Oxford, 1900]; it is summarized by K. Grobel, ". . . Whose Name was Neves," *NTS* 10 [1963–64] 373–82, and related to Jesus' parables by Jeremias, *Parables*, 178–79, 183). Jesus in the parable takes up the well-known story in order to give it a fresh application, namely the importance of giving heed to the testimony of Moses and the Prophets, which relates not alone to the after-life but to the kingdom of God which he proclaims and brings. In all these variants of the story, the contrast between the conditions of the godly and the godless in the life after death is an essential feature; that has not the remotest contact with the Lazarus story of John 11. Emphasis on the urgency of giving heed to the word of God is characteristic of Jesus; signs and wonders are without effect on those who reject it (hence his refusal to give the Pharisees a "sign from heaven," Mark 8:11–12). Now while the feature of faith and unbelief as to the word of Jesus is important to the present form of John 11, we should recall the widely accepted postulate of a more primitive form of the story that lay behind it; in that the emphasis is on *Jesus revealed through the miracle as the Lord over death;* this point was emphasized by the Evangelist through his inclusion of the revelation to Martha and his stress on the event as a means of the glorification of the Father and the Son (11:4); it is in connection with that last point that the significance of the miracle is developed as pointing to the glory of God and the Son through the death and resurrection of Jesus to which the miracle of Lazarus will lead. This is quite different from the lesson of the Lukan parable. The outstanding connection between the parable and the original miracle story is the name of Lazarus; yet, as is frequently observed, the oddity is not its presence in the miracle story but in the parable; for whereas Lazarus *of Bethany* firmly roots the man as Philip *of Bethsaida* (1:44) or Judas *Iscariot* (= Judas, *man of Kerioth*), Jesus never gives names in his parables! Understandably the conviction is gaining among scholars that the name Lazarus in the parable is a reflection of the miracle event, not vice versa; if it is due to Jesus the parable will have been told late in his ministry (as may well be true of a number of parables that are recorded in the synoptic Gospels, cf. Mark 12:1–12; Matt 21:28–22:14; 25:1–46).

2. As with all the signs of Jesus that he relates, the Evangelist recounts the significant event and seeks to unveil its meaning. The latter has already been adumbrated in 5:25, and it is more vividly stated in 11:25–26. For the Evangelist this forms the heart of the narrative. While admittedly its place in the story diverges from his usual procedure of relating first the sign and then the explanation, it is in harmony with his account of the sign that immedi-

ately precedes it; there the lesson of the story (9:5) is placed before the narrative that embodies it. That the revelation comes first does not make the narrative that follows superfluous; rather it prepares one to perceive with understanding the unfolding narrative. That is why the Evangelist set the Prologue before his account of the life, death, and resurrection of Jesus; it provides the key to the whole. "We beheld his glory" was the judgment of those who witnessed that unfolding story; it was written in hope that readers might grasp the truth and the wonder of it, and experience the life and power of him to whom the witness was borne. Such was the purpose of recounting the raising of Lazarus.

3. This consideration holds good of the Evangelist's concern to lay bare the final meaning of the Lazarus miracle, namely its aspect as an anticipation of the death and resurrection of Jesus. In the latter the glory of God in Christ is revealed in an ultimate manner, and therein the rationale behind 11:25–26 becomes plain: it is the crucified and risen Lord who is the Resurrection and the Life. In union with him the believer *has* the Life, and is assured of its consummation in the "last day." That message the Evangelist desired his contemporaries in the Church to grasp, and their successors, whom he could not have foreseen, and make their own. Whether the present commentator's generation has achieved it is dubious. In the increasingly secularized society of Western civilization, wherein God is a dogma without relevance to life, the Church's confidence in life after death has been gravely weakened. This, too, has become a dogma without relevance to life. Yet to all with ears to hear, the resurrection of Jesus spells "sure and certain hope," as John 11:25 states. And John 11:26 is positively startling: "He who *lives* and believes in me *shall never, never die*"! Since Jesus is the Resurrection and the Life, Christian existence in Christ is *life before death!* It is not primarily something awaited, but the principle of life in the present, and since it is life in union with the Lord who conquered death, death cannot touch it. The name Bishop Gore gave to the community he founded is an excellent characterization of the Church: "The Community of the Resurrection." Insofar as we who bear the name of Christian fail to recognize who we are, we do well to ponder again the sign of Lazarus, and grasp afresh the present relationship of faith as well as the joy of hope for the future.

H. Jesus the King, Triumphant
through Death (11:55–12:50)

Bibliography

Barbour, R. S. "Gethsemane in the Tradition of the Passion." *NTS* 16 (1960–70) 231–51. **Bertram, G.** ὑψόω. *TDNT* 8. 606–13. **Bevan, T. W.** "The Four Anointings." *ExpTim* 39 (1927–28) 137–39. **Blank, J.** *Krisis.* 264–96, 306–10. **Boismard, M. E.** "Le caractère adventrice de Jn 12:45–50." *Sac Pag* 2 (1959) 189–92. **Boman, T.** "Der Gebetskampf Jesu." *NTS* 10 (1963–64) 261–73. **Borgen, P.** "The Use of Traditions in John 12:44–50." *NTS* 26 (1979–80) 18–35. **Bruns, J. E.** "A Note on Jn 12:3." *CBQ* 28 (1966) 219–22. **Burkitt, F. C.** "On 'Lifting up' and 'Exalting.' " *JTS* 20 (1918) 336–38. **Caird, G. B.** "Judgment and Salvation. An Exposition of Jn 12:31–32." *CJT* 2 (1956) 231–37. **Derrett, J. D. M.** "The Anointing at Bethany." *SE* 2 (1964) 174–82. **Dodd, C. H.** *Interpretation.* 368–83. ———. *Historical Tradition.* 152–56, 162–73, 338–43, 352–57, 366–69. **Farmer, W. R.** "The Palm Branches in John 12:13." *JTS* 3 (1952) 62–66. **Feuillet, A.** *Johannine Studies.* 143–45. **Fortna, R. T.** *The Gospel of Signs.* 149–52. **Freed, E. D.** "The Entrance into Jerusalem in the Gospel of John." *JBL* 80 (1961) 329–38. **Hartingsveld, L. van.** *Die Eschatologie des Johannesevangeliums.* 40–45. **Kittel, G.** "אִזְדְּקֵף = ὑψωθῆναι = gekreuzigt werden." *ZNW* 35 (1936) 282–85. **Kossen, H. B.** "Who Were the Greeks of John XII 20?" *Studies in John.* FS J. N. Sevenster. 96–110. **Léon-Dufour, X.** "Trois Chiasmes Johanniques." *NTS* 7 (1960–61) 249–51. ———. "Père, fais-moi passer sain et sauf à travers cette heure." *Neues Testament und Geschichte.* FS O. Cullmann. 157–66. **McNamara, M.** "The Ascension and the Exaltation of Christ in the Fourth Gospel." *Scr* 19 (1967) 66–69. **Moloney, F. J.** *The Johannine Son of Man,* 172–85. **Moore, W. E.** " 'Sir, We Wish to See Jesus': Was This an Occasion of Temptation?" *SJT* 20 (1967) 75–93. **Munroe, W.** "The Anointing in Mark 14:3–9 and John 12:1–8." SBLASP (1979) 127–30. **Nestle, E.** "Die unverfälschte köstliche Narde." *ZNW* 3 (1902) 169–72. **Nicholson, G. C.** *Death as Departure: The Johannine Descent-Ascent Schema,* SBLDS Chico, CA: Scholars Press, 1983. 124–44. **Potterie, I. de la.** "L'exaltation du Fils de l'homme: Joh 12, 31–36." *Greg* 49 (1968) 460–78. **Sanders, J. N.** " 'Those Whom Jesus Loved': St John xi.5." *NTS* 1 (1954–55) 29–41. **Thüsing, W.** *Die Erhöhung und Verherrlichung Jesu.* 22–37, 75–89, 102–7, 128–31. **Torrey, C. C.** " 'When I Am Lifted up from the Earth,' John 12:32." *JBL* 51 (1932) 320–22. **Unnik, W. C. van.** "The Quotation from the OT in John 12:34." *NovT* 3 (1959) 174–79. **Vergote, A.** "L'Exaltation du Christ en croix selon le quatrième évangile." *ETL* 28 (1952) 1–23. **Wrege, H. T.** "Jesusgeschichte und Jüngergeschick nach Joh 12, 20–23 und Hebr 5, 7–10." *Der Ruf Jesu und die Antwortung der Gemeinde.* FS J. Jeremias. Ed. E. Lohse. Göttingen: Vandenhoeck & Ruprecht, 1970. 259–88.

Translation

[55] *Now the Passover of the Jews was near, and many went up to Jerusalem from the country before the Passover in order to purify themselves.* [56] *They were looking for Jesus and were talking with one another as they were standing in the temple: "What is your opinion? Surely he won't come to the festival, will he?"* [57] *But the chief priests and the Pharisees had given orders that if anyone should know where he was he should report it, so that they might arrest him.*

[12:1] *Six days before the passover Jesus came to Bethany where Lazarus[a] was, whom he had raised from the dead.* [2] *Accordingly they made a dinner for him there, and Martha was serving, but Lazarus was one of those reclining with him at the table.* [3] *Mary therefore took a pound of very expensive ointment, made from genuine nard,[b] and anointed the feet of Jesus, and she wiped his feet with her hair; and the house was filled with the fragrance of the ointment.* [4] *But Judas Iscariot,[c] one of his disciples, the one who was about to betray him, said,* [5] *"Why was this ointment not sold for three hundred denarii and given to the poor?"* [6] *But he said this, not because he was concerned for the poor but because he was a thief, and as he used to keep the collecting box he used to help himself[d] to what was put in it.* [7] *Jesus therefore said, "Let her alone; she had to keep it[e] for the day of my burial;* [8] *for the poor you always have with you, but you do not always have me."[f]*

[9] *When therefore the* [g] *great crowd of the Jews knew that he was there they came, not only on account of Jesus, but that they might see Lazarus also, whom he had raised from the dead.* [10] *The chief priests therefore planned to kill Lazarus also,* [11] *because on account of him many of the Jews were leaving them and believing in Jesus.*

[12] *The next day the* [h] *great crowd that had come to the festival, on hearing that Jesus was coming to Jerusalem,* [13] *took branches of palm trees and went out to meet him, and they shouted:*

Hosanna!
Blessed in the name of the Lord is he who comes,
        even the king of Israel!

[14] *And Jesus found a young donkey and sat upon it, according as it stands written:*

[15] *Don't be afraid, daughter of Zion!*
Look, your king is coming,
        sitting on a donkey's colt!

[16] *These things the disciples did not understand at first, but when Jesus was glorified they remembered that these things had been written about him, and that they had done these things to him.* [17] *The crowd that had been with him when* [i] *he called Lazarus out of the tomb and raised him from the dead bore testimony (to the fact).* [18] *This is the reason that the crowd met him, namely because they heard that he had performed this sign.* [19] *The Pharisees therefore said to one another, "You see that you are doing no good at all; look, the world has gone after him!"*

[20] *Now there were some Greeks among those who went up to worship at the feast;* [21] *so these approached Philip, who came from Bethsaida of Galilee,* [j] *and they made a request of him: "Sir, we want to see Jesus."* [22] *Philip comes and tells Andrew, and Andrew and Philip come and tell Jesus.*

[23] *But Jesus says in reply to them:*
"The hour has come that the Son of Man be glorified.

[24] *"Amen, amen I tell you, unless a grain of wheat falls into the ground and dies, it remains alone; but if it dies it produces a great harvest.*

[25] *"Anyone who loves his life loses* [k] *it, and anyone who hates his life in this world will preserve it for eternal life.*

[26] *"If anyone serves me he must follow me, and where I am my servant will be also; if anyone serves me my Father will honor him.*

[27] *"Now my heart is in turmoil. And what am I to say? 'Father, save me from this hour.' But for this purpose I came to this hour! 'Father, glorify your name!'"* [l]
[28] *A voice came out of heaven, "I have glorified it, and I will glorify it again."*

[29] *The crowd therefore that was standing there and heard the sound said that it had thundered; others were saying, "An angel has spoken to him."* [30] *Jesus said in reply, "This voice has not come about for my sake, but for yours.*

[31] *"Now is the judgment of this world, now the prince of this world* [m] *shall be thrown out,* [n] [32] *and I, if I am lifted up from the earth, will draw all* [o] *to myself."*

[33] *He said this to signify the kind of death he was about to die.* [34] *The crowd answered, "We have heard from the Law that the Christ remains forever; then how is it that you are saying that the Son of Man must be lifted up? Who is this Son*

of Man?" [35] *Jesus said to them, "Only for a little while is the light among you. Go on walking while you have the light, lest darkness overtake you; whoever walks in darkness does not know where he is going.* [36] *While you have the light, put your trust in the light, that you may become sons of light."*

These things Jesus said, and then he went away and hid himself from them.

[37] *Although he had performed such great signs before them they continued in unbelief toward him,* [38] *that the word spoken by the prophet Isaiah might be fulfilled when he said,*

> *Lord, who believed our report?*
> *And to whom has the arm of the Lord been revealed?*

[39] *On this account they could not believe, for again Isaiah said,*

> [40] *He has blinded their eyes.*
> *and calloused* [p] *their hearts,*
> *that they should not see with their eyes*
> *and perceive with their hearts and turn,*
> *and so I should heal them.*

[41] *Isaiah said these things because* [q] *he saw his glory, and he spoke about him.* [42] *Nevertheless many even of the authorities believed in him, but on account of the Pharisees they used not to confess it, in case they became thrust out of the synagogue;* [43] *for they loved the honor that men give beyond the honor that God gives.*

[44] *But Jesus cried out and said:*

"He who believes in me does not simply believe in me but in the One who sent me, [45] *and he who sees me sees the One who sent me.*

[46] *"I have come into the world as Light, in order that everyone who believes in me should not remain in darkness.*

[47] *"If any one hears my words and does not keep them, I am not the one to judge him, for I did not come in order to judge the world but in order to save the world.*

[48] *"He who sets me aside and does not receive my words has his judge: the word that I have spoken will judge him in the last day;* [49] *for I have not spoken on my own authority, but the Father who sent me has given me a command what to say and what to speak.* [50] *And I know that his command means life eternal. What therefore I speak, I speak just as the Father has told me."*

Notes

[a] Λάζαρος, without addition, is read by א B L W, MSS of the Syr., Coptic and Ethiopic versions; ὁ τεθνηκώς follows the name in P[66] A D K etc.—an early scribal addition?

[b] Nard is an oil taken from the root and spike of the nard plant, which is grown in India. Its description as πιστικῆς is hardly likely to reflect the Aram. פיסתקא (pîstaqaʾ), viz., the pistachio nut (Barrett, 412); πιστικός occurs elsewhere with the meaning "faithful" (from πιστός), and here = "genuine." Its appalling expense justifies the description; since a denarius was a day's wage for a laborer, this perfume represents a year's wages for a working man, hence the objection in v 5. (Curiously, Mark 14:5 reads, *"more than* 300 denarii"; contrast Mark 6:37, "200 denarii," with John 6:7, *"more than* 200 denarii"!).

[c] Judas' name in a number of MSS (A K Δ Θ Π Ψ etc.) is set after εἰς (ἐκ) τῶν μαθητῶν αὐτοῦ and then followed by Σίμωνος "son of Simon," in imitation of 6:71. The fuller "son of Simon Iscariot" occurs in X.

d ἐβάσταξεν = "used to take (away)"; the verb was used at times to mean take away (surreptitiously) money; the English term "lift" has both meanings!

e Ἄφες αὐτήν ἵνα . . . is ambiguous. Its simplest rendering would be, "Let her alone in order that she may keep it for the day of my burial," i.e., that she may use it on that day; but vv 3 and 5 imply that Mary had used the ointment (cf. Mark 14:3). Or it may be viewed as elliptical: "Let her alone; (she did this) in order to keep it. . . ." The sentence could be an example of the use of ἵνα to introduce an imperative sense: "Let her alone, let her keep it . . ."; in the context it could mean, ". . . she had to keep it." The reading in the koine text (omitting ἵνα and supplying the perfect τετήρηκεν, so A Γ Δ p⁶⁵ f¹ f¹³ etc.) is clearly an attempt to remove the difficulty, but approximates to the meaning of the text.

f V 8 corresponds exactly in wording (other than the position of πάντοτε) with Mark 14:7ac//Matt 26:11; it is omitted by D itᵈ syrˢ, and Brown considers the omission correct (449). On the other hand p⁷⁵* omits μεθ' ἑαυτῶν ἐμὲ δὲ οὐ πάντοτε ἔχετε, clearly by accident (through the twofold occurrence of ἔχετε), and 0250 omits both v 7 and v 8 for a similar reason (going from εἶπεν οὖν, v 7, to ἔγνω οὖν, v 8). In view of the all-but-universal inclusion of v 8 in the textual tradition it is unlikely that D's omission is original.

g The reading ὁ ὄχλος πολύς, with πολύς as predicative, is highly unusual (given by א B* L etc.), and is eased through the readings ὁ ὄχλος ὁ πολύς (p⁶⁶ᶜ W) and ὄχλος πολύς (p⁶⁶* p⁷⁵ A B³ etc.). In D OL syrᵖ copˢᵃ the sentence is simpler still: ὄχλος δὲ πολὺς ἐκ τῶν Ἰουδαίων ἤκουσαν. The UBS committee set the article in brackets as uncertain.

h The MS tradition has similar attempts to ease the expression ὁ ὄχλος πολύς as in v 9.

i ὅτε, read by א A B W etc., is better supported than ὅτι (p³⁶ D K L etc.); the latter may be due to a desire to clarify the account concerning the event (on the implications of the two readings see Schnackenburg, 2:377).

j Bethsaida lay east of the Jordan where the river flowed into Galilee; it was therefore in the tetrarchy of Philip, in Gaulonitis; but the Jews who settled on the shores of the lake viewed themselves as Galileans, not Gaulonites, as events in the Jewish-Roman war showed (see Schlatter, 267).

k ἀπολλύει can = "lose" or "destroy"; the contrast with "guard" may favor the latter meaning here (so Brown, 467; see also Dodd, *Historical Tradition*, 338–41).

l For τὸ ὄνομα L X f¹ f¹³ etc. read τὸν υἱόν, clearly through the influence of 17:1. D goes farther in this direction by adding after τὸ ὄνομα the clause ἐν τῇ δόξῃ ᾗ εἶχον παρά σοι πρὸ τοῦ τὸν κόσμον γενέσθαι, which is from 17:5.

m The "ruler of this world" = Satan. The expression occurs in the NT only in this Gospel (it is also in 14:30, 16:11), but note the related expressions "the god of this aeon" (2 Cor 4:4), "the ruler who has authority over the air" (Eph 2:2), and the claim made in Luke 4:6//Matt 4:8–9.

n The reading βληθήσεται κάτω in Θ OL syrˢⁱⁿ appears to be due to Luke 10:18 and Rev 12:9, 12.

o Instead of πάντας (אᶜ A B K L W X etc.) strong support is given to πάντα (p⁶⁶ א * D OL vg goth geo¹ etc.). The use of neuter for persons is not unknown in the Fourth Gospel (cf. 6:39–40 and 17:24, where neuter and masculine occur together), and the thought of cosmic redemption may have influenced the reading (cf. Col 1:16–17); the context and content of v 32 however do not favor the latter concept, and it is better to retain πάντας.

p For ἐπώρωσεν (A B* L X Θ etc.) ἐπήρωσεν is read by p⁶⁶ p⁷⁵ א K W Π etc. The two verbs are similar in meaning as well as form, and the latter is found elsewhere as a variant to the former. πωρόω = "harden, petrify," and with καρδία, which in Jewish thought indicates the mind, it means "make dull or obtuse, to blind"; πηρόω = "maim" or "mutilate," but with καρδία it = "blind" (BGD, 656); the meaning accordingly is the same for either verb.

q The attestation for ὅτι (p⁶⁶ p⁷⁵ א A B L X Θ etc.) is superior to that for ὅτε (D K Δ Π etc.) as for ἐπεί (W); as the more difficult reading ὅτι is to be accepted.

Form/Structure/Setting

1. 11:55–57 forms a bridge passage from the Lazarus narrative to the events of chap. 12, but it belongs essentially to the latter; it tells of the approach

of the final Passover of Jesus' ministry, and so provides the setting for the acts and discourses of chap. 12, which are concerned with the approaching death of Jesus.

The chapter consists of two narratives, a discourse, and an epilogue to the ministry of Jesus. Unlike the earlier sections of the Book of Signs the events narrated are not miraculous deeds performed by Jesus, but events wherein others perform actions for the honor of Jesus, and which are seen to be related to God's sovereign purpose, through him. They thus function as signs of the divine sovereignty (for a precedent, note that chap. 2 recounts a miraculous sign performed by Jesus, the Water into Wine, followed by a non-miraculous deed, the Cleansing of the Temple, the two together revealing the initiation of the saving sovereignty that comes through Jesus and also providing the themes for the discourses in chaps. 3–4).

2. The account of the anointing of Jesus in 12:1–8 invites comparison with those in Mark 14:3–9 and Luke 7:36–38. In Mark an unnamed woman anoints the head of Jesus with ointment of nard from an alabaster jar; in Luke a sinful woman comes with an alabaster jar of ointment, but overcome with emotion her tears wet the feet of Jesus, and she wipes his feet with the tresses of her hair and anoints them with the ointment; in John, Mary, the sister of Martha and Lazarus, anoints the feet of Jesus with ointment of nard from an alabaster jar and wipes his feet with her hair. Some scholars explain these phenomena of likeness and difference as due to the varied reporting in the evangelic traditions of a single incident in the life of Jesus (so, e.g., Dodd, *Historical Tradition,* 171–73; J. A. Fitzmyer, *The Gospel according to Luke* 1:686). It is more likely that two incidents have descended in the tradition, one of a sinful woman whose tears fell on the feet of Jesus and who wiped them with her hair, and another of one who brought expensive nard perfume and anointed the head of Jesus with it; in the transmission of the accounts the details of the two incidents became mixed (so A. Legault, "An Application of the Form-Critique Method to the Anointings in Galilee and Bethany," 131–41, followed by Brown, 450–52; see further the discussion in I. H. Marshall, *Commentary on Luke,* 304–7, who reaches the same conclusion).

3. The entry into Jerusalem (vv 12–19) is described in the synoptic Gospels also, but with considerable differences; Dodd affirmed, "They differ in every point where it is possible to differ in relating the same incident" (*Historical Tradition,* 155), but to him this underscores the independence of John's narrative from those of the other three. The event is described with unusual brevity, namely in vv 12–14 (strictly in vv 13–14); it is followed by a citation from Zech 9:9 (v 15), two comments of the Evangelist in vv 17–18, and a report of the Pharisees' reactions in v 19. No mention is made of the crowd of pilgrims that accompanied Jesus, only of those who went out of the city to meet him (vv 12–13). V 14 could imply that Jesus did not find the donkey till the crowds welcomed him, but that may be an unintended result of the Evangelist's mode of description in vv 12–13. The spreading of branches and clothes on the road by the crowd is not mentioned; this again may be due to the Evangelist's concentration of purpose: the waving of the palm fronds emphasizes the entry into the city as a sign of the coming acclamation by the world of Jesus as the Lord of the kingdom of God.

4. The discourse of vv 20–36 is sparked by the approach of Greeks who had come to the festival and requested to see Jesus (vv 20–22); their disappearance from the scene has led some to think that the brief narrative was an isolated piece of a larger whole. The function of the discourse is to show the necessity of the death and exaltation of Jesus for the establishment of the saving sovereignty of God that embraces all nations. A variety of sources has contributed to its compilation: vv 23 and 27–28 are closely connected in theme, yet the latter appears to be a separate tradition; vv 24–26 are parallel to elements within the synoptic Gospels (see *Comment*); vv 31–32 also have a close affinity with v 23, but like the other "lifting up" sayings (3:14–15; 8:28) they may well have been earlier independent. It has often been thought that vv 31–32 originally were linked with 3:14–21; MacGregor postulated an original order 12:31–32; 3:14–15; 12:34; 3:16–21; 12:35–36a, 44–50, 36b–43 (268–70). Gourbillon more simply proposed to set 3:14–21 between 12:31 and 32 ("La parabole du serpent . . . ," 213–26). Such suggestions are by no means impossible, but neither are they very convincing (see the discussion in Moloney, *The Johannine Son of Man,* 161–64).

The relation of vv 27–28 (and 29–30) to the accounts of the Agony in Gethsemane is of no little interest. V 27a echoes Ps 41(42):7, while Mark 14:34 cites the preceding verse of that psalm; the twice repeated Πάτερ = *Abba* in vv 27–28 reminds us of the prayer in Mark 14:35; the petition that Jesus be "saved" from the hour is parallel in content with that of Mark 14:36, but is verbally echoed in Heb 5:7; the latter passage states that Jesus was "heard," a feature not represented in Mark, but which may be obliquely in view in the longer text of Luke, which tells of the appearance of a strengthening angel (Luke 22:43); that, too, has a strange echo in John 12:29; the prayer of v 28a is the Johannine equivalent of Mark 14:36a. How are we to interpret this evidence? It could be that the Evangelist has simply transferred the Gethsemane scene to this point in illustration of the theme of the glorification of Jesus and the battle it involved (cf. his transferring the Cleansing of the Temple to the beginning of the ministry of Jesus as part of his programmatic representation of the work of Jesus). Another possibility has attracted some scholars, namely, that Mark united *two* narratives of the agony of Jesus, *one* of which was located in Gethsemane (see K. G. Kuhn, "Jesus in Gethsemane," *EvT* 12 [1952–53] 260–85), and that the Evangelist utilized an independent account of the agony that took place outside the garden of Gethsemane (see Brown, *CBQ* 23 [1961] 143–48, whose suggestion is acknowledged as plausible by R. S. Barbour, *NTS* 16 [1969–70] 232).

5. The last two paragraphs, 12:37–43 and 44–50, form a conclusion not alone to chap. 12 but to the whole account of the public ministry of Jesus in chaps. 2–12. The first paragraph gives a comment by the Evangelist on the effect of Jesus' ministry; the whole story is seen as an expansion of the statement in 1:11: "He came to his own domain and his own people did not accept him." The unbelief of the people fulfills the prophetic word of Isa 53:1 and entails the judgment of God on their obtuseness, as set forth in Isa 6:9–10. The second paragraph concludes the whole by repeating certain outstanding items in the proclamation of Jesus given in the earlier chapters (chiefly in 3:16–21; 5:19–47; 8:12–26).

Comment

THE APPROACH OF THE FINAL PASSOVER (11:55–57)

55 "The Passover . . . was near": this is the final and fateful Passover of Jesus, when he was to fulfill its deepest meaning (cf. 6:4). The paragraph is full of the tension of the approaching hour. "Consecration" for the festival is in harmony with the Israelite ceremonial system (cf. the demand that all be consecrated and cleansed at the giving of the Law, according to Exod 19:10). The period of cleansing, for such as needed it, was one week (see Schlatter, 261–62). Num 9:9–11 ordains that one unclean must still keep the Passover, but a month later. The occasion in Hezekiah's reign, when the Passover was held without due attention to the consecration of the people, is narrated in the consciousness of its exceptionable nature (2 Chron 30:15–20), and that kind of procedure was not permitted in later times.

56 The seeking for Jesus and questioning whether he would dare to come to the festival recalls 7:11 (at Tabernacles), and reflects the known hostility of the Jewish leaders to Jesus (cf. 7:25, 32; 8:59; 10:31, 39. The decision of the Sanhedrin in 11:47–53, 57, is assumed not yet to be known; cf. the secrecy implied in Mark 14:1–2, as in John 18:1–3). By contrast there is no hint of hostility to Jesus among the people who so spoke of him; they will have been among the crowd that went out to meet Jesus (12:12–13).

THE ANOINTING OF JESUS (12:1–8)

On the relation between this narrative and those of the anointings of Jesus in Mark 14:3–9; Luke 7:36–38; see above, p. 206. Unlike Mark, the Evangelist places the account prior to that of the Entry into Jerusalem instead of after it (see Mark 11:1–11; 14:3–9); doubtless this is primarily for the sake of the latter narrative. John wishes to show that Jesus enters Jerusalem as the king who has been anointed for burial, as one destined for exaltation via the suffering of death. While Mark highlights Mary's act of devotion by inserting it between the plot of the Jewish leaders to seize and kill Jesus and Judas' offer to betray him (Mark 14:1–2, 10–11), John achieves the same end through setting the Anointing after his account of the Sanhedrin's meeting and by naming Judas as the objector to Mary's "extravagance"; thereby Mary is contrasted both with Caiaphas and with Judas.

1 "Six days before the passover" will denote the time from Saturday evening to Sunday; a meal at which Martha *served* will have begun after the conclusion of the Sabbath, i.e., on Saturday evening. The introduction of Lazarus into the picture underscores the chief lesson of the story (v 7): he whom Jesus called from the grave reclines with Jesus designated for burial—and resurrection.

3–4 The description of the perfume as "very expensive" is no understatement; "300 denarii" should be reckoned in terms of a man's wages rather than of modern currency; since a denarius was the normal pay for a day's work, and the working week was six days, the sum represents a year's wages for a fully employed man. That Mary anointed the *feet* of Jesus, not his head, will have been interpreted by the Evangelist as a consecration of Jesus to royal service, i.e., to a death by which the saving sovereignty comes.

7 On the translation of the sentence see the *Notes;* ἵνα . . . τηρήσῃ relates to the action already performed by Mary, not to one that she might wish to take later; she had kept the perfume (as a family treasure?) to embalm the body of Jesus, and by her action had actually achieved it in advance of his death. Is this a motive imputed by Jesus to Mary without her being conscious of it, so that her act is accepted by him as having a more profound significance than she could have intended? Most scholars so interpret it (in Bultmann's estimate the Evangelist views the deed as an impressive prophecy, to be contrasted with that of Caiaphas, but equally without understanding of its deeper meaning, 415). Hoskyns, on the other hand, viewed Jesus' interpretation as bringing to light Mary's intention: "Mary consciously recognized the necessity of the death of Jesus, and also, recognizing that the hour had come, anticipated his burial by an act of intelligent devotion" (416). A. M. Hunter saw a confirmation of this view in Mary's breaking the neck of the alabaster jar, since it was customary, when anointing a dead body for burial, to break the neck of the flask before laying it in the coffin (*St. Mark,* TBC [London: SCM, 1948] 127); this latter point cannot be pressed, however, since an expensive perfume in an alabaster jar might be released only through breaking its long neck (so BGD, 34). There is no means of knowing whether Jesus attributed to Mary's action more than she knew; his comment, however, in v 8 shows that he saw in her act the expression of an unwavering faith and love: "Mary has recognized the dignity and greatness of Jesus and, in an exemplary action, has shown the others whom they have in their midst" (Schnackenburg, 2:370).

The Triumphal Entry of Jesus into Jerusalem (12:9–19)

9–11 The Evangelist's interpretation of the Palm Sunday event is indicated in his setting it in the context of the excitement engendered by the raising of Lazarus; the crowd (chiefly of pilgrims in the city?) came to Bethany to see Lazarus as well as Jesus, resulting in many of them "going away" from the Jewish leaders and believing in Jesus (NEB renders: "Many Jews were *going over* to Jesus . . ."); moreover the testimony of the "crowd" that had been present when Jesus raised Lazarus was a major factor in causing the "crowd" of pilgrims to go and meet Jesus (vv 17–18). Jesus accordingly is welcomed into the city as the King who is the conqueror of death.

12 The narrative records only the welcome given to Jesus by the people from the city, whereas the synoptists tell only of the pilgrims who accompanied Jesus to Jerusalem. *"Prima facie* Mark's account is the story which would be told by one of those who accompanied Jesus, and John's is the story which would be told by one of those who were at Jerusalem and heard of his approach" (Dodd, *Historical Tradition,* 156).

13 It is uncertain whether the palm branches were plucked by the people as they met Jesus or whether they were brought by them from the city. (Lagrange affirms that there must have been palms available, above all in the warmer eastern valley, where they were not high and were easy to reach, [325], whereas Schlatter stated that sheaves used at Tabernacles would have been preserved in every home, and so would have been taken out by the people when they set off to meet Jesus [265]). Their significance in any case was well known: they were a sign of homage to the victor.

It is recorded that when Simon the Maccabee drove out Gentile forces from the citadel in Jerusalem "he made his entry with a chorus of praise and the waving of palm branches, with lutes, cymbals and zithers, with hymns and songs, to celebrate Israel's final riddance of a formidable enemy" (1 Macc 13:51). Note also the vision in *Test. Naph.* 5: the sun and the moon were standing still, and Isaac told the sons of Jacob to lay hold of them: "And we all of us ran together, and Levi laid hold of the sun and Judah outstripped the others and seized the moon, and they were both of them lifted up with them. And when Levi became as a sun, lo, a certain young man gave to him twelve branches of palm; and Judah was bright as the moon, and under their feet were twelve rays. . . ." This is one of the many representations in the *Testaments* of the messianic salvation that was looked for through Levi and Judah, with priority accorded to the Levitical (priestly) messiah.

The cry "Hosanna" will have been linked with the palm fronds in the minds of the people. הושיעה־נא (*hôšíʿāh-nā*) is a strengthened form of the imperative "save"! ("do please save!"), but it came to be a greeting and even an ascription of praise. Its occurrence in Ps 118:25 was known to every Jew. In the feast of Tabernacles the Hallel (see Pss 113–118) was sung each morning by the temple choir; when the cry "Hosanna" was reached in Ps 118:25 every man and boy in the temple shook the *lulab* (a bunch of willow and myrtle tied with palm), and the cry was repeated three times. So deeply was this ingrained in the minds of the Jews they actually called the lulabs *hosannas*. It was therefore entirely natural for the crowd to repeat the cry of praise from Psalm 118 as they waved the palm leaves in welcome of Jesus. The greeting "Blessed in the name of the Lord is the coming one" originally applied to the pilgrims on entering the temple, but it came to have a particular application to the Messiah, as may be seen in the Midrash to Psalm 118 (244a) (see Str-B 1:150). The messianic application is reflected in the question of John the Baptist to Jesus, "Are you the Coming One, or are we to look for another?" (Matt 11:3), and yet more plainly in Jesus' citation of Ps 118:26. The additional line, "even the king of Israel" (v 13) makes the messianic application of Ps 118:26 explicit, and could be due to reflection on Zech 9:9, which is cited in v 15.

14–15 The enthusiasm of the crowd is uncomfortably reminiscent of the attempted messianic rising mentioned in 6:14–15. The Evangelist's stating at this point in the narrative that Jesus procured a donkey on which to ride into Jerusalem emphasizes the intention of Jesus to correct a false messianic expectation, for to enter the city on a donkey instead of on a horse, which was associated by Jews with war (cf. Isa 31:1–3; 1 Kings 4:26), was itself a demonstration of the peaceable nature of the mission of Jesus, and the relation of the event to Zech 9:9 makes that motive explicit; for Zech 9:9–10 describes the *joyous* coming of the King-Messiah—he is righteous, gentle, bringing salvation, riding on a donkey, proclaiming peace to the nations. Nothing further from a Zealotic view of the Messiah could be imagined.

16–18 This understanding of the significance of Jesus' action did not come to the disciples until Jesus was "glorified," i.e., after his death and resurrection. Then it was that they grasped the nature of the kingship of Jesus, as he himself had revealed it: the king of peace and salvation brought to the world the kingdom of peace and salvation precisely through his dying and rising.

19   The Pharisees' cry of dismay is a superb example of Johannine irony. An exaggerated utterance, it was prophetic of the inability of the Jewish opponents of Jesus to frustrate his task of bringing to humankind God's saving sovereignty; that applied both in the time of his ministry and in that of the Church, for it was in the post-Easter period that the "world" of nations was "going after" Jesus through the preaching of the gospel, and the endeavors of the Pharisees to nullify the witness of the Church were proving to be as unsuccessful as their opposition to Jesus himself.

THE COMING OF GREEKS AND THE DEATH AND GLORY OF JESUS (12:20–36)

20–22   The approach of Greeks to see Jesus was a confirmation of the Pharisees' exclamation in v 19. The Evangelist will have viewed these men as the firstfruits of the Gentile world that was to own Jesus as Lord. Their interest in Jesus will have been stimulated by his entry into Jerusalem, and possibly also by his cleansing of the temple (the latter will have taken place in the court of the Gentiles, which was the one part of the temple area open to them). Their contacting a disciple rather than Jesus reflects uncertainty as to whether Jesus would receive Gentiles, an uncertainty probably shared by Philip; hence his consultation with Andrew (cf. Matt 10:5–6).

23   The reply of Jesus indicates that the coming of the Gentiles heralds the climax of his ministry; his "hour" has at last arrived (contrast 7:30; 8:20), and it will witness his glorification. It is tacitly assumed that then will be the time for the Gentiles to come under the saving sovereignty of God. The connection between v 23 and vv 27–28, to say nothing of the intervening vv 24–26, shows that the hour of the "glorifying" of Jesus relates to his death; yet 13:31–32 and 17:1, 5 as clearly indicate that the glorifying includes his exaltation and return to the Father. The same idea applies to 12:31–32, except that the more specific term ὑψωθῆναι ("be lifted up") is used instead of δοξασθῆναι ("be glorified"); here the death-resurrection-exaltation of Jesus is concentrated into a single term, indicating the unity of the redemptive action of God in Christ as the means whereby the saving sovereignty of God comes for the world. It is a remarkable representation of the work of Christ for humanity, inasmuch as the death of Jesus on the cross is not regarded as the depth of shame from which he is raised to glory, but the death itself is his moment of glory wherein God is glorified (v 28) and one with his exaltation to the throne of God.

24–26   These vv provide an exposition of the law of the kingdom of God: life is given through death. The principle enshrined in v 23 is illustrated by the short parable in v 24. No explanation of it is given, but its meaning is transparent: so surely as a grain of wheat must be buried if it is to yield fruit for man, so the Son of Man must give himself in death if he is to produce a harvest of life for the world. The "law" to which the Son of Man submits is then applied generally in v 25, a saying which has parallels in the synoptic Gospels (Mark 8:35 par.; Matt 10:39; Luke 9:24; on their relationship see Dodd, *Historical Tradition,* 338–40): to love life is to destroy it, to hate life is to keep it (for "hate" as a Hebraic expression for "love less" see Gen 29:30–31; Luke 14:26 = Matt 10:37). Note, however, that the law of life through death in v 24 has in view making life possible for others, whereas in v 25 it is to gain life for oneself. V 26 gives a fresh formulation of another saying current in the synoptic tradition (Mark 8:32 par.; for their relationship see again Dodd, *Historical Tradition*, 352–53); the synoptic call to take up the cross is here characteristically paralleled with "where I am, there also my servant will be"; for the Christ draws men to fellowship with himself, alike in suffering and in the presence of God.

27–29 These verses describe the testing of the Son of Man. The brevity of this description of the agony of Jesus as he faces his "glorification" in no way diminishes its gravity in the eyes of the Evangelist.

27 The soul of Jesus "went into turmoil"; we recall the wrath and distress of his spirit when confronted with the havoc of death at the tomb of Lazarus (11:33–35), his horror over the triumph of evil in the soul of Judas (13:21), and the trauma facing his disciples through the events that lay ahead of them (14:1); the ταραχή of Jesus signifies an agitation, horror, convulsion, and shock of spirit (on this see esp. Thüsing, *Verherrlichung*, 79–89). The sentence, "Father, save me from this hour," should not be weakened through reading it as a question, as though Jesus refused to pray it (contrary to the UBS Greek Testament, RSV, JB, GNB, NIV); rather it should be read with a pause, and understood as expressing what Jesus really wanted to pray; hence it is a genuine prayer utterance (so WH, NEB). Jesus, in turmoil of spirit, shrinks from the fearful experience before him, and in his address to God seeks avoidance of it; yet he acknowledges that to endure it is the reason for his mission from God; in an act therefore of total obedience to the Father's will his spirit rises in unreserved affirmation, "Father, glorify your name." Hoskyns observed, "This obedience is the glorification of the Father's name, and constitutes the foundation of the Christian religion (Heb 5:7–10)" (425).

28 To this prayer of Jesus the answer is given from heaven, "I have glorified it, and will glorify it again." In view of the declaration of v 23 ("The hour has come . . .") and the twofold "now" of v 31, it is thought by some that "I have glorified it" is uttered from the same standpoint; i.e., "I have glorified it" embraces the ministry of Jesus *culminating in the death on the cross,* and the future "I will glorify it" relates to the resurrection of Jesus and its continuing consequences (so Thüsing, *Verherrlichung*, 196–97, and Blank, who however stresses the unity of the glorification of Jesus as a past which opens up the future, an end which is the beginning of glory [*Krisis,* 279–80]). It is, perhaps, more natural to interpret the statement as meaning that the Father's name has been glorified in the revelation that has taken place through the ministry of Jesus ("I have glorified it"), and that now the revelation is about to be climaxed in the obedience of the Son on the cross and in his exaltation by the Father (so Schnackenburg: "As in the past, so too in this hour he [the Father] will 'exalt' and 'vindicate' the holiness of his name . . . He will justify the Son, raise him above the power of evil and give him glory and saving power," 2:388).

29–30 The voice of God is interpreted by the crowd as a peal of thunder, or as an angel's voice. Neither explanation is adequate, but both imply a response from heaven to the prayer of Jesus (thunder is frequently associated with theophany, e.g., Ps 18:7–16; Rev 8:5; 11:19; 16:18). Jesus endorses this recognition, and says that the voice from heaven was for their sakes rather than his, hence they should believe (cf. the voice at the Transfiguration, addressed to the disciples rather than to Jesus, in Mark 9:7).

31–32 The declaration of v 31 must be taken at face value: the "lifting up" of the Son of Man (cf. vv 23, 34) signifies not *a* judgment (as Westcott, 128), nor the confidence that the *future* judgment has come near (van Hartingsveld, *Eschatologie des Johannesevangeliums* [42–45]), but that *the judgment of this world, both negatively and positively, takes place in the crucifixion-exaltation of the Son of Man-Jesus*. Moreover this judgment does not primarily denote the separation of believers and unbelievers that continually takes place before the revelation of God in the crucified Lord (contrary to Barrett, 426), however true it be that such a process does happen (cf. 3:20–21). The twofold "now" must be given its full force; it is the decision of God with reference to humankind, characterized as it is by rebellion against God and readiness to follow the "prince of this world," but specifically with respect to its rejection of the Son of Man and its putting him to death. Since the Son of Man is sent by God into the world as his representative and agent, rejection of the Son of Man is rejection of God himself. In the murder of the Son of Man sin is exposed in its most dreadful form. Insofar as the judgment of this world is a revelation of its sin and occasion of its condemnation, the death on the cross and exaltation by God to heaven is that moment. But it is more: *in that event God gave his Son.* Note that vv 31–32 follows closely on vv 23–28, just as the related 3:14–15 is set in immediate juxtaposition to 3:16–17. The sentence of judgment passed on this world is endured by the One whom this world murders. This turns the awful news of judgment on sin at the cross into the good news of deliverance from condemnation through the cross. It is an eschatological event in the fullest sense of the term: God acting in sovereign power to declare judgment, *both negatively and positively,* and to bring salvation through the Son of Man crucified and exalted to heaven.

As a consequence of this judgment, "the prince of this world shall be thrown out." The language is characteristic of apocalyptic; cf. Luke 10:18 ("I watched Satan fall, as lightning, out of heaven"), but still more the vision of Satan's ejection from heaven in Rev 12. The material of the latter vision is an ancient story, widespread in the Middle East, of the birth of one destined to slay the evil dragon; it was utilized by a Jewish apocalyptist to show its fulfillment in the Messiah of biblical promise (hence the introduction of Michael and his angels), but the Christian prophet shows how it came to fulfillment: the followers of the Lamb overcame the dragon "on account of the blood of the Lamb," i.e., *the dragon was overthrown through the death and exaltation of the Christ to reign with God;* hence the hymn was added, "Now have come the salvation and the power and the sovereignty of our God and the authority of his Christ, and the accuser of our brothers has been thrown down" (Rev 12:10). This prophetic "cartoon" will have been an independent composition of the Seer and in all likelihood will have been known by members of the Johannine school prior to its incorporation in the apocalypse. For the Evangelist, the utterance of Jesus employs a well-understood picture to show the change of situation for the world when Jesus was "lifted up" to heaven via the cross: Satan was *dethroned* and the Son of Man *enthroned* over the world for which he died.

32 The redemptive purpose of God in Christ is emphasized in the third clause of the sentence: "I, if I be lifted up from the earth, will draw all to myself." The lifting up is not simply on the cross, but via the cross to the throne of heaven. The thought is not that Jesus will draw all *to his cross*, but that he will draw all to *himself* as the crucified and exalted Redeemer. In virtue of his dying and rising the Son of Man brings the saving sovereignty to the world, and he exercises that sovereignty by drawing all to himself in the kingdom. The term πάντας, "all men," expresses the universal scope of the eschatological event disclosed in ὑψωθῶ ("if I be lifted up"); the saving sovereignty is for *all* humankind. But, as Schnackenburg remarked, "There is no limit to Jesus' saving power—except the resistance of unbelief. In spite of the universalistic overtone and intention of the statement, faith is still included as *a condition . . .*" (2:393).

The extent to which this understanding of ὑψωθῆναι was aided by the Semitic linguistic background has long been debated, but that this was a material factor appears to be reasonably clear. A variety of expressions were capable of combining the idea of death and lifting up. The old Aramaic זְקַף (*zeqaph*) means "set up," "lift up," "hang up," and could be used both of raising a criminal on a stake for his execution and for lifting up one who is bowed down (see G. Kittel's article in *ZNW* 35 [1936] 282–85). G. Bertram draws attention to the verb רוּם (*rûm*) "to be high, exalted," "to rise"; hiphil "to raise, remove"; its use in Ps 9:14, "thou who liftest me up (מְרוֹמְמִי, *me rômemî*) from the gates of death," LXX ὁ ὑψῶν με ἐκ τῶν πυλῶν τοῦ θανάτου, may well have helped to establish the rising belief in resurrection; the same term appears in 1QH 6:34; 11:12 of raising from death for resurrection; in Aramaic אָרִים (*ʾārîm*) = lift up, remove, take away (*TDNT* 8:606–7). M. McNamara was attracted to C. C. Torrey's suggestion that the term סְלַק (*slq*) used reflexively lay behind 12:32; its reflexive form meant "be raised up," more commonly "go away, depart, die" (the same range of meanings is evident in the Hebrew use of the term, hithpael and nithpael = "be dismissed, removed; rise; be called away from this world, die"; see "The Ascension and the Exaltation of Christ in the Fourth Gospel," 66–69). C. H. Dodd was impressed with the use of the expression נָשָׂא רֹאשׁ (*nāśā rôš*) in Gen 40:13, 19, recounting the dreams of the baker and butler imprisoned with Joseph: "lift up the head" for the former meant execution, for the latter restoration to office (*Interpretation*, 377).

More important than the linguistic precedents are intimations that the concept embodied in the Johannine use of ὑψοῦν was adumbrated in the primitive church. On the assumption that 1 Tim 3:16 is a stanza containing three couplets the line ἀνελήμφθη ἐν δόξῃ could combine the thought of death and exaltation, similarly as the unusual use of ἀνάλημψις in Luke 9:51. The echo of Isa 52:13 in the hymn citation of Phil 2:9, διὸ καὶ ὁ θεὸς αὐτὸν ὑπερύψωσεν, marks the ascent of the Christ from the death on the cross to the throne of God. Yet more significantly Heb 1:3, which probably embodies early confessional language, speaks of Christ as καθαρισμὸν τῶν ἁμαρτιῶν ποιησάμενος ἐκάθισεν ἐν δεξιᾷ τῆς μεγαλωσύνης ἐν ὑψηλοῖς ("having made a purgation of sins he sat down at the right hand of the majesty in the heights"); there is no suggestion here of Christ's death as entailing deepest humiliation, rather it expresses a majestic progression of events from pre-incarnation glory to post-incarnation glory. It is such a consciousness of the greatness and sublimity of the Son's willing offering of himself in death that led the Fourth Evangelist to associate the cross with the divine glory and to bracket the death and the exaltation in the single word ὑψωθῆναι.

33 The Evangelist interprets ὑψωθῶ not alone of death, but of a special form of death as one in which he will be "lifted up" from the earth in order to be "lifted up" to heaven; crucifixion is clearly in view, and Christian readers are expected to understand its pointer to the throne of heaven.

34 The crowd voices a difficulty which the representatives of Jesus were to face from Good Friday onward. The "Law" (= the OT, supremely represented by the Law) says that the Messiah remains "for ever." The scripture passage is likely to be Ps 89:37, "His seed shall remain for ever, his throne as long as the sun before me" (so van Unnik, *NovT* 3 [1959] 174–79). For most Jews the perpetuity of the kingdom of God included the continuance of the Messiah (contrary to the later view represented in 4 Ezra 7:28–29, that the messianic kingdom will be temporary and will end with the death of the Messiah and all flesh with him). The crowd therefore asks, "How can the Son of Man-Messiah be 'lifted up,' and so removed from the earthly scene by death?" Their further query, "Who is this Son of Man?" means, "What sort of a Son of Man is this, of whom such an unheard of fate is spoken?"

35–36a Jesus declines to answer the question; certainly the Son of Man "remains for ever," but this is neither the time nor the audience for an extended discussion on the relation of the death and exaltation of the Son of Man to the Kingdom of God and the ministry of the Paraclete-Spirit. Instead Jesus gives a warning and an appeal. For only a little longer will he, the Light, be among them; the darkness is shortly to fall, and they are in danger of being engulfed by it. The appeal is made therefore, "Believe in the Light and become sons of light," i.e., possessors of the nature of light and destined to enjoy the light of the divine kingdom (contrast the characterization of Judas as the "son of perdition," 17:12; the language was contemporary. The Qumran group viewed themselves as sons of light over against the sons of darkness).

36b So ends the public ministry of Jesus. He now hides himself from the populace. Their next sight of him will be on his way to his glorification.

Epilogue on the Public Ministry of Jesus (12:37–50)

37 This opening sentence summarizes the paragraph of vv 37–43: the response to the ministry of Jesus by his people was persistent unbelief. It climaxed the rejection of the Logos throughout Israel's history (1:11), including the word through the prophets, and specifically fulfilled words written in the Book of Isaiah.

38 The question in Isa 53:1 expresses the astonishment of the nations concerning the Servant of the Lord, rejected of men but exalted by God (it follows directly on Isa 52:13–15). The question could fittingly be so understood here, for it relates to the whole ministry of word and deed of Jesus ("what we have heard" = the word of Jesus, "the arm of the Lord" = God's powerful action through his signs); or it could be thought of as spoken by the believing remnant, or even by Jesus himself ("what we have heard" then represents what Jesus has received from the Father; cf. 3:11, 34; 7:16–17; 8:26; 12:49).

39 Not only did the people not believe, they *could* not believe because of what Isaiah said (in Isa 6:10): God had blinded their eyes and made their heart (= mind) obtuse in case they should see, and understand, and turn, and the Christ should heal them.

The statement sounds like naked predestinarianism, even irresistible reprobation, but it was neither so intended nor would it have been so understood. The language used has a long history in biblical thought. In Exodus it is frequently said that God hardened Pharaoh's heart (e.g., Exod 4:21), and as frequently that Pharaoh hardened his own heart (e.g., 8:15, 32); the relation between the two actions is never explained. Deut 29:2–4 laments that God has not given Israel a mind to understand, or eyes to see, or ears to hear, but appeal is made that the people "be careful to do the words of this covenant" (v 9). Isa 6:9–13 represents the Lord as commanding the prophet to make the people obdurate, blind, and deaf by his proclamation, lest they see and understand and turn, and that the process continue until the judgment of God overwhelms the cities and their people. There is bitter irony here, reflecting the prophet's experience of rejection of his message and declaration of the judgment that the rejection must bring; further, it affirms the prophet's *call* to bring to pass by his fruitless ministry the "strange work" that God has in view (cf. Isa 28:21 f.), which relates to the fulfillment of God's ultimate purpose. Von Rad rightly perceived, "We must learn to read the saying about the hardening of the heart with reference to the saving history" (*The Message of the Prophets* [London, 1969] 126). The same applies to the use of the saying by Jesus. Mark 4:11–12 relates to the whole ministry of Jesus ("all things" = word and action of Jesus); it all takes place "in parables" = "riddles," "in order that they may look and look and not see . . . lest they should turn and be forgiven." The guilt of the people in their repudiation of the ministry of Jesus matched the predestination of God, their rejection of his message matched the concealment of the secret of the kingdom, the judgment on their blindness entailed the divine rejection of the rejectors. But as in Isaiah's day the hardening of the nation was qualified by the creation of an obedient remnant, so the blindness of Israel in Jesus' day was qualified by the calling of a remnant of believers, with the prospect of a redemption that includes all peoples, a day when the hidden shall be revealed (Mark 4:22) and the rule of God shall be universally manifested. Such is the conclusion of Paul in his discussion of the problem (Romans, chaps. 9–11, esp. 11:28–31).

The reproduction of Isa 6:9–10 by our Evangelist makes its tone appear stronger through his attribution of the hardening action to God (not the prophet): he omits reference to deafness and sets first the people's blindness, perhaps through reflection on the healing of the blind man and his emphasis on Jesus as the Light of the world (note the parallel statement to this passage in 9:39–41, couched in terms of blindness and sight); moreover the paragraph preceding this ends with an appeal to walk in the light (vv 35–36), and that which follows makes an even more explicit appeal to believe in the Light which is Christ (v 46). This is important; the Evangelist interprets the course of events in the ministry of Jesus, as in the time of the Church's ministry to Israel, in the light of Isa 6:9–10, and in so doing implicitly calls on his Jewish contemporaries to come out from their situation of judgment on their unbelief and turn to the One who can bring them healing.

41 The glory of God that Isaiah saw in his vision (Isa 6:1–4) is identified with the glory of the Logos-Son, in accordance with 1:18 and 17:5. (8:56 is a little different; Abraham had a vision of the day of Jesus *in the future,* i.e., in the time of the coming kingdom of God, see *Comment* ad loc.). This means that the healing mentioned in v 40c is that which the Christ bestows (cf. 5:17).

42 Note the strong qualification of vv 38–40: "Nevertheless *many"—even of the authorities*—"believed in him." We have heard only of Nicodemus, and we shall hear of Joseph of Arimathea (19:38); there must have been others, of whose belief in Jesus the Pharisees knew nothing (7:48). But the faith of these men was not allowed to come to maturity: they did not confess their faith lest they be excluded from the synagogue. The inclusion of this statement will have had a double purpose. It shows that "they could not believe" of v 39 is no cast-iron fate from which people cannot break out; if "many" of the rulers believed, one may be sure that many more of the ordinary people did also. The statement is likely to reflect the situation of many in the synagogues of the Evangelist's day, and it makes a silent appeal that they too should count honor in the sight of God of greater consequence than honor in the sight of men, and so be bold enough to confess Jesus as the Christ.

44 The opening clause Ἰησοῦς δὲ ἔκραξεν . . . is paraphrased by Dodd as, "This is the content of the kerygma of Jesus" (*Interpretation,* 382; for κράξω as signifying proclamation cf. 1:15; 7:28, 37). Jesus has completed his public teaching. Having stated and explained in relation to scripture the unbelief of the Jews toward that teaching the Evangelist now closes the Book of Signs with an exposition of the grounds of faith in Jesus and the salvation that results from believing in him. This he does by selecting major emphases of the teaching of Jesus earlier recorded. The two parts of the sentence set forth in synonymous parallelism the well-known Jewish maxim, "One sent is as he who sent him"; it occurs again in 13:20, and also in the synoptic tradition (a comparison of Matt 10:40 with Luke 10:16 reveals a positive and negative statement of the principle, cf. also Mark 9:37 = Luke 9:49). This principle of representation lies behind the reiterated statements of the gospel that Jesus is the Sent One of God, commissioned to speak and act with authority in his Father's name (cf., e.g., 3:31–36; 6:36–40; 7:27–29, 33–34; 8:14–17, 28–29, 42–43; 10:34–36). The expression "he who sees" (v 46) is in parallelism with "he who believes," and clearly means "he who sees with faith." The Evangelist is fond of using varied expressions for believing in Jesus (cf. 6:40, 44, 45, 47, 51, where "seeing," "coming," "hearing," "believing," "eating" are different representations of the one reality of faith). Seeing with faith above all enables the believer to see in Jesus the Father himself (14:9).

46 The saying harks back to 8:12, but also echoes the theme in the prologue (1:4, 5, 9), and to 3:19–21, and to the whole episode of the healing of the blind man (esp. 9:5, 39–41).

47 Hearing and "guarding" the words of Jesus denotes persisting in faith and obedience in relation to that which is declared in the words, hence *living*

by the Word (cf. 8:51, 55; 14:23–24; 17:6; Rev 1:3). The main thought of
the sentence reproduces that of 3:17, which receives a necessary qualification
in 8:15–16 (cf. 5:21–22), as also in the statement that follows.

48 Since Jesus is the representative of God who makes known the revelation in words and deeds given by God (v 49), rejection of his message is
rejection of God, and so entails the judgment of God. This is assumed in
12:31–32 which locates the judgment in the death and exaltation of Jesus.
Here we learn that the word spoken by Jesus is the standard of judgment
by God, the giver of the word, and that such a judgment faces any who
persist in rejection of the word, including its proclamation after the cross
and offer of forgiveness (such we must assume to be the extended meaning
in the Evangelist's inclusion of the saying at this point). For the relation of
judgment "in the last day" to that enacted and revealed in the "lifting up"
of Jesus, see pp. 76–77, 213–14, 219–20.

49–50 The final affirmation of the summary of Jesus' proclamation reiter-
ates his sending by the Father and the origin of his message in God. This
has been a constant theme of the Gospel from the prologue on (cf. 1:14–
18; 3:31–36; 7:14–17; 8:26–29, and for v 50a see also 3:16; 5:19–29, 39–
40; 6:38–40, 68).

There are clear connections between this representation of the mission of Jesus
and the expectation of the coming prophet like Moses in Deut 18:18–19. Moses
gave the people the words and commands of God, and in the light of these commandments he called on them to choose between life and death (see esp. Deut 30:15–
20). This acknowledged link should be set within the larger frame of the hope of
the second Exodus. While Moses was known as the First Redeemer, Jesus is not
simply the Second but the final, eschatological Redeemer, who by his living, dying,
exaltation, and sending of the Spirit brings in the kingdom of God and the new
covenant for the renewed people of God. Hence arises the yet greater urgency to
"give heed to my words which he shall speak in my name" (Deut 18:19) and so
receive the life eternal of the saving sovereignty. (On this theme see further M. J.
O'Connell, "The Concept of Commandment in the Old Testament," *TS* 21 [1960]
351–403, esp. 352; Brown, 491–93; Schnackenburg, 2:424–25.)

Explanation

1. The great subject of chap. 12 is the meaning of the death and resurrection
of Jesus. The binding of the two events as an indissoluble action of God in
Christ, together with the unswerving obedience of Jesus as the Son, enables
the Evangelist to portray the redemptive act in terms of glory: the glory of
the Father and of the Son.

The accounts of the Anointing of Jesus and his Entry into Jerusalem are
presented as signs of the exaltation of Jesus via his cross to heaven. Mary's
costly anointing of Jesus for his burial reminds us of the prodigiously costly
anointing of the body of Jesus by Joseph of Arimathea and Nicodemus as
an offering fit for a king (19:38–39). The poor are ever with the Church,
but Mary took the opportunity while she had it of presenting Jesus with a
gift that marked him out as the Lord on his way to his redemptive death (v
8). So also the Entry of Jesus into Jerusalem signified the pilgrim's welcome
of the King who ascends his throne via his cross, though they had no understanding of the mode of his coronation. Their welcome nevertheless prefigured

the recognition by the nations of the Lord who gave himself for the life of the world. In like manner the testing of Jesus in his hour of agony comes to its climax in the prayer of Jesus, "Glorify your name!", and in the Father's response "I have glorified it, and will glorify it again" (v 28), i.e., through the death and exaltation of the Son (v 28).

The most vivid expression of the death of Jesus as exaltation ("lifting up") is in vv 31–32, which is also the most notable representation in the Gospels of the death and resurrection of Jesus as the eschatological event which forms the turning point of the ages. It is alike the hour of the judgment of the world, the overthrow of Satan's power, and the exaltation of Christ as Lord of the saving sovereignty of God. As such it is the climax of the work of the incarnate Son to bring the kingdom of God to humankind. The utterance is fitly set at the conclusion of the Book of Signs and at the end of the public ministry of Jesus; for the signs all exhibit the saving sovereignty which Jesus brought to the world, and the coming of the kingdom of God and its accompanying judgment through the death and resurrection of Jesus is the heart of God's good news, both for Israel and for the nations.

2. This recognition of the death and exaltation of Christ as the eschatological event of judgment and establishment of the saving sovereignty of God raises a question of crucial importance: does this eschatological action of God through the Son of Man *demand* or *exclude* further eschatological action of God through the Son of Man? The most famous answer to that question was given by Bultmann in his exposition of John 12:31–32: "The turn of the ages results now. . . . No future in this world's history can bring anything new, and all apocalyptic pictures of the future are empty dreams" (431). The first sentence is impeccably correct. One would think, however, that it should lead to a different conclusion from that of the second sentence, namely, that *the incursion of the saving sovereignty into this world's history indicates that all history is to be made new through the Son of Man.* Undoubtedly John 12:31–32 is the most dramatic expression in the Bible of so-called "realized eschatology," i.e., of the eschatological action of God through Christ in the present time. Nevertheless it did not lead the Evangelist to look on the world through rose-colored glasses. He records words of Jesus that make it plain that the world will continue to reject his message and to oppose his followers, just as it did him (15:18–16:4), and despite 12:31 he includes a prayer of Jesus that God will protect his disciples from the power of the Evil One (17:15). It is therefore altogether comprehensible that he represents Jesus as saying, after the declaration that the judgment of the world takes place through the event of his death and exaltation, "He who rejects me and does not receive my sayings has a judge; the word that I have spoken will be his judge on the last day" (12:48). The rejection of the kingdom brought by the Christ can only end in exclusion from it, i.e., by act of judgment; and the judgment at the end will be a revelation of God's action in Christ in accordance with the judgment that took place at the lifting up of the Son of Man.

The like applies to the issue of appropriating the life of the kingdom of God; to believe in the crucified and risen Lord is to know the life of his kingdom now with a view to resurrection in the consummated kingdom. This is expressed variously in the Gospel, e.g., in 6:40, "This is the will of

my Father, that everyone who sees the Son and believes in him may have
eternal life, and I will raise him in the last day." It is arbitrary to exclude
the last clause of that sentence as alien to the Gospel; it affirms that present
participation in the saving sovereignty (eternal life) anticipates fullness of
participation in the final revelation of that sovereignty (resurrection). The
same concept is set forth in 6:44 in terms closely similar to those of 12:32,
and such is the burden of 11:25. The statements in the Gospel relating to
the Parousia show a similar relation of the sovereign action of God in Christ
in the present and that in the future (see 14:3, 18, 23, and *Comment* on
these passages).

This Gospel shows that the sovereign action of God embraces the entire
work of the incarnate Son. As seen in the words and deeds in the ministry,
its most critical revelation is in the "lifting up" of the Son of Man, but it is
not ended thereby, for the exalted Lord continues his work of judgment
and salvation in the world through the Paraclete-Spirit. As the death of the
Son of Man marked his return to the glory that he had with the Father
before the foundation of the world, so the end of the process will be the
uniting of all whom the Father has given to the Son in the glory of the
divine sovereignty (17:24–26).

3. The contemporary situation of the Evangelist is reflected in every section
of the passage. The faith and love of Mary expressed itself in the most costly
gift that she could give to Jesus. A Jewish saying runs, "Good anointing oil
goes from the inner chamber right into the dining hall; but a good name
goes from the one end of the world to the other" (*Midr. Qoh.* 7:1 [31a]).
Mary's example of devotion to the Lord is recorded that all Christians should
follow it. The exposition of the death of Jesus in vv 24–26 is intended to set
the obedience unto death of Jesus as the pattern for true discipleship, much
as Mark 8:34–37. So also the resolution of the conflict of Jesus in vv 27–28
serves as a pattern for all Christians in their own circumstances of testing.

The main appeal of the chapter, however, is to the Evangelist's Jewish
contemporaries who know the message of Jesus and are attracted to him
but have not had the courage wholeheartedly to commit themselves to him
in the obedience of faith. To an unusual extent the Evangelist calls attention
throughout the chapter to the many Jews who "believed in" Jesus in the
last days of his ministry. The raising of Lazarus to life, he records, made a
deep impression on the Jews in Jerusalem, so that many of them forsook
their leaders and went over to Jesus (v 11), and it inspired the "great crowd"
to go out from the city and hail him as "the Coming One, even the king of
Israel" (v 13), while the Pharisees helplessly acknowledged that the world
had gone after Jesus (v 20). The Evangelist was even able to affirm that
many of the authorities believed in Jesus (v 42). But in spite of all this the
general verdict over Israel was the failure of the nation to respond in faith
to God's word through him (v 37), and thereby the nation fulfilled God's
word through the prophet (vv 38–41). The tragic mistake of "the great crowd"
of Jerusalem was their failure to advance beyond excitement over the signs
of Jesus to authentic faith in him to which the signs pointed, and so to
follow faith's beginnings with confession of Jesus as Lord and Messiah. John
accordingly points out the major obstacle of faith among his people—in the

time of Jesus and in his own time love of the praise of men more than the praise of God (v 43). To experience ejection from the synagogue was undoubtedly a fearful price for a Jew to pay for confessing Jesus as Messiah, but to face rejection from the kingdom of God through denial of Jesus as Messiah is far more to be dreaded. All this is recorded in hope that the readers of the Gospel to whom this was a burning issue should share no longer their compatriots' failure of faith, but give heed to the message of Jesus, which is summarized in vv 44–50, and so inherit the eternal life which is for those who truly obey the commandment of God (v 50).

III. The Passion and Resurrection of Jesus (13:1–20:31)

A. The Ministry of Jesus to the Disciples in the Upper Room (13:1–17:26)

Introductory Note on the Composition of the Farewell Discourses

1. The synoptic Gospels tell of Jesus instructing his disciples at points throughout his ministry (see, e.g., Mark 4:10–20; 6:7–13, expanded by Matthew to 10:1–42; Mark 8:14–21, 27–33; 9:1–13, 33–41; 10:23–45). Such instruction is intensified in the closing days of Jesus' ministry, as may be seen in Mark 13 (expanded by Matthew to chaps. 24–25) and Mark 14:3–42par. By contrast the Fourth Evangelist has set virtually the whole instruction of Jesus to his disciples in the context of the Last Supper. This has at least some counterpart in Mark's procedure relating to the eschatological discourse in Mark 13 and the words of Jesus at the Last Supper in Mark 14, for there are many parallels in John to these chapters. Luke affords a stronger precedent in placing teaching given by Jesus to his disciples, recorded by Mark at an earlier point in his Gospel, in the context of the Last Supper (Luke 22:14–38); again, some elements of this teaching have contacts with John's record (notably in chap. 13). In fashioning discourses by combining sayings of Jesus from various contexts, the Evangelist has followed a path trodden by his predecessors, especially by Matthew, whose discourses have all been constructed by bringing together related teaching of Jesus. But why should John have set it all in the Last Supper context? In part it was because the tradition before him handed down teaching given in that setting, and he has expanded it. More importantly, there was no more likely context wherein this teaching was communicated to the churches than in celebrations of the Lord's Supper. Dodd deduced from Paul's declaration in 1 Cor 11:26, "Show forth the Lord's death!" (an imperative, not indicative) that the fundamental Passion tradition took shape in the context of the Lord's Supper; and he further suggested that in the common plan that lay behind all the Gospels the Passion narrative began with the incidents of the Last Supper (*Historical Tradition*, 28, 59). It is accordingly not surprising that the instructions of Jesus at his last meal with his disciples should have been recounted at celebrations of the Lord's Supper, and that related teaching should have been associated with it. Schürmann rightly observed, "All regulations for the community have their ground here in the Eucharist and are ordered to it. For a life of faith and brotherly love among the disciples of Jesus is a life in the brotherhood of a community that celebrates the Lord's Supper" (*Der Abendmahlsbericht Lukas 22.7–38 als Gottesdienstordnung, Gemeindeordnung, Lebensordnung* [Paderborn: 1957] 95).

2. Apart from the preservation and communication of the teaching of Jesus in the Lord's Supper there was an important precedent in the ancient world for the discourses of John 13–17, namely the genre of *farewell discourses* or *testaments* of famous men. This was known in literature of the Hellenistic world, but was prominent in Jewish writings. We see it already in the Old Testament, e.g., in the blessings

of Jacob on his sons (Gen 49), Joshua's address to his people (Josh 22–24), and David's to Solomon and the nation (1 Chron 28–29). The same feature occurs in the writings of early Judaism, the best-known instance of which is *The Testaments of the Twelve Patriarchs*, which is wholly composed of the supposed last words of each of the patriarchs to their people. The most important example of this kind of writing, however, is the Book of Deuteronomy, which could well have been in the Evangelist's mind when composing the discourses of the Upper Room. This work in its entirety consists of the farewell discourses of Moses to Israel. The concept of Jesus as the new (or rather, greater than) Moses, bringing about a second Exodus for life in the kingdom of God is a major theme of the Evangelist's. Moreover the situation of Israel addressed in Deuteronomy is curiously similar to that of the disciples addressed in John 13–17: Israel is on the point of entering the promised land as the chosen people of God, and the disciples are about to be launched as the new Israel in order to be the instruments of the divine sovereignty in the world. There is also a surprising number of connections between the farewell discourses of Moses and those of Jesus (on this whole theme see A. Lacomara, "Deuteronomy and the Farewell Discourse," *CBQ* 36 [1974] 65–84). J. Blank, in endorsing this link between John 13–17 and Deuteronomy, observed that as Deuteronomy helped to make the original situation of Israel under Moses a continuing challenge to the Jews for decision—a "re-presentation" of the message to them—so the farewell discourses of Jesus in John make the authority of Jesus decisive for the life of the ongoing Church: "The farewell discourses are at the center of the Johannine 'theology of re-presentation, and are even to some extent the key to it" (Commentary, 2:13–14).

Here above all in the Gospel we need steadfastly to bear in mind that the Speaker is not simply the Christ who presided over the meal in the Upper Room, but the risen Lord in the midst of his people. If the Last Discourses are to be viewed as his last Testament, it is bound to be unique by that very fact. "It is not like other last testaments," said R. E. Brown, "which are the recorded words of men who are dead and can speak no more: for whatever there may be of *ipsissima verba* in the Last Discourse has been transformed in the light of the resurrection and through the coming of the Paraclete into a living discourse delivered, not by a dead man, but by the one who has life (6.57), to all readers of the Gospel" (2:582).

3. The structure of the Last Discourses may be set forth as follows: (*i*) 13:1–30, the Washing of the Disciples' Feet and Statement of the Betrayal; (*ii*) 13:31–14:31, a discourse concerned primarily with the departure and return of Jesus, reaching its conclusion in 14:31 and finding its natural continuation in 18:1 ff.; (*iii*) 15–16, a further discourse which subdivides into three: (a) 15:1–17, the allegory of the Vine and its Branches, (b) 15:18–16:4a, the world's hatred for Jesus and his disciples, (c) 16:4b–33, the ministry of the Paraclete, and the joy of the disciples despite tribulation; (*iv*) chap. 17, the prayer of Jesus in light of his impending death.

The once popular idea that chaps. 15–17 were uttered on the way from the Upper Room to Gethsemane is hardly to be countenanced. The statement in 18:1, "After saying these things Jesus *went out* with his disciples . . . ," clearly intimates that Jesus left the house at *that* point. Nor will it do to interpret 14:31 in terms of a resolution of the spirit rather than a physical movement. Dodd renders the main clause, "Up, let us march to meet him!" (i.e., the ruler of this world), thus allowing chaps. 15–17 to follow on without a break. On the contrary, 14:31 is most naturally translated "Rise up; *let us be on our way from here*" (Bruce, 306). It would appear, then, that chaps. 13–14 form a self-contained portrayal of the events in the Upper Room and Jesus' Farewell Discourse, and that chaps. 15–17 give a further representation of the Lord's instruction on that occasion.

The question arises how it came about that *two* Farewell Discourses are set side by side in the Gospel instead of being integrated as one discourse. Some have attributed this to a sheer accident, by which a disarrangement of the original sheets of the MS took place; Bernard, e.g., proposed that chaps. 15–16 originally preceded 13:31 ff., which were followed by 14 and 17 (1:xx), while Bultmann suggested the order 17, 13:31–35, 15–16, 13:36–38, 14 (459–61). Proposals of this kind have not met with favor, for they create fresh problems (it is, e.g., a strange procedure to set chap. 17 prior to the discourses, since it seems so clearly to indicate their climax). The main alternative suggestions are that the Evangelist so arranged previously existing materials that were before him, or that a later editor added chaps. 15–17 to an original farewell discourse consisting of chaps. 13–14. It is difficult to believe that the Evangelist himself, who composed with meticulous care the earlier discourses in the Gospel, left the last discourses in their present order; it is altogether more comprehensible that a later editor left undisturbed the discourse that came from the Evangelist (in 13–14), and then added the rest of his material as a self-contained whole. Such is the conclusion of most recent exegetes, and it is confirmed by the reappearance in chaps. 15–16 of a number of elements within the first discourse (see the listing of them in the chart drawn up by Brown, 2:589–591). Whereas some consider that the additions reflect a different theological viewpoint from that of the Evangelist (see, e.g., Becker, 2:477, and his article "Die Abschiedsreden im Johannesevangelium," *ZNW* 61 [1970] 215–46), it seems to the present writer that one fundamental theological standpoint is maintained through all the chapters (so Bultmann, emphatically, 459), and that the later editor(s) utilized material from the same source as that available to the Evangelist (so Schnackenburg, 2:90–91, and essentially Brown, who postulates two collections belonging to different periods or different circles of the Johannine community, 2:594. H. Thyen holds a distinctive view: there *are* differences of theological stance observable in the discourses, but the "redactor" of this diverse material is none other than the Evangelist! See "Johannes 13 und die 'kirchliche Redaktion' des vierten Evangeliums," 356).

4. The last discourse opens with a statement of time: "It was just before the Passover festival . . . during the meal Jesus rises. . . ." The Evangelist appears to suggest that the farewell meal in which Jesus instructed his disciples took place on the *eve* of the Passover, i.e., the day *before* the feast. He later reports the anxiety of the high priests, in the trial before Pilate, not to defile themselves and thereby be prevented from celebrating the Passover (18:28). The synoptic Gospels, on the other hand, indicate that Jesus celebrated with his disciples the Passover (Mark 14:12; Luke 22:15). There appears to be a clash of dates here, and scholars divide themselves over which tradition is right and which wrong. Not infrequently it is maintained that the Fourth Evangelist knowingly altered the date of the trial and death of Jesus in the interests of his theology, namely to show that Jesus died as God's Passover Lamb (1:29; 19:31–37). Lindars states, "The death of Jesus on the eve of the Passover is a purely Johannine invention, dictated by his theological interests" (446). That is a difficult assertion in view of the Jewish tradition that Jesus died on that very day (*Sanh.* 43a: "It was taught: On the eve of the Passover they hanged Jeshu. And an announcer went out in front of him,' for forty days [saying], 'He is going to be stoned, because he practiced magic and enticed and led Israel astray. Anyone who knows anything in his favor, let him come and plead in his behalf.' But not having found anything in his favor, they hanged him the eve of the Passover"). The elaboration of the tradition (by giving opportunity

for Jesus' defense) is doubtless due to the desire to defend the Jews for their action; but the tradition as to the occasion of his death is old ("It was taught").

The difference between the synoptic and Johannine representations of date of the Last Supper and its relation to the Passover celebration has been endlessly discussed without a solution being found that meets all the evidence. Mme. A. Jaubert's proposal has attracted considerable attention; she affirms that Jesus celebrated the Passover on the Tuesday evening of Passover week, in accordance with a *solar* calendar that was followed also by the Essenes, but John reports the observance of the Passover by the Jewish authorities on Friday, in accordance with the official *lunar* calendar; the time between the two observances was taken up with the trial and crucifixion of Jesus (see *The Date of the Last Supper* [New York: Alba, 1965]). It is an ingenious suggestion, but it hardly fits John's representation of the course of events from the beginning of the supper to the death of Jesus; Jeremias after reviewing it wrote, "I can only regard this as unfounded" (*The Eucharistic Words of Jesus*, 25).

Some features in the representations of the Last Supper in the four Gospels suggest a different line of thought. It is a curious fact that the synoptic Gospels, in their varied records of the words and acts of Jesus in the Last Supper, make virtually no mention of the Passover (e.g., there is no mention of the Passover Lamb); on the other hand some elements in the Fourth Gospel intimate an agreement of the tradition *behind* its account with the synoptic dating of the Last Supper; e.g., Jesus and the disciples *recline* at the meal, a feature unusual in Jewish evening meals, but mandatory for the Passover celebration in early Judaism. More importantly, John 19:14 must represent the same date as 19:31, and that has implications for 18:28, since 19:31 denotes *the eve of the sabbath in the Passover week*, not the eve of the Passover meal (see J. B. Segal, *The Hebrew Passover* [London: 1963] 36–37, and C. C. Torrey, "The Date of the Crucifixion according to the Fourth Gospel," *JBL* 50 [1931] 227). Bultmann pointed out that if the "high Sabbath" of 19:31 was the day of the sheaf offering, that would make it Nisan 16, which in turn implies that Jesus was crucified on Nisan 15, as represented in the synoptic Gospels (676 n.6). One can but acknowledge that further patient investigation of the traditions behind the Last Supper accounts of the four Gospels is clearly required. Fortunately, despite the intrinsic interest of the matter, it is of secondary importance, inasmuch as the synoptic Gospels and the Fourth Gospel alike are concerned to show the relation of the *death* of Jesus with the Passover; in this primary matter all agree that the latter finds its fulfillment in the offering of the Lamb of God, slain as God's Passover Lamb.

5. The question continues to perplex readers of the Fourth Gospel why the author omitted all reference to the words of Jesus concerning the bread and wine in the Supper. In the light of the foregoing we find unacceptable the suggestion that the Evangelist regarded the Lord's Supper as irrelevant (as, e.g., Bultmann, who believed that the Evangelist set the high-priestly prayer of Jesus *in place of* the Last Supper, 485–86). The entire narration of chap. 6 reflects the importance to the Evangelist of the Lord's Supper, and especially of the bread and wine taken in the Supper. Moreover, scholars have for long been convinced that the preservation of the last discourses of Jesus is due to the frequent use of the material in them in celebrations of the Lord's Supper. The brief accounts of the words of Institution in the synoptic Gospels are undoubtedly a reflection of their use in the churches' worship; it is not surprising, then, that the Fourth Evangelist, instead of repeating those brief words known throughout the churches, chose to reproduce *teaching that gave their meaning*. This indeed is the most plausible reason for John's recounting at the beginning of the discourse the detailed narrative of the foot-washing; he

gave this, not to replace the eucharistic acts and words of Jesus, but rather to interpret them, and so (in Schnackenburg's words) "to impart a doctrine to the community that celebrated the Eucharist" (3:46). A similar answer was given by Lacomara to the question why, in view of the similarities between the Last Discourses of Jesus and Deuteronomy, no mention is made of the (new) covenant, which is so prominent in all the other accounts of the Last Supper; in his view John reproduced the teaching which gave the significance of the covenant, in a manner comparable to his procedure in the discourse on the Bread of life in chap. 6: "As in John 6 we have an extended commentary on the words "This is my body . . . this is my blood," so in the chapters of the Farewell Discourse we have an extended commentary on the words 'of the new covenant' " ("Deuteronomy and the Farewell Discourse," 84).

6. The sayings on the "Paraclete" in the Upper Room discourses are of particular importance and have been intensively studied. There are five of these: 14:15–17, 25–26; 15:26–27; 16:7–11, 12–15. H. Windisch, in a celebrated essay (now included in *The Spirit-Paraclete in the Fourth Gospel* [Philadelphia: Fortress, 1968] 1–26), maintained that these sayings are small units, complete in themselves, and can be removed from their contexts without leaving a gap; the Evangelist took them over, interpreted, and expanded them as he applied them to the Spirit in the Church, and focused his witness on Jesus. Many have been persuaded by Windisch's arguments, but his belief that the Paraclete sayings are *alien* entities in the discourses has aroused opposition to his whole thesis. Some scholars, indeed, have been so impressed with the close relation of the Paraclete sayings to their contexts that they believe the sayings could not have existed apart from their present setting. Brown, from this standpoint, adduces the parallel of the Servant Songs of Deutero-Isaiah: "The Study of the Paraclete passages in isolation is something like the study of the Suffering Servant passages in Isaiah—the isolation of the information is essential, but there is no evidence that such figures were thought of apart from their respective contexts" ("The Paraclete in the Fourth Gospel," *NTS* 13 [1966–67] 114). The comparison is illuminating, but most scholars are now convinced that the Servant Songs were composed independently of their present contexts and were subsequently inserted into them (by the prophet? See the discussion in C. R. North, *The Suffering Servant in Deutero-Isaiah* [Oxford: OUP, 1948] 156–88). North believed that the prophet composed the songs at intervals. C. Westermann considers that another composed the fourth song (Isa 52:13–53:12), and that the earlier songs were extended in their contexts (e.g., 42:1–4 was expanded by vv 5–8(9); 49:7–12, following vv 1–6, was later interpreted of the Servant; and 50:10–11, 52:1–8 were added to 50:4–9; see *Das Buch Jesaja 40–66, ATD* [Göttingen: Vandenhoeck & Ruprecht, 1966] 26–27). The parallel illustrates how previously existing material of a closely related kind can be incorporated into fresh contexts and become wholly one with them. There is no doubt that the Paraclete sayings do form a coherent body of utterances concerning the Spirit. Each one can be abstracted from its present context, leaving the latter reading smoothly, but each one fits well into its context. This is particularly clear in the first two, 14:15–17 and 25–26, and perhaps even more strikingly the third, 15:26–27; this is significant, for the third saying is the key to the origin of the rest; it is closely parallel to the synoptic saying on the Spirit's aid to the disciples when they are on trial, which is found in Mark 13:11 and in Q, Luke 12:11–12 ∥ Matt 10:19–20. Significantly, the saying is without context in Q (in Luke 12 the saying owes its position to its contiguity with another saying on the Holy Spirit). The same is true of Mark 13:11; the latter is part of a sentence into which v 10 has been inserted (because of the mission slant of the saying), and it is without connection with what precedes and what follows it; it

owes its place in Mark 13 to its eschatological import, denoting the Church's mission by the aid of the Holy Spirit in the time of distress that presses on to the consummation. So also John 15:26–27, like Mark 13:11, is set in a context of persecution, intensified through the disciples carrying out their mission. It is likely that this fundamental saying was the center around which the rest of the Paraclete sayings were gathered as variations on one great theme, and which led to their incorporation into the other discourses. Whether they were added subsequently to the composition of the discourses, or whether they were constituent elements that formed the discourses is uncertain. On either reckoning their prior existence as instruction on the Paraclete-Spirit's ministry is assumed.

1. The Footwashing and the Betrayal of Jesus (13:1–30)

Bibliography

Bacon, B. W. "The Sacrament of Footwashing." *ExpTim* 43 (1931–32) 218–21. **Barton, G. A.** "The Origin of the Discrepancy between the Synoptics and the Fourth Gospel as to the Date and Character of Christ's Last Supper with His Disciples." *JBL* 43 (1924) 28–31. **Bishop, E. F. F.** " 'He That Eateth Bread with Me Hath Lifted Up His Heel against Me': John 13:18." *ExpTim* 70 (1958–59) 331–33. **Boismard, M. E.** "Le lavement des pieds." *RB* 71 (1964) 5–24. **Braun, F. M.** "Le lavement des pieds et la réponse de Jésus à saint Pierre (Jean xiii, 4–10)." *RB* 44 (1935) 22–23. **Campenhausen, H. von.** "Zur Auslegung von Joh 13, 6–10." *ZNW* 33 (1934) 259–71. **Christie, W. M.** "Did Christ Eat the Passover with His Disciples?" *ExpTim* 43 (1931–32) 515–19. **Derrett, J. D. M.** "Domine, tu mihi lavas pedes?" *BeO* 21 (1979) 13–42. **Dodd, C. H.** *Interpretation.* 390–423. **Dunn, J. D. G.** "The Washing of the Disciples' Feet in John 13:1–20." *ZNW* 61 (1970) 247–52. **Fridrichsen, A.** "Bemerkungen zur Fusswaschung Joh 13." *ZNW* 38 (1939) 94–96. **Grossouw, W. K.** "A Note on Joh 13:1–3." *NovT* 8 (1966) 124–31. **Haring, N. M.** "Historical Notes on the Interpretation of John 13:10." *CBQ* 13 (1951) 355–80. **Kelly, J.** "What Did Christ Mean by the Sign of Love?" *AFER* 13 (1971) 113–21. **Knox, W. L.** "John 13:1–10." *HTR* 43 (1950) 161–63. **Lohmeyer, E.** "Die Fusswaschung." *ZNW* 38 (1939) 74–94. **Michl, J.** "Der Sinn der Fusswaschung." *Bib* 40 (1959) 697–708. **Moffatt, J.** "The Lord's Supper in the Fourth Gospel." *Exp* 8th ser. 6 (1913) 1–22. **Mussner, F.** "Die Fusswaschung." *GeistLeb* 31 (1958) 25–30. **Richter, G.** *Die Fusswaschung im Johannesevangelium.* Regensburg: Pustet, 1967. **Robinson, J. A. T.** "The Significance of the Footwashing." *Neotestamentica et Patristica.* FS O. Cullmann. 144–47. **Thyen, H.** "Johannes 13 und die 'kirchliche Redaktion' des vierten Evangeliums." *Tradition und Glaube.* FS K. G. Kuhn. 343–56. **Weiser, A.** "Joh 13, 12–20—Zufügung eines späteren Herausgebers?" *BZ* 12 (1968) 252–57. **Wilcox, M.** "The Composition of John 13:21–30." *Neotestamentica et Semitica.* FS M. Black. Ed. E. Earle & M. Wilcox. Edinburgh: T&T Clark, 1969. 143–56.

Translation

[1] *It was just before the Passover festival;* [a] *Jesus, in full awareness that his hour had come that he should pass from this world to the Father, although he had*

always loved his own who were in the world, now showed his love for them to the limit. [2] *The Devil had already put into the heart*[b] *of Judas, son of Simon Iscariot,*[c] *that he should betray him. During the evening meal,*[c] *then,* [3] *Jesus, knowing that the Father had given all things into his hands, and that he had come from God and was going away to God,* [4] *rises from the meal and lays aside his robe, and taking a towel he tied it round him.* [5] *Then he poured water into the basin and began to wash the disciples' feet and to wipe them with the towel that was wrapped around him.* [6] *He comes therefore to Simon Peter; he says to him, "Master, are you going to wash my feet?"* [7] *Jesus answered him, "What I am doing you do not realize now, but you will come to know later."* [8] *Peter says to him, "Never, never shall you wash my feet!"*[d] *Jesus answered him, "Unless I wash you, you will have*[e] *no part with me."* [9] *Simon Peter says to him, "Master, not my feet only, but my hands and my head also!"* [10] *Jesus says to him, "He who has bathed does not need to wash (except for his feet),*[f] *but is clean all over; and you men are clean, but not all of you."* [11] *For he knew who was about to betray him; that is why he said, "Not all of you are clean."*

[12] *When therefore he had washed their feet (and) taken his robe he reclined at table again, and said to them, "Do you know what I have done to you?"* [13] *You address me, "Teacher!" and "Master!"*[g] *and you speak rightly, for I am.* [14] *If then I, the Teacher and Master, have washed your feet, you also ought to wash one another's feet.* [15] *For I have given you an example, that you should do just as I have done to you.* [16] *Amen, amen, I tell you, a slave is not greater than his master, nor is one sent greater than he who sent him.* [17] *If you know these things happy are you if you put them into practice.*

[18] *I am not speaking about all of you; I know whom I have chosen. But the scripture must be fulfilled,*[h] *'He who eats my*[i] *bread has lifted up his heel against me.'* [19] *Of a truth, I am telling you before it happens, in order that when*[j] *it does happen you may believe that I am he.* [20] *Amen, amen, I tell you, he who receives anyone I send receives me, and he who receives me receives the One who sent me."*

[21] *After saying these things Jesus became agitated in spirit. He bore witness and said, "Amen, amen, I tell you, one of you will betray me."* [22] *The disciples looked at one another, at a loss to know of whom he was speaking.* [23] *One of his disciples was reclining at table close to the breast of Jesus—the one whom Jesus loved.* [24] *Simon Peter therefore made signs to him that he should inquire who it was*[k] *of whom he was speaking.* [25] *That disciple therefore leaned back on Jesus' chest and said to him, "Master, who is it?"* [26] *Jesus answers, "It is he for whom I shall dip*[l] *this piece of bread in the dish and give it to him." After dipping the bread he (takes it and)*[m] *gives it to Judas, son of Simon Iscariot.*[n] [27] *Then after the piece of bread Satan entered into him. Jesus says to him, "What you are going to do, do quickly."* [28] *Now none of those reclining at table knew for what purpose he said this to him;* [29] *for some of them were supposing, since Judas used to keep the money-box, that Jesus was saying to him, "Buy what we need for the festival," or that he should give something to the poor.* [30] *After taking the bread, therefore, he went out at once; and it was night.*

Notes

[a] The relation of this temporal clause to the other verbs in the sentence has puzzled exegetes. Bultmann, e.g., thought that to relate it to ἀγαπήσας . . . ἠγάπησεν would be absurd—as though

one could *date* the love of Jesus in this way! He therefore restricted the clause to limit εἰδώς. . . . :"Since Jesus, before the feast of the passover, knew that his hour had come" (463). On the contrary the time statement of vv 1a and 2a most naturally provides the context for the discourses of chaps. 13–17 and especially to the event about to be described; ἀγαπήσας relates to the whole ministry of Jesus, ἠγάπησεν to the footwashing. Grossouw, taking εἰς τέλος as meaning "to the limit," rather than "to the end," renders ἠγάπησεν . . . as, "he gave them the perfect love token" ("A Note on Joh 13:1–3," 128)

b Grammatically it is possible to translate this clause as "the devil having put into his (own) heart . . . ," i.e., he made up *his* mind that Judas should betray Jesus (so Barrett, 439); but the grammatical *possibility* is intrinsically unlikely; the statement anticipates v 27.

c The variants in Judas' name and its relation to ἵνα παραδοῖ are numerous and are best seen as attempts to ease the reading adopted in the UBS text. Ἰούδας Σίμωνος Ἰσκαριώτου (= "Judas son of Simon Iscariot") is read by L Ψ 0124 1241 etc., and is to be preferred to Ἰούδας Σίμωνος Ἰσκαριώτης (= "Judas Iscariot, son of Simon"), which is read by P⁶⁶ ℵ B etc., since it is more difficult and accords with John's usage elsewhere (6:71; 13:26). Both these readings make Ἰούδας the subject of παραδοῖ. The common reading Ἰούδα . . . (read by A K Δ Θ etc.) sets the name Judas in the gen. case, but curiously in English the sentence may then be rendered in the same way as in the first reading.

d Jeremias has pointed out that οὐ μή in the Gospels commonly occurs in oath-like assurances (cf. Mark 14:25, 31; Matt 16:22; John 20:25) and is so intended here (*Eucharistic Words of Jesus*, 209–10).

e ἔχεις is a present with a future meaning (Braun, "Le lavement des pieds," 27–28, comparing 12:8, 48; 16:33).

f The question whether the original text of v 10 included εἰ μὴ τοὺς πόδας or omitted it is a *cause célèbre* of NT textual criticism. The phrase is omitted by ℵ it^aur,c vg Origen; Tatian and Tertullian omit also νίψασθαι, which Boismard thinks is correct ("Le lavement des pieds," 10). The longer reading was accepted by most older scholars (e.g., Westcott, 2:150; Bernard, 2:462; Schlatter, 282–83), but also recently by Haenchen (457) and Bruce (282–83). The UBS committee included it in view of its superior external attestation; they assumed that the phrase was omitted either by accident or through the difficulty of reconciling it with the immediately following clause (ἀλλ' ἔστιν καθαρὸς ὅλος, see Metzger, 240). Nevertheless the overwhelming majority of modern scholars believe the short reading is correct (so Lagrange, 353–55; Bultmann, 469–70; Hoskyns, 438–39; Boismard, 353–56; Braun, 25 n.1; Lohmeyer, 81–83; Wikenhauser, 250–51; Barrett, 441–42; Lightfoot, 273; Brown, 566–68; Lindars, 451; Schnackenburg, 3:20–22; Becker, 2:424; Thyen, 348; Schulz, 173–74; Michl, 702–3; Dunn, 250–51). The omission appears to be demanded by the context. (*i*) V 8 clearly relates to Jesus' act of washing, and in v 10 that is viewed as a bath (ὁ λελουμένος . . .) which results in a person becoming *completely* clean, hence without need of further washing. (*ii*) It is easier to understand the addition of "except for the feet" than its omission. Scribes did not realize that the act of washing the feet = a *bath*, and had to justify Jesus' washing *feet*. But this makes the act of Jesus of secondary importance, which is irreconcilable with v 7. (*iii*) The additions made in some MSS to the primary addition are significant of the way in which *that* addition arose through attempting to relate the statement of v 10 to the actions of Jesus: P⁶⁶ Θ syr^s,p bo^ms add μόνον to εἰ μὴ τοὺς πόδας. D reads οὐ χρείαν ἔχει τὴν κεφαλὴν νίψασθαι εἰ μὴ τοὺς πόδας μόνον.

g Observe that ὁ διδάσκαλος and ὁ κύριος are nominative for vocative. The former = רב (*rab*), the latter = מר (*mār*). Str-B point out that in address an individual says רבי ומרי (*rabbî umārî*), "My teacher and my master," while a group says, רבן ומרן (*rabban umāran*) or רבנא ומרנא (*rabbannā› umāranā›*), "Our teacher and our master." It was not permitted to a pupil to name the teacher by his name (2:558). This is an indication that the majority of appearances of κύριος in this Gospel have this significance rather than the full meaning of "Lord" (see, e.g., 6:34, 68(?); 11:3, 12, 21, 27, 32, 34, 39; 13:6, 9, 25, 36, 37; 14:5, 8, 22; even 20:2, 13, 18, 25; but contrast 20:28; many instances are less than "master" and merely = "sir," e.g., 4:11, 15, 19, 49; 5:7; 8:11; 9:36; 12:21; 20:15).

h On the possibility that ἵνα ἡ γραφὴ πληρωθῇ represents an imperative, see the note on John 9:3.

i μου is less well supported (by B C L etc.) than μετ' ἐμοῦ (in P⁶⁶ ℵ D K W etc.); but the latter could be due to the influence of the LXX (which reads μετ' ἐμοῦ) and to Mark 14:18.

j ἀπ' ἄρτι normally = "from now on"; but in several passages of the NT it should probably be read as ἀπαρτί, "assuredly," "definitely," and is comparable to Jesus' use of "amen" at the beginning of a sentence (cf. especially Rev 14:13; Debrunner would add Matt 23:39; 26:29, 64; John 14:7, see "Über einige Lesarten der Chester Beatty Papyri des Neuen Testaments," in *ConNT* 11:45–49. The reading ἀπαρτί is recommended in BDF § 12, 3. Otherwise we must assume that ἀπ᾽ ἄρτι = νῦν, "now."

ᵏ τίς ἂν εἴη is the only occurrence of an optative in our Gospel, but it is well supported here (P⁶⁶ A D K W etc.), and the various attempts to replace it with simpler language confirm its originality.

ˡ The reading βάψω . . . καὶ δώσω αὐτῷ (B C Origen, etc.) is typically Sem. and Johannine (especially the use of the superfluous αὐτῷ, a Hebraism, omitted by many MSS). βάψας . . . ἐπιδώσω (P⁶⁶ ℵ Δ Θ Ψ etc.) is "a stylistic modification, introduced by copyists in the interest of elegance" (Metzger, 241).

ᵐ λαμβάνει καὶ is included in a limited number of MSS (ℵ ᵃ B C L* X Origen etc.). The words could have been added by copyists in recollection of the accounts of the Institution of the Lord's Supper ("Jesus *took* bread. . . ," Mark 14:22; Matt 26:26; Luke 22:19; 1 Cor 11:23; Mark and Matthew add the additional words of Jesus, *"Take,* this is my body . . ."). Or the words may have been omitted by copyists as apparently needless.

ⁿ The variations in the name "Iscariot" after "Judas son of Simon" are similar to those in v 2 (see note thereon). The support for "son of Simon Iscariot" (Σίμωνος Ἰσκαριώτου) is stronger than in v 2 (read by ℵ B C L X Θ Ψ etc.), and the reading appears to be in accord with Johannine usage.

Form/Structure/Setting

1. The passage vv 1–30 falls into two major sections: vv 1–20 describing the footwashing of the disciples by Jesus, and vv 21–30 the announcement by Jesus of his impending betrayal by a disciple.

The narrative is preceded by a lengthy introductory statement in vv 1–3. Brown regards v 1 as an introduction to the whole "Book of Glory" (i.e., chaps. 13–20), and vv 2–3 as introducing specifically the narrative of the footwashing (2:563). It may, however, be better to regard vv 1–3 as forming a prelude to the upper room discourses, but with special reference to the footwashing (note how Heb 1:1–3 forms an exordium to the epistle, but flows without a break into the author's demonstration of the superiority of Jesus to the angels, 1:4 ff. W. K. Grossouw points out that the Book of Signs ends with an epilogue in 12:36–50; hence a new beginning was indispensable, "A Note on Joh 13:1–3," 129).

2. The story of the footwashing is contained in vv 4–11 and is followed by an interpretation of its significance in vv 12–20, which underscores its nature as a ὑπόδειγμα, an "example" (v 15). The narrative section itself, however, contains hints of profound dimensions, notably in the statement to Peter, "Unless I wash you, you have no part with me" (v 8), and the indication in v 10 that the footwashing is tantamount to a bath that makes one completely clean.

For centuries Christians have read a sacramental meaning in those words, seeing therein a reference to the efficacy of baptism, or even to baptism and the Lord's Supper together. This has led more recent scholars to the belief that the narrative as we now have it is composite, consisting of a primary, shorter, account, expanded to include a secondary meaning. The scholars in question, however, do not agree on which section was first and who added the second. Bultmann considered that the Evangelist had a source, consisting of the brief account in vv 4–5 and the interpretation in vv 12–20, the two together forming an apophthegm (story ending in significant teaching); to that the Evangelist added the interpretation given in vv 6–10 (462–63). Boismard went further and postulated a complete separation between the two interpretations; he saw in vv 1–2, 4–5, 12–15, 17–19 a *moralistic* account of the footwashing; in vv 3, 4–5, 6–10, 21–30 he found a *sacramental* account of the event, which presents the footwashing as a necessary rite for participating in the eschatological realities of life eternal, and so prefigures baptism; the two interpretations are thought to be independent of each other and combined without adjustment ("Le lavement des pieds," 5–24).

This solution of the problem set by the passage has been influential, although subsequent writers have felt compelled to modify it. Brown thinks that the idea of two parallel narratives combined into one is sound, but he prefers to view the first as a prophetic action, symbolic of the Lord's suffering unto death for others, and the second a moralistic interpretation. The former (i.e., vv 4–11) he believes to be prior and deriving from the Evangelist, the latter (vv 12–20) a later interpretation, deriving from an editor of the Johannine school, perhaps the same one as he who added chaps. 15–17 to 13:31–14:31 (2:560–62). This kind of solution is viewed with favor by recent exegetes, and will be found in Schnackenburg (3:10–15), Becker, who views the editor as the "ecclesiastical redactor" (2:419–30), and Thyen, who however judges "ecclesiastical redactor" to be a misnomer, and thinks that the "editor" was none other than the Evangelist ("Johannes 13 und die 'kirchliche Redaction' . . . ," 343–56).

It is a complicated matter. Not all have been persuaded of the rightness of rigorously distinguishing two diverse interpretations and then of assigning them to different writers. Lindars considers that all the editing is the work of the Evangelist, as elsewhere in this Gospel (447), and Barrett likewise affirms, "The combination of the two themes is a characteristic piece of Johannine theology" (437). Bultmann himself stressed that the two interpretations are not mutually exclusive, and that far from wishing to exclude the earlier interpretation the Evangelist desired to establish it: "It is the task of the exegesis to demonstrate the inner unity of the two interpretations" (462). This is the more clearly perceived when we see that "sacramental," or even "theological" over against "moralistic" is a false way of relating the two parts of the narrative; if the act of the footwashing is a parable of the stooping of the Son of God to the self-sacrifice on the cross, the call to the disciples is to walk in the same steps, much as in Mark 8:34. With this Haenchen agreed, and commented, "To say that this is only something ethical, but lies beneath the religious, is to bring the whole Johannine theology into confusion" (466). We have in brief compass in John 13:1–20 a phenomenon similar to the Evangelist's procedure in the "Book of Signs," where events are narrated and interpreted through dialogue and discourse; but the events are significant *in themselves*, and the discourses expound their inherent meaning (this is especially plain in the highly significant events of the turning of water into wine and the cleansing of the temple in chap. 2, as also in the two signs of 6:1–20). The account in vv 4–20 in its totality is a ὑπόδειγμα, an "example" with a theological significance of infinite dimensions. With Dodd we may view it as akin to the early "pronouncement stories," with emphasis, however, on the *action* rather than on the words which apply the action (*Historical Tradition,* 62–63).

3. In vv 21–30 a brief dialogue of dramatic intensity takes place, wherein Jesus both makes known that one of the disciples at the table will betray him and actually precipitates the act of betrayal by his words in v 27b.

On the assumption that the passage is based on the passion narrative available to the Fourth Evangelist, Bultmann regarded the source as containing vv 21b–27a, 30, the additions being due to the Evangelist (these include v 21a; the phrase

"whom Jesus loved" in v 23; the comment of vv 28–29, which Bultmann considered
to clash with vv 23–26; and the concluding comment in v 30, "It was night,"
479–81). Haenchen was dissatisfied with this. On the one hand he suspected the
concept of "a disciple whom Jesus loved" (in his estimate a curious idea, as though
Jesus loved only *one* disciple!), and on the other hand he found repulsive the
notion that Jesus gave to Judas a "magical morsel," with which Satan entered
into Judas. He stated that through the insertion of vv 23–27a "one of the most
astounding scenes of the Fourth Gospel has been ruined through a foolishly operative redaction" (463). For him, therefore, the original narrative consisted simply
of vv 21–22, 28–30. Becker inclines to a similar view, but more cautiously defines
the narrative as consisting of vv 21–22, 26–27, 30, characterizing it as "a tradition-
historical variant of Mark 14:18–21" (2:431). The views of these latter authors
are bound up with wider convictions on the impossibility of the Gospel deriving
from one so close to the historical Jesus as the Beloved Disciple, especially as
depicted in v 23. But the narrative is susceptible of a simpler reading than they
(especially Haenchen) have given it. The suggestion that the account had its origin
in the Johannine passion narrative is widely accepted (including by Becker); the
conviction that it was amplified by the Evangelist in the light of information available
to him is plausible, not least in the light of other passages in the Gospel wherein
the Beloved Disciple features (for a review of the references in the Gospel to the
Beloved Disciple and a discussion of their significance, see the Introduction,
pp. lxx–lxxv).

Comment

JESUS WASHES THE FEET OF HIS DISCIPLES (13:1–20)

The introductory clauses (vv 1–3) are frequently viewed as abnormally
overloaded, due to the work of an editor or editors on an earlier simple
text (cf. Becker: "Vv 1–3 as a single sentence-period is a monster that can
hardly have come from one hand," 2:419). Its length and complicated nature
are due in part, as Grossouw pointed out, to its forming "a minor prologue,
introducing the second 'book' of the gospel" ("A Note on John 13:1–3,"
127), but also to the author's desire to emphasize the extraordinary nature
of the event now to be described. It is evident that vv 1–3 contain the chief
elements of the Johannine theology: Jesus' knowledge of "the hour" (cf. 12:23;
17:1), his love for his own (1:11), the Father's placing all things into his
hands (3:35), the fact that he had come from God and was going to God
(16:28), the devil's opposition to God's work in Christ, particularly through
Judas Iscariot (12:31; 13:27). R. H. Strachan commented, "John makes use
of this massing of theological propositions in order to bring out the great
truth that this divine self-consciousness of Jesus, confronted by the final assault
of the devil directed through his instrument Judas, manifested itself not in
a sovereign display of omnipotence, but in an amazing act of self-humiliation,
described in vv 4–5" (265).

1 The "hour" of Jesus was that for which he came into this world (12:27);
the hour wherein God would glorify Jesus and Jesus would glorify God through
a death for the world's salvation (12:24–26); the hour of judgment for the
world and defeat of the devil and of the exaltation of Jesus to exercise the
divine sovereignty (12:31–32); hence the hour of his "crossing over" from

this world to the Father's side (17 5). Such is the context wherein he shows to his own his "love to the limit." Inasmuch as "his own" include all who belong to him, this demonstration of love embraces them as well as those who immediately received this ministry of love.

2 For an instructive parallel to the language of v 2 cf. Rev 17:17. In the NT "heart" primarily relates to man's thinking, but includes his volition; hence "a heart moved by the devil wills what the devil wills" (Schlatter, 279). The reference to Judas in this "minor prologue," anticipating his further mention in vv 18–19 and the scene in vv 21–30, is an indication of the shock to the primitive Church that Jesus was betrayed to his enemies by an *apostle*, who proved to be an instrument of the devil. His appearance in this introduction serves to contrast his appalling action with the humble and loving service of Jesus, and sets the latter in yet greater relief.

3 The knowledge of Jesus that his hour had come to depart to the Father (v 1) is repeated with two significant variations: he had *come from God*, with the Father's commission and authority; and *the Father had put all things in his hands*, therefore he was empowered to fulfill the sovereign will of God in judgment and salvation, a sovereignty which the world and the devil himself cannot destroy but only subserve.

4–5 The menial nature of footwashing in Jewish eyes is seen in its inclusion among works which Jewish slaves should not be required to do (*Mekh Exod.* 21.2.82a, based on Lev 25:39); the task was reserved for Gentile slaves and for wives and children. (It is recounted in *Pe'a* 1.15c.14 that the mother of Rabbi Ishmael wished to wash his feet on his return from the synagogue, but he refused to allow her to perform so demeaning a work; she on her part requested the court of rabbis to rebuke him for not allowing her the honor! See Str-B 1:707.) The action of Jesus in removing his outer garment and tying a towel around him underscores the humiliation of his action; the Midrash on Gen 21:14 states that when Abraham sent Hagar away he gave her a bill of divorce, and took her shawl and girded it around her loins "that people should know that she was a slave" (Str-B 2:557).

6 The opening words in Peter's statement produce an extraordinary sequence: κύριε, σύ μου . . . , "Master, you—my . . . !" The impression is given of Peter spluttering in astonishment and incomprehension! It is strangely akin, however, to his objection to Jesus' announcement of his impending rejection, sufferings, and death through the Jewish leaders (Mark 8:32–33); both occasions manifest a real concern for the Master but a total lack of understanding of his actions.

7 To what point of time does μετὰ ταῦτα refer? After completing the footwashing (cf. vv 12–15)? After Easter (cf. 2:22; 12:16)? Or after Pentecost (cf. 16:12–13)? In all probability the Evangelist had all these in mind; the words of Jesus in vv 12–15 required the cross and resurrection and increasing illumination by the Holy Spirit to bring out their full significance for thought and life.

8 In response to Peter's emphatic rejection of Jesus' service to him Jesus gives a startling revelation of the gravity of his action: "If I do not wash you, you will have no part with me" (μετ' ἐμοῦ, not ἐν ἐμοί, as, e.g., in 15:2–10). μέρος is used among Jews of having a part in an inheritance, notably in the promised land, and then eschatologically in the kingdom of God (cf. Luke 15:12; Matt 24:51; Rev 20:6; and for the thought here, Luke 22:29–30). The concept of "a part with me" is developed in 14:3; 17:24.

9–10 Peter's plea that Jesus wash his hands and head, as well as his feet, simply compounds his failure to perceive the nature of Jesus' action. Jesus' reply to him indicates that the washing of his feet is the equivalent of a bath: "He who has had a *bath* does not need a *wash*, for he is completely clean"; it is therefore wholly needless for Jesus to wash his hands and head. The action of Jesus is parabolic of the greater cleansing that he is about to achieve through his redemptive death, by which his disciples (and all who are to believe through them, 17:20) will be granted not only remission of guilt, but a part with him in the eternal kingdom.

For the distinction, generally acknowledged by scholars, between λούω (= bathe) and νίπτω (= wash or rinse) see F. Hauck, *TDNT* 4:946–47 and BGD, 480–81. The linguistic distinction is admittedly not always maintained by Greek writers, and in view of the Evangelist's fondness for synonyms it is denied by Barrett to obtain here; nevertheless Barrett acknowledges the chief point of the utterance in v 10: he who has been truly washed by Christ needs no further washings (442).

It is significant that Jesus qualifies the statement, "You are clean" with the words "but not all of you." All the disciples received the sign of cleansing and a part with Jesus through his death and resurrection; why was it not effective for Judas? Here we must recall that the assertion ὑμεῖς καθαροί ἐστε occurs once more (and only once!) in this Gospel, namely, in 15:3: "You are already clean *on account of the word that I have spoken to you.*" The two applications of the statement are complementary; they illustrate a fundamental assumption of the Gospel that the "word" and the "service" of Jesus are inseparable; the revelation that he brings from God is through word and deed—through incarnation, sign, death, and resurrection as exegeted by the Lord and by the Spirit he sends. Self-evidently, the word spoken and enacted must be *received* and *believed* if its effect is to be for life in the kingdom of God and not for loss of the kingdom (cf. 3:16–21). So it comes about that while all the disciples are "washed" by Jesus, not all are "clean," for among them stands the betrayer, who has rejected the word both spoken and enacted by Jesus.

Does the Evangelist wish the reader of the Gospel to see in the footwashing a reference to baptism and/or the Lord's Supper? An ancient (but by no means unanimous) tradition has seen allusions to both, notably in v 10, which is thought to speak of *two* washings: the first a bath by which one is made wholly clean, and which refers to the decisive cleansing from sin in baptism, without which one has no part with Jesus, the other a lesser cleansing, which (on the basis of the longer reading) is needful for sins committed subsequent to baptism and which are remitted through the Lord's Supper. This interpretation is believed by Cullmann to be so luminously clear that (in his estimate) it demonstrates the authenticity of the longer reading of v 10 (*Early Christian Worship* [London: SCM, 1953] 108–9). As we have seen (in the *Notes* on v 10), most textual critics have not been convinced of this luminous clarity. In particular, it is difficult to recognize any reference to the Eucharist, even in the longer reading of v 10. As J. Michl observed, "A footwashing would be a quite remarkable symbol for the tasting of the flesh and blood of Jesus" ("Der Sinn der Fusswaschung," 707). But what of baptism? Westcott was content to see in the footwashing a "foreshadowing" of Christian baptism (2:150). Bauer echoed a sentiment of earlier writers: this action was needful for the apostles, for otherwise they were not baptized (167, a thought to be pondered by any who fail to see baptism in the footwashing)! Bousmard ("Le lavement des pieds," 13–17), Dodd (*Interpretation,* 401), Barrett (436), and Brown (566–68, apparently) agree that the footwashing mirrors the sacramental act of baptism. Others find it needful to make modifications of this view. Sanders interprets the footwashing seen as a "bath," the (primary) cleansing accomplished through the death of Jesus, but in the footwashing viewed as a "wash," the token sacramental washing of baptism (308). Von Campenhausen argued that the footwashing suitably represents Christian baptism, since from the beginning it was administered by affusion, with the candidate standing in water up to his ankles: the desire for the application of more water (head and hands) reflects the objection by followers of John the Baptist that true baptism should be by immersion of the whole body; the footwashing by Jesus affirmed the necessity of baptism for all, and the adequacy of baptism as practiced in the Church ("Zur Auslegung von Joh 13, 6–10," 261–70). J. A. T. Robinson believed that if there is any sacramental reference in the footwashing it should be seen as "the act of universal baptism that Jesus is about to accomplish in his death, which in turn is to be the ground of the Church's sacramental action (the 'washing') and will make it sufficient for salvation"; in his view, however, the primary meaning of the passage is the necessity for disciples to drink the cup of Jesus and be baptized with his baptism, as Mark 10:32–45 teaches ("The Significance of the Footwashing," 144–45). Lohmeyer rejected all these interpretations and saw in the footwashing the eschatological word and deed of Jesus that brings cleansing, over against Jewish priestly action and the inheritance of temple and nation; by this act the disciples were *consecrated* to be companions of Jesus in the eschatological fulfillment and set apart for the calling of apostleship ("Die Fusswaschung," 83–86); Dodd inclined to a similar view (in his review of Cullmann's *Early Christian Worship* in *JEH* [1952] 219).

A secondary reference to baptism in the Evangelist's presentation of the footwashing is certainly possible, but in the view of an increasing majority of expositors improbable. On the one hand it smacks too much of the tendency to read baptism wherever water is mentioned—not only in the Gospel but in the Bible (Cullmann, for example, finds allusions to baptism in John 4:14 and 7:37–38, recalling that in certain Gnostic sects the baptismal water was *drunk* [*Early Christian Worship,* 82]; it is true that baptismal water came to be popularly regarded as good medicine, but can we seriously believe that the Evangelist had such thoughts in mind in those passages?). On the other hand it is evident that the emphasis in the narrative is Christological rather than sacramental in a narrow sense; it points directly to the redemptive death of Jesus rather than the rite which is a reflection of it. Interestingly Schnackenburg, who once advocated the baptismal interpretation of the footwashing, subsequently abandoned it; he wrote, "His external act has a very deep inner meaning, as Peter begins to sense, but it would be wrong to infer more from Jesus' suggestion than the fact that his giving of himself in death and the saving activity of that death are represented in this 'washing.' . . . The washing of the disciples' feet is interpreted in the Christological and soteriological sense as a symbolic action in which Jesus makes his offering of himself in death graphic and effective, not in a sacramental manner, but by virtue of his love, which his disciples experience to the extreme limit" (3:19–20). Such is the conclusion reached by G. Richter in his review of the interpretation of the footwashing through the centuries (*Die Fusswaschung im Johannesevangelium*), esp. 295–98; similarly Hoskyns, 436–37; Bultmann, 469–70; Lightfoot, 273; Blank 2:24; Haenchen, 458; Becker 2:425).

12–15 What Jesus has *done* for the disciples (v 12) is explained in terms of example: if he whom they acknowledge as "Teacher" and "Master" (revered terms) stooped to perform a slave's task for them, how much more readily should the disciples do the like for each other! The καθὼς ἐγώ . . . καὶ ὑμεῖς ("just as I . . . you also") recalls the use of the formula in 13:34: Christlike, Christ-inspired love will enable fellow believers so to act toward one another.

16 The comparison of v 13 is deepened by a saying drawn from the tradition of Jesus' sayings (cf. Matt 10:24); here "student" and "teacher" are replaced by "slave" and "master," and "one sent" along with the "superior who sends" him.

17 The beatitude follows on v 15 (v 16 is by way of parenthesis); it declares the (eschatological) happiness of those who not only *know* the significance of what Jesus has done for them, but who *live* in the light of it and in obedience to his call. The necessity of both knowing (hearing) and doing the will of God is emphasized throughout the Bible, not least by Jesus himself (cf., e.g., Matt 7:21–23, 24–27, which applies to the whole range of Jesus' teaching; Matt 23:1–3 and the woes of vv 13–36; and cf. James 1:22–25—and his whole letter!).

18 The first clause calls to mind the last clause of v 10. The scripture cited (Ps 41:9) aptly expresses the terrible truth that it was none other than one who "shared bread" with the Lord, i.e., a close companion of his, who handed him over to his enemies. In Eastern culture, where sharing bread and salt bound people together in covenant support, such betrayal signified the depth of depravity. E. F. F. Bishop interprets (through his experience in Israel) "lifting up the heel" as signifying "a revelation of contempt, treachery, even animosity"; if this were applied to Judas, as well as his sharing bread with Jesus, it would suggest that "in his inmost attitudes he really despised his Master" ("He That Eateth Bread with Me," 382–83).

19 Nevertheless the Lord was not taken by surprise by this treachery; he knew his betrayer (cf. 6:71), and declared it, and did not turn aside from his path, for he knew also that the Father had "given all things into his hands" (v 3); Judas and the powers of evil could but contribute to the accomplishment of God's saving purpose for which Jesus was sent.

How is the explanation of vv 12–20 to be related to that in vv 6–10? Schnackenburg observes that the thought of Jesus' death and the disciples' share in his glory has no place in vv 12–20; it appears to have been forgotten; this second explanation is independent of the first and is to be attributed to a later editor (3:23). This is a doubtful deduction from the evidence. However much redaction has taken place in vv 12–20, the writer could no more have forgotten the content of vv 6–10 than the reader who reads the passage now. It must have been present to his mind. The paradoxical nature of the footwashing remains transparent in vv 13–20: first it is the Teacher and the Master who performs the slave's task; then the Master of his slaves and the Sender of the messenger; and finally the reminder is given that behind the Sender, Jesus, stands none other than the Father who sent him. Every Jew would recognize in the last utterance (v 20) the maxim, "One who is sent is as he who sent him." The saying fittingly concludes the pericope, for it harks back to the introductory sentences that place the footwashing on the background of the mission of Jesus, who came from God and goes back to God. When the second explanation is seen as *complementary* to the first, the aspect of the footwashing as ὑπόδειγμα, "example," is given an immensity of height and depth, and of motive and urgency, for the example of humble service is seen to be that of the Lord who has stooped from the glory of heaven to the death of the cross for the salvation of mankind; the καθὼς ἐγὼ ἐποίησα . . . καὶ ὑμεῖς ποιῆτε of v 15 ("that you should do just as I have done to you") then becomes a colossal, awe-inspiring example to follow. Moreover it is more than example and model; it provides the possibility of acting in accordance with it. "Know what I have done to you!" says Jesus (reading for the moment the question as an imperative!). The cleansing and the gift of a "part" with him is redemptive and renewing, enabling the model to be reduplicated. Moreover, the gift of a "part" with Jesus means *koinonia* with him in the kingdom of God; carrying out like action among the disciples strengthens and deepens the *koinonia* with each other created by the Lord's redemptive act and gift of his Spirit. Bultmann is therefore right in seeing that *both* interpretations of the footwashing have to do with the community (*koinonia*) created by Jesus' "service": "The explicit theme of the first section is the fellowship with Jesus; this is shown to be grounded in . . . the service rendered by Jesus. . . . The second section adds that this fellowship of the disciples with Jesus at the same time opens up a fellowship amongst themselves, and that for the former to exist the latter must be made a reality through the disciples' action. . . . Thus *13:1–20 describes the founding of the community and the law of its being*" (478–79). The unity of the passage, accordingly, must be retained.

THE EXPOSURE OF THE BETRAYER (13:21–30)

21 A vague announcement of the impending betrayal of Jesus has already been made in vv 18–19. Jesus now makes a clear and emphatic statement (he "bore witness"), impelled by an overwhelming horror and agitation of spirit as he contemplated what was to take place (on ἐταράχθη τῷ πνεύματι see *Comment* on 12:27, the "Johannine Gethsemane"). The earlier passage showed that the intentions of Judas were known to Jesus; here the betrayer is exposed, and confronted in such a manner as to precipitate a decision either to renounce his deadly purpose or to proceed with it without delay.

23 It is in this context that the Evangelist makes his first explicit mention of the "beloved disciple." Two observations may be made at this juncture: first, he is introduced through Peter addressing a question to him; most of the subsequent appearances of this disciple are in association with Peter, generally to his advantage, but never denigrating Peter; secondly, the first thing said about him is not that Jesus loved him, but that he reclined ἐν τῷ κόλπῳ τοῦ Ἰησοῦ, "close to the breast of Jesus." This (to us) curious statement is explained by the situation of the company sharing in the meal. Instead of being seated about a table (*à la* Leonardo da Vinci!) the custom of reclining on cushions around a low table was being observed (this occurred only on special occasions, but it was mandatory for the Passover meal); the participants reclined on their left sides, supporting themselves with their left arm, leaving the right arm free; Jesus as the host would have been slightly forward of the rest; if the Beloved Disciple, who will have been on his right, leaned back to speak to Jesus he would literally have had his head at his breast. That he made such a movement at Peter's behest is implied in v 25: ἀναπεσών (literally "falling up") clearly means "leaning back." The use of the phrase ἐν τῷ κόλπῳ Ἰησοῦ, however, almost certainly is intended to recall the similar phrase in the prologue, where it is stated, "The only Son ὁ ὢν εἰς τὸν κόλπον τοῦ πατρός ('who is in the bosom of the Father') has expounded him." The Evangelist introduces the Beloved Disciple as standing in an analogous relation to Jesus as Jesus to the Father with respect to the revelation he was sent to make known; behind this gospel is the testimony of one who was "close to the heart" of Jesus. (For further discussion on the Beloved Disciple, see the *Introduction*, pp. lxx–lxxv).

In response to Peter's signs to inquire of Jesus as to whom he was referring, the disciple leans back to put the question to him. The fact that he so changed his position, along with the subsequent incomprehension of the disciples as to the import of Jesus' words to Judas (vv 28–29), suggests that both the disciple's question and Jesus' answer were spoken quietly; the rest of the group accordingly did not learn the identity of the betrayer, and Peter did not have his curiosity satisfied at that time.

26 There is some uncertainty as to the nature of τὸ ψωμίον, literally "the little bit," that Jesus dipped in the dish. The term was commonly used of bread, sometimes of meat. In the Passover meal green and bitter herbs were dipped in a dish of fruit puree, but this took place in an introductory course, prior to the main meal, and the impression is given by the Evangelist that the meal by this time was well advanced (cf. v 2). It is likely that Jesus dipped a piece of bread into the dish and gave that to Judas (possibly we are meant to recall the citation in v 18: "He who eats my bread lifted up his heel against me").

27 On the ground of the Evangelist's comment, "After the piece of bread Satan entered into him," it is assumed by some exegetes that the action and the word of Jesus had a negative intention. Schlatter, for example, thought that by this means Jesus nullified his fellowship with Judas, with the effect virtually of handing him over to Satan (exactly as in 1 Cor 5:5, *Das Evangelium nach Johannes*, 286). Similarly, Wrede viewed the bread given to Judas as a kind of Satanic sacrament (cited by Bultmann, 482 n.6). More recently Haenchen spoke contemptuously of "the magical morsel with which Satan entered into Judas," viewing the incident as an intrusion due to a "coarse editing" (463), while Becker considers that Judas is made "a marionette in the plan of salvation" (2:432). Such interpretations are highly unlikely. That Jesus, the host, handed to Judas bread that he had dipped in the dish is more plausibly a sign of favor than of hostility. In such a setting the action and the word would have been deeply significant. Jesus gives to Judas a sign of friendship, despite knowing the intention of his heart. His statement, "What you are about to do, do quickly," has the effect of setting Judas in the place of decision: he must make up his mind either to respond to Jesus' goodwill, and so repent of his plan to betray him, or to spurn it and carry out his intentions. If this be a correct reading of the situation, no man in all history was more truly "put on the spot" than Judas in that moment. But with the morsel "Satan entered. . . ." Newbigin commented, "The final act of love becomes, with a terrible immediacy, the decisive moment of judgment, which has been the central theme in John's account of the public ministry of Jesus. . . . So the final gesture of affection precipitates the final surrender of Judas to the power of darkness" (173).

30 The decision taken, Judas goes out. The Evangelist adds, "and it was night," on which W. F. Howard remarked, "Yet the paschal moon was shining at the full!" (*IB* 8:690). Judas was enveloped in an unillumined night, never to be relieved. He was on the way to his own place (Acts 1:25).

Explanation

1. Our consideration of the footwashing shows that we are not compelled to select a theological or moral interpretation of the event. We have here a clear case of "both-and" rather than "either-or" (the New Testament in any case does not know a theology without ethics, or ethics without theology). The necessity of submission to the service of the Servant of the Lord (v 8) carries with it the corollary of walking in the Servant's way. So also the mutual service of love between the followers of the Servant is rooted in his redemptive service, alike as source, inspiration, and pattern.

2. The footwashing is rightly seen as denoting the *katabasis,* the "descent," of the Word. If there is a parallel here with the Gnostic descent of the Redeemer, its nature and purpose are vastly different from the latter: the *katabasis* of the Lord is a descent to the death of the cross, that the world may be delivered from sin—its defilement, guilt, and bondage, and so released for life in the kingdom of God, which entails adoption of the pattern of service displayed in the Redeemer. It is noteworthy that in this pictorial presentation of the mission of Jesus we have the one clear approach in this Gospel to the concept of the death of Jesus, as a humiliation (in contrast to its depiction in terms of glory). The *anabasis* ("ascent") is not mentioned, but is presupposed in the reference to the disciples' having a "part" with Jesus in the kingdom of God. In this respect the footwashing is clearly parallel to Phil 2:1–11, the hymn of the descent and ascent of the Servant-Redeemer set in the context provided by the Apostle; the latter makes it clear that the way of the Servant is the way of his followers also (cf. Phil 2:3, 4, 5; G. F. Hawthorne, *Philippians,* WBC 43 [Waco, TX: Word Books, 1983] 78).

3. It is not to be overlooked that the footwashing is more than a simple parable of the greater act of cleansing achieved by Jesus through his death; it is itself an act of love to the limit, as the Evangelist recognized (13:1). Whereas its suitability to represent the love that gave itself on the cross is evident, the act may also be viewed as representative of all the actions of the love of Jesus in his ministry (so Michl, "Der Sinn der Fusswaschung," 701). It is precisely because it is a concrete embodiment of the love that gave itself to people and for people that we must not limit the "example" to acts of literally washing people's feet. Such a mode of obeying the injunction of vv 14–15 has admittedly been carried out by groups of Christians through the centuries, and is done by some to this very day, regardless of the unsuitability of the action in lands outside the Middle East and for people wearing

different clothing from that of first-century disciples. The example of "love to the limit" calls for love in action that expresses itself in limitless ways.

4. The enigma of Judas has inspired a multitude of endeavors to explain the riddle of his behavior. We may doubt that the Evangelist would have been impressed by most of them. He saw in Judas a fearful example of one who walked with the Lord but finally obeyed the voice of the Tempter. While he recognized in the actions of Judas an unwitting means of fulfilling the redemptive purpose of God, it may be assumed that the apologetic purpose was not the primary motive in recording the scene of 13:21–30; more likely it was the desire to warn readers to beware of taking a like path as Judas did. That there were those in the churches linked with the Evangelist who listened to voices viewed as of Antichrist is apparent from the Johannine epistles (cf. esp. 1 John 2:15–27; 3:4–10; 4:1–6). The story of Judas epitomizes for the readers of the Gospel the message of the Pauline dictum: "Let anyone who thinks that he stands take heed lest he fall" (1 Cor 10:12).

2. The Departure and the Return of Jesus (13:31–14:31)

Bibliography

Bacon B. W. " 'In My Father's House Are Many Mansions' (John 14.2)." *ExpTim* 43 (1931–32) 477–78. **Barrett, C. K.** " 'The Father Is Greater than I' (John 14:28): Subordinationist Christology in the New Testament." *Neues Testament und Kirche.* FS R. Schnackenburg. 144–59. **Boismard, M. E.** "L'évolution du thème eschatologique dans les traditions johanniques." *RB* 68 (1961) esp. 518–23. **Borgen, P.** "God's Agent in the Fourth Gospel." *Religions in Antiquity.* FS E. R. Goodenough. Leiden: Brill, 1968. 137–47. **Boring, M. E.** "The Influence of Christian Prophecy on the Johannine Portrayal of the Paraclete and Jesus." *NTS* 25 (1978) 113–23. **Caird, G. B.** "The Glory of God in the Fourth Gospel: An Exercise in Biblical Semantics." *NTS* 15 (1968–69) 265–77. **Cerfaux, L.** "La charité fraternelle et le retour du Christ (Jn xiii.33–38)." *ETL* 24 (1948) 321–32. **Charlier, C.** "La presence dans l'absence (Jean 13, 31–14, 31)." *BVC* 2 (1953) 61–75. **Dodd, C. H.** *Interpretation.* 390–423. **Fensham, F. C.** " 'I am the Way, the Truth and the Life': John 14:6." *Neot* 2 (1968) 81–88. **Fischer, G.** *Die himmlische Wohnungen: Untersuchungen zu Joh 14.2f.* Bern/Frankfurt: Lang, 1975. **George, A.** "L'Evangile Jn 14, 23–30: Les venues de Dieux aux croyants." *AsSeign* 51 (1963) 63–71. **Gollwitzer, H.** "Ausser Christus kein Heil? (Joh 14.6)." *Antijudaismus im Neuen Testament?* München: Kaiser, 1967. 171–96. **Gundry, R. H.** "In My Father's House Are Many Monai." *ZNW* 58 (1967) 68–72. **Johnston, G.** *The Spirit-Paraclete in the Gospel of John,* SNTSMS 12. Cambridge: 1970. **Kugelman, R.** "The Gospel for Pentecost (Jn. 14:23–31)." *CBQ* 6 (1944) 259–75. **Kundsin, K.** "Die Wiederkunft Jesu in den Abschiedsreden des Johannesevangelium." *ZNW* 33 (1934) 210–15. **Lazure, N.** "Louange à Fils de l'homme et commandement nouveau: Jn 13:31–33a.34–35." *AsSeign* 26 (1973) 73–80. **McCasland, S. V.** "The Way." *JBL* 77 (1958) 222–30. **Moloney, F. J.** *Son of Man.* 186–202. **Pas, H. L.** *"The Glory of the Father: A Study in St. John 13–17.* London: 1935. **Porsch, F.** *Pneuma und Wort: Ein exegetischer Beitrag zur Pneumatologie* *des Johannesevangeliums.* Frankfurt: Knecht, 1974. Esp. 240–67, 305–24. **Potterie, I. de la.** "L'Esprit Saint des l'évangile de Jean." *NTS* 18 (1972) 448–51. ———. "Je suis la voie, la vérité et la vie (Jn 14,6)." *NRT* 88 (1966) 917–42. **Reese, J. M.** "Literary Structure of John 13.31–14.31, 16.5–6, 16.16–33." *CBQ* 34 (1972) 321–31. **Riossetto, G.** "La route vers e Père: Jn 14,1–12." *AsSeign* 26 (1973) 18–30. **Schaefer, O.** "Der Sinn der rede Jesu von den vieler Wohnungen in seines Vaters Haus und von dem Weg zu ihm (Joh 14, 1–7)." *ZNW* 32 (1933) 210–17. **Schnackenburg, R.** "Johannes 14,7." *Studies in NT Language and Text.* FS G. D. Kilpatrick. Ed. J. K. Elliott. Leiden: Brill, 1976. 345–56. **Segovia, F. F.** "The Structure, *Tendenz* and *Sitz-im-Leben* of John 13:31–14:31." *JBL* 104 (1985) 471–93. **Smalley, S. S.** "The Christ-Christian Relationship in Paul and John." *Pauline Studies.* FS F. F. Bruce. Ed. D. A. Hagner & M. J. Harris. Exeter: Paternoster Press, 1980. 95–105. **Stagg, F.** "The Farewell Discourses: John 13–17." *RevExp* 62 (1965) 458–72. **Widengren, G.** "En la maison de mon Père sont demeures nombreuses (Jn 14 2)." *SEÅ* 37/38 (1972–73) 9–15.

Translation

[31] *When he went out Jesus said,*
Now the Son of Man has been glorified,
and God has been glorified in him;
[32] *if God has been glorified in him* [a]
God will also glorify him in himself,
and he will glorify him immediately.

[33] *"My children, I am with you only a little longer; you will look for me, and just as I told the Jews, 'Where I am going you cannot come,' I now say it to you also.* [34] *I give you a new command: Love one another;* [b] *as I have loved you, you also must love one another.* [35] *By this everyone will come to know that you are my disciples, if you have love among one another."*

[36] *Simon Peter says to him, "Master, where are you going?" Jesus replied to him, "Where I am going, you cannot follow me now, but you will follow later."* [37] *Peter says to him "Master,* [c] *why cannot I follow you now? I will lay down my life for your sake."*

[38] *Jesus replies, "You will lay down your life for my sake? Amen, amen I tell you, the cock will not crow before you deny me three times."*

[14:1] *"Do not let your hearts* [d] *continually be in turmoil; keep on believing in God, and keep on believing* [e] *in me.* [2] *In my Father's house there are many dwellings: if it were otherwise I would have told you, for I am going to make ready a place for you.* [3] *And if I go and make a place ready for* [f] *you I shall come again and take you with me to my home, that you also may be where I am.* [4] *And the way to where I am going you know."* [g] [5] *Thomas says to him, "Master, we don't know where you are going to; how can we know the way?"*

[6] *Jesus says to him, "I am the way, and the truth, and the life; none comes to the Father except through me.* [7] *If you men have come to know* [h] *me, you will know* [h] *my Father also; and assuredly* [i] *you do know him and have seen him."* [8] *Philip says to him, "Master, show us the Father, and that will be enough for us."* [9] *Jesus says to him, "Have I been so long a time with you and you have not come to know me, Philip? Anyone who has seen me has seen the Father. How is it that you are saying, 'Show us the Father'?* [10] *You do believe, don't you, that I am in the Father, and the Father is in me? The words that I am telling you all I am not speaking of my own accord; but it is the Father dwelling in me who is doing*

his works. [11] *Believe me that I am in the Father and the Father is in me; otherwise, believe*[j] *because of the works themselves.*

[12] *"Amen, amen I tell you, whoever believes in me will do the works that I do; indeed, he will do greater works than these, because I am going to the Father,* [13] *and whatever you ask in my name I will do, in order that the Father may be glorified in the Son;* [14] *if you ask me anything in my name I will do it.*[k]

[15] *"If you love me, you will keep*[l] *my commands;* [16] *and I shall ask the Father and he will give you another Paraclete that he may be with you forever,* [17] *the Spirit of truth, whom the world cannot receive, because it does not see him nor does it know him; but you are to know*[m] *him because he will dwell*[m] *with you and will be*[m] *in you.*

[18] *"I shall not leave you orphans,*[n] *I shall come back to you.* [19] *After a little while the world will see me no longer, but you will see me; because I live you too will live.* [20] *On that day you will come to know that I am in my Father, and you in me and I in you.*

[21] *"Whoever has my commands and keeps them is the one who loves me; and whoever loves me will be loved by my Father, and I shall love him and reveal myself to him."*

[22] *Judas, not the Iscariot,*[o] *says to him, "Master, whatever has happened, that you are about to reveal yourself to us and not to the world?"*

[23] *Jesus replied to him, "If anyone loves me he will keep my word, and my Father will love him, and we shall come to him, and we shall make our dwelling with him.* [24] *Whoever does not love me does not keep my words; and the word that you are hearing is not mine, but the word of the Father who sent me.*

[25] *"I have spoken these things to you while remaining with you;* [26] *"But the Paraclete, the Holy Spirit, whom the Father will send in my name, will teach you everything, and will remind you of everything that I have said to you.*

[27] *"Peace—I bequeath it to you. My peace I give to you. Not as the world gives it do I give it to you. Stop letting your heart be disturbed, and don't let it be cowardly.* [28] *You heard me say 'I am going away, and I am coming back to you.' If you loved me you would have been glad, because I am going to the Father, for the Father is greater than I.*

[29] *"And now I have told you before it happens, that when it does happen you may believe.* [30] *I shall not talk much longer with you, for the prince of this world is coming; he has no claim over me,* [31] *but the world must know*[p] *that I love the Father, and do just as the Father commanded me. Rise up, let us go from this place!"*

Notes

[a] The first clause of v 32 is omitted by the important MSS P[66] ℵ* B C* D L W etc. The omission, however, could well have occurred through homoioteleuton, or the clause may have been deleted through considering it redundant. Metzger points out that "there is a logical connection between the earlier and subsequent glorification, and the step-parallelism is characteristically Johannine" (242).

[b] ἵνα ἀγαπᾶτε is best viewed as imperatival in force; cf. 14:31.

[c] Κύριε is omitted by ℵ* 33 565 vg syr[s] cop[mss]. The strong and early support for its inclusion suggests that the omission was accidental, or that it was thought to be needless after Κύριε in v 36.

ᵈ The verbs in 14:1–4 are pl. since the disciple group is being addressed; the sing. ἡ καρδία instead of pl. is Sem. (Moulton and Turner, *Grammar* 3:23).

ᵉ While πιστεύετε in both clauses can be indicative, or first indicative and then imperative (as AV/KJV), the clear imperative suggests that the same sense is to be understood through the whole sentence.

ᶠ The translation is uncertain. ὅτι is omitted by P⁶⁵* c²ᵛⁱᵈ Δ Θ 28 700 etc., some OL MSS, Origenˡᵃᵗ TR, possibly because copyists viewed ὅτι as recitative, which is often omitted as superfluous (Metzger, 243). Interpreting it as recitative, many view the sentence as interrogative; "If it were not so, *would I have told you that* . . . ?" (so RSV, Moffatt, Bultmann, Bernard, Bauer, Hoskyns, Strathmann, Haenchen, Becker, Bruce); the difficulty of this rendering is that no clear assertion of the statement is found on the lips of Jesus earlier in the Gospel (12:26 is sometimes adduced as its basis). English versions tend to view it as a statement, either following the TR and omitting ὅτι (so AV/KJV, JB, NIV) or understanding ὅτι as "because" (so RV, NEB, NAS, Lagrange, Barrett, Morris, Lightfoot, Lindars). GNB assumes that v 2b relates both to that which precedes and to that which follows; for the justification of this see Newman and Nida, *A Translator's Handbook on the Gospel of John,* 455.

ᵍ The short reading, supported by P⁶⁶ᶜ ℵ* B C* D L W etc., appears somewhat abrupt and has been expanded so as to correspond with Thomas' observation and question in v 5. The short reading appears to be original.

ʰ ἐγνώκατε . . . γνώσεσθε has early attestation (P⁶⁶ ℵ D and the versions) and suitably balances the rest of the sentence. ἐγνώκειτε . . . ἐγνώκειτε ἄν represents an unfulfilled condition and result ("if you had known me, which you haven't, you would know my Father also, and you don't"). Has the latter formulation been due to the influence of 8:19? Or to Philip's question and Jesus' counter-question in vv 8–9?

ⁱ This is one of the instances where ἀπ᾽ ἄρτι should be read as a single term ἀπαρτί = "assuredly"; see A. Debrunner, "Über einige Lesarten der Chester Beatty Papyri des Neuen Testaments," *ConNT* 11:48.

ʲ The majority of MSS add μοι at the end of the sentence in imitation of its beginning; "the temptation is resisted" (Metzger, 244) by some of our earliest witnesses, including P⁶⁶ P⁷⁵ ℵ D L W itᶜ,ᵈ,ᵉ,ʳˡ vg syrᶜ,ᵖᵃˡ copᵐˢˢ.

ᵏ V 14 is omitted by various MSS (X f¹ 565 etc. itᵇ vgᵐˢˢ syrᶜ ˢ ᵖᵃˡ arm geo Diatessaronᶠ ˡ ᵗ). Λ* omits also the last seven words of v 13 (through homoioteleuton, passing from ποιήσω v 13 to ποιήσω v 14). The same phenomenon can have caused v 14 to be omitted (passing from ἐάν v 14 to ἐάν v 15). Was a scribe troubled that it appeared to contradict 16:23? That motive could have caused the omission of με, which has strong support (P⁶⁶ ℵ B W D θ etc.).

ˡ τηρήσετε is read by B L Ψ 1010 etc., with apparent support from MSS reading aor. subj. τηρήσητε (P⁶⁶ ℵ 060 33 etc); the imperative τηρήσατε is read by A D K W X Δ Θ Π etc.; the former agrees better with the immediately following κἀγὼ ἐρωτήσω . . . .

ᵐ There is confusion over the tenses of the verbs in the last clause of the sentence. Some important early MSS (P⁶⁶* B D* W f¹ many OL MSS syrᶜ,ᵖ,ᵖᵃˡ) read ἐστιν instead of ἔσται and understand all three verbs as present. ἔσται is supported by P⁶⁶ᶜ P⁷⁵ᵛⁱᵈ ℵ A Dᵇ f¹³ 28 etc. syrˢ,ʰ etc. Various versions go on to read μένει (present) as μενεῖ (future) along with ἔσται (it aur vg cop arm eth). The sense is best understood in reading the future tense for the last two verbs and γινώσκετε as a present with future meaning (see BDF § 33).

ⁿ ὀρφανούς lit. = "orphans," whether of deceased parents or abandoned by parents. The figure of speech was known to the Greeks (BGD cite *Phaedo* 65, p. 116a re the feelings of Socrates' friends, p. 583) and to the Jews (R. Jehoshua, *ca.* A.D. 90, on hearing an interpretation of the scripture by R. Eleazar ben Azaria, exclaimed, "Praise to you, our father Abraham, that Eleazar ben Azaria came from your loins! The generation is not orphaned in whose midst R. Eleazar dwells!" (Str-B 2:562).

ᵒ The usual variations that appear whenever the name Ἰσκαριώτης is mentioned in the text are to be seen here also. See *Notes* on 6:71 and 13:2. The Coptic reading "Judas the Cananite" evidently identifies him with Simon the Cananean (of Mark 3:18 = Matt 10:4); the Sinaitic Syriac calls him Thomas; this may well reflect the legend that makes Thomas the twin brother of Jesus, on the ground that this Judas = the brother mentioned in Mark 6:3 (also identified with the Jude who wrote the Epistle in the NT).

ᵖ ἵνα γνῷ is one of the possible examples of ἵνα introducing an imperatival clause; see the discussion in C. F. D. Moule, *An Idiom Book of NT Greek,* 144–45.

Form/Structure/Setting

1. The chief features of the discourse, 13:31–14:31, have been discussed in the introduction to the Upper Room Discourses (see pp. 222–27). Its form is that of a farewell discourse, beginning with an announcement of the glorification of Jesus in death (13:31–32) and ending with a call to depart from the Upper Room to face the final assault upon him (14:30–31). The setting is the Last Supper, which, however, is nowhere described. The structure in its broad outline is clear: 13:31–38 forms an introduction, 14:1–26 the main body of the discourse, 14:27–31 an epilogue. The detailed working out of the main themes of 14:1–26 is more controverted.

2. There is a widespread tendency to see in chap. 14 the working out of a single theme, viz., the departure and return of Jesus, stated in order to reinterpret the Church's traditional hope of the Parousia of Jesus (for a brief exposition of this view see Dodd, *Interpretation*, 395–96, 403–6). Becker ("Die Abschiedsreden im Johannesevangelium," 222–23), followed by Schnackenburg (3:58) and Segovia ("The Structure, Tendenz, and Sitz im Leben of John 13:31–14:31," 477–78) comprehend vv 4–17 under the theme of the departure of Jesus and vv 18–26 under the theme of the return of Jesus. Segovia prefers the division vv 1–3, which states the theme of the discourse; 4–14, an exposition of the departure of Jesus; 15–27, an exposition of the return of Jesus; 28–31, an epilogue. He sees in the two central sections highly intricate structures: vv 4–14 consist of three cycles (vv 4–6, 7–9, 10–14), each of which gives (*a*) a Christological statement (in vv 4, 7, 10), (*b*) a statement concerning the disciples' faith (vv 5, 8, 11) and (*c*) an expansion of the first Christological statement (vv 6, 9, 12–14); the second section has a fourfold series of three elements, (*a*) a definition of love for Jesus (vv 15, 21a, 23ab, 24), (*b*) promises to those who love Jesus (vv 16–17a, 21bc, 23cd, 25–26), (*c*) differentiation between those and the world (vv 17b-d, 18–20, 22, 27ac); the exposition accordingly presents a series of four parallel cycles, vv 15–17, 18–21, 22–23, 24–27. This analysis of the discourse is believed to make evident the Evangelist's purpose in showing that the primitive hope of the Parousia, stated in its traditional form in vv 2–3, is fulfilled in the coming of the Paraclete, through whom Jesus and the Father abide in the disciples ("Structure . . . ," 481–87).

3. The exposition of the passage must be left till later, but it should be stated here that the structural basis for this interpretation appears to be very dubious. The division of vv 4–14 into three cycles of three themes and of vv 15–27 into three cycles of four themes is artificial and requires some very implausible interpretations of the text. It is to be observed that the structure in vv 4–14 is controlled by a dialogue between Jesus and the disciples; Jesus speaks, and the disciples twice question him (through misunderstanding), thereby evoking clarifications of Jesus' meaning (note especially how vv 10–14 expand Jesus' answer to Philip in v 9). Vv 7–11 should not be brought under the rubric of the "departure" of Jesus; the passage sets forth the relation of Jesus to the Father in a manner reminiscent of the earlier discourses of the Gospel and relates to the revelation in the *earthly* life of Jesus. Certainly

vv 12–14 envisage the future, when Jesus will be with the Father, but the emphasis is on the continuing mission of the disciples in the future. Hence, the first promise of the Paraclete is set at this point (vv 15–16); the latter is given not in order to provide a restatement of the coming of Jesus, but as an encouragement of disciples in carrying out their mission. They are to have the assistance of another Paraclete, who is the *representative* of Jesus in his continuing ' absence." Undoubtedly the theme of the "coming" of Jesus binds together vv 18–23, but the concept is complex, not simple. The "coming" referred to in v 18 is explained in vv 19–20 in terms of the resurrection of Jesus: "You (unlike the world) will *see* me; because I *live,* you too will live." The language envisions the Easter event and its significance for the disciples (cf. Rev 1:17–18); in virtue of that experience the disciples will comprehend what to this point they have failed to grasp, namely the relation of Jesus to the Father (v 20, contrast vv 9–10), and they will then know the reality of life in union with the risen Lord. How this comes to pass is explained in vv 21–23: the Father in his love and the Son (in like love) will "come" to the believer and make their home (their μονή, cf. v 2) with him. Fittingly this section of the discourse (like the former) also comes to a conclusion in a promise of the sending of the Paraclete (vv 25–26); note however that he comes not in order to make this "coming" of the Father and the Son to the believer possible, but in order to *reveal* its reality and its significance ("he will teach you all things. . . .").

4. It is noteworthy that the epilogue, which takes up the language of consolation, trust, and the departure and return of Jesus, used in vv 1–3, bids the disciples to rejoice not in prospect of the return of Jesus but of his departure, since it means his return *to the Father.* Possibly there may be an echo of vv 12–14, but this conclusion forcibly reminds us that we have here a *farewell* discourse, the purpose of which is to prepare the disciples for the shock that lies ahead of them (v 29), and at the same time to encourage them. The departure of Jesus is his glorification, revealed in the Easter event, leading to the abiding of the Father and the Son in the believer, alike a perpetuation of Easter and anticipation of the Parousia, to which Jesus pledges his promise.

5. The discourse accordingly may be divided thus:

13:31–38   Introduction
    31–33   The glorification of Jesus
    34–35   The command to love
    36–38   The prediction of Peter's denial
14:1–26   The Discourse proper
    1– 3   The departure and return of Jesus
    4– 6   Jesus, the Way to God
    7–11   Jesus, the Revelation of God
    12–14   Jesus, the Power of the disciples' mission
    15–17   The coming of another Paraclete
    18–20   The coming of Jesus at Easter
    21–24   The coming of Jesus to the believer
    25–26   The Paraclete Teacher
14:27–31   Epilogue: The Bequest of Peace

Comment

INTRODUCTION (13:31–38)

The Glorification of Jesus (13:31–33)

31–32 The reaction of Jesus to the departure of Judas into the night is to be compared with his reaction to the arrival of the Greeks desiring to see him (12:20–32): the departure of the one and the arrival of the others signified the beginning of the end, the consciousness of which is inevitably intensified on the present occasion (cf. Caird: "With the departure of Judas all the actors in the drama, and Jesus in particular, are committed to their courses of action, which make the crucifixion virtually accomplished," "The Glory of God in the Fourth Gospel," 266). The sayings of Jesus in 12:23, 27, 31–32 are closely related to 13:31–32. The "now" of 12:23 is explicitly that of the "hour" of Jesus; but the hour includes not alone suffering and death but exaltation, as 12:31–32 makes clear: the glorification of the Son of Man takes place in his "lifting up" on the cross and to the throne of heaven; hence the "ruler of this world" is dethroned ("now"!) and believers are drawn to the exalted Savior. Similarly the past and future tenses of vv 31–32 are closely held together by the "Now" of v 31 and the "immediately" of v 32. It is doubtful that the first clause means that the Son of Man—Jesus—was glorified by God in his death on Good Friday and that the fourth and fifth clauses denote a later and separable glorifying of Jesus by God on Easter Sunday. God glorified the Son of Man in making his self-offering effective for the race; therein God was glorified in the perfect obedience and love of the Son, which was however at the same time a revelation of the love of God to humankind; in virtue of that act God glorifies the Son "in himself," i.e., in (his own) person, and he does it "immediately"—in the death and in the exaltation. In the whole event (note the singular!) the saving sovereignty of God is operative; it "comes" in the dying and the rising, and the redemptive dying is inconceivable apart from the rising, as the rising is from the dying. Hence it is "in Christ," crucified and risen, that we have justification (Rom 8:1), redemption (Eph 1:7) and reconciliation (2 Cor 5:17–21).

33 Twice it is recorded that Jesus told the Jews, "You will seek me . . . and where I am going you cannot come" (7:34; 8:21); on both occasions the Jews were perplexed and misunderstood the purport of the saying. The disciples are now told that they are to find themselves in a similar position, and they too are puzzled, but there the similarity ends. Jesus addresses them affectionately as "My children," an expression frequently used by Jewish teachers to their pupils (Str-B 2:559). Jesus does not tell them, as he did the Jews, that they will not find him (cf. 7:34), nor that they will die in their sins (8:21); on the contrary the discourse that follows sets forth promises which are the reverse of those warnings. Peter is told that though he cannot follow Jesus now, one day he will (v 36); the whole disciple group is assured that the departure of Jesus has in view the goal of their being with him in the Father's house forever (14:2–3); they will shortly see him again, for he will live, and so will they (14:19); this experience of the Easter revelation is to be extended to all who believe (14:21), which will be no less than an anticipation of the presence of the Lord in the Parousia (14:23). Thus "this developing train of thought links the farewell discourse to the fundamental statement in v 33" (Schnackenburg, 3:52–53).

The Command to Love (13:34–35)

The "new command" is further elaborated in 15:12–17. That its inclusion here breaks the flow of thought between vv 33 and 36–38 is no reason to consider it to be an editorial intrusion (as some maintain). Vv 31–32, 33, 34–35, 36–38 form an "agglomeration," to use a term of synoptic Gospel criticism, i.e., a series of sayings brought together by the Evangelist; here they illuminate the situation and in turn are illuminated by it. The situation and connection enable us to understand why the command to love one another is described as "now," although we know it to be rooted in the OT (Lev 19:18), and that Jesus himself drew attention to its importance as forming, with the *Shema* (Deut 6:4), the most important command of the OT (Mark 12:28 par.). Its "newness" would appear to consist in its being the Law of the new order, brought about by the redemption of God in and through Christ, intimated in vv 31–32.

The expression "new order" is deliberately ambiguous. We have in mind the era of the new covenant, established through the sacrificial self-giving of Christ and his resurrection to rule. The establishment of the new covenant is integral to the traditions of the Last Supper (cf. Mark 14:24 par.), which were perpetually remembered in the celebrations of the Lord's Supper, and therefore will have been assumed in this record of the Last Discourse of Jesus. The commands of the law were issued to Israel as their part in God's covenant with them, involving their response to his taking them to be his people whom he had "redeemed" from the slavery of Egypt (cf. esp. Exod 19:3–6). So the "new command" may be viewed as the obligation of the people of the new covenant in response to the redemptive act of God and his gracious election which made them his new people.

This basic understanding of new covenant, election, and new law is assumed in Matthew's presentation of the Sermon on the Mount (Matt 5–7). It is likely that the Sermon was compiled as a catechetical summary of the teaching of Jesus for new converts in the churches served by Matthew; he presents the teaching as given by the new and greater than Moses from a "mount," as the OT law was delivered at Sinai, and setting forth the messianic "law" for the heirs of the kingdom of God. In the spirit of Mark 12:28–31, the messianic law is reduced in our Gospel to one comprehensive law which fulfills all laws.

To speak of the *messianic* law is to be reminded that the very concept of new covenant brings to view the concept of new Exodus which introduces the kingdom of God. The new command is the rule of life for the new age, the kingdom of God, the saving sovereignty that makes people new for God's new world. This concept binds the presentation of the ministry of Jesus ("the Book of Signs") and that of his passion, death, and resurrection in the Fourth Gospel. It is not alone the law for a new *time*, but a law for a new *life*. It is the outcome of the peculiar redemption that initiates the kingdom and brings sinful men and women into it. The command follows the gift, and is possible of fulfillment only by reason of the gift.

This is part of the significance of the command to love one another "as I have loved you." It is no denigration of the OT command to love one's neighbor as oneself to acknowledge this new dimension of the command given in the Upper Room; not even love of self can possibly rise to the heights of the divine love for humankind revealed in the cross of Christ, and the noblest self-regarding love cannot compare with the outflow of love from the Redeemer who draws his own to him. The newness of the command, accordingly, springs from the eschatological reality of Christ's redemption, which is an eternal reality and holds its people in the eternal order. This is the fulfillment of the intimation in Jeremiah's prophecy, that the new covenant in the last days will be accompanied by a law written "upon their hearts"; it will be for a redeemed *and* renewed people. Such a community of Christly love will be a revelation to the world of the reality of Christ's redemption, a witness to the presence and power of the kingdom of God in the midst of the world (v 35, cf. 17:21, 23).

The Prediction of Peter's Denial (13:36–38)

The Evangelist appears to have woven two separate themes together here: (*i*) the familiar prediction that Peter is shortly to deny having any connection with Jesus; (*ii*) a prediction, unknown in other sources, that Peter one day will follow Jesus in laying down his life for him. Whereas the latter has no counterpart in the synoptic Gospels, its language and thought are reminiscent of 12:26, and it is repeated more fully in 21:18–19. The synoptic evangelists also link other sayings of Jesus with the prophecy of Peter's denial (see Mark 14:27–28; Matt 26:31–32; Luke 22:31–38); Brown suggested that "elements of what was once a larger scene have been transmitted in each of the various traditions" (2:616). Peter's questions in vv 36 and 37 show that he still fails to grasp that Jesus is about to go to the Father, and the reason for his going. But both questions reveal that he really wishes to follow Jesus, cost what it may (all the gospel accounts mention Peter's readiness to die with or for Jesus). Jesus accordingly acknowledges Peter's desire and promises that he will "follow" him, but only "later," with similar implications as the "afterwards" in v 7: Jesus must first "go away," for Peter's sake, as for that of the whole world, since what Jesus has to accomplish (for Peter, and for the rest) does not lie in Peter's power. Peter's impetuous utterance in v 37b echoes Jesus' description of the marks of a good shepherd (10:11, 15). Hoskyns commented, "Some speech of Peter such as is preserved in Mark—*If I must die with thee I will not deny thee*—seems to have been recast by the Fourth Evangelist so as to bring out a double significance: its eventual truth as well as its present falsehood" (452). By the power of the Good Shepherd's sacrifice Peter finally became a good shepherd, and followed in his Lord's footsteps.

THE DISCOURSE PROPER (14:1–26)

The Departure and Return of Jesus (14:1–3)

1 The appeal to faith, expressed first negatively and then positively, runs through the whole discourse. The "turmoil" in which the disciples could be ensnared (μὴ ταρασσέσθω) is of the kind Jesus endured as he approached the grave of Lazarus (11:23), as he faced the cross (12:27), and as he contemplated the betrayal of Judas (13:21, see *Comment* on these sayings). The distress in view is bound up with their loss (through death) of Jesus. The conjunction of the passage with the previous paragraph increases its intensity: if Peter's faith is to collapse to the point of denying his Master, what will happen to the rest of the disciples? In the face of such agitation the caution μὴ ταρασσέσθω would perhaps be fittingly rendered, "Stop letting your hearts be in turmoil." The following imperative "keep on believing in *God*" is entirely in place (rather than an indicative statement); the world may appear to have gone mad, but the disciples must continue to believe in God as the sovereign Lord of creation. "Keep on believing in *me*" will be much more difficult; how can the disciples continue to believe in Jesus as the Messiah, Son of God and Son of Man, when he is dragged off to the courts, condemned by the rulers, nailed to a cross, and mocked by the onlookers? Only the kind of faith seen in Abraham —"who against all hope, in hope *believed*" (Rom 4:18)—can prevail in such circumstances, and that is why they are bidden, "*keep on believing* in me.*" The remaining part of the discourse rings the changes on this call to believe.

2 A primary reason for maintaining faith in Jesus, precisely as the *Crucified*, is now given. The picture portrays a large house with many subsidiary living quarters (the AV/KJV translation of μοναί as "mansions" goes back to Tyndale [echoing the Vulgate *mansiones*] in whose time the term simply denoted a dwelling; Luther's *Wohnungen* is apt: in modern times the term is used not only for dwellings, but for "apartments," "flats"). Some exegetes have interpreted οἰκία in a corporate sense, in the light of the concept of the Church as a spiritual house or temple of God (cf, e.g., 1 Cor 3:16–17; Eph 2:20–22; 1 Pet 2:5, also John 2:19–21); the promise in vv 2–3 is then thought to relate to the fellowship which will be possible through Christ's departure and return through the Spirit (so R. H. Gundry, "In My Father's House Are Many Monai," 69–71. O. Schaefer viewed the Father's house as "the Father's realm of power and love that embraces heaven and earth," and the return of Jesus to his disciples as for mutual fellowship within that "home" in the present, "Der Sinn der Rede Jesu von den vielen Wohnungen . . . ," 213–16). On the contrary, the Father's "house" with its many dwellings is most plausibly a pictorial representation of the transcendent dwelling of God, such as is depicted under the figure of "the city of the living God, the heavenly Jerusalem" in Heb 12:22, a symbol which is greatly elaborated in the apocalyptic vision of the City of God in Rev 21:9–22:5. Naturally the figure in John 14:2–3 is wholly *unapocalyptic;* rather it is *eschatological,* as the related comparison of tent and house in 2 Cor 5:1 (see the full discussion of the possibilities of interpretation in G. Fischer, *Die himmlische Wohnungen: Untersuchungen zu Joh 14,2f,* 58–74). The departure of Jesus is for the purpose of preparing a place for the disciples within that "home"; the latter is viewed as existing already, but by his death and exaltation the Lord is to make it possible for his own to be there with him.

3 καὶ ἐάν is not to be rendered "And *when* I go . . ." but is truly conditional: "And *if* I go . . ." (cf. 8:16; 12:32; 12:47; Fischer points out that in John καὶ ἐάν each time leads the thought further, *Die himmlischen Wohnungen,* 89, n.89). "I am coming again" (πάλιν ἔρχομαι) in English and Greek alike expresses a genuine future, as the immediately following παραλήμψομαι, "I shall take you with me," shows (ἔρχομαι, present with a future sense, is common in the Fourth Gospel, cf. 1:15, 30; 4:21, 23, 25, 28; 14:18, 28; 16:2, 13, 25; note the use of ἔρχομαι in Rev 1:4, 7, 8; 22:20, and see BDF §323 [1]). The saying appears to be a clear promise of the Parousia of Jesus, although in simpler and more "homey" language (literally so!) than representations of the event such as those of Mark 13:24–27; 1 Thess 4:15–18. This appears to be demanded by the natural intent of καὶ παραλήμψομαι ὑμᾶς πρὸς ἐμαυτόν. A. L. Humphries' comment on the expression has been widely accepted: παραλαμβάνω in the NT commonly means "to take along with one's self" (cf. Matt 17:1; Mark 5:40; Luke 19:23; Acts 15:39) and the additional πρὸς ἐμαυτόν is a special use of the reflexive pronoun denoting "my home" (cf. 20:20; Luke 24:12); hence we should here translate, "I will come again and take you with me to my home" ("A Note on πρὸς ἐμαυτόν [John xiv.3] . . . ," 356). The clause that follows carries on the thought therein expressed: "that you also may be where I am"; the picture thus is completed of the Lord leaving the earth scene to prepare a place in the Father's house for his disciples, and of his coming again to take them away to that "house" that they may be with him always.

Insofar as a "common view" of John 14:2–3 exists the above may be said to represent it, and it will be found expressed in various ways in R. H. Charles's *A Critical History of the Doctrine of a Future Life* (London: Black, 1913[2]) 420–22; Bernard, 2:535; Schlatter, 293; Strathmann, 206; W. F. Howard, *IB* 8:700; Morris, 639; Boismard, "L'évolution du thème eschatologique," 522; G. Stählin, "Zum Problem der johanneischen Eschatologie," *ZNW* 33 (1934) 241–42; Bruce, 297–98; Schulz, 183 (apparently; his excursus on eschatology in John, 220–23, amounts to a retraction of his exposition). For many years it has been popular, however, to affirm that vv 2–3 include *all forms of the coming of Christ*—the appearances of the risen Lord, the coming of the Paraclete, the coming of Jesus at death, and the Parousia; this is very clearly represented by Westcott, 2:168, and with various nuances by Lagrange, 373–74; Hoskyns, 454; Strachan, 280; Barrett, 457; Gundry views the coming as in the Spirit and at the Parousia ("In My Father's House Are Many Monai," 68–72). From the viewpoint of exegesis, in distinction from a comprehensive view of the relation of Christ to humanity in history, this is not to be countenanced. Nor is the view, revived from time to time, that the coming of Jesus to the believer in death is here specifically in mind (so, e.g., Lightfoot, 275–76, and strangely, Bultmann, who saw the root of this as the individualistic eschatology of Gnosticism rather than Jewish-Christian hope, 602); Fischer regards this as a desperate solution, which overlooks the collective style of the promise and that the death in view is that of Jesus, not that of his disciples (310–11).

A view widely canvassed among critical scholars today sees in vv 2–3 an expression of the traditional Christian hope of the second coming of Christ, deliberately reproduced by the Evangelist with a view to correcting it by means of the unfolding of the discourse in chap. 14. Its best-known exponent is C. H. Dodd; to him the development of the discourse shows how vv 2–3 should be understood: Christ is the way to the Father, and so to the vision of God; he will continue his work through the disciples (vv 12–14) and the Spirit's dwelling in them (vv 15–16), and they are to know the mutual indwelling of Father and Son (vv 19–24). Thus the "coming" of the Lord means entering into union with him as their living

Lord and through him with the Father (*Interpretation*, 405–5). This interpretation was earlier succinctly stated by Heitmüller (824), is assumed by J. L. Martyn (147), Brown (2:624–27), Haenchen (474), and strongly argued by Becker (2:460–61, also in "Die Abschiedsreden Jesu im Johannesevangelium," *ZNW* 61 [1970] 222–28). Becker considers that the logion in vv 2–3 embodies an early Johannine apocalyptic revelation, and is characteristic of the primitive Christian Son of Man Christology; it assumes that the present is marked by the absence of the Lord, and so it is a time "empty of salvation," and removes fellowship with the exalted Lord to the end time; this view finds correction in vv 6–10, 12–17, 18–24, wherein it is revealed that the time of the exalted Lord is the time of salvation for the Church; by the Spirit he comes to his own and is ever present with them, hence through Christ the future has become present (462–66). This whole procedure seems to the present writer highly improbable. If the Evangelist wished to counter the Church's teaching on the Parousia, why did he put it on the lips of Jesus rather than, say, of a disciple (cf. 11:24–27)? As Fischer pointed out, it is a strange procedure that makes vv 2–3 the decisive ground of consolation and then drastically corrects it, since otherwise it will certainly be misunderstood (*Wohnungen*, 15–16). One may add that the "correction" has been largely unsuccessful, since the vast majority of Christians to this day haven't so understood it! It is a curious reading of vv 2–3 that deduces from it the present as a time "empty of salvation"; this is due to a failure to recognize the pictorial nature of language when attempting to express eschatological realities, whether in the Bible or in modern thought; the "going away" of Jesus to the Father's house to prepare a place for his own and his "coming again" to take them to it is as truly pictorial imagery as the descent of the Bride-City to a mountain for the benefit of earth's inhabitants in Rev 19–21; it does grave injustice to the Evangelist and Seer alike to impute to them wooden literalness in their symbolic descriptions. Every NT writer is aware that the "departure" of Jesus through death and resurrection and his "coming" signify God's saving sovereignty at work in and through the exalted Christ in the intervening time. In their varied ways of expressing it John and Paul are at one in this basic tenet of faith, as they are with the synoptic evangelists.

The relation of the "coming" of Christ in vv 2–3 to the "coming" in vv 18–20 and that in vv 22–23 will become clear as we proceed; suffice it to say at this point that the picture of being with the Lord in the Father's house is different from that of being in the Father and in the Son, consequent on the death and resurrection of Jesus (vv 18–20), just as the Easter revelation is distinguishable from the Parousia glory, though it is the one Christ who "comes" in both events. It is accordingly a mistake to try to interpret v 3 as a description of the post-Easter relation of the Lord to his disciples (as Lindars, 471, and at great length Fischer, 93–105, 305–334). It entails unnatural interpretations of some very clear language, and in the end it leads either to a denial of any real eschatology in the Fourth Gospel (expressions to the contrary being due to redactors) or to its reduction to such secondary importance that it plays no role in the Evangelist's theology (Schnackenburg, 2 540 [German ed.]; 2:434 [Eng. ed.]) reduces the statement to "the things of the future are unimportant for John."

For a brief, positive evaluation of these issues see especially M. de Jonge's essay, "Eschatology and Ethics in the Fourth Gospel," in *Jesus: Stranger from Heaven and Son of God*, 169, 191, esp. 173–74).

Jesus, the Way to God (14:4–6)

The passage continues the call to believe in v 1 and the assurance given in vv 2–3 by developing the thought of the *way* to the goal of Jesus' "going" and "coming" (note how v 4 emphasizes "the way" by placing the term *last* in the sentence; we placed it *first* for the same reason!).

5   Thomas, the loyal but undiscerning disciple (cf. 11:16), voices the incomprehension of the rest of the group. His question echoes that of Peter in 13:36, and reflects a complete failure to grasp the implications of vv 2–3. He seems to want to know precisely where the Father's house is located and where Jesus is going to prepare a place for them (cf. Hort: "In his eyes the journey must be like one from land to land, or, as we might say, from planet to planet"; *The Way, the Truth and the Life,* 15).

6   The disciple's lack of understanding, as so often, provides opportunity for Jesus to clarify the revelation. The saying is commonly recognized as ranking with 3:16 as an outstanding expression of the Gospel. "It forms a classical summary of the Johannine doctrine of salvation that is based entirely on Jesus Christ" (Schnackenburg, 3:65). Despite the coordination of the three terms the Way, the Truth, and the Life, the emphasis clearly falls on the first, for the statement explains the assertion of v 4 ("You know the way"), and concludes with a deduction from the main clause: "no one *comes to the Father* except through me." To say this is not to denigrate the importance of the second and third terms, for they explain how it is that Jesus is the Way: he is the Way because he is the truth, i.e., the revelation of God, and because the life of God resides in him (in the context of the Gospel that includes life in creation and life in the new creation, 1:4, 12–13; 5:26). Insofar as the saying is related to vv 2–3 it signifies that Jesus leads his own to the Father's house, revealing the truth about the goal of existence and how it may be reached, and making its attainment possible by granting entrance on to life in the Father's house. But the second clause of v 6 goes beyond the eschatological goal of life in the Father's house; "No one comes to the Father except through me" indicates that Jesus is the way *to the Father,* and therefore the way to the Father's house; that means that Jesus is the way to God in the present. De la Potterie points out that v 6 acts as a "hinge" in the section 14:1–11; while vv 1–6 look to the future opened up by Jesus, vv 6–11 have in view his present significance for faith; Jesus leads his own to the Father now because he is the Way, the Truth, and the Life in the present; "It is one of the many cases of anticipation of eschatological events in John" ("Je suis la voie, la vérité et la vie," 927–28). The saying, moreover, requires to be set in the context provided by this Gospel as a whole; it is as the Incarnate One who "goes" to the Father through the obedient offering of himself in death and through resurrection that he leads to the Father in the present and secures a place for his own in the Father's house. "I am the Way" accordingly depicts Jesus in his mediatorial role between God and man; as the Truth he is the mediator of the revelation of God, and as the Life he is the mediator of the salvation which is life in God; "these are two equally essential aspects of the person and work of the Christ and may not be separated" (de la Potterie, 938).

It is evident that v 6 presupposes the teaching on the Christ as the Logos, the Word of God made flesh. The latter clause of v 6 must then be related to the Prologue, where it is stated that the Christ is the Life, the Light of men, who enlightens every one (1:4, 9). That function he retains prior to, during, and after the Incarnation (though the preposition "after" in such a context requires care, since the Word made flesh remains the Incarnate One, even at the right hand of the Father). The negative form of v 6b has in mind the resistance to the Way, the Truth, and the Life suffered by the Word, but the reality to which it points is positive for humanity. "Jesus' claim, understood in the light of the prologue to the gospel, is inclusive, not exclusive. All truth is God's truth, as all life is God's life; but God's truth and God's life are incarnate in Jesus" (Bruce, 298–99; see further *Comment* on vv 7–9).

Jesus, the Revelation of God (14:7–11)

7 Since Jesus as the Way is the mediator of the truth of God and of life from God, to know him is to know the Father. The statement follows naturally on v 6a and puts positively what is negatively stated in v 6b. The future γνώσεσθε ("you will know") is logical rather than temporal, as is apparent from the latter clause: "Assuredly you do know him and you have seen him!"

8 "*Seen* him?" Philip is astonished; if only Jesus were to *show* them the Father, that would scatter all their doubts and fears! If this is to be classed as a "Johannine misunderstanding," enabling the revelation to be further clarified, it yet expresses the deepest yearning of the human race and of all its religions. We recall the desire of Moses on Mount Sinai: "Show me your glory," and the reply of God, "You cannot see my face, for no one may see me and live"; Moses was nevertheless allowed to glimpse God's *back* as his glory passed by him (Exod 33:18–23). Philip had failed to grasp that in Jesus the glory, grace, and truth of God, whom none has seen or can see, stands unveiled (John 1:18). For one whose spiritual sight is clear, the revelation is indeed "enough."

9 A gentle rebuke from Jesus leads to another peak point in the mountain ranges of revelation: "He who has seen me has seen the Father." Here is the needed counterpart to v 6b: that which humankind seeks through its religions, and partially finds, stands revealed in its completeness in Jesus. But the question posed to Philip, "How is it that you are saying, 'Show us the Father'?" challenges all would-be disciples. As Bultmann observed: "The implication behind the reproachful question is that all fellowship with Jesus loses its significance unless he is recognized as the one whose sole intention is to reveal God, and not to be anything for himself; but it also implies that the possibility of seeing God is inherent in the fellowship with Jesus. What need is there for anything further?" (608–9).

10 The basis of the revelation in v 10 is now made known. It is not simply that Jesus has been sent by God, and so according to Jewish definition, "One sent is as he who sent him," though that is uniquely true of Jesus in relation to God; nor is it solely because the revelation of God, made known "in many times and in various ways," is now made known in its completeness (cf. Heb 1:1); the affirmation holds good because Jesus is in the Father and the Father is in him. This so-called formula of reciprocal immanence is, as Schnackenburg puts it, "a linguistic way of describing . . . the complete unity between Jesus and the Father" (3:69). Significantly it was earlier stated to Jewish opponents of Jesus in justification of a statement closely related to that in v 9, namely, "I and the Father are one" (10:30, 37–38). The reality is greater than human language can express, but that to which it points is sufficiently clear: in the depths of the being of God there exists a *koinonia,* a "fellowship," between the Father and the Son that is beyond all compare, a unity whereby the speech and action of the Son are that of the Father in him, and the Father's speech and action come to finality in him.

11 If such assertions transcend understanding and therefore are difficult to grasp in faith, appeal is made to "believe the works," i.e., the signs of Jesus. The major part of this Gospel is taken up with the narration of the signs performed by him and expositions of their meaning. They who penetrate the significance of Jesus turning water into wine, of his healing miracles, of the feeding of the multitude in the wilderness and the walking on the water, and of the raising of Lazarus, will perceive in Jesus the saving sovereignty of *God* in action and his utterances as "words of eternal life" (6:68). In the words and works of Jesus the eschatological purpose of God is both declared and fulfilled.

Jesus, the Power of the Disciples' Mission (14:12–14)

12–14 The appeal for faith in Jesus, which has run through the discourse thus far, is continued in this passage and is given an encouragement which is nothing less than breathtaking. In order to understand it rightly, certain observations require to be grasped. First, throughout vv 12–14 the future tense is used; the period in view is that following the "lifting up" of Jesus to the throne of God, and so refers to the post-Easter era of the Church. Second, the passage is a single sentence and has a single dominant theme. The significance of this will appear shortly. Third, "the works that I do," in v 12a are clearly his miraculous works, the "signs" of the ministry which have featured so largely in the so-called "Book of Signs," chaps. 2–12. It is illegitimate to identify them with the "word" of Jesus on the ground of the close connection of word and works in v 10bc (as Bultmann did, 610–11; followed by Haenchen, 475, and Becker, 2:464); v 11b, with its parallel in 10:37–38, shows quite plainly that works performed by Jesus that confirm the word spoken by him are in mind. The assertion then is made that the believer in Jesus will (in an unspecified future, but in light of vv 3, 13 f., and the rest of the chapter, after the "departure" of Jesus through death-resurrection) will have power to perform the works such as those done by Jesus in his earthly ministry. Note that the participle ὁ πιστεύων, "whoever believes," is general, and not confined to the apostolic group. But further, the believer "will do *greater* works than these." Reflection will show that the "greater works" here mentioned are not more miraculous miracles than the miracles of Jesus (the Evangelist has stressed the motif of abundance in the signs of the new age in the water into wine and the feeding of the multitude, the divine power in the walking on the water, and the extraordinary nature of giving sight to the man born blind and the raising of Lazarus four days in the tomb). Nor is it likely that the first thought is that of the greater success of the disciples in their subsequent mission to Israel and the nations. Is the point in view not rather *the conveying to people of the spiritual realities of which the works of Jesus are "signs"?* All the works of Jesus are significant of the saving sovereignty of God at work among humankind through the eschatological Redeemer.

The main reality to which they point, and which makes their testimony a set of variations on a single theme, is the life eternal of the kingdom of God through Jesus its mediator. This is confirmed by the striking parallel to v 12 in 5:20 and its following exposition: the Father shows the Son all (*sc.*, the works) that he himself does, "and greater works than these he will show him, that you may be amazed." The context reveals that the "greater works" that the Father is to "show" the Son, greater than those given him to do thus far, are manifestations of resurrection and judgment, but with emphasis on the former (as 5:24–26 in relation to v 17 shows). Thus the "greater works" that the disciples are to do after Easter are the actualization of the realities to which the works of Jesus point, the bestowal of the blessings and powers of the kingdom of God upon men and women which the death and resurrection of Jesus are to let loose in the world.

The fourth observation is the continuity between vv 12c and 13a, and their connection with the performing of the greater works by the disciples. The fundamental ground by which the greater works are made possible is the "going" of Jesus to the Father, i.e., his death and resurrection to sovereignty which releases the powers of the kingdom of God in the world; the second ground is the prayer of the disciples in the name of Jesus, i.e., prayer with appeal to his name, in response to which *the risen Lord himself will do what is asked.* The continuity of thought demands that the prayer that is made is in relation to the disciples' ministry, and the Lord on high will through his disciples perform the greater works. The contrast accordingly is not between Jesus and his disciples in their respective ministries, but between Jesus with his disciples in the limited circumstances of his earthly ministry and the risen Christ with his disciples in the post-Easter situation. Then the limitations of the Incarnation will no longer apply, redemption will have been won for the world, the kingdom of God opened for humanity, and the disciples equipped for a ministry in power to the nations. Nothing has been said thus far about the sending of the Spirit, but that is shortly to be made known. Here the emphasis is on the continuing ministry of the Lord with and through his disciples, by whom the glorification of the Father in the Son will be continued.

In view of the extension of the sentence of vv 12–13 into v 14 it is likely that prayer in the service of the saving sovereignty of God is still primarily in mind, though a secondary extension to more general prayer is not to be ruled out (for a helpful comparison of the sayings on prayer in the Gospel and First Epistle of John see Brown, 2:633–36). The important additional feature in v 14 is its reference to prayer to Jesus: "If you ask *me* anything in my name I will do it." In view of the tightness of the context it is possible that the prayer in v 13 is of the same kind, i.e., directed to Jesus. If otherwise the prayer in v 13 is to the Father in the name of Jesus, to which Jesus himself responds. In both cases prayer "in the name of Jesus" denotes petition with invocation of his name or appeal to his name; while there are evident differences of nuance, accordingly as prayer is addressed to Jesus or the Father, the fundamental factor is the role of Jesus as mediator between God and his people. (For illuminating discussions of the concept see especially Heitmüller, *Im Namen Jesu,* 77–80; Bietenhard in *TDNT* 5:258–61, 276.)

The Coming of Another Paraclete (*14:15–17*)

15 Love for Jesus will lead to keeping the commands of Jesus: what are they? The interchange of "my commands" with "my word" and "my words" in vv 21, 23, 24 suggests that they include the full range of the revelation from the Father, not simply ethical instructions (cf. 8:31–32; 12:47–49; 17:6); the lover of Jesus will live in the light of their guidance and their power (for a similar usage see Rev 1:3; 22:7).

16 The first of the five Paraclete sayings is inserted at this point (see further 14:26; 15:26; 16:7–11, 12–15). The term παράκλητος is a verbal adjective with a passive sense and has the same meaning as ὁ παρακεκλημένος, "one called alongside." In secular Greek it was used especially of one called to help another *in court,* but it never became a technical term (unlike the Latin *advocatus,* meaning a professional legal adviser and representative). Behm summarized the linguistic evidence as follows: "The history of the term in the whole sphere of known Greek and Hellenistic usage outside the NT yields the clear picture of a legal adviser or helper or advocate in the relevant court. The passive form does not rule out the idea of the παράκλητος as an active speaker 'on behalf of someone before someone,' nor is there any need of recourse to the active of παρακαλέω in this connection" (*TDNT* 5:803). The law court connotation of the term is clear in 16:8–11, and while such associations may be present in the other passages (including this one), it is doubtful that they should control the meaning of them all (note esp. 14:25–26 and 16:13–14, wherein the teaching, recalling, and interpreting function of the Paraclete to the disciples is emphasized).

That the Spirit-Paraclete is introduced as "*another* Paraclete" implies that Jesus himself is also a Paraclete. It has been common to interpret this in the light of 1 John 2:1, "If anyone sins we have a Paraclete with the Father, Jesus Christ the Righteous One." Here the ascended Lord is viewed as a Paraclete *in* the court of heaven, pleading the cause of his own; the Holy Spirit is then understood as the Paraclete *from* heaven, supporting and representing the disciples in the face of a hostile world. Blank has recently upheld this interpretation on the ground that the stance of the Last Discourses is that of the post-Easter situation of the Church; the *present* ministries of the Lord and the Spirit are in view, so that the two Paracletes exercise parallel functions, not successive, and the Spirit as the agent of Christ makes Christ present in the Church (*Krisis,* 324: *Commentary,* 79). This is surely mistaken. The genius of the Evangelist throughout the Gospel is to hold together the past and present of Jesus and view the one in the light of the other, not allowing the present to swallow up the past (see the discussion on this in the *Introduction,* pp. xlvii–xlviii). The implication of v 16 is that Jesus has performed the role of a Paraclete during his earthly ministry, and after his departure he will ask the Father to send another Paraclete to perform a like ministry for his disciples. This holds good whether the Paraclete function is thought of in general terms as that of helping, or specifically as that of acting on behalf of the disciples before a hostile world (cf. 17:12). Porsch would see here a reference to the role of Jesus as the Accused, the Accuser, and the Judge in the trial that takes place in the world by reason of the revelation that he brought from the Father (the concept of a "trial" relating to the authenticity cf Jesus and his message is a thread running through the Gospel from beginning to end); a similar task is assigned to the Spirit after his departure, who acts as a Paraclete on behalf of the disciples as they suffer the hostility of the world formerly directed to Jesus (*Pneuma und Wort*, 243). This may perhaps define the Paraclete's task too narrowly, but with Porsch we may agree that the saying underscores the parallelism between *the activity of Jesus in his ministry* and that of *the Spirit in the era initiated by Easter-Pentecost*, plus *the continuity* of the one saving work in and through them. It is false to interpret the saying as affirming the Spirit to be the presence of Jesus in the new age.

"The Spirit of truth" designates the person of "the other Paraclete." The expression was already current in Judaism. *Test. Jud.* 20:1–5 states "Two spirits await an opportunity with humanity: the spirit of truth and the spirit of error. . . . And the spirit of truth testifies to all things and brings all accusations. He who has sinned is consumed in his heart and cannot raise his head to face the judge." 1QS 3:18–21 similarly reads, "He allotted unto man two Spirits that he should walk in them until the time of his visitation; they are the spirits of truth and perversity. The origin of Truth is in a fountain of light, and the origin of Perversity is from a fountain of darkness. Dominion over all the sons of righteousness is in the hand of the Prince of Light; they walk in the ways of light. All dominion over the sons of perversity is in the hand of the Angel of darkness; they walk in the ways of darkness." Barrett holds that these passages are irrelevant for the Gospel since the "spirits" merely denote good and evil inclinations (463). The connection with the Prince of light and the Angel of darkness, however, seems to demand a personal dualism here. It is not suggested that the concept of "Spirit of truth" originated among the Qumran group, still less that of the Paraclete-Spirit, but that these citations illustrate the familiarity of these notions in contemporary Judaism. The expression "Spirit of truth" in our Gospel could even have a secondary polemical intention (so G. Johnston, *The Spirit-Paraclete in the Gospel of John,* 121–22), since it defines the Paraclete as the Spirit who bears witness to the truth *which is Jesus* (14:6).

The "world" (humankind in opposition to God) cannot receive, see, or know the Spirit by reason of its nature. As Bultmann observed, "The world *qua* world cannot receive the Spirit; to do so it would have to give up its essential nature, that which makes it the world" (626). In John to "receive," "see," "know" in relation to God are all faith terms, and imply receiving the revelation, seeing it embodied in Jesus, and entering into the communion with God which knowledge of God entails. The incapacity of the world to receive or see or know the Spirit is due to its rejection of the revelation in Jesus and a consequent blindness under the judgment of God; to bring this home to those who belong to the godless world is part of the task of the Paraclete (16:8–11). When such receive the testimony they enter a new world, and begin to see and know the Spirit revealed in Jesus and his people.

In contrast to the world the disciples are to know the Paraclete because "he will remain alongside you" (παρ' ὑμῖν) "and will be in you" (ἐν ὑμῖν); for the future tenses see *Notes*). It is better not to distinguish the prepositions too sharply but, with Schnackenburg, to see in the two brief clauses a single figure of speech, affirming the presence of the Spirit with the disciples, while yet recognizing that the latter points to the Spirit's inner presence in individual believers (3:76).

The Coming of Jesus at Easter (14:18–20)

18–20   The relationship of v 18 with vv 2–3 (cf. the ἔρχομαι of vv 3 and 18) and its proximity to vv 15–17 have led to the belief that originally the "coming" of v 18 denoted the Parousia, but the Evangelist has reinterpreted the saying to affirm the coming of Jesus in the Spirit (so Bultmann, 617– 18, etc.; less radical scholars simply assume that v 18 was intended to apply to the Spirit's coming). Despite the increasing popularity of this view, most scholars rightly resist it. Windisch affirmed, "The idea that Jesus comes back to his own *in the Spirit* is nowhere to be found. This is a later combination which rests solely on the fact that the promise of his return, in vv 18f and in v 23 in the modern text, is imbedded between two Paraclete promises" (*The Spirit-Paraclete*, 2). We shall have to return to this issue later, meanwhile it is important to note that the Evangelist's intention in v 18 is made known in vv 19–20: Jesus is to "come" because he is to withdraw for a time from human sight—virtually for all time from the "world," but temporally from the disciples; these, however, are to "see" him, because he "lives," and so will they—in a new way, and then they will understand the true relation of Jesus to the Father and their own new relation to him. Clearly this points to Easter, with its manifestations of the risen Lord in mind, as the expansion of this passage in 16:16–30 confirms beyond cavil (note esp. 16:20, 22–23 and their link with 14:13–14). When Jesus so appears to his disciples they will "see" him with eyes of faith quickened into new perception. This they will do because Jesus "lives"—after his execution—and they will live in a new dimension by virtue of the resurrection life of their Lord (it is the same concept of life as that in 11:26—"he who *lives* and believes in me shall never die"). "On that day" the relation of Jesus to the Father ("I am in my Father"), which Jesus sought to make plain in vv 7–11, will become luminously clear; moreover they will then understand that a new union with their risen Lord has become possible, reflecting that of the Son with the Father ("you in me and I in you," v 20).

Naturally this renewal of spiritual life and perception is not confined to the Easter Day experiences. Easter initiates a new era or, in biblical language, the new age, which is that of the saving sovereignty of God, and which Jesus called the kingdom of God. That is why the passage is replete with eschatological terminology ("I come," in relation to the resurrection, is as truly eschatological as "I come" of the Parousia, v 3; "yet a little while" in v 19 echoes Isa 26:20 and Hab 2:33–34, cited in Heb 10:27–28 with reference to the end of the age; "in that day," v 20, commonly refers in the Bible to the last day, cf., e.g., Isa 2:11; 4:12; Mark 13:32). The resurrection of Jesus, along with the death from which it is inseparable, is the eschatological event which brings to a climax the eschatological ministry of "signs" of the kingdom into the world. Hence Jesus may say at the beginning of this paragraph, "I will not leave you orphans"; he comes at Easter to be reunited with his disciples and to lift to a new plane his relationship with them, for which that in the ministry could be only a preparation. How that will come about is more fully explained in vv 21–24.

The Coming of Jesus to the Believer (14:21–24)

21 The thought of v 15 is again reiterated: one who loves Jesus lives by the word of Jesus. Two further declarations are then made regarding such a person. First, he will be "loved by my Father"; this in no way lessens the reality of the Father's love for the world, manifest in Christ (3:16), but that love becomes revealed and experienced in a new depth by the lover of Jesus. (Cf. Haenchen: "This means that for the Christian the separation from the Father is abolished. The Father is no more the Unknown, the great X which in the end can also be the 'Nothing.' Rather behind the mask of the 'Nothing' there stands the great Lover," 477.) Second, the promise is made that to one who loves Jesus and seeks to follow him, Jesus will "reveal" himself.

The term ἐμφανίζω is used in Exod 33:13, 18, where Moses prays, "Show yourself to me" (ἐμφάνισόν μοι σεαυτόν), and Yahweh answers his prayer. In the NT the verb and its cognates are (along with other meanings) used of resurrection appearances; in Matt 27:53 of appearances of risen saints; Acts 10:40, in Peter's proclamation, God raised up Jesus and "gave him to become manifest" (ἔδωκεν αὐτὸν ἐμφανῆ γενέσθαι); Mark 16:9, Jesus appeared (ἐφάνη) to Mary Magdalene. Following the sayings on the Easter appearances and the era they initiated in vv 18–20, it is evident that what is here promised is a counterpart in the believer's life to the Easter appearances of the risen Lord to the disciples.

22 On "Judas, not Iscariot," see *Notes*. Judas is both surprised and perplexed at the utterance in v 21—another "misunderstanding." It is scarcely likely that the later Church's problem of the restriction of the resurrection appearances to believers is here mirrored (as is frequently suggested). Rather "Judas . . . is looking for another theophany that will startle the world" (Brown, alluding to the theophany to Moses on Sinai, 2:647). The theophany that Judas expects, however, is that of the greater Exodus, of the Messiah when he manifests his power in the judgment of the nations and the glory of his kingdom (in Hab 3:3–15 the theophany of Sinai and that of the Day of the Lord merge in vision; for the publicity of the Messiah's appearing cf. Isa chaps. 9, 11; Zech 9).

23 The misunderstanding is rectified with a repetition of the necessity for keeping the word of Jesus if the Father's love is to be experienced. It is to such as keep that word that the desired theophany is given; the Father himself, and Jesus, will come to such a person and "make their home" (μονή) with him. The connection with vv 2–3 is immediately apparent: Jesus goes in death to prepare in the Father's house a "dwelling," a "home" (μονή) for those who, like the disciples, keep his word, and he will come again to take them with him to the prepared home; in v 23 the Father and the Son come to the believer in his earthly existence and make their home with him *here*. Whereas not a few exegetes see in v 23 the climax of the reinterpretation of the Parousia hope in terms of the indwelling of the believer by the Father and the Son (through the Spirit?), it would seem that the Evangelist would teach us to distinguish these realities. We have already seen that the "coming" of Jesus to his disciples in v 18 relates to the Easter appearances of the risen Lord and the era they initiated. The promise in v 21 extends the Easter experience to the believer in the post-Easter era: Jesus will "manifest" himself to any who respond to the gospel proclamation. In reply to the question of Judas, that essentially eschatological reality is represented under a different eschatological image, namely that of the "coming" of the Father and Son to the believer to dwell with him (cf. Ezek 37:26–27; Zech 2:10; Rev 21:3). As in v 21 the Easter experience is post-dated, so in v 23 the Parousia is anticipated, but neither the resurrection nor the Parousia of Jesus is thereby brought into question. That Jesus in the Upper Room looks forward to the goal of redemption beyond this world is seen in 17:24, in the prayer that his followers "may be with me, where I am, that they may see my glory which you gave me" (cf. 12:25–26); the approximation of the language to 14:3 ("that where I am, you also may be") indicates that that goal is in the Father's "house," and the event that completes the reunion is the Parousia.

24 The paragraph concludes with an emphatic expression of the authority of the revelation just made known, with an implicit appeal to receive it in faith.

The question as to the relation of the coming of the Father and the Son to that of the Paraclete is frequently discussed. Very commonly it has been assumed that the text teaches that the former is actualized in the latter; the Father and the Son "come" to and are present with the believer *in* the Spirit. We have already questioned that interpretation, and our consideration of vv 18–25 has justified the query, for this paragraph relates to the action of the Christ in his dying and rising and the revelation of himself to his disciples; this describes his personal action, and in extending it to later followers there is no hint that it will be less direct. "I will love him . . . and my Father will love him" is the unmediated attitude of God to the believer. "I will manifest myself to him . . . We will come to him" is the direct action of God. "I am in my Father, and you in me and I in you" is of the same order. "I shall ask the Father and he will give you another Paraclete that he may be with you forever" is the promise of the distinctive ministry of the Spirit following Easter. It is not surprising that the Church Fathers interpreted these sayings as promising the indwelling of *the Trinity* in the believer (as Augustine: "The Holy Spirit also makes a dwelling with the Father and the Son; he is at home in every way, like God in his temple. The God of the Trinity, the Father, the Son and the Holy Spirit, come to us when we come to them," *In Jo.* 76.4). Since the ministry of the Paraclete-Spirit continues that of the Paraclete Jesus, and is perpetually represented in relation to him, it is natural that there should be many parallels in describing the functions of both and the conditions of receiving both. The same is evident in the Pauline letters (cf. Smalley, "The Christ-Christian Relationship in Paul and John," 98), but it is not legitimate to deduce therefrom that the Evangelist and the Apostle were representing the presence and action of the risen Lord as mediated by the Spirit. If that sets a problem for the theologian it is necessary to resolve it through reflection on the text, not to interpret the text in the light of speculative theology.

The Paraclete Teacher (14:25-26)

25 "I have spoken these things to you" is an expression frequently appearing in the Last Discourses, sometimes relating to the immediate context (e.g., 16:1, 4) and sometimes with a wider reference (e.g., 16:25, 33). Here it appears to refer to the word of Jesus in its totality, as in vv 23–24. "While I am with you" indicates that Jesus is on the point of departure, and the Paraclete-Spirit is about to assume his task. Coming at the close of the Last Discourse of 13:31–14:31 these words imply that Jesus' teaching ministry in the world now comes to an end (so Schnackenburg, 3:82).

26 The Spirit is to be "sent" by the Father "in the name of Jesus," a remarkable declaration which binds the Spirit closely to Jesus. Constantly in this Gospel Jesus is represented as the Sent One of God, having his origin in God, a mission from God, and an authority from God (cf., e.g., 4:34; 5:23, 24, 30, 37; 6:38–40; 7:16; 8:16, 18, 26; 12:44–49); that the Spirit is *sent* by the Father carries similar implications. Jesus affirmed that he had come "in the name of" his Father (5:43; 1:25), as his representative; the Spirit, however, is sent in the name of *Jesus;* he comes as *his* representative. The Spirit no more comes in his own name than Jesus came in his own name. (For an interesting parallel, in content though not in language, see Gal 4:4–6.) The task of the Paraclete-Spirit then is to *"teach* you everything and *remind* you of everything" that Jesus has said. The two tasks are strictly complementary, almost identical. The term "remind" ($ \dot{\upsilon}\pi o\mu\iota\mu\nu\dot{\eta}\sigma\kappa\omega $) occurs here alone in the Gospel, but the simpler $ \mu\iota\mu\nu\dot{\eta}\sigma\kappa\omega $ is used in the passive with the sense of "remember"; it occurs in two significant passages in the Gospel: first in 2:17, 22 it is said that after Easter the disciples *remembered* the enigmatic saying regarding the destruction of the temple and the formation of a new one (2:19), together with the relevance of Psalm 69:9 concerning the cleansing of the temple and the saying itself, and so the meaning of the whole event; the second is in 12:16, where it is stated that "after Jesus was glorified" the disciples *remembered* the triumphal entry of Jesus into Jerusalem and the scriptures which illuminated the meaning of the event. These two occasions of "remembering" in the time following Easter and the coming of the Spirit provide illustrations of what is meant by the Spirit "reminding" the disciples of what Jesus said: he not only enables them to *recall* these things but to perceive their significance, and so he *teaches* the disciples to grasp the revelation of God brought by Jesus in its richness and profundity.

Two observations accordingly are in place regarding this saying about the Paraclete: first, it is clear that the Spirit brings no new revelation; his task is to point to that which Jesus brought and to enable the disciples to understand it; second, alike the language used of the Paraclete-Spirit (e.g., $ \dot{\epsilon}\kappa\epsilon\tilde{\iota}\nu o\varsigma $, "he," in v 26), his role as representative of Jesus and his task of recalling and interpreting the revelation brought by Jesus make very clear the personal nature of the Spirit. The trinitarian implications of v 26, as of the rest of the Paraclete sayings, are evident.

Epilogue: The Bequest of Peace (14:27–31)

The discourse ends on the note with which it began: a word of assurance, a statement on the implications of Jesus' departure and return, and an encouragement to have faith. The conclusion of the farewell discourse in chaps. 15–16 (16:33) is virtually equivalent in meaning, though not in language.

27 "Peace" is the rendering of *shalom*. The term was used both in greeting and for farewell. This, however, is no ordinary farewell. "My peace" is Jesus' bequest of the peace which is no less than the salvation of the kingdom of God ("The new order is simply the peace of God in the world," Hoskyns, 461). It was to bring this into being that Jesus came, was departing, and was to come again. (For the concept of the Messiah as the bringer of peace cf. Isa 9:6–7; 52:7; 57:19; Ezek 37:26; Hag 2:9; Acts 10:36; Rom 14:17.) Jesus' gift of shalom is given "not as the world gives it"; its greetings of "shalom" have no power (cf. Jer 6:14), and its attempts to establish it in the world come to naught. A striking example of the latter is the famous *Ara Pacis,* altar of peace, erected in Rome by Augustus, the first of its emperors, to celebrate his establishment of the age of peace proclaimed by the prophets; it still stands in Rome, a monument to the skill of its sculptors and to the empty messianic pretensions of its emperors.

28 The encouraging explanation of the reason for Jesus' impending death and promise of his return, given in vv 2–3, should have brought joy to the disciples, since it is a departure to be with the Father; real love to Jesus would mean rejoicing with him in that prospect. A further ground of such joy is the reminder that the Father, who sent Jesus, and gave him his words to say and works to do, is greater than Jesus, and so *everything is under control;* God will work out his beneficent purpose through the terrifying events of the coming hours, and the disciples may be sure that he will do the like for them in *their* hours of testing (an encouraging word for the post-Easter Church, see Lindars, 484–85).

The intent of "the Father is greater than I" is clear in the context, but the statement has caused immense discussion through the history of the Church, and it played a prominent part in the Arian controversy. The problem has been to reconcile the declaration with intimations in the Gospel of Jesus' oneness with the Father in the Godhead (e.g., 1:1–18; 10:30; 20:28) and with the Church's creedal affirmations of the co-equality of the Father and the Son. Without doubt the statement in v 28 is one with many representations in the Fourth Gospel as to the obedience of the Son to the Father (e.g., 4:34; 8:29) and his dependence on the Father for every aspect of his ministry (e.g., 5:19; 12:48–49), as well as of the origin and end of the Son's mediation in revelation and redemption as being in the Father (e.g., 1:14, 18; 5:21–27). It is doubtful therefore if the reference of v 28 can be limited solely to the conditions of the Incarnation (as maintained, e.g., by Cyril of Alexandria, Augustine, etc.), but respect must also be had to the relations within the Godhead (so Tertullian, Athanasius, etc.). Barrett endeavors to take into account both aspects: "The Father is *fons divinitatis* in which the being of the Son has its source; the Father is God sending and commanding, the Son is God sent and obedient" (468; see further Barrett's article, "The Father Is Greater than I (Jo 14:28)"; for discussions in the early centuries see T. E. Pollard, *Johannine Christology and the Early Church* [Cambridge: CUP 1970] passim).

29–30 The same utterance appears in 13:19 in relation to the betrayal of Jesus by a disciple; here it refers to his impending death. Both the language and content of vv 30–31 echo Mark 14:41–42, but with characteristic Johannine nuances. Mark speaks of the approach of Judas, John of the approach of "the Prince of this world," for Judas is but the tool of the devil. "He has nothing over me" reflects the Hebrew אֵין לוֹ עָלַי (ʾayin lô ʿālî), commonly used in a legal sense. The devil has no claim over Jesus, for Jesus is not of this world (8:23), he has ceaselessly resisted the devil, and has never played into his hand (cf. 8:46). On the contrary the world must learn that Jesus loves *the Father* and that he does *his will;* hence he will make no compromise now and take an easy way out (the devil's way!), but he will do as the Father commanded: he will confront the world and the devil, lay down his life, and thereby win redemption for the world (cf. 3:16; 10:17–18). Accordingly Jesus bids his disciples to rise and go with him to meet the foe.

The epilogue (vv 27–31) assumes that the end of Jesus' farewell discourse is now reached and that the continuation of the narrative is in 18:1 ff. (see the *Introduction* to the Last Discourses of Jesus). C. H. Dodd suggested a different interpretation of vv 30–31, whereby the discourse of chap. 14 could continue into chap. 15: in his view the passage depicts the spiritual aspect of the conflict mentioned in Mark 14:41–42; he rendered v 31, ". . . to show the world that I love the Father and do exactly what he commands— up, let us march to meet him!", on which he commented, "There is no movement in space; the advance on the enemy is Christ's own resolve to do the Father's will" (*Interpretation,* 409; *Historical Tradition,* 72). The interpretation is highly ingenious, but hardly natural, and is generally regarded as implausible.

Explanation

1. The farewell discourse, unlike the discourses that have preceded it, is addressed to disciples of Jesus. Some elements of it relate uniquely to them, e.g., 13:33, 36–38 (addressed to Peter), 7–9 (to Philip), 18–20 (to those who were to witness resurrection appearances of Jesus), 27–31. The bulk of the discourse, however, is addressed to the disciples as representatives of the Church that is to be, and most of the passages just named have obvious relevance to the Church. While some elements admittedly can be incorporated into the Church's proclamation of the good news to the world (e.g., 14:1–3, 6, 8–11, 18–24, 27) the discourse is fundamentally *the Testament of Jesus to his Church.* In writing it the Evangelist will consciously have had in view the churches about him in their concrete situations; the modern reader will have no difficulty in relating it to the churches not only of the first century but of subsequent and present times.

2. The command to love one another in the light of Christ's love for his own (13:34–35) is a conspicuous example of such instruction. It is not an appeal to love all in the world, but a direction to members of Christian churches to become fellowships of Christly love; by this means a demonstration will be given of the power of Christ's love in the world. It may be observed, on the one hand, that Christians need love as much as anyone else, particularly when, as in the Johannine churches, the opposition of Jewish authorities

had become intense, and Gentiles were not exactly welcoming; in such circumstances they needed havens of deep and supportive love. That need never changes, even when the churches' problem is not opposition but apathy. But, on the other hand, those outside the churches need love also. The consideration "that the world may know that you are my disciples" may reflect the OT tradition of mission by attraction ("centripetal" rather than "centrifugal," to use the jargon of missiologists; for a striking example of this cf. Zech 8:20–23). The attractive power of communities of love is no less evident in our age, where such communities are increasingly uncommon.

3. Perhaps the most important feature of this Testament of Jesus is its exposition of the eschatological dimension of the redemptive revelation of God in Christ. To disciples shattered by the prospect of their Master's death and the disclosure of their own weakness, to churches which follow the crucified Messiah and experience the world's hostility formerly directed to him, and to Christians of later times confused by a secularism that sees no ground for faith or hope, the revelation in chap. 14 comes as the breath of heaven in an airless room. The prospect for the future, opened up in vv 2–3, is of sharing in the joyous fellowship of the Father's house; the individual believer finds his goal in the perfected fellowship of redeemed humanity with the Son of God and his Father. But the journey to that future is by a Way characterized by the Life of the Father's house, the expansive life of the coming glory scaled down to the dimensions of existence in this present world. Here the duality of perspective that binds the disciples in the Upper Room and the churches of the post-Easter period is clear; what to the disciples is a puzzling revelation of a future reunion with the Lord becomes the foundation stone of the Church's relation with the living Lord. Easter has happened! With it the life of the age to come has become the life of the Church today. The present reality and intensely personal nature of the fellowship with Christ in his Church is expounded in terms of Easter manifestations in the past and Parousia revelation anticipated for the future. The risen Lord discloses himself to *anyone* who loves him and keeps his word (v 21); to such the Father and the Son will come and anticipate the fellowship of the Father's house in present dwelling with the believer. In these pictorial representations the individual and corporate aspects of the Christian life are perfectly harmonized.

4. The brief statements in the discourse relating to the ministry of the Spirit convey the concept of the presence of God with the Church of the risen Lord in another key; in particular, they emphasize the continuity of the mission to humanity initiated by Jesus. The saying in vv 16–17 may well have in view the ministry of the Paraclete on behalf of disciples in a hostile world, acting as their Advocate, whereas that in v 26 is concerned with the Paraclete's ministry *to* the disciples in relation to the revelation in Jesus. It is assumed that the revelation of God through the Son has been made known once for all in its completeness; the Paraclete unfolds it to the minds of the original disciples for the Church, but by implication his continuous presence in the Church will be for the continuous unfolding of the revelation to the churches through all time. Thereby the revelation is made relevant to every generation.

3. Jesus the True Vine—The Hatred of the World for the Church—The Joy That Overcomes Tribulation (15:1–16:33)

Bibliography

Bammel, E. "Jesus und der Paraklet in Joh 16." *Christ and Spirit in the New Testament.* FS C. F. D. Moule. Cambridge: 1973. 199–217. **Berrouard, M. F.** "Le Paraclet, défenseur du Christ devant la conscience du croyant (Jean 16, 8–11)" *RSPT* 33 (1949) 361–89. **Blank, J.** *Krisis.* 316–440. **Borig, R.** *Der wahre Weinstock.* München: Kösel, 1967. **Bream, H. N.** "No Need to Be Asked Questions: A Study of John 16:30." *Search the Scriptures.* FS R. T. Stamm. Ed. J. M. Myers, O. Reimherr, & H. N. Bream. Leiden: Brill, 1969. 49–74. **Bruns, J. E.** "A Note on John 16:33 and 1 John 2:13–14." *JBL* 86 (1967) 451–53. **Bussche, H. van den.** "La Vigne et ses fruits." *BVC* 26 (1959) 12–18. **Carson, D. A.** "The Function of the Paraclete in John 16:7–11." *JBL* 98 (1979) 547–66. **Dibelius, M.** "Joh 15:13. Eine Studie zum Traditionsproblem des Johannesevangeliums." *Festgabe für Adolf Deissmann.* Tübingen: Mohr, 1927. 169–89; also in Dibelius, M. *Botschaft und Geschichte.* Vol. 1. Tübingen: Mohr, 1953. 204–20. **Fascher, E.** "Johannes 16, 32." *ZNW* 39 (1940) 171–230. **Hatch, W. H. P.** "The Meaning of John 16:8–11." *HTR* 14 (1921) 103–5. **Grundmann, W.** "Das Wort von Jesu Freunden (Joh xv 13–16) und das Herrenmahl." *NovT* 3 (1959) 62–69. **Hawkins, D. J.** "Orthodoxy and Heresy in John 10:1–21 and 15:1–17." *EvQ* 47 (1975) 208–13. **Jacobs, L.** " 'Greater Love Hath No Man . . .': The Jewish Point of View of Self-Sacrifice." *Judaism* 6 (1957) 41–47. **Jaubert, A.** "L'image da la Vigne (Jean 15)." *Oikonomia.* FS O. Cullmann. Ed. F. Christ. Hamburg: Reich, 1957. 93–99. **Johnston, G.** "The Allegory of the Vine." *CJT* 3 (1957) 150–58. **Kremer, J.** "Jesu Verheissung des Geistes: Zur Verankerung der Aussage von Joh 16:13 im Leben Jesu." in *Die Kirche des Anfangs.* FS H. Schürmann. Ed. R. Schnackenburg, J. Ernst, J. Wanke. Leipzig: St. Benno-Verlag. 1977. 247–76. **Lee, G. M.** "John 15:14, 'Ye are my Friends.' " *NovT* 15 (1973) 260. **Lindars, B.** "Δικαιοσύνη in Jn 16:8 and 10." *Mélanges Bibliques.* FS R. P. B. Rigaux. Ed. A. Decamps and R. P. André de Halleux. Gembloux: Duculot, 1970. 275–86. **O'Grady, J. F.** "The Good Shepherd and the Vine and the Branches." *BTB* 8 (1978) 86–88. **Patrick, J G.** "The Promise of the Paraclete." *BS* 127 (1970) 333–45. **Porsch, F.** *Pneuma und Wort.* 215–303. **Rosscup, J. E.** *Abiding in Christ: Studies in John 15.* Grand Rapids: Eerdmans, 1973. **Potterie, I. de la.** "Le Paraclet." *AsSeign* 47 (1963) 37–55; also in de la Potterie and Lyonnet, S. *La vie selon l'Esprit.* Paris: Cerf, 1965. 88–105. **Sandvik, B.** "Joh 15 als Abendmahlstext." *TZ* 23 (1967) 323–38. **Smith, D. M.** "John 16:1–15." *Int* 33 (1979) 58–62. **Schwank, B.** " 'Da sie mich verfolgt haben werden sie auch euch verfolgen' (Joh 15:18–16:4a)." *SeinSend* 28 (1963) 292–301. ———. "Es ist gut für euch dass ich fortgehe' (16, 4b–15)." *SeinSend* 28 (1963) 388–400. ———. "Sieg und Friede in Christus (16, 16–33)." *SeinSend* 28 (1963) 388–400. **Stenger, W.** "Δικαιοσύνη in Joh 16, 8.10." *NovT* 21 (1979) 2–12. **Thüsing, W.** *Erhöhung und Verherrlichung im Johannesevangelium.* 109–10, 117–26. **Thyen H.** " 'Niemand hat grössere Liebe als die, dass er sein Leben für seine Freunde hingibt' (Joh 15, 13)." *Theologia crucis—Signum crucis.* FS E. Dinkler. Ed. C. Andersen & G. Klein. Tübingen: Mohr, 1979. 467–81. **Wiefel, W.** "Die Scheidung von Gemeinde und Welt im Johannesevangelium auf dem Hintergrund der Trennung von Kirche und Synagoge." *TZ* 35 (1979) 213–27. **Zerwick, M.** "Vom Wirken des Heiligen Geistes in uns (Joh 16, 5–15)." *GeistLeb* 38 (1965) 224–30.

Translation

¹ "I am the true Vine, and my Father is the Vinedresser. ² Every branch in me that yields no fruit he cuts off, but every one that yields fruit he cuts clean[a] in order that it may yield more fruit. ³ Now you are clean on account of the word that I have spoken to you. ⁴ Remain in me and I in you. Just as the branch is unable to yield fruit by itself, unless it remains in the vine, so neither can you yield fruit unless you remain in me. ⁵ I am the vine, you are the branches. He who remains in me and I in him yields much fruit, for apart from me you can do nothing. ⁶ If anyone does not remain in me he is like a branch that is thrown away[b] and becomes withered;[b] men gather them and throw them into a fire, and they are burned. ⁷ If you remain in me and my words remain in you, ask whatever you wish and it will be done for you. ⁸ My Father becomes glorified[c] in this, that you yield much fruit and become disciples[d] of mine. ⁹ As the Father has loved me, so I have loved you; remain[e] in my love. ¹⁰ If you keep my commands you will remain in my love, just as I have kept my Father's commands and I remain in his love.

¹¹ "I have said these things to you that my joy may be in you and your joy may be complete. ¹² This is my command: Love one another, as I have loved you. ¹³ No one has greater love than this, that one lays down his life for the sake of his friends. ¹⁴ You are my friends if you do the things I command you. ¹⁵ No longer do I call you servants, because a servant does not know what his master is doing; but I have called you friends, because all that I have heard from my Father I have made known to you. ¹⁶ You did not choose me, but I chose you and set you aside that you should go forth and yield fruit and that your fruit should remain, so that the Father should give you whatever you ask in my name. ¹⁷ This is my command to you: Love one another.

¹⁸ "If the world hates you, realize[f] that it has hated me before[g] it hated you. ¹⁹ If you belonged to the world the world would love you as its own;[h] but because you do not belong to the world, but I chose you out of the world, the world hates you. ²⁰ Remember the statement I made to you: 'The servant is not greater than his master.' If they have persecuted me, they will persecute you also; if they have kept my word, they will keep yours also. ²¹ But they will do all these things because they do not know the One who sent me. ²² If I had not come and spoken to them they would not be guilty of sin; but now they have no excuse for their sin. ²³ He who hates me hates my Father also. ²⁴ If I had not done among them the works which no one else had done, they would not be guilty[i] of sin; but now they have both seen and hated both me and my Father. ²⁵ However, the saying that is written in their law had to come true:[j] 'They hated me for no reason.'

²⁶ "When the Paraclete comes, whom I will send to you from the Father, the Spirit of truth who comes forth from the Father, he will bear witness concerning me; ²⁷ and you also are to bear witness, because you have been with me from the beginning.

16:1 "I have spoken these things to you to prevent you from falling from faith. ² They will put you out of the synagogue; indeed the hour is coming when anyone who kills you will suppose that he is offering a service to God. ³ And these things they will do[k] because they never knew[l] the Father, nor me. ⁴ But I have said these things to you so that when their hour comes you may remember that I told you of them.[m]

"I did not tell you these things at the beginning because I was with you. [5] But now I am going away to him who sent me, and none of you asks me, 'Where are you going?' [6] But because I have said these things to you anguish has filled your hearts. [7] But I am telling you the truth; it is to your advantage that I am going away. For if I do not go away the Paraclete will not come to you; but if I go away I will send him to you. [8] And he, when he comes, will expose the world with respect to sin, and righteousness, and judgment; [9] with respect to sin, in that they are not believing in me; [10] with respect to righteousness, inasmuch as I am going away to the Father, and you no longer will see me; [11] with respect to judgment, inasmuch as the prince of this world has been judged.

[12] "I have many things to say to you, but you cannot endure them now; [13] but when he, the Spirit of truth, comes, he will guide you in[n] the entire truth; he will not speak on his own authority, but he will speak all that he hears, and he will disclose to you the things that are coming. [14] He will glorify me, inasmuch as he will receive what is from me and disclose it to you. [15] All that the Father has is mine; this is why I said that he will take what is from me and disclose it to you.

[16] "A little while, and you will no longer see me; and again a little while, and you will see me[o]" [17] Some of his disciples therefore said to one another, "What is this that he is saying to us, 'A little while and you will not see me, and again a little while and you will see me'? And again, 'Because I am going to the Father'?" [18] So they kept saying. "What is this 'little while' that he is speaking of? We do not know what he is talking about." [19] Jesus knew that they were wanting to question him, and he said to them, "Are you inquiring with one another about this, that I said, 'A little while and you will not see me, and again a little while and you will see me'? [20] Amen, amen I tell you, you will weep and make lamentation, but the world will be glad; you will be plunged into anguish, but your anguish will be turned to joy. [21] When a woman is in labor she has anguish, because her hour has come; but when the child is born she no longer remembers the anguish because of the joy that a human being has been born into the world. [22] You, too, now have anguish;[p] but I shall see you again, and your heart will be gladdened, and your gladness no one will take[q] from you. [23] On that day you will not put any questions to me. Amen, amen I tell you, whatever you ask the Father in my name[r] he will give it you. [24] Up to the present you have asked nothing in my name; ask, and you will receive, that your gladness may be complete.

[25] "I have said these things to you in the obscure speech of metaphor; the hour is coming when I will no longer use obscure language to you but will speak to you openly about the Father. [26] In that day you will ask in my name, and I do not say to you that I shall ask the Father on your behalf, [27] for the Father himself loves you, because you have loved me and have come to believe that I came forth from God.[s] [28] I came forth from the Father[t] and have come into the world; again I am leaving the world and am going to the Father." [29] His disciples say, "Look, now you are speaking plainly, and are not using obscure language at all. [30] Now we know that you know all things, and you have no need that anyone should question you. By this we believe that you have come forth from God." [31] Jesus replied to them, "Do you now believe?[u] [32] Listen, the hour is coming, and it is here, when[v] you will be scattered, each to his own place, and you will leave me alone. And yet I am not alone, for the Father is with me. [33] I have spoken these things to you so that you may have peace in me. In the world you will have trouble, but take heart, I have conquered the world."

Notes

[a] There is a play on words in *αἴρει* and *καθαίρει*, which is maintained in *καθαροί* of v 3. *αἴρει* means "take away, remove," in this context "clear away"; *καθαίρει* primarily means "cleanse," frequently in a religious sense, but it is used also in the sense of "clear" (i.e., the earth of weeds). *αἴρει* denotes the removal of dead branches, *καθαίρει* the removal of unwanted shoots from living branches. We may render therefore, he "clears away" the useless branches and "clears clean" the living ones, or, as in our tr., he "cuts off" the dead branches and "cuts clean" (of unwanted growth) the living ones.

[b] *ἐβλήθη* and *ἐξηράνθη* are often viewed as gnomic aorists, indicating what always happens in such cases (cf. James 1:11, so BDF § 333m1). Bernard (2:483) and Moulton-Turner (3:74) see here examples of a "proleptic aorist"; Barrett views them as "timeless aorists" (474). We do better perhaps in view of Johannine usage (cf. 13:31–32; 15:8 and examples given by Bauer, 185) to see the aorist here as expressing "a sequence introduced immediately with absolute certainty" (so also Bultmann, 537–38 n.3; Schnackenburg, 3:419 n.34).

[c] See previous note for the aorist *ἐδοξάσθη*.

[d] *γένησθε* along with the preceding *φέρητε* depends on *ἵνα*; such is the reading of P^{66vid} B D L X Θ π OL vg cop etc. and is perhaps to be preferred, on the basis of breadth of external support, to *γενήσεσθε* (so ℵ A K Δ ψ syr^{mss} etc.); the latter will require to be understood as an independent clause (see Metzger, 246).

[e] If the aorist *μείνατε* is not used for emphasis (Bernard, 2:484), it may be seen as "a summons to enter into, and so abide in, the love of Jesus" (Barrett, 476).

[f] *γινώσκετε* is indicative or imperative; both suit the context, but the latter is generally preferred.

[g] *πρῶτον* (*ὑμῶν*) is comparative, "before you," as in 1:15 and 30 (see BDF § 62).

[h] *τὸ ἴδιον*: for the use of the neuter to represent a collective whole, cf. 6:37, 39; 17:2, 24.

[i] Mixed tenses in conditional sentences are common in John; the imperf. in the apodosis after aorist signifies present time: "If I had not come . . . they would not (now) be in a condition of guilt." So also in v 24. The omission of *ἄν* in the apodosis in such sentences is frequent in Hellenistic Gr. (see BDF § 360).

[j] This could be an example of *ἵνα* introducing an imperative: "Let the saying . . . in their law be fulfilled"; otherwise, the sentence is elliptic, "It was that . . ." See *Notes* on 9:3 and on 12:7.

[k] After *ποιήσουσιν* some MSS (D etc.) add *ὑμῖν* or *εἰς ὑμᾶς* (33), or even simply *ὑμᾶς* (73 259); the additions appear to be due to the influence of 15:21.

[l] *οὐκ ἔγνωσαν* may be an ingressive aorist: "they did not begin to recognize" (so Moulton-Turner, 3:71).

[m] The second *αὐτῶν* is omitted by ℵ A L Π^{2} f^{13} OL vg etc.; others omit the first *αὐτῶν*, so K Ψ Δ Diat etc., while ℵ* D* etc. omit both. P^{66vid} A B Θ Π* etc. include *αὐτῶν* in both places; this is the most likely reading, since the omission is natural in view of the apparent superfluity of the term.

[n] *ἐν* (*τῇ ἀληθείᾳ*) is read by ℵ* D L W Θ etc., whereas *εἰς* (*τὴν ἀλήθειαν*) is read by A B K Δ Π etc. The latter is often thought to be a correction of the former, but *ἐν* and *εἰς* are often confused in Hellenistic Gr., indicating little sense of difference in meaning (see BDF § 205, 206, 218). For implications that have been drawn from the two readings see the *Comment.*

[o] After *ὄψεσθέ με* some MSS add *ὅτι ὑπάγω πρὸς τὸν πατέρα* (so A Γ Δ Θ Ψ vg syr^{c,s,p,h,pal} cop^{bo} etc.). This would appear to be in order to provide for the disciples' question at the end of v 17 (Metzger, 247).

[p] *ἔχετε*, supported by P^{22} ℵ* B C K W^{c} f^{1} f^{2} etc., is preferable to the future *ἕξετε* (P^{66} ℵ^{c} A D W Θ Ψ etc.) which is apparently due to the future tenses in v 20.

[q] *αἴρει* (P^{22} P^{66vid} A C D^{b} K L Δ Θ Π etc.) is more likely to be original than *ἀρεῖ* (P^{5} B D* and versions), since the latter may have been influenced by the future tenses of the immediately preceding verbs.

[r] The position of *ἐν τῷ ὀνόματί μου* varies in the textual tradition; it comes after *δώσει ὑμῖν* in P^{5vid} ℵ B C * L X Δ etc., but before the verb in P^{22vid} A C^{3vid} D K W Θ Π Ψ f^{1} f^{13} etc. The latter accords more easily with the context of prayer, but the former is possible, and by virtue of its difficulty may be original; see the *Comment.*

[s] (*τοῦ*) *θεοῦ* found in P^{5} ℵ^{*,b} A C^{3} K W Δ Θ Π etc. and widely supported in the versions, is the more difficult reading than *τοῦ πατρός*, which appears in B C* D L X etc., and is probably due to correction in the light of the context, especially v 28.

ᵗ ἐξῆλθον παρὰ τοῦ πατρός is omitted by D W itᵇ ᵈ ff²syrˢ copᵃᶜʰ², probably by accident. The support for παρά (p⁵ p²² ℵ A C² K Δ Θ Π etc.) is somewhat stronger than for ἐκ (B C* L X etc.). Metzger suggests that the latter has arisen through assimilation to the compound verbs in the context (249).

ᵘ The utterance of Jesus could be either a question or an affirmation. The comparable utterance in 13:38 favors the former as intended.

ᵛ After the expression ἔρχεται ὥρα, ὅτε and ἵνα are interchangeable; see 4:21, 23, 25; 13:1; 16:2, and Brown, 2:~26.

Form/Structure/Setting

We have earlier recognized the likelihood that chaps. 13–14 consist of an introduction (13:1–30) and a complete Farewell Discourse of Jesus (13:31–14:31), and that chaps. 15–16 were composed from material left by the Evangelist and form an amplification of the original discourse (see "Introductory Note on the Composition of the Farewell Discourses of Jesus," pp. 223–24). In this supplementary instruction three clear divisions, if not actual discourses, may be discerned: (*i*) 15:1–17, (*ii*) 15:18–16:4a; (*iii*) 16:4b–33. These three sections we shall consider in order.

1. The discourse of 15:1–17 falls naturally into two subdivisions, marked by two related themes: namely, the Vine and its branches and the command to the disciples to love one another. The two themes are so closely connected, however it is possible to place the dividing line at different points: e.g., vv 1–6, 7–17 (Brown, 2:665–66); 1–8, 9–17 (Bultmann, 539–40); 1–10, 11–17 (Borig, 19); 1–11, 12–17 (Schnackenburg, 3:108). It is not vitally important to determine the precise point of division. There is much to be said, however, in favor of Schnackenburg's observation that the formula "I have said these things to you" in v 11 appears to bring the previous section to a close, much as 16:1 does to 15:18–27, and 16:4a for the second division of the discourse, and 16:33 the third division (3:91–93). It is entirely consonant with this suggestion to acknowledge, with Brown (and Schnackenburg following him), that vv 1–6 consist of a *māšāl*, a kind of parable, that finds exposition and application in vv 7–17, much as the "parable" of the Shepherd and his flock in 10:1–5 is developed in the discourse of 10:6–18 (2:665–67). It is also not impossible that the *māšāl* originally had a context earlier in the ministry of Jesus and that it was incorporated in the Last Discourse, along with sayings relative to the Vine and its branches and other themes traditional in the Last Discourse material. These purely critical observations lead to some interesting reflections on the interpretation of the passage: the discourse harks back directly to the introduction to the Last Supper in 13:1–30; the imagery of the Vine and its branches not unnaturally recalls the words of the Institution regarding "the fruit of the vine," which Jesus gave his disciples but which he would not again drink (Mark 14:25); the thought of sharing in the body and blood of Christ inevitably entails the concept of unity with the Christ in his dying and rising (as Paul explicitly states in 1 Cor 10:16–17), a theme which lies at the heart of the Vine parable. The very idea that the parable originated earlier than the Last Supper suggests that the link with the *Lord's Supper* is at best secondary, not primary, but its transfer to the *Last Supper* and its affinity of thought with the latter suggests that the Evangelist's successor and his churches saw the inner connection of the parable and the Eucharist.

2. 15:18–16:4a is a closely unified section, with the theme of the world's hatred for the Church. Some, it is true, have noted differences of emphasis within the passage. Becker divides it into two parts, vv 18–27, in which the world in its hatred to the Church is the subject, and 16:1–4a, wherein the reaction of the Church to its persecution is primary (2:488). Blank prefers a division of three: vv 18–25 sets forth the theological principles governing the Church's situation in the world; vv 26–27 is a Paraclete saying relating to this situation; and 16:1–4a deals with the urgent problem of the exclusion of Christians from the Jewish community (122). While these are helpful guides to the content of the whole, the unitary nature of 15:18–25; 16:1–4a is evident. The *whole* passage treats of the relation of "world" and Church, with an especial eye on the Jewish synagogue as representative of the unbelieving world. The theological principles expounded in 15:18–25 continue in 16:1–4a. The purpose of Jesus declaring "these things" in 16:1 manifestly relates to 15:18–25, and the sentence similarly introduced in 16:4a has the same motive, viz., persistence in faith in Jesus. The Paraclete saying in 15:26–27 is the clearest example in the Last Discourses of the interruption of the flow of thought by the insertion of a previously existing saying on the Spirit. The connection between 15:18–25 and 16:1–4a is unmistakably clear. Moreover the saying in 15:26–27 has the closest parallel of all Paraclete sayings with the synoptic tradition, namely with the logion relating to the Spirit's inspiration of the disciples on trial in Mark 13:9, 11 par. (a detailed comparison of the sayings is given by Porsch, *Pneuma und Wort,* 269). The Markan saying itself is also an independent saying; a version of it occurs in a Q passage (Luke 12:11–12). This declaration about the Spirit evidently circulated in the primitive Church, commonly (though not uniformly) in a context of persecution of disciples by reason of their witness to Jesus. While we may recognize that John 15:26–27 was inserted into its present context, there is no warrant for regarding it as an interpolation subsequent to the composition of the Gospel (as some followers of Windisch have maintained); it is part of the Johannine tradition of the instruction on the Paraclete-Spirit, and is integral to the Gospel's emphasis on witness to Jesus and unity with him in his sufferings.

3. The discourse of 16:4b–33 is closely related in substance and expression to that of 13:31–14:31, and like the earlier discourse is dominated by the departure of Jesus. In this connection three themes come to the fore. (*i*) In vv 4b–6, 16–24, the anguish of the disciples at the prospect of Jesus going to the Father is both elaborated and contrasted with the joy that will be theirs through their reunion with the risen Jesus; since the former will prove to be only temporary and the latter permanent the real emphasis in the passage falls on the abiding joy that the disciples will possess ("Your gladness no one will take from you," v 22), and the discourse concludes on the triumphant note, "Take heart, I have conquered the world" (v 33). (*ii*) It is likely that 16:4b–6, 16–24 at one time formed a continuous section. Into this context *three* statements about the Paraclete have been inserted. The first in v 7 contains a promise concerning the sending of the Spirit, consequent on the departure of Jesus, and links well to the introductory saying about the bestowal of the Spirit in 14:16–17. The second statement in vv 8–11 describes the Paraclete's

ministry with respect to the *world,* and follows well on the third Paraclete passage in 15:26–27 concerning the witness of the Paraclete and the disciples before the hostile world. The third Paraclete passage in vv 12–15 deals with the ministration of the Spirit to the disciples in relation to their ministry within *the Church;* it is reminiscent of the second Paraclete saying in 14:25–26, expanding its description of the Spirit's instruction to the disciples as to the content and meaning of the revelation brought by Jesus. All three sayings are independent, including the first. (That the Paraclete's coming is for the "good" of the disciples leads one to expect a statement of his gracious ministry, such as is given in vv 12–15, rather than his role as a prosecuting attorney, as in vv 8–11. Insofar, however, as the disciples are the agents of the Paraclete in his "exposure" of the world and share in the vindication of Jesus, vv 8–11 can be brought within the scope of v 7.) (*iii*) The final section of the discourse, vv 25–33, contrasts the obscurity of the teaching of Jesus during his ministry with the plain speech that he will use in the future. This must refer to the instruction that Jesus will give to his disciples by means of the Paraclete after his death and resurrection. The implications of v 25 are wide-ranging; while it probably relates especially to vv 16–24, it extends to the entire earthly teaching of Jesus, including the significance of his life, death, and resurrection, and underscores the necessity of the Spirit's illumination to grasp the revelation of God in and through his Son. As such it is an indirect allusion to the nature and purpose of this Gospel.

Comment

Jesus as the True Vine (15:1–17)

1 We have here the last of the ἐγώ εἰμι, "I am," sayings of the Gospel. It is the only one to which an additional predicate is conjoined ("and my Father is the Vinedresser"). In the unfolding of the "parable" it is the opening affirmation ("I am the true Vine") that is to the fore, but the Father as the Vinedresser stands in the background throughout (in the "parable" itself, in vv 2 and 6; in the discourse, in vv 7–11). This latter feature is comprehensible, since the redemptive action of the Son is always that of Mediator, through whom God speaks his word and does his works (cf. 14:10), and the relation of the Son to the believer, which is the chief theme of the passage, is both patterned on that of the Father and the Son and is the means of relating the believer to the Father (cf. 14:10; 17:21–23). It is a feature of the Vine discourse that the symbol and the reality symbolized tend to coalesce, the latter at times affecting the presentation of the former (as, e.g., in the emphasis on "and I in you," which does not strictly derive from the vine symbol).

Why is Jesus the *true* Vine? It is hardly intended to signify the spiritual reality which is symbolized by the Vine (Dodd, *Interpretation,* 139, adducing for comparison the Platonic notion of the ideal world of reality). Bultmann is nearer the mark in seeing Jesus as the true Vine in contrast with whatever also claims to be the Vine (529–30). In Bultmann's view the background is the Gnostic idea of the vine as the tree of life, as seen in the Mandaean literature (cf. *Ginza* 59:39–60:2, "We are a vine of life, a tree on which there is no lie . . . from the odour of which each man receives life," and 301:11–14, "I am a tender vine . . . and the great Life [= God] was my planter"). If such ideas were in circulation in the Evangelist's time the assertion of v 1 would be deeply significant: in Jesus what was purely mythological has become reality in flesh and blood and through death and resurrection. But the vine imagery in the OT and in Judaism, reflected also in the teaching of Jesus in the synoptic Gospels, is closer to hand and more obviously pertinent. Israel is frequently represented in the OT as a vine or a vineyard (cf. Hos 10:1–2; Isa 5:1–7; Jer 2:21; Ezek 15:1–5, 17:1–21; 19:10–15; Ps 80:8–18). The tradition was continued in Judaism; an elaborate allegorical portrayal of Israel as a vine is found in *Lev. Rab.* 36 (133a) (reproduced in Str-B 2:563–64); the vine is a frequent figure on coins and ceramics from the Maccabaean era on; Josephus relates that a large golden vine was set at the sanctuary entrance in the temple built by Herod (*Ant.* 15.395). It is striking that in every instance when Israel in its historical life is depicted in the OT as a vine or vineyard, the nation is set under the judgment of God for its corruption, sometimes explicitly for its failure to produce good fruit (e.g., Isa 5:1–7; Jer 2:21). The parable of Jesus in Mark 12:1–11 has a different point, but it is in harmony with these representations of judgment. It seems likely therefore that the description of Jesus as the *true* Vine is primarily intended to contrast with the failure of the vine Israel to fulfill its calling to be fruitful for God. That the Vine is *Jesus,* not the Church, is intentional; the Lord is viewed in his representative capacity, the Son of God–Son of Man, who dies and rises that in union with him a renewed people of God might come into being and bring forth fruit for God. (There may be precedent for this in Ps 80:14–18, where a prayer for the vine Israel is paralleled with prayer for "the man at your right hand, the son of man whom you have raised up for yourself," so Dodd, *Interpretation,* 411.) At all events it is not the Church but Jesus who is the true Vine. He is the Vine, not the trunk over against the branches; the latter are *in him* as part of the plant. The image is feasible prior to the death and resurrection of Jesus, in terms of fellowship and discipleship, but its full meaning is possible only on the basis of the Easter event and the sending of the Holy Spirit. So understood it is remarkably similar to the figure of Christ as the Body that includes the Church (as expounded in 1 Cor 12:12–13, 14–27, but differently developed in Col 1:18; 2:19; Eph 1:22–23). For the comparison between Israel and Jesus as the Vine see A. Jaubert, "L'image de la Vigne," in *Oikonomia,* FS Cullmann, 93–99).

2–4 On the word play in these sentences see the *Notes;* and on the link between cleansing through the word of Jesus and that through his redemptive action see the *Comment* on 13:10. To "remain" in Jesus has a deeper significance than simply to continue to believe in him, although it includes that; it connotes continuing to live in association or in union with him. Μείνατε (aorist tense), could signify "Step into union with me," which would be a suitable injunction for readers of the Gospel, and not wholly unsuitable for the group in the Upper Room in prospect of the new relationship with the Lord about to be initiated through his death and resurrection. "And I in you" may be viewed as the apodosis of a conditional sentence: *"If* you remain in me, I shall remain in you"; but the emphasis in the passage is on *Jesus,* the Vine, hence it is more likely that a note of encouragement is intended here, "and be assured, I am remaining in union with you." In the divine relationship grace is alike the source and support of faith. On this condition alone fruitbearing is possible, as the image of a branch broken from a vine vividly illustrates ("neither can you yield fruit unless you remain in me").

5 The application of the figure is clear: to "remain" in Christ is to become fruitful, but "without me you can do nothing." The statement echoes that of Jesus' relating to his own dependence on his Father and his helplessness without him (5:19, 30); the utterance is even more plainly applicable to the believer in relation to the Redeemer: apart from Christ "nothing," in Christ "much fruit." If we are to ask what fruitbearing signifies, the broad answer of Bultmann is adequate: "every demonstration of vitality of faith, to which, according to vv 9–17, reciprocal love above all belongs" (532–33); we may add, in the light of v 16, "to which also effective mission in bringing to Christ men and women in repentance and faith belongs" (so esp. Hoskyns: "Those who have believed in Jesus through the apostolic preaching are the fruit of the vine and its branches," 476).

6 The *māšāl* concludes by recounting what happens to unproductive branches of a vine: they are thrown away, become withered, are collected and used as firewood. The picture is realistic (the parable depicts what happens on the farm) and is not applied to the judgment of Gehenna, rather it vividly portrays the uselessness of such as do not remain in the Vine and their rejection by the Vinedresser (for similar applications of the imagery, see Ezek 15:1–5; Matt 3:10; 13:30). While the statement is general, it will have been difficult for the Evangelist and his readers not to think of Judas, and later of the "many Antichrists" who led out members from the Church and formed heretical groups (cf. 1 John 2:18–19; 4:1–6; Schnackenburg thinks rather of those who commit a "sin unto death" [1 John 5:16–17] 3:101).

7–10 These vv draw out and illustrate the meaning of "remaining" in Jesus. If in vv 1–6 the emphasis is on *faith* that trusts in Christ, opens life to Christ, and remains in union with Christ, v 7 emphasizes remaining in the *words* of Christ, i.e., the revelation that he brought (cf. Brown: "Jesus and his revelation are virtually interchangeable, for he is incarnate revelation," 2:662). Such a believer is assured that his prayers will be answered, for his prayers will be dominated by the desire for the service of the kingdom of God (see 14:12–14).

8 In such fruitbearing the Father is glorified in the believer, as he is in the Son in his redemptive work (12:23, 28, 31–32; 13:31–32; 17:1), and so doing the believer becomes a true follower of his Lord (a "disciple"; Brown aptly cites Ignatius, on his way to Rome for martyrdom: "Now I am beginning to be a disciple," Rom 5:3).

9–10 To "remain" in Jesus is also to remain in his *love,* just as Jesus throughout his life remained in the Father's love. This must mean primarily remaining in the love that Jesus has for his disciples—rejoicing in its reality, depending on its support, doing nothing to grieve it, but on the contrary engaging in that which delights the Lover. Not surprisingly, then, to "remain" in Jesus further entails *keeping the commands* of Jesus, as he kept his Father's commands and remained in his love. In this Gospel the obedience of Jesus to his Father is frequently mentioned (e.g., 4:34; 6:38; 8:29, 55), and that obedience reaches its climax in his yielding his life for the salvation of mankind (10:17–18; 12:27–28; 14:31). Bultmann accordingly defines the Son's "remaining" in the Father's love as a "being for" the Father, fulfilled in his obedient work as Revealer; even so the believer's "remaining in" the love of the Son consists in a "being for" him, fulfilled in the service of love as he commanded (541).

11 Such a relationship of love leads to joy to the uttermost. Jesus experienced it, even when facing the dread hour of sacrifice; he revealed these things to his disciples that they might have the same joy in fullest measure; they, too, are to know it as they walk in the same path as he (12:24–26; cf. Hoskyns' comment: "The delightful divine merriness of the Christians, which originates in the Son and is deposited in his disciples, is matured and perfected as they love one another, undergo persecution, and readily lay down their lives for the brethren, 1 John 3:16," 477).

12 The commands of Christ laid on those who would remain in his love (v 10) are comprehended in the one command to love one another. In it the call to love God (Deut 6:4–5), recited daily by the Jews and conjoined by Jesus with the command to love one's neighbor (Lev 19:18; cf. Mark 12:29–31), is subsumed, for the fulfillment of this command is the condition of remaining in the love of the Son and of showing authentic love to God (so 1 John 4:11–12, 20–21). The addition "as I have loved you" is important; it includes the manifestation of Christ's love in his death for others, and so reveals the standard of love that should be maintained among believers; it further hints of the motive of such love (again as perceived in 1 John 4:19), and its source in the redemptive love that frees us from restrictive love of self. (On the command to love in relation to the old covenant and its law and the new covenant and Christ's redemption see the *Comment* on 13:34–35.)

13 The giving of one's life for one's friends is the greatest measure of altruistic human love. Not surprisingly this sentiment appears in classical literature, where "a whole library has grown up around the theme of friendship" (G. Stählin, *TDNT* 9:153). Aristotle, e.g., writes, "To a noble man there applies the true saying that he does all things for the sake of his friends . . . and, if need be, he gives his life for them" (*Eth. Nic.* 9.8, 1169a). Plato stated "Only those who love wish to die for others" (*Symposium,* 179B). It was said of the Epicurean Philonides that "for the most beloved of his relatives or friends he was ready to offer his neck" (*Vita Philonidis,* 22, cited Deissmann, *Light from the Ancient East,* 120). Stählin suggested that in v 13 the Evangelist "is clothing an ancient rule of friendship in biblical speech in order to apply it to the relation of Jesus to his disciples and also to that of the disciples with one another" (*TDNT* 9:166). Possibly so, but the context of mutual love and sacrifice for others, as well as the Jewish tradition relating to the friends of God, makes it needless to look for the inspiration of the saying elsewhere.

14 Abraham was noted as a "friend of God" (Isa 41:8; 2 Chron 20:7; *Jub.* 19:9, etc.; James 2:23), as also was Moses (Exod 33:11). In rabbinical literature the reference to "my brethren and friends" in Ps 122:8 was viewed as uttered by God with reference to the people of Israel (so *Mek. Exod.* 14:15, 35b, see Str-B 2:564–65). Jesus refers to "Lazarus, our friend" in 11:11. The disciples are declared to be his friends by virtue of his love for them manifest in his death on their behalf (v 13) and their obedience to him. That Jesus "no longer" calls the disciples servants intimates a new relationship in the light of his revelation to them and his death for them. The mark of difference between a servant and a friend is precisely the confidence which is extended to the latter; so far as Jesus and his disciples are concerned this is especially manifest in the Upper Room discourses, wherein he made known to them what he had heard from the Father. The same contrast is assumed in 8:31–36, and is in harmony with Jewish belief regarding the outstanding friends of God, Abraham and Moses (cf. Gen 18:17; Exod 33:11; both passages led the Jews to speculate further on the revelations of God to the patriarch and the lawgiver, for Abraham see Str-B 2:525–26, for Moses see Wayne Meeks, *The Prophet-King, Moses Traditions and the Johannine Christology* [Leiden: Brill, 1967], especially chaps. 3–4).

16 The privilege bestowed on the disciples was not on account of their worth but through electing grace. As always in the Bible, the election was for a purpose: "I set you aside that you should go forth and yield fruit. . . ." The verb ἔθηκα, "set aside," is used in v 13 of Jesus "setting aside" his life for others. The term appears in Num 8:10 for the ordination of Levites; in Num 27:18 for Moses setting aside Joshua for his task; in Acts 13:47 it denotes the setting aside of the Servant of the Lord for his ministry as light and salvation of the nations (a citation from Isa 49:6), and in 1 Tim 1:12 it is used of Paul's being set aside for the apostolic ministry. While the general scope of fruitbearing, noted in the *Comment* on v 5, obtains here, the employment of ἔθηκα ("I have set you aside") and ὑπάγητε ("that you should go forth") suggests that the sending of the disciples on mission is to the fore here (so Westcott, 2:207; Bernard, 2:489; Lagrange, 408; Barrett, 478, etc.); to this end assurance is given that prayer in the name of Jesus (as they engage in seeking fruit for the Lord's glory) will be answered by the Father.

17 The paragraph ends as it began (v 12) with the reiterated command for mutual love, and so brings the discourse on the Vine fittingly to its conclusion. The injunction to love is the first and last word of Christ to his friends.

The Hatred of the World for the Church (15:18–16:4a)

18–19 The world's hatred for the disciples is a factor with which the disciples have to come to terms. Two roots of that hatred are here mentioned: the world's prior hatred for *Jesus,* which inevitably becomes directed to the disciples through their connection with him; and its perception that the disciples are not "of" the world, i.e., that their *origin* is in another world and that they *belong* to that other world (on the two "worlds" cf. 3:31; 8:23; 18:36–37).

20 The saying of which the disciples are reminded is in 13:16, "A servant is not greater than his master." It occurs also in the Q tradition (Matt 10:24 // Luke 6:40; its context in Matthew indicates that that evangelist also saw its implication for believers sharing in the rejection and persecution of Jesus). It is uncertain whether the two clauses following the citation are in synonymous or contrasted parallelism. NEB assumes the former, and so renders the second clause, ". . . they will follow your teaching *as little as they have followed mine*" (similarly Lagrange: "The observance of the teachings of Christ was only a hypothesis contradicted by the sad reality," 411; and Dodd: the statement is made *per impossibile; Historical Tradition,* 409). On this basis Becker drew the conclusion: "The chance of changing is taken from the world, it can only reproduce itself over against Jesus and the Church (cf. v 19). The chance of mission is taken from the Church, it can only endure hatred as the Church that is foreign to the world. It is the isolated little group . . ." (490). Such a deduction does injustice to the presentation of both world and Church in our Gospel. It appears to assume that in John the "world" is and can only be *always* irrevocably evil and hostile to Jesus, but this is not so, as may be seen in such passages as 6:33, 51; 8:12; 9:5, and notably 3:16–17; 4:42; 17:21. If the Jews are especially in mind as representatives of the world (as is the case), we should also recall instances wherein positive response among them to Jesus is recorded, e.g., 2:23 (however unsatisfactory!); 3:1–2; 8:31; 12:9, 11. Barrett's comment accordingly is justified: "The Mission of the Church will result in the same twofold response as the work of Jesus himself (cf. 12:44–50)" (480; similarly Bultmann, 549; Lindars, 494; Schnackenburg, 3:115; Bruce, 313).

21 "All these things they will do" relates to the content of vv 18–20 and pinpoints the causes of the opposition, namely "on account of my name" (cf. Mark 13:13), and "because they do not know him who sent me." The thought is expanded in vv 22–24. The guilt of the world consists in its rejection of the revelation brought by Jesus, and since that revelation is from God it entails the rejection of God himself, which is direst sin (v 22). Moreover the works of Jesus are God's works in and through him; hence it can be said that the world has "seen" God, i.e., seen him in action in the person of his Son, but its response has been to hate both the Son and the Father in him (v 24).

25 So the scripture finds its ultimate fulfillment: "they hated me *for nothing*" (δωρεάν). The saying occurs both in Ps 35:19 and in Ps 69:4; it is likely, however, that the latter passage is in mind, since that psalm is frequently cited in the NT in connection with the sufferings of Jesus ("Psalm 69 has been quarried for quotations by NT writers more than any other OT passage," so Lindars [on John 2:17] 140). On the usage whereby the "law" stands for the OT as such, cf. 12:34, and for the unusual expression *"their* law," cf. 8:17 and 10:34, which refer to *"your* law." This mode of speech does not indicate a dissociation of Jesus from the OT revelation, as may be seen in 5:39, 45–47; rather it implies that the Jews stand condemned by that very law in which they glory as theirs, since it was given by God to them alone.

26–27 The clauses relating to the Paraclete, "whom I will send from the Father," and "who proceeds from the Father," are set in synonymous parallelism, and so express the same idea in variation (Schnackenburg, 3:118, with most modern writers). This means that the latter clause must be interpreted of the sending of the Spirit *on mission* to humankind, and not of the so-called "procession" of the Spirit from the Father, as many Greek Fathers maintained, and as is represented in the historic creeds. The sending of the Spirit in many respects corresponds to the sending of the Son (cf. 8:42; 13:3; 17:8. On "the Spirit of truth" see 14:16–17, and the *Comment* on that passage, pp. 256–58). The Spirit's task is to "bear witness" concerning Jesus (περὶ ἐμοῦ). His witness therefore is not here conceived of as that of an advocate, speaking in defense of *the disciples* (contrary to Dodd, who considered the procedure to be the same as that in 9:35–41, with the Spirit in place of the Christ, *Interpretation,* 414); nor is it that of a prosecuting attorney, giving evidence *against* the world (contrary to Porsch, *Pneuma und Wort,* 270). The witness of the Spirit, conjoined with that of the disciples, is to bring to light the truth of the revelation of Jesus in his word and deed, and death and resurrection; it takes place with and through the witness of the disciples to *Jesus in the Gospel.* Clearly this witness of the Paraclete is not a phenomenon apart from that of the disciples, but inseparably associated with it. "The Spirit is the power of the proclamation in the community" (Bultmann, 553–54). The Spirit thus illuminates the hearers' minds as to the reality of that which is proclaimed by the disciples and brings its truth to bear on their consciences (cf. 16:8–11). The saying, accordingly, is one in intention with Mark 13:9 and 11. Since the latter is reproduced as a single, unbroken sentence in Luke 12:11–12, it would appear that Mark himself inserted the declaration between the two halves of the saying about the Spirit, the declaration that the gospel must be preached to all nations. In so doing he indicated that the disciples' appearances in court would be occasions for declaring the good news to the persecutors (Luke's paraphrase brings out that aspect even more clearly, Luke 21:13–15). The disciples will be capable of doing this because they have accompanied Jesus "from the beginning," i.e., from the outset of the ministry of Jesus to its close (cf. the echo of this condition of apostolic witness in Acts 1:21–22). The concept of "the beginning," however, is a flexible one; in 1 John 1:1; 2:13 the beginning is Christ himself, and in 1 John 2:24; 3:11 it relates to the beginning of the believer's experience of Christ, i.e., his conversion.

16:1 The purpose of making known "these things," described in 15:18–27, is to prevent the disciples from being "trapped" or "made to stumble," and so fall away from faith in Jesus and forsake his people (cf. 6:61; 1 John 2:10, and the parallel statement in Mark 14:27. For the interesting history of the concept σκάνδαλον see Stählin's article in *TDNT* 7:339–58).

2 It has become almost a critical *sententia recepta* that the statement, "they will put you out of the synagogue," reflects the *birkath ha-minim,* the twelfth of the Eighteen Benedictions of the Jews, which is believed to have been formulated toward the end of the first century of our era in order to exclude Jewish Christians from the Synagogue. (The benediction reads: "For the apostates let there be no hope, and let the arrogant government [= Rome] be speedily uprooted in our days. Let the Nazarenes and the Minim [= heretics] be destroyed in a moment and let them be blotted out of the Book of Life and not be inscribed with the righteous. Blessed art thou, O Lord, who humblest the arrogant." For a fascinating and typical discussion on the relation of this to the Fourth Gospel see Martyn, *History and Theology in the Fourth Gospel,* 37–62). Despite the popularity of this view its legitimacy is quite uncertain, and we would refer the reader to our discussion on the issue in connection with John 9:22, pp. 153–54. Holding together, as we have sought to do throughout this commentary, the twofold perspective of this Gospel in the setting of the ministry of Jesus and that of the Evangelist's day, we consider it important to note that the prospect of exclusion is held before the disciples exactly as in the beatitude of Luke 6:22; from this Dodd concluded that such a prospect was early enough to have entered the common tradition behind Luke and John, i.e., well before the decision of the Jewish authorities at Jamnia to include the curse on the Christians (see *Historical Tradition*, 410). Bultmann similarly considered that the historical circumstances reflected in v 2 belong to "the period which stretches approximately from Paul to Justin, and one cannot pinpoint it any more exactly than that" (555).

The introductory clause to the main sentence of v 2, "the hour is coming," applies to the disciples—language which is repeatedly used in this Gospel of the destiny of Jesus (cf. 2:4; 7:30; 8:20; 12:23, 27; 13:1; 17:1). The same language is employed of the eschatological hour that ushers in the kingdom of God (4:21, 23; 5:25; 12:31–32). Whether intentional or otherwise, it is reminiscent of the prophetic-apocalyptic expression "the days are coming," which frequently relates to the onset of the judgments of the Lord (as, e.g., in Jer 7:32; 9:25, and often in Luke, 17:22; 19:43; 21:6; 23:29) but also to God's deliverance and kingdom (e.g., Jer 16:14–15; 31:31–40). The statement in v 2 is further related to the description of the disciples' sufferings in Mark 13:9–13, which is set alongside Israel's tribulation and Jerusalem's day of the Lord. V 2 accordingly belongs to the strain of future expectation in the Fourth Gospel that coexists with its emphasis on the presence of the eschatological hour in the ministry and crucifixion-exaltation of Jesus (e.g., as in 6:40 etc., 11:25; 12:31–32, 48; 14:1–6, 18–23). The notion that to slay "heretics" could be an act of divine worship is attested in rabbinic literature. NuR 21 (191a) comments on the action of Phinehas in putting to death an Israelite man and Moabite woman who had cohabited, by which he "made atonement for the people of Israel" (Num 25:13): "Did he then offer a sacrifice, since it is said that atonement was made by him? This alone will teach you that everyone who pours out the blood of the godless is like one who offers a sacrifice." Comparable statements are made in *Sanh* 9.6, see Str-B 2:565. Examples of action on the basis of this conviction may be seen in the martyrdom of Stephen, recounted in Acts 7; the death of James the brother of Jesus, who according to Josephus was stoned at the instigation of the high priest Ananus II (*Ant.* 20.200); and the execution of Polycarp by the Romans, when the Jews were said to be zealous in gathering wood for the fire, although it was a Sabbath (*Mart. Polycarp*, 13.1). Justin, in his *Dialogue* with Trypho the Jew, declared: "Your hands are still raised to commit crime! Even after putting Christ to death you are not converted. You even hate and kill us, who through him believe in God, the Father of the universe, as often as you have the power to do so" (133.6). The Christians, alas, were to repay this treatment with interest a thousandfold. Both Jews and Christians have cause to repent of perverted ways of offering God "worship."

3–4 The affirmation that unbelieving Jews who so act know neither the Father nor Jesus follows on from 15:18–25, and is to be understood in that context of hatred of Jesus and rejection of the revelation in his words and works. (A similar judgment on individual synagogues in Roman Asia is implied in Rev 2:9 and 3:9, which should not be universalized as though it were applicable to all synagogues of that time and place.) The sufferings which the disciples are to endure should serve as confirmation of their Lord's knowledge of the future and therefore of their faith in him.

THE JOY THAT OVERCOMES GRIEF AND TRIBULATION (16:4b–33)

4b ταῦτα ("these things") appears to refer to 16:1 and 4a, and to relate to the persecution ahead of the disciples. But the addition, "because I was with you," makes explicit what is assumed in vv 1–4a—that Jesus is about to leave his disciples.

6 It is the prospect that he is now on the point of going to the Father, rather than the persecution, that causes the disciples' anguish (the point is elaborated in vv 16–24). The gentle reproach in v 5, "None of you asks me, 'Where are you going?'", has caused perplexity in view of Peter's earlier asking this very question (13:36; cf. also Thomas's reference to the issue in 14:5). Various explanations have been offered to solve the problem. (*i*) The text is thought to have suffered dislocation. Bernard, e.g., placed chaps. 15–16 after the opening clause of 13:31, following them with 13:31b–14:31 (I,xx). Bultmann modified the suggestion by postulating the primitive order as chap. 17, 13:31–35, chaps. 15–16, 13:36–38, chap. 14 (459–61). Such suggestions raise difficulties of their own and are not generally favored. (*ii*) It is maintained that there is no contradiction between 13:36 and 14:5. Lagrange, for example, urged that since Jesus explained where he was going it was needless for the disciples to ask further on that point "now" (νῦν); "the intellectual trouble is dissipated, but the sadness remains" (417–18). Dodd has essentially the same view: "The disciples are in full possession of Christ's disclosure of his (and their) goal. . . . Consequently they are no longer puzzling themselves about the destination, and that is as it should be; but that being so, it is quite unreasonable to be sad about it" (*Interpretation,* n.1, 412–13). Hoskyns, by contrast, maintained that the lesson had *not* been grasped by the disciples: "Grief at his departure remains only when the disciples fail to persist in asking, *Domine, quo vadis?*" (483). (*iii*) The different representations in 13:36 and 14:5 are thought to be due to the work of an editor. For some that simply means that different uses have been made of the tradition without concern to reconcile them (so Brown, 2:710; Schnackenburg, 3:126). That is not unreasonable, when it is recalled that 13:31–14:31 is a complete farewell discourse and that chaps. 15–16 are built on related material. This common material is particularly apparent when comparing the first discourse with 16:4b–33. We saw that 13:33, 36–38 forms a continuous series of sayings; there is a close relation between them and 16:4b–5, 16–18. Had the final editor chosen to form one continuous discourse out of chaps. 13–16 he would doubtless have set 16:5 before 13:36; but he chose not to disturb the Evangelist's work in chaps. 13–14, expecting the reader to contemplate the teaching as preserved in the units of tradition. The main point of v 5 is in any case plain: the disciples were too concerned about their own loss to ponder the implications of Jesus going to the Father (contrast 14:28); if they were to do so their pain and doubt would be set to rest.

7 The statement that Jesus must depart before the Paraclete can come has led to some questionable exegesis. It is viewed as affirming "the impossibility of a concurrent ministry of the two Paracletes," and implies that "so long as the dominant personality of their Master was at their side the disciples could not grow to their full stature" (W. F. Howard, *Christianity According to St.*

John, 76, also in *IB* 7:730–31). Neither assertion is justifiable. If it be true, as Porsch holds, that the future presence of the Paraclete is better than the bodily presence of Jesus, it is unlikely that its intention is to express that. What Porsch has in mind is more carefully stated: "Only after Jesus' departure to the Father can the Paraclete demonstrate who he really is. To that extent full faith was possible only after the completion of the work of Jesus" (*Pneuma und Wort*, 279; the same interpretation is given by Brown, 2:710–11; Blank, *Commentary*, 135). Schnackenburg advances on this by maintaining that the statement "really points to the appointment of Jesus in his full effectiveness, since all that the Spirit does is to express Jesus and set his saving power free" (3:127). Haenchen expounds the astonishing idea that in this passage the Evangelist makes his understanding of the atonement plain: the gift of the Spirit is the sole means of taking away sin (493–94). Fundamentally the statement affirms the gracious continuance of the salvation history (Bammel, "Jesus und der Paraklet," 209). The key to its meaning is in the two clauses "if I do not go away . . . but if I go . . ." seen in light of the total teaching of the Gospel on the departure of Jesus. When 16:7 is set alongside 7:39; 12:23, 27–28, 31–32; 13:31–32 and 20:22, it is evident that the "lifting up" of Jesus via his cross to the throne of God brings about the turn of the ages that ushers in the saving sovereignty of God in fullness. From that time on the salvation of the kingdom of God in Jesus may be freely appropriated, in accordance with the ancient promises that *the Spirit of the kingdom of God* will be given for the renewal of man and the cosmos (see above all Joel 2:28–32, also Isa 32:14–18; 44:1–5; Jer 31:31–34; Ezek 11:17–20; 36:24–27; 37:1–14, and the passages that associate the Spirit with the saving rule of the Messiah, e.g., Isa 11:1–10; 42:1–4). The teaching on the Paraclete-Spirit is part and parcel of the eschatology of the Fourth Gospel that is centered in Christology. The Redeemer Son of God and Son of Man mediates the saving sovereignty of God through the Spirit of Life.

8 The role of the Paraclete in relation to the world that has rejected and continues to reject the revelation of God in Jesus is briefly announced in v 8 and explained in vv 9–11.

The brevity of the statement in v 8 and of the explanation in vv 9–11 has led to a variety of interpretations of the passage; its right understanding can be gained only in light of related teaching in the Gospel. The key term in v 8 is ἐλέγξει. In secular Gr. the verb's use is very broad. Büchsel summarized it as follows: In Homer ἐλέγχειν signifies "to scorn, to bring into contempt"; in later literature it means (*a*) to "shame" by exposure, opposition, etc.; (*b*) "to blame"; (*c*) "to expose," "to resist"; (*d*) to "interpret, expound"; (*e*) "to investigate." In the NT the usage is more restricted; basically it means "to show someone his sin and to summon him to repentance" (*TDNT* 2:473–74). Guidance as to its meaning in our passage is provided by its two other appearances in the Fourth Gospel: in 3:20 it is stated that the evil person hates the light and avoids it "in case his evil deeds be exposed" (NEB "should be shown up"); and in 8:46 Jesus asks his opponents, "which of you can prove me in the wrong?", i.e., demonstrate that Jesus is a sinner. Hoskyns was right in maintaining that in the passage before us ἐλέγχειν is almost exactly equivalent to the English term "expose" (484). The Oxford English Dictionary classifies the meanings of the word under two heads: (*i*) "put out into the open" (as the exposure of a plant or an infant); (*ii*) "to put forth, present to view," hence make known, disclose (secrets, etc.), set forth, and "unmask, show up an error or misrepresentation or impostor." It is this latter group of meanings which is evident in v 8 and its exposition in vv 9–11. The Paraclete is to *expose* the world and *demonstrate its error* with reference to sin, righteousness, and judgment. Observe that this exposure is not primarily related to specific acts of sin, righteousness, and judgment, but as to what sin, righteousness, and judgment *are*. The context of this exposure is the kerygma that sets forth God's action in Jesus, to which the Paraclete and the disciples bear witness before the world (15:26–27). This relationship of the Paraclete's "exposure" of the world calls into question Carson's valiant attempt to bring consistency into the understanding of v 8: "He will convict the world of *its* sin, *its* righteousness (showing its inadequacy) and *its* judgment (its false assessment of spiritual reality," "The Function of the Paraclete in John 16:7–11," 547–66); the Paraclete's exposure of the world is specifically in his witness to Jesus in the Gospel. The same factor makes implausible the view that the work of the Paraclete in this passage is directed to the illumination of *the disciples,* not of the world; the Paraclete is held to demonstrate to the disciples what sin, righteousness, and judgment are in face of the continuous accusations of the world that they, like Jesus, are guilty men, deserving of judgment; the Spirit consoles the disciples by showing that it is the world that is sinful, that true righteousness is in Jesus, and that the world stands condemned (so Berrouard, "Le Paraclet, défenseur du Christ devant la conscience du croyant," 361–89; followed by de la Potterie, "Le Paraclet," 101–3; S. Lyonnet, *La vie selon l'Esprit, condition du chrétien,* 85–105; Brown, 2:711–14; Porsch, *Pneuma und Wort,* 280–89). This rather sophisticated interpretation does not comport with the indications within the text that the Paraclete's ministry is here directed to the world itself, using the disciples' proclamation as his instrument, as in 15:26–27. The process in mind is strikingly illustrated in Acts 24:24–25, as well as in 1 Cor 14:24; Eph 5:11. Moreover it is likely that the "exposure" of the world through witness to Jesus is not restricted to bringing to light the *fact* of the world's condemnation but to enable individuals within the world to grasp it; i.e., it is an existential revelation, "at the same time both a disclosure of reality and as the realization of the revelation" (Schnackenburg, 3:129).

The fundamental concept of v 8 and its elaboration in vv 9–11 is that of a trial of the world before God. The "world" had already conducted its own trial of Jesus; therein he was declared to be guilty of heinous sin—sedition against Caesar and blasphemy against God, hence a man without righteousness and worthy of death. Significantly the accounts of the trial of Jesus, alike in the Fourth Gospel as in the Synoptics, are written to show that in reality *Jesus* was the innocent one and the "world" was condemned by its action. The task of the Paraclete is to expose the reality of this situation, and the trial before the Sanhedrin and Pilate's judgment hall in Jerusalem gives place to the tribunal of God in heaven. The Paraclete, through the witness of the disciples to Jesus in the gospel and its exemplification in the Church, unveils to the world the real nature of sin and righteousness and judgment in the light of what God was doing in Jesus, and its implications for men and women. The elements of this exposure are itemized in vv 9–11. The function of ὅτι in each clause is not to indicate cause ("To take ὅτι causally is artificial," Büchsel, 474 n.7), but to explicate the assertion in v 8: "in that, inasmuch as . . ." (so Bultmann, 563; Schnackenburg, 3:129).

9 The recognition that the prime *sin* is unbelief in relation to God's revelation in Christ runs through our Gospel (cf. 1:11; 3:19; 15:22). Such unbelief entails rejection, not ignorance, of the proclamation of Christ in the Gospel. Since the "exposure" of the world is one of a continuing situation, it has to do not only with the vote of the Jewish Sanhedrin and the decision of Pilate but with the attitude of the "world" as such. On this Blank commented: "Through the event of revelation and salvation, as through its continuing presence in the Church and its proclamation, the love that gives itself to the uttermost meets the *cosmos* itself, hence any πρόφασις περὶ ἁμαρτίας, i.e., any pretext or sophistry to remain further in sin, as also any excuse, is taken away. Thereby the sin in unbelief becomes naked, unveiled sin. . . . The condemnation is then the not-loving and the not-willing-to-live-out-of-love, which becomes a no-more-able-to-love" (*Krisis,* 336).

10   The nature of *righteousness* is brought to light in that Jesus "goes away" to the Father and his disciples "see him no more." This attestation is bound up with the mode of Jesus' departure: the lifting up of Jesus on the cross, which in the world's eyes was the demonstration of Jesus' unrighteousness, was none other than the means of his exaltation to heaven by the Father; it was at once God's reversal of the verdict of men, and so his attestation of the innocence of Jesus over against the world's allegations against him, and his installation of Jesus into the spendor of the session at his right hand; the justification of Jesus thus is the vindication of his righteousness in life and his entrance upon *righteousness in glory* with the Father (cf. 12:23; 13:31–32; 17:1, 5; and 1 Tim 3:16).

The addition of "and you no longer see me" is surprising, since the third person is used in vv 9 and 11; one would have expected "and the world no longer sees me." *Both* statements occur elsewhere in the Gospel (14:19; 16:16; the same idea is otherwise expressed in 7:33; 8:21; 13:33); here it underscores the finality of the departure of Jesus to the Father. What to the world was the end of Jesus, his disappearance forever from the earth scene, the disciples came to know as none other than the reception of Jesus by the Father into glory. This was the heart of the Easter proclamation and the disciples' task was to bear witness of it to the world. Where the world rejects the testimony, their "joy" at being rid of Jesus (16:20) is "the joy of the damned" (Blank, *Krisis,* 338); where it is received they experience the joy of the forgiven.

11   The reality of *judgment* and the world's entailment in it is exposed by the Spirit through the revelation in the Gospel that "the prince of this world has been judged." Again we are pointed back to 12:31: the judgment of the world took place when the Son of Man was lifted up on the cross and to heaven and its prince was "thrown out." The ejection of the latter from his vaunted place of rule took place as the Son of Man was installed by God as Lord of creation and Mediator of the saving sovereignty of God to the world. Hence the song of heaven in Rev 11:15 is appropriated as already proleptically realized: "The sovereignty of the world has passed to our Lord and his Christ, and he shall reign for ever and ever." The Paraclete brings to light that this involves the judgment *of the world* in that its submission to the "prince of this world" led not only to its rejection of the Son of God, but to becoming the tool of its prince to his murder; its continued failure to acknowledge Jesus as the rightful Lord of the world, installed by God, implicates it in the judgment that took place in the cross and resurrection of Jesus. Like the prince of this world, its cause is lost; *it has been judged.*

12   The last Paraclete passage forms a fitting climax to the rest, and brings together the intimations regarding the Spirit's ministry for the Church. Its opening sentence is fully in harmony with the situation of Jesus' farewell to the disciples, but it raises the question as to how it is related to the second Paraclete saying (14:26). Becker asserts that it is in flat contradiction to the earlier saying; that speaks of the Paraclete reminding the disciples of a *finished* revelation from the Lord on earth, whereas this one has in view the task of the Spirit as communicating *revelation yet to be received* from the risen Lord in heaven (2:498). This position is characteristic of an attitude that wherever a tension in utterances of this Gospel is observable we must be dealing with the work of an editor with a different theology. It is possible, however, that the tension at times may be deliberate, in order to cater to different aspects of the revelation and to different needs of the recipients. Such appears to be the case here, where Jesus speaks of a future which is beyond the ability of the disciples to imagine, and therefore the relevance of his teaching to those circumstances also beyond their present grasp. So Bultmann interprets: "The believer can only measure the significance and claims of what he has to undergo when he actually meets it. . . . Thus the apparent contradiction between v 12 and 15:15 is comprehensible: Jesus cannot state all that the future will bring, and yet he has said it all, everything, that is, that makes the believer free and ready for it" (572; similarly Porsch, "What is meant is not "*more*" in revelation, but *a new mode* of imparting it," *Pneuma und Wort,* 291).

13 The "Spirit of truth" will lead the disciples to grasp "all the truth." De la Potterie, preferring the reading εἰς (τὴν ἀλήθειαν πᾶσαν) understands it as showing the goal of the Spirit's leading, "to the very heart of all truth" ("Le Paraclet," 45 n.1); Brown, on the basis of ἐν (τῇ ἀληθείᾳ πάσῃ), understands the leading as "along the way of truth" (2:703); Barrett explains it as "guidance in the whole sphere of truth" (489). In any case the emphasis is on the term "all": the truth has been made known by Jesus to the disciples, but their grasp of it has been limited; the task of the Paraclete will be to lead them that they may comprehend the depths and heights of the revelation as yet unperceived by them. It is explicitly stated that the revelation mediated by the Paraclete will not be his own, but one that he will receive ("all that he will hear"). Its source is stated in vv 14–15: the Paraclete will receive from Jesus what he imparts to the disciples, just as Jesus received it from the Father. The latter point is emphasized throughout this Gospel with respect to the message of Jesus (e.g., 3:32–35; 7:16–18; 8:26–29, 42–43; 12:47–50), and it extends to the revelation in his works (5:19–27), for the revelation in his words and works is one (14:9–10). So constant is this emphasis, it is to be presumed that *the one revelation of God in Christ* is the content of that which the Spirit is to convey to the disciples. The significance of v 13 is its acknowledgment that the Spirit participates in the task of communicating the revelation to the Church by virtue of his relation to Jesus, just as Jesus communicated it by virtue of his relation to the Father. Porsch states the content of v 13 concisely: "Jesus brings the truth, and makes it present through his coming into the world; the Spirit-Paraclete opens up this truth and creates the entrance into it for the believers" (300).

The statement that the Paraclete "will disclose to you the things that are coming" has caused no little discussion. Popularly it has been understood as the inspiration of a prophetic ministry regarding the future of the kingdom of God, with the notable example of the Book of Revelation in mind (so Schlatter, 314; Bernard, 2:511; Wikenhauser, 295; Windisch, *Spirit-Paraclete*, 12; Johnson, *Spirit-Paraclete*, 38–39; Betz, *Der Paraklet*, 191–92). The difficulty about relating such a prophetic ministry *exclusively* to the future is that it is out of harmony with the general outlook of this Gospel. Thüsing makes the interesting suggestion that "the things that are coming," from the standpoint of the company in the Upper Room, most naturally refer to the "hour" that is coming, of which Jesus in the Gospel often speaks, i.e., the hour of his death and resurrection (*Erhöhung und Verherrlichung Jesu*, 149– 53). Most recent exegetes broaden the application to include the significance of Jesus' teaching for the time of the Church ("the new order which results from the departure of Jesus," Hoskyns, 487). Bultmann simply views the last clause of v 13 as stating "the essential significance of the word . . . : it illuminates the future"(575). The expression "prophetic ministry," accordingly requires to be taken in its classic biblical meaning as disclosing the word of God as it relates to *all* times: that word interprets the past, discloses the will of God for the present, and reveals the purpose of God that determines the future. There is a striking parallel to v 13 in Isa 41:21–29, where Yahweh challenges the idol-gods of the nations to present their case by uttering genuine prophecy: "Let them declare the meaning of past events, that we may give our minds to it; let them predict things that are to be that we may know their outcome. Declare what will happen hereafter; then we shall know you are gods" (vv 22–23). Porsch considers that the Evangelist was inspired by this passage in his whole presentation of the "law-suit" of Jesus against the world, and rightly points out the eschatological significance of the original passage, together with the eschatological nature of its "fulfillment" in the revelation in Jesus. This is undoubtedly right, providing that we acknowledge that the fulfill- ment of the hope of the kingdom of God is in the *total* revelatory and redemptive work of Jesus, i.e., in his ministry, death, and resurrection, sending of the Spirit of the kingdom, and the consummation of life and judgment at the end. In that context Porsch's conclusion as to the "prophetic" ministry of the Spirit is illuminating: "He will teach an understanding of the 'signs of the times' in the specific, concrete historical hour in light of the revelation of Jesus, especially of its eschatological significance" (*Pneuma und Wort*, 298). The unusual repetition of the term "disclose" (ἀναγγελεῖ) in vv 13, 14, 15 confirms the reference of all three sentences to the eschatological significance of the entire revelation of God in Christ—in the word and deed of his ministry, in his death and resurrection, and in the consummation of the divine sovereignty.

14–15 The singular use of the term "glorify" in relation to the death and resurrection of Jesus in this Gospel (esp. 12:23, 27–28; 13:31–32; 17:1, 5) suggests that the revelatory work of the Spirit, described as "he shall glorify me," has a special relation to the *redemptive* work of Jesus, wherein the revelation of God in Christ reaches its apex. In the Spirit's unfolding of that revelation the glorification of Jesus in his death and exaltation continues. For the revela- tion of God is supremely Jesus, given in incarnation, death, and resurrection, for the life of the world (3:16).

16–19 The paragraph of vv 16–24 follows on the reference to the sadness of the disciples at Jesus' announcement of his departure to the Father in vv 4b–6 (while the Paraclete sayings theologically belong to this context they interrupt the sequence of vv 4b–6, 16–24). The instruction of Jesus as to his departure and return is succinctly stated in v 16. The "little while" of the departure has been intimated more than once (to the Jews, 7:33, and then to the disciples, 13:33a); now, however, it is stated that the "little while" prior to the departure is followed by a "little while" that precedes his disciples' seeing him again. They are perplexed by both utterances, just as they were by the reference (in v 5) to Jesus' "going away" to the Father. They voice their bewilderment to one another, and so provoke a response from Jesus.

20 The disciples will both weep and make the lamentation for death (in Matt 11:17 = Luke 7:32: θρηνεῖν indicates the singing of funeral dirges; in Luke 23:27 it is conjoined with the beating of breasts by women as they follow Jesus to his crucifixion). By contrast "the world" will rejoice at the death of one whom it viewed as its enemy. But the situation of the disciples will speedily be transformed; their anguish will be turned to joy—after another "little while"!

21–22 To clarify the nature of the change a brief parable is adduced: a woman in labor has anguish, but when her child is born her anguish is turned to joy; so too the anguish of the disciples will give place to gladness, for the Lord who has died will appear to them ("I shall see you"), and thereafter their joy will be perpetual. The statement that *Jesus* will see the disciples, replacing that of v 16 ("*You* will see me"), shows that more is in view than simply a fresh spiritual insight on their part. The disciples will know joy instead of sadness because Jesus, having left them in death, will meet them in resurrection life. It is the Easter resurrection that is in view. Consequent on that no man will have power to rob the disciples of their joy, because Easter is not an isolated event but the beginning of the new creation (20:22), wherein disciples will know the presence of the Lord in a manner impossible in the days of his flesh. From that time on, therefore, life for them is existence in the shared fellowship of Father, Son, and Holy Spirit (14:21, 23, 26).

23–24 The joy of the new time introduced by Easter is to be characterized by two notable features: first, the joy of understanding; the disciples will no longer have to question Jesus in the kind of bewilderment which they had just known (vv 16–18), for Easter will be as a shaft of light from heaven on the way of Jesus, and the Spirit will be their leader into "all truth"; second, the joy of efficacious prayer, since the Father will hear and grant their prayers "in the name of Jesus." (The reference of "in my name" is uncertain, as is illustrated by its different positions in the early manuscripts. If the reference is to prayer *asked* in the name of Jesus, it assumes the naming of his name as Redeemer-Lord and presenting petitions for his sake and glory. If the reference is to the Father *giving* in the name of Jesus, it signifies giving in virtue of the achieved redemption of Jesus and the relation of the petitioners to him. In either case the promise assumes the role of Jesus as Mediator of the saving sovereignty of God for man.)

The parable of v 21, despite its simplicity and naturalness, is replete with echoes of OT prophecy, and it has the important function of emphasizing the eschatological nature of the event in view, namely the death and resurrection of Jesus. The figure of the pangs of childbirth is frequent in the OT for the swift coming of God's judgment upon wrongdoers (cf. e.g., Isa 21:2–3; Jer 13:21; Mic 4:9–10). Isa 66:7–14 is an example of the same image applied to bringing to birth the new age of salvation. Moreover the phrase "a little while" also frequently occurs in passages anticipating the eschatological action of God (e.g., Isa 10:25; 29:17; Jer 51:33; Hos 1:4). In this connection

Isa 26:16–21 is particularly important, since it combines the "little while" of
God's coming for judgment with the figure of a woman writhing in her labor
pains and a startling promise of resurrection ("Your dead will live; their
bodies will rise. You who dwell in the dust, wake up and shout for joy!"). In
view of these associations the whole passage, vv 16–24, has been interpreted
as primarily relating to the appearance of Jesus as Son of Man at the end
of the age (as early as Augustine, *In Jo.*, 101.5–6). Barrett believes that the
language is intended to apply both to the resurrection of Jesus and his Parousia
(491–92). Brown considers that the original teaching of Jesus as to his vindication was vague, and that the distinction between his resurrection and Parousia
was due to teachers within the Church; the Evangelist interprets the tradition
before him as indicating the presence of Jesus in his Church through the
coming of the Paraclete-Spirit (730). The majority of exegetes, however, recognize that this passage has in view the coming of Jesus to his disciples in the
Easter appearances and the new age which it introduces. There is no thought
of the Parousia in vv 16, 20–22, as the sequel in vv 23–24 surely makes
plain, nor does the Evangelist wish to depict in this passage the sending of
the Paraclete. His intention is one with his representations throughout this
Gospel that the death and resurrection of Jesus bring to a climax the eschatological action of God in him through which the promised saving sovereignty of
God comes to humankind (see esp. Hoskyns, 487–89; Lindars, 506–10;
Schnackenburg, 3:155–60).

25 A contrast is drawn between speech given "in proverbs" and instruction
that is plain, without concealing anything. The former relates to the ταῦτα
("these things") that Jesus has just uttered. That must signify the immediately
preceding paragraph, in particular the enigmatic saying of v 16 (cf. the puzzled
questioning in vv 17–18), its expansion in v 20, and the parable of v 21.
Without doubt, however, the Evangelist wishes us to see its pertinence to
the whole discourse in which it is set (vv 4b–33) and to the rest of the Last
Discourses of Jesus. Inasmuch as the revelation through Jesus remains hidden
from those who reject his claims, the entire story of Jesus, his life and death,
his words and deeds, come under the rubric "the obscure speech of metaphor."
The concept is closely akin to the presentation of the ministry of Jesus in
this Gospel as a book of "signs."

"The obscure speech of metaphor" is, of course, a paraphrastic rendering of
ἐν παροιμίαις. The term παροιμία is used in the Bible to translate the Heb. מָשָׁל
(*māšāl*), along with παραβολή which must be seen as synonymous with παροιμία.
That παραβολή does not occur in this Gospel is simply a predilection of the Evangelist.
The chief meanings of *māšāl* are (*i*) proverb, (*ii*) riddle, (*iii*) parable. In the Semitic
mind these three are closely interrelated. The author of the Book of Proverbs
writes his work to enable the man of understanding "to understand a proverb
(*māšāl*) and a parable, the sayings of the wise and their riddles" (Prov 1:6). Ben
Sira similarly speaks of the wise man as one who "researches into the hidden
sense of proverbs (ἀπόκρυφα παροιμιῶν) and ponders the obscurities of parables (ἐν
αἰνίγμασι παραβολῶν)" (Sir 39:3). The enigmatic quality of proverbs and parables
is taken for granted. An important development of the *māšāl* was its use as a
vehicle of prophecy, as may be seen in the well-known "love song" of the vineyard
(Isa 5) and still more in the prophetic allegories of Ezekiel (e.g., chaps. 15, 16,
17, 19, 23). It was natural for the apocalyptists to take up this mode of proclaiming

their message; the most significant example of this is the so-called *Parables of Enoch* (Enoch 37–71) which are extended apocalyptic visions regarding the judgment, the resurrection, the kingdom of God, and the Son of Man, and are represented to be "the words of the Holy One" (Enoch 37:2). That the aphorisms, similes, and parables of Jesus have an enigmatic quality about them is reflected in Mark 4:11: "To you the secret (μυστήριον) of the kingdom of God has been given, but for those outside everything takes place in parables," where the term "parables" comes close to meaning "riddles." The saying could easily have found a home in the Fourth Gospel, for, as the term γίνεται ("happens, takes place") shows, "everything" (τὰ πάντα) includes not alone the words of Jesus but his whole ministry, his action as well as his teaching; Jesus is a riddle to those who fail to perceive his role as mediator of the kingdom of God. It is comprehensible therefore that the revelation in Jesus should be described in our passage as given ἐν παροιμίαις. By contrast in the "hour" that is coming, i.e., following the hour of Jesus' suffering, he is to speak *plainly* of the Father. This can only signify his instruction mediated through the Spirit-Paraclete, as indicated in 16:12–15 (observe: "I have many things to say to you . . . when *he* comes he will guide you . . . *he* will receive what is mine and disclose it to you"). The threefold appearance of ἀναγγελεῖ in vv 12–15 corresponds to the ἀπαγγελῶ of v 25.

26–27 As was intimated in vv 23–24, the coming "hour," to be ushered in by the resurrection of Jesus, will be characterized by a new understanding of his revelation and by a new freedom and effectiveness in prayer. Here the emphasis lies on the fellowship with the Father which they will know, a fellowship rooted in that which they have with Jesus, who is one with the Father. While we may contrast this statement with assertions of the mediatorial role of Jesus in heaven (Rom 8:34; Heb 7:25; 1 John 2:1), it is clear that the emphasis in this passage is on the freedom of access which the disciples will have to the Father. There will be no need for Jesus to persuade the Father to listen to their prayers, still less to turn aside his wrath from them, for the Father himself loves them. Barrett points out that vv 26–27 elaborate the thought of 15:13–15; the disciples are called the "friends" of Jesus and with him form a unique circle of love: "In the present passage the point is that the Father himself stands within this circle (as indeed is implied by 15:9 f.)" (496).

28 The promise of plain speech is now adumbrated in a terse utterance which is at once a summary of Johannine Christology and the heart of this Gospel. The purpose of the "coming forth" and returning to the Father is assumed rather than stated, viz., the restoration of man to fellowship with God in the saving sovereignty. (So Schlatter: "Through the entrance into the world he establishes fellowship with men, through his departure from it he consummates his fellowship with God. Therein his greatness consists, that on both sides he perfects the fellowship; it gives him his royal power," 316.)

29–30 The disciples assume that the time of "plain speech" has begun. They are excited—now they understand it all! Clearly Jesus knows everything about God and man, and all that pertains to judgment and salvation and the kingdom; he has no need for anyone to put questions to him and test his knowledge, as the episode in vv 16–24 has demonstrated; he has in truth "come forth from God"!

31–32 Their enthusiastic confidence is shattered by Jesus. In his piercing question of two words the first bears the emphasis, *"Now (ἄρτι) believe?"* They have leaped to the conclusion that the time of plain speech has arrived, but the darkest hour of all time looms ahead before that hour can come, and in it their frailty of faith will be revealed. In them the prophecy of Zech 13:7 will be fulfilled: "Awake, O sword, against my shepherd, against the man who is close to me!" declares the Lord Almighty. "Strike the shepherd, and the sheep will be scattered. . . ." But if Jesus is to be forsaken by his friends he will not be abandoned by his Father: "the Father is with me," supporting him in his hour of testing as in every crisis of his ministry (8:29).

The question is raised whether v 32b implies a rejection of the tradition of the cry of desolation, recorded in Mark 15:34. In our judgment the affirmation that it does entails a misunderstanding of the Evangelist's intention. He is contrasting the faithlessness of the disciples in his hour of trial with the faithfulness of his Father. It has nothing to do with the experience of Jesus at one terrible moment on the cross, wherein he expressed his agony of spirit by quoting Ps 22:1. We should hesitate either to ascribe to Jesus in that moment a false judgment of his situation, or to equate the cry of desolation with the triumphant "It is finished" (on the ground that Ps 22 also concludes on a triumphant note; Hoskyns, 492, 531). The expression of confidence in his Father's presence when his followers desert him is entirely comprehensible in v 32. If a comparison with Mark 15:34 is legitimate the latter becomes yet more terrible in significance, but must be seen as the unfathomed depth of the descent of the Son of God prior to his ascent to the Father's right hand—a figure which is not inharmonious with the paradox of John 12:31–32!

33 Jesus' last word to his disciples is not of condemnation but encouragement, for he anticipates their speedy recovery. He has spoken "these things" (i.e., the discourse, not simply v 32) that *in him* they may have peace. He has already assured them of the possession of joy (vv 22, 24); peace and joy are two primary realities of the saving sovereignty that Jesus brings, and they are gifts of the present—even in tribulation! If the latter is the disciples' lot in this world, tribulation (θλῖψις) is the precursor of the triumphant kingdom of God. And the victory that brings the kingdom has already been won! "I have conquered the world" is the word of the Victor who, by his enduring θλῖψις in obedience and unwavering love, conquered the evil in the world, as he overcame the "prince" of this world (12:31). And *in him* every disciple shares his victory (a conviction strongly emphasized in 1 John: the believer conquers the evil one, 2:13–14, the Antichrists of this world, 4:4, and the world itself, 5:4–5).

Explanation

The relation of the time of Jesus and his disciples with that of the risen Lord and his Church in the Gospel becomes acute in the Last Discourses of chaps. 15–16, particularly in view of their forward look, which is concerned with the future relations of the disciples to the "world," especially as represented by the Jews, and the anticipated ministry of the Paraclete.

1. The relation to Israel of Jesus and his disciples and of the Lord and his Church is ambivalent. It is remarkable that the allegory of the Vine contains

no polemic. Its utilization of the imagery of vine and vineyard, so familiar from the OT, is compatible with the continuation of Israel-Church as the people of God. Even the epithet *"true* Vine" does not exclude that observation, since the prophets used the figure almost uniformly to denounce the *false* vine, Israel (Jer 2:21 is characteristic: "I planted you as a choice red vine, true stock all of you, yet now you are turned into a vine debased and worthless!" [NEB]). If, as F. C. Burkitt once remarked, the Church in the teaching of Jesus is to be seen as "Israel made new in the Remnant," the Vine imagery is thoroughly compatible with his consciousness of mission to Israel, in the Fourth Gospel as well as in the synoptics. The *true* Vine can emerge only through the redemptive ministry of him in whom Israel may be made new. It is the Redeemer with those united in him through faith and love. By definition this excludes from the true Vine those in Israel who rejected Jesus and his revelation, represented above all in the leaders who finally brought about his death. From the beginning the consciousness of this divorce between believing and unbelieving Israel could not be erased from the Church's mind, not even from that of the wholly Jewish Church. In the time of the Fourth Evangelist's ministry it will have been particularly vivid in view of the churches' experience of opposition from the synagogue leadership, comparable to that which Jesus suffered. The difference between the later and earlier churches on this issue will have been the clearer understanding of the later community that the true Vine includes believers from all nations (as 10:16; 12:12–32 envisages), whereas unbelieving Jews numbered themselves with the Gentiles who oppose the gospel and the Church that preaches it.

So within the Fourth Gospel a clear recognition comes about that the "world" in its opposition to Jesus and his Church finds its prime representatives in Israel's leaders. We have already observed that in our Gospel the concept "world" has a similar ambiguity to "Israel." The world as created by God through the Logos is the scene of the incarnation of the Logos, and the object of the divine love and redemptive work of the Son of God (e.g., 3:16–21; 4:42; 12:47); hence the Redeemer is "lifted up" to heaven in order to draw *all* in the world to him (12:31–32). But the world is also the scene where its "prince" holds sway. The passages that mention him show that he is a defeated power (12:31; 14:30; 16:11), but he is still able to inspire hostility to the followers of Jesus, as he did to Jesus himself. In such passages as 15:18–19, 25 the "world" and unbelieving Israel are virtually identified, as in 16:1–4 the militant opposition to the disciples is attributed to the synagogue. When opposition of this order was experienced by the churches of the Evangelist's time, the concept of "false" Israel as representatives of the world and its prince that fight Jesus and his Church would have been intensified. The modification of the Twelfth of the Eighteen Benedictions to include a curse on the Christians, at whatever date that may have taken place, will have seemed to the Christians the topstone that crowned their convictions. That in the vastly changed situation of the twentieth century, when the boot has been on the other foot and the Church's traditions have led to literally annihilating persecutions of Jews, this evaluation requires drastic modification goes without saying; but it needs to be said, loudly and clearly, as the Evangelist himself would undoubtedly have acknowledged.

2. The function of the Spirit in the Church is placed firmly in the future

in the Last Discourses, and his role is more extensively described in the discourses of chaps. 15–16 than anywhere else in the Gospel. The Paraclete sayings raise the question as to the relation of the Paraclete-Spirit to the revelation in Jesus in the continuing life of the Church.

In 16:25 the teaching of Jesus to his disciples is acknowledged to be obscure, and the full revelation of his teaching promised for the future. There is a certain tension here, inasmuch as in 18:20 Jesus declares to the chief priest Annas that he had "spoken openly (παρρησίᾳ) in the world," had always taught in the synagogues and in the temple, and had said nothing in secret. Yet the elusiveness of his teaching and the exasperation of at least some of his hearers is illustrated in the occasion when "the Jews" surrounded Jesus in the temple and asked him, "How long are you going to provoke us? If you are the Christ, tell us plainly (παρρησίᾳ)" (10:24). Jesus replied that he had done so, and they had not believed. The necessity for faith to grasp the truth made known by Jesus is similarly asserted in 8:46–47. It is evident that if the teaching of Jesus is to be understood there must be a readiness to receive it, and equally a readiness to progress in understanding. The disciples were willing enough, but their grasp of the revelation in Jesus was fragmentary, and therefore they were apt to misunderstand it. They were in need of a translation of the message and a continual illumination of its meaning, in other words of being "led" in the *entire* truth. The Paraclete's task is to disclose the truth of the gospel as he constantly draws on the fullness of the revelation made known in Jesus. The heart of his instruction is indicated in 16:14: "He will glorify me, inasmuch as he will receive what is from me and disclose it to you." The revelation, then, is Jesus; not a system of doctrines, but *him*. That the teaching of Jesus, with his life, death, and exaltation, entail doctrine is evident, and dogmatic formulation that endeavors to do justice to what was said and done by him is immensely important. But dogmatic formulations and exposition can never take the place of the revelation in Christ; they can never exhaust that revelation; of necessity they are always relative to the times in which they are expressed and they have to be restated for different ages and cultures. More importantly, the knowledge of the revelation is intended to lead to the experience of it, for through it the living Christ confronts the believer with the demand for faith and obedience, and for life in union with him (cf. "Abide in me, and I in you . . ."). It is in this context that the "prophetic" ministry of the Spirit-Paraclete is to be understood. The Spirit enables not only an understanding of the revelation, but also the expression of it in such a manner that both believer and unbeliever may grasp it and respond to it. All are ready to acknowledge that the greatest monument to the presence of this prophetic inspiration of the Spirit in the Church is the Fourth Gospel itself. It was early perceived to be the "spiritual" Gospel, in that it enables the believer to penetrate beyond the exterior of the life and teaching of Jesus to its heart—one is inclined to say to *his* heart. And at the same time it constantly demands the response of reader and hearer to the Christ so presented. It was surely part of the Evangelist's intention to make it plain that the Paraclete who illumined the minds of those about Jesus continues the same ministry in the church, that the revelation in Christ may constantly be freshly perceived and powerfully expressed. Of this ministry Blank wrote,

Prophecy liberates the Christian message from the fetters and incrustations of a paralyzing traditionalism. Its primary function is to relate the Christian message to the present age with its experiences and problems and to interpret it for the people of every today. If the message is to remain alive or to become alive again, the Church of every age and especially of today needs authoritative, Spirit-filled prophecy. Part of the task is to bring to light the contradiction between the message and the wretched reality of Church and world (*According to St. John*, 150–51).

4. The Prayer of Consecration (17:1–26)

Bibliography

Agourides, S. C. "The 'High-Priestly Prayer' of Jesus." *SE* 4 (1968) 137–43. **Becker, J.** "Aufbau, Schichtung und theologiegeschichtliche Stellung des Gebets in Joh 17." *ZNW* 60 (1969) 56–83. **Bornkamm, G.** "Zur Interpretation des Johannesevangeliums: Eine Auseinandersetzung mit E. Käsemanns Schrift, 'Jesu letzter Wille nach Johannes 17.'" *EvT* 28 (1968) 8–25. **Cadier, J.** "The Unity of the Church: An Exposition of Jn 17." *Int* 11 (1957) 166–76. **Delorme, J.** "Sacerdoce du Christ et ministère: semantique et théologie biblique." *RSR* 62 (1974) 199–219. **Feuillet, A.** *The Priesthood of Christ and His Ministers.* New York: Doubleday, 1975. **George, A.** "L'heure de Jean XVII." *RB* 61 (1954) 392–97. **Giblet, J.** "Sanctifie les dans la vérité Jn 17, 1–26." *BVC* 19 (1957) 58–73. **Käsemann, E.** *The Testament of Jesus according to John 17.* Tr. G. Krodel. Philadelphia: Fortress, 1968. **Laurentin, A.** "*We 'attah—καὶ νῦν*: Formule caractéristique des textes juridiques et liturgiques." *Bib* 45 (1964) 168–97, 413–32. **Lloyd-Jones, D. M.** *The Basis of Christian Unity: An Exposition of John 17 and Ephesians 4.* Grand Rapids: Eerdmans, 1963. **Malatesta, E.** "The Literary Structure of John 17." *Bib* 52 (1971) 190–214. **Minear, P.** "Evangelism, Ecumenism, and John 17." *TToday* 35 (1978) 353–60. ———. "John 17:1–11." *Int* 32 (1978) 175–79. **Morrison, C. D.** "Mission and Ethic: An Interpretation of John 17." *Int* 19 (1965) 259–73. **Pollard, T. E.** "'That They All May Be One' (John xvii 21)—and the Unity of the Church." *ExpTim* 70 (1958–59) 149–50. **Randall, J. F.** "The Theme of Unity in John 17:20–23." *ETL* 41 (1965) 373–94. **Schnackenburg, R.** "Strukturanalyse von Joh 17." *BZ* 17 (1973) 67–78, 196–202. **Thüsing, W.** *Herrlichkeit und Einheit: Eine Auslegung des Hohepriesterlichen Gebetes Jesu (Joh.17)* Düsseldorf: Patmos, 1962.

Translation

[1] *Jesus spoke these things, and raising his eyes to heaven he said, "Father, the hour has come; glorify your Son, that the[a] Son may glorify you,* [2] *according as you gave him authority over all flesh, in order that, with regard to everything[b] you have given to him, he should give them eternal life.* [3] *And this is the eternal life, that they may know you, the only true God, and Jesus Christ whom you sent.* [4] *I have glorified you on the earth, in that I have completed what you gave me to do;* [5] *and now,[c] Father, glorify me alongside yourself with the glory which I had with you before the world was.*

[6] *I manifested your name to the men whom you gave to me out of the world. They were yours, and you gave them to me, and they have kept your word.* [7] *Now they have come to know[d] that everything you have given to me is from you;* [8] *for I*

have given them the words that you gave to me, and they have received them, and come to know^c *in truth that I came forth from you, and they have believed that you sent me.* ⁹ *I pray for them; I am not praying for the world, but for those whom you have given to me, because they are yours;* ¹⁰ *and all mine are yours and yours are mine, and I have been glorified in them.* ¹¹ *And no longer am I in the world, but they are in the world, and I am on my way to you.*

"Holy Father, keep them in your name, the name^f *that you have given to me, that they may be one, just as we are one.* ¹² *While I was with them I kept them in your name*^g *that you have given to me, and I guarded them, and none of them has been lost except the one destined to be lost, that the scripture may be fulfilled.*

¹³ *"But now I am on my way to you, and I am saying these things in the world that they may have my joy completed in themselves.* ¹⁴ *I have given them your word, and the world hated them, because they do not belong to the world, just as I do not belong to the world.* ¹⁵ *I am not asking that you should take them out of the world, but that you should keep them out of the clutches of the evil one.*^h ¹⁶ *They do not belong to the world, just as I do not belong to the world.*

¹⁷ *"Consecrate them in the truth; your word is truth.* ¹⁸ *As you sent me into the world I also have sent them into the world;* ¹⁹ *and for their sakes I consecrate myself, that they also may become consecrated in (the) truth.*

²⁰ *"I am not making request for these alone, but also for those who are to believe in me on account of their word,* ²¹ *that they all may be one, just as you, Father, are in me and I am in you, that they also may be*ⁱ *in us, that the world may believe that you sent me.* ²² *And the glory which you have given me I have given them, that they may be one, just as we are one,* ²³ *I in them and you in me, that they may be perfected into one, that the world may know that you sent me, and have loved them just as you have loved me.*

²⁴ *"Father, with regard to what*^j *you have given me, it is my will that where I am they also may be with me, that they may look on my glory that you have given me, because you loved me before the foundation of the world.* ²⁵ *Righteous Father, although*^k *the world has not known you, yet I have known you, and these have come to know that you sent me;* ²⁶ *and I have made known to them your name, and will continue to make it known, that the love with which you have loved me may be in them, and I in them."*

Notes

^a ὁ υἱός is so read by P^{60vid} ℵ B C* W etc. To it σου is added in D Θ etc. Whereas the omission could have been due to copyists viewing σου as superfluous, the external attestation for the shorter reading is superior to that for the longer.

^b The overliteral translation calls attention to the unusual mode of referring to the people of God as a collective whole, represented by the neuter gender. The same language appears in v 24, where it was "corrected" by many copyists to the more conventional οὓς δέδωκάς μοι.

^c καὶ νῦν appears to reflect a technical phrase, common in judicial and liturgical contexts, to introduce a result that should follow on the facts made known (cf. Exod 19:5; 2 Sam 7:25–26); that it can introduce a forceful repetition of a plea already made is of pertinence here (cf. v 1; see the discussion of this idiom by Laurentin, *We'attah—kaì nûn*, 168–95, 413–32).

^d Instead of ἔγνωκαν (read by A B C D L Y Θ etc.) the first person sing. ἔγνων appears in ℵ it^{a b c e ff2} syr cop goth. This latter modification is viewed by the UBS committee as "a mistaken correction of a copyist influenced by the first person in v 6, or (in the case of ἔγνωκα) as an accidental error in transcription (loss of horizontal line over α representing final ν)," Metzger, 249.

ᵉ καὶ ἔγνωσαν is omitted in ℵ* A D W, so making the sentence to read, "they have received in truth that I came forth from you." This could have been due to a feeling that the statement contradicts 6:69 (so Metzger, 249).

ᶠ ᾧ δέδωκάς μοι, read by ⁶⁰ᵛⁱᵈ p⁶⁶ᵛⁱᵈ ℵ A B C D etc., was found difficult by copyists; the attracted relative ᾧ was replaced by ὁ in D* ℵ etc. and by οὕς in Dᵇ etc. (cf. v 6), with various omissions in p⁶⁶* itᵃ,ᵇ,ᶜ,ᵉ,ff² syrˢ etc. The greater difficulty of ᾧ δέδωκας . . . and superiority of its attestation tell in favor of its originality.

ᵍ The same phenomena regarding ᾧ δέδωκάς μοι appear as in v 11.

ʰ ἐκ τοῦ πονηροῦ may be either masc. ("the evil one") or neuter ("the evil" that is in the world). As in the comparable clause of the Disciples' Prayer, "Rescue us from the evil (one)" (Matt 6:13) as also in 1 John 2:13–14; 3:12; 5:18–19, the masc. is almost certainly to be understood.

ⁱ ὦσιν is read by p⁶⁶ᵛⁱᵈ B C* D W it syr cop etc. The addition of ἐν before ὦσιν in ℵ A C³ K L X Δ Θ etc. appears to be due to its occurrence earlier in the verse; the attestation for the shorter reading is stronger.

ʲ On ὁ δέδωκάς μοι Black commented, "The *casus pendens* gives emphasis to the Johannine neuter phrase, and the employment of the neuter is not ineffective as a generalization—'Thy gift to me'—explained more fully in the sequel" (*Aramaic Background*, 62).

ᵏ The construction καὶ . . . δὲ . . . καὶ . . . has created difficulty. Barrett (515) viewed the first as intended to coordinate the statement about the world and the disciples: "It is true *both* that the world did not know thee . . . *and* that these men knew . . ."; but that entails treating ἐγὼ δέ σε ἔγνων as a parenthesis, which is very doubtful. The suggestion of Sanders-Mastin is more plausible, viz. that the καὶ . . . δὲ construction has been combined with the καὶ . . . καὶ construction used to introduce a contrast, so giving the sequence καὶ . . . δὲ . . . καὶ . . . , which should be rendered "*although* . . . *yet* . . . *and* . . ." (379 n.1).

Form/Structure/Setting

1. The prayer of chap. 17 is no everyday prayer, but is conditioned by its position at the conclusion of the farewell discourse of Jesus. The inclusion of a prayer is not uncommon in descriptions of farewell discourses in the OT and in later Jewish writings. The book of Deuteronomy, itself a series of farewell discourses in form, concludes with the Song of Moses (chap. 32) and Moses' blessings of the tribes (chap. 33); the former is a psalm, the latter a kind of prophetic prayer. In Jewish apocalyptic literature we may note the prayer of Ezra in 4 Ezra 8:19b–36, the prayer of Baruch in 2 Bar 48, and in the Book of Jubilees the prayers ascribed to Moses (1:19–21), Noah (10:3–6), Abraham (chaps. 20–22) and Isaac (36:17). Attention is frequently called to comparable prayers in the Hermetic literature, notably that at the end of Poimandres (1:31–32) and that at the end of the work "Concerning Regeneration" (13:21–22; see Dodd, *Interpretation*, 236–39); others are also impressed with those found in Mandaean writings, especially the Book of John, 236–39 (so Bauer, 208, and Bultmann, as reflected in the footnotes of his exposition, 490–522). The distinctiveness of the prayer of John 17, over against other related compositions, lies in the uniqueness of him who prays and the setting of his prayer: Jesus, the Son of God, is about to depart to his Father through a death and resurrection for the life of the world; in that circumstance he prays that the purpose of God may be perfectly fulfilled through what he now does and through his followers.

2. That the prayer has a didactic intention in the Gospel has been recognized from early times. S. Agourides has pointed out that, in the early exegetical tradition of the Church, chap. 17 is viewed as "teaching in the form of prayer." He observed that as the prayer at the grave of Lazarus was for the sake of

the people, so the prayer of chap. 17 is made for the benefit of the disciples; hence, "the consolatory discourse is changed into a prayer" ("The 'High-Priestly Prayer' of Jesus," 137, 144). Westcott described the prayer as "at once a prayer, and a profession, and a revelation" (2:239). The title "High-Priestly Prayer" of Jesus goes back to a Lutheran theologian of the sixteenth century, David Chytraeus, and has been widely adopted; from this viewpoint the prayer is regarded as a supreme example of the intercession of the risen Lord alluded to in 1 John 2:1; Heb 7:25; 9:14; Rom 8:34, not least on the ground that it is the risen Lord, not the earthly Jesus, who speaks in this prayer. Illuminating as the concept is, the opening words of the prayer indicate the stance of the *earthly* Jesus, who has arrived at the hour to which his whole ministry has moved, and in that momentous hour he seeks his Father's face, for himself as well as for his disciples. On that basis Hoskyns strongly favored the title given by Westcott, "The Prayer of Consecration"; seeing in v 19 the focal point of the prayer, he characterized it as "The Consecration of Jesus to death and of his disciples to the mission—*ad gloriam dei*" (494). There is no need for a controversy as to whether the prayer is offered on behalf of Jesus or of his disciples; it is for both. On no account should the weight of personal prayer in vv 1 and 19 be discounted; yet those very petitions embrace the disciples also—that life may be available for them, as for the rest of humankind, and that they may participate in the consecration of Jesus.

The question of the relation of the prayer to that in Gethsemane, recounted in the synoptic Gospels, is frequently raised, more often than not, to contrast them as impossibly distant (cf. e.g., Brown, 2:748). If, however, one compares the narrative of 12:27–28, the so-called "Johannine Gethsemane," it is natural to view the two prayers in the Johannine presentation as complementary. The prayer of chap. 17 may be considered as an expansion of the final element of the "Gethsemane" prayer, "Father, glorify thy name," and the response from heaven, "I have glorified it and will glorify it again" (12:28). The reversal of order of the Gethsemane prayer and that in the upper room belongs to the Johannine structure of composition. Chaps. 12 and 13–17 are carefully constructed theological documents; neither would have appeared to the Evangelist as distortions of the story of Jesus' ministry.

3. The original setting of the composition (*Sitz im Leben*) of the prayer is not infrequently identified with celebrations of the Lord's Supper in the early churches. The view has more in its favor than is sometimes acknowledged, inasmuch as the prayer is set in the context of the *Last* Supper, and the materials of the farewell discourses will themselves have been frequently employed in celebrations of the *Lord's* Supper. It is scarcely conceivable, however, that the prayer itself would have been recited during observances of the Lord's Supper, but it is possible that *elements* of the prayer were so used; note especially the petitions that the disciples be kept faithful in a hostile world, that they may share in the consecration of Jesus for the salvation of the world, that they may be one in Christ, that the world may see the love of the Lord embodied in them, that they at the last may behold the glory of Jesus in the company of the Father and share in it. It is, of course, not the only section of the Fourth Gospel that will have formed the subject of meditation in the worship of the Johannine churches; on the contrary one may

wonder what parts of it were *not* so used in the Evangelist's circle, prior to their incorporation in the Gospel.

4. The structure of the prayer has been much discussed. The threefold division, proposed by Westcott, has been widely adopted, namely, vv 1–5, 6–19, 20–26 (Jesus prays for *himself*, for his *disciples*, for the *Church*). Feuillet saw in this division confirmation of his thesis that the prayer has in view the procedures of the Jewish Day of Atonement: the High Priest in Lev 16:17 makes atonement for himself, for his family, for the people, but the interpretation is somewhat attenuated (see *The Priesthood of Christ and His Ministers*, [62–79]). Since vv 6–8 do not strictly contain a petition for the disciples, they are sometimes included with vv 1–5, thereby producing a better balance in the length of the sections, i.e., vv 1–8, 9–19, 20–26 (so Bernard, 2:559; Brown, 2:749–50). The same consideration led Dodd to a fourfold division: vv 1–5, 6–8, 9–19, 20–26 (*Interpretation*, 417–18). Others have opted for a fourfold analysis that divides the final paragraph of the prayer, e.g., vv 1–5, 6–19, 20–23, 24–26 (Lagrange, 449–51; Strathmann, 231–35), or vv 1–5, 6–19, 20–24, 25–26 (Barrett, 499). These divisions are based on considerations of content. Some have sought to obtain a more objective analysis of the prayer by examining its formal characteristics. E. Malatesta proposed an elaborate literary structure in the prayer which includes external elements, such as repetition, and chiasmus, both in major sections (A—B—A) and in minor (a—b—c—b¹—a¹), and carefully balanced length of lines, words, and syllables. On this basis he produced a fivefold analysis of the prayer: vv 1–5, 6–8, 9–19, 20–24, 25–26 (see his article, "The Literary Structure of John 17," provided with charts illustrating the schematic arrangement of the prayer and its thematic structure). A. Laurentin analyzed the prayer on the basis of the formula καὶ νῦν ("and now"), which reflects the Semitic ועתה *wᵉʿattāh*. He thereby produced the following analysis: vv 1–4 (introduction to the prayer), 7–12 (part 1), 13–23 (part 2), 24 (transition), 25–26 (conclusion) ("*Wᵉʿattāh—καὶ νῦν*," *Bib* 45 [1964] 168–95, 413–32). J. Becker used the category of genre in his investigation of the chapter. He found a fourfold repetition of the succession (*i*) report of one's right, (*ii*) introduction to a petition, (*iii*) the petition itself, (*iv*) the basis of the petition. After the announcement of the theme of glory, authority, and life eternal in vv 1b–2 he saw its development as follows: vv 4–5, the Son prays for his glorification; 6–13, revelation of the name of God and prayer for the Church in its unity; 14–19, revelation of the word of God and healing of the Church in the truth; 22–26, vision of the heavenly glory of Jesus, ("Aufbau, Schichtung und theologiegeschichtliche Stellung des Gebetes in Joh 17," 56–83; more briefly in Becker's commentary, 2:508–17).

While these more detailed analyses of the prayer are impressive, they schematize the alleged structures of the text too much (for an evaluation see Schnackenburg's article, "Strukturanalyse von Joh 17," 67–68). Schnackenburg's own analysis, which seeks to take into account both the formal elements of structure and the content of the prayer, does not differ greatly from those of his forerunners, but it seems to us to accord well with the text and its content, and we shall follow it in our own exposition (a summary of his position, in light of his article, is set forth in his commentary, 3:167–69, 197–202). It may be reproduced as follows: (*i*) vv 1–5, prayer for the glory of the Son that he may give life to those given to him; (*ii*) vv 6–19, prayer for the disciples (*a*) 6–11a, reason for praying for them, (*b*) 11b–16, prayer that they may be kept, (*c*) 17–19, prayer that they may be consecrated with Jesus; (*iii*) vv 20–23, prayer that all believers may be one; (*iv*) vv 24–26, prayer that believers may be perfected in the glory of Jesus.

Comment

Prayer for the Glory of the Son (17:1–5)

1 "The hour has come"; it is the event to which the whole life and mission of Jesus has moved (contrast 2:4; 7:6, 8, 30; 8:20 with intimations of the arrival of the hour in 12:23, 27–28, 31–32; 13:1, 31). The petition, "Glorify your Son that the Son may glorify you," strikes the keynote of the prayer ("The first petition is in fact its whole contents," Bultmann, 490). Its significance is complex; in the context it expresses the desire of Jesus that his life, now to be devoted to God in death (v 19), may be an acceptable sacrifice; that God may raise him to the throne of his glory (cf. 13:31–32); that the honor that comes from God alone may be his, and that all may recognize it; that thereby this event may constitute the coming of the saving sovereignty, the kingdom of God for the life of the world, and so the revelation of the Father's glory in terms of redeeming love and power.

2 The glory of the Father and the Son is expressed in the bestowal of eternal life upon humankind. The authority of the Son to convey this gift is inherent in his position as Mediator of the saving sovereignty (cf. 5:21–27), and by his exaltation as Lord of the kingdom it extends to "all flesh." The redemption of Christ is universal in scope (cf. 3:16; 12:31–32), the kingdom of God is universe wide, hence the authority of the Son has the same limitless bounds; but the gifts of the saving sovereignty, summed up in eternal life, are for those whom the Father has "given" to the Son. This intimates that kingdom and judgment go together, and both accord with the electing purpose of God. Divine election and human responsibility are variously expressed in the Gospel (see esp. 6:37, 39–40, 44, 64–65; 12:37–42) and they are to be held together as truly as God's sovereignty and human freedom must be so held. (Hoskyns seeks to do this in his comment, "In the contrast between *all flesh* and *whatsoever thou hast given* is expressed the inevitable tragedy of the mercy of God; it is offered to all, but received by the few, and those the elect," 498. But how justified is he in this contrast of "all" with "the few"? Contrast Rom 11:32!)

3 V 3 is a parenthesis (Barrett remarks that it would have been a footnote, had such been available to the Evangelist, 503). As a definition of eternal life it reads remarkably like a confession of faith: the eternal life, of which the Gospel speaks, consists in the knowledge of God and of Jesus the Son, the Christ he has sent. The objectivity of the statement, especially its reference to Jesus the Messiah, led the orthodox Lagrange to surmise that it may be a gloss of the Evangelist (44). Certainly its confessional ring accords well with Jewish tradition, both Palestinian (Bar Qappara saw the essence of the Law in Prov 3:6: "Acknowledge, i.e., *know*, him, and he will direct your paths," *Ber.* 63a) and Hellenistic (e.g., Philo: The end of wisdom's way is "knowledge and understanding of God," *Deus* 143; see Barrett's excellent exposition, 503–4). Yet the utterance reflects more closely the gospel tradition of Jesus' teaching, above all as expressed in Matt 11:27 in its context of kingdom of God sayings in Matt 11:2–14, 20–24, 25–26: none "knows" the Son save the Father, and none "knows" the Father except the Son, and he to whom the Son wills to reveal him. Such knowledge advances beyond the intellect to include relationship and communion; its revelation by the Son entails entry into the *koinonia* (fellowship) of the Father and the Son, which is the heart of life in the saving sovereignty, (cf. Rev 21:3; 22:3–5). If v 3 is a gloss of the Evangelist, it is yet one with our Lord's teaching in the Gospel and with the prayer in particular. Blank even goes so far as to conclude, "It is upon this acknowledgment of God and his Revealer that the prayer and all it has to say is based" (200).

4 The affirmation of v 4 is the basis of the petition in v 5 and anticipates it. "I glorified you *on the earth*" sets the ministry of Jesus in the light of his return to the Father's side *in heaven* (v 5). As in 4:34 the work given by the Father to Jesus to do is inclusive; in 5:36 the plural "works" relate to the diverse works that the Father has given to the Son to accomplish; in 19:30 the last work of Jesus has now been completed in the yielding of his life to God in death. Is this final "work" included in the τελειώσας, "the accomplishing," of v 4? Lindars, on the basis of 12:24, distinguishes between the work of Jesus in his ministry and the glorification of the Son of Man in death and resurrection, and so eliminates the latter from view here (520). From Chrysostom onward most writers have included the death with the works of the ministry as a unity, and it is difficult to avoid that conclusion; one should not, however, thereby assume that the standpoint of the prayer, in contrast to that of the discourses, is after the death and resurrection have taken place (as Brown, 2:742). Admittedly the entire Last Discourses and the prayer have been written from the Evangelist's position of the post-Pentecostal period; but the distinctive stance of the prayer is that Jesus stands not *after* the hour, but *in* the hour wherein his final work for God and man takes place, as v 19 makes plain. If a certain oscillation within the prayer is visible, the fundamental standpoint is nevertheless consistent, so that "I am no more in the world" of v 11a must be controlled by the immediately succeeding "I am on my way to you" of v 11b (as also v 13). In that setting the Christ, now committed to the cross, seeks that response of the Father which will bring him to the Father's side (see the discussions of A. George, " 'L'heure' de Jean XVII," 394–96, and Dodd, *Interpretation*, 419–20; both expositions are highly illuminating but require some modification).

5 The prayer for glory, accordingly, is for a restoration of that which the Son enjoyed with the Father prior to creation (cf. 1:1–5). Haenchen points out that this prayer assumes that the incarnation entailed a *forfeiture* of the glory that the Son once possessed; it calls into question therefore Käsemann's contention that the Evangelist's representation of the glory of Jesus in his ministry undermines the reality of the incarnation, and made of Jesus a "god walking about the earth" (see Käsemann's *Testament of Jesus*, 8–26, and Haenchen, 502). Perhaps we should heed Schnackenburg's observation, that the glory of Jesus "before the world was made" characterizes not the *pre-mundane* but the *supra-mundane* existence of the Logos, and therefore ultimately the superiority of the Revealer to and his transcendence over the world (3:174). Such an interpretation of the Son in relation to the Father in no way cancels out the fundamental utterance of 1:14, "The Word *became* flesh."

PRAYER FOR THE DISCIPLES:
REASON FOR PRAYING FOR THEM (17:6–11a)

6–9 While the whole prayer of Jesus has relation to the disciples (and the Church they represent) the central section explicitly makes mention of them and their situation in the world. A series of reasons for the necessity of such intercession is stated. The first is that assumed in v 2, and now clearly stated in the second clause of v 6: God "gave" the disciples to Jesus; i.e., he chose them out of the world for the possession and the service of his Son. Second, to these men Jesus revealed God's "name," i.e., his nature, his character. Schlatter thought that this has primary reference to the name "Father" (319–20); while this doubtless is of central importance in the revelation of the Name, the full range of the revelation of God's character must also be included, not least that which is entailed in the saving sovereignty of the Father. Third, the disciples have "kept" the word brought by Jesus; i.e., they have adhered to it, and sought to live in its light.

Fourth, they have come to know (especially in light of the revelation in the Last Discourses?) that all that God gave to Jesus has come from the Father. This is faith-knowledge coming to maturity. Fifth, these gifts of God to Jesus are none other than the *words* that Jesus has spoken. The disciples have "received" them, and so recognized them as authoritative and normative for life. Sixth, they have realized that Jesus has come from God, and so is the Incarnate One on mission from God, a mission to reveal the Father and to establish his saving sovereignty.

Jesus accordingly prays for the disciples, not for the world. The exclusion of the world from his prayer must be understood in its context; the disciples have been chosen to help the Church to fulfill its calling, which is none other than to reveal and to continue the mission of its Lord to the world (v 18); it is as the Church fulfills its calling in the unity of the divine love that the world will recognize that Jesus has been sent to them by God (vv 21, 23). To this extent the prayer of Jesus for the disciples is indirectly prayer for the world also (as is generally acknowledged, see esp. Hoskyns, 500, and Bultmann, 500).

11a Precisely because Jesus is "on his way" to the Father his prayer for the disciples has become an urgent necessity (for the stance of Jesus assumed in v 11a see *Comment* on v 4).

PRAYER FOR THE DISCIPLES:
THAT THEY MAY BE KEPT IN GOD AND OUT OF THE CLUTCHES
OF THE EVIL ONE (17:11b–16)

11b "Holy Father" in address to God is found here alone in the Gospel; in view of the elements of otherness, awesomeness, and splendor conveyed by the biblical concept of holiness the expression here combines the two notions of transcendence and intimacy characteristic of Jesus' personal attitude to God and of his teaching about God (cf. Matt 11:25: "I thank you, *Father* [*Abba*], *Lord of heaven and earth* . . ."). Its use here befits the petition so introduced, as also that in vv 17–19, but the precise meaning of the petition is variously construed. It is possible to translate ἐν τῷ ὀνόματί σου as "*by* your name," and to interpret as in the NEB, "Protect *by the power* of your name" (so Heitmüller, *Im Namen Jesu*, 132–34; Schlatter, 321; Hoskyns, 500; Bultmann, 503. Bruce cites the parallelism seen in Ps 54:1, "Save me, O God, by your *name*, and vindicate me by your *might*," 332). It is, however, even more natural to translate ἐν as "in," and to interpret the prayer, "Keep them *in* your name," as in NEB margin, "Keep them *in loyalty* to thee," or, more fully, *in adherence to* what Jesus has revealed to the disciples of the character of God (so Lagrange 445; Lindars, 524; Barrett, 507; Schnackenburg, 3:180). It is not impossible that both thoughts are implied, as Brown believes (2:759), but the context appears to have in view primarily the latter concept. The petition follows on vv 6–8, wherein "the name which you gave me" is anticipated by "the words which you gave me"; they denote the revelation of the Father which Jesus has received and passed on to his disciples; it is only as the disciples are maintained in adherence to that revelation that they can be one as the Father and the Son are one, which is the purpose of the petition, "Keep them in your name." The like applies to the prayer in vv 17–19: only as the disciples persist in the truth revealed can they participate in the sanctification of Jesus and so in his redemptive ministry.

12 The petition of v 12 is strengthened by reference to the impending departure of Jesus. Hitherto he has maintained the disciples in the revelation of the Father; henceforth they will have special need of the Father's aid. One alone has been lost, Judas "the son of perdition," and that not through fault of Jesus, but through the ingrained evil of the man. His destiny is to fulfill the scripture referred to in 13:18, namely Ps 41:9; and indeed he has already set in motion that fulfillment; having "lifted up his heel" against his Master, the death of the Lord and his own destruction are already on the way.

"Son of perdition (υἱὸς τῆς ἀπωλείας) is a Hebraism in which the genitive is ambiguous. It can denote the person's character, as in Ps 57:4, where "children of unrighteousness' is rendered in the LXX τέκνα ἀπωλείας; or the person's destiny, as in Isa 34:5, where "the people I have doomed" appears in the LXX as τὸν λαὸν τῆς ἀπωλείας (in 2 Sam 12:5 "a son of death," i.e., one doomed to be put to death, is rendered lit. as υἱὸς θανάτου). The same expression, "the son of perdition," ὁ υἱὸς τῆς ἀπωλείας, is applied to the Antichrist in 2 Thess 2:3 in parallelism with "the man of lawlessness," presumably to denote his evil nature, but it may also include the thought of his sure destruction, which is mentioned in 2 Thess 2:8. A similar duality of meaning could attach to the expression in our passage.

13–15 "These things," uttered by Jesus in his prayer, indicate that through his departure to the Father the saving sovereignty of God comes to its climactic action, and in their communion with the Father the disciples are to experience a unity such as that which exists between the Father and the Son. In this the joy of Jesus reaches its perfection (cf. 13:28). For the disciples to be reminded of these things should suffice to enable them to share his joy to the fullest (cf. 15:11).

Jesus has spoken these things "in the world," but on the point of departure from it; the disciples are to remain in the world, and the world hates them because (*a*) they have received the word of Jesus, which is the revelation of the Father, and (*b*) they thereby show that they, like Jesus himself, belong to God and not to them, for the revelation condemns the world's ways and the world is characterized by its rejection of the revelation in Christ (cf. 3:19–21). Jesus therefore renews the prayer of v 11, that the disciples be kept out of the clutches of "the evil one," who is behind the world's opposition to God manifest in Christ. Yet the Lord explicitly disavows a prayer that the disciples may escape the evil one by their removal from the world. That should never be, for the Father, far from abandoning the world in its rebellion, is engaged in the process of delivering the world and through the Son establishing a sovereignty that spells salvation for the world (3:16; 12:31–32); the disciples accordingly are to be in the world as witnesses to the sovereign rule in the grace that forgives the rebels and gives life to the full (10:10).

16 The consciousness of this mission of the disciples is not annulled by the repeated mention (in v 16) of the world's hostility to Jesus and his disciples; rather that utterance forms a bridge to a prayer for the disciples to share in a consecration by which the salvation of God might be conveyed to the world (vv 17–19).

PRAYER FOR THE DISCIPLES:
THAT THEY MAY BE CONSECRATED WITH JESUS (17:17–19)

17 "Consecrate them in the truth" deepens and develops the petition of v 11b, "Keep them in your name" (so Schnackenburg, 3:185, who notes the parallel between "your name" in v 11, i.e., the revelation of God in Jesus, and "the truth" in vv 17 and 19). The verb ἁγιάζειν, "consecrate," is defined by Bultmann as "to take out of the sphere of the profane and place in the sphere of the divine" (509 n.1). That is right, but the word is peculiarly biblical, and stamped with its own associations. In the OT it is especially used of dedication, whether of man or beast, to the service of God. "Consecrate them in the truth" will have in view a separation from the world's ways to God, and so for a life in conformity with his revelation in Christ and in dedication to his service.

18 Precisely because the consecration of the disciples is for the service of God in the discipleship of Jesus, they are sent into the world as Jesus was sent by the Father. The parallelism between his sending and theirs is to be observed. Jesus is the one uniquely consecrated by the Father and sent by him into the world (10:36) to bring to the world the revelation of the Father and his saving sovereignty. His entire ministry was a fulfillment of that calling, and now he stands in the hour of the final accomplishment of both ends; he therefore hands over the mission to his men whom he has prepared for this task. If the aorist ἀπέστειλα ("I sent") reflects the Evangelist's post-Easter standpoint, its setting in the Upper Room is nevertheless of fundamental importance. For the disciples' consecration is dependent on that of

Jesus' in the Last Supper, and it makes explicit that his mission is for the sake of the world, and therefore that their mission, as that of the Church, must be directed to the same end. As Bultmann expressed it, "The community takes over Jesus assault on the world, his ἐλέγχειν ("exposure") and κρίνειν ("judging," 16:8–11)—the assault which is at the same time the paradoxical form of his courtship of the world (3:16), and which continually opens up for the world the possibility of faith (vv 21, 23)," (510).

19 This verse brings this thought to its logical climax. We cannot but recall the sayings of Jesus at the Last Supper, recorded by the synoptists and Paul: "My body . . . ὑπὲρ ὑμῶν ("on your behalf," Luke 22:19; 1 Cor 11:24); "My blood . . . ὑπὲρ πολλῶν ("on behalf of many," Mark 14:24). These are the clearest words of Jesus relating to the significance of his death: it is seen as a sacrifice for others, whereby a new covenant is initiated for the inheritance of the kingdom of God, and so the fulfillment of the passover hopes of another Exodus. The like significance attaches to the utterance, "On their behalf I consecrate myself." It accords with the OT meaning of "consecrate" in sacrificial contexts, whereby "consecrate" can be synonymous with "sacrifice" (cf. Deut 15:19, 21). That Jesus should consecrate *himself* for such a purpose is a highly unusual mode of speech, but it reflects his consciousness, attested elsewhere in this Gospel, of performing his service for the saving sovereignty of God by virtue of the authority given him by God (cf. esp. 10:17–18; 18:11; 19:30). This self-consecration of Jesus to death brings his mission of mediating the saving sovereignty to the world to its climax, accordingly it represents a sacrifice of eschatological proportions. We have already noted, however, that the term "consecrate" is used of the setting aside of persons to priestly or prophetic ministry (for the former cf. Exod 28:41; for the latter Jer 1:5). This aspect of meaning is plainly present throughout vv 17–19, but there is a special nuance in its application in v 19b: following on v 19a, "that *they also* may be consecrated . . . ," must surely indicate an overlap in the meaning of the consecration of Jesus and that of his disciples; his dedication unto death is made in order that they too may be dedicated to the same task of bringing the saving sovereignty to the world *in like spirit as he brought it.* Certainly he alone through his unique obedience unto death and exaltation to sovereignty can introduce the saving sovereignty into the world and open its gates for all; but his disciples can, and must, serve as its instruments and embodiment as they proclaim the good news to the world. This they will best do as they exemplify the suffering love of the Redeemer.

PRAYER THAT ALL BELIEVERS MAY BE ONE (17:20–23)

This section of the prayer is an expansion of that in v 11b for the unity of the disciples. The emphasis laid upon the theme by its repetition and by the terms used indicates its importance. It is the only explicit petition within the prayer on behalf of the Church in its historical existence (v 24 relates to the future).

20–21 That Jesus should pray for those "who are to believe through their word" assumes the success of the disciples' mission (alluded to in v 18) and the reality of their consecration to the task (v 19). The unity for which Jesus prays, "that they may be *one*," is defined in the clauses that follow: "just as you, Father, are in me, and I in you, that they may be in us." If the Evangelist was aware, as he may well have been, that the members of the Qumran Community called themselves "the unity" (*yaḥad*), he could have viewed their claim to be "the one" only in polemical (or at least corrective) terms. For the unity with heaven to which those Covenanters aspired was a unity of saints below and "saints" (i.e., angels) above; they believed in a fellowship of men and angels. By contrast the unity of Christian believers, for which prayer is here made, is more radical and fundamental: it is rooted in the being of God, revealed in Christ, and in the redemptive action of God in Christ. The prayer "that they may be *one*" accordingly is defined as "that they may be *in us*."

22–23 In the development of the prayer the nature of this unity is clarified. Its possibility proceeds from the declaration of Jesus, "The glory which you have given me I have given them." Unfortunately the precise nature of that "glory" given to believers is uncertain. Whether we view it, with Bultmann (513), as the *name* of God and the *words* of God given to Jesus, by which Jesus is known and confessed as Revealer and Redeemer (cf. vv 8, 11, 14); or as the incarnate glory, which is his divine glory, at once veiled and revealed in his ministry (Lagrange, 427–28); or the divine life which is the eternal life brought by Jesus, anticipating its fullness in the world to come (Schnackenburg, 3:22); or the unity with the death and resurrection of Jesus from which that life flows (Barrett, 513), on any such interpretation the "glory" is plainly the *gift* of the Redeemer-Revealer, the Son of God, who by his incarnation, death, and resurrection brings to humankind the saving sovereignty of God. It is in virtue of this that sinful men and women may attain a unity with their fellows such as that which exists within the Godhead; or, more precisely, that they may together participate in that unity within the Godhead. That such may come to pass is the purpose of the redemptive ministry of the Son of God (v 22).

The nature of the relationship between the Father and the Son that determines the unity of redeemed humanity has already been stated in 14:10–11, 20: "I in the Father and the Father in me"; it is a mutual indwelling of persons. In the prayer the relationship of the redeemed to the Father and the Son is stated in slightly different ways: in v 21, "As you are in me, and I in you, *that they may be in us*"; in v 23, "*I in them, and you in me*." In the former case the redeemed become one by participating in the *koinonia* of the Father and the Son; in the latter case that participation is through their union with the Son, a concept which is in harmony with representations within the entire Gospel of the mediatorial role of the incarnate Son of God. By this means redeemed men and women become "perfected into one" (τετελειωμένοι); in this Gospel the latter term is chiefly used of Jesus *achieving* his work, so 4:34; 5:36; 17:4. Accordingly, the unity envisaged is possible only through the accomplished redemptive action of God in Christ, while it yet calls for an appropriate ethical response from those drawn into it. This is indicated in the closely related command of Christ, to love "as I have loved you" (13:34). On this Schnackenburg observed: "The unity that is desired is brought about in reciprocal love. The two belong together like the two sides of the same coin" (3:191).

Both in vv 20–21 and 22–23 the petitions for the unity of the Church conclude with virtually identical words: "so that the world may believe (v 23, 'know') that you sent me" (v 23 adds, "and that you have loved them as you loved me"). The parallelism in the construction of the two sentences is striking:

"that they all may be one . . . that they may be in us, that the world may believe . . ."

"that they may be one . . . that they may be perfected into one, that the world may know . . ."

Are the three clauses, introduced in each case by ἵνα ("in order that"), strictly parallel in both sentences, stating the *purpose* of the prayer? Or is the third clause in both sentences to be viewed not as coordinate with the first two petitions (which are really one), but as stating the *consequence* of the prayer for the miracle of unity? On this the exegetes cannot agree, but even on the second alternative the petition is of first importance: the unity of the Church, sought for and achieved by the redemption of the Son of God, is brought about "that the world may believe." The Church is to be the embodiment of the revelation and the redemption of Christ before the world, so that the world may not only *hear* that Jesus is the Christ, who has achieved redemption for all, but they may *see* that the redemptive revelation of the Christ has power to transform fallen men and women into the likeness of God and to bring about the kind of community that the world needs. (On the missionary intention of the prayer see esp. Bultmann, 515; Brown, 2:773; Schnackenburg, 3:190–91; and on the implications of the prayer for the modern search for Christian unity see the *Explanation*).

Some scholars, notably Becker, "Aufbau . . . des Gebetes in Joh 17," 74–76, and his commentary, 2:509, and Schnackenburg, 3:188–89, have maintained that the prayer for future believers in vv 20–21 is a later editorial addition. The chief ground for this view is that the entire prayer up to v 19 has in view the disciples, who are manifestly representatives of the Church to be, and that in vv 22–23 the prayer reverts to the disciples; prayer for "all believers" accordingly is needless, and it disturbs the flow of the prayer (there is a good connection between vv 17–19 and 22–23). This argument actually overstates the position. Vv 1–5 have in view *all believers* (see esp. v 2), and the prayer of vv 22–23 is followed in v 24 by one for *all* whom the Father has given the Son. *If* the petition of vv 22–23 does relate primarily to the disciples we may have here an instance where the "editor" is likely to be the Evangelist, who incorporates at this point (viz., vv 20–21) a prayer for all believers from the materials from which the prayer was composed. We have seen the like phenomenon in the Last Discourses, which the prayer concludes. But it must be observed that vv 22–23 may have in view not the disciples alone but all believers; v 22a links on to v 2, especially if the "glory" relates to the life bestowed through Christ's redemptive death and resurrection; and the mutual indwelling of v 23, with its impact on the unbelieving world, suits better the whole company of believers than the group of eleven disciples in the Upper Room. The issue is not of major importance, but neither is its basis clear. With Bultmann, who denies the change of viewpoint in vv 20–23 (515 n.1), and with most exegetes we provisionally adhere to the unity of this section of the prayer.

PRAYER THAT BELIEVERS BE PERFECTED IN THE GLORY OF THE SON (17:24–26)

24 The concluding paragraph of Jesus' prayer clearly echoes its beginning, including also certain of the later petitions, and in its final sentence we perceive allusions to the ministry of the Paraclete-Spirit promised in the farewell discourses. Whereas Schnackenburg maintains that the prayer continues to have in view the original disciples as representatives of the Church, and not the Church itself (3:194), the emphatic opening clause, which defines those for whom Jesus prays, denotes all whom the Father has given to Jesus: "with regard to what you have given me" echoes the related phrase in v 2: "everything that you have given me," i.e., the whole company of those from among "all flesh" given by the Father to Jesus. Moreover the content of the prayer in v 24 is related to that of v 2: in the earlier v Jesus speaks of his authority to grant eternal life to all those given to him, and in v 24 he makes known his will that those given him by the Father be with him, beholding his glory, and so sharing in it. Admittedly v 25 refers to "these" who have known that the Father has sent him, i.e., the disciples, but in v 26 the petition appears to extend the horizon beyond them to the whole Church. The oscillation between original disciple group and Church, which we saw in vv 20–23, is apparent here also; as Blank puts it, "the contours are blurred" (2:242).

The thought of the prayer is remarkably similar to that in 1 John 3:2: "Beloved friends, now we are God's children, and it has not yet been revealed (οὔπω ἐφανερώθη) what we shall be. We know that (ἐὰν φανερωθῇ) we shall be like him, for we shall see him as he is." The untranslated Greek is ambiguous (see S. S. Smalley, *1, 2, 3 John* WBC 51 [Waco: Word, 1984] 145, 146); it may be rendered as "when *it* is revealed" or "when *he* is revealed." In its context, however, the ambiguity is resolved by the opening sentence in the paragraph: "And now, my children, abide in him, in order that *when he is revealed* (ἐὰν φανερωθῇ) we may have confidence and not shrink in shame from him at his coming" (2:28). The parallel is instructive for our passage. Of itself the prayer that Christ's people may be with him and behold his glory is without indication of time, other than that it follows his "glorification"; inasmuch, however, as the prayer has the Church in view, and Jesus, by his death and exaltation goes to prepare a place for his own and will return to welcome them to the Father's house (14:2–3), it is likely that the glory of the Parousia and the consummation of God's sovereign saving action are primarily in mind. Admittedly the language is capable of application to individual believers as they pass through death to the world beyond this, but it is doubtful that it should be so limited. Becker, following Bultmann, affirms that the author of this prayer knows no Parousia, and has here individualized the Christian hope (2:528); Schnackenburg also is confirmed by this passage in his belief that the writer in his eschatology occupies a theological position between the Evangelist and the author of 1 John (3:195). In light of our exposition of John 14, and of vv 2–3 in particular, these interpretations are unacceptable. If v 24 is an expression of the ultimate will of Jesus for his Church, then the ultimate horizons of the perfected kingdom which his Parousia will make possible will be in view. In that context the "beholding" of the glory of Jesus will result in the participation by his people in that glory. That such a prospect does not eliminate prior enjoyment of the vision of the Lord's glory is illustrated by Paul, who sets such experience in the present (2 Cor 3:18), anticipates the fellowship of the Lord's presence after death (2 Cor 5:6–8; Phil 1:21), and looks forward to the perfection of such grace in the Parousia (1 Cor 15:51–52; Phil 1:6; 3:20–21).

25–26 The petition of v 24 is grounded in vv 25–26, which Barrett views as summarizing the substance of the Gospel (514). The world has not known the Father, but Jesus has known him, in virtue of his unique relationship to the Father (1:18), and his own have come to know that he has been sent into the world from the Father. These, therefore, are in a relationship to God in Christ that marks them off from the world (for the unusual linguistic construction that expresses this thought see *Notes* on v 25). Having so begun the communication of the Father's "name" to his own, Jesus affirms that he will continue to make it known. The reader can hardly forget the related statements concerning the Paraclete's ministry, e.g., in 16:12–15, and esp. 16:25. The goal of the process of revealing the Father's name is disclosed in v 26: "that the love with which you loved me may be in them, and I in them." That statement of the goal has a variety of significations: (*i*) it implies an ever increasing understanding of the love of the Father for the Son; (*ii*) an ever fuller grasp of the wonder that that love is extended to believers also; and (*iii*) an ever more responsive love on their part toward the Father, issuing in an increasingly profound fellowship with him. All these proceed from an ever deepening experience of abiding in the Son and he in them. In this way the love command in 13:34 receives its deepest expression and attains its ultimate fulfillment. And hereby the prayer of v 24 receives its final exposition: the glory of the Christ is the glory of God's love, beheld by his people, and transforming them into bearers of Christly love. The final fulfillment of that prayer can only be in that perfection which will be established in the consummation of the saving sovereignty brought by the Son of God: Revealer and Redeemer in the past, the present, and the future.

Explanation

1. The farewell prayer of Jesus is uttered not on a sickbed but at the close of the Last Supper, in prospect of a death for the salvation of the world. The self-consecration of Jesus in v 19 recalls the words of the Institution

as conveyed in the synoptic Gospels and in the tradition cited by Paul: "My body . . . My blood of the covenant. . . ," a tradition which the Evangelist most surely knew, as 6:51–58 give evidence. Jesus, consecrated by the Father and sent into the world (10:36), consecrates himself for a sacrifice that will complete that mission, a mission to bring to the world the life of God's saving sovereignty. The action brings to a climactic expression the many intimations in the Gospel of his vocation to achieve redemption through his obedient death (cf. 1:29; 3:14–16; 6:51–62; 10:10–18; the Lazarus episode, chap. 11, followed by chaps. 12, 13–16, 18–20). In view of the crescendo of emphasis in the Gospel on the redemptive death of Jesus it is strange that E. Käsemann should conclude that the Fourth Evangelist had no theology of the death of Jesus (*Testament of Jesus*). By contrast H. Thyen recalled Martin Kähler's famous description of Mark's Gospel as "a passion story with a detailed introduction," but only to urge that the Fourth Gospel *from beginning to end* represents the Passion of Jesus as the divine action in him ("Johannes 10 im Kontext des vierten Evangeliums," a seminar paper delivered to the SNTS in Atlanta, 1986). Whereas in the synoptic Gospels the understanding of the death of Jesus as redemptive most clearly comes to expression in their accounts of the Last Supper, in our Gospel the sayings at the Supper simply bring to a climax the many significant utterances that have gone before them.

2. The prayer of Jesus for the unity of his followers has assumed an important place in the strivings after the unity of the Church in the modern ecumenical movement. It is desirable to clarify the relationship between the intent of the prayer and the desire to bring about a fulfillment of it in the concrete relations of the churches.

(*i*) It is of fundamental importance to recognize that in the prayer the basis of the unity of the Church is the nature of God and the reality of his redemptive activity. More specifically, it is an outflow of the relations within the Triune God and of his action in and through the incarnate Son, whereby his saving sovereignty became operative in the world. That unity of God's people became a reality when the Son bestowed on those who believed in him the glory that the Father had given to him (v 22), and it is to find its perfection in the consummation of the saving sovereignty (vv 24–26). The unity of the Church for which Jesus prayed accordingly proceeds from God and belongs essentially to his redemptive work in Christ. As such it transcends all human efforts at reconciling the conflicting interests of people, including those of Christians in their endeavors to harmonize their own interests.

(*ii*) Since the unity of the Church is rooted in the unity of God and the redemption achieved in Christ, we are to understand that the prayer of Jesus was answered: God has made the Church one in Christ. It finds the locus of unity in the Temple of his body (2:17–19) and has become one flock under the one Shepherd (10:16). In this miracle of reconciliation within a renewed humanity the earliest Christians rejoiced. For them it was a miracle both of faith and of experience. In Christ the deepest divisions of humankind had been done away. No longer were Jews and Gentiles sundered from one another in life and in death; no longer were slaves and free separated by an unbridgeable gulf; no longer were male and female viewed as on different planes of existence, for all were one (Body) in Christ (Gal 3:28). The fellowship created by the Spirit of Christ was a new phenomenon in the world, and it remains an experienced reality to this day. There is no gulf created by the cultures, traditions, social mores, and political orders that cannot be bridged in Christ. That is good news for telling in a nuclear and space age, wherein the divisions of nations who cannot trust one another threaten to destroy them all.

(*iii*) It is characteristic of our existence in a fallen world that the new-creation unity brought into being by God in Christ has itself become marred. It was not long after Pentecost that the harmony of the earliest believers became disturbed by a dissension between Aramaic-speaking Jewish Christians and Greek-speaking Jewish Christians in Jerusalem (Acts 6:1). If such could happen among Christian *Jews* of differing cultural backgrounds, it was sure to occur on a larger scale when the Church became a fellowship embracing all nations. The NT bears witness to the struggles to maintain the unity of the Church in face of such tensions. The Letters of John reveal the existence of deep divisions within the Johannine communities; while there is no hint of reference to them in the prayer it is scarcely conceivable that the Evangelist did not have them in mind as he penned the prayer. Christians from Pentecost on are called to give expression to their unity in Christ, as truly as they are called to give expression to their new life in Christ, and in both cases this has to happen before the eyes of the world. The re-creation of believers as one Body in Christ should determine their common life. It is a principle which requires us to begin within the life of the local church, then extend outward, both to relations with communities of the same order as ourselves and to fellowships of Christians of other confessions. In the light of the divisions that have arisen between Christian churches through the centuries, it was inevitable that a movement should arise to call the churches to reverse the trends of the centuries and to seek to experience and express anew their unity in Christ. It was equally natural that this movement should begin within the missionary agencies of the churches (as at Edinburgh, 1910), since the divisions were hindering the carrying out of the missionary task; the nations frequently saw the reconciling power of the gospel less clearly than its divisive power. That the World Council of Churches in process of time has made mistakes, and at times even adopted policies that have alienated Christians rather than brought them closer together, is a reminder that churches are composed of sinners saved by grace, and sometimes the sins are more apparent among them than the grace. For this the churches and their agencies have need to repent—again and again, and again. But they also have need to listen to the prayer of Jesus—again, and again, and again! For reflection on the prayer of necessity leads to urgent consideration how the unity which embraces all Christians within one Body can be expressed within their mutual relations, and how it should become a principle of action in the churches' mission to the world. Perhaps then reflection on the fact that the unity of the Church was the subject of Jesus' prayer to God rather than exhortation to disciples may drive us to our knees in prayer for grace that his prayer may be answered in us, and in our own churches, that the world may be able to perceive in us the reconciling power of God in Christ.

B. *The Death and Resurrection of Jesus* (18:1–20:31)

1. *The Passion Narrative: The Arrest, Trial, Crucifixion, and Burial of Jesus* (18:1–19:42)

Introduction to the Passion Narrative of the Fourth Gospel

1. From the earliest days of Form Criticism it was recognized that the first continuous narrative about Jesus to be written was that which told of his suffering and death. "The Passion Story," said Martin Dibelius, "is the only piece of Gospel tradition which in early times gave events in their larger connection" (*From Tradition to Gospel* [London: Nicholson & Watson, 1934] 179). The necessity for such an account is clear. On the one hand, the gospel makes known the redeeming acts of God in Christ, emphasizing above all the death and resurrection of Jesus; the first written Gospel, that of Mark, is controlled by that message, and provides the setting for the account of Jesus' death and resurrection (we recall the definition of a Gospel as a passion narrative provided with an introduction). On the other hand, it was imperative to explain, especially to Jews, who were the first to hear the gospel, how the Messiah came to be rejected by their leaders and to suffer the accursed death of crucifixion, a necessity which in later times was hardly less needful for the Gentile world. For this reason the events of the passion story were early linked with OT passages, which were calculated to show that these extraordinary happenings took place "by the deliberate will and plan of God" (Acts 2:23). Dodd pointed out that these "testimonies" were not mere embroidery to the narratives, but formed the scaffolding supporting the structure (*Historical Tradition*, 31). Accordingly, while Mark cites no less than seventeen passages in his passion narrative, each of the other evangelists includes some of these and adds other citations which each deems to be of importance, so giving his narrative a particular slant. Of the dozen passages quoted by Mark after the Upper Room account, John has four, but of the six used in John's description of the crucifixion and death of Jesus, three are not in Mark or in Matthew and Luke. It should be observed that these testimonies were drawn from the OT in order to shed light on the events of the Passion, not to provide inspiration for fictitious elaborations of it. There were many passages viewed by contemporary Jews as messianic which are not referred to in the Gospels; it was the story of the life and death of Jesus, not to say his teaching, which led the earliest Christian teachers to the texts they chose. As Dodd pointed out, the early Church searched the Scriptures not to find support for teaching that they had already formulated but "to find an explanation of attested facts" (*Historical Tradition*, 49).

2. The historicity of the trial narratives, especially of that before the Jewish leaders, has been meticulously examined in this century. H. Lietzmann gave impetus to this questioning, having become convinced that the early Christians were moved by a tendency to place (unwarrantably) the blame for the death of Jesus squarely on the shoulders of the Jewish leaders. On the basis of investigations by the French jurist J. Juster (in *Les juifs dans l'empire romain* [Paris: 1914]) he maintained that John's representation that the Jews did *not* have power to try offenders accused of capital offenses (John 18:31) is unhistorical. In his view the Sanhedrin could

have sentenced Jesus to death, and if they had done so he would have been *stoned;* as it was he was *crucified,* which shows that he was tried and condemned by a Roman court, as indeed the Gospels themselves attest. So out of a brief meeting of the Sanhedrin the Christians constructed a full-blown trial scene, as described in Mark 14:55–65, and the other evange ists followed in this path ("Der Prozess Jesu," in *Sitzungsberichte der Preussischen Akademie der Wissenschaft* [Berlin: 1934] 313–22). Lietzmann's arguments were immensely influential; they were taken up and developed by other scholars, so that today it is commonly maintained, especially among Jewish researchers, that the Gospels give a perverted version of the trial and death of Jesus, particularly in their reports of the part played by the Jews in bringing about his death.

This is an unfortunate controversy, into which one reluctantly enters. The sensitivity of Jews regarding any possible source of anti-semitism is comprehensible; in so far, however, as the gospel reports have contributed to anti-semitic violence, that is a reflection of the failure of the Church (and those who have no business to number themselves with the Church) to be Christian, not of the historicity of the gospel narratives. We do no service to Jews or Christians or to the world at large to evade the tragic facts of the episode in which, according to the NT, *all* kinds of people were involved. Lietzmann's arguments were buttressed by contentions which are contested by scholars today and which in the present writer's judgment are untenable. To state a few of them: Lietzmann held that the threat against the temple in Mark 14:58 cannot be reconciled with Jesus' cleansing of the temple; that the High Priest's question, "Are you the Messiah, *the Son of the Blessed One?*" reflects a Christian, not a Jewish view of the Messiah; that the Jews would not have held a confession to be the Messiah as blasphemy, and so a cause for execution, as is represented in Mark 14:62. By contrast, it is now generally recognized that the cleansing of the temple is to be viewed as an act of prophetic symbolism embodying warning and threat, in harmony with Jer 7:11; that the expression "Son of God" was used among Jews contemporary with Jesus as a messianic title, notably in the Qumran Community, but by others also; see, e.g., M. Hengel, *The Son of God: The Origin of Christology and the History of Jewish-Hellenistic Religion,* trans. J. Bowden (London: SCM, 1976) 41–56. The offense given by Jesus to the High Priest was not his simple answer "I am" (the Messiah), but his additional statement that the High Priest and his court would see him seated at the right hand of God, enthroned in the presence of God as no man could be, and coming with the clouds of heaven, i.e., in a theophany as God alone can come from heaven; that would certainly appear as blasphemy to Jewish minds. As to the right of the Jews to pass sentence of death, there is a baraita in the Talmud, *pSanh.* 1.18a, 37, which states that criminal jurisdiction was taken from the Israelites forty years before the destruction of the temple (see Str-B 1:1027, who, however, thought that the right to pass the death sentence was taken from the Jews starting with the year A.D. 6, and that what transpired in the year A.D. 30 was due to other considerations). The Palestinian Talmud contains a similar but more specific statement: "A baraita says, 'Forty years before the destruction of the Temple they took from Israel the right to inflict capital punishment'" (*jSanh.* 1.1; 7.2). The British jurist A. N. Sherwin-White has strongly criticized Juster's arguments, and in particular Lietzmann for not checking the evidence for himself. He affirmed, "Capital power was the most jealously guarded of all attributes of government (i.e., among the Romans), not even entrusted to the principal assistants of the governors"; certain concessions were made to the Sanhedrin in its police powers regarding the temple and its violators, and beyond that "anything else should either belong to the jurisdiction of the procurator or require his sanction"; the statement in John 18:31 accordingly should be accepted as accurate (*Roman Society and Roman Law in the New Testament,* 24–47; the citations are from this book 36, 42; see further the same writer's article, "The Trial of Christ," in *Historicity and Chronology in the New Testament,* Theological Collections no. 6 [London: SPCK, 1965] 97–116).

The same fundamental position, acknowledging the correctness of John 18:31, is maintained by Blinzler, *Der Prozess Jesu,* 4th ed. 229–44; Bammel, "Die Blutgerichtsbarkeit in der römischen Provinz Judaa," *JJS* 25 (1974) 35–49; D. R. Catchpole, *The Trial of Jesus* (Leiden: Brill, 1972); A. Dauer, *Die Passionsgeschichte im Johannesevangelium,* 143–45; C. H. Dodd, *Historical Tradition,* 105–6; A. E. Harvey, *Jesus on Trial,* 54–55; Jeremias, "Zur Geschichtlichkeit des Verhörs Jesu vor dem hohen Rat," *ZNW* 43 (1950–51) 145–50; G. D. Kilpatrick, *The Trial of Jesus,* 16–21; E. Lohse, *TDNT* 7:865–66; J. A. T. Robinson, *The Priority of John,* 254–58. So also in the commentaries of Becker, 2:563–64; Bernard, 2:607–8; Brown, 2:849–50; Bruce, 351–52; Haenchen, 534–35; Lindars, 556–57; Sanders-Mastin, 395; Schnackenburg, 3:245–56. Support for the viewpoint of Juster and Lietzmann will be found in T. A. Burkill, "The Competence of the Sanhedrin," *VC* 10 (1956) 80–96; idem, "The Trial of Jesus," *VC* 12 (1958) 1–18; idem, "The Condemnation of Jesus: A Critique of Sherwin-White's Thesis," *NovT* 12 (1970) 321–42; P. Winter, *On the Trial of Jesus,* 75–90; and Barrett's commentary, 533–35.

Much of the discussion regarding the trial of Jesus relates to the synoptic accounts of his appearance before the Sanhedrin (the Fourth Gospel is distinguished from the synoptics in briefly describing Jesus' appearance before the High Priest Annas and passing over completely his appearance before Caiaphas and the Sanhedrin). The observation has often been made that the procedure of the Jewish authorities in the trial accounts is in crass contradiction to the rules laid down in the tractate *Sanhedrin* concerning the conduct of trials for capital offenses. No less than twenty-seven deviations from the latter have been reckoned in the synoptic records! On this, two observations may be made. First, it is exceedingly difficult to determine whether the interrogation of Jesus before the Jewish authorities is rightly described as a proper legal trial. The examination of Jesus by Annas is clearly not viewed by the Evangelist as a regular trial, but as an occasion for providing a ground of accusation for more formal legal proceedings. It is possible that the trial before the Sanhedrin is to be understood in a similar manner. (The decision that Jesus must be put to death was recorded by the Fourth Evangelist in 11:47–53.) A further observation was made by Blinzler, in light of his conviction that the interrogation before Caiaphas was a trial: the Mishnah was codified toward the end of the second century of our era and gives the regulations according to the *Pharisaic* understanding, whereas in the time of Jesus the *Sadducees* played the leading role in the Sanhedrin; they had a stricter code than the Pharisees, and supported themselves on a literal interpretation of OT law. Blinzler pointed out that those prescriptions of the Mishnah which were acknowledged by the Sadducees were observed in the trial of Jesus before the Sanhedrin, they and no other (see his article, "Zum Prozess Jesu," *Lebendiges Zeugnis,* 1 [1966] 13–16). The Fourth Evangelist gives no account whatever of the appearance of Jesus before the Sanhedrin presided over by Caiaphas; he tells of Jesus being taken first to Annas, the father-in-law of Caiaphas, and after a brief hearing Jesus was then sent on to Caiaphas, but without describing what then took place (see John 18:12–14, 19–24). The reason for this is clear: in the Evangelist's view the essential decision about Jesus had already been taken by the Sanhedrin under Caiaphas, namely on the occasion narrated in 11:45–53. The assembly of Jewish leaders who had Jesus before them after his arrest was implementing the statement recorded in 11:53, and formulating a case that would be acceptable to the Roman governor.

3. As in earlier sections of the Fourth Gospel the relation between the synoptic accounts of the passion narrative and that in our Gospel have been lengthily discussed, with similar results, namely, the assertion by some of the dependence of John on the synoptists and the contrary view of John's independence of them. The issue is the more complicated by the nature of the history narrated, its length, the early date of its compilation, and the closeness of accord between the four accounts. If we divide the events concerned into (i) the Arrest, (ii) the Trial, and (iii) the Execution of Jesus we find that all four Gospels include (i) the departure of Jesus with his disciples to a place by the Mount of Olives and the coming of Judas with a crowd to arrest him there; (ii) the trial, or at least examination of Jesus by the Jewish High Priest; the trial by Pilate, wherein the question is asked, "Are you the king of the Jews?" and the answer of Jesus; Pilate's statement to the Jews as to the innocence of Jesus; their demand for the release of Barabbas rather than Jesus; Pilate's sentencing of Jesus to death; (iii) the crucifixion of Jesus along with two other men; the dividing and casting lots for the clothes of Jesus by the soldiers; the offering of wine to Jesus; his death; Joseph of Arimathea's request of Pilate for the body of Jesus and his placing him in his own tomb.

With this common material in mind two things are apparent in the Fourth Evangelist's narrative. First, there are many passages which come from the Evangelist himself, e.g., in 18:12–14 the reference to 11:49–50 (Caiaphas was High Priest "that year," and his advice to the Sanhedrin as to the "advantage" in having Jesus put to death); Jesus' answer to the High Priest, and his answer to the official who slapped him for it, 18:4–9; the conversations between Pilate and Jesus and between Pilate and the Jews; the affirmation that Jesus bore the cross for himself, 19:16b; the emphasis on the significance of the inscription on the cross, 19:20–22; Jesus' committal of his Mother to the Beloved Disciple, 19:26–27; the cry from the cross, 19:30. Second, the remainder of the narrative goes back to an earlier tradition. The moot question is to determine its source, whether it was identical with that on which the synoptists drew, or an independent tradition, and on either solution whether it drew on the synoptic Gospels. Anton Dauer, in a monograph devoted to the elucidation of these issues, concluded that the marked dissimilarities between the Johannine and the synoptic accounts, including differences that do not reflect the Fourth Evangelist's redaction, indicate an independence of tradition behind the Fourth Gospel passion narrative; on the other hand, the pre-Johannine tradition has many similarities with all three synoptic Gospels, including passages that show redaction of Mark by Matthew and Luke. This situation is explicable if we postulate *a passion tradition in which the written and the oral traditions flowed together,* whereby the oral tradition was enriched by the synoptic Gospels. Dauer accordingly concluded that the passion narrative that was at the disposal of the Fourth Evangelist was an independent tradition, but it was variously influenced by the synoptic reports, so that in individual places parallels with the earlier Gospels arose (see *Die Passionsgeschichte im Johannesevangelium,* especially 60, 99, 164, 226, and the summary in 334–36). It is of interest to compare this solution with that of D. Moody Smith in relation to the Gospel as a whole, namely, that the Evangelist did not use any of the synoptic Gospels as his sources, but neither did his Gospel take shape in isolation from them ("John and the Synoptics," 443–44; see our Introduction pp. xxxvii). Dauer is more specific, but he recognizes that the passion narrative is a special case. His solution is virtually the same as that of N. A. Dahl, "Die Passionsgeschichte bei Matthäus," *NTS* (1955–56) 22, and of P. Borgen, "John and the Synoptics in the Passion Narrative," *NTS* 5 (1958–59) 246–59, especially 247. It is worthy of consideration as a working hypothesis.

4. It is evident that John's narrative, which flows without a break into his account of the resurrection of Jesus, is controlled by the understanding of the passion of

Jesus as his "lifting up" to the divine glory; accordingly the kingship of Jesus
runs as a thread through the entire narrative, even to his burial. We shall observe
the appearances of this motif in its various manifestations in our exposition, and
consider it finally in the concluding *Explanation* of the passage.

Bibliography

Allen, J. E. "John 18:31b." *The Trial of Jesus.* FS C. F. D. Moule. 83–87. **Bajsic, A.**
"Pilatus, Jesus und Barabbas." *Bib* 48 (1967) 7–28. **Bammel, E.** "φίλος τοῦ καίσαρος
(John 19:12)." *TLZ* 77 (1952) 205–20. **Bampfylde, G.** "John 19:28: A Case for a
Different Translation." *NovT* 11 (1969) 247–60. **Barton, G.** " 'A Bone of Him Shall
Not be Broken': John 19:36." *JBL* 49 (1930) 13–19. **Blank, J.** "Die Verhandlung vor
Pilatus: Joh 18:28–19:26 im Lichte der joh. Theologie." *BZ* 3 (1959) 60–81. **Blinzler,
J.** *Der Prozess Jesu.* Regensburg: Verlag Pustet, ⁴1969. **Bonsirven, J.** "Hora Talmudica:
La notion chronologique de Jean 19,14, aurait-elle un sens symbolique?" *Bib* 33 (1952)
511–15. **Borgen, P.** "John and the Synoptics in the Passion Narrative." *NTS* 5 (1959)
246–59. **Bornhauser, K.** *The Death and Resurrection of Jesus Christ.* Tr. A. Rumpus.
Bangalore: C. L. Press, 1958. **Braun, F. M.** *Mother of God's People.* Staten Island, NY:
Alba, 1968. **Brown, R. E.** "The Passion according to John: Chapters 18–19." *Worship*
49 (1975) 126–34. **Buse, I.** "St. John and the Marcan Passion Narrative." *NTS* 4
(1957–58) 215–19. ———. "St. John and the Passion Narratives of St. Matthew and
St. Luke." *NTS* 7 (1960–61) 65–76. **Chevalier, M. A.** "La comparution de Jésus devant
Hanne et devant Caiphe (Jean 18, 12–14 et 19–24)." *Neues Testament und Geschichte.*
FS O. Cullmann. Zürich: Theologischer Verlag, 1972. 179–85. **Corssen, P.** "ἐκάθισεν
ἐπὶ βήματος." *ZNW* 15 (1914) 338–40. **Dauer, A.** *Die Passionsgeschichte im Johannesevange-
lium: Eine traditionsgeschichtliche und theologische Untersuchung zu Joh 18, 1–19, 30.* Munich:
Kösel, 1972. **Dodd, C. H.** *Interpretation.* 423–43. ———. *History and Tradition in the
Fourth Gospel.* 21–151. **Edwards, W. D., Gabel, W. J., and Hosmer, F. E.** "On the
Physical Death of Jesus Christ." *JAMA* 255 (1986) 1455–63. **Evans, C. F.** *The Passion
of Christ.* London: 1977. 50–66. **Fenton, J. C.** *The Passion according to John.* London:
1961. **Fitzmyer, J. A.** "Crucifixion in Ancient Palestine, Qumran Literature, and the
New Testament." *CBQ* 40 (1978) 493–513. **Ford, J. M.** "Mingled Blood from the
Side of Christ." *NTS* 15 (1969) 337–38. **Fortna, R. T.** "Jesus and Peter at the High
Priest's House: A Test Case for the Question of the Relation between Mark's and
John's Gospel." *NTS* 24 (1978) 371–83. **Haenchen, E.** "Historie und Geschichte in
den johanneischen Passionsberichten." In *Die Bibel und Wir,* by E. Haenchen. Tübingen:
Mohr, 1968. 182–207; ET in *Int* 24 (1970) 198–219. ———. "Jesus vor Pilatus (Joh
18, 28–19, 15). Zur Methode der Auslegung." In *Gott und Mensch,* by E. Haenchen.
Tübingen: Mohr, 1965. 144–56. **Hart, H. S. J.** "The Crown of Thorns in John 19:2–
5." *JTS* 3 (1952) 66–75. **Harvey, A. E.** *Jesus on Trial: A Study in the Fourth Gospel.*
London: SPCK, 1976. **Jaubert, A.** "The Calendar of Qumran and the Passion-Narrative
in John." *John and Qumran.* Ed. J. H. Charlesworth. London: Chapman, 1972. 62–
75. **Jeremias, J.** "A Comparison of the Marcan Passion Narrative with the Johannine."
Eucharistic Words of Jesus. London: SCM, 89–96. **Kilpatrick, G. D.** *The Trial of Jesus.*
London: Williams' Library, 1953. **Klein, G.** "Die Verleugnung des Petrus." *ZTK* 58
(1961) 285–328. **Kurfess, A.** "ἐκάθισεν ἐπὶ βήματος (Joh 19, 13)." *Bib* 34 (1953) 271.
Langkammer, H. "Christ's 'Last Will and Testament' (John 19:26–27) in the Interpretation of the Fathers of the Church and the Scholastics." *Anton* 43 (1968) 99–109.
Lietzmann, H. "Der Prozess Jesu." *Sitzungsberichte der Preussischen Akademie der Wissen-
schaften in Berlin, philos.-hist. Klasse.* Berlin: 1931. 313–22. ———. "Bemerkungen zum
Prozess Jesu." *ZNW* 30 (1931) 211–15; 31 (1932) 78–84. **Lindars, B.** "The Passion
in the Fourth Gospel." *God's Christ and His People.* FS N. A. Dahl. Oslo: Universitätsverla-

get, 1977. 71–86. **Mahoney, A.** "A New Look at an Old Problem (John 18:12–14, 19–24)." *CBQ* 27 (1965) 137–44. **Mein, P.** "A Note on John 18:6." *ExpTim* 65 (1953–54) 286–87. **Michaels, J. R.** "The Centurion's Confession and the Spear Thrust (John 19:34 ff)." *CBQ* 29 (1967) 102–9. **Nestle, W.** "Zum Ysop bei Johannes, Josephus und Philo." *ZNW* 14 (1913) 263–65. **Potterie, I. de la.** "La passion selon S. Jean." *AsSeign* 21 (1969) 21–34. ———. "Jesus roi et juge d'après Jn 19, 13: ἐκάθισεν ἐπὶ βήματος." *Bib* 41 (1960) 217–47; tr. in *Scr* 13 (1961) 97–111. ———. "Das Wort 'Siehe, deine Mutter' und die Annahme der Mutter durch den Jünger (Joh 19, 27b)." *Neues Testament und Kirche.* FS R. Schnackenburg. Freiburg: Herder, 1974. 191–219. **Richter, G.** "Blut und Wasser aus der durchbohrten Seite Jesu (Joh 19, 34b)." *Studien zum Johannesevangelium.* Ed. J. Hainz. Regensburg: Pustet, 1977. 120–42. ———. "Die Gefangennahme Jesu nach dem Johannesevangelium (18, 1–12)." *Studien zum Joh.* 74–87. **Sabbe, M.** "The Arrest of Jesus in John 18:1–11 and Its Relation to the Synoptics." BETL 44 (1977) 203–34. **Sava, A. F.** "The Wound in the Side of Christ." *CBQ* 19 (1957) 343–46. **Schnackenburg, R.** "Die Ecce-Homo-Szene und der Menschensohn." *Jesus und der Menschensohn.* FS A. Vögtle. Freiburg: Herder, 1975. 371–86. **Schneider, J.** "Zur Komposition von Joh 18, 12–27; Kaiphas und Hannas." *ZNW* 48 (1957) 111–19. **Schürmann, H.** "Jesu letzte Weisung: Joh 19, 26–27a." In Schürmann, *Ursprung und Gestalt.* Düsseldorf: Patmos, 1970. 13–28. **Sherwin-White, A. N.** *Roman Law and Roman Society in the New Testament.* Oxford: OUP, 1963. ———. "The Trial of Christ." *Historicity and Chronology in the New Testament.* Ed. D. Nineham. London: SPCK, 1965. 97–116. **Stanley, D. M.** "The Passion according to John." *Worship* 33 (1958–59) 210–30. **Temple, S.** "The Two Traditions of the Last Supper, Betrayal and Arrest." *NTS* 7 (1960) 77–85. **Twomey, J. J.** "Barabbas Was a Robber." *Scr* 8 (1956) 115–19. **Wead, D. W.** " 'We Have a Law': John 19:7." *NovT* 11 (1969) 185–89. **Winter, P.** *On the Trial of Jesus.* Studia Judaica 1. Berlin: de Gruyter, 1961. ———. "The Trial of Jesus and the Competence of the Sanhedrin." *NTS* 10 (1964) 494–99. **Wilkinson, J.** "The Incident of the 'Blood and Water' in John 19:34." *SJT* 28 (1975) 149–72.

Translation

¹ *After Jesus had said these things he went out with his disciples to the other side of the Kedron torrent,*[a] *where there was a garden, into which he and his disciples entered.* ² *Now Judas also, his betrayer, knew the place, because Jesus had often stayed there with his disciples.* ³ *Judas therefore, after receiving a detachment of soldiers and some police from the chief priests and Pharisees, comes there with lanterns and torches and weapons.* ⁴ *Knowing all that was coming upon him Jesus went out, and says to them, "Who is it you are looking for?"* ⁵ *They replied to him, "Jesus the Nazarean."*[b] *He says to them, "I am he."*[c] *Judas, his betrayer, was also standing there with them.* ⁶ *When therefore he said to them, "I am he," they moved backward and fell to the ground.* ⁷ *Again he questioned them, "Who are you looking for?" And they said, "Jesus the Nazarean."* ⁸ *Jesus replied, "I told you that I am he; if therefore you are looking for me, let these men go."* ⁹ *This was in order that the saying he had spoken might be fulfilled, "Of those whom you have given me I have lost not one."* ¹⁰ *Simon Peter then, since he had a sword, drew it and struck the High Priest's slave and cut off his right ear. Now the slave's name was Malchus.* ¹¹ *Jesus therefore said to Peter, "Put the sword back into its sheath. Am I not to drink the cup which the Father has given me?"*

¹² *So the detachment of soldiers and their commander and the Jewish police*

seized Jesus and bound him, [13] *and*[d] *they took him first to Annas, for he was the father-in-law of Caiaphas, who was High Priest that year.* [14] *Now Caiaphas was the man who gave counsel to the Jews that it was to their advantage that one man should die for the people.*

[15] *Simon Peter, along with another disciple, was following Jesus. Now that disciple was a friend*[e] *of the High Priest, and he went with Jesus into the High Priest's courtyard,* [16] *but Peter remained standing outside at the gate. The other disciple therefore, the High Priest's friend,*[f] *went out and spoke to the girl who kept the gate and brought Peter in.* [17] *The maid who kept the gate therefore says to Peter, "You aren't by chance one of the disciples of this man, are you?" He says, "I am not."* [18] *Now the slaves and the temple police had made a coal fire, because it was cold, and they were warming themselves; but Peter also was standing with them and warming himself.*

[19] *The High Priest*[g] *questioned Jesus about his disciples and about his teaching.* [20] *Jesus replied to him, "I have spoken openly to the world; I always taught in the synagogue and in the temple, where all Jews come together, and I have said nothing in secret.* [21] *Why do you question me? Question the hearers as to what I said to them; surely they know what I said."* [22] *On saying this one of the constables who was standing by gave Jesus a slap in the face and said, "Is that how you answer the High Priest?"* [23] *Jesus replied to him, "If I spoke wrongly, give evidence about the wrong; but if I spoke rightly, why do you hit me?"* [24] *So Annas sent him bound to Caiaphas, the High Priest.*

[25] *Meanwhile Simon Peter was still standing and warming himself. They said to him therefore, "You're not by chance one of his disciples, are you?" He denied it and said, "I am not."* [26] *One of the High Priest's slaves, a relative of the man whose ear Peter had cut off, says to him, "I saw you in the garden with him, didn't I?"* [27] *Again Peter denied it; and immediately a cock crew.*

[28] *They took Jesus from Caiaphas to the Governor's residence. It was early,*[h] *and they did not enter the Governor's residence*[i] *so as not to become defiled, but that they might eat the passover lamb.* [29] *Pilate therefore went outside to them, and said, "What accusation are you bringing against this man?"* [30] *They replied to him, "If he were not committing evil*[j] *we would not have handed him over to you."* [31] *Pilate therefore said to them, "You take him yourselves, and judge him in accordance with your law." The Jews said to him, "It is not permitted to us to put anyone to death,"* [32] *in order that the saying of Jesus might be fulfilled when he signified what sort of death he was going to die.*

[33] *Again therefore Pilate entered his residence and asked him, "Are you the king of the Jews?"* [34] *Jesus replied, "Are you saying this of your own accord, or did others tell you about me?"* [35] *Pilate answered, "I'm not a Jew, am I? Your nation and the chief priests handed you over to me. What have you done?"* [36] *Jesus replied, "My kingdom is not of this world; if my kingdom were of this world my subjects would now be fighting that I should not be handed over to the Jews; but as it is, my kingdom comes from elsewhere."* [37] *Pilate therefore said to him, "So you are a king, then?" Jesus replied, "You say that I am a king!*[k] *For this purpose I have been born, and for this I have come into the world, that I should bear witness to the truth. Everyone who is of the truth listens to my voice."* [38] *Pilate says to him, "Truth? What is that?"*

After saying this he went out again to the Jews and said to them, "I find no ground for a charge against this man. [39] But you have a custom that I should release someone for you in the Passover. Do you wish that I release for you the king of the Jews?" [40] They shouted again and said, "Not this man, but Barabbas." Now Barabbas was a rebel.

[19:1] Then Pilate took Jesus and had him flogged. [2] And the soldiers wove a crown out of thorns, and they placed it on his head, and they put around him a purple cloak, [3] and they kept coming to him and saying, "Hail, you 'King of the Jews'!" And they slapped him in the face time and again.

[4] Pilate went out again and said to them, "Look, I am bringing him out to you, that you may know that I find no ground for complaint against him." [5] Jesus therefore came outside, wearing the crown of thorns and the purple cloak, and he says to them, "Look, the Man!" [6] When therefore the chief priests and the officials saw him they shouted, "Crucify! Crucify!" Pilate says to them, "Take him yourselves and you crucify him! For I find no ground for a charge against him." [7] The Jews replied to him, "We have a law, and according to that law he ought to die, because he made himself the Son of God."

[8] When Pilate heard that statement he became yet more afraid, [9] and he went into his residence again, and said to Jesus, "Where are you from?" But Jesus gave him no answer. [10] Pilate therefore says to him, "Are you not going to talk to me? You know, don't you, that I have authority to release you, and I have authority to crucify you?" [11] Jesus replied to him, "You would possess no authority at all against me unless it were given you from above to have it; for this reason the man who handed me over to you has a greater sin." [12] From this moment on Pilate tried to release him; but the Jews kept shouting and saying, "If you release this man you are no 'Friend of Caesar.' Anyone who makes himself a king is in opposition to Caesar."

[13] Pilate therefore, on hearing these words, brought Jesus out, and he sat on the judge's seat in the place called "Stone Pavement," but in the language of the Jews "Gabbatha."[l] [14] It was the Preparation Day for the Passover, the hour was about midday,[m] and he says to the Jews, "Look, your king!" [15] They shouted, "Take him away! Take him away! Crucify him!" Pilate says to them, "Your king! Am I to crucify him?" The chief priests replied to him, "We have no king except Caesar." [16] Then he handed him over to them to be crucified.

They took over Jesus, accordingly, [17] and carrying the cross for himself he went out to the place called "the Skull," which in the Jews' language is called Golgotha.[n] 18 There they crucified him, and with him two others, one on each side and Jesus in the middle.

[19] And Pilate wrote an inscription: "Jesus the Nazarene, the King of the Jews." [20] Many of the Jews read this inscription, for the place where Jesus was crucified was near the city; and it was written in Hebrew, in Latin, and in Greek.[o] [21] The Jewish chief priests therefore said to Pilate, "Don't leave it written,[p] 'The King of the Jews,' but write what he himself said, 'I am King of the Jews.' " [22] Pilate answered, "What I have written, I have written."

[23] The soldiers, then, when they had crucified Jesus, took his clothes and divided them into four parts, one part for each soldier. They also took the tunic, but the tunic was seamless, woven throughout from the top to the bottom. [24] They said therefore to one another, "Don't let us tear it, but let us cast lots for it and see who will get it"—that the scripture might be fulfilled (which says):

> They divided my clothes among themselves,
> and for my clothing they cast lots.

The soldiers therefore did these things.
[25] But there stood beside the cross of Jesus his mother, and his mother's sister, Mary the wife of Clopas, and Mary Magdalene. [26] Jesus therefore, on seeing his mother and the disciple whom he loved standing near her, says to his mother, "Mother, look, your son." [27] Then he says to the disciple, "Look, your mother." And from that hour the disciple took her into his own home.

[28] After this Jesus, knowing that all was now accomplished, in order that the scripture might be fulfilled said, "I am thirsty." [29] A jar stood there, full of cheap wine; they therefore put a sponge full of the wine on a hyssop plant[q] and brought it to his mouth. [30] When he had taken the wine Jesus said, "It is accomplished!" And he bowed his head and handed over his spirit.

[31] Accordingly, since it was the Preparation Day, and in order to prevent the bodies from remaining on the cross on the sabbath, for that sabbath was a great day, the Jews requested Pilate that the legs of the men might be broken, and that they be taken away. [32] The soldiers therefore came, and they broke the legs of the first man, and those of the other one who had been crucified with him; [33] but when they came to Jesus and saw that he was dead already they did not break his legs, [34] but one of the soldiers pierced his side with a lance, and immediately blood and water came out. [35] The man who saw this has borne witness to it—and his witness is authentic, and he knows that he tells the truth—that you, too, may believe.[r] [36] For these events happened in order that the scripture might be fulfilled, "Not a bone of his is to be broken." [37] And again another scripture says, "They will look on him whom they pierced."

[38] After this Joseph of Arimathea, a disciple of Jesus, but a secret one through fear of the Jews, requested Pilate that he might remove the body of Jesus, and Pilate gave permission. He came therefore and removed his body. [39] Nicodemus also came, the man who at the first went to him at night, bringing a mixture[s] of myrrh and aloes, about a hundred pounds in weight. [40] They took the body of Jesus therefore and bound it with cloth wrappings and with the spices, in accordance with the custom of the Jews to bury people. [41] Now in the place where he was crucified there was a garden, and in the garden a new tomb in which no one had ever yet been laid. [42] Since therefore it was the Preparation Day of the Jews and the tomb was near, they laid Jesus there.

Notes

[a] Kedron was a χείμαρρος, lit. "winter-flowing," as a noun denoting a torrent that flowed during the rainy season of winter. Like Luke, our Evangelist does not name the place to which Jesus went with his disciples ("Gethsemane" = "oil press"), but he alone mentions that it was a garden. Early expositors could not resist linking the garden wherein man fell into sin with the garden of the Savior's struggle to obey his Father, which was also the scene of his arrest, and that garden where he burst the bands of death at Easter. The connection, however, is scarcely to be viewed as intended by the Evangelist.

[b] ὁ Ναζωραῖος, like Mark's ὁ Ναζαρηνός, without doubt is the equivalent of ὁ ἀπὸ Ναζαρέτ of 1:45; for other derivations and meanings that have been proposed, see H. H. Schaeder, TDNT 4:874–79.

ᶜ After λέγει αὐτοῖς various MSS read ὁ Ἰησοῦς (so ℵ A C K L W etc.), while B places ὁ Ἰησοῦς after ἐγώ εἰμι; the shorter reading (without ὁ Ἰησοῦς) is found in P⁶⁰ D it ᵇ ᵉ ʳˡ syrˢ·ᵖᵃˡᵐˢ copᵇᵒᵐˢˢ Origen. Whereas the name could have been omitted accidentally (it was usually contracted to ΙΣ) the temptation to identify the speaker and the differing position of the name favors the short reading, which also happens to be an impressive one.

ᵈ The differences between the Johannine account of Jesus before the High Priest and that in the synoptic Gospels set copyists wondering whether the order of the text was correct. The MS 225 puts v 24 into v 13 after πρῶτον, 1195 sets v 24 *after* v 13, but the Sinaitic Syr. rearranges the text boldly, thus: vv 13, 24, 14–15, 19–23, 16–18, 25–27. If the latter were original the order in the rest of MSS would be inexplicable; the changes are clearly due to a desire to harmonize the Fourth Gospel with the other three.

ᵉ The expression γνωστὸς τῷ ἀρχιερεῖ has a slight but significant modification in v 16, ὁ γνωστὸς τοῦ ἀρχιερέως, "the acquaintance of the High Priest." Barrett points out that in the LXX of 2 Kings 10:11 and Ps 55:14 it renders מְיֻדָּע (*meyuddāʾ*), "familiar friend"; and the related form γνωτὸς can = "kinsman," and even "brother." In view of this usage C. H. Dodd concluded that in v 15 "the person so described was a member of the High Priest's circle, possibly a kinsman and himself of priestly birth, or at any rate one who stood in intimate relations with the governing high priestly family" (*Historical Tradition*, 87).

ᶠ The textual variants in the description of "the other disciple" are of minor significance. The addition of ἐκεῖνος in K*ᵛⁱᵈ Ψ f¹³ 1241 etc. appears to be due to an assimilation to v 15.

ᵍ On the variations in the order of the passage see n. d on vv 13–27.

ʰ πρωΐ = "it was early in the morning." Its technical use for the fourth watch in the night according to Roman reckoning, i.e., 3:00–6:00 A.M., is hardly likely in view of 20:1 (the only other occurrence of πρωΐ in our Gospel).

ⁱ πραιτώριον originally denoted the praetor's tent in camp, with its surroundings; hence, it came to be used for the Governor's official residence. In Palestine, that was situated in Caesarea, but there was one also in Jerusalem. It is uncertain whether this was Herod's palace in the western part of the city, near the Jaffa gate, a suitable location since it dominated the city, or whether it was the Antonia fortress, north of the temple area, where the praetorian cohort was stationed during festivals to quell potential riots. The latter identification is adopted by most recent scholars in view of the discovery of a pavement of great flagstones in the Antonia area, thought to be the *Lithostrotos* of 19:13; but others favor the former, since according to Philo and Josephus the Roman procurators usually stayed there when in Jerusalem (see Blinzler, *Der Prozess Jesu* ⁴1969, 256–59).

ʲ The noun κακοποιός (A C³ Dˢᵘᵖᵖ K X Δ Θ etc.) instead of κακὸν ποιῶν (ℵᶜ B L W etc., adopted in the UBS text) could have been suggested by 1 Pet 2:12; 4:15 (Metzger, 252).

ᵏ The precise significance of σὺ λέγεις has been disputed. C. H. Dodd affirmed, "That 'You say' is either in Greek or Aramaic a recognized form of expression for an affirmative reply to a question is a theory for which I have been able to find no sufficient support in actual examples" (*Historical Tradition*). On the contrary, the reply of Jesus to Judas in Matt 26:25 appears indubitably to mean "Yes." So also the σὺ εἶπας in Matt 26:64 for ἐγώ εἰμι in Mark 14:62 has a clearly affirmative intention, even if it implies that the confession has a greater significance than the questioner realizes (the rest of the saying explains that deeper significance). The single parallel to the expression that Str-B found is, despite its singularity, quite clear: A certain Simeon the virtuous told R. Eliezer (ca. A.D. 90) that he had gone between the porch and the altar of the Temple without having washed his hands and feet. Eliezer answered, "Who is more esteemed, you or the High Priest?" Simeon was silent. Eliezer continued, "Are you not rightly ashamed to say that the very dog of the High Priest is more esteemed than you?" Simeon replied, "Rabbi, you have said it," i.e., *You are right* (Str-B 1:990). So also the context in John 18:37 shows that an affirmation is intended in the σὺ λέγεις of Jesus; he has just spoken of the nature of his kingdom, which led Pilate to exclaim, "So you are a king, then?" Jesus proceeds to explain further the nature of his sovereignty in terms of his vocation to bear witness to the truth (so Bultmann: "The continuation shows that in Jn 18:37 σὺ λέγεις = 'Yes,' for the continuation becomes senseless if one attempts to understand it otherwise," 654 n.6).

ˡ The "stone pavement" will have been a platform in front of the praetorium where people gathered. *Gabbatha* does not translate Λιθόστρωτος but means "an elevated place"; both the Antonia fortress and Herod's palace were on high ground, so the term would have suited either location.

ᵐ Whereas virtually the whole MS tradition reads ἕκτη, "*sixth* hour," a few MSS have τρίτη (*third* hour, so D[supp] L X[txt] Δ Ψ etc.). This is clearly due to an accommodation of the text to Mark 15:25, where some MSS change *third* hour to *sixth*, to agree with John 19:14.

ⁿ Golgotha (Hebrew גלגלת, *Golgolet,* Aramaic גלגלתא, *Gulgultāʾ*) means "skull." Luke 23:33 does not cite the Sem. name but simply reads, "they came to the place that is called Skull." John 19:17 could be translated in the same way, the gen. then being regarded as one of apposition. Presumably the name was given by reason of the shape of the ground (hence the tradition that it was a hill; for the legends associating it with the burial of Adam's skull see Brown, 2:900). The hillock behind the bus station in Jerusalem, Gordon's Calvary, is undoubtedly reminiscent of a skull in shape, but the traditional site of Golgotha in the Church of the Holy Sepulchre is favored by recent archaeologists (see, e.g., J. Jeremias, *Golgotha* [Leipzig: E. Pfeiffer, 1926]; A. Parrot, *Golgotha et Saint-Sepulchre* [Neuchâtel-Paris: Delachaux et Niestlé, 1955]; K. M. Kenyon, *Digging up Jerusalem* [New York: Praeger, 1974] 226–34, 261–67; J. Finegan, *The Archeology of the New Testament* [Princeton: Princeton Univ. Press, 1978] 156–68 [with bibliography]).

ᵒ The order of languages, "Hebrew, Latin, Greek" has strong attestation (א[a] B L N X it[e,ff2] syr[pal] cop[sa,boh] arm eth etc.) and indicates the national language, the official language, and the common language. Many later MSS (including most minuscules and MSS of the Lat. tradition) read "Hebrew, Greek, Latin," viewing the languages as spoken in order from East to West (Metzger, 253).

ᵖ Μὴ γράφε is a call to *stop* letting the writing continue to remain (N. Turner interprets the expression, "alter what you have written," Moulton's *Grammar of NT Greek,* 3:76). The chief priests apparently ask Pilate simply to add the word εἰμι, "I am," to the *titulus,* so making it the claim of Jesus and not a proclamation.

q The sixteenth-century writer J. Camerarius suggested that instead of ὑσσώπῳ, "on a hyssop plant," we should read ὑσσῷ, "on a javelin." He had no idea that two cursives, 476* and 1242, actually have that reading. It is hardly likely that the original reading survived in these two late MSS, but it is considered possible that they may reflect an astute correction back to the original text. A confusion in the wording is also discernible: the usual reading in early MSS would be ΥΣΣΩΠΩΠΕΡΙΘΕΝΤΕΣ, the shorter variant ΥΣΣΩΠΕΡΙΘΕΝΤΕΣ; the question is whether the latter is due to omitting the third syllable or the former due to lengthening it, perhaps on account of the unusual term ὑσσός and the familiarity of scribes with hyssop at Passover. Many modern translators have adopted the reading ὑσσῷ, "javelin" (Moffatt, Goodspeed, Phillips, Rieu, Williams, NEB) and a number of exegetes also (e.g., Lagrange, 496; Bernard, 2:640; Bultmann, 674 n.2; Dodd, *Historical Tradition,* 124 n.2; J. A. T. Robinson, *The Priority of John,* 279). G. D. Kilpatrick has objected that the term ὑσσός denotes the Lat. *pilum,* used by Rom. *legionary* troops, whereas in the six decades before the Jewish War (A.D. 66) only *auxiliary* troops were used in Judea ("The Transmission of the NT and Its Reliability," *Transactions of Victoria Institute,* 89 [1957] 98–99). The question then arises whether the Evangelist was aware of the restriction of the term in this fashion. Certainly a sprig of hyssop could not support a sponge, though Str-B maintained that a hyssop *stem* could do so (2:581; see further E. Nestle, "Zum Ysop bei Johannes, Josephus und Philo," *ZNW* 14 [1913] 263–65). The possibilities should be acknowledged and left open.

ʳ On πιστεύ[σ]ητε see *Notes* on 20:31.

ˢ Instead of μίγμα (= "mixture"), attested by P[66vid] א[c] A D[supp] K L X Δ Θ etc., ἕλιγμα, "a fold, wrapping" appears in א* B W cop[boms], σμῆγμα, "ointment," in 1242*, and σμίγμα, a variation of μίγμα, in Ψ etc. The first reading has superior attestation and probability.

Form/Structure/Setting

1. The fundamental form of the passion narrative of the four gospels was supplied by the kerygma, the primitive proclamation of the good news. We see it in briefest compass in such pregnant summaries as 1 Cor 15:3–4 (cf. also Rom 3:25; 4:25; 2 Cor 5:19; 1 Peter 3:18, 22). Formulations like these encapsulated the heart of the gospel and required fuller exposition. Peter's address on the Day of Pentecost (Acts 2:14–36) may be viewed as an exposition of the passion and resurrection of Jesus related to the outpouring

of the Holy Spirit. To make the needful proclamation specific in the general preaching "a short narrative of historical reminiscence about the Arrest, Condemnation, and Execution of Jesus" was drawn up for use in preaching and teaching (the cited words are from Bultmann, *The History of the Synoptic Tradition*, 275). The manner in which this primitive passion narrative was developed in the Fourth Gospel has been explained in our introduction to the Johannine passion narrative. (For further discussions of the passion narrative in the primitive preaching of the Church see especially C. H. Dodd's *Apostolic Preaching and Its Developments*, chaps. 1 and 2, and more briefly his *History and the Gospel* [London: Nisbet, 1938] 80–84).

2. The setting of the passion narrative in the life of Jesus requires no explanation, except that every Christian preacher and teacher who recounted it did so in the knowledge that this "end" of the ministry of Jesus in Judea and Galilee was its beginning for the world of nations. Ministry is service: the death of Jesus was the climax of his service of God and man, whereby the saving sovereignty of God was brought to humanity. No one knew this better than the Fourth Evangelist, who penned his narrative in the consciousness that every step of Jesus in those hours constituted part of *the* hour, whereby the Father was glorified in the Son and the Son was in process of exaltation to the throne of God.

The Evangelist, however, was not publishing a tract for all times and peoples without regard for his own time and people. The churches to whom his Gospel was first addressed were under pressure, and their faith was being attacked precisely at the point of the passion narrative. The modern Jewish desire to dissociate the Sanhedrin from responsibility for the death of Jesus was not shared by Jews in the early centuries of our era. Part of the polemic against the Christian preaching of Jesus as Messiah and Son of God was precisely his rejection and condemnation by the Jewish leaders of his time. There is a well-known *baraita* in the Talmud which tells when and why Jesus died:

> On the eve of the Passover Jeshu was hanged. For forty days before the execution took place a herald went forth and cried, "He is going forth to be stoned because he has practiced sorcery and enticed Israel to apostasy. Anyone who can say anything in his favor, let him come forward and plead on his behalf." But since nothing was brought forward in his favor he was hanged on the eve of the Passover.

> Ulla retorted: "Do you suppose that he was one for whom a defense could be made? Was he not a *Mesith* (enticer), concerning whom Scripture says, 'Neither shalt thou spare, nor shalt thou conceal him'?" (*Sanh.* 43a).

It is considered likely that this text has expanded an earlier one which stated simply that Jesus was hanged on the eve of the Passover because he practiced sorcery and deceived and led Israel astray. Since it was known that such offenses were punished by stoning, it was assumed that the "hanging" of Jesus was that which followed on stoning. The point of interest to us is its continuance of a tradition that the Jewish leaders condemned Jesus to death as *a false prophet*. (On the history of the text see W. Horbury, "The Benediction of the Minim," *JTS* 33 [1982] 56–58.)

The sentiment voiced by Ulla in the above citation, namely, that Jesus received his just due in his execution, was early elaborated in Jewish criticism of Jesus, whether based on purely Jewish traditions of the trial and death of Jesus or on an early Christian passion narrative reproduced in garbled form. Celsus, the early pagan opponent of Christianity, reports a Jew as saying,

> How could we have held him for a God who, as we heard, produced none of the works which he proclaimed, and when we had convicted him, and condemned him, and wanted to punish him, he hid himself and tried to escape, and in a most ignominious way was seized and betrayed by none other than those whom he called his disciples? If he were God he could neither have fled, nor be led off bound, least of all be left in the lurch and abandoned by his companions, who shared everything with him and had him as teacher, and held him to be the Savior and Son and Messenger of the Most High God" (Origen, *Contra Celsum*, 2.8–9).

G. Richter believed that reports of this kind must have circulated among the Jews long before the time of Celsus; he thought it likely that they were not simply known to the Fourth Evangelist, but that he felt obliged to counter them in his passion narrative. The Evangelist, for example, tells how Jesus, far from seeking to run away from those sent to arrest him, actually *went forth* to meet them (18:4); the Jewish allegation that Jesus tried to escape is the reverse of the truth! He goes on to show that it was the soldiers and Jewish police who were seized with fear, not Jesus who was afraid of them (18:6). He also makes it plain that the disciples did not run off in panic; they were allowed to depart because Jesus told his captors to let them go (18:8–9; the loyalty of the disciples as a group had already been shown in Thomas's exclamation, "Let us also go with him that we may die with him!" 11:16). Other elements of Jewish propaganda against Jesus may have influenced the shaping of John's account of the last hours of Jesus; e.g., the scoffing at Jesus' "lamentation" in prospect of his death, and his prayer to God that he may escape it (*Contra Celsum*, 2.24; contrast John 12:27–28); and the observation that Jesus could not even endure thirst, but "greedily turned to drink," whereas the best of men often endure it (*Contra Celsum*, 2.37); in this last case the Evangelist related the cry of Jesus, "I thirst," to the fulfillment of the Scripture (19:28). Just as Matthew felt constrained to counter contemporary Jewish allegations that the disciples' of Jesus stole his body (Matt 28:13–15), so it is well possible that our Evangelist in his narrative had in view contemporary Jewish representations of unworthy conduct of Jesus in his last hours and sought to correct them. (See the treatment of this theme in Richter, *Studien zum Johannesevangelium*, 74–87. Richter, while showing considerable insight relating to this theme, considered that the Evangelist had no independent information concerning Jesus' conduct in this time, and that the Evangelist composed his descriptions freely, as the Gnostics did in their representations of Jesus. This suggestion does not accord with the Evangelist's general dealing with the traditions of Jesus' history, which in the judgment of most are especially sound in the accounts of the trial and death of Jesus.)

3. The structure of the passion narrative is perspicuously clear; it proceeds

through the stages of the arrest of Jesus (18:1–11), his interrogation by the Jewish High Priest (18:12–27), trial by Pilate (18:28–19:16a), crucifixion and burial (19:16b–42). The steps by which the narrative advances are also plainly marked in successive paragraphs. If the arrest and examination of Jesus by Annas are bracketed as a unit, the narrative divides itself into three sections, each containing seven paragraphs. Whether the Evangelist constructed the narrative in accordance with such a plan it is hard to say (his friend John the Seer produced much of the Book of Revelation in that manner); at least it is helpful for the reader to observe the construction. It may be set forth as follows:

1. The Arrest of Jesus and Examination by the High priest: 18:1–27
   i. Judas leads a detachment of soldiers and Jewish police, vv 1–3
   ii. Jesus confronts the group, vv 4–9
   iii. Peter attempts to defend Jesus, vv 10–11
   iv. Jesus is led to the High Priest Annas, vv 12–14
   v. Peter's first denial of Jesus, vv 15–18
   vi. The interrogation of Jesus before Annas, vv 19–24
   vii. Peter denies Jesus twice more, vv 25–27
2. The Trial of Jesus before Pilate: 18:28–19:16a
   i. Jesus is handed over to Pilate, vv 28–32
   ii. Pilate's first interrogation of Jesus, vv 33–38a
   iii. Pilate's declaration of the innocence of Jesus, vv 38b–40
   iv. Jesus is flogged and mocked by the soldiers, 19:1–3
   v. Jesus is presented as a mock-king and further declared innocent, vv 4–7
   vi. Pilate's second interrogation of Jesus and attempt to release him, vv 8–12
   vii. Jesus is sentenced to death by crucifixion, vv 13–16a
3. The Crucifixion, Death, and Burial of Jesus: 19:16b–42
   i. The crucifixion of Jesus, vv 16b–18
   ii. The title on the cross and Jewish objections to it, vv 19–22
   iii. The dividing of Jesus' clothes, vv 23–24
   iv. Jesus gives his Mother to the Beloved Disciple, vv 25–27
   v. The death of Jesus, vv 28–30
   vi. The piercing of Jesus' side, vv 31–37
   vii. The burial of Jesus, vv 38–42

Comment

THE ARREST OF JESUS (18:1–11)

1–2 The opening clause is intended to convey the meaning: "After Jesus had uttered the preceding discourses and prayer he went out of the house with his disciples" (see *Comment* on 14:31). This, along with the observation in v 2b cf. Luke 22:39, indicates that Jesus and his disciples were accustomed to staying at night in the garden during the period leading up to the festival (on the Passover day itself Jews were required to stay within an extended city limit, which would have included Gethsemane but not Bethany).

3 Commentators have not infrequently regarded the episode in vv 3–9 as a theological distortion of what is recorded in the synoptic Gospels (Mark 14:43–50 par.). A cohort commonly consisted of 600 men under the command of a superior officer (a "chiliarch," commander of a thousand). Haenchen interpreted v 3 as meaning that Judas was *given charge* of the entire Roman occupying force of Jerusalem with its tribune, plus "servants" (= temple police) sent by the High Priest, and that is an impossible circumstance to envisage (517). Certainly it is impossible, but it is unlikely that we were meant to read it so. The Evangelist should not be credited with stupidity when he wrote that Judas "took" a force of Roman soldiers and Jewish constables (as Bultmann recognized: "λαβών does not signify that Judas commands the troops, but only that he shows the way," 639, n.1). Apart from the fact that a cohort (σπεῖρα) could denote a "maniple" of 200 soldiers, there is no need to understand that the entire company of soldiers in the Antonia garrison was dispatched. The troops were stationed in the Antonia during festivals precisely to prevent riots; it is comprehensible that the Jewish leaders asked for their presence in case of violent resistance when their own police attempted to arrest Jesus (see among others Bernard, 2:584; Gardner-Smith, *St. John and the Synoptic Gospels*, 57–58; Brown, 2:807; Dodd, *Historical Tradition*, 73–74, 112–20). That the Evangelist wished, through his mention of Roman soldiers, to emphasize that representatives both of the Gentile world and the Jewish nation joined forces to arrest Jesus may be freely admitted (Hoskyns is typical: "In the Johannine account the forces of darkness, the Roman and the Jewish authorities, and the apostate disciple are arrayed against the Christ from the beginning," 509). But this does not require the deduction that the Evangelist has manipulated his sources in an unhistorical manner. The whole passion narrative is told in order that the reader may grasp its theological significance. Dodd's comment on the implications of v 9 is noteworthy: "The action of Jesus in the Garden was a σημεῖον of his action upon a larger scale and a higher plane; and this action upon a larger scale and a higher plane is the true meaning of his action in the Garden" (*Interpretation*, 432). To throw light on that "larger scale and higher plane" of the events of the passion story is the Evangelist's purpose through the whole narration.

4–6 It is in accordance with this intention that the Evangelist states that Jesus knew "all that was coming upon him." It was the hour ordained by the Father—hence *he* takes the initiative; Judas' betrayal by a kiss is not mentioned, and Jesus himself advances toward the soldiers and the police to ask whom they want. The reply of Jesus, "*I am* (*he*)," may be seen as a normal self-identification, but we are almost certainly intended to recognize its overtones, as throughout this Gospel (cf. esp. 6:20; 8:28, 54). Bultmann is right in rejecting the notion that the *psychological* effect of the personality of Jesus caused the reaction of the crowd, but questionable in speaking of the *miraculous* effect produced by the words of Jesus (639). The reality of the *mysterium tremendum* before the presence of God (especially through a vision) is frequently illustrated in the Bible (e.g., Ezek 1:28; Dan 10:9; Acts 9:4; Rev 1:17), and it is not a phenomenon limited to Jews. It is entirely comprehensible that the Jewish constables of the temple were awed by the "I am" uttered by Jesus in the garden (cf. the reaction to him in the temple, reported in John 7:46), and their shrinking back could have produced what is described in v

6; moreover, we should not dismiss as absurd an awesome effect of Jesus on the Roman soldiers in that situation (note the unexplained 19:8—"Pilate was *the more* afraid"). Was the Evangelist mindful of some pertinent sayings in the Psalms (e.g., Pss 27:2; 34:4; 56:9)?

7–9 Jesus manifests not only his spiritual authority before his antagonists but also his concern as Shepherd for his own: "Let these men go." In this solicitude the Evangelist recognizes the fulfillment of a saying of Jesus. It is characteristic of the Evangelist's style that he does not report a saying precisely in these words, but the sentiment is clearly expressed in 17:12 (cf. also the related 6:69; 10:28); it belongs to the basic concept of Jesus as the good Shepherd of his sheep. It will not go unnoticed that the Evangelist parallels Jesus' sayings and their fulfillment with OT sayings that find fulfillment in Jesus' life and work (cf. 12:38; 13:18; 15:25; 19:24, 36), a datum of significance relating to the authority of the words of Jesus.

10–11 The identification of the disciple who struck the High Priest's slave as Peter (cf. Mark 14:47 par.) has no special significance for the Evangelist and may be assumed to have been in the tradition he received (the same applies to the name of the slave, Malchus). But when we recall the synoptic testimony we see Peter here as having as little comprehension of the passion of Jesus in its unfolding as he did when Jesus first announced it (Mark 8:31–33; similarly in John 13:6–10). The readiness of Jesus to drink the "cup" given him by his father is reminiscent of the Gethsemane tradition (Mark 14:36; more closely Matt 26:39, 42; and cf. John 12:27–28).

The Interrogation of Jesus by Annas and Peter's Denials (18:12–27)

12–14 The Fourth Evangelist alone reports that Jesus was taken first to Annas. In all probability it will have been the temple police who delivered him; their task will have been to make the arrest, that of the Roman soldiers to prevent trouble at the arrest; the latter will have returned to the Antonia barracks after seeing Jesus safely handed over. That Jesus should have been delivered to Annas need occasion no surprise. Naturally the procedure must have been agreed on between Caiaphas and Annas, but the latter was clearly an immensely influential person among the Jewish leadership. He had been high priest A.D. 6–15. His deposition by Valerius Gratus, Pilate's predecessor, will not have diminished his respect in Israel, for no less than five of his sons and a grandson became high priests, and Caiaphas was his son-in-law; his family thus had a monopoly of the high-priestly office during the period A.D. 17–41. Annas accordingly will have held a patriarchal position in the high-priestly circles, not least in the period when Caiaphas held office. (The references to Annas in Luke's writings are significant: the elaborate dating of John the Baptist's ministry includes the phrase, "during the high-priesthood of Annas and Caiaphas"—both viewed as high priests, and Annas placed first; so also in Acts 4:6 the assembled company of the Sanhedrin has among them "Annas the High Priest and Caiaphas and John and Alexander and all who were of the high-priestly family.")

There is no necessity therefore to resort to textual emendation to avoid the interrogation of Jesus by Annas rather than Caiaphas. A. Mahoney, observing that Caiaphas is called High Priest in vv 13 and 24, considered that Caiaphas must be the person designated as High Priest in v 19; in that case Jesus was interrogated by *Caiaphas* in the presence of Annas, not by Annas himself. A difficulty, however, arises for this interpretation from v 24: how should Annas, after this interrogation by Caiaphas, send Jesus bound to Caiaphas? Mahoney answered by proposing a slight emendation: instead of reading ἀπέστειλεν αὐτὸν ὁ Ἄννας δεδεμένον ("Annas sent him *bound* to Caiaphas") he suggested that the text originally read ἀπέστειλεν αὐτὸν ὁ Ἄννας δὲ μένων ("But Annas sent him to Caiaphas, *while he himself continued to remain*") (the phenomenon of dittography is a common mistake among copyists of the NT). With this correction it is assumed that Caiaphas went on from Annas to the meeting of the Sanhedrin, to which Annas sent Jesus but refrained from going himself (see "A New Look at an Old Problem," 140–41). Like most emendations of the NT text, this too is possible, but needless and implausible.

15–16   The story of Peter's denials of Jesus is told in all four Gospels, with variations on the main theme. R. A. Culpepper justly observed that the theme is not that Peter denied that Jesus is Lord or Messiah, but that he himself was his disciple (*Anatomy of the Fourth Gospel,* 120). The information that Peter was accompanied by another disciple, who was a "friend" of the High Priest and who secured his entry into the High Priest's courtyard, is unique to our Gospel (on the significance of γνωστός see the *Notes*). Why the Evangelist refrains from making known in clearer fashion the identity of the other disciple is a mystery, for he does not hesitate to give the names of Joseph of Arimathea and of Nicodemus. It is noticeable that the mode of reference is akin to the Evangelist's oblique manner of referring to "the disciple whom Jesus loved," as also to the unnamed eyewitness who told of the soldiers' decision not to break the legs of Jesus on the cross and of one who pierced his side (19:31–35). The possibility that the Evangelist intends us to identify the persons mentioned as *one,* namely, as the Beloved Disciple, is strong, not least in view of the Beloved Disciple's association with Peter (cf. 13:23–24; 20:2–10; 21:20–24). On this issue the exegetes are divided (see the *Introduction,* lxxii–lxxv; F Neirynck considered it anew and inclined to see in 19:15–16 the Beloved Disciple ["The 'other disciple' in John 18:15–16," 113–41]).

17–18   All the Gospels state that it was a girl who precipitated Peter's first denial; our Gospel alone tells us that she was the maid (παιδίσκη) who kept the gate, whom the other disciple persuaded to let him in. It would appear then that the conversation took place at the gate, not by the fire, to which Peter moved afterward (contrast Mark 14:67; Luke 22:55).

19–21   The interrogation of Jesus by Annas and the sharp answer of Jesus to him call for some explanation. In any court inquiry among Jews the correct procedure was to call witnesses, not to question the accused. (So Bornhäuser: "Jewish judges did not enquire of the accused, but of the witnesses. On their testimony everything depended. If two witnesses agreed in essentials, then the accused was doomed, no matter what he might say in his defence," *The Death and Resurrection of Jesus Christ,* 98.) Jesus accordingly was justified in objecting to the procedure and demanding a proper trial. Moreover, the questions of Annas about Jesus' disciples and his teaching are likely to be linked with the tradition perpetuated in the Talmud that Jesus was convicted of being a false prophet (note the citation from *Sanh.*

43a cited on p. 319). The mark of the false prophet is that he "secretly entices" or "leads astray" the people to apostatize from the God of Israel, the punishment for which is death (see Deut 13:1–10). It looks as if Annas was endeavoring to make Jesus incriminate himself on this issue. Jesus sees through this attempt and declares that his teaching of the people has been in public places, in the temple, and in synagogues, not in secret with a view to promoting apostasy among the people (observe that the charge that Jesus "leads astray" the people appears earlier in the Gospel, e.g., 7:12, 47).

22–24 The key word is actually spoken to the officer who struck Jesus for his answer to the High Priest: "If I spoke wrongly, state the evidence for it," on which J. A. T. Robinson commented: "In other words he is denying any secret or subversive activity and demanding that they produce witnesses prepared to testify on oath in open court" (*The Priority of John,* 249). In other words, Jesus is calling for a just trial. Annas therefore brings the examination to an end and sends Jesus on to Caiaphas to see what he can do.

25–27 The Evangelist returns to Peter in the High Priest's courtyard, where the Apostle continues to stand before the fire. His interlocutors this time are described as "they," which in the context would most naturally denote the servants and the police, though admittedly the term could be indefinite (in Mark "the same maid" addresses Peter, 14:69, in Luke 22:58 it is "another person," a masculine reference). The third address to Peter in the synoptists is vague; "the bystanders" speak to him (Mark 14:70, similarly Matt 26:73), "another" (Luke 22:59), but our Evangelist is specific: it was a relative of Malchus, whose ear Peter had cut off, who identified Peter as a companion of Jesus in the garden; this led to his third and final denial of Jesus, followed by the cock's crow.

The differences in the Evangelists' accounts of this event are characteristic of those observable in the Gospels generally in their reports of the ministry of Jesus: variations in details but clearly attested occurrences. The most important difference between the account in the Fourth Gospel and those in the synoptics is the location of the event: in the courtyard of the High Priest Annas, not in that of the High Priest Caiaphas. The episode will, of course, have been narrated separately and as a *unit* in the early gospel tradition, as Luke has reproduced it (22:54–62). Mark, followed by Matthew, separates off the introduction to the narrative, telling of Peter's following Jesus at a distance and arriving at the High Priest's court; he then reports the examination of Jesus before the Sanhedrin, and follows that by the account of Peter's denials (14:53–54, 66–71, the denials; 55–65, the interrogation). The Fourth Evangelist goes further in the direction of Mark's treatment: he describes how Peter came to be in the High Priest's courtyard and his first denial (18:15–18), and sets the account of the interrogation of Jesus by Annas between that and the second and third denials (18:18–24, 25–27). This procedure was almost certainly followed in order to emphasize that Peter's denials took place at the same time as Jesus faced the High Priest, and so to contrast the faithlessness of the disciple with the fearlessness of the Master (so Brown: "By making Peter's denials simultaneous with Jesus' defence before Annas, John has constructed a dramatic contrast wherein Jesus stands up to his questioners and denies nothing, while Peter cowers before his questioners and denies everything," 2:842).

The historicity of Peter's denials has been questioned by some scholars. Bultmann pronounced the story to be "legendary and literary" (*History of the Synoptic Tradition,* 269), chiefly on the basis that Luke 22:31–32 (in his view) presupposes that all the disciples *except Peter* are to desert Jesus, and that only Peter will remain unwavering. G. Klein followed Bultmann in this, and further suggested that the story arose from a group who resented Peter's prominence in the post-resurrection Church and circulated this story of his denials to discredit him ("Die Verleugnung des Petrus," 324). Haenchen saw the inspiration of the story in the prophecy of Zech 13:7, interpreted as showing that *all* the disciples would take offense at Jesus (Mark 14:27), and Peter's denials were created as an illustration, or better, concretization, of their failure; he further agreed with Klein that if Peter had been suspected of being a follower of Jesus he would not have escaped by merely denying it (530). Suggestions of this kind, which are largely speculative, cannot be disproved, but neither can they justly be said to be plausible. Luke 22:31–32 would appear to indicate that Satan's "request" to sift the disciples as wheat (note the plural ὑμᾶς, "you all"), like that in the story of Job, is successful, but that Jesus intercedes more powerfully for Peter that he may not utterly fall; not, as Klein maintained, that Satan will have no success with Peter, but that Satan will not have the power to destroy Peter's faith. The saying in vv 31–32 is in complete harmony with the prediction that Peter will deny Jesus before cockcrow, which is added in v 34, and with the tradition that he did so (see the discussion in I. H. Marshall, *Commentary on Luke*, 820–23). We do not know of any militant hostility to Peter in the primitive Church that would have inspired a group to invent so malicious a slander as would be involved in creating the story of the denials. Nor is it likely that the prophecy of Zech 13:7 led to the notion that the whole disciple group denied Jesus, and prompted an early teacher to epitomize their behavior in this fictitious account. The portrayal of Peter's actions on the night of Jesus' arrest, as well as his following Jesus to the High Priest's courtyard and his failure within it, is in character with what is recorded of Peter in the NT. In our judgment it is unlikely that early preachers and teachers of the Church would have made known far and wide this story of the leading apostle's appalling failure without special cause; the ground for its circulation surely lies in the man himself. In his proclamation of the good news he will have freely confessed his disgraceful behavior, and his subsequent forgiveness and restoration, as an example of the readiness of the crucified and risen Lord to forgive sinners, even when they are as unworthy as the man who denied his Master.

THE TRIAL OF JESUS BEFORE PILATE (18:28–19:16a)

In striking contrast to the meager account of Jesus' appearance before the High Priest Annas, and the absence of any report on his appearance before Caiaphas and the Sanhedrin (hinted at in vv 24, 28), the description of the trial by Pilate is lengthy, fuller by far than any of the synoptic accounts. For John this is the *real* trial of Jesus, wherein the Jewish rulers are the accusers and the representative of the Roman State the judge. Strangely, the primary charge of the Jews against Jesus is not articulated at the beginning of the account; it first emerges in Pilate's question in v 33: "Are you the King of the Jews?" Self-evidently that is based on information supplied by the Jewish leaders to Pilate, but it is not so stated (contrast the "charge sheet" in Luke 23:2). Further references to the interrogation of Jesus under Caiaphas are probably to be seen in the ambiguous description of Jesus as "one who does evil" (v 30) and the allegation that he made himself the Son of God (19:7). Both these charges appear earlier in this Gospel (cf. esp. 5:18; 7:12,

47; 8:48; 9:16, 24), and are closely related to the synoptic accounts of the examination by the Sanhedrin (Mark 14:55–65 par.). The trial scene in the Fourth Gospel, however, is dominated by the claim of Jesus to be King and the nature of his sovereignty. Hence the trial before Pilate becomes "Jesus' witness and self-confession as the hidden King," and thereby his last revelatory pronouncement (Schnackenburg, 3:241).

Jesus Is Handed over to Pilate (18:28–32)

28 The laconic "They bring Jesus . . . to Pilate" does not mention the identity of those who bring Jesus to the governor. While the temple police will naturally be included, Pilate's statement in v 31, *"You* take him and judge him," assumes that "they" are prominent members of the Sanhedrin, some of whom were quite certainly of high-priestly rank (so explicitly 19:6, 15). They came "early in the morning," and that of necessity. Pilate, as all Roman governors, will have begun his day very early, as judged by modern customs, and will have concluded it at a fairly early hour. (Sherwin-White illustrates: "The emperor Vespasian was at his official duties even before the hour of dawn, and the elder Pliny, most industrious of Roman officials, had completed his working day, when Prefect of the Fleet, by the end of the fourth or fifth hour. In Martial's account of daily life at the capital, where two hours are assigned to the protracted duty of *salutatio,* the period of *labores* ends when the sixth hour begins. Even a country gentleman at leisure begins his day at the second hour": *Roman Law in the New Testament,* 45). Moreover, if the Jewish leaders were to carry through their plan of expediting the execution of Jesus before the passover festival, there was no time to be lost.

Bultmann, following a suggestion of H. Schlier, saw a further, symbolic significance in the term πρωί, "early." "If the ἦν δὲ νύξ ("It was night") of 13:30 is pondered, one could well suppose that the mention of the time could have a deeper meaning here also: the day of victory of Jesus over the world is breaking" (651). So also J. Blank, "Die Verhandlung vor Pilatus . . . ," 66. The thought is interesting, but it may credit too much to the solitary word of time here, in contrast to the dramatic utterance of 13:30.

The Jewish deputation refuse to enter the governor's residence in order to avoid contracting defilement, and thereby disqualify themselves from sharing in the passover meal. They are acting in accordance with the dictum, "The dwellings of non-Jews are unclean," *Ohol.* 18:7. The precise ground for this uncleanness is uncertain, but it appears to be founded on the fear of Jews that abortions and premature babies who die may be buried within the area of Gentile houses, so rendering the homes subject to the uncleanness of the dead (see Str-B 1:838–39). It is stated in Num 9:6–12 that anyone who comes into contact with a corpse may not celebrate the passover at the appointed time (since such contact renders a person unclean for seven days, Num 19:11), but must celebrate it a month later. On the basis of Levitical ceremonial law the regulation is comprehensible, but the insistence of the high priests on maintaining it in this circumstance entails the extreme of irony; they hold fast to the ceremonial law while they seek the execution of the promised Deliverer of Israel, the Son of God and Savior; and in their zeal to eat the passover lamb they unwittingly help to fulfill its significance through their demanding the death of the Lamb of God, at the same time shutting themselves out from its saving efficacy.

No more eloquent example than this can be found of the ability of religious people to be meticulous about external regulations of religion while being wholly at variance with God. One result of this decision of the Jewish leaders, however, should be noted: by remaining outside the praetorium they occasion the interchange of scenes wherein Pilate goes into his residence to speak with Jesus and comes out to confer with them. The trial of Jesus before the governor thus is played out like a drama on two stages, front and back (Dodd's imagery, *Historical Tradition,* 96). The effect of this is not only to enhance the dramatic quality of the narrative, but to exclude the Jewish leaders from the revelation of truth given to the Roman governor.

29–30 While it may be assumed that some conversation had taken place between the Jewish leaders (Caiaphas?) and Pilate concerning Jesus (cf. the assistance of Roman soldiers at the arrest of Jesus), Pilate naturally asks for the official charge to be presented against Jesus by the high priests. Their response is extraordinarily vague (Brown regards it as insolent, 866). It is possible that, having already consulted Pilate concerning Jesus, they anticipated that he would not trouble to investigate further, but would simply rubber-stamp their decision. If such was their hope they were mistaken. Pilate decided to make an investigation of his own. Bruce rightly concludes, "It was evident that Pilate was in effect opening a new trial, instead of simply confirming the death penalty which, as they had maintained, Jesus had incurred in terms of Jewish law" (350).

31 Pilate's reply, accordingly, was both ironic and humiliating for the Jewish leaders. If by their answer they wished to give the impression that Jesus was offending against their laws, let them judge him according to those laws. If however they wanted to bring about his death they must speak up and state their case clearly, for, as they themselves acknowledged, they had no power to carry out the death penalty; that authority lay in the hands of the governor alone. (For further discussion on this issue see the *Introduction to the Passion Narrative,* 308–10.)

32 With the Evangelist's comment cf. his similar one in 12:33. He was fully aware that had the Jews been given an exceptional permission to put Jesus to death on the basis of a serious breach of their law, they would have done it by stoning. But the Jews expressly wanted Jesus to die at the hands of the Romans (cf. the later cries of *"Crucify* him!"); for *their* mode of execution entailed the curse of the Law: "Anyone who is hung on a tree is under God's curse" (Deut 21:23). The chief priests clearly wished to ensure that Jesus was not viewed as a martyr for God's cause, but as an impostor who died under the curse of God. By contrast the Evangelist sees in the death of Jesus by crucifixion God's way of fulfilling his purpose to "lift up" Jesus in the glory of divine love to enthronement with himself; thereby the saving sovereignty is opened for all the world, and the exalted Lord can draw all who will into the eternal life of the kingdom of God. (See further the *Comment* on 12:31–32).

Pilate's First Interrogation of Jesus (18:33–38a)

33 Pilate's first words to Jesus, "Are you the king of the Jews?" appear in all four Gospels. In the three synoptics Jesus replies at once, "You say it" (σὺ λέγεις), whereas our Evangelist delays that till v 37; the intervening passage supplies a crucial exposition of the nature of Jesus' kingship, an exposition which finds yet further expansion after the σὺ λέγεις of v 37a. The governor's question manifestly reflects a fresh formulation by the Jewish leaders, after the dismissal of their inadequate statement in v 30; their charge is based on the confession of Jesus in response to Caiaphas' demand, "Are you the Messiah, the Son of the Blessed One?" to which Jesus gave an affirmative answer (Mark 14:61–62 par.). While our Evangelist is silent about the latter episode, he clearly links Pilate's question with the allegations of the chief priests (v 35), and probably alludes in 19:7 to Caiaphas' question and Jesus' answer (note that Mark 14:62 expounds the affirmation of Messiahship in terms of the Son of Man of Dan 7:13, who is to come in theophanic glory, and to be revealed as the Lord at God's right hand of Ps 110:1, a status indistinguishable to Jewish ears from that of Son of God, except that it implies being more exalted than is suggested by their usual concept of the title). The expression "King of the Jews" is a translation for the benefit of the Roman governor, not unknown in Jewish recent history (according to Josephus, Herod the Great had the title, *Ant.* 14:385); Pilate naturally could interpret it only in political terms, as was intended by the Jewish authorities. His question to Jesus, accordingly, was to elicit whether or not he claimed to be such: was he guilty, or not guilty? (So Bruce, 352.)

Expositors have frequently noted that in all four Gospels Pilate's question begins with the pronoun, Σύ, which is unnecessary in Greek and could indicate emphasis, as though to ask, "Are *you* the king of the Jews?" That could express surprise, not to say astonishment. Pilate already had one revolutionary on his hands, Barabbas, a murderer; one alleged to call himself *king* of the Jews must be an even more extreme example of the same kind! But the instant impression made on him by Jesus was of an altogether different kind of person; hence his astonished question. While one must acknowledge the nuance as possible, it is at least doubtful. N. Turner, in Moulton-Turner's *Grammar of NT Greek* 3:37, points out that the use of nominative pronouns for emphasis is not strictly observed in the NT and papyri, and he includes the σὺ εἶ of v 33 as an example of this tendency. In the synoptic Gospels the question introduced by σὺ εἶ is answered by σὺ λέγεις, where again the pronoun is unlikely to indicate emphasis (the same applies to John's v 37, despite arguments to the contrary; see *Notes* on the latter passage). Pilate's question is best understood as a straightforward commencement of interrogation of the prisoner, in accordance with Roman trial procedure (see Sherwin-White, "The Trial of Christ," 105, who alludes to the usage by which the direct question was put to the defendant three times before his case was allowed to go by default, and who sees the custom observed in vv 33–37).

34–35 Jesus asks whether Pilate's question proceeds from "a spontaneous recognition that he is in the presence of royalty," or whether he is simply echoing the Jewish accusations (Hoskyns, 520). Pilate responds with an indignant, not to say contemptuous, exclamation, "I'm not a Jew, am I?" He at once disclaims any interest in peculiar Jewish notions and denies any reason to know anything about Jesus other than what people have told him. Both persons in this confrontation wish to get behind the façade. Jesus wants to know whether Pilate has any insight of his own which he can lead on to further understanding; if he has merely received the complaints of the Jewish leaders, he is already on the wrong track and has no understanding of what kingship in its ultimate sense (i.e., as applied to Jesus) means. Pilate, on the other hand, by his further statement about Jesus' being handed over to him by the representatives of his nation and his further question, indicates that he is dissatisfied with the Jewish accusations. What has Jesus done to make the rulers so intent on his execution? Is his offense simply against Jewish traditions, or has he actually committed a crime that Roman law must punish? (On this see Morris, 769.)

36 Jesus takes up Pilate's question (v 33) and answers it by defining *negatively* the nature of his kingdom. Bultmann is right when he observes, "Jesus does not speak directly about himself; rather he speaks about his βασιλεία," i.e., his kingdom (654; so also Brown, 868). But the moot word there is "directly"; for if Jesus talks about his "kingdom" he really means his sovereign rule, his kingly activity, i.e., his action in his capacity as the king who brings salvation. Schnackenburg, curiously (for he is as well informed as anyone about the eschatology of Jesus), writes: "Jesus' βασιλεία does not signify his 'kingdom' but, in accordance with Pilate's question, it is a designation of function, 'kingship' " (3:249). By this Schnackenburg wishes to distinguish the term here from its use in John 3:3, 5. One is constrained to ask, however, where in the four Gospels βασιλεία, when referring to God's kingdom, means anything other than "kingship." It is commonplace that βασιλεία, like the Hebrew *malkûth* and the Aramaic *malkûtha*, means "sovereign rule." K. G. Kuhn stated that when contemporary Jews spoke of "the kingdom of heaven" (in which "heaven" is a periphrasis for God) they really meant, "God is king" (*TDNT* 1:571). In the synoptic Gospels the kingdom of God in the proclamation of Jesus denotes the dynamic activity of the sovereign Lord for the salvation of men and women; characteristically it relates especially to the saving sovereignty of God operative in and through Jesus himself. Time and again in our study of this Gospel we have observed that the "signs" of Jesus and the teaching related to them set forth the saving sovereignty of God manifest in Jesus; hence despite the fact that the expression βασιλεία τοῦ θεοῦ, "kingdom of God," occurs only in John 3:3 and 5, the whole Gospel is concerned with the kingship of God in Jesus. And that is what Jesus was referring to in his utterance to Pilate; his kingship is the sovereign action of the Son through whom God performs his saving works and speaks his saving words.

It is worthy of note that the original meaning of the English term "kingdom" was identical with that of the Hebrew *malkûth* and the Greek *basileia*. The first definition of kingdom in the Oxford English Dictionary defines it as "kingly function, authority or power; sovereignty, supreme rule; the position or rank of a king, kingship." An illuminating illustration of its use is given from Hobbes, *Rhet.* 8 (1681) 19, wherein monarchy is referred to as ". . . which Government, if he limit it by law, is called *Kingdom;* if by his own will *Tyranny*." The contrast of "kingdom" and "tyranny" perfectly illustrates the active force of the former term. The translators of the KJV/AV labored half a century before Hobbes, and would have been conscious of this significance of the word "kingdom" when they used it in their rendering of the Gospels.

In Jesus' statement to Pilate his sovereignty is defined in a negative fashion through the necessities of the situation. The meaning of the opening clause is made clear through its repetition in the final clause of the sentence: "My kingdom is not of this world. . . . My kingdom is not ἐντεῦθεν," i.e., "from here" (so Bauer in his *Lexicon*, 536); the Kingdom of Jesus, that is, does not have its *origin* in this world, defined by Barrett as "the field in which humanity and the spiritual world are organized over against God" (536). If the sovereignty of Jesus does not originate in this world it is self-evidently not like the kingdoms of this world, as Jesus proceeds to state: if his rule were exercised in the manner of the kingdoms of this world he would have an army, as they do, and his followers would do battle to prevent him from falling into the hands of his enemies, whether Jews or Romans; but he has no army! Pilate therefore must recognize that his rule is wholly different from that of the political powers of this world, and wholly different from anything that Pilate has experienced; hence *he constitutes no threat to Roman authority*.

It is essential that Jesus' statement should not be misconstrued as meaning that his kingdom is not *active* in this world, or *has nothing to do with* this world. The utterance attributed to the grandsons of Jude, the brother of Jesus, to the emperor Domitian comes close to that position; according to Eusebius (*Hist.* 3.29.4) "they said that it was not worldly, nor on earth, but heavenly and angelic, and that it would be established at the end of the world." The fundamental concept of the kingdom of God in the Bible is that it denotes God's "coming" *to this world* to bring judgment and salvation to humankind. When the Gospels depict Jesus powerfully active among people, delivering them from Satan's thrall and bringing to them the blessings of God's beneficent rule, they purpose to describe the kingdom of God in action in this world. Such is the import of the crucial utterances of Jesus about the kingdom of God, like Matt 11:5, 12–13; 12:28; 13:16–17; Mark 4:11–12, in conjunction with the parables of the kingdom; Luke 4:16–20; 17:20–21. That the Fourth Gospel is one with the rest in this respect is seen in its accounts of the signs of Jesus and their interpretations. Brown's comment, accordingly, is pertinent: "Jesus does not deny that his kingdom or kingship affects this world, for the world will be conquered by those who believe in him (1 John 5:4). But he denies that his kingdom belongs to this world; *like himself, it comes from above*" (869; see further Bultmann's strong statement, 657).

37 Pilate rightly perceives that when Jesus declares that his kingdom is not of this world, then he is claiming to be a king of some sort, hence his exclamation, "So you are a king, then?" Jesus' reply, "You say that I am a king," affirms the rightness of Pilate's perception; in no way does it constitute a diminution or evasion of the governor's statement (not even as Dodd would paraphrase it: " 'King' is *your* word, not mine," *Historical Tradition*, 99; see our *Notes* on σὺ λέγεις). Naturally Pilate's understanding of "king," as applied to Jesus, falls far short of reality. Jesus therefore, having explained what his kingdom is *not*, now declares what it *is*: his kingdom is *the Kingdom of Truth*. He was born and came into the world (a double expression to signify his coming from the presence of God, in incarnation) to bear witness to this kingdom. Manifestly, Jesus is not speaking of truth in an abstract, or even general way, but specifically in relation to his ministry. He came among men with a mission from God to bear witness to the truth of God's saving sovereignty, and to reveal it in word and deed. This kingdom-mission of his entails bearing witness to judgment and salvation, differing in application to people accordingly as they "listen," i.e., give heed to his testimony. At this point, however, the positive aspect of his mission alone is stated. As Lagrange pointed out, "To reveal the truth was a way of making subjects (French, *partisans*) and of creating a kingdom" (477).

> The same balance of emphasis on the saving sovereignty of God that brings life eternal in the kingdom of God or judgment for the rejectors of the Redeemer-Son of God, and the authoritative witness to the truth that he brings who has come from God, is observable in the two kerygmatic passages of John 3:16–21 and 3:31–36; the first illuminates the Nicodemus discourse on life eternal and the second the witness of John the Baptist to the Bridegroom of the kingdom. The close link between Truth and Kingdom in revelation is succinctly expressed in *Jer. Sanh.* 18a: "The seal of God is truth. What is truth? that he is the living God and the King eternal" (cited by Schlatter, 341; also by Westcott, from Lightfoot, 2:285).

38 Jesus' positive statement to Pilate about the kingdom of truth does more than describe the subjects of his kingdom; it implicitly conveys an invitation to join their number; accordingly it placed Pilate in a situation of decision as to the truth that gives men a part in the kingdom of salvation. Jesus the prisoner sets his judge in the dock! Pilate's answer indicates that he has no intention of occupying that position: "Truth, what is that?" His turning on his heel without waiting for an answer shows that he doesn't believe that Jesus, or anyone else for that matter, could give one. And that means that he foreclosed the possibility of his coming under the Kingdom of truth and life. As Haenchen observed, "If Pilate, face to face with this Truth standing before him, asks, 'What is truth?' it is evident that he does not belong to 'those whom the Father has given to Jesus'" (536–37). Nevertheless one fact was made clear to Pilate from this interview with Jesus: this man was not the threat to Roman rule that the Jewish leaders made him out to be. His kingdom, in truth, was not "of this world."

Pilate's Declaration of the Innocence of Jesus (18:38b–40)
38–39 Pilate goes outside the praetorium to address "the Jews." In light of the shouting described in vv 40; 19:6, 12, 14, 15, and the mention of the "officials" in 19:6, we are to assume that the Jewish leaders had been joined by supporters whom they had summoned (we do not hear of any sympathizers with Jesus present also). The declaration of Pilate in v 38b should have brought to a close the business at hand. If the governor, after interrogation of Jesus, had really found no ground for a charge against him he should have dismissed the case forthwith—and the Jewish leaders also. But he made a grave mistake: after referring to the custom of releasing a prisoner at the Passover festival he asked them if *they* wished him to release "the king of the Jews" (possibly an ironic use of the title, since it was obvious that Jesus was no aspirant to political rule). Why did Pilate resort to this expedient? It has been suggested

that he wanted to make it possible for the Jewish leaders to save face, for by acting on this custom Jesus would not have been formally acquitted of the charges they had brought against him, but he would have been given an amnesty. A. Bajsic thought otherwise. He considered that Pilate, on the one hand, took the kingship of Jesus seriously, in the non-political sense, and hoped that the people would recognize the compliment; and on the other hand, he saw in Barabbas a dangerous rebel, whose supporters had already arrived to seek the customary release in his favor. He hoped that sufficient support for Jesus would be forthcoming to justify releasing Jesus, an action which would entail the execution of Barabbas. On that basis the Jewish rulers would have no ground for complaint to higher authority through his release of "the king of the Jews," since the people would have been responsible for the choice, and it would have rid the nation of the really dangerous revolutionary ("Pilatus, Jesus und Barabbas," 7–28). The thesis is by no means impossible, but if Pilate acted on such a motivation he underestimated the ability of the Jewish leaders to outwit him, for as the trial proceeded they set him in the very position of danger that he had wished to avoid.

40 The chief priests had no intention of letting Pilate get away with his scheme, and the crowd had no intention of leaving Barabbas to his fate; together they clamored for the release of Barabbas. So it came about that the leaders of Israel, their henchmen, and the supporters of the popular hero asked for the release of one who had been guilty of violent political assault against the state, entailing murder, and demanded the death of him who came to realize the nation's true destiny through the almighty but peaceful divine love.

The tragic irony of the situation runs deeper, the more it is examined, for the term used in description of Barabbas (λῃστής, lit. "one who takes booty") was used especially of violent men, whether robbers, or pirates, or rampaging soldiers on the loot. Josephus consistently uses it of the Zealots. From the Roman point of view these latter were guerrillas who had to be exterminated; from the popular Jewish point of view such men were heroic freedom fighters. In Mark 15:7 Barabbas is said to be one of "the insurrectionists who had committed murder in the uprising." He will have been a leader among those who sought to make way for the kingdom of God through violence (some versions in v 40 called him an ἀρχιλῃστής, i.e., a leader of freedom fighters). The very name of the man is intriguing. "Barabbas" is a patronymic, meaning "son of the father" (abba), though some early exegetes interpreted it as "son of the rabbi," reading the name as though it were Barrabbas. There is a variant reading in Matt 27:16–17 which gives his name as Jesus Barabbas; the omission of the first name, as indeed its presence, could be accidental (through contracting Ἰησοῦν to ΙΝ); but the comment of Origen, who knew the reading, gives a clue as to its absence in most MSS: "In the whole range of the scriptures we know that no one who is a sinner is called Jesus." The Bible Societies' committee concluded that the full name, Jesus Barabbas, was original, and that the name Jesus was suppressed on theological grounds (see Metzger, 67–68). So the Jews, at the instigation of the high priests, who normally repudiated the Zealots and all like them, asked for the release of Jesus Barabbas the epitome of messianic Jewish nationalism, and called for the death of Jesus of Nazareth, whose fulfillment of the messianic promises was through the redemptive path of the Servant of the Lord and the Son of Man. It was the greatest tragedy of the ancient people of

God for all time. (On the significance of Barabbas see the article of J. J. Twomey, "Barabbas Was a Robber," 115–19.)

As to the custom of setting free a prisoner at the Passover feast, scholars have been perplexed at being unable to trace reference to it in secular or Jewish literature, and it has led some to suppose that there never was any such custom. For some time, however, an ambiguous passage in the Talmud, *Pesah.* 91a, has been cited as of uncertain significance; but C. B. Chavel appears to have succeeded in demonstrating from it Jewish acquaintance of the custom and its probable origin. The passage reads: "A mourner, and one who is removing a heap (of debris which had fallen upon a person, without knowing whether he is dead or alive), and *one who has received a promise to be released from a prison,* and an invalid, and aged person who can eat as much as an olive, one slaughters (the lamb) on their behalf. Yet in the case of all these, one may not slaughter for them alone, lest they bring the Passover-offering to disqualification." It may, of course, happen that for various reasons none of these may be able to participate in the Passover feast (in particular, the hoped-for release from prison might not materialize), and so they must be registered for the Passover-offering with others. A comment follows in *Pesahim* on the reference to one promised release from prison. "The Sages learned this only of a heathen prison, one slaughters for him separately, since he was promised, he will (definitely) be released, as it is written, 'The remnant of Israel shall not do iniquity, nor speak lies.' " Here two different conditions are in view: the situation when Roman power operated through the criminal courts of Palestine, and that when Jews exercised that power for themselves. So the release of a prisoner on the eve of the Passover applied both to the period of Roman rule and to the earlier time when the Jews were independent, i.e., under the Hasmonean rulers. Chavel suggested that the custom in question arose in that earlier period. The Jewish ruler released a political prisoner when Jews assembled for the Passover from all parts of the land and from the diaspora to placate the people and as a gesture of goodwill that was to characterize the festal season. The Roman administration continued the custom for a similar purpose—to give a token assurance to the people that they would not be molested during the feast (Chavel: "The Releasing of a Prisoner on the Eve of Passover in Ancient Jerusalem," *JBL* 60 [1941] 273–78; Str-B thought the association of *Pes.* 91a likely; so also Blinzler, *Prozess,* 317–20; Barrett, 538; Schnackenburg, 3:252, strongly so; Bruce, 355). That Mark 15:8 mentions that *the crowd* asked Pilate to make a release according to custom, while John tells of *Pilate* reminding them of it is of small consequence; a request could have been made to Pilate prior to his public statement. The important matter is that in all the Gospel traditions Pilate makes the offer of releasing Jesus and the crowd ask for Barabbas.

Jesus Is Flogged and Mocked by the Soldiers (19:1–3)

1 "Pilate took Jesus and had him flogged." Why? If we begin with our Evangelist's understanding there can be little doubt: it is a fresh strategy to have Jesus set free. Having failed with the plan to release him through the amnesty custom (18:39–40) Pilate now seeks to satisfy the Jews' desire that Jesus be punished, but in a less drastic way than by crucifixion. Such is the clear intimation of Luke 23:16: Pilate declares that after examination neither he nor Herod found any basis for the Jewish charges, nor ground for inflicting the death penalty. Accordingly he adds: "I will punish him and then release him." This was proposed as an alternative to crucifixion, not, be it noted, as an accompaniment of it.

John's record and the proposal mentioned in Luke 23:16 appear to differ from the setting of the flogging in Mark and Matthew. In the latter the crowd's clamor for the release of Barabbas is reluctantly granted, Pilate sets Barabbas free and hands Jesus over to be crucified after having him flogged (Mark 15:15 par.). The impression is given that the flogging takes place *after* the sentence of crucifixion and as part of the punishment inflicted on Jesus, which accords with general Roman practice. Blinzler, however, dissents from this interpretation. He cites L. Wenger (*Die Quellen des römischen Rechts* [1953] 287 n.11) as maintaining that the expression, "he delivered him to be crucified," which appears not only in Mark 15:15 but in the other Gospels also, is the equivalent of announcing the death penalty; it means, "he condemned him to the death of the cross." Mark's past participle, φραγελλώσας ("after flogging him"), indicates that the *death sentence was passed only after his scourging* (Blinzler, 334). If that be so Mark, Matthew, and John all record the events in question (including the mocking by the soldiers) in the same order—only John interposes other happenings, of which the synoptists appear to know nothing, between the mocking by the soldiers and the crucifixion. It is easy to see how a fuller record of the events, such as the Fourth Evangelist has, can change the aspect of earlier accounts. Dodd, in discussing this matter, is content to observe that if John is independent of Mark at this point (which accords with his position generally) "we must suppose that more than one strain of tradition preserved this sequence of events" (*History and Tradition,* 103). A point in favor of our Evangelist's positioning of the beating of Jesus is its connection with the *Ecce Homo* scene which immediately follows; the latter is inseparable from the mocking of Jesus by the soldiers, which presumably took place *after* they had flogged him, and is represented as yet another attempt by Pilate to set Jesus free.

One issue that arises from the different possible settings of the flogging of Jesus is the nature of the punishment. As administered by Romans it could be one of three kinds: the *fustigatio,* a beating of a less severe kind, *flagellatio,* a flogging, or *verberatio,* a scourging, which was the most terrible of all and was always associated with other punishments, including crucifixion. The first punishment was given for lighter offenses, often accompanied by a magisterial warning; Sherwin-White states that it was ordered, e.g., in connection with accidental fires, and by provincial governors when dealing with the ancient equivalent of youth gangs (*Roman Society and Roman Law,* 27). He himself believes that this was what was in Pilate's mind in Luke 23:16; the latter statement indicates that Pilate intended to "teach Jesus a lesson" (παιδεύσας) and then release him, but in reality Luke gives no record of Pilate carrying it out. Is this the punishment that the Fourth Evangelist wishes us to understand was inflicted upon Jesus? In the light of Luke 23:16 one may be inclined to think so, but Blinzler denies it. He is impressed with the coincidence of order of events in Mark and in John, and considers it unthinkable that the flogging administered to Jesus was repeated; accordingly we must understand that the severest kind of scourging was inflicted on Jesus in the narrative of 19:1. If that be so, Pilate's action, even if intended for the ultimate good of Jesus, was in flagrant contradiction to his admission of Jesus' innocence, and reflects the cruel streak in Pilate which other sources attribute to him. It is rarely realized how terrible was the Roman mode of flogging, the *verberatio.* Blinzler describes it thus:

> The delinquent was stripped, bound to a post or a pillar, or sometimes simply thrown on the ground, and beaten by a number of torturers until the latter grew tired and the flesh of the delinquent hung in bleeding shreds. In the provinces this was the task of soldiers. Three different kinds of implements were customary. Rods were used on freemen; military punishments were inflicted with sticks, but for slaves scourges or whips were used, the leather thongs of these being often fitted with a spike or with several pieces of

bone or lead joined to form a chain. The scourging of Jesus was carried out with these last-named instruments. . . . . It is not surprising to hear that delinquents frequently collapsed and died under this procedure, which only in exceptional cases was prescribed as a death sentence. . . . Josephus records that he himself had some of his opponents in Galilean Tarichae scourged until their entrails were visible. The case of Jesus bar Hanan, the prophet of woe, whom the procurator Albinus had scourged until his bones lay bare . . . also makes one realize what the little word φραγελλώσας in Mark (15:15) means (*Prozess Jesu*, 321–22; John's word ἐμαστίγωσεν is more precise).

It is generally believed that the suffering of this severe scourging was the reason why Jesus was unable to carry his cross all the way to his execution, and why he died so soon after being crucified (see the illuminating description of the death of Jesus by an inter-disciplinary group in *JAMA* 255 [1986]: "On the Physical Death of Jesus Christ").

2–3 The mockery of Jesus by the soldiers was motivated by a spontaneous desire for some crude and cruel horseplay. (It is entirely improbable that a reflection of ancient rites of human sacrifice lies behind the narrative, as was once maintained by Sir James Frazer, *The Golden Bough* III [London: Macmillan, [2]1914] 186–98; Bultmann provides further titles on this theme, *History of the Synoptic Tradition*, 272 n.3.) The crown that the soldiers made, though primarily intended as a caricature and not as an instrument of torture, will have been unspeakably painful. Its form will have been an imitation of the radiate crown of the divine rulers, such as had figured on coins in the east for centuries prior to the episode in the Gospels. It was most likely made from great thorns of the date palm, which were easily available. The appearance of the crown was not as commonly represented in modern attempts to make a crown of twigs with thorns, but will have appeared more like an American Indian's headdress, with thorns as large as the feathers (see the illustrations in H. St. J. Hart's article, "The Crown of Thorns in John 19:2–5," esp. 71–74, where the largest of thorns depicted is twelve inches long). The use of such a crown signifies that Jesus was decked out as a king who was God. We are to assume that he was seated, like a king on his throne. His purple cloak (it may have been only an old shaggy rug) represented the royal dress of a king. According to Mark and Matthew, Jesus was also given a stick—a royal diadem! But his crown was most royal of all: "He was, as it were, *divus Iesus radiatus*" (Hart, 74), i.e., "the radiant god Jesus." So the soldiers bowed the knee to him, as they would before a Hellenistic ruler of that time. They cried, "Hail, King of the Jews!" in imitation of the greeting accorded to the Roman emperor, *"Ave, Caesar!"* But instead of the kiss of homage they spat at him and slapped his face (according to Mark and Matthew they also hit him on the head with the rod in his hand, Mark 15:15 par.).

Almost certainly John recorded this incident with a similar motive as when he recounted the prophecy of Caiaphas (11:49–52), and the immediately following *Ecce Homo* scene, and Pilate's title of Jesus on the cross, with his refusal to change it when requested. Mockery it certainly was, accompanied by cruel despising and hate, but back of their enthronement of Jesus and mocking worship of him as King of the Jews stood the God who was the prime mover in the whole process, and who made their crude acknowledgment a profound reality. For it is precisely in that suffering, culminating in the cross on which he hung, that Jesus revealed his royalty and the glory of a love that gives itself to the uttermost for the redemption of a world that knows not what it does. (On this aspect of the kingship of Jesus in this passage, see J. Blank, "Die Verhandlung vor Pilatus," 62, 73–74; A. Dauer, *Die Passionsgeschichte im Johannesevangelium*, 262–63.)

Jesus Is Presented as a Mock-King and Further Declared Innocent (19:4–7)

4–5   No mention is made of Pilate's awareness as to what has happened to Jesus. We must presume either that Pilate had witnessed at least part of the soldiers' pantomime, or that an officer had brought Jesus, wearing the soldiers' costume, to him. In any case the episode gave Pilate the idea of a new attempt to win the Jews' approval of releasing Jesus (instead of Barabbas?—the Evangelist gives no clue as to when the governor gave Barabbas to the people; in view of Mark 15:15 it is likely to have been when he pronounced the death sentence on Jesus; the fact that it was the prerogative of *the people* to select the man who should receive the amnesty illuminates Pilate's otherwise inexplicable repeated appeals to them; see Bajsic, "Pilatus, Jesus und Barabbas," 11–12). His statement on bringing out Jesus, "that you may know that I find no ground of complaint against him," and his cry, "Look, the Man!" must be to demonstrate the harmlessness of Jesus. Dressed in his wretched clothes that made him look more like a clown than a king, bleeding profusely, in pain and with bruised face through the additional beatings, Jesus must have looked a shocking sight, enough to horrify any who knew him. Yet, as with his description of the mockery of the soldiers, the Evangelist will have wished his readers to recognize that the pathetic figure on whom the Jews are bidden to gaze is the Man sent from God, who, in that state of humiliation and woe, was in the process of bringing the kingdom of heaven for all humankind, including those thirsting for his blood and those who were shedding it.

Bultmann's comment on the presentation of Jesus to the Jews is noteworthy: "Clearly the purpose in this is to make the person of Jesus appear to the Jews as ridiculous and harmless, so that they should drop their accusation. Hence Jesus has to step forth as the caricature of a king, and Pilate presents him with the words, 'That is the man! Look at the pitiful figure!' But to the mind of the Evangelist the entire paradox of the claim of Jesus is in this way fashioned into a tremendous picture. In very truth, it is just such a man who asserts that he is the king of truth! The declaration ὁ λόγος σὰρξ ἐγένετο ('The Word became flesh') has become visible in its extremest consequence" (659). Barrett further draws attention to the striking saying in Zech 6:11–12, without affirming that the Evangelist will necessarily have had it in mind (541).

6   Once more Pilate experiences the failure of his stratagem with the Jews. Far from their changing their minds about Jesus, the high priests and their followers shouted that he should be crucified. This unexpected reaction infuriated Pilate: he shouted back, "Take him yourselves and crucify him! For *I* (whatever *you* think!) find no ground for your charges against him." Naturally this is no authorization for the Jewish leaders to crucify Jesus (he knew that they could not do it anyway); it indicates both his anger and disgust at their unrelenting attitude toward Jesus and himself, and his own refusal to do what they asked, since he knows that Jesus is not guilty of their charges.

7   The Jewish leaders respond to Pilate's fury with a new charge, which, if it were pressed, would change the nature of the trial, since it fell within the compass of their own laws. The law to which they refer is that of blasphemy, incurred because Jesus had "made himself" the Son of God. The synoptists record that the blasphemy was the ground of his condemnation in the trial before Caiaphas (note, not the simple admission that he was the Messiah, but his further exposition of it in relation to himself, Mark 14:61–64 par.). While the Fourth Evangelist refrains from recording the trial before Caiaphas, this may be viewed as a clear echo of it; moreover he has earlier referred to the Jewish charge that Jesus made himself the Son of God and the Jews' desire to put him to death for it (see esp. 5:17–18 and 10:30–39). Significantly the former passage links the claim to be Son of God with Jesus' performing "signs" on the sabbath day (5:16–18); in the eyes of the Jewish teachers and rulers this brought him within the orbit of Deut 13:1–6 and made him a false prophet, for whose activities the death penalty is laid down. We recall that this view of Jesus as a false prophet appears to lie behind the interrogation of Jesus by Annas (18:19–23), and that a reminiscence of it has been preserved in the Talmud (Yeshu was hanged "because he practiced sorcery and enticed Israel to apostasy," *Sanh.* 43a). In setting forth this charge to Pilate the chief priests were not abandoning their accusation that Jesus claimed to be the king of the Jews, but rather supporting it with a religious charge of sufficient gravity to warrant his death on the basis of their law, a consideration that Pilate should not view lightly (had they so wished they could have strengthened the accusation by declaring that Jesus had made his claim to kingship in blasphemous terms). The reader, however, recognizes at once that the new charge betrays the real reason for the remorseless quest of the chief priests and Pharisees for his death. The messianic pretension was serious enough, but the claim to be Son of God, with its accompanying roles of Redeemer and Revealer, was intolerable. It remains the great stumblingblock to Israel to this day. (On the issues bound up with v 7 see D. W. Wead's article, "We Have a Law," 184–89.)

Pilate's Second Interrogation of Jesus and Attempt to Release Him (19:8–12)

This second questioning of Jesus by Pilate should be compared with the first (18:33–37), for similar issues and emphases appear in both (notably regarding Jesus' origin and the nature of his authority), and the reactions of both Pilate and Jesus in the second interrogation become more comprehensible in the light of the first (so Schnackenburg, 3:259–60).

8 On hearing that Jesus "made himself the Son of God" Pilate "became the more afraid." Why *more*? Although fear on Pilate's part has not been mentioned earlier, it is evident that he became increasingly unnerved by the trial, in a manner unusual for him. The impression made by Jesus upon him in face of the accusations of his enemies, which he knew were groundless, and his bearing after the flogging and the cries of the crowd for his death filled him with increasing awe. Then to hear that this man, the like of whom he had never encountered, claimed to be the Son of God caused him to be seized with sudden fear. The idea that gods could come down and appear in the likeness of men was common enough in the pagan society of his time. (An example is seen in Acts 14:11: when the inhabitants of Lystra witnessed

a healing by Paul, accompanied by Barnabas, they cried, "The gods have come down to us in human form." See also Bultmann, 661 n.4, for examples of the effect of a "divine man" on a ruler.) Thus Pilate's reaction to Jesus at this point may be seen as "the numinous terror before the divine, which falls upon the representative of earthly power" (Schnackenburg, 3:260). Doubtless this fear would be increased by the thought of the vengeance that could be taken by a divine being on one who had maltreated him (Pilate had had Jesus flogged!).

9 The governor therefore takes Jesus away from the crowd to question him again. His opening words, "Where are you from?" are surely no mere rewriting by the Evangelist of Luke 23:16 (*contra* Barrett, 542, who has a low view of the historicity of John's passion narrative). They express Pilate's anxiety to know whether Jesus was of earth or from heaven, whether he was a man or a god. But to his astonishment Jesus gives him no answer. The silence of Jesus in this setting recalls Isa 53:7 (cf. also Mark 14; 61; 15:5); not that it should be viewed as the inspiration for *composing* this element of the narrative (*contra* Haenchen, 539), nor as expressing the Evangelist's view that the divine does not communicate with man directly (again Haenchen—a curious idea in the Evangelist's description of the trial of the *Revealer!*). That Jesus so behaved in his trial is preserved as an element in the tradition John received, but it has a limited application for him, since Jesus speaks again to his judge (as in the synoptics he does to his Jewish judges [Mark 14:62 par.] and as he did earlier to Pilate [Mark 15:2 par.]). The reason for Jesus' silence is doubtless due to Pilate's reactions to Jesus' revelation in the first interrogation; after Pilate's skeptical response to Jesus' statement that he had come into the world to bear witness to the truth, how should Pilate now comprehend Jesus' origin? And if his present motive for asking was fear for his skin, what hope was there of his serious attention to the revelation of Jesus' relationship to God? Only faith can grasp the mystery of Jesus (cf. Rev 19:12).

10–11 Pilate's fear turns to annoyance. He was not used to people declining to answer his questions, least of all a prisoner whose life was in his hands. He was conscious of possessing authority from the most powerful man on earth and representing the most powerful nation on earth. He therefore reminds Jesus that he has authority to release him and authority to destroy him. Jesus, however, was also conscious of authority, and that of an infinitely greater power than the emperor of Rome, namely, the almighty God, who in that very moment was granting Pilate the authority to dispose of his life, but in accordance with his own will, not that of his unwitting instrument (note the imperfect tenses of the conditional sentence, indicating the present time in which the authority is delegated). The authority to which Jesus refers, accordingly, is specifically related to the present situation, regarding Jesus in this trial; he is not speaking in general terms of the relation of the state to God, in the manner of Paul in Romans 13, although this interpretation is as old as Augustine (*In Jo* 116.200.648). Interestingly, Bultmann, who interprets all Pilate's dealings with the Jews in the trial as typical of the relations of the state to the world, retracts his earlier view that v 11 applies to the God-given authority of the state; it has in view "the fact that Jesus has been given by God into Pilate's hands" (662, n.4). This gives added point to his observation that Jesus shows little concern as to what may become of him through Pilate's judgment, but Pilate is bidden to ponder his own situation and its responsibility.

The identity of him who has "the greater sin" than Pilate is uncertain. It is natural to think of Judas, in view of 13:21 (the same verb is used in both sentences, παραδώσει, the future in prospect, παραδούς, the past tense, since it has happened); yet Judas disappears after leading the soldiers and police to Jesus (18:13), and he had no part in handing over Jesus to Pilate. Since the Jewish leaders are mentioned in 18:28 as together bringing Jesus to Pilate, it is suggested that they collectively are in mind (e.g., Bultmann, 662; Lindars, 569; Schnackenburg, 3:261–62). Yet the contrast between ὁ παραδούς and Pilate more naturally applies to an individual, in which case Caiaphas, the head of the Jewish hierarchy that delivered up Jesus to Pilate, is the most likely person in view. He was the prime mover in instigating Jesus' death (11:49–53), and he was responsible for eliciting and formulating the charge that Jesus was king of the Jews and guilty of blasphemy (Mark 14:61–64), of which the Evangelist shows his awareness. Like Pilate, he was given authority over Jesus, but he abused it, and for political expediency handed Jesus over to Pilate on a trumped-up charge of sedition to secure his death. For this reason Pilate, though a guilty man, was not so guilty as the High Priest of God.

12 Pilate was clearly deeply affected by what Jesus had said, so he makes another attempt to secure Jesus' release (through the amnesty?). The Jewish leaders respond by playing their trump card. "Friend of Caesar" he makes himself out to be; if he releases Jesus he becomes Caesar's *enemy!* The threat to denounce Pilate before Caesar if he sets Jesus free is evident. And that really was something for Pilate to fear! For Tiberius was notoriously suspicious of any who threatened his position, and he dealt with them ruthlessly and savagely. Pilate knew that an accusation of aiding and abetting a revolutionary king in turbulent Palestine would be highly dangerous. He was caught in a trap of his own making, unable to escape.

It is the height of irony that the Jewish leaders, of all people, should succeed in embarrassing the Roman governor in this way. "What a grotesque situation!" commented Blinzler. "The highest Roman official in Judea has to endure being accused of lack of loyalty to the emperor by the representatives of a nation more passionately seething with hatred for the Roman yoke than almost any other in the empire" (*Prozess Jesu,* 337). Grotesque, indeed—yet there are factors that point to Pilate's utter helplessness in this situation. Building on a suggestion going back to Deissmann (in *Light from the Ancient East,* 383, n.3), E. Bammel gave compelling evidence to show that "Friend of Caesar" was a title accorded to persons of honor among the leading men of Rome (the Latin *amicus Caesaris* may be compared with the British "Companion of Honour," bestowed on a very limited group of people by the British sovereign). The title "Friend of Caesar" was given to all Roman senators, but also to certain other selected individuals. A fascinating issue arises from the fact that Pilate was a favored acquaintance of the highly influential Aelius Sejanus, through whom he probably gained the coveted status of Friend (Brown cites Tacitus as saying, "Whoever was close to Sejanus had a claim on the friendship of Caesar," *Annals* 6.8). But on October 18, A.D. 31, Sejanus was overthrown and many of his supporters were executed with him. Bammel considers that Caiaphas was too good a politician not to know the situation in Rome, and that it was *this* circumstance that made the threat to Pilate as a sharp sword (see the article, "φίλος τοῦ καίσαρος," 205–10, esp. 207–9). The difficulty of being so precise as this lies in the uncertainty of the year of the crucifixion of Jesus; it is frequently reckoned as A.D. 30, but many would set it in A.D. 33. Bammel appears to favor Stauffer's belief that the overthrow of Sejanus is an important datum in this matter and so the true date should be seen as A.D. 32 (col. 208, n.10 of article). In view of the lack of agreement in determining the date of our Lord's death, we can only view the relation of the high priests' threat to Pilate and the Sejanus affair as a possible but unprovable factor. But the importance of the threat remains, even without this particular strengthening of it, in light of the severity of Tiberius' punishment of *"lèse majesté"* crimes. It broke down Pilate's resistance. "His fear of the sinister and suspicious emperor was even greater than his awe of the mysterious personality of the Accused; his own safety appeared to him more important than a passing triumph over the accusers who were unsympathetic to him" (Blinzler, 338).

Jesus Is Sentenced to Death by Crucifixion (19:13–16a)

The trial by Pilate now draws to its climax. In form it resembles the scene in 19:4–7, but the situation has radically changed through the threat to Pilate made in v 12. Pilate has been decisively defeated, and when the Jews see him ascending the tribunal they know that they have won the day. But Pilate has not finished with them; he has his own mode of revenging himself on the Jews for his humiliation at their hands.

13–14 Pilate brings out Jesus from the praetorium. He takes his place on the tribune, a raised platform from which he can survey the area and make his public pronouncements. It is likely that Jesus is made to stand beside him, for the sentence is about to be passed publicly, in the presence of the accusers and the accused. The place, the day, and the hour are all mentioned, for the Evangelist is conscious of the momentous nature of the event now taking place. The governor is on his judgment seat in the "Stone Pavement" area; it is the seat rather than the pavement that is important; the representative of the Roman empire is about to deliver his official judgment on Jesus. It is the sixth hour (noon) of the Preparation Day; at this hour three things take place: Jews cease their work, leaven is gathered out of the houses and burned, and the slaughtering of the Passover lambs commences. The Passover festival, for all practical purposes, now begins (see J. Bonsirven, "Hora Talmudica" for references in Jewish literature, esp. 513–15). The Evangelist's thought is plain: Passover is the great celebration of Israel's deliverance from slavery by God's almighty power; then it was that he showed himself as King, and they became his people. In *this* celebration the Jews gathered before Pilate are about to play a decisive part in the fulfillment of the Passover, a second Exodus, wherein God would achieve an emancipation for all nations, not for Israel alone, giving them life in the promised land of his eternal kingdom. The crucial hour of destiny for Jew and Gentile has arrived.

Pilate's statement to the Jews, however, was unexpected. They were awaiting the announcement of a decision, i.e., the death sentence of Jesus. Instead of announcing the crime for which Jesus is now to be put to death (e.g.,

"This man made himself king"), Pilate calls to the crowd, "Look, your king!" He makes the moment of condemnation of Jesus one of proclamation of his kingship, and that in a formal yet dramatic way. Unlike the presentation of Jesus in 19:4–6, this was not intended to ridicule Jesus. Since that occasion, Pilate had been moved by Jesus and defeated in his attempt to rescue him. Now he makes the moment of *his* decision the moment of decision *for the Jews*. They have a final and crucial opportunity of declaring their mind on Jesus and recanting, if they will, on their unjust and bitter accusations of him.

Our exegesis of v 13 has proceeded on the assumption that ἐκάθισεν means that Pilate *sat* upon the judgment seat. Such is the interpretation of the majority of exegetes. But from the time of Harnack a line of scholars has urged that the verb ἐκάθισεν should be viewed not as intransitive, but as transitive: "he (Pilate) *set* him (Jesus) on the judgment seat" (so Boismard, Bonsirven, Corssen, de la Potterie, Gardner-Smith, Haenchen, Lightfoot, Loisy, Meeks—for references see the excursus by Dauer, 169 n.188). The most impressive exposition of this point of view is undoubtedly that of de la Potterie (in his article "Jésus, roi et juge," *Bib* 41 [1960] 217–47, translated and slightly abbreviated in *Scripture* 13 [1961] 97–111). He has succeeded in disposing of the linguistic objections to it, and sought to ease the historical objections also (e.g., he admits that Pilate would not have placed Jesus on his own seat, but since βῆμα means "tribunal," the platform on which the governor sat, along with the assessors and clerks, it would have been simple for Jesus to sit on another chair on the platform). The strongest argument adduced for this interpretation is the theological intention of the passage. Emphasis on the kingship of Jesus obviously dominates John's account of the trial before Pilate. It comes to its climax in 19:14: "Behold your King"—on the *bēma!* But, says de la Potterie, another emphasis of the Evangelist's is judgment (as in 3:18–21; 5:22, 27; 9:39; 12:48); in v 13 the two themes of Jesus as King and Jesus as Judge come together; in the moment when the Jews cry, "Away with him . . . Crucify him," *Jesus faces them as their Judge:* "He is their Judge because they will not have him as their King" (so de la Potterie, 108, ET).

One must admit that all this is very possible, but on balance doubtful. While, for example, the term βῆμα can denote the tribunal in its entirety, in John 19:13 it is most natural to understand it of the governor's seat, and that ἐκάθισεν ἐπὶ βήματος means that he sat upon it; the expression is so interpreted in Matt 27:19, and in comparable passages in Acts of kings and governors (see Acts 12:21; 25:6, 17). Moreover even on de la Potterie's understanding of βῆμα, it is highly unlikely that the governor would have set Jesus on another chair on the tribunal and cried, "Behold your King!" More importantly, the emphasis of the Evangelist throughout the trial is on Jesus as King (as de la Potterie admits), but *not* on Jesus as Judge. The Evangelist consistently portrays the trial with the intention of emphasizing the passion of Jesus as his glorification. This takes place through the whole process of the mocking, scourging, presentation of Jesus as king by Pilate, and even the cries of "Crucify," till it reaches its completion in the lifting up of Jesus on the cross. The high point in the trial is the call of Pilate, "Look, your King!" and it is confirmed in Pilate's composition of the inscription on the cross. All this plainly relates to the kingship of Jesus, not his role as judge (see Dauer, 273). It is therefore simplest, most natural, and in keeping with the theological emphasis of the Evangelist to interpret ἐκάθισεν ἐπὶ βήματος of Pilate taking his seat on the *bēma* to deliver his judgment relating to Jesus (so Blinzler in his excursus on this issue, *Prozess*, 346–56; Dauer in a similar excursus, *Passionsgeschichte*, 269–74; and the commentaries of Bauer, Bernard, Bruce, Brown, Bultmann, Hoskyns, Lagrange, Morris, Schnackenburg).

15 The Jews' response was resoundingly clear—a furious expression of revulsion against Jesus, stronger than before; "Take him away! Take him away! Crucify him!" Pilate exclaims, "Your *king!* Am I to *crucify* him?" He will have had no doubt as to their answer to this last appeal of his, but he makes it to rivet on them their responsibility for Jesus' death. The shame they heap on their king they will heap on their own heads. The high priests state their response in terms reminiscent of their earlier declaration to Pilate (v 12): "We have no king except Caesar." The implications of this statement are to be weighed. In the context of the trial of Jesus, of the Man who proclaimed to the nation the kingdom of God, and manifested it in his deeds, and called on Israel to repent and believe, it is nothing less than the abandonment of the messianic hope of Israel. For it is not Jesus alone whom they reject; *any* claimant to the messianic office is excluded on the basis of the slogan, "No king but Caesar." Their repudiation of Jesus in the name of a pretended loyalty to the emperor entailed their repudiation of the promise of the kingdom of God, with which the gift of the Messiah is inseparably bound in Jewish faith, and Israel's vocation to be its heir, its instrument, and its proclaimer to the nations.

16 No more remains to be said, other than Pilate's sentencing of Jesus to die by crucifixion. Curiously, the sentence is not actually reported (not in any of the Gospels), although it is plainly inferred. The usual formula for sentence to crucifixion was *Ibis in crucem*, "You shall go to the cross." It would have been simple enough for the Evangelists to have written that, but they were evidently not particularly concerned with legal formulae. Mark and Matthew wrote, "He handed over Jesus to be crucified" (Mark 15:15 par.). The term "handed over" (παρέδωκεν) clearly indicates a judicial sentence to crucifixion; a similar official and quasi-legal meaning of the term is seen in the very different saying of Matt 5:25. In the context of the trial of Jesus no object of the verb is given (i.e., to whom Pilate handed over Jesus), but neither was it necessary. Luke 23:25 however states, "He handed Jesus over *to their will*," i.e., to the will of the Jews. To whom does Pilate hand over Jesus in John 19:16? The context, taken literally, should mean that he handed over Jesus to the high priests, but that is obviously not meant. Dauer suggests that the Evangelist is simply repeating the statement contained in his source, and that he deliberately refrained from correcting it; he thereby suggested that the Jewish leaders had achieved their purpose (as in Luke 23:25), but at the same time brought about the fulfillment of the saying of Jesus, *"You will lift up the Son of Man"* (John 8:28; see Dauer, *Passionsgeschichte im Joh.*, 131–32, 269).

THE CRUCIFIXION, DEATH, AND BURIAL OF JESUS (19:16b–42)

A comparison of the accounts of the death of Jesus in the Fourth Gospel with those in the synoptic Gospels may well give two surprises: first, that they have so much in common, and second, that John omits so many features that are in the other Gospels, yet has striking features that are not in them. The most important elements in Mark but not in John are the mocking of Jesus (by the passersby, and by the chief priests and scribes, Mark 15:29–32), the darkness over the land (15:33), the cry of desolation (15:34), the tearing of the curtain in the temple (15:38), and the centurion's confession upon the death of Jesus (15:39). These are common to Matthew also. Luke adds a few points: the weeping women on the way to Golgotha (Luke 23:27–31), the prayer of Jesus for his enemies (23:34), the conversation of the two crucified with Jesus and the repentance of one (23:39–43), the mourning of the crowd standing by (23:47–49).

John's own special features include the inscription on the cross and the controversy it caused (19:19–22), his scripture quotations (vv 24, 28–29, 36–37), the care of Jesus for his mother (vv 25–27), his last cry from the cross (v 30), and the piercing of his side (vv 31–36). It is evident that, as in his account of the ministry of Jesus, the Evangelist has been very selective in his story of the death of Jesus. As he made choice of seven signs, and made much of their significance, so he has concentrated on a few features in the tradition that he received of Jesus' death which appeared to him most significant. The controlling motif in his account is that which dominated his narration of the arrest and trial of Jesus, namely, the kingship of Jesus. The anticipations in the Gospel of Jesus being "lifted up" are here fulfilled, so that the crucifixion is seen as the enthronement of Jesus.

One element in John's account, shared incidentally by the three synoptic Gospels, is the brevity of his description of the actual crucifixion: it is contained in a sub-clause consisting of three words (v 18: ὅπου αὐτὸν ἐσταύρωσαν, "where they crucified him"). This is in marked contrast to the tendency of Christian devotion through the ages to meditate on the sufferings of Jesus on the cross. The evangelists' laconic statements were hardly due to their indifference to the pain of crucifixion; this mode of killing people was frequently spoken of in the ancient world as one of the most terrible of punishments that human cruelty had devised (see Blinzler for citations from Cicero, Tacitus, Josephus, and Callistratus, *Prozess Jesu*, 357; M. Hengel, *Crucifixion*, tr. J. Bowden [Philadelphia: Fortress, 1977]). The strong consciousness of the early Christians that the will of God for the world's salvation was being achieved through Jesus on the cross will doubtless have powerfully affected them in their view of the cross. This especially applied to our Evangelist, who more than any other in his time seized on the crucifixion of Jesus as his "lifting up" to highest heaven, his hour of glory and truest exaltation, one with his enthronement in resurrection at the right hand of God. That conviction controls his completion of the story of the arrest, trial, and death of the Son of God.

The Crucifixion of Jesus (19:16b–18)

16b–17 Despite the ambiguity of the pronoun in v 16a, "*They* took over Jesus," it must relate to the four soldiers who formed the execution squad (cf. v 23). They will have commanded Jesus to carry his cross, as did every man so condemned (cf. Plutarch: "Each criminal as part of his punishment carries his cross on his back," *The Divine Vengeance*, 554 A/B). The "cross," however, was not the whole instrument of crucifixion but the cross-beam on which the crucified hung. (The usual procedure was for the condemned person to have his outstretched arms nailed to the cross-beam as he lay on the ground; it was then lifted up with his body on it and affixed to the vertical post which was already in the ground; at Golgotha such posts will presumably have been standing permanently.)

The term ἑαυτῷ is often viewed as an ethic dative, "for himself," but it is now more commonly viewed as meaning "by himself" (Brown, 898; Bultmann follows Radermacher in rendering it "alone," 668 n.3). It calls our attention to the contrast with the account in the synoptic Gospels, that Simon of Cyrene was commandeered to carry the cross for Jesus (Mark 15:21 par.). Traditionally it has been thought that Jesus set out for Golgotha, carrying the cross for himself, and that he collapsed on the way, so Simon was press-ganged into carrying it for him (Luke 23:26 was often interpreted as indicating that Simon carried the cross *with* Jesus, from behind). This harmonization is favored by many recent exegetes (e.g., Dodd, who sees it as "a perfectly reasonable interpretation of the evidence," *Historical Tradition*, 125 n.2). While accepting that, we should also recognize that the intention of the Evangelist must be taken into account. It may well be that his overriding concept of Jesus as King may have been in mind here also (so Brown: Jesus sets out for the cross as "sole Master of his destiny," heading for his enthronement on the cross, 2:917). Other motifs may conceivably have been operative. The significance of Isaac carrying the wood for his sacrifice was much in the minds of the Church Fathers, and not alone in theirs but in the minds of the rabbis also. For many of the latter the offering of Isaac made acceptable the offerings of the altar in the temple, and even of the Passover lamb ("When I see the blood I shall pass over you: I see the blood of the binding of Isaac," *Mek.* of Rabbi Ishmael). It was further said that Isaac carried the wood "as one bears the cross on one's shoulder" (*Gen. Rab.* 56.4, on Gen 22:6). It would be no wonder if our Evangelist paralleled Jesus setting out for Golgotha and Isaac setting out for the mount with his Father. Christians have also very understandably linked Jesus bearing his cross to Golgotha with his call to take up the cross and follow him (note esp. the closeness of Luke's language in Luke 14:27 with John 19:17). Haenchen observed: "Jesus can be an example of discipleship . . . only if he himself has carried the cross" (550). Again, we should like to know how early was the notion, expressed by the Gnostic Basilides in the commentary on John, that Simon of Cyrene died on the cross instead of Jesus (cf. the Nag Hammadi evidence, *The Second Treatise of the Great Seth*, VII, 56, in *The Nag Hammadi Library in English*, ed. J. M. Robinson [New York: Harper & Row, 1977] 332). The motive for such an idea is obvious, and the legend spread far and wide (eventually it became part of Mohammedan dogma, as it is to this day). It is not inconceivable that various stories gathered around Simon's name in the Evangelist's time, and for that reason he omitted reference to him (so Hoskyns, 528). Such concerns could have been entertained by our Evangelist, but we have no means of knowing, and their plausibility is limited.

18 The place of crucifixion was a public area near the city (cf. v 20; on Golgotha see the *Notes*). The site was clearly chosen for all to see, that they might take warning from the fate of law-breakers. (Josephus tells us that Titus had men crucified "opposite the wall" as a spectacle for those in the city, *B.J.* 5.449). The Evangelist, however, had a more encouraging thought:

Golgotha was a place where all the world might see Jesus lifted up, not least where they might read the inscription on his cross!

The two men crucified with Jesus are described by Mark as λησταί (Mark 15:27); that was John's term for Barabbas (18:40); it suggests that they were associates of Barabbas, fellow freedom fighters or revolutionaries. The point may have seemed too obvious for John to mention. More important to him, apparently, was the fact that the men were set "one on this side and one on the other, and Jesus in the middle." By this rather fulsome expression John may have wished to draw attention to Jesus' position, for with Jews "when three persons are present the most honored shall take his place in the middle" (see Str-B, 1:835). Conceivably the Evangelist considered that the central place between these revolutionaries befitted the real Deliverer, the King (cf. Schlatter, 348; Dauer, 173; Schnackenburg, 3:270). It is even more probable that the Evangelist, with the primitive Church generally, saw in Jesus crucified between such men a fulfillment of Isa 53:12. This Scripture may even have had an influence on preserving the memory of these fellow prisoners of Jesus (so Brown, 2:900).

The Title on the Cross and Jewish Objections to It (19:19–22)

19–20   It was customary for one doomed to be crucified to have a tablet or placard stating the cause for his execution hung about him, or carried by another before him, and then affixed to his cross. (Eusebius, *H.E.* 6.44, relates how in the reign of Marcus Aurelius a Christian named Attalus was led round the amphitheatre in Lyons with a tablet attached to him, on which it was written, "This is Attalus the Christian," cited Blinzler, 362.) In other circumstances one would expect that the placard that Jesus wore would have recorded the charge of sedition made against him. Pilate, however, deliberately used the wording that emanated from the chief priests, and that he himself had repeatedly taken up during the trial: "Jesus the Nazarene, the King of the Jews." Its repetition in three languages also accorded with custom (Bauer cites a title erected by Roman soldiers over the tomb of Gordian, "in Greek, Latin, Persian, Jewish and Egyptian writing, that it might be read by all," [173]. That this one should prove to be provocative, not to say infuriating, to the Jews goes without saying. It was Pilate's last act of revenge upon them. For the Evangelist the action of Pilate was the climax of the whole series of events that culminated in the crucifixion of Jesus: Pilate, the judge and representative of the dominion that ruled the world, hereby declares that Jesus on his cross is King of his people. It was written in Hebrew that the Jews might understand it; in Latin that the Romans might know it; in Greek, the *lingua franca* of the world, that all nations might learn of it. "Thus did Pilate tell it out among the nations that the Lord is king" wrote Hoskyns, in the words of Ps 96:10. Here the irony of John reaches its apex: the two men who were most responsible for the death of Jesus became the unwitting prophets of the death of Jesus: the one declaring it as the means of redemption for Israel and the nations (11:49–50) the other proclaiming it the occasion of his exaltation to be King of Israel and Lord of all.

21–22   The indignation and rage of the chief priests over the inscription was inevitable. They demanded that Pilate should alter it, but their request was represented as a modest one: let the governor insert the little word εἰμι, "I am"; that would show that it was Jesus who claimed to be king of the Jews, and that he was now dying because *it was a criminal lie*. Pilate, however, was ready for them. For the first time in the whole sequence of events leading to the death of Jesus, he remained adamant to the Jewish leaders: "What I have written, I have written" was his reply, and no further discussion was allowed. On that Dauer commented: "Pilate in no way yielded to their objections: *he refuses to change the truth into a lie;* the Kingship of Jesus stands unalterably fast" (275).

The Dividing of Jesus' Clothes (19:23–24)

23–24 By custom the clothes of an executed person were the property of his executioners. since they were viewed as "spoil." Jesus will have had an outer garment (i.e., a robe), a tunic, a belt, sandals, and presumably a head covering. It is the tunic to which attention is called; it was seamless. That was not particularly unusual in Palestine (it could have been made by his mother), but clearly it would have been foolish to divide it into four, and so the soldiers cast lots for it. All the other Evangelists tell the story (Mark 15:24 par.), though more briefly than John. The synoptists echo the language of the psalm (22:18) without citing it explicitly, and without distinguishing between the dividing of the clothing from casting lots for the tunic. It has frequently been suggested that John's story has arisen through developing the earlier account on the basis of the parallelism of the Scripture (cf. Matt 21:12–14 for a like phenomenon). It should be observed nevertheless that the parallel lines in the psalm do not distinguish different kinds of clothing, as John's narrative demands; the account of the seamless tunic could hardly have developed on the basis of the psalm. It was treasured by the Evangelist as another example of the events of the passion of Jesus fulfilling the purpose of God made known in the scriptures.

Is there any further meaning that the Evangelist wished his readers to perceive in this event? Various additional interpretations have been offered through the centuries. Josephus describes the High Priest's χιτών as seamless: "This garment consists not of two parts, so that it would be sewn around the shoulders and at the side, but it is woven from a single length of thread" (*Ant.* 3.161). Philo saw in it a symbol of the robe that the Logos fashions out of the various powers and elements of the world and that is untearable (*De fuga et inv.,* 110–12). The former statement has led some to consider that the seamless garment is reminiscent of the High Priest's robe, and points to Jesus' high priestly ministry (e.g., Macgregor in his commentary, 346; Spicq in *Epître aux Hébreux,* 1:122). The latter is consonant with the more popular view (going back to Cyprian, *De Unitate Ecclesiae,* chap. 7) that the seamless garment represents the unity of the Church. It should be acknowledged, however, that the garment in question is a tunic, not a *robe*, as Josephus and Philo had in view. And while one may view the tunic as close to the body of Jesus, and eloquent of the unity of the Church over against division of the Jews because of Jesus (so Hoskyns, appealing to the contrasting picture in 1 Kgs 11:29–30), the interpretation overlooks that *Jesus has his tunic taken from him!* Such is Schnackenburg's view. He suggests that it is simpler to see here a parallel with Jesus laying aside his garments in the footwashing, an event which the Evangelist views as a picture of Jesus laying aside his glory and giving himself to the death of the cross. In these hours Jesus' last possessions, and his life, are taken from him, but he remains under the protection of God, even as the tunic is not destroyed (3:274).

Jesus Gives His Mother to the Beloved Disciple (19:25–27)

25 The οἱ μὲν οὖν στρατιῶται, "the soldiers therefore," of v 24c appears to be linked with εἱστήκεισαν δὲ . . . "but there stood," of v 25. The soldiers and the women are being contrasted: the former are occupied with sharing Jesus' clothes, the latter are watching and waiting with devotion, and doubtless prayer. The mention of the women at *this* point (rather than after the death of Jesus, as in the synoptics) is primarily to introduce the following scene in vv 26–27. The contrast, therefore, between the soldiers and the women extends to Jesus: the soldiers dispose of his clothes among themselves, Jesus directs the relations of those he loves.

The list of women in v 25 creates problems, in part to determine how many they are, in part to define their relationship to the synoptic lists of women standing afar as Jesus dies (Mark 15:40; Matt 27:55–56; Luke 23:49 gives no names). John's list may be understood as denoting two women, or three, or four. On the first interpretation we read of "his mother and his mother's sister, namely Mary of Clopas and Mary Magdalene, "thereby identifying the mother of Jesus with Mary of Clopas. This is hardly natural. The second interpretation reads the list as Jesus' Mother, her sister Mary of Clopas, and Mary Magdalene; but that means that Mary the mother of Jesus had a sister named Mary, which is not very likely. The third mode of interpretation is most straightforward. It sees the list as composed of two pairs, the first without names and the second named.

The relationship of the women mentioned by the Fourth Evangelist to those in the synoptics is more difficult to determine. Traditionally it has been assumed that the same persons appear in John as in Mark and Matthew. The mother of Jesus is excepted, since she is in John's list only. Mary Magdalene appears in all the lists. So that leaves two mentioned by John to be accounted for. The easiest solution is to identify Mary (wife?) of Clopas with Mary mother of James and Joses (Joseph). The unnamed sister of Jesus' mother could be Salome, mentioned by Mark alone; she could also be the unnamed mother of the sons of Zebedee, who is included in Matt 27:56. This last suggestion greatly attracts a number of expositors, since it makes James and John, the sons of Zebedee, the cousins of Jesus. The traditional identification of John the son of Zebedee with the Beloved Disciple helps to explain his close relationship with Jesus in the ministry. Moreover, it makes more comprehensible the immediately following scene, in which Jesus commits his mother to the Beloved Disciple.

It must be admitted that the above series of identifications is speculative. Bultmann considered the procedure to be "arbitrary" (672). Schnackenburg speaks of it as "extremely problematical" (3:277); he holds that the mention of Jesus' mother in John points to his tradition as a different one from that in the synoptics. The other women, therefore, apart from Mary Magdalene, could be persons not mentioned in the synoptics (3:277). In support of this it should be noted that the persons named by Mark and Matthew are "among" those standing afar; there is no compulsion then to restrict those who drew near to Jesus to the persons named by Mark and Matthew.

What of the fact that the synoptics describe the women as standing at a distance from the cross, whereas in John the women are near the cross? Westcott's answer was that the latter were the more courageous of those who stood afar (2:312). Whether "courageous" is the appropriate word is uncertain. It is not unreasonable to suppose that at some point those closest in affection to Jesus drew near to him at his end. Contrary to those who maintain that Roman soldiers would not allow it (to prevent attempts to rescue the crucified), E. Stauffer reproduces evidence to show that crucified persons were often surrounded by their relatives and friends, and even enemies (*Jesus and His Story*, tr. D. M. Barton [London: SCM, 1960] 111, 179 n.1). Barrett's objections to Stauffer's position are not convincing (551).

26–27 Jesus speaks, not to the women as a group, but to his mother, and to the Beloved Disciple, of whose presence by the cross we now learn. Jesus is conscious that the end is near (v 28). His brief words to his mother and the disciple are not just a commendation or suggestion; they are more like a testamentary disposition, in language reminiscent of adoption. Stauffer was very definite about the form of the statements; he wrote, "A crucified man has the right to make testamentary dispositions, even from the cross. Jesus now makes use of this right, and with the official formula of the old Jewish family law he places his mother under the protection of the apostle John: 'Woman, behold your son! Son, behold your mother!' " (*Jesus and His Story*, 113). An example of the formula-like language, not applied to real adoption, is seen in *Tobit*, when Tobit is engaged to Sarah; to him it is said, "From now on you are her brother, behold she is your sister" (7:12).

Stauffer speaks of Mary coming under the protection of the Beloved Disciple ("Woman, behold your son!"). What is intended in the words, "Behold your mother"? Roman Catholic exegesis through many centuries has interpreted the clause in terms of the disciple *coming under the care of Mary*. That led to the belief that Mary was appointed the mother, not only of the Beloved Disciple, but of all disciples, hence of the Church. Brown finds the exegetical key to this interpretation in the link between vv 26–27 and 2:4: "If Mary was refused a role during the ministry of Jesus as it began at Cana, she finally received her role in the hour of Jesus' passion, death, and resurrection. . . . In becoming the mother of the Beloved Disciple (the Christian) Mary is symbolically evocative of Lady Zion who, after the birth pangs, brings forth anew people in joy (John 16:21; Isa 49:22; 54:1; 66:7–11)." He further sees in Mary, in accord with long tradition, the new Eve who, in imitation of her prototype, the "woman" of Gen 2–4, can say: "With the help of the Lord I have begotten a man." In harmony with most Catholic exegetes he sees this appointment of our Lord as the climax of his work on earth; the comment of the Evangelist immediately following vv 26–27 ("Jesus, knowing that all things had now been completed") is held to imply that the Evangelist regarded this episode as "the completion of the work that the Father had given to Jesus to do, in the context of the fulfilment of Scripture" (2:925–

26). Not all Catholics subscribe to this view. Dauer maintains that the emphasis in vv 26–27 is not that Mary receives new rights and duties of mother regarding the disciples, but that the disciple takes over the rights and duties of a grown son as regards Mary. He cites in support H. Schürmann's paraphrase of the Lord's words: "Woman, see your son who now cares for you! Son, see your mother to be cared for by you!" That is to say, the passage must be interpreted from the standpoint that the mother of Jesus is entrusted to the disciple, and not conversely he to the mother of Jesus (*Die Passionsgeschichte im Joh.- ev.*, 322–26). That interpretation seems to me to accord precisely with the intention of the text. Brown protests that an understanding of the passage simply in terms of the solicitude of Jesus for his mother does not fit the context, with its highly symbolic episodes (923). Perhaps, however, the episodes surrounding vv 25–27 are not so "highly symbolic" as is maintained (e.g., the significance of the tunic of Jesus, thought to symbolize the unity of the Church, vv 23–24).

It may not be amiss to recall Schlatter's comment on this passage: "Its naturalness gives a depth to the last word of Jesus to his mother, with which a last word to John was bound, which is only destroyed through allegorical reinterpretation" (351). Granting, however, that an added symbolic meaning may have been intended by the Evangelist, what might that be? Here the judgment of Schnackenburg, another Roman Catholic, is worth pondering. With Brown he also links vv 25–27 to John 2:4, and comments thus: "H. Schürmann may have indicated the way to the right understanding: Mary with her confident behaviour at the wedding represents those who expect salvation from Jesus. She stands begging for Jesus' gift. If her plea at that time was fulfilled in such a way that the gift of wine pointed symbolically into the future, then at this moment she is granted lasting fulfilment. She is to receive the disciple whom Jesus loved in place of her son, and remain with him. He will obtain for her what she longs for, unfold that which Jesus leaves behind" (3:278). Schnackenburg also considers it possible that Mary may represent that part of Israel that is receptive to messianic salvation, as against the representatives of unbelieving Judaism. "In this way the tendency to refer (in the person of Mary) all those who expect the messianic salvation to the Beloved Disciple and the Christian community is not weakened but rather confirmed and clarified for the true Israelites." And this is true because with this last disposition Jesus ensures that his revelation is passed on and made to bear fruit, i.e., through the Beloved Disciple, who takes Mary to himself and with her all who seek salvation (278–79). It will be observed that in this view the significance of the Beloved Disciple is assumed to be his position in relation to the Lord; as the Son of God through his intimate fellowship with the Father was able to reveal the Father (1:18), so the Beloved Disciple, through his intimate fellowship with Jesus (13:23), was able to comprehend and explain the revelation through Jesus. That revelation Mary and all other believers should rejoice to receive, and live in its light.

The Death of Jesus (19:28–30)

28   The giving of a drink to Jesus on the cross is variously described in the Gospels. The offering of wine mixed with myrrh, mentioned by Mark

(15:22) is a quite different incident; it preceded the act of crucifying, and was prepared by women to dull the senses and lessen the pain; this drink Jesus refused to take. Luke records the mockery of Jesus by the rulers and the soldiers, and in that context states that the soldiers gave Jesus ὄξος, cheap wine, to drink (23:36). Mark and Matthew place the event immediately following the cry of desolation (Mark 15:34–36 par.); the impression is given that bystanders thought that Jesus was calling on Elijah for help, and they gave the drink to help him, as they waited to see if Elijah came to save him. It is clear that the precise setting of this happening was uncertain in the tradition, but we may acknowledge that (i) it happened just before Jesus died; (ii) the giving of the wine was the action of a soldier; the wine belonged to the guard standing by, and no one would have dared to take some of it and give it to a man on a cross. Both these points are taken up by John. He introduces the event with the words, "Jesus knew that all was now accomplished," i.e., the work that he had come from heaven to achieve. A sign is now given that this "accomplishment" was at its end. It happened, not that the entire revelation of God in the Scriptures be brought to fulfillment, but that a particular Scripture passage (γραφή) be fulfilled. Jesus cries, "I thirst." Both the thirst and the action in seeking to satisfy it belong to the fulfillment of the Scripture, namely Ps 69:22: "They gave me vinegar for my thirst." (The term חמץ [homes] was used of vinegar, but the Greek rendering of it ὄξος [oxos] denoted a drink, whether a watered-down vinegar or cheap wine, which was popular among soldiers.)

The saying is part of the lengthy description of the desolation, isolation, and scorn experienced by the Righteous Sufferer, and in the psalm the giving of the drink appears to be part of the torment inflicted upon the sufferer. If Mark cites the event as linked with the cry of desolation from the cross (Ps 22:11), John underscores the reality of the desolation by his specific citation of the scripture, for the thought of Ps 69 is closely parallel to that of Ps 22. Dodd indeed thought that the cry "I thirst" was a symbolical equivalent of the cry of desolation (Historical Tradition, 42 n.1). Dauer thought likewise; he hazarded the suggestion that John's source ended with the cry of thirst and the description of Jesus' death, and added: "Jesus' cry of thirst, which stands in close connection with the attached giving of a drink, as in Mark/ Matthew it does with the cry 'My God . . . ,' appears to leave no further place for the latter in the Johannine source" (Passionsgeschichte, 210). If it leaves no further room it is because it is thought needless, not because there is no room for it in Johannine theology. One may no more assume that John's emphasis on the cross as the exaltation of Jesus excludes his desolation of spirit than his emphasis on the deity of the Son excludes the Son's true humanity. That Jesus hung on the cross as King was not in spite of his agony, epitomized in the thirst of crucifixion, but through his agony endured in obedience and love to the glory of God.

The parenthetical "in order that the scripture might be fulfilled" could have been inserted to show the link between the event and the purpose of God made known in the scripture without suggesting that Jesus knowingly uttered the cry in order that the scripture may be fulfilled. It could, however, conceivably relate to the consciousness of Jesus that he was experiencing the desolation described in

the psalm in order that the purpose of God might be carried through to its completion. Significantly, Ps 69, as Ps 22, concludes with a cry of triumph:

> Let heaven and earth praise him . . .
> the seas and all that move in them,
> for God will save Zion,
> and all who love his name will dwell there.

29 The use of a sponge for the wine, fixed on an implement, need not
have been due to the cross-beam standing high, for it was often no more
than the height of a man; the soldier presumably did not wish to use his
own cup. Mark and Matthew record that the sponge was fixed on a κάλαμος,
i.e., "a reed," or stalk or staff (Mark 15:36 par.). John's source may have
had the same word, in which case he himself changed it to *hyssop* (ὑσσώπῳ)—
or to *javelin* (ὑσσῷ)?

The possibilities are discussed in the *Notes*. The mass of MSS have the former
reading. It is commonly assumed that the change was made by the Evangelist in
order to indicate that Jesus died as God's Passover Lamb (1:29). In Exod 12:22
the use of hyssop is prescribed for sprinkling blood of a lamb on the door frame
of a house on the night of the Exodus from Egypt. But the giving to Jesus a
drink from a sponge on a hyssop stalk is a remote parallel to the sprinkling of
blood of a lamb on the door of a house. The Evangelist's pointers to the death of
Christ as the fulfillment of Passover are clearer than this (e.g., 1:29, 36; chap 6;
19:31–36). Recent exegetes therefore are inclined to dismiss the association here
(e.g., Bultmann, 674 n.2; Schnackenburg, 3:284; Haenchen, 553). The use of a
javelin on which to place the sponge is favored by the fact that the giver of the
drink was a soldier. Whether, however, he used his javelin or a stick is of no
consequence for the meaning of the event in relation to the Scripture cited by
the Evangelist, and so far as the soldier was concerned his action was simply a
spontaneous response to the cry of Jesus. The action was certainly unusual for a
member of a Roman execution squad on behalf of a crucified Jew he was guarding,
not least in view of the treatment meted out to Jesus by his group—and he may
well have been one of them who engaged in the sport! Not surprisingly, some
have wondered whether there is a link here with the synoptic account of the centurion
who confessed Jesus as υἱὸς θεοῦ, "Son of God," in Mark 15:39.

30 After drinking the wine, Jesus uttered his last word known to the
Evangelist, τετέλεσται. The rendering, "It is finished!" conveys only half the
meaning. For the verb τελέω fundamentally denotes "to carry out" the will
of somebody, whether of oneself or another, and so to fulfill obligations or
carry out religious acts. "It is *accomplished!*" renders that aspect of the word.
Doubtless both meanings of the term, the temporal and the theological, are
intended here. "So the last word of Jesus interprets his suffering and dying
as the crowning conclusion and high point of the work that he has performed
in obedience—the obedience of the Son finds here its most radical expression—
and enables the believing eye to see the glorifying of the Son through the
Father" (Dauer, *Passionsgeschichte*, 20).

Dodd considered that τετέλεσται in its Johannine context conveys the notion
of the completion of *rites of sacrifice and initiation*, for the death of Christ is conceived
of as both sacrifice and initiation. This he substantiates from the use of the term
τελέω in the Hermetic literature. In *De Regeneratione* (*Corp. Herm.* 13) Tat, the
son of Hermes, in the final stage of the initiation utters a prayer, "O God . . .

receive the spiritual sacrifices which thou desirest of me, for by thy will all things are completed (τετέλεσται)." This last utterance, says Dodd, "may be compared with the τετέλεσται which is the last word of the dying of Jesus in the Fourth Gospel" (*Interpretation*, 421). It may be compared, indeed, but hardly viewed as comparable with the sacrifice of the incarnate Son of God for the unleashing of the divine sovereignty in the world.

More important is the relation of the final word of Jesus in the Fourth Gospel to that in Mark's gospel. It is of interest to note that Mark records another "loud cry" of Jesus, but does not know what it was (15:37). Schnackenburg urges that we should not attempt to construct a historical combination of the last sayings of Jesus in the Gospels but allow each to speak to us. The τετέλεσται of John 19:30 is "a counterpoint to the synoptic description of Jesus forsaken by God. . . . The two ways of looking at things are close together, equally justified and not untenable; both meet in the *mysterium* of Jesus' person, and both reveal something to us of the secret of our own death" (3:285). We have here a singular illustration of the mercy and wisdom of God in providing us with more than one Gospel.

The death of Jesus took place as Jesus "bowed his head and handed over his spirit." This is close to the synoptic descriptions of the event: Jesus "breathed his last" (lit., "breathed out" [his spirit], ἐξέπνευσεν; Mark 15:37; Luke 23:46); Jesus "gave up (lit., "sent away") the spirit" (Matt 27:50). Bultmann viewed these expressions as having the same meaning (675 n.1). The term παρέδωκεν, however, is stronger than the verbs used in the synoptic Gospels, and it is possible that it reflects the thought in 10 18, "I have authority to lay down (my life). . . ." The death of Jesus is then 'a conscious act . . . a self-offering to the Father" (Schnackenburg, 3:285). By contrast it is unlikely that the Evangelist wished us to interpret his language as meaning, "He handed over *the Spirit*"—to Mary and the Beloved Disciple as representing believers in Jesus (so Hoskyns, 532; Bampfylde, "John 19:28 . . . ," 252–54; Brown, 2:931). In v 30 τὸ πνεῦμα clearly means the spirit of Jesus himself; and the fulfillment of the promise of the Spirit in 7:37–39, as in the Paraclete passages, belongs to the resurrection activity of Jesus, as is made abundantly plain in 20:22.

The Piercing of Jesus' Side (19:31–37)

31 The scene is set by the request of "the Jews" (the Jewish leaders) that the bodies of the crucified men should not remain on the crosses on the sabbath, and that their legs be broken. The note of time gives the clue: it was the Preparation Day. In v 13 that denoted the day before Passover; here it signifies the day before the sabbath (cf. Mark 15:42), but a very special sabbath—a "great" day (cf. 7:37), for it coincided with the Passover. Since the day begins in the evening, it is now on the point of commencing.

The request to Pilate was comprehensible. Romans left crucified men to linger till their death, sometimes for several days, and then the vultures finished them off. If there was any reason for hastening the death of crucified men, their legs were smashed with an iron mallet, so causing great loss of blood and asphyxia. Jewish law laid it down that one that is hanged (usually after execution) should not remain on a gibbet overnight, since a hanged man is accursed in God's sight and pollutes the land (Deut 21:22, 23). It was doubly important to the Jewish leaders for that law to be observed on this occasion, inasmuch as it was both a sabbath and the day of the Passover; possibly also

they wished Jesus to undergo this mutilation, so making him plainly accursed
in the sight of God and abandoned by him. (It is of interest that the bones
of a man crucified in this period, discovered in the area north of Jerusalem,
had been broken; one leg was simply fractured, the other was smashed to
pieces, see N. Haas, "Anthropological Observations on the Skeletal Remains
from Giv‘at ha-Mivtar," *IEJ* 20 [1970] 38–59.)

32–34 The soldiers (of the execution squad?), after receiving their order,
began with the men on either side of Jesus. On seeing that he had already
died, they realized that there was no need to smash his legs, but why, in
such circumstances, a soldier should thrust a spear into the side of Jesus is
not clear. The term νύσσω means "to prick, stab (especially with a dagger),
pierce"; the soldier could have simply pricked the flesh of Jesus to test whether
he was really dead, or, more likely, he thrust the spear deeply into his side
to ensure that he did die, "that he should not have a spark of life when
taken down from the cross" (Blinzler, 391). At all events the result of the
spear thrust was an immediate efflux of blood and water. Both the physiological
significance of this happening and its theological meaning have been long
discussed, and we leave both questions till the end of this section. Our interpretation will be affected by our view of the origin of v 35.

35 The sentence plainly emphasizes the signal importance both of what
the soldiers refrained from doing and of what they did. An eyewitness
(ὁ ἑωρακώς) guarantees the truth of what has just been stated; it is simplest
to view him as the person referred to as ἐκεῖνος (lit. "that one," but often simply "he"). The suggestion that "he" here denotes the Christ, or even God, on
the ground that ἐκεῖνος sometimes means the one (e.g., 3:5, 16) and sometimes
the other (e.g., 1:33; 5:19, 37; 8:42) is insufficient to support either application
here, for ἐκεῖνος is used of many different individuals in this Gospel (e.g.,
John the Baptist, 5:35; Moses, 5:46; Peter, 18:17, 25; the Beloved Disciple,
13:25; 21:7, 23). The context determines the meaning, and here it appears
to be the eyewitness. The statement is noticeably similar to that in 21:24,
affirming the identity of the witness as the Beloved Disciple and confidence
in his trustworthiness. Most exegetes have considered 21:24 to be an editorial
addition to chap. 21, and viewed it as the earliest attestation of authorship,
or at least the source of, this Gospel. There is a growing consensus that v
35 comes from the same editorial hand, and that it was inserted as a recollection
of the Beloved Disciple's witness to this event, thereby underlining its importance (and his). Of this, however, we cannot be sure; the issue is bound up
with the origin of chap. 21, whether it was integral to the Gospel, or an
appendix or an epilogue, whether it was added by the Evangelist or by an
editor, and so whether or not it indicates the Evangelist's own testimony to
the Beloved Disciple's witness. If the last idea holds good, it follows that
19:35 also comes from the Evangelist. In a situation of uncertainty, at least
v 35 gives the impression of an addition to the narrative; it is likely that
John's source ran straight on from vv 32–34 to vv 36–37. If that be so, the
importance of the refraining from breaking the legs of Jesus and the piercing
of his side lay, in the earliest tradition, in the fulfillment of the scriptures
cited in vv 36–37.

36 Three passages fall to be considered as source of the quotation: Exod

12:46, in the midst of prescriptions concerning the Passover, requires that "each lamb must be eaten inside the one house . . . you must not break a bone of it" (καὶ ὀστοῦν οὐ συντρίψετε ἀπ' αὐτοῦ). Num 9:12 similarly states, "no bone of it shall be broken" (καὶ ὀστῶν οὐ συντρίψουσιν ἀπ' αὐτοῦ). Ps 34:20, describing God's care for the Righteous Sufferer, says: "He guards every bone of his body, not one of them is broken" (ἓν ἐξ αὐτῶν οὐ συντριβήσεται). The Evangelist's wording does not precisely concur with any of these, but both typologies accord with the interest of the early churches and of the Evangelist himself: Jesus in his death brings to fulfillment the significance of the Passover and the eschatological hope of a second Exodus. He also fulfills the role of the Righteous Man who suffers but is under the care of God (a care that will extend to resurrection to his presence, see especially Wisd Sol 2:10–5:23). It is not impossible that *the source* had in view the latter figure and *the Evangelist*, with his marked interest in the Exodus typology, the former (so Bultmann, 676–77; Barrett, 558; Schnackenburg [tentatively], 3:292; Lindars thinks that the Evangelist had both typologies in mind, 590).

37 Zech 12:10 was an important testimony in the primitive Church, as its use in Matt 24:30; Rev 1:7, and this passage shows. The Masoretic Hebrew text reads, "They will look upon *me*, on *him* whom they have pierced"; the speaker is God, but the change of person supports the belief that he has been "pierced" when his representative, the "Shepherd," is stricken with the sword (13:7; so P. Lamarche, *Zacharie IX–XIV, Études Bibliques* [Paris: Gabalda, 1961] 80–83; W. Rudolph, *Haggai-Sacharja-Maleachi* [KAT 1976] 224, who believes that the "piercing" of the Messiah is in view; for other interpretations see R. A. Mason, *The Books of Haggai, Zechariah and Malachi* [Cambridge: CUP, 1977] 118–19, who thinks that Zechariah's language relates to the ill-treatment of the prophet and his circle, in rejecting whom the people reject God). The "looking" at the pierced one in Zechariah is in contrition as a result of God's pouring on the people "a spirit of grace and supplication"; hence they grieve bitterly as for a firstborn son. In Matthew and Revelation the lamentation takes place at the coming of the Son of Man, and it is unclear whether it is through remorse or in repentance. The application in John 19:37 is not to be restricted to the end of the age; in statements in the Gospel concerning "seeing" the Son of Man lifted up, the primary emphasis is on salvation. The link between this citation and that concerning the Lamb who brings deliverance at the second Exodus (or the Righteous Man whose sufferings bring salvation) suggests that the salvation aspect is to the fore here also. Naturally the obverse of judgment for those who persist in looking on the Redeemer in unbelief is not excluded. Brown considers that in our passage two groups are in mind, the "Jews" who are the enemies of Jesus and are defeated through the event which they instigated, and those represented by the Beloved Disciple, who look in faith to Jesus (2:954–55); that is less suitable to the context than the primary looking with eyes of faith to the crucified Savior (so Schnackenburg, 3:292–94).

The relation of the spear thrust to the emission of blood and water and the death of Jesus has been of interest to many physicians. Recently an illuminating article appeared in *JAMA* (255 [1986] 1455–63), jointly written by consultants of the departments of Pathology and Medical Graphics of the Mayo Clinic, Rochester,

MN, and a pastor ("On the Physical Death of Jesus Christ," by W. D. Edwards, W. J. Gabel, F. E. Hosmer); among other things it contains a useful bibliography on the subject. On the theme of our interest, the authors appear to support the view of Pierre Barbet (ET, *A Doctor at Calvary: the Passion of our Lord Jesus Christ as Described by a Surgeon* [Garden City, NY: Doubleday, 1953]), that is, that the heart of Jesus was pierced, and that the blood came from the heart and the water from the pericardial sac. Their statement runs: "The water probably represented serous pleural and pericardial fluid, and would have preceded the flow of blood and been smaller in volume than the blood. Perhaps in the setting of hypovolemia and impending acute heart failure, pleural and pericardial effusions may have developed and would have added to the volume of apparent water. The blood, in contrast, may have originated from the right atrium or the right ventricle or perhaps from a hemopericardium" (1463). A. F. Sava, however, in an article not cited by these writers ("The Wound in the Side of Christ," *CBQ* 19, 343–46) objects to the idea that the blood came from within the heart and the water from the pericardial sac: "Any fluid that leaves the pericardial sac cannot skip across the space between the lining of the lung and the outer surface of the pericardial sac. Because of this, a fluid thus evacuated from the pericardium as well as from inside the heart, will flood the space around the lung rather than ooze its way slowly across the pierced lung. This is what I observed in my experiments with fresh cadavers." He similarly doubts that a spontaneous rupture of the heart, followed by decomposition of the blood, evacuated into the heart of Jesus (contrary to a well-known work by W. Stroud: *Treatise on the Physical Cause of the Death of Christ and Its Relation to the Principles and Practice of Christianity,* [London: Hamilton & Adams, [2]1971]). Sava's own proposal is that the blood and water were present just inside the rib cage between the pleura lining the chest and that lining the lung. Severe chest injuries show that nonpenetrating injuries of the chest are capable of producing an accumulation of hemorrhagic fluid in the space between the ribs and the lung—it may amount to as much as two liters. Sava relates that he has collected into glass cylinders blood from different cadavers from two to four hours after death; on standing, the contents separated into a lower (half by volume) layer of deep red, while over it the serum appeared clear, pale straw-colored. "I submit, therefore, that the brutal scourging of Christ several hours before his death upon the cross, was sufficient to produce a bloody accumulation within the chest, so that the settling by this fluid into layers and its ultimate evacuation by opening the chest below the level of separation must inevitably result in the 'immediate' flow of blood followed by water" (344–45).

The discussion among the physicians will doubtless go on, but this contribution appears to be reasonable. We, of course, are especially interested to know what the Evangelist wished his readers to learn, beyond the fulfillment by Jesus of the scriptures that he cites in vv 36–37. Almost certainly he desired them to recognize *the reality of the death of Jesus, and so the reality of his humanity as a man of flesh and blood* (cf. 1:14: "the Word *became* flesh"). That Docetism was already perceived as a danger in the Johannine churches is seen in 1 John 4:1–6 (cf. 2:18–24); the closely parallel utterance to our passage, 1 John 5:6–9, has as its primary intention the witness of the water and blood to the real incarnation of the Son of God. The truth of that witness is attested by the Holy Spirit, hence the three witnesses of vv 7–8. G. Richter has urged that in 1 John 5:6 "this is he who came through water and blood . . . not in the water only but in the water and in the blood" relates not to two different events, viz., the baptism and the death of Jesus, but to two elements of a single condition: Jesus came from God as *a man having both water and blood* ("Blut und Wasser: Joh 19, 34b," 125). This interpretation is in harmony with the ancient view, current alike in the Jewish and Hellenistic worlds, that man consists of blood and water, even as he was born of blood and water, and that an imbalance of either signifies a diseased condition. The Jewish view is expressed in *Lev. Rab.* 15, 115c (see Str-B, 2:582–83). Of the wider world E. Schweizer wrote, "From Heraclitus (*ca.* 500 B.C.) to Galen (in the 2nd century A.D.) it is taught that the right relation of water and blood, together with black and yellow gall in the human body, guarantees good health." He pointed out that a distinction was made by the pagans between gods and humans: "Homer reports how from a goddess wounded through a lance, 'blood-water' alone streamed out instead of blood and water, because the gods, who neither eat bread nor drink wine, have no blood" (*Iliad* 5.340 f.). Similarly Plutarch related that the wounded Alexander told those who regarded him as a god, "This is blood, as you see, and not blood-water, as it flows in the holy gods" (*Moralia* 180e; see Schweizer, "Das Herrenmahl im Neuen Testament," in *Neotestamentica* [Zürich: Zwingli Verlag, 1963] 382–83). It is easy to see how these ideas found their way among the Gnostics and influenced their views of Jesus, as also why the Evangelist laid such emphasis on the phenomenon of blood and water at the death of Jesus, as reported by the eyewitness. This understanding of v 34 was recognized as early as Irenaeus, who linked the efflux of water and blood with other features of the life of Jesus, such as his hunger and thirst and weariness. "All these," he said, "are signs of the flesh that was taken from the earth and that he recapitulated in himself in order to save his creation" (*Adv. Haer.* 3.22.2). This intention of the Evangelist is acknowledged by many modern commentators (e.g., by Bernard, 2:647; Schlatter, 354; Bultmann, 678 n.1; Barrett, 556; Schnackenburg, 3:291; Bruce, 376; Smalley, *1, 2, 3 John* [WBC 51, 1984] 277–79).

Are there other levels of symbolic meaning seen by John in this happening? From Chrysostom on it has been common to see in the water and the blood the true initiation of the sacraments of baptism and the Lord's Supper (for evidence from the Fathers see Westcott's excursus, 2:328–33; also Hoskyns, 534–36). Many modern expositors have also been persuaded of this view. For Cullmann, for example, v 34 shows that in the two sacraments Christ gives to his Church the atonement accomplished in his death: "Scarcely is the historical Jesus dead . . . when he shows in what form he will from now on be present upon earth, in the sacraments, in baptism and the Lord's Supper" (*Early Christian Worship,* tr. A. S. Todd & J. B. Torrance [London: SCM, 1953] 115. For related expositions see Westcott, 2:320; Bauer, 176; Hoskyns, 533; Barrett, a secondary reference, 557; Bultmann, 678 n.1). Despite the popularity of this view it is not without difficulties. Brooke pointed out that the term "blood" is never by itself used in the NT as a designation of the Lord's Supper (*Commentary on The Johannine Epistles,* ICC [Edinburgh: T & T Clark, 1912] 132). In the discourse on the Bread of Life, the eucharistic application becomes clear in the statements about eating *the flesh* and drinking *the blood* of the Son of Man (6:53–56), and only by virtue of them can one look back into the discourse and its signs for further reflections of eucharistic thinking. The statement about birth from water and the Spirit in 3:5, set in juxtaposition with a discourse on the baptism of John and Jesus (3:22–30), makes the reference to baptism transparent. Admittedly blood from the side of Jesus can be linked with the blood of Jesus as true drink in 6:55, but water from the side of Jesus can hardly be equated with baptism in water, not even when the water of baptism came to be viewed as excellent medicine (see W. Heitmüller, *Im Namen Jesu,* 283). For reasons such as these, caution is now being used in linking this passage with the sacraments. Brown for example wrote, "At most we can give a probability to the double sacramental reference of 19:34b (on a secondary level)" (2:952); Schnackenburg sees the *probabil-*

ity of a sacramental reference in 1 John 5:6–8 and the *possibility* of its presence in John 19:34–35 (3:291); Richter rules it out altogether ("It cannot come into question, even on a second or third level of thought," 139).

It is of interest to note that Dodd viewed the flowing of blood and water from the side of Jesus as a "sign" of the life that flows from the crucified and risen Christ (*Interpretation*, 428; *Historical Tradition*, 133–35). That is the direction in which Schnackenburg looks: "The blood is, presumably, a sign of Jesus' saving death (cf. 1 John 1:7) and the water is symbolic of Spirit and life (cf. John 4:14; 7:38), but both are most intimately connected" (3:294). That is a cautious yet deeply significant conclusion in relation to the meaning of the death of Jesus. On that interpretation the Johannine account of the life and death of Jesus reaches a fitting τέλος, its climactic end.

The Burial (19:38–42)

38 All four Gospels tell of Joseph of Arimathea's going to Pilate and requesting that he might remove the body of Jesus. The synoptic Gospels yield information not in John: that Joseph was a member of the Sanhedrin (Mark 15:43 par.), and so a resident of Jerusalem; that he was one who looked for the kingdom of God (Mark 15:43; Luke 23:51); that he was rich (Matt 27:57); and that he dissented from the policy and actions of the Sanhedrin regarding Jesus (Luke 23:50–51). Matthew also speaks of him as a disciple of Jesus (27:51); John alone adds, "but a secret one through fear of the Jews." In view of 12:42–43 that was no compliment to Joseph. In ordinary circumstances it would rather have condemned him in the Evangelist's eyes, but this was no ordinary situation. Romans added to the shame of crucifixion refusal to allow those so put to death a decent burial. Commonly the crucified were left to vultures. Exceptions could be made only as an act of grace by the authorities, and that gesture to relatives who so petitioned. Usually the body was granted, but never when the offense was *lèse-majesté*. The Jews could not bring themselves to deny those they executed a burial, but neither did they allow such to be buried in family tombs, for fear of the executed contaminating those already buried in them. Accordingly they provided a burial place for executed criminals away from the city (so Jos. *Ant.* 5.44; in Mishnaic times they provided two such places, one for those stoned and burned, and another for those beheaded and strangled). The request of the Jewish leaders in v 31 would have carried with it permission to bury the crucified men in the common grave (on this see Blinzler, *Prozess Jesu*, 385–94). It was therefore an uncommonly courageous act for Joseph to dissociate himself from the Sanhedrin and to show his sympathy with Jesus, who had been so ignominiously condemned and killed. He will have been aware that he had no right to make the request, since he was unrelated to Jesus. But he was equally aware that none of the brothers of Jesus would attempt to take this step. His position and wealth naturally will have commended him to Pilate; nevertheless he should have been denied what he asked in view of the nature of Jesus' offense against Caesar. That Pilate acceded to it is in line with John's whole account of the trial of Jesus. Pilate knew well that the charge against Jesus was unfounded, and so he released the body to Joseph.

39 Whereas all the synoptists report Joseph's action, none of them knows of Nicodemus' part in the burial of Jesus. His introduction into the Passion tradition of the Johannine churches will have been due to the Evangelist. (For an interesting summary of what may be gleaned from Jewish sources regarding Nicodemus and his family, see J. A. T. Robinson, *The Priority of John*, 284–87.) Self-evidently Nicodemus would not normally have on hand the amount of spices here mentioned. There must have been an urgent collaboration with Joseph while Jesus was dying, and so Joseph procured the grave clothes and Nicodemus the spices. "Thus," commented Hoskyns, "the two timorous believers are publicly and courageously drawn to the Christ after his exaltation upon the cross (12:32)" (526).

Mixture of myrrh and aloes was well known among Jews. Myrrh is a fragrant resin, often used by Egyptians in embalming, but by Jews rendered into powdered form; so also aloes are a powdered aromatic sandalwood. We read of them together in the OT, e.g., in Ps 45:8 "Your robes are all fragrant with myrrh and powder of aloes"; in Prov 7:17 a prostitute spreads her bed and night clothes with them: in Cant 4:14 the cheeks of the loved one are like "myrrh and aloes with all the choicest spices." Their use in connection with burial of the dead has nothing to do with embalming, but is to combat the inevitable putrefaction of the corpse and to keep it sweet smelling for a time. Nicodemus certainly intended to achieve that! The amount of spices that he is reported to have brought appears to us staggering in quantity. One hundred λίτραι is the equivalent of 65.45 pounds (hence the NEB rendering, "more than half a hundredweight," the latter being a British measure of 112 pounds). Lagrange thought that an error must have arisen in the tradition and that the original quantity will have been much less (503), while Dodd thought it "an extravagant touch introduced by the Evangelist" (*Historical Tradition*, 139 n.2). There is no need for such suggestions. The family of Nicodemus appears to have been enormously wealthy, and the bringing of huge amounts of spices at royal funerals was familiar to Jews. It is related in 2 Chron 16:14 that when King Asa was buried he was "laid on a bier which had been heaped with all kinds of spices skillfully compounded; and they kindled a great fire in his honor." That was eclipsed in the funeral of Herod the Great; according to Josephus (*Ant.* 17.199) five hundred slaves bore spices in the funeral procession as they followed the army to the king's burial place. More closely related is the action of the proselyte Onkelos, who is recorded as having burned eighty pounds of spices at the death of Gamaliel the elder. When asked why he had done so, he replied, citing the words of Jeremiah to Zedekiah, king of Judah: "You shall die in peace, and with the burnings of your fathers (the former kings) who were before you. Is not R. Gamaliel far better than a hundred kings?" (Str-B, 2:584. The incident is dated *ca.* A.D. 40–50). One may imagine the Teacher of Israel, a contemporary of Onkelos, echoing, "Is not Jesus far greater than all other kings?" The Evangelist thus continues the theme of the kingship of Jesus into the account of his burial.

40 Joseph and Nicodemus therefore take the body of Jesus and bind it with the cloth wrappings and spices. The term ἀρώματα, while used in Mark's account of the women's hope of *anointing* the body of Jesus on Easter morning (16:1), also denotes *spices*, and here it clearly denotes the myrrh and aloes mentioned in v 39. The spices will have been spread the length of the wrappings, and these wound round the body of Jesus. They will also have been spread on the bank of the tomb. The process is well described by Robinson: "The Mishnah (Shab. 23.5) makes specific provision for the corpse to be laid on sand over the sabbath 'that it may be the longer preserved' until it could be attended to. The spices, in powdered or granule form, were doubtless a more effective (if much more costly) preservative, and if the corpse was to be underlaid with them and perhaps packed around, as their binding in with the ὀθόνια suggests, then a considerable amount would have been required" (*Priority of John*, 283).

A difficulty arises when comparing John's description of the binding of Jesus' body for burial with that of the synoptists. Mark states that Joseph brought a σινδών and wrapped the body of Jesus in it (Mark 15:46 par.). John says that Nicodemus bound the body with ὀθόνια, "linen clothes" or "wrappings." Various considerations have been adduced to ease the problem. The term σινδών can denote the material (linen cloth) or a single article of clothing. Brown maintains that the plural ὀθόνια can be "a plural of category designating no more than one object, or a plural of extension indicating the size of the piece (see BDF, § 141)"; he disputes that ὀθόνια should be translated as "linen strips," or "bandages," and denies that the Jews ever wrapped their corpses with bands or strips like those used for Egyptian mummies (2:942). Thus it is possible to make the two traditions say the same thing. This, however, may be a case where the possible may not be the probable. Schnackenburg holds that the analogy with John 11:44 and 20:6–7 points to a plurality of cloths being used in the burial of Jesus; we have two different early traditions with apparently diverging details, and are not in a position to resolve the problem (3:298). For enthusiastic contenders for the genuineness of the Turin shroud, the question is acute, but for most others not so. Blinzler concludes that the purpose of the synoptists was to show that Jesus was not buried naked, but in costly clothing and with a worthy burial. John represents Jesus as bound in a number of cloths, and this he stated since for him it played an important role in the manifestation of the resurrection (20:3–9) (*Prozess Jesu*, 396–97).

41–42 Our Evangelist alone mentions that there was a garden in the place where Jesus was crucified; accordingly the place where Jesus died was the place of his burial and the scene of the manifestation of his resurrection. Without doubt John in his whole account of the burial of Jesus has his eye on the resurrection morning. The tomb is stated to be a new one in which no one had been laid. The Jewish leaders would have been satisfied to learn of that, in view of the prohibition against burying executed criminals in a grave with ordinary people. The Evangelist will have had other thoughts: in the providential ordering of God, Jesus was not buried in the common criminals' grave, but in a tomb that was at hand, unused and therefore fit for the Holy One of God, and one that could be an unmistakable witness to the victory of the Lord of life over death.

Explanation

1. Following on the work of C. H. Dodd it has been common to see the Gospel of John as consisting of two main divisions: the Book of Signs and the Book of the Passion (or, as Brown prefers, the Book of Glory). Dodd himself, however, recognized that the Book of the Passion records the *supreme*

sign, to which all the lesser signs point, and in which they find their ultimate significance: "We find in the story of the arrest, trial and crucifixion of Jesus Christ a σημεῖον (sign) on the grand scale, to whose significance each detail contributes." All the signs in the Gospel are related to the supreme sign, above all as revelations of the divine sovereignty which comes through Christ in his total ministry, culminating in his "lifting up" on the cross and to heaven. Precisely because it is the final and all-inclusive sign, it transcends all others. The preliminary signs had only temporary effects, and that within a limited area; the wine that was so lavishly provided at the wedding feast finally ran out, the multitude which ate the loaves in the wilderness grew hungry again, and Lazarus was raised, but to die once more. When, however, the Son of Man was lifted up on his cross all the world was affected and history was changed for ever. Thus the cross is a sign, but a sign which is also the thing signified. The preliminary signs set forth so amply in the gospel are not only temporal signs of an eternal reality; they are also signs of this Event, in its twofold character as word and as flesh. They are true—spiritually, eternally true—only upon the condition that this Event is true, both temporally (or historically) and spiritually or eternally" (*Interpretation,* 439). We thereby see the unity of the Fourth Gospel as the exposition of the Word made flesh for the accomplishment of eternal salvation through his ministry and lifting up via his cross to the throne of God. "For God so loved the world that he *gave* his only Son"—to us and for us.

2. While we now recognize that all four Evangelists are theologians in their own right, the Fourth Evangelist has labored more than all to bring to the clear light of day the theological significance of the passion narrative handed on to the churches. Our study has made it evident that in so doing he has made one underlying theme to dominate his whole presentation, namely, the kingship of Jesus, the Messiah who "came to his own and his own received him not." The motive for this clarification is apparent: the task of the Son of God is to reveal the Father in words and works that bring *the divine sovereignty* to man; it is therefore essential for the believer to grasp that every step of the Via Dolorosa trodden by the Son is part of the fulfillment of that purpose. The Lord of history works through the machinations of men as they humiliate and finally put to death the representative of the divine sovereignty. But not for one moment does the divine purpose fail, nor does the instrument of the divine sovereignty swerve from it. The unity of the process whereby the Son of Man is "lifted up" is made evident at every stage in the story, so that, as Dauer puts it, "his Passion is itself already shot through with the brilliance of the Easter glory" (*Passionsgeschichte,* 336). The opening scene in the garden reveals the majesty of the King incognito, before whom the men sent to arrest him retreat and fall back in awe. But since the King is the obedient Son of God, he at once takes the initiative in stepping forth to his captors, and stays the sword of his follower as he declares his intention to drink the cup prepared for him by the Father; for kingship, obedience, and suffering are inseparable in the establishment of the saving sovereignty of God for man. The silken thread that unites sovereignty and humiliation is seen in the examination of Jesus by the High Priest Annas, for as prisoner Jesus sets right alike judge and

the official who smites him, and his very refusal to speak further is a judgment upon his judge for ignoring the Word of God that he was sent to bring to his nation.

It is, however, in the trial before Pilate that this theme is uniquely developed, from the opening conversation to the title on the cross that Pilate composed and would not alter. Through all the vacillations of Pilate, the unrelenting demands of the Jewish leaders for his death, and the cruel mockery of the soldiers, the divine will was working its way. If Pilate's vaunted authority, so appallingly misused in the trial, is given him by God, the same applies to the Jewish leaders as they exercise their authority over the nation to bring about the execution of the Son of God. It all remains under the sovereign control of God, who holds in his hand the Son as he achieves the salvation of humankind. That aspect of the Passion is underscored by the Evangelist as he punctuates his narrative with citations from the scriptures. These show the accord of the sufferings which bring the kingdom with the revealed will of God. Summarizing this element of the Evangelist's presentation Dauer wrote, "If the Evangelist in the passion story adheres far more closely to the tradition than elsewhere in the Gospel, this section of the life of Jesus is nevertheless entirely stamped by his spirit; it forms, together with the chapters that precede and that follow, a great unified whole, and proclaims the glory of the Son of God incarnate and now returning to the Father" (*Passionsgeschichte*, 338).

3. Does this "spirit" that stamps the Johannine passion narrative include an anti-Jewish bias that lays an unjust burden of guilt on the Jewish people for their part in the death of Jesus? We have already considered this question from the viewpoint of sensitive Jewish objectors, but there are others who need to be addressed. Our examination of John's narrative has brought to light some significant features. Remarkably enough, no account of a trial of Jesus by the Sanhedrin is given by the Evangelist, only a brief interrogation by Annas; the Evangelist knows of the Sanhedrin's meeting and of the charge that issued from it, that Jesus made himself king, but he chose not to describe it. More importantly, there is no equivalent in the Gospel of the cry of the people in general, recorded in Matt 27:25: "His blood be on us and on our children." The weight of responsibility for the death of Jesus is placed on the shoulders of *the Jewish leaders*, and above all on Caiaphas; he it is who gave the decisive counsel to the Sanhedrin that determined its course, alike in its meeting with Jesus and its dealings with Pilate (11:50; cf. also 19:11). The group before Pilate's judgment seat that first called for Jesus to be crucified is identified by John as "the chief priests and their henchmen" (19:5); they presumably were "the Jews" who kept up the cry in 19:12, 14–15, strengthened doubtless by supporters whom they rounded up. It is noteworthy that this interpretation of the situation is reflected in the primitive preaching of the gospel in Acts, epitomized in Peter's address to fellow Jews on the Day of Pentecost: "When he (Jesus) has been given up to you, by the deliberate will and plan of God, you used heathen men to crucify and kill him" (Acts 2:23). Significantly, Josephus, in his famous passage about Jesus in *Ant.* 18.63–64, used language that implies the same understanding of the event; he was, says Josephus, "accused before Pilate *by the leading men among us*" (τῶν

πρώτων ἀνδρῶν παρ' ἡμῖν). Whatever therefore may be thought about other sections of the Fourth Gospel (notably chap. 8) there is no anti-Semitism in John's passion narrative. J. A. T. Robinson interprets the Evangelist's intention similarly: "Writing as a Jew for other Jews, he is concerned from beginning to end to present the condemnation of Jesus, the *true* king of Israel, as the great betrayal of the nation by its own leadership" (*Priority of John*, 273–74). It should further be recognized that there is no question of the Evangelist whitewashing Pilate. On the contrary, he is portrayed as a man who caught a glimpse of the greatness of Jesus, but who had not the moral strength to see that justice was done for him. In that respect he shared in the guilt of those who failed to listen to the truth that Jesus was born to reveal (18:37–38a).

Now here is something on which Christians, whether ecclesiastical leaders, scholars, or the Church at large, should reflect. Israel's misfortune at this time in its history has been paralleled in the Christian Church more times than it may care to think, when the authentic apostolic faith has been more apparent among the humble people of God (the counterpart to those contemptuously viewed by the Pharisees as a rabble under the curse of God, 7:49) than it was among its leaders. There have been periods when the Church would have been unjustly judged by outside observers had they assessed the quality and reality of its faith in the light of the conduct of its highest authorities. So also the realities of the historical situation of the Jewish people, as represented in the Gospel that more fully depicts the inside story of the passion of Jesus than the others, require to be taken into account alike by Christians and Jews. This seems not to have been done by a number of recent scholars, who follow Bultmann's lead in their interpretation of the utterance of the chief priests, "We have no king apart from Caesar" (19:15). On this Bultmann comments: "The answer of the ἀρχιερεῖς (chief priests), and so of the nation's representatives . . . surrenders the messianic claim of the people, *and in that moment the Jewish people surrender themselves*" (665); i.e., they surrender their claim to be the people of God. Acknowledging that a nation cannot be wholly divorced from its leaders' actions, this particular deduction goes beyond warrant. (Many in Bultmann's own nation have been very anxious that others should not identify their people wholly with the Nazi leaders in their policies and actions during the Nazi regime.) Admittedly it is important to recognize that the Fourth Evangelist's account of the relations between Jesus and Jewish leaders of his day is presented in light of the contemporary controversy between the Church and the Synagogue, which was especially acute and painful for Jewish Christians. But it is plain that the Evangelist's own circumstances did not blind him to the fact that the Church's roots, even salvation itself (4:22), were in Israel; and moreover, that up to his time the Church's history was largely that of *Jewish* believers in Jesus as the Messiah of Israel and Savior of the world, together with members of the nations drawn into the Church by *Jewish* preachers. Further, the polemic in his Gospel against "the Jews" who opposed Jesus was not made solely to enable Christians to defend themselves against Jewish polemics, but in hope that many of their opponents might be convinced of the truth of the revelation in Jesus. "New Israel" is not an expression used in the Fourth Gospel for the Church; "Israel made new in the Remnant" would accord better with the standpoint of all four Gospels. But both expressions begin with recognition of the covenant people of God and see the eschatological fulfillment brought about through the crucified Lord as embracing believing Israel and believing Gentiles. John would most surely have had a fellow feeling with Paul in his attitude to his nation that persecuted him, but which he still passionately loved: "God has not given up on his people" (Rom 11:1). Neither did Jesus, who gave himself up for them. Nor did the Fourth Evangelist—his church was mainly Jewish. Nor should we, for they have the promises as well as we, and we belong to one another.

2. The Resurrection of Jesus (20:1–31)

Bibliography

Auer, E. G. *Die Urkunde der Auferstehung Jesu.* Wuppertal: Brockhaus, 1959. **Balagué, M.** "La prueba de la Resurrección (Jn 20, 6–7)." *EstBib* 25 (1966) 169–92. **Beare, F. W.** "The Risen Jesus Bestows the Spirit: A Study of John 20:19–23." *CJT* 4 (1958) 95–100. **Benoit, P.** "Marie-Madeleine et les Disciples au Tombeau selon Joh 20, 1–18." *Judentum, Urchristentum, Kirche.* FS J. Jeremias. Berlin: Töpelmann, 1960. 141–52. ———. *The Passion and Resurrection of Jesus Christ.* New York: Herder, 1969. **Bode, E. L.** *The First Easter Morning: The Gospel Account of the Women's Visit to the Tomb of Jesus.* Rome: Biblical Institute Press, 1970. 72–86. **Cadbury, H. J.** "The Meaning of John 20:23: Matt 16:10 and Matt 18:18." *JBL* 58 (1939) 251–54. **Cassian, Bishop (S. Besobrasoff.)** *Le Pentecôte Johannique.* Paris: Éditeurs Réunis, 1939. **Dodd, C. H.** "Some Johannine 'Herrenworte' with Parallels in the Synoptic Gospels." *NTS* 2 (1955–56) 85–86. ———. "The Appearances of the Risen Christ: An Essay in Form-Criticism of the Gospels." *Studies in the Gospels.* FS R. H. Lightfoot. Ed. D. E. Nineham. Oxford: Blackwell, 1955. 8–35. **Dunn, J. D. G.** *Baptism in the Holy Spirit.* SBT 2d ser. 15. London: SCM, 1970. 173–82. **Evans, C. F.** *The Resurrection and the New Testament.* SBT 2nd series 12. London: SCM, 1970. 116–28. **Fowler, D. C.** "The Meaning of 'Touch Me Not' in John 20:17." *EQ* 47 (1975) 16–25. **Fuller, R. H.** "John 20:19–23." *Int* 32 (1978) 180–84. ———. *The Formation of the Resurrection Narratives.* London: 1972. **Grass, H.** *Ostergeschehen und Osterberichte.* Göttingen: Vandenhoeck & Ruprecht, 1964. 51–73. **Hartmann, G.** "Die Vorlage der Osterberichte in Joh 20." *ZNW* 55 (1964) 197–220. **Hooke, S. H.** *The Resurrection of Christ.* London: Darton, Longman & Todd, 1967. **Künneth, W.** *The Theology of the Resurrection.* London: SCM, 1965. **Lindars, B.** "The Composition of John xx." *NTS* 7 (1960–61) 142–47. **McNamara, M.** "The Ascension and Exaltation of Christ in the Fourth Gospel." *Scrip* 19 (1967) 65–73. **Mahoney, R.** *Two Disciples at the Tomb: The Background and Message of John 20:1–10.* Bern/Frankfurt: 1974. **Mantey, J. R.** "The Mistranslation of the Perfect Tense in John 20:23: Matt 16:19 and Matt 18:18." *JBL* 58 (1939) 243–49. **Michaelis, W.** *Die Erscheinungen des Auferstandenen.* Basel: Majer, 1944. **Neirynck, F.** "Les femmes au Tombeau: Étude de la rédaction Mathéenne." *NTS* 15 (1968–69) 168–90. **Richter, G.** "Der Vater und Gott Jesu und seiner Bruder in Joh, 29, 17." *Studium zum Johannesevangelium.* 266–80. **Riesenfeld, H.** "Zu den johanneischen *ina*-Sätzen." *ST* 19 (1965) 213–20. **Seidensticker, P.** *Die Auferstehung Jesu in der Botschaft der Evangelisten.* Stuttgarter Bibelstudien 26. Stuttgart: Katholisches Bibelwerk, 1968. 122–44. **Turner,**

M. M. B. "The Concept of Receiving the Spirit in John's Gospel." *VoxEv* 10 (1977) 24–42. **von Campenhausen, H.** *Der Ablauf der Osterereignisse und das leere Grab.* Heidelberg: Winter, [3] 1966. **Yates, J. E.** *The Spirit and the Kingdom.* London: SPCK, 1963.

Translation

[1] *Now on the first day of the week* [a] *Mary Magdalene comes to the tomb early,*[b] *while it is still dark, and she sees the stone removed from the tomb.* [2] *So she runs, and comes to Simon Peter and to the other disciple, the one whom Jesus loved, and says to them, "They have taken the Master out of the tomb, and we do not know where they have put him."* [3] *Peter therefore and the other disciple came out*[c] *and went toward*[d] *the tomb.* [4] *The two of them were running together, and the other disciple ran ahead more speedily than Peter, and was the first to reach the tomb.* [5] *Bending down to look in he sees the linen wrappings lying there; he did not, however, go in.* [6] *Simon Peter therefore comes following him, and he went into the tomb, and he saw the linen wrappings lying there,* [7] *and the napkin which had been on his head; it was not lying with the linen wrappings but rolled up in a separate place by itself.* [8] *Then the other disciple, who was the first to come, also went into the tomb, and he saw, and believed;* [9] *for they did not yet understand the Scripture (which said) that he must rise from the dead.* [10] *So the disciples returned again to their homes.*

[11] *But Mary was standing by the tomb, outside,*[e] *crying. While she was still crying she bent down to look into the tomb,* [12] *and she sees two angels in white sitting there, one at the head and the other at the feet where the body of Jesus had been lying.* [13] *They say to her, "Woman, why are you crying?" She says to them, "They have taken away my Master, and I do not know where they have put him."* [14] *After saying this she turned back, and she saw Jesus standing, and she did not know that it was Jesus.* [15] *Jesus says to her, "Woman, why are you crying? Who is it you are looking for?" She, thinking that he was the gardener, says to him, "Sir, if you are the one who carried him away, tell me where you put him, and I will take him away."* [16] *Jesus said to her, "Mary!" She turned and said to him in Hebrew, "Rabbouni!" (which means, "Teacher").*[f] [17] *Jesus said to her, "Do not keep on trying to hold me,*[g] *for I have not yet ascended to the Father.*[h] *But go off to my brothers and tell them, 'I am ascending to my Father and your Father, my God and your God.'"* [18] *Mary Magdalene went and reported to the disciples, "I have seen the Master!" and she told them these things that he had said to her.*

[19] *On the evening of that day, the first of the week, when the doors were locked where the disciples were for fear of the Jews, Jesus came and stood in the midst of them, and said to them, "Peace to you!"* [20] *And on saying this he showed them his hands*[i] *and his side. The disciples therefore became filled with joy when they saw the Lord.* [21] *(Jesus) then said to them, "Peace to you! As the Father has sent me, I also am sending you."* [22] *And after saying this he breathed into them and said to them, "Receive (the) Holy Spirit.* [23] *Whoever's sins you forgive they stand forgiven them;*[j] *whoever's sins you hold back, they remain held back."*

[24] *But one of the Twelve, Thomas, whose name means "Twin," was not with them when Jesus came.* [25] *The other disciples therefore tried to tell*[k] *him, "We have seen the Master!" But he told them, "If I do not see in his hands the marks of the nails, and put my finger into the place where the nails were, and put my*

hand into his side, I will never believe!" ²⁶ *Eight days later the disciples were
again in the house, and Thomas was with them. Jesus comes, though the doors
were locked, and he stood in the midst of them and said, "Peace to you!"* ²⁷ *Then
he said to Thomas, "Bring your finger here, and see my hands; and bring your
hand, and put it into my side, and stop being unbelieving, but believe!"* ²⁸ *Thomas
answered him, "My Lord, and my God!"* ²⁹ *Jesus says to him, "Because you have
seen me you have believed. Happy are they who have not seen, and yet have believed!"*

³⁰ *Now there were many other signs that Jesus did in the presence of his* ^l *disciples
that are not recorded in this book;* ³¹ *but these have been written so that you may
believe* ^m *that Jesus is the Christ, the Son of God, and that through believing you
may have life in his name.*

Notes

^a μιᾷ τῶν σαββάτων. The use of cardinal for ordinal (μιᾷ for πρώτῃ) is Sem. σάββατον in Gr.
means both sabbath and week; this is not so for the Heb. שַׁבָּת (*šabbāt*) in the OT, but it so
developed in later Heb. σάββατα reflects the Aram. שַׁבְּתָא; it should be indeclinable, but as it
looks like a Gr. pl. it became declined like one.

^b πρωΐ is variously interpreted in the Gospels. Mark defines it "the sun having risen" (16:12),
Luke, "at deep dawn" (24:11), Matthew with an ambiguous phrase which may mean "as it was
dawning towards the first day" (28:11).

^c The sing. ἐξῆλθεν with Peter first as subject, followed by ὁ ἄλλος μαθητής, is a frequent
construction in the Gospel. The following ἤρχοντο is also common usage, and should not be
made the basis of conjecture that the reference to "the other disciple" was added later.

^d εἰς can be used in later Gr. for πρός, with the meaning "toward" (Brown, citing ZGB § 97).

^e The presence of ἔξω in the text is uncertain. In ℵ^c B W X etc. it precedes κλαίουσα, in
Dgr^{supp} K L etc. it follows the verb, and it is omitted in ℵ* A and MSS of the OL and OS.
Normally that would suggest that the omission is original, but ℵ has ἐν τῷ μνημείῳ instead of
πρὸς τῷ μνημείῳ, which suggests that ἔξω may have been omitted accidentally. The UBS committee
therefore accepted the first reading as most likely.

^f A good example of conflation is provided in the alternative readings for the translation of
Ῥαββουνί. The overwhelming MS tradition reads Διδάσκαλε, but it^{a r¹} have κύριε, so D it^d read
κύριε διδάσκαλε, and others give that in reverse order. Some MSS add καὶ προσέδραμεν ἅψασθαι
αὐτοῦ (ℵ^a Θ Ψ etc.), clearly a gloss to explain the command of Jesus in v 17.

^g μή μου ἅπτου. Commonly μή with the present imperative calls for the cessation of an act in
progress. BDF speak of the action here as one that has already happened or has been attempted
(§ 336.3). Our translation, "Don't keep on trying to hold me," allows for the situation in which
Mary attempts to do so.

^h τὸν πατέρα alone is read by ℵ B D W it^{b,d,e} etc., but many more MSS add μου after πατέρα
(so p⁶⁶ A K L X Δ Θ etc.). It is most likely that the shorter reading is original and that μου has
been added to match the words of Jesus in v 17b.

ⁱ That Jesus showed his "hands" is an over-literal translation which it is difficult to avoid.
When crucified men were *nailed* (which was not always the case) to a cross the nails were driven
through their wrists, since hands could not bear the weight of the body. But both the Heb.
word for hand (יָד, *yād*) and the Gr. term (χείρ, *cheir*) can include the wrist and the forearm.
One could translate "Jesus showed his hands and wrists," or even use the term "wrists" only,
but showing the hands would reveal the marks in the wrists, and it may be best to leave it so
and explain it in terms of the extension of meaning.

^j Among the profusion of variants for the term ἀφέωνται (read by ℵ^c A D [L] X etc.) the
most important are the present ἀφίενται (B³ K W Δ Θ etc.) and the future ἀφεθήσεται (ℵ^a supported
by MSS of the Latin, Syriac, Coptic, Armenian, and Ethiopic versions). It is likely that the
reading of B* ἀφείονται is a slight corruption for ἀφέωνται (ιο instead of ω). The alternative
readings are best viewed as simplifications that weaken the sense (so the UBS committee).

The meaning of ἀφέωνται in the light of subsequent use of v 23 in church history was raised
by J. R. Mantey in an article "The Mistranslation of the Perfect Tense in John 20:23, Mt 16:19

and Mt 18:18." He maintained that the usual meaning of the perfect tense in Gr., a past action that affirms an existing result, should be recognized as applying to the verbs in the perfect tense in the parallel passages of Matt 16, 18, and John 20. He admits that there are a few rare usages in Gr. literature where a perfect may be translated to imply immediate *future* action, but there are no such usages in the NT. The Matthaean passage should be translated, "Whatever you bind on earth shall have been bound in heaven, and whatever you loose on earth shall have been loosed in heaven." The sentence shows that God does not concur in man's decisions; man is to ratify and obey God's decrees. Presumably the same principle applies to John 20:23. H. J. Cadbury wrote a rejoinder to Mantey's article, "The Meaning of John 20:23, Matthew 16:19, and Matthew 18:18." He pointed out that the six verbs in the perfect tense in the sentences quoted are in the apodosis of a *general condition,* and general conditions are extremely difficult to limit to present, past, or future. The question here is whether a perfect in the apodosis indicates an action or condition prior to the time of the apodosis, and the answer is that it does not. This is seen in 1 John 2:5; James 2:20; Rom 14:23; Rom 13:8, as the grammarians acknowledge. In the two passages of Matthew the future perfects seem to imply a permanent condition rather than a condition prior to the time of the relative clause, and they mean, "Whatever you bind or loose on earth will prove thereafter to have been bound or loosed in heaven." Or, to paraphrase, Matthew's future perfects imply "shall be once for all," and John's perfects "shall be at once." If not the angels, at least the grammarians appear to be on Cadbury's side in this debate.

^{k} ἔλεγον may be an imperf. with conative force, hence "tried to tell."

^{l} The attestation for αὐτοῦ after μαθητῶν is evenly matched with that of its omission; for the inclusion P^{66} ℵ C D L W X Θ Ψ etc., for the omission A B K Δ Π etc. For this reason the UBS committee placed the term in brackets.

^{m} Rarely has the absence of the letter σ in a word caused so much discussion as here. πιστεύσητε, aorist subjunctive, is read in ℵ^c A C D K L W X Δ Π etc., and πιστεύητε, present subjunctive, in P^{66vid} ℵ* B Θ etc. The aorist suggests the action of *taking the step of faith,* the present a *continuance in believing;* the difference has bearing on the purpose of the writing of the Gospel. While the external attestation may be held to support the former rather than the latter reading, the intrinsic likelihood of the reading is bound up with the supposed intention of the Evangelist. The UBS committee therefore set the σ in brackets and left the decision to the reader.

Form/Structure/Setting

1. On the analogy of the summaries of the kerygma that were current in the early Church and its hymns (e.g., 1 Cor 15:3–4; Acts 10:36–43; Phil 2:6–11), it is likely that the account of the sufferings and death of Jesus was already followed by an account of the resurrection. And just as the passion narrative was based on the memory of individual incidents, which were also told separately (e.g., Jesus in Gethsemane and Peter's denials), so there would have been early connected narratives of resurrection appearances of Jesus, and individual stories circulating independently. In the nature of the case, the variety of experiences of the risen Lord gave room for greater diversity in the accounts of the Resurrection. Recent scholars tend to agree that the narratives of the Resurrection in the Fourth Gospel reflect earlier accounts in a pre-Johannine tradition, as well as the Evangelist's revision of them in accordance with his own knowledge and theological understanding.

2. Apart from the conclusion in vv 30–31, chap. 20 describes events of Easter Sunday that took place in the morning, vv 1–18, and in the evening, vv 19–29. Each section can be again divided into two: (*i*) the discovery of the empty tomb, vv 1–10, and the appearance of Jesus to Mary, vv 11–18; (*ii*) the appearance of Jesus to the disciples, vv 19–23, and the appearance to Thomas, vv 24–29. Critical analysis has been directed especially to the

first two narratives (vv 1–10 and 11–18), on the ground that elements within them indicate a complex use of sources.

3. It is immediately obvious that while Mary is described as going to the tomb of Jesus alone, in v 2 she speaks of *"we* do not know . . . ," recalling the synoptic stories of the women at the tomb (but see later, p. 371). Whereas Mary goes back to the disciples to tell them about the stone rolled away from the tomb, she is at the tomb in v 11, with no indication of her return. The faith of the "other disciple," the one whom Jesus loved, is emphasized in v 9, with no hint of its effect on anyone else. Varied suggestions have been made as to the development of the passage. P. Benoit recognized in vv 1–2 a tradition parallel to those in the synoptics, but older. He observed that Luke 24:12 tells of a visit of Peter alone to the tomb, after the report of the women, and returning he "wondered at what had happened." Benoit considers that the Lukan sentence is based on an early pre-Johannine tradition, which lies behind vv 3–10; it told of Peter alone visiting the tomb. Yet Luke 24:24 speaks of "some of those with us" going to the tomb after the report of the women—a hint that Peter was not alone! John has developed his story in a double manner: (*a*) he depicts a "race" between Peter and John to the tomb; this is to be viewed as an explication, not simply an addition ("Here, as elsewhere, the shadow of the other disciple is seen"). (*b*) An apologetic turn is given to the narrative—the sight of the grave clothes shows that there was no mere robbery here. In Benoit's view, the story of Mary Magdalene has also been enlarged by the Evangelist. Earlier it was independent of the preceding narrative and consisted of an appearance to Mary at the tomb; v 11a was followed immediately by vv 14b–18; some parallels are observable with the synoptics (e.g., Matt 28:9–10), but there are original traits which depict not the kerygma of the Resurrection and the empty tomb, but a manifestation of a new state of the risen Lord. The additional vv 11b–14a recount a tradition of an angelic appearance to women at the tomb, parallel to the synoptic accounts (Benoit, "Marie-Madeleine et les disciples au tombeau," 141–49).

This interpretation of Benoit was taken up and developed in various ways. G. Hartmann thinks that *a single story* lies behind vv 1–18. The narrative told of Mary going to the disciples, after which *she and Peter* went to the tomb. Since the Beloved Disciple was introduced by the Evangelist, v 8 originally told of the lack of comprehension of both Peter and Mary. Peter went back to the house, and Mary stayed at the tomb, hence the continuation of the narrative in v 11. The appearance of the angel and that of Jesus are in tension: vv 11b–14a are a later addition by a redactor, vv 14b–16 from the tradition, v 17 from the Evangelist ("Die Vorlage der Osterberichte," 197–209). Schnackenburg follows closely on Hartmann; he agrees that in the narrative Peter and Mary went to the tomb, and that v 8 replaced something like Luke 24:12. The appearance to Mary came from the source; that of the angels was an addition by the Evangelist, their presence giving a heavenly confirmation of vv 6–7 (3:304). Brown makes a minor modification of this approach by suggesting that *three* narratives lay behind the present one; vv 1–2 and 11–13 are thought to be two different forms of a single story; hence, we have (*a*) a visit to the tomb by several women, vv 1–2, 11–13; (*b*) a visit to the tomb by several disciples, including Peter, vv 3–10; the appearance to Mary Magdalene, vv 14–18, parallel to Matt 28:9–10, Mark 16:9–11 (2:999–1004).

Reconstruction of this kind can never be more than tentative, but development of the tradition along these lines is quite plausible, so long as it is recognized that the Evangelist had due reason for his editing. The unity of the passion narrative and resurrection tradition speaks for this; as John supplemented his narrative of the Passion on the basis of his knowledge of events and his theological insight, so he has proceeded in his account of the Resurrection. As a disciple of the Beloved Disciple he would have had good reasons for identifying the other disciple with Peter at the tomb.

4. The appearances of Jesus to the disciples and to Thomas have been subjected to similar critical analysis. The starting point has been the conviction that the two narratives of vv 19–23 and 24–29 are a development from a single narrative. It is urged that (*a*) in vv 19–23 the presence of *all* the disciples is presupposed, (note especially the commission of the disciples in v 21 and the endowment with the Holy Spirit in v 22); (*b*) the story of Thomas develops elements of vv 19–23; (*c*) above all, the episode of Thomas epitomizes the motif of the disciples' unbelief that is present in all the synoptic accounts of the Resurrection (cf. Matt 28:17; Luke 24:11, 27–28, 41; Mark 16:14). Not surprisingly the Thomas story is considered by some to be a creation of the Evangelist to dramatize this theme of doubt (so Dodd, *Historical Tradition,* 145; Lindars, "The Composition of John xx," 143; Brown, 2:1031). The latter deduction does not follow the former. Thomas could have been singled out because he so outrageously embodied the early unbelief of the disciples. Bultmann, followed by Hartmann ("Vorlage der Osterberichte," 216), and Schnackenburg (3:322) believed that the substance of the story was already in the Johannine tradition. Hartmann sought to recreate the story from John's account by observing that v 20a appears unmotivated (contrast Luke 24:39). He suggests that the announcement of Mary Magdalene in v 18 was followed by the blank expression of unbelief in v 25, but set in the plural since it gave the reaction of all the disciples. Then came the account of the appearance of the risen Lord in v 19 (of which v 26 is a doublet), and the invitation in v 27 to all the disciples. In v 20 the Lord shows his hands, etc., and the disciples react with the confession of v 28. The Lord then gives his commission (v 21), imparts the Spirit (v 22), and authorizes the disciples (v 23; "Vorlage," 210–14). This is an ingenious and complicated proposal, and it treats the tradition behind the text with seriousness. Nevertheless it is implausible to represent all the disciples as expressing themselves in Thomas's words, which strike one as a highly individual expression of depressed unbelief that gives way to adoring faith.

A different solution suggests itself, one that arises out of the compressed nature of the narrative in vv 19–23 and its content. The paragraph contains the cardinal elements of the Lord's dealing with his disciples in the Resurrection. He appears to them in such fashion that they know who he is, and rejoice in his presence and his triumph over death (vv 19–20). He gives them a commission to continue his mission which the Father gave to him (v 21). He fulfills the promise of the sending of the Holy Spirit by bestowing him on them (v 22). He authorizes them to declare forgiveness and guilt as they make known his saving grace to man (v 23). These varied elements are set forth in five sentences. It is altogether probable that they were derived from various traditions of the appearances; the last three sayings will have been independent, but together with vv 19–20 they provide a remarkably complete summary of the instruction and actions of the risen Lord. With them the story of Jesus in the Fourth Gospel reaches a genuine τέλος, "conclusion," and vv 30–31 could suitably have followed at once. The Evangelist, however, chose to do otherwise. He added the Thomas episode with two considerations in mind: on the one hand, he wished to epitomize the unbelief of the disciples in the face of the news of the resurrection of Jesus, for such unbelief was a common reaction to the message of the Resurrection (cf. the expostulation of Festus [Acts 26:24] to Paul on hearing his testimony: "Paul, you're mad!"); on the other hand, in recording Thomas's ardent confession of faith he both matched the exposition of Christ the Word of God (1:1–18) in his conclusion of the Gospel and exemplified the faith that the Gospel was intended to elucidate, so fittingly preparing for his declaration of purpose in vv 30–31. The story of Thomas must not be swallowed up in the narrative of vv 19–23. It is a work of art through which the Gospel concludes with dramatic power and an effective appeal to respond to its message.

5. The setting of the events is Jerusalem. Those connected with the tomb of Jesus can be nowhere else, and the link includes the appearance to Mary Magdalene (note the misunderstanding that Jesus was the gardener, a feature which is not secondary and is related to Jewish objections to the Christian proclamation of the Resurrection). This has important bearing on the much debated question as to the location of the resurrection appearances of the Lord. The Evangelist states that the appearance to the disciples took place that evening. Admittedly, it is not connected with a location in the same manner as the events of the morning (Dodd observes that of itself the incident could equally well have happened in Galilee), but the Evangelist has his reasons to set it on Easter Day, in Jerusalem. We may be content to follow his guidance (see Dodd's discussion, *Historical Tradition*, 149–50).

6. The contents of the chapter may be simply stated:

    i.   Mary Magdalene and two disciples visit the tomb of Jesus, 20:1–10.
    ii.   Jesus appears to Mary Magdalene, 20:11–18.
    iii. Jesus appears to the Disciples, 20:19–23.
    iv. Jesus appears to Thomas, 20:24–29.
    v.   Conclusion, 20:30–31.

Comment

MARY MAGDALENE AND TWO DISCIPLES VISIT THE TOMB OF JESUS (20:1–10)

1 The time is given as the first day of the week, not the third day after the crucifixion, as in the early kerygma (1 Cor 15:3–4). Brown suggests that the time of finding the tomb empty was fixed in Christian memory, possibly before the third-day symbolism was perceived (2:980). Strictly, that is correct, but the third-day language will speedily have become current through the memory of Jesus' passion predictions (Mark 8:31 etc.) and the contemporary Jewish significance of the expression. The third day, or after three days, was not necessarily intended literally (cf. Hos 6:2. an important saying for Jews and Christians), but through its use in the OT it was perceived by the rabbis as expressive of deliverance (cf. the dictum in the Midrash on Gen 42:17: "The Holy One, blessed be he, never leaves the righteous in distress more than three days"). If it be asked why the disciples did not recall Jesus' intimations of his coming death and resurrection after three days, some considerations spring to mind at once Despite all that Jesus said about his coming sufferings and the necessity for bearing the cross after him, it would seem that the disciples approached Jerusalem with him in high expectation of the speedy coming of the kingdom of God (Luke explicitly states that, Luke 19:11; consider also the effect of the entry into Jerusalem on the disciples). The dreadful reality of the crucifixion crushed the followers of Jesus beyond measure, and their faith also (cf. Luke 24:21a). Moreover, it is highly probable that Jesus' predictions regarding his resurrection after three days were understood to refer to the resurrection when the kingdom of God came in glory in a short time (note Martha's response to "Your brother will rise," 11:24). The disciples would not have envisaged a personal resurrection of Jesus, apart from the resurrection to the kingdom of God in the last day.

Was Mary alone at the tomb? It is difficult to say. The "we do not know" of v 2 suggests that others were with her. But Bultmann (684 n.1) was persuaded that οὐκ οἴδαμεν is not a genuine plural; it reflects an Oriental mode of speech whereby plural can be used for singular (so G. Daman for Galilean Aramaic, *Grammatik des jüdisch-palästinischen Aramäisch* [Darmstadt: Wissenschaftliche Buchgesellschaft, 1960] 265; and for similar Greek usage E. C Colwell, who provides many instances, *The Greek of the Fourth Gospel,* [Chicago: University of Chicago Press, 1931] 111–12). E. L. Bode thinks that it is a regular mode of the Evangelist's writing, seen, e.g., in 3:2, 11; 9:31; 14:5; 21:24 (*The First Easter Morning,* 73–75). Some of these examples are ambiguous, but it is by no means certain that the Evangelist intended Mary's "we know" to indicate the presence of other women at the tomb with her, as in the synoptic tradition. The impression given by the text is that Mary took one look at the tomb and fled, without looking inside. If she had been joined by the other women, she must have left before they did. Moreover, if the synoptic testimony is to be received, her message was very different from that which they were told to take to the disciples (Mark 16:7 par.).

2 Mary's report suggests the fear that either enemies or robbers had taken the body of Jesus. The robbing of tombs was sufficiently common for official action to be taken against it. A decree of the emperor Claudius (A.D. 41–54), a copy of which was found at Nazareth, ordered capital punishment for those destroying tombs, or removing bodies, or displacing the sealing or other stones (the text is in Barrett's *The New Testament Background, Selected Documents* [London: SPCK, 1957] 15). The Jewish allegation that the body of Jesus was removed by his disciples, mentioned in Matt 28:13–15, is not hinted at in this account, but the theme of robbery continues in the narrative.

3–5 Peter and the Beloved Disciple, in their anxiety, run as speedily as they can to the tomb. The latter runs ahead of Peter and reaches the tomb first. The Evangelist may well have wished to hint that this was not simply

because the Beloved Disciple was a faster runner than Peter; he who was
especially loved by the Lord loved him especially also, and love made him
more fleet of foot. His speedy arrival, however, did not make much difference;
he waited for Peter to arrive before entering the tomb. What prompted the
reticence is not said, but at all events Peter did not share it. His immediate
entry into the tomb accords with his character. He surveys the scene and
observes what is there. The linen wrappings that were around the body of
Jesus were lying in one place, and the napkin was rolled up apart from
them. The details will have been significant to the writer of the source, as
to the Evangelist. Their apologetic implications were noted from early times.
Chrysostom saw their pertinence to the notion of robbery of the tomb: "If
anyone had removed the body, he would not have stripped it first, nor would
he have taken the trouble to remove and roll up the napkin and put it in a
place by itself" (*In Jo. Hom.* 85.4). One may add, nor would he have left
those costly cloths and spices!

Some scholars wish to go further in their deductions from the grave cloths.
Early in this century H. Latham expounded the view that the wrappings
that had been around Jesus lay flat on the tomb's shelf, vacated by him
without disturbing them, and that the napkin that had been about his head
retained its shape; he had an artist draw an impressionist picture to illustrate
the point (*The Risen Master,* [Cambridge: Deighton Bell, 1901] 29–56). This
interpretation has been freshly presented by M. Balagué, who has sought
to set it on a firm exegetical basis ("La prueba de la Resurrección (John 20,
6–7)" *EstBib* 25 [1966], 169–92). E. G. Auer goes further: like K. Bornhäuser
before him (*Die Leidens-und Auferstehungsgeschichte Jesu* [Gütersloh: Bertels-
mann, 1947] 140–41; ET: *The Death and Resurrection of Jesus Christ* [Bangalore:
C. I. Press, 1958] 190–91), he believes that the cloths around the body of
Jesus remained firm on account of the aromatic oils and spices mixed with
them, so retaining their shape as when he occupied them (*Die Urkunde der
Auferstehung Jesu* [Wuppertal: Brockhaus, 1959]). Auer's interpretation clearly
goes beyond the meaning of the Evangelist's language, and with Brown one
must ask. If the evidence was as clear as that, why did Peter not grasp its
meaning at once? (2:1008). The view of Latham and Balagué is consonant
with the text, but whether the Evangelist intended it to be so understood is
more than we can say. The apologetic significance of the narrative could
have a different slant: in Jewish eyes the testimony of women was unacceptable,
hence their report of the empty tomb of small account. That *two men* should
verify the evidence was important, since they could fulfill the Jewish require-
ment of valid testimony according to Deut 19:15. So far as the Evangelist
himself was concerned, he may well have had a simpler interest: Jesus has
forsaken his burial clothes for ever, for he is risen! The Evangelist had penned
the story of Lazarus, and recorded how Lazarus, at the bidding of Jesus,
came forth from his tomb, with the wrappings of the dead still binding him
hand and foot, and the napkin on his head; he had to be freed to take up
life again in this world. Jesus on the contrary left his wrappings in the grave
as a sign of his resurrection into the life of God's eternal order. If this was
plain to the Evangelist, it was otherwise with Peter. As he stood and gazed
on the grave clothes in the tomb, he was totally uncomprehending. The
sign was a mystery beyond his fathoming.

8 To the Beloved Disciple the mystery was of a different dimension. On entering the tomb "he saw, and believed"; he saw not only the wrappings, but their significance: he "believed"! There has been an understandable reluctance of exegetes to give that statement full value. G. Stählin, for example, regarded it as signifying an embryonic and incomplete faith ("On the Third Day," 286). In our Gospel, however, πιστεύω ("believe") when used absolutely, as here, means genuine faith (see, e.g., 5:44; 6:47; 19:35; 20:29). The seeing and believing in the empty tomb is akin to the seeing and believing the "signs" of Jesus (cf. 4:48, and by contrast 10:25–26), and this was a sign from the Lord. That John writes, "*he* saw, and believed" clearly distinguishes the faith of the Beloved Disciple from the incomprehension of Peter (contrary to Bultmann, who maintained that the faith of the Beloved Disciple was shared by Peter, 684).

9 The observation that the disciples did not know or understand the Scripture is so unexpected after v 8 that some have pronounced it a scribal gloss (so Bultmann, 682). That is needless. The lack of understanding of the Scriptures concerning the Messiah's redemptive work is beautifully illustrated in the Emmaus story (Luke 24:25–27, 32) and extended to the whole disciple group in Luke 24:44–47. The plural ἤδεισαν shows that the ignorance of the Scriptures applied to both disciples; in the context, however, it appears to emphasize the disparity between the faith of the one and the incomprehension of the other.

Schnackenburg observes (3:313) that v 9 almost certainly stood in the Evangelist's source, for the formula δεῖ . . . ἀναστῆναι "he must rise," is not found elsewhere in John but is frequent in the synoptic Gospels (note especially the passion predictions, Mark 8:31, etc., and its use in the Lukan resurrection narrative, Luke 24:7, 25–26, 46). In the Lukan passage the death and resurrection is "according to the Scriptures," plural; "the Scripture" in our passage is likely to have the same import, i.e., the testimony of the entire Scripture, rather than that of a single passage.

10 The disciples went "to their homes"; note the plural. In view of 19:27, where εἰς τὰ ἴδια has the same meaning as πρὸς αὐτούς, Bernard assumed that the Beloved Disciple took the news of the empty tomb to Mary, the Mother of Jesus (2:662). The lack of mention of the disciple's sharing his faith at once with his fellow disciples is often mentioned by the commentators. We do not, of course, know that he did *not* do so. The brevity of the resurrection accounts must be remembered. What we do know is the skepticism with which the disciples as a whole met with any notion that Jesus was alive—they even found it difficult to believe when they actually *saw* Jesus (Luke 24:36)! The Beloved Disciple would not have made much of a dent in their armor that morning. It is conceivable that he waited to see what further events should happen that might confirm his intuitive faith before making it known widely.

Are there other motives in the report of the visit of the two disciples to the tomb, beyond those we have mentioned? It is fashionable to talk about the "rivalry" existing between Peter and the Beloved Disciple, and between the churches that adhered to them, and to see this reflected in the episode at the tomb (this view is largely derived from chap. 21). More specifically 20:3–10 is regarded as an attempt to play down that rivalry: the Beloved Disciple reaches the tomb first, but Peter enters it before him. Peter is the first to see the evidence of the grave clothes; the other disciple is the first to believe their testimony (though some would place

them on equality here—they both believed). Bultmann, following Loisy, held that
Peter represented Jewish Christianity and the Beloved Disciple Gentile Christianity.
The Jewish Church was first in time (Peter entered the tomb first), but that does
not signify precedence over the Gentile Church. They both stand equally near
the risen Lord—indeed, faith is even greater with Gentiles than Jews, for the
Beloved Disciple ran faster to the grave! (see Bultmann, 685). There is no warrant
for such an application of the passage. Brown is right in urging that the contrast
between the two disciples should not be magnified; they are represented as friends,
not rivals, throughout the Gospel. There is no depreciation of Peter, not even in
21:15–17, where he is commissioned to care for the Lord's sheep. But admittedly
Peter is not the hero of the Fourth Gospel; the Beloved Disciple has that role,
but his is a primacy of love, and that does not exclude a different primacy of
Peter (2:1006–7; see further R. Mahoney, *Two Disciples at the Tomb*, 250–60; J.
Blank, *Johannes* 3:163).

JESUS APPEARS TO MARY MAGDALENE (20:11–18)

11–12   Mary is at the tomb again. Her weeping now is not because Jesus
is dead, but because his body has disappeared. That kind of loss would be a
concern to anyone at any time, but among Jews of the near Orient at that
time, abuse or outrage of the dead was a shocking thing (cf. the Philistines'
exposure of the bodies of Saul and his sons, and the bravery of the men of
Jabesh-Gilead in recovering them and giving them a proper burial, 1 Sam
31:9–13). It was natural for Mary to fear the worst concerning Jesus. She
now stoops to look into the tomb. For the first time? We do not know. Her
attention, however, is caught not by the grave clothes, as with Peter and
John, but by the sight of two angels. The scene recalls the synoptic accounts:
in Mark 16:5 a "young man" (νεανίσκος) dressed in white appears to the
women; in Luke 24:4 two "men" in flashing clothing; in Matt 28:2–3 an
angel with the appearance of lightning and wearing a garment white as snow.
In all cases (including Mark) the appearance is of angelic beings, for "shining
white garments are the symbol of the heavenly world" (Blank, *Johannes* 3:167).
The presence of the angels is a witness that the powers of heaven have been
at work here. Their position in the tomb, one at the head and the other at
the feet where Jesus had lain, is a reminder of the silent testimony of the
grave clothes, but of another order; it witnesses that *God*, not robbers, has
taken Jesus, for a purpose yet to be revealed.

13–14   The angels do not at once announce the good news that Jesus is
risen. In each of the synoptic narratives they refer in some way to the seeking
of the women for Jesus (in Mark 16:6, Matt 28:5, it is a statement; in Luke
24:5 a question, "Why are you seeking the living among the dead?"). Here
they ask Mary why she is crying, to elucidate the same quest for Jesus. She
tells them, but then turns away from them. Why? Surely there is a better
reason than a clumsy joining of two episodes by the Evangelist, as some
suggest. We are to understand that Mary suddenly becomes aware of the
presence of another near the tomb, and she turns to see who it is. In harmony
with other resurrection narratives, Mary does not recognize the Lord. The
Emmaus couple returning home from Jerusalem had no idea of the identity
of the Stranger who joined them, any more than the disciples fishing in the

lake of Tiberias knew who the man was standing on the shore. Two complementary concepts are involved here In the longer ending of Mark, it is said that the Lord appeared to the two walking to Emmaus "in a different form" (ἐν ἑτέρᾳ μορφῇ, Mark 16:12); and of the Emmaus couple Luke says, "Their eyes were *held* so as not to recognize him," 24:16 (the counterpart to which is that when Jesus breaks bread "their eyes were *opened* and they recognized him," 24:31). Both concepts are of importance for interpreting the resurrection narratives. Westcott made a penetrating observation on the first: "A little reflection will show that the special outward forms in which the Lord was pleased to make himself sensibly recognizable by his disciples were no more necessarily connected with his glorified person than the robes which he wore" (*The Gospel of the Resurrection* [London: Macmillan, [8]1906] 95).

The latter feature is bound up with the revelation of Christ by the Spirit, not without relation to the preparedness of the human spirit. On this Bultmann commented: "It is possible for Jesus to be present, and yet for a man not to recognize him until his word goes home to him" (686). So with Mary: although the question of Jesus was calculated to draw her attention to him, it was insufficient for her to realize that he who addressed her was the one she sought. She assumed that at so early an hour during the Feast only the gardener would be there. She may further have thought that since the tomb was new, he may have removed the body of Jesus from it to another place, without ill will: hence her plea to know where he had placed it that she may take him away. Then it was that the revelation took place. It needed no more than the utterance of her name, in the way Jesus used to speak to her. Mary correspondingly answered Jesus in the way she used to address him, marked only with the astonishment that suited the circumstance: *"Rabbouni!"* All the love and faith and joy of which her illuminated heart and mind were capable were poured into that word: *"Teacher!"* The Shepherd had called his sheep by name, and the sheep heard and joyfully responded (John 10:3). Jesus thereby re-established the personal relationship that Mary thought she had forever lost; only now it was to be set on a deeper level than had been possible when Mary knew Jesus as "Rabbi."

Hoskyns, in an unaccustomed lapse, seriously misleads in his note on *Rabbouni* through an unguarded use of Str-B (2:25). He states that in the older Jewish literature *rabboni* (an alternative form of the term) is hardly ever used in reference to men, *never* in addressing them, but is reserved for address to God; Mary's use of the term therefore is parallel to Thomas' confession of faith in v 28 (543). Hoskyns omitted to mention that the term is used in address to men in the Palestinian and Jerusalem Targums. *Rabbouni* is one of various extended forms of *rabbi*. According to Lindars it indicates greater respect and deference than the simple form, and he adds, "John is quite correct in supposing that a woman would use this form, whereas male disciples use the simple *rabbi* (1:38)" (606). Albright said that *rabbouni* is a caritative of *rabbi*, implying "my dear (or little) rabbi" ("Recent Discoveries in Palestine and the Gospel of St. John," in the Dodd FS, *The Background of the NT. . . ,* 158). This meaning would not, however, suit the only other instance of *rabbouni* in the New Testament, Mark 10:51, where Bartimaeus asks Jesus for his sight. The Evangelist translates Mary's use of it simply as "Teacher." That suits the context perfectly, and should be accepted. (It confirms that κύριος in v 2 should not be rendered "Lord" but "Master"; Mary was not in a position to ascribe to Jesus at that point the significance contained in *Kurios* in the Church's confessions.)

The apparently innocent confusion of Mary about the gardener may have been an important feature of the story in the estimate of the Evangelist. H. von Campenhausen saw it as related to a Jewish alternative to the allegation that the disciples stole the body of Jesus, mentioned by Matthew as current in his day (Matt 28:12–14). Tertullian cites a passage in which Jews scoff at Jesus and his disciples, who believed that their Master had risen from the dead, whereas in fact the gardener had taken him away in order that the many visitors should not spoil his salad plants! (*Spect.* 30). Another more developed form of the incident tells that "Juda the gardener," as an honest man, foresaw the threatening swindle and therefore took the body away. When the disciples went around with their tales about the resurrection, causing the Jews great embarrassment, he was able to produce the missing body. This was then publicly dragged through the streets of Jerusalem, and the Christian lies became obvious to everybody (see Krauss, *Das Leben Jesu nach jüdischen Quellen* [1902] 170 ff.). Von Campenhausen thought that the simpler version of the story is earlier than the longer one, and that the Jews saw that it was more likely to be believed than that the disciples stole the body of Jesus. The Evangelist, knowing of it, told the story of Mary and the disciples at the tomb, drawing attention to the testimony of the grave clothes, and the appearance of *the risen Lord,* not the gardener, to her. See *Der Ablauf der Osterereignisse und das leere Grab,* 32–35.

17 There is a clear contact between Mary's attempt to take hold of Jesus and the scene in Matt 28:9, where the women to whom Jesus appears "seized" (ἐκράτησαν) the feet of Jesus and prostrated themselves before him. In this context the term κρατέω is virtually synonymous with ἅπτομαι (so Bultmann, 687 n.1). It is even possible that Matthew's statement about the women generalizes the action of Mary. Remembering Eastern customs, we are probably to assume that Mary did just what Matthew describes: she prostrated herself before Jesus and sought to clasp his feet. It was an act of joyful adoration combined with a simple desire to hold Jesus, not because she feared to lose him again, but in a perfectly normal expression of affection. Blank remarks, "Contact belongs to the primary ways in which man in this world becomes aware of outward reality. But meeting and contact with the risen Jesus takes place on another plane, namely in faith, through the Word, or in the Spirit" (170–71).

Bernard's suggested emendation of μή μου ἅπτου to read μή πτόου "do not be afraid," to avoid the difficulty entailed in the next clause and the comparison with the Thomas episode (671) is ingenious and plausible, and is even supported by the μή φοβεῖσθε of Matt 28:10. Nevertheless, like all other suggested emendations of the NT text, it should not be resorted to if sense can be made of the extant passage.

The rest of v 17 is one of the most perplexing sections in the Gospel. The difficulty relates especially to the concept of ascension presented in it. Mary is given a message to the disciples that Jesus is about to ascend to the Father; why not rather that he is risen from the dead? If ascension is Jesus going to the Father, how can that be separated from his death and resurrection as a "lifting up" to the Father? Mary is told not to attempt to hold on to Jesus because he has not yet ascended; Thomas is invited to thrust his hand into the wounds of Jesus. Does the ascension take place between the two occasions?

We begin with the observation that v 17 is reminiscent of Matt 28:10. There the message for the disciples is that they are to go into Galilee to meet Jesus (it is in the angelic declaration of 28:7 that the women are to tell them that Jesus is risen). Matthew's message thus *assumes* the resurrection of Jesus; *so does the message through Mary*. The last thing that the disciples have learned about Jesus is that his body is missing; here they are to learn that he is alive, and on his way to his Father to complete his saving task.

We should further observe that the emphasis in the word to Mary is not the negative "I am not ascended," but the positive "I am ascending." Lagrange pointed out that v 17 should not be split into two halves, as was done by Westcott and others, but be seen as one, and its unity maintained. He wrote: "There is only a phrase with an opposition (indicated by the time) between ἀναβέβηκα, 'I have ascended' and ἀναβαίνω, 'I am ascending.' The message given to Mary Magdalene is but a parenthesis, and the force of δέ must apply to ἀναβαίνω, thus: 'Do not insist on touching me, for I am not yet ascended to my Father; however, I will not delay much to go. . . . This is what you must say to my brothers, that they may be better prepared than you have been to understand the nature of my presence' (511). The paraphrase "I will not delay much to go" is better rendered *"I am on my way,"* since the force of ἀναβαίνω is "I am in process of going" (so BDR § 324, 3, modifying BDF § 323, 3). That suggests that the "ascension" to which Jesus refers, which has not happened but which is on the way, relates especially to the *work* that Jesus is accomplishing in the completion of his saving task, i.e., in his mediation of the saving sovereignty of God to the world. This work of his, for which he dies and rises and ascends to the Father, has been made known to the disciples, especially in the Upper Room discourses. We recall his promise to prepare a place for the disciples in the Father's house (14:2); to banish their sadness and fill them with joy through reunion with them (14:18–19; 16:16–22); the new relationship whereby the Father and the Son will make their home with them (14:21–23); the new era of effective prayer and power in their service for God (14:12–14; 16:23–24); and above all the bestowal of the Paraclete-Spirit, who will take the place of Jesus and expound his revelation to them and enable them to carry out their mission.

The virtual replacement of the language of resurrection with that of ascension is an indication that the two are fundamentally one, and indissolubly bound with the death of Jesus. Schnackenburg thinks it possible that in the Evangelist's source the exhortation of Jesus to Mary not to keep holding him was that she might go and tell the disciples that he was *risen,* and that the Evangelist modified the language to convey the full import of Jesus' resurrection as one with Jesus' total saving work: "For him, everything is compressed into Jesus 'hour', therefore it is not really possible to dissect the event into death, resurrection, lifting up and installation in heavenly glory" (3:318–19). The ascension in this sense, accordingly, is not to be located at a date in the future; it is in process. It is noteworthy that the vision of ascension narrated in Acts 1:9 is set by Luke in the Gospel in closest association with Easter Day (Luke 24:50–51; the impression is given that it happened on Easter Day, but that is through Luke's compression of his narrative). The Acts narrative is a parabolic action, signifying the conclusion of the Easter appearances. For John the "ascending" of Jesus is the conclusion of his "hour" whereby the salvation of the kingdom of God is wrought. (See further the excellent expositions of this passage by Brown, 2:1011–17, and Schnackenburg, 3:317–20.)

The message through Mary is more than the simple announcement that Jesus ascends. "Go to my brothers," Jesus says, "and say, 'I am ascending to my Father and your Father, and my God and your God.'" Clearly the "brothers" are not the brothers of the flesh (contrary to Dodd, *Historical Tradition*, 147, 324), but the disciples (as Mary understood, v 18). We may therefore interpret them as believers who by virtue of the "lifting up" of Jesus and the impending bestowal of the Spirit are to become sharers in his sonship with the Father. The distinction between the only Son of the Father and the sons who by the Spirit share his sonship is naturally assumed. But as Brown points out, it is not the difference but the likeness that is proclaimed here: "The statement of the Johannine Jesus is one of identification and not of disjunction" (2:1016). By way of illustration, Brown cites Ruth 1:16: "Your people shall be my people and your God my God." The parallel is apt, but it should be noted that while it is Ruth who chooses to come under Naomi's God, it is the Redeemer who has chosen to come to us, and in virtue of his total saving activity, living, dying, rising and ascending, makes us the sons of the Father and the people of God.

18 Mary departs and delivers her message to the disciples. How did they receive it? According to the tradition in Mark 16:10, they refused to believe her, just as in Luke 24:13 the women's story of seeing Jesus alive appeared to them as "idle tales." It was urgently necessary for Jesus himself to deal with them!

JESUS APPEARS TO THE DISCIPLES (20:19–23)

19 The occasion is closely paralleled in Luke 24:36–42, also set on Easter evening, after the arrival of the Emmaus couple to report that they had seen the Lord. The feature of the locked doors, mentioned at the beginning, shows the ability of Jesus to presence himself in any place; "passing *through* locked doors," however, is hardly appropriate to denote that power, or the ability of the risen Jesus to "materialize" himself (Barrett, 567); the Lord reveals himself where he wills, in a mode beyond comprehension, and it is well for us to acknowledge the limits of our understanding here. The reference to the disciples' fear of the Jews as motive for the locked doors may have been added by the Evangelist; the greeting of Jesus is then the more significant: "*Peace* to you!" It is well known that that was (and still is) the everyday greeting of Jews in Palestine—"*Shalom* to you!" But this was no ordinary day. Von Rad wrote, "Seldom do we find in the Old Testament a word which to the same degree as *shalom* can bear a common use, and yet can also be filled with the concentrated religious content far above the level of the average conception" (*TDNT* 2:402). Never had that "common word" been so filled with meaning as when Jesus uttered it on Easter evening. All that the prophets had poured into *shalom* as the epitome of the blessings of the kingdom of God had essentially been realized in the redemptive deeds of the incarnate

Son of God, "lifted up" for the salvation of the world. His "Shalom!" on Easter evening is the complement of "It is finished" on the cross, for the peace of reconciliation and life from God is now imparted. "Shalom!" accordingly is supremely the Easter greeting. Not surprisingly it is included, along with "grace," in the greeting of *every* epistle of Paul in the NT.

20 Similarly here, as in Luke 24:39, Jesus shows the disciples his hands (and his *feet!*), but in order to allay the terror of the disciples. Bultmann thought that the action is unmotivated in this context, where no mention of fear is made (691). On the contrary, the revelation of the wounds of Jesus was a means of letting the disciples realize that it was he himself, their crucified Lord, who stood before them. That clear identification was to become critically important for the Church to maintain; the Crucified is *the risen Lord*, in the fullest sense of the term, and the risen Lord is *the Crucified*, the flesh and blood Redeemer, whose real death and real resurrection accomplished salvation for the whole person and the whole world. The disciples therefore were "filled with joy" as they grasped that he who stood before them was their own Master, alive from the dead. The promise of Jesus, made to them in the Upper Room, that he would "come" to them (14:18) and turn their grief into joy (16:20–22) was now fulfilled. Joy is a fundamental blessing of the kingdom of God (e.g. Isa 25:6–9; 54:1–5; 61:1–3), and "Joy is the basic mood of Easter" (Blank, 178).

21 Each Gospel ends with a commission of the risen Lord. The forms of these commissions are given by the Evangelists, who convey their content with emphases that accord with their own insights and situations. This manifestly applies to the compressed version of the commission made known by our Evangelist, not least by reason of its echo of 17:18. It is introduced by the repeated greeting, "Peace to you"; the Lord had already bequeathed his peace to his disciples in prospect of his impending death (14:27), and now he communicates it as he sends them to proclaim its accomplishment for all and gift to all. The special contribution made by the Evangelist in this form of the commission is indicated in two words, "As . . . so . . . ." "*As* the Father . . . *so* the Son." The sending of the Son into the world by the Father is a constant theme of this Gospel It reflects in measure the principle of Jewish authorization "One who is sent is as he who sends him." In the person of the Son, in his words and deeds, the Father himself is present, his words declared and his actions performed. The time has now come for the disciples to go forth into the world as the representatives of the Lord; thereby the declaration of 13:20 will become operative as men and women receive the Christ in the mission of the disciples and the God and Father who sent him. This concept, however, is deepened in two respects. The mission of the Son has not finished with his "lifting up" to heaven. "As the Father has sent me" implies a sending in the past that continues to hold good in the present. Such is the force of the Greek perfect tense, and Westcott perceived this long ago: "The mission of Christ is here regarded not in the point of its historical fulfilment (*sent*), but in the permanence of its effects (*hath sent*). The form of the fulfilment of Christ's mission was now to be changed, but the mission itself was still continued and still effective. The apostles were commissioned to carry on Christ's work, and not to begin a new one" (2:349–

50). That insight has been freshly appreciated by recent scholars. The risen
Lord does not hand over his mission to his disciples and leave them to it;
"he only gives the disciples a share in it . . . with the assistance of the Paraclete"
(Schnackenburg, 3:324). It is this setting that is presupposed in the striking
words of 14:12–14: the disciples go forth to their mission and seek the Lord's
aid therein, and in response to their prayers *he* will do through them "greater
things" than in the days of his flesh, "that the Father may be glorified in
the Son"—in the powerful mission that *he* continues! The second point of
added depth is the link established in the juxtaposition of the declaration of
mission and the bestowal of the Spirit. The Paraclete-Spirit was promised
earlier to the disciples, assuring them that they would thereby be enabled to
carry out their task of witness in a hostile world (see especially 15:25–26;
16:8–11). The risen Lord, in associating his disciples with his continuing
mission in the world, bestows the Spirit, through whom his own ministry in
the flesh was carried out in the power of God.

This interpretation, shared by most exegetes, is severely modified by P. Seidensticker, who understands v 21 in the light of v 23. Admitting that "this sending
of Jesus by the Father is all-encompassing," he adds, "the pericope, however, views
it mainly as conveying special authority to forgive sins." In his conviction the motif
of forgiveness is not to be linked with the picture of Jesus in the synoptic Gospels,
for love of sinners is not the characteristic of the Fourth Gospel but rather the
exaltation of the Revealer; the saying of Jesus (in v 21) is spoken within the fellowship
of the disciples and does not extend beyond the area of the Church: "It answers
to a pastoral concern of the Johannine churches." "While Matt 28:16 ff. has understood the universal spread of the Church as the decisive content of the sending
of Jesus, the Johannine church concentrates on its own spiritual life in the fellowship
with Christ and God" (*Die Auferstehung Jesu in der Botschaft der Evangelisten,* 132).
The rooting of the commission of the disciples in the mission of Jesus *to the world*
alone suffices to put this view out of court, for the Son was sent with a revelation
and for a redemption to be accomplished for the whole world, as cardinal utterances
like 1:29; 3:16; and 12:31–32 show. Moreover, the Spirit who is given with the
commission is the Spirit who is to testify with and through the disciples to the
world that is not only beyond the Church, but hostile to it, and at times actively
opposed to it. Seidensticker has interpreted v 21 in the light of v 23; it would
appear methodologically more correct to interpret v 23 in the light of vv 21–22.

22 "After saying this" links the saying with the commission given in the
previous verse; the accomplishment of the mission is the primary purpose
of the giving of the Spirit. The unusual vocabulary of the sentence suggests
that it came from the Evangelist's source; that probably explains the reference
to the Spirit as πνεῦμα ἅγιον, "holy Spirit," without the definite article. Whatever
the reason for that in the source, in the Gospel it is not to be interpreted in
an impersonal sense, or simply as *a* gift of the Spirit (contra Westcott, 350).
The important saying, 7:39, also has "spirit" without the definite article, following a clause in the same sentence with it.

"He breathed *in*" is perhaps needlessly literal, but it harks back to the
unusual term in Gen 2:7 and Ezek 37:9–10. In the former passage God
"breathed into the nostrils of Adam the breath of life," so completing the
creation of man. In the latter the prophet calls to the wind to "breathe into
these slain that they may live," after which "breath came into them, they

came to life and rose to their feet, a mighty host." This is a vision of the return of the Jewish people from the lands ("the graves") to which they had been transported, and their quickening by the Spirit on their return to their own. The symbolism is a clear application of the notion of resurrection, and that in an eschatological context (deliverance for the kingdom). It is not surprising that it came to be viewed as a representation of resurrection in the time of the kingdom. In v 22 the symbolic action primarily represents the impartation of life that the Holy Spirit gives in the new age, brought about through Christ's exaltation in death and resurrection. New age and new creation are complementary ideas in eschatological contexts. Strictly speaking, one should not view this as the *beginning* of the new creation but rather as the beginning of the *incorporation of man* into that new creation which came into being *in the Christ* by his incarnation, death, and resurrection, and is actualized in man by the Holy Spirit (cf. 2 Cor 5:17).

The significance of this act, accordingly, is not to be limited as though it were solely for the disciples in relation to vv 21 and 23. All three sentences have to do with the whole Church, like the promises of the Spirit earlier in the Gospel. Neither is v 22 to be regarded as a symbolic promise of the gift of the Spirit later to be bestowed, i.e., at Pentecost (as Theodore of Mopsuestia maintained; his view was condemned by the fifth ecumenical Council at Constantinople in A.D. 553). Likewise it is inadequate to view the gift of Christ as a *partial* bestowal of the Spirit who is to be *fully* given at Pentecost, an idea expressed in a variety of ways. Calvin considered "the Spirit was given to the apostles now in such a way that they were only *sprinkled* with his grace and not *saturated* with full power" (*Gospel according to St. John, 11–21* [Edinburgh: Oliver and Boyd, 1961] 205, cited by Turner, "Receiving the Spirit in John's Gospel," 32). Bengel viewed the gift as an "earnest" of Pentecost, Westcott as *the power of new life* anticipating the *power for ministry* (350–51); Bruce inverts the order, seeing the Easter gift as *empowerment for ministry*, to be followed by the Spirit's *gift of new life* at Pentecost.

It would appear that the fundamental mistake in the examples of exegesis in regard to this passage is the dividing of Easter from Pentecost, and the consequent placing of a wedge between the Fourth Evangelist and Luke. Barrett expressed the view that it is impossible to harmonize the account of a special bestowal of the Holy Spirit with that contained in Acts 2 (570). But who said that it was "special"? It is commonly conceded that we have two representations of the sending of the Holy Spirit to the Church, because of two ways of looking at Christ's redemptive deeds: (*a*) that in the Fourth Gospel, which sees his death, resurrection, and ascension as essentially one, and the gift of the Spirit bound up with the three in the Easter event; (*b*) and that in Luke, which places the Ascension forty days after the Resurrection and the outpouring of the Spirit on the day of Pentecost. The differences appear so marked, it has seemed to many either that one Evangelist has modified the tradition in the interests of his theology, or (more commonly) that there were two occasions of the Spirit's coming. On the latter hypothesis it is thought that the Fourth Evangelist was aware of this, for he has made no mention of the Paraclete in his resurrection narrative, knowing that that enduement came in the Pentecostal event (so Porsch, 376–77; J. D. G. Dunn,

Baptism in the Holy Spirit, 177–78; M. M. B. Turner, who sees John 20:22 as the complement and fulfillment of 17:17–19, "Receiving the Spirit," 34). By contrast to these views it is a questionable procedure to distinguish the coming of the *Spirit* to the disciples from the coming of the *Paraclete* to the Church. If the Spirit is bestowed, the Paraclete has come. The gift of the Spirit is made to the disciples in the context of the handing to them of the commission; the Paraclete was promised to enable them to fulfill it; accordingly the Spirit who is given is the Paraclete. That the Evangelist has not used the term is of no consequence; the reality without the word is plain.

Here we should recall what was written in the section on the composition of this chapter. John is not recording in vv 19–23 something that took place in five minutes on the first Easter Sunday evening. In briefest compass he summarizes the acts of the risen Lord, bringing together sayings and happenings uttered and performed in the Easter period. The gift of the Spirit could have been at any time within the Easter period. Significantly, Luke binds the sending of the Spirit on the Day of Pentecost to Easter; Peter's explanation as to what has taken place states: "The Jesus we speak of has been raised by God, as we can all bear witness. Exalted thus at God's right hand, he received the Holy Spirit from the Father and poured out this which you see and hear" (Acts 2:32–33). *The outpouring of the Spirit on the Day of Pentecost is the act of the risen Lord!* It is important to note that both John and Luke are capable of accommodating chronology to theology when it seems right to do so. John's setting the cleansing of the temple in his programmatic chap. 2 is a singular example, done for the best of theological reasons. And Luke has taken a leaf out of John's book, by concentrating his resurrection narratives into his account of Easter Day without any hint of extension of time, *even including the story of the Ascension in the Easter narrative.* If we did not have the Acts of the Apostles we would most surely assume that Luke, like John, set the Ascension within Easter. Theologically he has done so, for the Ascension to him is the last Easter appearance of Jesus.

What, then, is our conclusion? The Fourth Evangelist does not specify the Easter events according to chronology. He could perfectly well have been aware of the Pentecostal tradition and write exactly as he has done. But there is no question of viewing the sending of the Spirit as taking place at Easter *and* at Pentecost. It is one or the other, in view of the nature of each Evangelist's presentation of the event. In the judgment of the present writer, the Lukan narrative in Acts 2 is an authentic account of the coming of the Spirit at the celebration of the giving of the Law, when the company of the new covenant received power to proclaim the message of the new covenant in tongues for the whole world to hear, just as the word of the old covenant was so proclaimed amidst flames of fire (the narrative is shot through with the symbolism of the festival, just as John 7–8 reflects the celebration of Tabernacles; see J. H. E. Hull, *The Holy Spirit in the Acts of the Apostles,* 48–56). The Fourth Evangelist wrote one volume only, not two, as Luke. What he wrote concerning the coming of the Spirit was theologically and historically sound, as, I am persuaded, was that written by his brother in the Lord, Luke.

23 One cannot deal with this saying without recalling the similar Matt

16:19b, with its parallel in Matt 18:18. The saying is clearly independent, and has been given varied contexts by the Evangelists, or their sources. Our Evangelist has set it in the context of the resurrection commission of Jesus. Significantly its appearance in Matt 16:19b has the nature of a charge to an apostle.

The majority of commentators still interpret the Matthaean saying in the light of the rabbinic use of the terms "binding" and "loosing" for determining whether actions are "forbidden" or "allowed" by the Law, and so view the saying as relating to a kind of magisterial office. Certainly that usage was current in Rabbinism, but the terms were also applied to imposing or relieving the "ban" on offenders, i.e., their exclusion from or readmittance to the synagogue (see Str-B, 1:738–47). There is increasing conviction among other scholars, however, that Schlatter's judgment is right, that "this mode of speech plainly shows that originally the formula 'loose and bind' describes the activity of the judge" (*Der Evangelist Matthäus*, 511). The language refers to the judge's declaration of the guilt or innocence of persons brought before him, who are "bound" to or "loosed" from the charges made against them. In Matt 16:19b it would denote Peter's authority to declare people forgiven or condemned according to their response to the message of the kingdom of God. With this Jeremias agrees: "The authority of the messengers includes both the communication of salvation and the imposition of judgment. It is the judge's authority to acquit and to pronounce guilty that is described by this pair of opposites and the synonymous phrases 'bind and loose' and 'forgive and retain sins.' As pairs of opposites are used in Semitic languages to describe the totality, these pairs of words mean that the messengers receive total authority" (*New Testament Theology*, 238). The saying therefore, alike in Matthew and in John, is fittingly placed in a context of commission to disciples. Interestingly, while the Matthaean saying is set in the ministry of Jesus, it has in view Peter's work in the era following the Resurrection (Peter was certainly no rock-man on whom the Lord could build his church in the period approaching his passion!). John's context is specifically that of the commission of the *risen* Lord in v 21 and the gift of the Spirit in v 22. It entails therefore the double context of the continuance of the mission of Jesus through his disciples in the world, and the continuance of that mission through the Holy Spirit to the world in and with the disciples. (This latter aspect is the theme of 15:25–26; 16:8–11.) With the double context, there is a double aspect of the mission: that of declaring salvation and judgment. The Gospel makes it plain that Jesus was sent primarily to reveal God and to redeem mankind: "God did not send the Son into the world to condemn the world, but that the world might be saved through him" (3:17). But the rejection of the revelation and of the Revealer inevitably entails a negative judgment upon the rejectors. So we have the paradoxical saying, at the close of the narrative of the healing of the blind man: "For judgment I came into this world, that those who do not see should see, and that those who see should become blind" (9:39). The ministry itself concludes in the lifting up of Jesus, which is declared to be the judgment of this world and its prince (12:31)—condemnation for those who range themselves with the crucifiers of the Christ, and forgiveness for those who receive his word. This process of judgment continues through the witness of the followers of Christ and through the Spirit of Christ who works with and through them. Disciples proclaim forgiveness of sins and so entry into the saving sovereignty of God through the redemption of Christ, and judgment on those who reject the revelation and redemption of Christ.

The question is often raised whether any allusion to baptism is present in v 23. In the light of the missionary commission of Matt 28:19, the record of the mission preaching in the Acts of the Apostles, and the association of forgiveness of sins with baptism in the letters of the NT, it is likely that baptism is *assumed* here, as in Luke 24:46–47; cf. Acts 2:38. Some interpreters are more emphatic. Gardner-Smith wrote: "The apostles are here commissioned to grant or refuse remission of sins, that is, to grant or withhold the privilege of baptism. It is in keeping with what we know of early Christian mission preaching to suppose that its aim was to secure candidates for baptism, so that here we have in other words the exact equivalent of the commission recorded in the first gospel" (*The Narratives of the Resurrection* [London: Methuen, 1926] 84). The language of the first sentence requires revision in light of the link in the NT between proclamation of the gospel, hearing of faith, repentance, and baptism, but the sentiment of the quotation is otherwise sound. That raises a further question, namely, whether the saying is limited to entry into the Church or whether it applies also to life within the Church. Undoubtedly it has the mission to the world primarily in mind, but this Gospel is directed to the Church, wherein believers stand continually in need of forgiveness of sins, and discipline at times has to be exercised regarding offending members. For that reason the parallel Matthaean saying is placed also in a church context (Matt 18:18). How John 20:23 operated in the Johannine churches we cannot tell, but it is not impossible that it followed an application like that in the Matthaean communities. There is no evidence that the power to forgive sins or discipline offenders attached to officers in the churches, but we do recall the role played by Peter in the incident of Ananias and Sapphira (Acts 5:1–11) and the demand of Paul that the Corinthian church come together to discipline an immoral member in the congregation (1 Cor 5:1–5). When church organization is sufficiently developed to ordain officers, it is inevitable that they play a part in such processes. From this statement in v 23 the Roman Catholic Church has evolved the sacrament of Penance. Protestants find this difficult to accept, not to say repugnant to their thinking. It is significant, however, that in the area of pastoral counseling, when dealing with sin and guilt, an authoritative word of forgiveness is required from a representative of the Lord of the cross and resurrection. The churches have need to learn from one another.

JESUS APPEARS TO THOMAS (20:24–29)

24–26 Thomas has featured in the Gospel before, in 11:16 and 14:5. There he is seen as less a skeptic than a loyal but pessimistic follower of Jesus, ready to die with him if need be, but slow to comprehend and ready to say so (14:5). His response to his fellow disciples concerning the resurrection of Jesus is an exaggerated expression of the attitude they manifested to the

women who said that they had seen Jesus. But the conditions he lays down
for believing are unreasonable. They are an example of the attitude condemned by Jesus in 4:48. "After eight days" the Lord appears in the same
manner as before, or on the "eighth" day, i.e., the following Sunday (this
according to the Jewish mode of reckoning, counting the first and the last
days in the period). The language will have reminded early readers of their
own meetings for worship on the first day of the week, marking the day
when Jesus rose from the dead.

The expression "the Lord's Day" (Rev 1:10) had just such a nuance of worship.
It arose out of a custom in the Middle East, in Asia Minor as well as Egypt, of
naming a day in honor of a ruler. In Egypt, in the time of Ptolemy Euergetes,
the twenty-fifth day of each month was called "king's day," in honor of his ascending
the throne of his father on the twenty-fifth day of Dios. In various areas of Asia
Minor a day was named "Sebaste," i.e., "Emperor's Day," at first one day in the
month and then, in some parts at least, a day a week (Thursday). This precedent
led Christians to claim Sunday as the day when the real *kurios* rose from death to
the sovereignty of the universe. "The Lord's Day" became the day for celebrating
the accession of Jesus, the risen Lord, to the throne of God. The slightly later
Epistle of Barnabas is witness to this: "We celebrate with gladness the eighth day in
which Jesus also rose from the dead and appeared and ascended into heaven"
(15:9).

27 The Lord whose care extends to his people at all times has heard
the declaration of Thomas, and takes up his challenge. As he extends his
hands, with the invitation to touch them and for Thomas to put his hand in
his side, he adds a saying which is half rebuke and half appeal: "Stop being
unbelieving, and show yourself a believer!" Did Thomas extend his finger
and hand, as he was invited? The tradition early arose that he did, and that
others did so with him. Ignatius wrote: "I know and believe that he was in
the flesh even after the resurrection; and when he came to Peter and his
company he said to them, 'Lay hold and handle me, and see that I am not
a demon without body.' And straightway they touched him, and they believed,
being joined to his flesh and his blood" (*Smyrn.*, 3.2). The scene in which
Thomas extends his hand to touch the Lord became a favorite theme for
later artists. Nevertheless it is unlikely that Thomas did any such thing; otherwise the Evangelist would have made the point that Thomas became convinced
when he *touched* the body of the risen Lord. But v 29 speaks only of Thomas
seeing the Lord. The impression given by the narrative is that Thomas was
overwhelmed by the appearance of the Lord and his words to him, and
without any further demonstration he burst out with his confession.

28 His statement is not simply a mode of address to Jesus, in the vocative
("O my Lord and my God!"), still less an exclamation, to the praise of God,
according to Theodore of Mopsuestia ("My Lord and my God!"); that view
was proscribed at the fifth ecumenical Council in A.D. 553. Rather it is a
confession issuing from the depths of Thomas' soul: "You are my Lord and
my God" (so Bruce, 394). So it comes about that the most outrageous doubter
of the resurrection of Jesus utters the greatest confession of the Lord who
rose from the dead. His utterance does not simply acknowledge the reality
of the resurrection of Jesus, but expresses its ultimate meaning, i.e., as revelation of who Jesus is. Yet it is not an abstract theological definition concerning

the person of Christ. The personal pronoun is of vital importance: "*my* Lord, and *my* God." He confesses *to* the risen Jesus that he belongs to him as his willing subject; he adores him and henceforth will serve him as he deserves. And if the flash of inspiration in this moment of revelation extended so far, he may have included the thought that this revelation of who Jesus is has taken place in his exaltation to the right hand of God through his death and resurrection and ascension, and that he, Thomas, is included in the redemption achieved by that event. Certainly the reader is expected to take that further step of acknowledgment of Jesus. At all events, in so confessing Jesus "Thomas fulfils the Lord's words, 'That all may honour the Son, even as they honour the Father' (5:23), and human faith perceives the truth stated in the first verse of the Prologue to the gospel, 'and the Word was God' " (Hoskyns, 548).

29 With AV/KJV, RV, ASV, NEB, NIV, we have translated the opening words of Jesus to Thomas as a statement. The USB text, in agreement with WH, Nestle[26], RSV, read it as a question. Lindars considers that 1:50 and 16:31 favor understanding v 29a also as a question (646), but the present context is different. Barrett remarked, "In this solemn and impressive pronouncement Jesus does not ask questions but declares the truth" (573). Schnackenburg agrees, and points out that with Thomas' confession the theme of doubt is over. The saying of Jesus describes the faith of Thomas and that of believers who have not "seen" in verbs in the perfect tense, which indicates a firm faith; and v 19b better follows on a statement than on a question (334). The emphasis in v 29, of course, is not on Thomas but on those who have not "seen." They have not had the privilege of the disciples in seeing Jesus alive from the dead, nor of having their faith quickened in the extraordinary manner granted to Thomas. Theirs is a faith called forth by the word of the Gospel; but it is none the worse for that, for their trust in the Lord revealed through the Word is of special worth in his eyes. Their commendation is set forth in a beatitude, a declaration of happiness in the sight of God that conveys a revelation. There is a number of such in the synoptic Gospels, especially in Matt (in addition to those in the Sermon on the Mount, see 11:6; 13:16; 24:46; and note Acts 20:35). The Fourth Gospel contains only one other beatitude besides this, namely 13:17, and curiously both have an admonitory note (in this case directed to the privileged like Thomas). Yet the effect of this beatitude is to apply the lesson of Thomas to all readers of the Gospel: Happy are they who, without having had Thomas' experience share Thomas' faith! Happy, indeed, for "faith has an immediate access to the person of Jesus Christ, the Revealer, and on that account has its own certainty" (P. Sickenberger, 138).

    An appealing statement attributed to Rabbi Simeon ben Laqish (*ca.* A.D. 250), is worthy of inclusion, although frequently cited. "The proselyte is dearer to God than all the Israelites who stood by Mount Sinai. For if all the Israelites had not seen the thunder, and the flames, and the lightnings, and the quaking mountain, and the sound of the trumpet, they would not have accepted the Law and taken upon themselves the kingdom of God. Yet this man has seen none of all these things, yet comes and gives himself to God. Is there any who is dearer than this man?" (*Tanḥ*. 6, 32a; see Str-B, 2:586).

CONCLUSION (20:30–31)

30 Scholars who believe that the Evangelist incorporated a "signs source" into his Gospel usually view this passage as the conclusion of that source. Bultmann thought that the Evangelist had no difficulty in using it for the conclusion of the whole Gospel, since for him "signs" and word are interchangeable; the whole Gospel therefore can be comprised under the term "signs" (698). This is a questionable position to take. The "signs" of the first twelve chapters are specifically actions of Jesus, generally miraculous, which find their exposition in discourses; it is a confusion of terminology to place the discourse material under the umbrella of signs. Where, then, are the signs of the second part of the Gospel? Apart from Dodd's belief that the "lifting up" of the Son of Man in death and resurrection is the supreme sign, there is much to be said in favor of viewing the resurrection appearances as signs, particularly the last appearance to Thomas. The statement that Jesus did "many other signs" is then comprehensible. It is evident from a comparison of this Gospel with the synoptics that other miracles were known in the circles of those who fashioned the traditions, and it is only to be expected that there were others that they did not record. John restricted his choice of signs to a group that were especially instructive. (To a lesser extent, the synoptic Evangelists pursued a similar policy; cf. S. H. Hooke: "The authors of the Synoptic Gospels, although they have not explicitly stated it, as the Johannine author has, have selected with the same end in view, out of a great body of material preserved orally in the kerygma, or in writing, certain acts which Jesus was believed to have done" [*The Resurrection of Christ*, 75]).

31 "These have been written *that you may believe*"; the Gospel is a testament of faith, written to quicken faith. But in what sense? In the *Notes* mention was made of the uncertainty as to whether the verb "believe" was originally an aorist subjunctive ($\pi\iota\sigma\tau\epsilon\acute{\upsilon}\sigma\eta\tau\epsilon$) or a present subjunctive ($\pi\iota\sigma\tau\epsilon\acute{\upsilon}\eta\tau\epsilon$); the evidence is evenly balanced. Strictly speaking, the former should indicate making an act of faith, putting one's trust in Jesus as the Messiah, etc.; the latter, a continuing to hold the faith already reposed in Jesus. The former represents an evangelistic intention in writing the book; the latter, a desire to build up Christians in the faith. It is increasingly recognized, however, that a decision like this can hardly rest on a fine point of Greek grammar, not least in view of the fact that the Evangelist does not always keep the rules in his use of tenses. H. Riesenfeld pursued another path, in the area of syntax. He examined the sentences in the Gospel and I John which use ἵνα to express purpose; he found that in the latter the sentences were intended to show the Christian readers the true meaning and implications of their faith in Jesus (see 1 John 1:3,4; 3:11, 23; 5:13, and 2 John 5, 6). In the Gospel similar statements appear in the Upper Room discourses (13:15, 19, 34; 14:19; 15:11, 12, 17; 16:33; 17:13). These would imply that the Gospel, like the letter, was written for the benefit of Christians ("Zu den johanneischen ἵνα-Sätzen," 213–20). Scholars have been impressed with this argument and have increasingly inclined to believe that John's Gospel was primarily directed to the edification of Christians. It is hardly necessary to oppose that view. The Gospel, like the Bible as a whole, was written for the sake of the people of God, and it has been preserved by them through the centuries. But the Bible is also a very powerful witness to the Christian faith for non-believers, as the Bible Societies throughout the world can testify; and so is the Gospel of John, as a multitude of evangelistic agencies have experienced. The primary and the secondary purposes run close together. Bultmann, however, considered that the Evangelist would not have been greatly concerned whether his readers were Christians or not, inasmuch as faith can never be taken for granted, but must be perpetually renewed, and therefore must continually hear the word anew (698–99). That is a consideration that Christians must ever bear in mind with regard to their own commitment and growth.

The confession that the Evangelist would lead the uncommitted to make and the committed to maintain is that *Jesus is the Christ, the Son of God*. That may appear as an unexpected reduction of the confession of Thomas, but it depends on the content read into the titles. For Jews, "Messiah" and "Son of God" would be synonymous, the latter being understood in adoptionist terms in line with the second Psalm, where the king at his coronation enters on the status of the Son of God. In this Gospel *Son of God* is the key concept of the relation of Jesus to God, being strictly synonymous with the absolute use of "the Son"; consequently the term *Messiah* also is raised in significance. He is the king of the saving sovereignty who belongs to the new creation, and the inscription on the cross implies that he achieves his kingdom in the exaltation via the cross to the right hand of God. The content of Christological faith in v 31 is not to be viewed as a lower Christology than that of Thomas' confession, but must be understood in its light and filled out by it. And the end of such confession of Jesus, Messiah and Son of God, is "life in his name": the eternal life of the new age, "eschatological life," the life of the world to come lived in this life by virtue of the Redeemer's gift and in union with him.

J. Blank wrote of vv 30–31: "This is the shortest summary of Johannine theology. If one wished to explain every concept of this concluding remark in its full significance one would have to read through the whole Gospel again" (191). And yet again! The end of the Gospel, as the beginning, leads into still, deep waters.

Explanation

1. The resurrection narratives of John 20 end with a beatitude on those who have not seen but have believed. Such confessors of Christ are viewed to be like the proselyte who has not been given to stand at the foot of Sinai and see its awful wonders, yet who worships God. Bultmann found in the episode of Thomas and the command to Mary, "Stop trying to touch me," an implied critique of the Easter narratives: "The miracles of the substantial and mundane appearance of the Risen Lord, which in v 30 are comprehended under the term σημεῖα, 'signs,' have only the relative worth of *semeia* generally, and their real significance is a symbolic one. Consequently there is something peculiarly ambiguous and contradictory attaching to the Easter narratives. For in truth, if contact with physical hands is denied, how can seeing with physical eyes be permitted?" Bultmann concluded that as a miracle is a conces-

sion to the weakness of man, so is the appearance of the risen Jesus a concession to the weakness of the disciples. The Easter stories can claim only a relative worth. Their significance is symbolic of the fulfillment of the promise "I am coming to you" (14:18). The event is not the fulfillment itself; the "day" when disciples "see" Jesus and know that he is in the Father and they in him (14:20) is *the eschatological day that breaks in at any time for the believer* (687–91, 695–96).

This view of the resurrection narratives is due to Bultmann's existentialist approach to theology. His stress on encounter with the living Lord is accompanied by a lack of interest in the event itself, from which nevertheless, Christian experience takes its rise. His answer to the question 'How, then, do we come to believe in the resurrection as an event of salvation?" is "Because it is proclaimed as such." "The crucified and risen Christ encounters us in the word of proclamation, nowhere else. It is precisely faith in this word that is the true Easter faith" (*Kerygma and Myth*, tr. R. H. Fuller, ed. H. W. Bartsch [London: SPCK, 1953] 50).

Bultmann wished to be rid of the dependence of Christian faith on historical proofs, which in the nature of things can never be final. But this should not lead to devaluing the witness given in the Gospel to the resurrection of Jesus. Naturally the Gospels do not claim that the disciples *saw* the Resurrection take place; they saw the Lord after the event; the event and the witness to it must be distinguished. W. Künneth called the Resurrection "the primal miracle," God's act in Jesus that established the new reality of life in Christ. It was a creative act, parallel to the primal miracle of creation. But such an act of God calls for its revelation, *and it has been given*. "The primal miracle of the resurrection has also a face towards history" (*The Theology of the Resurrection*, 73–81). The Lord therefore revealed himself to witnesses, able to attest to the world the good news of God's redemptive act for the life of the world. That redemptive "act," of course, was not confined to Easter; it included the life, ministry, and death of the Son of God. But Easter let in a shaft of life from heaven upon the whole. The resurrection appearances were not concessions to human weakness; they were revelations of God's action in Christ for eternal salvation. Through the witness borne to those revelations we may learn of God, be emancipated from the shackles of sin, and begin to live in his fellowship.

2. The confession of Thomas to Jesus "My Lord and my God," is startling in its starkness, and is rightly regarded as the culmination of the revelation of God in Christ recorded in the Fourth Gospel. It needs to be set in its context, for it is by no means isolated. The affirmation "The Word was with God and the Word was God" is followed by the equally startling statement *"And the Word became flesh . . .* and we saw his glory, such glory as befits *the Father's only Son"* (1:14), but we are so accustomed to the saying it ceases to have its impact on us. In this Gospel we have been made aware that the account of the ministry of Jesus is the unfolding story of *how* the Word made flesh revealed his glory. He is shown as the Son of Man, and Son of God, come from God to reveal God and redeem man. Those who "saw" but did not believe alleged that he made himself equal with God (5:18). The mistake of such people lay in assuming that he gave himself that status,

whereas he emphasized his total dependence on the Father, who accomplished
his works and made known his words in and through him (5:19–26). The
nature of the relationship of the Father and the Son is expressed in the
dictum "I and the Father are one" (10:30), and is explained in terms of
mutual indwelling, "the Father in me and I in the Father" (14:9–11). By
consequence, "Anyone who has seen me has seen the Father" (14:9). This
revelation of the Father in the Son reaches its apex in the "hour" of Jesus,
which in the light of Easter proves to be his death-resurrection-ascension to
the presence of God. The eschatological nature of that event (cf. 12:31–32)
means that the "return" to the Father entails the assumption of sovereignty
with the Father. It is no accident that the status of Jesus as "Messiah" is
emphasized in his Passion; it is as King of the Jews that he is lifted up and
enters on his reign at the right hand of God, where he is King not alone of
Jews, but of all nations. Jesus thus is seen to be the Mediator between God
and man—in revelation, redemption, and rule.

Thomas' confession, accordingly, could be made only after the Easter event
and the revelation of the risen Lord. The key term of his confession is really
kurios, Lord. For that elastic term, which can extend from polite address to
one's fellow ("Sir") to the acclamation of God Almighty (*kurios* = *adonai* =
yahweh), receives its fullest connotation when applied to Jesus in the Resurrection. It is instructive to observe the progress in the use and significance
of *kurios* in chap. 20. Mary says to the disciples, "They have taken away *the
Lord"* (v 2), where *kurios* is equivalent to *rabbi,* "teacher"; it is an identification
of the Jesus whom they knew. Mary even addresses Jesus with such a word
when she recognizes him as risen from the dead (v 16). Her report after
the appearance of Jesus to her, "I have seen *the Lord,"* still keeps within that
orbit. Only its significance has grown, certainly for the reader, since Jesus is
now the *risen* Master. John's record of the joy of the disciples on seeing *the
Lord* is, of course, his own report, suitable to the context. Finally the utterance
of Thomas shows who the Risen One is: the Lord who is God. The Son of
God-Son of Man-King of Israel is now seen to be the *kurios* in the fullest
meaning of the term as applied to God.

The background to this application of *kurios* to God is complex. Of prime
importance is its appearance in the translation of the OT into Greek, where
it renders various terms for God (אדון, *ʾādôn;* אדני, *adônāi;* אלהים, *ʾelohîm;*
יהוה, *yahweh*); the expression κύριος ὁ θεός frequently renders יהוה אלהים,
yahweh ʾelohîm. Of particular importance is its use in Jewish worship and
prayer, for *kurios* was early applied in Christian confessions and hymns (cf.
the primitive confession, "Jesus is Lord" [*kurios*] used at baptism, Rom 10:9,
and the hymn in Phil 2:6–11, where the confession "Jesus Christ is Lord" is
to be the universal acclamation). The use of the term in the Hellenistic world,
alike for gods and men, could not but be present to the consciousness of
Christians, and that not only in the Gentile churches. Their answer to the
claims made on behalf of the pagan divinities is recorded in 1 Cor 8:5–6:
"If there be so-called gods, whether in heaven or on earth—as indeed there
are many 'gods' and many 'lords'—yet for us there is one God, the Father,
from whom all being comes, toward whom we move; and there is one Lord,
Jesus Christ, through whom all things came to be, and we through him."

That answer applied with especial seriousness to the claims of the emperors of Rome, especially in Asia Minor, where emperor worship was enthusiastically espoused and the Church was numerically strong. Domitian, who was emperor when the Fourth Gospel and the Book of Revelation were written, demanded recognition of himself as *dominus et deus noster*, "Our Lord and God" (a favorite title of his when announcing executions: "It has pleased our Lord and God . . ."). The Christian use of *kurios* naturally did not arise through the clash of loyalties to Christ and Caesar, but it was firmly set over against the claims of Caesar. The Book of Revelation was written to strengthen Christian resolution, and to make known what it means that Jesus is "King of kings and Lord of lords" (Rev 19:16). It is not to be forgotten that the book emerged from within the Johannine school! In the churches served by the Gospel and the Apocalypse, the confession of Thomas played a significant part in strengthening the faith of the Christians and directing them to the Lord of the cross and resurrection. It performs a similar service to this day.

IV. Epilogue: The Mission of the Church and Its Chief Apostles (21:1–25)

Bibliography

Ackroyd, P. R. "The 153 Fishes in John XXI.11—A Further Note." *JTS* 10 (1959) 10. **Agourides, S.** "The Purpose of John 21." *Studies in the History and Text of the New Testament.* FS K. W. Clark. Ed. B. L. Daniels & M. J. Suggs. Salt Lake City: University of Utah, 1967. 127–32. **Bacon, B. W.** "The Motivation of John 21:15–25." *JBL* 50 (1931) 71–80. **Benoit, P.** *The Passion and Resurrection of Jesus Christ.* 289–312. **Boismard, M. E.** "Le chapître xxi de saint Jean: essai de critique littéraire." *RB* 54 (1947) 473–501. **Brown, R. E.** "John 21 and the First Appearance of the Risen Jesus to Peter." *Resurrexit, Actes du Symposium international sur la Résurrection de Jésus.* Rome: 1970; Rome: Libreria Editrice Vaticana, 1974. 246–60. ———. Donfried, K. P., Reumann, J. eds. *Peter in the New Testament: A Collaborative Assessment by Protestant and Roman Catholic Scholars.* Minneapolis: Augsburg; New York: Paulist, 1973. **Braun, F. M.** "Quatre 'signes' johanniques de l'unité chrétienne." *NTS* 9 (1962–63) 153–55. **Cassian, Bishop (S. Besobrasoff).** "John xxi." *NTS* 3 (1956–57) 132–36. **Chapman, J.** "We Know That His Testimony Is True." *JTS* 31 (1930) 379–87. **Cullmann, O.** "The Breaking of Bread and the Resurrection Appearances." In *Essays on the Lord's Supper* by O. Cullmann & F. J. Leenhardt. Ecumenical Studies in Worship. Ed. J. G. Davies and A. R. George. London: Lutterworth, 1958. 8–16. ———. *Peter: Disciple, Apostle, Martyr.* New York: Meridian Books, 1958. **Dodd, C. H.** "Note on John 21.24." *JTS* 4 (1953) 212–13. **Emerton, J. A.** "The 153 Fishes in John xxi.11." *JTS* 9 (1958) 86–89. ———. "Some NT Notes." *JTS* 11 (1960) 329–36. **Grant, R. M.** "One Hundred Fifty-three Large Fishes." *HTR* 42 (1949) 273–75. **Grass, H.** *Ostergeschehen und Osterberichte.* Göttingen: Vandenhoeck & Ruprecht, ³1964. 74–85. **Jonge, M. de.** "The Beloved Disciple and the Date of the Gospel of John." *Text and Interpretation.* FS M. Black. Ed. E. Best and R. McL. Wilson. Cambridge: CUP, 1979. 99–114. **Klein, G.** "Die Berufung des Petrus." *ZNW* 58 (1967) 1–44. **Lee, G. M.** "John 21.20–23." *JTS* 1 (1950) 62–63. **Marrow, S. B.** *John 21—An Essay in Johannine Ecclesiology.* Rome: Gregorian University, 1968. **McEleny, N. J.** "153 Great Fishes-Gematriachal Atbash." *Bib* 58 (1977) 411–17. **Pesch, R.** *Der reiche Fischfang.* Düsseldorf: Patmos, 1969. **Rissi, M.** " 'Voll grosser Fische, hundertdreiundfunfzig': Joh 21, 1–14." *TZ* 35 (1979) 73–89. **Romeo, J. A.** "Gematria and John 21:11—The Children of God." *JBL* 97 (1978) 263–64. **Shaw, A.** "The Breakfast by the Shore and the Mary Magdalene Encounter as Eucharistic Narratives." *JTS* 25 (1974) 12–26. ———. "Image and Symbol in John 21." *ExpTim* 86 (1975) 311. **Smalley, S. S.** "The Sign in John 21." *NTS* 20 (1974) 275–88. **Spicq, C.** ʼΑΓΑΠΗ *dans le Nouveau Testament.* Paris: Gabalda. 3:230–37. **Thyen, H.** "Aus der Literatur zum Johannesevangelium." *TR* 42 (1977) 211–70. ———. "Entwicklungen innerhalb der johanneischen Theologie und Kirche im Spiegel von Joh 21 und der Lieblingsjünger Texte des Evangeliums." *L'Évangile de Jean.* Ed. M. de Jonge. 259–99.

Translation

[1] *After this Jesus again revealed himself to the disciples at the sea of Tiberias; and he revealed himself in this way.* [2] *Simon Peter and Thomas (whose name*

means "Twin"), Nathanael of Cana in Galilee, the sons of Zebedee, and two others of his disciples were together. [3] Simon Peter says to them, "I'm going fishing." They say to him, "We'll come with you too." They went out and got into the boat, and that night they caught nothing. [4] Now when day had broken, there stood Jesus on[a] the shore; the disciples, however, did not know that it was Jesus. [5] Jesus then says to them, "Boys, you haven't by chance caught any fish, have you?"[b] They replied to him, "No." [6] He said to them, "Throw the net to the right side of the boat, and you will find some."[c] They threw it therefore, and now they did not have the strength to haul it in because of the number of the fish. [7] That disciple whom Jesus loved said to Peter, "It is the Lord!" Simon Peter on hearing that it was the Lord, tied[d] his outer garment around himself, for he was practically naked, and threw himself in the sea. [8] But the other disciples came with the boat, for they were not far from land, about one hundred yards, dragging the net with the fish. [9] When they got ashore they saw a charcoal fire there, with fish[e] lying on it, and bread. [10] Jesus says to them, "Bring some of the fish that you have just now caught." [11] Simon Peter, therefore, went aboard and dragged the net to land full of great fish, one hundred and fifty-three of them, and although there were so many the net was not torn. [12] Jesus says to them, "Come and have breakfast." Now none of the disciples dared to inquire, "Who are you?" for they knew that it was the Lord. [13] Jesus comes and takes the bread and gives it[f] to them, and similarly the fish. [14] This was now the third occasion that Jesus was revealed to the disciples after he had been raised from the dead.

[15] When they had finished breakfast Jesus says to Simon Peter, "Simon, son of John, do you love me more than these others do?"[g] He says to him, "Yes, Lord, you know that I love you." He says to him, "Take care of my lambs." [16] He says to him again, a second time, "Simon, son of John, do you love me?" He says to him, "Yes Lord, you know that I love you." He says to him, "Look after my sheep." [17] He says to him the third time, "Simon, son of John, do you love me?" Peter was pained that he had said to him for the third time, "Do you love me?" And he says to him, "Lord, you know everything, you know that I love you." Jesus says to him, "Take care of my sheep."

[18] Amen, amen I tell you, when you were young,[h] you used to put on your own belt and you used to walk where you wanted to; but when you grow old you will stretch out your hands, and someone else[i] will put on your belt, and take you where you do not want to go." [19] Now he said this to signify the kind of death by which he was to glorify God. And after saying this he told him, "Follow me."

[20] Peter turned round and saw following them the disciple whom Jesus loved, the one who at the supper had leaned back against his breast and asked, "Master, who is the one who is to betray you?" [21] Peter then, on seeing him,[j] says to Jesus, "Lord, and what about him?" [22] Jesus says to him, "If I should will that he remain[k] until I come, what is that to do with you? You follow me." [23] The report therefore spread abroad among the brothers that that disciple was not going to die. But Jesus did not say to him that he was not going to die, but, "If I should will that he remain till I come, (what is that to do with you?)"[l]

[24] This is the disciple who bears witness about these things and who wrote these things, and we know that his witness is true.

[25] Now there are many other things which Jesus did as well; if they were written one by one, I do not think that the world would have room for the books that would be written.[m]

Notes

ᵃ For εἰς τὸν αἰγιαλόν (read by B C E G H K P S W etc.) some MSS have the more "correct" ἐπὶ τὸν αἰγιαλόν (so ℵ A D L M U X etc.); the latter is clearly a scribal improvement.

ᵇ μή expects a negative answer, or expresses a doubt, or both. See Moulton, *Prolegomena*, 170 n.1. He cites a modern Gr. ballad for παιδία addressed to soldiers, meaning "lads." For τί . . . ἔχετε as meaning "have you *caught* anything?" see Bernard, 2:696.

ᶜ After εὑρήσετε P66 ℵ Ψ vgᵐˢˢ add οἱ δὲ εἶπον· δι' ὅλης νυκτὸς ἐκοπιάσαμεν καὶ οὐδὲν ἐλάβομεν· ἐπὶ δὲ τῷ σῷ ῥήματι βαλοῦμεν, i.e., "but they said, We toiled through the whole night and caught nothing, but at your word we shall throw it," clearly introduced from Luke 5:5.

ᵈ While it is possible to translate τὸν ἐπενδύτην διεζώσατο as "he put on the outer garment," i.e., a tunic, the verb διαζώννυμι more properly means "gird oneself," i.e., tuck one's clothes in a girdle or belt. Lagrange (525) suggests that Peter, while fishing, was wearing a kind of smock or overall and nothing else (hence "virtually naked") and that he belted himself so as to be able to swim better, as well as to be more presentable ashore.

ᵉ The author of this chapter uses προσφάγιον (v 5), lit., "something to eat," but usually a fish relish eaten with bread, ὀψάριον, a diminutive of τὸ ὄψον, cooked food, tidbit, but most commonly of fish, taken with bread, and ἰχθύς (v 10) as synonymous in meaning. Brown suggests that the variety of terms for fish reflects the combination of the two different stories of the miraculous catch of fish and the meal of fish and bread (2:1073). Certainly the ὀψάριον of v 9 represents fish for eating, but in the next sentence it is used for fish caught, just as in v 5 προσφάγιον denotes fish which the disciples had *not* caught! The interchangeability of terms is a feature of the author's style and is observable in a complex manner in vv 15–17.

ᶠ Instead of καὶ δίδωσιν, D f r¹ (syrˢ) read εὐχαριστήσας ἔδωκεν, an interesting accommodation of the text to the Lord's Supper by one who viewed it as a eucharistic meal; cf. Mark 14:23 par. and John 6:11.

ᵍ The difference between the terms for love in the conversation between Jesus and Peter led Westcott to assume that the changes were deliberate: whereas Jesus uses the higher term for love (ἀγαπάω) Peter lays claim only to the feeling of natural love (φιλέω). But when Jesus puts the question the third time, he adopts Peter's word, as though he would test the truth of even the lower love that Peter professed, and it was for this reason that Peter was grieved, namely that Jesus appeared to doubt the reality of even that love which he had professed (2:367–69). Bernard examined the use of the two verbs in the Fourth Gospel and concluded that whatever distinction they may have had elsewhere, in the Gospel they are synonymous. Both terms are used of God's love for man (3:16; 16:27), of the Father's love for the Son (3:35; 5:20), of Jesus' love for men (11:5; 11:3), of the love of men for men (13:34; 15:19), and of the love of men for Jesus (8:42; 16:27). Since the LXX Syr., and OL translations use both verbs indifferently, Bernard drew the inference that "we must treat ἀγαπᾷς and φιλεῖς in vv 15–17 as synonymous, as all patristic expositors do" (2:702–4). With this almost all exegetes concur, with two recent exceptions. J. Marsh asserted that whereas Bernard proved the point of rough synonymity, that does not prove that the words are used synonymously in this passage (*Saint John*, 672). Spicq also insisted that the distinction should be maintained here: "The subject is not a private conversation or a moral lesson given to a disciple, but the establishment of Peter at the head of the Church, his primacy; and the Saviour claims from him not an affection of a friend but the religious love of ἀγάπη, which constitutes the life itself of his Church" ('ΑΓΑΠΗ, 3:233). Lofty as this sounds, it does not take seriously the habit of the author of this chapter to use synonyms. We have already noticed his treatment of προσφάγιον, ὀψάριον, and ἰχθύς as equivalents, despite their original differences in meaning. So also in vv 15–17, apart from the use of the two verbs for love, we find two verbs used for the shepherd's care for his sheep, βόσκω and ποιμαίνω, and two or even three nouns for the sheep, ἀρνία, πρόβατα, and προβάτια (the MS support for the last is good, but not unanimous). It is difficult to believe that the author intended any distinction of meaning in these varied verbs and nouns; the same applies to the two verbs for love.

ʰ νεώτερος frequently loses its comparative sense and simply = "young man"; see Bauer's *Lexicon*, 536.

ⁱ For the singular ἄλλος σε ζώσει καὶ οἴσει (B C*ᵛⁱᵈ K X etc.) the plural is read by some MSS, ἄλλοι σε ζώσουσιν και οἴσουσιν (so C² MSS of syr and cop), presumably on the assumption that several will engage in the task; yet others substitute either ἀποίσουσιν (ℵᶜ W³³,⁵⁶⁵) or ἀπάγουσιν (D itᵈ), "will lead you off" as a criminal.

k For Ἐὰν αὐτὸν θέλω μένειν, "If I wish him to remain . . ." the Clementine Vulgate with b c r¹ Tat read Sic eum vole manere . . . , "I wish him to remain *thus*," (*sic* for *si*); d ff² VgWW read *si sic,* similarly D reads οὕτως after μένειν. On this see Metzger, 256–57.

¹ τί πρὸς σέ, is omitted in ℵ* 565 etc. itᵃ ᵉ syrˢ, but it is included in ℵ¹ A B C* W Θ Ψ and the majority of MSS. The shorter text may be due to the desire of copyists to emphasize the main element in the sentence. While most in the UBS committee wished to retain the phrase, it is put in brackets to show its uncertainty in the text.

ᵐ At various times in Christian history v 25 has been thought to be a marginal note which became incorporated in the text (so in various scholia prior to the eighth century, Westcott, 2:377; Brown, 2:1125). Tischendorf thought that it was originally omitted from Codex Sinaiticus (ℵ) and added by a corrector. Closer examination of the text has shown that the addition was by the original scribe, who corrected himself. Whether his omission had been accidental or due to his using another MS cannot be known. There is, however, insufficient reason for viewing the passage as a later addition to the original text of chap. 21.

Form/Structure/Setting

1. In the estimate of the majority of NT scholars, chap. 21 is an addendum to the Gospel, whether it be described as an appendix, a postscript, or an epilogue, and whether it be put to the account of the Evangelist or to a later editor of the Johannine school. It is emphasized that the beatitude of 20:29 fittingly closes the accounts of the resurrection appearances of Jesus and that 20:30–31 seems clearly to bring the Gospel to its close. So sure was Lagrange of the latter feature that he proposed that 20:30–31 be moved to its present place (250). Reasonable as this suggestion may appear, it merely serves to clarify the realities of the situation. For 21:1–23 would not be in place after the Thomas incident, and still less immediately after 20:19–23. Chap. 20 has been carefully structured to give a brief but *total* picture of the Easter story: the finding of the empty tomb by Mary and its confirmation by two disciples; the appearance of Jesus to Mary and that to the disciple group; their commission by the risen Lord, reception of the Holy Spirit, and solemn authorization in the proclamation of the gospel—all this forms a succinct summary of the events of the First Easter. The appearance to Thomas has a special motive: with his confession of Jesus the theology of the prologue is given definitive expression, and the beatitude on all readers of the Gospel who believe is pronounced; this naturally leads to a statement making known the purpose of the Gospel—that Thomas' faith might be shared by its readers, and so the eternal life which is at the heart of the revelation in the Gospel might be gained by all who believe. Accordingly, it is not merely the unsuitability of chap. 21 following on 20:30–31 that has to be faced: it is rather that the twentieth chapter in its form, structure, and purpose is conceived as a complete presentation of Jesus in the resurrection. It needs no complementation. The remark in 20:30 about the many other *signs* that Jesus did could extend to the resurrection *appearances* also, for the Evangelist chose not to write more than he has done. Had he planned to record the appearance(s) to Peter and his colleagues narrated in chap. 21 he would have composed chap. 20 differently.

If therefore the Evangelist himself added chap. 21, there must have been an important reason for its composition, not apparent when he wrote the Gospel. The most compelling ground could have been the death of the Beloved Disciple after the writing of chaps. 1–20 and the consequent dismay that it

caused among the Johannine churches; questions may also have arisen concerning the distinctive nature of the Johannine witness in relation to that of
churches in which Peter was viewed as the leader of the Church. It is, however,
simpler to assume that another than the Evangelist wrote the chapter, since
it has an emphasis on the situation of the Church and its leaders beyond
anything in the body of the Gospel. This includes the meaning of the "sign,"
which relates to the mission of the Church, not to the Christ and his salvation,
as in the signs recorded and explained in the ministry of Jesus (see A. Shaw,
"Image and Symbol in John 21," 311). The issues admittedly are complex,
as is apparent in the differences of opinion as to the linguistic phenomena
of chap. 21 in relation to those of 1–20, and the significant challenge to
contemporary critical views from H. Thyen (see his discussion in "Aus der
Literatur zum Johannesevangelium," *TR* 42 [1977] 213–61, and "Entwicklungen innerhalb der johanneischen Theologie . . . ," in *L'Évangile de Jean*, ed.
M. de Jonge, *BETL* 44 [1977] 259–99), who believes that the Evangelist himself
is the "redactor" who penned the chapter as an integral part of the Gospel.
On the question of the authorship of chap. 21 we refrain from offering any
further judgment.

2. The structure of the chapter is clear: (*i*) an appearance of Jesus to the
disciples by the sea of Tiberias (= Galilee), when a miraculous catch of fish
takes place and Jesus invites the disciples to a meal, vv 1–14; (*ii*) a painful
conversation between Peter and Jesus, vv 15–17; a prophecy of Peter's martyrdom, vv 18–19; a statement as to the destiny of the Beloved Disciple, vv
20–23; (*iii*) a conclusion to the chapter, which also rounds off the whole
Gospel. The impression is given that the entire narrative takes place as a
continuous single event, but as in chap. 20 that may be due to the compressed
presentation of the writer. There are indications that more than one episode
may have been brought together here. It is increasingly believed that vv 1–
14 may be composed of *two* appearances of Jesus, one telling of a fishing
miracle and the other of a meal of Jesus with his disciples. The conversation
of Jesus with Peter may well have taken place in the "appearance to Peter"
referred to in 1 Cor 15:5 and Luke 24:34; the prophecy of his martyrdom
is perhaps more likely to have been given apart from his rehabilitation by
Jesus; the saying about the future of the Beloved Disciple would certainly
have very suitably followed on the prophecy of the martyrdom, but it is
eminently likely that it circulated in the churches as a separate tradition and
could have been brought to its present position by the editor.

3. The analysis of vv 1–14 is sufficiently complex to call for separate mention.
That it formed a complete section in itself is indicated by v 14. Bauer proposed
a simple division: vv 1–8, telling of the catch of fish at the risen Lord's direction;
vv 9–13, describing a meal of the risen Jesus with his disciples (213). Bultmann
thought that the original narrative told of one event only, namely, in vv 2–
3, 4a, 5–6, 8b–9, 10–11a, 12; this includes the catch of fish but excludes the
prepared meal and special role of Peter (702–4). R. Pesch, in a monograph
devoted to 21:1–14 (*Der reiche Fischfang*), proposed an analysis entailing
two sources that have been interwoven by the author: a fishing tradition in
vv 2, 3, 4a, 6, 11, and an appearance with a meal, vv 4b, 7–9, 12–13; in
Pesch's view the former was not originally an Easter story but an event in
the ministry of Jesus (cf. Luke 5:1–11). Apart from the dissociation of the

miraculous catch of fish from the Easter narratives, this approach has found acceptance with many scholars. The setting beside the sea will have been common to the two accounts, with elements of vv 1–4 in each; the fishing narrative will have followed with vv 5–8, 10, 11, and the meal narrative with vv 9, 12, 13; the beginning and the end (vv 1, 14) were provided by the editor. If the Beloved Disciple were included in the "two other disciples" of v 2, there is no need to suggest that he added the reference to the Beloved Disciple in v 7a, but he may have used v 10 as a connection for the two stories. The bringing together of the two accounts is presumably due to the fact that both report appearances of the Lord by the sea of Tiberias; the postulate that there are *two* explains the tension between the large catch of fish and the meal already prepared by Jesus on the shore. The setting of a resurrection appearance at a meal reminds of Luke 24:41–43, (Acts 1:4? so RSV[mg], GNB[mg], JB, NIV), Acts 10:41, but especially the revelation of the risen Lord to the Emmaus Disciples (Luke 24:28–31). The extraordinarily large supply of wine in the Cana miracle is to be compared; it indicates the fullness of the risen Lord's power, but has various other motives of importance to the writer. The meal is narrated in such a way as to suggest eucharistic overtones.

4. The setting of the resurrection narrative(s) in vv 1–14 is in Galilee, beside the lake. Because of the disciples' lack of recognition of Jesus in vv 4, 7, the nature of the conversation with Peter in vv 15–17, and the fact that the *Gospel of Peter* (of which we have only a fragment) begins an account of Peter going fishing with others on *the last day of the feast of unleavened bread*, it is assumed by many scholars that this account records the *first* appearance of Jesus to the disciples; the statement that it was the *third* appearance is set to the account of the editor. The analysis of the chapter that we have given, however, does not necessarily favor that conclusion. On the contrary *two* appearances are recorded in the tradition behind vv 1–14, and in all likelihood vv 15–17 give the substance of an *earlier* appearance to Peter. The setting of this latter appearance is not stated in the Gospel accounts, and all possible locations have been suggested—Jerusalem or its environs, Galilee, and on the way from Jerusalem to Galilee. Clearly Luke 24:34 is recorded on the assumption that it took place in or around Jerusalem; this is often thought to be due to Luke's bringing together all the resurrection appearances in Jerusalem and therefore does not rule out an appearance of Jesus to Peter in Galilee. That is correct, but we must not overlook that Paul as well as Luke states that the appearance to Peter took place before any appearance to the Twelve, and Paul has it in association with "raised on the third day" (1 Cor 15:3–5). The appearance to Peter obviously was very early after the appearance to Mary Magdalene in the garden, and if it did take place in the Jerusalem area, it is likely that the first appearance to the disciples will have taken place there also. (R. H. Fuller suggested that the appearance to Peter occurred when Peter was on the way from Jerusalem to Galilee and that the "Quo Vadis" legend arose from it ["The Formation of the Resurrection Narratives," 35]; he points out [202 n.51] that F. C. Burkitt maintained the same view, in *Christian Beginnings* [London: University Press, 1924] 87–88.)

The context of vv 18–19 can only be stated to be in the Easter period.

The ambiguous announcement of Peter's future martyrdom (cf. 13:36) is perhaps more likely to have been made on a later occasion than his reinstatement by the Lord, but admittedly that is a subjective judgment. The core of vv 20–23 is the saying of v 22, which doubtless circulated among the Johannine churches independently, but is here given its setting in a manner reminiscent of the "pronouncement stories" of the synoptic Gospels. The rectification of misunderstanding to which it gave rise will have been an important factor in the decision to add this chapter to the Gospel. The conclusion in vv 24–25 was for the purpose of bringing the chapter to an end and to enable an important statement to be made regarding the authority of the Gospel as a whole, thereby integrating the epilogue into the Gospel.

5. The exposition that follows will be based on the following outline:

  i.   The risen Lord appears to the disciples by the Sea of Tiberias (21:1–14)
  ii. The risen Lord addresses Peter (21:15–23)
      a. Jesus rehabilitates Peter and confirms him in his pastoral calling, 21:15–17
      b. A prophecy of Peter's martyrdom, 21:18–19
      c. The destiny of the Beloved Disciple, 21:20–23
  iii. Conclusion (21:24–25)

Comment

THE RISEN LORD APPEARS TO THE DISCIPLES BY THE SEA OF TIBERIAS (21:1–14)

1 The author begins and ends the narrative with the statement, "Jesus revealed himself" (or "was revealed," v 14). The term is not used of resurrection appearances in chap. 20, nor in any recorded in the synoptic Gospels, other than Mark 16:12, 14 (the longer ending). Whereas the verb φανεροῦν ("reveal") occurs in the synoptics only at Mark 4:22 (of the revelation of men's deeds in the judgment), it is frequent in the Fourth Gospel with reference to Jesus (see esp. 1:31, John the Baptist came "that he might be revealed to Israel"; 2:11, "he revealed his glory"; 17:6, "I revealed your name"); it is accordingly fitting that at Easter the risen Lord "revealed *himself.*" "The whole verse makes the effect of an announcement of a theme" (Schnackenburg, 3:352).

2 The group of disciples is described in an unusual manner. Simon Peter heads the list. Thomas follows, and we are again told that his name means "the Twin" (cf. 20:24); his mention is doubtless to link what follows with the immediately preceding narrative. Nathanael is described as "the man from Cana of Galilee"—an item of information not given earlier. So also the two sons of Zebedee have not been mentioned in the Gospel, but are assumed to be well known. "Two other disciples" conclude the list; their names are not given, but since the disciple whom Jesus loved is referred to in v 7, the author clearly wishes us to realize that he is one of the two unnamed. On this Hanechen remarked: "They (the two unnamed) make the identification of the Beloved Disciple impossible. Only in this way is his secret kept" (595).

So seven disciples have come together, doubtless a symbolical number, representing the whole disciple group, and indeed the whole Body of disciples, the Church.

3 "I'm going fishing," says Peter, and the rest agree to go also. Never has a fishing trip been so severely judged! "The scene is one of complete apostasy, and is the fulfillment of 16:32," wrote Hoskyns (552). Brown more mildly commented: "The scene is rather one of aimless activity undertaken in desperation" (2:1096). One is constrained to ask how the learned professor knows that. There is not a hint of "aimlessness" or "desperation" in the text. That a one-time fisherman should tell his friends one evening, "I'm going fishing," does not imply, "I'm finished with preaching the kingdom of God, and I'm going back to my old job." Even though Jesus be crucified and risen from the dead, the disciples must still *eat!* A night on the lake, when fish are best caught, is an obvious recourse for such men. One should ask first what Peter and company are doing in Galilee: the answer, of course, is given in Mark 14:28 and 16:7: the disciples were told that Jesus would go ahead of them to Galilee and that they would see him there. Acknowledging the complexity of the resurrection accounts and the difficulty of sorting out the traditions that lie behind them, let us also bear in mind that two of them report that Peter saw the empty tomb, and that certain women saw Jesus alive; that could well have led Peter to being baffled but hardly to despair. The narrative of chap. 21 can be read differently from the way commonly advocated. According to Luke 24:34 Peter has already seen the risen Lord, a report in harmony with the tradition recorded by Paul in 1 Cor 15:5. The deduction of the Beloved Disciple recorded in v 7 of this chapter implies knowledge of at least *that* disciple that Jesus was risen from the dead; the fact that Peter does not expostulate but leaps into the water to reach him as soon as possible assumes that it was not news to him also. We moderns are extraordinarily unimaginative in our endeavors to understand the thinking of the disciples in a situation that had never existed in the world before. The only thing that they knew about the resurrection of the dead was that it comes at the end of the world; and one place where it may confidently be expected *not* to be revealed was Galilee! The heart of the world was Jerusalem, the navel of the earth, the place where Messiah's throne would be set up, and all nations would flow to it and seek him. The disciples needed to understand before the death of Jesus that his conquest of death would not mean *finis* to history, and they needed to be told that even more urgently after the resurrection of Jesus; for in truth, the end of all things *had* come into history, not as its conclusion, but for its remaking. The new eon was proving to be different from anything that any Jew, including prophets and apocalyptic seers, had grasped, so it is not surprising that Peter and his friends were finding it difficult to come to terms with what they were experiencing. Acts 1:6 is completely comprehensible on the lips of Jewish disciples of the risen Jesus; hence the wisdom of H. B. Swete, who long ago commented on Mark 16:7: "It was important to dispel at the outset any expectation of an immediate setting up of the kingdom of God in a visible form at Jerusalem" (*The Gospel according to St. Mark* [London: Macmillan, [3]1927] 398). In the somewhat confused narrative of vv 3–14 we glimpse something of the perplex-

ity of followers of Jesus in the unique period between Easter Sunday and
Pentecost.

4 The failure of the disciples to recognize Jesus on the shore is not to
be taken as an indication that they had not seen him since his resurrection;
rather it points to the mystery of Jesus in his resurrection state. It is, as
Brown suggested, another instance of the transformed appearance of Jesus
(2:1070). Whether we should also add, with Bultmann, that the eyes of the
disciples were "held," like those of the Emmaus disciples (707), is less certain.
What is plain is that the Jesus whom they were meeting in his Easter glory
was living in a different mode of existence from that of his former earthly
conditions, which his followers of necessity shared, and therefore that all
his communications with them were accommodations to the earthly plane
which they occupied.

5–6 That Jesus directed the disciples to throw their net on the *right* side
of the boat is hardly likely to be due to the notion that the right side is the
lucky one (a banal suggestion! The Greeks so viewed it, see BGD, 174); we
are to assume a knowledge of the risen Lord beyond that of this order (lit.,
"*super*natural"!—"transcending the powers of the ordinary course of nature,"
Oxford English Dictionary).

7 The Beloved Disciple recognizes by the miracle that the Man on the
shore is the risen Lord. Characteristically, he tells Peter of his intuition, and
equally characteristically Peter throws himself into the sea—not to bring the
fish to shore, but to reach the Lord as quickly as he can. The scene is curiously
akin to the episode at the empty tomb (20:4–8); if this chapter comes from
another than the Evangelist, we are clearly dealing with a Johannine tradition
at one with the former narrative and with a writer whose mind is at one
with the Evangelist's.

8–11 The narrative at this point is held up by the statement in v 9 that
the disciples, on coming to land, see fish and bread prepared by Jesus for
them. We have suggested that vv 9, 12, 13 portray a separate scene, which
is here conjoined with the conclusion of the fishing miracle. If v 9 for the
moment be removed and connected with vv 12–13 it will be seen that the
fishing narrative moves naturally, even speedily. Peter hurries to get ashore
to be with Jesus (v 7), while the rest of the disciples bring the boat to land,
dragging the net with them (v 8). Jesus at once tells Peter to bring some of
the fish that have been caught (v 10), whereupon he goes to the boat and
hauls in the net (v 11). The question that is often asked, "What was Peter
doing when he reached the shore?" has no place in this sequence. There is
no question of his standing around, whether in embarrassment or joy, or of
a conversation taking place between him and Jesus in anticipation of vv 15–
17. The narrative is brief and to the point. If v 10 originally was integral to
the fishing story (as seems to be demanded by v 11), then it will have concluded
with the report of a meal with Jesus *which the disciples provided*.

9, 12–13 The provision of a meal of fish and bread by Jesus, particularly
in light of the language used in v 13, imparts to the occasion something of
the quality of the Last Supper. Dodd observed, "The meal of bread and fish
is treated in early Christian art as an alternative expression of the eucharistic
idea," but he added, "the text of the gospel gives no hint of this" (*Interpretation*,

431 n.1). If we confine ourselves to the text of chap. 21 this is true, but the link between this narrative and that of the feeding of the multitude in John 6 adds another dimension. In early Christian art, meals of bread and fish are frequently depicted as representations of the Lord's Supper, but it is unclear whether the feeding of the multitude or the resurrection meal of the disciples with Jesus has provided the symbolism. Perhaps that is not important, for the two events were intended to be linked in the Christian's mind. Alan Shaw maintained that the eucharistic significance of our present passage is shown by "the similarity of 21:13 to 6:11 and by the contents of the meal (21:9), fish and bread (or *a* fish and *a* loaf); for only two meals are described in the Fourth Gospel, and they are both meals of bread and fish, and with the former is associated the eucharistic teaching of chap. 6" ("The Breakfast by the Shore . . . ," 12). At this point we may recall that chap. 6 can be read on two levels: the one recounts the signs of the feeding of the multitude and walking on the water, leading to an exposition of Jesus as the Bread of Life, whom one must receive as the Crucified and Exalted Lord to gain the life he brings; the other conveys a portrayal through sign and word of the significance of the Lord's Supper. A similar understanding of the narrative in vv 9, 12, 13 probably accords with the author's intention.

One curious feature of v 12 is its statement that the disciples did not dare to ask the name of their host, because, or although, they knew it was the Lord. It is, in fact, a characteristic feature of the resurrection appearances in the Gospels. It is related to, yet different from, the experience of the Emmaus disciples, who did not know the identity of the Lord until he broke the bread; here the disciples know the Lord as he invites them, before participating in the meal, yet there is a peculiar reticence in their relationship toward him, which we presume must have disappeared during the meal. Bultmann caught the mood of the narrative well: "Since they have indeed recognized him, the meaning of the question obviously must be, 'Is it *really* you?' This is intended to describe the peculiar feeling that befalls the disciples in the presence of the risen Jesus: it is he, and yet it is not he; it is not he, whom they hitherto have known, and yet it is he! A peculiar wall is erected between him and them. This partition is set aside, as Jesus now distributes bread and fish among the disciples to eat. For even though he, as the risen Lord, does not himself participate in the meal, the sense can hardly be other than that table fellowship between the Risen Jesus and the disciples is now established" (709–10).

Few statements in the Fourth Gospel have teased the minds of its readers so much as that in v 11, namely, that the fish caught in the disciples' net numbered 153. It could, of course, be simply an exact reminiscence, a genuine fisherman's story—153 great fish, and the net unbroken! Almost certainly, however, the writer intended some further significance to be seen in the number, as with all the signs performed in the ministry of Jesus and in the record of the meal in vv 9, 12, 13.

The most popular solution of the conundrum among modern scholars goes back to Jerome. In his commentary on Ezek 47 he links the miracle of the fish with the prophet's vision of the stream of living water that flows from the Temple to the Dead Sea, making the latter teem with life, and he states: "Writers on the nature and properties of animals, who have learned 'fishing' in either Latin or Greek (one of whom is the most learned poet Oppianus Cilix) say that there are one hundred and fifty-three species of fish" (*Comm. xiv in Ezechiel*, Migne, *PL* 25, 474C). On the basis of this information it is natural to assume that the author of John 21 saw in the miraculous catch of fish an acted parable of the mission of the apostles and of the Church after them to all nations, and its success as it proceeds in obedience to the risen Lord. R. M. Grant, however, queried whether this could have been in the author's mind. He maintained that Jerome's reference to "writers" in the plural was a generalization from Oppian's writing; Oppian does not give the number of fish as 153, but states that there are countless myriads of species of fish; when, however, the various kinds of fish which he describes are counted up they number 157 (see "One Hundred Fifty-Three Large Fish," 273). Grant admitted that it is difficult to be confident in counting Oppian's named species, but he assumed that Jerome must have reached his figure with John 21 already in mind. This has led recent scholars to believe that Jerome's information must be discounted.

An alternative theory, to which scholars have been attracted, was propounded by none other than Jerome's friend Augustine. He pioneered the mathematical solutions to the problem by observing that 153 is the sum of the numbers one to seventeen which is a triangular number. (If one represents the numbers 1 to 17 by dots on separate lines, they form a triangle, see Hoskyns' diagram, 553.) Augustine then pointed out that $17 = 10 + 7$; the former represent the ten commandments, the latter the sevenfold Spirit of God (*Tract. in Jo.*, 122). More simply, it is evident that ten and seven were important numbers in Jewish tradition. *Pirqe 'Abot* 5:1–9 lists features of the sacred history in which ten occurs: e.g., by 10 sayings the world was created; there were 10 generations from Adam to Noah, and 10 from Noah to Abraham; by 10 trials Abraham was tested; 10 wonders were done for Israel in Egypt, 10 by the sea, and 10 in the sanctuary. Verses 10–11 go on to speak of significant sevens: seven things concern a rude man, and seven concern a wise man (they are listed); so also seven kinds of punishment come upon the world for seven transgressions—the punishments and the transgressions are itemized. Grant, accordingly, sees in the number 153 a symbol whose significance derives from its components, 17 as the sum of the two most sacred numbers, the importance of which is increased when it is triangulated. From this it is deduced that 153 is a numerical symbol for perfection, and so for the perfection of the Church.

Augustine added to this mathematical meaning an allegorical interpretation of the number: $153 = 3 \times 50 + 3$, the number of the Trinity. Cyril of Alexandria modified that by proposing that 100 represents the fullness of the Gentiles, 50 the remnant of Israel, and 3 the Trinity (*In Jo.* XII: *PG*, 74, col.745). Rupert of Deutz brought the idea closer to home; 100 represents the married, 50 the widows, and 3 the virgins (cited by Brown, 2:1075)! Such proposals hardly commend themselves to the modern mind.

The modern mind, however, has its own esoteric expressions, among which gematria exercises a fascination for some. *Gematria* is a term derived from geometry, but it makes play with words in languages wherein numerals are represented by letters of the alphabet ($a = 1$, $b = 2$, $c = 3$, etc.). Both the Greeks and the Hebrews represented numbers in this way; accordingly any name (or even any word) could be added up and represented by its total. Deissmann cites an example from the graffiti of Pompeii which reads, "I love the girl whose name is 545" (*Light from the Ancient East*, 276). The most famous example of gematria is the number of Antichrist, given in Rev 13:18 as 666; all kinds of names have been found to total 666, but the most likely candidate is *Nero Caesar* written in Hebrew letters, for the cipher almost certainly originated in a Jewish apocalyptic circle. J. A. Emerton, perceiving the weaknesses of the traditional explanations of 153, sought a solution along this path. He observed that Ezek 47, and especially v 10, could have been in the mind of the author of John 21: the stream of living water from the temple is to bring life to the Dead Sea, which will be full of fish; fishermen will stand along the shore and they will spread their nets from En-gedi to En-eglaim. "En" (עַיִן) is the Hebrew for "spring"; *gedi* (גְּדִי) provides the total 17, *eglaim* (עֶגְלַיִם) 153. These two numbers are mathematically related. Emerton suggested that the number of fish may thus represent the places where, according to prophecy, fishermen are to stand and spread their nets in the time of messianic fulfillment ("The Hundred and Fifty-Three Fishes in John XXI.11," 86–89). P. R. Ackroyd followed up Emerton's suggestion; he pointed out that in a Greek gospel an allusion to the place names in Ezek 47 would have been more understandable if they had been written in Greek; among the varied modes of spelling the two names in the LXX he noted that ηγγαδι = 33, and 'Αγαλλειμ = 120; the two together give the desired number 153 ("The 153 Fishes in John XXI.11—A Further Note," 94). Emerton was not impressed, for the two transliterations cited by Ackroyd come from different MSS of the LXX; no one MS offers them both; in any case the link between 17 and 153, provided in the Hebrew text, disappears in the Greek ("Gematria in John XXI.11," 335–36). He accordingly preferred to keep to his original proposal based on the Heb. text.

Other interpretations of 153 based on gematria have been suggested. H. Kruse proposed two possible explanations; the one קָהָל הָאַהֲבָה, "the church of love," the other בְּנֵי הָאֱלֹהִים, "the children of God" ('Magni Pisces Centum Quinquaginta Tres," 143–47). He did not know that the former had earlier been proposed by D. R. Ahrendts (*ZWT* 41 [1898] 480); and J. A. Romeo, working by the same method, independently suggested the latter ("Gematria and John 21:11," 263–64). Kruse preferred his first solution, but the expression nowhere occurs in the Johannine writings. Romeo felt justified in adhering to the latter one, for the expression occurs in John 1:12 and 11:52, and in his view it is well suited to the context of 21:1–14.

An altogether more complicated proposal was made by N. J. McEleny on the basis of what he called "Gematriachal Atbash." The latter term refers to a replacing of letters in words by a reverse order of the alphabet; in English it would mean reading z for a, y for b, x for c, and so on.

The Jews apparently were acquainted with this kind of substitute writing in OT times (an example is given in turning *Babel* [בָּבֶל] into *sesek* [שֵׁשַׁךְ] in Jer 25:26; 51:41). When gematria is applied to "atbash" then z represents 1, y = 2, x = 3, etc. On this principle McEleny found that IXΘ, an abbreviation of IXΘΥΣ (*ichthus*, fish), has the value of 153. *Ichthus*, of course, is the well-known acrostic for Ἰησοῦς Χριστὸς Θεοῦ υἱὸς σωτήρ, "Jesus Christ, God's Son, Savior"; the short term McEleny assumed to represent "Jesus Christ, God." So the author of John 21 is thought to have concealed the holy name of the Risen in acrostic fashion under gematriachal atbash; those with eyes to see will understand that Christ, as the first of his brethren going up from the waters of baptism and later from the tomb of the Father, is identified with his Church under the symbolism of the fish ("153 Great Fishes [John 21:11] . . . ," 413–17). This example of gematria from McEleny illustrates in an extreme manner the unlikelihood of this type of esoteric writing being employed by the author of John 21. It is altogether too complicated for the ordinary reader of the Gospel to perceive, and too much even for most modern scholars to guess without being initiated into this particular mystique.

M. Rissi, in an article on Joh 21, turned from all these notions and urged that one presupposition alone suffice to provide the clue to the fishing miracle, namely, the observation of Augustine that 153 was the triangular number of 17. There is

a clear link between the narrative of vv 1–14 and the feeding of the multitude in
John 6. In the latter we read of *five* loaves, multiplied, from which *twelve* baskets
full of broken pieces were taken up: 5 + 12 = 17! The figure 153 thus builds a
bridge between the feeding miracle of the ministry and that of the Resurrection,
and enables the theological weight of the one to be carried over to the other. In
the ancient world fish were a symbol of fruitfulness, life, and immortality. If the
eucharistic taking of bread and wine celebrated Jesus' *death,* the eating of bread
and fish was a celebration of his *resurrection,* which made fellowship with the Lord
after his death possible. So the eucharistic meal in chap. 21 depicts *an epiphany
celebration of the risen Lord* ("Voll grosser Fische . . . ," esp. 81–86). This is a down-
to-earth interpretation which seeks to do justice to the theological significance of
the narrative. Its elucidation of the eucharistic element in the narrative is actually
independent of the interpretation offered, for the link with John 6 is given in the
narrative itself. But it is questionable whether justice is done by Rissi to the sign
of the great catch of fish, and to the combination of *two* major motifs in the single
narrative. The epiphany of the Lord by the lake, manifest in the granting of so
great a haul of fish, should not be submerged in the eucharistic manifestation.
When two such motifs are combined, it is not surprising that a clash of symbolism
arises, namely, the ingathering of a multitude of fish, symbolizing the success of
the Church's mission to the nations, and the giving of fish with bread to eat in a
eucharistic meal. We do not ask for consistency in the symbolism of parables, still
less in descriptions of the eschatological hope voiced by prophets of the Old and
New Testaments; we should not be offended by the like in the composite representation of John 21:1–14.

Accepting Rissi's contribution we may yet see in the sign of the catch of fish a
symbol of "the breadth or even the universality of the Christian mission" (Brown,
2:1075). Despite Grant's objections, we are not sure that Jerome should be dismissed
out of hand. He did, after all, refer to "writers" in the plural, not solely to Oppian,
whose work was in any case a century later than the Fourth Gospel, and yet whose
description of varieties of fish came very close to 153. It is possible that one of
these days some ancient writing will come to light containing a comparable tradition
to the varieties of fish attested by Jerome. Till then we must allow the secret of
153 to remain, yet acknowledging its attestation to the greatness of the sign it
emphasizes.

THE RISEN LORD ADDRESSES PETER (21:15–23)

Jesus Rehabilitates Peter and Confirms Him in His Pastoral Calling (21:15–17)

The situation in vv 15–23 is quite different from that in vv 1–14. Whereas in
the earlier passage Jesus appears to the disciple group, from v 15 on he deals
with Peter alone, who is later joined by the Beloved Disciple; the rest of the disciples
disappear entirely from the scene. Verses 1–14 form "a disciple pericope," vv 15–
19 "a Peter fragment" (Schnackenburg, 3:361). The threefold questioning of Peter
by Jesus is highly unusual. The impression is given that Jesus is not satisfied with
Peter's avowals of his love for him, so that even after apparently restoring him to
fellowship with himself, and enjoining on him ministry in the Church, the renewed
questions of Jesus query the reality of Peter's protestations of love. Most students
of the Gospel agree that the procedure stands in relation to Peter's repeated denials
of Jesus. Some, it is true, have sought a different explanation for this threefold
repetition. P. Gaechter saw in it a reflection of a near-Orient custom of making a
declaration three times before witnesses, notably in relation to contracts and legal
dispositions (see "Das dreifache 'Weide meine Lämmer,' " 328–44). Undoubtedly

such a legal slant to the threefold declarations to Peter would give a peculiar authority to Peter's installation as Shepherd of Christ's sheep, but it imputes to the narrative a more formal nature than the context warrants and to the Lord's words a questionable notion of the pastoral ministry to which he appoints. Similar objections apply to the notion that the threefold question and answer reflect a liturgical form, such as would be used in an ordination (G. Stählin in *TDNT* 9:134 n.194). The question of Jesus is conditioned by the relationship that had existed between Jesus and Peter during the ministry of Jesus and the peculiar rupture of it at the trial of Jesus together with Peter's undoubted grief, not to say shock, caused by the crucifixion of Jesus and the guilt that must have haunted him on account of his own behavior. Peter must have been conscious of the fact that he had forfeited all right to be viewed as a disciple of Jesus, let alone a close associate of his in his ministry, through his repeated disavowal of any connection with him. When one contemplates how Jesus had prepared Peter for responsible leadership among the people of the Kingdom and for the mission to Israel and the nations, this was a profoundly serious failure, which called for a process of re-establishment commensurable with the seriousness of the defection.

15 The opening phrase is an editorial link with the preceding paragraph. The one issue that Jesus must clarify with Peter is his relation to him after the debacle in the High Priest's court; the sole element of that relationship concerns Jesus' love, for without it all else is vain (cf. 1 Cor 13:1–3). The question, "Do you love me *more than these?*", in the context must surely mean, ". . . more than your fellow disciples do?" (rather than, "more than you love them," or "more than you love your fishing equipment"). It is not that Jesus would distinguish the depth of Peter's love from that of the others, but that Peter had brashly asserted his loyalty to Jesus as more steadfast than theirs (see Matt 26:33, which has no real counterpart in John 13:36–37, but which in some form could well have been known in the Johannine circles). The question is whether he is prepared to make such a statement now. Peter does not attempt to answer it in relation to his friends, but in his embarrassment he appeals to the Lord's knowledge that he truly loves him, despite his failure. To his relief the Lord accepts his avowal, and indicates his reinstatement with the declaration, "Take care of my lambs"; Peter's love for his Lord is to be made manifest in his care for the Lord's flock.

16–17 The unexpected repetitions of the Lord's question to Peter have the effect of searching him to the depths of his being. We have seen (in the *Notes*) the improbability of the variety of terms having any major significance, alike in the repeated question of Jesus, the answer of Peter, and the Lord's commission to him. The pain or grief of Peter was not due to Jesus' framing his question with the use of Peter's own word ($\phi\iota\lambda\epsilon\hat{\iota}\varsigma$ instead of $\dot{\alpha}\gamma\alpha\pi\hat{\alpha}\varsigma$), but is explained by Jesus' act when for the *third* time he put the same question to him, as though to ask whether there was any substance in his avowal of love, any ground for his accepting its reality. By this time all the old self-confidence and assertiveness manifest in Peter before the crucifixion of Jesus had drained away. He could only appeal to the Lord's totality of knowledge, which included his knowledge of Peter's heart; he more than all people could tell that he was speaking the truth. He really did love him, and more than that he could not say. More than that was not necessary; the Lord accepted his protestation of love.

How, then, are we to understand the commission given to the penitent and chastened Peter? The endeavor to answer that question appears to be the one issue in the entire Gospel where members of different Christian confessions not only divide, but find difficulty in understanding the answers of the others. Lagrange, for example, speaks of "some narrowly confessional Protestants, lagging behind the times," who hold that Peter only figures here as representing the apostles, and so a *primus inter pares*, a first among equals, in contrast to more independent critics who acknowledge the ancient Catholic exegesis and recognize that Jesus is choosing Peter as the sole repository of his pastoral authority (528, 530). Hoskyns cites a typical expression of this view given by Cornelius à Lapide: "On his departure into heaven Christ here designates his Vicar upon earth and creates Peter the Supreme Pontiff, in order that one Church may be governed by one Pastor" (557). The key issue is the meaning of the term "shepherd" in the statement to Peter. J. F. X. Sheehan urged that it has to be understood in the light of its use in the OT. Sheehan has no difficulty in demonstrating its association in Israel's history with rulers and with ruling. For example, it is recounted how the elders of Israel came to David and said, "The Lord told you, 'You shall shepherd my people Israel and you shall be prince over them'" (2 Sam 5:2); on this Sheehan commented, "The position of shepherd and prince in such a citation makes the two words almost equal in meaning" ("Feed my Lambs," 22–23). On that basis, said Sheehan, it is comprehensible to interpret the Lord's commission to Peter to "shepherd" the flock as meaning that he should "rule" over it. With this Brown agrees, and believes that it is in line with fundamental principles. God is Shepherd; he delegates authority to rule; as in 20:21 Jesus sends his disciples in the manner that he was sent, so here he, as the model Shepherd, makes Peter the same. "The ideal of 10:16 is carried over into chapter 21: one sheep herd, one shepherd." In harmony with this Matt 16:19 is interpreted as meaning that "the gift of the keys makes Peter the Prime Minister of the Kingdom" (2:1114–16).

What is so surprising in this discussion is the neglect to observe the significance for our passage of the concept "shepherd," with its closely similar term "bishop," in the NT Church (here Schnackenburg is a conspicuous exception, 3:364). In 1 Pet 2:25 Jesus is said to be "the Shepherd and Bishop of your souls"; in context this denotes Jesus as the one who gave his life for the sheep and cares for them in the present. In the hortatory part of the letter (5:2) Peter as "a fellow elder" (= bishop, pastor) appeals to the elders: "Shepherd the flock of God that is among you" (ποιμάνατε τὸ . . . ποίμνιον τοῦ θεοῦ), so virtually citing the words of the risen Lord to him, "Shepherd my sheep" (ποίμαινε τὰ πρόβατά μου). By way of expounding his meaning he adds, "Watch over it (ἐπισκοποῦντες), not because you have to, but willingly . . . not acting as lords over God's people (τῶν κλήρων), but becoming examples to the flock" (1 Pet 5:3). A similar charge by Paul to the elders of Ephesus is recorded in Acts 20:28: "Keep watch over yourselves and over all the flock (ποίμνιον) of which the Holy Spirit has made you guardians (ἐπισκόπους) to shepherd the Church of the Lord" (ποιμαίνειν τὴν ἐκκλησίαν τοῦ κυρίου). Both passages speak in the same manner as the risen Lord spoke to Peter on restoring him to fellowship and to the service of pastor. The verbs are the same, ποιμαίνω or variants of it; the scope of the ministry is the same—"my lambs, my sheep

. . . the flock of God, the Church of the Lord." There is no formal difference of meaning in the language by which the risen Lord confirmed Peter in his calling to be a shepherd of his sheep from that by which Peter and Paul exhorted the pastor-elders to fulfill their calling as shepherds of the flock of God in 1 Pet 5:1–3 and Acts 20:28. This applies also to the representative nature of the shepherd's office and the authority which it carries. There is no ground for denying that Jesus in the resurrection scene of John 21:15–17 entrusted his sheep to Peter as the Father entrusted them to him, and that thereby he gave him the authority that goes with the shepherd's office. But that is an essential element of the concept of ministerial calling within the Church. The risen Lord as supreme Shepherd of his sheep exercises his ministry through those whom he calls to be his under-shepherds, and to them he delegates authority over the flock. This is apparent not only in the apostolic exercise of authority in the NT Church (particularly plain in the Pauline letters), but in that assumed also for the presbyter-bishops of the churches (e.g., 1 Tim 3:4–5; Heb 13:17). It is the *exclusive* authority claimed to be given to Peter in John 21:15–17 that is so puzzling to one not in the Christian tradition that assumes it as self-evident, for there is not a hint of such a singular authority in the text. Part of the explanation for the interpretation, especially among modern exegetes, has been the tendency to interpret John 21:15–17 in light of Matt 16:18–19a, but that is surely a mistake in hermeneutics. The functions and figures employed in the Matthaean passage are quite different from those in the Johannine passage.

This is not the place to enter into a detailed discussion of Matt 16:18–19a, but we content ourselves with two observations: First, the unique role of Peter in the *founding* of the Church, according to Matt 16:18, is not in question, but that is of no help to elucidate John 21:15–17. Second, the figure of the keys given to Peter requires more than Isa 22:19–25 for understanding its application in Matt 16:19a. In Matt 23:13, with its parallel in Luke 11:52, and in Rev 1:18; 3:7–12, the notion of keys of the kingdom has the thought of persons authorized to open the door into the kingdom of God, so allowing others to enter upon the eternal life of the kingdom, and *that* is to the fore in Matt 16:19a (see the author's exposition in *Jesus and the Kingdom of God* [Grand Rapids: Eerdmans, 1986] 179–85). The one clear connection between the figures employed in Matt 16:19a and John 21:15–17 lies in the aspect of the Shepherd's calling to seek the lost sheep and gather them into the flock, hence the aspect of *mission*. By general consent that is not the primary emphasis of John 21:15–17, where the concern is rather for the care of those who belong to the flock of Jesus. By reason of his devastating experience of fall and restoration to the fellowship of his Lord, Peter is peculiarly fitted to carry out that aspect of the pastoral office, referred to by Jesus in Luke 21:32: "Once you have recovered, you in your turn must strengthen your brothers" (JB). The letter known as 1 Peter is an excellent example of the Apostle's fulfillment of that commission.

A Prophecy of the Martyrdom of Peter (21:18–19)

18 We have earlier stated that the prophecy of v 18 may have circulated independently in the churches. Bultmann observed that it has no inner connection with vv 15–17 (713); Brown agreed, adding that the fact that vv 15–17 deal with Peter's future made appropriate the addition of an independent saying concerning his death (2:1117). Two utterances of Jesus would have helped to make this connection: "The good shepherd lays down his life for the sheep" (John 10:11), and, "No one has greater love than this, that one lays down his life for the sake of his friends" (15:13).

The contrast between Peter's freedom in his youth and the limitations imposed on him in later life has led to the belief that such is the prime intent of the saying. Bernard interprets it thus: "The words 'you girded yourself . . . another will gird you' may point only to the contrast between the alertness of youth and the helplessness of old age, which cannot always do what it would; and 'you will stretch you hands' may refer merely to the old man stretching out his hands that others may help him in putting on his garments, whereas the young man girds himself unassisted, before he sets out to walk," (2:708). On that understanding v 19 is viewed as affirming that Peter will glorify God through a life of obedience till ripe old age, with the possibility of an added interpretation given by the editor, in applying it to the outstretched arms of the crucified. Bultmann modifies this approach in an ingenious manner; he saw the saying as a prophecy by parable, at the base of which lay a proverb: "In youth a man is free to go where he will; in old age a man must let himself be taken where he does not will." But the proverb is cited with a special application to Peter: whereas at one time he freely chose his way, he will be unwillingly led to his last journey by martyrdom; the details of the picture, however, belong to the proverb, and are not to be taken as a forecast of death by crucifixion (713–14). Bultmann's view of an adapted proverb in v 18 is widely accepted, but it must be recognized as pure hypothesis, without any evidence behind it, and its application to Peter's death is hardly convincing (so Haenchen, emphatically, 590). The "stretching out" of the hands has proved the main difficulty. The expression was actually employed by classical writers with reference to the crucified man (illustrations gathered by Wettstein may be found in commentaries, most fully in Haenchen, 590), and Christian writers from the second century on so interpreted it, not only in this passage, but in what seemed to them pertinent OT passages; e.g., Moses lifting up his arms to pray in the battle with Amalek (Exod 17:12) was viewed as a type of Christ on the cross (so *Barn.* 12; Justin, *Trypho,* 90, 91); and Isa 65:2, "I have spread out my hands all the day to a rebellious people" was taken as a prophecy of the crucifixion of Jesus (*Barn.* 12; Justin, *Apology* 1, 35; Irenaeus, *Dem.* 79). Modern exegetes have frequently observed that the application of v 18 to crucifixion is contrary to the text order, which places the stretching out of the hands *prior* to one being girded and being led away to death. The clue to the language, however, was noted by Bauer, who recognized that it has in view the binding of the *patibulum,* the crossbeam, to the outstretched arms of the delinquent, who had then to carry it to the place of crucifixion (232). The hesitation of exegetes to accept this interpretation is a mystery. Schnackenburg, citing Bauer's view, remarked, *"refuted* by Wellhausen, who already knew this explanation, as 'antiquarian sophistry' " (482 n.75). Antiquarian sophistry indeed! It has become common knowledge of late that what Bauer described was the general procedure for crucifixion by the Romans (see M. Hengel, *Crucifixion,* on methods of crucifying). This is what happened to Jesus; John 19:17 states that he "carried the cross for himself," i.e., he carried the cross-beam, which will have been placed on his neck, and he will have held it in position as his outstretched arms and hands were bound to it on either side. Bornhäuser, with this in mind, commented on our passage: "This understanding of the stretching out of the hands makes it quite plain that Jesus predicts to Peter that he will die for him as an old man on the stake of shame. Then is clear also why the mention of being guided by another comes after the spreading out of the hands. Not 'others,' but 'one other' will gird him and guide him to a place to which Peter does not want to go. This 'other' is he among those who carry out the death sentence, who girds the garment of the condemned and leads him to the place of execution ' (*The Death and Resurrection of Jesus Christ,* 250–51).

The explanation in v 19, therefore, is in accord with the saying it seeks to explain. "The kind of death by which he was to glorify God" echoes 12:33 (cf. 18:32 also); that Peter's death will be for the glory of God recalls the teaching in the Gospel that God is to be glorified through the death of Jesus (cf. 12:27–28; 13:31–32; 17:1). In a manner akin to the glorification of God in Jesus, though not to the same degree, God is glorified in those who lay down their lives for the name of Jesus (see further 1 Pet 4:16; the language is frequent in early Christian martyrologies).

The final word to Peter, "Follow me," forms a transition to the next paragraph, for it is evident that its meaning is in the first place literal: Peter is asked to *go along with* Jesus. But in view of the drift of the entire context it is likely that a further meaning is to be understood. Peter is to "follow" Jesus' undeviating discipleship for the rest of his days, and at the last in death. It will be as Peter so follows Jesus that the declaration in 13:36b will receive its fulfillment. By the time that this chapter was written Peter had indeed glorified God by a martyr's death, and that on a cross. The obscurity of the saying was clarified by the event, and thereby it becomes the earliest witness we possess to the death of Peter by crucifixion. More importantly, Peter's martyrdom will have been known among the churches; the shame of Peter's denials of Jesus will have been obliterated by his blood, and the renown of his leadership in the Church brought to a notable climax with the gaining of the martyr's crown. That may be of significance for the next paragraph, vv 20–23.

The Destiny of the Beloved Disciple (21:20–23)

20 The previous paragraph ends with the command of Jesus to Peter, "Follow me"; the present paragraph is linked to it through Peter's observation that the Beloved Disciple was also "following." While the themes of vv 20–23 are closely related to that of vv 18–19, the introduction of the Beloved Disciple with reference to the Last Supper (13:24), which was not felt necessary when mentioning him in v 7, suggests that this is an independent paragraph. The recollection of 13:24 is significant, inasmuch as it reminds the reader that this disciple was in closest relation to Jesus, in a manner reminiscent of the relation of Jesus to the Father in revelation (1:18), and that his request to know the identity of the betrayer was due to *Peter's* wanting to know it;

Peter went to Jesus via the Beloved Disciple. It is a reminder, along with other related passages, of this disciple's special place alongside Peter. That is of importance in a passage that deals with the contrasting destinies of the two disciples.

21–22 While Peter's question is sometimes viewed as trifling, posed merely to enable the saying of Jesus to be announced in v 22, it is comprehensible enough, given the frequent association of Peter and the other disciple in the Gospel. If Peter's path in life has now been made known to him, it is natural for him to be curious as to what is in store for his colleague. But the answer of Jesus is unexpectedly sharp in tone. He makes it plain that his will for his friend is of no concern to Peter, not even if that disciple is called to tread a quieter and less demanding way than his; if instead of the call to martyrdom it be the Lord's will for the Beloved Disciple to remain till the Lord himself shall come, that should make no difference to Peter in the pursuit of his vocation. The one thing that matters is that he should follow his Lord—in the present moment—to hear what further word may yet be addressed to him, and in the days and years ahead, as the risen Lord guides him and reveals his unfolding task, till the final call to follow him in a death to the glory of God. Accordingly the command given in v 19 is repeated, only yet more emphatically: "As for you, *you follow me.*"

It is evident that this issue is of importance to the author of chap. 21. The way in which he has presented the scene shows that he was not *solely* concerned to correct the misapprehension about the survival of the Beloved Disciple till the Parousia of Christ. He is at pains to remind the reader of the unique relation to the Lord of this disciple, and therefore his special ministry to the rest of the disciples and to the Church: his record of the Lord's brusque correction of Peter, when he wanted to know what service was appointed for that disciple and what would happen to him, is part of that representation. On the other hand, there is no hint of a desire to denigrate Peter in the interest of the Beloved Disciple; the author has just penned vv 15–17 and 18–19, and he will have been responsible for joining all three paragraphs together. Peter's humiliation was recorded to show that the shameful past was all forgiven, and that the Lord had recommissioned him with the pastoral care of his flock. Moreover, vv 18–19 should be read with thought for the reaction of early Christians to the passage: Peter was being given the privilege of laboring for Christ to old age, and to complete it with the crown of martyrdom. No such honor was given to the Beloved Disciple. By the time chap. 21 was written and the Gospel went into circulation both disciples had died, one with the glory of martyrdom and one with a peaceful end at Ephesus (we would certainly have heard to the contrary had it been otherwise).

Is it reasonable to suggest that this presentation of the relations of Peter and the Beloved Disciple, to the Lord and to each other, was made for the benefit of churches which were inclined to exalt one over against the other? The tendency to favor one apostle more than another is seen in the Corinthian correspondence of Paul—an all-too-human tendency, as Paul himself wryly remarked (1 Cor 3:3–4). And that would be the more natural in circles where one apostle was known and loved, and others were known only through secondhand reports. The anonymity of the Beloved Disciple indicates that he was so well known in the churches he served that there was no need to use his proper name, but it is well possible that he was quite unknown in many areas of the Church, whereas Peter was known to all. It was desirable therefore for Christians elsewhere to learn how the famous Peter and the comparatively unknown Beloved Disciple were related. So the author endeavors to show that both men were gifts of the risen Lord to the churches, very different in gifts and calling, but with important tasks to perform for the benefit of all. In Cullmann's words, "He sets the two disciples face to face and shows how the Risen One assigns a unique position to each one of them for the future, but gives each of them a different role" (*Peter: Disciple, Apostle, Martyr* [New York: Meridian Books, 1958] 29). If it be asked precisely what the different roles were, the answers diverge somewhat. The authors of *Peter in the New Testament: A Collaborative Assessment by Protestant and Roman Catholic Scholars* state that Peter was called to feed the sheep and the Beloved Disciple to "remain"; "In the Johannine tradition this command to feed the sheep is specifically addressed to Peter and not to the Beloved Disciple (or to anyone else)" (143). That sentence is strictly true, but it is misleading. Not only were others in the NT Church called to be shepherds, it is evident that the Beloved Disciple was the notable Shepherd of the sheep in the churches of his area. Peter's commission to serve the Lord as a shepherd of his sheep is part of his rehabilitation as a leading disciple or apostle; but he needed a fresh commission, and the Beloved Disciple did not. We come closer to the heart of the Fourth Gospel, clearly shared in this respect by the author of chap. 21, when we recognize the calling of the disciples to be *witnesses* (cf. 15:16, 26–27; 16:7–11; observe that the verb μαρτυρέω, "witness," occurs 33 times in the Fourth Gospel, as compared with once in Matthew, once in Luke, and not at all in Mark; see J. Chapman, "We Know That His Testimony Is True," 380). However much or little may have been known about the Beloved Disciple in churches beyond his area, all knew that Peter was the great witness to Christ, that through his witness the Church was launched on its mission, and that his faithful testimony was completed in a martyr's death (*martyr* = "witness"). The Beloved Disciple appears to have walked in a quieter way and in a more restricted area; he, too, was a witness for Christ, but in a different manner. Having uniquely associated with the Lord in his ministry, he was uniquely taught by the Paraclete-Spirit, thereby gaining comprehension of God in Christ, and his witness was completed in the Gospel of which he was the inspiration. The vocations of Peter and the Beloved Disciple thus were immensely important to the Church; the author of chap. 21 wrote to enable the churches to recognize both, and to be grateful for both.

22–23 That the saying of v 22 circulated among the Johannine churches is evident from the reference to "the brothers," who understood it as a promise from the Lord that the Beloved Disciple would survive till the Parousia. The saying has caused some commentators as much perturbation as "the brothers," to judge from their anxiety to empty it of real eschatological content. Westcott, for example, was anxious to show that the coming of Christ includes the thought of his coming in death to the believer, to the Society, and to Jerusalem in judgment (to which the Beloved Disciple "remained"!), and that the Beloved Disciple abides still, insofar as the history of the Church is imaged in the history of the apostles (2:373; cf. also the interpretation by Hoskyns of "remain" = "abide" in the sense of John 15 and 1 John 3:14, 558–59). J. A. T. Robinson offered a more realistic view in suggesting that v 22 reflects the imminent expectation of the first generation Church, and that it was possible to maintain it in the Johannine churches since *the Beloved Disciple was still alive;* the correction in v 23 suits best the time shortly after Peter's death, about A.D. 65, when the Gospel was written (*The Priority of John,* 70, 71). Critical scholars are not inclined to share this inference from our passage as to the date of the Gospel, but they tend to agree that the imminent expectation of the coming of Christ in the first generation Church was fostered in some minds by the continuance of the Beloved Disciple into old age. Surely the Lord was to come before he, the last of the original disciples, should die! It is not demonstrable, but it is likely that the emphasis on the mistaken nature of this belief indicates that the Beloved Disciple *has now died,* and that this resulted in bitter disappointment and was a blow to faith. The contrary notion, that there would have been no reason to combat the expectation if the disciple had died, is the reverse of the truth. The history of such groups as the Millerites in the nineteenth century illustrates the terrible offense to faith when hopes nourished by misguided prophets prove false. What, then, has the author of the epilogue done to counteract the mistaken belief of "the brothers"? One thing he did not do: he did not state that belief in the promise of the Lord's coming is a mistake. The promise stands, and it must be cherished still. The author contented himself rather with correcting the wording of the statement that had been in circulation, and refrained from any further comment: the Lord said, not, "*I will* that he remain . . . ," but, "*If I will* that he remain. . . ." That is, he announced a possibility of the future, in harmony with the eschatological hope of the entire NT, gospels and epistles, in order to etch indelibly on Peter's mind that the future of the Beloved Disciple was not his concern but that of the risen Lord, and of him alone.

This interpretation of v 23 does not satisfy some modern exegetes. Schnackenburg has been severely critical of it, judging that it makes the saying sophistic. After the death of the disciple it is clear that Jesus did *not* want the disciple to live to the Parousia, and prior to his death it has no weight (3:371); accordingly he follows those who wish to interpret "remain" in a figurative manner; *the Beloved Disciple "remains" in his Spirit-borne proclamation embodied in the Gospel* (3:371). This latter is an attractive interpretation, but it appears to us more sophistic than the simple reading of the saying. It imports the meaning of v 24 into v 23, but v 24 was added for different reason, and is more pertinent to the issue of the relation of Peter and the Beloved Disciple than to the time of the Parousia.

Not infrequently the question as to the relation of the eschatology of vv 22–23 to that of the Gospel has been raised. In the view of some the eschatology which has been jettisoned by the Evangelist has here been re-established by the author of the epilogue. On this view two observations may be made. First, it is illegitimate to evaluate the eschatology of an author on the basis of one sentence—as truly as it is to interpret Paul's eschatology solely by 1 Thess 4:13–18; that passage was directed to a single problem in the community, and so also is John 21:22–23. How the writer would have related future expectation to present realization of the blessings of the kingdom of God cannot be known from this one sentence (assuming that he was not the Evangelist). Second, the view that *the Evangelist* rejected the fundamental elements of Christian eschatology and transmuted them into something different can be held only on a selective reading of the Gospel. In our exegesis we have seen how eschatology is fundamental to the entire Gospel, for it is the gospel of *life*—the life of the kingdom of God! The Evangelist has emphasized beyond all other NT writers present eschatological realities, which are important also in the synoptic Gospels and the epistles. But he has given clear expression to the cardinal elements of eschatological hope, judgment, resurrection, and Parousia, while omitting expressions that could imply an *imminent* coming of the kingdom of God (for example, he has nothing comparable to the parables of "watching" in the synoptic Gospels, Mark 13:33–37; Matt 24:32–33, 36–41, 42–44, 45–51). Yet the Evangelist at no point presents eschatological hope as dogma without reference to life; both present and future aspects of resurrection to eternal life, judgment, and Parousia are related to the individual and to the Church. On this Schlatter has a down-to-earth comment we do well to heed. Noting the reserve of the Evangelist, alike regarding the eschatological glory of the Church and its condition in the present, it is clear where the emphasis lies, namely, "*that* and *how* the work of Jesus is continued through the disciples, and the Vine becomes fruitful through its branches. The Church is not thereby given a substitute for prophecy, but rather the capacity to treasure that which she has received and to do that which she has to do now in the name of Jesus for the fulfillment of his will" (375).

Conclusion (21:24–25)

These two sentences are appended to the narratives of vv 1–23 to attest the origin of the Gospel in the Beloved Disciple (v 24), and to round off the epilogue and give the book a final conclusion (necessitated through the addition of chap. 21 after the conclusion of 20:30–31). In view of the different nature and purpose of the two sentences, it is possible that they come from two different sources. The prior question, however, is to determine who the subject is of "we know" in v 24.

24 The following answers are possible as to the identity of the person or persons.

(*i*) The elders of the church at Ephesus. So Westcott believed—he thought that the form of v 24, as contrasted with that of 19:35, shows that it was not from the Evangelist, and that v 25, spoken in the first person *singular,* came from one who perhaps had heard the Apostle say something like this (2:374).

(*ii*) The author, using the "editorial 'we,'" as he does at times in the Gospel (e.g., 3:2, 11; 20:2) and in his epistles (1 John 1:2, 4; 3 John 11). J. Chapman, convinced of this view, wrote, "The writer uses ἡμεῖς (we) and the plural verbs for the sake of solemnity, and *always does so when referring to his* μαρτυρία, (witness)" ("We know that his Testimony is true," 379–85).

(*iii*) The writer and others closely linked to him. So, e.g., Schlatter: "The speaker stands in this 'we' in the first place, but he knows that he is not alone, but sees himself in a greater circle of such as share his knowledge with him" (376). This accords with the famous passage in the Muratorian

Canon, which states that John wrote the Fourth Gospel at the entreaties of his fellow disciples and bishops, but not until he had asked them to pray with him concerning the matter; then "it was revealed to Andrew, one of the Apostles, that John should write down all things in his own name *with the recognition of all.*"

(*iv*) The author and the church to which he belonged. So Bultmann: "The idea is that the community knows that the testimony of the Beloved Disciple is always true . . . accordingly the readers of the gospel will receive as true the testimony that is borne in the gospel" (717–18).

(*v*) "We know" is an indefinite expression meaning "as is well known," or "it is a matter of common knowledge," therefore, virtually, "one knows" (so Dodd, "Note on John 21.24," 212–13).

The plausibility of each of these solutions leads to some uncertainty, but perhaps the second one should be taken more seriously than it has been in recent times (see *Comment* on 20:2). Its implications, however, vary according to one's ideas about the author. J. Chapman, for example, believed that the writer is none other than John the son of Zebedee, the Beloved Disciple. He paraphrases v 24 thus: *"This person* (n.4: in the Chinese sense; 'this person' = I) is the Apostle, who is the witness of these things and is the writer of this book, and I, even I (whose high place among the Apostles has been described in it) know that it is all perfectly accurate" (385). We have already given our reasons why we find this position difficult to receive (see *Introduction*, p. lxx, and this paraphrase well exemplifies the inconceivability of the Beloved Disciple writing of himself like this. From a very different viewpoint, H. Thyen considers that v 24 provides the key to all the Beloved Disciple passages in the Gospel: the writer is the Evangelist, who introduced all the passages relating to the Beloved Disciple into the earlier form of the Gospel, and who *created this figure for the purpose of giving a divine authorization for his work* (Thyen's developing views on this subject may be seen in his *TR* article, "Aus der Literatur zum Johannesevangelium" 42 [1977] 211–70; "Entwicklungen innerhalb der johanneischen Theologie und Kirche im Spiegel von Joh 21 und der Lieblingsjünger Texte des Evangeliums," *L'Evangile de Jean*, ed. M. de Jonge, BETL 44 [1977] 259–99; his views on John 21 were summarized in a SNTS seminar paper in 1984 bearing the significant title, "Joh 21: Nicht 'Nachtrag,' sondern 'Schlüssel' zum Vierten Evangelium" = "John 21: Not 'Supplement' but 'Key' to the Fourth Gospel"). Here we have swung to the opposite pole of criticism, attaching great significance to John 21 and to v 24 in particular. The view that the Beloved Disciple is the creation of the Evangelist or Redactor of the Gospel, is, however, extremely unlikely. His frequent association with Peter indicates that we are dealing with an individual among the earliest disciples of Jesus. (On his role in the Johannine Circle, see J. Roloff, "Der Johanneische 'Lieblingsjünger' und der Lehrer der Gerechtigkeit," *NTS* 15 [1968–69] 129–51). We go on to investigate the meaning of the statement that the Beloved Disciple is the one "who bears witness of these things and wrote these things." Dodd's idea that "these things" denote the narrower context of vv 20–23, or at most chap. 21 ("Note on John 21:24," 212–13; *Historical Tradition,* 12) has little to commend it; there is general agreement that the entire Gospel is in view here. The *Gospel,* then, is stated to be a *transcription* of the *witness* of the Beloved Disciple to Jesus, the Christ and Son of God (cf. 20:31). Did the author of 21:24 mean to say that the "transcript," i.e., *the written Gospel,* as well as *the witness it bears* was the work of the disciple? That was the conviction of most scholars in earlier years. Barrett stated it to be "the most natural meaning of these words, and therefore the meaning to be adopted unless very strong reasons are brought against it" (587). Strong reasons do exist against this view, not least the unlikelihood that the author was claiming that the Beloved Disciple *wrote* 21:1–23 (vv 21–23 may well imply his death!) The Disciple could, of course, have supplied materials for the chapter. And that may well apply to a great deal of chaps. 1–20 (we have observed the difficulty of accepting that the Beloved Disciple *wrote* the Farewell Discourses as they now exist in the two versions, chaps. 13–14, 15–16, as distinct from acknowledging that they reflect his testimony). For this reason many have followed Bernard in interpreting "wrote" as having a causative sense, "caused to be written." Bernard cited 19:19 as an example of this; that "Pilate wrote a title and put it on the cross" presumably means that Pilate was responsible for its wording; so also the apostles in the NT letters speak of their "writing" them, whereas we know that they consistently used amanuenses (2:713). The suggestion should not be dismissed out of hand, as H. P. V. Nunn did, in pointing out that any scribe who ventured to put into shape Pilate's words would have got into serious trouble, and in affirming that scribes who wrote apostolic letters will always have written the *exact* words dictated to them (*The Authorship of the Fourth Gospel* [1952] 8, cited by Morris, 880 n.63). On the contrary, considerable freedom was accorded amanuenses in the ancient world, who often were left to convey in their own language the substance of what they were told to write, especially in letters (there is no other way of linking the pastoral Epistles with Paul except on such a basis, unless one took the contrary view and maintained that they were the *only* letters that he actually wrote, all the rest reflecting the language and style of amanuenses; so M. P. Prior, in an unpublished dissertation, "Second Timothy: A Personal Letter of Paul," King's College, London, 1985). This mode of composition in the ancient world was so common a phenomenon that it is not necessary to change the meaning of "wrote" in v 24 to "caused to write"; but the statement may be understood simply as "an assertion of spiritual responsibility for what is contained in the book" (G. Schrenk, *TDNT* 1:743). More specifically, it asserts that the book reproduces the *witness* of the Beloved Disciple; it is this which most concerns the author of v 24; hence he adds, "We know that his *witness* is true." The saying is remarkably close to 5:32, which refers to the witness that God bears concerning Jesus (extended through 5:33–40; cf. also 8:14, 18). The Fourth Gospel is supremely a book of witness to Jesus, based on the witness borne *by* Jesus, and *to* Jesus by the Paraclete Spirit, who enabled the Beloved Disciple to grasp it and hand it on to the Church.

25 So the epilogue, and the Gospel to which it is added, come to a formal conclusion. Its similarity with the Evangelist's conclusion in 20:30–31 is apparent when one sets them side by side:

Jesus loved. R. A. Culpepper summarized them in the following manner: "The Paraclete was to remain with the disciples (14:7), teach them everything (14:26), remind the disciples of all that Jesus had said (14:26), declare what he has heard (16:13), and glorify Jesus, because he will 'receive from me (Jesus) and declare to you' (16:14). From all indications this is exactly what the Beloved Disciple has done. He has come from the bosom of Jesus and has made him known to those who now affirm his testimony. He has taught, reminded, and borne a true witness. The words of Jesus in the gospel are the words that he has received from the Lord and written or caused to be written. . . . The Beloved Disciple is therefore not only the authority and representative of the Johannine tradition vis-à-vis Peter, he is *the epitome of the ideal disciple*. In him belief, love, and faithful witness are joined. He abides in Jesus' love, and the Paraclete works through him" (*Anatomy of the Fourth Gospel,* 122–123). So surely as the early church needed the ministry of the Beloved Disciple to complement that of Peter, so surely does the Church at all times need the ministry of those who ponder the revelation of the Lord attested in the Gospel and seek the guidance of the Paraclete-Spirit who made it possible. Perhaps it needs even more urgently shepherds who *unite* in their ministries the qualities of Peter and the Beloved Disciple. If they ask as well they may, "Who is equal to such a calling?" (2 Cor 2:16), they may also echo the words of the apostle who raised the question: "Our competence comes from God. *He* has made us competent as ministers of a new covenant" (2 Cor 3:4–5).

5. In the thrilling but stormy generation that saw the birth and advance of the Christian Church and ended in the terrible events of the fall of Jerusalem, Christians needed to understand rightly the eschatological teaching of Jesus. That necessity remains in every generation, not least in light of the constant clamor of voices claiming to give the last word of the Spirit on the end times. In the period when the Gospel was sent on its way there was need for one particular problem to be cleared up, and this the author sought to do in vv 20–23. His example is to be followed, and that in two respects: to listen carefully to what the Lord actually said, and not to be content with secondhand repetitions of his word and opinions about it; and to give heed to its content, letting the teaching of the kingdom of God and the coming of Christ have its due effect on our life and service. In this endeavor the author was at one with the spirit of the Evangelist, even if his accent was more Galilean than Jerusalemite. Happy is the congregation whose shepherd interprets the word of the Lord for today's world in its truth and power!

Index of Ancient Authors

Aquinas 138
Aristotle
  Eth. Nic. 9.8 274
  Eth. Nic. 1169a 274
Athanasius 262
Augustine 6, 12, 140, 143, 144, 262, 402, 403
  Confessions 9.13–14 6
  De Conuig. Adult. 2.6 144
  In Ioan. Ev. Tract. 9.1 162
  In Ioan. Ev. Tract. 76.4 260
  In Ioan. Ev. Tract. 101.5–6 286
  In Ioan. Ev. Tract. 116.200.648 339
  In Ioan. Ev. Tract. 122 402

Basil
  Corderius-Catena 295 195

Callistratus 344
Chrysostom 139, 357
  Hom. in Ioan. 9.6.7 155
  Hom. in Ioan. 85.4 372
Cicero 344
  1 Clement lxxv
Clement of Alexandria lxvii, lxviii, lxxxviii
  The Rich Man's Salvation 42.1–2 lxvii
Clementine Recognitions 23
Cyprian 85, 143
  De Unitate Ecclesiae 7 347
Cyril of Alexandria 262, 402
  In. Jo. XII: PG 74 402

Didache lxxv

Egerton Papyrus 2 lxxv, lxxix, 192
Ephraim the Syrian lxxix
Epiphanius
  Pancrion 51.25.6 107
Epistle of Barnabas lxxv, lxxix
  12 408
  15:9 385
Epistle of Diognetus lxxix
Eusebius lxvii, lxviii, 143, 144
  Ecclesiastical History 3.29.4 331
  Ecclesiastical History 3.31.3 lxvii
  Ecclesiastical History 3.39.3–4 lxviii
  Ecclesiastical History 3.39.17 143
  Ecclesiastical History 4.14.7 lxvii
  Ecclesiastical History 5.4–8 lxvii
  Ecclesiastical History 6.44 346

Gospel of Peter 397

Heraclitus 6
Hippolytus 151
Homer
  Iliad 5.340–341 357

Ignatius lxxv, lxxix
  Romans 5.3 273
  Smyrn. 3.2 385
  Smyrn. 7:1 95
Irenaeus lxvi, lxvii, lxviii 143
  Against Heretics 2.22.6 139
  Against Heretics 3.1.2 lxvi, lxxix
  Against Heretics 3.3.4 lxvi
  Against Heretics 5.22.2 357
  Against Heretics 5.33.4 lxvii
  Against Heretics 15.2 55
  Dem. 79 408

Jerome 145, 165, 401, 402, 404
Josephus 16, 69, 88, 125, 317, 318, 336, 344, 362
  Jewish Antiquities 3.151 347
  Jewish Antiquities 5.44 358
  Jewish Antiquities 17.74 34
  Jewish Antiquities 8.100 106
  Jewish Antiquities 11.2 lxxxv
  Jewish Antiquities 12.325 173
  Jewish Antiquities 14.37 44
  Jewish Antiquities 14.107 198
  Jewish Antiquities 15.395–97 165
  Jewish Antiquities 15.395 272
  Jewish Antiquities 14.385 329
  Jewish Antiquities 17.199 359
  Jewish Antiquities 18.63–64 362–363
  Jewish Antiquities 20.200 278
  Jewish Antiquities 21.38 24
  The Jewish War 2.166 196
  The Jewish War 3.505 84
  The Jewish War 3.375 130
  The Jewish War 5.449 345
  Vita 59

Justin Martyr
  Apology 1:35 408
  Apology 26:1 136
  Apology 26:4–5 135
  Apology 25:1 24
  Apology 61 lxxv, 47
  Dialogue with Trypho 69 107
  Dialogue with Trypho 94 408
  Dialogue with Trypho 143.6 278

Marcion lxvii, lxviii
Muratorian Fragment lxvii–lxviii, 413–414

Origen x, 20, 48, 69, 114–115, 135, 165, 333
  Contra Celsum 2.8–9 320
  Contra Celsum 2.24 320
  Contra Celsum 2.37 320
  Contra Celsum 6.11 136
  In Jo. 28.12 197

$\mathfrak{p}^{45}$ 164, 165, 183, 184
$\mathfrak{p}^{52}$ lxxv, lxxix
$\mathfrak{p}^{66}$ 2, 33, 38, 45, 58, 69, 70, 85, 103, 121, 126, 151, 165, 183, 184, 204, 205, 229, 230, 242, 243, 268, 293, 318, 366, 367, 394
$\mathfrak{p}^{75}$ 2, 38, 45, 58, 69, 70, 84, 85, 103, 121, 126, 151, 164, 165, 183, 205, 243
Papias lxvii, lxviii
  Exposition of the Oracles of the Lord lxviii
Philo liv–lv, lxvi, lxxix, 6–7, 60, 317, 318
  De Fuga et Inventione 110–112 347
  De Posteritate Caini 144 416
  De Somniis 2.242 60
  Quod Deus sit immutabilis 143 297
  De Vita Mosis 2.65 lxxxv
     2:134 liv
  Legum Allegoriae 1:31–32 liv
  Legum Allegoriae 3:79ff 35–36
  De Mutatione Nominum 92
Philonides Vita 22 274
Plato
  Phaedo 65 243
  Symposium 179b 274
Plutarch
  The Divine Vengeance 554 A/B 344
  Moralia 180e 357
Polycarp lxvi, lxvii, lxviii
  Martyrdom of Polycarp 13.1 278

Shepherd of Hermas lxxv

Tacitus 344
  Annals 6.8 340
Tatian (including Ephraem's Commentary) 151
  Harmony of the Gospels lxxv, 47, 58, 66, 106
Tertullian 2, 85, 143, 262, 376
  De Bapt. 1 162
  Spect. 30 376
Theodore of Mopsuestia 381, 385

Valentinus lxxv

Apocryphal and Pseudepigraphal Writings

Assumption of Moses
  12:6   79

2 Baruch
  48   293

Ben Sirach
  4:10   25, 179
  24   8
  24:6–8   8

24:21   60, 92
24:24–27   60
39:3   164, 286
43:10   23

1 Enoch
  37–71   164, 287
  37:2   287
  42:2   8

48:6   110
49:2–4   26
62:1–10   112

4 Ezra
  2:14   138
  7:28–29   215
  8:19b–36   293
  13:51–52   110

Jubilees
1:19–21   293
1:23   49
1:24–25   25, 179
10:3–6   293
16:20–31   114
19:9   274
20–22   293
36:17   293

1 Maccabees
1:9   173
4:36–59   173
4:59   172
13:51   210

2 Maccabees
1:9   148, 173
5:19   196
10:6   114

Odes of Solomon   lxxv, lxxix, 7
7   7

Psalms of Solomon
18:6   49

Testament of the Twelve
Patriarchs   223
Benjamin 3   24
Joseph 19:8–9   24
Judah 20:1–5   257

24:3   49
Naphtali 5   210
Tobit 7:12   349

Wisdom of Solomon   lx
2:10–5:23   355
2:10–24   112
2:18   25, 179
2:24   135
5:1–5   112
7:20   27
7:22–8:1   lx
8:19–20   155
9:1   8
9:1–4   lx
18:14–16   8

Qumran Materials

IQH
3:19–23   lxii
6:34   214
11:7–14   lxii
11:10–12   lxi
11:12–14   49
11:12   214
16:8–12   lxii
16:11–12   lxii

1QS lxiii
1:20   21
3:1–12   lxi
3:6–9   49
3:6–8   lxii
3:15–4:26   lxii
3:18–21   257
3:21–24   lxii
9:6   lxii

9:11   24, 117
10:19–21   120
11:2–9   lxii
12:10   21
1QSa 2:11ff   25, 179
4QDan   25, 179
4QFlor
1:6–7   25, 179
11QMelch   176

Jewish Targums and Rabbinic Writings

Aboda. Zara. 5a   176
Abot
2 (1d)   62
2.5   120
5:19   158
B. Abod. Zar
14d   157
28b   156
B. Bat. 126b   155
Ber. 28b   lxxvii, 153
63a   296
Ber. Rab. 70:12   28
Besa 32b   134
Chag. 5b, 32   15
Eighteen Benedictions   xlvi, lxxvii, lxxviii
Benediction 12   xlvi, lxxvii, 153, 154, 277, 289
Exod. Rab.
19.81c   134
21:3   120
Gen. Rab.
1   9
1.19   79
11.8c   74
44.28a   138
56.4   345
65 (41b)   47
91 (58a)   196–197
94 (60a)   197
100 (64a)   189
Ger. Rab. 63:939c   155
J. Ber. 5a   118
Jerusalem Targum on Deuteronomy
21:20   154
jSanh.
1.1   309
7.2   309
18a   332
Ketub 2.9   129
96a   20
Lev. Rab.
15.2   53
15:115c   357

36 (133a)   272
Mek. of Rabbi Ishmael   345
Mek. Exod
13:17   92
14:15   274
14:35b   274
15   198
15:32 (15b)   47
17 (41a)   198
21.2.82a   233
Memar Markah (Samaritan Writing)   lv
3:3   lxiv
4:1   lxiv
111.3   65
Midr. Gen. 21:14   233
Midr. Gen. 42:17   371
Midr. Ps. 82   176
Midr. Ps. 118   210
244a   210
Midr. Qoh.
1:9   91
7:1 (31a)   220
11:5   47
Midr. Rabba   118
51   118
Midr. Rab. Exod. 32:7   176
Midr. Sam.
5:9   120
Ohaloth 18:7   327
Pe'a l.15c.14   233
Pesah 91a   334
Pirqe R. El. 3[2b]   118
Pirqe 'Abot
2.15   152
5:1–9   402
27   78
pSanh
1.18a 37   309
Qidd. 70a   62
Rabbi Aha   53
Rabbi Akiba   lxi
Rabbi Chijja   15
Rabbi Eleazar   lxi
Rabbi Jehoshua b.Levi   20

Ruth Rab. 2:14   190
Sabb.   69
7.2   157
19:2   109
Sanh.
6b–7a   176
9.6   278
38b   138
43a   108, 224, 319, 325, 338
99a   99
107a   108
Sem. 8   189
Shab. 23.5   360
S. OlamRab
21   121
Sota
22a   108, 136
47a   108
47b   176
Sukk.
5:1   113, 127
5:55a   117
27b   121
Tanh.
6   386
1Qb   109
32a   386
Tanh. B   75
6. (60a)   138
9(13a)   176
Tg. on Isaiah 44:3   60
Tg. Ps. J.   176
Toledoth Jeshu   135
Tos. Sanh. 12:10   155
Tr. Sopherim 16:8   416
T. Shabb
15   109
16   109
Yalkut Shimoni 2, 480   59
Yoma
4a   158
85b   109

Gnostic, Mandaean and Hermetic Writings

Basilides Commentary on John	345	Gospel of Thomas	137	P. Oxyr. 1	73
Concerning Regeneration		18	137	Poimandres	lvi
13	352	19	137	1:31–32	293
13:21–22	293	31	73	The Second Treatise of the	
Ginza		38	112	Great Seth	345
59:39–60:2	271	85	137		
301:11–14	272	Gospel of Truth	lvi, lxxv, lxxix		

Index of Modern Authors

Abbott, E. A. xxviii
Ackermann, J. S. 162
Ackroyd, P. R. 392, 403
Adam, J. 6
Agourides, S. C. 291, 293, 392
Ahrendts, D. R. 403
Aland, K. lxxv, 1
Albright, W. F. 58, 375
Alford, H. 38
Allen, J. E. 312
Allen, W. C. 100
Argyle, J. 56, 63
Arndt, F. W. (See W. Bauer for the entries of BGD)
Auer, E. G. 364, 372

Bacon, B. W. 227, 240, 392
Bajsic, A. 312, 334, 337
Balagué, M. 364, 372
Balz, H. 189
Bammel, E. 18, 28, 162, 178, 180, 196, 198, 199, 265, 280, 310, 312, 340, 341
Bampfylde, G. 312, 353
Barbet, P. 356
Barbour, R. S. 201, 207
Barclay, W. xxvi
Barker, M. 180
Barrett, C. K. xi, xxvi, xxviii, xxxv–xxxvii, xli, xlii, lvi, lxxv, lxxxiv, lxxxviii, 18, 21, 33, 35, 45, 50, 63, 64, 73, 81, 84, 87, 94, 106, 107, 108, 110, 115, 125, 126, 130, 131, 135, 153, 154, 159, 165, 166, 169, 170, 173, 174, 188, 190, 192, 193, 194, 196, 197, 204, 213, 229, 231, 234, 235, 240, 243, 250, 257, 262, 268, 275, 276, 283, 286, 287, 293, 295, 296, 297, 299, 302, 305, 310, 317, 331, 334, 337, 339, 349, 355, 357, 366, 371, 378, 386, 415
Barton, G. A. 227, 312
Bauer, W. xxvi, 45, 58, 69, 115, 126, 151, 159, 170, 171, 192, 193, 197, 209, 234, 243, 250, 268, 293, 331, 342, 346, 357, 394, 396, 400, 408
Baur, F. C. lxxv
Beare, F. W. 364
Beasley-Murray, G. R. 43, 407
Becker, J. xxvi, xxxviii, 21, 22, 34, 38, 40, 43, 45, 47, 50, 51, 59, 71, 87, 132, 156, 166, 167, 174, 185, 190, 192, 194, 197, 224, 229, 231, 232, 235, 238, 243, 244, 251, 254, 270, 275, 283, 291, 295, 303, 305, 310
Becker, U. 144, 145
Behm, J. 256
Bell, H. I. lxxv
Bengel, J. A. 49, 381
Benoit, P. 364, 368, 392
Berger, K. 18, 27
Bernard, J. H. xxvi, xc, 3, 21, 38, 45, 46, 47, 48, 58, 89, 125, 126, 131, 165, 166, 191, 192, 196, 197, 224, 229, 243, 250, 268, 275, 279, 284, 295, 310, 318, 322, 342, 374, 376, 394, 408, 415

Berrouard, M. F. 265, 281
Bertram, G. 201, 214
Betz, O. 284
Bevan, E. 180
Bevan, T. W. 201
Bietenhard, H. 255
Billerbeck, P. lx, lxxvi, 15, 20, 27, 35, 47, 48, 53, 60, 62, 63, 70, 74, 75, 76, 99, 106, 108, 109, 116, 118, 119, 120, 121, 127, 128, 134, 136, 145, 151, 155, 157, 158, 173, 180, 190, 195, 196, 198, 210, 233, 243, 246, 272, 274, 278, 309, 317, 318, 327, 334, 346, 359, 375, 383, 386, 416
Birdsall, J. N. 162, 165
Bishop, E. F. F. 162, 169, 227, 236
Black, M. 164, 193
Blank, J. xxvi, xxviii, lxxxiv, 43, 50, 66, 77, 123, 128, 129, 131, 135, 136, 138, 139, 141, 156, 160, 161, 201, 212, 223, 235, 256, 265, 270, 280, 282, 290, 297, 312, 327, 337, 374, 376, 379, 388
Blass, F., Debrunner, A., Funk, R. W. 3, 125, 126, 240, 360, 366, 377
Blenkinsopp, J. 100, 115
Bligh, J. 56, 66, 81, 152, 156
Blinzler, J. 144, 145, 195, 310, 312, 317, 334, 335, 340, 342, 343, 346, 354, 358, 360
Bode, E. L. 364, 371
Boice, J. M. xxvi
Boismard, M.-E. xxvi, 2, 3, 22, 32, 34, 43, 86, 100, 162, 201, 227, 229, 231, 235, 240, 250, 342, 392
Boman, T. 1, 8, 9, 201
Bonner, C. 180
Bonsirven, J. 312, 341, 342
Borgen, P. xxviii, xli, 1, 43, 50, 81, 86, 87, 91, 201, 240, 312
Borig, R. 265, 269
Boring, M. E. 240
Bornhäuser, K. 199, 324, 372, 402
Bornkamm, G. 81, 149, 155, 160, 192, 291
Bouyer, L. xxvi
Bowker, J. W. xxviii
Bowman, J. xxviii, lxiii, lxv, 56, 136
Braude, W. G. 176
Braun, F. M. 2, 37, 56, 100, 180, 192, 227, 229, 312, 392
Bream, H. N. 265
Bright, J. 149
Brooke, A. E. 48, 357
Brooks, O. S. 81
Brown, R. E. xi, xxvi, xxviii, xxxvi, xlii, lxi, lxxviii, xc, 20, 21, 22, 32, 45, 46, 53, 59, 67, 81, 84, 86, 87, 90, 105, 107, 108, 118, 119, 126, 131, 135, 146, 148, 151, 153, 162, 165, 166, 167, 170, 174, 177, 190, 191, 193, 197, 205, 206, 207, 218, 223, 224, 226, 229, 230, 231, 235, 248, 251, 255, 259, 269, 273, 279, 280, 281, 283, 286, 294, 295, 297, 299, 303, 310, 312, 318, 322, 325, 328, 331, 340, 342, 345 349, 350, 353,

355, 357, 360, 366, 368, 369, 370, 372, 374, 378, 392, 394, 395, 399, 400, 402, 404, 406, 407
Brownlee, W. H. xxviii, lxxvii, lxxix
Bruce, F. F. xxvi, 94, 125, 131, 134, 138, 165, 191, 192, 223, 229, 243, 250, 253, 276, 299, 310, 328, 329, 330, 334, 342, 357, 381, 385
Bruns, J. E. xxviii, 162, 202, 265
Buchanan, G. W. xxviii, lxiv
Büchsel, F. xxvi, 192, 280, 281
Bultmann, R. xi, xxvi, xxxiv, xxxvi, xxxviii, xxxix, xlii, xliii, lv, lvii, lxxiii, lxxv, lxxix, lxxxvi, 3, 5, 11, 12, 14, 20, 21, 24, 26, 31, 33, 38, 40, 41, 45, 46, 47, 48, 50, 52, 53, 59, 60, 62, 63, 67, 71, 74, 75, 76, 78, 84, 87, 88, 89, 90, 92, 93, 97, 103, 105, 110, 112, 116, 118, 128, 130, 131, 132, 133, 135, 137, 138, 139, 145, 148, 156, 160, 165, 166, 168, 174, 185, 190, 192, 196, 197, 209, 219, 224, 225, 228, 229, 230, 231, 232, 235, 237, 238, 243, 250, 253, 254, 257, 258, 268, 269, 271, 273, 276, 277, 278, 279, 281, 283, 284, 293, 296, 298, 299, 300, 301, 302, 303, 305, 318, 319, 322, 326, 330, 331, 336, 337, 339, 340, 342, 345, 348, 352, 355, 357, 363, 369, 371, 373, 374, 376, 379, 387, 388, 389, 396, 400, 401, 407, 408, 414
Burkill, T. C. 310
Burkitt, F. C. 141, 202, 289, 397
Burney, C. F. lxxix, 2, 3, 28, 100
Buse, I. 37, 312
Bussche, H. Van De 265

Cadbury, H. J. 364, 367
Cadier, J. 291
Cadman, W. H. 180, 190
Caird, G. B. 202, 240, 246
Calvin, J. 381
Camerarius, J. 318
Campenhausen, H. von 144, 227, 235, 365, 376
Carroll, K. L. 149
Carson, D. A. xxviii, xli, 41, 265, 281
Cassian, Bishop (S. Besobrasoff) 364, 392
Catchpole, D. R. 310
Cerfaux, L. 162, 164, 240
Chapman, J. 392, 411, 413, 414
Charles, R. H. 250
Charlesworth, J. H. xxviii, lxii
Charlier, C. 240
Charlier, J. P. 123
Chavel, C. B. 334
Chevalier, M. A. 312
Christie, W. M. 227
Chytraeus, D. 294
Cilix, Oppianus 401, 404
Coleman, B. W. 144
Colpe, C. xxviii
Conybeare, F. C. lxxix
Conzelmann, H. xxxiv, 128
Cortes, J. B. 100

Corssen, P. 312, 342
Cottam, T. 100
Cribbs, F. L. xxviii, lxxvi, lxxvii
Cullmann, O. xxviii, xli, xlvii, lvii, lxxiv,
   lxxviii, 18, 25, 37, 41, 56, 59, 64,
   136, 234, 235, 272, 357, 392, 411,
   417
Culpepper, R. A. xxviii, lxxiv, 1, 4, 324,
   418

Dahl, N. A. xxviii, 123, 311
Dalman, G. 371
Daniélou, J. 100, 117
Danker, F. (See W. Bauer for the entries
   of BDG)
Daube, D. 56, 58, 90, 180, 197
Dauer, A. 310, 311, 312, 337, 342, 343,
   346, 347, 350, 351, 352, 361, 362
Davies, W. D. xlvi
Debrunner, A. 126, 230, 243 (also see
   Blass, F. for BDF and BDR entries)
Deissmann, A. 151, 274, 340, 402
Dekker, C. 100
Delorme, J. 291
Demke, C. xxviii, 1, 3
Derrett, J. D. M. 32, 34, 144, 146, 162,
   202, 227
Dibelius, M. 192, 265, 308
Dodd, C. H. x, xi, xxvi, xxviii, xxxiii,
   xxxvi, xli, xlii, xliii, xliv, xlv, li, liv,
   lvi, lvii, lix, lxxi, lxxii, lxxvii, xc, 1,
   10, 12, 15, 18, 21, 22, 31, 32, 34,
   35, 36, 37, 39, 43, 45, 46, 47, 50,
   52, 58, 59, 63, 66, 67, 71, 73, 74,
   75, 87, 88, 90, 92, 97, 98, 104, 123,
   128, 131, 132, 134, 149, 152, 165,
   166, 167, 169, 173, 179, 180, 184,
   190, 191, 198, 202, 205, 206, 209,
   211, 212, 214, 217, 222, 223, 227,
   231, 235, 240, 244, 250, 263, 271,
   272, 275, 276, 277, 279, 293, 295,
   297, 308, 310, 312, 317, 318, 319,
   322, 328, 331, 335, 345, 351, 352,
   353, 358, 359, 360, 364, 369, 370,
   378, 387, 392, 400, 414
Dunkerley, R. 181
Dunn, J. D. G. 81, 227, 229, 364, 381
Dupont, J. 2, 123
Dürr, L. 7

Edwards, R. A. xxvi
Edwards, W. E. 312, 356
Emerton, J. A. 162, 176, 392, 402, 403
Evans, C. F. 312, 364

Farmer, W. R. 202
Farrer, A. lxxviii
Fascher, E. 265
Fee, G. D. 100
Fensham, F. C. 240
Fenton, J. C. xxvi, 312
Feuillet, A. 67, 81, 149, 162, 166, 202,
   291, 295
Filson, F. V. xxviii, lxxxii
Findlay, J. A. xxvi, 66
Finegan, J. 318
Fischer, G. 240, 249, 250, 251
Fitzmyer, J. A. 206, 312
Flusser, D. 26
Ford, J. M. 312
Foretell, I. T. 181
Fortna, R. T. xxix, xxxix, xl, 34, 67, 71,
   81, 88, 90, 149, 152, 181, 185, 202,
   312
Fowler, D. C 364

Fraser, J. 336
Freed, E. D. xxix, lxiv, lxv, 202
Fridrichsen, A. 227
Fuller, R. H. xxxiv, 181, 185, 194, 364,
   397

Gabel, W. J. 312, 356
Gaechter, P. 67, 75, 404
Gardner-Smith, P. x, xxix, xxxvi, 322,
   342, 384
Gärtna, B. 81
Gärtner, E. 41
George, A. 165, 240, 291, 297
Geyser, A. 32
Giblet, J. 81, 163, 291
Gifort, G. 81, 89
Gingrich, F. W. (See W. Bauer for the
   entries of BGD)
Gnilke, J. xxvi, 145
Godet, F. xxvi
Collwitzer, H. 240
Goodspeed, E. J. 318
Gore, A. 201
Gourbillon, J. G. 207
Grant, R. M. lxxvi, 392, 402, 404
Grass, H. 364, 392
Griffith, F. L. 200
Grimm, W. 181
Grelot, P. 100
Green-Armytage, A. H. N. xxix
Grobel, K. 200
Grosscuw, W. K. 227, 229, 230, 232
Grundmann, W. xxvi, 265
Gundry, R. H. 240, 249, 250
Guthrie, D. 43

Haenchen, E. xi, xxvi, xxix, lxxix, 10,
   21, 22, 36, 47, 48, 56, 58, 59, 72,
   74, 87, 103, 115, 151, 132, 137, 139,
   152, 166, 174, 192, 196, 197, 229,
   231, 232, 235, 238, 243, 251, 254,
   259, 280, 297, 310, 312, 322, 326,
   332, 339, 342, 345, 352, 398, 408,
   416
Hahn, F. 101, 163, 190
Hanson, A. T. 163, 177
Hare, D. R. A. lxxvii
Haring, N. M. 227
Harris, R. 101
Hart, H. S. J. 312, 336
Hartungsveld, L. Van xxix, 202, 213
Hartmann, G. 364, 368, 369
Harvey, A. E. 310, 312
Haas, N. 354
Hatch, W. H. P. 265
Hauck, F. 234
Hawkins, D. J. 265
Hawthorne, G. F. 239
Heer, J. 132
Hegermann, H. xxix, lxxxvi
Heitmüller, W. xxvi, 67, 192, 251, 255,
   299, 357
Hendriksen, W. xxvi
Hengel, M. 26, 179, 309, 344, 408
Hennecke, E. 143
Héring, J. 191
Hiers, R. H. 37, 39
Higgins, A. J. B. xxix
Hobbes, T. 330, 331
Hobbs, H. H. xxvi
Hofrichter, P. 2, 14
Holland, H. S. xxix, xxxiii
Holtzmann, O. lxxv
Hooke, S. H. 101, 364, 387
Hooker, M. D. 1

Horbury, W. 149, 154, 320
Horsley, R. A. 81, 88
Hort, F. J. A. lxix, 252
Hoskyns, E. C. x–xi, xxvi, 1, 5, 10, 13,
   18, 45, 47, 53, 61, 67, 73, 74, 78,
   84, 87, 91, 107, 110, 113, 130, 131,
   132, 135, 139, 159, 169, 170, 177,
   188, 193, 196, 197, 209, 212, 229,
   235, 243, 248, 250, 262, 273, 274,
   279, 280, 284, 286, 288, 294, 296,
   298, 299, 322, 330, 342, 345, 347,
   353, 357, 359, 375, 386, 399, 402,
   406, 412
Hosmer, F. E. 312, 356
Howard, J. K. 81
Howard, W. F. xxvi, xxix, xxxviii, 132,
   166, 239, 250, 279, 417
Huckle, J. xxvi
Hulen, A. B. 18, 26
Hull, J. H. E. 72, 382
Hull, W. E. J. xxvi
Humphries, A. L. 250
Hunter, A. M. xxvi, xxix, lxi, 45, 209

Ibuki, Y. 46
Iersel, B. M. F. Van 18, 21

Jacobs, L. 265
Jaubert, A. xxix, lxiii, 225, 265, 272, 313
Jeremias, J. xxix, 1, 67, 81, 116, 120,
   144, 145, 146, 163, 166, 196, 200,
   225, 229, 310, 313, 318, 383
Jocz, J. xxix, lxxvii, 149
Johnson, E. D. 82, 284
Johnston, G. 240, 257, 265
Jonge, M. De xxix, lxxxviii, 18, 24, 43,
   47, 101, 176, 251, 392, 396, 414
Jülicher, A. lxxv
Juster, J. 308, 310

Kähler, M. xxxiii, 306
Käsemann, E. xxix, xxxix, lv, lxxxi, xc,
   1, 3, 13, 79, 291, 297, 306
Keim, T. lxxv
Kelly, J. 227
Kenyon, F. C. lxxv
Kenyon, K. M. 318
Kern, W. 123
Kilmartin, E. J. 82
Kilpatrick, G. D. xxix, liv, 67, 69, 101,
   115, 310, 313, 318
Kimelman, R. 149
Kittel, G. 202, 214
Klein, G. 313, 326, 392
Klos, H. 82
Knox, R. A. 190
Knox, W. L. 197, 227
Kossen, H. B. 202
Kraeling, C. H. 18, 43
Kragerud, A. xxix
Krauss, H. 376
Kreitzer, L. xi
Kremer, J. 265
Kruse, H. 403
Kugelman, R. 240
Kuhn, H.-W. lxii
Kuhn, K. G. 149, 207, 330
Kuhn, K. H. 101
Kümmel, W. G. lxi, lxvi, lxxix, lxxxiv,
   67, 191
Kundsin, K. xlv, 240
Künneth, W. 364, 389
Kurfess, A. 313
Kysar, R. xxvi, xxix, xxxvi, lxxvii, lxxxiv

Lacomara, A. 223
Lagrange, M. J. xxvi, 103, 165, 170, 192, 209, 229, 243, 250, 275, 279, 295, 296, 299, 302, 318, 332, 342, 359, 377, 394, 406
Lake, K. lxxix
Lamarche, P. 355
Lamouille, A. xxvi
Langkammer, H. 313
Lapide, C. 406
Lategan, B. C. 123
Latham, H. 372
Laurentin, A. 291, 292, 295
Lazure, N. 240
Lee, G. M. 265, 392
Leenhardt, F. J. 82, 86
Legault, A. 206
Lehman, K. 41
Léon-Dufour, X. xxix, xlix, l, li, 37, 40, 41, 67, 72, 82, 85, 98, 99, 202
Leroy, H. 41, 137
Lewis, F. W. 166
Lietzmann, H. 308, 309, 310, 313
Lightfoot, R. H. xxvi, lxix, lxxx, 115, 177, 229, 235, 243, 250, 332
Lindars, B. xxvi, xxix, xxxvi, xlii, 3, 32, 33, 35, 40, 41, 45, 58, 59, 73, 82, 94, 108, 115, 134, 135, 137, 139, 145, 158, 165, 177, 192, 197, 224, 229, 231, 243, 251, 262, 265, 276, 286, 297, 299, 310, 313, 340, 355, 364, 369, 375, 386
Linnemann, E. 32
Lloyd-Jones, D. M. 291
Lofthouse, W. F. lxxxiii
Lohmeyer, E. xlv, 227, 229, 235
Lohse, E. 310
Loisy, A. xxvi, 342, 374
Lorenzen, T. xxix
Luther, M. 192, 249
Lyonnet, S. 281

MacDonald, J. xxix, lxiii–lxiv, 56, 62, 65
MacGregor, G. H. C. xxvi, 82, 207, 347
Macneil, B. 181
Macrae, G. W. xxvi, xxix, 101, 106
Macuch, R. lvii
Mahoney, A. 313, 324
Mahoney, R. 364, 374
Malatesta, E. x, xxix, 291, 295
Malina, B. J. 82
Manson, T. W. xxix, lxxx, lxxxii, 144, 146
Mantey, J. R. 364, 366, 367
Marrow, S. B. 392
Marsh, J. xxvi, 177, 192, 394
Marshall, I. H. 56, 206, 326
Martin, J. P. 163, 181
Martyn, J. L. xxix, xlii, xliv, xlvii, xlix, l, li, lxvi, lxxvii, lxxviii, lxxx, 73, 101, 117, 123, 136, 149, 152, 153, 159, 251, 277
Mason, R. A. 355
Mastin, B. N. xxvi, xxxvi–xxxvii, 293, 310
McCasland, S. V. 240
McEleny, N. J. 392, 403
McNamara, M. 202, 214, 364
Meeks, W. xxix, xliv, xlv, lxiv, lxv, lxxvii, lxxviii, 50, 79, 112, 275, 342
Mein, P. 313
Mendner, S. 37, 40
Metzger, B. 21, 45, 70, 84, 85, 126, 151, 165, 183, 229, 230, 242, 243, 268, 269, 292, 293, 317, 318, 333, 395

Meyer, P. W. 163
Michaelis, W. xlii, 364
Michaels, J. R. 313
Michl, J. 227, 229, 234, 239
Minear, P. S. 163, 291, 417
Miranda, J. P. xxix, lxxxiv
Moffatt, J. lxxv, 166, 227, 243, 318
Mollat, D. 82, 149, 163
Moloney, F. J. 202, 207, 240
Montefiore, H. 82, 88
Moore, G. F. 120
Moore, W. E. 202
Moreton, M. J. 67
Morgan, G. C. 169
Morris, L. xxvi, xxxvi, lxxvi, 169, 170, 192, 243, 250, 330, 342, 415
Morrison, C. D. 291
Moule, C. F. D. xxx, 18, 151, 243
Moulton, J. H. 58, 126, 132, 151, 243, 268, 318, 329, 394
Müller, K. 149
Munck, J. xxx
Munroe, W. 202
Mussner, F. xxx, l, li, lii, liii, 227

Neirynck, F. xxx, xxxvii, 324, 364
Nestle, E. 202, 318
Nestle, W. 313
Neugebauer, F. lxxxviii
Newbigin, L. xxvi, 177, 238
Newman, B. 243
Nichol, W. xxx, xxxix, xlii, 34, 67, 181, 185
Nicholson, G. C. 202
Nida, E. 243
Noetzel, H. 32, 35
North, C. R. 226
Nunn, H. P. V. 415

Odeberg, H. xxvi, xxx, 43, 48, 59, 92, 128
Oke, C. C. 101
O'Connell, M. J. 218
O'Grady, J. F. 265
O'Neill, J. C. 18, 24
Osborne, B. 181, 195
Osborne, R. E. 144

Pancaro, S. xxx, 181, 198
Painter, J. 18
Parrot, A. 318
Pas, H. L. 240
Patrick, J. G. 265
Pauly, A. F. Von 189
Pesch, R. 392, 396
Phillips, J. B. 318
Pollard, T. E. xxx, lxxxiii, 163, 174, 262, 291
Porsch, F. xxx, 56, 82, 240, 256, 257, 265, 270, 277, 280, 281, 283, 284, 381
Porter, C. L. 149, 151
Potterie, I. De la 43, 48, 202, 241, 252, 265, 281, 283, 313, 342
Prior, M. P. 415
Pusey, E. B. 6

Quasten, J. 163
Quispel, G. lviii

Rad, G. Von lx, 156, 216, 378
Radermacher, L. 345
Randall, J. F. 291
Reese, J. M. 241
Reiser, W. E. 181, 195

Richardson, A. xxvi
Richter, G. 1, 13, 43, 227, 235, 313, 320, 356, 358, 364
Riedl, J. 123, 132
Riesenfeld, H. 144, 364, 387
Riosetti, G. 241
Rissi, M. 32, 392, 403, 404
Robinson, J. A. xxx, xxxiii
Robinson, J. A. T. xxx, xxxv, lxxvi, lxxvii, 1, 18, 23, 56, 163, 166, 227, 235, 310, 318, 325, 359, 360, 363, 412
Roloff, J. xxx, lxxiv, 37, 82, 149, 414
Romaniuk, K. 181
Romeo, J. A. 392, 403
Romero, Archbishop 417
Rosscup, J. E. 265
Ruckstuhl, E. xxx, xxxix, xl
Rudolph, W. 355

Sabbe, M. 313
Sanders, J. N. xxvi, xxx, xxxvi–xxxvii, lxxvii, lxxix, 21, 40, 94, 135, 165, 166, 174, 178, 181, 183, 192, 194, 195, 202, 293, 310
Sanders, J. T. xxx, 1, 9
Sandvik, B. 265
Sass, G. 181, 193
Sava, A. F. 313, 356
Schaeder, H. H. 317
Schaefer, O. 241, 249
Schilling, F. A. 144
Schlatter, A. xi, xxvi, 45, 52, 62, 63, 69, 78, 79, 95, 138, 165, 174, 188, 190, 191, 197, 205, 208, 209, 229, 233, 238, 250, 284, 287, 298, 299, 332, 346, 350, 357, 383, 413
Schmiedel, P. W. lxxv
Schlier, H. 327
Schmithals, W. xxxviii, lvii, lxxv, lxxix
Schnackenburg, R. xi, xxvii, xxxvi, lx, lxxi, lxxii, lxxx, lxxxii, lxxxiv, 3, 13, 21, 26, 27, 32, 34, 35, 38, 41, 43, 46, 50, 52, 53, 58, 59, 61, 64, 71, 76, 82, 84, 85, 88, 90, 94, 95, 96, 107, 111, 115, 116, 119, 130, 132, 133, 135, 139, 140, 145, 159, 162, 165, 166, 170, 174, 178, 184, 185, 190, 192, 193, 194, 196, 197, 205, 209, 212, 214, 218, 224, 226, 229, 231, 235, 236, 241, 244, 247, 251, 252, 253, 257, 261, 268, 269, 273, 276, 279, 280, 281, 286, 291, 295, 297, 299, 300, 302, 303, 304, 305, 310, 313, 327, 330, 334, 338, 339, 340, 342, 346, 347, 348, 352, 353, 355, 357, 358, 360, 368, 369, 373, 377, 378, 380, 386, 398, 404, 406, 408, 412, 416
Schneider, J. xxvii, 101, 163, 166, 170, 313
Schottrof, L. xxx, lv
Schrage, W. lxxvi, 149
Schrenk, G. 415
Schulz, S. 67, 77, 192, 229, 250
Schürmann, H. lxxi, 82, 85, 94, 96, 222, 313, 350
Schwank, B. 265
Schwartz, E. lxxv
Schweitzer, A. xxxiv
Schweizer, E. xxx, xxxix, lxxix, 67, 82, 90, 357
Scobie, C. H. H. xxx, lxiv, 18, 23
Scott, E. F. xlviii, 37, 39
Seidensticker, P. 364, 380
Segal, J. B. 225

Segovia, F. F. 244
Sevenster, G. xxx
Shaw, A. 392, 396, 401, 417
Sheehan, J. F. X. 406
Sherwin-White, A. N. 309, 310, 313,
    327, 329, 335
Sickenberger, P. 386
Sidebottom, E. M. 99
Sjöberg, E. 110
Skeat, T. C. lxxv
Skemp, J. B. 9–10
Smalley, S. S. xxx, 18, 241, 260, 304,
    357, 392
Smith, C. W. F. 101
Smith, D. M. xxvii, xxx, xxxvii, xxxviii,
    xxxix, xliii, xlvii, 265, 312
Smith, G. A. 58, 168, 169
Smith, M. lxxviii
Smothers, E. R. 101, 123, 125
Solages, B. De xxx
Spicq, C. 347, 392, 394
Stagg, F. 241
Stählin, G. 250, 274, 277, 373, 406
Stanley, D. M. 313
Stauffer, E. 43, 144, 341, 349
Stenger, W. 181, 185, 265
Strachan, R. H. xxvii, xlii, 192, 232, 250
Strack, H. L. lx, lxxvii, 15, 20, 27, 35,
    47, 48, 53, 60, 63, 70, 74, 75, 76,
    99, 106, 108, 109, 116, 118, 119,
    120, 121, 127, 128, 134, 136, 145,
    151, 155, 157, 158, 173, 180, 190,
    195, 196, 198, 210, 233, 243, 246,
    272, 274, 275, 278, 309, 317, 318,
    327, 334, 346, 359, 375, 383, 386,
    416
Strathmann, H. xxvii, 74, 192, 243, 250,
    295
Stroud, W. 356
Swete, H. B. 399

Tasker, R. V. G. xxvii
Teeple, H. M. xxx, xxxviii
Temple P. J. 97
Temple S. 32, 67, 313
Temple W. xxvii, cxxv, 192
Tenney, M. C. xxvii
Theissen, G. 32
Thompson, F. 30–31
Thüsing, W. xxx, 43, 23, 202, 212, 265,
    284, 291
Thyen, H. x, xxx, lxxi, lxxiii, lxxiv,
    lxxxiii, xc, 1, 2, 3, 5, 46, 82, 98, 224,
    227, 229, 231, 265, 306, 392, 396,
    414
Tischendorf, N. 396
Titus, E. L. xxx
Topel, L. J. 43
Torrey, C. C. xxx, 164, 202, 214
Trocmé, E. 37, 38
Trudinger, P. 181
Turner, C. H. 101
Turner, H. E. W. lvii
Turner, M. M. B. 364, 381, 382
Turner, N. 125, 151, 213, 265, 318, 329
Twomey, J. J. 313, 53–
Tyndale, W. 249

Unnik, W. C. Van xxx, xxxviii, 202, 215

Vanhoye, A. 67, 72
Vergote, A. 202
Vermes, G. 26, 179
Vielhauer P. 143
Visokay, E. xxvi
Vögels, H. 37
Volkmar, G. lxxv

Walker, R. 56
Watson, G. W. E. 56, 64
Wead, D. W. 313, 338

Wedel, A. F. 56
Weiser, A. 227
Wellhausen, J. xxvii, 408
Wenger, L. 335
Westcott, B. F. xxvii, lviii, lxix, lxx, lxxii,
    45, 111, 132, 170, 174, 177, 191,
    193, 213, 229, 234, 250, 275, 294,
    295, 332, 349, 357, 375, 377, 379,
    380, 381, 394, 395, 411, 413
Westermann, C. 226
Wettstein, J. J. 408, 416
White, H. J. 37
Widengren, G. 241
Wieand, D. J. 67, 70
Wiefel, W. 265
Wilcox, M. 181, 194, 227
Wiles, M. F. xxx
Wilkenhauser, A. xxvii, 229, 284
Wilkens, W. xxxi, lii, 181, 185
Wilkinson, J. 313
Williams, A. T. P. 318
Williams, F. E. 18, 21
Wilson, R. MacL. xxxi
Windisch, H. xxxi, lxxxviii, 226, 258, 284
Wink, W. 18, 23
Winter, P. 310, 313
Woodhouse, H. 101
Woude, A. S. Van De 176
Wrede, W. 238
Wroge, H. T. 202

Yamauchi, E. xxxi, lvii
Yates, N. B. 365
Ysebaert, J. lxxxv

Zahn, T. xxvii
Zerwick, M. 126, 265
Zimmermann, H. 90
Zinzendorf, N. Von lxxxi

Index of Principal Topics

Authorship xxxv, xlii, xlv, lxvi–lxxv, 143–44, 395–96

Christology xxxiv, xliv, lv, lxv, lxxvi, lxxxi–lxxxiv, lxxxix, 3, 6–10, 18–19, 42, 55–56, 74–75, 79–81, 86, 88, 89–90, 98, 131, 139–40, 178, 186, 235, 245, 251, 262, 280, 380

Date of the Gospel lxxv–lxxxi
Docetism xc, 14, 95, 356

Eschatology xxxiv, lxxx, lxxxiv, lxxxv–lxxxvii, 40, 54, 62, 63–66, 73, 76–77, 79–80, 92, 93, 116, 117, 130, 131, 190–91, 213, 218, 219, 251, 258, 285, 305, 381, 388, 389, 412, 413

Gnostics/Gnosticism xxxviii, xxxix, lv–lviii, lxv, lxxv, lxxix, lxxx, lxxxviii–xc, 2, 7, 13, 135, 179, 239, 250, 271, 293, 321, 357

Hellenistic Background xliv, xlv, liii–lviii, lxv–lxvi, 6–10
Hermetic Literature lvi, 352

Jamnia xlvi, lxxvii, lxxx
Jerusalem xlv, lxxxi, 20, 22, 37–42, 59, 72, 73, 104, 145, 208, 209–10
Jewish/Christian tensions xlvi–xlviii, lxxxviii–xc, 104, 106, 122, 141–42, 153, 158, 362–363
John the Baptist xxxviii, xlv, lii, lviii, lxv, lxxii, lxxvi, lxxxviii, 4, 11–12, 15, 18, 22, 23–26, 28, 46, 49, 52–53, 58, 64, 72, 78, 79, 111, 199, 210, 332, 398
Johannine School xliv, 29–30

Kingdom of God lxxx, lxxxii–lxxxiii, lxxxv–lxxxvii, 15, 24, 33, 36, 39, 40, 42, 45, 46, 48–49, 50, 52, 55, 58–59, 61–62, 64, 65, 66, 74, 76, 79–80, 88–89, 92, 93, 98, 106, 116, 117, 128, 130, 133, 137, 143, 147, 164, 169, 170, 172, 173, 191, 198, 199, 206–7, 210, 215, 216, 218–21, 234, 237, 239, 248, 255, 258, 262, 273, 278, 280, 284, 287, 288, 296, 329, 330–31, 332, 371, 378, 379, 381, 399, 413

Literary sources behind John xxxviii–xliii
Logos liv, lv, lvi, lxxxi–lxxxiv, 2–17, 128, 139–40, 177, 199, 215, 217, 219, 252, 289, 297, 337, 356, 389, 416
Lord's Supper (Last Supper) 94–96, 98–99, 222–23, 225, 226, 230, 231, 234–35, 247, 269, 294, 301, 305, 306, 357, 400, 401, 409

Mandaism lvii–lviii, 271, 293
Muratorian Canon lxvii, lxviii, 413–14

Nag Hammadi lvi

Palestinian Background xliv, xlv
Paraclete xlviii, l, li, liii, lxii, 16, 29, 215, 220, 223, 226, 227, 245, 256–57, 258, 261, 264, 270–71, 276, 277, 279, 280, 281, 282, 283, 284, 288, 290, 304, 353, 377, 380, 382, 411, 416, 417
Parousia lxxxvii, 198, 220, 244, 245, 247, 250, 251, 258, 259–60, 264, 286, 304, 305, 410, 411, 412, 413
Purpose of Writing lxxxviii–xc

Qumran xlv, lxi–lxiii, lxxiv, lxxvi, lxxx, 25, 42, 70, 120, 176, 179, 215, 257, 302, 309

Rabbinic Judaism lx–lxi, lxiv
Revelation (The Book of) (Relationship of John to) lxix–lxx, xc–xcii
Revelation-discourse xxxiii–xxxix, lv

Samaritan Religion lxiii–lxv, 64–65
Signs-source xxxix, xl–xlii, xc–xcii, 22, 33–34, 71, 104, 185, 206, 217, 219, 230, 231, 247, 254, 286, 360
Son of David xlvii
Son of God xlvii, lvi, lxv, lxxxi–lxxxiv, 4, 5, 14–15, 16, 17, 22, 26, 27, 30, 33, 36, 41, 46, 51, 54–55, 75–77, 79–80, 85, 93, 95, 129, 134, 140, 151, 170, 171, 172, 174, 175–78, 179–80, 185, 187, 192, 200, 212, 245, 249, 254, 255, 260, 262, 271, 272, 273, 276, 280, 282, 289, 295, 296, 297, 300, 302, 303, 305, 309, 319, 329, 338, 344, 350, 351, 352, 356, 361, 362, 379, 388, 389, 390, 416
Son of Man liv, lvi, lxv, lxxxi–lxxxiv, lxxxv, 22, 28, 30, 35, 46, 49, 50, 75–77, 79–80, 96, 131, 132, 151, 154, 159, 160, 161, 172, 175, 179–80, 211, 212, 213, 214, 215, 219, 246, 249, 251, 272, 280, 282, 287, 297, 327, 328, 333, 343, 355, 361, 389
Soteriology lxxxiv–lxxxv, 46–47, 50, 51, 252
Structure of Gospel (Outline) xc–xcii
Synoptic Gospels (Relationship of John to) xxxii–xxxiii, xxxv–xxxvii, xl–xli, xliv, lxiii, lxxvi, lxxviii, 33, 36, 38–39, 50, 71–73, 87–88, 104, 141–42, 143, 160, 167, 168, 169, 173, 211, 217, 222, 224, 225, 226, 248, 275, 306, 310–12, 325–26, 335, 336, 338, 347, 348, 360

Wisdom lx, 8–9, 11–12, 60–61, 98

Index of Biblical Texts

A. Old Testament

Genesis

1	6, 10
1:1	10
1:3	7
1:6	7
1:9	7
2–4	349
2	liv, 6
2:2	74
2:7	151, 155, 380
3	135
4	135
5:1	138
9:5	130
12:1–4	134
17:17	138
18:17	275
22	51, 158
22:2	14
22:4	41
22:6	345
22:10–13	25
22:12	14
22:15–18	134
22:16	14
24:1	lxi, 138
25:22	155
27:35	27
29:30–31	211
40	50
40:13	214
40:19	214
42:17	40
49	223
49:10	156

Exodus

	24
3:12	33
3:14	90, 139
4:1–9	33
4:21–22	177
4:22–23	25
4:22	135
4:21	216
7:1	lxv, 75
8:15	216
8:32	216
12:22	352
12:46	lix, 87, 355
13:21–22	128
14:19–25	127
15:24	93
16:2	93
16:15	86, 91
17:1–6	114, 116
17:3	93
17:12	408
19:3–6	247
19:5	13, 292
19:10	208
19:16–25	78
20:15	154
20:22	180

23:1b	146
23:7	146
28:41	301
32:30–32	79
33:7–11	14
33:11	158, 274, 275
33:13	259
33:18–23	253
33:18	259
34	lxiv
34:6	14
34:18–20	15
34:21–23	15
40:34–38	14

Leviticus

	327
16:17	295
18:5	156
19:18	247, 274
23:34–36	106, 114
25:39	233
26:16	64

Numbers

4:2–3	139
4:39	139
7:10–11	177
8:10	275
8:24–25	139
9:6–12	327
9:9–11	208
9:12	87, 355
11:1	93
11:4–6	93
11:13	84
14:1–3	93
19:11	327
20:3	94
21:4–9	50
25:13	278
27:18	275
29:12–39	114

Deuteronomy

	223, 226
1:16–17	120
1:17	176
4:11–12	78
4:33	78
5:9	154
6:4–5	274
6:4	70, 135, 247
11:29	61
12:1–4	61
13:1–10	325
13:1–6	107, 338
13:1–5	40, 157
14:1–2	135
15:19	301
15:21	301
16:13	114

16:15	114
17:2–5	120
18:15–18	62, 79, 65
18:15	lxiv, 24, 88, 103, 117, 157
18:18–19	218
18:18	lxiv, 24, 117, 157
18:19	218
18:20–22	40
19:15–19	120
19:15	70, 78, 129, 372
21:22	353
21:23	328, 353
27:3	61
27:15–26	120
28:30	64
29:2–4	216
30:15–20	218
32	293
32:39	lix
32:47	78
33	293
34:10–12	157

Joshua

7:19	151
12:25	85
22–24	223

Judges

11:12	34
11:34	14

Ruth

1:16	378

1 Samuel

10:1–9	33
31:9–13	374

2 Samuel

5:2	406
7:14	25
7:25–26	292
12:5	299
20:1	197
21:17	78

1 Kings

	189
4:26	210
8:63	177
11:29–30	347

2 Kings

	189
3:13	34
4:42	84
5:10–14	155

6:8–12	27	80:14–18	272
7:24–41	60	82	172, 176, 179
10:11	317	82:1–4	176
14:25	121	82:1	176
17:30–31	61	82:1b	176
		82:6–7	176
1 Chronicles	189	82:6	75, 175, 176, 177
28–29	223	89:26–27	25
		89:37	215
2 Chronicles	189	89:48 [88:49]	137
16:14	359	90:2 [89:2]	139
20:7	274	96:10	346
30:15–20	208	105:40–41	116
35:21	34	110:1	329
		113–118	113, 210
Ezra		118	113, 210
5:16	38	118:20	169, 170
6:16 [7:7]	177	118:21	194
10:2	120	118:25	113, 131, 210
10:11	120	118:26	20, 192, 210
		122:8	274
Nehemiah		132:17–18	78
3:1	69	139:17	138
9:15	91		
		Proverbs	8, 286
Job	154	1:6	286
9:8	89	3:19	lx
14:11–12	189	3:6	296
14:14	48	6:5	92
		7:17	359
Psalms	81	8	10
2:7	25	8:22	9
7:9–11	136	8:22–31	8
9:14	214	8:27–31	8
18:7–16	213	10:27	128
22	288, 351, 352		
22:11	351	*Ecclesiastes*	
22:18	347	1:9	118
22:1	288	8:15	99
23:2	27		
27:1	128	*Song of Solomon*	
27:2	323	4:14	359
33:6	7		
34:4	323	*Isaiah*	lvi
34:20	lix, 355	2:11	258
35:19	276	4:12	258
35:22–28	136	5	164, 286
40:10	95	5:1–7	272
41:7 [42:7]	207	6:1–4	217
41:9	236, 299	6:9–13	216
44:3	128	6:9–10	207, 216
45:8	359	6:10	216
54:1	299	7:10–16	33
55:14	317	8:6	155
56:9	323	8:9	40
57:4	299	9	259
58:4	155	9:6–7	262
60	352	10:25	285
69	276, 351	11	259
69:4	276	11:1–10	280
69:9	39, 41, 261	11:1–2	25
69:22	351	12:3	113, 114, 117
77:16	89	21:2–3	285
77:19	89	22:19–25	407
78:24	91	25:6–9	88, 379
78:15–16	116	25:6	195
80:1–7	128	26:16–21	286
80:8–18	272	26:20	258
80:14–19	128	27:12	63
		28:21–22	216
		29:17	285

31:1–3	49, 210
32:14–18	280
34:5	299
40:3	20
41:4	lix
41:8	274
41:21–29	284
42:1–4	226, 280
42:1	25, 26
43:3	65
42:5–8	226
42:8–13	78
42:9	226
43:10–13	lix, 29
43:10–11	90
43:10	90, 130
43:11–13	139
43:11	130, 65
43:25	90
44:1–5	280
44:6–11	78
44:6	180
44:7–9	29
45:5–6	90
45:18	90
45:21–22	65
46:4	139
46:9	97
48:12	139, 140
49:1–6	226
49:6	275
49:7–12	226
49:22	349
50:4–9	226
50:4	29
50:10–11	226
52:1–8	226
52:7	262
52:13–53:12	26, 226
52:13–15	216
52:13	lxxxiv, 50, 131, 214
53	25
53:1	207, 215
53:7	339
53:12	346
54:1–5	379
54:1	349
54:13	93
55:1	92
55:11	8
57:19	262
60:14	xlvii
60:19–22	128
61:1–3	379
62:4–5	53
63:8–9	65
65:2	408
66:7–14	285
66:7–11	349
66:19	33
Jeremiah	177, 248
1:5	155, 301
1:18	120
2:13	60
2:21	272, 289
6:14	262
7:11	309
7:21	40
7:32	278
9:25–26	134
9:25	278
13:21	285
16:14–15	278

17:10	47	34	lv, 168, 178, 179
17:15	60, 146	36:24–27	280
25:26	403	36:25–27	49
31:1–4	280	37:1–14	280
31:31–40	278	37:9–10	380
31:34	93	37:26–27	260
51:33	285	37:26	262
51:41	403	45:25	114
		47	401, 402
		47:1–12	41, 114
Lamentations		47:1–11	116
1:16	118		
		Daniel	
Ezekiel	61, 177	7	lxxxii, 77
1:4	128	7:13	110, 131, 329
1:13	128	10:9	323
1:26–28	128	12:2	189
1:28	323		
8	41	*Hosea*	
8:1–18	27		
10:15–19	41	1:4	285
11:17–20	280	2:14–20	53
11:22–23	41	6:2	371
13:7	288, 326	10:1–2	272
13:17	326		
15	286	*Joel*	
15:1–5	272, 273		
16	286	2:28–32	280
17	286	3:18	118
17:1–21	272	4:13	63
19	286		
19:10–15	272	*Amos*	
21:21–23	27		
22:29	120	3:1–2	170
23	286	4:4	40

Micah	
4:9–10	285
5:2	110, 118, 119
6:15	64
Habakkuk	
2:33–34	258
3:3–15	259
3:3–4	128
Haggai	262
Zechariah	39
2:10	260
6:11–12	337
8:20–23	264
9	259
9:9–10	210
9:9	206, 210
12:10	355
13:7–9	168
13:7	355
14:5b–7	128
14:8	114
14:11	116
14:16–17	114
Malachi	
3:1	23
4:5	23

B. New Testament

Matthew	xxxiii, xxxv–xxxvii, xlvii, lxxviii, 119, 308, 311, 336, 343, 349, 351	8:13	71	11:27	lxxxii, 54, 80, 297
		8:20	77	12–13	29
		9:18	159	12:18	192
		8:27–29	xxxvii	12:28	xxxiv, 331
2:4–6	110	9:30	192	13:16–17	331
2:5–6	118	9:37	63	12:38–40	40
3:7–12	25	10	xlvi	13:16	386
3:9	134	10:1–42	222	13:24–30	63
3:10	273	10:4	243	13:30	273
3:11–12	29	10:5–15	xlvi	14:25	89
3:11	15	10:5–6	211	14:33	85
4:1–4	63	10:17–23	xlvi	16	367
4:5–7	106	10:16	xlvi	16:13	159
4:8–9	205	10:19–20	226	16:16	85
4:12	58	10:23	xlvi	16:18–19a	407
5–7	247, 386	10:24–31	xlvi	16:18	407
5:3–12	48	10:24	236, 275	16:19	366, 367, 406
5:6	36	10:32–38	xlvi	16:19a	407
5:11–12	154	10:32–33	80, 154	16:19b	383
5:17	lix, 160	10:37	211	16:22	229
5:20	45	10:40	217	17:1	250
5:25	343	11:2–14	297	18	367
6:13	293	11:2–3	29	18:3	45, 47
7:1	147	11:3	20, 192, 210	18:12–14	168
7:21–23	236	11:5	xxxiv, 199, 331	18:18	367, 383, 384
7:21	45	11:6	386	19:23	45
7:24–27	236	11:12–13	331	19:28	lxxxv, 48
7:28–29	119	11:12	xxxiv	21:12–14	347
8:2	159	11:17	285	21:22–14	200
8:5–13	69, 71, 73	11:18–19	28, 77	23	141, 142
8:7	69, 73	11:20–24	297	23:1–3	236
8:11–12	36	11:25–26	297	23:13–36	236
8:12	92, 134	11:25	299	23:13	156, 170, 407

23:32	40
23:35–36	40
23:38	41
23:39	230
24–25	222
24:26–27	110
24:30	355
24:32–33	413
24:36–41	413
24:42–44	413
24:45–51	413
24:46	386
24:51	234
25:1–46	200
25:26	64
25:31–46	28, 77, 80
25:31–33	51
26:11	205
26:25	317
26:26	230
26:29	230
26:31–32	248
26:33	405
26:39	323
26:42	323
26:61	38, 40
26:64	21, 230, 317
26:73	325
27:16–17	333
27:19	342
27:25	362
27:40	38, 40
27:50	353
27:51	358
27:53	lxxxvii, 259
27:55–56	348
27:56	348
27:57	358
27:66	53
28:2–3	374
28:5	374
28:7	377
28:9–10	368, 369
28:9	376
28:10	376, 377
28:11	366
28:12–14	376
28:13–15	320, 371
28:17	369
28:18–20	171
28:19	lxxxii, 384
Mark	xxxiii, xxxiv–xxxvii, lxxviii, 20, 199, 308, 311, 317, 336, 349, 351
1:1	11
1:3	21
1:4	11
1:5	110
1:7	15
1:11	14
1:14	89
1:16	148
1:22	108, 119
1:29	21, 25
1:40	159
1:43	192
2:1–3:6	104, 105, 141
2:1–12	147
2:5	74
2:10	28
2:14	148
2:17	160
2:19	36
2:28	28
3:1–6	71
3:18	243
3:20–21	107
3:21	109
3:22	91, 109
3:31–35	35
3:32–35	107
4:1–9	63
4:10–20	222
4:11–12	216, 331
4:11	287
4:22	216, 398
4:26–29	63
5:21–43	184, 199
5:22	159
5:23	151, 189
5:34	189
5:39	189
5:40	250
6	87
6:3	10, 106, 243
6:7–13	222
6:31	87
6:32	87
6:36	87
6:37	204
6:47	89
6:51	85
7:3–4	35
7:24–30	71
7:27	73
7:33	155
8:1–8	87
8:2–3	88
8:11–12	200
8:11	40, 87, 91
8:14–21	87, 222
8:23	155
8:27–33	222
8:27–30	21, 87
8:27	159
8:29	85
8:31–33	323
8:31	lxxxiii, 28, 41, 50, 77, 131, 159, 172, 371, 373
8:32–33	233
8:32	212
8:33	97
8:34–37	220
8:34	129, 189, 231
8:35	211
8:37	154
8:38	lxxxii, 23, 77, 80, 180
9:1–13	222
9:1	137
9:7	213
9:14–27	184
9:19	71, 73, 125
9:31	131, 172
9:33–41	222
9:37	217
10:15	47
10:17	lxxxv
10:21	lxxxv
10:23–45	222
10:23	lxxxv
10:27	lxxxv
10:29–30	lxxxv
10:32–45	235
10:32	131, 172
10:45	160, 165
10:51	375
10:52	189
11:1–11	208
11:9	20, 169
11:15–19	38
11:17	37
11:27–12:40	104, 105
11:27–12:37	141, 145
11:27–33	38
11:30	52
12:1–12	200
12:1–11	272
12:10–11	169
12:13–37	38
12:17b	119
12:18–27	190
12:24–27	189
12:28–31	247
12:28	247
12:29–31	274
12:32–34	119
12:37b	119
12:41	125
13	lxxviii, 222, 227
13:9–13	278
13:9	270, 277
13:10	226
13:11	226, 227, 270, 277
13:13	276
13:18	173
13:21–22	110
13:24–27	250
13:27	198
13:32	lxxxii, 80, 180, 258
13:33–37	413
13:34–36	169
13:34	167
14	222
14:1–2	112, 187, 199, 208
14:3–42	222
14:3–9	206, 208
14:3	205
14:5	192, 204
14:6	175
14:7	205
14:10–11	208
14:12	224
14:17	lxx
14:18–21	232
14:18	229
14:22	230
14:23	394
14:24	247, 301
14:25	229, 269
14:27–28	248, 326
14:27	168, 277
14:28	399
14:31	229
14:34	207
14:35	207
14:36	207, 323
14:36a	207
14:41–42	263
14:43–50	322
14:47	323
14:53–54	325
14:55–65	309, 325, 327
14:58	38, 40, 309
14:61–64	175, 338, 340
14:61–62	173, 329
14:61	179, 339
14:62	lxxxiii, 28, 77, 131, 309, 317, 329, 339
14:66–71	325
14:67	324
14:69	325
14:70	325
15:2	339

15:5	339	12:36	167	24:27–28	369
15:7	333	12:49	160	24:28–31	397
15:8	334	13:1–5	152	24:31	375
15:15	335, 336, 337, 343	13:10–17	71	24:32	373
15:21	345	13:12	71	24:34	396, 397, 399
15:22	351	14:1–6	71	24:35–36	373
15:24	347	14:26	211	24:36–42	378
15:25	318	14:27	345	24:36	373
15:27	346	16:19–31	199	24:39	369, 379
15:29–33	343	15:1–7	168	24:41–43	397
15:29	38, 40	15:12	234	24:41	369
15:33	343	17:20–21	331	24:44–47	373
15:34–36	351	17:22	278	24:46–47	384
15:34	288, 343	17:23–24	110	24:46	373
15:36	352	19:10	28, 160	24:50–51	377
15:37	353	19:11	371		
15:38	344	19:23	250	*John*	xlvii
15:39	344, 352	19:43	278		
15:40	348	19:47–48	145	1	xc, 18, 30, 31, 45, 64
15:42	353	20:1–2	145	1–20	lxxii, lxxiii, 395, 396, 415, 417
15:43	358	21:6	278	1:1–18	xxxviii, lxxii, xc, xci, 1–17, 262,
15:46	360	21:13–15	277		370
16:1	359	21:32	407	1:1–5	xxxviii, 3, 5, 10, 11, 297
16:5	374	21:37–38	145	1:1–2	4
16:6	374	21:38	143	1:1	lxxxi, lxxxiii, 3, 9, 10, 125, 139
16:7	371, 399	22:14–38	222	1:1c	3, 11
16:9–11	369	22:15–18	36	1:2	3, 11
16:9	259	22:15	224	1:3–4	80, 159
16:10	378	22:16	88	1:3	2, 4, 11
16:12	366, 375, 398	22:18	88	1:4	lxxxiii, 2, 11, 12, 128, 217, 252
16:14	398	22:19	94, 230, 301	1:4–5	4, 161
16:20	171	22:20	88	1:5	lxxxiii, 11, 53, 217
16:24	369	22:29–30	88, 234	1:6	11, 111
		22:29–30a	36	1:6–8	xxxviii, 3, 4, 5, 11, 15, 18, 22
		22:29	80	1:6–8a	3
Luke	xxxiii, xxxv-xxxvii, xlvii, lxiii,	22:31–38	248	1:6–7	78
	lxxviii, 20, 119, 308, 311, 317, 351	22:31–32	326	1:7	51, 178
		22:34	326	1:7a	22
2:26	137	22:39	88, 322	1:7c	22
2:49	39	22:40	88	1:8	lxxxix
3:15–16	21	22:43	207	1:8a	22
3:15	23	22:44	81	1:8c	22
3:23	139	22:54–62	425	1:9–13	5, 12
4:6	205	22:54	88	1:9–12	xxxviii, 11
4:16–30	39	22:55	324	1:9–10	4
4:16–20	331	22:58	325	1:9	lxxxiii, 3, 12, 51, 217, 252
4:22	108	22:59	325	1:10–13	53
4:30	126	22:67	173	1:10–12	3, 4, 11, 12
5:1–11	397	23:2	327	1:10–12b	3
5:5	394	23:8–9	40	1:10–11	3
5:10	416	23:16	334, 335, 339	1:10	lxxxiii, 3, 12
6:22–23	154	23:25	343	1:10a	12
6:22	xxvii, 277	23:26	345, 351	1:10b	12
6:40	275	23:27–31	344	1:10c	12
7:1–10	69, 71, 73	23:27	285	1:11	4, 12, 207, 215, 232, 281
7:10	71	23:29	278	1:12–14	11
7:11–17	199	23:33	318	1:12–13	3, 12, 252
7:13	71	23:34	344	1:12	lxxxiii, 2, 13, 403
7:32	285	23:39–43	344	1:12a	4
7:36–38	206, 208	23:46	353	1:12b	4
8:3	21	23:47–49	344	1:12c	4
8:15	175	23:49	348	1:13	lxxxiii, 2, 4, 6, 12, 13, 14
9:24	211	23:50–51	358	1:14–18	3, 4, 5, 13, 218
9:49	217	23:51	358	1:14	li, liv, lv, lix, lxxxi, xc, 3, 4, 5, 13,
9:51	214	24:4	374		14, 15, 35, 94, 262, 298, 356, 389
9:53	64	24:5	374	1:14e	3
10:16	217	24:7	373	1:15	3, 4, 15, 18, 22, 25, 217, 250, 268
10:18	205, 213	24:10	21	1:15a	2
10:22	lxxxii, 80	24:11	366, 369	1:16	lxxxiii, 4, 14, 15
10:38–42	183	24:12	250, 368	1:16–17	3, 11, 35
11:29–30	40	24:13	378	1:17	lix, lxi, 4, 14, 15, 36, 87, 92
11:52	156, 170, 407	24:16	375	1:18	lxxxi, lxxxii, lxxxiii, xci,
12	226	24:21a	371		2, 3, 4, 11, 15, 18, 93, 217, 253,
12:8–9	23, 77, 80, 154	24:24	368		262, 305, 350, 409
12:11–12	226, 270, 277	24:25–27	373	1:19–12:50	xci
12:35–38	169				

1:19–2:1 34
1:19–51 xci, 18–31, 67
1:19–37 12
1:19–36 78
1:19–34 21, 46
1:19–28 21, 23–24, 78
1:19–24 22
1:19–23 lxxxix, 52
1:19–21 22
1:19 20, 23
1:19b 21, 22
1:19c–22a 21
1:19ff 11, 22
1:20 23
1:21 21, 23
1:22–24 21
1:22–23 22
1:23 20
1:24–25 24
1:24–25a 21
1:25–28 22
1:25–26 21
1:25 21, 22, 117, 261
1:25b–26 21
1:26–27 24
1:26 21, 22, 24, 26
1:26c 22
1:27 21
1:28–34 178
1:28–30 21
1:28 21, 183
1:29–36 29
1:29–34 22, 24–26
1:29–31 lxxxix
1:29 li, lii, lix, lxxxi, lxxxiv, lxxxv, xc, 24, 85, 87, 94, 224, 306, 352, 380
1:30–34 22
1:30 15, 21, 25, 250, 268
1:30b 22
1:31 21, 22, 24, 398
1:32–43 lvi
1:32–34 24
1:32–33 29
1:32 21, 25
1:33–34 21
1:33 21, 22, 66, 354
1:33b–34 21
1:33b 22
1:34 li, lxxxi, 21, 22, 25, 26, 27
1:35–51 26
1:35–50 22
1:35–40 lxx, lxxii, lxxiii
1:35–36 21
1:35ff 22
1:36–39 26
1:36 lii, lxxxi, lxxxvi, 24, 87, 352
1:37 26
1:38–39 26
1:39 21
1:41 lxxxi, 26
1:42 27, 192
1:43–46 27
1:43 26
1:44 70, 200
1:45 317
1:46 73
1:47–50 27
1:48–49 63
1:48 61
1:49 lxxxi, 192
1:50 34, 386
1:51 lx, lxxxi, lxxxiii, xci, 22, 23, 28, 30, 31, 34, 35, 80
2–12 xlii, xc, 207, 254

2–4 31, 67
2:1–4:42 xci, 31
2:1–3:6 105
2 31, 58, 67, 206, 231
2:1–12 xxxii, 31, 32–37
2:1–11 22, 31, 67
2:1–3a 33
2:1 31, 34, 36, 39, 45, 67
2:2–3 34
2:3b–5 33
2:4 34, 73, 103, 107, 188, 278, 296, 349, 350
2:6–8 33
2:6 35
2:8 35
2:9–10 33
2:10 35
2:11 xl, 5, 14, 33, 35, 398
2:12 33, 71
2:13–22 37–43
2:13–14 223
2:13 39
2:14–17 39
2:14–16 38
2:14–15 38
2:15–17 39
2:15b 40
2:16 38
2:17–19 117, 306
2:17 38, 41, 261, 276
2:18 38, 40
2:19–22 lxxxv
2:19–21 lxii, 40, 172, 249
2:19–20 37
2:19 38, 40, 41, 42, 198, 261
2:20–21 38
2:21 40
2:22–23 135
2:22 38, 41, 233, 261
2:23–3:36 43–56
2:23–3:21 46
2:23–3:12 52
2:23–32 80
2:23–25 xl, 31, 45, 46, 47, 70, 73
2:23 33, 39, 132, 276
2:24 47
2:25 47, 61
2:28 160
3–4 xl, 206
3 lii, 31, 46, 58, 67
3:1–21 13
3:1–12 46, 47
3:1–10 119
3:1–2 276
3:1 20
3:2–3 73
3:2 lxxxi, lxxxii, 47, 49, 70, 152, 371, 413
3:3–8 50
3:3–7 129
3:3 lxxv, lxxxv, 13, 47, 48, 52, 117, 330
3:4 48
3:5 xxxviii, xli, lxxxv, 47, 48, 52, 117, 330, 354, 357
3:6–8 49
3:6 49, 117
3:7 47
3:8 47, 49, 117
3:9 55
3:11–12 49
3:11 216, 371, 413
3:12 lii, 46
3:13–21 46, 47, 50, 53, 55, 94
3:13–16 46
3:13 lii, lv, lix, 45, 46, 50, 55

3:14–21 207
3:14–16 lxxxv, 55, 80, 306
3:14–15 lii, lxxxii, lxxxiii, lxxxiv, lxxxv, lxxxviii, 46, 49, 50, 131, 159, 172, 207, 213
3:14 lix, 46, 96, 131, 137
3:15 51, 54
3:16–21 lii, lxxxiii, lxxxv, 46, 76, 77, 207, 234, 289, 332
3:16–17 lxxxi, 213, 276
3:16 xliv, lxxx, lxxxi, lxxxii, lxxxiv, lxxxvii, lxxxviii, 4, 5, 12, 14, 46, 51, 66, 76, 159, 171, 198, 218, 252, 259, 263, 274, 284, 296, 300, 301, 354, 380, 394
3:17–21 46, 51, 55, 142, 161
3:17 lxxxi, lxxxii, 51, 129, 147, 160, 218, 383
3:18–21 lxxxvii, 147, 160, 342
3:18 lxxxi, lxxxii, 14, 51, 76
3:19–21 12, 51, 119, 129, 159, 217, 300
3:19–20 235
3:19 45, 129, 281
3:20–21 213
3:20 280
3:21 lxxxvii
3:22–30 46, 357
3:22–24 46, 51
3:22 39, 51, 58
3:23 52, 236
3:25–30 lxxxix, 46, 49, 52
3:25–26 52
3:25 20, 45, 52
3:26 xxxix, 52, 53, 106
3:27–29 52
3:28 159
3:29–42 47
3:30 lii, 53
3:31–36 lii, 46, 50, 53, 55, 217, 218, 332
3:31–35 55
3:31–34 158
3:31 45, 46, 53, 111, 192, 275
3:32–35 283
3:32 29, 53
3:33–35 53
3:33 53
3:34 lxxxi, 216
3:35 232, 394
3:36 lxxxi, lxxxv, lxxxvii, 54, 76, 159
4 xxxii, 31, 66, 67
4:1–42 56–66
4:1–6 59
4:1–3 58
4:1–2 xxxix, 52, 59
4:1 39, 52, 73, 106
4:2 187
4:3 58
4:4 59
4:5–6 59
4:6–18 59
4:7–26 59, 60
4:7–18 60
4:9 20, 60
4:10–11 191
4:10 60
4:11–12 60
4:11 229
4:12 137
4:13–14 60
4:14–15 59
4:14 235, 358
4:15–18 61
4:15 92, 229

4:19–26 59, 61
4:19 lxxxi, lxxxii, 27, 61, 157, 229
4:21–26 42
4:21 61, 250, 269, 278
4:22–24 151
4:22 lviii, 13, 20, 62, 171, 363
4:23–24 lxxx
4:23 36, 62, 250, 269, 278
4:24 62
4:25 62, 64, 250, 269
4:26 62, 159
4:27–30 59, 62
4:27 62
4:28–30 59
4:28–29 63
4:28 250
4:29 lxxxi, 27, 64
4:31–38 59, 63
4:31–34 63
4:32 59
4:34 xl, lxxxiii, 59, 261, 262, 273, 297, 302
4:35–38 63
4:35–36 63
4:35 lxiii
4:35a 63
4:35b–36 63
4:36 58, 63
4:37–38 63
4:37 63
4:38 63, 64
4:39–42 59, 64
4:39 59, 64
4:41 132
4:42 li, lxiii, lxxx, lxxxii, xci, 65, 70, 171, 276, 289
4:43–5:57 xci
4:43–5:47 xcii, 66–81
4:43–54 xxxii
4:43–45 70, 73
4:43 73
4:44 70, 73
4:45 73, 80
4:46–5:47 79
4:46–5:9 76, 80
4:46–54 xliii, 67, 71, 73
4:46 69, 71
4:47 69, 73
4:48–49 71
4:48 71, 73, 373, 385
4:49 229
4:49ff 71
4:50 69, 71, 73
4:51 73
4:51ff 71
4:53 69, 73
4:54 xliii, 33, 71, 73
5–8 179
5–6 104
5 xl, xliii, 67, 72, 73
5:1–9 xliii, lx, 67, 71, 72, 109
5:1–9b 73
5:1–5 71
5:1 xliii
5:2 lxxvi
5:3 70
5:4 70
5:6–8 74
5:6 34
5:7 229
5:8 76
5:9 74
5:10–18 109
5:9c–18 72, 74
5:10–29 xliii

5:13 74
5:14 74
5:16–18 338
5:17–47 67
5:17–30 74, 79, 80, 122, 174
5:17–29 lxxxiii
5:17–18 74, 175, 338
5:17 xl, lx, lxxxiii, lxxxvii, 72, 75, 217
5:18 72, 74, 137, 327, 389
5:19–47 lxxxix, 207
5:19–30 72, 75, 172, 175
5:19–29 218
5:19–27 lxxxi, 283
5:19–26 390
5:19–24 lxxxii
5:19–23 xl, lxxxiii
5:19–21 72
5:19–20 53, 75, 188
5:19–20a 75
5:19 lxxxiii, 75, 76, 77, 137, 262, 273, 354
5:19a 75
5:20 76, 255, 394
5:20b 75
5:21–29 28, 37, 191
5:21–27 262, 296
5:21–23 76
5:21–22 lx, 218
5:21 lxxxvi, lxxxvii, 67, 73, 75, 80, 189, 190
5:22–30 72
5:22 75, 76, 342
5:23 261, 386
5:24–27 77
5:24–26 72, 76, 255
5:24 lv, lxxxv, lxxxvi, 73, 76, 137, 261
5:25–27 77
5:25–26 lxxxiii, 73
5:25 lxxxii, lxxxvi, 36, 62, 76, 80, 190, 195, 200, 278
5:26–27 75, 77, 159, 189
5:26 lxxxii, 80, 93, 190, 252
5:27–29 72
5:27 lxxxiii, 79, 342
5:28–29 xxxviii, lxxxiii, lxxxvi, 62, 73, 77, 80
5:28 79
5:29 77
5:30 lxxxi, 53, 75, 77, 108, 129, 137, 261, 273
5:30a 72
5:30b 72
5:31–47 29, 73, 77, 80
5:31–32 78
5:31 70, 129
5:32 78, 415
5:33–40 415
5:33–35 78
5:34–47 lxiii
5:34 78
5:35 354
5:36 78, 297, 302
5:37–40 78
5:37 70, 130, 261, 354
5:38 78, 79, 273
5:39–40 30, 81, 93, 96, 218
5:39 lxi, 78, 79, 276
5:40 79
5:41–47 78
5:41–44 79
5:42 79
5:43 79, 261
5:43b 79
5:44 373
5:45–47 lxv, 79, 276

5:45–46 109, 158
5:45 109
5:46 354
6–7 xxxviii
6:1–7:1 xcii
6 xxxii, xl, xliii, lix, lxxxi, lxxxv, xci, 60, 87, 99, 225, 226, 352, 401, 404
6:1–71 81–99
6:1–21 86, 92
6:1–20 231
6:1–15 85, 88
6:1–13 86
6:1–5a 85
6:1 xliii
6:2 84
6:3 87
6:4 84, 87, 88, 94, 177, 208
6:5–8 27
6:5 88
6:5b–9 85
6:5ff 34
6:6 88
6:7 204
6:10–11 85
6:11 88, 394, 401
6:12–13 85
6:14–15 47, 85, 86, 88, 118, 196, 210
6:14 lxxxi, 88, 147
6:15 lxxxi, 73, 87, 88, 89, 196
6:16–21 85, 86, 89
6:16–18 85
6:16 87, 89
6:19–21 85
6:19 89
6:20 lxxxiv, 13, 62, 86, 89, 322
6:21 85, 97
6:22–35 86
6:22–26 85, 86, 90
6:22–24 90
6:22–23 187
6:22 90
6:23–24 90
6:23 58, 90
6:24–33 196
6:25–27 47
6:25–26 86
6:25 86, 90
6:26–51 85, 94
6:26 90
6:27–31 85, 86, 91
6:27 lxxx, 53
6:28–29 xliii
6:30–59 lix
6:30–31 86
6:30 87
6:31–33 lxxxv, 88
6:31–58 xli
6:31–59 85
6:31–33 86
6:31 86, 93, 95, 96
6:32–58 lxxxii
6:32–51 93, 94
6:32–40 47
6:32–35 86, 87, 91, 93, 96, 99
6:32–33 91
6:32b 85
6:33 lxxxv, 192, 276
6:34–40 86
6:34–35 92
6:34 92, 229
6:35–50 87
6:35–47 85
6:35 lxxxiv, 60, 85, 89, 92, 94, 95, 96, 98, 113, 115
6:36–47 86

6:36–40   86, 92, 217
6:36–37   92, 174
6:37–39   171
6:37   93, 268, 296
6:38–40   92, 218, 261
6:38   93
6:39   xxxviii, lxxxvi, 92, 93, 165, 190, 268
6:39–40   lxxxv, 205, 296
6:40   xxxviii, li, lxxxv, lxxxvi, 92, 95, 190, 217, 218, 278
6:41–48   86
6:41–47   86, 93
6:41–42   96
6:41   20, 85, 86, 89, 91, 93, 94, 97, 107
6:44–45   171
6:44   xxxviii, lxxxvi, 92, 93, 174, 190, 217, 220, 296
6:45   217
6:47–51   lxxxv
6:47   89, 93, 137, 217, 373
6:48–71   86
6:48–58   85
6:48–51   86, 93
6:48   89
6:49–58   87
6:49–51   lxxxv, 93
6:49   85, 93
6:50   93, 95
6:51–62   306
6:51–58   xc, 47, 87, 98, 306
6:51   lxxxv, 60, 89, 93, 94, 95, 171, 191, 192, 217, 276
6:51b–58   xxxviii, xli
6:51c   94
6:52–59   86, 94
6:52–58   85, 99
6:52   86, 91, 94, 97, 99
6:53–58   lxxxv, 94, 96
6:53–57   96
6:53–56   357
6:53   85, 94
6:54   xxxviii, lxxxvi, 92, 95, 190
6:55   93, 95, 357
6:56   95
6:57   95, 99, 191, 223
6:58   lxxxv, 26, 94, 95
6:59   86, 87
6:60–71   86, 96
6:60–69   xc
6:60–65   85
6:60   99
6:61   86, 107, 277
6:62–63   96, 97
6:62   96
6:63   96, 137
6:64–65   171, 296
6:66–71   xxxvii, 85, 87
6:66–70   xci
6:66–69   157, 196
6:66   86, 88, 97
6:67–71   86
6:67–69   5, 97
6:68   lxxxi, lxxxv, 137, 218, 229, 254
6:69   lxxxi, lxxxii, 97, 137, 293, 323
6:70–71   97
6:71   204, 229, 236, 243
7–10   166
7–8   xl, xci, 104, 105, 141, 142, 144, 147, 149, 153, 382
7   lix, 100, 104, 106, 115, 121, 122, 123, 140, 141, 142
7:1–8:59   xcii, 100
7:1–8:11   100
7:1–52   100

7:1–13   105, 106
7:1   xliii, 106, 121
7:2   106
7:3–9   35, 188
7:3–5   106
7:4   107
7:5   107
7:6–7   107
7:6   103, 296
7:6ff   34
7:7   45
7:8   103, 107, 296
7:9   147
7:10–13   196
7:10–11   147
7:10   103, 104, 107
7:11–13   20, 172
7:11–12   107
7:11   20, 208
7:11bff   34
7:12–13   106, 119, 157
7:12   119, 121, 325, 327
7:13   106, 142, 157
7:13b   107
7:14–18   105, 108
7:14–17   218
7:14–16   158
7:14–15   108
7:14   129
7:15–19   107
7:15   122, 142
7:16–18   lxxxi, 283
7:16–17   108, 129, 216
7:16   129, 261
7:17   108, 116, 122, 132
7:18–30   21
7:18   108, 122
7:18b   108
7:19–24   105, 109
7:19   109, 122, 142
7:20   109, 110
7:21–23   lx, 109
7:21   108, 121
7:22–23   122
7:24   122, 129, 144
7:25–31   105, 110
7:25–27   110
7:25   107, 208
7:26–27   110, 118
7:26   104, 106, 110
7:27–29   217
7:27   110, 112
7:28–30   130
7:28–29   111, 122
7:28   75, 217
7:29   111
7:30–32   196
7:30–31   111, 119, 157
7:30   35, 110, 119, 178, 211, 278, 296
7:31   110, 172
7:32–36   105, 112
7:32   107, 142, 157, 172, 208
7:32a   106
7:33–36   105
7:33–34   112, 130, 217
7:33   105, 112, 282, 284
7:34   52, 105, 246
7:35–36   112
7:35   130, 142
7:35b   113
7:36   105, 143
7:37–44   141
7:37–39   96, 105, 113, 353
7:37–38   41, 60, 61, 106, 113, 114,

   115, 116, 117, 119, 122, 127, 128, 129, 140, 142, 173, 177, 235
7:37   114, 217, 353
7:37a–38b   115
7:38   191, 358
7:38b   116
7:39   lxxxv, 49, 60, 115, 116, 117, 133, 280, 380
7:40–52   104, 127
7:40–44   105, 117, 196
7:40–43   114, 122, 172
7:40–41   117, 118
7:40–41a   129
7:40   lxxxi, 147
7:41–42   121
7:41   118
7:42   111, 119, 122
7:43–44   119
7:43   157
7:44   119, 143
7:45–52   105, 119
7:45–46   119, 142
7:46–52   142, 144
7:46   114, 119, 129, 157, 323
7:47–52   106, 196
7:47–48   119
7:47   119, 121, 325, 327
7:48   119, 217
7:49   lxi, 119, 120, 363
7:50–51   120
7:50   47
7:52   73, 121, 122
7:53–8:11   100, 127, 143–147
7:53–8:3   145
8   100, 104, 105, 121, 140, 141, 142, 363
8:1–8   87
8:3   145
8:4–6   146
8:7–9   119, 146
8:7   145
8:11   87, 229
8:12–59   123
8:12–26   207
8:12–20   105, 126, 141
8:12   xlix, lxxxiv, 5, 89, 106, 125, 126, 127, 128, 130, 140, 141, 142, 148, 152, 155, 173, 177, 217, 276
8:13–20   140
8:13–18   78
8:13   125, 129, 144, 157
8:14–21   87
8:14–18   130
8:14–17   217
8:14   125, 129, 140, 415
8:15–16   129, 144, 218
8:15   141
8:16   78, 125, 140, 141, 249, 261
8:17–18   78, 129
8:17   125, 165, 276
8:18   261, 415
8:19   129, 140, 243
8:20   35, 119, 130, 178, 211, 278, 296
8:21–29   105, 130
8:21–22   105, 130
8:21   105, 246, 282
8:22   20, 105, 130, 157
8:23–29   158
8:23–24   130
8:23   lv, 263, 275
8:24   lxxxi, 89, 105, 130, 139, 140
8:25   131
8:25b   125

8:26–29	131, 218, 283	9:5	148, 152, 155, 160, 161, 201,	10:10–18	306
8:26	131, 141, 216, 261		217, 276	10:10	lxxxv, 174, 300
8:27–30	87	9:6	151, 155	10:11–18	166
8:27	131	9:7	151, 155	10:11–13	166, 170
8:28–29	132, 134, 217	9:8–12	152, 156	10:11	lxxxiv, 89, 94, 166, 169, 170,
8:28	li, lxxxi, lxxxiii, lxxxiv, 50,	9:8	152		171, 173, 175, 248, 408
	62, 75, 78, 89, 131, 133, 139, 140,	9:8–41	xlix	10:12–13	170
	172, 207 322, 343	9:11–12	161	10:12	174
8:29–40	134	9:11	156	10:14–18	166
8:29	lxxxiii, 131, 262, 273, 288	9:13–17	152, 156	10:14–15	170, 174
8:30–59	132, 133	9:13	157	10:14–15a	171
8:30–36	105, 132	9:14–16	156	10:14	89, 166, 175
8:30–32	132, 133, 141, 142	9:15	156, 157	10:15	94, 165, 166, 169, 170, 171,
8:30	132	9:16	119, 157, 161, 327		248
8:31–59	105, 148	9:17	157, 161	10:16–17	174
8:31–36	275	9:18–23	152, 157	10:16	lxxx, 148, 169, 171, 289,
8:31–32	133, 256	9:18–21	157		306, 406
8:31	132, 137, 139, 276	9:19	lxxxi, lxxxii	10:17–18	lxxxv, 38, 170, 171, 199,
8:32	132, 134	9:22–23	xlii, 157		263, 273, 301
8:33–59	141, 142	9:22	lxxvi, 153, 154, 158, 277	10:17	165, 166, 171
8:33	132, 133, 142	9:24–34	152, 158	10:18	103, 166, 171, 353
8:33a	134	9:24	161, 327	10:19–29	166
8:34–36	133, 134, 142	9:24–25	158	10:19–21	166, 167, 172
8:35–36	134	9:25–26	134	10:19	119, 157
8:35	134	9:26–29	158	10:20	109
8:37–40	105, 133, 134	9:28	109	10:21–39	179
8:37–38	134	9:29	161	10:22–42	167, 172
8:37	132, 142	9:30–38	158	10:22–39	148, 149, 166, 167, 172
8:41–47	105, 135	9:31–38	160	10:22–38	xci
8:41	126, 133, 135	9:31	371	10:22–30	167, 172
8:42–43	135, 217, 283	9:33	161	10:22–29	166
8:42	111, 276, 354, 394	9:34	159, 161	10:22–27	169
8:43	132	9:35–41	277	10:22	177
8:44	126, 135	9:35–38	152, 159	10:24–39	172
8:45–47	136	9:35–36	159	10:24–25	173, 174
8:46–47	290	9:35	154, 159	10:24	20, 172, 175, 290
8:46	263, 280	9:36	229	10:25–26	175, 373
8:47	136	9:37–38	159, 161	10:25	174
8:48–59	105, 109, 136	9:37	151	10:26–39	148
8:48	133, 136, 142, 157, 327	9:38–39	151	10:26–30	92, 174
8:49–50	136	9:38	151, 160	10:26–29	166
8:50	137, 141	9:39–10:9	148, 151	10:26	166
8:51	137, 139, 142, 218	9:39–41	76, 148, 152, 159, 160,	10:27–29	166
8:52–53	138		161, 166, 216, 217	10:27	174
8:52	133	9:39	129, 151, 160, 161, 342, 383	10:28–29	174
8:54–55	137	9:40–41	169, 172	10:28	323
8:54	lxi, 322	9:41	160	10:29–30	lxxix
8:54a	137	9:51–55	lxiii	10:29	171
8:55	218, 273	10	xl, lvi, lix, xxxi, 104, 148, 166,	10:30–39	338
8:56	138, 139, 217		167, 179, 180, 186	10:30	lvi, lxxxiii, 79, 149, 172,
8:57–58	139	10–11	xxxviii		174, 175, 176, 180, 253, 262, 390
8:57	133, 142, 157	10:1–42	162–180	10:31–39	167, 175
8:58–59	xci	10:1–21	148, 149, 167, 168	10:31–32	175
8:58ff	lxxix	10:1–18	165, 166, 172	10:31	20, 188, 208
8:58	lxxxi, lxxxiv, 13, 62, 89, 131,	10:1–10	166	10:32	175
	140, 149, 175	10:1–5	167, 168	10:33	175, 176
8:59	100, 104, 119, 140, 178, 208	10:1–5	166, 167, 171, 269	10:34–36	175, 176, 217
9–10	xci, 148	10:1–3a	166, 167	10:34	276
9:1–10:42	xcii, 148–180	10:1	167, 169	10:35	176, 177
9:1–10:21	149	10:2–4	167, 169	10:36	lxxxi, 97, 172, 177, 300, 306
9	xl, xlix, l, lxxvii, 104, 148, 149, 151,	10:2–3	169	10:37–39	177
	153, 154, 161, 162, 166	10:2	170	10:37–38	174, 253, 254
9:1–41	149–162	10:3–4	169	10:38	85, 132, 180
9:1–38	148, 160	10:3	170, 375	10:39	178, 188, 208
9:1–7	xlix, 151, 152, 154	10:3b–5	166, 167	10:40–42	xci, 166, 167, 178
9:1–4	74	10:4	148	10:41–42	199
9:1	126, 148, 151, 153	10:5	lxiii, 167	11	xl, xci, 104, 184, 193, 195, 199,
9:2	154	10:6–18	269		200, 306
9:2–5	151	10:7–18	167, 169	11:1–54	xcii, 180–201
9:2–3	152	10:7–10	166, 169	11:1–16	187
9:3–4	152	10:7	lxxxiv, 89, 166, 169, 170	11:1–2	187
9:3	155, 187, 229, 268	10:7b	169	11:1	184, 185, 186
9:3b	155	10:8	lxxxviii, 170	11:2	58, 185, 187
9:4–5	152	10:9–11	92	11:3–4	185
9:4	xl, 152, 155	10:9	89, 164, 166, 170	11:3	184, 185, 186, 229, 394

11:4	151, 184, 185, 187, 188, 193, 194, 200	11:38a	194	12:23–24	lxxxv, 107, 137
11:5–6	185, 188	11:39–40	194	12:23	50, 131, 187, 207, 211, 212, 213, 232, 246, 273, 278, 280, 282, 284, 296
11:5	lxxiv, 183, 185, 187, 188, 394	11:39	190, 229		
11:6	184, 186, 188	11:41–44	185		
11:7–16	184	11:41–42	184, 194	12:24–26	64, 129, 207, 211, 232, 274
11:7–10	185	11:41	194		
11:7–8	188	11:41a	185	12:24	171, 212, 213, 297
11:8–9	187	11:41b	194	12:25–26	260
11:9	152, 188	11:43–44	xci, 185, 186, 195	12:25	212
11:10	47	11:44	360	12:26	212, 243, 248
11:10a	188	11:45–54	196	12:27–29	212
11:10b	188	11:45–53	187, 311	12:27–28	lxxxiii, 187, 207, 211, 220, 273, 280, 284, 294, 296, 320, 323, 408
11:11–15	184, 185, 186	11:45–46	188, 196		
11:11–12	188	11:45	178, 185, 186		
11:11	lxxxi, 189, 274	11:46–53	185, 187	12:27	193, 212, 232, 237, 246, 249, 278
11:12	189, 229	11:47–53	186, 208, 310		
11:13	187	11:47–48	196	12:27a	194, 207
11:14–15	189	11:48	196	12:27b	194
11:14	61, 188	11:49–53	340	12:28	211, 212, 219, 273, 294
11:15	188	11:49–52	336	12:28a	207
11:16	185, 187, 189, 252, 320, 384	11:49–50	112, 130, 196, 311, 346	12:29–30	207, 212
11:17–27	187, 189	11:49	196, 197	12:29	207
11:17–19	185	11:50–52	lxxx, 171	12:30–31	36
11:17	185, 186, 188, 189, 194	11:50–51	94	12:31–34	lxxxiii, 80
11:18–30	185	11:50	xxxiii, 362	12:31–33	137
11:18–19	190	11:51–52	lxxxii, 197, 198	12:31–32	lv, lxix, lxxix, 5, 16, 29, 76, 96, 107, 119, 131, 157, 159, 171, 172, 187, 188, 198, 207, 211, 213, 218, 219, 232, 246, 273, 278, 280, 282, 288, 289, 296, 300, 329, 380, 390
11:18	185, 187	11:51–52	16, 94, 403		
11:19	185	11:52	198, 311		
11:20–27	184, 185	11:53	187, 199		
11:20–21	186	11:54	xcii, 201–221		
11:20	lxxxi, 190	11:55–12:50	xci, 186, 205, 208		
11:20a	185	11:55–57	208		
11:21–22	188, 190	11:55	208	12:31	lix, lxxxiii, lxxxiv, lxxxvi, 94, 130, 207, 212, 213, 219, 232, 282, 288, 289, 383
11:21	192, 229	11:56	208		
11:22	190	11:57	199, 208		
11:23–24	190	12	xl, xc, 205, 206, 207, 218, 294, 306		
11:23	194, 249			12:32	51, 131, 205, 207, 214, 220, 249, 359
11:24–27	251	12:1–8	206, 208		
11:24–25	195	12:1	208	12:33	215, 328, 409
11:24	183, 371	12:2	185	12:34	lxi, 131, 159, 175, 207, 215, 276
11:25–26	188, 189, 190, 191, 194, 200, 201	12:3–4	208		
		12:3	205	12:35–36	216
11:25	lxxxi, lxxxiv, lxxxvi, lxxxvii, 5, 80, 89, 128, 191, 201, 220, 278	12:5	204, 205	12:35–36a	207, 215
		12:7	205, 208, 209, 268	12:35	11
		12:8	205, 209, 218, 229	12:36–50	230
11:25a	190	12:9–19	209	12:36–43	lii
11:25b	190	12:9–13	196	12:36b–50	xci
11:26	137, 201, 258	12:9–11	209	12:36b–43	207
11:26a	191	12:9–10	187	12:36b	215
11:26b–27	188, 188	12:9	178, 205, 276	12:37–50	215
11:27–12:40	105	12:11	220, 276	12:37–43	119, 207, 215
11:27	229	12:12–32	289	12:37–42	296
11:28–44	192	12:12–19	206	12:37	xl, 215, 220
11:28–37	187	12:12–14	206	12:38–41	220
11:28–32	184, 192	12:12–13	208	12:38–40	217
11:28–30	186	12:12	209	12:38	215, 323
11:28–29	195	12:13–14	206	12:39	216, 217
11:28	185	12:13	lxxxi, 192, 209, 210, 220	12:40c	217
11:30	185, 187	12:14–15	210	12:41	5, 217
11:31	lxxxi	12:14	206	12:42–43	358
11:32–34	185	12:15	206, 210	12:42	lxxvi, 217, 220
11:32	188, 229	12:16–18	210	12:43	221
11:33–35	186, 212	12:16	233, 261	12:44–50	46, 207, 208, 221, 276
11:33–34	185	12:17–19	178, 187, 196	12:44–49	261
11:33–39a	185	12:17–18	206, 209	12:44	217
11:33	189, 192, 193	12:19	206, 211	12:46–49	119
11:33b	193	12:20–36	207, 211	12:46	216, 217
11:34	229	12:20–32	66, 246	12:47–50	283
11:35–37	185	12:20–23	lxxx	12:47–49	256
11:35	193	12:20–22	207, 211	12:47	217, 249, 289
11:36–38	194	12:20	171, 220	12:48–49	262
11:36	lxxiv, 194	12:21–22	26, 27	12:48	lxxxvi, 190, 218, 219, 278, 342
11:37	172, 194	12:21	229	12:49	75, 78, 216, 218, 229
11:38–44	187	12:23–28	213	12:49–50	218
11:38–39	185, 186	12:23–26	lxix	12:50	221
				12:50a	218
				13–20	xc, 230

Reference	Pages
13–17	xc, 222, 223, 229, 294
13–16	279, 306
13–14	223, 224, 269, 279, 415
13	lxx, 222
13:1–20:31	xcii, 222–391
13:1–17:26	xcii, 222–307
13:1–30	xcii, 223, 227–240, 230, 269,
13:1–20	230, 231, 232, 237
13:1–3	230, 232
13:1–2	231
13:1	lxx, 35, 119, 230, 232, 233, 239, 269, 278, 296
13:1a	229
13:2–3	230
13:2	97, 230, 233, 238, 243
13:2a	229
13:3	lvi, 112, 129, 231, 233, 236, 276
13:4–20	231
13:4–11	230, 231
13:4–5	231, 232, 233
13:6–10	231, 236, 323
13:6	229, 333
13:7	229, 233
13:8	229, 230, 239
13:9–10	234
13:9	229
13:10	229, 230, 234, 236, 272
13:12–20	230, 231, 236
13:12–15	231, 233, 235
13:12	235
13:13–20	236
13:13	236
13:14–15	239
13:15	230, 236, 237, 387
13:16	236, 275
13:17–19	231
13:17	236, 386
13:18–19	233, 237
13:18	95, 236, 238, 299, 323
13:19	89, 236, 263, 387
13:20	217, 236, 379
13:21–30	97, 230, 231, 232, 237, 240
13:21–26	lxx
13:21–22	232
13:21	193, 212, 237, 249, 340
13:21a	231
13:21b	231
13:23–27a	232
13:23–26	lxx, 232
13:23–24	324
13:23	lxx, lxxiii, 4, 16, 232, 237, 350
13:24	409
13:25	229, 238, 354
13:26–27	232
13:26	229, 238
13:27	229, 232, 237
13:27a	231
13:27b	231
13:28–30	232
13:28–29	232, 238
13:28	299
13:30	47, 173, 231, 232, 239, 327
13:31–14:31	xcii, 223, 231, 240–264, 244, 261, 269, 270, 279
13:31–38	244, 245, 246
13:31–35	224, 279
13:31–33	245, 246
13:31–32	lxxxiv, 50, 54, 131, 187, 211, 244, 246, 247, 268, 273, 280, 282, 284, 296, 409
13:31	lxxxiv, 50, 246, 279, 296
13:31b–14:31	279
13:31ff	224
13:32	29, 242, 246
13:33–36	112
13:33	246, 247, 263, 279, 282
13:33a	284
13:34–35	245, 247, 263, 274
13:34	236, 303, 305, 387, 394
13:35	248
13:36–38	224, 245, 247, 248, 263, 279
13:36–37	406
13:36	229, 246, 248, 252, 279
13:36b	409
13:37	165, 229, 248
13:37b	248
13:38	61, 165, 269
14–16	xliii, 117
14	224, 244, 250, 263, 264, 279, 305
14:1–26	244, 245, 248
14:1–11	252
14:1–6	252, 278
14:1–4	243
14:1–3	244, 245, 248, 263
14:1	193, 212, 248, 251
14:2–3	26, 244, 246, 249, 250, 251, 252, 258, 259, 262, 264, 304, 305
14:2	130, 245, 249, 377
14:2b	243
14:3	lxxxvi, lxxxvii, 28, 220, 234, 249, 251, 254, 258, 260
14:4–17	244
14:4–14	244
14:4–6	244, 245, 251
14:4	112, 244, 252
14:5	229, 243, 244, 252, 279, 371, 384
14:6–11	252
14:6–10	251
14:6	lxxxi, lxxxiv, 89, 244, 252, 257, 263
14:6b	253
14:7–11	244, 245, 253, 258
14:7–9	244, 253, 263
14:7	230, 244, 248, 253, 418
14:8–11	263
14:8–10	27
14:8–9	243
14:8	229, 244, 253
14:9–11	390
14:9–10	245, 283
14:9	244, 253, 390
14:10–14	244
14:10–11	175, 178, 302
14:10	xl, 75, 244, 253, 271
14:10bc	254
14:11	244, 254
14:11b	254
14:12–17	251
14:12–14	244, 245, 250, 254, 273, 377, 380
14:12–13	1, 255
14:12	33, 155, 254
14:12a	254
14:12c	255
14:13–14	254, 258
14:13	243, 255
14:13a	255
14:14	243, 255
14:15–27	244
14:15–17	226, 244, 245, 256, 258
14:15–16	245, 250
14:15	243, 244, 256, 259
14:16–17	264, 270, 276
14:16–17a	244
14:16	lxxxi
14:17	255
14:17b–d	244
14:18–26	244
14:18–25	260
14:18–24	251, 263
14:18–23	245, 278
14:18–21	244
14:18–20	244, 245, 251, 258, 259, 263
14:18–19	258, 377
14:18	lxxxvii, 220, 245, 250, 258, 260, 379, 389
14:19–24	250
14:19–20	245, 258
14:19	246, 258, 282, 387
14:20	lxxxvii, 245, 258, 302, 389
14:21–24	245, 259
14:21–23	245, 377
14:21	lxxxvii, 247, 256, 259, 260, 264, 285
14:21a	244
14:21bc	244
14:22–23	244, 251
14:22	229, 244, 259
14:23–24	218, 261
14:23	lxxxvii, 26, 220, 247, 256, 258, 259, 260, 284
14:23ab	244
14:23cd	244
14:24–27	244
14:24	244, 256, 260
14:25–31	xliii
14:25–26	226, 244, 245, 256, 261, 271
14:25	261
14:26	li, 256, 261, 264, 283, 285, 418
14:27–31	244, 245, 262, 263
14:27	193, 262, 263, 379
14:27ac	244
14:28–31	244
14:28	lxxxiii, 79, 112, 262, 279
14:29–30	263
14:29	245
14:30–31	244, 263
14:30	205, 289
14:31	132, 151, 223, 242, 263, 273
15–17	223, 224, 231
15–16	223, 224, 262, 269, 279, 288, 290, 415
15:1–16:33	265–291
15	lix, 263, 412
15:1–17	xcii, 16, 223, 269, 271
15:1–11	269
15:1–10	lxxxi, 269
15:1–8	269
15:1–6	269, 273
15:1	lxxxiv, 89, 271
15:2–10	233
15:2–4	272
15:2	271
15:3	234, 268
15:5	89, 273, 275
15:6	271, 273
15:7–17	269
15:7–11	271
15:7–10	273
15:7	133, 273
15:8	268, 273
15:9–17	269, 273
15:9–10	273, 287
15:10	274

15:11–17	269	16:22	270, 288	17:24–26	xci, 220, 295, 296, 304,
15:11	269, 274, 299, 387	16:23–24	285, 286, 287, 377		306
15:12–17	247, 269	16:23	243	17:24	lxxxii, 198, 205, 234, 260,
15:12	274, 275, 387	16:24	288		268, 292, 295, 301, 303, 304, 305
15:13–15	287	16:25–33	271	17:25–26	295, 305
15:13	165, 274, 275, 408	16:25	164, 250, 261, 271, 286, 287,	17:25	304, 305
15:14	274		290, 305	17:26	304, 306
15:15	283	16:26–27	287	18–20	306
15:16	273, 275, 411	16:27	394	18:1–20:31	xcii, 308–391
15:17	275, 387	16:28	232, 268, 287	18:1–19:42	308–364
15:18–16:4	219	16:29–30	287	18:1–27	321
15:18–16:4a	xcii, 223, 269, 270, 275	16:31–32	287	18:1–11	xcii, 321
15:18–27	269, 270, 277	16:31	386	18:1–3	208, 321
15:18–25	270, 278	16:32	lxxi, 288, 399	18:1–2	321
15:18–20	276	16:32b	288	18:1	223
15:18–19	275, 289	16:33	xci, 29, 229, 261, 262, 269, 270,	18:1ff	223, 263
15:19	276, 394		288, 387	18:2b	322
15:20	275	17	112, 223, 224, 293, 294	18:3–9	322
15:21	268, 276	17:1–26	xcii, 291–307	18:3–6	119
15:22–24	276	17:1–8	295	18:3	322
15:22	276, 281	17:1–5	295, 296, 303	18:4–9	311, 321
15:24	268, 276	17:1–4	295	18:4–6	322
15:25–26	380, 383	17:1	29, 35, 54, 119, 131, 172, 187,	18:4	320
15:25	151, 175, 276, 289, 323		205, 211, 232, 273, 278, 282, 284,	18:6	320, 323
15:26–27	16, 226, 227, 270, 271,		292, 294, 296, 409	18:7–9	323
	276, 281, 411	17:1b–2	295	18:8–9	320
15:26	256	17:2	165, 268, 296, 298, 303, 304	18:9	322
15:27	125	17:3	111, 296, 297	18:10–11	321, 323
16:1–4	xlvii, 289	17:4	xl, 63, 297, 298, 302	18:11	301
16:1–4a	270, 279	17:4–5	295	18:12–27	xcii, 321, 323
16:1	261, 269, 270, 277, 279	17:5	lxxxii, 5, 54, 172, 205, 211, 217,	18:12–14	311, 321, 323
16:2	lxxvi, lxxvii, lxxix, 17, 250, 269,		233, 282, 284, 297	18:13–27	317
	277, 278	17:6–19	5, 295, 296	18:13–24	xxxvi
16:3–4	278	17:6–13	295	18:13	317, 324, 340
16:4	261	17:6–11a	296, 298	18:14–15	317
16:4a	269, 270, 279	17:6–9	298	18:14	20
16:4b–33	xcii, 223, 269, 270, 279,	17:6–8	295, 299	18:15–18	321, 325
	286	17:6	218, 292, 293, 298, 398	18:15–17	lxxii
16:4b–6	270, 284	17:7–12	295	18:15–16	lxx, lxxiii, 324
16:4b–5	279	17:8	111, 276, 302	18:15	317
16:4b	279	17:9–19	295	18:16–18	317
16:5	112, 279, 285	17:11	13, 172, 293, 300, 302	18:16	lxxii
16:6	279	17:11a	297, 298	18:17–18	324
16:7–11	226, 256, 281, 411	17:11b–16	296, 298	18:17	354
16:7	270, 271, 279, 280	17:11b	297, 298, 300, 301	18:18–24	325
16:8–11	5, 29, 256, 257, 270, 271,	17:12	215, 256, 299, 323	18:19–24	311, 321
	277, 301, 380, 383	17:13–23	295	18:19–23	317, 338
16:8–9	130, 136, 160	17:13–15	299	18:19–21	324
16:8	280, 281	17:13	297, 387	18:19	324
16:9–11	137, 280, 281	17:14–19	295	18:20	290
16:9	281, 282	17:14	302	18:22–24	325
16:10	112, 282	17:15	219	18:24	317, 323, 326
16:11	lxxxvi, 130, 205, 282, 289	17:16	300	18:25–27	317, 321, 325
16:12–15	li, 226, 256, 271, 287, 305	17:17–19	296, 299, 300, 301, 303,	18:25	354
16:12–13	233		382	18:28–19:16	xxxvi
16:12	282, 283	17:17	177, 300	18:28–19:16a	xcii, 321, 326
16:13–14	256	17:18	lxxx, 298, 300, 302, 379	18:28–32	321, 327
16:13	250, 283, 284, 418	17:19	lxxxv, 94, 97, 177, 294, 296,	18:28	224, 225, 326, 327, 340
16:14–15	283, 284		297, 300, 301, 302, 303, 305	18:29–30	328
16:14	284, 290, 418	17:19a	301	18:30	327, 329
16:15	284	17:19b	301	18:31–33	lxxv
16:16–30	258	17:20–26	295	18:31	20, 308, 310, 327, 328
16:16–24	lxxxvii, 270, 271, 279, 284,	17:20–24	295	18:32	328, 409
	286, 287	17:20–23	lxxx, lxxxii, 295, 296, 301,	18:33–38a	321, 329
16:16–22	112, 377		304	18:33–37	329, 338
16:16–19	284	17:20–21	302, 303	18:33	326, 329, 330
16:16–18	279, 285	17:20	234	18:34–35	329
16:16	282, 284, 285, 286	17:21–23	271	18:35	329
16:17–18	286	17:21	lxxxvii, 170, 178, 248, 276,	18:36	20, 330
16:17	112, 268		298, 301, 302	18:37–38a	363
16:20–22	286, 379	17:22–26	295	18:37	lxxxii, 318, 327, 329, 331
16:20	258, 268, 282, 285, 286	17:22–23	302, 303, 304	18:37a	329
16:21–22	285	17:22	302, 306	18:37–38	lxxv
16:21	285, 286, 349	17:22a	303	18:38–39	332
16:22–23	258, 284	17:23	248, 298, 301, 302, 303, 304	18:38b–40	321, 332

18:38	20, 332
18:38b	136, 332
18:39–40	334
18:40	332, 333, 346
19:1–3	321, 334
19:1	334, 335
19:2–3	336
19:4–7	321, 337, 341
19:4–6	136, 342
19:4–5	337
19:5	lxxi, 362
19:6	327, 332, 337
19:7	327, 329, 337, 338
19:8–12	321, 338
19:8	323, 338
19:9	339
19:10–11	339
19:10	103
19:11	52, 339, 362
19:12	332, 340, 341, 343, 362
19:13–16a	321, 341
19:13–16a	321, 341
19:13–14	341
19:13	342, 353
19:14–15	362
19:14	225, 318, 332, 342
19:15–16	324
19:15	327, 332, 343, 363
19:16	343
19:16b–42	xcii, 321, 343
19:16b–18	321, 344
19:16b–17	344
19:16a	344
19:16b	311
19:17	318, 345, 409
19:18	344, 345
19:19–22	321, 344, 346
19:19–20	346
19:19	xxxi, 415
19:20–22	311
19:20	345
19:21–22	346
19:23–24	321, 347
19:23	344
19:24	323, 344
19:24c	348
19:25–27	lxx, lxxi, 321, 344, 348, 350
19 25	348
19:26–27	311, 348, 349, 350
19:26	34
19:27	373
19:28–30	321, 350
19:28–29	344
19:28	320, 349, 350, 353
19:29	352
19:30	36, 297, 301, 311, 344, 352, 353
19:31–37	xli, 25, 39, 116, 177, 224, 321, 353
19:31–36	344, 352
19:31–35	324
19:31	225, 353, 358
19:32–34	354
19:34	xc, 94, 116, 353, 357
19:34–37	lxx, lxxi
19:34–35	358
19:34b–35	xxxviii, 357
19:34b	357
19:35	xxxviii, 14, 354, 373, 413
19:36–37	3–4, 354, 356
19:36	37, 323, 354
19:37	lix, 355
19:38–42	321, 358
19:38–40	47
19:38–39	218
19:38	217, 358
19:39	358, 360
19:40	359
19:41–42	360
20	xxxvi, 195, 367, 388, 390, 395, 396, 398
20:1–31	xcii, 364–391
20:1–18	367, 368
20:1–10	lxx, lxxi, 367, 368, 370
20:1–2	368
20:1	317, 370
20:2–10	324
20:2	lxxii, 229, 368, 371, 375, 390, 413, 414
20:3–10	368, 369, 373
20:3–9	360
20:3–5	371
20:4–8	400
20:4	lxxii
20:6–7	195, 360, 368
20:8	lxxii, 368, 373
20:9	lxxi, 373
20:10	373
20:11–13	367, 370, 374
20:11–13	368
20:11–12	374
20:11a	368
20:11b–14a	368
20:13–14	374
20:13	229
20:14–18	369
20:14b–18	368
20:14b–16	368
20:15	229
20:16	lxxxi, 390
20:17	lvi, 306, 307, 366, 368, 376, 377
20:17b	366
20:18	lxxxi, 229, 369, 378
20:19–23	367, 369, 370, 378, 382, 395
20:19–20	369, 370
20:19	369, 378
20:19b	386
20:20	250, 369, 379
20:20a	369
20:21–22	380
20:21	lxxx, 66, 155, 369, 379, 380, 381, 383, 406
20:22	xli, 116, 117, 280, 285, 353, 369, 370, 380, 381, 382, 383
20:23	366, 367, 369, 370, 380, 381, 382, 384
20:24–29	14, 367, 369, 370, 384
20:24–28	xci
20:24–26	384
20:24	398
20:25	229, 369
20:26	369
20:27	369, 385
20:28	lxxxi, lxxxiv, 229, 262, 369, 375, 385
20:29	li, xc, 373, 385, 386, 395
20:30–31	x, xl, lii, lxxxviii, xc, xci, 5, 53, 152, 170, 192, 367, 370, 387, 388, 395, 413, 415, 416
20:30	xl, 5, 29, 387, 388, 395
20:31	lxxxiv, lxxxv, 16, 318, 387, 388, 415
21	xxxviii, lxxi, lxxii, lxxiii, lxxvi, xc, 66, 354, 375, 395, 396, 399, 401, 402, 403, 404, 406, 410, 411, 413, 414, 416, 417
21:1–25	xcii, 392–418
21:1–23	395, 413, 415
21:1–20	lxxi
21:1–14	lxx, lxxii, 396, 397, 398, 403, 404, 416, 417
21:1–11	lxxx
21:1–8	396
21:1–4	397
21:1	89, 397, 398
21:2–3	396
21:2	396, 397, 398
21:3–14	399
21:3	396, 398
21:4	89, 397, 400
21:4a	396
21:4b	396
21:5–8	397
21:5–6	396, 400
21:5	394
21:6	396
21:7–9	396
21:7	lxxi, lxxxi, 354, 397, 398, 399, 400, 409
21:7a	397
21:8–11	400
21:8	400
21:8b–9	396
21:9–13	396
21:9	394, 397, 400, 401, 402
21:10–11	396
21:10–11a	396
21:10	394, 397, 400, 403
21:11–14	396
21:11	396, 397, 400, 401
21:12–13	396, 400
21:12	396, 397, 400, 401
21:13	397, 400, 401
21:14	397, 398
21:15–23	398, 404
21:15–19	404
21:15–17	374, 394, 396, 397, 398, 400, 407, 410, 417, 404, 405
21:15	404, 405
21:16–17	405
21:18–23	417
21:18–19	248, 396, 398, 407, 409, 410
21:18	407, 408
21:19	408, 409, 410
21:20–23	lxxi, 396, 398, 409, 414, 418
21:20–24	lxx, 324
21:20	409
21:21–24	lxxiii
21:21–23	lxxii, lxxxvi
21:21–22	410
21:22–23	411, 412
21:22	398, 410, 411, 412
21:23	lxxi, 354, 412
21:24–25	xci, 398, 413
21:24	lxxi, lxxii, lxxiii, 354, 371, 412, 413, 414, 415
21:25	143, 395, 413, 415, 416
Acts	xlvii, lxxx, 39, 384
1:4	397
1:6	399
1:9	377
1:21–22	277
1:25	239
2	381, 382
2:14–36	319
2:17	190
2:23	308, 362
2:32–33	382

2:38	384
4:6	324
4:11	169
4:12	97
5:1–11	384
5:12	165
5:31	65
6	xlv
6–7	lxxvii
6:1	307
6:13	196
7	278
8	xlv
8:32–35	25
9:4	323
10:6	89
10:25	159
10:36–43	367
10:36	262
10:37	11
10:40	259
10:41	397
10:45	132
13:13	183
13:23	65
13:47	275
13:50	lxxvii, 154
14:11	338
15:39	250
17:23	10
18:24–19:7	23
19:1–7	lxxxix
20:28	406
20:35	386
20:38	407
21:8–9	lxviii
21:20–24	xlvi
21:20	132
24:24–25	281
26:24	370

Romans

1–11	147
1:3	118
2:28–29	134
3:25	319
4:18	249
4:25	319
5:12–21	171
8:1	246
8:34	287, 294
9–11	216
9:6–8	134
10:9	390
11:1	364
11:28–31	216
11:32	296
12:1–2	147
13	339
13:8	367
14:7	262
14:9	191
14:23	367
15:8	13

1 Corinthians

1:14–17	58
3:3–4	410
3:16–17	249
5:1–5	384
5:5	238
8:5–6	390
10:4	114

10:12	240
10:16–17	269
11:23	230
11:24	94, 301
11:26	222
12:12–13	272
12:14–27	272
13	3
13:1–3	405
14:24	281
15:3–4	liii, 319, 367, 370, 397
15:5	396, 399
15:51–52	305

2 Corinthians

2:7	151
2:16	418
3:4–5	418
3:12–18	1
3:18	305
4:4	205
4:10	189
5:1	249
5:6–8	305
5:14–21	171
5:14–15	191
5:15	191
5:17–21	246
5:17	lxxxvi, 31, 48, 191, 381
5:19	319

Galatians

1:6–9	132
2:19–20	95
3:28	307
4:4–6	261

Ephesians

1:7	246
1:22–23	272
2:2	205
2:11–18	171
2:20–22	249
3:18	11
5:11	281
5:25–27	53
5:33	151

Philippians

1:6	305
1:21	305
2:1–11	239
2:3	239
2:4	239
2:5	239
2:6–11	xxxiv, xliv, lxxvi, 3, 54, 367, 390
2:9	50, 214
3:12	11
3:20–21	305
3:20	65

Colossians lxxx

1:13	76
1:15–20	xxxiv, xliv, lxvi, lxxvi, 3
1:16–17	205
1:18	272
2:19	272

1 Thessalonians

2:14–16	lxxvii
4:13–18	412
4:13	193
4:15–18	250
4:17	198
5:4	11

2 Thessalonians

2:1	198
2:3	299
2:8	299

1 Timothy lxxx, 65, 415

1:12	275
3:4–5	407
3:16	3, 13, 214, 282
4:6	175
6:13	30

2 Timothy lxxx, 65, 415

2:8	118
2:11–13	3, 129
3:1	190
3:16	xliv

Titus 65, 415

3:5	48

Hebrews 176

1:1–3	xliv, 230
1:1	253
1:3	214
1:4ff	230
5:7–10	212
5:7	207
5:17	194
7:13	xxxii
7:25	287, 294
9:14	294
10:27–28	258
11:5	137
11:17	14
12:22	249
13:7	407

James 236

1:22–25	236
2:20	367
2:23	274
5:3	190

1 Peter

1:1	198
1:11	268
1:23	48
2:4	169
2:5	249
2:7	169
2:12	317
2:25	406
3:18	319
3:22	319
4:15	317
4:16	409
5:1–3	407
5:2	406
5:3	406

2 Peter	lxxx	4:11–12	274	3:8	137
		4:16	137	3:9	lxxx, 142, 159, 278
1:4	11	4:19	14, 274	3:21	13
		4:20–21	274	5	25
Jude	lxxx, 243	5:1	135	7:17	194
		5:4–5	288	8:5	213
1 John	xxxix, lvi, lxxx, lxxxi, 13,	5:6–9	356	11:5	38
	255, 288, 305	5:6–8	xc, 358	11:15	282
		5:6	356	11:19	213
1:1	277	5:7–8	356	12	213
1:2–3	10	5:8–12	78	12:1–17	lxix
1:2	413	5:13	387	12:4	38
1:3	387	5:16–17	273	12:9	205
1:4	387, 413	5:18–19	293	12:10	213
1:5	62			12:12	205
1:7	358	*2 John*	lxxiv, lxxx, lxxxi	13:14	191
2:1	255, 287, 294			13:18	402
2:3–5	137	5	387	14:13	230
2:5	367	6	387	14:14–16	63
2:13–14	288, 293			16:18	213
2:15–27	240	*3 John*	lxxiv, lxxx, lxxxi	17:17	233
2:18–24	179, 356			19–21	251
2:18–27	97	11	413	19:7	53
2:18–22	168	15	169	19:12	339
2:18–19	273			19:16	391
2:10	277	*Revelation*	xlv, xlvii, lvi, lxxviii, lxxx,	20:4–5	191
2:13	277		284, 321, 391	20:6	234
2:24	277			20:9	38
2:28	304	1:1–3	lxviii	21:2–4	198
3:2	304	1:2	30	21:2	53
3:4–10	240	1:3	137, 218, 256	21:3	260, 297
3:7–10	97	1:4	250	21:4	194
3:9	48	1:5	30	21:9–22:5	249
3:11	277, 387	1:7	250, 355	21:9–10	53
3:12	293	1:8	250	21:13–14	lxx
3:14	412	1:10	385	21:22	41, 61
3:16	137	1:17–18	25	22:1–3	41
3:17	70	1:17	323	22:1–2	116
3:23	387	1:18	25, 407	22:3–5	297
4:1–6	97, 168, 179, 240, 273, 356	2–3	lxxx	22:7	137, 256
4:2	xc	2:7	13	22:9	lxviii, 137
4:4	288	2:8	191	22:10	53
4:5–6	136	2:9–10	xlvi	22:17	53
4:7–12	70	2:9	lxxx, 142, 278	22:18	lxviii
4:8	62	3:7–17	xlvii	22:20	250
		3:7–12	407		